# Dictionary

Latin – English
English – Latin

**Berlitz Publishing**
Springfield, NJ · Munich · Singapore

Original edition by
S. A. Handford
Reader in Classics at King's College, University of London
and Mary Herberg
Formerly Assistant Lecturer in Classics at King's College,
University of London
Inset cover photo: © Punchstock/Medioimages

Berlitz Publishing
193 Morris Avenue
Springfield, NJ 07081
USA

Printed in Germany
ISBN 981-246-415-8

08 07 06 05
5.
4.
3.
2.

# PREFACE

The Latin-English section of this dictionary is an entirely revised edition of Professor K. Feyerabend's well-known dictionary, which went through several editions.

Our special thanks are due to Mr. S. A. Handford for the present revision, which takes account of recent scholarship and increases the number of entries by 2200 words.

A special feature is the marking of 'hidden' quantities. There is an introductory account of the development of the Latin language, and just before the main text there is a list of the Roman authors whose vocabulary is included, and information on the arrangement of the dictionary.

The English-Latin section of the dictionary, compiled by Mrs. Mary Herberg, offers a Classical prose vocabulary. Equivalents have been drawn wherever possible from Cicero and Caesar, and where notes on a word's construction are given they are likewise based on the best prose usage.

In a dictionary of this size it is not possible to distinguish fully between the different meanings of one English word. Often the notes on construction will help to show which sense is being translated, but if there is any doubt the word must be checked in the Latin-English section, and this rule holds good wherever the Latin word is unfamiliar.

# Some Remarks on the Latin Language

I. Latin is one of several Italic languages, the most important of the others being Oscan — spoken by the Samnites, Campanians, Apulians, Lucanians, and other peoples of central and southern Italy — and Umbrian, which was spoken in the district called Umbria, and at one time, probably, in other parts of north-central Italy. Italic is one branch of the great family of languages known as Indo-European, which includes nearly all European languages — Greek, Celtic, Germanic, and Balto-Slavonic — and some of the languages of India and Persia, the oldest of these being Sanskrit, the sacred language of the Indian Brahmins.

Of the non-Italic branches of Indo-European, Latin shows most affinity to Celtic, which, besides the languages of ancient Gaul and Britain, includes Welsh, Breton, Manx, Irish, and Gaelic. This may mean that people speaking languages from which Latin and some Celtic languages (especially Irish) are derived lived at one time in close contact. We have no means of knowing when the Italic group of languages was brought into Italy — presumably from some part of central Europe —, except that it was certainly before 1,000 B.C. The oldest Latin inscriptions in existence date from the sixth century B.C., but inscriptions earlier than about 200 B.C. are few and short. The earliest extant Latin literature is the comedies of Plautus, who began to write in the last decade of the third century B.C.

II. **The Alphabet.** The ultimate source of the Latin alphabet, and of those of the other Italic languages, is the 'western' Greek alphabet used in parts of the Greek mainland, in the island of Euboea, and in some of the Greek colonies in southern Italy and Sicily. The Latin alphabet has a particularly close resemblance to that in use at Cumae in Campania, a colony founded from Chalcis in Euboea. The Romans probably derived it, however, not from these Campanian Greeks, but from the Etruscans of north-central Italy, who used a variety of the western Greek alphabet, although their language was not Indo-European[1].

---

[1] Nevertheless, Etruscan had a considerable influence upon the vocabulary of Latin. Not only are many Latin proper names of Etruscan origin (including, most probably, the name of Rome itself), but also a number of words connected with religion, the state, and the theatre.

In the later Republican period the Latin alphabet consisted of the following twenty-one letters:

a b c d e f g h i k l m n o p q r s t u x

In the time of Augustus two new letters were introduced for use in words borrowed from Greek or other languages; *y* (for the Greek υ) and *z* (for the Greek ζ).

Notes: (1) The letter *c*, derived from the Greek γ, was at first used both for the sound of English *g* in *go*[1], and for the sound of *k*. As it continued to be used for *k*, the letter *k* eventually went almost out of use[2]. For the *g*-sound, a new letter, *G*, was formed in the third century B.C. by the addition of a small stroke to *C*.

(2) The letter *i* represented not only a vowel sound, but also a semivowel sound like that of the English *y* in *yet*. When the letter is used for this *y*-sound, it is generally called 'consonantal *i*', and is sometimes written *i̯*. In medieval texts it was often written as *j* — a practice still sometimes followed, though it has now become rare.

(3) The letter *u* (capital *V*) represented a vowel sound, and also a semivowel sound like that of the English *w*. In the latter case it is generally called 'consonantal *u*', and is sometimes written *u̯*. The medieval practice of writing it as *v* still remains common, but modern editors are tending to revert to the Roman practice of using *u* (capital *V*).

III. **Pronunciation.** No system of writing can be, and remain, entirely phonetic; but Latin spelling in the classical period was very nearly phonetic — more so even than modern Italian is. The classical pronunciation is known with a fair degree of accuracy. The ancient writers themselves, especially the grammarians, tell us something about it. Something can be inferred from the development of Latin sounds in Romance languages; for instance, most of the pure vowel sounds represented by Latin *a e i o u* are similar to those represented by these letters in Italian and French (with a few exceptions: e.g. the *u* of the French *plume* is quite different from the *u* of the Latin *pluma*). Another kind

---

[1] A survival of the original use of Latin *c* for *g* is seen in the abbreviations *C.* for *Gāius* and *Cn.* for *Gnaeus*.

[2] It was retained only in a very few words, e. g. *Kalendae* (abbreviated *Kal.* or *K.*).

of evidence is transliterations of Greek words into Latin, e.g. *cithara* (for κιθάρα), and, in particular, transliterations of Latin names into Greek, in the Greek authors who wrote on Roman history — e.g. Κικέρων (*Cicerō*), Βροῦτος (*Brūtus*), Ἰούλιος (*Iūlius*), Γερμανικός (*Germānicus*), Οὐαλέριος (*Valerius*).

Single vowels in any given Latin word are either long by nature (e.g. *fās, nūbēs*) or short by nature (e.g. *lăpĭdĕ, pĭŭs* — though the quantity of short vowels is not usually marked). The difference between the sounds of long and short vowels is partly a matter of actual length — i.e. the time taken in pronouncing them — and partly a matter of quality or timbre. The following is a list of the Latin long and short vowels, together with some English, French, and German words containing approximately similar vowel-sounds:

| Latin | English | French | German |
|---|---|---|---|
| ā | father | page | Vater |
| ă | aha | patte | Mann |
|  | footpath |  |  |
| ē |  | église | Weh |
| ĕ | fed | avec | Bett |
| ī | machine | livre | ihn |
| ĭ | pit |  | mit |
| ō |  | dos | Sohn |
| ŏ | not | botte | Gott |
| ū | brute | rouge | du |
| ŭ | full |  | und |
| ȳ |  | dur | über |
| y̆ |  |  | Hütte |

When two vowels come together in a Latin word, they are often pronounced quite separately, as in *ăēnĕŭs, ăĭt, rĕmĕăt, crĕĕt, dēīs, ĕōs, rĕŭs, pĭăs, dīĕī, dŭbĭōs, gĕnĭŭs, clŏācă, rĕbŏĕt, sŭās, stătŭĕt, mŏnŭĭt, strēnŭŏs, tŭŭs*[1]. Sometimes, however, two vowels form a diphthong. Each keeps its proper sound as nearly as possible, but they are run together by means of a "glide" so as to make a monosyllable. The following are the Latin diphthongs, with

---

[1] The first of the two vowels which come together is nearly always short. Moreover, in compound words, a naturally long vowel, or the diphthong *ae*, is shortened in this position: e. g. *deamat* (*dē + amat*), *dehīscēns, prohibet* (*prō + habet*), *praeacūtus* (*prae + acūtus*), *praeeunte, praeustus.* The rule, however, does not apply to Greek words adopted into Latin, e. g. *Aenēās, āēr, hērōus.* Exceptions in genuine Latin words are *diēī, rēī* (and some other nouns of the fifth declension); *fīŏ; Gāī; nullīus* (and other genitives in *-ius*, though in most cases the *i* can also be scanned short).

English and German words containing similar sounds (French has no diphthongs):

| Latin | English | German |
|-------|---------|--------|
| ae | f*i*nd | St*ei*n |
| au | h*ou*se | H*au*s |
| ei | gr*ey* | |
| eu | | |
| oe | t*oi*l | h*eu*te |
| ui | | pf*ui* |

Notes: (1) Latin *ae* should probably be pronounced more broadly than the diphthong in *find* — more like the *ai* commonly heard in *Isaiah*.

(2) In certain words, *au* tended to be pronounced in colloquial Latin as *ō*, and it was often so written: e.g. *Clōdius* for *Claudius*, *cōpa* as a feminine corresponding to the masculine *caupō*.

(3) The diphthong *ei* is very rare. It occurs in the interjection *ei*, and in *Pompei*, vocative of *Pompēius*.

(4) The sound of the Latin *eu* was perhaps similar to that of the *eu* in Italian *neutro* — though this is not a true diphthong, the two vowels being pronounced more or less separately. This Latin diphthong is rare. It occurs in *ceu*, *heu*, *neu*, *seu*, and *neuter*.

(5) The diphthong *ui* is rare. It occurs in the interjection *hui*, and in *huic* and *cui*. (In *quis*, *quī*, *quid*, &c., the *u* is consonantal.)

The Latin consonants, except as noticed below, were pronounced more or less as they generally are in English.

Notes: **bs** (e.g. *urbs*) was pronounced as *ps*; **bt** (*obtineō*) as *pt*.

**c** (*cīvis*) was always 'hard', as *k* (never as *s*); **ch** (*pulcher*) as *kh* (as in English *deck-hand*).

**g** (*gemma*) was always 'hard', as in English *go* (never as in English *gem*).

Consonantal **i** (*iaciō* — sometimes written *jaciō*) was pronounced as the *y* in English *young*.

**m** at the end of a word (*bellum*) was not sounded, but the preceding vowel was slightly nasalized, somewhat as in the French *un*. Compare the forms *circuit*, *circuitiō* for *circumit*, *circumitiō*.

**ng** (*angulus*) was pronounced as in English *angle*.

**q** was used only before consonantal *u* (*quaerō*); the combination *qu* was pronounced *kw*, as in English.

**s** (*rosa*) was always 'hissed', as in the English *sit* (never as in English *rose*).

**t** (*ratiō*) always had its proper sound; *ra-ti-ō* was pronounced as it is written (not with the sound of *sh* as in English *rational*, nor with the sound of *ts*, although in many Italian words *t* has been replaced by a *z* which is pronounced as *ts* — e.g. *giustizia* from Latin *iūstitia*).

Consonantal **u** (*uīuō* — often written *vīvō*) was pronounced as the *w* in English *wet*; **gu** (*anguis*) as in English *anguish*.

**x** was pronounced *ks*, as in English *extra* (not *gz* as in *examine*, nor *kz* as in *exonerate*).

**ph** and **th** were used in words borrowed from Greek (e.g. *philosophia*, *theātrum*) to represent the Greek letters φ and θ. Properly speaking, each of these Latin consonants should have its normal sound — *ph* as in the English *loophole*, *th* as in *hothouse*. But *ph* is generally pronounced as *f* (a sound which it acquired only about the fifth century A.D.), and even *th* is often pronounced as in the English *thin*.

**IV. Accent.** A syllable is said to be accented either because it is pronounced at a higher musical pitch than the neighbouring syllables (pitch-accent or musical accent), or because, in pronouncing it, the breath is expelled with more force (stress-accent or 'exspiratory' accent). In practice, both kinds of accent are often used together, and it is not easy to demonstrate that any accent is purely a matter of pitch or purely a matter of dynamic stress. However, accentuation in various languages is easily recognizable as being mainly pitch-accent or mainly stress-accent. In Greek and some other Indo-European languages, and — it can be confidently assumed — in the parent Indo-European itself, it was mainly pitch-accent. In English and in German it is mainly stress-accent.

The nature of Latin accent is debatable. The ancient grammarians are unanimous in describing it as a pitch-accent. But there is reason to think that they can not have been altogether right. In some period preceding that of the earliest extant Latin literature, it is clear that the main accent of most Latin words, however many syllables they contained, was on the first syllable. And some of the changes which took place in the following — i.e. the unaccented — syllables suggest strongly that there was at any rate a considerable element of dynamic stress in this first-syllable accent. These changes are mainly of two kinds:

(1) *Weakening of vowels.* Unaccented short vowels in middle syllables were frequently weakened. Under certain conditions, *a, e, o, u* could all become *i*; *a* and *o* could also become *u*; and *a* could become *e*. Long vowels resisted weakening, but the diphthong *ae* became *ī*, and *au* became *ū*. These changes are especially common in verbs compounded with prepositions. Thus, *a'bigō* from *ab + agō*; *ob'sideō* from *ob + sedeō*; *ī'licō* for *in locō*; *ob'stipuī* for *obstupuī*; *sur'rupuī*, later *surripuī*, from *sub + rapuī*; *e'pistula* for *epistola* (from the Greek ἐπιστολή); *re'periō* from *re + pariō*; *oc'cīdō* from *ob + caedō*; *in'clūdō* from *in + claudō*.

(2) *Syncope.* In words of three or more syllables, a short vowel in the second syllable, immediately following the accented first syllable, was often 'syncopated' — i.e. the second syllable disappeared as a separate syllable, although it might leave traces behind. Thus *auceps*, 'bird-catcher', stands for *\*a'vi-cap-s* (formed from *avis* and *capiō*); *vīndēmia*, 'vintage', is for *\*vī'ni-dēmia* (from *vīnum* and *dēmō*); *quīndecim* is formed from *quīnque* and *decem*; *reppērī* is for *\*re'-peperī*, *rettulī* for *\*re'-tetulī*, the double consonants preserving a trace of the unsyncopated forms. This process continued to some extent in the historical period. Plautus wrote *balineum* ('bath', from the Greek βαλανεῖον), while a little later the word appears as *balneum*; similarly, Plautus' *columen*, 'summit', became *culmen*. It is difficult to imagine that syncope on such a large scale could take place except under the influence of an accent having a considerable stress-element.

As to the nature of the Latin accent in the literary period, there is no agreement. Some think it was, as the grammarians say it was[1], a pitch-accent (in which case, the stress-element which appears to have been present in a pre-literary period must have been merely a temporary phenomenon); some think it was a stress-accent; and some think that it may ave contained both elements, the stress-element being the more prominent in the popular speech, and the pitch-element in the consciously refined speech of the educated class, most of whom knew some Greek.

---

\* The asterisk indicates that these forms are not found in manuscripts or inscriptions, but are assumed to have preceded the extant forms.

[1] Cicero himself (*Orator* 58) calls the Latin accent *acuta vox*, which would most naturally describe a pitch-accent.

However that may be, there is general agreement that, if the accent was a stress-accent, it was a much less vigorous stress than is used in English or German, and that, in speaking Latin, quantity is more important than accent. Every effort should be made to observe the proper length of each syllable, and un-accented syllables, whether long or short, must never be slurred over as they often are in English.

About the *position* of the accent in historical times there is no doubt at all. Its position was bound up with the quantity of the penultimate syllable in any given word. The rules are very simple:

(a) Words of two syllables are accented on the first syllable: *dū'-rī, bi'-bit, Rō'ma, fe'-rās.*

(b) Words of more than two syllables are accented
   (i) on the penultimate syllable, if it is long: *lē-gā'-tus, hor-tā-ban'-tur, sol-li-ci-tā'-re;*
   (ii) on the antepenultimate syllable, if the penultimate is short: *cōn'-fe-rō, ha-bu'-e-ris, mi-se-ri-cor'-di-a.*

These rules apply to words lengthened by the addition of an enclitic — *-que, -ve, -ne, -ce*: thus, *vi-rum'-que, de-us'-ve, po-test'-ne, hū-ius'-ce.* The following are only apparent exceptions: *tan-tōn'* (= *tan-tō'-ne*), *dī-xīn'* (= *dī-xī'-ne*), *il-līc'* (= *il-lī'-ce*).

## V. Division of syllables. 1. A single consonant goes with the following vowel: *de-li-be-ra-bo.* (Notice that *qu, ch, ph, th* count as single consonants: *a-qua, e-chi-nus, e-le-phas, Ce-the-gus.*) This rule holds good for compounds such as *a-bi-go, i-ne-o,* although, in dictionaries and grammars, such words are often written *ab-igo, in-eo,* in order to show their etymology. Syllables ending with vowels are known as open syllables.

**2** (*a*). Two consonants coming together are generally divided between syllables: *col-lum, ma-gis-ter, om-nes, in-gen-ti-a.* The first of the two syllables in question, ending with one of the two consonants, is called a closed syllable.

(*b*). This rule is subject to an important exception. Consonant-groups consisting of a mute (*p, b, t, d, c, g*) or *f,* followed by *l* or *r,* are generally (always, in prose and in the earliest poetry) left undivided: thus, *a-pri-cus, a-gros, re-flu-o.* This does not apply, however, to compound words in which the first of the two consonants belongs to a preposition; in this case, the two consonants are *always* divided: e.g. *ab-rupi, ad-latus* (= *al-latus*), *sub-ripuit* (= *sur-ripuit*).

**3.** When three consonants come together, they are divided either 2 + 1 or 1 + 2: e.g. *sanc-tus*, *cons-tat*, *sump-se-ro*, *im-bris*, *e-ques-tris*. Four consonants are divided 2+2: *mons-trum*.

**VI. Length of syllables.** The length of syllables, which is important both for correct pronunciation and for the scanning of verse, is not the same thing as the length of the vowels contained in the syllables. In a given word a vowel is either short or long, and its length can not be altered by the presence of consonants. What consonants *can* do is to make *syllables* long. The following are the main rules for determining the length of syllables:

(1) *Open* syllables containing a short vowel are short: *dĕ-ōs*, *ă-mās*, *flō-rĕ*, and generally *pă-trēs*.

(2) *All* syllables containing a long vowel or a diphthong[1] are long: *gra-dū*, *pēs*, *lēx*, *rē-gis*, *ā-ēr*, *bo-nae*, *lau-dī*.

(3) *All* closed syllables — i.e. those which, according to the principles explained above, end with a consonant — are long, irrespective of the quantity of their vowels. In practice, this means that, when a vowel is followed by two or more consonants (excluding the particular consonant-groups mentioned above under Section V, **2** (*b*)), the syllable containing that vowel is long: e.g. *pan-dō*, *trac-tus*, *mis-sus*. The two consonants need not be both in the same word; the same principle applies when a word ending with a consonant is followed by a word beginning with a consonant: e.g. *dī-vi-di-mus mū-rōs*.

(4) When the consonant-groups mentioned under Section V, **2** (*b*) occur inside a word, the classical poets often treat them just like other consonant-groups — i.e. they divide them between syllables. Thus, the words ordinarily pronounced *vo'-lu-crēs*, *te'-ne-brae* can, if it suits a poet's convenience, be pronounced *vo-luc'-rēs*, *te-neb'-rae*. In this case the syllables *-luc-*, *-neb-* are closed, and are therefore long syllables. As explained above, in compounds such as *ab-ri-pi-ō*, *sub-le-vā-re* the consonants are *always* divided.

In scanning verse, it is usual to place a 'long' mark over all vowels in closed syllables (*pāndō*, *trāctus*, *mīssus*). Although this is a convenient way of indicating the length of the syllables, it is, strictly speaking, incorrect, because it involves marking as long many vowels which are in fact short. A better method would be to indicate the length of the syllables by placing a stroke over both the vowel and the consonant following it.

---

[1] The *ae* of *prae* is short when it is compounded with a word beginning with a vowel or *h*. (See above, Section III.).

Observe that the letter *h* does not count as a consonant, and has no effect on syllable length. On the other hand, syllables in which a vowel is followed by *x* or *z* are always long, these being regarded as double consonants (*x* stands for *cs*, *z* probably for *ds* or *dz*).

In compounds of *iaciō* the *a* is weakened into *i*, and the consonantal *i̯* is omitted in writing: thus, *abiciō, adiciō, coniciō, iniciō, subiciō*. The first syllable however is generally scanned as a closed, and therefore long, syllable, just as though the *i̯* were present; and the words were probably pronounced *ab-i̯iciō*, etc.

**VII. 'Hidden' quantities.** Since a closed syllable is necessarily scanned long, we often have no means of knowing the quantity of the vowel which it contains. Sometimes other forms of the word make it clear. Since the *e* of *necem* is short, it is a safe deduction that the *e* of *nex* is also short, although the syllable, being closed because of the *x*, is scanned long; conversely, since *ultrīcem* has *ī*, the *i* of *ultrīx* must also be long; similarly, *iūs* shows the quantity of the *u* in *iūstus*. Ancient authors give us some information on the subject. Cicero (*Orator* 159), for example, tells us that the vowels of *in* and *con* were always long before *s* or *f* (*īnsānus, īnfēlix, cōnsuēvit, cōnfēcit*), and this probably applies to all vowels before *ns* and *nf*. Some evidence is supplied by inscriptions, on which long vowels may be found indicated in various ways: e.g. PAASTORES (i.e. *pāstōrēs*); QVEINCTIVS (*Quīnctius*); QVA'RTO (*quārtō*). The evidence obtained from these sources can often be confirmed (though sometimes, unfortunately, it is contradicted) by an examination of the forms assumed by Latin words when they passed into Romance languages. In this dictionary, vowels in closed positions are marked long when it is fairly certain that they are long; but in many cases the quantity is uncertain or unknown.

# Notes on this Dictionary

I. **Vocabulary.** This dictionary presents a substantially complete vocabulary of the most widely read authors of classical Latin, down to A.D. 140. The following are the chief authors:

T. Maccius **Plautus**\* (c. 251 — 184 B.C.); P. **Terentius** Afer (Terence: ? 195 — 159); M. Tullius **Cicerō** (106 — 43); C. Iūlius **Caesar** (? 102 — 44); Cornēlius **Nepōs** (c. 99 — c. 24); T. **Lucrētius** Cārus (? 94 — ? c. 51); C. **Sallustius** Crispus (Sallust: 86 — c. 34); C. Valerius **Catullus** (c. 84 — c. 54); P. **Vergilius** Maro (Virgil: 70 — 19); Q. **Horātius** Flaccus (Horace: 65 — 8); T. **Līvius** (Livy: 59 B.C. — A.D. 17); Albius **Tibullus** (? c. 50 to 19 B.C.); Sex. **Propertius** (? c. 50 — after 16 B.C.); P. **Ovidius** Nāso (Ovid: 43 B.C. — A.D. ? 17); Phaedrus (c. 15 B.C. to A.D. c. 50); L. Annaeus **Seneca** (Seneca the Younger: c. 5 B.C. — A.D. 65); Ti. **Sīlius Italicus** (A.D. c. 26 — c. 101); A. **Persius** Flaccus (34 — 62); M. Annaeus **Lūcānus** (Lucan: 39 — 65); M. Valerius **Martiālis** (Martial: c. 40 — c. 104); P. Papinius **Stātius** (c. 45 — 96); D. Iūnius **Iuvenālis** (Juvenal: between 45 and 65 — after 127); Cornēlius **Tacitus** (c. 55 — after 115); C. **Valerius Flaccus** (? c. 60 — 92 or 93); C. **Plīnius** Caecilius Secundus (Pliny the Younger: 61 or 62 — before 114); C. **Suētōnius** Tranquillus (c. 69 — c. 140).

The following are not included: (1) some words which occur only in surviving fragments of lost works; (2) most of the words found only in inscriptions, in technical writers (e.g. Cato, Varro, Seneca the Elder, Columella, Pliny the Elder, Quintilian), or in Petronius; (3) a few rare technical terms occurring only in certain authors of the first and second centuries of the Christian era.

II. **Spelling.** The consonantal *i* is printed as *i*, and is treated as forming one letter with the vowel *i*. In deference, however, to the usage of most printed texts, consonantal *u* is printed as *v*, and is listed separately from the vowel *u* — although to the Romans they were one and the same letter.

---

\* This dictionary contains a more complete list of Plautine words than is to be found in other Latin-English dictionaries. Practically all the words whose authenticity is reasonably certain have been included — generally with the spelling given by W. M. Lindsay in his *Oxford Classical Text* of Plautus.

The standardization of spelling in most languages is comparatively recent, having resulted chiefly from the invention of printing and the compilation of full and accurate dictionaries. Since the entire life of the Latin language falls within a period when these things did not exist, it is not surprising that many words are variously spelt. It must be remembered, too, that classical Latin literature covers a period of some centuries, and that all the manuscripts we possess were written centuries later than the literature which they preserve.

Many of the variations in spelling are indicated in the dictionary by means of cross-references. The following are some of the most important:

(1) Compounds formed with prepositions: e.g. *ac-curro* or *ad-curro* (and similarly in words beginning with *f, g, l, n, p, r, s, t*); *a-scribo* or *ad-scribo*; *a-spicio* or *ad-spicio*; *a-sto* or *ad-sto*; *col-laudo* or *con-laudo*; *il-lido* or *in-lido* (and similarly in words beginning with *m* or *r*); *im-buo* or *in-buo*; *im-pello* or *in-pello*; *op-secro* or *ob-secro*; *op-tineo* or *ob-tineo*; *sum-mitto* or *sub-mitto* (and similarly in words beginning with *c, f, g, p, r*); *trans-duco* or *tra-duco* (and similarly in words beginning with *i, l, m, n, v*).

(2) Some words were spelt with or without an initial *h* — e.g. (*h*)*arena*, (*h*)*erus*, (*h*)*olus*, (*h*)*umerus*, (*h*)*umidus*.

(3) Many spellings varied in different periods:

    (a) The early Latin forms *servos, volnus, voltus* were later replaced by *servus, vulnus, vultus*.

    (b) Early spellings such as *equos, equom, antiquos, antiquom, aquola* were afterwards replaced by *ecus, ecum, anticus, anticum, acula*, and later still by *equus, equum, antiquus, antiquum, aquula* (most of these words are listed in the dictionary in the latest forms, because they are the forms most commonly found in printed texts).

    (c) The verbs *verro* and *verto* (and their compounds) were in early Latin spelt *vorro, vorto*; the same variation of spelling occurs in words derived from these verbs — e.g. *devorticulum, revorsio*.

    (d) Many words show a variation between *i* and *u*, the spellings with *u* being the older — e.g. *optimus, optumus*; *monimentum, monumentum*; *recipero, recupero*; *manifestus, manufestus*; *sacrifico, sacrufico*; *carnifex, carnufex*.

III. Many Latin participles are used as adjectives. Some of the more important are separately listed; some others will be found at the end of the articles on the verbs to which they belong.

To save space, regularly formed adverbs are not listed, unless they have meanings different from those of the corresponding adjectives.

In the alphabetical word-list (but not always in the course of the articles), long vowels are marked thus: ā. Short vowels (ă) are marked only when it is desired to call particular attention to their quantity.

The figures 1, 2, 3, 4, placed after verbs, indicate the conjugation to which they belong. The figures 2, 3 placed after adjectives, participles, or pronouns, indicate the number of different terminations which they have in the nominative singular.

## Abbreviations

| | | | |
|---|---|---|---|
| *abbr.* | abbreviation | *gram.* | grammatical |
| *abl.* | ablative | *hort.* | horticultural term |
| *acc.* | accusative | *imperat.* | imperative |
| *acc.c.inf.* | accusative with infinitive | *impers.* | impersonal(ly) |
| | | *indecl.* | indeclinable |
| *adj.* | adjective | *indef.* | indefinite |
| *adv.* | adverb | *indic.* | indicative |
| *alci* | *alicui* | *int.* | interjection |
| *alcis* | *alicuius* | *intens.* | intensive |
| *alqa* | *aliqua* | *interr(og).* | interrogative |
| *alqd* | *aliquid* | *intr(ans).* | intransitive |
| *alqm* | *aliquem* | *jur.* | juridical term |
| *alqo* | *aliquo* | *lit.* | literally |
| *alqos* | *aliquos* | *liter.* | literary term |
| *c.* | *circa* | *loc.* | locative |
| *cj.* | conjunction | *m* | masculine |
| *coll.* | collective | *med.* | medical term |
| *comp.* | comparative | *metaph.* | metaphorical |
| *dat.* | dative | *mil.* | military term |
| *depon.* | deponent | *mus.* | musical term |
| *dim(in).* | diminutive | *n(eut).* | neuter |
| *esp.* | especially | *nom(in).* | nominative |
| *exclam.* | exclamatory | *opp.* | opposed to |
| *f* | feminine | *P.* | passive |
| *fig.* | figuratively | *part.* | participle |
| *fut.* | future | *pers.* | personal |
| *gen.* | genitive, generally | *pf.*, *perf.* | perfect |
| *genit.* | genitive | *pl.* | plural |

| | | | |
|---|---|---|---|
| *poet.* | poetical | *subst.* | substantive (noun *or* pronoun) |
| *pol.* | political term | | |
| *pos.* | positive | *sup.* | supine |
| *poss.* | possessive | *superl.* | superlative |
| *prep.* | preposition | *thea.* | theatrical term |
| *pron.* | pronoun | *trans.* | transitive |
| *reflex.* | reflexive | *usu.* | usually |
| *rel(at).* | relative | *vb.* | verb |
| *rhet.* | rhetorical term | *v/i.* | verb intransitive |
| *sc.* | *scilicet* (that is to say) | *v/t.* | verb transitive |
| *sg.* | singular | *vulg.* | vulgar |
| *subj.* | subjunctive | *w.* | with |

⚔ military term　　⚓ nautical term　　⚘ botanical term

# Latin-English Dictionary

# A

**A** *abbr.* **1.** = **Aulus; 2.** = **antiquo** (*legem*) *or* **absolvo; 3. a. d.** = **ante diem; 4. a.u.c.** = **anno urbis conditae.**

**ā, āh** *int.* alas!, ah!

**ā, ab** (**abs te** = **a te**) *prep. with abl.* **1.** (*of space*) from, away from, out of, down from; distant from a point; at, on, in (*a tergo, a latere, a dextra parte*); **2.** (*of time*) after, from, since, since the time of; **3.** (*of relation*) by, from, of, on the part of, in respect of, on account of, in consequence of, from, against (*defendere*).

**abacus, ī,** *m* table; counting *or* play board.

**ā-baetō** 3 = **abito.**

**ab-aliēnātiō, ōnis** *f* alienation (*of property*).

**ab-aliēnō** 1 to alienate; **a)** to sell, withdraw (*rem*); to deprive (*alqm re*); **b)** to estrange (*ab alqo*).

**ab-avus, ī,** *m* great-great-grand-father; ancestor.

**ab-dicātiō, ōnis** *f* abdication, resignation.

**ab-dicō[1]** 1 to renounce; **a)** to disown, reject (*alqm*); **b)** to resign, abdicate (*se magistratu*).

**ab-dicō[2]** 3 to forbid; to disapprove of. [secret.]

**ab-ditus** 3 hidden, concealed,}

**ab-dō, didī, ditum** 3 **a)** to remove, put aside, withdraw; **b)** to hide, conceal, bury (*alqd in locum, in loco*): **c) se abdere** to hide oneself, withdraw, retire, escape; to plunge oneself (*in rem, in re, re*).

**ab-dōmen, inis** *n* belly, paunch.

**ab-dūcō** 3 to lead *or* conduct away from, take away, carry off, rob (*alqd ab, de, ex re, alqm ab alqo*): **a)** to separate, seduce, alienate, remove, draw away (*a re, ab alqo, ad alqm*): **b)** to reduce, degrade.

**ab-eō, iī, itum, īre** to go away *or* off (*ab alqo, de, ex, a re, in or ad alqd*); **a)** to resign, retire from (*an office, magistratu*); **b)** to come off, turn out, end; **c)** to pass away, disappear; **d)** to turn aside, deviate from (*ab re ad* or *in alqd*); **e)** to be transformed, changed into (*in alqd*): **f) abi** begone! be off!

**ab-equitō** 1 to ride away.

**ab-errātiō, ōnis** *f* escape, relief.

**ab-errō** 1 to wander, go astray, lose one's way (*ab* or *ex re*): to deviate, wander in thought, forget for a time (*a re ad alqd*).

**ab-hibeō** 2 to keep off.

**ab-hinc** *adv.* (*with acc., seldom abl.*) from this time, ago.

**ab-horrēns, tis** incongruous, inappropriate.

**ab-horreō, uī, —** 2 to shrink back from, abhor (*a re*); **a)** to be averse *or* disinclined to (*a re*); **b)** to vary *or* differ from, be inconsistent with, be opposed to (*a re*).

**āb-iciō** (*and* **ăb-**), **iēcī, iectum** 3 **1.** to throw *or* cast away *or* down; **a)** to squander; **b)** to fling away, give up, abandon; **2.** to strike to the ground; **se ābicere** to prostrate oneself (*ad pedes alcis*); to degrade, humble.

**ab-iectiō, ōnis** *f* dejection.

**ab-iectus** 3 cast away *or* down; **a)** dispirited, low; **b)** common, mean, contemptible; **c)** cowardly, despondent.

**abiegnus** 3 of fir-wood.

**abiēs, etis** *f* fir(-tree); **a)** ship; **b)** spear; **c)** writing-tablet.

**ab-igō, ēgī, āctum** 3 to drive away *or* off; **a)** to procure abortion; **b)** to banish, expel; **c)** to repel.

**ab-itiō, ōnis** *f* a going away.

**ā-bitō** 3 to go away.

**ab-itus, ūs** *m* a going away, departure; egress, outlet.

**ab-iūdicō** 1 to deprive of by judicial decree (*alqd ab alqo, alci alqd*).

**ab-iungō, iūnxī, iūnctum** 3 to unyoke, detach.

**ab-iūrō** 1 to abjure, deny by *or* on oath.

**ab-lēgātiō, ōnis** *f* a sending away.

**ab-lēgō** 1 to send away *or* off; **a)** to remove, banish; **b)** to dismiss, dislodge (⚔).

**ab-ligŭr(r)iŏ** 4 to squander.
**ab-locŏ** 1 to lease, farm out.
**ab-lūdŏ** 3 to differ from.
**ab-luŏ, luī, lūtum** 3 to wash (away), cleanse.
**ab-natŏ** 1 to swim away.
**ab-negŏ** 1 **a)** to deny, refuse; **b)** to disown, abnegate.
**ab-nepōs, pōtis** m, **ab-neptis, is** f great-great-grandson or -daughter.
**ab-noctŏ** 1 to sleep out.
**ab-normis, e** irregular.
**ab-nuŏ, nuī, nuitūrus** 3 to deny, refuse, decline (by a sign) (*alci alqd* or *de re*); **a)** to reject; **b)** to deny, disclaim (*alqd*; *acc. c. inf.*).
**ab-nūtŏ** 1 = abnuo.
**ab-oleŏ, ēvī, itum** 2 **a)** to destroy, annihilate, to do away with, abolish (*alqd*); **b)** to take away, remove.
**ab-olēscŏ, lēvī, —** 3 to disappear, vanish.
**ab-olitiŏ, ōnis** f abolition; amnesty.
**abolla, ae** f thick cloak.
**ab-ōminor** 1 **a)** to deprecate as an evil omen; **b)** to detest, execrate, abominate.
**ab-orior** 4, **ab-orīscor** 3 to fail, perish.
**ab-ortiŏ, ōnis** f, **ab-ortus, ūs** m miscarriage.
**ab-ortīvus** 3 prematurely born.
**ab-rādŏ, rāsī, rāsum** 3 to scrape or shave off (*alqd ab alqo*).
**ab-ripiŏ, ripuī, reptum** 3 to snatch away, tear off, drag off; **se abr.** to hurry away.
**ab-rogātiŏ, ōnis** f repeal (*of a law*).
**ab-rogŏ** 1 **a)** to repeal, annul, abrogate (*alqd*); **b)** to take away (*alci alqd*).
**abrotonum, ī,** n southernwood (*a plant*).
**ab-rumpŏ, rūpī, ruptum** 3 **1.** to break off or away; **2.** to tear, rend, burst; **a)** to sever, end; **b)** to violate.
**ab-ruptiŏ, ōnis** f a breaking off; divorce.
**ab-ruptus** 3 tòrn or broken off; precipitous, steep; **abruptum, ī** n precipice.
**abs-cēdŏ, cessī, cessum** 3 to go away, withdraw, retire (*ab alqo, ab, ex, de re*); **a)** to desist from, abandon, give up (*re*); **b)** to disappear, to be lost.

**abs-cessiŏ, ōnis** f a going away, diminution.
**abs-cessus, ūs** m a going away, departure, absence.
**abs-cīdŏ, cīdī, cīsum** 3 to cut off, hew off (*alci alqd*); **a)** to separate; **b)** to take away.
**ab-scindŏ** 3 to take or break off (*alqd a* or *de re*); **a)** to rip open (*venas*); **b)** to divide, separate; **c)** to hinder. [tous, steep; **b)** short.]
**abs-cīsus** 3 cut off; **a)** precipi-⌐
**abs-conditus** 3 concealed, hidden; **a)** secret; **b)** abstruse.
**abs-condŏ, con(di)dī, conditum** 3 to conceal, hide (*alqd in loco*); to make a secret of.
**ab-sēns, tis** absent, remote.
**ab-sentia, ae** f absence; want.
**ab-siliŏ** 4 to leap away.
**ab-similis, e** unlike.
**absinthium, ii** n wormwood.
**absis, īdis** f arch, vault.
**ab-sistŏ, stitī, —** 3 to go away, withdraw (*a re, re*); **a)** to desist from; **b)** leave off (*with inf.*).
**ab-solūtiŏ, ōnis** f **a)** acquittal; **b)** perfection.
**ab-solūtōrius** 3 belonging to acquittal.
**ab-solūtus** 3 **a)** complete, perfect; **b)** unconditional.
**ab-solvŏ** 3 to loosen; **a)** to set free, release (*alqd alqa re, ab alqo*); **b)** to acquit, absolve; **c)** to complete, finish, bring to an end; **d)** to relate.
**ab-sonus** 3 inharmonious, discordant (*a re* or *w. dat.*); incompatible.
**ab-sorbeŏ, uī, —** 2 to swallow down, devour.
**absque** *prep. with abl.* apart from, without.
**abs-tēmius** 3 abstemious, temperate.
**abs-tergeŏ** 2 **a)** to wipe off, dry by wiping; ⚓ to break off; **b)** to remove.
**abs-terreŏ** 2 to frighten away, drive away (*alqm a re*); to deter.
**abs-tinēns, tis** abstinent, continent; chaste.
**abs-tinentia, ae** f abstinence; integrity; self-denial, contentedness.
**abs-tineŏ, tinuī, (tentum)** 2 **a)** to keep off or back (*alqm* or *alqd a re* or *re*); **b)** to abstain, refrain (*re, a re*); **c)** to spare.
**ab-stŏ** 1 to stand at a distance.

**abs-trahō** 3 to draw *or* drag away *or* off *(alqm or alqd ab, de, ex re, ad or in alqd)*; **a)** to pull away, remove, detach *(alqd a re)*; **b)** to carry on *(ad alqd)*; **c)** to estrange.

**abs-trūdō** 3 to thrust away, conceal *(alqd in rem or in re)*.

**abs-trūsus** 3 **a)** concealed, hidden, secret; **b)** abstruse.

**ab-sum, ā-fuī (ā-futūrus) ab-esse 1.** to be away from, be absent *(a re)*; **a)** *(alci or ab alqo, a re)* to stand off, take no part, to be missing *or* wanting, to abandon, not to help; **b)** to be inconvenient, inconsistent with, different *(a re)*; **c)** to be free from *(a re)*; **2. haud multum (longe) abest, quin** it is not far from being the case that; **tantum abest, ut ... ut** so far is it from ... that.

**absūmēdō, inis** *f* a consuming.

**ab-sūmō** 3 **a)** to take away, diminish, consume; **b)** to waste; **c)** to destroy; **d)** to spend *(time)*. **P.** to perish, be killed.

**ab-surdus** 3 unmelodious, out of tune, harsh; **a)** foolish, silly, unreasonable; **b)** incongruous, inconsistent.

**ab-undāns, tis** overflowing; **a)** abundant, rich, abounding *(w. abl. or gen.)*; **b)** living in abundance, plentiful; **c)** overloaded.

**ab-undantia, ae** *f* abundance, plenty, fulness; an overcharging.

**ab-unde** *adv.* plentifully, more than enough, copiously.

**ab-undō** 1 to overflow, stream over; **a)** to abound *(re)*, be rich in; **b)** to enjoy.

**ab-ūsiō, ōnis** *f* incorrect use of a figure of speech.

**ab-usque** *(w. abl.)* = **usque ab.**

**ab-ūsus, ūs** *m* a using up.

**ab-ūtor** 3 **a)** to use up, consume, to use fully *(with abl.)*; **b)** to abuse, use wrongly, misapply, waste.

**ac,** *see* **atque.**

**acalanthis, idis** *f* goldfinch, thistle-finch.

**acanthus, ī** *m* *(and f)* **1.** bear's-breech *(a plant)*; **2.** gum arabic.

**a-capnus** 3 smokeless.

**ac-cantō** 1 to sing beside.

**ac-cēdō** 3 **1.** to go *or* come to, to approach, come near *(ad alqm, ad alqd, with acc., with dat.)*; **a)** to approach as an enemy *(ad alqd, with*

*dat.)*; **b)** to enter upon some work, to undertake *(ad alqd)*; **c)** to assent, agree *(ad alqm, ad alqd)*; **d)** to come near, be like *(ad alqd)*; **2.** to be added *(ad alqd, with dat.)*; **accēdit ut** *or* **quod** = moreover.

**ac-celerō** 1 **a)** to accelerate; **b)** *intr.* to hasten.

**ac-cendō, cendī, cēnsum** 3 to kindle, set on fire, light; **a)** to lighten up; **b)** to inflame, excite, arouse, stir, provoke; **c)** to increase.

**ac-cēnseō** 2 to reckon to.

**ac-cēnsus, ī** *m* **1.** apparitor, attendant of a magistrate; **2.** light-armed soldier.

**ac-centus, ūs** *m* accent.

**ac-ceptiō, ōnis** *f* a receiving, accepting.

**ac-ceptō** 1 to receive *(repeatedly)*.

**ac-ceptor, ōris** *m*, **ac-ceptrix, īcis** *f* receiver, approver.

**ac-ceptus** 3 welcome, pleasing, agreeable *(alci)*.

**ac-cersō** 3 = **arcesso.**

**ac-cessiō, ōnis** *f* **1.** a coming to, approach; audience, admission; **2.** increase, addition, appendage; progress.

**ac-cessus, ūs** *m* **1.** = **accessio**; **2. a)** entrance; **b)** inclination *(ad alqd)*.

**ac-cidō[1], cidī, — 3** *[cado]* **1.** to fall down, to fall to; **a)** to fall at the feet of; **b)** to reach, strike *(the senses)*; **2.** to come to pass, happen, take place; **accidit ut** it happens that; **a)** to occur; **b)** to fall out, turn out.

**ac-cidō[2], cidī, cīsum** 3 *[caedo]* to cut *or* hew at; **a)** to consume; **b)** to weaken, ruin.

**ac-cingō** 3 **1.** to gird to *or* on; **2.** to equip with *(abl.)*, arm, furnish, provide; **se acc.** *or* **P.** to gird oneself, make oneself ready, to be ready *(ad, seldom in rem, dat., acc., inf.)*.

**ac-ciō** 4 to call to, summon, send for; **accītus** outlandish.

**ac-cipiō, cēpī, ceptum** 3 **1.** to take, receive, get, accept *(alqd ab alqo)*; **acceptum, ī** *n* what is received *(money)*; **a)** *alci alqd acceptum referre* to enter to the credit, to give credit for; **b)** to suffer, bear; **c)** to admit, approve of; **2.** to receive as a guest; **a)** to entertain; **b)** to treat, deal with; **3.** to hear, perceive; **a)** to learn, understand; **b)** to feel; **c)** to take, interpret, explain (*in bonam partem, in omen, falsa pro veris*); **4.** a) to obtain; b) to suffer (*detrimentum, cladem*).

**accipiter, tris** *m* a hawk, bird of prey.

**accipitrīna, ae** *f* hawk's talon.

**ac-cītus, ūs** *m* summons, call.

**ac-clāmātiō, ōnis** *f* cry, shout.

**ac-clāmō 1** a) to call, cry, shout at; b) to name by acclamation.

**ac-clārō 1** to make clear, reveal.

**ac-clīnis, e** leaning on, inclined to (*dat.*).

**ac-clīnō 1** to lean on, incline to (*se in alqm* or *ad alqd*).

**ac-clīvis, e** *and* **-vus 3** inclined upwards, ascending, sloping.

**ac-clīvitās, ātis** *f* acclivity, ascent.

**ac-cognōscō 3** to recognize.

**ac-cola, ae** *m* one who dwells near, neighbour.

**ac-colō 3** to dwell near (*alqd*).

**ac-commodātiō, ōnis** *f* a) an adjusting, accommodation; b) complaisance.

**ac-commodātus 3** adapted, fitted, fit, suitable (*alci, ad alqd*).

**ac-commodō 1** to put on, apply, fit; a) to adjust, adapt (*alci alqd, ad alqd*); b) to attribute, ascribe; c) to make use of.

**ac-commodus 3** fit for (*with dat.*), suitable.

**ac-crēdō 3** to give credence.

**ac-crēscō 3** a) to grow, increase; b) to come as an addition.

**ac-crētiō, ōnis** *f* increase.

**ac-cubitiō, ōnis** *f*, **ac-cubitus, -us** *m* a lying at table.

**ac-cubō 1** to lie at, recline at table.

**ac-cubuō** *adv.* lying near.

**ac-cūdō 3** to coin.

**ac-cumbō, cubuī, cubitum 3** to lie down, to lie beside; to lie at table. [heaps up.]

**ac-cumulātor, ōris** *m* one who

**ac-cumulō 1** a) to heap up, amass, to give in abundance, to heap upon; b) to overwhelm (*alqm re*).

**ac-cūrātiō, ōnis** *f* accuracy, exactness, carefulness.

**ac-cūrātus 3** exact, careful; nice, precise.

**ac-cūrō 1** to do carefully.

**ac-currō, (cu)currī, cursum 3** to run to *or* up, to hasten to (*ad alqm, ad* or *in alqd*).

**ac-cursus, ūs** *m* a running to.

**accūsābilis, e** worthy of blame.

**accūsātiō, ōnis** *f* a) accusation, complaint; prosecution, indictment; b) bill of indictment.

**accūsātor, ōris** *m* accuser, prosecutor.

**accūsātōrius 3** like an accuser.

**accūsātrix, īcis** *f* female accuser.

**ac-cūsitō 1** to accuse.

**ac-cūsō 1** a) to accuse, prosecute (*alqm rei* or *de re*); b) to complain of, blame, reproach (*alqd, alqm de re, in re*; with *quod*).

**acer**[1], **eris** *n* maple(-tree).

**ācer**[2], **ācris, ācre** sharp, cutting, piercing; a) penetrating, pungent, biting, shrill; b) acute, sagacious, subtle; c) violent, energetic, active, ardent, spirited, brave; d) passionate, hot, fierce; e) severe, cruel.

**acerbitās, ātis** *f* bitterness, sourness; a) severity, harshness; b) bitterness, painfulness; c) misery, affliction, distress.

**acerbō 1** to make bitter *or* worse.

**acerbus 3** bitter, sour; a) raw, unripe; b) harsh, severe, rough, angry, morose; c) grievous, distressing.

**acernus 3** of maple (wood).

**acerra, ae** *f* casket for incense.

**acersecomēs, ae** *m* long-haired youth.

**acervālis, e** like a heap.

**acervātim** *adv.* by heaps, in heaps; to sum up, briefly.

**acervō 1** to heap up.

**acervus, ī** *m* heap, pile; a) mass, multitude; b) (*in logic*) argument by accumulation.

**acēscō, — 3** to become sour.

**acētābulum, ī** *n* (vinegar-)bowl, cup.

**acētum, ī** *n* sour wine, vinegar; wit.

**acidus 3** sour, sharp; disagreeable.

**aciēs, ēī** *f* **1.** sharp edge, point; a) keenness, piercing look, sight; b) eye, pupil; c) insight, acuteness; **2.** a) line of battle, battle-array; army; b) battle; c) battle in words, disputation.

**acina, ae** *f* = **acinus.**

**acīnacēs, is** *m* Persian sabre.

**acinus, ī** *m and* **-um, ī** *n* berry (*of the grape*).

**acipēnser, eris** *m* a sea-fish, sturgeon.

**aclys, ydis** *f* small javelin.

**acoenonoëtus 3** curmudgeonly (*or* stupid ?).

**aconītum** (*and* **-on**), **ī** *n* a poisonous plant, aconite; poison.

**acosmos** unadorned.

**ac-quiēscō 3 1.** to come to rest, to repose (*a re*); **a)** to die; **b)** to have peace; **2. a)** to be content with (*re*); **b)** to find comfort in.

**ac-quirō, quīsīvī, quīsītum 3 a)** to acquire in addition; **b)** to obtain, gain, win.

**acrāto-phorum, ī** *n* vessel for unmixed wine.

**acrēdula, ae** *f* a bird.

**ācriculus 3** irritable; hothead.

**ācrimōnia, ae** *f* sharpness; energy.

**ācriter** *adv. of* **ācer.**

**acroāma, atis** *n* **a)** anything heard with pleasure; **b)** musician, singer, reader, actor.

**acroāsis, is** *f* lecture.

**acta[1], ae** *f* sea-shore, beach.

**ācta[2], ōrum** *n*/*pl.* actions, deeds; **a)** public *or* legal acts, proceedings, ordinances; **b)** register, minutes, records; **c)** journal, gazette (*diurna*).

**āctiō, ōnis** *f* a doing, performing, action; **1.** enterprise, business; **a)** public action; **b)** office; **2. a)** a performing, rendering (*of an orator or actor*); **b)** action in a court of justice, suit at law, process; **c)** permission *or* right to bring an action.

**āctitō 1** to do *or* perform often.

**āctivus 3** active, practical.

**āctor, ōris** *m* **1.** driver, shepherd; **2.** agent, performer; **a)** manager, executor; **b)** accuser, plaintiff; **c)** actor, player.

**āctuāriola, ae** *f* a small boat.

**āctuārius[1]** **1** easily driven, swift; **āctuāria, ae** *f* swift-sailing vessel.

**āctuārius[2], i** *m* shorthand writer; registrar of documents.

**āctum, ī** *n*, *see* **acta[2], orum.**

**āctuōsus 3** active, full of life, effective; passionate.

**āctus, ūs** *m* **1.** a driving, motion, impulse; **a)** driving of cattle; **b)** right of way for driving cattle; **2. a)** movement of the body, gesture; **b)** recital, presentation of a play; **c)** division of a play, act. [rectly.]

**actūtum** *adv.* immediately, di-

**acula, ae** *f* = **aquula.**

**aculeātus 3** provided with prickles *or* stings, stinging; cunning.

**aculeus, ī** *m* sting, point; **a)** sagacity, cunning; **b)** sarcasm; **c)** spur, goad.

**acūmen, inis** *n* point, sharpness; spear-point; **a)** cunning, trickery; **b)** acuteness.

**acuō, uī, ūtum 3** to point, sharpen, whet; **a)** to exercise, practise; **b)** to spur, stimulate; **c)** to tease, grieve; **d)** to raise, enhance.

**acus, ūs** *f* needle; *acu pingere* to embroider.

**acūtulus 3** somewhat sharp, rather subtle.

**acūtus 3** pointed, sharpened, sharp; **a)** cutting, pungent, piercing, hot; **b)** acute, cunning, penetrating, sagacious; **c)** crafty, subtle.

**ad** *prep.* with *acc.* **1.** (*of space*) **a)** to, towards, in the direction of, to the vicinity of, against, before; **b)** up to (*ad unum omnes* all, to a man); **c)** at, near, close by; **2.** (*of time*) **a)** about, toward; till, to, even to, up to, *ad tempus* for some time, in due time, temporarily, for a certain time; **b)** at, on; **3.** (*of relation*) **a)** (*with numbers*) about, near to, almost; **b)** for the purpose of; **c)** with respect to; **d)** according to, in consequence of; **e)** compared with; **f)** besides, in addition to (*ad hoc, ad haec*).

**ad-āctiō, ōnis** *f* enforcing.

**ad-āctus, ūs** *m* a driving in.

**ad-aequē** *adv.* in like manner.

**ad-aequō 1** to make equal (*alqd alci rei*); **a)** to compare to, to put on a par (*alqd cum re*, or with *dat.*); **b)** to come near to (*with acc.*).

**ad-aestuō 1** to surge.

**adamantēus 3**, **-tinus 3** of steel; hard as steel.

**adamās, antis** *m* steel; adamant; hardness, inflexibility.

**ad-ambulō 1** to walk near.

**ad-amō 1** to fall in love with.

**ad-aperiō 4** to throw open, open fully.

**ad-apertilis, e** capable of being opened.

**ad-aptō 1** to adjust to.

**ad-aquō 1** to water.

**ad-auctus, ūs** *m* growth.

**ad-augeō 2** to increase.

**ad-augēscō 3** to begin to grow.

**ad-bibō, bibī, — 3** to drink (in); *fig.* to listen eagerly to.

**ad-bītō, —, — 3** to go near.

**adc...,** see **acc...**

**ad-decet** 2 it befits.

**ad-dēnseō** 2 to make compact.

**ad-dīcō** 3 **1.** to assent, to be propitious; **2.** a) to award, adjudge (in servitutem; alci alqd); **addictus, ī** m 3 debtor, bondsman; b) to knock down to (in auctions, alci alqd); c) to sell, make over; d) to dedicate, devote, consecrate (alci alqd); **se add.** to give oneself up to.

**ad-dictiō, ōnis** f an adjudging, award.                          [(alqd).]

**ad-discō** 3 to learn in addition

**additāmentum, ī** n addition, accession.

**ad-dō, didī, ditum** 3 to give or put to; **1.** a) to bring to, add to, increase; b) to impart, bestow; **2.** to add (in reckoning); to say or write in addition; **adde** moreover (alci alqd, in rem).

**ad-doceō** 2 to teach in addition.

**ad-dormīscō** 3 to fall asleep.

**ad-dubitō** 1 to incline to doubt, to hesitate (de re, in re); trans. to doubt.

**ad-dūcō** 3 **1.** to draw (tight) to oneself, to stretch, draw together; **2.** to lead to, bring to or along (alqd or in alqd), in iudicium or in ius to bring to justice; c) to bring to a certain condition or state of mind; b) to induce, prevail upon (alqm in or ad alqd, with ut); **P.** to be influenced, persuaded.

**ad-ductus** 3 drawn together, wrinkled; severe, stern.

**ad-edō, ēdī, ēsum** 3 to gnaw at; to consume.

**ad-ēmptiō, ōnis** f a taking away.

**ad-eō[1], iī, itum, īre** to go or come to or up, to approach (ad, in alqd, with acc.); a) to draw near; a) to accost, address, apply to; b) to travel to, to visit; c) to approach as an enemy, to attack; d) to undertake, enter on (alqd or ad alqd), take in hand; to undergo, incur (alqd).

**ad-eō[2]** adv. to that point, thus far, so far; a) so long; b) so much, to that degree; c) even, indeed, truly, just, precisely; **atque adeō** and what is more.

**adeps, ipis** m and f soft fat of animals.

**adeptiō, ōnis** f an obtaining.

**ad-equitō** 1 to ride up to (with dat. or ad alqm, in alqd).

**ad-errō** to wander or travel to (with dat.).

**ad-ēsuriō** 4 to hunger after.

**adf...,** see **aff...**

**adg...,** see **agg...**

**ad-haereō** 2 to cleave, stick or hang to, to adhere (with dat.); a) to border on, be near; b) to be attached, to cling to.

**ad-haerēscō, haesī, haesum** 3 to stick to, adhere; a) to cling to, remain (ad alqd or in re, with dat.); b) to stick fast, stop.

**ad-haesiō, ōnis** f a clinging to.

**ad-hibeō, uī, itum** 2 to bring to, hold to, lay on (alqd ad alqd or with dat.); a) to apply to, use, show, employ; b) to summon, call, invite (in convivium); to consult; c) to treat, handle.

**ad-hinniō** 4 to neigh to (alci); to crave, long for (ad alqd).

**ad-hōc** adv. = **adhuc.**

**ad-hortātiō, ōnis** f exhortation, encouragement.

**ad-hortātor, ōris** m one who exhorts.

**ad-hortor** 1 to exhort, encourage, rouse (alqm ad alqd or with ut, ne).

**ad-hūc** adv. **1.** thus far, hitherto; **2.** a) till now, up to the present time; b) as yet, still, even now; **3.** still more, besides, in addition.

**ad-iaceō** 2 to lie at, by the side of; to adjoin (ad alqd, with dat. or acc.).

**ād-iciō** (and ăd-), **iēcī, iectum** 3 **1.** to throw to, cast to, to direct to (alqd in, ad alqd, with dat.); **2.** to apply to, to add.

**ad-iectiō, ōnis** f, **ad-iectus, ūs** m addition.

**ad-igō, ēgī, āctum** 3 to drive to; a) to drive home; b) to thrust or push to (alqd in or ad alqd, in re, with dat.); c) to compel, urge (alqm ad alqd; with ut), alqm ad ius iurandum to bind by oath.

**ad-imō, ēmī, ēmptum** 3 to take away, to take from (alci alqd).

**adipātus** 3 a) fatty, greasy; **-ta, ōrum** n/pl. food made with or cooked in fat; b) turgid, bombastic.

**ad-ipīscor, adeptus sum** 3 to reach, come up to, overtake (alqm); to obtain, get, attain (alqd ab alqo).

**ad-itiālis, e** connected with an entry into office, inaugural.

**ad-itiō, ōnis** *f* a going to, approach.
**ad-itus, ūs** *m* a going to, approach (*ad rem, ad alqm*); **a)** entrance, entry, access (*in rem, ad alqm*); **b)** audience; admittance; **c)** beginning, commencement; **d)** possibility of entrance; opportunity, chance.
**ad-iūdicō** 1 to award, adjudge, adjudicate (*alci alqd*); to assign, ascribe.
**ad-iūmentum, ī** *n* help, assistance, support.
**ad-iūnctiō, ōnis** *f* a joining to, union (*rei ad alqd*); **a)** addition, connexion; **b)** restriction.
**ad-iūnctor, ōris** *m* one who adds.
**ad-iūnctus** 3 closely joined, connected, united; belonging to (*with dat.*); **adiūnctum, ī** *n* **a)** characteristic *or* essential attribute; **b)** accessory circumstance.
**ad-iungō** 3 to yoke, harness, *or* bind to (*alqd alci rei*); **a)** to join, connect, attach (*alqd ad alqd* or with *dat.*); **adiūnctum esse** to border on; **b)** to add, annex, associate (*alqd ad alqd* or with *dat.*); **c)** to win as a friend *or* ally; **d)** to unite; **e)** to give, attribute, confer; **f)** to direct to.
**ad-iūrō** 1 **a)** to swear in addition; **b)** to swear to; **c)** to confirm *or* promise by oath.
**adiūtābilis, e** helping.
**ad-iūtō** 1 to help, assist (*alqm*).
**adiūtor, ōris** *m* helper, assistant; **a)** aid, adjutant; **b)** deputy, secretary; **c)** secondary player (*in the theatre*).
**adiūtōrium, ī** *n* help.
**adiūtrīx, īcis** *f* female helper *or* assistant.
**ad-iuvō, iūvī, iūtum** 1 to help, assist, aid (*alqm in re, ad alqd*); **a)** to encourage, further (*alqd*); **b)** to be of good service, to avail, be useful.
**adl...**, *see* **all...**
**ad-mātūrō** 1 to hasten still more.
**ad-mētior** 4 to measure out to.
**ad-migrō** 1 to be added to.
**adminiculō** 1 to support by props.
**adminic(u)lum, ī** *n* prop, support, stake; **a)** aid, help; **b)** instrument.
**ad-minister, trī** *m* assistant, helper, servant, attendant; *fig.* tool.
**ad-ministra, ae** *f* female helper *or* assistant.
**ad-ministrātiō, ōnis** *f* help, aid;

**a)** management, direction; **b)** administration, government.
**ad-ministrātor, ōris** *m* manager, administrator.
**ad-ministrō** 1 to direct, administer, manage, execute (*alqd*).
**ad-mīrābilis, e a)** admirable, wonderful; **b)** strange, astonishing.
**ad-mīrābilitās, ātis** *f* admirableness.
**ad-mīrandus** 3 = **admirabilis.**
**ad-mīrātiō, ōnis** *f* **a)** admiration; **b)** wonder, astonishment.
**ad-mīrātor, ōris** *m* admirer.
**ad-mīror** 1 **a)** to admire; **b)** to wonder at, be astonished at (*alqd, in alqo, alqm in* or *de re*, with *acc. c. inf.* or *quod*).
**ad-misceō** 2 **1.** to mix with, admix; **a)** to add to by mixing (*alqd alci rei*); **b)** to join, mingle (*alqa re*); **2.** to implicate (*alqm ad alqd*).
**ad-missārius, ī** *m* stallion.
**ad-missiō, ōnis** *f* audience.
**ad-missum, ī** *n* trespass, crime.
**ad-missūra, ae** *f* breeding, breeding-stud.
**ad-mittō** 3 **1.** to let go, let loose, set in motion (*alqd in alqm*), to put to a gallop (*equum*); **2. a)** to admit (*alqm in* or *ad alqd*), to give audience; **b)** to give a share in; **c)** to allow, permit; **d)** to commit (*a crime*); **3.** to grant, to be propitious.
**ad-mixtiō, ōnis** *f* admixture.
**ad-moderātē** suitably.
**ad-moderor** 1 to moderate.
**ad-modum** *adv.* **a)** (*with numbers*) to full measure, at least; **b)** (*of degree*) wholly, entirely; completely, quite, altogether; *non* ~ not at all, ~ *nihil* nothing at all; **c)** (*in answers*) certainly.
**ad-moeniō** 4 to blockade.
**ad-mōlior** 4 to move *or* bring to.
**ad-moneō** 2 **1.** to remind, to call to mind (*alqm alcis rei* or *de re*; with *acc. c. inf.*); to put in mind of a debt; **2.** to admonish, warn (*alqm*); **a)** to advise, suggest; **b)** to urge, incite (*alqm, ut* or *ne*).
**ad-monitiō, ōnis** *f* **a)** a reminding; **b)** admonition, suggestion, exhortation.
**ad-monitor, ōris** *m* admonisher.
**ad-monitrix, īcis** *f* female admonisher.
**ad-monitum, ī** *n* = **admonitio.**

**ad-monitus, ūs** *m* = admonitio.

**ad-mordeō, momordī, morsum** 2 to gnaw at, bite at.

**ad-mōtiō, ōnis** *f* digitorum application (*to a stringed instrument*).

**ad-moveō** 2 to move *or* bring to *or* near (*alqm or alqd ad alqd or dat.*); **a)** to bring up, lead on, conduct; *se ad alqd* to draw near; **b)** *calcaria or stimulos* to give the spur, to goad; **c)** to bring up (*war-machines*); **d)** *fig.* to apply, direct to.

**ad-mūgiō** 4 to low *or* bellow to (*dat.*). [muring.]

**ad-murmurātiō, ōnis** *f* a mur-

**ad-murmurō** 1 to murmur.

**ad-mutilō** 1 to fleece.

**adn...,** *see* ann...

**ad-oleō**[1] 2 to smell.

**ad-oleō**[2]**, uī,** — 2 to pile up on *or* with; to burn.

**ad-olēscēns, tis** growing up, young; *subst.,* *see* adulescens.

**ad-olēscentia, ae** *f* = adulescentia.

**ad-olēscō, olēvī, (ultum)** 3 to grow up, grow; to be piled high.

**ad-operiō** 4 **a)** to cover, veil; **b)** to close, shut.

**ad-opīnor** 1 to conjecture.

**ad-optāticius** 3 adopted.

**ad-optātiō, ōnis** *f* = adoptio.

**ad-optiō, ōnis** *f* adoption.

**ad-optīvus** 3 belonging to adoption; adopted; *hort.* grafted.

**ad-optō** 1 **a)** to choose in addition, to select; **b)** to adopt; **c)** *hort.* to graft.

**ador, ōris** (*and* ŏris) *n* spelt.

**adōrea** (*or* -ia)**, ae** *f* praise, glory, reward of valour.

**adōreus** 3 of spelt.

**ad-orior** 4 to rise against; **a)** to attack, assail, assault (*alqm, alqd*); **b)** to address (*with entreaties*); **c)** to undertake, attempt (*alqd; inf.*).

**ad-ōrnō** 1 **a)** to fit out, equip, prepare, provide; **b)** to adorn, embellish.

**ad-ōrō** 1 to speak to; **a)** to implore, entreat; **b)** to reverence, worship; **c)** to ask for.

**adp...,** *see* app...; **adqu...,** *see* acqu...; **adr...,** *see* arr...

**ad-rādō** 3 to scrape at; to cut.

**ads..., adsc...; adsp..., adstt..., ad-...,** *see* ass..., asc..., asp..., ast..., att...

**ad-sum,** *see* as-sum.

**adūlātiō, ōnis** *f* a fawning; flattery.

**adūlātor, ōris** *m* flatterer; servile person.

**adūlātōrius** 3 flattering, cringing.

**adulēscēns, entis** *m* young man, youth; *f* young woman, maiden.

**adulēscentia, ae** *f* youth; young people.

**adulēscentulus, ī** *m,* **ula, ae** *f* a young man, woman.

**adūlō** 1 to fawn; to wipe off.

**ad-ūlor** 1 to fawn on (*alqm*); to flatter, cringe, to revere in a servile manner (*alqm, alci*).

**adulter, erī** *m* **a)** adulterous; adulterer; **b)** gallant, paramour.

**adultera, ae** *f* adulteress.

**adulterīnus** 3 forged, counterfeit, false, not genuine.

**adulterium, ī** *n* adultery.

**adulterō** 1 **a)** to commit adultery; **b)** to falsify, corrupt; **c)** to seduce to adultery.

**adultus** 3 grown up, adult, mature.

**adumbrātim** in outline.

**adumbrātiō, ōnis** *f* sketch, outline.

**ad-umbrō** 1 to sketch, to shade; **a)** to represent vaguely; **b)** to imitate; **ad-umbrātus** 3 sketched, shadowed; **a)** vague, dim, imperfect; **b)** unreal, feigned, vain, fictitious.

**ad-uncitās, ātis** *f* hooked shape.

**ad-uncus** 3 bent inwards, hooked.

**ad-ūnō** 1 to unite.

**ad-urgeō** 2 to press to; to pursue eagerly.

**ad-ūrō, ussī, ustum** 3 to set on fire, kindle; **a)** to scorch, singe; **b)** to nip, freeze.

**ad-usque** *prep.* with *acc.* = usque ad; *adv.* all the way.

**advectīcius** 3 imported, foreign.

**ad-vectō** 1 to convey continually.

**ad-vectus, ūs** *m* a conveying.

**ad-vehō, vexī, vectum** 3 to carry *or* bring to a place; **P.** to be brought, conveyed, borne to; to arrive, land.

**ad-vēlō** 1 to veil; to crown.

**ad-vena, ae** *m* stranger, foreigner, immigrant; novice.

**ad-veneror** 1 to honour.

**ad-veniō** 4 to come to, to arrive at (*in locum, ad alqd*); **a)** to approach, appear; **b)** to happen (*ad alqm*).

**adventīcius** 3 coming in addition; foreign, strange.

**adventō** 1 to approach, advance, draw near.

**ad-ventor, ōris** *m* visitor, guest.

**adventus, ūs** *m* approach, arrival.

**ad-verberō** 1 to strike.

**adversārius 1.** *adj.* 3 opposed, contrary, hostile, noxious (*with dat.*); **2.** a) ~ ī *m* opponent, adversary, enemy, antagonist; b) **adversāria, ōrum** *n/pl.* arguments of an opponent; memoranda; notebook.

**ad-versātrīx, īcis** *f* female adversary.

**ad-versiō, ōnis** *f* direction.

**ad-versitor, ōris** *m* slave who goes to meet his master.

**ad-versō** 1 *animum* to watch.

**ad-versor** 1 to resist, oppose, withstand (*with dat.* or *quominus*).

**ad-versus¹** 3 turned towards, fronting, opposite, in front; **dentes** front teeth; (*vulnus*) on the breast; **in adversum os** full in the face; **flumine adverso** up stream; **ex adverso** over against; **in adversum** against; a) opposed, hostile; **adverso senatu** against the will of the senate; b) odious; unfavourable, unpropitious (*with dat.*) — *subst.* **adversa, ōrum** *n/pl.* a) misfortune, calamity, disaster; b) the contrary, contrast.

**ad-versus²** *or* **-sum 1.** *adv.* in the opposite direction, to meet; **2.** *prep.* with *acc.* a) opposite, over against, towards; b) in respect of; contrary to; compared with.

**ad-vertō** 3 to turn to *or* towards (*alqd in alqd*); a) to steer, land; b) **animum advertere** to direct one's attention to, to heed, notice (*ad alqd,* with *acc.* or *dat.*); to perceive (*alqd; acc. c. inf.*); to punish (*in alqm*); c) to draw *or* direct to oneself (*omnium oculos, odia*).

**ad-vespeiāscit, āvit,** — 3 evening approaches.

**ad-vigilō** 1 to watch, guard.

**ad-vocātiō, ōnis** *f* 1. a summoning to advise; a) legal advice; b) the bar, body of advocates; 2. delay for consultation.

**ad-vocātus, ī** *m* a) one who is called to aid in a trial; b) advocate, witness.

**ad-vocō** 1 to call, summon (*alqm in, ad alqd*); a) to call as an adviser *or* witness; b) to call to aid, ask for help (*with acc.*).

**ad-volātus, ūs** *m* a flying to.

**ad-volō** 1 to fly to *or* towards; to hasten towards (*ad, in alqd*).

**ad-volvō** 3 to roll to *or* towards; **P.** to throw oneself at the feet of, to fall prostrate before.

**ad-vors-, -vort-** = **ad-vers-, -vert-.**

**adytum, ī** *n* the holiest part of a temple, inmost recess (*generally in pl.*).

**aedēs** (*or* **aedis**), **is** *f* 1. a) room, chamber, apartment; b) temple, chapel, sanctuary; 2. *pl.* a dwelling, house, habitation.

**aedicula, ae** *f* small building, temple, *or* room.

**aedificātiō, ōnis** *f* a) act of building; b) building, edifice.

**aedificātiuncula, ae** *f* a small building.

**aedificātor, ōris** *m* builder, architect; one who is fond of building.

**aedificium, ī** *n* building, structure, edifice.

**aedi-ficō** 1 to build, erect, construct, establish; to build houses.

**aedīlicius** 3 of an aedile; *subst.* ex--aedile.

**aedīlis, is** *m* aedile, superintendent of public works.

**aedīlitās, ātis** *f* office of an aedile.

**aedis,** *see* **aedes.**

**aedituus, ī, aedituēns, entis** *m* guardian of a temple.

**aēdōn, onis** *f* nightingale.

**aeger, gra, grum** sick, ill, suffering; a) feeble, weak, frail; b) troubled, dejected, dissatisfied; c) painful, sad.                                   [aegis.]

**aegis, idis** *f* shield of Jupiter,⌋

**aegi-sonus** 3 sounding with the aegis.

**aegocerōs, ōtis** (and **-os, ī**) *m* the wild goat (*sign of the zodiac*).

**aegrē** *adv.* **1.** painfully, distressingly, annoyingly; **aegre facere alci** to mortify, grieve; **aegre ferre** to be grieved, distressed (*alqd*); **2.** a) with difficulty, hardly, scarcely; b) reluctantly, unwillingly.

**aegreō,** —, — 2 to be sick.

**aegrēscō,** —, — 3 to fall sick; a) to become worse; b) to be grieved, mortified.

**aegrimōnia, ae** *f* sorrow, distress, grief.

**aegritūdō, inis** *f* a) sickness; b) grief, uneasiness.

**aegror, ōris** *m* illness.

**aegrōtātiō, ōnis** *f* sickness.

**aegrōtō 1** to be sick *or* ill; to suffer.

**aegrōtus 3** sick, ill, suffering.

**aelinos, ī** *m* dirge.

**aelūrus, ī** *m* cat.

**aemulātiō, ōnis** *f* a) emulation, rivalry; b) envy, jealousy.

**aemulātor, ōris** *m* rival; imitator.

**aemulātus, ūs** *m* = **aemulatio.**

**aemulor 1** a) to strive after, emulate, vie with, rival (*with acc.*); b) to envy (*alci*).

**aemulus 3** a) striving after, vying with (*alci*); imitator (*alcis*); b) envious, jealous.

**aēneus 3** of copper, bronze(-coloured); hard as metal.

**aenigma, atis** *n* riddle, mystery, allegory, enigma.

**aēni-pēs, edis** bronze-footed.

**aēnus 3** = **aēneus; aēnum, ī** *n* bronze vessel.

**aequābilis, e** uniform, similar, equal; equable; impartial, just.

**aequābilitās, ātis** *f* equality, uniformity; impartiality.

**aequaevus 3** of equal age.

**aequālis, e** like, equal; **1.** even, level; **2.** a) uniform, steady; b) equal in size, growth, *or* height; c) equal in age, coeval, contemporary (*alcis*).

**aequālitās, ātis** *f* a) equality (*of age, of rights*); b) evenness.

**aequanimitās, ātis** *f* fairness, impartiality; calmness, kindness.

**aequātiō, ōnis** *f* a making equal; equal distribution.

**aequē** *adv.* equally, in like manner; a) fairly, justly; b) **aeque ... ac** as ... as, just as, equally with.

**aequi-lībritās, ātis** *f* equipoise.

**aequi-noctiālis, e** relating to the equinox, equinoctial.

**aequi-noctium, ī** *n* equinox.

**aequiperābilis, e** comparable.

**aequi-perō 1** a) to compare (*alqd alci*); b) to equal, rival (*with acc.*).

**aequitās, ātis** *f* uniformity, evenness; a) equanimity, patience, calmness; b) impartiality, fairness, justice; c) equality of rights.

**aequō 1 1.** to make even, level, smooth; to make straight; **2.** to make equal (*alqd alci rei*); **solo aequare** to level with the ground; a) to distribute equally; b) to compare (*alqd cum re* or *dat.*); **se aequare** *or* **P.** to become equal, come up to, reach (*with acc.*).

**aequor, oris** *n* even surface, level; a) flat field, plain; b) surface of the sea, sea, ocean.

**aequoreus 3** belonging to the sea.

**aequus 3** equal; **1.** even, level; *subst.* **aequum, ī** *n* level ground, plain; a) favourable, advantageous; b) friendly, propitious; **aequi** friends; **2.** equal in size *or* height; indecisive; a) even-tempered, calm; b) impartial, fair; **aequum est** it is just; **aequi boni(que) facere** to be content with; *subst.* **aequum, ī** *n* equity, equal degree *or* right; fairness, what is right; **ex aequo** equitably (*also* = *aeque*); **in aequo** in the same condition.

**āēr, āeris** *m* a) air, atmosphere; b) mist, cloud.

**aerārius 3 1.** of copper *or* bronze; a) relating to mining; b) belonging to money, pecuniary; **tribunus aerārius** paymaster; **2.** *subst.* a) **aerārius, ī** *m* citizen of the lowest class; b) **aerāria, ae** *f* copper-mine; c) **aerārium, ī** *n* public treasury, public funds, finances.

**aerātus 3** covered *or* fitted with brass; supplied with money, rich.

**aereus 3** = **aēneus; = aeratus.**

**aeri-fer 3** bearing bronze cymbals.

**aeri-pēs, pedis** brazen-footed.

**aeri-sonus 3** sounding with bronze.

**āērius 3** belonging to the air, aerial; lofty, high.

**aerūgō, inis** *f* rust of copper, verdigris; a) envy; b) avarice.

**aerumna, ae** *f* toil, hardship, suffering.

**aerumnōsus 3, aerumnābilis, e** full of hardship, troubled, miserable.

**aes, aeris** *n* **1.** copper, bronze, brass; **2.** anything made of copper *or* bronze; a) copper vessel, image, statue, tablet; b) money, coin, the as; c) meanś, fortune; **aes alienum** another's money, debt; d) pay, fee, salary.

**aesculētum, ī** *n* oak-wood *or* -forest.

**aesculeus 3** of the oak.

**aesculus, ī** *f* the winter oak.

**aestās, ātis** f summer; summer heat or weather; year.

**aesti-fer** 3 heat-bringing.

**aestimābilis, e** valuable.

**aestimātiō, ōnis** f 1. an appraising, valuation, estimation; assessment of damages, fine; 2. true value, esteem.

**aestimātor, ōris** m appraiser; one who values a thing according to its worth.

**aestimō** 1 1. to appraise, estimate (alqd, with gen. or abl. of value), to assess a penalty; 2. to value, esteem, judge (alqd, re, ex re).

**aestivō** 1 to pass the summer.

**aestivus** 3 relating to summer, of summer, summer-like; **aestiva, ōrum** n/pl. a) summer camp; b) campaign; c) summer pastures, cattle in summer pastures; d) summer-time.

**aestuārium, ī** n a) lagoon, shallow water; b) inlet of the sea, creek, bay.

**aestumō** = aestimo.

**aestuō** 1 1. to blaze; to burn, glow, be hot, boil, seethe; 2. to swell, heave; a) to be agitated, excited; b) to hesitate, be in doubt.

**aestuōsus** 3 a) glowing, hot; b) surging, agitated.

**aestus, ūs** m 1. fire, heat, glow, sultriness; summer heat, fever; 2. a raging, seething; a) tide, surge, swell; b) passion, rage, fervour; c) unrest, anxiety, hesitation.

**aetās, ātis** f 1. age, life of man, life-time; a) **aetas prima** childhood, youth; b) **aetas constans, media, confirmata** manhood, middle age; c) **aetas extrema, exacta** old age; d) men of a certain age; 2. time of life, generation; time at which a person lives; 3. age of the world.

**aetātula, ae** f youthful age.

**aeternitās, ātis** f eternity, endless duration, immortality.

**aeternō** 1 to immortalize.

**aeternus** 3 eternal; a) immortal, imperishable; b) everlasting, permanent.

**aethēr, eris** m the upper air, sky, heaven; heavenly things, upper world.

**aetherius** 3 relating to the upper air; a) etherial, celestial, heavenly; b) airy; c) of the upper world.

**aethra, ae** f the clear sky.

**aevitās, ātis** f = aetas.

**aevum, ī** n (aevus, ī m) 1. eternity; 2. = aetas.

**af-fābilis, e** affable, approach-/ **af-fābilitās, ātis** f affability. [able.\

**af-fabrē** adv. cunningly, in a workmanlike manner.

**af-fatim** adv. sufficiently, enough, abundantly (with gen.).

**af-fātus, ūs** m a speaking to, address.

**affectātiō, ōnis** f a striving, eager desire.

**affectātor, ōris** m one who strives after a thing.

**affectiō, ōnis** f; a) disposition, condition, state of mind; b) inclination, partiality, predilection; c) influence.

**affectō** 1 to grasp (alqd); to pursue, aim at, strive after, to enter on; a) = afficere; b) to try to get, to win over; to influence; c) to affect, feign, simulate.

**affectus¹, ūs** m condition, state, disposition; a) passion, feeling, emotion; b) affection.

**affectus²** 3 1. furnished, provided, gifted, endowed (with abl.); disposed, inclined, affected; 2. indisposed, impaired, weakened, disordered; ending.

**af-ferō, attuli, allātum, afferre** to carry, bring, convey to (alci alqd); **manus** to lay hands on, to do violence (with dat.); **manus sibi** to commit suicide; a) to bring, carry; b) to report, announce, relate (alqd ad alqm or alci, de re, with acc. c. inf.); c) to produce; allege; to cause (alci alqd); d) to contribute, help, assist, be of use (alqd ad alqd); e) to bring as an addition.

**af-ficiō, fēci, fectum** 3 to treat in a certain way (alqm or alqd alqa re), **vulnere** to wound, **poena** to punish, **iniuria** to outrage, **honore** to honour, **timore** to frighten, **laude** to praise, **muneribus** to present with, **praemio** to reward, **supplicio** to behead, **dolore** to give pain; P. **vulnere affici** to be wounded; **morbo** to fall sick; a) to influence, affect, dispose; b) to weaken, impair, afflict, attack, oppress.

**af-fīgō** 3 to fasten to, attach, affix (alqd ad alqd or with dat.); to pin fast; to imprint (memoriae).

**af-fingō** 3 to form in addition (*alci alqd*); to feign *or* invent in, addition to add falsely.

**af-fīnis, e** adjoining, bordering on, neighbouring (*alci*); **a)** connected with, privy to, accessory to; **b)** related by marriage (brother-, sister-, father-in-law).

**af-fīnitās, ātis** *f* **a)** relationship by marriage; **b)** neighbourhood.

**af-firmātē** *adv.* with positive assurance.

**af-firmātiō, ōnis** *f* affirmation, solemn assurance.

**af-firmō** 1 to strengthen; **a)** to confirm, assert; **b)** to assure.

**af-flātus, ūs** *m* a blowing *or* breathing on; **a)** blast, breath; **b)** inspiration.

**af-fleō** 2 to weep at.

**af-flictātiō, ōnis** *f* pain, torture.

**af-flictō** 1 to beat *or* strike repeatedly; **a)** to damage, trouble, harass, torment; **b)** to afflict, grieve.

**af-flictor, ōris** *m* a damager, destroyer.

**af-flictus** 3 **1.** beaten, shattered, damaged; **a)** cast down, miserable, wretched, distressed; **b)** discouraged, spiritless; **c)** vile, contemptible.

**af-flīgō, xī, ctum** 3 to strike *or* dash against; **a)** to strike to the ground, throw down; **b)** to damage, shatter, injure, ruin, distress; **c)** to weaken, discourage, humiliate; **d)** to dash to pieces.

**af-flō** 1 **1. a)** to blow *or* breathe on; to scorch; **b)** to impart by breathing (*alci alqd*); **2.** *intr. and* **P.** to blow (*propitiously*).

**af-fluēns, tis a)** affluent, abounding, abundant, plentiful; **b)** provided copiously, rich, full of.

**af-fluentia, ae** *f* abundance, plenty.

**af-fluō** 3 to flow to *or* towards; **a)** to come imperceptibly, to glide on; **b)** to flow with, abound (*with abl.*).

**af-for** 1 to accost, address, implore (*alqm*).

**af-fore, af-forem,** *see* **assum.**

**af-formīdō** 1 to be in fear.

**af-frangō** 3 to dash *or* press against.

**af-fremō** 3 to roar *or* murmur at.

**af-fricō** 1 to rub on.

**af-fulgeō** 2 to shine against *or* upon (*alci*); to beam, glitter, appear bright.

**af-fundō** 3 **a)** to pour into (*alqd alci rei*); **P.** to be washed by, to be spread out; **b)** to add; **affūsus** prostrate.

**af-futūrus** 3, *see* **assum.**

**afluō = affluō.**

**ā-fore, ā-forem,** *see* **absum.**

**agāsō, ōnis** *m* groom, hostler; churl.

**agellus, ī** *m* little field *or* estate.

**agēma, atis** *n* Macedonian horseguards.

**ager, grī** *m* field, arable land, estate; open *or* flat country; **a)** territory, district; **b) in agrum** in depth (*opp. in breadth*).

**ā-gerō** (?) 3 to take *or* carry away.

**ag-gemō** 3 to groan *or* sigh at.

**agger, eris** *m* **1.** heap, mound, pile, rubbish, soil; **2. a)** rampart, dike, dam, mole; **b)** fortification, wall; **c)** rampart marking a boundary; **d)** causeway constructed with logs; **e)** elevation, bank of a river; **f)** funeral pile.

**aggerō**[1] 1 to form a mound, to heap up; to pile up, amass, increase.

**ag-gerō**[2] 3 **a)** to carry, bring, *or* convey to; **b)** to bring forward, utter.

**ag-gerō**[3] **= agero.**

**ag-gestus, ūs** *m* a bringing to, accumulation.

**ag-glomerō** 1 to attach.

**ag-glūtinō** 1 to glue to, stick on.

**ag-gravēscō, —, —** 3 to become worse.

**ag-gravō** 1 **a)** to make heavier *or* worse; **b)** to molest, oppress.

**ag-gredior, gressus sum** 3 to step *or* go to, to approach (*ad alqm or alqm*); **a)** to apply to, address (*with acc.*); **b)** to attack, assail, fall upon (*alqm*); **c)** to begin, undertake, attempt, try (*ad alqd, alqd, with inf.*).

**ag-gregō** 1 to add to, join to (*alqm alci, in or ad alqd*); **se a.** to attach oneself to.

**ag-gressiō, ōnis** *f* attack (*on a subject*), introduction.

**agilis, e** easily moved; **a)** quick, nimble; **b)** active, busy, lively.

**agilitās, ātis** *f* quickness, agility.

**agitābilis, e** easily moved.

**agitātiō, ōnis** *f* motion, movement; **a)** agitation; pursuit, management; **b)** activity.

**agitātor, ōris** *m* driver; charioteer.

**agitō** 1 to set in violent *or* constant motion, to drive about *or* onward, to drive, chase, hunt, shake, toss up and down; **1. a)** to incite, spur, pursue; **b)** to trouble, vex; to ridicule; **c)** to stir, rouse, disturb; **2.** to practise, exercise, prosecute, occupy oneself with; **a)** to celebrate, keep (*a festival*); **b)** to pass (*time*), to live; **c)** to discuss, debate (*alqd, de re*); **d)** to consider, think, deliberate (*alqd, alqd animo, in or cum animo, secum*).

**agmen, inis** *n* **1.** a driving, movement, stream; **2.** what is driven *or* moved; **a)** band, throng, crowd, troop, multitude; **b)** army on the march, column, phalanx, army in line of battle; ∼ **primum** vanguard, ∼**medium** the centre, ∼ **extremum** *or* **novissimum** rear; **c)** war, battle.

**agna, ae** *f* ewe-lamb.

**agnālia, ium** *n/pl.* feast of the ewes.

**a-gnāscor, agnātus sum** 3 to be born in addition.

**a-gnātiō, ōnis** *f* blood-relationship on the father's side.

**a-gnātus** 3 born after; related on the father's side.

**agnellus, ī** *m* little lamb.

**agnīnus** 3 of a lamb; **agnīna** (*caro*) lamb's flesh.

**agnitiō, ōnis** *f* recognition.

**a-gnōscō, agnōvī, agnitum** 3 **a)** to perceive, observe (*alqd or acc. c. inf.*); **b)** to recognize, acknowledge, identify, approve (with *acc.*, with *acc. c. inf.*).

**agnus, ī** *m* lamb.

**agō, ēgī, āctum** 3 **1.** to drive, lead, conduct, chase, hunt, urge; to set in motion (**P.** to go, march); **a)** to drive away, rob, **ferre atque agere** to rob and plunder; **b)** to accuse, arraign, impeach, *alqm reum* to bring an action against; **c)** to impel, excite, prompt (*alqm ad alqd*); **se agere** to behave, bear oneself; **2.** to put in motion (*things*); **a)** to drive, lead, direct, draw, steer, push, pull, advance; to strike (*root*); **b)** to construct, build (*roads*); **animam agere** to expire; **c)** to pass, spend, live; **3.** to pursue, practise, undertake, act, perform, execute, transact, manage; **aliquid agere** to be active *or* busy, **nihil agere** to be inactive, idle, **quid agis?** how are you?, **id agere ut (ne)** to aim at,

take care, to have as one's purpose; **bene mecum agitur** I am well; **actum est de me** I am done for; **res agitur** is at stake, is concerned; **4. a)** to keep (*a festival*), observe, celebrate; **b)** to act (*a play or part*), to deliver, declaim; **c) gratias agere** to thank, give thanks; **d)** to treat, consider, discuss, speak, transact (*alqd cum alqo*); (*causam*) **agere** to plead, conduct a lawsuit; **e)** to live, dwell, pass time, do service; *adj.* **agēns** effective, powerful; **age, agite** well then! come!

**agōn, ōnis** *m* contest, combat in the public games.

**agorā-nomus, ī** *m* inspector of the market.

**agrārius** 3 relating to land *or* fields *or* country; **lex** law for the division of land; **triumvir** officer for the division of land; *subst.* **agrāriī, ōrum** *m/pl.* the agrarian party.

**agrestis, e** living in the fields *or* country; **a)** wild, savage; **b)** rustic, uncultivated, boorish, clownish, brutish; **c)** agricultural; *m* countryman, peasant.

**agri-cola, ae** *m* tiller of the field, husbandman, farmer.

**agri-cultiō, -cultor, -cultūra,** *see* **ager** *and* **cultiō** *etc.*

**agri-peta, ae** *m* colonist, settler.

**āh, ā** *int.* ah! alas!

**ahēneus, ahēnus = aēneus, aēnus.**

**ai** *int.* alas!

**ain' = aisne,** *see* **aio.**

**āiō 1.** to say yes, affirm, assent; **āiēns, tis** affirmative; **2.** to assert, say, state, aver; **ain' = aisne** indeed? really? is it possible?, **quid ais** what is your opinion?

**āla, ae** *f* **a)** wing (*of a bird or army*); **b)** armpit, shoulder; **c)** squadron, troop (*of cavalry*).

**alabaster, trī** *m*, **-trum, ī** *n* unguent-flask.

**alacer, cris, cre** lively, quick, brisk, eager, excited, active, cheerful.

**alacritās, ātis** *f* liveliness, quickness, eagerness, cheerfulness, ardour.                    [on the cheek.]

**alapa, ae** *f* box on the ear, slap

**ālārius** 3, **ālāris, e** belonging to the wing of an army; *pl.* **ālāriī, ōrum** *m/pl.* auxiliary troops.

**ālātus** 3 winged.

**alauda, ae** *f* lark.

**alāzōn, onis** *m* braggart, boaster.

**albātus** 3 clothed in white.

**albeō, uī,** — 2 to be white *or* pale.

**albēscō, buī,** — 3 to become white; to dawn.

**albi-capillus** 3 white-haired.

**albicō** 1 to be white.

**albidus** 3, **albulus** 3 white.

**albitūdō, inis** *f* whiteness.

**albus** 3 white (*without lustre*); a) clothed in white; b) pale, grey; c) bright, fortunate, propitious; *subst.* **album, ī** *n* white colour; white tablet (*for advertisements*); register, list.

**alcēdō, inis** *f* kingfisher.

**alcēdōnea, ōrum** *n/pl.* winter calm.

**alcēs, is** *f* elk.

**alcyōn, onis** *f* kingfisher.

**ālea, ae** *f* a) game with dice, die; b) hazard, risk, chance.

**āleārius** 3 relating to gambling.

**āleātor, ōris** *m* dicer, gambler.

**āleātōrius** 3 of a dicer *or* gambler.

**ālēc, ēcis** *n* = allec.

**āleō, ōnis** *m* = aleator.

**āles, itis** 1. winged; swift, quick; 2. *subst.* bird; prophetic bird; a) omen, augury; b) poet.

**alēscō** 3 to grow.

**alga, ae** *f* sea-weed.

**algeō, alsī,** — 2 to be *or* feel cold.

**algēscō, alsī,** — 3 to catch cold.

**algidus** 3 cold, icy.

**algor, ōris** (*and* **algus, ūs**) *m* cold.

**aliā** *adv.* (*sc.* **viā**) by another way.

**aliās** *adv.* 1. at another time; **aliās ... aliās** at one time ... at another time; 2. elsewhere; in another way.

**āliātus** = **alliātus**.

**alibī** *adv.* elsewhere, at another place; **alibī ... alibī** here ... there; **alius alibī** one here ... another there; with some other person; in other respects.

**alica, ae** *f* spelt grits, drink made of spelt.

**alicāria, ae** *f* wench, prostitute.

**alicubī** *adv.* anywhere, somewhere.

**alicula, ae** *f* cape.

**alicunde** *adv.* from somewhere, from any place.

**alid** = **aliud**.

**aliēnātiō, ōnis** *f* 1. alienation (*of property*), transfer; 2. separation, desertion, breach, enmity.

**aliēni-gena, ae** *m* alien, foreign; foreigner.

**aliēnō** 1 1. to make a thing another's, to make over, transfer; a) to cast off, disown; b) to sell; c) to make subject to another; d) to cause one to lose his reason (*mentem*), to drive mad; 2. to estrange, set at variance, alienate (*alqm* or *alod ab alqo*); **P.** to have an aversion, to shrink from.

**aliēnus** 3 belonging *or* relating to another; **aes aliēnum** another's money, debt; **nomina a.** debtors; **aliēnissimus** not related at all; *subst.* **aliēnus, ī** *m* stranger, foreigner; **aliēnum, ī** *n* another man's property, affair of a stranger; a) not acquainted with, not related to, strange to (*ab alqo* or *dat.*); b) averse, unfavourable, hostile (*ab alqo, a re,* also with *dat.* or *gen.*); strange, unsuitable, unseasonable, disadvantageous.

**āliger, gera, gerum** bearing wings.

**alimentārius** 3 belonging to nourishment.

**alimentum, ī** *n* 1. food, nourishment, provisions; 2. return due to parents for the bringing up of children.

**alimōnium, ī** *n* nourishment.

**aliō** *adv.* to another place; **alius aliō** one in this direction, another in that; to another person *or* thing.

**aliō-quī(n)** *adv.* 1. in other respects, otherwise, for the rest; 2. besides, moreover, in general, in any case.

**aliō(vo)rsum** *adv.* in another direction, in a different sense.

**āli-pēs, pedis** wing-footed, swift-footed.

**ālipilus, ī** *m* slave who removes superfluous hair.

**aliptēs, ae** *m* anointer, wrestling master.

**aliquā** *adv.* (*sc.* **viā**) by any way; somehow. [long time.]

**aliquam-diū** *adv.* for a pretty]

**aliquam multī** a good many.

**aliquandō** *adv.* 1. at any time, at some time, once, ever; 2. finally, at length, sometimes.

**aliquantillum** a little bit.

**aliquantisper** for a while.

**aliquantulus** 3 very little *or* small.

**aliquantus** 3 some, considerable; *subst.* **aliquantum, ī** *n* a good deal, a considerable amount, not a little (*with gen.*).

aliquātenus to some extent.

ali-quī, a, od some, any.

ali-quis, a, id some one, something, anyone, anything; aliquid (adv.) in some degree.

ali-quō adv. to some place, somewhere.

ali-quot some, a few, several.

ali-quotiē(n)s adv. several times.

aliquō-vorsum adv. to some place.

alis = alius.

aliter adv. 1. otherwise, in another way (with ac, atque, et, quam); non aliter, haud aliter not otherwise, just as (ac si, quam si exactly as if); alius aliter one in this way, another in that; 2. in the contrary manner, in other respects.

aliubi = alibi.

ālium, ī n = allium.

ali-unde adv. from another direction, from elsewhere.

alius, a, ud (gen. alīus and alterius, dat. aliī) a) another, other; aliī — aliī some — others; alius aliud fecit one did this, another that; alius aliō more vivit people live in different ways; alius ex aliō one after the other; alius ac, atque, et other than, different from; nihil aliud nisi or quam nothing else but, only; b) different, of another kind.

al-lābor 3 to glide or flow to or towards (with dat. or acc.).

al-labōrō 1 to add to by toil.

al-lacrimō 1 to weep at.

al-lāpsus, ūs m a gliding up to.

al-lātrō 1 to bark at; to rail at.

al-laudābilis, e praiseworthy.

al-laudō 1 to praise.

allēc, ēcis n fish-sauce.

allectō 1 to allure, entice.

al-lectus 3, see allego² and allicio.

al-lēgātiō, ōnis f a sending of negotiators.

allēgātus, ūs m instigation.

al-lēgō¹ 1 a) to send on business, as a negotiator, or deputy (alqm alci or ad alqm); b) to adduce, allege.

al-legō² 3 to choose in addition, select.                   [alleviation.]

al-levāmentum, ī n means of

al-levātiō, ōnis f alleviation.

al-levō 1 to lift up, raise, erect; to lighten, alleviate; P. to recover.

allex¹, icis m little man.

allēx², ēcis f = allec.

alliātus 3 provided with garlic.

al-licefaciō 3 to entice.

al-liciō, lexī, lectum 3 to allure, entice, draw to oneself (alqm or alqd ad alqd, ad se).

al-līdō, sī, sum 3 to dash or strike against; P. to suffer damage, to be ruined.

al-ligō 1 1. to bind or tie to (alqd ad alqd); a) to make fast, hold fast; b) to fetter, shackle; c) to bind, oblige by kindness; d) to bind, make responsible; se all. scelere to become an accomplice in a crime (in scelere alligātus involved in a crime); 2. (vulnus, oculum) to bind up, dress.

al-linō, lēvī, litum 3 to smear on, bedaub.

allium, ī n garlic.

al-locūtiō, ōnis f = alloquium.

al-loquium, ī n a) a speaking to, address; b) exhortation, encouragement, consolation.

al-loquor 3 a) to speak to, address; b) to exhort, comfort (alqm).

al-lubēscit it begins to please.

al-lūceō 2 to shine at or upon.

al-lūdiō 1 to play or sport with.

al-lūdō 3 to play or sport with; a) to approach in play or by stealth; b) to wash (the shore); c) to add in sport.

al-luō, luī, — 3 to wash (against).

al-luviēs, ēī f inundation.

al-luviō, ōnis f alluvial soil.

almus 3 a) nourishing, giving food; b) kind, gracious, bountiful, sweet.

alnus, ī f alder; ship, boat.

alō, aluī, altum or alitum 3 to nourish, feed, bring up, rear; a) to support, maintain; b) to promote, strengthen, increase.

aloē, ēs f aloe; bitterness.

alogia, ae f folly.

alpha the first letter of the Greek alphabet, A.

als(i)us 3 cold, cool.

altāria, ium n/pl. (high) altar.

alter, era, erum a) one of two, the one, the other; the opposite; b) the second, alter Marius a second M.; alter ego one's second self; c) neighbour, fellow-man; unus et alter the one and the other, one or two, a few; alterum tantum as much again.

alterās at any other time.

**altercātiō, ōnis** f dispute, debate, quarrel.

**altercor** (and **cō**) 1 to dispute, quarrel (cum alqo).

**alternō** 1 to do by turns or alternately; to change; to hesitate.

**alternus** 3 one after the other, alternate, reciprocal; **alternīs** (adv.) by turns; (in poetry) elegiac, in couplets.

**alter-uter, utra, utrum** one of two, one or the other.

**alti-cinctus** 3 high-girt.

**altilis, e** fat; subst. fattened fowl.

**alti-sonus** 3 sounding from on high.

**alti-tonāns, tis** high-thundering.

**altitūdō, inis** f height; a) sublimity, grandeur; b) depth; c) reserve, secrecy.

**altiusculus** 3 a little too high.

**alti-volāns, tis** high-flying.

**altor, ōris** m nourisher, sustainer.

**altrin-secus** adv. at or on the other side.

**altrix, īcis** f foster-mother, nurse.

**altrō-vorsum** adv. on the other side.

**altus** 3 1. a) high; subst. **altum, ī** n height; heaven; depth, deep sea; b) lofty, elevated, great; 2. deep; **altum, ī** n depth, far distance; **ex altō repetere** to fetch from afar; a) secret, profound, unfathomable; b) ancient, remote.          [mind.]

**alucinātiō, ōnis** f wandering of the]

**alucinor** 1 to wander in mind, to ramble in speech.

**alumna, ae** f foster-daughter, pupil.

**alumnus, ī** m foster-son, nursling; pupil; a young one.

**alūta, ae** f soft leather; shoe; purse; face-patch.

**alv(e)ārium, ī** n beehive.

**alveolus, ī** m small trough; gaming board, play at dice; bed of a small river.

**alveus, ī** m hollow, cavity; a) trough, basin, bathing-tub; b) boat, ship; c) bed of a river; d) beehive; e) dice-board.

**alvus, ī** f belly, abdomen; a) womb; b) stomach; c) hold of a ship; d) beehive.

**ama, ae** f = **hama**.

**amābilis, e** lovely, lovable.

**amābilitās, tātis** f lovableness.

**ā-mandātiō, ōnis** f a sending away.

**ā-mandō** 1 to send away, remove (alqm in locum).

**amāns, tis** loving (with gen.), fond, affectionate, friendly, kind; lover.

**ā-manuēnsis, is** m secretary.

**amāracinum, ī** n marjoram ointment.

**amāracus, ī** m marjoram.

**amarantus, ī** m amaranth, unfading flower.

**amāritiēs, ēī** f = **amaritudo**.

**amāritūdō, inis** f, **amāror, ōris** m bitterness; exasperation.

**amārus** 3 bitter, pungent; morose.

**amāsius, ī** m lover.

**amātiō, ōnis** f love-affair.

**amātor, ōris** m, **amātrix, īcis** f lover.

**amātorculus, ī** m little lover.

**amātōrius** 3 loving, amorous, amatory.

**ambactus, ī** m vassal.

**amb-adedō** 3 to eat round, consume.

**amb-āgēs, um** f/pl. (abl. sing. **āge**) roundabout way; a) digression, diffuseness; b) evasion, subterfuges; c) riddle, ambiguity.          [sume.]

**amb-edō** 3 to eat round, con-]

**amb-ēstrix, īcis** f gluttonous woman.

**amb-igō, —, —** 3 a) to doubt, waver, hesitate; b) to dispute, contend, argue, debate.

**ambiguitās, ātis** f ambiguity.

**ambiguus** 3 inclined to both sides; of uncertain nature, hybrid; a) wavering, hesitating, uncertain, doubtful; b) obscure, ambiguous; c) untrustworthy; d) irresolute, timid; subst. **ambiguum, ī** n = **ambiguitas**.

**ambiō, īvī and iī, ītum** 4 to go round; a) to avoid, shun; b) to surround (alqd re); c) to go round canvassing for votes, for help; to entreat, solicit (alqm).

**amb-itiō, ōnis** f a going about; a) display, pomp; b) canvassing for an office; c) a striving after honours or for favour, courting, flattery; d) desire for popularity, ambition; e) striving after something.

**ambitiōsus** 3 1. encompassing, twining around; 2. a) eager for favour, striving after honours; b) competing for an office; c) vain, ostentatious, pretentious.

**amb-itus, ūs** m 1. a going round; a) circuit, revolution, circular course, circle, edge, orbit; b) circumlocution; c) period (*in grammar*); **2.** a) illegal canvassing for an office; b) = **ambitio.**

**ambō, ae, ō** both, the two.

**ambrosius 3** divine; *subst.* **ambrosia, ae** *f* ambrosia, food of the gods.

**ambūbāia, ae** *f* Syrian flute-player.

**ambulācrum, ī** *n* walk.

**ambulātiō, ōnis** *f* a walking about; promenade.

**ambulātiuncula, ae** *f* a little walk; little promenade.

**ambulātor, ōris** *m* pedlar.

**ambulātōrius 3** movable.

**ambulō 1** to walk about, take a walk; **a)** to strut, stalk; **b)** to march, travel; **c)** to traverse, travel over (*alqd*).

**amb-ūrō 3 a)** to burn round, scorch, burn up; consume; **b)** to nip, benumb; **P.** to be injured, damaged.

**ambustulātus 3** burnt round.

**amellus, ī** *m* purple Italian starwort.

**ā-mēns, tis** senseless, mad; foolish, stupid. [strap.]

**āmentātus 3** furnished with a]

**ā-mentia, ae** *f* senselessness, madness, folly.

**āmentō 1** to hurl, whirl.

**āmentum, ī** *n* strap, thong.

**ames, itis** *m* fork for a fowler's net.

**amethystinātus 3** clad in clothing of amethyst-purple.

**amethystinus 3 a)** of amethyst-purple (*n/pl.* purple garments); **b)** set with amethysts.

**amethystus, ī** *f* amethyst.

**amīca, ae** *f* female friend; mistress.

**amiciō —, ictum 4** to clothe, wrap round, to cover, envelop.

**amīciter,** in a friendly way.

**amīcitia, ae** (*and* **tiēs, ēi**) *f* friendship; **a)** alliance; **b)** friends.

**amīcō 1** to make friendly.

**amictus, ūs** *m* garment, covering.

**amīcula, ae** *f* sweetheart.

**amiculum, ī** *n* cloak, mantle.

**amīculus, ī** *m* (dear) friend.

**amīcus 3 a)** friendly, loving, kindly, well-wishing; **b)** favourable, propitious, pleasing; *subst.* **amīcus, ī** *m* **a)** friend; **b)** ally, minister.

**ā-migrō 1** to wander away.

**ā-missiō, ōnis** *f*, **ā-missus, ūs** *m* loss.

**amita, ae** *f* aunt (*father's sister*).

**ā-mittō 3 1.** to send away, dismiss, let go; to let slip, to loose; to break one's word (**fidem a**); **2.** to lose, to suffer the loss of. [near a river.]

**amni-cola, ae** *m and f* dwelling]

**amniculus, ī** *m* streamlet.

**amnis, is** *m* river, stream; **a)** torrent; **b)** current, flood; **c)** water.

**amō 1** to love, **se am.** to love oneself; **a)** to be in love, to love passionately; to have an amour; **b)** (*with inf.*) to be wont, to be fond of; **c)** **ita** *or* **sic me di ament** *or* **amabunt** so help me the gods!; **amabo** (**te**) be so good, I entreat you; **d)** (*alqm de*, or *in re*) to be obliged for, to owe gratitude.

**amoenitās, ātis** *f* pleasantness, delightfulness, loveliness, charm.

**amoenus 3** pleasant, delightful, lovely, charming; luxurious.

**ā-mōlior 4** to move (away) with effort, to remove; **a)** to put away, avert, get rid of; **b)** to refute, repel.

**amōmum, ī** *n* an aromatic shrub.

**amor, ōris** *m* love, affection (*alcis* or *in, erga alqm*); **a)** amour, love--affair, amorous intrigue; **b)** object of love, darling; **c)** desire, passion, longing (*alcis rei*); **d)** the god of love, Cupid.

**ā-mōtiō, ōnis** *f* a removing.

**ā-moveō 2** to move away, remove (*alqd ab, ex re*), **se a.** to retire, withdraw, depart; **a)** to steal; **b)** to banish; **c)** to lay aside, to sway (away) from, get rid of (*alqd a re*).

**amphi-bolia, ae** *f* ambiguity.

**amphi-theātrālis e** of the amphitheatre.

**amphi-theātrum, ī** *n* amphitheatre.

**amphora, ae** *f* **a)** two-handled vessel (*for wine*), jar, pitcher; **b)** a measure for liquids, *or* of the tonnage of a ship.

**ampla, ae** *f* handle; opportunity.

**am-plector, plexus sum 3** to encircle, surround, encompass, embrace; **a)** to embrace lovingly, to love, esteem, value, welcome, receive; **b)** to embrace with the mind, to consider, understand; **c)** to discuss, comprehend, comprise.

**amplexor** (*and* **ō**) **1** = **amplector.**

**amplexus, ūs** *m* a surrounding, encircling; embrace.

**ampli-ficătiō, ōnis** *f* an enlarging, increasing; amplification.

**ampli-ficător, ōris** *m* one who enlarges, amplifier.

**ampli-ficē** *adv.* splendidly.

**ampli-ficō** 1 a) to enlarge, increase, extend, make wide; b) to magnify, amplify, glorify.

**ampliō** 1 a) = **amplifico;** b) to adjourn, delay a judgment.

**ampliter** *adv.* amply, fully; splendidly.

**amplitūdō, inis** *f* wide extent, width, size; a) greatness, grandeur; b) dignity, high rank.

**amplius** *adv.* 1. (*of time*) more, longer, further; 2. in a higher degree; 3.(*with numbers*) more than; besides, further, more, in addition; **nihil amplius** nothing further; **hoc amplius** besides this.

**ampliusculē** *adv.* a little too much.

**amplus** 3 of large extent, ample, large, spacious, roomy; a) great, full, copious, abundant, numerous; *subst.* **amplius** *n* a greater amount, larger sum; b) strong, violent; c) splendid, magnificent, glorious, honourable; d) esteemed, distinguished, honoured, illustrious, excellent, noble.

**ampulla, ae** *f* a) a flask for unguents; b) bombast, inflated speech.

**ampullārius, ī** *m* flask-maker.

**ampullor** 1 to write *or* talk bombastically.

**amputātiō, ōnis** *f* a cutting off.

**amputō** 1 a) to cut around, to cut off (*alqd, alci alqd*); b) to lop, prune; c) to curtail.

**amurca, ae** *f* scum *or* dregs of oil.

**amygdala, ae** *f* almond-tree.

**amygdalum, ī** *n* almond (kernel).

**amystis, idis** *f* the emptying of a cup at one draught.

**an** *cj.* 1. *in disjunctive* (*direct* or *indirect double*) *questions:* or; **utrum** — **an** whether — or; **annon** (*direct,* **necne** *indirect*) or not; 2. *in indirect simple questions* = **num** whether; **haud scio, nescio, dubito, dubium** *or* **incertum est an** (= whether not) I almost think, I might almost say, perhaps, probably; 3. *in simple direct questions:* or then, or rather.

**anabathrum, ī** *n* raised seat.

**anadēma, atis** *n* headband.

**anaglypta, ōrum** *n/pl.* work in relief.

**ana-gnōstēs, ae** *m* a reader.

**ana-lecta, ae** *m* slave who removes food left over at table and gathers up waste fragments.

**analectis, idis** *f* shoulder-pad.

**anancaeum, ī** *n* large drinking cup.

**ana-paestus** 3 anapæstic; *subst.* **~, ī,** anapæst; **-um, ī** *n* poem in anapæsts.

**anas, atis** (and **itis**) *f* duck.

**anaticula, ae** *f* little duck.

**anatīnus** 3 of a duck.

**anatocismus, ī** *m* compound interest.

**an-ceps, cipitis** two-headed; a) two-sided, twofold; amphibious; from *or* on both sides; b) doubtful, undecided, **ancipiti Marte** with uncertain success; c) wavering; d) ambiguous; e) dangerous.

**ancīle, is** *n* the shield said to have fallen from heaven in the time of Numa; shield.

**ancilla, ae** *f* maidservant.

**ancillāriolus, ī** *m* maidservant's lover.

**ancillāris, e** of a maidservant.

**ancillula, ae** *f* a young maidservant.

**ancipes** = **anceps.**

**an-cīsus** 3 cut round.

**ancora, ae** *f* anchor.

**ancorāle, is** *n* (anchor-)cable.

**ancorārius** 3 belonging to an anchor.

**andabata, ae** *m* gladiator who fought blindfold; a blind man.

**andro-gynus, ī** *m* man-woman, hermaphrodite.

**andrōn, ōnis** *m* passage between two walls.

**ānellus, ī** *m* a little ring.

**aneō** 2 to be an old woman.

**anet-,** *see* **anat-.**

**anēthum, ī** *n* dill.

**ān-frāctus, ūs** *m* a turning, bending round; a) circuit, revolution; b) circuitous way; diffuseness, prolixity; c) intricacies.

**angellus, ī** *m* small corner.

**angina, ae** *f* quinsy.

**angi-portus, ūs** *m or* **-um, ī** *n* narrow lane; by-street.

**angō, (anxī), — 3** 1. to press tight, squeeze, compress; 2. to choke, strangle; to vex, trouble, torment; **P.** to feel pain, be grieved.

**angor, ōris,** *m* **a)** strangling, suffocation; **b)** anguish, torment, trouble.

**angui-comus 3** with snaky hair.

**anguiculus, ī** *m* a small snake.

**angui-fer 3** serpent-bearing.

**angui-gena, ae** snake-born.

**anguilla, ae** *f* eel.

**angui-manus 3** snake-armed.

**anguineus 3, anguīnus 3** of serpents, snaky.

**angui-pēs, pedis** serpent-footed.

**anguis, is** *m and f* serpent, snake; the Dragon (*constellation*).

**Angui-tenēns, tis** *m* the Serpentholder (*constellation*).

**angulātus 3** with corners, angular.

**angulus, ī** *m* corner; **a)** angle; **b)** secret place, corner, nook, recess, lurking-place.

**angustiae, ārum** *f|pl.* narrowness, straitness; narrow place; **a)** defile, narrow passage; **b)** shortness (*of breath, of time*); **c)** difficulty, scarcity, poverty, want; distress, perplexity, trouble; **d)** narrowmindedness, meanness; **e)** captiousness.

**angusti-clāvius 3** wearing a narrow stripe of purple.

**angustō 1** to make narrow.

**angustus 3** narrow, strait, contracted; **a)** short, brief; **b)** confined, slight, faint, limited, needy, scant; **c)** critical, difficult; **d)** base, low, mean; **e)** narrow-minded.

**an-hēlitus, ūs** *m* a panting, short breath, asthma; **a)** breath, breathing; **b)** exhalation, vapour.

**an-hēlō 1 a)** to pant, gasp, breathe with difficulty; **b)** to roar, crash; **c)** to breathe out *or* forth; **d)** to pant for (*alqd*).

**an-hēlus 3 a)** panting, gasping; **b)** causing to pant.

**anicula, ae** *f* little old woman.

**anilis, e** of an old woman.

**anīlitās, ātis** *f* old age (*of a woman*).

**anima, ae** *f* **1.** current of air, wind; **a)** air; **b)** breath, breeze; **2.** soul, vital principle, life; **animam efflāre, edere** to expire, give up the ghost; **animam agere** to breathe one's last; **a)** departed spirit, shade (in the nether world); **b)** living being, person; **c)** lifeblood; **d)** dear heart, good soul; **e)** mind.

**anim-adversiō, ōnis** *f* **1.** perception, observation, investigation, inquiry; **2. a)** censure; **b)** punishment.

**anim-adversor, ōris** *m* observer.

**anim-advertō 3 1.** to attend to, pay attention, consider, notice, observe, perceive, discern, apprehend; **2. a)** to blame, censure; **b)** to punish, chastise (*alqd, in alqm*).

**animal, ālis** *n* living being, creature; beast, monster.

**animālis, e 1.** of air; **2. a)** animate, living; **b)** enlivening.

**animāns, tis** animate, living; *subst. m and f* = **animal.**

**animātiō, ōnis** *f* an animating.

**animātus 3 a)** animate, living; **b)** disposed, minded; **c)** courageous.

**animō 1** to animate, quicken, give life; **a)** *in alqd* transform into; **b)** to dispose, inspirit, to endow with a certain disposition; to encourage.

**animōsus 3 a)** breathing, living; **b)** courageous, bold, spirited; **c)** audacious, passionate, furious.

**animula, ae** *f* a little soul, life.

**animulus, ī** *m* little life, little heart.

**animus, ī** *m* (*locat.* **animi** in the heart) **1.** *poet.* = **anima; 2.** soul, mind; **a)** intellect, mental powers, reason; **b)** thought, memory, consciousness, self-possession; **c)** judgment, opinion, belief; **d)** feeling, sentiment, affection, inclination, heart; **e)** disposition, character, nature; **f)** courage, heart, spirit; **g)** haughtiness, arrogance, pride; **h)** passion, vehemence, wrath; **i)** desire, will, wish; **k)** purpose, design, intention, resolve; **l)** inclination, pleasure.

**annālis, e a)** relating to a year, annual, **lex ~** law fixing the age required for an office; **b)** *subst.* **annālēs, ium** *m|pl.* yearly records, chronicles, annals.

**an-narrō 1** to relate.

**annatō 1** to swim to.

**an-ne = an.**

**an-nectō 3** to tie, bind *or* fasten to (*alqd ad alqd,* or with *dat.*); to connect, unite, add (*with dat.*).

**an-nexus, ūs** *m* connexion.

**anniculus 3** a year old.

**an-nītor** 3 to lean upon *or* against (*ad alqd*); to exert oneself, take pains (*de re, pro alqo*, with *ut*, with *inf.*).

**anni-versārius** 3 returning every year, yearly.

**an-nō** 1 to swim up to (*ad alqm, dat., acc.*).

**annōna, ae** *f* a) yearly produce, crop, corn-supply; b) corn, grain; c) price of grain and other provisions; market-price; high price of corn, dearness.

**annōsus** 3 full of years, aged.

**an-notātiō, ōnis** *f* a noting down, remark.

**annōtinus** 3 of last year, a year old.

**an-notō** 1 a) to note down, mark; b) to remark, observe, take notice of.

**an-nūbilō** 1 to bring up clouds.

**an-numerō** 1 a) to count among, reckon, consider (*alqm alci* or *in re*); b) to count out, pay (*alci alqd*).

**an-nūntiō** 1 a) to announce; b) to relate in addition.

**an-nuō, nuī,** — 3 to nod to, make a sign; a) to nod assent *or* approval, to agree, assent, grant, promise; b) to point out by a nod.

**annus, ī** *m* a year; **anno** in *or* for a year, a year ago; **annum** during a whole year; **ad annum** for the coming year, **in annum** for a year; a) (*pl.*) time of life, age; b) season (= **tempus anni**); c) produce of the year, harvest.

**an-nūtō** 1 to nod to.

**annuus** 3 a) of a year, lasting a year; b) returning every year, yearly.

**an-quirō, sīvī, sītum** 3 to seek *or* search carefully (*alqd*); a) to inquire into, examine (*alqd, de re*); b) to conduct judicial inquiry *or* examination; to accuse, impeach (*de re, gen.* or *abl.*).

**ānsa, ae** *f* a) handle, haft; b) opportunity, occasion (with *gen.* or *ad alqd*).

**ānsātus** 3 with handles *or* ears.

**ānser, eris** *m* (*and f*) goose.

**ante** 1. *adv.* in front, before, forwards; previously, before; 2. *prep.* with *acc.*; a) (*of space*) before, in front of; b) (*of time*) before; c) (*of relation*) before, more than, above,

beyond; **esse ante aliquem** to be superior to; **ante omnes, ante alios** above all others; **ante omnia** before all other things = especially.

**anteā** *adv.* before, formerly, earlier, previously.

**ante-ambulō, ōnis** *m* footman (*running before his master*).

**ante-capiō** 3 to take beforehand, preoccupy; a) to receive, obtain previously; b) to be beforehand, anticipate.

**ante-cēdēns, tis** foregoing, preceding.

**ante-cēdō** 3 to go before, precede (with *acc.* or *dat.*); a) to be in the van; b) to overtake (*acc.*); c) to excel, surpass, to have the precedence *or* advantage of (with *acc.* or *dat.*).

**ante-cellō,** —, — 3 a) to be prominent; b) to surpass, excel, distinguish oneself (*alci rei* or *in re, alqa re*).

**ante-cessiō, ōnis** *f* a) a preceding, going forward; b) antecedent cause.

**ante-cessor, ōris** *m* skirmisher.

**ante-cursor, ōris** *m* forerunner; advanced guard, skirmisher.

**ante-eō** to go before, precede (with *dat.*, with *acc.*); a) to anticipate, be beforehand; b) to surpass, excel (*acc.*); c) to prevent.

**ante-ferō** 3 a) to bear *or* carry before, in front; b) to place before, prefer (*alqm* or *alqd alci rei*).

**ante-fīxus** 3 fastened before, in front; **antefīxum, ī** *n* ornament affixed to the frieze of a house *or* temple.

**ante-gredior, gressus sum** 3 = antecedo.

**ante-habeō** 2 to prefer.

**ante-hāc** *adv.* before this time, before now, hitherto.

**ante-logium, ī** *n* prologue.

**ante-lūcānus** 3 before daybreak.

**ante-merīdiānus** 3 before midday.

**ante-mittō** 3 to send before.

**antenna (-mna), ae** *f* (sail-)yard.

**ante-occupātiō, ōnis** *f* anticipation of an opponent's point.

**ante-pertus** 3 previously acquired.

**ante-pēs, pedis** *m* forefoot.

**ante-pīlānus, ī** *m* soldier who fought before the triarii.

**ante-pōnō** 3 a) to place before; b) to prefer (*alqd alci*).

**ante-potēns, tis** very rich.
**ante-quam** *cj.* before; **non ante quam** not until.
**antēs, ium** *m/pl.* rows *of vines.*
**ante-signānus, ī** *m* a) soldier who fought before the standards; b) leader.
**ante-stō,** *see* **antisto.**
**an-testor** 1 to call as a witness.
**ante-veniō** 4 to come *or* arrive before; a) to anticipate; b) to exceed, surpass; c) to prevent.
**ante-vertō** 3 to precede; to get the start of; a) to anticipate; b) to prevent, frustrate (*alqd*); c) to prefer to (*dat., ut*).
**ante-volō** 1 to fly before (*acc.*).
**anticipātiō, ōnis** *f* preconception, innate notion.
**anticipō** 1 to take *or* receive before; to anticipate; **viam** to take a shorter way.
**antīcus** 3 1. in front; 2. = **antiquus.**
**antid-eā** *adv.* = **antea.**
**antid-eō** = **anteeo.**
**antid-hāc** *adv.* = **antehac.**
**anti-dotum, ī** *n* antidote.
**antīquārius** 3 antiquarian; *subst.* ~, **ī** *m* antiquary.
**antīquitās, ātis** *f* ancient time, antiquity; a) men of ancient times, the ancients; b) events of ancient times, the history of ancient times; c) the good old times, primitive virtue.
**antīquitus** *adv.* a) from antiquity; b) in former times.
**antīquō** 1 to make obsolete, to reject (*a law*).
**antīquus** 3 (**antīcus**) 1. what is in front, *comp. and superl.* preferable, of more value *or* importance, more *or* most celebrated; 2. old, ancient, former; a) of old times, venerable, long-established, oldfashioned; **antīquī, ōrum** *m* the ancients, ancient writers; **antīqua, ōrum** *n/pl.* old customs, obsolete things; b) of the good old times, of primitive virtue.
**anti-stes, itis** *m and f* overseer of a temple, chief priest(ess).
**anti-stita, ae** *f* = **antistes** *f.*
**anti-stō, stetī, — 1** a) to stand before; b) to be superior, to excel, be prominent.
**anti-theton, ī** *n* antithesis.

**antlia, ae** *f* machine for pumping water.
**antrum, ī** *n* cave, cavern, grotto.
**ānulārius** 3 belonging to a seal-ring; *subst.* ~, **ī** *m* ringmaker.
**ānulātus** 3 wearing a ring.
**ānulus, ī** *m* finger-ring, seal-ring.
**anus¹, ūs** *f* old woman; old hag.
**ānus², ī** *m* ring.
**ānus³, ī** *m* fundament.
**anxietās, ātis** *f* anxiety, solicitude, trouble, grief.
**anxi-fer** 3 bringing anxiety.
**anxitūdō, inis** *f* = **anxietas.**
**anxius** 3 a) anxious, troubled, uneasy, solicitous (*re, de re, pro alqo*); b) tormenting, troublesome.
**ap-age** away with you, begone, be off!
**apēliōtēs, ae** *m* east-wind.
**aper, prī** *m* wild boar.
**aperiō, ruī, rtum** 4. 1. to uncover, lay bare, to open, unclose, to make accessible; 2. to discover, unveil, display, unfold, make known; to reveal, explain, disclose (*alci alqd*, with *acc.c.inf.*).
**apertō** 1 to lay bare.
**apertus** 3 1. uncovered, bare; without deck exposed; 2. not shut, open; a) accessible, free, unobstructed; **apertum, ī** *n* open space; open field; b) clear, manifest, plain, evident; not obscure, intelligible; c) practicable; d) frank, open, candid, straightforward.
**apex, icis** *m* point, extremity, top, summit; a) top of the helmet; b) conical hat, cap; cap of a priest; crown, tiara; c) highest ornament.
**a-phractus, ī** *f* (*and* **-um, ī** *n*) ship without deck.
**apicātus** 3 adorned with a priest's cap.
**apicula, ae** *f* bee.
**apis, is** *f* bee.
**apīscor, aptus sum** 3 to reach, obtain, get.
**apium, ī** *n* celery.
**aplustre, is** *n* stern.
**apo-clētī, ōrum** *m/pl.* committee of the Aetolian league.
**apo-dytērium, ī** *n* undressing room in a bath.
**apo-lactizō** 1 to kick away, spurn.
**apo-logō** 1 to reject.
**apo-logus, ī** *m* narrative; fable.
**apo-phorēta, ōrum** *n/pl.* presents given at the Saturnalia

**apo-proēgmena, ōrum** *n/pl.* what is rejected.

**apo-sphrăgisma, atis** *n* image of a seal-ring.

**apo-thēca, ae** *f* store-room, magazine, warehouse.

**ap-parātiō, ōnis** *f* a) preparation; **b)** a preparing.

**ap-parātus¹, ūs** *m* a) a preparing; **b)** tool, implement, instrument, engine; **c)** magnificence, splendour, pomp.

**ap-parātus²** 3 a) well prepared, ready; **b)** splendid, sumptuous.

**ap-părĕo** 2 to appear, become visible, make one's appearance; **a)** to be clear, manifest, evident, perceptible (**appāret** *with acc.c.inf.* it is clear, plain); **b)** to appear as a servant, to attend, serve.

**ap-pariō** 3 to gain.

**ap-păritiō, ōnis** *f* a) a waiting upon, service, attendance; **b)** servants.

**ap-păritor, ōris** *m* public servant, lictor.

**ap-parō** 1 to prepare, make ready, equip, provide.

**appellātiō, ōnis** *f* a) an addressing, speaking to; appeal; **b)** a naming, name, title; **c)** pronunciation.

**appellātor, ōris** *m* appellant.

**appellitō** 1 to name habitually.

**ap-pellō¹** 1. to address, accost, speak to, greet; **a)** to apply to, entreat, request (*alqm de re*); **b)** to appeal to (*alqm*); **c)** to press (*for money*); **d)** to summon (*alqm*); **e)** to call by name, to name, entitle; to mention; 2. to pronounce.

**ap-pellō², pulī, pulsum** 3 to drive, move, bring to *or* towards (*alqd ad alqd*), navem, classem to bring to land (*ad or in locum*); **P.** (*and intrans. active*) to reach land.

**appendicula, ae** *f* a small appendage.

**ap-pendix, icis** *f* appendage, supplement, addition.

**ap-pendō, ndī, nsum** 3 to weigh out.

**ap-petēns, tis** a) striving after, eager for; **b)** grasping, avaricious.

**appetentia, ae** *f* = **appetitio.**

**ap-petitiō, ōnis** *f* a) a grasping at; **b)** desire, longing for.

**ap-petitus, ūs** *m* = **appetitio.**

**ap-petō** 3 to strive after, long for; **a)** to desire, seek; **b)** to seek to go

to, to approach, arrive (*with acc.*); **c)** to draw near (*of time*); **d)** to attack, assail (*alqd alqa re*).

**ap-pingō** 3 to paint in (*alqd alci rei*); to add in writing.

**ap-plaudō** 3 a) to strike one thing upon another (*with dat.*); to strike with (*abl.*); **b)** to applaud.

**ap-plicātiō, ōnis** *f* attachment, inclination.

**ap-plicō, cāvī, cātum** (*or* **cuī, citum**) 1 to apply, attach, add, join to, to place near (*alqd ad alqd or alci rei*); **a)** (*navem*) to steer to, bring to land, **P.** to land; **b)** to turn to, direct towards, **se applicāre** *ad alqd* to devote oneself to; *ad alqm* to associate with; **applicātus** *ad alqd* inclined to; **c)** to add (*alqd ad rem*).

**ap-plōrō** 1 to weep at, bewail.

**ap-pōnō** 3 to put *or* place at, by, beside, near (*alqd ad rem or with dat.*); **a)** to serve, set before, put on the table; **b)** to add to, put to; **c)** to procure.

**ap-porrēctus** 3 stretched out near.

**ap-portō** 1 a) to carry, convey, bring to; **c)** to cause.

**ap-poscō** 3 to demand in addition.

**ap-positus** 3 a) placed *or* situated near, contiguous; **b)** appropriate, proper.

**ap-pōtus** 3 drunk, intoxicated.

**ap-precor** 1 to pray to, worship.

**ap-prehendō** 3 to seize, take hold of.

**ap-prīmē** *adv.* chiefly, exceedingly.

**ap-prīmō, pressī, pressum** 3 to press to (*alqd alci rei*).

**ap-probātiō, ōnis** *f* a) approval, assent; **b)** proof.

**ap-probātor, ōris** *m* one who approves, assents.

**ap-probē** *adv.* fully, very well.

**ap-probō** 1 a) to approve, assent to, favour; **b)** to bless; **c)** to make acceptable; **d)** to prove.

**ap-prōmittō** 3 to promise besides.

**ap-properō** 1 a) to hasten, accelerate; **b)** to make haste.

**ap-propinquātiō, ōnis** *f* approach.

**ap-propinquō** 1 to approach, draw near (*ad alqd or with dat.*) (*of place and time*). [assault.]

**ap-pugnō** 1 to fight against, attack,]

**ap-pulsus, ūs** *m* a) a driving towards, approach, landing; **b)** influence.

**aprīcātiō, ōnis** *f* a basking in the sun.

**aprīcitās, ātis** *f* sunniness, warmth of the sun.

**aprīcor** 1 to bask in the sun.

**aprīcus** 3 open to the sun, sunny; fond of sunshine; *subst.* **-um, ī** *n* sunlight.

**Aprīlis, e** belonging to April; *subst.* *m* April.

**aprūgnus** 3 belonging to a wild boar.

**aps..., see abs...**

**aptō** 1 a) to fit *or* adapt to, to adjust, accommodate; b) to prepare, make ready.

**aptus** 3 a) fastened, connected, joined, allied; b) depending upon; c) adhering together; d) prepared, equipped, fitted out; e) suitable, appropriate, fit, proper.

**apud** *prep.* with *acc.* 1. at, near, by, with (*of places and persons*); before, in the presence of, among; at the house of; 2. in the opinion of; in the writings of.

**aqua, ae** *f* water; **aquā et igni interdicere** alci to exclude from society, to banish; a) sea, lake, river, rain, tears; b) *pl.* baths, bathing-place; c) water-conduit; d) water-clock.

**aquae-ductus, ūs** *m* a) aqueduct, conduit; b) the right of conducting water (*to a place*).

**aquāliculus, ī** *m* stomach.

**aquālis, e** of water; *subst.* *m* water-jug.

**aquārius** 3 belonging to water; *subst.* **~, ī** *m* a) inspector of conduits; b) the Aquarius *or* Water-carrier (*constellation*).

**aquāticus** 3 *and* **aquātilis, e** growing *or* living in the water; watery.

**aquātiō, ōnis** *f* a fetching of water.

**aquātor, ōris** *m* one who fetches water.

**aquila, ae** *f* eagle; the eagle as the standard of a Roman legion.

**aqui-lex, legis** *m* water-finder.

**aquili-fer, ferī** *m* eagle-bearer.

**aquilīnus** 3 relating to an eagle.

**aquilō, ōnis** *m* the north-wind; a) storm; b) north.

**aquilōnius** 3 northerly.

**aquilus** 3 dark-coloured, blackish.

**aquola, ae** *f* = aquula.

**aquor** 1 to fetch water.

**aquōsus** 3 full of water, watery, rainy, moist.

**aquula, ae** *f* a little water, small stream.

**ar = ad.**

**āra, ae** *f* altar, hearth; refuge, shelter.

**arānea, ae** *f* a) spider, b) spider's web.

**arāneola, ae** *f* (*and* us, ī *m*) little spider.

**arāneōsus** 3 full of cobwebs.

**arāneum, ī** *n* a spider's web.

**arāneus, ī** *m* = aranea.

**arātiō, ōnis** *f* 1. a ploughing; agriculture; 2. arable land.

**arātiuncula, ae** *f* small farm.

**arātor, ōris** *m* a) ploughman, husbandman; farmer; b) cultivator of public lands.

**arātrum, ī** *n* plough.

**arbiter, trī** *m* 1. spectator, beholder, eyewitness; 2. arbiter, umpire; a) judge; b) lord, master, ruler, governor.

**arbitra, ae** *f* female witness.

**arbitrārius** 3 matter of opinion.

**arbitrātus, ūs** *m* free-will, choice, pleasure; a) full discretion; b) direction; maxim.

**arbitrium, ī** *n* 1. decision of an arbiter, judgment; = **arbitratus**; 2. a) **~ funeris** funeral expenses; b) dominion, mastery, authority.

**arbitror** 1 (*and* **arbitrō** 1) a) to decide as an arbiter, to give judgment; b) to consider, think, believe.

**arbor** (*and* **ōs**), **oris** *f* tree (*coll.* trees); mast, oar, ship.

**arboreus** 3 of a tree; tree-like.

**arbustus** 3 full of trees; **-um, ī** *n* plantation, orchard, vineyard; trees, shrubs.

**arbuteus** 3 of the strawberry-tree.

**arbutum, ī** *n* fruit of the strawberry-tree.

**arbutus, ī** *f* strawberry-tree.

**arca, ae** *f* chest, box; a) box for money, coffer; b) coffin; c) cell.

**arcānus** 3 secret, private, hidden; silent, trusty; *subst.* **arcānum, ī** *n* a secret.

**arceō, uī,** — 2 to shut in *or* up, enclose, confine; a) to restrain, hinder, prevent, keep at a distance; b) to protect from.

**accessītor, ōris** *m* one who fetches.

**arcessītus, ūs** *m* a calling for, summons.

**arcessō, īvī, ītum** 3 to call, summon, fetch, send for; **a)** to summon before a court of justice (*alqm capitis, crimine, alcis rei*), accuse; **b)** to bring, procure; **c)** to derive, fetch, seek from.

**arche-typus** 3 original.

**archi-magīrus, ī** *m* chief cook.

**archi-mīmus, ī** *m* chief mime-actor.

**archi-pīrāta, ae** *m* pirate chief.

**archi-tectōn, onis** = architectus.

**archi-tector** 1 to build; to devise, invent.     [architecture.]

**architectūra, ae** *f* art of building,]

**architectus, ī** *m* master-builder, architect; **a)** inventor, deviser, maker; **b)** plotter, schemer.

**archōn, ontis** *m* archon (*of Athens*).

**arci-potēns, tis** skilful in archery.

**arci-tenēns, tis** holding a bow; *subst.* **A~** *m* the Archer (*constellation*).

**Arcto-phylax, acis** *m* (*a constellation*) Boötes.

**Arctos, ī** *f* the Great Bear; the two Bears; the north; night.

**arctōus** 3 northern.

**Arctūrus, ī** *m* the brightest star of Boötes; the rising of Boötes.

**arcuātus** 3 bent like a bow.

**arcula, ae** *f* small box, casket.

**arculārius, ī** *m* casket-maker.

**arcus, ūs** *m* a bow; **a)** rainbow, triumphal arch, vault; **b)** circle, curve.

**ardaliō, ōnis** *m* a busybody.

**ardea, ae** *f* heron.

**ardēns, tis** burning, glowing, hot; **a)** glittering, sparkling; **b)** fiery, impassioned.

**ardeō, ārsī, ārsum** 2 to burn, be on fire; **a)** to sparkle, flash; **b)** to be inflamed, excited, to burn with passion, with love, to desire ardently (*alqm, in alqo, ad* or *in alqd*).

**ardēscō, ārsī,** — 3 to take fire, become inflamed; **a)** to flash, glitter; **b)** to become furious.

**ardor, ōris** *m* flame, fire, heat; **a)** brightness, gleam; **b)** eagerness, zeal, desire; **c)** love; a beloved one.

**arduus** 3 **a)** steep, elevated, lofty; *subst.* **arduum, ī** *n* a steep place, height; **b)** difficult, troublesome, hard.

**ārea, ae** *f* open space; **a)** building ground, site for a house; **b)** threshing-floor; **c)** playground, racecourse; **d)** bald spot.

**āre-faciō** 3 to dry.

**arēna, ae** *f* sand; **a)** sandy place; **b)** sandy desert; **c)** sea-shore, strand, beach; **d)** arena in an amphitheatre.

**arēnāria, ae** *f* sand-pit.

**arēni-vagus** 3 wandering in sandy deserts.

**arēnōsus** 3 sandy.

**ārēns, tis** dry, arid; thirsty.

**āreō, uī,** — 2 to be dry or arid.

**āreola, ae** *f* small open space.

**ārēscō, āruī,** — 3 to become dry, dry up.

**aretā-logus, ī** *m* babbler about virtue.

**argentārius** 3 **a)** of silver; **b)** of money; (*taberna*) **argentāria, ae,** *f* banker's shop; *subst.* **argentārius, ī** *m* money-changer, banker.

**argentātus** 3 ornamented with silver.

**argenteolus** 3 of silver.

**argenteus** 3 made of silver; *subst.* **~, ī** *m* silver coin; **a)** ornamented or covered with silver; **b)** of a silver colour, silvery; **c)** of the Silver Age.

**argentum, ī** *n* silver; silver plate; silver money, money.

**argīlla, ae** *f* white clay, potter's clay.

**argītis, idis** *f* vine with white grapes.

**argūmentātiō, ōnis** *f* a proving, argumentation, reasoning.

**argūmentor** 1 **a)** to adduce proof; **b)** to adduce in proof.

**argūmentum, ī** *n* 1. subject, story, representation, statement; theme, matter, contents; plot, drama, tale; reality; 2. proof, conclusion; mark, token.

**arguō, uī, ūtum** 3 to make clear or known, to manifest, show, prove; **a)** to betray; **b)** to confute, disprove; **c)** to accuse, charge, censure, blame (*alqm alcis rei* or *de re*, with *acc. c. inf.*).

**argūtātiō, ōnis** *f* creaking.

**argūtiae, ārum** *f/pl.* 1. significance; quick movement; 2. cleverness, sagacity, acuteness, wit; subtlety, cunning.

**argūtor** (*and* ō) 1 to talk much.

**argūtulus** 3 somewhat subtle.

**argūtus** 3 1. significant, expressive; piercing, noisy, melodious; 2. a) clear, explicit; b) sagacious, acute, witty; c) sly, cunning, subtle, artful.

**argyr-aspides, um** *m/pl.* soldiers armed with a silver shield.

**āridulus** 3 somewhat dry.

**āridus** 3 dry, arid, parched; *subst.* **āridum, ī** *n* dry land; a) thirsty; b) poor, meagre, scanty, unadorned.

**ariēs, etis** *m* ram; battering-ram.

**arietātiō, ōnis** *f* butting.

**arietō** 1 to butt like a ram, to strike violently.

**arista, ae** *f* a) beard of an ear of corn; b) ear of corn; cereals.

**aristolochia, ae** *f* (*a plant useful in childbirth*).

**arithmētica, ōrum** *n/pl.* (and **-ca, ae** *f*) arithmetic.

**āritūdō, inis** *f* dryness.

**arma, ōrum** *n/pl.* 1. tools, implements, tackle, outfit; 2. weapons, arms, armour; a) shield; b) war, battle; c) warriors, armed men; d) defence.

**armamaxa, ae** *f* Persian travelling-coach.

**armāmenta, ōrum** *n/pl.* tackling, equipment of a ship.

**armāmentārium, ī** *n* arsenal, armoury.

**armāriolum, ī** *n* little chest.

**armārium, ī** *n* chest, cupboard.

**armātūra, ae** *f* armour; a) branch of the service; b) armed soldiers.

**armātus¹, ūs** *m* = **armatura**.

**armātus²** 3 armed, equipped; *subst.* **armātī, ōrum** *m/pl.* armed men, soldiers.

**armentālis, e** grazing in herds *or* flocks; belonging to a herd.

**armentārius, ī** *m* herdsman.

**armentum, ī** *n* herd, cattle (for ploughing).

**armi-fer** 3 bearing arms, warlike.

**armi-ger** 3 a) bearing arms; b) shield-bearer; man of the body-guard; attendant.

**armilla, ae** *f* bracelet, arm-ring.

**armillātus** 3 adorned with a bracelet.

**armi-potēns, tis** mighty in arms.

**armi-sonus** 3 resounding with arms.

**armō** 1 1. to furnish with implements, to equip, fit out (*a ship*); 2. to make ready for battle, to arm (*alqm alqa re, in* or *contra alqm, ad* or *in alqd*); to strengthen, help.

**armus, ī** *m* shoulder, shoulderblade, upper arm; flank.

**arō** 1 to plough, till; a) to furrow; b) to farm, cultivate; c) to gain by agriculture.

**arquātus** 3 jaundiced.

**ar-rēctus** 3 upright; steep, precipitous.

**ar-rēpō** 3 to creep to, steal to, to approach gently (*ad alqd* or with *dat.*).

**arr(h)abō, ōnis** *m* deposit, security.

**ar-rīdeō** 2 a) to laugh or smile at, to laugh with; b) to be favourable, to please (*alci*).

**ar-rigō, rēxī, rēctum** 3 a) to erect, lift up; b) to excite, animate, rouse.

**ar-ripiō, ripuī, reptum** 3 to snatch, catch; a) to seize, lay hold of; b) to drag into a court, to accuse; c) to seize with violence.

**ar-rīsor, ōris** *m* fawner.

**ar-rōdō** 3 to gnaw at.

**arrogāns, tis** assuming, arrogant, presumptuous, haughty.

**arrogantia, ae** *f* assumption, arrogance, pride, haughtiness.

**ar-rogātiō, ōnis** *f* adoption of an adult.

**ar-rogō** 1 1. to associate with (*alqm alci*); 2. a) to appropriate, claim; b) to confer upon (*alci alqd.*).

**ar-rōsor, ōris** *m* one who gnaws *or* nibbles.

**ars, artis** *f* 1. skill; 2. a) profession, business, trade; b) fine *or* liberal art, letters; c) science, knowledge; theory, principles of art; manual *or* text-book of any art *or* science; conduct, practice, method, work of art; 3. character, habit; artificial means, artifice, cunning, trick, fraud, intrigue.

**artē** *adv.* of **artus²**.

**artēria, ae** *f* a) artery; b) windpipe.

**arthrīticus** 3 gouty.

**articulātim** *adv.* a) limb by limb, piecemeal; b) distinctly.

**articulō** 1 to speak distinctly.

**articulus, ī** *m* 1. a) joint; a) limb; finger; b) knot (*of plants*); 2. a) part, division; b) point, moment, crisis.

**arti-fex, icis** *m and f* 1. *adj.* clever, skilled, ingenious (*alcis rei*); 2. artist, master of an art; a) author, maker, contriver; b) cunning deceiver.

**artificiōsus** 3 a) skilful, full of art; b) artistic, skilfully wrought; artificial.

**artificium, ī** n 1. skill, knowledge, ingenuity, art; a) work of art; b) trick, cunning, craft; c) theory, system; 2. trade, profession, handicraft.

**artō** 1 to straiten, press or draw together; to contract, limit.

**artolaganus, ī** m cake.

**artopta, ae** f baking-pan.

**artua** n/pl. limbs.

**artus¹, ūs** m joint, limb (mostly pl.).

**artus²** 3 a) tight, narrow, close; subst. **artum, ī** n narrow space; b) dense, firm; c) straitened, scanty, small, needy; subst. **artum, ī** n scantiness, difficulty, precarious position.

**artūtus** 3 strong-limbed.

**ārula, ae** f small altar.

**arundō**, see **harundō**.

**aruspex**, see **haruspex**.

**arvīna, ae** f grease, fat, lard.

**arviō = rāviō**.

**arvum, ī** n ploughed land, arable field; a) crop; b) country, field, plain; c) pasture-ground.

**arvus** 3 arable, ploughed.

**arx, arcis** f 1. castle, citadel, fortress, stronghold; height, eminence; 2. protection, bulwark, refuge.

**as, assis** m 1. the whole or unity (divided into twelve parts), **heres ex asse** sole heir; 2. a copper coin, the as.

**asarōtum, ī** n mosaic floor.

**ascaulēs** m bagpiper.

**a-scendō, ndī, ēnsum** 3 a) to mount, ascend, go up (in or ad alqd); b) to rise, reach.

**ascēnsiō, ōnis** f = ascensus.

**a-scēnsus, ūs** m a going or climbing up, ascent; a) a rising; b) place of ascending, approach, step, degree.

**ascia, ae** f carpenter's axe.

**a-sciō** 4 to take to oneself, to adopt.

**a-sciscō** 3 to take to oneself, receive, adopt (alqm or alqd in or ad alqd, inter alqos, sibi socium); a) to appropriate or associate with oneself; b) to assume, arrogate; c) to approve of.

**ascop(ēr)a, ae** f leather wallet.

**ā-scrībō** 3 to add in writing, to write in addition (alqd alci rei, in alqd, in alqa re); a) to enter in a list; b) to appoint, assign (alqm tutorem liberis); c) to reckon or number among (alqm in or ad alqd); d) to attribute, ascribe (alci alqd).

**āscrīpticius** 3 enrolled in the list of citizens.

**ā-scrīptiō, ōnis** f addition in writing.

**āscrīptīvus, ī** m supernumerary soldier.

**ā-scrīptor, ōris** m one who adds his name, supporter.

**asella, ae** f little she-ass.

**asellus, ī** m little ass.

**asīlus, ī** m gadfly.

**asina, ae** f she-ass.

**asinārius, ī** m donkey-driver.

**asinus, ī** m ass; blockhead.

**asōtus, ī** m libertine.

**asparagus, ī** m asparagus.

**a-spectābilis, e** visible.

**a-spectō** 1 to look at attentively or with respect; 1. to lie towards (alqd); 2. to observe (alqd).

**a-spectus, ūs** m 1. a looking at, glance, look; a) limit of vision; b) faculty of seeing; 2. appearance.

**as-pellō, pulī, pulsum** 3 to drive away.

**asper, era, erum** rough, uneven, stormy; a) cold, harsh, hard, sharp, coarse; b) bitter, abusive; c) cruel, severe, unkind, violent; d) troublesome, difficult, adverse, dangerous.

**a-spergō¹, rsī, rsum** 3 1. to sprinkle, scatter on (alqd alci); 2. to besprinkle, taint (alqa re).

**a-spergō², inis** f a sprinkling; drops, spray.

**asperitās, ātis** f roughness, unevenness; a) sharpness, sourness, harshness; b) rudeness; c) fierceness, severity, austerity; d) calamity, difficulty, adversity, violence.

**aspernātiō, ōnis** f disdain, contempt.

**a-spernor** 1 to despise, reject.

**asperō** 1 a) to make rough or uneven; b) to sharpen; c) to excite, exasperate.

**aspersiō, ōnis** f a sprinkling, a laying on of colours.

**a-spiciō, spexī, spectum** 3 to look at or upon; 1. to behold, see, observe; 2. to face; a) to lie towards; b) to inspect, examine, survey; c) to consider, weigh, ponder, respect.

**a-spīrāmen, inis** *n* something breathed on; favour, gift.

**a-spīrātiō, ōnis** *f* a breathing upon; exhalation.

**a-spīrō 1 1.** to breathe at *or* upon; to exhale; **a)** to be favourable (*with dat.*), to assist; **b)** to strive for, seek to reach, aspire to (*in, ad alqm or alqd*); **2.** *trans.* to breathe *or* blow something upon a person; to infuse, instil.

**aspis, idis** *f* viper, adder.

**as-portātiō, ōnis** *f* a carrying away.

**as-portō 1** to carry *or* bring away.

**asprētum, ī** *n* rough, uneven, stony place.

**assecla, ae** *m* = **assectator.**

**as-sectātiō, ōnis** *f* attendance.

**as-sectātor, ōris** *m* attendant, follower; disciple.

**as-sector 1** to follow, accompany.

**assecula, ae** *m* = **assectator.**

**as-sēnsiō, ōnis** *f* **a)** an assenting, assent, applause; **b)** belief in the reality of sensible appearances.

**as-sēnsor, ōris** *m* one who assents.

**as-sēnsus, ūs** *m* = **assensio;** echo.

**assentātiō, ōnis** *f* **a)** an assenting; **b)** flattering assent, flattery, adulation.

**assentātiuncula, ae** *f* base flattery.

**assentātor, ōris** *m* flatterer.

**assentātōriē** *adv.* in a flattering manner.

**as-sentātrīx, īcis** *f* female flatterer.

**as-sentior, sēnsus sum** (*and* **as-sentiō**) **4** to assent, agree (*alci de re, in re*).

**as-sentor 1** to assent; to flatter (*alci*).

**as-sequor 3** to overtake, reach (*with acc.*); **a)** to become like, to equal; **b)** to obtain, gain; **c)** to comprehend, understand.

**asser, eris** *m* stake, pole, post.

**as-serō[1], seruī, sertum 3** to join to; **a)** to lay hold of, claim; to assume; **b)** to set free, liberate; **c)** (*in servitutem*) to claim as a slave.

**as-serō[2], sēvī, situm 3** to sow *or* plant near.

**assertiō, ōnis** *f* declaration of a person's free status.

**assertor, ōris** *m* one who asserts a person's free state or servile status; defender, champion.

**as-serviō 4** to help, assist (*with dat.*).

**as-servō 1** to keep carefully, to preserve; to watch.

**as-sessiō, ōnis** *f,* **as-sessus, ūs** *m* a sitting near.

**as-sessor, ōris** *m* **a)** assistant; **b)** assessor (of a judge).

**as-sevēranter** *adv.* earnestly.

**as-sevērātiō, ōnis** *f* **a)** earnestness, perseverance; **b)** earnest assertion *or* affirmation.

**as-sevērō 1 1.** to do with earnestness; **2. a)** to affirm *or* assert earnestly; **b)** to show, prove.

**as-sideō, sēdī, sessum 2** to sit near, by the side of; **a)** to attend, watch, wait upon; **b)** to encamp before, to besiege, blockade.

**as-sīdō, sēdī, sessum 3** to sit down.

**assiduitās, ātis** *f* a sitting at; **a)** constant attendance, presence, attention; **b)** continual intercourse; **c)** constant repetition; **d)** perseverance, persistence, constancy.

**assiduus 3** sitting near; **a)** established, well-off, (man) of substance; **b)** untiring, incessant, unremitting; **c)** perpetual, continuous.

**assignātiō, ōnis** *f* an assigning, allotment.

**as-signō 1** to assign, allot, to commit, intrust; to ascribe, attribute (*alci alqd*).

**as-siliō, siluī,** (**sultum**) **4** to leap *or* spring at *or* upon; to assail.

**as-similis, e** like, similar.

**as-simulātiō, ōnis** *f* comparison.

**as-simulō 1** to make like, copy (*alqd alci rei*); **a)** to compare; **b)** to imitate, counterfeit, feign, pretend (*alqd,* with *acc.c.inf.,* with *quasi*).

**as-sistō, stitī,** — **3 a)** to stand at, by, near; **b)** to help, defend.

**as-soleō,** —, — **2** to be wont, accustomed; **ut assolet** as is usual.

**as-sonō,** —, — **1** to resound, answer.

**as-sūdāscō 3** to get into a perspiration.

**as-suēfaciō 3** to accustom to (*alqm alqa re or ad alqd,* with *dat.* or with *inf.*).

**as-suēscō 3 1.** to become accustomed (*alqa re, ad alqd*); **2.** to make familiar; **3.** to accustom; **assuētus 3 a)** accustomed; **b)** usual, customary, familiar.

**assuētūdō, inis** *f* custom, habit, intercourse.

**as-sūgō 3** to suck in.          [plank.|

**assula, ae** *f* splinter of wood; board,|

**assulātim** *adv.* in splinters *or* fragments. [(*alqd* or with *dat.*).]
**as-sultō** 1 to leap at, assault, attack
**assultus, ūs** *m* assault, attack.
**as-sum, affuī, adesse** (**afforem** = **adessem, affore** = **affutūrum esse**); to be at, by, near; to be at hand, be present; **a)** to appear, arrive; **b)** to appear before a tribunal (*in iudicio, ad iudicium*); **c)** to share, participate, assist (*alci rei*); **d)** to be present to witness *or* to support, defend (*alci in re*); **e)** to give attention (*animo*).
**as-sūmō** 3 to take to oneself, receive; **a)** to take in addition to (*alqd ad alqd* or with *dat.*); **b)** to take for one's assistance; **c)** to appropriate to oneself, to claim, assume, arrogate.
**as-sūmptiō, ōnis** *f* a taking to one; **a)** approval; **b)** minor proposition of a syllogism.
**as-sūmptīvus** 3 resting on external evidence.
**as-suō** 3 to sew on.
**as-surgō** 3 to rise up, stand up; to mount.
**assus** 3 roasted; (*nutrix*) dry-nurse; *subst.* **assum, ī** *n* **a)** roast meat; **b)** dry heat bath.
**ast** = **at**.
**a-sternō** 3 to strew on, scatter upon.
**asticus** 3 of a city, city-.
**a-stipulātor, ōris** *m* **a)** one who joins in accepting a verbal contract; **b)** supporter.
**a-stipulor** 1 to agree with (*alci*).
**a-stituō** 3 to add, place to.
**a-stō, stitī,** — 1 **a)** to stand at, by, near; **b)** to stand upright *or* erect; **c)** to assist, aid.
**a-strepō, puī, pitum** 3 to make a noise at; **a)** to shout; **b)** to applaud, assent loudly (*alci*).
**a-strictus** 3 drawn together, tight; **a)** sparing, parsimonious; **b)** concise, brief.
**a-stridō** 3 to hiss (at).
**astri-fer** 3 and **astri-ger** 3 starry.
**a-stringō** 3 to draw together, contract, bind together (*alqd ad alqd*); **a)** to cause to freeze *or* congeal; **b)** to bind, fetter, oblige (*alqm alqa re*); **c)** to circumscribe, condense.
**astro-logia, ae** *f* astronomy.
**astro-logus, ī** *m* **a)** astronomer; **b)** astrologer.

**astro-nomia, ae** *f* astronomy.
**astrum, ī** *n* star, constellation; (*pl.*) heaven, immortality, glory.
**a-struō** 3 to build to, in addition; to add.
**astu** *n* (*indecl.*) city (Athens).
**a-stupeō,** —, — 2 to be astonished *or* amazed at (*alci rei*).
**astus, ūs** *m* cunning, craft; stratagem.
**astūtia, ae** *f* **a)** skill, adroitness; **b)** cunning, craft, astuteness.
**astūtus** 3 **a)** shrewd, sagacious; **b)** crafty, cunning.
**asȳlum, ī** *n* place of refuge, sanctuary, asylum.
**asymbolus** 3 contributing nothing (to an entertainment).
**at** *cj.* but, yet, but on the other hand, moreover, but meanwhile; **at contra** but on the contrary, **at vero** *or* **at certe** but certainly, **at tamen** and yet; *si non* — **at** (*certe, tamen*) if not — but yet *or* nevertheless; but at least.
**atābulus, ī** *m* south-east wind, sirocco.
**atat** *int.*, *see* **attat**.
**at-avus, ī** *m* great-great-great-grandfather; ancestor.
**āter, ātra, ātrum** black, dead black, dark; **a)** clothed in black; **b)** gloomy, sad, unfortunate, dismal, unlucky; **c)** malicious, virulent, deadly.
**āthlēta, ae** *m* wrestler, athlete.
**āthlēticē** like an athlete.
**a-tomus, ī** *f* indivisible body, atom.
**atque** *cj.* (*before consonants* **ac**) **a)** and, and also, and moreover, and even, and especially; **b)** *after words of comparison* (*aequus, similis, talis, alius, contra, dissimilis* etc.): as, than; **c)** and so, and thus, and consequently; **atque adeo** and in fact.
**at-quī** *cj.* yet, however, nevertheless, notwithstanding, rather; (*in syllogisms to introduce the minor proposition*): but, now.
**ātrāmentum, ī** *n* black liquid, blacking, ink.
**ātrātus** 3 clothed in black.
**ātri-color** black.
**ātriēnsis, is** *m* house-steward.
**ātriolum, ī** *n* small hall *or* forecourt.
**ātritās, ātis** *f* blackness.
**ātrium, ī** *n* forecourt, hall; **a)** principal room of a house; **b)** house, palace.

**atrōcitās, ātis** *f* a) fierceness, harshness, atrociousness; **b)** severity, barbarity.

**atrōx, ōcis** a) repulsive, horrid, terrible; **b)** savage, fierce, cruel, harsh, severe; **c)** violent, perilous; **d)** morose, gloomy.

**at-tāctus, ūs** *m* a touching, touch.

**attagēn, ēnis** *m* (*and* **attagēna, ae** *f*) woodcock.

**at-tamen** *cj.* but yet, but nevertheless.

**attat, attatae** *exclamation of surprise, pain, warning etc.:* oh! alas!

**attegia, ae** *f* hut, tent.

**at-temperātē** *adv.* appropriately, seasonably.

**at-temperō** 1 to fit on; to direct, point at.

**at-temptō** 1 to make a trial of; a) to try to corrupt; **b)** to attack, assail.

**at-tendō, dī, tum** 3 to stretch to, direct to, (*animum*) to give attention to (*ad alqd*), give heed, to mind (*alqd, alci rei* or with *acc.c.inf.*).

**at-tentiō, ōnis** *f* attentiveness, attention.

**at-tentō = attempto.**

**at-tentus** 3 a) attentive, engaged; **b)** intent on, striving after; **c)** economical

**at-tenuō** 1 to make thin; a) to lessen, diminish; **b)** to weaken, reduce, impair; **attenuātus** 3 concise, meagre, dry, affected.

**at-terō** 3 a) to rub against; **b)** to rub away, wear away; **c)** to destroy, waste, injure.

**at-testor** 1 to bear witness *or* testimony, to attest.

**at-texō** 3 to weave *or* plait to; to join closely (*alqd ad alqd* or with *dat.*).

**atticissō** 1 to be in the Attic manner.

**at-tineō, tinuī, (tentum)** 2 1. to hold fast, detain; a) to delay, keep (*re*); b) to hold, have possession of; 2. *intr.* to reach, pertain to, a) to concern; **quod attinet ad me** for my part, as far as I am concerned; b) **non** or **nihil attinet** it is of no use, does not matter.

**at-tingō, tigī, tāctum** 3 to touch against, come in contact with (*alqd*); a) to arrive at, reach; b) to border on; **c)** to touch, strike, lay hands on, seize, attack; d) to come in contact with, belong to, be related to; e) to engage in, undertake, manage, be occupied in; f) to touch, mention, refer to.

**at-tollō, —, —** 3 a) to raise up, lift up; to erect; to raise (*alqd ad* or *in alqd*), elevate, exalt, distinguish, aggrandize; **b) P.** to rise up.

**at-tondeō, ndī, nsum** 2 a) to shear, shave, cut; b) to lessen, depreciate.

**at-tonitus** 3 thunder-struck; a) stunned, terrified, senseless; b) inspired, frantic.

**at-tonō** 1 to thunder at, strike with thunder; a) to stun, terrify; b) to inspire. [whirl upwards.]

**at-torqueō, —, —** 2 to hurl *or*]

**at-trahō** 3 a) to draw to, attract; a) to pull tight; b) to drag; c) to allure, take with one.

**at-trectātus, ūs** *m* touching, feeling.

**at-trectō** 1 to touch, handle; a) to lay hands on; b) to appropriate; c) to busy oneself with.

**at-tremō** 3 to tremble at (*dat.*).

**at-trepidō** 1 to go to tremblingly.

**at-tribuō** 3 to allot, assign to, make over; a) to commit, confer, bestow; b) to pay out; c) to attribute, ascribe, impute; d) to add, annex; e) to attribute words to.

**at-tribūtiō, ōnis** *f* a) an assigning, assignment; b) predicate, attribute. (*also* **attribūtum**).

**at-trītus** 3 worn; shameless.

**au** *int.* oh! ah! now!

**au-ceps, cupis** *m* bird-catcher, fowler; **syllabarum** quibbler, wordcatcher.

**auctārium, ī** *n* addition.

**aucti-ficus** 3 promoting increase.

**auctiō, ōnis** *f* a) public sale, auction; b) goods sold at an auction.

**auctiōnārius** 3 pertaining to an auction.

**auctiōnor** 1 to hold an auction.

**auctitō** 1 to increase greatly.

**auctō** 1 to increase, augment.

**auctor, ōris** *m* (and *f*) **1.** guarantor, attesting witness (*alcis rei*); a) example, model, teacher, authority; b) narrator, historian, writer, author; c) voucher, security, d) guardian (*of a woman*); e) witness; f) promoter, producer; **2.** adviser, counsellor; originator, doer, beginner, causer; founder, maker, inventor; progenitor.

**auctōrāmentum, ī** *n* contract; wages, pay, earnest-money.

**auctōritās, ātis** *f* **1.** warrant, security, attestation; a) credibility; b) legal ownership, right of possession, property; c) full power, authorisation; d) legal document *or* deed; **2.** a) model, pattern, example, precedent; b) weight, dignity, influence, importance, power, worth, consequence, estimation; c) influential person; **3.** a) counsel, advice, encouragement; b) will, pleasure, decision, bidding, command; c) decree *or* will (*of the Senate*).

**auctōrō** 1 to bind, oblige, pledge; to hire.

**auctumnus, ī** *m, see* **autumnus.**

**auctus¹, ūs** *m* a) an increasing, augmenting; b) increase, growth, thriving.

**auctus²** 3 increased, enlarged.

**aucupium, ī** *n* a) bird-catching, fowling; b) the hunting after a thing; **verbōrum** a quibbling.

**aucupor** (*and* **aucupō**) 1 to strive for, hunt after, lie in wait for (*alqd*).

**audācia, ae** *f* a) courage, daring, boldness, bravery; b) temerity, presumption, insolence; c) bold action.

**audāx, ācis** (*adv.* **audācter**) a) courageous, daring, bold, intrepid; b) foolhardy, audacious, rash, insolent.

**audēns, tis** daring, bold, courageous.

**audentia, ae** *f* boldness, courage.

**audeō, ausus sum** 2 a) to have a mind, to be willing; b) to dare, venture, risk.

**audiēns, tis** *m* hearer, listener.

**audientia, ae** *f* a hearing, listening; attention; **-am facere alci** to procure a hearing for.

**audiō** 4 **1.** to hear, to have the faculty of hearing; **2.** to perceive, understand, learn; *subst.* **audītum, ī** *n* hearsay, report; **audītō** on hearing; a) to listen to; b) to hear a case, to examine; c) to lend an ear to a prayer, to grant; d) to approve of, give credence to; e) to obey, follow, **dicto audiēns esse** to obey; **3.** to be called, named, reported, pass for, **bene** (**male**) **audire** to be well (ill) spoken of, to be in good (bad) repute (*ab alqo*).

**audītiō, ōnis** *f* a) a hearing, listening; b) hearsay, report.

**audītō** 1 to hear often.

**audītor, ōris** *m* hearer, listener; pupil, scholar.

**audītōrium, ī** *n* lecture-room, (place of) audience.

**audītus, ūs** *m* a) sense of hearing; b) = **audītio.**

**au-ferō, abstulī, ablātum** 3 **1.** to carry away, bring away (*alqd ab, ex, de re*); **se auferre** to remove oneself, withdraw; **P.** to hurry *or* run away, to disappear; **2.** to take away, carry off, snatch away (*alqd de or ab re, alci alqd*); to rob, steal; to destroy, kill; **3.** to gain, obtain, get (*alqd ab alqo,* with *ut*).

**au-fugiō** 3 to flee away, to flee from (*alqd*).

**augeō, xī, ctum** 2 to cause to grow; **1.** to increase, augment, enlarge, extend; a) to exaggerate; b) to magnify, extol; **2.** to furnish abundantly, to enrich, load (*alqm re*); to advance, honour; **P.** to grow, become greater.

**augēscō, —, —** 3 to begin to grow, to become greater.

**augmen, minis** *n* increase, bulk.

**augur, uris** *m* augur, diviner.

**augurālis, e** pertaining to an augur; *subst.* **augurāle, is** *n* the general's tent in a camp.

**augurātiō, ōnis** *f* a divining.

**augurātus, ūs** *m* office of an augur.

**augurium, ī** *n* a) interpretation of omens, divination, augury; prophecy; b) presentiment, foreboding; c) omen, sign.

**augurius** 3 = **auguralis.**

**augurō** 1 *and* **auguror** 1 **1.** to act as an augur, to interpret omens; **augurātō** after taking the auguries; **2.** a) to consecrate, dedicate; b) to predict, foretell, prophesy; c) to conjecture, forebode.

**augustus** 3 a) consecrated, sacred, reverend, venerable, majestic, elevated; b) **Augustus** 3 relating to the month of August; (*mensis*) *m* August.

**aula¹, ae** *f* **1.** yard, forecourt; **2.** a) royal court, palace; b) royal dignity; c) courtiers.

**aula², ae** *f* = **olla.**

**aulaeum, ī** *n* hangings, canopy, curtain (*esp. in a theatre*).

**aulicus** 3 belonging to a princely court.

**auloedus, ī** *m* one who sings to the flute.

**aura, ae** *f* breath of air, breeze, gentle breeze; a) air (*pl.* the upper air, heaven, the upper world); b) breath, wind; odour, exhalation; c) breath of favour (**aura popularis**); d) scent, slight indication.

**aurārius** 3 relating to gold; *subst.* **aurāria, ae** *f* gold-mine.

**aurātus** 3 gilded, ornamented with gold; golden.

**aureolus** 3 = **aureus**.

**aureus** 3 of gold, golden; (*nummus*) gold coin (*worth 25 denarii*); a) gilt, ornamented with gold; b) of the colour of gold, glittering like gold; c) beautiful, magnificent, excellent; lovely.

**auri-chalcum, ī** *n* a) imaginary precious metal; b) = **orichalcum**.

**auricilla, ae** *f* lobe of the ear.

**auri-comus** 3 with golden hair, with golden foliage.

**auricula, ae** *f* lobe of the ear; ear.

**auri-fer** 3 carrying gold.

**auri-fex, ficis** *m* goldsmith.

**aurīga, ae** *m* charioteer, driver (*also* **A~** *a* constellation); pilot, helmsman.

**aurīgārius, ī** *m* driver in a chariot--race.

**aurīgātiō, ōnis** *f* a driving in a chariot-race.

**auri-gena, ae** sprung from gold.

**auri-ger** 3 bearing gold.

**aurīgō** 1 to drive a racing-chariot.

**auris, is** *f* the ear; **aures alci praebere** *or* **dare** to give attention to; a) (*pl.*) sense of hearing, critical judgment; b) earth-board of a plough.

**auri-scalpium, ī** *n* ear-pick.

**aurītulus, ī** *m* long-eared animal, ass.

**aurītus** 3 long-eared; listening.

**aurōra, ae** *f* dawn, daybreak; the east.

**aurufex** = **aurifex**.

**aurum, ī** *n* gold, a) vessel *or* ornament of gold, b) coined gold, money; c) golden lustre, brightness; d) the Golden Age

**ausculor** 1 = **osculor**.

**auscultātiō, ōnis** *f* an obeying

**auscultātor, ōris** *m* listener

**auscultō** 1 to hear with attention, listen to (*alqd*); to obey (*alci*).

**ausim** *subjunctive of* **audeō**.

**au-spex, icis** *m* bird-seer; interpreter of omens; a) director, leader, protector; b) witness at a marriage.

**auspicātus** 3, *see* **auspico**.

**auspicium, ī** *n* 1. a) divination by means of birds, auspices; b) the right to take auspices; c) command, guidance, power, authority, inclination, will; the beginning; 2. sign, omen.

**(auspicō** 1 *and*) **auspicor** 1 1. to take the auspices, **auspicātō** after taking the auspices; 2. to begin *or* undertake under good auspices; to begin (*alqd*); **auspicātus** 3 inaugurated, consecrated; favourable, fortunate, lucky, auspicious.

**auster, strī** *m* the south wind; the south.

**austēritās, ātis** *f* severity.

**austērus** 3 sour, harsh; a) severe, strict; b) morose, gloomy, sad, hard.

**austrālis, e** southern.

**austrīnus** 3 due to the south wind.

**ausum, ī** *n* (*and* **ausus, ūs** *m*) venture, bold undertaking.

**aut** *cj.* or, or else; **aut ... aut** either — or; **neque aut ... aut** and neither — nor.

**autem** *cj.* (*never at the beginning of a clause*) 1. but, however, on the other hand, moreover; 2. and now, besides, further.

**authepsa, ae** *f* cooking-apparatus.

**auto-graphus** 3 written with one's own hand.

**auto-maton, ī** *n* self-moving machine.

**autumnālis, e** autumnal.

**autumnus** 3 autumnal; *subst.* **autumnus, ī** *m* autumn.

**autumō** 1 to assert, affirm.

**auxiliāris, e, -ārius** 3 a) aiding, helping, assisting; b) auxiliary; **auxiliārēs, ium** *m/pl.* auxiliary troops.

**auxiliātor, ōris** *m* helper, assistant.

**auxiliātus, ūs** *m* aid

**auxilior** 1 to help, succour, assist (*alci*).

**auxilium, ī** *n* help, assistance, aid, **alci auxiliō esse** *or* **auxilium ferre** to come to one's assistance, to help; **auxiliō alcis** with the aid of; *pl.* a) expedients, resources; b) auxiliary troops, military power.

avāritia, ae (and tiēs, ēi) f avarice, covetousness, greediness.

avārus 3 greedy, covetous, avaricious; eagerly desirous; adv. avārē, avāriter.

ā-vehō 3 to carry or convey off or away (alqd ab alqo, ex re in alqd). P. to ride, sail, drive away.

ā-vellō, vellī or vulsī, vulsum 3 a) to tear, rend, pluck, pull off, snatch away (alci alqd); b) to separate by force (alqd ab or de re).

avēna, ae f 1. oats, wild oats; 2. straw; oaten or pastoral pipe.

aveō[1], —, — 2 to long for, desire earnestly, crave (alqd).

aveō[2] 2 to fare well; avē, avēte hail! farewell!

ā-verrō, verrī, — 3 to sweep away.

ā-verruncō 1 to avert (evil).

ā-versābilis, e abominable.

ā-versātiō, ōnis f dislike, aversion.

ā-versiō, ōnis f a turning away; ex āversiōne from behind.

ā-versor[1] 1 to turn oneself from, to shrink from; to repulse.

ā-versor[2] ōris m embezzler.

ā-versus 3 turned away or backward; back; subst. āversa, ōrum n/pl. the back part; — disinclined, unfavourable, hostile, averse (with dat.).

ā-vertō 3 to turn away or off, to avert, divert (alqm or alqd ab, ex re ad or in alqd); P. to turn oneself away from (with acc.); intr. to turn away; a) to put to flight; b) to carry off, purloin, steal, embezzle; c) to estrange, alienate; d) to keep off, ward off.

avia, ae f grandmother.

aviārium, ī m haunt of birds, aviary.

aviditās, ātis f eagerness, vehement desire, longing; covetousness, greediness.

avidus 3 eager, desirous, longing (alcis rei, in or ad rem); a) greedy, voracious, gluttonous; b) avaricious, covetous; c) ardent, fiery.

avis, is f bird; omen, portent.

avītus 3 of a grandfather, ancestral, hereditary; very old.

āvius 3 a) out of the way, remote, unfrequented; subst. āvia, ōrum n/pl. solitude; b) wandering.

āvocāmentum, ī n distraction, recreation.

ā-vocātiō, ōnis f a calling away, diversion.

ā-vocō 1 to call away; a) to withdraw, remove (a re, in rem); b) to divert, distract. [vanish.]

ā-volō 1 to fly away; to flee away,]

ā-vors-, -vort- = ā-vers-, -vert-.

avunculus, ī m maternal uncle; great-uncle.

avus, ī m grandfather; ancestor.

axicia, ae f pair of scissors.

axis[1], is m 1. axle-tree; wagon, car, chariot; 2. the North Pole; 3. the heaven; region, clime.

axis[2], is m board, plank.

axula, ae f = assula.

# B

babae *int.* wonderful! strange!
bāca (bacca), ae *f* 1. berry; round fruit, olive; 2. pearl.
bācātus 3 adorned with pearls.
baccar, aris *n* cyclamen.
bacchābundus 3 raving like the Bacchantes.
Bacchānal, ālis *n* place devoted to Bacchus; feast of Bacchus.
Bacchānālia, ium *n/pl.* feast of Bacchus.                [gies.\
bacchātiō, ōnis *f* bacchanalian or-/
bacchor 1 to celebrate the festival of Bacchus; a) to revel, rave, rage; b) to run about wildly.
bāci-fer 3 bearing berries *or* olives.
bacillum, ī *n* a little staff; the lictor's wand.
baculum, ī *n* (*and* baculus, ī *m*) stick, staff.
badizō 1 to walk, march.
bāi(i)olō, -olus = bāiulō, -ulus.
bāiulō 1 to carry a burden.
bāiulus, ī *m* porter, carrier.
balanātus 3 perfumed with balsam.
balanus, ī *f* 1. balsam-nut; 2. a shell-fish.
balatrō, ōnis *m* jester, buffoon.
bālātus, ūs *m* a bleating.
balbus 3 stammering.
balbūtiō 4 to stammer, stutter; to stammer out.
balineum, ī *n* = balneum.
bālitō 1 to bleat.
ballaena, ae *f* whale.
ballista, ae *f* military engine for hurling stones.
ballistārium, ī *n* = ballista.
balneārius 3 belonging to a bath; *subst.* balneāria, ōrum *n/pl.* bathing-rooms.
balneātor, ōris *m* bath-keeper.
balneolum, ī *n* small bathroom.
balneum, ī *n* bathroom, bath; balnea, ōrum *n/pl. or* balneae, ārum *f/pl.* public baths.
bālō 1 to bleat; *subst.* bālantēs, ium, um *f/pl.* sheep.
balsamum, ī *n* balsam(-tree).
balteus, ī *m* (*and* -um, ī *n*) sword--belt, baldric.

balūx, ūcis *f* gold-dust.
baptistērium, ī *n* bath.
barathrum, ī *n* abyss, chasm, belly.
barba, ae *f* beard.
barbaria, ae (*and* barbariēs, ēī) *f* 1. foreign country (of the barbarians); 2. rudeness, roughness, savageness, want of culture.
barbaricus 3 barbarian, foreign.
barbarus 3 1. foreign, strange; *subst.* barbarus, ī *m* foreigner, barbarian; 2. rude, savage, uncivilized, cruel.
barbātulus 3 with a small beard.
barbātus 3 bearded; *subst.* ~, ī *m* an old Roman.
barbi-ger 3 bearded.
barbitos, ī *m* lyre, lute.
barbula, ae *f* small beard.
bardītus, ūs *m* = barritus.
bardocucullus, ī *m* (Gallic) hooded cloak.
bardus 3 stupid, dull.
bāris, idos *f* Egyptian rowing-barge.
bārō, ōnis *m* simpleton.
barritus, ūs *m* war-song of the Germans; war-cry.
barrus, ī *m* elephant.
bascauda, ae *f* bowl (*or* basket?).
bāsiātiō, ōnis *f* a kissing, kiss.
bāsiātor, ōris *m* one who kisses.
basilicus 3 royal, princely; *subst. m* a 'royal' (highest) throw at dice; *f* basilica, public building (*law-court, exchange*).
bāsiō 1 to kiss.
basis, is *f* base; a) pedestal; b) foundation; c) base of a triangle.
bāsium, ī *n* kiss.
batillum, ī *n* = vatillum.
batioca, ae *f* cup.
battuō, —, — 3 to beat, strike.
baubor 1 to bark.
baxea, ae *f* a kind of sandal.
bdellium, ī *n* a fragrant gum.
beātitās, ātis *and* beātitūdō, inis *f* happiness, felicity.
beātus 3 happy; 1. prosperous, rich, wealthy, beātī the rich; fertile, abundant, excellent; 2. blessed, fortunate; making happy (*dimin.* beātulus).

bellāria, ōrum n/pl. dessert, fruit.

bellātor, ōris m warrior; warlike.

bellātōrius 3 pertaining to war.

bellātrix, īcis f warlike.

bellāx, ācis f warlike.

bellē adv. of bellus.

belliāt(ul)us = bellus.

bellicōsus 3 warlike, martial; fond of fighting or war.

bellicus 3 1. belonging to war, of war; subst. bellicum, ī n war-signal; bellicum canere to blow the war-trumpet; 2. = bellicosus.

belli-ger 3 warlike.

belli-gerō 1 to wage war, to fight.

belli-potēns, tis mighty in war.

bellō 1 (and bellor 1) to wage war, fight (cum alqo, adversus alqm, pro alqo).

bellum, ī n war; in bello or belli in war, during war; domi bellique in peace and in war; combat, fight, contest.

bellus 3 pretty, charming (dimin. beñlulus).

bēlua, ae f wild beast, monster, brute. [of animals.]

bēluātus 3 ornamented with figures/

bēluōsus 3 abounding in monsters.

bene adv. (melius, optimē) 1. well (better, best), properly, rightly, exactly, prosperously; bene agere to do or act well, (cum alqo to treat kindly); bene dicere to speak well of (alci), to commend, praise; bene facere to do or make well or rightly (alci to do good, to benefit); bene factum good deed, favour; bene est it is well, I am glad or satisfied; bene te (or tibi) good health to you!; 2. thoroughly, fully, very much (bene impudens, bene sanus, bene notus, bene mane).

benedicē adv. with friendly speech.

bene-ficentia, ae f kindness, liberality.

bene-ficiārius, ī m privileged soldier (exempt from menial work).

bene-ficium, ī n a) kindness, favour, benefit, service; beneficiō alcis rei by means of; b) distinction, honour, promotion, grant; c) privilege.

bene-ficus 3 kind, generous, liberal.

bene-volēns, tis = benevolus.

bene-volentia, ae f a) good-will, benevolence (erga or in alqm); b) favour.

bene-volus 3 well wishing, benevolent, kind (alci).

benignitās, ātis f a) kindness, friendliness, mildness, courtesy; b) liberality, bounty (in alqm).

benignus 3 kind; a) goodnatured, friendly, pleasing, benignant; b) beneficent, liberal, obliging; fruitful, copious, rich (benignē facere alci = bene facere); benignē you are very kind, much obliged to you!

beō 1 to make happy, bless, gladden.

bēryllus, ī m a precious stone, beryl.

bēs, bessis m two thirds.

bēsālis, e weighing eight ounces.

bēstia, ae f beast, animal; beast of prey.

bēstiārius 3 of wild beasts; subst. m one who fights with wild beasts.

bēstiola, ae f small animal.

bēta¹, ae f (a vegetable) beet.

bēta² the second letter of the Greek alphabet, B.

bētāceus, ī m beetroot.

biblio-pōla, ae m book-seller.

biblio-thēca, ae f library.

biblus, ī f papyrus.

bibō, bibī, — 3 to drink; to imbibe, absorb, drink in.

bibulus 3 fond of drinking; absorbent.

bi-ceps, cipitis two-headed; with two peaks.

bi-clīnium, ī n dining sofa for two persons.

bi-color, ōris two-coloured.

bi-corniger 3 and bi-cornis, e two-horned; two-pronged.

bi-corpor, oris with two bodies.

bi-dēns, tis with two teeth or prongs; subst. m hoe, fork; f sheep.

bidental, ālis n place struck by lightning.

bīduum, ī n space of two days; bīduō in two days.

bi-ennium, ī n space of two years.

bi-fāriam adv. in two ways or parts.

bi-fer 3 bearing (fruit) twice.

bi-fidus 3 split into two parts.

bi-foris, e having two doors or openings.

bi-fōrmātus 3 double-formed.

bi-fōrmis, e two-formed; two-shaped.

bi-frōns, tis with two foreheads.

bi-furcus 3 two-pronged.

bīgae, ārum f/pl. (also bīga, ae) pair of horses; two-horsed chariot.

**bīgātus** 3 bearing the figure of a pair of horses; ~, ī *m* silver coin so stamped.

**bi-iugis, e** *and* **bi-iugus** 3 yoked two together; *subst.* **biiugī, ōrum** *m/pl.* = **bigae.**

**bi-lībra, ae** *f* two pounds.

**bi-lībris, e** weighing *or* holding two pounds.

**bi-linguis, e** having two tongues; **a)** speaking two languages; **b)** double-tongued, false.

**bīlis, is** *f* bile, bilious effusion; **a)** anger, wrath; **b)** melancholy, sadness.

**bi-lix, īcis** with a double thread.

**bi-lūstris, e** lasting ten years.

**bi-maris, e** lying on two seas.

**bi-marītus** 3 husband of two wives.

**bi-māter, tris** having two mothers.

**bi-membris, e** with double members; *subst.* ~, **is** *m* centaur.

**bi-mē(n)stris, e** of two months.

**bīmulus** 3 only two years old.

**bīmus** 3 two years old.

**bīnī, ae, a** **a)** two by two, two for each; **b)** a pair, two.

**bi-noctium, ī** *n* space of two nights.

**bi-nōminis, e** having two names.

**bi-palmis, e** two palms long.

**bi-partītus, bi-pertītus** 3 (*adv.* -ō), in two parts, in two ways.

**bi-patēns, tis** with two doors open, wide open.

**bi-pedālis, e** two feet long.

**bipenni-fer** 3 bearing a two-edged axe.

**bi-pennis, e** double-edged; *subst.* ~, **is** *f* double-edged axe.

**bi-pertītus** 3 = **bipartitus.**

**bi-pēs, edis** two-footed, biped.

**bi-rēmis, e** two-oared; *subst.* **bi-rēmis, is** *f* ship with two sets of oars.

**bis** *adv.* twice; in two ways.

**bi-sulcus** 3 (*or* **cis, ce**) forked, split.

**bītō** 3 to go.

**bitūmen, inis** *n* mineral pitch, asphalt, bitumen.

**bitūmineus** 3 bituminous.

**bi-vertex, icis** with two peaks.

**bi-vius** 3 having two ways; *subst.* **bivium, ī** *n* place where two roads meet.

**blaesus** 3 lisping, stammering.

**blandi-dicus** 3, **blandi-loquus** 3, **blandi-loquentulus** 3 smooth-tongued.

**blandi-loquentia, ae** *f* flattery.

**blandīmentum, ī** *n* = **blanditia.**

**blandior** 4 **a)** to flatter, caress, coax; **b)** to please, gratify, to be favourable (*with dat.*).

**blanditia, ae** *f* **a)** flattery, caress; **b)** blandishments, allurements; **c)** delight, enticement, charm; **d)** dainty.

**blandus** 3 **a)** flattering, fondling, caressing; **b)** charming, agreeable, enticing, alluring; — *adv.* **blandē, -diter, -dītim.**

**blaterō** 1 *and* **blatiō** 4 to babble, prate.

**blatta, ae** *f* moth, cockroach.

**blennus** 3 stupid.

**bliteus** 3 insipid, silly.

**blit(e)um, ī** *n* a tasteless kitchen-vegetable.

**boārius** 3 relating to cattle.

**boia, ae** *f* collar.

**bōlētātiō, ōnis** *f* mushroom-eating.

**bōlētus, ī** *m* mushroom.

**bolus, ī** *m* throw of dice; gain, profit, advantage.

**bombax** *int.* strange! indeed!

**bombus, ī** *m* a humming.

**bombȳcinus** 3 of silk.

**bombȳx, ȳcis** *m* silk-worm; silk.

**bonitās, ātis** *f* **a)** goodness; **b)** virtue, integrity, kindness.

**bonum, ī** *n* **a)** a good, the good; **b)** excellence; **c)** profit, advantage; **bonō esse** *alci* to be of advantage; **bonum publicum** the common weal; **d)** *pl.* **bona** goods, property.

**bonus** 3 (*comp.* **melior, us,** *superl.* **optimus** 3, *adv.* **bene**) good; **1. a)** excellent, perfect; **b)** fit, proper, suitable, able, clever; **c)** brave, courageous; **d)** noble, distinguished, genteel, aristocratic, **optimī** *m/pl.* = **optimates;** **e)** rich, wealthy; **f)** considerable, large; **g)** fair, nice, delicate; **h)** favourable, propitious, kind; **bonae res** good fortune; **2. a)** honest, righteous, virtuous, faithful, chaste; **bonus vir** man of honour; **bonae artes** good qualities, fine arts, liberal sciences; **b)** kind, auspicious, favourable; **c)** patriotic, loyal, aristocratic.

**boō** 1 to roar, to echo.

**boreās, ae** *m* the north-wind; the north.

**borēus** 3 northern.

**bōs, bovis** *m* and *f* ox, bull, cow.

**botryō, ōnis** *m* bunch of grapes.
**botulārius, ī** *m* sausage-maker.
**botulus** (*and* **botellus**), ī *m* sausage.
**bovārius** 3 = **boarius**.
**bovīle, is** *n* = **bubīle**.
**bovillus** 3 = **bubulus**.
**brācae, ārum** *pl.* (*and* **brāca,** ae) *f* breeches, trousers.
**brācātus** 3 a) wearing breeches; b) foreign; Transalpine.
**bracchiālis, e** of the arm.
**bracchiolum, ī** *n, dim. of* **bracchium.**
**bracchium, ī** *n* the whole arm; a) lower arm, fore-arm; b) branch of the sea, of trees; yard of a sail.
**brassica, ae** *f* cabbage.
**brattea** *and* **bratteola, ae** *f* gold-leaf.
**bratteātus** 3 gilded; fair-seeming, deceptive.
**breviārium, ī** *n* summary.
**breviculus** 3 shortish.
**brevi-loquēns, tis** short in speaking.
**brevis, e** short; 1. a) small, narrow, shallow, *subst.* **breve, is** *n* shallow place, shoal; b) little, indifferent, brief, concise; **brevī** *adv.* in short, shortly; 2. short in time, **brevī** (*tempore*) in a short time.
**brevitās, ātis** *f* shortness; brevity, conciseness.
**breviter** *adv. of* **brevis.**
**brūma, ae** *f* the shortest day in the year, the winter solstice; winter time, wintry cold.
**brūmālis, e** belonging to the winter solstice; wintry.
**brūtus** 3 heavy, inert; stupid.
**būbīle, is** *n* ox-stall.
**būbō, ōnis** *m* (*f*) owl.
**bubulcitor** 1 to be a cowherd.

**bubulcus, ī** *m* ox-driver, one who ploughs with oxen
**būbulus** 3 of cattle, of oxen; *subst.* **būbula, ae** *f* beef
**bū-caeda, ae** *m* one who is whipped with thongs of ox-hide.
**bucca, ae** *f* cheek. mouth.
**buccella, ae** *f* small mouthful.
**buccō, ōnis** *m* babbler, fool.
**buccula, ae** *f* cheek; cheek-piece.
**bucculentus** 3 puffy-cheeked.
**bū-cer(i)us** 3 ox-horned.
**būcētum, ī** *n* cattle-pasture.
**būcina, ae** *f* horn, crooked trumpet; a) shepherd's horn; b) trumpet-call; c) Triton's-horn.
**būcinātor, ōris** *m* trumpeter.
**būcolicus** 3 belonging to shepherds, bucolic.
**būcula, ae** *f* young cow, heifer.
**būfō, ōnis** *m* toad.
**bulbus, ī** *m* onion, garlic.
**būlē, ēs** *f* Greek council.
**būleuta, ae** *m* councillor.
**būleutērium, ī** *n* senate-house.
**bulla, ae** *f* a) bubble; b) boss, stud; c) amulet.
**bullātus** 3 wearing a *bulla* (*i. e.* a boy).
**bū-mastus, ī** *f* large grape.
**būris, is** *m* crooked beam holding the ploughshare.
**busti-rapus, ī** *m* robber of tombs.
**bustuārius** 3 belonging to a place for burning the dead.
**bustum, ī** *n* place for burning the dead; pyre, tomb.
**bū-thysia, ae** *f* sacrifice of oxen.
**buxētum, ī** *n* plantation of box-trees.
**buxeus** 3 yellowish.
**buxi-fer** 3 bearing box-trees.
**buxus, ī** *f and* **buxum, ī** *n* box(tree); a) boxwood; b) box flute, pipe, comb, spinning-top.

# C

**C.** *abbr.* a) = **Gaius;** b) = **con-demno;** c) = **centum;** d) **Cn.** = **Gnaeus;** e) **CIↃ** = 1000.

**caballus, ī** *m* pack-horse, nag.

**cacāturiō** 4 to want to evacuate the bowels.

**cachinnātiō, ōnis** *f* = **cachinnus.**

**cachinnō**[1] 1 to laugh aloud.

**cachinnō**[2]**, ōnis** *m* scoffer.

**cachinnus, ī** *m* loud laugh.

**cacō** 1 to evacuate the bowels; to defile.

**caco-ēthes, is** *n* disease.

**caco-zēlus, ī** *m* bad imitator.

**cacula, ae** *m* servant of a soldier.

**cacūmen, inis** *n* point, extremity, top, height.

**cacūminō** 1 to make pointed.

**cadāver, eris** *n* dead body, corpse; a) carcass; b) ruins.

**cadāverōsus** 3 like a corpse.

**cadō, cecidī, cāsum** 3 to fall; **1.** to fall down, sink down (*de* or *ex re in alqd*), to descend; a) to flow down; b) to slip, drop; c) to be thrown; **2.** to go down, set, to fall down prostrate; a) to be killed, be slain; b) to be conquered, captured, destroyed; c) to lose strength, be overthrown, decline, vanish, decay, cease; **animō cadere** to lose courage, **causā** or **in iūdiciō cadere** to lose a law-suit; d) to fall flat, fail (*of theatrical representations*); **3.** to fall into (*in alqd*); a) to get into, to incur, fall under, be subject or exposed to; b) to belong, agree, refer, be suitable, fit; c) to happen; d) to terminate, end (*words*); **4.** to occur, come to pass, turn out.

**cādūceātor, ōris** *m* herald, officer bearing the flag of truce.

**cādūceus, ī** *m* a herald's staff.

**cādūci-fer, feri** *m* bearer of the herald's staff.

**cādūcus** 3 **1.** falling, fallen; hurled (*flash of lightning*); **2.** inclined to fall; a) frail, perishable, transitory; b) *in law:* rendered void, having no heir or owner.

**cadus, ī** *m* wine-jar.

**caeci-genus** 3 born blind.

**caecitās, ātis** *f* blindness.

**caecō** 1 a) to make blind, to blind; b) to make obscure.

**caecus** 3 blind, not seeing; a) mentally or morally blind; b) dark, obscure; c) invisible, hidden; d) unintelligible, unknown; e) vague, uncertain, doubtful, aimless.

**caedēs, is** *f* **1.** a cutting off or down; **2.** a killing, slaughter; a) murder; b) massacre, bloodshed; c) persons slain.

**caedō, cecidī, caesum** 3 to cut, hew; **1.** to strike, beat, cudgel; **2.** a) to fell, cut down or off, cut to pieces; b) to slay, kill, murder.

**caelāmen, inis** *n* bas-relief, chased work.

**caelātor, ōris** *m* chaser, engraver, carver.

**caelātūra, ae** *f* (art of) engraving.

**caelebs, libis** unmarried, single.

**caeles, itis** heavenly; *m/pl.* the gods.

**caelestis, e** a) belonging to heaven, heavenly, celestial; *subst.* god, deity; **caelestia, ium** *n/pl.* heavenly things or bodies; b) divine, superhuman, glorious.

**caelibātus, ūs** *m* celibacy.

**caeli-cola, ae** *m* dweller in heaven, god.

**caelicus** 3 heavenly; magnificent.

**caeli-fer** 3 bearing the heavens.

**caeli-potēns, tis** mighty in heaven.

**caelō** 1 to engrave in relief, to chase, carve; to adorn.

**caelum**[1]**, ī** *n* the sky, the heaven; **de caelo tangi** to be struck by lightning; **de caelo servare** to observe the signs of heaven; a) the home of the gods, the upper world; b) clime, zone, region; c) air, atmosphere, weather; d) height, highest joy, immortality.

**caelum**[2]**, ī** *n* engraver's chisel.

**caementum, ī** *n* unhewn stone.

**caenōsus** 3 muddy.

**caenum, ī** *n* dirt, mud; lowest strata of society.

**caepa, ae** *f and* **caepe, is** *n* onion.

**caerimōnia, caeremōnia, ae** *f*
a) holy dread, reverence, veneration; **b)** sanctity, sacredness; **c)**
religious action *or* usage, ceremony.
**caeruleus** *and* **caerulus** 3 dark-
-blue, blue-black; black; (blue-)-
green, dark, *subst.* **caerula, ōrum**
*n/pl.* the blue sea.
**caesariātus** 3 long-haired.
**caesariēs, ēi** *f* the hair of the head,
bushy hair.
**caesicius** 3 cut, tailored (?).
**caesim** *adv.* by cutting; in short
sentences.
**caesius** 3 (with) bright blue (eyes).
**caespes, itis** *m* turf, grass; altar of
turf.
**caestus, ūs** *m* boxing-glove made of
thongs.
**caetra, ae** *f* short Spanish shield.
**caetrātus** 3 armed with a short
shield.
**calamārius** 3 pertaining to a
writing-reed.
**calamister, trī** *m* = **calamistrum.**
**calamistrātus** 3 curled with the
curling-iron.
**calamistrum, ī** *n* curling-iron for
the hair; artificial ornament in
speech.
**calamitās, ātis** *f* a) loss, damage,
injury, disaster, calamity, ruin;
**b)** defeat, misfortune in war.
**calamitōsus** 3 ruinous, disastrous,
destructive; suffering damage, exposed to injury, unhappy.
**calamus, ī** *m* a) reed, cane; **b)** reed-
-pen, reed-pipe, arrow, fishing-rod,
lime-twig.
**calathiscus, ī** *m, dim. of* **calathus.**
**calathus, ī** *m* a) wicker-basket;
**b)** bowl, cup.
**calātor, ōris** *m* attendant (*of
priests*).
**calcar, āris** *n* spur; incitement.
**calceāmentum, ī** *n* shoe.
**calceārium, ī** *n* shoe-money.
**calceātus, ūs** *m* shoes, sandals.
**calceō** 1 to furnish with shoes.
**calceolārius, ī** *m* shoemaker.
**calceolus, ī** *m* little shoe.
**calceus, ī** *m* shoe, half-boot.
**calcitrō[1]** 1 to kick; to be stubborn,
refractory.
**calcitrō[2], ōnis** *m* a kicker.
**calcō** 1 to tread, to tread on; a) to
tread down, trample upon; **b)** to
despise, abuse.

**calculātor, ōris** *m* teacher of arithmetic.
**calculus, ī** *m* small stone, pebble;
**1.** stone used a) in reckoning; b) in
playing draughts; c) for voting;
**2.** a computing, calculating; **3.** stone
(*in the bladder*).
**caldārius** 3 belonging to warmth;
supplied with warm water; *subst.*
**-um, ī** *n* room for taking warm
baths.
**caldus** 3 = **calidus.**
**cale-facio** 3 to make warm *or* hot;
to heat, to excite.
**cale-factō** 1 to make warm.
**cale-fiō, P.** *of* **calefacio.**
**Calendae, ārum** *f/pl.* the calends,
first day of each month.
**calendārium, ī** *n* debt-book,
account-book.
**caleō, uī, calitūrus** 2 to be warm
*or* hot; a) to glow, be inflamed,
enamoured; **b)** to be urged on
zealously; **c)** to be yet fresh *or* new.
**calēscō, luī, — 3 to grow warm *or*
hot, to glow.
**cal-faciō = calefacio.**
**calidus** 3 a) warm, hot; **b)** fiery,
rash, eager; *subst.* **calida, ae** *f*
warm water.
**caliendrum, ī** *n* wig for women.
**caliga, ae** *f* half-boot of soldiers.
**caligātus** 3 wearing soldier's shoes.
**cāliginōsus** 3 dark, obscure, gloomy.
**cālīgō[1], inis** *f* darkness, obscurity,
night; a) mist, vapour, fog; **b)** mental darkness; **c)** calamity, affliction.
**cālīgō[2]** 1 a) to cover with darkness,
to obscure; **b)** to be dark, gloomy,
blind.
**calix, icis** *m* a) cup, goblet, drinking-vessel; **b)** pot.
**callainus** 3 emerald-green.
**calleō, uī, — 2 a) to be thick-
skinned, callous; **b)** to be clever,
experienced, versed, skilful; **c)** to
know by experience *or* practice.
**calliditās, ātis** *f* a) shrewdness,
skill; **b)** cunning, craft, slyness,
artfulness.
**callidus** 3 dexterous, skilful;
a) practised, versed, shrewd;
**b)** well-wrought, ingenious; **c)** crafty, cunning, artful.
**callis, is** *f* (*and m*) **a)** stony foot-
way, foot-path, mountain-path;
**b)** alpine meadow.
**callōsus** 3 thick-skinned.

**callum, ī** *n* thick skin; insensibility.

**calō**[1] 1 to call together.

**cālō**[2], **ōnis** *m* horse-boy, groom, soldier's servant.

**calor, ōris** *m* a) warmth, heat, glow, summer heat; b) heat of passion, fire of love, zeal.

**caltha, ae** *f* marigold.

**calthula, ae** *f* yellow robe.

**calumnia, ae** *f* a) artifice, chicanery, deceitful pretence, malicious prosecution; b) penalty for false accusation; c) false statement, sophistry.

**calumniātor, ōris** *m* contriver of tricks, intriguer, malicious prosecutor, false accuser.

**calumnior** 1 a) to contrive tricks, to intrigue; b) to prosecute maliciously, to censure, depreciate, calumniate.

**calva, ae** *f* bald head, scalp.

**calvitium, ī** *n* baldness.

**calvor, —, —** 3 to deceive.

**calvus** 3 bald, without hair.

**calx**[1], **cis** *f* (*m*) a) limestone, lime; b) goal in a race-course; c) counter in a game.

**calx**[2], **cis** *f* (*m*) heel, hoof.

**camella, ae** *f* goblet, cup.

**camēlus, ī** *m* (*f*) camel.

**camera, ae** *f* a) vault, arch; b) flat boat with a covering.

**camīnus, ī** *m* a) fire-place; b) furnace, forge, smithy.

**cammarus, ī** *m* lobster.

**campester, stris, stre** a) pertaining to a field *or* plain, flat, level; b) of the Campus Martius, used in sport; *subst.* **campestre, is** *n* leathern apron used in wrestling.

**campus, ī** *m* a) field, plain, level place, open country, level of the sea; b) the Campus Martius, place of assemblage for the people in Rome, athletic grounds.

**camur, a, um** crooked.

**canālis, is** *m* (*f*) water-pipe, conduit, channel, canal.

**cancellī, ōrum** *m/pl.* lattice, enclosure, balustrade, grating, railings; boundaries.

**cancer, crī** *m* a) crab (*also* **C~** *sign of the zodiac*); b) cancer; c) south, summer heat.

**candē-faciō** 3 to make shining white.

**candēla, ae** *f* a) wax-light, candle; b) cord covered with wax.

**candēlābrum, ī** *n* candlestick, lamp-stand.

**candeō, uī, —** 2 to be shining white, to glitter, glow.

**candēscō, duī, —** 3 to become glittering white; to glow.

**candidātōrius** 3 pertaining to a candidate.

**candidātus** 3 clothed in white; *subst.* **~, ī** *m* candidate.

**candidulus** 3 shining white.

**candidus** 3 shining white, glittering, white; a) clothed in white; b) bright, clear, fair, beautiful, lucid; c) artless, honest, upright; d) happy, fortunate, lucky, joyful.

**candor, ōris** *m* dazzling whiteness, lustre, brightness; a) dazzling beauty; b) clearness; c) integrity, sincerity, frankness.

**cāneō, uī, —** 2 to be grey, white, hoary.

**cane-phoros, ī** *f* basket-bearer.

**cānēscō, —, —** 3 to become grey, white, hoary, old.

**canīcula, ae** *f* little dog; **C~** the Dog-star, Sirius.      [dog.]

**canīnus** 3 relating to a dog, of a dog.

**canis, is** *m and f* dog; a) malicious, insolent, shameless person; b) parasite; c) sea-dog; d) the Dog-star; e) the worst throw (*in dice*).

**canistra, ōrum** *n/pl.* plaited basket.

**cānitiēs, ēī** *f* a) grey colour; b) grey hair.

**canna, ae** *f* reed, cane, reed-pipe.

**cannabis, is** *f* hemp.

**canō, cecinī, (cantum)** 3 to sound 1. a) to sing; b) to crow, croak, hoot; c) to play on a musical instrument (*abl.*); 2. *trans.* to utter; a) to sing, compose (*poems*); b) to celebrate, praise; c) to prophesy, announce; d) **bellicum, classicum, signum canere** to give the signal for battle; **receptuī canere** to sound the signal for retreat.

**canor, ōris** *m* song, sound.

**canōrus** 3 melodious, harmonious; *subst.* **canōrum, ī** *n* melodious sound.      [charm.]

**cantāmen, inis** *n* incantation,

**cantātor, ōris** *m* singer.

**cantērinus** 3 of a horse.

**cantērius, ī** *m* gelding (*horse*).

**cantharis, idis** *f* Spanish fly.

**cantharus, ī** *m* a) tankard; b) a sea fish.

**canthērius, ī** *m* = canterius.

**canthus, ī** *m* tire; wheel.

**canticum, ī** *n* musical monologue; song; singsong.

**cantilēna, ae** *f* old song, silly prattle, gossip. [tation.]

**cantiō, ōnis** *f* a) song; b) incan-

**cantitō 1** to sing often *or* usually.

**cantiuncula, ae** *f* an alluring song.

**cantō 1** a) = cano; b) to recite incantations, to enchant.

**cantor, ōris** *m* singer; poet; a) reciter, player; b) eulogist.

**cantrīx, īcis** *f* female singer.

**cantus, ūs** *m* a) song, a crowing, croaking; b) music, sound; c) incantation; d) prophecy.

**cānus 3** a) whitish-grey, white; *subst.* **cānī, ōrum** *m/pl.* grey hair; b) old, venerable.

**capācitās, ātis** *f* room for holding, capacity.

**capāx, ācis** a) wide, large, spacious, roomy, capacious; b) able to grasp, capable, apt, fit for.

**capēdō, inis** *f* sacrificial bowl.

**capēduncula, ae** *f* small bowl used in sacrifices.

**capella, ae** *f* (little) she-goat.

**caper, prī** *m* he-goat; smell in the arm-pits.

**caperrō 1** to be wrinkled.

**capessō, sīvī, sītum 3** to seize eagerly, to lay hold of, snatch at; a) to take in hand, busy oneself with, enter upon, engage in, **rem publicam** to enter public life; b) to strive to reach, to repair to, resort to *(alqd)*.

**capillāmentum, ī** *n* wig; plant-hair.

**capillāre, is** *n* hair-oil.

**capillātus 3** hairy, having hair.

**capillus, ī** *m* hair of the head *or* of the beard.

**capiō, cēpī, captum 3** 1. to take, seize, grasp; **arma** to take up arms; a) to capture, take, occupy, hold; b) to arrive at, reach *(alqd, portum)*; c) to take possession of, catch, make prisoner, take by force of arms; d) to win, gain *(gloriam virtutibus)*; e) to undertake, enter upon, engage in, **fugam capere** to flee, **consilium c.** to resolve, plan, propose; f) to win, fascinate, enchain, charm, allure, deceive, mislead, betray,

delude; g) to harm, lame, injure, attack, weaken **(mente captus** distracted, mad, lunatic); 2. to choose, select *(locum, sibi tabernaculum, alqm socium)*; 3. to receive, get, obtain, acquire *(alqd ab alqo, ex re)* **pecuniam** *ab alqo* to accept a bribe; to enjoy, reap *(fructum)*, to suffer, be subjected to; 4. to contain, hold, suffice for; to allow of, comprehend; to comprehend mentally.

**capis, idis** *f* sacrificial bowl with one handle.

**capistrō 1** to harness, halter.

**capistrum, ī** *n* halter, muzzle.

**capital, ālis** *n* capital crime.

**capitālis, e** relating to the head, to life; a) capital, deadly, endangering life, **hostis ~** a deadly enemy; b) chief, pre-eminent, distinguished.

**capitō, ōnis** *m* one who has a large head.

**capitulātim** *adv.* summarily, briefly.

**capitulum, ī** *n* small head.

**cāpō, ōnis** *m* capon.

**capparis, is** *f* ♀ caper.

**capra, ae** *f* she-goat *(also a star)*; smell under the armpits.

**caprea, ae** *f* wild goat, roe.

**capreāginus 3** goatish.

**capreolus, ī** *m* 1. roebuck; 2. support, prop.

**Capri-cornus, ī** Capricorn *(sign of the zodiac)*.

**capri-fīcus, ī** *f* wild fig-tree.

**capri-genus 3** born of goats.

**capri-mulgus, ī** *m* goat-milker, countryman, herdsman.

**caprīnus 3** of goats.

**capri-pēs, pedis** goat-footed.

**capsa, ae** *f* chest, box, case.

**capsārius, ī** *m* slave who carried the books of schoolboys.

**capsula, ae** *f* smal lbox *(for personal property)*.

**captātiō, ōnis** *f* a catching at, eager seizing; **verborum** a quibbling.

**captātor, ōris** *m* one who seizes eagerly; legacy-hunter.

**captiō, ōnis** *f* a) deceit, fraud, chea·; b) fallacy, sophism; c) injury, loss.

**captiōsus 3** a) deceitful; b) sophistical, captious; *subst.* **captiōsum, ī** *n* sophism.

**captiuncula, ae** *f* fallacy, sophism.

**captīvitās, ātis** *f* a) captivity; b) conquest, capture.

captīvus 3 taken in war, *subst.*
  captīvus, ī *m* prisoner, captive;
  a) pertaining to a prisoner; b) captured, conquered.
captō 1 to strive to seize (*alqd*); a) to
  catch *or* snatch at; b) to try to obtain,
  desire, seek, hunt for (*alqd aure to*
  listen eagerly).          [wages.]
captūra, ae *f* prey, booty; day's
captus, ūs *m* a) a taking, seizing,
  catching; b) power of comprehension, understanding, capacity.
capūdō, inis *f* = capedo.
capulāris, e ready for a coffin.
capulus, ī *m* a) handle; hilt of a
  sword; b) coffin.
caput, itis *n* the head; a) man,
  person, individual, animal; b) top,
  summit, point, end, extremity;
  origin, source, mouth (*of a river*);
  c) life; **capitis accusare** to
  prosecute on a capital charge;
  **causa** *or* **iudicium capitis** trial
  of a capital crime; d) civil
  rights, political life, citizenship;
  e) the chief point; chief, leader,
  author, contriver; chief thing, leading principle, most important part;
  principal place, capital; principal
  sum, stock; division, chapter.
carbaseus 3 of linen.
carbasus, ī *f*, carbasa, ōrum *n/pl.*
  linen garment, sail, awning.
carbō, ōnis *m* coal, charcoal.
carbōnārius, ī *m* charcoal-burner.
carbunculus, ī *m* small coal; grief,
  sorrow.
carcer, eris *m* barrier, starting-
  place; prison, jail.
carcerārius 3 of a prison.
carchēsium, ī *n* drinking-cup; top
  of a mast.
carcinōma, atis *n* cancerous ulcer.
cardaces, um *m/pl.* class of Persian
  soldiers.
cardiacus 3 suffering from a disease
  of the stomach.
cardō, inis *m* door-hinges, pivot and
  socket of doors; a) pole, turning
  point; b) chief circumstance, crisis.
carduus, ī *m* thistle.
cārectum, ī *n* place full of reeds.
careō, uī, — 2 to be without, be free
  from, be destitute of (*alqa re*), a) to
  abstain from, deny oneself, make no
  use of; b) to be deprived of, to want,
  miss.
cārex, icis *f* reed-grass, sedge.

cariēs, ēī *f* decay, rottenness.
carīna, ae *f* a) keel of a ship;
  b) vessel, ship.
carinārius, ī *m* dyer with nut-
  -brown.
carinum, ī *n* nut-brown garment.
cariōsus 3 rotten, decayed.
cāris, idis *f* crab.
cāritās, ātis *f* dearness, high price;
  a) scarcity; b) high esteem, regard,
  respect, love, affection.
carmen, inis *n* a) song, tune;
  b) poem, poetry, lyric poetry; poetic
  inscription; c) formula (*religious or
  legal*); incantation, prediction,
  oracle.
carnārium, ī *n* frame of meat-
  -hooks; larder, pantry.
carnārius, ī *m* a lover of flesh.
carni-fex, icis *m* executioner, hangman; a) tormentor, murderer;
  b) villain.
carnificīna, ae *f* a) the hangman's
  office; b) rack, torture, torment.
carnificius 3 of an executioner.
carnificō 1 to cut to pieces, behead.
carnu-, *see* carni-.
carō, carnis *f* flesh.
carpatinus 3 of raw hide.
carpentum, ī *n* two-wheeled carriage, coach.
carpō, psī, ptum 3 to pluck; a) to
  pluck off; b) to graze on, eat; c) to
  crop, gather; to enjoy, make use of;
  d) to divide into parts, to take
  one's way, to pass over, sail along *or*
  through; e) to select, choose out;
  f) to gnaw at (*alqd*); to lacerate; to
  tear *or* pull to pieces; to weaken,
  enfeeble; to blame, censure, slander,
  revile; to harass, alarm.
carptim *adv.* by pieces; a) repeatedly; b) singly; c) by degrees.
carptor, ōris *m* carver.
car(r)ō 3 to card (wool).
carrūca, ae *f* four-wheeled carriage.
carrus, ī *m* cart, wagon.
caruncula, ae *f* a piece of flesh.
cārus 3 dear, valued, loved.
caryōta, ae (*and* caryōtis, idis) *f*
  a kind of date.
casa, ae *f* hut, cottage, cabin.
cascus 3 very old.
cāse(ol)us, ī *m* cheese.
casia, ae *f* a) cinnamon; b) spurge-
  -laurel.
cassida, ae *f* helmet of metal.
cassis[1], idis *f* helmet of metal.

**cassis²**, is *m* (*mostly* **cassēs, ium** *m*/*pl.*) hunting-net; a) snare; b) spider's web.

**cassō** 1 to tumble.

**cassus** 3 empty, hollow; a) *with gen.* or *abl.* devoid of, deprived of, without; b) vain, futile, useless, fruitless (*adv.* **in cassum** *or* **incassum**).

**castanea, ae** *f* chestnut (tree).

**castellānus** 3 pertaining to a castle *or* fortress; *subst.* **~, ī** *m* occupant of a castle.

**castellātim** *adv.* in single fortresses.

**castellum, ī** *n* castle, fort, stronghold; refuge.

**castēria, ae** *f* sleeping room for rowers.

**castigābilis, e** deserving punishment.

**castigātiō, ōnis** *f* a) a correcting, censure, reproof; b) punishment.

**castigātor, ōris** *m* corrector, reprover.

**castigātōrius** 3 reproving.

**castigō** 1 a) to correct, reprove; b) to punish; c) to amend; d) to restrain, hold in.

**castimōnia, ae** *f* purity, chastity; abstinence.

**castitās, ātis** *f* chastity, purity of morals.

**castor, oris** *m* beaver.

**castoreum, ī** *n* secretion of the beaver, castoreum.

**castrēnsis, e** of a camp.

**castrō** 1 to emasculate, castrate; enervate.

**castrum, ī** *n* 1. = **castellum**; 2. *pl.* military camp, encampment; a) military service; b) a day's march; c) political party, philosophic school.

**castus** 3 pure, innocent; a) chaste; b) pious, religious; c) continent, disinterested.

**casula, ae** *f* cottage.

**cāsus, ūs** *m* a falling; 1. fall; a) false step; destruction; b) end; 2. a) accident, event, occurrence, chance; b) disaster, misfortune, calamity, death; 3. (*in grammar*) case.

**cata-dromus, ī** *m* tight-rope.

**cata-gelasimus** 3 exposed to ridicule.

**cata-graphus** 3 painted, coloured.

**catamītus, ī** *m* catamite.

**cata-phractēs, ae** *m* a coat of mail with iron scales.

**cata-phractus** 3 mailed.

**cataplēxis** *f* a wonder.

**cataplūs, ī** *m* ship(s) coming to land.

**cata-pulta, ae** *f* engine of war for throwing arrows.

**catapultārius** 3 of a catapulta.

**cata-racta, ae** *f* *and* -**tēs, ae** *m* a) waterfall; sluice; b) portcullis.

**cataractria, ae** *f* a kind of spice.

**cata-scopus, ī** *m* spy-ship.

**cata-sta, ae** *f* stage for the sale of slaves.

**catēia, ae** *f* a wooden spear.

**catēlla, ae** *f* (*and* **catēllus, ī** *m*) a little chain.

**catellus, ī** *m* (*and* **catella, ae** *f*) little dog.

**catēna, ae** *f* chain, fetter; a) barrier, restraint, check; b) bond.

**catēnārius** 3 kept on a chain.

**catēnātus** 3 chained, fettered.

**caterva, ae** *f* crowd, troop, band, throng; company of actors.

**catervārius** 3 belonging to a troop.

**catervātim** *adv.* in companies, in troops.

**cathedra, ae** *f* arm-chair, sedan--chair.

**cathedrārius** 3 professorial, academic.

**catillō** 1 to lick plates.

**catillus, ī** *m* small bowl, dish.

**catīnus, ī** *m* bowl, dish.

**catōmum** back (?).

**catulus, ī** *m* young animal, whelp; young dog. [wise.]

**catus** 3 intelligent, sagacious,]

**cauda, ae** *f* tail, **caudam trahere** to be mocked; appendage.

**caudeus** 3 of rushes.

**caudex, icis** *m* a) trunk of a tree, log; b) wooden tablet for writing, book, notebook, account-book.

**caudicālis, e** relating to wood.

**caulae, ārum** *f*/*pl.* 1. spaces, pores; 2. sheep-fold.

**caulis, is** *m* stalk, stem of a plant; cabbage.

**caupō, ōnis** *m* innkeeper.

**caupōna, ae** *f* inn, tavern.

**caupōnius** 3 of a tavern.

**caupōnor** 1 to traffic *or* trade in.

**caupōnula, ae** *f* wretched tavern.

**caurus, ī** *m* the north-west wind.

**causa, ae** *f* 1. cause, reason, motive, inducement, occasion (*with gen.* or *quod, cur, ut, inf.*); a) **causā** *with* *gen.* on account of, for the sake of, with respect to, **meā causā** for my sake, on my behalf; b) good reason, **cum causā** with good reason; c) well founded excuse; d) pretext, feigned cause, pretence, **per causam** under a pretext; **2.** cause, affair, business; a) lawsuit, judicial process; **causam agere, defendere** to carry on *or* conduct a law-suit, to defend a case; **causam perdere = causā cadere** to lose a lawsuit; question, matter for discussion; b) party, side, faction; c) condition, circumstances, situation; d) relation of friendship (*cum alqo*).

**causārius** 3 sickly, invalid.

**causia, ae** *f* broad-brimmed hat.

**causi-dicus, ī** *m* advocate.

**causi-ficor** 1 to plead an excuse.

**causor** 1 to give as a reason, to pretend (*alqd*, with *acc. c. inf.*, with *quod*).

**caussa, ae** *f* = **causa**.

**causula, ae** *f* petty lawsuit *or* cause.

**cautēla, ae** *f* caution.

**cautēs, is** *f* sharp rock, crag.

**cautim** *adv.* = **caute (cautus)**.

**cautiō, ōnis** *f* a) precaution, circumspection; precautionary measure; b) security, bond, bail, obligation, warranty.

**cautor, ōris** *m* a) one who is on his guard; b) surety.

**cautus** 3 a) circumspect, wary, careful; b) secured, safe.

**cav-aedium, ī** *n* inner yard of a house.

**cavea, ae** *f* hollow place, cavity; a) den, cave, stall, bird-cage, beehive; b) auditorium in a theatre, theatre, the spectators.

**caveō, cāvī, cautum** 2 **1.** to be on one's guard, take care, take heed (*alqm, ab alqo, alqd, a re, ne, ut*); **cavē** (*with following subj.*) take care lest, see that ... not; **2.** to provide for, have a care for (*alci a re*); a) to lend aid to; b) to give security *or* bail for (*alci alqa re, de re*); c) to make oneself secure, to procure bail for oneself (*ab alqo*); d) to stipulate, order, decree.

**caverna, ae** *f* hollow, cave, cavern; a) hold of a ship; b) tank.

**cavilla, ae** *f* jesting, raillery.

**cavillātiō, ōnis** *f* a jeering, jesting, railing, scoffing, sneering.

**cavillātor, ōris** *m* jester, jeerer, humourist.

**cavillor** 1 a) to jest, jeer, rail, scoff, mock (*alqd* or *cum alqo*); b) to shuffle.

**cavō** 1 to make hollow, to hollow out; to pierce through.

**cavus** 3 hollow, excavated, concave; enveloping; *subst.* (*and* **cavum, ī** *n*) a hollow, hole.

**cedo**[1] (*pl.* **cette**) a) here with it! give here! (*with acc.*); b) out with it! let us hear!; c) only look!

**cēdō**[2], **cessī, cessum** 3 **1.** to go, move, go along (= **incedo**); a) *in alqd* to take the place of, to change to, to become; b) *alci* or *in alqm* to fall to the lot of, to accrue; c) *alci* to turn out, result; d) *pro re* to pass for; **2.** to give place, go away, withdraw (with *abl.* or *ex, de re*); a) to give up (*property*), to yield, cede; b) to pass away, vanish; c) to retreat before, submit to; **3.** to comply with, yield to, obey.

**cedrus, ī** *f* cedar, juniper; cedar-wood, cedar-oil.

**cēlātor, ōris** *m* concealer.

**celeber, bris, bre** (*also* **celebris, bre**) much visited, frequented, populous; a) renowned, distinguished, celebrated; b) solemn, festive; c) well-known, common, usual; d) numerous, frequent.

**celebrātiō, ōnis** *f* a) numerous assembly; b) festival.

**celebrātor, ōris** *m* one who celebrates.

**celebrātus** 3 = **celeber**.

**celebritās, ātis** *f* a) numerous concourse *or* attendance at; b) festivity, celebration; c) multitude, large assembly; d) frequency, repetition; e) fame, renown.

**celebrō** 1 **1.** to visit frequently *or* in great numbers, to frequent; a) to accompany in great numbers, to crowd round; b) to celebrate, keep a festival; **2.** to do frequently, to practise, engage in, repeat; a) to make known, publish, proclaim; b) to praise, honour, make famous; c) to fill with (*alqd alqa re*).

**celer, eris, ere** swift, quick, speedy; *subst.* **Celerēs, um** *m/pl.* Roman knights; a) quick in mind, lively; b) hasty; *adv.* **celeriter** (*and* **celere**).

**celeri-pēs, pedis** swift-footed.

**celeritās, ātis** f swiftness, quickness; adroitness.

**celerō** 1 a) to quicken, hasten, accelerate; b) to make haste.

**celeuma, atis** n coxswain's command (giving the time to a crew).

**cella, ae** f cell; a) chamber, room, closet; b) granary, cellar, store-room; c) cell of a beehive; d) sanctuary.

**cellārius** 3 of a store-room; subst. storekeeper.

**cellula, ae** f dimin. of cella.

**cēlō** 1 to conceal, hide from (alqd, alqm), to keep secret; P. cēlor de re to be kept ignorant of.

**celōc(u)la, ae** f dimin. of celox.

**celōx, ōcis** f swift-sailing ship, yacht.

**celsus** 3 a) raised high, lifted, towering; b) high, lofty, elevated; c) noble, high-spirited; d) haughty.

**cēna, ae** f principal meal, dinner; inter cēnam at dinner-time.

**cēnāculum, ī** n a) dining-room; b) tenement, flat; attic.

**cēnāticus** 3 pertaining to a dinner.

**cēnātiō, ōnis** f, **cēnātiuncula, ae** f (little) dining-room.

**cēnātōria, ōrum** n pl. dinner dress.

**cēnāturiō** 4 to want one's dinner.

**cēnitō** 1 to be accustomed to dine often or repeatedly.

**cēnō** 1. to dine, eat; cēnātus 3 having dined, after dinner; 2. trans. to eat up, dine upon.

**cēnseō, suī, sum** 2 1. a) to tax, value, estimate, assess, to take an account of the names and property of Roman citizens; to take the census; capite cēnsī the lowest class of Roman citizens, whose persons only were counted; b) to make a return to the censor, P. to be assessed; 2. to value, appreciate, weigh; a) to be of opinion, think, hold, judge; b) to vote, propose, recommend by vote; to decree, resolve, order (alqd, with ut, ne, acc. c. inf.); c) to adjudge to.

**cēnsiō, ōnis** f taxation; opinion.

**cēnsor, ōris** m a Roman magistrate, censor, commissioner of assessment, censurer, critic.

**cēnsōrius** 3 relating to a censor; censorial; rigid, severe; one who has been a censor.

**cēnsūra, ae** f censorship.

**cēnsus, ūs** m a) a registering of citizens and property, census; b) register of the census, censor's list; c) amount of property.

**centaurium and -rēum, ī** n a plant, centaury.

**Centaurus, ī** m centaur (half man, half horse).

**centēnī** 3 one hundred each.

**centēsimus** 3 the hundredth; subst. **centēsima, ae** f the hundredth part, one per cent.    [ed.]

**centi-ceps, cipitis** hundred-head-

**centiē(n)s** adv. a hundred times.

**centi-manus** 3 having a hundred hands.

**centō, ōnis** m a covering of rags, patch-work.

**centum** a hundred; many.

**centum-geminus** 3 a hundred-fold.

**centum-plex, icis** a hundred-fold.

**centum-pondium, ī** n weight of a hundred pounds.

**centum-virālis, e** pertaining to centumviri.

**centum-virī, ōrum** m/pl. the centumviri (a college of judges).

**centunculus, ī** m patchwork.

**centuria, ae** f a division of one hundred; company of soldiers.

**centuriātim** adv. by centuries.

**centuriātus[1], ūs** m office of a centurion; division into centuries.

**centuriātus[2]** 3 divided into centuries.

**centuriō[1], ōnis** m centurion, commander of one hundred soldiers.

**centuriō[2]** 1 to divide into centuries.

**centuriōnātus, ūs** m election of centurions.

**centussis, is** m a hundred asses.

**cēnula, ae** f a little or frugal meal.

**cēpa, ae** f = caepa.

**cēra, ae** f wax; a) writing-tablet covered with wax; b) seal of wax; c) image of wax, ancestral portrait; d) waxen paint for the face.

**cērārium, ī** n fee for sealing.

**cerastēs, ae** m horned snake.

**cerasus, ī** f cherry(-tree).

**cērātus** 3 covered with wax.

**cerco-pithēcus, ī** m long-tailed monkey.    [cutter.]

**cercūrus, ī** m swift-sailing vessel,

**cerdō, ōnis** m workman.

**Cereālis, e** belonging to Ceres.

**cerebellum, ī** n brain.

**cerebrōsus** 3 hot-brained, hotheaded.

**cerebrum, ī** *n* a) brain; **b)** understanding; **c)** hot temper.

**cěreus** 3 of wax, waxen; **a)** wax-coloured; **b)** pliant, soft; *subst.* **cěreus, ī** *m* wax-light.

**ceriāria, ae** *f* caterer (?).

**cěrintha, ae** *f* honeywort.

**cěrinthus, ī** *n* wax-coloured garment.

**cernō, crēvī, crētum** 3 to separate, sift; **1. a)** to distinguish, discern, see distinctly, perceive (*alqd*); **b)** to understand, comprehend; **P. cerni re, in re** to be shown, show oneself; **c)** to have regard for; **2.** to decide; **a)** to resolve, determine (*alqd*); **b)** to contend, fight (*de, pro re, rem*); **c) hereditatem** to accept *or* enter upon an inheritance.

**cernulō** 1 to knock down.

**cernuus** 3 head-foremost.

**cěrōma, atis** *n* wrestler's ointment; wrestling; **cěrōmaticus** 3 smeared with *ceroma*.

**cerrītus** 3 frantic, mad.

**certāmen, inis** *n* contest, contention, struggle (*de re or gen.*); **a)** rivalry, competition; **b)** prize; **c)** fight, battle, combat, war.

**certātim** *adv.* in rivalry, emulously.

**certātiō, ōnis** *f* (and **-tus, ūs** *m*) **a)** a contending, contest, competition; **b)** public discussion.

**certē** *adv.* surely, certainly; **a)** really, undoubtedly; **b)** yet surely; **c)** at least. [ly, really.]

**certō**[1] *adv.* with certainty, sure-

**certō**[2] 1 to fight, struggle, contend, contest (*cum alqo, de or pro re*); **a)** to emulate, vie with (*cum alqo, de re, with inf.*); **b)** to contend at law.

**certus** 3 decided **1. a)** determined, resolved, *mihi certum est* (*with inf.*) I have made up my mind; **b)** resolved upon; **2. a)** settled, established, fixed; **b)** sure, true, to be depended on; **c)** informed, assured, *alqm* **certiorem facere** to inform *or* apprise one (*alcis rei, de re*); **d)** definite, positive, undoubted.

**cerūchus, ī** *m* halyard.

**cěrula, ae** *f* a little piece of wax; **miniata** red pencil.

**cěrussa, ae** *f* white-lead; (white) paint for the face: **cěrussātus** 3 painted with *cerussa*.

**cerva, ae** *f* hind, deer.

**cervical, ālis** *n* pillow, cushion for the head.

**cervicula, ae** *f* a little neck.

**cervīnus** 3 of a stag *or* deer.

**cervīx, īcis** *f* (*mostly pl.*) **a)** the nape, neck; **esse in cervīcibus alcis** to be in dangerous proximity; **b)** courage, boldness.

**cervus, ī** *m* **a)** stag; **b)** forked stakes (*in a fortification*).

**cěryx. ȳcis** *m* herald.

**cessātiō, ōnis** *f* a delaying; inactivity.

**cessātor, ōris** *m* loiterer, idler.

**cessiō, ōnis** *f* a giving up, cession.

**cessō** 1 to delay, loiter (*with inf.*); **a)** to be remiss, to be inactive (*in, a re*), idle; **b)** to cease, stop, rest; **c)** to be unemployed, out of action.

**cestro-sphendonē, ēs** *f* war-engine for hurling stones.

**cestus, ī** *m* girdle of Venus.

**cētārium, ī** *n* fishpond.

**cētārius, ī** *m* fishmonger.

**cētē** *n* (*pl. of* **cētus**).

**cēterō-quī(n)** in other respects, otherwise.

**cēterus** 3 the other, the rest, remainder; (**et**) **cētera** and so on; *adv.* **a) cēterum** *and* **cētera** for the rest, in other respects; **b) cēterum** however, but. [tratus.]

**cētra, cētrātus,** *see* **caetra, cae-**

**cētus, ī** *m* (*pl.* **cētē** *n*) sea-monster, whale, dolphin, shark.

**ceu** *adv* **a)** as, like as, just as; **b)** (*with subj.*) as if.

**cēveō** 2 to move the haunches; to fawn.

**chalc-aspides, um** *m/pl.* soldiers with brazen shields.

**chalybēïus** 3 of steel.

**chalybs, ybis** *m* steel.

**chaos** *n* (*abl.* **chaō**) **a)** boundless, empty space; the nether world; **b)** the shapeless mass out of which the universe was made.

**chara, ae** *f* plant with edible root.

**charistia, ōrum** *n/pl.* festival of family reconcilement.

**charitōn mia** (χαρίτων μία) one of the Graces.

**charta, ae** *f* **a)** Egyptian papyrus, paper; **b)** writing, book, letter, poem.

**chartula, ae** *f* paper, letter.

**Chēlae, ārum** *f/pl.* the arms of Scorpio, *the constellation* Libra.

**çhelydrus, ī** *m* a water-snake.

**chelys** *f* tortoise-shell lyre.

**cheragra** = chiragra.

**chersos**, ī *f* land-turtle, tortoise.

**chīli-archus**, ī *m*, **-ēs**, ae *m* commander of 1000 soldiers; *in Persia:* the grand vizier.

**chimaeri-fer** 3 producing the chimera.

**chiragra**, ae *f* gout in the hand.

**chīro-graphum**, ī *n* a) handwriting, autograph; b) bond.

**chīro-nomōn**, ūntis *m* gesticulator.

**chīrūrgia**, ae *f* surgery.

**chīrūrgus**, ī *m* surgeon.

**chlamydātus** 3 dressed in a cloak.

**chlamys**, ydis *f* (*military*) cloak.

**chor-āgium**, ī *n* preparation of a chorus.

**chor-āgus**, ī *m* supplier of a chorus.

**chor-aulēs**, ae *m* flute-player in a chorus.

**chorda**, ae *f* a) string; b) cord.

**chorēa** (*and* **chorēa**), ae *f* dance in a ring.

**chorēus** (*and* **-īus**), ī *m* trochee.

**choro-citharistēs**, ae *m* cithara-player in a chorus.

**chors**, chortis *f* = cohors.

**chorus**, ī *m* dance in a ring, choral dance; dancing troop, chorus; band, crowd.

**chrīa**, ae *f* sentence used as a theme for logical development, as a rhetorical exercise.

**chrȳs-anthus**, ī *m* a golden flower.

**chrȳs-endetus** 3 inlaid with gold.

**chrȳso-colla**, ae *f* substance used for soldering gold.

**chrȳso-lithus**, ī *m* chrysolite.

**chrȳsos**, ī *m* gold.

**cibārius** 3 1. pertaining to food; *subst.* **cibāria**, **ōrum** *n/pl.* victuals, food, provisions; a) fodder; b) allowance (*of corn*); 2. common, ordinary.

**cibātus**, ūs *m* food.

**cibō** 1 to feed.

**cibōrium**, ī *n* drinking-cup.

**cibus**, ī *m* food, victuals, nutriment, fodder; a) nourishment, sustenance; b) bait.

**cicāda**, ae *f* cicada, tree-cricket.

**cicātricōsus** 3 full of scars.

**cicātrix**, īcis *f* scar, cicatrice.

**ciccum**, ī *n* pomegranate core, trifle.

**cicer**, eris *n* the chick-pea.

**cichorēum** ī *n* chicory.

**cicōnia**, ae *f* stork.

**cicur**, **uris** tame, domesticated.

**cicūta**, ae *f* a) hemlock; b) flute of hemlock-stalks.

**cieō**, cīvī, citum 2 to move, stir, set in motion; a) to call to aid, summon; b) to call by name, mention by name; c) to produce, cause, excite.

**cīmex**, icis *m* bug.

**cinaedicus** 3 lewd, unchaste.

**cinaedus**, ī *m* sodomite, unchaste person.

**cincinnātus** 3 with curled hair.

**cincinnus**, ī *m* a) (*artificial*) curl of hair; b) artificial ornament (*in rhetoric*).

**cincticulus**, ī *m* little girdle.

**cinctus**, ūs *m* (*and* **cinctūra**, ae *f*) a) a girding; b) girdle, apron.

**cinctūtus** 3 girded.

**cine-factus** 3 reduced to ashes.

**cinerārius**, ī *m* hairdresser (*with hot irons*).

**cingō**, cinxī, cinctum 3 to gird (*with acc.*), gird on; a) to gird up, to make ready; P. to be girded, encircled, to gird oneself; b) to surround, enclose (*aliqd alqa re*), invest; c) to accompany, escort; d) to protect, to cut off on all sides.

**cingulus**, ī *m* zone (of the earth).

**cingulum**, ī *n* and **cingula**, ae *f* girdle, belt; zone.

**cini-flō**, ōnis *m* hair-curler.

**cinis**, eris *m* (*f*) ashes; a) ashes of a burnt corpse; ruins of a city; b) destruction.

**cinnamum** (*and* **-on**), ī *n* cinnamon.

**ciō**, cīvī, citum 4 = cieo.

**cippus**, ī *m* a) post; b) tomb-stone; c) sharpened stake.

**circā** 1. *adv.* around, round about, all around; in the neighbourhood; 2. *prep.* with *acc.* a) (*of space*) about, round, on the side of, near to, near by; among; b) (*of time*) about) c) (*of number*) about; d) in respect to.

**circā-moerium**, ī *n* space about a wall.

**circēnsis**, e belonging to the circus; (*ludi*) **circēnsēs** *m/pl.* the circus-games.

**circinō** 1 to fly through in a circle.

**circinus**, ī *m* a pair of compasses.

**circiter** 1. *adv.* about, near; 2. *prep.* with *acc.* = circa.

**circitō** 1 to perambulate, wander through.

**circius**, ī *m* north-west wind.

circu-eō = circumeo.

circu-itiō, ōnis f a going round; a) a patrolling; b) circumlocution, indirect manner.

circu-itus, ūs m a going round in a circle; a) revolution; b) circuit, compass; c) digression, circumlocution; d) period.

circulātim adv. in a circle.

circulātor, ōris m one who runs about; itinerant vendor.

circulātrix, īcis (f) of a mountebank or cheap-jack.

circulor 1 a) to form a circle of persons; b) to converse, to gossip.

circ(u)lus, ī m circular figure, circle; a) circular course, orbit; b) ring, chain; c) company, social gathering.

circum adv. and prep. = circa (1 and 2a).

circum-āctus, ūs m revolution.

circum-agō 3 1. to drive, lead, turn round, in a circle; 2. to turn round, change, turn about, drive about, mislead; P. to turn oneself round, to be driven or led about; to pass away, be spent.

circum-arō 1 to plough around.

circum-caesūra, ae f circumference.

circum-cīdō, cīdī, cīsum 3 to cut around, to cut, clip; to diminish, abridge, cut off.

circum-circā adv. round about.

circum-cisus 3 cut off around; a) steep, precipitous, inaccessible; b) abridged, short.

circum-clūdō, sī, sum 3 to shut in, enclose, surround.

circum-colō 3 to dwell round about (alqd).

circum-cursō 1 to run round.

circum-dō, dedī, datum 1 a) to put or place around (alqd alci rei); b) to surround with, encompass, enclose (alqd re), to invest, besiege; P. to place oneself around.

circum-dūcō 3 to lead, move, draw around; to lengthen, prolong.

circum-ductiō, ōnis f a) cheating; b) rhetorical period

circum-eō to go round, travel, march, drive around (alqd); a) to surround, encircle, to outflank; b) to visit, inspect (alqd).

circum-equitō 1 to ride round.

circum-ferō 3 to bear or carry round; a) to pass around, hand

round; b) to publish, proclaim, spread around; P. to go round, revolve, to move about.

circum-flectō 3 to bend round, turn about.

circum-flō 1 to blow round about.

circum-fluō 3 a) to flow round (alqd); to surround, encompass; b) to overflow; to abound in, be rich (alqa re).

circum-fluus 3 a) flowing around; b) flowed around.

circum-fodiō 3 to dig round.

circum-forāneus 3 a) round the forum; b) frequenting markets.

circum-fremō 3 to make a noise round.

circum-fundō 3 a) to pour around (alqd alci rei), P. to flow round (alci rei); b) to cover, enclose, overwhelm with (alqa re); to surround, encompass, P. to be crowded, surrounded by.

circum-gemō 3 to roar around.

circum-gestō 1 to carry round.

circum-gredior, gressus sum 3 to go round, surround (in a hostile manner).

circum-iaceō, —, — 2 to lie or dwell round about.

circum-iciō, iēcī, iectum 3 to throw or cast round, to put round (alqd alci rei), to enclose with; adj. circumiectus 3 a) surrounding; b) surrounded.

circum-iectus, ūs m encompassing.

circum-itiō, -itus = circuitio, -itus.

circum-lātrō 1 to bark or roar round about.

circum-ligō 1 a) to bind round or to (alqd alci rei); b) to bind with, encompass (alqd alqa re).

circum-linō, --, — 3 a) to smear around, b) to spread all over, cover

circum-litiō, ōnis f a coat (e.g. of varnish) spread over something

circum-luō, —, — 3 to wash round, flow around

circum-luviō, ōnis f island formed by a river flowing in a new channel

circum-mittō 3 to send round.

circum-mūniō (or moeniō) 4 to fortify, to enclose by a wall.

circum-mūnītiō, ōnis f an investing, circumvallation.

**circum-padănus** 3 about the river Po.

**circum-pendeō** 2 to hang around.

**circum-plaudō** 3 to applaud on all sides.

**circum-plector** (*and* **-ō**), **plexus sum** 3 to embrace, enclose.

**circum-plicō** 1 to wind around.

**circum-pōnō** 3 to place round.

**circum-pōtātiō, ōnis** *f* a drinking round in turn.

**circum-rētiō** 4 to enclose in a net, ensnare.

**circum-rōdō** 3 a) to gnaw round; b) to slander.

**circum-saepiō** 4 to hedge *or* fence around.

**circum-scindō** 3 to tear off around.

**circum-scrībō** 3 **1.** to describe a circle round (*alqd*); to enclose in a circle; **2.** a) to define, fix the boundaries of (*alci alqd*), limit; b) to restrain, confine; c) to circumvent, deceive, cheat, defraud; d) to cancel, annul, set aside.

**circum-scriptē** *adv.* a) by precise definition; b) in periods.

**circum-scriptiō, ōnis** *f* an encircling; a) circumference; b) boundary, limit, compass; c) period; d) a deceiving, cheating, overreaching.

**circum-scriptor, ōris** *m* deceiver, cheat.

**circum-scriptus** 3 bounded; concise; in periods.

**circum-secō** 1 to cut around.

**circum-sedeō** 2 a) to sit around; b) to besiege, blockade, invest.

**circum-sessiō, ōnis** *f* a beleaguering, besieging.

**circum-sīdō, sēdī, — 3** to besiege.

**circum-siliō** 4 to leap around.

**circum-sistō, stetī, — 3** to stand round, surround.

**circum-sonō** 1 a) *intr.* to resound on all sides; b) *trans.* to make echo, surround with noise.

**circum-sonus** 3 sounding around.

**circum-spectātrix, īcis** *f* she who looks round.

**circum-spectiō, ōnis** *f* caution, circumspection.

**circum-spectō** 1 (*intens.*) = **circumspicio**.

**circum-spectus¹, ūs** *m* consideration; prospect, view.

**circum-spectus²** 3 cautious, circumspect, considerate.

**circum-spiciō, spexī, spectum** 3 to look round; **1.** to look about (*cautiously* or *attentively*); **2.** a) to see, observe; b) to view on all sides, to survey; c) to look for, seek for, wait for; d) to consider, weigh, survey.

**circum-stō, stetī, — 1** a) *intr.* to stand round; b) *trans.* to surround, encircle (*alqd*); to threaten, beset.

**circum-strepō** 3 a) to surround with noise; b) to shout (*alqd*) round about.

**circum-struō** 3 to build round.

**circum-tentus** 3 encased.

**circum-terō** 3 to crowd round.

**circum-textus** 3 woven all around.

**circum-tonō** 1 to thunder round.

**circum-tōnsus** 3 shorn all around.

**circum-vādō, sī, — 3** to attack, assail on every side.

**circum-vagus** 3 flowing around.

**circum-vallō** 1 to surround with a wall, to blockade.

**circum-vectiō, ōnis** *f* a) a carrying around; b) circuit, revolution.

**circum-vectō** 1 to carry round.

**circum-vector** 1 to ride *or* sail round (*alqd*); to go through, describe.

**circum-vehor** 3 *trans.* to ride *or* sail round (*alqd*).

**circum-vēlō** 1 to veil around, envelop.

**circum-veniō** 4 to come around, surround, flow round; a) to encircle, enclose; b) to invest, to beset, to oppress, distress, overthrow; c) to ensnare, cheat, deceive.

**circum-vertō** 3 to turn *or* twist round; **P.** to turn oneself round.

**circum-vestiō** 4 to clothe round.

**circum-vinciō** 4 to bind all round.

**circum-vīsō** 3 (*intens.*) to look all round.

**circum-volitō** 1 to fly round (*alqd*).

**circum-volō** 1 to fly round (*with acc.*).

**circum-volvor** 3 to roll round; to revolve through (*annum*).

**circus, ī** *m* a) circular line, circle; b) race-course, circus.

**cīris, is** *f* an unknown sea-bird.

**cirrātus** 3 curly-haired.

**cirrus, ī** *m* curl; fringe.

**cis** *prep.* with *acc.* a) on this side of; b) within.

**cis-alpīnus** 3 lying on the Roman side of the Alps, Cisalpine.

**cisium, ī** *n* two-wheeled carriage.

**cis-rhēnānus** 3 on the left side of the Rhine.

**cista, ae** *f* chest, box.

**cistell(ul)a, ae** *f* little box.

**cistellātrīx, īcis** *f* female slave in charge of the money-box.

**cisterna, ae** *f* cistern, reservoir.

**cisto-phorus, ī** *m* Asiatic coin stamped with a cista.

**citātim** *adv.* quickly, hastily.

**citātus** 3 speedy, swift, rapid.

**citerior, ius a)** on this (*the Roman*) side; **b)** nearer, closer.

**cithara, ae** *f* cithara, lyre.

**citharista, ae** *m and* **citharistria, ae** *f* player on the cithara.

**citharizō** 1 to play on the cithara.

**citharoedicus** 3 of a *citharoedus.*

**cithar-oedus, ī** *m* one who sings to the cithara.

**citimus** 3 nearest.

**citō** *adv. of* **citus.**

**citō²** 1 to put in quick motion, to excite, rouse; **a)** to call, summon, cite; **b)** to call a defendant, a witness; to accuse (*capitis*); **c)** to name, appeal to, quote, recite.

**citrā 1.** *adv.* nearer, on this side; **2.** *prep.* with *acc.*; **a)** on this side of, within; **b)** short of, without, except, setting aside.

**citreus** 3 of citrus-wood.

**citrō** *adv.* to this side; **ultrō et citrō** hither and thither, to and fro, reciprocally

**citrum, ī** *n* (article made of) citrus--wood.

**citrus, ī** *f* citrus-tree.

**citus** 3 swift, quick, rapid; *adv.* **citō; non cito** not easily; **citius** sooner, rather.

**civicus** 3 = **civilis** 1.

**cīvīlis, e 1.** pertaining to citizens, of citizens; **a) ius cīvīle** civil law, private rights; **b)** civil, civic, patriotic, political, public; **2.** affable, courteous, polite

**cīvīlitās, ātis** *f* politeness, courteousness.

**cīvis, is** *m and f* citizen, **a)** fellow--citizen, countryman; **b)** subject

**cīvitās, ātis** *f* citizenship; **a)** condition *or* rights of a citizen; **b)** the citizens; city, state, commonwealth.

**cīvitātula, ae** *f* citizenship of a small town.

**clādēs, is** *f* damage, injury, disaster, destruction, defeat, slaughter, massacre.

**clam 1.** *adv.* secretly, privately, in secret; **2.** *prep.* with *abl.* (and *acc.*) without the knowledge of, unknown to.

**clāmātor, ōris** *m* shouter.

**clāmitātiō, ōnis** *f* loud crying.

**clāmitō** 1 *intens. of* **clamo.**

**clāmō** 1 to cry aloud, shout (*trans.* and *intr.*); **a)** to proclaim, to call aloud to (*alci*); **b)** to call upon, invoke; **c)** to call by name; **d)** to declare.

**clāmor, ōris** *m* loud shout, call, cry; **a)** acclamation, applause, rejoicing; **b)** outcry, complaint, cry of sorrow, war-cry; **c)** noise, sound, din, echo.

**clāmōsus** 3 noisy.

**clanculārius** 3 concealed, anonymous.

**clanculum = clam.** [ed, hidden.]

**clandestīnus** 3 secret, conceal-

**clangō** 3 to resound, peal.

**clangor, ōris** *m* sound, clang, noise.

**clāreō, —, —** 2 to be bright *or* clear; to shine.

**clārēscō, ruī, —** 3 to become bright *or* clear; **a)** to become audible; **b)** to become brilliant, illustrious.

**clārigātiō, ōnis** *f* demand of satisfaction; fine for transgressing limits.

**clāri-sonus** 3 clear-sounding.

**clāritās, ātis** *f* clearness, brightness; **a)** distinctness; **b)** renown, fame, celebrity.

**clāritūdō, inis** *f* = **claritas.**

**clārō** 1 to make clear; to make famous.

**clārus** 3 bright, clear, shining; **a)** distinct, loud, audible; **b)** plain, clear, evident; **c)** illustrious, renowned, notorious

**classiārius** 3 belonging to the navy; *subst.* **~, ī** *m* soldier on a ship, marine, sailor

**classicula, ae** *f* little fleet.

**classicum, ī** *n* trumpet-call for battle; war-trumpet

**classicus** 3 belonging *or* pertaining to the fleet *or* navy; *subst.* **~, ī** *m* = **classiarius.**

**classis, is** *f* **1.** class *or* division of citizens; **2. a)** army; **b)** fleet, navy; naval service.

**clătrātus** 3 latticed.

**clătrī, ōrum** *m*/*pl.* bar, lattice.

**claudeō** 2 *and* **claudō** 3 = claudico.

**claudicātiō, ōnis** *f* a limping.

**claudicō** 1 a) to limp, be lame; b) to waver, halt.

**claudō, sī, sum** 3 **1.** to shut, close, shut up; *subst.* **clausum, ī** *n* enclosure, confinement; a) to close, end, conclude, **agmen claudere** to bring up the rear; b) to round (*a period*); **2.** to shut in, imprison, confine (*alqd in rem, in re, re*); a) to make inaccessible, to intercept, dam up, stop; b) to surround.

**claudus** 3 a) limping, halting, lame; b) wavering; c) crippled, defective.

**claustra, ōrum** *n*/*pl.* (*sg. rare*) a) lock, bolt, bar, barrier; b) gate, dam, dike, barricade; c) confinement, den, cage; d) key (*of a position*), bulwark, entrenchment.

**clausula, ae** *f* close, conclusion.

**clāva, ae** *f* cudgel, club; staff.

**clāvārium, ī** *n* (*mil.*) money for shoe-nails.

**clāvātor, ōris** *m* cudgel-bearer.

**clāvĭcula, ae** *f* a) small key; b) vine tendril.

**clāvi-ger** 3 a) [*clava*] club-bearer; b) [*clavis*] key-bearer.

**clāvis, is** *f* a) key; b) lock.

**clāvus, ī** *m* **1.** nail; **2.** a) rudder, helm; b) purple stripe on the tunic.

**clēmēns, tis** mild, placid, calm, gentle, kind, merciful.

**clēmentia, ae** *f* mildness, benignity, kindness, forbearance, moderation.

**clepō, psī, (ptum)** 3 to steal.

**cleps-ydra, ae** *f* water-clock.

**clepta, ae** *m* thief.

**cliēns, tis** *m* dependant, client; adherent, retainer, follower, vassal.

**clienta, ae** *f* female client.

**clientēla, ae** *f* a) clientship, patronage; b) clients, dependants, vassals.

**clientulus, ī** *m* a poor client.

**climactēricus** 3 critical, climacteric.

**clīnāmen, inis** *n* inclination (of atoms).

**clīnātus** 3 inclined, bent.

**clīnicus, ī** *m* a) physician; b) undertaker, bearer of a bier.

**clipeātus** 3 bearing a shield.

**clipeus, ī** *m* (*and* **clipeum, ī** *n*) round brazen shield; a) disk of the sun; b) oval medallion.

**clītellae, ārum** *f*/*pl.* pack-saddle.

**clītellārius** 3 bearing a pack-saddle.

**clīvōsus** 3 hilly, steep.

**clīvus, ī** *m* gentle ascent, slope, declivity; eminence, hill.

**cloāca, ae** *f* sewer, drain.

**clōstra,** *see* claustra.

**clūdō, cluēns,** *see* claudo, cliens.

**clueō** (*and* **clueor**) 2 to hear, be spoken of, to be reputed, famed.

**clūnis, is** *f* or *m* buttock.

**clupeus** = clipeus.

**clūrīnus** 3 of apes.

**clystēr, ēris** *m* enema; syringe.

**Cn.** (*abbr.*) = **Gnaeus.**

**co-acervātiō, ōnis** *f* a heaping up.

**co-acervō** 1 to heap together, heap up, accumulate.

**co-acēscō, acuī, —** 3 to become sour.

**co-āctiō, ōnis** *f* a collecting.

**co-āctō** 1 to constrain, force.

**co-āctor, ōris** *m* collector of money; rear man (in a column).

**co-āctum, ī** *n* felt.

**co-āctus, ūs** *m* compulsion.

**co-aedificō** 1 to build on.

**co-aequō** 1 a) to make equal, even, level; b) to place on the same footing.

**co-āgmentātiō, ōnis** *f* a joining, connection.

**co-āgmentō** 1 to join, connect, cement together.

**co-āgmentum, ī** *n* a joining together, joint.

**co-āgulum, ī** *n* rennet.

**co-alēscō, aluī, alitum** 3 to grow together, to become united by growth; a) to join together, to unite; b) to grow, to take root, become strong.

**co-angustō** 1 to compress, confine, narrow.

**co-arguō** 3 to prove fully, to demonstrate, show, establish; a) to convict, prove guilty; b) to prove to be wrong, to refute.

**co-artātiō, ōnis** *f* a pressing together.

**co-artō** 1 a) to pack. confine; b) to abridge, shorten.

**coaxō** 1 to croak.

**coccinātus** 3 clad in scarlet.

**coccin(e)us** 3 scarlet-coloured.

**coccum, ī** *n* scarlet dye *or* cloth.

**cochlea, coclea, ae** *f* snail, snail-shell.

coc(h)lear(e), is *n* spoon.

cocles, itis one-eyed.

coctilis, e baked, burned; of burned bricks.

cocus, i *m* = coquus.

cōda, ae *f vulg.* = cauda.

cōdex, icis *m* = caudex.

cōdicārius 3 made of tree trunks.

cōdicillus, ī *m* 1. small wooden block; 2. (*pl.*) writting tablet; a) note, billet; b) petition; c) imperial rescript; d) addition to a will, codicil.

co-emō 3 to buy up.

co-ēmptiō, ōnis *f* a) marriage by fictitious sale; b) fictitious marriage.

co-ēmptiōnālis, e bought up with others (as being valueless).

co-eō, ii, (itum), īre 1. to go *or* come together, to meet, assemble; a) to meet in battle, to encounter; b) to be united, to combine; to copulate; to unite in marriage; c) to heal up, close; d) to congeal, curdle; e) to agree; 2. *trans.* so-cietatem to form an alliance (*cum alqo*).

(coepiō), coepī, coeptum 3 to begin.

coeptō 1 (*intens.*) = incipio.

coeptum, ī *n* an undertaking, work begun.

coeptus, ūs *m* a beginning, undertaking.      [a dinner.)

co-epulōnus, ī *m* companion at|

co-erceō, cuī, citum 2 to enclose on all sides, to hold together; a) to enclose, encompass; b) to restrain, confine, control, keep in order, to check, curb, correct, tame.

co-ercitiō, ōnis *f* a) a restraining; b) (right of) punishing

coetus, ūs *m* a) a coming together, meeting; b) assembly, company

cōgitābilis, e conceivable.

cōgitātiō, ōnis *f* a thinking; 1. a) a considering, deliberating, meditation, b) power of thinking, reflection, imagination; 2. thought; a) idea, notion; b) purpose, plan, design.

cōgitō 1 1. a) to think, reflect upon, ponder, weigh (*de re*); to be disposed; b) to think of, have in mind, intend, purpose (*de re* or with *inf.*); 2. to design, plan (*alqd* or with *inf.*); *adj.* cōgitātus 3 well-considered, deliberate, intended; *subst.* cōgitā-tum, ī *n* thought, idea; purpose.

cognātiō, ōnis *f* blood-relationship; a) kindred, relations; b) resemblance, affinity, agreement.

co-gnātus 3 a) related by blood (*with dat.*); b) connected, related, similar; *subst.* ~, ī *m* kinsman, blood-relation.

cognitiō, ōnis *f* a becoming acquainted with; a) a knowing, knowledge, acquaintance (*with gen.*); b) notion, idea; c) legal inquiry *or* examination, trial.

cognitor, ōris *m* a) advocate, procurator, attorney, protector; b) witness to identity.

cognitūra, ae *f* public prosecutor's office.

cognitus 3, *see* cognosco.

cognōmen, inis *n* surname; a) family name; b) name.

cognōmentum, ī *n* = cognomen.

cognōminis, e of the same name.

cognōminō 1 to surname; cognō-minātus synonymous.

co-gnōscō, gnōvī, gnitum 3 to become acquainted with, learn, perceive, understand; see; *pf.* to know; a) to read, peruse; b) to inquire into, investigate, examine, study; c) to examine judicially; d) to recognize, identify; e) to reconnoitre, act as a scout; *adj.* cognitus 3 known, tried, proved.

cōgō, coēgī, coāctum 3 1. to drive together, bring together (*alqm* or *alqd ab, ex re in, ad alqd*); a) to contract, condense; b) to gather together, assemble, collect, summon; to collect (*money*); (*agmen*) to bring up the rear; 2. to urge, force, compel (*ut,* or with *inf.*); a) to constrain; b) to drive, press; c) to conclude; coāctus 3 constrained, compelled, forced.

co-haerentia, ae *f* coherence, connection

co-haereō, haesī, — 2 to hang together (*cum re, inter se*); a) to be united, cohere, adhere; b) to hold together, subsist, consist of (*abl.*).

co-haerēscō, haesī 3 to stick together.

co-hērēs, ēdis *m* and *f* co-heir.

co-hibeō, buī, bitum 2 to hold together; a) to hold, contain, comprise; b) to restrain, confine; c) to hinder, hold back; d) to control, repress.

**co-honestō** 1 to honour, celebrate.
**co-horrēscō, horruī, —** 3 to shudder, shiver.
**co-hors, tis** f 1. enclosure, cattle-yard; 2. a) division of soldiers, cohort, **praetoria** body-guard of a general; b) retinue or suite of a governor; c) troop, crowd, multitude. [encouragement.]
**co-hortātiō, ōnis** f exhortation,
**cohorticula, ae** f a small cohort.
**co-hortor** 1 to exhort, encourage,
**cŏ-iciō = conicio.** [incite.]
**co-inquinō** 1 to defile, pollute.
**co-itiō, ōnis** f a coming together; a) conspiracy, plot; b) agreement.
**co-itus, ūs** m meeting; sexual union.
**colaphus, ī** m box on the ear.
**cōleus, ī** m sack; scrotum.
**cōliculus, ī** m young stalk, young greens.
**col-labāscō** 3 to totter.
**col-labefactō** 1 to cause to totter.
**col-labefīō, factus sum, fierī** to be made to totter, to fall to pieces, collapse, be ruined.
**col-lābor** 3 = **collabefio.**
**col-lacerātus** 3 torn to pieces.
**col-lacrimātiō, ōnis** f a weeping.
**col-lacrimō** 1 to bewail.
**col-lactea, ae** f foster-sister.
**collāre, is** n collar.
**col-lātīcius** 3 contributed, lent.
**col-lātiō, ōnis** f a bringing together, **signorum** hostile encounter, collision; a) contribution of money, collection; b) comparison, similitude.
**col-lātīvus** 3 into which much is collected, i. e. fat, distended.
**col-lātor, ōris** m contributor.
**col-lātrō** 1 to bark at, abuse.
**col-lātus, ūs** m = **collatio;** esp. engagement, attack.
**col-laudātiō, ōnis** f warm praise.
**col-laudō** 1 to praise very much.
**col-laxō** 1 to make loose.
**col-lēcta, ae** f contribution.
**col-lēctāneus** 3 collected.
**col-lēctīcius** 3 gathered in haste.
**col-lēctiō, ōnis** f a) a gathering; b) a summing up; c) inference.
**col-lēctus, ūs** m collection.
**collēga, ae** m partner in office, colleague.
**collēgium, ī** n 1. colleagueship; 2. association, guild, corporation, college, company, fraternity.

**col-lēvō** 1 to make smooth.
**col-lībertus, ī** m fellow-freedman.
**col-libet** 2 it pleases, is agreeable.
**col-līdō, sī, sum** 3 a) to strike or dash together; P. to meet in a hostile manner; b) to dash to pieces.
**col-ligātiō, ōnis** f a binding together, connection.
**col-ligō**[1] 1 to bind together; tie, connect, bind (alqd cum re, inter se); a) to combine, unite; b) to fasten, fetter; c) to restrain, hinder.
**col-ligō**[2], **lēgī, lēctum** 3 1. a) to bring together, collect, gather, **vasa** to pack up for a march; b) to put together, to enumerate, reckon; c) to assemble, bring together, concentrate; 2. a) **se** or **animum** to collect one's mind, recover one's senses or courage; b) to gain, obtain, acquire; c) to consider, reckon; to infer, conclude.
**col-līneō** 1 to direct in a straight line; to hit the mark.
**col-linō, lēvī, litum** 3 to besmear; to defile (alqd alqa re).
**col-liquefactus** 3 made liquid, dissolved.
**collis, is** m hill, elevation.
**col-locātiō, ōnis** f a) a putting, placing; b) a giving in marriage.
**col-locō** 1 to place, lay, set (alqm or alqd in re); a) to station, quarter, settle; b) to lay out, invest, advance (money); c) to settle (a woman) in marriage (alqm in matrimonio); d) to employ, occupy, manage (alqd in re).
**col-locuplētō** 1 to enrich greatly.
**col-locūtiō, ōnis** f conversation.
**colloquium, ī** n conversation, talk.
**col-loquor** 3 to speak, talk, converse with (cum alqo de re), to treat or negotiate with; to accost.
**col-lubet = collibet.**
**col-lūceō, —, —** 2 to shine on all sides, to shine, to be illuminated, to be clear or bright.
**col-luctor** 1 to wrestle with.
**col-lūdō** 3 to play or sport with (dat.); to have a secret understanding with (cum alqo).
**collum, ī** n (and **collus, ī** m) the neck. [to rinse.]
**col-luō** 3 to wash thoroughly,
**col-lūsiō, ōnis** f secret understanding (cum alqo).
**col-lūsor, ōris** m playmate, playfellow.

col-lūstrō 1 a) to light up on all sides, illuminate; b) to survey, review.

col-lutulentō 1 to defile.

col-luviēs, ēi f = colluvio.

col-luviō, ōnis f conflux, collection of filth, washings, dregs, offscourings; medley, rabble.

collybus, ī m moneychanging.

collȳra, ae f a kind of bread.

collȳricus 3 made with collyra.

collȳrium, ī n eye-salve.

colō, coluī, cultum 3 to care for; a) to till, cultivate, farm; b) to tend, adorn; adj. cultus 3 cultivated, tilled (culta, ōrum n/pl. tilled land, gardens, plantations), adorned, elegant, polite, accomplished; b) to abide, dwell in a place; c) to bestow care upon, to guard, protect, honour, revere, worship, cherish, love.

colocāsium, ī n waterlily.

cōloephia, ōrum n/pl. = colyphia.

colōna, ae f country-woman.

colōnia, ae f 1. farm, estate; 2. colony, settlement; colonists.

colōnicus 3 colonial; levied in the colonies.

colōnus, ī m 1. peasant, farmer; 2. colonist; inhabitant.

color (and colōs), ōris m colour, hue, tint; a) complexion; b) outward show, external appearance or condition; c) colouring, style, character.

colōrō 1 to colour, dye, tan.

colossēus 3 gigantic.

colossus, ī m gigantic statue.

coluber, brī m serpent, snake.

colubra, ae f female serpent.

colubri-fer 3 serpent-bearing.

colubrīnus 3 snake-like.

cōlum, ī n sieve, strainer.

columba, ae f pigeon, dove.

columbar, āris n collar like a pigeon-hole.

columbīnus 3 of a pigeon or dove.

columbus, ī m male pigeon or dove.

columella, ae f small column.

columen, inis n column, pillar; a) highest part, top; b) prop, support

columis, is = incolumis (?).

columna, ae f column, pillar; prop.

columnāriī, ōrum m/pl. rascals, thieves.

columnārium, ī n tax on pillars.

columnātus 3 supported by pillars.

colurnus 3 made of hazel-wood.

colus, ūs and ī f (m) distaff.

colustrum, ī n beestings.

colūtea, ōrum n/pl. pod-like fruit.

cōlȳphia, ōrum n/pl. meat for athletes.

coma, ae f the hair of the head; foliage, leaves.

comāns, tis hairy, covered with hair; having leaves.

cōm-archus, ī m ruler of a village.

comātus 3 long-haired; having leaves.

combardus 3 stupid.

com-bibō[1], ōnis m drinking-companion.

com-bibō[2], bibī, — 3 to drink up, imbibe, to swallow.

comb-ūrō 3 to burn up, consume, destroy.

com-edō 3 to eat up, consume; to waste, squander, dissipate.

comes, itis m and f companion, associate, comrade; a) guardian, tutor, teacher; b) attendant, client; c) pl retinue.

comētēs, ae m comet.

cōmicus 3 of comedy, comic; subst. ~, ī m comic poet or actor.

cōmis, e affable, courteous, kind, amiable, obliging.

cōmissābundus 3 revelling, carousing.

cōmissātiō, ōnis f a revelling, riotous banquet.

cōmissātor, ōris m drinking-companion, reveller, rioter.

cōmissor 1 to revel, riot, carouse.

cōmitās, ātis f affability, kindness, friendliness, gaiety.

comitātus, ūs m a) attendance; b) train, escort, retinue; c) travelling company; d) imperial court or suite.

comitiālis, e pertaining to the comitia, of an election; morbus epilepsy.

comitiātus, ūs m assembly of the people in the comitia.

com-itium, ī n place of assembly; n/pl. -ia, iōrum assembly of the people for electing magistrates, etc.: election.

com-itor (com-itō) 1 to accompany, attend, follow (alqm, alqd); comitātus alqo attended by.

com-maculō 1 to spot, stain, pollute.

**com-manipulāris, is** *m* one belonging to the same maniple, comrade.
**com-marītus, ī** *m* fellow-husband.
**com-meātus, ūs** *m* a going to and fro, free passage; **a)** leave of absence; **b)** transport, convoy, supply-train, caravan; c) provisions, supply, food, forage.
**com-meditor** 1 to imitate.
**com-meminī, isse** to remember, recollect.
**com-memorābilis, e** memorable.
**com-memorātiō, ōnis** *f* a) a mentioning, reminding; **b)** remembrance.
**com-memorō** 1 **1.** to keep in mind, remember; **2.** a) to remind of (*alqd*); b) to mention, recount, relate (*alqd* or *de re*).
**commendābilis, e** worthy of praise, commendable.
**commendātīcius** 3 of recommendation.
**commendātiō, ōnis** *f* **a)** recommendation; **b)** that which recommends, excellence.
**commendātor, ōris** *m*, and **-trīx, īcis** *f* one who recommends.
**com-mendō** 1 to commit to the care of, to intrust to; to recommend (*alci alqd, se alci*); to make agreeable.
**commentāriolum, ī** *n* short treatise, sketch.
**commentārium, ī** *n* = **commentārius.**
**commentārius, ī** *m* notebook, diary, memorandum, notes, sketch, paper, commentary; *pl.* memoirs, records.
**commentātiō, ōnis** *f* **a)** careful consideration, deep reflection, meditation, study, preparation; **b)** treatise, dissertation.
**commentīcius** 3 invented, fictitious; **a)** ideal; **b)** feigned, false.
**commentor**[1] 1 to consider thoroughly, to meditate, think over (*alqd, de re*); **a)** to discuss; **b)** to study, prepare (*mentally*), to practise, exercise in speaking *or* writing; c) to compose, sketch, write down.
**commentor**[2], **ōris** *m* inventor, deviser.
**commentum, ī** *n* **a)** invention, thought, device; **b)** fiction, falsehood.
**com-meō** 1 **a)** to come and go, go to and fro, go about; **b)** to visit frequently, to resort to.

**com-mercium, ī** *n* **a)** commercial intercourse, trade, traffic; **b)** the right of trade; c) communication, correspondence, communion.
**com-mercor** 1 to traffic together, to buy up, purchase.
**com-mereō** (*and* **eor**) 2 **a)** to deserve fully; **b)** to be guilty of.
**com-mētior** 4 to measure; to measure with, compare.
**com-mētō**[1] 1 to measure.
**com-mētō**[2] 1 to go frequently.
**com-migrātiō, ōnis** *f* wandering.
**com-migrō** 1 to migrate; to remove to.
**com-militēs, um** *m/pl.* fellow-soldiers.
**commilitium, ī** *n* a serving together as soldiers, comradeship.
**com-militō, ōnis** *m* fellowsoldier, comrade.
**com-minātiō, ōnis** *f* a threatening, threat.
**com-mingō** 3 to make water on; to defile, pollute.
**com-mīniscor, mentus sum** 3 to devise, invent; to feign.
**com-minor** 1 to threaten (*alci alqd*).
**com-minuō** 3 to break into small pieces, to crush; **a)** to lessen, diminish; **b)** to weaken, enervate, reduce.
**com-minus** *adv.* hand to hand; at close quarters; close by, near; face to face.
**com-misceō** 2 **a)** to mix *or* mingle together (*alqd cum re* or with *abl.*); **b)** to unite, join.
**com-miserātiō, ōnis** *f* appeal to compassion; pathetic speech.
**com-miserēscō** 3 to pity.
**com-miseror** 1 to lament, bewail, excite pity.
**com-missiō, ōnis** *f* contest, struggle; prize composition.
**com-missum, ī** *n* **1.** an undertaking; transgression, offence, crime, fault; **2.** secret, trust.
**com-missūra, ae** *f* connection, joint, knot, juncture.
**com-mītigō** 1 to make soft.
**com-mittō** 3 **1.** to bring together, join, combine, connect, unite (*alqd alci rei*); to set *or* bring together in a fight; **2.** to engage in, begin, carry on; **a) proelium** to commence *or* fight a battle; **b)** to commit, be guilty of (*alqd in, erga, adversus*

alqm); c) to give cause, allow it to happen (ut, ne, cur, quare); d) to forfeit; **3.** to give, intrust, commit to; to resign to, expose, abandon.

**commoditās, ātis** f a) just proportion, symmetry, fitness, convenience, comfort, advantage; **b)** courtesy, kindness, indulgence.

**commodō** 1 a) to adapt oneself to suit another person (alci); to accommodate; **b)** to furnish, lend, give (alci alqd).

**commodulē** (and **lum**) adv. conveniently, nicely.

**commodum**[1] adv. opportunely; just, just now.

**commodum**[2], **ī** n a) convenience, opportunity; **b)** use, advantage, profit; **c)** favour, privilege, prerogative; **d)** reward, pay; **e)** loan.

**com-modus** 3 **1.** proper, fit, convenient, suitable, appropriate; a) good, agreeable; b) easy, useful, serviceable, pleasant; **2.** obliging, friendly, polite.

**com-mōlior** 4 to set in motion.

**com-monefaciō** 3 = **commoneo.**

**com-moneō** 2 a) to remind, bring to one's recollection (alqm alcis rei, de re); **b)** to warn, to exhort (with ut, ne).

**com-mōnstrō** 1 to show or point out distinctly.

**com-morātiō, ōnis** f a tarrying, abiding, dwelling on.

**com-mordeō** 2 to bite; to abuse, slander.

**com-morior** 3 to die together.

**com-moror** 1 to tarry, linger, abide, sojourn.

**com-mōtiō, ōnis** f excitement, agitation, commotion.

**commōtiuncula, ae** f slight indisposition.

**com-moveō** 2 to put in violent motion (alqm, alqd); **a)** to remove, drive away, carry away, displace, castra to decamp; **b)** to shake, excite, stir, agitate, disturb; **c)** to rouse, make an impression upon, produce (alci dolorem), **d)** to disquiet, **commōtus** 3 moved, excited, agitated, disordered.

**commūnicātiō, ōnis** f imparting, communication.

**commūnicō** (and **-or**) 1 **1.** to make common, to unite (alqd); a) to share with, have in common with (alqd

cum alqo); **b)** to communicate, impart, give a share in, grant; **2.** to inform, take counsel with, confer with (cum alqo, de re).

**com-mūniō**[1] 4 to fortify on all sides, to strengthen, secure.

**commūniō**[2], **ōnis** f communion, mutual participation.

**com-mūnis, e** a) common, ordinary, general, usual, universal, public; **b)** affable, courteous, condescending; subst. **commūne, is** n a) common property; **b)** commonwealth, state, community, **in commūne** for common use, for all, in general, generally.

**commūnitās, ātis** f **1.** community; **2.** a) public spirit; b) condescension.

**com-mūnitiō, ōnis** f a paving a way.

**com-murmuror** (and **ō**) 1 to murmur, mutter.

**com-mūtābilis, e** (ex)changeable.

**com-mūtātiō, ōnis** f (and **-tus**, **-ūs** m) a changing, change, alteration.

**com-mūtō** 1 a) to change, alter; **b)** to exchange, change for.

**cōmō, cōmpsi, cōmptum** 3 **1.** to unite; **2.** to adorn, arrange; dress; **cōmptus** 3 adorned, embellished, neat, pretty.

**cōmoedia, ae** f comedy.

**cōmoedicē** as in a comedy.

**cōmoedus, ī** m comic actor.

**cōmōsus** 3 hairy.

**com-pacīscor, pactus sum** 3 to make an agreement, form a compact; **compactō** adv. according to agreement.

**com-pāctiō, ōnis** f a joining together.

**com-pāctus** 3 sturdy, compact.

**compāgēs, is** f a) a joining together; **b)** connection, joint; c) structure.

**compāgō, inis** f = **compages.**

**com-pār, aris** like, similar, equal; subst. m companion, comrade, compeer.

**comparābilis, e** comparable.

**comparātiō, ōnis** f **1.** a) a preparing, preparation; b) a procuring, acquiring; **2.** a comparing, comparison; a) relation; b) agreement, contract.

**comparātīvus** 3 comparative.

**com-parcō** 3 to save, lay up; to abstain from (inf.).

**com-păreō, ruĭ,** — 2 to appear, be visible, exist.

**com-parŏ[1] 1** [*par*] to bring together as equals, to pair, match; **a)** to bring together for a combat, to oppose; **b)** to compare, make a comparison, to consider by comparing.

**com-parŏ[2] 1** [*parare*] to prepare, make ready, arrange; **a)** to get ready, equip (*soldiers*); **b)** to make arrangements *or* preparations; **c)** to appoint, ordain, establish, settle, institute, **ita comparātus** of such a constitution; **d)** to procure, provide, furnish, obtain, acquire (*alci alqd*).

**com-pāscō 3** to feed together.

**com-pāscuus 3** for common pasturage.

**com-pectus sum, com-pectō = compactus sum, compacto;** *see* **compaciscor.**

**com-pediŏ 4** to fetter.

**compellātiō, ōnis** *f* **a)** an accosting, addressing; **b)** a rebuking, reprimand.

**com-pellŏ[1] 1** to accost, address; **a)** to rebuke, reproach, abuse, chide; **b)** to arraign, accuse.

**com-pellŏ[2] pulĭ, pulsum 3** to drive together, to one place (*alqd in* or *ad alqd*); **a)** to force together; **b)** to drive; **c)** to impel, incite, urge, compel (*alqm in* or *ad alqd*).

**compendiārius 3** saving time, shortened; **compendiāria via** (*also* *f and n* as *subst.*) short cut.

**compendium, ĭ** *n* a shortening, abridging; **a)** short way; **b)** a sparing, saving, profit.

**compēnsātiō, ōnis** *f* equivalent, compensation.

**com-pēnsō 1 a)** to balance, weigh together, counterbalance (*alqd cum re*); **b)** to compensate, make good (*alqd re*).

**com-percō = comparco.**

**comperendinātus, ūs** *m and* **-tiō, ōnis** *f* an adjourning a trial to the third day.

**com-perendinŏ 1** to adjourn a trial to the third day, to summon a defendant for the third day.

**com-periŏ** (*and* **-ior), perĭ, pertum 4** to find out, learn, discover, get information; **compertus 3 a)** known, heard; **b)** ascertained, certain; **c)** convicted. [(*for the feet*).]

**com-pēs, edis** *f* fetter *or* shackle

**compescō, uĭ,** — 3 to restrain, check, repress, suppress.

**com-petitor, ōris** *m* rival, competitor.

**com-petītrix, icis** *f* female competitor.

**com-petŏ 3 a)** to coincide (*cum re*); **b)** to be adequate, capable, suitable, fit; to correspond.

**com-pilātiō, ōnis** *f* a pillaging, plundering; compilation.

**com-pilŏ 1** to plunder, pillage, rob.

**com-pingŏ[1], pēgĭ, pāctum 3 a)** to join together, frame, construct; **b)** to drive *or* thrust into; to fasten up.

**com-pingŏ[2], pinxĭ,** — 3 to paint over, bedaub.

**compitālicius 3** belonging to the *Compitalia.*

**compitālis, e** belonging to a *compitum; subst.* **Compitālia, iōrum** *n/pl.* festival in honour of the *Lares compitales,* celebrated on the cross-roads.

**compitum, ĭ** *n* cross-roads.

**com-placeō 2** to please well.

**com-plānō 1** to make level *or* even; to raze to the ground.

**com-plector, plexus sum 3** to clasp, embrace; **a)** to surround, encircle, enclose; **b)** to comprehend, comprise; **c)** to understand, grasp mentally; **d)** to esteem, value, honour, care for; **e)** to take into possession, lay hold of.

**complēmentum, ĭ** *n* complement.

**com-pleō, ēvĭ, ētum 2** to fill up, fill full, make full (*alqd with gen.* or *abl.*); **a)** to complete, fill with men; **b)** to accomplish, fulfil, finish; **c)** to live through, pass.

**complexiō, ōnis** *f* connection, combination; short summary; sentence; period; syllogism; dilemma.

**complexus, ūs** *m* embrace, affection; close grip (of an enemy).

**com-plicō, uĭ, ātum 1** to fold together *or* up; **complicātus 3** confused, intricate.

**com-plōdō 3** to strike together, clap (*the hands*).

**com-plōrātiō, ōnis** *f* (*and* **-us, ūs** *m*) loud complaint, wailing, lamentation.

**com-plōrō 1** to bewail, lament loudly.

**com-plūrēs, a, ium** several, very many.

**com-plūriēs** *adv.* several times.

**com-plūsculi** 3 a good many.

**com-pluvium, ī** *n* open space in the middle of a Roman house.

**com-pōnō** 3 **1.** to bring, place, put together (*alqd in loco*); a) to collect, unite, concentrate; b) to inter, bury; c) to take in (*sails*); d) to oppose, confront; e) to compare, contrast (*alqd cum re* or with *dat.*); **2.** to compose, compound, make up, construct, form, fashion, make by joining together (*alqd ex re*); a) to compose, write; b) to agree upon together, to appoint, fix, settle; c) to invent, devise, contrive; **3.** to arrange, dispose, regulate, set in order, adjust; to allay, settle, appease, quiet.

**com-portō** 1 to carry *or* bring together.

**com-pos, otis** a) partaking of, possessing, participating in, sharing in (with *gen.*, seldom *abl.*); b) having the mastery of.

**com-positiō, ōnis** *f* a putting together, adjusting; matching; composition, arrangement; settlement, reconciliation.    [maker.]

**com-positor, ōris** *m* arranger,

**com-positūra, ae** *f* putting together; fabric, texture.

**com-positus** 3 put together; a) well arranged, carefully adjusted *or* assumed; b) suitable, prepared; c) quiet, calm; (ex) **compositō** by agreement.

**com-pōtātiō, ōnis** *f* drinking party.

**com-potiō** 4 to put in possession of (*alqm alqo*).

**com-pōtor, ōris** *m*, **-trīx, trīcis** *f* drinking-companion.

**com-prānsor, ōris** *m* dinner-companion.

**com-precātiō, ōnis** *f* an imploring.

**com-precor** 1 to implore, supplicate, pray to.

**com-prehendō** 3 **1.** a) to comprise, express, describe; b) to embrace with kindness; **2.** to take hold of, seize, grasp, catch; a) to arrest, apprehend, capture; b) to detect, discover; c) to perceive, comprehend.

**com-prehēnsibilis, e** perceptible; conceivable, intelligible.

**com-prehēnsiō, ōnis** *f* a) a seizing, laying hold of; b) comprehension,

perception; c) arrest, hostile seizing; d) period, sentence, style.

**com-prēndō** = **comprehendo**.

**com-pressiō, ōnis** *f and* **-ssus**[1], **ūs** *m* a) a pressing together, pressure, compression; b) embrace; c) conciseness.

**com-pressus**[2] 3 pressed together; concise.

**com-primō, pressī, pressum** 3 **1.** to press *or* squeeze together; a) to compress, to close; b) to embrace, ravish; **2.** to hold back; a) to restrain, check, repress, hinder, subdue; b) to keep to oneself, conceal.

**com-probātiō, ōnis** *f* approval.

**com-probātor, ōris** *m* approver.

**com-probō** 1 a) to approve of, assent to, acknowledge; b) to prove, confirm.

**com-prōmissum, ī** *n* mutual agreement to accept an award.

**com-prōmittō** 3 to agree to abide by the decision of an arbiter.

**comptiōnālis** = **coemptionalis.**

**cōmptulus** 3 elegant, foppish.

**cōmptus, ūs** *m* a) union; b) neatness.

**com-pungō, (nxī), nctum** 3 to prick *or* sting.

**com-putātiō, ōnis** *f* a) reckoning; b) stinginess.

**com-putātor, ōris** *m* reckoner.

**com-putō** 1 to sum up, reckon, compute.

**com-putrēscō** 3 to rot.

**cōnāmen, inis** *n* a) effort, attempt; b) support.

**cōnātum, ī** *n* attempt, undertaking, venture; effort, exertion; impulse.

**cōnātus, ūs** *m* = **conatum.**

**con-cacō** 1 to defile with filth.

**con-caedēs, ium** *f/pl.* barricade of trees, abattis.

**con-calefaciō** 3 to warm thoroughly.

**con-caleō** 2 to be warm.

**con-calēscō, luī, —** 3 to become warm, to glow.

**con-callēscō, luī, —** 3 a) to become callous, insensible; b) to become shrewd.

**con-camerātus** 3 vaulted over.

**con-castīgō** 1 to chastise severely.

**con-cavō** 1 to curve.

**con-cavus** 3 hollow, concave, curved.

**con-cēdō** 3 1. (*intr.*) to go away, give way; a) to depart, retire; withdraw, remove (*abl.*, *ab*, *ex*); to resort to, to pass (*in alqd*), **in sententiam** *alcis* to assent to; b) to yield (*alci*), to submit, be inferior, give precedence (*with dat.*); 2. (*trans.*) to concede; to pardon; grant, allow; to hand over, resign.

**con-celebrō** 1 to visit a place often; to celebrate a festival; a) to pursue eagerly; b) to publish, proclaim; c) to praise, honour, extol.

**con-cēnātiō, ōnis** f a dining together.

**con-centiō, ōnis** f = **concentus.**

**con-centuriō** 1 to assemble in centuries.

**con-centus, ūs** m a singing together; a) harmony, music, concert; b) unanimity, concord.

**con-ceptiō, ōnis** f, a) = **conceptus;** b) drawing up of a legal formula.

**con-ceptus, ūs** m a) a becoming pregnant, conception; b) catching; c) collection.

**con-cerpō, psī, ptum** 3 to tear in pieces, rend; to criticize.

**con-certātiō, ōnis** f contest, dispute, controversy.

**con-certātor, ōris** m rival.

**con-certātōrius** 3 controversial.

**con-certō** 1 to contend eagerly, to dispute (*cum alqo de re*).

**con-cessiō, ōnis** f a yielding, concession; admission.

**con-cessō** 1 to leave off.

**con-cessus, ūs** m only in *abl.* **-u** *alcis* = by permission of.

**concha, ae** f mussel; a) mussel shell, Triton's trumpet; b) purple-fish; c) pearl; d) vessel or box for unguents; e) the vulva.

**concheus** 3 belonging to a shell-fish.

**conchis, is** f bean.

**conchīta, ae** m gatherer of mussels.

**conchȳliātus** 3 dyed with or dressed in purple.

**conchȳlium, ī** n shell-fish; a) oyster; b) purple-fish; purple dye, purple clothing.

**con-cidō¹, cidī, —** 3 to fall or tumble down; a) to sink down, drop; b) to fall, be slain, overthrown, defeated, to perish; c) to get discouraged.

**con-cidō², cidī, cīsum** 3 to cut up, cut to pieces; a) to cut down,

destroy, kill; b) to beat severely; c) to prostrate, strike down; *see also* **concīsus.**

**con-cieō, cīvī, citum** 2 = **concio.**

**conciliābulum, ī** n place of assembly, market-place, court.

**conciliātiō, ōnis** f union, connection; a) a making friendly, winning over; b) inclination; c) recommendation; d) an acquiring.

**conciliātor, ōris** m author, promoter, mediator.

**conciliātrīcula, ae** f = **conciliatrix.**

**conciliātrīx, īcis** f a female promoter, match-maker.

**conciliātū** m by union.

**conciliātūra, ae** f match-making.

**conciliō** 1 to bring together, unite; a) to reconcile, make friendly, win over; b) to recommend; c) to cause, mediate, bring about; d) to procure, acquire, gain (*alci alqd*); to play the match-maker. — **conciliātus** 3 a) beloved by (*alci*); b) inclined to (*ad alqd*).

**concilium, ī** n a) union; b) assembly, meeting; assembly of the people; council.

**concinnitās, ātis** f symmetry of style; elegance.

**concinnitūdō, inis** f = **concinnitas.**

**concinnō** 1 to arrange carefully; to cause, produce, make.

**con-cinnus** 3 a) harmonious, elegant, pretty, tasteful, polished; b) courteous, obliging.

**con-cinō, cinuī, (centum)** 3 a) to sing or sound together; b) to sing in harmony, in a chorus; c) to celebrate, praise; d) to agree together.

**con-ciō, cīvī, cītum** 4 1. to bring together, assemble, summon; 2. to stir up, move violently; a) to rouse, excite; b) to produce, cause, promote.

**concipilō** 1 to cut to pieces.

**con-cipiō, cēpī, ceptum** 3 1. to take or hold together; to express in words, in a certain form; 2. to take in, draw in, suck (*fluids*); to catch or take (*fire*); a) to conceive, become pregnant; *subst.* **conceptum, ī** n foetus; b) to perceive, comprehend, understand; to imagine, think, fancy; entertain (*odium in alqm*); c) to receive, incur, commit.

**con-cīsiō, ōnis** *f* a separating *or* cutting up.

**con-cīsūra, ae** *f* a dividing, distribution.

**concīsus** 3 concise, brief, short, abrupt.

**con-citāmentum, ī** *n* incentive.

**con-citātiō, ōnis** *f* quick movement; **a)** sedition, tumult; **b)** violent passion.

**con-citātor, ōris** *m* exciter, agitator.

**con-citō** 1 to move quickly; **a)** to stir up, excite, rouse up, instigate; **b)** to summon; **c)** to cause, produce, occasion; **concitātus** 3 rapid, swift, violent.

**concitor, ōris** *m* = concitator.

**con-clāmātiō, ōnis** *f* loud shouting together.

**con-clāmō** (*and* -**mitō**) 1 **1.** to shout together *or* loudly; **vasa** to give the signal for packing; **2.** to call together; to bewail.

**conclāve, is** *n* room, chamber, apartment.

**con-clūdō, sī, sum** 3 **1.** to shut up, close, confine; to compress, condense, comprise; **2.** to bring to an end; to conclude, argue, infer; **conclūsum, ī** *n* conclusion (*in a syllogism*).

**con-clūsē** in rounded phrases.

**con-clūsiō, ōnis** *f* **1.** a shutting up, blockade; **2.** a) close, end; b) conclusion (*in a syllogism*).

**conclūsiuncula, ae** *f* paltry conclusion.

**con-color, ōris** of the same colour.

**con-comitātus** 3 escorted.

**con-coquō** 3 to boil thoroughly; **a)** to digest; **b)** to bear, endure, brook; **c)** to consider maturely, revolve in mind.

**concordia, ae** *f* concord, unity, harmony; intimate friend.

**concordō** 1 to be of one mind, be in union, to agree.

**con-cors, dis** of one mind, concordant, agreeing.

**con-crēbrēscō, bruī** 3 to grow strong.

**con-crēdō** 3 to intrust, commit, consign (*alci alqd*).

**con-cremō** 1 to burn up.

**con-crepō, uī,** — 1 **a)** to sound violently; to resound, rattle, clash, grate, creak; **b)** to cause to sound.

**con-crēscō** 3 to grow together; **a)** to condense, harden, stiffen, congeal curdle; **b)** to grow, be formed; **con-crētus** 3 **a)** condensed, hardened, thick, hard; **b)** composed of.

**con-crētiō, ōnis** *f* a condensing, congealing, materiality.

**con-crīminor** 1 to make an accusation.

**con-cruciō** 1 to torture.

**con-cubīna, ae** *f* concubine.

**con-cubīnātus, ūs** *m* concubinage.

**con-cubīnus, ī** *m* bedfellow, one living in concubinage.

**con-cubitus, ūs** *m* a lying together; copulation; coition.

**con-cubius** 3: -**ā nocte** in the silence of night, at midnight; -**um** *subst. n* the dead of night.

**con-culcō** 1 to trample upon, to maltreat, despise.

**con-cumbō, cubuī, cubitum** 3 to lie down; to lie with.

**con-cupiēns, tis** desirous.

**con-cupīscō, pīvī** *and* **piī, pītum** 3 to long for, covet (*alqd*).

**con-cūrō** 1 to take great care of.

**con-currō, (cu)currī, cursum** 3 **a)** to run together, flock together (*ex re in* or *ad alqd*); **b)** to meet in conflict, rush together, engage in combat; **c)** to meet together (*cum alqo*); **d)** to happen at the same time.

**con-cursātiō, ōnis** *f* a running together, concourse; a running about, skirmishing.

**concursātor, ōris** *m* skirmisher.

**con-cursiō, ōnis** *f* **a)** a running together, concurrence; **b)** emphatic repetition of words.

**con-cursō** 1 **a)** *intr.* to run to and fro, to go about; to skirmish; **b)** *trans.* to visit.

**con-cursus, ūs** *m* **a)** a running together, concourse, throng, tumult; **b)** a meeting together; an encountering, attack, assault; **c)** combination.

**con-cussiō, ōnis** *f* a shaking, concussion.

**con-cussū** *m* by a shaking.

**con-custōdiō** 4 to watch *or* guard closely.

**con-cutiō, cussī, cussum** 3 **1.** to strike together; **2.** to shake violently, agitate; **a) se concutere** to examine oneself carefully; **b)** to disturb, alarm, trouble; **c)** to impair, weaken.

**condalium, ĭ** *n* little ring.

**con-decet** 2 it is proper *or* decent.

**con-decorŏ** 1 to adorn carefully.

**condemnātor, ōris** *m* prosecutor, accuser.

**con-demnŏ** 1 **a)** to sentence, condemn, find guilty (*alqm alcis rei, de re*); to accuse of, charge with, blame, disapprove; **b)** to effect the condemnation of a person.

**con-dēnsŏ** 1 to press close together.

**con-dēnsus** 3 very dense, close, thick.

**con-diciŏ, ōnis** *f* **1.** agreement; stipulation; a) proposition, condition, terms; b) marriage-contract, marriage; **2.** state, position, situation; place, circumstances, rank, relation, nature, manner.

**con-dīcŏ** 3 to agree upon, to appoint (*alci alqd*).

**con-dīgnus** 3 very worthy.

**condimentum, ĭ** *n* spice, seasoning.

**condiŏ** 4 **a)** to make savoury, to prepare (*food*) carefully; to soften, temper; **b)** to pickle, preserve; to embalm; **conditus** 3 savoury, seasoned.

**condiscipulātus, ūs** *m* companionship in school.

**con-discipulus, ĭ** *m* (*and* **-la, ae** *f*) schoolfellow.

**con-discŏ** 3 to learn thoroughly.

**conditĭŏ, ōnis** *f* a seasoning, pickling, preserving.

**conditīvum, ĭ** *n* tomb.

**conditor, ōris** *m* founder, maker, authoı, contriver, composer.

**conditōrium, ĭ** *n* tomb, coffin, urn.

**conditūra, ae** *f* **a)** preserving; **b)** seasoning.

**con-dŏ, didī, ditum** 3 **1.** to put together; a) to found, establish, build; b) to compose, write, describe; **2.** to put in, preserve; a) to store up, hide (*alqd in rem, in re*); b) to bury, inter; c) to pass (*time*); d) to hide, conceal, plunge (*a sword*).

**con-docefaciŏ** 3 (*and* **con-doceŏ** 2) to teach, instruct, train.

**con-dolēscŏ, luī,** — 3 to feel pain, suffer.

**con-dōnātĭŏ, ōnis** *f* a giving away.

**con-dōnŏ** 1 to give away, present (*alci alqd*); **a)** to remit; **b)** to give up to, surrender, deliver up; **c)** to forgive, pardon.

**con-dormiŏ** 4 to fall asleep.

**con-dormiscŏ, mivī** 3 to fall asleep.

**con-dūcibilis, e** profitable, advantageous.

**con-dūcŏ** 3 **1.** to lead *or* draw together, to assemble, gather (*alqd in locum*), to unite, combine; **2.** to hire, rent, employ, to hire for use, contract for, farm; *subst.* **conductī, ōrum** *m/pl.* hired soldiers, mercenaries; **conductum, ĭ** *n* hired apartment *or* house; **3. conducit** it is useful, profitable (*alci, ad alqd*).

**con-ductīcius** 3 hired.

**con-ductĭŏ, ōnis** *f* **a)** a bringing together; **b)** a hiring, farming.

**con-ductor, ōris** *m* **a)** hirer, farmer, tenant; **b)** contractor.

**con-duplicātĭŏ, ōnis** *f* a doubling; embrace.

**con-duplicŏ** 1 to double.

**con-dūrŏ** 1 to harden.

**condus, ĭ** *m* store-keeper.

**cō-nectŏ, nexuī, nexum** 3 to bind together; **a)** to connect, join, link (*alqd cum re* or with *dat.*); **b)** to subjoin a logical conclusion.

**cō-nexĭŏ, ōnis** *f* logical conclusion.

**cō-nexus, ūs** *m* a joining.

**cŏn-fābulor** 1 to talk.

**cŏn-farreŏ** 1 to marry by the ceremony of *confarreatio* (*an offering of bread*).

**cŏn-fātālis, e** determined by the same fate.

**cŏn-fectĭŏ, ōnis** *f* **1.** a composing, finishing, completing; **2.** consumption, a chewing; **3.** exaction of money.

**cŏn-fector, ōris** *m* **1.** finisher, executor; **2.** destroyer.

**cŏn-ferciŏ, rsī, rtum** 4 to cram together; **cŏnfertus** 3 closely compressed, dense, thick, crowded, in close array; filled full.

**cŏn-ferŏ, tulī, collātum, cŏnferre** **1.** to carry *or* bring together (*alqd ex re, in alqd, in* or *ad alqm*); **a)** to unite, join, connect (**P.** to be concentrated); **b)** to place together *or* near; to exchange (*words*), to discuss; to bring into hostile contact, set together (*arma, manus, signa*); **signis collātis** in a pitched battle; **collātō pede** foot to foot; **c)** to pay in, contribute, to be profitable, of use; **d)** to compare, contrast (*alqd cum re,* or with *dat.*); **2.** to bring to a place, remove, transfer (*alqd ex re* *in rem*); a) **se cōnferre** to betake oneself to, to devote oneself to, join oneself to; b) to put off, defer, postpone; c) to change, transform; d) to bestow on (*alci alqd*); to ascribe, attribute, impute; to transfer, assign (*alqd ad alqm*); e) to direct, apply to, to use.

cōnfertim *adv. of* confertus.

cōn-fervēfaciō 3 to melt.

cōn-fervēscō, buī, — 3 to begin to boil *or* to glow.

cōn-fessiō, ōnis *f* confession, acknowledgment.

cōn-festim *adv.* without delay, immediately.

cōn-ficiēns, tis effecting, efficient (*with gen.*).

cōn-ficiō 3 1. to make, make ready, prepare, bring about, accomplish, execute, fulfil; a) to compose, write; to settle, finish, bring to an end; to pass over, complete (*of time or space*); b) to produce, cause, procure, provide; c) to get, collect, contribute; d) to infer, show (*in a logical conclusion*); 2. to grind, chew, digest, waste, consume, weaken, lessen, diminish, kill, destroy, subdue.

cōn-fictiō, ōnis *f* an inventing.

cōn-fidēns, tis self-reliant, confident, bold, daring; audacious, impudent.

cōn-fidentia, ae *f* a confiding, confidence; boldness, arrogance, impudence.

cōnfidenti-loquus 3 speaking boldly.

cōn-fidō, fisus sum 3 to trust, confide, rely on (*with dat.* or *abl.*); to be assured, believe firmly, to hope (*with acc. c. inf.*).

cōn-figō 3 a) to fasten *or* nail together; b) to pierce through.

cōn-findō 3 to cleave asunder.

cōn-fingō 3 to invent, devise, fabricate.

cōn-finis, e bordering, adjoining (*with dat.*); neighbouring, nearly related, similar.

cōn-finium, ī *n* a) common boundary; b) confine, border, bordering-line; c) nearness, intermediate state.

cōn-fiō, —, fierī to be brought together, to be accomplished, brought about.

cōn-firmātiō, ōnis *f* a making firm;

a) encouragement, consolation; b) a confirming, affirmation.

cōn-firmātor, ōris *m* one who confirms, a surety (*alcis rei*).

cōn-firmitās, ātis *f* obstinacy.

cōn-firmō 1 to make firm, establish, a) to strengthen, make lasting; to support, confirm, prove; b) to encourage, console, cheer, make bold; c) to assert, corroborate, affirm, protest.

cōn-fiscō 1 to lay up in a chest; to confiscate.

cōn-fisiō, ōnis *f* confidence.

cōn-fiteor, fessus sum 2 a) to confess, avow, own, acknowledge (*alqd, de re*; with *acc. c. inf.*); b) to reveal, make known; **cōnfessus 3** a) who pleads guilty; b) confessed, acknowledged.

cōn-flagrātiō, ōnis *f* a burning.

cōn-flagrō 1 to be in flames.

cōn-flictiō, ōnis *f* collision, conflict.

cōn-flictō 1 to strike together; a) to ruin; b) *intr. and* P. to struggle, contend, fight; to be tormented, afflicted, harassed (*alqa re, ab alqo*).

cōn-flictus, ūs *m* a striking together.

cōn-flīgō, xī, ctum 3 a) to strike together; b) *intr.* to be in conflict, to struggle, fight.

cōn-flō 1 a) to blow together, blow up, kindle; b) to melt (*metals*); to bring together, make up, bring about; c) to forge, invent; to cause, produce, occasion.

cōn-fluō, fluxī, — 3 to flow *or* pour together; *subst.* **cōnfluēns, tis** (*also pl.*) confluence.

cōn-fodiō 3 to pierce through, transfix, stab.

cōn-fore (*and* cōn-futūrum) to be about to happen.

cōn-fōrmātiō, ōnis *f* a forming, shaping, form, shape; a) notion, conception; b) figure of speech.

cōn-fōrmō 1 to form, shape; to arrange, fashion, educate.

cōn-frag(ōs)us 3 uneven, rough.

cōn-fremō, uī, — 3 to murmur loudly, to roar.

cōn-fricō 1 to rub.

cōn-fringō, frēgī, frāctum 3 to break in pieces, shiver, shatter; to destroy, undo.

cōn-fugiō 3 to flee, take refuge.

cōn-fugium, ī *n* place of refuge.

cŏn-fulgeō 2 to shine, glitter.

cŏn-fultus 3 driven together.

cŏn-fundō 3 to pour together; **a)** to mix, mingle, join, unite (*alqd in alqd*); **b)** to confound, confuse, throw into disorder, disturb, obscure; **c)** to disconcert, perplex; **cŏnfūsus** 3 confused, disorderly; disturbed, disconcerted, blushing, disfigured.

cŏn-fūsīcius 3 mixed together.

cŏn-fūsiō, ōnis *f* **a)** a mingling, mixing, union; **b)** confusion, disorder.

cŏn-fūtō 1 **a)** to silence; **b)** to check, repress; **c)** to confute, refute.

con-gelō 1 **a)** *trans.* to freeze, harden; **b)** *intr.* to freeze, congeal.

con-gemīnātiō, ōnis *f* a doubling, embrace.

con-geminō 1 to (re)double.

con-gemō 3 to sigh *or* groan loudly.

conger, grī *m* sea-eel, conger-eel.

congeriēs, ēī *f* heap, pile, mass.

con-gerō 3 to carry *or* bring together, to collect; **a)** to heap up, pile up; to build, construct; **b)** to heap upon, load; **c)** to build a nest.

con-gerrō, ōnis *m* companion in amusement.

congestīcius 3 heaped up.

con-gestus, ūs *m* **a)** a bringing together, heaping up; **b)** heap.

congiālis, e holding a *congius*.

congiārium, ī *n* donation, distribution, largess (*in wine, oil, money etc.*).

congius, ī *m* a measure for liquids (6 pints).

con-glaciō 1 to freeze, congeal.

con-glīscō 3 to blaze up anew.

con-globātiō, ōnis *f* a pressing *or* crowding together.

con-globō 1 to gather into a ball, to make round; to press together in a mass *or* crowd.

con-glomerō 1 to roll into a mass.

con-glūtinātiō, ōnis *f* a gluing *or* cementing together.

con-glūtinō 1 to glue *or* cement together, to unite, join, bind closely,

con-graecō 1 to squander in Greek manner.

con-grātulor 1 to wish joy, congratulate one another.

con-gredior, gressus sum 3 **a)** to come together, meet; **b)** to meet in combat, to fight.

congregābilis, e social, sociable.

congregātiō, ōnis *f* union, society.

con-gregō 1 to collect into a flock, to collect, gather together, associate, unite.

con-gressiō, ōnis *f* = congressus.

con-gressus, ūs *m* a meeting; **a)** intercourse, conversation, conference; **b)** onset, encounter, fight.

congruēns, tis agreeing, fit, appropriate; accordant, consistent, harmonious (*cum re,* or with *dat.*).

con-gruentia, ae *f* consistency, symmetry.

con-gruō, uī, — 3 to come together, meet; **a)** to coincide; **b)** to agree, harmonize, suit, correspond (*cum re,* or with *dat.*); to be of one mind (*de re, in rem*).

con-gruus 3 in agreement.

cŏn-iciō (and cŏn-), iēcī, iectum 3 **1.** to throw together, bring together; to conjecture, guess, infer (*ex, de re*); **2.** to throw, cast, thrust, drive; to direct, turn, urge, force (*in or intra alqd*), **se cōnicere** to rush, run, hasten away.

con-iectiō, ōnis *f* **a)** a hurling, throwing; **b)** conjecture, interpretation. [infer.]

con-iectō 1 to conjecture, guess,

coniector, ōris *m* (*and* -trīx, īcis *f*) interpreter of dreams, soothsayer.

coniectūra, ae *f* **a)** conjecture, guess, inference; **b)** interpretation of omens, soothsaying.

con-iectūrālis, e conjectural.

con-iectus, ūs *m* **a)** a throwing together; **b)** a throwing, casting, hurling; **c)** a turning, directing; **teli** reach of a shot.

cōni-fer 3, cōni-ger 3 cone-bearing.

cō-nītor 3 **a)** to lean *or* push against; **b)** to strive, struggle, exert oneself, ascend; **c)** to bring forth, give birth.

con-iugātiō, ōnis *f* relationship of words.

con-iugātor, ōris *m* uniter.

coniug(i)ālis, e conjugal.

con-iugium, ī *n* **a)** marriage, wedlock; **b)** husband, wife.

con-iugō 1 = coniungo.

con-iŭnctim *adv.* jointly.

con-iŭnctiō, ōnis *f* union, connection; **a)** friendship, intimacy; **b)** marriage, relationship; **c)** connecting particle.

**con-iūnctus** 3 connected, joined, united (*cum re*, or with *dat.*); **a)** adjoining, bordering on; **b)** near, associated, intimate, allied, kindred; agreeing with.

**con-iungō** 3 **a)** to connect, join, unite (*alqd cum re*, or *dat.*); **b)** to add (*alqd alci rei*); **c)** to contract (*a union*).

**con-iūnx, iugis** *f* wife, spouse, consort (*more rarely m* husband); **a)** female; **b)** bride, mate.

**con-iūrātiō, ōnis** *f* **a)** a swearing together; union confirmed by oath; **b)** conspiracy, plot; conspirators.

**con-iūrō** 1 to swear together; **a)** to take the military oath; **b)** to combine under oath; **c)** to conspire, plot; **coniūrātus** 3 united by an oath; *subst.* conspirator.

**coniux,** *see* **coniunx.**

**cō-niveō, (nivī** *or* **nīxī),** — 2 to wink, shut the eyes (*of the eyes:* to be shut); **a)** to be languid, drowsy; **b)** to overlook, leave unnoticed, connive.

**conl...,** *see* **coll...**

**con-nectō,** *see* **conecto.**

**con-nitor,** *see* **conitor.**

**con-niveō,** *see* **coniveo.**

**cōnōpēum (and cōnōpium), ī** *n* mosquito-net.

**cōnor** 1 to attempt, try, undertake, venture, endeavour (*alqd*; with *inf.*).

**con-quassātiō, ōnis** *f* a violent shaking, shattering.

**con-quassō** 1 to shake violently, to shatter, disturb.

**con-queror** 3 to bewail, lament; to complain (*alqd, de re*, with *acc. c. inf.*).

**con-questiō, ōnis** *f* a bewailing, complaint.

**con-questus, ūs** *m* complaint.

**con-quiēscō** 3 to rest, repose (*ab, ex re*); **a)** to find rest; **b)** to be still, quiet.

**con-quīnīscō** 3 to squat down.

**con-quīrō, sīvī, sītum** 3 to seek for, bring together; to search out, to collect; **conquīsitus** 3 sought out, choice.

**con-quīsītiō, ōnis** *f* a seeking out, search for; a collecting; a levying, conscription.

**con-quīsītor, ōris** *m* recruiting officer.

**conr...,** *see* **corr...**

**cōn-saepiō** 4 to fence in, hedge in.

**cōn-saeptum, ī** *n* enclosure.

**cōn-salūtātiō, ōnis** *f* a greeting.

**cōn-salūtō** 1 to greet, salute.

**cōn-sānēscō, nuī,** — 3 to become healed, to recover.

**cōn-sanguineus** 3 related by blood, of a brother *or* sister; brother *m*, sister *f*.

**cōn-sanguinitās, ātis** *f* blood-relationship.

**cōn-sauciō** 1 to wound severely.

**cōn-scelerātus** 3 wicked, villainous.

**cōn-scelerō** 1 to defile with a crime.

**cōn-scendō, dī, sum** 3 to ascend, mount, climb (*alqd*), to go on board (*navem*).

**cōn-scēnsiō, ōnis** *f* an ascending, embarking.

**cōn-scientia, ae** *f* **1.** joint knowledge, a being privy to (*with gen.*); **2.** consciousness, **a)** feeling; sense; **b)** good *or* bad conscience, remorse.

**cōn-scindō** 3 to tear *or* rend to pieces.

**cōn-sciō** 4 (*sibi*) to be conscious.

**cōn-scīscō** 3 **a)** to resolve jointly *or* publicly; **b)** *sibi alqd.* to bring *or* inflict upon oneself, **mortem** to commit suicide.

**cōn-scius** 3 **a)** knowing with another (*alci rei or alcis rei; alci alcis rei*), conscious; **b)** self-conscious; conscious of guilt (*gen.*); *subst.* **~, ī** *m* partaker, accomplice.

**cōn-screor** 1 to clear the throat.

**cōn-scrībillō** 1 to scribble on.

**cōn-scrībō** 3 to write together; **1.** to enrol; **2. a)** to levy, enlist; **b)** to enrol in a particular class (**cōn-scriptus** newly chosen senator); **c)** to write, compose; **d)** to write all over.

**cōn-scriptiō, ōnis** *f* a drawing up in writing, composition, treatise.

**cōn-secō** 1 to cut to pieces.

**cōn-secrātiō, ōnis** *f* consecration, dedication; **a)** execration; **b)** apotheosis.

**cōn-secrō** 1 to dedicate, consecrate (*alqd alci*); **a)** to execrate; **b)** to deify, to make immortal.

**cōnsectārius** 3 following logically, consequent.

**cōn-sectātiō, ōnis** *f* a striving after.

**cōn-sectātrix, īcis** *f* she who pursues eagerly, friend, adherent.

**cōn-sectiō, ōnis** *f* a cutting to pieces.

**cŏn-sector 1** to follow, attend (*with acc.*); **a)** to pursue (*alqm*); **b)** to overtake, catch; **c)** to strive after, emulate.

**cŏn-secūtiō, ōnis** *f* effect, consequence; **a)** sequence; **b)** conclusion.

**cŏn-senēscō, senui, —** 3 to become old *or* grey; to become weak *or* infirm, to decay, fade, degenerate, grow obsolete.

**cŏn-sēnsiō, ōnis** *f* = **consensus**.

**cŏn-sēnsus, ūs** *m* agreement, unanimity, harmony; **a)** common accord; **b)** conspiracy, plot.

**cōnsentāneus** 3 agreeing, fit, suitable (*cum re;* with *dat.*); reasonable, consistent.

**cŏn-sentiō** 4 to agree, be of one mind, accord, harmonize (*cum alqo, de re*); **a)** to resolve unanimously (with *inf.* or *ut*); **b)** to conspire, plot (*contra alqm, ad alqd*); (*of things*) to harmonize, suit, fit; **cōnsentiēns, tis** agreeing, accordant, harmonious.

**cŏn-sequē** *adv.* consecutively.

**cŏn-sequēns, tis** according to reason, reasonable, appropriate, consequent; *subst.* **cōnsequēns, tis** *n* consequence.

**cŏn-sequentia, ae** *f* consequence, succession.

**cŏn-sequor** 3 **1.** to follow up, to follow, go after (*alqm* or *alqd*); a) to pursue; b) to imitate, copy, obey; c) to follow as an effect, to result; **2.** to overtake, reach, attain to (*alqm, alqd*); a) to become like *or* equal; b) to express adequately; b) to understand, perceive, learn.

**cŏn-serō¹, sēvī, situm** 3 a) to sow, plant; b) to plant in *or* with.

**cŏn-serō², seruī, sertum** 3 to connect, twine together; **a)** to join, fit, bind, tie; **b)** to bring together in a hostile manner (*manus cum alqo* to come to close quarters), to engage (*in battle*); **c)** *in law:* **manum** to lay hands on a thing in dispute.

**cōnsertē** *adv.* connectedly.

**cŏn-serva, ae** *f* (*female*) fellow--slave.

**cŏn-servātiō, ōnis** *f* preservation, a keeping.

**cŏn-servātor, ōris** *m* preserver, keeper, defender.

**cŏn-servātrīx, īcis** *f* preserver.

**cŏn-servitium, ī** *n* joint servitude.

**cŏn-servō** 1 to keep, preserve; a) to maintain, observe; b) to save, keep safe, keep intact, spare.

**cŏn-servus, ī** *m* fellow-slave.

**cŏn-sessor, ōris** *m* one who sits near *or* by; neighbour, assessor.

**cŏn-sessus, ūs** *m* a sitting together, assembly, spectators, audience.

**cōnsīderātiō, ōnis** *f* consideration, reflection.

**cōnsīderātus** 3 a) well considered, maturely reflected upon; b) thoughtful, prudent, cautious.

**cŏn-sīderō** 1 to look at, regard, contemplate; to consider, weigh, reflect)

**cōn-sidium, ī** committee. [upon.∫

**cŏn-sīdō** 3 **1.** to sit down together, to settle (*in loco*); **2.** to sit down, be seated, take a seat; a) to hold sessions, be in session; b) to take up a position, to encamp, station oneself; c) to settle, stay; d) to land; e) to sink down, give way, subside, abate, cease.

**cŏn-signō** 1 **1.** to seal, sign, subscribe; to attest, certify, vouch for; **2.** to write down, note, register.

**cŏn-silēscō** 3 to become silent.

**cōnsiliārius** 3 counselling; *subst.* ~, ī *m* counsellor, adviser.

**cōnsiliātor, ōris** *m* adviser, counsellor.

**cōnsilior** 1 to take *or* give counsel, hold a consultation.

**cōnsilium, ī** *n* **1.** a taking counsel; a) deliberation, consultation; b) assembly *or* body of counsellors, council, senate, council of war, body of judges; **2.** consideration, understanding, foresight, prudence, judgment; wisdom; a) resolution, plan, determination, measure, design, intention (**cōnsiliō** on purpose); stratagem, device; b) advice, suggestion.

**cōn-similis, e** similar, like.

**cŏn-sipiō** 3 to be of sound mind.

**cŏn-sistō, stitī, —** 3 **1.** to take one's stand *or* place oneself in company with others, be together (*in loco*); a) to exist, occur, take place; b) to be based upon (*in re*), depend on, consist of; **2.** to place oneself; a) to stand still, stop, halt, stay, to anchor; b) to establish oneself, to settle; to stand firmly; to keep one's ground *or* footing, to continue, endure; c) to stop, dwell, abide, tarry; d) to falter; e) to come to a stand, to rest, cease; f) to contain *or* collect oneself.

cōnsitiō, ōnis f a sowing, planting.

cōnsitor, ōris m sower, planter.

cōnsitūra, ae f = consitio.

cōn-sobrīnus, ī m and -a, ae f cousin.

cōn-socer, erī m joint father-in-law.

cōn-sociātiō, ōnis f union, association.

cōn-sociō 1 to unite, associate, to make common, share with (alqd cum alqo); cōnsociātus 3 united, harmonious.

cōn-sōlābilis, e consolable.

cōn-sōlātiō, ōnis f a consoling, consolation, comfort; consolatory treatise.

cōn-sōlātor, ōris m comforter.

cōn-sōlātōrius 3 of consolation.

cōn-sōlor 1 to console, comfort, encourage (alqm de or in re); to mitigate, alleviate, relieve.

cōn-somniō (?) 1 to dream.

cōn-sonō 1 to sound together, to resound, echo; to agree.

cōn-sonus 3 sounding together, harmonious; agreeing.

cōn-sōpiō 4 to lull to sleep.

cōn-sors, tis having an equal share (with gen.); a) partaking of; b) brotherly, sisterly; c) common; subst. partner, sharer, associate, comrade.

cōnsortiō, ōnis f companionship, community.

cōn-sortium, ī n = consortio.

cōn-spectus[1] 3, see conspicio.

cōn-spectus[2], ūs m 1. a seeing; a) look, sight, view; b) an appearing, becoming visible, in cōnspectū within sight, in cōnspectum venīre to come in sight; 2. mental view, survey, consideration.

cōn-spergō, sī, sum 3 to sprinkle, moisten, besprinkle; to cover.

cōn-spicillum, ī n look-out.

cōn-spiciō, spexī, spectum 3 1. a) to look at, behold, view; b) to descry, perceive, observe, P. to attract notice, to be conspicuous, distinguished, admired; 2. to perceive mentally; — cōnspectus 3 visible, distinguished, remarkable; cōnspiciendus 3 worth seeing.

cōn-spicor 1 to see, behold.

cōn-spicuus 3 visible; striking, remarkable, conspicuous, eminent.

cōn-spīrātiō, ōnis f a) union, harmony; b) conspiracy.

cōn-spīrō 1 1. to breathe together, to sound together; 2. a) to agree, harmonize (cum alqo); b) to conspire, plot; cōnspīrātus 3 of one mind; subst. conspirator.

cōn-spōnsor, ōris m a joint surety.

cōn-spuō 3 to spit upon.

cōn-spurcō 1 to defile.

cōn-spūtō 1 to spit upon.

cōn-stabiliō 4 to establish.

cōn-stāns, tis standing firm; a) firm, steady, immovable, constant, unchanging, regular, consistent, harmonious; b) resolute, constant, steadfast, faithful.

cōnstantia, ae f a) firmness, steadiness, constancy, perseverance; agreement, harmony, consistency; b) steadfastness, self-possession.

cōnsternātiō, ōnis f a) dismay, alarm, fright, consternation; b) mutiny, tumult.

cōn-sternō[1] 1 a) to cause confusion, to confound, perplex; b) to terrify, alarm, frighten; c) to excite, cause a revolt.

cōn-sternō[2] 3 a) to strew over, cover, to thatch, pave; b) to throw down, prostrate.

cōn-stipō 1 to press or crowd together.

cōn-stituō, uī, ūtum 3 1. a) to place or put together, b) to cause to stand, to place, put; 2. a) to station, post, moor; b) to appoint, settle, fix by agreement; c) to erect, set up; d) to draw up in line, arrange; e) to settle, establish, to found, build, construct; f) to set in order, organize, manage; g) to undertake, make, effect, constitute; h) to designate, assign; i) to determine at law, decide; k) to resolve, take a resolution (with inf., acc. c. inf.); — cōnstitūtus 3 constituted, arranged, disposed.

cōnstitūtiō, ōnis f constitution, condition; a) regulation, arrangement; b) disposition, nature.

cōnstitūtum, ī n a) regulation, order; b) agreement, appointment; fixed time or place for meeting.

cōnstitūtus 3, see constituo.

cōn-stō, stitī, stātūrus 1 to stand firm, to exist; a) to stand still or firm, to remain, to remain the same, to be unaltered (in re); b) to agree, be consistent, correspond (alci rei, cum or in re); sibi cōnstāre to be consistent; ratio cōnstat the reckoning is right; c) to be certain, ascertained, known, **inter omnes cŏnstat** everybody knows; **d)** to exist, be extant; e) to consist of, be composed of, be derived from (*ex* or *in re*; *abl.*); to cost (with *abl.* or *gen.*).

cŏn-strātum, ĭ *n* a covering, floor.

cŏn-strĭngō 3 to bind together; a) to fetter, confine; b) to strengthen, fortify; c) to bind, restrain, limit, compress.

cŏnstructiō, ōnis *f* a putting together, construction, building.

cŏn-strŭō 3 to heap up together, to pile up; a) to construct, build up, to erect; b) to arrange.

cŏn-stŭprātor, ōris *m* debaucher, ravisher.

cŏn-stŭprō 1 to ravish, violate.

cŏn-suādeō 2 to advise emphatically.

cŏn-suāsor, ōris *m* adviser.

cŏn-sūcidus 3 juicy.

cŏn-sūdō 1 to sweat profusely.

cŏn-suēfaciō 3 to accustom, habituate (*alqm* with *inf.*).

cŏn-suēscō 3 to accustom oneself to (*inf.*), *pf.* to be accustomed, be wont; a) *cum alqo* **cŏnsuēvisse** to be intimate with; **b) cŏnsuētus** 3 accustomed, usual.

cŏn-suētiō, ōnis *f* love-affair.

cŏnsuētūdō, inis *f* custom, habit, usage, way, usual practice; a) form of speech; b) social intercourse, intimacy; correspondence (*epistularum*); c) love-affair.

cŏnsul, ulis *m* consul.

cŏnsŭlāris, e relating to a consul, consular; *subst.* ⁓, is *m* a) one who has been a consul, ex-consul; b) governor of consular rank; *adv.* cŏnsŭlāriter in a manner worthy of a consul. [sul, consulship.]

cŏnsŭlātus, ūs *m* the office of con-]

cŏnsŭlō, lui, ltum 3 1. to deliberate, consider, consult (*de re*); a) to take care for (*dat.*), have regard, be mindful; **sibi cŏnsulere** to look to one's interest; b) to take a resolution, resolve, take measures (*against*) (*de re*, *in alqm*); 2. a) to ask the advice of, to consult (*alqm de re*); b) to consult an oracle; *alqd boni* to take in good part; *see also* cŏnsultus.

cŏnsultātiō, ōnis *f* a) deliberation; **b)** a consulting, asking for advice, inquiry; c) subject of consultation.

cŏnsultō 1 a) to consider maturely, to weigh, **in medium** for the common good; to provide for (*with dat.*), have a care; b) to consult (*alqm*).

cŏnsultor, ōris *m* a) adviser; **b)** one who asks advice.

cŏnsultrīx, īcis *f* she who cares for.

cŏnsultum, ĭ *n* deliberation; resolution, decree, measure; answer of an oracle.

cŏnsultus 3 a) well considered, weighed, deliberated upon; b) knowing, experienced, learned; **iuris** or **iure cŏnsultus** learned in the law, lawyer, counsellor; *adv.* cŏnsultō (*and* -tē) deliberately, purposely.

cŏn-summābilis, e capable of completion or perfection.

cŏn-summātiō, ōnis *f* completion.

cŏn-summō 1 a) to sum up; b) to finish, accomplish, complete, perfect; **cŏnsummātus** 3 complete.

cŏn-sūmō 3 1. to use up, consume; a) to eat up; b) to spend, employ, waste, destroy, annihilate, exhaust; 2. to use, spend upon (*alqd in re*).

cŏn-sūmptiō, ōnis *f* a consuming.

cŏn-sūmptor, ōris *m* consumer, destroyer.

cŏn-suō 3 to stitch together; to plan.

cŏn-surgō 3 a) to rise, stand up (*together*); b) to rise for an action; to strive upwards, aspire.

cŏn-surrēctiō, ōnis *f* a rising in a body.

cŏn-susurrō 1 to whisper together.

con-tābēfaciō 3 to consume.

con-tābēscō, bui, — 3 to waste away.

con-tābulātiō, ōnis *f* a covering with planks; wooden floor or story.

con-tābulō 1 to cover with boards; a) to build towers in stories; b) to bridge over.

con-tāctus, ūs *m* = **contagio**.

con-tāgēs, is *f* contact.

con-tāgiō, ōnis *f* (*also* -gium, ĭ *n*) a) a touching, contact; b) contagion, infection; contamination, bad example.

con-tāminō 1 to pollute, contaminate; to blend together.

con-technor 1 to devise.

con-tegō 3 to cover; a) to protect; b) to conceal, to bury.

con-temerō 1 to violate, defile.

**con-temnō, psī, ptum** 3 to despise, contemn, to slight, esteem lightly.

**contemplātiō, ōnis** f a viewing, surveying, contemplation.

**contemplātīvus** 3 speculative, theoretical.

**contemplātor, ōris** m observer.

**contemplātus, ūs** m = **contemplatio.**

**contemplor** (*and* -ō) 1 to look at, view, survey, consider.

**contemptim** *adv.* contemptuously, scornfully.

**contemptiō, ōnis** f contempt, disregard, disdain.

**contemptor, ōris** m despiser.

**contemptrīx, īcis** f she who despises. [able.)

**contemptus¹** 3 despised, despic-/

**contemptus², ūs** m = **contemptio.**

**con-tendō, tendī, tentum** 3 1. to stretch together; a) to put together, to compare, contrast; b) to strive with some one else, to contend, dispute; 2. to stretch forcibly, to draw tight, strain; a) to hurl, b) to exert oneself, to strive, to pursue earnestly (*in, ad alqd*), to hasten on a journey, try to reach; c) to strive to obtain, to demand (*alqd ab alqo*; *with ut, ne*), ask; d) to assert, affirm, maintain (*alqd; acc. c. inf.*).

**con-tentē¹** energetically.

**con-tentē²** sparingly.

**contentiō, ōnis** f 1. a) comparison, contrast; b) contest, combat, contention; dispute, controversy.; 2. a) exertion, zealous pursuit; b) vehemence, passion.

**contentiōsus** 3 contentious.

**contentus¹** 3 [*contendo*] a) stretched, strained, tense; b) eager, zealous.

**contentus²** 3 [*contineo*] contented, satisfied (*alqā re*).

**con-terminus** 3 bordering on, neighbouring.

**con-terō** 3 to grind, bruise; a) to rub away, wear away, waste, consume, spend, destroy; b) to esteem lightly; **conteri** *or* **se conterere** (*in re*) to be wearied, to drudge; **contrītus** 3 trite, common.

**con-terreō** 2 to terrify, frighten.

**con-testor** 1 a) to call to witness; b) **litem** to introduce a lawsuit; **contestātus** 3 tried, proved.

**con-texō** 3 to weave *or* twine to-

gether; a) to connect, unite (*alqd cum re*); b) to continue; c) to devise, build, compose.

**con-textus¹** 3 woven together, closely connected, continuous.

**con-textus², ūs** m connection, coherence; sequel.

**con-ticēscō, ticuī, — 3** to become silent, still *or* dumb.

**con-ticinium** (*or* -cinnum), ī n sleeping time, night.

**con-tignātiō, ōnis** f a joining together of beams; floor, story.

**con-tignō** 1 to construct of beams.

**contiguus** 3 a) contiguous, near; b) within reach.

**con-tinēns, tis** 1. holding together; moderate, temperate; 2. a) bordering, neighbouring (*with dat.*); b) following, continuous, in unbroken succession; — *subst.* **continēns, tis** f mainland, continent; n main point (of a case).

**continentia, ae** f temperance, abstinence, self-restraint.

**con-tineō, tinuī,** (**tentum**) 2 1. to hold *or* keep together; a) to bind together, connect, join; b) to keep, maintain, retain, preserve; 2. to surround; a) to shut in, enclose, limit; b) to contain, comprise, comprehend, involve, P. to depend upon, consist of; 3. to keep in a place *or* situation, to hold back, stay, stop; a) to check, repress, restrain, curb; b) to keep some one from something.

**con-tingō, tigī, tāctum** 3 1. to touch; a) to reach, take hold of, seize; b) to arrive at, come to; c) to border on, touch, be near, be related to; d) to concern, affect; *part.* **contāctus** 3 defiled, polluted, tainted; 2. *intr.* to happen, turn out, come to pass.

**continuātiō, ōnis** f unbroken succession; a) continuance, prolongation, series; b) period.

**continuō¹** *adv.* immediately, at once, directly; continuously.

**continuō²** 1 to join in unbroken succession; a) to connect, unite, make continuous (*alqd alci rei*), P. to be adjacent, border on; b) to extend (*alqd alqā re*); c) to carry on, draw out, continue, do uninterruptedly, P. to follow close upon; d) to prolong.

**continuus** 3 hanging together; **a)** uninterrupted, continuous, successive, following on; **b)** connected with, near; **c)** incessant, unremitting.

**contiō, ōnis** *f* meeting, assembly, convocation; **a)** public meeting (*of the people* or *of the soldiers*); **b)** speech made to an assembly, public address, harangue. [public.]

**contiōnābundus** 3 speaking in]

**contiōnālis, e** *and* **-nārius** 3 relating to a public assembly; vulgar.

**contiōnātor, ōris** *m* demagogue, popular orator.

**contiōnor** 1 **a)** to speak in public; **b)** to form an assembly.

**contiuncula, ae** *f* **a)** small assembly; **b)** petty speech.

**con-tollō** 3 = **confero**. [ly.]

**con-tonat** it 'thunders violent-]

**contor** 1 to inquire.

**con-torqueō** 2 to twist, whirl, contort; **a)** to turn, direct, influence (*alqm ad alqd*); **b)** to hurl, brandish; **contortus** 3 intricate, confused, complicated; vigorous, vehement.

**con-tortiō, ōnis** *f* complicated expression. [tricate.]

**contorti-plicātus** 3 entangled, in-]

**con-tortor, ōris** *m* perverter.

**contortulus** 3 somewhat intricate.

**contrā** **1.** *adv.* opposite, over against; **a)** on the other side; **b)** on the contrary (*contrā ac* otherwise than), in return; against; **2.** *prep.* with *acc.* opposite to, over against; against, contrary to.

**con-tractiō, ōnis** *f* a drawing together; **a)** abbreviation, shortness; **b)** dejection.

**contractiuncula, ae** *f* dejection, sadness. [against (*alci*).]

**contrā-dīcō** 3 to gainsay, speak]

**contrā-dictiō, ōnis** *f* a speaking in opposition.

**con-trahō** 3 to draw together; **1.** to draw in, shorten (*orationem*), to make narrow; **a)** to reduce, confine; **b)** to check, restrain; **2.** to collect, unite, assemble, concentrate; **a)** to bring about, accomplish, execute, cause, produce; **b)** to transact, contract, bargain, complete a business--arrangement; — **contractus** 3 drawn in, contracted, narrow, limited, short; living in retirement; **res contracta** contract.

**contrārius** 3 lying over against, opposite (*alci rei*); **a)** opposed; **b)** hostile, contrary to, inimical, conflicting; injurious; — *subst.* **contrārium, ī** *n* the opposite, reverse, opposite direction.

**con-trectābiliter** so as to be felt.

**contrectātiō, ōnis** *f* a touching, handling.

**con-trectō** 1 to touch, handle, feel; **a)** to violate, dishonour; **b)** to consider, survey.

**con-tremīscō** *and* **-ēscō, muī**, — 3 to tremble violently, shake, shudder at (*alqd*); to waver.

**con-tremō** 3 to quake.

**con-tribuō** 3 **a)** to unite, incorporate, add, annex.

**con-trīstō** 1 to make sad *or* sorrowful, to make gloomy.

**con-trītus** 3 worn out, trite.

**contrōversia, ae** *f* **a)** quarrel, dispute, debate, question, controversy; **b)** lawsuit; **c)** contradiction.

**contrō(-versiōsus,)-versus** 3 controverted, disputed.

**con-trucīdō** 1 to cut down *or* to pieces.

**con-trūdō** 3 to thrust into, crowd into (*alqm in alqd*).

**con-truncō** 1 to cut to pieces.

**contubernālis, is** *m* (*and f*) tent-companion, comrade; **a)** personal follower, attendant of a general; **b)** companion, mate, husband (*f* wife).

**con-tubernium, ī** *n* **1.** common tent, common dwelling; **a)** abode of a male and female slave; **b)** marriage of slaves, concubinage; **2.** tent--companionship, comradeship; intercourse, attendance.

**con-tueor, (tuitus sum)** 2 (*and* **con-tuor**) 3) to look on *or* at attentively, to regard,. behold, survey.

**contuitus** *or* **-tūtus, ūs** *m* a beholding, sight.

**contumācia, ae** *f* **a)** obstinacy, stubbornness; **b)** constancy, firmness.

**con-tumāx, ācis** **a)** stubborn, obstinate; **b)** unyielding.

**con-tumēlia, ae** *f* **a)** injury, violence, damage; **b)** insult, affront, contumely.

**contumēliōsus** 3 **a)** insulting, abusive; **b)** reproachful.

**con-tumulō** 1 to cover with a mound, to bury.

**con-tundō, tudī, tū(n)sum** 3 a) to crush, bruise, break to pieces; b) to put down, subdue, destroy.

**con-turbātiō, ōnis** f confusion, consternation.

**con-turbātor, ōris** m ruinously expensive.

**con-turbō** 1 to throw into disorder, disturb, confound; a) to fail (in business), be bankrupt; b) to disquiet, cause anxiety.

**contus, ī** m pole; spear, pike. [jugal.)

**cō-nūbiālis** (and -**nūb**-), e con-)

**cō-nūbium** (and -**nūb**-), ī n marriage, wedlock; a) nuptials; b) right of intermarriage.

**cōnus, ī** m cone; apex of a helmet.

**con-vador** 1 to bind over to appear in court.

**con-valēscō, luī,** — 3 a) to become strong or valid; b) to recover, regain health. [all sides.)

**con-vallis, is** f a valley shut in on)

**con-vāsō** 1 to pack up.

**con-vectō** 1 intens. of **conveho**.

**con-vector, ōris** m fellow-passenger.

**con-vehō** 3 to carry together to one place; to convey; P. to be conveyed or carried.

**con-vellō** 3 a) to pull or tear away, to pluck up, **signa** to decamp; b) to shake, overthrow, destroy.

**con-vena, ae** meeting together; subst. -**nae, ārum** m/pl. assembled multitude, strangers, vagabonds.

**con-veniēns, tis** a) agreeing, unanimous, harmonious; b) convenient, corresponding, fit, becoming, appropriate.

**con-venientia, ae** f agreement, harmony, symmetry.

**con-veniō** 4 1. to come together, assemble, meet (in locum, ad alqm); a) to come into the power of a man, to marry; b) to visit, meet, address, accost (alqm); 2. to come about, to a decision, be agreed upon; **convenit** it is agreed or decided upon; 3. to be fit, suitable, appropriate (ad alqd); to consist, apply, be adapted to; **convenit** it is suitable, proper, becoming.

**conventicium, ī** n money paid for attendance in an assembly.

**con-venticius** 3 casually met.

**conventiculum, ī** n a coming together, assembly.

**con-ventiō, ōnis** f and **con-ventum, ī** n agreement, convention, contract.

**con-ventus, ūs** m a coming together, assembly; a) congress, council, judicial session, court of justice; b) assembly of the inhabitants of a province, provincial corporation; c) union, agreement.

**con-verberō** 1 to beat severely.

**con-verrō** 3 to sweep together, to scrape together; to beat.

**con-versātiō, ōnis** f intercourse, conversation.

**con-versiō, ōnis** f a turning round; a) periodical return; b) revolution, change.

**con-versō** 1 to turn round; -**sor** to keep company (with).

**con-vertō** 3 1. a) to turn round, back, to the other side, to reverse, **signa** to wheel round, change the direction; **se, terga convertere** to flee; b) to turn in a circle; c) to throw back, to cause to yield; d) to change, alter, transform; e) to convert, pervert; f) to exchange; g) to translate; 2. to direct, turn (alqd in or ad alqd); to apply to; P. to turn round; intr. to turn, return, change.

**con-vestiō** 4 to clothe, cover.

**convexus** 3 a) vaulted, arched; b) sloping, steep; subst. **convexum, ī** n vault, arch.

**conviciātor, ōris** m slanderer, reviler.

**convicior** 1 to revile, rail at, reproach.

**convicium, ī** n loud cry, noise, clamour; a) altercation, contention; b) loud disapprobation or contradiction; c) a reviling, reproach, abuse, censure, reproof.

**con-victiō, ōnis** f = **convictus**.

**convictor, ōris** m table-companion, familiar friend.

**con-victus, ūs** m a) a living together, social intercourse; b) familiar friends; c) = **convivium**.

**con-vincō** 3 a) to convict, refute, prove guilty (alqm alcis rei) or wrong; b) to prove or demonstrate clearly.

**con-vīsō** 3 to survey, examine; to shine upon.

**conviva, ae** m table-companion, guest.

**convivālis, e** belonging to a banquet.

convīvātor, ōris *m* host, entertainer.

convīvium, ī *n* feast, banquet, entertainment; company at table, guests.

con-vīvō 3 to live with; to eat with.

con-vīvor 1 to feast *or* banquet together.

con-vocātiō, ōnis *f* a calling together.

con-vocō 1 to call together, assemble.

con-volō 1 to fly *or* run together.

con-volūtor 1 to go round, go about.

con-volvō 3 a) to roll together, roll up *or* round; b) to wrap.

con-vomō 3 to vomit upon.

con-vorr-, -vors-, -vort- = con-verr-, -vers-, -vert-.

con-vulnerō 1 to wound severely.

co-operiō, ruī, rtum 4 to cover over, to overwhelm.

co-optātiō, ōnis *f* election by way of supplement, co-optation, election.

co-optō 1 to choose, elect (*to an office*).

co-orior 4 to arise, break out *or* forth, to appear.

co-ortus, ūs *m* rising.

cōpa, ae *f* hostess of a tavern.

cophinus, ī *m* basket.

cōpia, ae *f* plenty, abundance (*alcis rei*); a) wealth, riches, resources; b) provisions, supplies, victuals; c) multitude, throng, number; d) body of men, troop, band, *pl.* troops, forces; e) fulness, copiousness; f) ability, power, opportunity, means.

cōpiolae, ārum *f/pl.* small forces.

cōpiōsus 3 well supplied *or* provided, wealthy; a) abounding, plentiful, copious (with *abl.* or *a re*); b) eloquent.

cōpis, e = copiosus.

coprea, ae *m* dirty joker.

copta, ae *f* a very hard cake.

cōpula, ae *f* band; a) rope, thong, tie; b) grapnel; c) connection.

cōpulātiō, ōnis *f* a coupling, union.

cōpulō (*and* -or) 1 to bind *or* join together, to couple, connect, unite, fasten.

coquinō 1 = coquo.

coquinus 3 of cooks.

coquō, xī, ctum 3 to cook, bake, boil, roast; a) to burn, parch, dry up; b) to ripen, make mature; c) to digest; d) to disturb, torment; e) to meditate.

coquus, ī *m*, coqua, ae *f* cook.

cor, cordis *n* 1. the heart; a) soul, feeling, *alci* cordi *esse* to be dear to, be agreeable, please; b) courage; c) judgment, mind; d) person; 2. stomach.

corallium, ī *n* red coral.

cōram 1. *adv.* a) openly, publicly. before the eyes of all, face to face; b) personally, in one's own person; 2. *prep.* with *abl.* in the presence of.

corbis, is *f* (*m*) basket.

corbīta, ae *f* ship of burden.

corbula, ae *f* small basket.

corcodīlus, ī *m* = crocodilus.

corcōtārius = crocotarius.

corculum, ī *n* a little heart.

cordātus 3 prudent, wise.

cordāx, ācis *m* a lascivious dance.

cor-dolium, ī *n* heartache, grief.

coriandrum, ī *n* coriander.

corium, ī *n* (*and* corius, ī *m*) hide, skin; leather.

corneolus 3 horny.

corneus 3 a) horny, of horn; b) of cornel-wood.

corni-cen, inis *m* horn-blower.

cornīcor 1 to caw like a crow.

cornīcula, ae *f* crow.

corniculārius, ī *m* promoted soldier.

corniculum, ī *n* a little horn; ornament on the helmet.

corni-ger 3 horned.

corni-pēs, pedis horn-footed.

cornix, icis *f* crow.

cornu, ūs *n* 1. horn, antler; a) excrescence on the head; b) horn of the moon; c) branch of a river; d) tongue of land; e) ends of the sail-yards; f) top of a helmet; g) end of a staff round which writings were rolled; h) wing of an army; i) horn of plenty; 2. horn as a material; a) bugle-horn, trumpet; b) bow; c) funnel; d) horn holding the strings of a lyre.

cornum, ī *n* a) = cornu; b) cornel-berry; javelin of cornel wood.

cornus¹, ī *f* cornel(-tree); javelin.

cornus², ūs *m* = cornu.

cornūtus 3 horned.

corōlla, ae *f* small wreath.

corōllārium, ī *n* garland, chaplet; gift, present.

**corōna, ae** *f* wreath, garland, chaplet; **a)** crown, diadem; **b)** circle, assembly, audience; **c)** surrounding army, besiegers.

**corōnārius** 3 of a wreath *or* crown; **aurum corōnārium** present of gold for a victorious general.

**corōnis, idis** *f* final flourish; end.

**corōnō** 1 to wreathe, crown with a garland, to surround.

**corporātus** 3 material.

**corporeus** 3 *and* **corporālis e** bodily, corporeal, composed of flesh.

**corpulentus** 3 stout, corpulent.

**corpus, oris** *n* body; **a)** flesh; **b)** corpse, shade, soul of a dead one; **c)** trunk; **d)** person, individual, being; **e)** substance, essential matter; **f)** mass, frame, system, structure, corporation; collection of writings.

**corpusculum, ī** *n* little body.

**cor-rādō** 3 to scrape together.

**corrēctiō, ōnis** *f* improvement, amendment; correction.

**cor-rēctor, ōris** *m* improver, amender; corrector, censor.

**cor-rēpō** 3 to creep, slink.

**correptus** 3 pronounced short.

**cor-rīdeō** 2 to laugh aloud.

**corrigia, ae** *f* shoe-string, -tie.

**cor-rigō, rēxī, rēctum** 3 to make straight; **a)** to set right; **b)** to correct, improve, amend, reform.

**cor-ripiō, ripuī, reptum** 3 to snatch up, seize, grasp, take up; **a)** to snatch away violently; **b)** to arrest; **c)** to carry away, catch, attack, seize; **d)** to blame, rebuke, reproach, chide, accuse; **e)** to hasten, quicken, shorten.

**cor-rīvō** 1 to conduct (*streams*) together.

**cor-rōborō** 1 to strengthen, invigorate; **P.** to gain strength.

**cor-rōdō, sī, sum** 3 to gnaw to pieces.

**cor-rogō** 1 to collect by begging.

**cor-rūgō** 1 to wrinkle.

**cor-rumpō** 3 to break completely; to destroy, annihilate, ruin, spoil, waste; **P.** to perish; **a)** to make worse, deteriorate, injure, mar, corrupt; **b)** to falsify, adulterate; **c)** to pervert, degrade; to seduce, entice, mislead; **d)** to gain by gifts, to bribe. — **corruptus** 3 spoiled, bad, marred, corrupted; perverted, perverse.

**cor-ruō** 3 to fall together, fall down; to be ruined; to cause to fall in a heap.

**cor-ruptēla, ae** *f* a corrupting, seducing, bribing.

**cor-ruptiō, ōnis** *f* a corrupting; **a)** corruption; **b)** bribery, seduction.

**cor-ruptor, ōris** *m* corrupter, seducer, briber.

**corruptrix, īcis** *f* she who seduces.

**cors, tis** *f* = **cohors.**

**cortex, icis** *m* (and *f*) bark, shell; bark of the cork-tree.

**cortīna, ae** *f* kettle, caldron; **a)** the Delphic tripod; **b)** oracle.

**corulus, ī** *f* hazel(-tree).

**cōrus, ī** *m* = **caurus.**

**coruscō** 1 1. *trans.* to move quickly, vibrate; 2. *intr.* to be in quick motion, to flash, glitter.

**coruscus** 3 **a)** shaking, trembling, waving, vibrating; **b)** flashing, glittering.

**corvus, ī** *m* raven; grappling-iron.

**cōrycus, ī** *m* sand-bag for athletes.

**corylētum, ī** *n* hazel-thicket.

**corylus, ī** *f* = **corulus.**

**corymbi-fer** 3 bearing clusters of ivy-berries. [*berries*].)

**corymbus, ī** *m* cluster (*of ivy-*)

**coryphaeus, ī** *m* leader, chief, head.

**cōrytus, ī** *m* quiver; quiverful of arrows.

**cōs, cōtis** *f* a) flint-stone; **b)** whetstone, grindstone.

**cosmētēs, ae** *m* wardrobe-keeper.

**cosmicos, ī** *m* citizen of the world; **-ca, ōrum** *n/pl.* worldly things.

**costa, ae** *f* rib; side.

**costum, ī** *n* (*and* **costos, ī** *f*) balsam-shrub; unguent.

**cōtēs, is** *f* = **cautes.**

**cothurnātus** 3 with the cothurnus; lofty, tragic.

**cothurnus, ī** *m* high shoe of tragic actors, cothurnus; **a)** hunting-boot; **b)** tragic style, tragedy.

**cottabus, ī** *m* clap, stroke.

**cottana(-ona), ōrum** *n/pl.* figs.

**cot(t)īdiānus** 3 daily

**cot(t)īdiē** *adv.* daily, every day.

**cotula, ae** *f* small cup (holding one hemina).

**cōturnix** (*and* **cŏ-**), **īcis** *f* quail.

**coturnus, ī** *m* = **cothurnus.**

**covinnārius, ī** *m* one who fights from a chariot (**covinnus, ī** *m*).

**coxa, ae** *f* the hip.

**coxendix, īcis** *f* hip, hip-bone.

**crābrō, ōnis** *m* hornet.

**crambē, ēs** *f* cabbage.

**crāpula, ae** *f* intoxication.

**crāpulārius** 3 for intoxication.

**crās** *adv.* to-morrow; in the future.

**crassitūdō, inis** *f* thickness; density.

**crassus** 3 thick, dense, solid; a) fat, stout; b) rude.

**crāstinus** 3 of to-morrow; *subst.* **-um, ī** *n* the morrow.

**crātēr, ēris** *m and* **crātēra, ae** *f* mixing-vessel, wine-bowl; a) basin; b) crater of a volcano; c) the Cup (*a constellation*).

**crāticula, ae** *f* gridiron.

**crātis, is** *f* (*mostly pl.*) wicker--work, hurdle; a) fascines; b) joint; rib; honeycomb.

**creātiō, ōnis** *f* election.

**creātor, ōris** *m* creator, begetter, founder.

**creātrīx, īcis** *f* mother.

**crēber, bra, brum** thick, crowded together, close, frequent, numerous; a) abundant, abounding (*re*); b) repeated; *adv.* **crēbrō** frequently, repeatedly.

**crēb(r)ēscō, b(r)uī, —** 3 to become frequent, to increase; to spread abroad.

**crēbritās, ātis** *f* frequency.

**crēdibilis, e** worthy of belief, credible.

**crēditor, ōris** *m* creditor.

**crēdō, didī, ditum** 3 1. to commit, consign, intrust; to lend, give as a loan; 2. to trust, confide in (*alci*); a) to believe, give credence to (*alci alqd*); b) to think, be of opinion, suppose, imagine; **crēdō** (*parenthetic*) I suppose, believe, think.

**crēdulitās, ātis** *f* easy belief, credulity.

**crēdulus** 3 easy of belief, confiding, unsuspecting.

**cremō** 1 to burn.

**cremor, ōris** *m* thick juice.

**creō** 1 to produce, make, create; a) to beget, bring forth; b) to cause, effect (*alci alqd*); c) to choose, elect.

**creper, era, erum** dark; uncertain.

**crepida, ae** *f* sole, sandal.

**crepidātus** 3 wearing sandals.

**crepidō, inis** *f* a) pedestal; b) mound, pier, mole, dam.

**crepidula, ae** *f* little sandal.

**crepitācillum, ī** *n* rattle.

**crepitō** 1 (*intens. of* **crepo**) to rattle, clatter, creak, rustle.

**crepitus, ūs** *m* a rattling, clattering, creaking, rustling.

**crepō, uī, itum** 1 1. *intr.* to rattle, clatter, creak, rustle, crack; 2. *trans.* to cause to sound, to talk much of, to make ado about.

**crepundia, ōrum** *n/pl.* a child's rattle; toys.

**crepusculum, ī** *n* (evening-) twilight.

**crēscō, crēvī, (crētum)** 3 to grow, grow up; a) to spring up, to rise; b) to increase, thrive, swell, prosper, become great, increase in power and fame; **crētus** 3 born, sprung from.

**crēta, ae** *f* chalk; white earth, clay, paint for the face.

**crētātus** 3 chalked.

**crēterra, ae** *f* = **crater(a).**

**crēteus** 3 of clay.

**crētiō, ōnis** *f* declaration about accepting an inheritance.

**crētōsus** 3 abounding in chalk or clay.

**crētula, ae** *f* clay for sealing.

**crētus** 3, *part. pf.* P. *of* **cerno** *and* **cresco.**

**cribrum, ī** *n* sieve.

**crīmen, inis** *n* accusation, reproach, charge; a) object of reproach, guilty person *or* thing; b) fault, offence, crime, guilt.

**crīminātiō, ōnis** *f* accusation, calumny.

**crīminātor, ōris** *m* accuser, slanderer.

**criminor** (*and* **-ō**) 1 a) to accuse, charge with a crime, to calumniate; b) to complain of, denounce.

**criminōsus** 3 slanderous, reproachful, backbiting.

**crīnālis, e** relating to the hair, of the hair; *subst.* **crīnāle, is** *n* hair-band, diadem.

**crīni-ger** 3 = **crinitus.**

**crīniō** 4 to cover with hair (i. e. leaves).

**crīnis, is** *m* (*and f*) the hair; tail (*of a comet*).

**crīnitus** 3 having hair, hairy.

**crisis** (*acc.* **-im**) *f* crisis.

**crīsō** 1 to move the thighs.

**crispi-sulcāns, tis** winding, serpentine.

crispō 1 a) to swing, brandish; b) to curl.

crisp(ul)us 3 curly, curly-headed; quivering.

crista, ae f a) crest, comb (of a bird); b) plume of a helmet.

cristātus 3 a) crested; b) having a plume.

criticus, ī m judge, critic.

croceus 3 of saffron; yellow, orange.

crocinus 3 saffron-coloured; -num, ī n saffron-oil.

crōc(c)iō 4 to croak.

crocodīlus, ī m crocodile.

crocōt(ul)a, ae f saffron-coloured robe.

crocōtārius 3 of saffron robes.

crocum, ī n and crocus, ī m a) saffron; b) saffron-colour.

crotalistria, ae f castanet-dancer.

crotalum, ī n rattle, castanet.

cruciābilitās, ātis f torture.

cruciābiliter with torture.

cruciāmentum, ī n = cruciatus.

cruciātus, ūs m torture, torment; a) execution; b) instrument of torture.

cruciō 1 a) to torment, put to the rack; b) to afflict, grieve.

cruci-salus, ī m cross-dancer.

crūdēlis, e cruel; unfeeling, hard, severe, fierce.

crūdēlitās, ātis f cruelty, hardness, severity.

crūdēscō, —,— 3 to become violent, grow worse.

crūditās, ātis f indigestion.

crūdus 3 raw, bloody, uncooked, unbaked; unripe; a) fresh, vigorous; b) with full stomach; undigested; c) unprepared, undressed; d) unfeeling, cruel.

cruentō 1 to make bloody, stain with blood; to wound.

cruentus 3 bloody; a) blood-red; b) blood-thirsty.

crumēna (and -mīna), ae f purse; money.

crumilla, ae f small purse.

cruor, ōris m blood from a wound, gore; a) drop of blood; b) blood-shed; murder.

cruppellārius, ī m mail-clad Gallic soldier.

crūri-crepida, ae m slave with legs chained.

crūri-fragius, ī m slave with legs broken.

crūs, ūris n leg, shin.

crūsma, atis n music played on a stringed instrument.

crusta, ae f crust, rind, bark, shell; inlaid or embossed work.

crustō 1 to encrust.

crustulārius, ī m confectioner.

crust(ul)um, ī n cake, confectionery.

crux, crucis f cross, gallows; a) crucifixion; b) torture, trouble, misery; c) gallowsbird, good-for--nothing.

crypta, ae f vault, crypt.

crypto-porticus, ūs f walled passage.

crystallinus 3 of crystal.

crystallum, ī n and -us, ī f ice; crystal.

cubiculāris, e belonging to a sleeping-room.

cubiculārius, ī m valet.

cubiculāta, ae f (sc. navis) ship furnished with cabins.

cubiculum, ī n a) sleeping-room, bedroom; b) apartment.

cubīle, is n resting-place, den, bed, seat.

cubital, ālis n elbow-cushion.

cubitālis, e a cubit long.

cubitō 1 to be accustomed to lie.

cubitum, ī n and -tus, ī m a) elbow, b) cubit (1½ feet).

cubitūra, ae f lying.

cubitus, ūs m = concubitus.

cubō, buī, bitum 1 to lie down, rest, repose; a) to lie asleep; b) to recline at table; c) to lie sick; d) to slope, slant.

cucullus, ī m hood.

cucūl(l)us, ī m cuckoo.

cucumis, (er)is m cucumber.

cucurbita, ae f gourd; cupping--glass.

cūdō¹, (dī, sum) 3 to beat, strike, knock, hammer, stamp, coin.

cūdō², ōnis m helmet of raw hide.

cūiās, ātis of what country?, whence?

cuicui-modī of whatever kind.

cūius 3 (interrog.) of whom?, whose?; (rel.) of whom, whose.

cūius-modī of what kind?

cūiusque-modī of every kind.

culcit(ul)a, ae f mattress, pillow.

culex, icis m gnat, midge.

culillus, ī m = culullus.

culīna, ae f kitchen; food, fare.

**culleus, ī** *m* (leather-) bag, sack.

**culmen, inis** *n* top, summit; culmination; roof, height.

**culmus, ī** *m* stalk, straw.

**culpa, ae** *f* guilt, error, fault, defect; **in culpā esse** to be to blame; a) mischievous thing, cause of fault; b) unchastity.

**culpitō** 1 to blame, reproach.

**culpō** 1 a) to reproach, accuse, find fault with; b) to blame, disapprove.

**cultellus, ī** *m* little knife.

**culter, trī** *m* knife; razor.

**cultiō, ōnis** *f* cultivation.

**cultor, ōris** *m* cultivator; a) planter, husbandman, farmer; b) inhabitant; c) friend, worshipper, lover.

**cultrārius, ī** *m* sacrificer.

**cultrix, īcis,** *fem. of* **cultor.**

**cultūra, ae** *f* = **cultus²**.

**cultus¹** 3, *see* **colo.**

**cultus², ūs** *m* cultivation, labour, tilling; a) cultivated land; b) care, training, education; c) culture, civilization, refinement; d) veneration, adoration, worship; e) way of life; luxury, wantonness; dress, attire, splendour, adornment.

**culullus, ī** *m* drinking-vessel.

**cūlus, ī** *m* the fundament.

**cum¹** *prep.* with *abl.* with, together with, in the company of, in connection with, on the side of, at the same time with.

**cum²** *cj.* 1. when (*gen. with subj. of past time, with indic. of present or future time*); at the time when (*with indic.*); whenever (*with indic.; later, with subj.*); 2. as, since (*with subj.*); 3. although, whereas (*with subj.*); — **cum primum** as soon as; **cum praesertim** especially when *or* as; **cum maxime** precisely when; at this *or* that very moment; **cum ... tum** both ... and; while ..., especially.

**cūmatile, is** *n* sea-green garment.

**cumb(ul)a, ae** *f* small boat.

**cumera, ae** *f* box, corn-chest.

**cumīnum, ī** *n* cumin.

**cum-que** *adv.* 1. at any time, always; 2. = **et cum.**

**cumulātus** 3 heaped up, increased, augmented, perfect, complete, full.

**cumulō** 1 to heap up, accumulate, pile; a) to fill, load, cover (*alqd alqa re*); b) to augment, increase; c) to crown, complete, bring to perfection.

**cumulus, ī** *m* heap, pile, mass; a) addition, increase, surplus, summit, point, crown; b) immense number.

**cūnābula, ōrum** *n/pl.* cradle; resting-place, dwelling.

**cūnae, ārum** *f/pl.* cradle; nest.

**cūnctābundus** 3 lingering much.

**cūnctāns, tis** lingering, delaying, slow; tenacious.

**cūnctātiō, ōnis** *f* a lingering, delaying, tarrying.

**cūnctātor, ōris** *m* delayer, lingerer, loiterer.

**cūnctor** (*and* **-ō**) 1 to linger, loiter, delay; to hesitate, doubt.

**cūnctus** 3 (*mostly pl.*) all collectively, all in a body, all together, the whole; *subst.* **cūncta, ōrum** *n/pl.* all things, everything at once.

**cuneātim** *adv.* in the form of a wedge.

**cuneātus** 3 pointed like a wedge.

**cuneō** 1 to wedge.

**cuneolus, ī** *m* little wedge.

**cuneus, ī** *m* wedge; a) troops drawn up in form of a wedge; b) wedge-formed division of seats in a theatre, the spectators.

**cunīculōsus** 3 full of rabbits.

**cunīculus, ī** *m* a) rabbit, cony; b) underground passage, mine, canal.

**cunila, ae** *f* a sort of plant.

**cunnus, ī** *m* the vulva; unchaste woman.

**cunque** = **cumque.**

**cūpa, ae** *f* tub, cask, tun.

**cupiditās, ātis** *f* a longing, desire, passion; lust; a) covetousness, avarice; b) desire for love; c) ambition; d) party-spirit.

**cupīdō, inis** *f* (*m*) = **cupiditas.**

**Cupīdō, inis** *m* Cupid, (God of) Love.

**cupidus** 3 longing, desiring, desirous, wishful, eager, passionate; a) covetous (*with gen.*); b) lustful, amorous; c) ambitious; d) eager, fond; e) partial, factious.

**cupiēns, tis** longing, desiring.

**cupiō, īvī** *and* **ii, ītum** 3 to long for, desire, wish (*alqd*; *with inf.*); to be favourable, wish well, be devoted (*alci*).

**cupītor, ōris** *m* one who desires.

**cuppēdia¹, ōrum** *n/pl.* dainties.

cuppēdia², ae f daintiness.
cuppēdinārius, ī m confectioner.
cuppēdō, inis f desire.
cuppēs m one fond of delicate food.
cupressētum, ī n cypress-grove.
cupresseus 3 of cypress-wood.
cupressi-fer 3 cypress-bearing.
cupressus, ī (and ūs) f the cypress; box of cypress wood.
cūr adv. why?
cūra, ae f 1. care; carefulness, attention, diligence, pains (alcis rei); a) an attending, caring, minding, healing, cure; b) administration, management, oversight, command, office, business; c) written work, writing, book; d) guardian, overseer; protégé(e); 2. care, anxiety, trouble, disquiet, grief; a) disquiet of love; b) object of love, mistress.
cūrābilis, e needing medical treatment (?).
cūralium, ī n = corallium.
cūrātiō, ōnis (and cūrātūra, ae) f a taking care (of), care, management; treatment.
cūrātor, ōris m manager, superintendent; overseer, keeper.
cūrātus 3 anxious, earnest; cared for.
curculiō, ōnis (dimin. curculiunculus, ī) m corn-weevil.
cūria, ae f curia 1. senate-house; senate; 2. the tenth part of a tribus or division of the Roman people; meeting-place of the curiæ.
cūriālis, is m member of the same curia.
cūriātim adv. by curiæ.
cūriātus 3 relating to the curiæ; comitia cūriāta assembly of the people in curiæ; lex cūriāta law passed in the comitia curiata.
cūriō¹, ōnis m priest or head of a curia.
cūriō² (ōnis) wasted by care.
cūriōsitās, ātis f desire for knowledge; curiosity.
cūriōsus 3 a) careful, attentive, diligent; b) inquisitive, curious, prying; c) careworn.
curis, is f lance, spear.
cūrō 1 to care for, pay attention to, look or attend to (alqd; with ut or inf.); a) to be solicitous for, think of (with acc.; de re; inf.); b) to administer, manage, govern, command; c) to tend, cure, heal; to refresh; d) to procure, provide.
curriculum, ī n a running, course; a) race, race-course; b) orbit; c) race-chariot; d) career, course, race-ground.
currō, cucurrī, cursum 3 a) to run, hasten; to sail, fly, move quickly, flow; to spread; b) to traverse, pass over (with acc.).
currus, ūs m chariot, car; the horses, team; a) war-chariot; b) triumphal car; c) plough; d) ship.
cursim adv. hastily, quickly.
cursitō and cursō 1 to run constantly, to run to and fro.
cursor, ōris m runner; a) racer, charioteer; b) courier.
cursūra, ae f a running.
cursus, ūs m a running; a) rapid motion, course, march, voyage, passage, journey; b) direction, way; c) flow, progress, speed; d) flow of words; e) race-course; career.
curtō 1 to shorten, abridge.
curtus 3 shortened, mutilated; circumcised; castrated.
curūlis, e belonging to a chariot; curule; (sella) ~ f curule chair.
curvāmen, inis n and curvātūra, ae f a bending, bend, arching.
curvō 1 to bend, curve, crook, round.
curvus 3 bent, bowed, crooked, curved, arched.
cuspis, idis f point, sting; head of a spear; lance, javelin.
custōdēla, ae f = custodia.
custōdia, ae f a watching, guarding, watch, guard, protection, care; a) guard, watch, sentinel; watch-station; b) custody, confinement, imprisonment, prison; c) captive, prisoner.
custōdiō 4 to watch, guard, keep; a) to preserve, heed; b) to observe, take care of, se custōdīre to be on the watch; c) to hold in custody.
custōs, ōdis m and f watchman, keeper; a preserver, protector, defender; b) body-guard; watch, spy; c) jailer.
cutīcula, ae f skin.
cutis, is f skin; coating, outside.
cyathissō 1 to fill the cups.
cyathus, ī m a) ladle for filling drinking-cups; b) a measure for liquids (= ¹/₁₂ sextarius).

**cybaea, ae** *f* transport-vessel (*navis*).
**cybiosactēs, ae** *m* dealer. in salt-fish.
**cybium, ī** *n* (dish made of) tunny-fish.
**cycladātus** 3 wearing a cyclas.
**cyclas, adis** *f* circular robe.
**cyclicus** 3 belonging to a cycle, cyclic.
**Cyclōps, ōpis** *m* Cyclops (*one-eyed giant*).
**cycnēus** (*and* **cyg-**) 3 of a swan.

**cycnus** (*and* **cyg-**) **ī** *m* swan.
**cydōnium, ī** *n* quince.
**cylindrus, ī** *m* cylinder, roller.
**cymba, ae** *f* = **cumba**.
**cymbalum, ī** *n* cymbal.
**cymbium, ī** *n* drinking-vessel.
**cynicus** 3 doglike, Cynic.
**cyno-cephalus, ī** *m* ape with a dog's head.
**cyparissus** = **cupressus**.
**cytisus, ī** *f* a kind of clover, snail-clover.

# D

**D** *abbr.* a) = **Decimus**; b) **Divus**; c) 500 (= half of **CIƆ**).

**dactylicus** 3 dactylic.

**dactyliothēca, ae** *f* casket for rings.

**dactylus, ī** *m* a dactyl.

**daedalus** 3 skilful, artfully constructed.

**dāmiūrgus, ī** *m* = demiurgus.

**damma, ae** *f* deer; venison.

**damnātiō, ōnis** *f* condemnation.

**damnātōrius** 3 condemnatory.

**damni-ficus** 3, **damni-gerulus** 3 causing damage, injurious.

**damnō** 1 to condemn, declare guilty (*alqm alcis rei*), **votidamnare** to grant one's wish and exact fulfilment of a vow; a) to sentence, doom; b) to disapprove, reject, blame (*alqd*); c) to consecrate, condemn as a sacrifice; d) to bind *or* oblige.

**damnōsus** 3 a) causing damage, injurious, destructive (*alci*); b) prodigal.

**damnum, ī** *n* loss, damage, injury; a) fault; b) something lost; c) fine, penalty.

**danista, ae** *m* money-lender.

**danisticus** 3 money-lending.

**danunt** = **dant** (*see* do).

**daphnōn, ōnis** *m* grove of bay-trees.

**dapinō** 1 to serve up.

**daps, dapis** *f* (*mostly pl.*) sacrificial feast; a) banquet; b) food, victuals.

**dapsilis, e** sumptuous, costly.

**datārius** 3 belonging to gifts.

**datātim** *adv.* by giving, by tossing from one to the other.

**datiō, ōnis** *f* a giving; the right to give away.

**'datō** 1 to give away.

**dator, ōris** *m* giver.

**datū** (*abl.*) by gift.

**dē** *prep.* with *abl.* 1. (*of space*) from, down from, away from, out of; 2. (*of time*) from, immediately after, during, in the course of; 3. (*of relation*) from, out of a number *or* class (*unus de multis*); on account of; according to, in accordance with; with relation to; concerning; **dē integro** anew, **dē improviso** unexpectedly, **dē industria** purposely.

**dea, ae** *f* goddess.

**de-albō** 1 to whitewash.

**de-ambulātiō, ōnis** *f* a walking, promenading.

**de-ambulō** 1 to take a walk.

**de-amō** 1 to love very much.

**de-armō** 1 to disarm.

**de-artuō** 1 to tear limb from limb, to ruin.

**de-asciō** 1 to cheat.       [rave.]

**dē-bacchor** 1 to revel wildly, to)

**dē-bellātor, ōris** *m* conqueror.

**dē-bellō** 1 a) to finish a war, fight out (*cum alqo*); b) to subdue, vanquish.

**dēbeō, uī, itum** 2 to owe, be indebted; a) to be in debt; b) to remain indebted; c) to be under obligation; d) to be bound *or* pledged, one ought, must, should; e) to be destined, fated; f) to have to thank for; — **dēbitus** 3 due, owing, becoming; destined, doomed; **dēbitum, ī** *n* debt.

**dēbilis, e** lame, infirm, frail, weak, feeble, helpless.

**dēbilitās, ātis** *f* lameness, debility, weakness.

**dēbilitātiō, ōnis** *f* a disabling.

**dēbilitō** 1 to lame; to weaken, debilitate, unnerve, disable.

**dēbitiō, ōnis** *f* indebtedness.

**dēbitor, ōris** *m* debtor; indebted for.

**dēbitum, ī** *n and* **dēbitus** 3, *see* debeo.

**dē-blaterō** 1 (*alci alqd*) to blab out.

**dē-cantō** 1 to sing; a) to repeat in singing, repeat often, harp on; b) to leave off singing.

**dē-cēdō** 3 to go away, depart (*ab, ex, de re*; with *abl.*); a) to march off, to evacuate, to leave a province, surrender (*office*), retire; b) **de vita** to depart from life, to die; c) to make way, give place (*alci*), yield (*de via*); to yield, be inferior, rank below; to depart, deviate; d) to cease, abandon; to disappear, abate, subside.

**decem** ten.

**december, bris, bre** belonging to December; *subst. m* December.

**decem-iugis, is** *m* chariot with ten horses.

**decem-peda, ae** *f* measuring-rod ten feet in length.

**decempedātor, ōris** *m* land-surveyor.

**decem-plex, plicis** tenfold.

**decem-scalmus** 3 having ten tholes *or* oars.

**decem-vir, ī** *m* one of a commission of ten men.

**decem-virālis, e** relating to the decemvirs.

**decemvirātus, ūs** *m* decemvirate, office of a decemvir.

**decēns, tis** becoming, seemly, decent; handsome, beautiful.

**decentia, ae** *f* comeliness, decency.

**deceō, uī, —** 2 to be comely, seemly, decent, to become, be suitable *or* proper (*alqm*).

**dē-ceptor, ōris** *m* deceiver.

**dec-ēris, is** *f* with oars worked by ten rowers.

**dē-cernō, crēvī, crētum** 3 1. to decide, determine, decree (*alqd; acc. c. inf.; ut*); **b)** to judge, vote for, resolve, fix, settle; **c)** to adjudge, award (*alci alqd*); **d)** to proclaim; **e)** to form a purpose *or* resolution; 2. **pugnam, proelium** to fight out (*cum alqo*), decide by combat.

**dē-cerpō, psī, ptum** 3 to pluck off; **a)** to take away; **b)** to enjoy.

**dē-certātiō, ōnis** *f* contest, decisive battle.

**dē-certō** 1 to fight to a decision, to fight out.

**dē-cessiō, ōnis** *f* a going away, departure; decrease.

**dēcessor, ōris** *m* predecessor.

**dēcessus, ūs** *m* a going away, departure; **a)** retirement of a magistrate; **b)** death.

**dē-cidō[1], cidī, —** 3 to fall down (*ab, ex, de re*), fall off; **a)** to sink down, die; **b)** to fail (*a spe*); **c)** to sink, perish.

**dē-cidō[2], cīdī, cīsum** 3 to cut *or* hew off; **a)** to decide, terminate, settle; to cut short; **b)** to agree, compromise (*cum alqo de re*).

**deciē(n)s** *adv.* ten times.

**decimānus** 3 1. belonging to tithes, **ager ~** land paying a tenth, **frumentum** a tithe of corn; *subst. ~, ī*

*m* tithe-farmer (**-na, ae** *f* tithe-farmer's wife); 2. belonging to the tenth cohort *or* legion; **porta** main gate of a Roman camp.

**decimō** 1 to take every tenth man for punishment.

**decimus** 3 the tenth; *subst.* **a)** **decimum, ī** *n* tenfold yield; **b)** **decima, ae** *f* a tenth part, tithe; largess.

**dē-cipiō, cēpī, ceptum** 3 to cheat, deceive (*alqm alqa r*[*r*]); **a)** to escape notice; **b)** to elude, beguile (*alqd*).

**dēcīsiō, ōnis** *f* agreement, settlement.

**dē-clāmātiō, ōnis** *f* practice in public speaking; loud talking.

**dē-clāmātor, ōris** *m* rhetorician, elocutionist. [rhetorical.]

**dē-clāmātōrius** 3 declamatory,]

**dē-clāmitō** 1, *intens. of* declamo.

**dē-clāmō** 1 1. *intr.* to practise public speaking, to speak loudly *or* violently; 2. *trans.* to declaim.

**dē-clārātiō, ōnis** *f* exposition, declaration.

**dē-clārātor, ōris** *m* announcer.

**dē-clārō** 1 to make clear *or* distinct; to declare, pronounce, explain, proclaim (*alci alqd; acc. c. inf.*).

**dēclīnātiō, ōnis** *f* a bending aside, turning away, inflection; **a)** an avoiding; **b)** rejection.

**dēclinis, e** turning aside, retreating.

**dē-clīnō** 1 1. *trans.* to bend aside, turn away (*alqd ab, de re in alqd*); to avoid, shun; 2. *intr.* to deviate, digress (*de, ab re*); to incline to (*in alqd*).

**dē-clīvis, e** sloping, inclined downwards; *subst.* **dēclīve, is** *n* declivity, slope.

**dēclīvitās, ātis** *f* declivity.

**dē-coctor, ōris** *m* spendthrift, bankrupt.

**dē-collō** 1 to behead.

**dē-cōlō** 1 to trickle away.

**dē-color, ōris** deprived of colour, discoloured; **a)** dark, tanned; **b)** degenerate.

**dēcolōrātiō, ōnis** *f* a discolouring.

**dē-colōrō** 1 to discolour; to stain.

**dē-condō** 3 to hide away.

**dē-coquō** 3 to boil; **a)** to boil down; *subst.* **dēcocta, ae** *f* a cold drink; **b)** to become bankrupt.

**decor, ōris** *m* **a)** comeliness, elegance; **b)** charm, beauty, grace.

**decorāmen, inis** *n* ornament.

**decorō** 1 **a)** to adorn, embellish; **b)** to honour, distinguish.

**decōrus** 3 **a)** fitting, seemly, becoming; **b)** beautiful, graceful, handsome; embellished, adorned.

**dē-crepitus** 3 very old, decrepit.

**dē-crēsco** 3 to become less *or* fewer, to decrease, lessen, disappear, vanish.

**dēcrētōrius** 3 decisive, final.

**dēcrētum, ī** *n* **a)** decree, decision, resolution; **b)** principle, doctrine.

**dē-culcō** 1 to kick *or* knock down.

**decuma, decumānus = decima, decimanus.**

**decumātēs agrī** *m/pl.* tributary *or* tithe-land.

**dē-cumbō, cubuī, cubitum** 3 to lie down; to fall down.

**decuria, ae** *f* a body *or* division of ten; division, class.

**decuriātiō, ōnis** *f and* -tus, ūs *m* a dividing into *decuriae*.

**decuriō**[1] 1 to divide (into *decuriae*).

**decuriō**[2], **ōnis** *m* **a)** commander of ten horse-soldiers; **b)** member of a municipal senate.

**decuriōnātus, ūs** *m* office of *decurio*.

**dē-currō, (cu)currī, cursum** 3 **1. a)** to run *or* hasten down, to fly, flow, sail, march down (*ab, ex, de re in or ad alqd*); **b)** to come away, hasten, travel; to march, manœuvre; **c)** to have recourse to, take refuge in; **2. a)** to run over, pass through; **b)** to discuss, treat.

**dē-cursiō, ōnis** *f and* -sus, ūs *m* **1. a)** a running down; **b)** military evolution, manœuvre; charge, attack; **c)** course, career; **2.** end of a course, completion.

**dē-curtō** 1 to curtail, mutilate.

**decus, oris** *n* **a)** ornament, beauty, splendour, glory, honour, dignity, worth, virtue; **b)** deed of honour, exploit.

**decussis, is** *m* coin worth ten *asses*.

**decussō** 1 to divide crosswise.

**dē-cutiō, cussī, cussum** 3 to shake off, strike down, throw down.

**dē-deceō** 2 to be unbecoming, unfitting, unseemly (*alqm*).

**dē-decor, oris** unseemly, shameful.

**dē-decorō** 1 to disgrace, dishonour, bring to shame.

**dē-decōrus** 3 disgraceful, shameful, dishonourable.

**dē-decus, oris** *n* disgrace, dishonour, infamy, shame; **a)** blot, blemish; **b)** crime, evil, vice.

**dē-dicātiō, ōnis** *f* consecration, dedication.

**dē-dicō** 1 **1.** to declare, specify; **2.** to dedicate, consecrate, inscribe, devote (*alci alqd*). [refusal.|

**dē-dignātiō, ōnis** *f* a scorning,|

**dē-dignor** 1 to disdain, reject, scorn.

**dē-discō** 3 to unlearn, forget.

**dēditīcius** 3 one who has surrendered *or* capitulated unconditionally; prisoner, subject.

**dēditiō, ōnis** *f* a giving up, surrender, capitulation.

**dēditus** 3 given up, surrendered; given to, devoted, addicted, engaged in (*with dat.*).

**dē-dō, didī, ditum** 3 **a)** to give up, surrender, deliver, consign, yield (*alci alqd*); **b)** **se dēdere** to surrender oneself, to capitulate; to apply, devote *or* dedicate oneself (*dat.*).

**dē-doceō** 2 to cause to unlearn.

**dē-doleō** 2 to cease grieving.

**dē-dolō** 1 to hew smooth.

**dē-dūcō** 3 **1.** to lead *or* bring down; to lead, fetch, draw down *or* away (*ab, ex, de re in or ad alqd*); **2. a)** to remove; **b)** to lead, conduct, escort, accompany; **c)** to lead forth, found a colony; **d)** to lead *or* turn away from, to dispossess; **e)** to seduce, mislead; **f)** to take away, subtract; **g)** to spin out (*a thread*); to compose; **3. a)** to conduct a bride to her husband; **b)** to conduct a young man to a public teacher; **c)** to divert, derive, deduce, reduce.

**dē-ductiō, ōnis** *f* a leading down *or* away (*alcis in alqd*); **a)** a leading forth, establishing, colonizing; **b)** ejection, expulsion; **c)** diminution, subtraction; **d)** inference.

**dē-ductor, ōris** *m* attendant, client.

**dē-ductus** 3 humble, weak, poor.

**de-errō** 1 to lose one's way, go astray.

**dē-faecō** 1 to cleanse, make clear.

**dē-faenerō** 1 to involve in debt.

**dē-fatīgātiō, ōnis** *f* weariness, fatigue, exhaustion.

**dē-fatīgō** 1 to weary out, fatigue, tire.

**dēfectiō, ōnis** *f* **1.** desertion, defection, rebellion, revolt; **2.** disappearance, eclipse; exhaustion, weakness.

**dēfector, ōris** *m* rebel, deserter.

**dēfectus¹, ūs** *m* = **defectio**.

**dēfectus²** 3, *see* **deficio**.

**dē-fendō, dī, sum** 3 1. to ward off, drive away, keep off, avert (*alci alqd*); 2. to defend, protect (*alqm ab alqo, in, adversus*); a) to maintain, sustain, support; b) to assert, allege in defence.

**dē-fēnerō** = **defaenero**.

**dēfēnsiō, ōnis** *f* a warding off; defence.

**dēfēnsitō** 1 *and* **dēfēnsō** 1 to (be wont to) defend; **causas** to be a lawyer.

**dēfēnsor, ōris** *m* a) one who wards off; b) defender, protector.

**dē-ferō** 3 1. to bring, bear, carry down, to throw down; 2. to remove, divert, drive off; 3. to carry *or* bring to a place (*pecuniam in aerarium*); to confer, transfer, deliver; a) to offer, grant, hand over; b) to bring *or* give an account of, to report, announce, tell; c) to inform against, indict, accuse; d) to register.

**dē-fervēscō, fervī (ferbuī), —** 3 to cease boiling *or* raging.

**dēfetīgō** 1 = **defatigo**.

**dē-fetiscor, fessus sum** 3 to become tired, grow weary *or* exhausted.

**dē-ficiō** 3 1. a) to rebel, revolt, desert, fall off (*ab alqo ad alqm*); b) to be wanting, fail, cease, become less, run out; c) to sink, faint, become weak, expire; d) (*animo*) to lose courage; to become eclipsed; 2. *trans.* a) to abandon, leave, desert; b) to fail; — **dēfectus** 3 abandoned; enfeebled, weak.

**dē-fīcō** = **defaeco**.

**dē-fīgō** 3 to fix *or* fasten into (*alqd in re*); a) to drive *or* fix down; b) to turn intently, direct (*oculos, lumina*); c) to render immovable, make fast, to fix in amazement, stupefy, astonish; to enchant; d) to imprint firmly; **P.** to fix oneself, to be deeply engaged in.

**dē-fingō** 3 a) to disfigure; b) to form, mould.

**dē-fīniō** 4 to bound, limit, terminate (*alqd re*); a) to define, determine, explain; b) to confine, restrict; c) to give a definition.

**dē-fīnītiō, ōnis** *f* a defining, limiting; a) a prescribing; b) definition.

**dē-fīnītīvus** 3 definitive, explanatory.

**dē-fīnītus** 3 a) defined, distinct; b) plain, perspicuous.

**dē-fīō, dēfierī** to fail, be wanting (*alci*).

**dē-flagrātiō, ōnis** *f* a consuming [by fire.

**dē-flagrō** 1 a) to burn down, be consumed by fire; b) to consume by fire; c) to cease burning, be allayed.

**dē-flectō, flexī, flexum** 3 1. to bend down *or* aside, to turn aside (*alqd de re in alqd, ad alqm*); 2. to turn away, lead astray; a) to alter; b) to turn oneself aside (*a, de re*).

**dē-fleō** 2 a) to weep for, bewail; to tell with tears; b) to weep violently.

**dē-floccō** 1 to depilate; **dēfloccātus** bald.

**dē-flōrēscō ruī, —** 3 to fade, wither.

**dē-fluō** 3 1. to flow down; a) to glide *or* fall down; b) to swim *or* sail down; c) to change to (*ad alqd*); 2. to flow away, cease flowing; to vanish.

**dē-fluus** 3 flowing down, descending, falling.

**dē-fodiō** 3 1. to dig up; 2. to dig in, cover with earth (*alqd in re, in rem*); to bury, hide.

**dē-fōrmātiō, ōnis** *f* a deforming, disfiguring; degradation.

**dē-fōrmis, e** 1. formless, without shape; 2. deformed, disfigured; a) hideous, ugly; b) disgraceful, shameful.

**dē-fōrmitās, ātis** *f* deformity, ugliness.

**dē-fōrmō** 1 1. to form, shape, delineate, depict; 2. to deform, disfigure; to disgrace, dishonour.

**dē-fraudō** 1 to deceive, cheat (*alqm alqa re*).

**dē-frēnātus** 3 unbridled.

**dē-fricō** 1 to rub down, rub hard; to lash, satirize.

**dē-fringō, frēgī, frāctum** 3 to break off.

**dē-frūdō** 1 = **defraudo**.

**dē-frūstror** 1 to cheat.

**dē-frutum, ī** *n* must boiled down.

**dē-fugiō** 3 to flee away; to flee from, avoid, shun (*with acc.*).

**dē-fundō** 3 to pour down *or* out, to empty.

**dē-fungor** 3 (*with abl.*) to have done with, to finish, complete, perform, discharge; to be discharged from office; to die.

**dē-futūtus** 3 worn out by debauchery.

**dē-gener, eris** degenerate, not genuine, unworthy of one's ancestors (*with gen.*); unworthy, ignoble, base.

**dē-generō** 1 1. *intr.* to become degenerate (*ab alqa re, in alqd*); to become unlike; 2. *trans.* to cause to degenerate, to dishonour, disgrace.

**dē-gerō** 3 to carry away.

**dē-glūbō** 3 to flay, skin.

**dēgō,** —, — 3 to pass (*time*), to live.

**dē-grandinat** 1 it hails violently.

**dē-grassor** 1 to assail.

**dē-gravō** 1 to press down, weigh down; to burden, distress.

**dē-gredior, gressus sum** 3 a) to go, march or walk down; to dismount; b) to go away.

**dē-grunniō** 4 to grunt out.

**dē-gustō** 1 to taste (*alqd*); to lick; a) to graze; b) to try, make a trial of, test.

**de-hibeō** 2 = **debeo.**

**dehinc** *adv.* from here; a) from this time, henceforth; b) thereupon, for the future; next.

**de-hīscō,** —, — 3 to gape, split open.

**de-honestāmentum, ī** *n* deformity, disgrace, dishonour.

**de-honestō** 1 to dishonour.

**de-hortor** 1 to advise to the contrary, to dissuade (*alqm ab re,* with *ne* or *inf.*); to alienate.

**dē-iciō, iēcī, iectum** 3 to throw, cast, hurl down; P. to rush down; a) to fell, prostrate, precipitate, tear down; b) to destroy, kill; to cast down (*oculos a re*), avert, turn away; c) to overthrow; d) to drive out, expel, drive from a position, drive off (*loco, re, ex* or *de re, in alqd*); to turn out of possession, dispossess; e) to prevent from obtaining, deprive (*abl.*); f) to remove, carry off.

**dē-iectiō, ōnis** *f* ejection, dispossession.

**dē-iectus¹** 3 low-lying, sunken; dejected, dispirited.

**dē-iectus², ūs** *m* a throwing down, hurling down; a) fall; b) declivity, depression.

**dē-ierō** 1 to swear solemnly.

**dein** *adv.* = **deinde.**

**deinceps** *adv.* successively, in order, in succession, following; immediately.

**deinde** *adv.* from there, then, next; thereafter, afterwards.

**dē-iungō** 3 to unyoke; to separate.

**dē-iuvō** 1 to deny help.

**dē-lābor** 3 a) to glide or fall down, sink; b) to glide away (*ab, de, ex re*); c) to be derived from (*ab alqo*); c) to fall into, to digress (*in, ad alqd*).

**dē-lacerō** 1 to tear to pieces.

**dē-lambō** 3 to lick.

**dē-lāmentor** 1 to bewail, lament.

**dē-lassō** 1 to weary, tire out.

**dē-lātiō, ōnis** *f* information against one, denunciation, accusation.

**dē-lātor, ōris** *m* informer, denoun-) **dēlēbilis, e** destructible. [cer.⌡

**dēlectābilis, e** delightful, pleasant.

**dēlectāmentum, ī** *n* delight, amusement. [amusement.⌡

**dēlectātiō, ōnis** *f* delight, pleasure,⌡

**dēlectō** 1 to delight, amuse, please, charm.

**dē-lēctus, ūs** *m* a) selection, choice; b) = **dilectus.**

**dē-lēgātiō, ōnis** *f* a delegating; assignment of a debt.

**dē-lēgō** 1 to send away, dispatch (*alqm in* or *ad alqd*); a) to transfer, give in charge, entrust; to assign, attribute; b) to refer to; c) to assign, make over a debt.

**dē-lēnificus** 3 soothing, winning.

**dē-lēnimentum, ī** *n* a) anything that soothes or charms; b) blandishment, charm, caress.

**dē-lēniō** 4 to soothe, charm, caress.

**dē-lēnitor, ōris** *m* soother, cajoler.

**dēleō, ēvī, ētum** 2 to blot out, obliterate; to destroy, annihilate, abolish, finish (*bellum*).

**dēlētrix, īcis** *f* she who destroys.

**dēlīberābundus** 3 reflecting, deliberating maturely.

**dēlīberātiō, ōnis** *f* deliberation, reflection, consideration.

**dēlīberātīvus** 3 deliberative; requiring deliberation.

**dēlīberātor, ōris** *m* one who deliberates.

**dē-līberō** 1 a) to weigh carefully, consider, consult (*de re, alqd*); b) to resolve, decide; c) to consult an oracle.

**dē-libō** 1 to take away a little, to take from; a) to enjoy; b) to detract, diminish (*alqd de re*).

**dē-librō** 1 to bark, peel.

**dē-libūtus** 3 besmeared, anointed.

**dēlicātus** 3 1. delightful, charming, pleasing; luxurious, voluptuous, tender, soft; 2. nice, dainty, effeminate, spoiled.

**dēliciae, ārum** *f/pl.* (*also* **-ia, ae** *f and* **-ium, ī** *n*) delight, pleasure, luxury, voluptuousness; a) favourite, darling, sweetheart; b) ornament.

**dēliciolae, ārum** *f/pl.* (*and* **dēliciolum, ī** *n*) darling.

**dē-licō** 1 to explain.

**dēlictum, ī** *n* fault, offence, crime, trespass.

**dēlicuus** (*or* **-uos**) 3 lacking.

**dē-ligō[1], lēgī, lēctum** 3 to pick, pluck; a) to choose, pick out, select; b) to separate, remove; **dēlēctī, ōrum** *m/pl.* picked men.

**dē-ligō[2]** 1 to bind *or* tie together, to fasten (*alqd ad alqd*).

**dē-lingō** 3 to lick.

**dē-linquō, līquī, lictum** 3 to fail, commit a crime, transgress.

**dē-liquēscō, licuī, —** 3 to melt, dissolve.

**dē-liquiō, ōnis** *f* lack, loss.

**dēlīrāmentum, ī** *n* folly, nonsense.

**dēlīrātiō, ōnis** *f* silliness, folly, madness.

**dē-līrō** 1 to be silly, mad, insane.

**dēlīrus** 3 silly, mad, insane, crazy.

**dē-litēscō, lituī, —** 3 to conceal oneself, lie hid.

**dē-lītigō** 1 to scold *or* rail.

(**delphin, inis** *and*) **delphīnus, ī** *m* dolphin.

**dēlūbrum, ī** *n* sanctuary, shrine, temple.

**dē-luctor** (*and* **-ō**) 1 to wrestle.

**dē-lūdificō** (*and* **-or**) 1 to mock, jeer, hoax.

**dē-lūdō, sī, sum** 3 to mock, delude, deceive.

**dē-lumbis, e** feeble.

**dē-lumbō** 1 to make lame, weaken.

**dē-madēscō, duī, —** 3 to become quite wet.

**dē-mandō** 1 to give in charge, intrust (*alci alqd*).

**dē-mānō** 1 to flow down.

**dēm-archus, ī** *m* ruler of a district, tribune of the people.

**dē-mēns, tis** out of one's senses, mad, insane, foolish.

**dēmentia, ae** *f* folly, madness, insanity.

**dē-mentiō** 4 to be mad.

**dē-mereor** (*and* **-reō**) 2 to earn; to deserve well of.

**dē-mergō, rsī, rsum** 3 a) to submerge, dip, plunge, immerse; b) to cast down, sink, overwhelm.

**dē-mētātus** 3 measured out, marked.

**dē-mētior, mēnsus sum** 4 to measure off *or* out.

**dē-metō, (messuī,) messum** 3 to mow, cut off, reap.

**dē-migrātiō, ōnis** *f* emigration.

**dē-migrō** 1 to migrate, emigrate, remove; to depart from.

**dē-minuō** 3 to make less *or* smaller, to diminish; to take away (*alqd de or ex re*).

**dē-minūtiō, ōnis** *f* a lessening, diminution; a) decrease, loss; b) loss of dignity, of civil rights.

**dē-miror** 1 to wonder at, be amazed.

**dē-missīcius** 3 hanging down.

**dē-missiō, ōnis** *f* a letting down, lowering.

**dē-mitigō** 1 to make mild.

**dē-mittō** 3 to send *or* let down, to lower, drop, to cast, thrust *or* put down; a) to sink down; to fix, drive *or* plunge into; to lead to a lower position; b) **se dēmittere** (*or* **P.**) to go, flow, let oneself down, to condescend, stoop, engage in; — **dēmissus** 3 lowered, hanging down, low; a) feeble, weak; b) modest, humble, unassuming; c) downcast, dispirited; d) poor, needy.

**dēmiūrgus, ī** *m* chief magistrate in some Greek states.

**dēmō, dēmpsī, dēmptum** 3 to take away (*alqd de re; alci alqd*), to withdraw, subtract, remove.

**dē-mōlior** 4 a) to pull *or* throw down, to destroy, demolish; b) to remove.

**dē-mōlītiō, ōnis** *f* a tearing down, demolition.

**dē-mōnstrātiō, ōnis** *f* a showing, pointing out; a) description, representation, explanation, proof; b) laudatory speech.

**dēmōnstrātīvus** 3·a) demonstrative; b) laudatory.

**dē-mōnstrātor, ōris** *m* one who points out, indicator.

**dē-mōnstrō** 1 to show, point out, indicate; **a)** to describe, explain, mention; **b)** to prove, demonstrate.

**dē-mordeō** 2 to bite (off).

**dē-morior** 3 to die; to be dying of love for (*alqm*).

**dē-moror** 1 **1.** to delay, linger; **2.** *trans.* to stop, hinder, delay.

**dē-moveō** 2 to move *or* put away, remove, drive out; to turn away, divert.

**dē-mūgītus** 3 filled with the noise of bellowing.

**dē-mulceō** 2 to stroke caressingly.

**dēmum** *adv.* **1.** at length, at last; **a)** now at last, then indeed, not till then; **b)** only; **2.** precisely, certainly.

**dē-murmurō** 1 to mutter over.

**dē-mūtō** 1 to change, alter.

**dēnārius** 3 containing ten (*asses*); *subst.* **dēnārius, ī** *m* a Roman silver coin.

**dē-nārrō** 1 to tell, relate exactly.

**dē-nāsō** 1 to deprive of the nose.

**dē-natō** 1 to swim down.

**dē-negō** 1 **a)** to deny; **b)** to refuse, reject a request.

**dēnī, ae, a** ten each, ten at a time, by tens,

**dē-nicālis, e** relating to the dead, funeral.

**dēnique** *adv.* at last, at length, finally; **a)** in short, in a word, in fine; **b)** then indeed; **c)** even, certainly, at least; just, precisely; only.

**dē-nōminō** 1 to name, call.

**dē-normō** 1 to make irregular.

**dē-notō** 1 to mark out, indicate, denote, point out; to stigmatize.

**dēns, tis** *m* tooth; **a)** the tooth of envy, of slander, of hatred, of time; **b)** spike, prong.

**dēnseō, —, — 2** *and* **dēnsō** 1 to make thick, to thicken, press together, condense; to crowd together.

**dēnsus** 3 thick, close, dense; **a)** crowded together, pressed together; **b)** frequent, following closely, uninterrupted.

**dentālia, ium** *n/pl.* share-beam of a plough, ploughshare.

**dentātus** 3 provided with teeth.

**denti-frangibulus** 3 breaking teeth.

**denti-frangibulum, ī** *n* instrument for breaking teeth, fist.

**denti-legus** 3 collecting teeth.

**dentiō** 4 to cut one's teeth; (of teeth) to grow (through lack of use).

**denti-scalpium, ī** *n* toothpick.

**dē-nūbō** 3 to marry (*of a woman*).

**dē-nūdō** 1 to lay bare, make naked; **a)** to uncover; **b)** to rob, plunder.

**dē-numerō** 1 to pay (down).

**dē-nūntiātiō, ōnis** *f* announcement, declaration, proclamation; threat, menace, warning, order.

**dē-nūntiō** 1 to announce, declare, proclaim; **a)** to menace, threaten; **b)** to foretell, prophesy; **c)** to direct, order, command; **d)** to give notice of.

**dēnuō** *adv.* anew, again.

**dēnus** tenth.

**de-onerō** 1 to unload, disburden.

**de-orsum** (*and* **-us**) *adv.* downwards, down.

**de-ōsculor** 1 to kiss affectionately.

**dē-paciscor** 3 = **depeciscor.**

**dē-pāctus** firmly fixed.

**dē-parcus** 3 niggardly.

**dē-pāscō** (*and* **-scor**) 3 to feed on, to consume.

**dē-peciscor, pectus sum** 3 **a)** to make an agreement (*cum alqo, ut*); **b)** to bargain for (*sibi alqd*).

**dē-pectō —, pexum** 3 to comb.

**dē-pecūlātor, ōris** *m* plunderer, embezzler.

**dē-pecūlātus, ūs** *m* swindling.

**dē-pecūlor** 1 to plunder, rob (*alqm alqa re*).

**dē-pellō, pulī, pulsum** 3 **a)** to drive down; **b)** to drive away, expel, remove (*alqm alqa re, ab, de, ex re*); **c)** to wean; **d)** to keep off; **e)** to displace, avert, to drive out of one's course.

**dē-pendeō, —, — 2** to hang down, hang from, to depend upon (*a re*).

**dē-pendō, ndī, nsum** 3 to pay.

**dē-perdō, didī, ditum** 3 to ruin, destroy; to lose.

**dē-pereō, —,** to perish, be lost, be ruined utterly; (*trans.*) to be desperately in love with.

**dē-pilō** 1 to depilate.

**dē-pingō** 3 to depict, paint, portray; to describe.

**dē-plangō** 3 to bewail, lament.

**dē-pleō** 2 to empty, exhaust.

**dē-plexus** 3 winding oneself round, gripping.

**dē-plōrābundus** 3 lamenting.

**dē-plōrātiō, ōnis** *f* lamentation.

**dē-plōrō** 1 **1.** to weep violently (*de re*); **2.** *trans.* to bewail, deplore; to give up as lost.

**dē-pluŏ** 3 to rain down.

**dē-poliŏ** 4 to smooth, polish.

**dē-pōnō** 3 to put, place, lay down (*alqd in re, in rem*), **arma** to lay down arms; **a)** to deposit, commit to the charge of (*alqd apud alqm, in re*), to intrust; **b)** to give up, lay aside, resign, get rid of, renounce; **dēpositus** 3 despaired of, given up, dead, **dēpositum, ī** n deposit, trust.

**dē-populātiō, ōnis** f a laying waste, pillaging.

**dē-populātor, ōris** m spoiler, pillager.

**dē-populor** (*and* -**lō**) 1 to lay waste, pillage.

**dē-portō** 1 **a)** to carry down or away (*alqd ex re in* or *ad alqd*), take away; **b)** to bring home; **c)** to banish, exile.

**dē-poscō, poposcī,** — 3 to demand or request earnestly (*alqd, sibi alqd, alqm alqd*); **a)** to demand for punishment; **b)** to challenge.

**dēpositum, ī** n, *see* depono.

**dē-postulō** 1 to demand.

**dē-prāvātē** wrongly.

**dē-prāvātiō, ōnis** f **a)** distorting; **b)** perversion, corruption.

**dē-prāvō** 1 to distort, pervert; **a)** to disfigure; **b)** to spoil, corrupt.

**dēprecābundus** 3 earnestly entreating.

**dē-precātiō, ōnis** f **1.** an averting by entreaty; **a)** apology; **b)** deprecation; **2.** appeal, intercession.

**dē-precātor, ōris** m intercessor, averter.

**dē-precor** 1 **1.** to avert by entreaty, deprecate, beg to escape (*alqd ab alqo*); to pray for forgiveness; **2.** to pray for, intercede in behalf of (*alqm* or *alqd ab alqo*; *ut, ne*).

**dē-prehendō** 3 to seize, lay hold of; **a)** to catch, snatch; **b)** to surprise, detect, overtake, apprehend, discover; **c)** to confine, bring into a difficulty; **d)** to perceive, understand, discover, find.

**dē-prehēnsiō, ōnis** f a catching, detection.

**dē-prēndō, ndī, nsum** 3 = deprehendo.

**dē-primō, pressī, pressum** 3 to press or weigh down; **a)** to sink (*a ship*); to place deep in the ground; **b)** to depress, oppress; **c)** to depreciate; **dēpressus** 3 sunken, low.

**dē-proelior** 1 to fight furiously.

**dē-prōmō** 3 to draw or bring forth, to bring out, to fetch (*alqd ex, de, ab re*); to derive, obtain.

**dē-properō** 1 to hasten.

**depsō, suī, stum** 3 to knead.

**dē-pudet, uit** — 2 to cease to be ashamed (*alqm* with *inf.*).

**dē-pūgis, e** with thin buttocks.

**dē-pugnō** 1 to fight out, to the end, decisively (*cum alqo*).

**dēpulsiō, ōnis** f a driving away or off; defence.

**dē-pulsō** 1 to drive away.

**dēpulsor, ōris** m one who drives away.

**dē-pungō** 3 to prick, mark.

**dē-purgō** 1 to clean out.

**dē-putō** 1 **1.** to cut off; **2.** to reckon, estimate.

**dē-pȳgis, e = depugis.**

**dēque** = et de; *see* susque.

**dē-questus** 3 (*pf. part. of dequeror*) complaining of (*with acc.*).

**dē-rādō** to scrape off.

**dērēctus** 3 = directus.

**dē-relictiō, ōnis** f a forsaking.

**dē-relinquō** 3 to forsake wholly, to abandon, desert.

**dē-repente** *adv.* suddenly.

**dē-rēpō** 3 to creep down.

**dē-rīdeō** 2 to laugh at, mock.

**dē-rīdiculus** 3 very ridiculous; *subst.* -**culum, ī** n object of ridicule, mockery.

**dē-rigēscō, riguī,** — 3 to become quite stiff.

**dē-rigō = dirigo.**

**dē-ripiō, ripuī, reptum** 3 to tear down or off (*alqd de re*); **a)** to snatch away (*alci alqd*), to pull down; **b)** to curtail, detract from.

**dē-rīsor, ōris** m derider, mocker.

**dē-rīsus, ūs** m mockery.

**dērīvātiō, ōnis** f diversion.

**dē-rīvō** 1 to lead off, turn away, divert (*alqd ex re in alqd*); to derive.

**dē-rogātiō, ōnis** f partial repeal.

**dē-rogō** 1 **a)** to take away; detract (*alqd de, ex re; alci alqd*); **b)** to repeal in part.

**dē-rōsus** 3 gnawed away.

**dē-runcinō** 1 to plane off; to cheat.

**dē-ruō** 3 to cast down, overturn.

**dē-ruptus** 3 precipitous, steep.

**dē-sacrō** 1 to dedicate.

**dē-saeviō** 4 to rage furiously.

**dē-saltō** 1 to dance.

**dē-scendō, ndī, nsum** 3 to go, come, climb down, to descend (*a, de, ex re* in or *ad alqd*); **a)** to sink down, penetrate; **b)** to descend, stoop, yield, agree to, lower oneself (*ad* or in *alqd*).

**dēscēnsiō, ōnis** *f and* **dēscēnsus, ūs** *m* a descending; descent, way down.

**dē-scīscō, scīvī** *and* **sciī, scītum** 3 to revolt from, desert (*ab algo ad alqm; a re*), to go over; to withdraw, depart, deviate.

**dē-scrībō** 3 1. to copy, transcribe; 2. to sketch, draw, depict, describe, delineate; a) to define, explain, assign, allot, appoint, fix, prescribe; b) = **discribo**.

**dē-scrīptiō, ōnis** *f* delineation; a) transcript, copy; b) definition, disposition, division, arrangement; c) description, representation.

**dē-scrīptus** 3 well arranged, precisely ordered.

**dē-secō, cuī, ctum** 1 to cut off.

**dē-serō, seruī, sertum** 3 to forsake, abandon; a) to desert, leave; b) to give up, neglect; **dēsertus** 3 deserted, forsaken (*a re*), solitary, lonely, waste; *subst.* **dēserta, ōrum** *n/pl.* deserts, wastes, wilderness.

**dē-serpō** 3 to creep down.

**dēsertor, ōris** *m* a) deserter, runaway, fugitive; b) abandoning, neglecting (*gen.*).

**dēsertus** 3 *and* **-ta** *n/pl., see* **desero**.

**dē-serviō** 4 to serve diligently (*alci*).

**dēses, idis** inactive, idle, indolent.

**dē-siccō** 1 to dry up.

**dē-sideō, sēdī, sessum** 2 to sit idle.

**dēsīderābilis, e** desirable, to be longed for.

**dēsīderātiō, ōnis** *f* = **desiderium**.

**dēsīderium, ī** *n* a longing, desire, yearning; wish, request.

**dē-sīderō** 1 to long for, desire, wish for, require, ask (*alqd ab algo*; with *inf.* or *acc. c. inf.*); to miss, lack, lose; **P.** to be lost.

**dēsidia, ae** *f* inactivity, idleness.

**dēsidiābulum, ī** *n* lounging-place.

**dēsidiōsus** 3 idle, lazy, indolent; causing idleness.

**dē-sīdō, sēdī** *and* **sīdī, —** 3 to sink down, fall, settle.

**dē-signātiō, ōnis** *f* designing, describing; appointment.

**dē-signātor, ōris** *m* = **dissignator.**

**dē-signō** 1 to mark out, point out by signs; a) to allude to; b) to designate, represent, copy; c) to appoint to a magistracy.

**dē-siliō, siluī, (sultum)** 4 to leap down.

**dē-sinō, siī, situm** 3 to leave off, desist, cease (*alcis rei*; with *inf.*); a) to end, close (*in alqd*); b) to abandon.

**dē-sipientia, ae** *f* folly.

**dē-sipiō, —, —** 3 a) to be foolish *or* silly; b) to act foolishly.

**dē-sistō, stitī, —** 3 to desist, leave off, cease (*re, de* or *a re*, with *inf.*).

**dē-sōlō** 1 to make solitary, to forsake, leave alone.

**dē-spectō** 1 a) = **despicio**; b) to tower above.

**dēspectus**[1] 3 = **despicatus**.

**dēspectus**[2]**, ūs** *m* 1. view, prospect; 2. contempt.

**dēspēranter** *adv.* despairingly.

**dē-spērātiō, ōnis** *f* hopelessness, despair.

**dē-spērō** 1 to be hopeless, to despair (*de re, alqd*); with *acc. c. inf.*); **dēspērātus** 3 a) hopeless, desperate; b) given up, despaired of.

**dēspicātiō, ōnis** *f and* **-tus**[1]**, ūs** *m* contempt.

**dēspicātus**[2] 3 despised, contemptible.

**dēspicientia, ae** *f* contempt.

**dē-spiciō, spexī, spectum** 3 1. to look down upon; a) to overtop, command; b) to despise, disdain; 2. to look away.

**dē-spoliātor, ōris** *m* robber, plunderer.

**dē-spoliō** 1 to plunder, despoil.

**dē-spondeō, spondī, spōnsum** 2 1. to promise formally, pledge; to betroth, promise in marriage (*alci alqm*); 2. **animum** to lose courage, to despond.

**dē-spōnsō** 1 to betroth.

**dē-spūmō** 1 a) to skim; b) to dissipate the fumes of (*wine*); c) to shed scum; d) to cease foaming, abate.

**dē-spuō — —** 3 to spit out.

**dē-squāmō** 1 to scale (*fish*).

**dē-stertō, tuī, —** 3 to cease snoring *or* dreaming.

**dē-stillō** 1 to drop down, drip.

**dē-stimulō** 1 = **distimulo.**

**dēstinātiō, ōnis** f determination, resolution; appointment.

**dēstinō** 1 to make fast or firm (*alqd alqa re, ad alqd*); **a)** to fix, determine, settle, resolve; **b)** to aim at, to intend, choose; **c)** to betroth, designate as a wife for; **dēstinātus** 3 determined, fixed, intended; *subst.* **dēstinātum, ī** n plan, purpose.

**dē-stituō, tuī, tūtum** 3 **1.** to set down, place; **2.** to leave, forsake, abandon; to deceive, betray (*alqm in re*), **spe** and **a spe** to deprive of hope; **dēstitūtus** 3 forsaken, deceived, deprived, needy, helpless.

**dēstitūtiō, ōnis** f a forsaking; disappointment.

**dē-stringō** 3 to strip off; **a)** to draw, bare (*the sword*), brandish; **b)** to touch lightly, graze; **c)** to criticize, satirize; **dēstrictus** 3 sharp, severe, rigid.

**dē-structiō, ōnis** f a pulling down; refutation.

**dē-struō** 3 to pull down, tear down, demolish.

**dē-subitō** *adv.* suddenly.

**dē-sūdāscō** 3 to sweat profusely.

**dē-sūdō** 1 to sweat greatly; to exert or fatigue oneself.

**dē-suēfīō, fierī** to become unaccustomed, estranged (*a re*).

**dē-suēscō** 3 = **desuefio.**

**dēsuētūdō, inis** f disuse, want of practice.

**dē-suētus** 3 unused, out of use; unaccustomed (*with inf.*).

**dēsultor, ōris** m leaper, circus-rider.

**dēsultōrius** 3 (*equus*) circus-rider's horse.

**dē-sultūra, ae** f a leaping down.

**dē-sum, fuī, esse** to be absent or away, to be wanting (*alci rei, ad alqd*); **a)** to fail, abandon, desert, neglect; **b)** to lose the opportunity; **sibi deesse** to betray oneself, to be wanting in one's duty.

**dē-sūmō** 3 to choose, select.

**dē-super** *adv.* from above.

**dē-surgō** 3 to rise.

**dē-tegō** 3 to uncover, lay bare, unroof; to reveal, disclose.

**dē-tendō, —, tēnsum** 3 to unstretch, take down.

**dē-tergeō** 2 to wipe off; **a)** to break off, sweep away; **b)** to cleanse.

**dēterior, ius** *comp.* worse, inferior,

lower, poorer, meaner; *superl.* **dēterrimus** 3 worst, lowest, last.

**dē-terminātiō, ōnis** f boundary, end.

**dē-terminō** 1 to bound, limit.

**dē-terō** 3 to rub off or away, to file away; **a)** to wear away; **b)** to lessen, weaken, impair.

**dē-terreō** 2 to frighten off, deter (*alqm a, de re*; with *abl.*; with *ne* or *inf.*); **a)** to prevent, hinder, discourage (*alqm a re*); **b)** to keep off, ward off (*alqd ab alqo*).

**dētestābilis, e** detestable, execrable, abominable.

**dē-testātiō, ōnis** f a cursing, execration; an averting (*by sacrifice*).

**dē-testor** 1 to curse, execrate; **a)** to avert, ward off, deprecate (*alqd ab alqo*); **b)** to call down upon (*alqd in alqm*).

**dē-texō** 3 to weave, plait; to finish.

**dē-tineō, tinuī, tentum** 2 **a)** to keep back, detain, to check, hold away (*alqm a re*); **b)** to keep, occupy, engage; **c)** to withhold (*money*); **d) se dētinēre** to support existence.

**dē-tondeō, tondī, tōnsum** 2 to shear off, clip; to strip.

**dē-tonō, uī, —** 1 **a)** to thunder down; **b)** to cease to thunder or to rage.

**dē-torqueō** 2 **a)** to turn away or off, bend aside, to avert (*alqd a re ad* or *in alqd*); **b)** to twist, distort.

**dē-tractātiō, ōnis** f = **detrectatio.**

**dē-tractiō, ōnis** f a drawing or taking away; removal.

**dē-tractō** = **detrecto.**

**dē-tractor, ōris** m disparager, detractor.

**dē-trahō** 3 **1.** to draw or take down, pull down (*alqd de, a re, re*); to humiliate; **2.** to take away, remove, withdraw (*de, ex re, alci alqd*), drag; **a)** to disparage, detract, calumniate, slander; **b)** to drag away, take from; **c)** to drag or bring to (*alqd ad* or *in alqd*).

**dētrectātiō, ōnis** f a declining, refusal.

**dē-trectātor, ōris** m = **detractor.**

**dē-trectō** 1 **a)** to decline, refuse; **b)** to detract from, disparage.

**dētrīmentōsus** 3 hurtful, detrimental.

**dētrīmentum, ī** n damage, loss, injury; defeat.

**dē-trūdō** 3 **1.** to thrust down *or* away; a) to drive away, dislodge; b) to force away (*de, ex re*); **2.** a) to force, compel (*ad, in alqd*); b) to postpone, put off.

**dē-truncō** 1 to lop *or* cut off; to mutilate, behead.

**dē-tumēscō, muī,** — 3 to cease being swollen, to subside.

**dē-turbō** 1 to thrust down, cast down, drive away (*de, ex, a re*); to eject, dispossess.

**dē-turpō** 1 to disfigure.

**de-unx, cis** *m* eleven twelfths.

**de-ūrō** 3 to burn, destroy; to nip.

**deus, ī** *m* a god, deity, divine being; a) tutelary god; b) person in power.

**de-ūtor** 3 to misuse, maltreat.

**dē-vāstō** 1 to lay waste, devastate.

**dē-vehō** 3 to convey, carry *or* bear down *or* away (*alqd ex re in* or *ad alqd*); **P.** to sail.

**dē-vellō** 3 to pull, pluck *or* tear away.

**dē-vēlō** 1 to unveil, uncover.

**dē-veneror** 1 to venerate, worship.

**dē-veniō** 4 to come to, arrive.

**dē-verbeor** 1 to cudgel well.

**dē-versor**[1] 1 to lodge as a guest, put up.

**dē-versor**[2]**, ōris** *m* guest (*in an inn*).

**dēversōriolum, ī** *n* little inn.

**dēversōrium, ī** *n* inn, lodging; tavern; place of retreat.

**dēversōrius** 3 (fit) for lodging in.

**dēverticulum, ī** *n* 1. by-road; digression; refuge; 2. = deversorium.

**dē-vertō** 3 to turn away *or* aside (*trans.* and *intr.*); to go to lodge (*in alqd, ad* or *apud alqm*), to put up; to digress.

**dē-vēscor** 3 to devour.

**dēvexitās, ātis** *f* declivity.

**dēvexus** 3 inclining, sloping; sinking, steep.

**dē-vinciō** 4 to bind, tie fast; a) to fasten, connect (*alqd cum alqo*); b) to pledge, oblige, lay under obligation (*re*); c) to devote *or* attach to (*re*); **dēvinctus** 3 devoted to, strongly attached.

**dē-vincō** 3 to conquer completely, to overcome, subdue; to carry through, enforce (*ut*).

**dē-vītātiō, ōnis** *f* an avoiding.

**dē-vītō** 1 to avoid.

**dē-vius** 3 out of the way, off the road; a) retired, sequestered, secluded; b) solitary, wandering; c) inconstant, foolish; **dēvium** (*iter*) by-way.

**dē-vocō** 1 a) to call down; b) to call away *or* off, to recall (*alqm ab, ex, de re ad* or *in alqd*); c) to invite; d) to allure, seduce.

**dē-volō** 1 a) to fly down; to hasten down; b) to fly away.

**dē-volvō** 3 to roll down *or* downwards; **P.** to roll oneself down, to fall headlong.

**dē-vorō** 1 to swallow down, devour; a) to consume, waste; b) to bear patiently, endure; c) to devour eagerly, absorb; d) to enjoy.

**dēvortium, ī** *n* by-way.

**dē-vors-, -vort- = dē-vers-, -vert-.**

**dē-vōtiō, ōnis** *f* a devoting, consecrating; a) vow, curse, execration; b) incantation, spell.

**dē-vōtō** 1 to lay a spell on.

**dē-voveō** 2 to vow, devote, offer, consecrate; to devote to death (*alci alqd, se pro alqo*); a) to curse; to bewitch; b) to give up, destine. appoint; — **dēvōtus** 3 devoted (*alci*); accursed.

**dextāns, tis** *m* five sixths.

**dextella, ae** *f* a little right hand.

**dexter, t(e)ra, t(e)rum** right, on the right hand; a) propitious; b) suitable, fitting; c) skilful, handy, dexterous; — *subst.* **dext(e)ra, ae** *f* right hand, right side; fidelity, pledge of friendship, bravery; **dext(e)rā** *adv.* (and *prep.* with *acc.*) on the right (of); *comp.* **dexterior, ius,** *superl.* **dextumus** and **dextimus.**

**dext(e)rē** adroitly.

**dexteritās, ātis** *f* skilfulness, dexterity.

**dextrōrsum** (*or* -**sus**) *adv.* towards the right hand, to the right.

**dextrō-vorsum = dextrōrsum.**

**dextumus** 3, *see* dexter.

**diabathrārius, ī** *m* maker of low Greek shoes.

**dia-dēma, atis** *n* royal headdress, diadem.

**diaeta, ae** *f* a) mode of living (*prescribed by a physician*); b) room.

**dia-lecticus** 3 dialectical; *subst.* a) ~, **ī** *m*, dialectician, logician; b) -**a, ae** *f* dialectics, art of discussion.

**dialectus, ī** *f* dialect.

**diālis, e** of Juppiter.

**dia-logus, ī** *m* dialogue, conversation.

**dia-nomē, ēs** *f* distribution.

**dia-pasma, atis** *n* powder for sprinkling.

**diārium, ī** *n* daily ration *or* allowance.

**dia-trēta; ōrum** *n/pl.* cups decorated with filigree.

**di-baphus, ī** *f* purple-striped state-robe.

**dica, ae** *f* lawsuit, action; jury.

**dicācitās, ātis** *f* pungent wit, raillery.

**dicāculus** 3 witty, satirical.

**dicātiō, ōnis** *f* a settling as a citizen in another state.

**dicāx, ācis** satirical, witty.

**dichorēus, ī** *m* double-trochee.

**diciō, ōnis** *f* jurisdiction; authority, power, control.

**dicis causā** for form's sake, for the sake of appearance.

**dicō¹** 1 to dedicate, consecrate, devote to a god (*alci alqd*); to devote, give up to; **se civitati** *or* **in civitatem** to become a citizen of another state.

**dicō², dīxī, dictum** 3 1. a) to fix, appoint, settle; b) to name, appoint, proclaim (*alqm dictatorem*); 2. to say, speak, utter, tell, relate, mention, declare, affirm; a) to plead (*causam*), to pronounce judgment (*ius*); b) to deliver an oration, **ars dīcendī** art of eloquence; c) to name, call (*alqm nomine, alci nomen*); d) to sing, celebrate in verse; e) to describe, narrate.

**di-crotum, ī** *n* (*and* **-ta, ae** *f*) vessel with two banks of oars.

**dictamnus, ī** *f and* **-num, ī** *n* dittany (*a plant*).

**dictāta, ōrum** *n/pl., see* dicto.

**dictātor, ōris** *m* chief magistrate with absolute power, dictator.

**dictātōrius** 3 of a dictator.

**dictātrīx, īcis** *f* mistress.

**dictātūra, ae** *f* dictatorship.

**dictērium, ī** *n* witty remark.

**dictiō, ōnis** *f* a saying, speaking, uttering; **causae** defence; a) answer of an oracle; b) conversation; c) declamation, speech; diction, style.

**dictitō** 1 to say often, maintain, assert repeatedly.

**dictō** 1 1. to say often, reiterate (*alci alqd*); 2. a) to dictate; b) to compose, draw up; *subst.* **dictāta, ōrum** *n/pl.* dictation, lesson, precepts.

**dictum, ī** *n* a saying; a) word, remark; b) maxim, proverb, sentence; c) order, command; d) promise; e) witty saying.

**dī-dō, dīdidī, dīditum** 3 to distribute, spread, disseminate.

**dī-dūcō** 3 to draw apart; a) to separate, sever, divide; b) to expand, disjoin; c) to disperse, scatter, separate forcibly.

**diēcula, ae** *f* a little while.

**diērēctus** 3 (? = crucified) ruined, 'done for'; (ab)i **diērēctus** *or* **diērēctē** (*adv.*), go and be hanged!

**diēs, ēī** *m* (*and* *f*) 1. day; daylight, daytime; a day's march *or* journey; 2. fixed day *or* time, appointed time, term; birthday, day of death; 3. space of time, period, time.

**dif-fāmō** 1 to divulge, to spread abroad an evil report, to defame.

**differēns, entis** different.

**differentia, ae** (*and* **-feritās, ātis**) *f* difference, diversity.

**dif-ferō, distulī, dīlātum** 3 1. to carry different ways; a) to spread abroad, disperse; to publish, report, circulate; to defame; b) to put off, delay, postpone, protract; c) to separate, scatter; to distract; 2. *intr.* to differ, be different, vary (*ab alqo, inter se*).

**dif-fertus** 3 stuffed full (*abl.*).

**dif-fibulō** 1 to unclasp.

**dif-ficilis, e** difficult, hard, troublesome; a) dangerous, critical; b) morose, surly, captious, obstinate; *adv.* **difficulter, difficiliter, difficile.**

**difficultās, ātis** *f* difficulty, trouble; a) need, poverty, distress; b) moroseness, obstinacy.

**diffīdēns, tis** distrustful, uneasy.

**dif-fīdentia, ae** *f* distrust.

**dif-fīdō, fīsus sum** 3 to distrust.

**dif-findō** 3 to cleave asunder, split; to break off; to open; to interrupt.

**dif-fingō** 3 to transform, form anew.

**dif-fiteor, —, —** 2 to deny, disavow.

**dif-flāgitō** 1 to harass with demands.

**dif-flō** 1 to disperse by blowing.

**dif-fluō** 3 to flow in different directions, to flow away; to be dissolved, to melt away, disappear.

**dif-fringō, —, frāctum** 3 to break to pieces.

**dif-fugiō**, 3 to flee in different directions; to disperse, be scattered.

**diffugium**, ī *n* dispersion.

**dif-fulminō** 1 to scatter like a thunderbolt.

**dif-funditō** 1 to dissipate.

**dif-fundō** 3 to spread by pouring, to pour forth in all directions; **a)** to spread, scatter, diffuse; **b)** to extend, expand; **c)** to gladden, cheer up; — **diffūsus** 3 extended, extensive, spread out; prolix.

**dif-fūsilis**, e expansive.

**dif-fūsiō**, ōnis *f* expansion; *animi* cheerfulness.

**dif-futūtus** 3 exhausted by debauchery.

**di-gamma** *n* the digamma; investment- *or* interest-book.

**dī-gerō** 3 **a)** to separate, divide; **b)** to distribute (*alqd in alqd*); **c)** to put in order, arrange.

**dī-gestiō**, ōnis *f* (*and* -tus, ūs *m*) distribution, enumeration.

**digitulus**, ī *m* a little finger.

**digitus**, ī *m* 1. finger; extremus **digitus** tip of the finger; a finger's breadth, inch; 2. toe.

**dī-gladior** 1 to fight for life and death, to contend fiercely.

**dignātiō**, ōnis *f* reputation, honour, rank.

**dignitās**, ātis *f* worthiness, merit; **a)** dignity, grandeur, splendour, dignified exterior, majesty, distinction, eminence; **b)** personal dignity, honour, esteem, authority; **c)** rank, high office.

**dignō** 1 to deem worthy (*alqm alqa re*).

**dignor** 1 **a)** to be deemed worthy; **b)** to deem worthy *or* deserving; to deign, to condescend.

**di-gnōscō**, —, — 3 to distinguish, discern.

**dignus** 3 worthy, deserving (*abl.;* with *qui* and *subj.*); fitting, suitable, becoming, proper.

**dī-gredior**, **gressus sum** 3 to go apart *or* asunder, to depart; to deviate, digress (*ab alqo, de, ex, a re*).

**dī-gressiō**, ōnis *f* and **-sus**, ūs *m* a separating, parting, departure; digression.

**dī-iūdicātiō**, ōnis *f* a deciding.

**dī-iūdicō** 1 to decide, determine; to distinguish (*alqd a re*).

**dī-iungō**, **dī-iūnctiō**, *see* disiungo, disiunctio.

**dī-lābor** 3 **a)** to glide apart; to fall asunder, fall to pieces; to dissolve, disappear, melt away; **b)** to flee, escape, disperse; to slip away.

**dī-lacerō** 1 to tear to pieces, rend asunder; to ruin.

**dī-lāminō** to split in two.

**dī-laniō** 1 to tear to pieces.

**dī-lapidō** 1 to squander, waste.

**dī-largior** 4 to lavish, give liberally.

**dī-lātiō**, ōnis *f* a delaying.

**dī-lātō** 1 to spread out, extend; to enlarge.

**dī-lātor**, ōris *m* loiterer.

**dī-laudō** 1 to praise highly.

**dī-lēctus**[1] 3, *see* **diligo**.

**dī-lēctus**[2], ūs *m* a picking out; levy, recruiting; levied soldiers.

**dī-līdō** 3 to break to pieces.

**dīligēns**, tis **a)** careful, attentive, assiduous, accurate, diligent, scrupulous; **b)** careful in house-keeping, thrifty.

**dīligentia**, ae *f* **a)** carefulness, attentiveness, accuracy, diligence; **b)** frugality.

**dī-ligō**, **lēxī**, **lēctum** 3 to esteem highly, to prize, value, love; **dī-lēctus** 3 beloved, dear.

**dī-lōrīcō** 1 to tear open.

**dī-lūceō**, —, —2 to be clear, evident.

**dī-lūcēscō**, **lūxī**, — 3 to grow light, become day.

**dī-lūcidus** 3 clear, evident.

**dīlūculum**, ī *n* daybreak, dawn.

**dī-lūdium**, ī *n* interval (between plays *or* games).

**dī-luō** 3 to wash away; **a)** to dissolve; **b)** to weaken, lessen, impair; **c)** to refute; **d)** to remove.

**dīluviēs**, ēī *f and* **-vium**, ī *n* inundation, flood, deluge.

**dīluviō** 1 to flood.

**dī-madēscō**, **duī**, — 3 to melt away.

**dī-mānō** 1 to flow different ways, to spread abroad.

**dī-mēnsiō**, ōnis *f* a measuring.

**dī-mētior**, **mēnsus sum** 4 to measure out, lay out.

**dī-mētō** *and* **-tor** 1 to measure out, to bound by measuring.

**dīmicātiō**, ōnis *f* fight, struggle, combat.

**dī-micō** 1 to fight, contend, struggle (*cum alqo, pro, de re*); to strive; to be in conflict.

**dīmidiātus** 3 halved, half.  [a half.\]

**dīmidius** 3 half; **dīmidium**, ī *n\*

**dī-missiō, ōnis** f a sending away or out; a dismissing, discharge.

**dī-mittō** 3 to send in different directions, to send about, send forth; a) to dismiss, disband, dissolve, adjourn a meeting; b) to discharge; to let loose, let go, release; to repudiate; c) to renounce, give up, abandon, forgo.

**dim-minuō** 3 to break to pieces.

**dī-moveō** 2 to move asunder, part, separate; a) to remove, take away (*alqd a, de re, abl.*); b) to estrange.

**dī-nōscō** 3 = **dignosco**.

**dī-notō** 1 to distinguish.

**dī-numerātiō, ōnis** f enumeration.

**dī-numerō** 1 to count up, reckon, enumerate.

**dī-ōbolāris, e** worth two obols.

**di-oecēsis, is** f district of jurisdiction.

**di-oecētēs, ae** m overseer of finances, treasurer.

**diōta, ae** f two-handled winejar.

**diplōma, atis** n document, letter of recommendation.

**dipsas, adis** f a serpent whose bite causes thirst.

**di-pyrus** 3 twice burnt.

**dirae** f/pl., see **dirus**.

**dī-rēctus** 3 straight, direct; a) level; upright, steep; b) straightforward, plain, simple.

**dirēmptus, ūs** m separation.

**dīreptiō, ōnis** f a plundering, sack.

**dīreptor, ōris** m plunderer.

**dir-ibeō** 2 to separate, to sort (*voting-tablets*).

**diribitiō, ōnis** f a sorting of voting-tablets.

**diribitor, ōris** m a sorter of voting-tablets.

**diribitōrium, ī** n house for the sorting of voting-tablets.

**dī-rigō, rēxī, rēctum** 3 to set straight, arrange in a straight line; a) to direct, to send, aim, steer; b) to dispose, order.

**dir-imō, ēmī, ēmptum** 3 to take apart, to separate, divide; a) to interrupt, end, disturb, frustrate; b) to break up.

**dī-ripiō, ripuī, reptum** 3 to tear asunder, to tear to pieces; a) to plunder, pillage, rob; b) to snatch away.

**dīritās, ātis** f misfortune; cruelty.

**dī(r)rumpō** 3 a) to break in pieces, shatter; P. to burst; b) to break up (*amicitiam*).

**dī-ruō** 3 to pull down, destroy, demolish.

**dīrus** 3 ill-omened, ominous, portentous; awful, dreadful, horrible; *subst.* **dīrae, ārum** f/pl. a) bad omens; b) curses, execrations; c) the Furies.

**dis-,** see also **des-**.

**dīs, dītis** (*neut.* **dīte**) = **dives**.

**dis-calceātus** 3 unshod.

**dis-cēdō** 3 **1.** to go asunder, part, separate (*in alcis sententiam* to take sides with); to disperse; **2.** to go away; a) to march away, depart (*ab, ex, de re*); b) to desert, forsake; c) to get away, come off (*superior, victor, victus*); d) to depart, leave, abandon; e) to pass away, vanish.

**disceptātiō, ōnis** f discussion, debate; a) controversy, dispute; b) decision.

**disceptātor, ōris** m (f **-trīx, īcis**) arbitrator, judge, umpire.

**dis-ceptō** 1 to discuss, debate, dispute (*de re*); to decide, determine, arbitrate (*in re*).

**dis-cernō, crēvī, crētum** 3 to separate, divide, set apart; a) to distinguish, discern (*alqd a re*); b) to decide, settle.

**dis-cerpō, psī, ptum** 3 to pluck to pieces, to tear asunder; to scatter.

**dis-cessiō, ōnis** f and **-sus, ūs** m a) separation; b) a going away, marching away, departure; division in voting.

**discidium, ī** n separation; a) divorce; b) absence; c) disaffection, alienation.

**dis-cīdō** 3 to cut in pieces.

**dis-cinctus** 3, see **discingo**.

**dī-scindō** 3 to tear or cleave asunder, to rend asunder.

**dis-cingō** 3 to ungird; **discinctus** 3 ungirt, without a girdle; reckless, dissolute, extravagant.

**disciplīna, ae** f **1.** instruction, teaching; a) learning, knowledge, science; b) method of teaching, system, school; **2.** discipline, training, education; custom, habit, order, way of living.

**discipulus, ī** m (**discipula, ae** f) pupil, scholar, disciple.

**dis-clūdō, sī, sum** 3 to shut up apart, keep apart, separate.

**discō, didicī, —** 3 to learn (*alqd ab alqo*, with *inf.* or *acc. c. inf.*), become acquainted with, find out; to study; *pf.* to know.

**dis-color, ōris** of a different colour; party-coloured; different.

**dis-condūcō** 3 to be inconvenient *or* disadvantageous.

**dis-conveniō, —, —** 4 to disagree, be inconvenient.

**dis-cordābilis, e** discordant.

**dis-cordia, ae** *f* disagreement, dissension, discord.

**dis-cordiōsus** 3 quarrelsome.

**dis-cordō** 1 to disagree, quarrel.

**dis-cors, dis** disagreeing, discordant; **a)** different, at variance, inharmonious; **b)** mutinous.

**dis-crepantia, ae** *f* (*and* **discrepātiō, ōnis** *f*) disagreement, disunion, difference.

**dis-crepitō** 1 to differ.

**dis-crepō, uī (āvī), —** 1 to differ in sound; to disagree, be different (*cum* or *a re*, *inter se*); *impers.* **discrepat** there is a disagreement.

**dī-scrībō** 3 **a)** to divide (*alqd in alqd*); **b)** to distribute, classify, assign (*alci alqd*); **discrīptus** 3 well-arranged; **c)** = **describo.**

**dis-crīmen, inis** *n* that which divides; dividing line; **a)** interval, distance; **b)** intervening space; **c)** difference, distinction; (power of) discernment; **d)** turning-point, critical moment, crisis, peril, danger, hazard; turn, issue; trial.

**dis-crīminō** 1 to separate, divide; to mark out.

**dī-scriptiō, ōnis** *f* distribution, assignment.

**dis-cruciō** 1 to torture, torment.

**dis-cumbō, cubuī, cubitum** 3 to recline at table; to go to bed.

**dis-cupiō** 3 to desire greatly.

**dis-currō, (cu)currī, cursum** 3 to run different ways, run about.

**dis-cursus, ūs** *m* (*and* **-sātiō, ōnis** *f*) a running about, to and fro.

**discus, ī** *m* quoit.

**dis-cutiō, cussī, cussum** 3 to strike asunder, dash to pieces, to shatter; **a)** to disperse; scatter; **b)** to remove, destroy.

**disertē** (*and* **-im**) distinctly, lucidly.

**disertus** 3 well arranged; **a)** eloquent; **b)** well expressed, clear, clever, fluent.

**dis-iciō, iēcī, iectum** 3 to throw asunder, drive asunder, disperse; **a)** to tear asunder, ruin, destroy, frustrate; **b)** to squander; **disiectus** 3 scattered, dishevelled; extended.

**dis-iectō** 1 to toss about.

**dis-iectus, ūs** *m* scattering.

**dis-iūnctiō** (*or* **dī-iūnctiō), ōnis** *f* separation; logical dilemma.

**dis-iungō** (*or* **dī-iungō)** 3 to unyoke, unharness; **a)** to separate, sever, disunite, remove (*alqd a re*); **b)** to estrange; **disiūnctus** 3 **a)** separated, distant, remote; **b)** different; **c)** logically opposed.

**dis-marītus, ī** *m* twice married man.

**dis-pālēscō** 3 to be divulged.

**dis-pālor** 1 to wander about, straggle.

**dis-pandō** (*and* **-pennō), pandī, pānsum, pēnsum** *or* **pessum** 3 to stretch out, spread out.

**dis-pār, aris** unlike, different.

**dis-parilis, e** unlike, dissimilar.

**dis-parō** 1 to separate, divide; **disparātum, ī** *n* antithesis.

**dispectus, ūs** *m* examination, consideration.

**dis-pellō, pulī, pulsum** 3 to drive asunder, disperse.

**dis-pendium, ī** *n* expense; loss.

**dis-pēnsātiō, ōnis** *f* economical management; **a)** administration, direction; **b)** office of a steward.

**dispēnsātor, ōris** *m* steward, treasurer, paymaster.

**dis-pēnsō** 1 to distribute, disburse, pay out; to manage, arrange, regulate.

**dis-percutiō** 3 to knock to pieces.

**dis-perdō** 3 to ruin *or* destroy fully.

**dis-pereō** to perish *or* to be lost, undone, ruined.

**dī-spergō, sī, sum** 3 to disperse, scatter, spread abroad, spread out.

**dis-pertiō** (*and* **-ior**) 4 to divide, distribute.

**dis-pertītiō, ōnis** *f* dividing.

**dī-spiciō, spexī, spectum** 3 to open the eyes; to discern, perceive, descry, discover.

**dis-plicentia, ae** *f* dissatisfaction.

**dis-pliceō, uī, (itum)** 2 to displease; **sibi displicēre** to be dissatisfied with oneself, to be fretful.

**dis-plōdō** 3 to burst, cause to explode.

**dis-pōnō** 3 to set in different places; to arrange, dispose, draw up, assign, adjust; — **dispositus** 3 well-arranged, methodical.

**dis-positiō, ōnis** *f,* **-tūra, ae** *f,* **-tus, ūs** *m* regular arrangement.

**dis-positor, ōris** *m* disposer, arranger.

**dis-pudet** 2 it causes much shame.

**dis-pungō** 3 to check up, audit.

**disputābilis, e** arguable.

**disputātiō, ōnis** *f* a reasoning; discussion; *dimin.* **-tiuncula, ae** *f.*

**disputātor, ōris** *m* debater, disputer.

**dis-putō** 1 a) to clear up by reckoning; b) to discuss, argue, examine, dispute.

**dis-quīrō, —, —** 3 to investigate.

**dis-quīsītiō, ōnis** *f* inquiry, investigation.

**dis-rumpō** 3 = **dirumpo**.

**dis-saepiō** 4 to separate, divide.

**dis-saeptum, ī** *n* partition.

**dis-sāvior** 1 = **dissuavior**.

**dis-secō** 1 to cut asunder.

**dis-sēminō** 1 to sow; to scatter, spread.

**dis-sēnsiō, ōnis** *f (and* **-sus, ūs** *m)* disagreement, dissension; a) discord; b) opposition.

**dis-sentāneus** 3 contrary.

**dis-sentiō** 4 to differ in opinion, to dissent, disagree (*ab* or *cum alqo*); to be different (*ab re*), opposed.

**dis-serēnāscit, nāvit, —** 3 it clears up.

**dis-serō[1], sēvī, situm** 3 to scatter seed, to plant here and there.

**dis-serō[2], ruī, rtum** 3 to set asunder; to discuss, to argue (*alqd* or *de re; cum alqo*).

**dis-serpō** to steal abroad, spread.

**dis-sertiō, ōnis** *f* severance.

**dis-sertō** 1 to discuss, treat of.

**dissiciō** = **disicio**.

**dis-sideō, sēdī, sessum** 2 1. a) to sit apart; b) to be remote; 2. to disagree, be at variance, contrary.

**dis-signātiō, ōnis** *f* arrangement.

**dis-signātor, ōris** *m* a) usher in a theatre; b) funeral undertaker.

**dis-signō** 1 to arrange, regulate, dispose.

**dis-siliō, luī, —** 4 to leap or burst asunder.

**dis-similis, e** dissimilar, unlike (with *gen.* or *dat.*).

**dis-similitūdō, inis** *f* unlikeness, difference.

**dis-simulanter** (*and* **-lābiliter**) *adv.* secretly.

**dis-simulantia, ae** *and* **-lātiō, ōnis** *f* a dissembling, concealing.

**dis-simulātor, ōris** *m* dissembler, concealer.

**dis-simulō** 1 a) to dissemble, disguise; b) to conceal, hide, keep secret (*alqd; de re; acc. c. inf.*); c) to disregard.

**dissipābilis, e** that may be scattered.

**dissipātiō, ōnis** *f* a scattering, dispersion.

**dis-sipō** 1 to scatter, disperse; a) to spread abroad, to disseminate; b) to rout, put to flight; to overthrow, destroy; c) to squander.

**dis-sociābilis, e** dividing; incompatible.

**dis-sociātiō, ōnis** *f* separation.

**dis-sociō** 1 to disunite, separate; to estrange, set at variance.

**dis-solūbilis, e** that may be dissolved.

**dis-solūtiō, ōnis** *f* a dissolving, dissolution; a) an abolishing, destruction; b) refutation; c) dissoluteness.

**dis-solūtus** 3 disjointed, unconnected; a) loose, lax, remiss; b) negligent, careless; c) dissolute, licentious.

**dis-solvō** 3 to disunite, separate, dissolve; a) to abolish, abrogate, annul; b) to refute, reply to; c) to release, disengage; d) to pay (*alci alqd*).

**dis-sonus** 3 discordant, inharmonious, confused; disagreeing, different.

**dis-sors, tis** not in common, of a different lot or fate.

**dis-suādeō** 2 to advise against, resist, speak against (*alqd; de re,* with *acc. c. inf.*).

**dis-suāsiō, ōnis** *f* an advising to the contrary.

**dis-suāsor, ōris** *m* one who advises to the contrary, opponent.

**dis-s(u)āvior** 1 to kiss affectionately or to one's heart's content.

**dis-sultō** 1 to leap or burst asunder.

**dis-suō** 3 to unstitch, rip open; a) to open wide; b) to dissolve by degrees.

**dis-taedet** 2 it tires.

**di-stantia, ae** *f* distance, remoteness; diversity.

**dis-tendō, tendī, tentum** 3 to stretch asunder, extend; a) to fill full, distend; b) to divide; to disperse.

**dis-tentus** 3 [*distineo*] busy, occupied.

**dis-terminō** 1 to limit, separate by a boundary.

**dis-terminus** 3 separated.

**di-stichon, ī** *n* couplet.

**di-stimulō** 1 to squander.

**distinctiō, ōnis** *f and* **-tus, ūs** *m* a distinguishing; a) distinction; b) difference.

**distinctus** 3 separated; marked off, distinguished; a) decorated; b) adorned, embellished; c) distinct.

**dis-tineō, tinuī, tentum** 2 to keep asunder, separate, keep from uniting; a) to occupy, engage; b) to hinder, prevent, detain.

**di-stinguō, inxī, inctum** 3 to separate, divide, part; a) to decorate, adorn; b) to distinguish, discriminate (*alqd ab alqo*).

**di-stō, —, —** 1 to stand apart; a) to be distant *or* remote; b) to differ, to be different; **distat** there is a difference.

**dis-torqueō** 2 to twist, distort; to torture; **distortus** 3 distorted, misshapen, deformed; perverse.

**dis-tortiō, ōnis** *f* a distorting.

**dis-tractiō, ōnis** *f* a pulling asunder, separating; dissension, discord.

**dis-trahō** 3 to pull *or* draw asunder, to tear to pieces, divide; a) to sell in parcels; b) to end, adjust; c) to prevent, frustrate; d) to draw in different directions, to distract, perplex; e) to estrange, alienate.

**dis-tribuō** 3 to divide, distribute (*alci alqd, alqd in alqm*); a) to dislocate; b) to divide logically; **distribūtus** 3 well arranged.

**dis-tribūtiō, ōnis** *f* division, distribution.

**di-stringō** 3 to draw asunder, stretch out; a) to keep from uniting; b) to torture; c) to occupy, engage.

**dis-truncō** 1 to cut to pieces.

**dis-turbātiō, ōnis** *f* destruction.

**dis-turbō** 1 to drive asunder; to demolish, destroy; to disturb, confuse, frustrate.

**dite** *neut. of* **dis,** see **dives.**

**ditēscō, —, —** 3 to grow rich.

**dīthyrambicus** 3 dithyrambic.

**dīthyrambus, ī** *m* dithyramb, song in honour of Bacchus.

**dītiae, ārum** *f* riches.

**dītō** 1 to enrich.

**diū** *adv. (comp.* **diūtius, diŭtius,** *superl.* **diutissimē)** a) by day; b) a long time, long while; c) long since, long ago.

**diurnus** 3 belonging to the day, of the day; a) by day; b) daily, of one day, for one day; *subst.* **diurna, ōrum** *n/pl.* official gazette.

**dius** *adv.* by day.

**dius** 3 = **divus.**

**diūtinus (and diŭtinus)** 3 lasting, long, of long duration.

**diuturnitās, ātis** *f* long duration, length of time.

**diuturnus** 3 lasting, long, of long duration.

**dī-vāricō** 1 to spread asunder, stretch apart.

**dī-vellō, vellī (vulsī), vulsum** 3 to tear apart, rend asunder, tear in pieces, divide forcibly; to remove, separate, tear away (*alqd a re*).

**dī-vendō** 3 to sell in separate lots.

**dī-verberō** 1 to strike asunder, cut, divide.

**dī-verbium, ī** *n* dialogue (*on the stage*).

**dīversitās, ātis** *f* diversity, contrariety, contradiction.

**dī-versus** 3 1. turned away from, opposite, contrary; a) apart, separate, remote; b) different, various; c) opposed; — 2. turned *or* going in different directions; a) isolated; b) opposed in character, discordant.

**dī-vertō** to differ.

**dīves, itis** rich (with *abl.* and *gen.*), wealthy; fertile, copious; precious, costly.

**dī-vexō** 1 to tear asunder, to vex, trouble; to destroy.

**dīvidia, ae** *f* sorrow, grief.

**dī-vidō, vīsī, vīsum** 3 1. to part asunder, separate, divide; to remove from (*alqd ab alqa re*); 2. a) to divide into parts; b) to distribute, allot.

**dīviduus** 3 a) divisible; b) divided, separated.

**dīvinātiō, ōnis** *f* 1. gift of prophecy; divination, prophecy; 2. selection of a prosecutor.

**divīnitās, ātis** *f* divine nature, godhead, divinity.

**divīnitus** *adv.* by divine influence; excellently, admirably.

**divīnō** 1 to foretell, prophesy, divine, forebode.

**divīnus** 3 of a god *or* deity, divine; **res divīna** sacrifice; **res divīnae** religion, service of the gods; natural laws, physics; **a)** inspired, prophetic; *subst.* **divīnus, ī** *m* diviner, prophet; **b)** divine, excellent, admirable, godlike.

**divīsiō, ōnis** *f* division; distribution.

**divīsor, ōris** *m* divider, distributor of bribes.

**divīsus, ūs** *m* = **divisio.**

**divitiae, ārum** *f/pl.* riches, wealth, treasures; copiousness.

**di-vors-, -vort-** = **dī-vers-, -vert-.**

**di-vortium, ī** *n* separation; a) boundary line, water-shed; **b)** divorce.

**di-vulgō** 1 to make public, to publish, spread abroad, divulge.

**divus** 3 divine, godlike; deified; *subst.* **divus, ī** *m* god; **diva, ae** *f* goddess; **divum, ī** *n* the sky, the open air.

**dō, dedī, dătum, dăre** to give, offer, present (*alci alqd*); **datum, ī** *n* gift; **a)** to offer, dedicate (*to the gods*); to furnish, pay; **poenam** to suffer punishment; to give up, deliver, hand over, render, surrender; to confer, grant, yield, leave, abandon; to be ready to give; **b)** to devote, **operam dare** to bestow care *or* pains; **c)** to concede, resign, permit, allow (*alci alqd*); to forgive, let loose, release; to tell, communicate, relate, utter, announce; to attribute, impute, assign, ascribe, reckon (*alci laudi* or *crimini*); **d)** to bring, put, throw, **se dare in** to betake oneself to; **e)** to cause, produce, excite, make, display; to arrange.

**doceō, cui, ctum** 2 to teach, instruct (*alqm alqd* or *alqa re*), inform, tell; **a)** to show, prove, explain; **b)** to teach, rehearse (*a play*); **c)** to be a teacher, give instruction.

**dochmius, ī** *m* the dochmiac foot.

**docilis, e** easily taught, docile, tractable.

**docilitās, ātis** *f* docility.

**doctor, ōris** *m* teacher, instructor.

**doctrīna, ae** *f* instruction, teaching; **a)** learning, knowledge, erudition; **b)** science.

**doctus** 3 learned (with *abl.* or *inf.*), trained; **a)** skilled, experienced; **b)** versed in Greek letters; *subst.* **doctus, ī** *m* a learned man, literary man.

**documentum, ī** (*and* **-men, inis**) *n* lesson; **a)** example, instance, pattern, proof; **b)** a warning.

**dōdrāns, tis** three fourths.

**dōdrantārius** 3 of three fourths.

**dogma, atis** *n* philosophic principle, tenet, doctrine.

**dolābra, ae** *f* pickaxe.

**dolēns, tis** causing pain, painful.

**dolenter** *adv.* painfully.

**doleō, luī, litūrus** 2 **a)** to suffer pain, feel pain, to grieve, be sorry *or* afflicted (*alqd, de re, quod, acc. c. inf.*); **b)** to cause pain, be painful to (*alci*).

**dōliāris, e** like a barrel.

**dōliolum, ī** *n* little cask.

**dōlium, ī** *n* cask; wine-jar.

**dolō**[1] 1 to chip with an axe, to hew; to cudgel.

**dolō**[2]**, ōnis** *m* 1. iron-pointed staff, sword-stick; sting; 2. fore-topsail.

**dolor, ōris** *m* pain, smart, ache; **a)** sorrow, grief, affliction, distress, trouble, mortification; **b)** indignation, resentment.

**dolōsus** 3 deceitful, cunning, crafty.

**dolus, ī** *m* fraud, deceit, guile, deception, trickery, malice; fault.

**domābilis, e** tamable.

**domesticātim** *adv.* in private houses.

**domesticus** 3 belonging to a house *or* family; **a)** domestic; **b)** private, native; *subst. m* member of a household.

**domicēnium, ī** *n* meal eaten at home.

**domicilium, ī** *n* dwelling, abode, residence; home.

**domina, ae** *f* mistress of a household, lady, mistress.

**dominātiō, ōnis** *f* rule, dominion; despotism, tyranny; rulers.

**dominātor, ōris** *m* ruler, lord.

**dominātrix, īcis** *f* mistress.

**dominātus, ūs** *m* = **dominatio.**

**dominicus** 3 pertaining to a lord *or* ruler.

**dominium, ī** *n* property; feast, banquet.

**dominor** 1 to be lord *or* master, to rule; to domineer; to be ruled; **-āns, antis** (of words) having their ordinary sense.

**dominus, ī** *m* master, lord, head; owner, proprietor; ruler, lord, despot; entertainer, host.

**domi-porta, ae** *f* house-carrier, snail.

**domitō** 1, *intens. of* domo.

**domitor, ōris** *m* tamer, subduer.

**domitrix, īcis** *f* tamer, subduer.

**domitus, ūs** *m* a taming, subduing.

**domō, uī, itum** 1 to tame, break, subdue, conquer.

**domus, ūs** *f* house, dwelling; home, native town *or* country; household, family; philosophical school *or* sect; **domum** home, homewards; **domō** from home; **domī** at home, in the house; **domī bellīque** (*or* **militiaeque**) in war and peace.

**dōnābilis, e** deserving of (*alqa re*).

**dōnārium, ī** *n* altar, temple; votive offering.

**dōnātiō, ōnis** *f* a giving; gift, present.

**dōnātivum, ī** *n* largess, distribution of money.

**dōnātor, ōris** *m* giver.

**dōnec** *cj.* as long as, while; until.

**dōnicum, dōnique** = donec.

**dōnō** 1 a) to give as a present (*alcı alqd*), bestow, grant, confer; b) to sacrifice, give up; c) to pardon, forgive, remit; d) to present with, endow (*alqm re*).

**dōnum, ī** *n* present, gift; offering, sacrifice.

**dorcas, adis** *f* gazelle.

**dormiō** 4 to sleep; to be inactive, idle.

**dormī(tā)tor, ōris** *m* sleeper, dreamer.

**dormītō** 1 to be drowsy, to fall asleep.

**dormītōrius** 3 belonging to sleep.

**dorsum, ī** *n* (*and* **-us, ī** *m*) the back; ridge of a mountain.

**dory-phoros, ī** *m* lance-bearer.

**dōs, dōtis** *f* dowry, marriage-portion; gift, quality, talent.

**dōtālis, e** belonging to a dowry.

**dōtō** 1 to endow, to portion; **dōtātus** 3 endowed, richly provided.

**drach(u)ma, ae** *f* drachma (*a Greek coin* = **denarius**).

**drach(u)missō** 1 to hire oneself out for a drachma.

**dracō, ōnis** *m* serpent, dragon.

**dracōni-gena, ae** *m and f* dragon-born.

**drāpeta, ae** *m* runaway slave.

**draucus, ī** *m* sodomite.

**dromas, adis** *m* dromedary.

**dromos, ī** *m* the Spartan race-course.

**drōpax, acis** *m* depilatory plaster.

**Druidae, ārum**, *and* **-dēs, um** *m/pl.* druids.

**dubitābilis, e** doubtful, to be doubted. [itatingly.]

**dubitanter** *adv.* doubtingly; hes-

**dubitātiō, ōnis** *f* a) doubt, uncertainty; b) hesitation, wavering, irresolution.

**dubitō** 1 a) to doubt, be in doubt (*de re; quin*); to deliberate; b) to hesitate, waver, be irresolute, delay.

**dubius** 3 a) doubting, uncertain, wavering, irresolute; b) doubtful, doubted, undecided, uncertain, dubious; dangerous, precarious, critical; **sine dubiō** without doubt; **in dubiō esse** to be questioned, to be in danger; **in dubium vocāre** to make doubtful, call in question.

**ducātus, ūs** *m* leadership.

**ducēnārius** 3 relating to two hundred.

**ducēnī** 3 two hundred each.

**ducentēsima, ae** *f* tax of one half per cent (½ %).

**du-centī** 3 two hundred.

**ducentiē(n)s** *adv.* two hundred times.

**dūcō, dūxī, ductum** 3 1. to draw; a) to drag behind, to move by drawing; b) to draw out (*ferrum de vagina*); c) to draw in (*aëra, spiritum*); to quaff, drink in; d) to stretch, draw in, pull at (*frena, arcum*); e) to take, receive, admit (*colorem, cicatricem, formam, notam*); f) to incite, seduce, allure; g) to distort, make wry faces (*os*); h) to form by drawing, to spin; to form, fashion, shape, compose (*carmina, versus*); to hammer out; to construct, build, draw (*fossam, muros*); i) to extend, prolong, protract (*bellum, tempus, rem in noctem*); to keep off *or* in suspense; 2. to lead, guide, conduct, direct; a) to lead to, conduct, derive (*hostes ex aquam ex montibus in urbem, alqm secum in castra, ad mortem, originem ab alqo*);

to lead home as a wife, to marry;
b) to cause, produce (*soporem, somnum*); c) to take, lead away, carry
off; d) to lead, command, march
(*copias*); to lead in front, in advance,
take the lead, form the van; e) to
incite, move (*ad credendum*); **P.** to
be moved, incited; **3.** to calculate,
reckon, compute; to consider, think,
hold, account, esteem, regard (*alqd
in malis sive bonis, pro nihilo, alqm
victorem, alqd turpe* or *nefas, omnia
pericula levia;* with *dat. alqd honori*
or *laudi*).

**ductilis, e** (capable of being) led,
conducted.

**ductim** *adv.* in deep draughts.

**ductitō 1** to lead away; to marry
(*alqm*); to cheat.

**ductō 1,** *intens. of* **duco.**

**ductor, ōris** *m* leader, commander.

**ductus, ūs** *m* a leading, conducting;
a) **ōris** lineaments of the face;
b) command, leadership.

**dūdum** *adv.* a) a short time ago,
a little while ago, not long since;
b) formerly, of old; **iam dūdum**
now for a long time.

**duellum, duellātor, duellicus** =
**bellum, bellator, bellicus.**

**duim** = **dem** (*see* **do**).

**dulcēdō, inis** *f* sweetness, pleasantness, charm, delightfulness.

**dulcēscō, —, —** 3 to become sweet.

**dulciārius** 3 of confectionery.

**dulciculus** 3 sweetish.

**dulci-fer** 3 sweet.

**dulcis, e** sweet; pleasant, delightful,
charming, dear.

**dulcitūdō, inis** *f* = **dulcedo.**

**dūlicē** *adv.* like a slave.

**dum 1.** *cj.* a) while, as long as; until;
b) provided that; **2.** *adv.* (*joined to
other words*) now (*agedum, cedodum*).

**dūmētum, ī** *n* thicket, thorn-hedge.

**dum-modo** *cj.* = **dum** provided
that, if only.

**dūmōsus** 3 covered with thorn-
bushes, bushy.

**dum-taxat** *adv.* exactly, strictly
speaking, precisely; a) only, merely;
b) at least, in so far; c) of course.

**dūmus, ī** *m* thorn-bush; thicket.

**duo, ae, o** two; the two, both.

**duo-deciē(n)s** *adv.* twelve times.

**duo-decim** twelve.

**duo-decimus** 3 the twelfth.

**duo-dēnī** 3 twelve each.

**duo-et-vīcēsimānus, ī** *m* soldier of
the twenty-second legion.

**duo-virī** = **duumviri.**

**du-plex, icis** a) twofold, double;
b) double-tongued, false.

**duplicārius, ī** *m* a soldier who
receives double pay.

**duplicō 1** to double; a) to fold in
two, double up; to bend; b) to
enlarge, augment.

**duplus** 3 double, twice as large,
twice as much; *subst.* **duplum, ī** *n*
double.

**du-pondius, ī** *m* coin of two asses.

**dūrābilis, e** lasting, durable.

**dūracinus** 3 with a hard skin.

**dūrāmen, inis** *n* frozen state.

**dūrāmentum, ī** *n* durability,
firmness.

**dūrateus** 3 wooden.

**dūrēscō, ruī, —** 3 to grow hard.

**dureta, ae** *f* wooden bathing-tub.

**dūritās, ātis** *f* = **duritia.**

**dūriter** *adv.* = **dure** (*see* **durus**).

**dūritia, ae** (*and* **-tiēs, ēī**) *f* hardness;
a) austerity; b) absence of feeling,
insensibility; c) harshness, severity,
oppression.

**dūriusculus** 3 somewhat hard *or*
harsh.

**dūrō 1 1.** *trans.* to make hard; a) to
dry; b) to make hardy, insensible;
c) to bear, endure; **2.** *intr.* a) to
become hard *or* dry; b) to continue,
last, remain.

**dūrus** 3 hard; a) harsh, rough, ugly,
awkward; b) shameless; c) strong,
enduring; d) insensible, unfeeling,
rude, stern, severe, cruel; e) hard,
difficult, painful, toilsome, oppressive, distressing, adverse.

**duum-virātus, ūs** *m* office of a
duumvir.

**duum-virī, ōrum** *m/pl.* a commission of two men.

**dux, ducis** *m* (*and f*) leader; a) guide;
b) commander, general; c) prince,
ruler.

**dynamis, is** *f* plenty.

**dynastēs, ae** *m* ruler, prince.

# E

**ē, ex** *prep.* with *abl.* **1.** (*of space*) out of, from, from within (*ex castris venire, ex patria fugere, ē loco superiore impetum facere, Rhenus oritur ex Alpibus; pugnare ex equo* on horseback; *pendere ex arbore; ex alqo audire* or *cognoscere*); **2.** (*of time*) since, from, immediately upon (*ex Kalendis Martiis, ex eo tempore, ex praetura urbem relinquere; ex quo* from which time, since; *diem ex die* day after day); **3.** (*of relation*) from, of; a) *to denote origin* (*liberos habere ex femina, ex serva natus, soror ex matre*); from among, from, out of (*unus ex multis, ex ephoris quidam*); b) *to denote the material:* out of (*statua ex aere facta*); c) *to denote the cause:* from, on account of, by reason of, in consequence of, through (*Demetrius ex doctrina nobilis est, avem ex pennis cognoscere, ex pedibus laborare, ex vulnere aeger* or *mori, ex eadem causa*); d) *to denote a change:* (*ex beato miser, ex aratore orator factus est*); e) *according to* (*ex senatus consulto, ex edicto praetoris, ex consuetudine, ex sententia* satisfactorily); f) **ex contrario** on the contrary; **ē regione** opposite to; **ex composito** by agreement; **ex improviso** unexpectedly; **ex usu esse** to be advantageous; **ē re publica esse** to be for the public benefit; **magna ex parte** mostly; **ex itinere** straight from a march.

**eā** (*sc. via*) *adv.* there, that way.

**eādem** *adv.* by the same way.

**eā-propter** = **propterea.**

**eā-tenus** *adv.* so far, to such a degree.      [ebony.\

**ebenus, ī** *f* ebony-tree; **-num, ī** *n*)

**ē-bibō** 3 to drink up; to squander.

**ē-bītō** 3 to go out.

**ē-blandior** 4 to obtain by flattery.

**ēbrietās, ātis** *f* drunkenness, intoxication.

**ēbriolus** 3 tipsy.

**ēbriōsitās, ātis** *f* love of drink.

**ēbriōsus** 3 given to drink; drunkard.

**ēbrius** 3 drunk, intoxicated.

**ē-bulliō** 4 to bubble up; to boast of.

**ebulum, ī** *n* dwarf elder.

**ebur, oris** *n* ivory; work of ivory.

**eburātus** 3 adorned with ivory.

**eburneolus** 3 of ivory.

**eburneus (-nus)** 3 (made of) ivory.

**ē-castor** *int.* by Castor!

**ec-ce** *adv.* lo! behold!

**ecce-re** *int.* there! indeed!

**ec-clēsia, ae** *f* assembly of the Athenian people.

**ec-dicus, ī** *m* public attorney, prosecutor.

**ecf...,** *see* **eff...**

**eche-nēis, idis** *f* ('ship-holder') sucking-fish, remora.

**echidna, ae** *f* adder, viper.

**echīnus, ī** *m* a) sea-urchin; b) rinsing-vessel.

**ēchō, ūs** *f* echo.

**ec-loga, ae** *f* selection; eclogue.

**ec-quandō** *adv.* ever? whether ever.

**ecquis, quī, ecqua(e), ecquid, quod** (is there) any(one)? whether any(one); *also* **ecquisnam:** *adv.*

**ecquid** *interrog. particle* (whether) at all?; **ecquō** anywhere?

**eculeus, ī** *m* a) young horse, colt; b) wooden rack (instrument of torture).

**ecus** = **equus.**

**edācitās, ātis** *f* voraciousness.

**edāx, ācis** greedy, gluttonous; consuming.

**ē-dentō** 1 to knock out the teeth from.

**ēdentulus** 3 toothless, old.

**ede-pol** *int.* by Pollux!

**edera, ae** *f* = **hedera.**

**ē-dīcō** 3 a) to make known, publish, proclaim, declare (*alci alqd*); b) to decree, ordain, order, appoint (*alqd; ut, ne*).

**ē-dictiō, ōnis** *f* edict.

**ē-dictō** 1 to proclaim, publish.

**ē-dictum, ī** *n* decree, proclamation, edict.

**ē-discō, didicī, —** 3 to learn by heart, learn thoroughly.

**ē-disserō, ruī, rtum** 3 to relate fully, explain.

**ē-dissertō** 1, *intens. of* **edissero.**

**ēditīcius** 3 announced, proposed.

**ēditiō, ōnis** *f* a publishing; statement, proposal.

**ēditor, ōris** *m* producing.

**ēditus** 3 elevated, high, lofty; *subst.* **-um, ī** *n* height.

**edō¹, ēdī, ēsum** 3 to eat, consume.

**ē-dō², didī, ditum** 3 to give out, put forth; **a)** to breathe, to utter; **b)** to bring forth, give birth; **c)** to publish, make known; spread abroad; to proclaim, ordain, designate, name; **d)** to display, produce, perform, cause, furnish.

**ē-doceō** 2 to teach *or* instruct thoroughly (*alqm alqd*); to inform, relate.

**ē-dolō** 1 to hew out, to complete.

**ē-domō** 1 to tame thoroughly, to subdue.

**ē-dormiō** 4 to sleep out *or* off (*alqd*).

**ēdormiscō** 3 = **edormio.**

**ēducātiō, ōnis** *f* ,a bringing up, education.

**ēducātor, ōris** *m* foster-father, tutor.

**ēducātrix, īcis** *f* foster-mother.

**ē-ducō¹** 1 **a)** to bring up, rear; **b)** to educate.

**ē-dūcō²** 3 1. to draw out (*sortem*); **2.** to lead out; **a)** to march out (*alqm* or *alqd ex re in alqd*); to take out of port; to bring before a court; **b)** to take away; **c)** to raise up; to erect, build; **d)** to bring up, rear, educate.

**edūlis, e** eatable.

**ē-dūrō** 1 to last, continue.

**ē-dūrus** 3 very hard.

**ef-farciō, —, fertum** 4 to stuff full, fill out.

**ef-fātum, ī** *n* utterance; **a)** prophecy; **b)** axiom.

**effectiō, ōnis** *f* **a)** a practising; **b)** efficient cause.

**effector, ōris** *m* producer, author.

**effectrix, īcis** *f* she who effects, produces.

**effectus, ūs** *m* an effecting; **a)** execution, performance; operation; **b)** result, consequence.

**ef-fēminō** 1 **a)** to make a woman of; **b)** to make effeminate.

**efferciō** 4 = **effarcio.**

**ef-feritās, ātis** *f* savageness.

**ef-ferō¹** 1 [*ferus*] to make wild; to enrage.

**ef-ferō², extulī, ēlātum** 3 1. to bear, carry, bring, take out (*alqd ex, de re, ad* or *in alqd*); **a)** to carry to the grave, bury; **b)** to bring forth, produce, bear; **c)** to utter, express, spread abroad, make known; **d)** to carry away, transport; **P.** to be carried away (*studio, gaudio*); **2. a)** to raise, lift up, elevate; **b)** to make haughty; **c)** to extol, praise.

**ef-fertus** 3, *see* **effarcio.**

**ef-ferus** 3 very wild, savage.

**ef-fervēscō, ferbuī** (*or* **fervī**), — 3 to boil up *or* over; to burst forth.

**ef-fervō, —, —** 3 = **effervesco.**

**ef-fētus** 3 exhausted, worn out, weakened.

**efficācitās, ātis** *f* efficiency.

**efficāx, ācis** efficient, effective.

**efficiēns, tis** efficient, effective.

**efficientia, ae** *f* efficiency.

**ef-ficiō, fēcī, fectum** 3 to bring about, produce, effect, make; **a)** to bear (*fruit*); to make up (*of number*); **b)** to execute, finish, complete, accomplish; **c)** to cause, carry through (*alqd; ut, ne*); **d)** to prove, show.

**effigiēs, ēī** (*and* **-ia, ae**) *f* image, copy; **a)** likeness, portrait; **b)** ideal; **c)** phantom; **d)** form, shape.

**ef-fingō** 3 1. to wipe out *or* off; 2. to form, fashion, copy, imitate; to represent, express.

**ef-flāgitātiō, ōnis** *f* (*and* **-tātus, ūs** *m*) pressing request, solicitation, demand.

**ef-flāgitō** 1 to demand *or* ask urgently, to entreat (*alqd ab alqo; ut, ne*).

**ef-flictim** *adv.* desperately (*amare*).

**ef-flictō** 1 to strike dead.

**ef-flīgō, xī, ctum** 3 to kill, slay.

**ef-flō** 1 to breathe *or* blow out.

**ef-flōrēscō, ruī, —** 3 to blossom, bloom, flourish.

**ef-fluō, uxī, —** 3 to flow out *or* forth; **a)** to run over; **b)** to slip from, escape (*ex re*); to disappear, vanish, be forgotten.

**effluvium, ī** *n* outlet.

**ef-fodiō** 3 **a)** to dig out *or* up; to tear out; **b)** to rummage, ransack.

**ef-for, fātus sum** 1 to speak out, say, utter; **a)** to define *or* consecrate a place; **b)** to state a proposition.

**ef-frāctārius, ī** *m* housebreaker, burglar.

**ef-frēnātiō, ōnis** *f* unbridled impetuosity.

**ef-frēnātus** 3 unbridled, unrestrained, unruly.

**ef-frēnō** 1 to let loose.

**effrēnus** 3 = effrenatus.

**ef-fricō** 1 to rub off.

**ef-fringō, frēgī, frāctum** 3 to break open *or* away.

**ef-fugiō, fūgī, (fugitum)** 3 1. *intr.* to flee away (*ex re*); 2. *trans.* to escape from, avoid, shun; to escape observation.

**effugium, ī** *n* a fleeing away, flight; a) escape; b) means of escape, way of flight.

**ef-fulgeō, lsī,** — 2 to shine forth.

**ef-fultus** 3 supported by, resting upon.

**ef-fundō** 3 to pour out *or* forth, to shed; a) to waste, squander, exhaust; b) to send forth; to pour out, utter; c) to bring forth *or* produce abundantly; d) to loose, let go; *P.* (*also* se effundere) to pour out in a crowd; to let oneself go, give way to (*in alqd*).

**ef-fūsiō, ōnis** *f* a pouring out, shedding; a) a pouring forth; b) extravagance, profusion; c) excess of hilarity.

**ef-fūsus** 3 poured forth; a) widespread, extensive; b) let loose, disorderly; extravagant; c) unrestrained, immoderate.

**ef-fūtiō** 4 to chatter, babble forth.

**ef-futuō** 3 to waste in debauchery.

**ē-gelidus** 3 mild; cool.

**egēns, tis** needy (*with gen.*), poor.

**egēnus** 3 needy (*gen.* or *abl.*), in want, poor.

**egeō, uī,** — 2 a) to be in need, in want (*gen.* or *abl.*), to be needy, poor, to be without; b) to desire, wish for, want (*gen.*).

**ēgerō** (?), **ōnis** *m* one who carries off.

**ē-gerō** 3 to take *or* bring out; a) to discharge, vomit; b) to expel.

**egestās, ātis** *f* a) need, poverty; b) want.

**ē-gestiō, ōnis** *f* (*and* -tus, ūs *m*) carrying away; squandering.

**ē-gignō** 3 to produce.

**egǒ** (*and* egō) *pers. pron.* I.

**ē-gredior, gressus sum** 3 to go out, come forth (*ex re, re, in, ad alqd*); a) to march out; to land, to put to sea; to digress (*a re*); b) to go up, ascend; c) to go beyond (*acc.*), to overstep, pass.

**ē-gregius** 3 distinguished, select, extraordinary, excellent, admirable, honourable; *subst.* **ē-gregium, ī** *n* honour, glory.

**ē-gressus, ūs** *m* a going out, egress; a) departure; a landing; b) outlet, mouth.

**ē-gurgitō** 1 to pour out, squander.

**ehem** *int.* = hem.

**ēheu** (*and* ĕheu) *int.* ah! alas! woe!

**eho** *int.* ho! indeed!

**ei** *int.* = hei.

**ēia** *int.* ha! well then! quick!

**ē-iaculor** 1 to shoot out.

**ē-iciō, iēcī, iectum** 3 to throw, cast, *or* drive out, to expel, banish, drive into exile; **se ēicere** to rush out *or* forth; a) to cast forth, utter; b) to bring to shore; to run aground; ēiectus 3 shipwrecked; c) to hoot, hiss (*off the stage*), to reject, disapprove.

**ēiectāmentum, ī** *n* refuse.

**ēiectiō, ōnis** *f* banishment, exile.

**ēiectō** 1 (*intens. of* eicio) to throw out; to vomit forth.

**ē-iectus, ūs** *m* emission.

**ē-ierō** 1 = eiuro.

**ēiulātiō, ōnis** *f and* ēiulātus, ūs *m* a wailing, lamenting.

**ēiulō** 1 to wail, lament.

**ē-iūrātiō, ōnis** *f* a laying down, resigning.

**ē-iūrō** 1 to deny *or* refuse on oath; a) to resign solemnly, to abdicate; b) to abjure, disown, abandon, (*alqd*).

**ēius-modī** of that sort, of such a kind.

**ē-lābor** 3 to glide out of, slip away (*ex re in alqd*); to be dislocated (*artus*); a) to escape, be lost, fall out; b) to fall, glide.

**ē-labōrō** 1 a) to work out, elaborate, produce; b) to work hard, endeavour, strive.

**ē-lāmentābilis, e** lamentable.

**ē-languēscō, guī,** — 3 to become languid.

**ē-lātiō, ōnis** *f* elevation, transport, exaltation.

**ē-lātrō** 1 to bark out, cry out.

**ē-lātus** 3 a) elevated, exalted; b) haughty, proud.

**ē-lāvī** (*perf.*), *see* ēluō.

**ē-lecebra, ae** *f* seductress.

**ē-lēctilis, e** selected, choice.

ē-lēctiō, ōnis f (and -tus, ūs m) choice, selection.

ē-lectō 1 to wheedle out.

ēlectrum, ī n a) amber; b) alloy of gold and silver.

ē-lēctus 3 picked, select.

ēlegāns, tis choice, fine, tasteful, correct, elegant, refined.

ēlegantia, ae f taste, refinement, grace, elegance; correctness.

elegēa (also -īa, -iā, -ēïa), ae f elegy.

elegēon, ī n elegy.

elegī, ōrum m/pl. elegiac verses.

elegīdion, ī n little elegy.

elementārius 3 learning the elements.

elementum, ī n simple substance, first principle, element; pl. rudiments, beginnings.

elenchus, ī m a kind of pearl.

elephantus, ī (and elephās, antis) m elephant; ivory; (elephas) elephantiasis.

eleutheria, ae f liberty.

ē-levō 1 to raise, lift up; a) to alleviate; b) to lessen, impair.

ē-liciō, cuī, citum 3 to entice out, lure forth; a) to elicit, bring out; b) to search out, find out; c) to invite, induce; d) to call down, conjure up; e) to produce, cause.

ē-līdō, sī, sum 3 a) to strike, thrust or drive out; b) to dash to pieces, shatter, crush.

ē-ligō, lēgī, lēctum 3 to pick out, choose, select.

ē-līminō 1 to carry out of doors.

ē-līmō 1 to file off, polish.

ē-linguis, e speechless; without eloquence.

ē-linguō 1 to 'de-tongue'.

ē-liquō 1 to filter out, to let trickle out.

ē-līsiō, ōnis f a squeezing out.

ē-lix, icis m furrow for draining.

ē-lixus 3 boiled, soaked.

elleborum and -us = hell...

ē-locō 1 to farm out, let on hire.

ē-locūtiō, ōnis f oratorical delivery.

ēlogium, ī n inscription; a) epitaph; b) clause in a will; c) judicial record.

ē-loquēns, tis eloquent.

ēloquentia, ae f a) eloquence; b) a pronouncing.

ēloquium, ī n a) = elocutio; b) = eloquentia.

ē-loquor 3 to speak out, speak plainly; to utter, pronounce.

ē-lōtus 3 = ēlūtus (ēluō).

ē-lūceō, xī, — 2 to shine forth, gleam, glitter; to be conspicuous or manifest.

ē-luctābilis, e such as one can struggle out of.

ē-luctor 1 a) to struggle out, burst forth; b) to overcome with difficulty (alqd).

ē-lūcubrō, -or 1 to work out by lamplight, to compose at night.

ē-lūdificor 1 to fool completely.

ē-lūdō 3 1. to win at play; 2. to parry, elude; a) to avoid; b) to mock, jeer, ridicule (alqm); c) to frustrate (alqd).

ē-lūgeō, xī, — 2 to mourn; to have finished mourning.

ē-lumbis, e weak in the loins.

ē-luō, uī, lūtum 3 to wash out, to cleanse; to wash away, efface; intrans. (with pf. ēlāvī) to be cleaned out, ruined.

ē-lūtus 3 washed out; insipid.

ēluviēs, ēī and -viō, ōnis f a flowing off; inundation, flood, pond.

em int. there! see!

ēmacerātus 3 emaciated.

ēmācitās, ātis love of buying.

ē-mancipātiō, ōnis f emancipation of a son; transfer of property, surrender.

ē-mancipō 1 to release from the paternal authority; to transfer, make over (property).

ē-maneō 2 to remain outside.

ē-mānō 1 to flow out; a) to arise, spring, emanate; b) to spread abroad, become known.    [away.]

ē-marcēscō, rcuī, — 3 to wither]

ē-mātūrēscō, ruī, — 3 to become ripe; to grow mild.

emāx, ācis fond of buying.

em-blēma, atis n embossed or inlaid work, relief.

em-bolium, ī n interlude.

ēmendābilis, e that may be amended.    [correction.]

ēmendātiō, ōnis f amendment,]

ēmendātor, ōris m corrector.

ēmendātrix, īcis f she who amends.

ē-mendīcō 1 to obtain by begging.

ē-mendō 1 to free from faults, to correct, amend; ēmendātus 3 correct, faultless, perfect.

ē-mentior 4 to lie, feign, pretend.

ē-mercor 1 to buy up, bribe.

ē-mereō *and* -eor 2 1. to deserve, obtain by service; to deserve well of (*alqm*); 2. to serve out; ēmeritus 3 veteran.

ē-mergō 3 1. to cause to rise up; se ēmergere *or* P. to raise oneself up, rise (*ex re*); 2. *intr.* to come forth *or* up, to emerge, to extricate oneself.

ē-mētior, mēnsus sum 4 to measure out; a) to pass over, traverse (*alqd*); to live through, survive; b) to impart, bestow.

ē-metō 3 to mow down, reap.

ē-micō, uī, ātum 1 to spring forth, dart forth, to break out; to rush up; to project; to shine forth.

ē-migrō 1 to wander forth, emigrate.

ē-minātiō, ōnis *f* threatening.

ēminēns, tis projecting; a) lofty, eminent; b) prominent, illustrious, excellent.

ēminentia, ae *f* prominence; the lights of a painting.

ē-mineō, uī, — 2 to project; a) to be conspicuous; b) to be eminent, distinguish oneself.

ē-minor 1 to threaten.

ē-minus *adv.* at a distance, from afar.

ē-mīror 1 to wonder at, be astonished at (*alqd*).

ēmissārium, ī *n* outlet, drain.

ēmissārius, ī *m* emissary, spy.

ē-missīcius 3 prying.

ē-missiō, ōnis *f* (*and* ēmissus, ūs *m*) a sending forth, hurling.

ē-mittō 3 to send out; a) to send forth, hurl; to utter; b) to let loose, let go, set free; c) to send forth from oneself.

emō, ēmī, ēmptum 3 to buy, purchase; to pay, bribe.

ē-moderor 1 to moderate.

ē-modulor 1 to sing, praise, celebrate.

ē-mōlior 4 a) to heave up, agitate; b) to accomplish.

ē-molliō 4 to soften; to make mild; to make effeminate.

ē-molō 3 to use up by grinding.

ēmolumentum, ī *n* advantage, profit.

ē-moneō 2 to admonish.

ē-morior 3 to die off, to perish, pass away.

ē-mortuālis, e belonging to death.

ē-moveō 2 to move out *or* away, to remove, expel.

empīricus, ī *m* physician guided only by experience.

emporium, ī *n* place of trade.

emporus, ī *m* merchant.

ēmptiō, ōnis *f* a buying, purchase.

ēmptitō 1 to buy up, purchase.

ēmptor, ōris *m* buyer, purchaser.

ē-mūgiō 4 to bellow out.

ē-mulgeō, —, lsum 2 to empty, drain.

ē-mungō, mūnxī, mūnctum 3 a) to blow the nose; ēmūnctus 3 refined; b) to cheat.

ē-mūniō 4 to wall off, fortify; to make passable.

ēmussitātus 3 (made true with a workman's ruler) perfect.

ēn *int.* lo! behold! see! there! come!

ē-nārrābilis, e that may be related *or* told.

ē-nārrātiō, ōnis *f* a) exposition; b) scanning (of verse).

ē-nārrō 1 to explain fully.

ē-nāscor 3 to grow out of, to arise.

ē-natō 1 to swim from, to escape (by swimming).

ē-nāvigō 1 a) to sail away; b) to sail through (*acc.*).

encaustus 3 burnt in, encaustic.

endromis, idis *f* athlete's wrap.

ē-necō, cuī, ctum 3 to kill, destroy; to exhaust.

ē-nervis, e nerveless, weak.

ē-nervō 1 to enervate, weaken, make effeminate.

ē-nicō 1 = eneco.

enim *cj.* for; for instance, namely; truly, certainly, in fact.

enim-vērō *adv.* truly, certainly, to be sure; but indeed.

ē-niteō, tuī, — 2 to shine forth.

ē-nitēscō, tuī, — 3 to begin to shine forth.

ē-nītor, nixus *or* nīsus sum 3 1. to struggle up, force one's way out, to ascend; to strive; 2. to bring forth, bear.

ē-nixus 3 earnest, zealous.

enlychnium, ī *n* lamp-wick.

ē-nō 1 = enato.

ē-nōdātē plainly.

ē-nōdātiō, ōnis *f* explanation.

ē-nōdis, e without knots, smooth; clear.

ē-nōdō 1 to free from knots; to explain.

ē-normis, e a) irregular; b) exceedingly big.

**ē-nŏtēscō, tuī, —** 3 to become known.

**ē-notō** 1 to make notes on. [known.]

**ēnsiculus, ī** *m* little sword.

**ēnsi-fer** *and* **-ger** 3 sword-bearing.

**ēnsis, is** *m* sword.

**enterocēlē, ēs** *f* rupture, hernia; **-cēlicus** 3 suffering from hernia.

**entheātus** 3 divinely inspired.

**entheus** 3 **a)** divinely inspired; **b)** inspiring.

**enthȳmēma, atis,** *n* reflection; a type of logical argument.

**ē-nūbō** 3 to marry out of her station *or* town (of a woman).

**ē-nucleō** 1 to take out the kernel; to explain in detail; **ēnucleātus** 3 clean, clear.

**ē-numerātiō, ōnis** *f* a counting up, enumeration.

**ē-numerō** 1 to reckon, count up.

**ēn-umquam** (*in questions*) ever?

**ē-nūntiātiō, ōnis** *f and* **-tum, ī** *n* enunciation, proposition.

**ē-nūntiātīvus** 3 declaratory.

**ē-nūntiō** 1 to speak out, tell, to declare, announce, state; to disclose, betray.

**ē-nuptiō, ōnis** *f* a marrying out of the family.

**ē-nūtriō** 4 to nourish, bring up.

**eō¹** *adv.* **1.** thither, to that place (*rarely* in that place); **2.** so far, so much; **3.** on that account; therefore; *with comp.*: the ...

**eō², iī** (*and* **īvī**), **itum, īre** to go; **a)** to walk, march, to ride, sail, &c.; **in sententiam** to vote for, support; **b)** to proceed; **c)** to happen, turn out; **d)** to pass away.

**eōdem** *adv.* to the same place; in the same place. [East.]

**Eōs (ē-)** *f* (only *nom.*) dawn; the **Eōus** (**ē** *and* **ĕ**) 3 of the morning, of the East; *subst.* ~, **ī** *m* **a)** the morning-star; **b)** man of the East.

**epaphaeresis** (*acc.* **-in**) *f* repeated removal.

**ē-pāstus** 3 eaten up.

**ephēbus, ī** *m* a youth.

**ephēmeris, idis** *f* day-book, diary.

**ephippiātus** 3 riding with a saddle.

**ephippium, ī** *n* horse-cloth, saddle.

**ephorus, ī** *m* ephor.

**epi-bata, ae** *m* marine.

**epi-chysis, is** *f* vessel for pouring out.

**epi-cōpus** 3 provided with the oars.

**epi-crocus** 3 thin, transparent.

**epicus** 3 epic.

**epi-dīcticus** 3 for display.

**epi-dīpnis, idis** *f* dessert.

**epi-gramma, atis** *n* inscription; epigram.

**epi-logus, ī** *m* peroration, epilogue.

**epi-mēnia, ōrum** *n/pl.* month's rations.

**epi-nīcia, ōrum** *n/pl.* triumphal songs.

**epi-rēdium, ī** *n* strap attaching a horse to a carriage.

**epi-stolium, ī** *n* small letter.

**epi-stula, ae** *f* letter, epistle.

**epi-taphius, ī** *m* funeral oration.

**epi-thēca, ae** *f* addition.

**epi-toma, ae** *and* **-ē, ēs** *f* abridgment, epitome.

**epitonion, ī** *n* water-tap.

**epi-tȳrum, ī** *n* olive salad.

**epops, opis** *m* hoopoe.

**epos** *n* epic poem.

**ē-pōtō** 1 to drink up, absorb; *pf. part.* P. **ēpōtus** 3 drunk up, absorbed.

**epulae, ārum** *f/pl.* **a)** viands, food, dishes; **b)** feast, banquet; entertainment.

**epulāris, e** belonging to a feast *or* banquet.

**epulātiō, ōnis** *f* feasting.

**epulō, ōnis** *m* arranger of a feast; feaster.

**epulor** 1 to feast, dine.

**epulum, ī** *n* feast, banquet.

**equa, ae** *f* mare.

**eques, itis** *m* and *f* **1.** horseman, rider; **a)** horse-soldier, cavalry; **b)** rider and horse; **2.** knight; equestrian order.

**equester, tris, tre 1.** of a horseman, of cavalry, equestrian; **2.** of knights.

**e-quidem** *adv.* **a)** truly, indeed; of course; **b)** for my part.

**equīle, is** *n* stable for horses.

**equīnus** 3 of horses.

**equiria, ōrum** *n/pl.* horse-races.

**equitābilis, e** fit for riding.

**equitātus, ūs** *m* **1. a)** a riding; **b)** cavalry; **2.** knights, the equestrian order.

**equitō** 1 to ride on horseback, to be a cavalry-man.

**equola, ae** *f* young mare.

**equuleus, ī** *m* = **eculeus.**

**equus, ī** *m* horse, steed; stallion; chariot, horse-race; cavalry.

**era, ae** *f* mistress of a house; mistress.

ē-rādīcō 1 to uproot.

ē-rādō 3 to scrape off, scratch out; to erase, eradicate.

eranus, ī m a friendly society.

ē-rēctus 3 upright, erect; a) elevated, lofty, noble; b) haughty; c) attentive, eager, intent; d) lively, resolute.

ē-rēmigō 1 to row through.

ē-rēpō 3 a) to creep through or over; b) trans. to climb.

ēreptiō, ōnis f robbery.

ēreptor, ōris m robber.

ergā prep. with acc. towards, in relation to.

ergastulum, ī n house of correction, prison.

ergō (and -ŏ) 1. prep. with gen. on account of, because of; 2. adv. a) consequently, therefore, accordingly, then; b) well then, as I was saying.

ērīcius, ī m hedgehog; cheval de frise.

eri-fuga, ae m one who runs away from his master.

ē-rigō, rēxi, rēctum 3 to raise up, set up, place upright; a) to erect, build; b) to lead to a height; c) to arouse, stir, excite; d) to encourage, cheer.

erīlis, e of a master or mistress.

Erīnȳs, yos f goddess of revenge, Fury.

ē-ripiō, ripuī, reptum 3 a) to tear out, snatch away, tear or pluck out (alqd ex, a, de re); b) to take away, rob (alci alqd); c) to rescue, deliver, free; to remove from.

ē-rogātiō, ōnis f payment, expenditure.

ē-rogitō 1 to inquire.

ē-rogō 1 to pay out, expend; to bequeath.

erōmenion n (ἐϱωμένιον) darling.

errābundus 3 wandering about.

errāticus 3 wandering.

errātiō, ōnis f a wandering.

errātor, ōris m wanderer.

errātum, ī n error, mistake, fault.

errātus, ūs m a wandering.

errō[1] 1 to wander, stray, rove; to go astray; to err, be in error, be mistaken (in re).

errō[2], ōnis m vagabond.

errōneus 3 wandering.

error, ōris m 1. a wandering, roving, straying; a) uncertainty, doubt;

b) a going astray; 2. error, infatuation; a) deception; b) mistake, fault.

ē-rubēscō, buī, — 3 to grow red, to blush, to be ashamed of; to respect.

ērūca, ae f a plant.

ē-rūctō 1 to belch forth, vomit; to cast out.

ē-rudiō 4 to instruct, teach, educate (alqm re, de re); adj. ēruditus 3 instructed, learned.

ē-ruditiō, ōnis f instruction, learning, knowledge.

ē-ruditulus 3 somewhat skilled.

ē-rumpō 3 1. trans. to cause to break forth, to emit, se ērumpere to burst forth, break out; 2. intr. to break out or forth; a) to rush or sally forth; b) to come to light, become public; c) to turn out, result.

ē-ruō 3 to dig out; a) to dig up, to throw out; b) to pluck out; c) to bring out, search or rummage out; d) to root out, to destroy utterly.

ē-ruptiō, ōnis f a breaking out, bursting forth; sally.

erus, ī m master of a house, master; owner, proprietor.

ervum, ī n vetch.

ēsca, ae f food, victuals; bait.

ēscārius 3 of food; — ia, ōrum n/pl. dishes.

ē-scendō, ndī, ēnsum 3 to climb up, mount, ascend.

ē-scēnsiō, ōnis f a landing; climbing.

ē-scēnsus, ūs m a going up, climbing; ascent.

ēsculentus 3 eatable; subst. -a, ōrum n/pl. food.

essedārius, ī m fighter in a war-chariot.

essedum, ī n (and -da, ae f) war-chariot; travelling-chariot.

essentia, ae f essential being, essence.

ēssitō 1 to eat (habitually).

ēssuriālis, e belonging to hunger.

ēs(s)uriō[1] 4 to desire to eat, to be hungry.

ēssuriō[2], ōnis m starving person.

ēsurītiō, ōnis f a hungering, hunger.

ēsuritor, ōris m hungry man.

et cj. 1. and; a) and so, and then; b) and indeed, and in fact; c) and moreover, and besides; 2. and also, also (= etiam); 3. et ... et as well ... as, both ... and, not only ... but also.

**et-enim** *cj.* for, and indeed.
**etēsiae, ārum** *m/pl.* Etesian (summer) winds.
**etēsius** 3 Etesian.
**ētho-logia, ae** *f* portrayal of character.
**ētho-logus, ī** *m* imitator of manners.
**etiam** *cj.* 1. as yet, even yet, still; a) again, **etiam atque etiam** again and again, repeatedly; even now, even at this time; b) at once; 2. also; a) even, nay even, furthermore, besides, then too; b) still, even; c) certainly.
**etiam-num, -nunc** *adv.* yet, still, till now, even to this time.
**etiam-sī** *cj.* even if, although.
**etiam-tum** *and* **-tunc** *adv.* even then, till then.
**et-sī** *cj.* a) although, albeit; b) and yet, notwithstanding.
**etymologia, ae** *f* etymology.
**eu** *int.* well! well done!
**euǎn, euhǎn** *int. the Bacchic cry* eu(h)an.
**euǎns, tis** crying *euan.*
**euax** *int.* hurrah! bravo!
**euge** (*and* **eugē**), **eugepae** *int.* well done! bravo!
**euhǎn,** *see* **euan, euhoe,** *see* **euoe.**
**eunūchus, ī** *m* eunuch.
**euoe, euhoe** *int. the shout of the Bacchantes.*
**eurīpus, ī** *m* strait, channel.
**eurŏus** 3 eastern, south-eastern.
**eurus, ī** *m* south-east wind; the east.
**eu-schēmē** *adv.* becomingly.
**ē-vādō** 3 1. *intr.* to go *or* come out, go forth; a) to climb, ascend (*ex re, in alqd*); b) to escape, get away; c) to turn out, become, result, prove to be; 2. *trans.* a) to pass, travel over; b) to climb; c) to escape (*alqd*).
**ē-vagātiō, ōnis** *f* aberration, extension.
**ē-vagor** 1 a) *intr.* to wander, make evolutions; to spread, extend; b) *trans.* to transgress.
**ē-valēscō, luī, —** 3 to grow strong; to prevail; to be able (*with inf.*).
**ē-vānēscō, nuī, —** 3 to disappear, vanish.
**ēvānidus** 3 vanishing, passing away.
**ē-vāstō** 1 to devastate.
**ē-vehō** 3 to carry *or* convey out (*alqd ex re in* or *ad alqd*); a) to lead up, lift up, raise; b) P. to proceed, advance, sail out, ride away; to be

carried away *or* forth; to raise oneself up, to mount.
**ē-vellō** 3 to tear out, pluck out (*alqd ex re; alci alqd*); to root out, erase, remove.
**ē-veniō** 4 to come out, come forth; a) to come to pass, happen, occur (*ut*); b) to fall to the lot of (*alci; ut*); c) to proceed, turn out, result, issue (*prospere, bene, male; ut*).
**ēventum, ī** *n* (*mostly plur.*) = eventus.
**ēventus, ūs** *m* consequence, issue, result; a) end; b) occurrence, accident, event; c) success, fortune.
**ē-verberō** 1 to strike violently, to beat.
**ē-vergō** (?) 3 to pour *or* shoot out.
**ēverriculum, ī** *n* drag-net; that which sweeps up *or* together.
**ē-verrō, —, rsum** 3 to sweep out; to clean out, plunder completely.
**ē-versiō, ōnis** *f* an overthrowing; destruction, ruin.
**ēversor, ōris** *m* destroyer.
**ē-vertō** 3 to overturn, throw down; a) to turn upside down; b) to demolish, destroy, ruin; c) to turn *or* drive out, expel.
**ē-vestīgātus** 3 traced out.
**ē-vidēns, tis** manifest, clear, plain, evident.     [tinctness.]
**ēvidentia, ae** *f* clearness, dis-]
**ē-vigilō** 1 to watch through; a) *trans.* to elaborate carefully; b) *intr.* to be wakeful, vigilant.
**ē-vilēscō, luī, —** 3 to become vile, worthless.
**ē-vinciō** 4 to bind *or* wind round.
**ē-vincō** 4 to conquer completely, to subdue utterly; a) to prevail over *or* upon (*ut*); b) to prove (*acc.c.inf.*)
**ē-virō** 1 to emasculate, unman.
**ē-viscerō** 1 to take out the bowels; to mangle.
**ē-vītābilis, e** avoidable.
**ē-vītō**[1] 1 to avoid, shun.
**ē-vītō**[2] 1 to deprive of life.
**ē-vocātiō, ōnis** *f* the summoning of a debtor.     [arms.]
**ē-vocātor, ōris** *m* one who calls to]
**ē-vocō** 1 to call out *or* forth (*alqm ex re, ad se*); a) to challenge; b) to summon (*for military service*); **ē-vocātī, ōrum** *m/pl.* re-enlisted veterans; c) to summon to a place of honour, to raise; d) to call forth, produce, stir, elicit; e) to seduce.

ēvoe *int.* = euoe.

ē-volō 1 to fly out *or* away (*ex re*);
a) to rush forth; b) to hasten away,
escape; c) to fly up. [ing.]

ē-volūtiō, ōnis *f* an unrolling, read-

ē-volvō 3 1. to roll out *or* forth; to
spin out; 2. to unroll, unfold; to
strip; a) to read; b) to disclose,
make clear, narrate.

ē-vomō 3 to vomit forth, cast out.

ē-vors-, -vort- = ē-vers-, -vert-.

ē-vulgō 1 to make known, publish.

ēvulsiō, ōnis *f* a pulling out.

ex *prep., see* e.

ex-acerbō 1 to exasperate.

ex-āctiō, ōnis *f* 1. a driving out;
2. an exacting; a) a collecting of
debts, tax, tribute; b) management.

ex-āctor, ōris *m* 1. driver-out, expeller; 2. a) collector, exactor;
b) executioner.

ex-āctus 3 accurate, precise, exact;
perfect.

ex-acuō 3 to sharpen, make sharp *or*
pointed; to excite, stimulate, stir up.

ex-adversum (*or* -advorsum) *and*
-sus *adv.* and *prep.* with *acc.* over
against, opposite.

ex-aedificātiō, ōnis *f* a building up,
finishing.

ex-aedificō 1 to finish building, to
build up.

ex-aequātiō, ōnis *f* a making equal.

ex-aequō 1 to make equal, place on
a level (*alqd alci rei or cum re*); to
equal. [out.]

ex-aeresimus 3 that may be taken

ex-aestuō 1 to boil up, foam up;
to effervesce, glow.

ex-aggerātiō, ōnis *f* elevation.

ex-aggerō 1 to heap *or* pile up, dam
up; a) to accumulate; b) to amplify,
magnify, heighten.

ex-agitātor, ōris *m* censurer.

ex-agitō 1 to rouse, hunt, chase;
a) to disquiet, disturb, harass; b) to
censure, blame, reproach; c) to excite, stir up.

ex-agōga, ae *f* exportation (*of goods*).

ex-albēscō 3 to turn white.

ex-ambulō 1 to walk out.

ex-āmen, inis *n* 1. swarm (*of bees*),
multitude; 2. tongue of a balance;
examination, consideration.

exāminō 1 to weigh, consider, examine.

ex-amussim *adv.* (by a workman's
ruler) accurately, perfectly.

ex-anclō 1 to drain; to endure.

exanguis, e, *see* exsanguis.

ex-animālis, e 1. lifeless; 2. killing.

ex-animātiō, ōnis *f* breathless
terror.

ex-animis, e *and* -mus 3 lifeless,
senseless, frightened.

ex-animō 1 to deprive of breath;
a) to deprive of life, to kill; b) to
exhaust, weaken, discourage, dismay.

ex-antlō 1 = exanclo.

ex-ārdēscō, ārsī, — 3 to take fire;
a) to be kindled, inflamed, to glow
(*alqa re; ad* or *in alqd*); b) to break out.

ex-ārēscō, āruī, — 3 to become
quite dry; to be dried up, be gone.

ex-armō 1 to disarm; to dismantle.

ex-arō 1 a) to plough out *or* up, to
furrow; to obtain by ploughing;
b) to write, note, set down.

ex-asciātus 3 hewn out, well prepared.

ex-asperō 1 to make quite rough;
a) to stir up (*waves*); b) to make
savage, to exasperate.

ex-auctōrō 1 to dismiss from service, discharge; to cashier.

ex-audiō 4 to hear; to catch the
sound of; to overhear; to listen,
give heed to.

ex-augeō 2 to increase exceedingly.

ex-augurātiō, ōnis *f* deconsecration.

ex-augurō 1 to deconsecrate.

ex-auspicō 1 to take a good auspice.

ex-ballistō 1 to take by storm.

ex-bibō = ebibo.

ex-caecō 1 to make blind; to block.

ex-calceō 1 to remove the shoes
from; -ceātus 3 a) barefoot; b) not
wearing buskins, i.e. acting in comedy or mime.

ex-candēscentia, ae *f* heat, wrath.

ex-candēscō 3 to become hot, to
burn with anger.

ex-cantō 1 to charm up, bring forth
by incantations.

ex-carnificō 1 to torture to death.

ex-cavātiō, ōnis *f* hollowing out.

ex-cavō 1 to hollow out.

ex-cēdō 3 1. to go out, forth, away,
to go from; to depart, withdraw,
emigrate (*ex, de, a re, re, in* or *ad
alqd*); a) to disappear; b) to go
beyond, advance, proceed; c) to
result in; d) to die; 2. *trans.* a) to
transgress; b) to rise above, overtop;
c) to exceed, surpass, pass beyond;
d) to go out of, leave (*urbem*).

**ex-cellēns, tis** high, lofty; excellent, distinguished, surpassing, superior.

**excellentia, ae** *f* superiority, excellence, merit.

**ex-cellō** 3 to rise, be distinguished, eminent, excellent.

**ex-celsitās, ātis** *f* loftiness.

**ex-celsus** 3 elevated, lofty, high; *subst.* **-um, ī** *n* height, high rank, high station.

**ex-ceptiō, ōnis** *f* a) exception; b) restriction, limitation; c) protest, objection.

**ex-ceptiuncula, ae** *f* a limitation.

**ex-ceptō** 1 to take out *or* up; to catch, receive.

**ex-cernō** 3 to sift, sort.

**ex-cerpō, psī, ptum** 3 to take *or* pick out; a) to select; b) to separate, leave out, except.

**ex-cessus, ūs** *m* a going out *or* away; a) death; b) digression.

**excetra, ae** *f* viper.

**excidium, ī** *n* (*and* **-diō, ōnis** *f*) destruction, demolition, annihilation.

**ex-cidō¹, cidī, —** 3 to fall out *or* down, to fall from (*e, de re in alqd*); a) to slip out, escape; b) to fall away, perish, be lost; c) to be deprived of (*abl.*).

**ex-cidō², cidī, cīsum** 3 to cut out *or* off, to cut *or* hew down; a) to hollow out; b) to demolish, destroy, extirpate, banish.

**ex-cieō, cīvī, citum** 2 *and* **exciō** 4 to set in motion; a) to rouse, awake, excite, stir up, shake; b) to frighten; c) to summon, call forth, call to help; d) to provoke; e) to cause, produce.

**ex-cipiō, cēpī, ceptum** 3 1. to take out (*alqd ex re*), catch up; a) to withdraw, rescue, release; b) to except, make an exception; c) to make a condition, state expressly; 2. to catch, snatch; a) to capture, take prisoner; b) to catch with the ear, to listen to; c) to await, meet, be exposed to, sustain, obtain; 3. to receive; a) to welcome, entertain; b) to engage, claim; c) to interpret, take for; 4. to follow, succeed, take up, continue, prolong.

**excīsiō, ōnis** *f* a destroying.

**ex-citō** 1 1. to arouse, stir up; a) to awaken, excite; b) to call out *or* forth; c) to cause, produce; 2. to raise, summon up, call up; a) to erect, construct; b) to kindle; c) to

enliven, revive, encourage, comfort; d) to stimulate, excite; **excitātus** 3 excited, lively, vehement.

**ex-clāmātiō, ōnis** *f* exclamation.

**ex-clāmō** 1 to cry aloud; to call out *or* aloud; to call upon.

**ex-clūdō, sī, sum** 3 to shut out, exclude; a) to thrust out, remove; b) to separate; c) to prevent, hinder; d) to hatch.

**ex-clūsiō, ōnis** *f* a shutting out.

**ex-cōgitātiō, ōnis** *f* a devising, contriving.                                      [invent.]

**ex-cōgitō** 1 to devise, contrive,

**ex-colō** 3 to cultivate, tend, work carefully; a) to improve, ennoble, perfect; b) to honour, worship.

**ex-concinnō** 1 to arrange, to furnish (a house).

**ex-coquō** 3 to boil *or* melt out; to dry up.

**ex-cors, dis** silly, stupid.

**excrēmentum¹, ī** *n* excrement, spittle, mucus.

**excrēmentum², ī** *n* growth.

**ex-crēscō** 3 to grow out *or* up, increase.                                      [torture.]

**ex-cruciābilis, e** deserving of

**ex-cruciō** 1 to torture, torment, plague, afflict, trouble.

**ex-cubiae, ārum** *f/pl.* a lying out on guard; watch, sentries.

**excubitor, ōris** *m* watchman, guard, sentinel.

**excubitus, ūs** *m* guard-duty.

**ex-cubō** 1 to lie *or* sleep out; to keep watch.

**ex-cūdō, dī, sum** 3 to strike out, hammer out; a) to forge, mould; b) to hatch out; c) to prepare, compose.                              [stamp firm.]

**ex-culcō** 1 to tread down *or* out; to

**ex-cūrātus** 3 carefully attended to.

**ex-currō, (cu)currī, cursum** 3 to run out *or* forth, to hasten forward; a) to sally forth, make an incursion; b) to make an excursion; c) to issue forth; d) to spread; e) to project.

**ex-cursō** 1 to sally forth repeatedly.

**ex-cursiō, ōnis** *f* a running out *or* forth; a stepping forward; a) excursion; b) sally, attack, invasion; c) digression.

**ex-cursor, ōris** *m* skirmisher, scout.

**ex-cursus, ūs** *m* = **excursio**.

**excūsābilis, e** excusable.

**excūsātiō, ōnis** *f* a declining, excusing, excuse, plea.

**ex-cūsō** 1 a) to decline, refuse (*alqd*); b) to plead as an excuse, to apologize for, excuse, absolve from, dispense with; c) to pretend.

**ex-cutiō, cussī, cussum** 3 to shake out *or* off; a) to cast *or* drive out (*alci alqd*); b) to throw down, hurl, send forth; c) to drive out *or* away, expel, reject; d) to shake out, search, investigate, examine; e) to wrest, extort; f) to shake about; g) to extend; to discharge; **excussō lacertō**, *or* **excussē** (*adv.*), with extended arm.

**ex-dorsuō** 1 to bone (*fish*).

**exec...**, *see* **exsec...**

**ex-edō, ēdī, ēsum** 3 to eat up, consume; a) to corrode, hollow out; b) to destroy.                              [seats.]

**ex-edra, ae** *f* hall furnished with|

**ex-edrium, ī** *n* sitting-room.

**exemplar** (*and* **-āre**) **āris** *n* a) copy; b) image, likeness; c) model, pattern, example.

**exemplāris, is** *m* copy.

**exemplum, ī** *n* a) copy; b) tenor, purport, contents; c) imitation, image; d) pattern, model, specimen, instance, ideal; e) way, manner; f) example, warning, punishment; g) precedent.                              [ture.]

**ex-enterō** 1 to disembowel; to tor-|

**ex-eō** 1. to go out, forth, *or* away; a) to march out; to disembark, land; b) to turn out, result; c) to leave, withdraw; d) to pass away, run out, expire; e) to mount upwards, ascend, rise; f) to spread abroad, become known; 2. *trans.* a) to exceed; b) to avoid, evade (*alqd*).

**exequiae** *and* **exequor**, *see* **exs-**.

**ex-erceō, uī, itum** 2 1. to keep in motion; a) to keep busy, at work; to occupy, employ; b) to trouble, disturb, harass; 2. to exercise, practise, train, discipline (*alqm re, in re, ad alqd*); a) to follow, pursue, employ oneself about; b) to till, work (at), administer; **exercitus** 3 harassed; disciplined, trained; hard, distressing.

**exercitātiō, ōnis** *f* exercise, training.

**exercitium, ī** *n* exercise.

**exercitō** 1 to exercise often; **exercitātus** 3 a) practised, versed, trained (*in re*); b) troubled, vexed, harassed, worried (*re*).

**exercitor, ōris** *m* trainer.

**exercitus, ūs** *m* 1. exercise; 2. army, trained body of men, forces; a) land-army, infantry; b) multitude, host, swarm.

**ex-errō** 1 to wander away.

**ex-ēsor, ōris** *m* an erosive agent.

**exfāfillātus** 3 bared.

**ex-hālātiō, ōnis** *f* exhalation, vapour.

**ex-hālō** 1 to breathe out, exhale.

**ex-hauriō** 4 1. to draw out, empty; a) to take out, empty out (*alqd ex re*); b) to take away, remove (*alci alqd*); 2. to drink up, empty; a) to exhaust, bring to an end; b) to undergo, endure.

**ex-hērēdō** 1 to disinherit.

**ex-hērēs, ēdis** disinherited.

**ex-hibeō, uī, itum** 2 to hold forth, tender, present; to deliver, produce, show; a) to furnish; b) to display, exhibit (*alci alqd*); c) to maintain, support; d) to procure, occasion, cause.

**ex-hilarō** 1 to gladden.

**ex-horrēscō, ruī, —** 3 to tremble, shudder, be terrified (at).

**ex-hortātiō, ōnis** *f* exhortation.

**ex-hortor** 1 to exhort, encourage.

**ex-igō, ēgī, āctum** 3 1. to drive out, thrust out, expel (*alqm ex re*); a) to drive, plunge, thrust (*a weapon*); b) to sell, export; 2. to demand, require, enforce, exact (*money*); a) to inquire after, to ask (*alqd ab or de alqo*); b) to measure, estimate, weigh; c) to examine, consider, deliberate; 3. to complete, finish; a) to pass, live through; b) to establish, settle.

**exiguitās, ātis** *f* scantiness, littleness, shortness.

**exiguus** 3 a) scanty, small, little, petty, short; b) mean, poor, trifling.

**ex-īlis, e** a) thin, slender, meagre; b) poor, feeble, wretched; cheerless; destitute.

**exīlitās, ātis** *f* leanness, poorness.

**exiliō, exilium** *see* **exs-**.

**exim** *adv.*, = **exinde**.

**eximius** 3 1. excepted; 2. distinguished, extraordinary, excellent.

**ex-imō, ēmī, ēmptum** 3 to take out *or* away (*alqd de or ex re; alci alqd*); a) to separate, remove; b) to free, release, deliver; c) to consume, spend (*time*); d) to remove, banish; e) to except, make an exception.

**exin** *adv.* = **exinde**.

**ex-inániö** 4 to empty, make empty; to plunder.

**ex-inde** *adv.* from there; then, after that, next; since then.

**existimátiö, önis** *f* a) judgment, opinion; b) good name, reputation, honour; credit.

**existimátor, öris** *m* judge, critic.

**ex-ístimö** 1 a) to judge, consider, suppose, think, reckon; b) to value, estimate; c) to pass judgment on (*de re*); *subst.* **exístimantés, ium** *m/pl.* critics.

**existö,** *see* **exsistö.**

**exitiä(bi)lis, e** destructive, fatal.

**ex-itiö, önis** *f* a going out.

**exitiösus** 3 destructive, pernicious, deadly.

**ex-itium, í** *n* destruction, ruin, hurt.

**ex-itus, ús** *m* a) a going out, egress, departure; outlet, passage; b) end, close, conclusion; end of life, death; issue, result, event.

**ex-lecebra, ae** *f* = **elecebra.**

**ex-léx, légis** bound by no law, lawless.

**ex-obsecrö** 1 to beg earnestly.

**ex-oculö** 1 to knock out the eyes of.

**exodium, í** *n* after-play, interlude.

**ex-olésčö, lévi, (létum)** to grow out of use, become obsolete, pass away; *adj.* **exolétus** 3 a) grown up (*for prostitution*); b) obsolete, forgotten.

**ex-onerö** 1 to unload, disburden; a) to remove, send off; b) to discharge, release.

**ex-optábilis, e** very desirable.

**ex-optö** 1 to desire or wish greatly, to long for (with *inf.* or *ut*); **ex-optátus** 3 longed for, desired.

**ex-örábilis, e** easily entreated.

**ex-örábula, örum** *n/pl.* means of entreaty.

**ex-örátor, öris** *m* one who obtains by entreaty.

**ex-ördior** 4 to lay the warp, begin to weave; to begin, commence (*alqd; inf.*); *subst.* **exörsum, í** *n* = **exordium.**

**exördium, í** *n* a beginning, commencement; introduction.

**ex-orior** 4 to come out, spring up, rise; a) to come forth, appear; b) to arise, originate, begin, proceed.

**ex-örnátiö, önis** *f* an adorning.

**ex-örnátor, öris** *m* embellisher.

**ex-örnátulus** 3 rather smart.

**ex-örnö** 1 to fit out, equip, furnish, supply with (*alqd alqa re*); a) to arrange, instruct; b) to adorn, embellish, extol.

**ex-örö** 1 a) to prevail upon, persuade by entreaty; b) to obtain by entreaty; to soften, appease (*alqd; ut*).

**ex-örsum, í** *n* = **exordium.**

**ex-örsus, ús** *m* = **exordium.**

**ex-ortus, ús** *m* a rising.

**ex-os, ossis** boneless.

**ex-ösculor** 1 to kiss.

**ex-ossö** 1 to bone.

**ex-östra, ae** *f* movable stage in a theatre; open stage.

**ex-ösus** 3 hating, detesting (*with acc.*).

**exöticus** 3 outlandish, foreign.

**ex-pallésčö** 3 to turn pale; to shrink from (*alqd*).

**ex-palliátus** 3 deprived of a cloak.

**ex-pallidus** 3 very pale.

**ex-palpö** 1 to coax out.

**ex-pandö** 3 to unfold.

**ex-patrö** 1 to squander in debauchery.

**ex-pavésčö, pávi** 3 to be terrified, frightened (of).

**expectö** 1, *see* **exspecto.**

**ex-pectorö** 1 to banish from the mind. [perty.]

**ex-peculiátus** 3 deprived of pro-

**ex-pediö** 4 1. *trans.* to disengage, extricate (*alqd ex re*); a) to let loose, set free; **se expedire** to escape; b) to free from evil or obstacle, to bring through critical circumstances, to put in order, arrange, set right; c) to dispatch, hurl; d) to relate, narrate; e) to make ready, prepare, procure; 2. *intr.* to be serviceable, profitable, advantageous (*expedit alci*).

**expeditiö, önis** *f* enterprise, expedition, special mission; a getting rid of, despatch.

**expeditus** 3 disengaged; a) unimpeded, free, easy; b) ready, at hand, ready for action.

**ex-pellö, puli, pulsum** 3 to drive out or away, to thrust out (*alqd ex re, re, in alqd*); a) to expel, banish, eject; b) to repudiate, reject; c) to rob of (*alqm re*); d) to shoot.

**ex-pendö, ndi, énsum** 3 to weigh out, weigh; a) to ponder, consider, estimate; b) to pay out, pay, expend, lend out; c) to pay, suffer, undergo; *subst.* **expēnsum, ī** *n* payment; *alci alqd* **expēnsum ferre** to enter a sum as paid to someone.

**ex-pergĕfaciō** 3 to awaken, rouse.

**expergiscor, perrēctus sum** 3 to be awakened, to wake.

**expergō, gī, gitum** 3 to awaken, rouse.        [patient of (*alcis rei*).]

**experiēns, tis** enterprising, active;

**experientia, ae** *f* a) trial, proof; b) experience, practice.

**experimentum, ī** *n* a) trial, proof, test; b) experience.

**experior, pertus sum** 4 to try, prove, test; a) to undertake, attempt, risk, undergo, experience; b) to contend with (*cum alqo*); c) to learn *or* know by experience (*alqd in re*).

**ex-pers, tis** having no part in, not sharing in, devoid of, free from (*with gen.*).

**expertus** 3 a) experienced in (*gen.*); b) tried, proved.

**expetendus** 3 desirable.

**expetēns, entis** desirous.

**ex-petessō** 3 to desire, wish for.

**expetibilis, e** desirable.

**ex-petō** 3 a) to long for, seek after, strive for, aspire to, desire, wish (*alqd ab alqo*); b) to befall (*in alqm*).

**expiātiō, ōnis** *f* atonement.

**ex-pīlātiō, ōnis** *f* a pillaging.

**expīlātor, ōris** *m* plunderer.

**ex-pīlō** 1 to pillage, plunder.

**ex-pingō** 3 to paint, depict, describe to the life.

**ex-piō** 1 to atone for, make amends, purify (*alqd a re*); a) to expiate, avenge; b) to make good; c) to appease.

**ex-piscor** 1 to fish out; to search out (*alqd ab alqo*).

**explānābilis, e** intelligible.

**ex-plānātiō, ōnis** *f* explanation, interpretation.

**ex-plānātor, ōris** *m* interpreter.

**explānātus** 3 plain; distinct.

**ex-plānō** 1 a) to make plain *or* flat, to spread out; b) to explain; interpret.

**ex-plēmentum, ī** *n* filling, food.

**ex-pleō, plēvī, plētum** 2 to fill up *or* full (*alqd re*); a) to fill, make up, complete (*a number*); to supply, make good; b) to finish, ac-

complish; c) to fill, satisfy; d) to discharge, execute, perform; e) to pass over, live through; **explētus** 3 complete, perfect.

**ex-plētiō, ōnis** *f* a satisfying.

**explicātiō, ōnis** *f* an unfolding, uncoiling; exposition, explanation.

**explicātor, ōris** *m* explainer, expounder.

**explicātrix, īcis** *f* she that explains.

**explicātus, ūs** *m* an unfolding; exposition.

**ex-plicō, cāvī** *or* **cuī, cātum** *or* **citum** 1 to unfold, unroll, uncoil; a) to spread out, loosen, undo; b) to spread *or* stretch out, extend, display; c) to disentangle, arrange, regulate, settle, adjust, perform; d) to set free, release; e) to explain, exhibit, express, interpret; **ex-plicātus** 3 well-ordered, regular; plain, clear; **explicitus** 3 easy, plain.

**ex-plōdō, sī, sum** 3 to drive out, hiss off (*the stage*), explode; to disapprove.        [examination.]

**explōrātiō, ōnis** *f* investigation,]

**explōrātor, ōris** *m* scout, spy.

**explōrātōrius** 3 of a scout.

**ex-plōrō** 1 to search out, examine, explore (*alqd*; *de re*); to spy out, reconnoitre; **explōrātus** 3 ascertained, established, certain, sure.

**explōsiō, ōnis** *f* a driving off the stage.

**ex-poliō** 4 to smooth off, polish up; to finish, adorn, embellish.

**ex-polītiō, ōnis** *f* a polishing, finishing, embellishing.

**ex-pōnō** 3 to put *or* set out *or* forth; a) to expose (*children*); b) to set on shore, disembark; c) to offer (*cash*); d) to leave unprotected, to abandon (*alci alqd*); e) to publish; f) to exhibit, propose, relate, explain, expound; **expositus** 3 open, accessible; exposed, abandoned; common, vulgar.

**ex-porrigō** (and **-porgō**) 3 to stretch out.

**ex-portātiō, ōnis** *f* exportation.

**ex-portō** 1 to carry out, bring out (*alqd ex re*); a) to convey away, export; b) to send away, banish.

**ex-poscō, poposcī, — 3** to ask *or* beg earnestly (*alqd ab alqo, alqd alqm*); a) to request, entreat, implore; b) to demand the delivery of a person.

**ex-positicius** 3 exposed.

**ex-positiō, ōnis** *f* a) an exposing; b) exposition, narration, explanation.

**ex-postulātiō, ōnis** *f* a) demand, request; b) expostulation, complaint.

**ex-postulō** 1 a) to demand urgently (*alqd ab alqo; ut*), to insist on; b) to expostulate (*cum alqo alqd or de re; acc.c.inf.*), complain of.

**ex-pōtus** = **ēpōtus**.

**ex-primō, pressī, pressum** 3 to press *or* squeeze out; a) to force out; b) to carry up, raise; c) to pronounce, articulate; d) to extort, elicit; e) to form, represent, portray, express, imitate, copy; f) to translate, render; g) to describe; **ex-pressus** 3 clearly exhibited, distinct, visible, manifest, clear, plain; translated.

**ex-probrātiō, ōnis** *f* a reproaching, charge.

**ex-probrātor, ōris** *m*, **-trīx, īcis** *f* upbraider.

**ex-probrō** 1 to reproach with, blame for, to charge against (*alci alqd; de re*).

**ex-prōmō** 3 to bring forth *or* out; a) to show forth, exhibit, display; b) to utter, declare.

**expugnābilis, e** assailable.

**expugnātiō, ōnis** *f* a taking, storming.

**expugnātor, ōris** *m* stormer, conqueror.

**expugnāx, ācis** victorious, effectual.

**ex-pugnō** 1 to take by assault, to storm, capture; a) to subdue, overcome, conquer; b) to gain by force, to force (*alqd; ut*).

**expulsiō, ōnis** *f* a driving out, expulsion.

**ex-pulsō** 1 to knock away.

**expulsor, ōris** *m* expeller.

**expultrix, īcis** *f* she that expels.

**ex-pungō, nxī, nctum** 3 to strike out, blot out.

**ex-pūr(i)gātiō, ōnis** *f* excuse.

**ex-pūr(i)gō** 1 to purge, cleanse, purify; to exculpate, excuse.

**ex-pūtēscō** 3 to rot.

**ex-putō** 1 to consider, think.

**ex-quaerō** = **exquiro**.

**ex-quīrō, sīvī, sītum** 3 to search out, seek diligently; a) to examine;

b) to inquire out, make inquiry; investigate; c) to ask (*alqd ab or ex alqo*); to demand; **exquīsītus** 3 carefully studied, choice, refined.

**ex-rādīcitus** from the roots.

**ex-sacrificō** 1 to sacrifice.

**ex-saeviō** 4 to cease raging.

**ex-sanguis, e** a) bloodless; lifeless; b) pale, wan; c) weak, feeble.

**ex-saniō** 1 to drain (*a body*) of watery *or* bloody matter.

**ex-sarciō** 4 to patch, mend, make good.

**ex-satiō** = **exsaturo**.

**ex-saturābilis, e** that may be satiated.

**ex-saturō** 1 to satiate, satisfy.

**exscendō** *and* **exscēnsiō, ōnis** *f*, *see* **escendo** *and* **escensio**.

**ex-scindō** 3 to tear out; to extirpate, destroy.

**ex-screō** 1 to cough up, to clear the throat.

**ex-scrībō** 3 to write out *or* off; a) to copy; b) to write down.

**ex-sculpō** 3 a) to cut *or* chisel out, to carve; b) to scratch out, erase.

**ex-secō** 1 to cut out; a) to extort; b) to castrate.

**exsecrābilis, e** a) accursed, execrable; b) execrating.

**exsecrātiō, ōnis** *f* a) execration, curse; b) solemn oath.

**ex-secrātus** 3 cursed, execrable.

**ex-secror** 1 a) to curse, execrate; b) to take a solemn oath.

**ex-sectiō, ōnis** *f* a cutting out.

**ex-secūtiō, ōnis** *f* performance, execution; administration.

**ex-secūtor, ōris** *m* avenger.

**exsequiae, ārum** *f/pl.* funeral procession, funeral rites.

**exsequiālis, e** of a funeral.

**ex-sequor** 3 1. to follow to the grave; 2. to follow, pursue; a) to strive after; b) to investigate, examine; c) to assert, maintain; d) to prosecute, carry out, execute, perform, accomplish; e) to punish, avenge; f) to go through, describe, relate; g) to bear, suffer.

**ex-serciō** 4, *see* **exsarcio**.

**ex-serō, ruī, rtum** 3 a) to stretch out *or* forth, thrust out, put forth; b) to bare, uncover; **se exserere** to come forth.

**ex-sertō** 1 to stretch forth; to bare.

**ex-sībilō** 1 to hiss out, to hiss from the stage.

**ex-siccō** 1 to dry up, make quite dry.

**ex-sicō** 1 = exseco.

**ex-signō** 1 to write out, note down.

**ex-siliō, luī** (*and* **livī**), — 4 **a**) to leap out; **b**) to spring forth, start up.

**exsilium, ī** *n* **a**) exile; **b**) place of exile, retreat.

**ex-sistō, stitī,** — 3 to step out, come forth (*ab, ex re*); **a**) to emerge, appear, come to light; **b**) to spring, proceed, arise; **c**) to be visible, to exist, to be.

**ex-solvō** 3 to loose, unbind, untie; **a**) to deliver, release, set free (*alqm alqa re*); **b**) to discharge, pay (*debts*); **c**) to throw off, lay aside; **d**) to fulfil, keep; **e**) to repay; **f**) to solve, explain.

**ex-somnis, e** sleepless.

**ex-sorbeō, uī,** — 2 to suck out, suck up, drain, drink, swallow.

**ex-sors, tis** free from; deprived of (*with gen.*); chosen, choice.

**ex-spatior** 1 to wander from the course *or* out of the way; to spread, overflow.

**ex-spectātiō, ōnis** *f* an awaiting, expectation.

**ex-spectō** 1 to look out for, await, expect, wait for, wait (*with dum, si, ut; alqd ab* or *ex re; with acc.c.inf.*); to hope, long for, desire; to fear, apprehend, anticipate; **exspectātus** 3 expected, longed for, desired, welcome.

**ex-spergō** 3 to disperse.

**ex-spēs** (*indecl.*) hopeless (*with gen.*). [out, exhalation.]

**ex-spirātiō, ōnis** *f* a breathing]

**ex-spirō** 1 to breathe out; to expire, die, cease.

**ex-splendēscō, duī,** — 3 to shine forth, glitter.

**ex-spoliō** 1 to spoil, pillage, plunder, rob (*alqm alqa re*).

**ex-spuō** 3 to spit out; to cast out, expel.

**ex-sternō** 1 to terrify, dismay.

**ex-stillēscō,** —, —3 to begin to drip.

**ex-stillō** 1 to drop *or* trickle out (*re*).

**ex-stimulātor, ōris** *m* inciter.

**ex-stimulō** 1 to prick, goad; to excite.

**ex-(s)tinctiō, ōnis** *f* extinction.

**ex-(s)tinctor, ōris** *m* extinguisher; destroyer.

**ex-(s)tinguō, inxī, inctum** 3 to put out, quench, extinguish; **a**) to dry up; **b**) to destroy, kill, ruin; **c**) to abolish, annihilate, annul; **P.** to go out (*fire*); to die, perish, to be forgotten.

**ex-stirpō** 1 to root out, to eradicate.

**ex-stō,** —, — 1 to stand out *or* forth, to project (*ex* or *de re*); **a**) to be visible, appear; **b**) to be extant, to exist.

**ex-structiō, ōnis** *f* an erecting, building up.

**ex-struō** 3 to pile up; to erect, raise, build up, fill with buildings.

**ex-sūdō** 1 to sweat out; to sweat at (*acc.*), perform with sweating.

**ex-sūgō** 3 to suck out.

**ex-sul, ulis** *m and f* banished person, exile.

**ex-sulō** 1 to be banished, live in exile.

**exsultātiō, ōnis** *f* exultation.

**ex-sultim** *adv.* leaping about, frisking.

**ex-sultō** 1 to spring, jump, leap up; **a**) to move freely, gambol about; **b**) to exult, rejoice; **c**) to revel, to boast. [mountable.]

**ex-superābilis, e** superable, sur-]

**ex-superantia, ae** *f* superiority, pre-eminence.

**ex-superō** 1 to mount up, appear above (*alqd*); to surpass, surmount, excel, overcome.

**ex-surdō** 1 to deafen; to dull.

**ex-surgō** 3 to rise up, get up, stand up (*contra* or *adversus alqd*); to recover strength.

**ex-suscitō** 1 to awaken, rouse; to stir up.

**exta, ōrum** *n/pl.* the internal organs.

**ex-tābēscō, buī,** — 3 to waste away; to vanish, disappear.

**extāris, e** for cooking *exta*.

**ex-temp(u)lō** *adv.* immediately, straightway.

**ex-temporālis, e** extemporary, without preparation.

**ex-temporālitās, ātis** *f* faculty of extemporary speech.

**ex-tendō, tendī, tentum** *or* **tēnsum** 3 to extend, stretch out; **a**) to spread out (*alqd in* or *ad alqd*); **b**) to increase, enlarge, prolong, continue, lengthen; **c**) to spend, pass.

**extēnsus, extentus** 3 extensive.

**ex-tentō** 1 to stretch, exert.

**ex-tentus, ūs** *m* extent, width.

**ex-tenuātiō, ōnis** *f* diminution.

**ex-tenuō** 1 to make thin; a) to lengthen; b) to make small, reduce, diminish, lessen, weaken, extenuate; **extenuātus** 3 faint, weak, reduced.

**exter, a, um** on the outside, outward, foreign; *comp.* **exterior, ius** outward, outer, exterior, on the outer side; *superl.* (**extimus** *and*) **extrēmus** 3 outermost, utmost, extreme, furthest; a) remotest, last; b) highest, greatest, lowest, least, meanest, worst.

**ex-terebrō** 1 to bore out.

**ex-tergeō** 2 to wipe; to strip clean, plunder.

**ex-terminō** 1 to drive out *or* away; a) to expel, banish; b) to remove, put away.

**externus** 3 outward, external; foreign, strange; **externa, ōrum** *n/pl.* external things, foreign examples; *subst.* **externus, ī** *m* foreigner.

**ex-terō** 3 to rub out *or* away; to crush.

**ex-terreō** 2 to frighten, terrify, alarm; to rouse up.

**ex-tersus, ūs** *m* a wiping.

**exterus** 3 = **exter**.

**ex-texō** 3 to unweave; to plunder.

**ex-timēscō, muī, —** 3 to be greatly afraid (of).

**extimus** 3, *superl.* of **exter**.

**ex-tinguō** 3, *see* **ex(s)tinguō**.

**exti-spex, icis** *m* observer of entrails, diviner.

**exti-spicium, ī** *n* divination by inspection of entrails.

**extō, —, —** 1, *see* **exsto**.

**ex-tollō, —, —** 3 to lift out *or* up, to raise up; a) to raise, extol, elevate, praise; b) to excite, encourage; c) to adorn, beautify.

**ex-torqueō** 2 to twist *or* wrench out, wrest away (*alqd ex* or *de re*); a) to put out of joint, torture; b) to extort, obtain by force, tear away.

**ex-torris, e** exiled, banished.

**ex-tortor, ōris** *m* snatcher.

**extrā** *adv.* and *prep.* with *acc.* on the outside, without, externally; outside, without, beyond; except, besides.

**ex-trahō** 3 to draw *or* drag out (*alqd a, de, ex re in* or *ad alqd*); a) to draw forward; b) to release, extricate; c) to protract, prolong, draw out.

**extrāneus** 3 external, stranger.

**extra-ōrdinārius** 3 extraordinary, uncommon, unnatural.

**extrārius** 3 = **extraneus**.

**extrēmitās, ātis** *f* extremity, end; circumference.

**extrēmus** 3, *superl.* of **exter**.

**ex-trīcō** (*and* **-or**) 1 to disentangle, extricate, clear; to procure with difficulty, hunt up.

**extrīn-secus** *adv.* a) from without; b) outside.

**ex-trūdō** 3 to thrust out *or* forth, drive out *or* away (*alqd ex* or *a re in alqd*); to get rid of.

**extruō** 3, *see* **exstruo**.

**ex-tumefactus** 3 swollen up.

**ex-tumeō** 2 to swell up.

**extumus** 3 = **extimus**.

**ex-tundō, tudī, (tūsum)** 3 to beat out, strike out; a) to hammer *or* forge out; b) to form, devise, fashion; c) to drive out *or* away; d) to dash to pieces.

**ex-turbō** 1 to drive out *or* away; thrust away; to repudiate, divorce.

**ex-ūberō** 1 a) to grow luxuriantly; b) to abound, come forth in abundance (*abl.*).

**exul, ulis** = **exsul**.

**exulcerātiō, ōnis** *f* a making sore, inflammation.

**ex-ulcerō** 1 to make worse; to exasperate, embitter.

**ex-ululō** 1 to howl, cry out.

**ex-undō** 1 to flow out, overflow.

**ex-unguō** 3 to rub away by anointing; to squander on unguents.

**ex-uō, uī, ūtum** 3 to draw out, take off, pull off; a) to lay aside, shake off, put away, divest oneself of (*alqd*); b) to unclothe, bare (*alqm re*); c) to strip, despoil, deprive.

**ex-urgeō** 2 to squeeze out.

**ex-ūrō** 3 a) to burn out *or* up, consume by fire; b) to dry up; c) to inflame; d) to destroy.

**ex-ustiō, ōnis** *f* a burning, combustion.

**exuviae, ārum** *f/pl.* a) what is stripped off, skin of an animal; b) clothing, equipment, arms; c) spoils, booty.

# F

**F** *abbr.* = **filius**.

**faba, ae** *f* bean.

**fabālis, e** of beans.

**fābella, ae** *f* a) short story, fable, tale; b) short play.

**faber**[1], **brī** *m* workman, smith, artificer, carpenter; engineer, sapper.

**faber**[2], **bra, brum** skilful; workmanlike.

**fabrē-faciō** 3 to make artistically *or* skilfully.

**fabrica, ae** *f* 1. work-shop; 2. a) trade, profession, art; architecture; b) skilful production, fabric, structure; c) crafty device, trick.

**fabricātiō, ōnis** *f* a framing, construction.

**fabricātor, ōris** *m* artificer, framer, contriver.

**fabricor** (*and* **-cō**) 1 a) to frame, forge, construct, build; b) to form, fashion.

**fabrīlis, e** of a workman *or* artificer; **-lia, ium** *n/pl.* tools.

**fābula, ae** *f* 1. narration, account, tale, story; a) fable, fiction; b) dramatic poem, play; epic poem; c) affair, concern, matter; 2. common talk, conversation.

**fābulāris, e** fabulous, legendary.

**fābulātor, ōris** *m* narrator.

**fābulor** 1 to talk, chat, speak.

**fābulōsus** 3 fabulous.

**fabulus, ī** *m* bean.

**facessō, īvī** *and* **iī, itum** 3 1. to perform, execute, accomplish; to bring on, cause; 2. to go away, depart.

**facētia, ae** *f* drollery; *pl.* **-iae, ārum** *f* wit, pleasantry, humour.

**facētus** 3 fine, elegant; a) courteous, polite; b) merry, witty, humorous.

**faciēs, ēī** *f* external form, outward appearance, shape, figure; aspect; a) pretence, pretext; b) look, face, countenance; beauty.

**facilis, e** 1. easy to do, easy, without difficulty; favourable, prosperous; 2. a) ready, quick; b) good-natured, compliant, willing,

yielding, courteous, affable; 3. *adv.* **facile** easily, without trouble *or* difficulty; certainly, without contradiction, beyond dispute; readily, willingly; agreeably, well; **non** (**haud**) **facile** hardly.

**facilitās, ātis** *f* 1. easiness, ease, facility in doing; fluency of expression; 2. a) inclination (*with gen.*); b) willingness, courteousness, affability.

**facinorōsus** 3 criminal.

**facinus, oris** *n* (conspicuous) deed, action; a) bad deed, crime, misdeed; b) instrument of villainy; c) *pl.* criminals.

**faciō, fēcī, factum** 3 1. (*trans.*) to make, produce, effect, create, perform, carry out; a) to build, erect (*castra*); b) to compose, write; to coin, make, earn (*money*); c) to commit, execute, practise; exercise; to celebrate, offer; to suffer (*damnum, naufragium*); d) to cause, occasion; to give, procure (*alci magnas opes, nomen, potestatem*); to deal with (*quid facias hoc homine?* what is to be done with ...?); e) to take care, provide for (*with ut*); 2. (*trans.*) a) to make into, render, appoint (*with double acc.*); b) to represent, introduce (*with acc. part.*), feign, assert; c) to estimate, value, consider (*with gen.*); to suppose; d) to put under, in the power of (*gen.*); 3. (*intr.*) a) to do, deal, act in any manner; b) to side, take part (*cum alqo*); c) to be good, of use, of service.

**facteon** = **faciendum**.

**factiō, ōnis** *f* a making, doing, preparing; a) class, order, sect, party; b) faction, partisans, party--spirit, party-organization.

**factiōsus** 3 factious, seditious; partisan.

**factitō** 1 to do *or* make frequently, to practise. [nearer being done.]

**factius nihilō** (*factus*) not any]

**factor, ōris** *m* a) oil-presser; b) one who catches a ball (?).

**factus** 3 done, made, accomplished, created; *subst.* **factum, ī** *n* deed, action, exploit; event.

**facul** *adv.* = **facile** (*see* facilis 3).

**facula, ae** *f* little torch.

**facultās, ātis** *f* capability, possibility, opportunity; a) permission, power, means; b) skill, ability; c) plenty, abundance, supply, stock, property.

**fācundia, ae** *f* eloquence, command of language.

**fācunditās, ātis** *f* talkativeness.

**fācundus** 3 eloquent.

**faeceus** 3 of dregs; filthy.

**faecula, ae** *f* wine-tartar.

**faenebris, e** of interest, of usury.

**faenerātiō, ōnis** *f* usury.

**faenerātō** with interest (*i.e* 'you (he) shall pay for it').

**faenerātor, ōris** *m* capitalist, usurer.

**faeneror** (*and* **-rō**) 1 to lend on interest; to invest.

**faenilia, ium** *n*/*pl.* hay-loft.

**faeni-seca, ae** *m* hay-cutter, rustic.

**faenum, ī** *n* hay.

**faenus, oris** *n* produce; gain, profit; a) interest, usury; b) burden of debt, lent capital.

**faenusculum, ī** *n* a bit of interest.

**faex, cis** *f* sediment, lees, dregs; a) salt of tartar; b) refuse, rabble.

**fāgineus** *and* **fāginus** 3 of beech, beechen.

**fāgus, ī** *f* beech-tree; beechwood.

**fala, ae** *f* a scaffold used in besieging cities; wooden pillar.

**falārica, ae** *f* fire-dart.

**falcārius, ī** *m* sickle-maker.

**falcātus** 3 a) furnished with scythes; b) sickle-shaped.

**falci-fer** 3 sickle-bearing.

**fallācia, ae** *f* deceit, trick, artifice; intrigue (*pl.*).

**fallāci-loquus** 3 speaking deceitfully.

**fallāx, ācis** deceitful, deceptive, fallacious.

**fallō, fefellī, falsum** 3 to deceive, cheat, trick; **P.** to deceive oneself, be mistaken; a) to violate, break (*fidem*); b) to imitate, counterfeit; c) to cause to pass imperceptibly, to beguile, cheat, silence; d) to escape the notice of, be concealed, remain undiscovered; **mē fallit** I fail to observe.

**falsārius, ī** *m* forger.

**falsi-dicus** 3 speaking falsely.

**falsi-ficus** 3 acting falsely.

**falsi-iūrius** 3 swearing falsely.

**falsi-loquus** (*and* **-locus**) speaking falsely.

**falsimōnia, ae** *f* deceit.

**falsi-parēns, tis** having a pretended father.

**falsus** 3 false **1.** feigned, counterfeit, pretended; a) spurious, supposed; b) untrue, erroneous; **2.** deceitful, hypocritical; *subst.* **falsum, ī** *n* falsehood, deceit, fraud, error; *adv.* **falsō.**

**falx, cis** *f* a) sickle, scythe; b) wall-hook.

**fāma, ae** *f* a) report, rumour, fame, tradition; b) public opinion, popular voice; c) reputation, character, renown, infamy, scandal.

**famēlicus** 3 famished, starved.

**famēs, is** *f* hunger; a) famine; b) poverty; c) greed.

**fāmigerātiō, ōnis** *f* report.

**fāmigerātor, ōris** *m* talebearer.

**familia, ae** *f* household; slaves, servants; family property, estate; house, family; company, sect.

**familiāris, e** belonging to a household *or* family, *m* slave; **res ~** estate, property; a) familiar, intimate, friendly, *m* friend, companion; b) native, belonging to one's own people.

**familiāritās, ātis** *f* intimacy, familiar intercourse, friendship.

**fāmōsus** 3 a) famous, renowned; b) notorious, infamous.

**famul** = **famulus.**

**famula, ae** *f* female slave.

**famulāris, e** of slaves.

**famulātus, ūs** *m* servitude.

**famulor** 1 to serve, be a slave.

**famulus, ī** *m* servant, slave; *as adj.* serving, servile.

**fānāticus** 3 inspired, enthusiastic; frantic, furious.

**fandus,** *see* **for.**

**fānum, ī** *n* temple, sanctuary.

**fār, farris** *n* spelt, corn, grain; a) grits; b) bread.

**farciō, sī, tum** 4 to stuff, cram.

**farferum, ī** *n* colt's-foot.

**farīna, ae** *f* meal, flour; quality of material, character.

**farrāgō, inis** *f* mixed fodder; medley.

**farrātus** 3 filled with meal; *subst.* **-tum** *n* porridge.

**fartim** (*acc.*) stuffing, contents; **-tem** mincemeat.

**fartor, ōris** *m* sausage-maker; fattener of fowls.

**fās** *n* (*indecl.*) divine law; the dictates of religion; a) what is right, proper, allowable, lawful, permitted; b) divine will.

**fascia, ae** *f* band, bandage, head--band; sock; swaddling-band; brassière; bed-girth; wisp of cloud.

**fasciculus, ī** *m* small bundle *or* bunch.

**fascinō** 1 to enchant, bewitch.

**fascinum, ī** *n* (*and* **-us, ī** *m*) penis.

**fasciō** 1 to bandage.

**fasciola, ae** *f* small bandage.

**fascis, is** *m* bundle, parcel; a) burden, load; b) **fascēs** *pl.* bundle of rods with an axe; high office, consulship.

**fasēlus,** *see* **phaselus.**

**fāstī, ōrum** *m*/*pl.*, *see* **fastus².**

**fastīdiō** 4 to feel disgust *or* loathing; to dislike, disdain, despise.

**fastīdiōsus** 3 a) full of disgust, disdainful; fastidious, nice; b) cloying, disgusting.

**fāstīdium, ī** *n* a loathing, aversion; haughtiness; fastidiousness, nicety.

**fastīgātus** 3 sloping; descending; pointed.

**fastīgium, ī** *n* a) slope, declivity, descent, depth; b) top *or* gable-end of a building; c) height, summit, top; highest point *or* degree, high rank *or* dignity; d) chief point.

**fastōsus** 3 proud, lordly.

**fastus¹, ūs** *m* pride, haughtiness, disdain, contempt.

**fāstus²** 3 a) **dies ～** judicial day; b) *subst.* **fāstī, ōrum** (*and* **-ūs, uum**) *m*/*pl.* register of judicial days; calendar, almanac, annals.

**fātālis, e** a) ordained by fate *or* destiny, decreed, fated; b) fatal, dangerous, deadly.

**fateor, fassus sum** 2 a) to confess, own, acknowledge; b) to indicate, manifest.

**fāti-canus, fāti-cinus** 3 prophesying, prophetic.

**fāti-dicus** 3 prophesying; prophetic; *m* prophet.

**fāti-fer** 3 deadly.

**fatigātiō, ōnis** *f* weariness.

**fatigō** 1 a) to weary, tire, fatigue; b) to vex, harass, torment, plague; to importune; c) to pass without rest.

**fāti-legus** 3 death-gathering.

**fāti-loqua, ae** *f* prophetess.

**fatiscō** *and* **-or, —, —** 3 a) to open in chinks, to gape *or* crack open; b) to grow weak, become exhausted, faint.

**fatuitās, ātis** *f* silliness, folly.

**fātum, ī** *n* utterance; a) prophetic declaration; b) determination of the gods, divine will; destiny, fate, law of nature; ill fate, mishap; destruction, ruin, death.

**fatuor** 1 to talk foolishly.

**fatuus** 3 silly, foolish; *subst.* *m and f* fool, jester.

**faucēs, ium** *f*/*pl.* throat, gullet; a) defile, pass; b) gulf, abyss; c) narrow inlet, strait.

**Faunus, ī** *m* Faun.

**faustitās, ātis** *f* fertility, prosperity.

**faustus** 3 fortunate, favourable, auspicious.

**fautor (favitor), ōris** *m* favourer, furtherer, promoter, protector; applauder.     [tectress.)

**fautrīx, īcis** *f* patroness, pro-)

**faux, cis** *f*, *see* **fauces.**

**favea, ae** *f* favourite maidservant.

**faveō, fāvī, fautum** 2 to favour, to be favourable, promote, befriend (*alci*); a) to applaud; b) (*linguā*) to favour with the tongue, be silent.

**favilla, ae** *f* (glowing) ashes; spark (*metaph.*).

**favōnius, ī** *m* the west-wind.

**favor, ōris** *m* favour, good-will; applause.

**favōrābilis, e** winning favour, pleasing, agreeable.

**favus, ī** *m* honeycomb.

**fax, facis** *f* torch, firebrand; a) nuptial-torch, wedding; b) funeral-torch; c) fiery meteor, shooting-star; d) light, fire, flame; e) incitement, cause of ruin.

**faxim = fecerim, faciam** (*subj.*); **faxō = fecero, faciam** (*fut.*).

**febrīcitō** 1 to have a fever.

**febricula (ī ?), ae** *f* (slight) fever.

**febriculōsus** 3 sick of a fever.

**febris, is** *f* fever.

**Februārius** 3 belonging to February; *m* February.

**fēcunditās, ātis** *f* fertility.

**fēcundō** 1 to make fruitful.

**fēcundus** 3 a) fruitful, fertile; rich, abundant; b) fertilizing.

**fel, fellis** n gall, bile; choler; anger, bitterness.

**fēlēs** or **fēlis, is** f (wild) cat, marten.

**felicātus** 3 = filicatus.

**fēlicitās, ātis** f a) fruitfulness, fertility; b) happiness, good fortune, luck.

**fēlix, icis** a) fruitful, fertile; b) happy, fortunate; c) favourable, propitious.

**fēl(l)ātor, ōris** m sucker.

**fēl(l)ō** 1 to suck.

**fēmella, ae** f woman.

**fēmina, ae** f woman, female.

**feminālia, ium** n/pl. thigh-wrappings.

**fēmineus** 3 womanly, feminine; womanish.

**fēminīnus** 3 feminine (only gram.).

**femur, oris** or **inis** n thigh.

**fēnebris, e,** see **faenebris.**

**fēnerātiō, fēneror,** see **faen...**

**fenestella, ae** f small window or gate.

**fenestra, ae** f opening; a) window; b) loophole, entrance.

**fēniculum, ī** n fennel.

**fēnilia, fēnum, fēnus,** see **faen...**

**fera, ae** f, see **ferus.**

**fērālis, e** belonging to the dead, to a funeral; deadly, fatal; subst. **fērālia** (and **fĕr-**), **ium** n/pl. festival of the dead.

**ferāx, ācis** fruitful, fertile.

**ferculum, ī** n barrow, litter, bier; dish, course.

**ferē** adv. a) nearly, almost, about; **non ferē** scarcely, hardly; b) for the most part, in general, quite, entirely.

**ferentārius, ī** m light-armed spearman; energetic helper.

**feretrum, ī** n litter, bier.

**fēriae, ārum** f/pl. festival days, holidays.

**fēriātus** 3 keeping holiday, unoccupied, idle, at leisure.

**fericulum** = ferculum.

**ferīnus** 3 of wild beasts; (caro) **-a, ae** f game, venison.

**feriō, —, —** 4 to strike, beat, thrust, hit; a) to strike dead, kill, slay; b) **foedus** to make a compact or treaty; c) to cheat.

**fērior** 1 to idle, to keep holiday.

**feritās, ātis** f wildness, savageness.

**fermē** adv. = fere.

**fermentum, ī** n a) leaven, ferment; b) beer; c) anger.

**ferō, tulī, lātum** 3 1. to bear, carry, bring; a) **ventrem** to be pregnant; b) **prae se ferre** to manifest, show, display, profess; c) to carry about oneself; d) to bear, suffer, endure; **aegre, moleste, graviter** to be angry or vexed at; e) to report, make known, relate, say, tell; **ferunt** people say; **fertur** it is said; f) to celebrate, praise; g) to carry away, take off, snatch, plunder, spoil; h) to get, receive, obtain, earn, win; 2. to bring, carry (alci alqd); a) to take, lead, conduct; b) to offer; c) to propose, move (a law); d) to require, allow; e) to bring forth, produce, yield; to cause, create; f) to enter or note down (in an account-book); 3. to set in motion, move, drive, carry off, take away; **P.** or **se ferre** to rush, run, hasten, speed, flow, rise, mount up.

**ferōcia, ae** f high, defiant, or headstrong spirit; overbearing behaviour.

**ferōcitās, ātis** f = ferocia.

**ferōculus** 3 = ferox.

**ferōx, ōcis** a) bold, courageous; b) spirited, defiant, headstrong, overbearing.

**ferrāmenta, ōrum** n/pl. iron tools.

**ferrāria, ae** f iron-mine.

**ferrārius (faber), ī** m blacksmith.

**ferrātilis, e** fettered.

**ferrātus** 3 covered with iron, iron-clad; m soldier in armour.

**ferreus** 3 of iron; a) hard, unfeeling, hard-hearted, cruel; b) firm, rigid, unyielding.

**ferri-crepīnus** 3 clanking chains.

**ferri-terium, ī** n place of fettered slaves.

**ferri-terus, ī** m, **ferri-trībāx, ācis** m fettered slave.

**ferrūgin(e)us** 3 rust-coloured; rusty black, dusky; blue-green (like verdigris). [colour; verdigris.]

**ferrūgō, inis** f iron-rust; dark)

**ferrum, ī** n iron; a) iron-tool, e.g. axe, ploughshare, knife, scissors, chain, pen, curling-iron; b) weapon, sword, arrowhead; **ferrō ignique** with fire and sword.

**fertilis, e** a) fruitful, fertile, productive; **b)** fertilizing.

**fertilitās, ātis** f fertility.

**fertum, ī** n sacrificial cake.

**ferula, ae** f an umbelliferous plant; rod; goad.

**ferus 3** a) wild, untamed, uncultivated; **b)** rude, savage, cruel; *subst.* (**ferus, ī** m), **fera, ae** f wild animal.

**fervē-faciō 3** to make hot.

**fervēns, tis** = **fervidus.**

**ferveō, ferbuī, — 2** (*and* **fervō, —, — 3**) to boil; a) to boil up, foam, rage; **b)** to swarm forth; to be busy, go on busily; **c)** to glow, burn.

**fervēscō 3** to become hot, begin to glow.

**fervidus 3** a) boiling; **b)** burning, glowing, raging; fiery, hot,. vehement, impetuous.

**fervō, —, — 3,** *see* **ferveo.**

**fervor, ōris** m a) a boiling, violent heat; **b)** a raging; ardour, passion.

**fessus 3** tired, wearied, exhausted.

**festīnanter** *adv.* hastily.

**festīnātiō, ōnis** f haste, hurry.

**festīnātō** *adv.* = **festinanter.**

**festīnō 1** a) *intr.* to make haste, hasten, be quick; **b)** *trans.* to hasten, make haste with.

**festīnus 3** hasty, quick.

**festīvitās, ātis** f a) gaiety; **b)** humour, pleasantry.

**fēstīvus 3** festive, gay; a) pretty, agreeable, pleasant; **b)** humorous, witty; **c)** kind.

**festūca, ae** f rod used by a praetor in freeing slaves.

**festūcula, ae** f pile-driver.

**fēstus 3** solemn, festive, festal; *subst.* **fēstum, ī** n festival, holiday, feast.

**fēteō 2** to stink.

**fētiālis, e** belonging to the college of the. **fētiālēs (ium** m), diplomatic negotiators.

**fētidus 3** stinking, fetid.

**fētor, ōris** m stench.

**fētūra, ae** f a) a bringing forth, breeding; **b)** offspring.

**fētus¹ 3** pregnant, breeding; a) productive, fertile, full of (*abl.*); **b)** f -a that has brought forth, newly delivered.

**fētus², ūs** m a bringing forth, bearing; a) growth; **b)** production, offspring, progeny; **c)** fruit, produce.

**fiber, brī** m beaver.

**fibra, ae** f a) fibre, filament; lobe of lungs *or* liver; **b)** *pl.* entrails.

**fibula, ae** f clasp, buckle, brooch, brace.

**ficēdula** (*and* **ficē-), ae** f a small bird.

**ficētum, ī** n a) fig-orchard; **b)** a crop of piles.

**ficōsus 3** suffering from piles.

**fictilis, e** made of clay, earthen; *subst.* **-e, is** n earthen vessel *or* ware.

**fictiō, ōnis** f invention; formation.

**fictor, ōris** m, **fictrīx, īcis** f moulder; a) sculptor; **b)** baker of sacrificial cakes.

**fictūra, ae** f a forming, fashioning.

**fictus 3** formed, fashioned; a) feigned, fictitious; **b)** false, dissembling; **c)** = **fixus;** *subst.* **fictum, ī** n deception, fiction, lie.

**ficulnus 3** of a fig-tree.

**ficulus, ī** f little fig.

**ficus, ī** *and* **ūs** f a) fig-tree; **b)** fig; **c)** ~, ī m piles, haemorrhoids.

**fidēlia, ae** f earthen vessel, pot.

**fidēlis, e** a) faithful, trusty, sincere; **b)** sure, safe, strong.

**fidēlitās, ātis** f faithfulness, trustiness.

**fīdēns, tis** confident, bold.

**fīdentia, ae** f confidence.

**fidēs¹, ēī** (*and* **-ěī**) f 1. a) trust, faith, confidence, belief; **fidem habere** to place confidence in, **fidem facere** *alci* to produce confidence; (*in business*) credit; **b)** good faith, sincerity, trustworthiness, credibility, faithfulness, conscientiousness, **ex bona fidē** in good faith; **c)** fulfilment, assurance, confirmation, proof; 2. a) promise, engagement, word of honour, pledge; **b)** protection, safe-conduct, guardian care, **in alcis fidem venire** to surrender at discretion.

**fidēs², is** f 1. lyre-string; 2. (*mostly* **fidēs, ium** f/*pl.*) stringed instrument.

**fidi-cen, inis** m lute-player, harpist; lyric poet.

**fidi-cina, ae** f female lute-player.

**fidi-cinius 3** of lute-playing.

**fidicula, ae** f small lute; instrument of torture.

**fidius, ī** m the god of faith, **mēdius fidius!** by the god of truth!

**fidō, fīsus sum** 3 to confide, trust (*alci; alqa re*); to venture (*inf.*).

**fidūcia, ae** *f* **1.** trust, confidence, reliance, assurance; self-reliance; **2.** a) trustiness; b) deposit, pledge, mortgage.

**fidūciārius** 3 intrusted.

**fidus** 3 = fidelis.

**figō, xī, xum** 3 **1.** to fix, fasten, drive in (*alqd in re, in* or *ad rem*), attach, affix; a) to post up, bill; b) to hang up; **2.** a) to transfix, pierce through.

**figulāris, e** of a potter.

**figulus, ī** *m* potter; bricklayer.

**figūra, ae** *f* form, shape, figure; a) beauty; b) image, appearance; c) kind, nature, quality; d) figure of speech.

**figūrō** 1 to form, fashion.

**filātim** thread by thread.

**filia, ae** *f* daughter.

**filicātus** 3 adorned with fern.

**filiola, ae** *f* little daughter.

**filiolus, ī** *m* little son.

**filius, ī** *m* son, child.

**filix, icis** *f* fern, bracken.

**filum¹, ī** *n* thread, yarn; a) fillet of wool; **b)** string, cord, fibre, wick; c) texture.

**filum², ī** *n* figure, shape, outline; manner.

**fimbriae, ārum** *f/pl.* fringe, curl.

**fimbriātus** 3 fringed.

**fimum, ī** *n* and **fimus, ī** *m* dung, manure; dirt.

**findō, fidī, fissum** 3 to cleave, split, separate, divide.

**fingō, finxī, fictum** 3 to form, fashion, shape, frame; a) to make, mould, represent, **ars fingendī** sculpture, art of statuary; **b)** to arrange, set to rights, **se fingere** *ad alqd* to regulate oneself; c) to instruct, teach, train; d) to make into something; e) to imagine, conceive, think; f) to devise, invent, feign, pretend.

**finiēns, tis** *m* (*sc.* orbis) horizon.

**finiō** 4 to limit, bound, enclose; a) to restrain, check; b) to determine, prescribe, appoint; c) to put an end to, finish, terminate; d) to cease speaking; e) to cease, end, die; **P.** to come to an end; **finītus** 3 limited, restricted; rhythmical.

**finis, is** *m* (*and f*) boundary, limit, border; **fine** (*with gen.*) up to, as far as; a) *pl.* borders, territory, land, country; b) *fig.* limit, end, termination, limitation; c) end, purpose, aim, object; d) extremity, highest point *or* degree, **bonōrum** chief good; e) end, close, stop; death.

**finem facere** to make an end; death.

**finitimus (-umus)** 3 bordering upon, adjoining, neighbouring (*alci*); connected with, nearly related; *m* neighbour.

**finitor, ōris** *m* surveyor.

**fiō, factus sum, fieri** **1.** to grow, spring up; a) to be born *or* created; b) to happen, come to pass; **fieri potest, ut** it is possible that; **fieri non potest quin** it is indispensable, inevitable that; **2. P.** *of* **facere:** a) to be made; b) to be turned into, appointed; c) to be estimated.

**firmāmen, inis** *n* support.

**firmāmentum, ī** *n* support, prop, stay; main point.

**firmātor, ōris** *m* one who makes firm.

**firmitās, ātis** *and* **-tūdō, inis** *f* firmness, strength; steadfastness, constancy, endurance.

**firmiter** *adv. of* **firmus.**

**firmō** 1 to make firm *or* strong; a) to strengthen, fortify (*alqa re*); **b)** to encourage, animate; c) to confirm, assert, affirm, prove.

**firmus** 3 firm, fast, strong, powerful (*ad alqd*); steadfast, constant, trusty, lasting, faithful; *adv.* **firmē** (*and* **firmiter**).

**fiscālis, e** belonging to the state-treasury.

**fiscella, ae** *f* small basket.

**fiscina, ae** *f* basket.

**fiscus, ī** *m* money-basket, money-bag; a) treasury, public chest; **b)** imperial treasury.

**fissilis, e** (that may be) cleft.

**fissiō, ōnis** *f* a cleaving.

**fissum, ī** *n* cleft, fissure.

**fistūca, ae** *f* pile-driver.

**fistula, ae** *f* pipe; a) waterpipe; **b)** shepherd's pipe; c) ulcer, fistula; d) writing-reed.

**fistulātor, ōris** *m* piper.

**fistulātus** 3 fitted with tubes *or* pipes.

**fisus** 3, *see* **fido.**

**fītilla, ae** *f* pap, soft food used at a sacrifice.

**fixus 3** fixed, immovable.

**flābelli-fera, ae** *f* fan-bearer.

**flābellulum, ī** *n* little fan.

**flābellum, ī** *n* fan, fly-flap.

**flābilis, e** airy, breath-like.

**flābra, ōrum** *n/pl.* breezes, winds.

**flacceō, —, — 2** to be languid, flag.

**flaccēscō, —, — 3** to flag.

**flaccidus 3** feeble.

**flaccus 3** flabby; flap-eared.

**flagellō 1** to whip, scourge, lash.

**flagellum, ī** *n* whip, scourge; **a)** thong of a javelin; **b)** vineshoot; **c)** arm of a polypus.

**flāgitātiō, ōnis** *f* pressing demand, request, importunity.

**flāgitātor, ōris** *m* demander, dun.

**flāgitiōsus 3** shameful, disgraceful, infamous, profligate.

**flāgitium, ī** *n* **a)** shameful act, outrage; **b)** shame, disgrace; **c)** rascal, scoundrel.

**flāgitō 1** to ask *or* demand urgently, entreat (*alqd ab alqo* or *alqm alqd*; *ut, ne*); **a)** to require; **b)** to demand to know; **c)** to summon, accuse.

**flagrāns, tis** burning, flaming, blazing; **a)** glowing; **b)** hot, vehement, passionate, eager.

**flagrantia, ae** *f* glow, heat.

**flagri-triba, ae** *m* whipped slave.

**flagrō 1** to burn, flame, blaze; **a)** to glitter, shine; **b)** to glow, be inflamed with passion, be excited (*alqa re*).

**flagrum, ī** *n* whip, scourge.

**flāmen¹, inis** *n* a blowing, blast, breath, breeze, wind.

**flāmen², inis** *m* priest of a particular deity, *flamen*.

**flāminica, ae** *f* wife of a *flamen*.

**flāminium, ī** *n* office of a *flamen*.

**flamma, ae** *f* flame, blaze; **a)** torch, lightning, star; **b)** fire, glow, heat, glare; **c)** flame of passion, fire of love; **d)** destructive fire, ruin.

**flammārius, ī** *m* maker of bride's veils.

**flammeolum, ī** *n* bridal veil.

**flammēscō 3** to become fiery.

**flammeum, ī** *n* bride's veil.

**flammeus 3** flaming, fiery(-red).

**flammi-fer and -ger 3** = flammeus.

**flammō 1 a)** *intr.* to burn, flame; **b)** *trans.* to burn, consume; to heat, inflame.

**flammula, ae** *f* little flame.

**flāmōnium, ī** *n* office of a *flamen*.

**flātus, ūs** *m* a blowing, breathing; **a)** breeze, wind; **b)** breath, snorting; **c)** haughtiness.

**flāvēns, tis** = flavus.

**flāvēscō 3** to become yellow.

**flāvus 3** (golden-)yellow, brownish *or* reddish yellow.

**flēbilis, e a)** lamentable, deplorable, pitiable; **b)** weeping, tearful.

**flectō, xī, xum 3 1.** to bend, turn round, curve; **a)** to bend, move, persuade, prevail upon, influence; **b)** to double, pass round; to apply to; **2.** to wind, contort; **a)** to turn, direct, change (*alqd in alqd*); **b)** *intr.* to turn, go, march, direct one's course; **flexus 3** bent, curved, winding.

**flēmina, um** *n/pl.* swellings in the ankles.

**fleō, ēvī, ētum 2 a)** to weep, cry; **b)** to bewail, lament (*acc.*).

**flētus, ūs** *m* **a)** a weeping, wailing, lamenting; **b)** tears.

**flex-animus 3 a)** affecting, touching; **b)** touched, affected.

**flexibilis, e** flexible, pliant; **a)** tractable; **b)** inconstant, fickle.

**flexilis, e** pliant, pliable.

**flexi-loquus 3** ambiguous.

**flexiō, ōnis** *f* a bending; **a)** shift, excuse; **b)** modulation of the voice.

**flexi-pēs, edis** with crooked feet.

**flexuōsus 3** winding, tortuous.

**flexūra, ae** *f* a bending, winding.

**flexus, ūs** *m* a bending, turn; **a)** a winding, curve; **b)** crooked way; **c)** transition, change.

**flīctus, ūs** *m* a striking, collision.

**flō 1 a)** *intr.* to blow; to sound; **b)** *trans.* to blow at, out, up *or* away; to melt, cast, coin.

**floccus, ī** *m* flock of wool; trifle.

**flōrēns, tis** blooming, flowering, flourishing; **a)** shining, bright; **b)** in the prime, in repute, excellent; **c)** flowery.

**flōreō, uī, — 2** to bloom, blossom; **a)** to shine, glitter; to froth (*wine*); **b)** to flourish, be prosperous, in the prime, in repute, distinguished.

**flōrēscō 3** to begin to blossom.

**flōreus 3** of flowers, flowery.

**flōridulus 3** blooming.

**flōridus 3 a)** blooming; **b)** flowery.

**flōri-fer 3** flower-bearing.

**flōri-legus** 3 culling flowers.

**flōrus** 3 blond.

**flōs, ōris** *m* flower, blossom; a) flower-juice; honey; b) flourishing condition, prime, best part, top, crown, freshness, splendour, glory, ornament, innocence; downy beard.

**flōsculus, ī** *m* little flower, floweret; pride, ornament.

**flucti-fragus** 3 wave-breaking.

**flucti-sonus** 3 resounding with waves.

**flucti-vagus** 3 wandering *or* moving in waves.

**fluctuātiō, ōnis** *f* a wavering, agitation.

**fluctuō** 1 (*and* **-uor**) to wave, undulate; to waver, hesitate.

**fluctuōsus** 3 full of waves.

**fluctus, ūs** *m* a flowing; flood, billow, surge; commotion; disturbance.

**fluēns, tis** a) flowing, fluent; b) lax, enervated, effeminate; c) unrestrained.

**fluenti-sonus** 3 resounding with waves.

**fluentum, ī** *n* flow, stream.

**fluidus** 3 flowing, fluid; a) lax, languid; b) dissolving.

**fluitō** 1 to flow; a) to float, swim; b) to wave, undulate; c) to waver.

**flūmen, inis** *n* stream, flood, flowing water; b) river; c) flow of words.

**flūmineus** 3 of a river.

**fluō, uxī, (uxum)** 3 to flow, stream; a) to drip, run down (*alqa re*); b) to stream forth *or* along, to spread; c) to pass, pass away, proceed; to flow away, vanish, dissolve, perish; d) to fall down, flow down, sink.

**flūtō** 1 = **fluitō**.

**fluviā(ti)lis, e** of a river.

**flūvidus** (*and* **flŭvidus**) 3 = **fluidus**.

**fluvius, ī** *m* river.

**fluxus** 3 flowing; a) loose, slack; b) frail, weak, transient, perishable; c) impaired.

**fōcāle, is** *n* neck-cloth.

**fōcil(l)ō** 1 to warm, restore to life.

**fōculum, ī** *n* warming-pan.

**foculus, ī** *m* fire-pan; fire.

**focus, ī** *m* a) fire-place, hearth; b) fire-pan, altar; c) funeral pile; d) home, family.

**fodicō** 1 to dig, prick, wound.

**fodiō, fōdī, fossum** 3 a) to dig, dig up; b) to prick, pierce.

**foederātus** 3 allied.

**foedi-fragus** 3 league-breaking.

**foeditās, ātis** *f* foulness, hideousness, ugliness

**foedō** 1 to make foul; a) to defile, pollute; b) to disgrace, disfigure, mar.

**foedus¹** 3 foul, filthy, ugly, repulsive, detestable, horrible.

**foedus², eris** *n* compact, treaty, league, alliance; a) agreement, stipulation; b) promise.

**foetidus** 3 *and* **foetor, ōris** *m*, *see* **fet…**

**foliātum, ī** *n* unguent made from leaves of spikenard.

**folium, ī** *n* leaf; foliage.

**folliculus, ī** *m* little bag, sack; a) inflated ball; b) pod, shell; egg-shell.

**follis, is** *m* a) purse; b) bellows; c) punch-ball; d) puffed-out cheeks.

**follitus** 3 in a sack.

**fōmentum, ī** *n* poultice, bandage; alleviation, mitigation.

**fōmes, itis** *m* touchwood, tinder.

**fōns, tis** *m* a) spring, fountain, well, source; b) origin, cause.

**fontānus** 3 of a spring *or* fountain.

**fonticulus, ī** *m* little spring.

**for, fātus sum** 1 a) to say, speak; **fandō audīre** to know by hearsay; b) to foretell, prophesy; *subst.* **fandum, ī** *n* right.

**forābilis, e** that can be bored through, vulnerable.

**forāmen, inis** *n* hole, opening, aperture.

**forās** *adv.* out of doors, forth, out.

**for-ceps, ipis** *f* (*and* *m*) pair of tongs, pincers.

**forda, ae** *f* cow in calf.

**fore = futurum esse; forem = essem**.

**forēnsis, e** belonging to the forum *or* market-place; public, forensic.

**forfex, icis** *f* scissors.

**forica, ae** *f* public latrine.

**foris¹, is** *f* (leaf of a) door, gate, *pl.* folding-doors, entrance.

**foris²** *adv.* a) out of doors, without, abroad; in public; b) from without, from abroad.

fōrma, ae *f* form, shape, figure, appearance; a) fine form, beauty; b) quality, condition, sort, species; c) image, representation, outline, sketch; d) model, pattern, shoemaker's last; e) stamp, coin.

fōrmālis, e formal, official.

fōrmāmenta, ōrum *n/pl.* shapes.

fōrmātiō, ōnis *f* formation.

fōrmātor, ōris *m* former, fashioner.

fōrmātūra, ae *f* fashioning.

formīca, ae *f* ant.

formīcinus 3 ant-like.

formīdābilis, e terrible, formidable.

formīdō[1] 1 to fear (*alqd*), be afraid of *or* terrified; formīdātus 3 feared.

formīdō[2], inis *f* a) fear, terror, dread; b) that which produces fear, fright.

formīdolōsus 3 a) fearful, dreadful; b) afraid, timid.

fōrmō 1 to form, shape, fashion; a) to make, produce; b) to regulate, direct, prepare.

fōrmōnsus = formosus.

fōrmōsitās, ātis *f* beauty.

fōrmōsus 3 finely formed, beautiful.

fōrmula, ae *f* fine form, beauty; a) rule, prescription; b) form of contract, agreement, regulation; c) formula, lawsuit, judicial proceedings; d) principle.

fornācālis, e belonging to an oven.

fornācula, ae *f* furnace.

fornāx, ācis *f* furnace, oven, kiln.

fornicātus 3 arched, vaulted.

fornix, icis *m* arch, vault; a) vaulted opening; b) triumphal arch; c) brothel.

forō 1 to bore, pierce.

forpex, icis *f* tongs.

fors *f* (*only nom.* and *abl. sg.* forte) chance, hap, luck, hazard, accident; fors (as *adv.*) perhaps; forte by chance, as -it happens (happened).

(fors-an, forsit,) forsitan *adv.* perhaps.

fortasse (fortassis) *adv.* perhaps, probably, possibly.

forticulus 3 somewhat brave.

fortis, e strong, vigorous; a) enduring, firm; b) brave, bold, courageous, manly.

fortitūdō, inis *f* a) strength, force; b) manliness, firmness, fortitude, bravery, courage, boldness.

fortuītus 3 (*adv.* -ō) casual, accidental.

fortūna, ae *f* fate, fortune, luck; a) good *or* bad fortune; b) F ~ the Goddess of Fate; c) prosperity; misfortune, adversity; d) state, condition, circumstances, fate, lot, position, rank; e) (*mostly pl.*) property, possessions.

fortūnō 1 to make prosperous *or* happy; fortūnātus 3 prosperous, lucky, happy, fortunate; wealthy, rich.

forulī, ōrum *m/pl.* book-case.

forum, ī *n* a) open space; b) market-place, market, market-town; c) the forum; public affairs; d) the courts, jurisdiction; e) commerce.

forus, ī *m* (*mostly pl.*) a) gangway in a ship; b) row of seats in a theatre; c) row of bee-cells; d) dice-board.

fossa, ae *f* ditch, trench, canal; a) pit; b) furrow; c) watercourse, river-bed.

fossiō, ōnis *f* a digging.

fossor, ōris *m* digger, navvy.

fossūra, ae *f* a digging.

fovea, ae *f* pitfall, pit.

foveō, fōvī, fōtum 2 a) to keep warm, to warm; b) to cherish, foster, fondle, caress, love.

frāctus 3 broken; weakened, feeble, faint.

fragilis, e a) easily broken, brittle; weak, frail, perishable; b) crackling.

fragilitās, ātis *f* weakness, frailty.

fragmen, inis *n* = fragmentum.

fragmentum, ī *n* broken piece, fragment, remnant; *pl.* ruins, wreck; faggots.

fragor, ōris *m* a) crashing, crash, noise; b) breaking.

fragōsus 3 broken; a) rough, uneven; b) roaring; c) brittle.

fragrō 1 to smell (sweet).

frāgum, ī *n* wild strawberry.

framea, ae *f* spear, javelin.

frango, frēgī, frāctum 3 to break *or* dash to pieces, shiver, shatter; a) to grind, bruise, crush; b) to break (*a promise*); c) to break down, subdue; d) to weaken, diminish, violate; e) to soften, move, touch.

frāter, tris *m* brother (*pl.* brother and sister); a) cousin, brother-in-law; b) fellow, companion.

frāterculus, ī *m* little brother.

frāternitās, ātis *f* brotherhood.

**fräternus** 3 of a brother, brother-ly, fraternal; a) belonging to a relation *or* kinsman; b) friendly, allied.

**frātri-cīda, ae** *m* fratricide.

**fraudātiō, ōnis** *f* a cheating, deceit.

**fraudātor, ōris** *m* cheat, deceiver.

**fraudō** 1 a) to deceive, cheat, defraud (*alqm re*); b) to embezzle, purloin.

**fraudulentia, ae** *f* deceitfulness.

**fraudulentus** 3 deceitful.

**fraus, dis** *f* a cheating, deceit, imposition, fraud; a) self-deception, error, mistake; b) injury, damage; c) offence, crime.

**frausus sit** (*depon.*) = **fraudāverit.**

**fraxineus** (*and* **fraxinus**[1]) 3 of ashwood.

**fraxinus**[2], **ĭ** *f* ash-tree; spear, javelin.

**fremebundus** 3 roaring, snorting, murmuring.

**fremidus** 3 noisy.

**fremitus, ūs** *m* a roaring, rushing, noise, murmuring.

**fremō, uī, (itum)** 3 to growl, resound, roar, murmur, rage, howl, snort, mutter, neigh, grumble.

**fremor, ōris** *m* a roaring, murmuring.

**frēnātor, ōris** *m* bridler; hurler.

**frendō, —, frēsum** 3 (**frendeō, —, — 2**) to gnash the teeth.

**frēniger** 3 bearing bridles.

**frēnō** 1 to furnish with a bridle; to bridle, curb, restrain, check.

**frēnum, ĭ** *n* (*pl. usually* **-ī, ōrum** *m*) bridle, curb, bit.

**frequēns, tis** numerous, full, crowded; a) populous, much frequented, filled; b) frequent, repeated, common, usual.

**frequentātiō, ōnis** *f* piling up.

**frequentia, ae** *f* crowding together, concourse, throng.

**frequentō** 1 a) to visit often *or* in crowds; to frequent, attend; b) to assemble in numbers, bring together; to fill with a multitude, to crowd, people; c) to do often, to repeat. [of Sicily.)

**fretēnsis, e** belonging to the Straits)

**fretum, ĭ** *n* strait, sound, channel; sea; (*metaph.*) seething flood.

**fretus**[1], **ūs** *m* = **fretum.**

**frētus**[2] 3 leaning on, supported; relying on, trusting.

**fricō, cuī, c(ā)tum** 1 to rub.

**frictus** 3, *see* **frigo.**

**frīge-factō** 1 to make cold *or* cool.

**frīgeō, (xī), — 2** to be cold *or* chill; a) to be inactive, languid, lifeless; b) to be coldy received, disregarded.

**frīgerō** 1 to cool, refresh.

**frīgēscō, —, — 3** to grow cold.

**frīgidārius** 3 for cooling.

**frīgidulus** 3 somewhat cold *or* languid.

**frīgidus** 3 cold, cool, chill; *subst. f* cold water; a) chilling; b) remiss, inactive, indolent, feeble; c) dull, insipid, trivial.

**frīgō, xī, ctum** 3 to roast.

**frīgus, oris** *n* cold; a) frost; b) cold shudder; c) inactivity, slowness; d) cold reception; loss of favour.

**friguttiō** 4 to chatter, babble.

**fringillus, ĭ** *m* finch *or* sparrow.

**friō** 1 to crumble.

**frit** (*indecl.*) the tip of an ear of corn.

**fritillus, ĭ** *m* dice-box.

**frīvolus** 3 empty, trifling, worthless; *subst. n/pl.* paltry possessions.

**frondātor, ōris** *m* pruner.

**frondeō, —, — 2** to be in leaf, become green.

**frondēscō, —, — 3** to put forth leaves.

**frondeus** 3 covered with leaves.

**frondi-fer** 3 leafy.

**frondōsus** 3 full of leaves.

**frōns**[1], **dis** *f* leaves, foliage; leafy bough, garland of leaves.

**frōns**[2], **tis** *f* (*and m*) forehead, brow, front, countenance; b) forepart, face; c) outside, exterior; appearance.

**frontālia, ium** *n/pl.* frontlet.

**frontō, ōnis** *m* with a large forehead.

**frūctuārius** 3 liable to payment out of the produce.

**frūctuōsus** 3 fruitful, productive; profitable, gainful.

**frūctus, ūs** *m* a) enjoyment, satisfaction; b) fruit, produce; profit, gain, income, return.

**frūgālis, e** (*only comp.* **-lior** *and superl.* **-lissimus,** *adv.* **-liter**) = **frugi.**

**frūgālitās, ātis** *f* thrift(iness), orderliness; temperance.

**frūgēs, um** *pl.* of **frux.**

**frūgī** (*dat. of* **frux,** *used as adj.*) thrifty, frugal; temperate, honest, worthy, virtuous (*see* **frugalis**).

**frūgi-fer** 3 fruit-bearing.
**frūgi-ferēns, tis** fruitful.
**frūgi-legus** 3 grain-gathering.
**frūgi-parus** 3 corn-producing.
**frūmentārius** 3 of *or* producing corn, of provisions; *subst.* ~, **ī** *m* corndealer.
**frūmentātiō, ōnis** *f* a providing of corn, foraging, distribution of corn.
**frūmentātor, ōris** *m* purchaser of corn; forager.
**frūmentor** 1 to fetch corn, to forage.
**frūmentum, ī** *n* corn, grain, wheat.
**frūniscor** 3 to enjoy.
**fruor, (frūctus** *and* **fruitus sum)** 3, *fut. part.* **fruitūrus,** to make use of, enjoy, delight in (*abl.*); to have the use of.
**frustillātim** *adv.* in pieces.
**frūstrā** *adv.* a) in error; b) in vain, for nothing; c) without reason, groundlessly.
**frūstrāmen, inis** *f* deception.
**frūstrātiō, ōnis** *f* deception, disappointment; a delaying.
**frūstrātus, ūs** *m* deceiving.
**(frūstrō** *and)* **frūstror** 1 to deceive, disappoint, elude, frustrate.
**frustulentus** 3 full of morsels.
**frustum, ī** *n* piece, bit.
**frutex, icis** *m* a) shrub, bush; b) blockhead.
**fruticētum, ī** *n* thicket.
**(fruticō** *and)* **fruticor** 1 to put forth shoots.
**fruticōsus** 3 full of shrubs, bushy.
**frūx, ūgis** *f* (*usually pl.* **frūgēs, um)** fruit, produce; a) fruits of the earth *or* of trees; b) result, success, value.
**fuam, fuās, fuat** = **sim, sis, sit.**
**fūcō** 1 to dye (red), paint; to falsify.
**fūcōsus** 3 counterfeit, spurious.
**fūcus¹, ī** *m* rock-lichen; a) red colour; b) propolis, bee-glue; c) disguise, deceit, dissimulation.
**fūcus², ī** *m* drone.
**fuga, ae** *f* a fleeing, flight, running away; a) banishment, exile; b) desire to escape; c) an avoiding, shunning, aversion; d) swift motion, speed.
**fugāx, ācis** fleeing, swift, fleet; a) timid, shy; b) shunning, avoiding; c) transitory.
**fugiō, fūgī, fugitum** 3 1. to flee, fly, take flight, run away, escape, be off; a) to become an exile *or* fugitive, to leave the country;

b) to vanish, disappear, pass away, perish; 2. to flee from (*alqm*); a) to avoid, shun, desire to escape; b) to escape, flee away from, elude, forsake, omit, forbear; c) to escape the notice of, be unobserved by, unknown to; **me fūgit** I failed to notice.
**fugitīvus** 3 fleeing away, fugitive; *m* runaway slave.
**fugitō** 1 to flee in haste; to avoid, shun.
**fugitor, ōris** *m* runaway, deserter.
**fugō** 1 to put to flight, drive away.
**fulcīmen, inis** *n* prop, support, pillar.
**fulciō, lsī, ltum** 4 to prop up, stay, support; to secure, sustain, uphold.
**fulcrum, ī** *n* bedpost, foot of a couch; couch.
**fulgeō, lsī,** — 2 (*and* **fulgō** 3) to flash, lighten; a) to shine, glitter, gleam, glare; b) to be conspicuous.
**fulgidus** 3 flashing.
**fulgor, ōris** *m* a) lightning, flash of lightning; b) brightness, splendour; glory.
**fulgur, uris** *n* a) lightning, flash of lightning; b) brightness.
**fulgurālis, e** pertaining to lightning.
**fulgurātor, ōris** *m* interpreter of lightning.
**fulgurītus** 3 struck by lightning.
**fulgurō** 1 to lighten.
**fulica, ae** *f* coot (*or* cormorant?).
**fūligō, inis** *f* soot; black paint.
**fulix, icis** *f* = **fulica.**
**fullō, ōnis** *m* fuller.
**fullōnia, ae** *f* trade of a fuller.
**fullōnius** 3 pertaining to a fuller.
**fulmen, inis** *n* a) flash *or* stroke of lightning; thunderbolt; b) fiery flashing; c) destructive power, crushing blow.
**fulmenta, ae** *f* heel of a shoe.
**fulmineus** 3 belonging to lightning; a) sparkling, brilliant; b) destructive.
**fulminō** 1 to lighten.
**fultūra, ae** *f* prop, support.
**fulvus** 3 reddish yellow, tawny.
**fūmeus** 3, **fūmidus** 3, **fūmi-fer** 3 smoking, smoky.
**fūmi-ficō** 1 to burn incense.
**fūmi-ficus** 3 steaming, smoking.
**fūmō** 1 to smoke, steam.
**fūmōsus** 3 full of smoke, smoky, smoked.

**fūmus, ī** m smoke, steam, vapour.
**fūnāle, is** n a) thong of a sling;
b) wax-torch; c) candelabrum.
**fūnālis, e** tied by a rope.
**fūn-ambulus, ī** m rope-walker.
**fūnctiō, ōnis** f performance, execution.
**funda, ae** f sling; sling-stone;
casting-net.
**(fundāmen, inis** n and) **fundāmentum, ī** n foundation, base.
**fundātor, ōris** m founder.
**funditō 1** to shoot with a sling, to
hurl, pour out (words).
**funditor, ōris** m slinger.
**funditus** adv. from the bottom,
completely, entirely.
**fundō¹ 1** a) to make a foundation
for; b) to found, secure, establish,
confirm; **fundātus 3** established,
firm.
**fundō², fūdī, fūsum 3** to pour out,
shed; to melt, cast, found; a) to
pour forth, scatter, hurl, spread;
b) to utter; c) to bring forth,
produce, bear, yield; d) to
overthrow, overcome, rout, beat;
e) to throw down, prostrate.
**fundus, ī** m bottom, ground;
a) piece of land, farm; b) foundation; c) authority, one who
sanctions.
**fūnebris, e** a) belonging to a funeral,
funeral; b) deadly, mortal, fatal.
**fūnereus 3** = funebris.
**fūnerō 1** to bury; to kill.
**fūnestō 1** to pollute (by death).
**fūnestus 3** a) polluted by death; in
mourning; b) deadly; destructive,
fatal.
**fungīnus 3** of mushrooms.
**fungor, fūnctus sum 3** to busy
oneself with, be engaged (abl.);
a) to perform, execute, administer,
discharge; b) to complete, finish;
c) to suffer.
**fungus, ī** m mushroom; candle-snuff.
**fūniculus, ī** m cord, string.
**fūnis, is** m (and f) rope, cord, line.
**fūnus, eris** n funeral, burial, funeral
procession; a) bier; b) corpse, dead
body; c) death, murder; destruction, ruin.
**fur, fūris** m and f thief; rogue.
**fūrāx, ācis** thievish.
**furca, ae** f fork; forked prop.
**furci-fer, erī** m rascal.
**furcilla, ae** f hay-fork.

**furcillō 1** to pitchfork.
**furcula, ae** f a) forked prop;
b) narrow pass.
**furenter** adv. furiously.
**furfur, uris** m a) chaff; b) bran.
**furia, ae** f rage, fury, madness;
a) violent passion, desire; b) Goddess of Revenge, Fury.
**furiālis, e** of the Furies; a) furious,
raging; b) infuriating.
**furibundus 3** furious, raging; inspired.
**fūrīnus 3** of thieves.
**furiō 1** to madden, infuriate.
**furiōsus 3** mad, furious.
**furnāria, ae** f baker's trade.
**furnus, ī** m (baker's) oven, fireplace.
**furō, —, — 3** to rage, revel, be mad
or furious.
**furor¹, ōris** m rage, madness, fury,
passion; a) passionate love; b)
frenzy, inspiration.
**fūror² 1** to steal (alqd alci, ab alqo,
ex re), purloin, pilfer; to withdraw
secretly.
**fūrti-ficus 3** thievish.
**fūrtim** adv. by stealth, secretly.
**fūrtīvus 3** a) stolen; b) secret,
furtive.
**fūrtum, ī** n theft; a) a stolen thing;
b) secret action, deceit, trick,
artifice; c) stratagem; love intrigue.
**fūrunculus, ī** m petty thief.
**furvus 3** black, dark, gloomy.
**fuscina, ae** f trident.
**fuscō 1** to blacken.
**fuscus 3** a) dark brown; black;
dark; b) husky, indistinct.
**fūsilis, e** molten, fluid.
**fūsiō, ōnis** f an outpouring.
**fūstis, is** m cudgel, club.
**fūstitudīnus 3** cudgelling.
**fūstuārium, ī** n a cudgelling to
death.
**fūsus¹, ī** m spindle.
**fūsus² 3** poured out; a) stretched
out, prostrate, extended; b) flowing, diffuse, free; c) copious, full,
plump; broad.
**fūt(t)ilis, e** that cannot hold or
contain; brittle; vain, worthless,
futile.
**fūt(t)ilitās, ātis** f emptiness, silly
talk.
**futuō 3** to lie with (acc.); hence
**futūtiō, ōnis** f; **futūtor, ōris** m;
**futūtrix, īcis** f.

# G

**gabata, ae** *f* bowl, dish.
**gaesum, ī** *n* long javelin.
**galbaneus** 3 of galbanum.
**galbanum, ī** *n* resinous sap of a Syrian plant, galbanum.
**galbinus** 3 greenish-yellow; effeminate.
**galbinātus** 3 dressed in yellow.
**galea, ae** *f* helmet.
**galeō** 1 to arm with a helmet.
**galēriculum, ī** *n* = **galerum.**
**galēritus** 3 wearing a cap.
**galērum, ī** *n and* **galērus, ī** *m* skin }
**galla, ae** *f* gall-nut.  [cap; wig.}
**gall-iambus, ī** *m* song of the *galli* (priests of Cybele).
**gallica, ae** *f* Gaulish shoe.
**gallina, ae** *f* hen.
**gallināceus** 3 of hens, of fowls.
**gallinārius, ī** *m* poultry-keeper.
**gallus**[1], **ī** *m* cock.
**gallus**[2], **ī** *m* castrated priest of Cybele.
**gamēliōn, ōnis** *m an Attic month (January to February).*
**gānea, ae** *f and* **-eum, ī** *n* cook-shop; public house; brothel.
**gāneō, ōnis** *m* glutton, debauchee.
**ganniō** 4 to growl, snarl.
**gannitus, ūs** *m* growling, snarling.
**garriō** 4 to chat, prate, talk, chatter.
**garrulitās, ātis** *f* a chattering, babbling.
**garrulus** 3 chattering, talkative.
**garum, ī** *n* fish-sauce.
**gaudeō, gāvīsus sum** 2 to rejoice, be glad *(alqa re; quod; acc.c.inf.)*; to delight in.
**gaudium, ī** *n* joy, gladness, delight, enjoyment; darling.
**gaulus, ī** *m* round dish.
**gausape, is** *and* **-pum, ī** *n* thick woollen cloth; shaggy beard; *hence* **gausapātus** 3 clothed in woollen cloth; **gausapinus** 3 of woollen cloth, **-na, ae** *f* woollen garment.
**gaza, ae** *f* treasure, wealth.
**gelasīnus, ī** *m* dimple.
**gelidus** 3 icy cold; stiff, cold.
**gelō** 1 to freeze.
**gelū, ūs** *n* (also **gelum, ī** *n and* **gelus** *m*) frost, cold, ice.

**gemebundus** 3 groaning, sighing.
**gemelli-para, ae** *f* twin-bearing.
**gemellus** 3 = **geminus.**
**geminātiō, ōnis** *f* a doubling.
**geminō** 1 to double; **a)** to repeat; **b)** to pair, couple, unite.
**geminus** 3 double; **a)** twin; **b)** paired, twofold, both, two; **c)** of double nature; **d)** resembling, similar.
**gemitus, ūs** *m* a groaning, sighing; **a)** a roaring, roar; **b)** sorrow, pain.
**gemma, ae** *f* **a)** bud, eye; **b)** precious stone, jewel; goblet *(of precious stones)*: seal-ring.
**gemmātus** 3 set with jewels.
**gemmeus** 3 set with jewels; sparkling, brilliant.
**gemmi-fer** 3 producing gems.
**gemmō** 1 **a)** to put forth buds; **b)** to be adorned (as) with precious stones.
**gemō, uī, (itum)** 3 **a)** to groan, sigh; to moan, creak; **b)** to lament, bewail *(alqd).*
**gena, ae** *f* **a)** cheek; **b)** socket of the eye, eye.
**geneā-logus, ī** *m* genealogist.
**gener, erī** *m* **a)** son-in-law; **b)** brother-in-law.
**generālis, e** belonging to a kind *or* species, general, of all.
**generāscō** 3 to be generated.
**generātim** *adv.* by kinds, by species, by classes; generally, in general.
**generātor, ōris** *m* breeder, begetter.
**generō** 1 to beget, procreate, engender, produce.
**generōsus** 3 **a)** of noble birth, eminent; **b)** superior, excellent, generous, magnanimous.
**genesis, is** *f* constellation that presides over one's birth.
**genesta, ae** *f* = **genista.**
**genetīvus** 3 pertaining to generation *or* birth; original, native.
**genetrīx, īcis** *f* she who brings forth, mother.
**geniālis, e a)** nuptial, bridal; **b)** pleasant, delightful, joyous, genial.

**geniculātus** 3 knotty, knotted.
**genista, ae** f broom(-plant).
**genitābilis, e** generative.
**genitālis, e** pertaining to generation; fruitful, generative.
**genitīvus** 3 = **genetivus**.
**genitor, ōris** m begetter, father.
**genitrix, īcis** f = **genetrix**.
**genitūra, ae** f = **genesis**.
**genius, ī** m a) tutelar deity, guardian spirit; one's essential self; b) natural inclination, taste; c) talent, genius.
**genō** 3 = **gigno**.
**gēns, tis** f race, family, clan; a) descendant, offspring; b) kind, species; c) tribe, people; community; d) region, country; pl. **gentēs, ium** foreign nations, barbarians.
**genticus** 3 national.
**gentīlicius** 3 belonging to a clan or family.
**gentilis, e** a) of the same clan or family; b) national.
**gentilitās, ātis** f (relationship between) the members of a gens.
**genū (and genus), ūs** n knee.
**genuāle, is** n garter.
**genuīnus**[1] 3 innate, natural.
**genuīnus**[2] 3 of the cheek or jaw; subst. m back tooth.
**genus, eris** n 1. birth, descent, origin, family; a) high descent, noble birth; b) people, nation, tribe; c) race, line; d) posterity, descendants; 2. gender; 3. kind, class, sort, species; a) order, division; b) kind, description, character, (dicendi) fashion, manner, way, style; c) respect, relation.
**geō-graphia, ae** f geography.
**geō-metrēs, ae** m geometer.
**geō-metria, ae** f geometry.
**geōmetricus** 3 geometrical.
**geōrgicus** 3 agricultural.
**germānitās, ātis** f brotherhood, relationship.
**germānus** 3 full or own (brother or sister); a) brotherly, sisterly; b) genuine, real, true.
**germen, inis** n a) shoot, bud, graft; b) germ, seed; c) embryo.
**germinō** 1 to sprout, bud.
**gerō, gessī, gestum** 3 1. to bear, wear, carry, have, bring; a) **prae se** to exhibit, display; **persōnam alcis** to represent, act the part of;

b) to keep, entertain, cherish; c) to bring forth, produce; d) **se gerere** (with adv.) to act, behave, deport oneself, conduct oneself; 2. to carry out, administer, manage, rule, govern, regulate, transact, accomplish, perform; **rem bene gerere** to be successful, manage business well; **bellum gerere** to wage war; **res gestae** exploits; **alci morem gerere** to gratify, humour; P. to happen, take place, be done.
**gerrae, ārum** f/pl. trifles, nonsense.
**gerrēs, is** m a cheap kind of sea-fish.
**gerrinum(?)** = **cerinum**.
**gerrō, ōnis** m trifler, buffoon.
**geruli-figulus, ī** m accomplice.
**gerulus, ī** m carrier, porter.
**gestāmen, inis** n a) thing carried or worn; b) conveyance, carriage.
**gestātiō, ōnis** f a riding or driving for pleasure; carriage drive, promenade.
**gestātor, ōris** m (and **-trix, īcis** f) bearer; rider in a carriage.
**gestātōrius** 3 belonging to a gestator; **sella -a** sedan-chair.
**gesticulātiō, ōnis** f pantomimic motion, gesticulation.
**gesticulor** 1 to gesticulate.
**gestiō**[1], **ōnis** f a managing, performing.
**gestiō**[2] 4 to exult, be joyful, transported; to desire eagerly, long for passionately (inf.).
**gestitō** 1 to be wont to carry.
**gestō** 1 to carry, bear, wear; P. to ride, drive, sail; (in sinu, pectore) to cherish, love.
**gestor, ōris** m carrier.
**gestus, ūs** m bearing, carriage; gesture, action.
**gibba, ae** f (and **-us, ī** m) hunch, hump.
**gibber** 3 hunched, humped.
**gignō, genuī, genitum** 3 to beget, produce; to occasion, cause; **gignentia, ium** n/pl. growing things, vegetation.
**gilvus** 3 pale yellow.
**gingīva, ae** f gum (in the mouth).
**glaber, bra, brum** hairless, smooth; subst. m young slave, page.
**glabrāria, ae** f a) a lover of smooth-skinned boys; b) shorn bare, robbed.
**glaciālis, e** icy, frozen.
**glaciēs, ēī** f ice, frost.

glaciō 1 to turn into ice.

gladiātor, ōris *m* swordsman, gladiator; robber, bandit; *pl.* combat of gladiators.

gladiātōrius 3 of gladiators; *subst.* -ium, ī *n* pay of gladiators.

gladiātūra, ae *f* the fighting of gladiators.

gladius, ī *m* sword; a) weapon; b) murder.

glaeba, ae *f* clod; earth; lump.

glaebula, ae *f dimin.* of glaeba.

glaesum, ī *n* = glesum.

glandi-fer 3 acorn-bearing.

glandiōnida, ae *and* glandula, ae *f*, glandium, ī *n* gland (in meat, as a delicacy).

gláns, dis *f* acorn, nut; acorn-shaped ball.

glārea, ae *f* gravel.

glāreōsus 3 full of gravel.

glaucina, ōrum *n/pl.* a cheap ointment.

glaucōma, atis *n*, glaucūma, ae *f* cataract, blindness.

glaucus 3 grey-green; with light-coloured eyes.

glēba, ae *f* = glaeba.

glēsum, ī *n* amber.

glis, īris *m* dormouse.

gliscō, —, — 3 to blaze up, swell up; to grow, increase.

globōsus 3 globular, spherical.

globus, ī *m* ball, globe, sphere; a) round heap; b) crowd, mass; c) union, clique.

glomerāmen, inis *n* round body, ball.

glomerō 1 to form into a ball; to collect, crowd, assemble.

glomus, (*and* glō-), eris *n* ball of thread.

glōria, ae *f* glory; a) fame, renown; b) ornament, pride; c) glorious deed; d) thirst for glory, ambition, boasting.

glōriātiō, ōnis *f* vainglory.

glōriola, ae *f* little glory.

glōrior 1 a) to boast, vaunt (*de re*, *re*); b) to pride oneself (*in re*).

glōriōsus 3 a) glorious, famous; b) boasting.

glūbō (psī, ptum) 3 to bark, peel, rob.

glūten, inis *n* glue.

glūtinātor, ōris *m* bookbinder.

gluttiō 4 to swallow.

gluttus, ūs *m* gulp.

gnārus 3 (*and* gnāruris, e) a) knowing, skilled, practised; b) known.

gnātus, gnāvus etc., *see* natus, navus.

gōbius, ī (*and* -iō, ōnis) *m* groundling, gudgeon.

gomphus, ī *m* peg, pin.

gōrȳtus, *see* corytus.

grabātus, ī *m* couch, camp-bed.

gracilis, e (*and* -us 3) thin, slender, meagre, lean; a) scanty, poor; b) plain, simple, unadorned.

gracilitās, ātis *f* slenderness, thinness.

grāculus, ī *m* (jack)daw.

gradārius 3 slow, deliberate.

gradātim *adv.* step by step.

gradātiō, ōnis *f* climax.

gradātus 3 cut in steps.

gradior, gressus sum 3 to step, walk, go.

gradus, ūs *m* step, pace, gradum conferre to come to close combat; a) a stepping forward, approach, advance; b) station, position, stand; c) step, stage, degree; *pl.* stairs, ladder; d) dignity, rank.

graecissō 1 to copy the Greek style.

graecor 1 to imitate Greek manners.

grallātor, ōris *m* person that walks on stilts.

grāmae, ārum *f* discharge from the eye.

grāmen, inis *n* grass, blade of grass; plant, herb.

grāmineus 3 grassy; of bamboo.

grammaticus 3 of grammar; *subst. m* grammarian, philologist; grammatica, ae *f* (*and* -ca, ōrum *n/pl.*) grammar.

grānārium, ī *n* granary.

grand-aevus 3 old, aged.

grandēscō, —, — 3 to become great, to grow.

grandiculus 3 fairly big.

grandi-fer 3 productive.

grandi-loquus 3 boastful.

grandinat it hails.

grandiō 4 to make great, increase.

grandis, e a) full-grown, aged, old; b) great, tall, full, abundant, strong, weighty; c) lofty, dignified.

grandi-scāpius 3 with a large trunk.

granditās, ātis *f* greatness, grandeur.

grandō, inis *f* hail.

**grāni-fer** 3 grain-bearing.

**grānum, ī** *n* grain, seed, corn.

**graphiārius** 3 relating to a writing-style.

**graphicus** 3 masterly, exquisite.

**graphium, ī** *n* writing-style.

**grassātor, ōris** *m* rioter, footpad.

**grassātūra, ae** *f* a waylaying.

**grassor** 1 to move about; a) to prowl about for mischief, behave riotously; b) to act, proceed; c) to attack, use violence.

**grātēs** *f/pl.* thanks, thanksgiving.

**grātia, ae** *f* 1. a) charm, loveliness, grace; b) favour, credit, influence, regard; **grātiam inīre** *ab alqo* find favour; c) friendship, love; **in grātiam redīre** *cum alqo* to be reconciled; 2. favour, kindness, courtesy, service; **grātiam facere** to excuse (*alci alcis rei*); a) **in grātiam alcis** to please; b) thanks, thankfulness, gratitude, requital, recompense; **grātiās agere** to return thanks; **grātiam habēre** to be thankful; **grātiam referre** to requite, recompense; 2) *abl.* **grātiā** (*with gen.*) for the sake of, on account of, in favour of; d) **grāt(i)īs** out of kindness, for nothing, gratuitously.

**grātificātiō, ōnis** *f* obligingness, complaisance.

**grātificor** 1 to do a favour to, to oblige (*alci*); to make a present of, to sacrifice.

**grātiōsus** 3 obliging; a) given out of favour; b) in favour, popular, beloved; influential.

**grāt(i)īs,** *see* gratia.

**grātor** 1 = gratulor.

**grātuītus** 3 without pay *or* reward; free, spontaneous, gratuitous; *adv.* **grātuītō.**

**grātulābundus** 3 congratulating.

**grātulātiō, ōnis** *f* a) a wishing joy, congratulation; b) thanksgiving; joyful festival.

**grātulātor, ōris** *m* congratulator.

**grātulor** 1 a) to congratulate (*alci alqd, de* or *in re*; *acc. s. inf.; quod*); b) to rejoice; c) to render thanks (*alci*).

**grātus** 3 pleasing, agreeable; a) lovely, charming; b) acceptable, dear; **gratum alci facere** to do a favour; c) thankful, grateful.

**gravanter** *adv.* = **gravate.**

**grāvāstellus** (?) greyish-headed.

**gravātē** *and* **-tim** reluctantly, unwillingly.

**gravēdinōsus** 3 subject to colds *or* catarrhs.

**gravēdō, inis** *f* cold, catarrh.

**gravēscō, —, —** 3 to become burdened; to grow worse.

**graviditās, ātis** *f* pregnancy.

**gravidō** 1 to impregnate.

**gravidus** 3 pregnant, with child, with young; loaded, full.

**gravis, e** heavy, weighty; a) burdensome, burdening, oppressive, troublesome; b) hard, severe, unpleasant, harsh; c) strong (*of smell*), offensive; deep, low (*of sound*); d) unwholesome, noxious; e) important, weighty, grave, mighty, venerable, having authority; responsible; serious; f) loaded, burdened, heavy-armed; g) pregnant; h) grieved.

**gravitās, ātis** *f* heaviness, weight; a) importance, greatness; b) vigour, intensity; c) dignity, gravity, seriousness; d) oppressiveness, offensiveness; severity, harshness, violence, vehemence; e) dulness, slowness.

**gravō** 1 to make heavy, to load, burden, weigh down; a) to oppress; b) to make worse *or* more grievous.

**gravor** 1 a) to feel incommoded, annoyed, vexed (*abl.*); b) to do unwillingly, to shrink from doing (*alqd*), to refuse, decline.

**gregālis, e** belonging to a herd; a) of a common soldier; b) *subst. m/pl.* companions.

**gregārius** 3 belonging to a herd; (of soldiers) in the ranks, common, private.

**gregātim** *adv.* in flocks, in crowds.

**gregor** 1 to assemble (*intr.*).

**gremium, ī** *n* lap, bosom; the heart, centre.

**gressus, ūs** *m* a stepping; step, course.

**grex, gregis** *m* flock, herd; a) band, troop, crowd; b) company, society, clique.

**gruis, is** *f* = grus.

**grūmus, ī** *m* hillock.

**grundiō** *and* **grunniō** 4 to grunt.

**grundītus** *and* **grunnītus, ūs** *m* a grunting.

**grūs, uis** *f* (*m*) crane.

**gryps, pis** *f* griffin.

**gubernāc(u)lum, ī** *n* a) helm, rudder; **b)** guidance, direction.

**gubernātiō, ōnis** *f* a) a steering; **b)** direction, government.

**gubernātor, ōris** *m* a) steersman, pilot; **b)** ruler, governor.

**gubernātrix, īcis** *f* directress.

**gubernō 1** a) to steer, pilot; **b)** to direct, conduct, govern.

**gubernum, ī** *n* helm, rudder.

**gula, ae** *f* a) gullet, throat; **b)** appetite, gluttony, gormandizing.

**gulōsus 3** gluttonous, greedy.

**gumia, ae** *m* glutton.

**gurges, itis** *m* whirlpool; a) raging abyss, gulf; **b)** waters, stream, sea; **c)** spendthrift.

**gurguliō, ōnis** *m* **1.** gullet; windpipe; **2.** = **curculiō; 3.** penis.

**gurgustium, ī** *n* hovel, hut.

**gustātōrium, ī** *n* (dish containing) hors d'œuvres.

**gustātus, ūs** *m* (sense of) taste.

**gustō 1** to taste, take a little; to enjoy.

**gustus, ūs** *m* (preliminary) taste; sample; hors d' œuvres.

**guttātus 3** speckled.

**gutt(ul)a, ae** *f* drop; spot.

**guttātim** drop by drop.

**guttur, uris** *n* (*and m*) gullet, throat.

**gūtus, ī** *m* narrow-necked jug.

**gymnas, adis** *f* wrestling.

**gymnasi-archus, ī** *m* master of a gymnasium.

**gymnasium, ī** *n* physical training school; practice-ground; lecture-room.

**gymnasticus 3** gymnastic.

**gymnicus 3** gymnastic.

**gynaecēum** *and* **-īum, ī** *n,* **gynae-cōnītis, idis** *f* the women's apartments.

**gypsō 1** to plaster, cover with gypsum.

**gypsum, ī** *n* gypsum; plaster figure.

**gȳrus, ī** *m* circle, ring; a) circular course, circuit; **b)** place where horses are trained.

# H

**habēna, ae** f thong, strap; **a)** whip; **b)** rein, bridle; management, government.

**habeō, uī, itum** 2 to have **1.** to hold; **a)** to keep, retain, detain; **b)** to contain; **c)** to pronounce, deliver (*orationem*); **d)** to hold, conduct; **e)** to treat, use, handle; **f)** to believe, think, regard (*pro amico*); **sē habēre** (*or intrans.*) to be (in a certain condition); **2. a)** to own, possess, occupy, be master of; be rich; **b)** to know; **c)** to keep *or* breed (*animals*); **d)** to occupy, engage; **3.** to show, exhibit, be characterized by; to cause, produce; — **habitus** 3 **a)** in good condition, fit; **b)** in a certain humour.

**habilis, e** manageable, handy; **a)** suitable, fit, proper, apt (*ad alqd, alci rei*); **b)** nimble, swift; skilful.

**habilitās, ātis** f aptitude, ability.

**habitābilis, e** habitable.

**habitātiō, ōnis** f dwelling, habitation; house-rent.

**habitātor, ōris** m dweller, inhabitant, tenant.

**habitō** 1 **a)** to inhabit (*alqd*); **b)** to dwell, reside, abide; to be habitually, to stay, remain.

**habitūdō, inis** f form, appearance; condition.

**habituriō** 4 to desire to have.

**habitus, ūs** m **a)** appearance; **b)** dress, attire; **c)** condition, state, quality, nature, character; **d)** disposition, state of feeling.

**habrotonum = abrotonum.**

**hāc** *adv.* on this side, by this way.

**hāc-tenus** *adv.* **a)** to this place, thus far; **b)** up to this time, hitherto; **c)** to this extent, so far.

**haedilia, ae** f (**haedillus** *and* **haedulus, ī** m) little kid.

**haedīnus** 3 of a kid.

**haedus, ī** m young goat, kid.

**haereō, haesī, sum** 2 to hang, to stick, to cling to, adhere (*in re, ad rem, dat.*); **a)** to remain in a place; **b)** to remain attached, keep close to, keep firm, not to leave; **c)** to stand

still, cease; **d)** to be embarrassed, perplexed, at a loss.

**haerēscō, —, —** 3 to stick, adhere.

**haeresis, is** f philosophical sect; craft, trade.

**haesitābundus** 3 stammering, perplexed. [stammering.)

**haesitantia, ae** f a hesitating,)

**haesitātiō, ōnis** f a hesitating, stammering; irresolution.

**haesitātor, ōris** m one who is undecided.

**haesitō** 1 to stick fast, remain fixed; **a)** to stammer; **b)** to hesitate, be at a loss *or* irresolute.

**ha(ha)hae** *int.* ha ha!

**halagora** (?) salt-market.

**halcēdō, halcyōn,** *see* alc...

**hāl(l)ēc, ēcis** n, *see* allec.

**hali-aeetos, ī** m sea-eagle.

**hālitus, ūs** m breath, steam, vapour.

**hālō** 1 to breathe, be fragrant, exhale; to spread (*perfume*).

**halo-phanta, ae** m rogue, scoundrel.

**haltēr, ēris** m leaden weight, dumb-bell.

**halucinātiō, -nor,** *see* al-.

**hama, ae** f water-bucket, pail.

**hama-dryas, adis** f wood-nymph.

**hāmātilis, e** with hooks.

**hāmātus** 3 furnished with a hook; crooked.

**hāmiōta, ae** m angler.

**hāmulus, ī** m little hook.

**hāmus, ī** m **a)** hook; **b)** fishhook; **c)** talon; **d)** thorn.

**haphē, ēs** f fine sand (used by wrestlers for dusting the body); dust.

**hapsis = absis.**

**hara, ae** f pig-sty.

**harēna, ae** f, *see* arena.

**harēnōsus** 3, *see* arenosus.

**hariolātiō, ōnis** f soothsaying.

**hariolor** 1 to foretell, prophesy; to talk foolishly.

**hariolus, ī** m soothsayer.

**harmonia, ae** f consonance, concord. [pling-iron.)

**harpagō¹, ōnis** m hook, grap-)

**harpagō²** 1 to rob.

**harpastum, i** *n* ball for use in a game.

**harpē, ēs** *f* sickle-shaped sword.

**harundi-fer** 3 reed-bearing.

**harundinētum, ī** *n* reed-plot.

**harundineus** 3 reedy; made of reed; **carmen -um** a shepherd's song.

**harundinōsus** 3 full of reed.

**harundō, inis** *f* reed, cane; a) pen; b) shepherd's pipe; c) fishing-rod; d) arrow-shaft; e) hobby-horse; f) weaver's comb; g) splint.

**haru-spex, icis** *m* inspector of entrails, diviner.

**haruspica, ae** *f* a female haruspex.

**haruspicīnus** 3 relating to the inspection of entrails.

**haru-spicium, ī** *n* inspection of victims.

**hasta, ae** *f* staff, rod, pole; a) spear, lance, pike, javelin; b) auction; **sub hastā vendere** to sell by auction.

**hastātus** 3 armed with a spear; *subst.* soldier of the first line.

**hastīle, is** *n* spear-shaft, spear, shaft, stick.

**hau** = **haud**.

**haud** *adv.* not, not at all.

**haud-dum** *adv.* not yet.

**haud-quāquam** *adv.* not at all.

**hauriō, hausī, haustum** 4 1. to draw, draw up *or* out (*alqd ex, de, a re*); a) to spill, shed; b) to derive, borrow; c) to gather, collect; 2. to drink in, to drain; a) to swallow, devour, exhaust, consume; b) to traverse, pierce; c) to seize eagerly, enjoy, know thoroughly; d) to accomplish.

**haustor, ōris** *m* drinker.

**haustrum, ī** *n* bucket.

**haustus, ūs** *m* a drawing; a) the right of drawing; b) drawn water, a handful, draught; c) drinking, drink.

**haut** = **haud**.

**haveō, —, —** 2 = **aveō²**.

**hebdomas, adis** *f* the seventh day.

**hebenus, -num** = **ebenus, -num**.

**hebeō, —, —** 2 to be blunt, dull.

**hebes, etis** blunt, dull; a) dim; b) sluggish, weak, stupid.

**hebēscō, —, —** 3 to become blunt, dull, weak, faint.

**hebetātiō, ōnis** *f* dulness.

**hebetō** 1 to make blunt, dull, weak.

**hecatombē, ēs** *f* hecatomb, large-scale sacrifice.

**hedera, ae** *f* ivy.

**hederi-ger** 3 ivy-bearing.

**hederōsus** 3 full of ivy.

**hēdy-chrum, ī** *n* cosmetic balsam.

**hei** *int.* ah! woe!

**hēia** *int.* = **eia**.

**hēiulō** 1 = **eiulo**.

**helciārius, ī** *m* boat-hauler.

**helica, ae** *f* a spiral.

**Helicē, ēs** *f* *constellation of the* Great Bear.

**hēlio-camīnus, ī** *m* apartment exposed to the sun.

**helix, icis** *f* spiral.

**helleborōsus** 3 full of hellebore.

**helleborus, ī** *m and* **-rum, ī** *n* hellebore.

**helluātiō, ōnis** *f* gluttonous revelry.

**helluō, ōnis** *m* gormandizer, glutton, squanderer.

**helluor** 1 to gormandize, devour (*with abl.*).

**helops, opis** *m* a much-prized fish.

**hēlu-,** *see* **hellu-**.

**helvella, ae** *f* a small pot-herb.

**hem** *int.* oh! well! only see! indeed!

**hēmero-dromus, ī** *m* courier, fast runner.

**hēmi-cyclium, ī** *n* semicircle.

**hēmina, ae** *f* = ½ *sextarius*.

**hēmi-tritaeos, ī** *m* semi-tertian fever: *adj.* suffering from such a fever.

**hendeca-syllabī, ōrum** *m/pl.* hendecasyllabic verses.

**hēpatiārius** 3 pertaining to the liver.

**heptēris, is** *f* galley with oars worked by seven rowers (?).

**hera, ae** *f* = **era**.

**herba, ae** *f* a) grass, blade, herb, herbage, plant, turf; b) weeds.

**herbēscō, —, —** 3 to sprout.

**herbeus** 3 grass-green.

**herbidus** 3 grassy.

**herbi-fer** 3 producing grass.

**herbi-gradus** 3 going in the grass.

**herbōsus** 3 grassy; made of herbs.

**herbula, ae** *f* little herb.

**herciscō, —, herctum** 3 *and* **herctum ciēre** to divide an inheritance.

**hercle** *int.* by Hercules!

**here** *adv.* = **heri**.

**hērēditārius** 3 a) of an inheritance; b) hereditary, inherited.

**hērēditās, ātis** *f* inheritance.

**hērēdium, ī** *n* hereditary estate.

**hērēs, ēdis** *m and f* heir, heiress; successor; owner.

**herī** *adv.* yesterday.

**herīlis, e,** *see* **erīlis.**

**herm-aphrodītus, ī** *m* hermaphrodite.

**hērōicus** 3 heroic, epic.

**hērōĭnē, ae** *and* **hērōis, idis** *f* demigoddess.

**hērōs, ōis** *m* demigod, hero; distinguished man.

**hērōus** 3 = **heroicus.**

**herus, ī** *m* = **erus.**

**hesternus** 3 of yesterday.

**hetaeria, ae** *f* fraternity, club.

**hetaericē, ēs** *f* the Macedonian horse-guards.

**heu** *int.* oh! ah! ah! alas!

**heus** *int.* ho! there! hark!

**hexa-clīnon, ī** *n,* couch for six persons.

**hexa-meter, trī** *m* of six feet; *subst.* hexameter.

**hexa-phoron, ī** *n* litter borne by six men.

**hexēris, is** *f* vessel with oars worked by six rowers (?).

**hiātus, ūs** *m* a) an opening, aperture, cleft; open mouth; b) pompous language; c) eager desire; d) hiatus.

**hībernāculum, ī** *n* tent for winter-quarters; winter-residence.

**hībernō** 1 to pass the winter.

**hībernus** 3 wintry, winter-...; *subst.* **hīberna, ōrum** *n/pl.* a) winter-quarters; b) winter.

**hibiscum, ī** *n* the marsh-mallow.

**hibrida, ae** *m* and *f* halfbreed, mongrel, hybrid.

**hīc¹, (and hĭc), haec, hōc** a) this, this here; b) present, actual, **hic** ... **ille** the latter ... the former; c) the following; d) such.

**hīc²** *adv.* in this place, here; in this affair, on this occasion, herein, at this point.

**hice, haece, hōce** = **hic.**

**hīcine, haecine, hōcine** *interrog.* = **hic** + **ne.** [stormy.]

**hiemālis, e** wintry, of winter;

**hiemō** 1 a) to pass the winter, to winter; b) to be stormy.

**hiem(p)s, emis** *f* winter, cold; storm.

**hiero-nīcae, ārum** *m/pl.* victors in the sacred games.

**hietō** 1 to gape, yawn.

**hilariculus** 3 = **hilarus.**

**hilaris, e** = **hilarus.**

**hilaritās, ātis** (*and* **hilaritūdō, inis**) *f* cheerfulness, gaiety.

**hilarō** 1 to cheer, gladden.

**hilarulus** 3 merry.

**hilarus** 3 cheerful, glad, joyful.

**hilla, ae** *f* sausage.

**Hīlōta, ae** *m* Helot, serf of the Spartans.

**hīlum, ī** *n* a little thing, trifle.

**hinc** *adv.* a) from this place, hence; b) on this side, here; c) from this time, hereupon; d) from this cause, on this account.

**hinniō** 4 to neigh.

**hinnītus, ūs** *m* a neighing.

**hīn(n)uleus, ī** *m* young deer.

**hiō** 1 to stand open, gape, yawn; a) to be amazed, gape with wonder; b) to long for: c) to be badly connected.

**hipp-agōgus, ī** *f* a vessel for cavalry-transport.

**hippo-centaurus, ī** *m* hippocentaur (*half horse half man*).

**hippo-dromus, ī** *m* race-course.

**hippo-manes, is** *n* a) slimy discharge of a mare; b) membrane on the head of a newborn foal.

**hippo-pērae, ārum** *f/pl.* saddle-bags.

**hippo-toxota, ae** *m* mounted archer.

**hīra, ae** *f* empty gut, jejunum.

**hircīnus** 3 of a goat.

**hircōsus** 3 smelling like a goat.

**hircus, ī** *m* he-goat; smell of a goat; dirty fellow.

**hirnea¹, ae** *f* wine-jar.

**hirnea², ae** *f* rupture, hernia.

**hirsūtus** 3 a) shaggy, bristly, rough; b) rude, unpolished.

**hirtus** 3 = **hirsutus.**

**hirūdō, inis** *f* leech; bloodsucker.

**hirundinīnus** 3 of swallows.

**hirundō, inis** *f* swallow.

**hīscō, —, —** 3 to open, gape, yawn; to utter, speak.

**hispidus** 3 shaggy, rough.

**historia, ae** *f* a) inquiry, history, historical work; b) narrative, account, tale, story; c) theme of discourse.

**historicus** 3 historical; *subst.* **-, ī** *m* historian.

**histricus** 3 = **histrionalis.**

**histriō, ōnis** *m* actor, player.

**histriōnālis, e** of actors, like an actor.

**histriōnia, ae** *f* dramatic art.

**hiulcō** 1 to cause to gape.
**hiulcus** 3 gaping; greedy; with a hiatus.
**hōc** *adv.* = huc.
**ho-diē** *adv.* to-day, at this time, now; **hodiēque** even to this day, even now.
**hodiernus** 3 of this day, today's.
**holus(culum), holitor, holitōrius,** see **ol-**.
**homi-cīda, ae** *m* and *f* manslayer.
**homicīdium, ī** *n* manslaughter, homicide.
**homō, inis** *m* a man; a) human being, person; b) servant, slave; — *pl.* a) man, mankind, the human race; b) society, fellows; c) foot-soldiers.
**homoeo-merīa** (*acc.* an) *f* the homogeneousness of constituent particles.
**homullus, ī** *m* little man.
**homunciō, ōnis** *and* **homunculus, ī** *m* = homullus.
**honestāmentum, ī** *n* ornament.
**honestās, ātis** *f* a) honour, reputation, character; b) honesty, probity, integrity, virtue; beauty, grace; — *pl.* honourable men, notabilities.
**honestō** 1 to honour, dignify, adorn.
**honestus** 3 a) honoured, distinguished, noble; b) respectable, honest, worthy, virtuous, decent, proper; fine, beautiful.
**honor** *and* **-ōs, ōris** *m* a) honour, distinction, respect; **honōris causā** out of respect; b) esteem, praise; c) public honour, official dignity, office, preferment; d) honorary gift, reward, recompense, fee; e) glory, ornament, decoration, grace, charm, beauty.
**honōrābilis, e** honourable.
**honōrārius** 3 for the sake of honour, honorary; *subst.* **-ium, ī** *n* honourable gift.
**honōri-ficus** 3 honourable.
**honōrō** 1 to honour, respect; **honōrātus** 3 a) honoured, respected; b) high magistrate, dignitary; c) respectable, conferring honour.
**honōrus** 3 honourable, conferring honour.
**honōs, ōris** *m* = honor.
**hoplo-machus, ī** *m* heavy-armed fighter, gladiator.
**hōra, ae** *f* hour; a) time, season; b) *pl.* = horologium.

**hōraeum** (?) a pickle of young fish.
**hordēia, ae** *f* (?) a shell-fish (perhaps also *f adj.* = of barley).
**hordeum, ī** *n* barley.
**hōria** *and* **hōriola, ae** *f* fishing-boat.
**hōrnōtinus** *and* **hōrnus** 3 of this year.
**hōro-logium, ī** *n* sun-dial, water-clock.
**hōro-scopus, ī** *m* horoscope.
**horrendus** 3 = horribilis.
**horreō, uī, —** 2 to stand on end, bristle; **horrēns** bristly, shaggy, rough; a) to shake, tremble, shudder (at), be afraid; b) to be astonished, amazed at (*alqd*).
**horrēscō, ruī, —** 3 to rise on end, bristle up; to begin to shudder, to be terrified (at).
**horreum, ī** *n* storehouse, barn, granary.
**horribilis, e** a) terrible, dreadful, horrible; b) astonishing, wonderful.
**horridulus** 3 *dimin.* of horridus.
**horridus** 3 a) standing on end, rough, shaggy, bristly; b) unadorned, rude, wild, savage; c) unpolished, uncouth; stern, blunt; d) shuddering; e) terrible, frightful.
**horri-fer** 3 chilling, dreadful, horrible.
**horri-ficō** 1 to ruffle; to terrify; to make dreadful.
**horri-ficus** 3 dreadful, frightful.
**horri-sonus** 3 sounding dreadfully.
**horror, ōris** *m* a) a bristling, trembling, shuddering, dread; b) awe; thrill.
**hōrsum** *adv.* hither, this way.
**hortāmen, inis** *and* **hortāmentum, ī** *n* incitement, encouragement.
**hortātiō, ōnis** *f* encouragement, exhortation.
**hortātor, ōris** *m*, **-trīx. icis** *f* encourager, exhorter.
**hortātus, ūs** *m* encouragement, exhortation.
**hortor** 1 to incite, instigate, encourage, cheer, exhort (*alqm ad alqd; ut, ne*); to harangue.
**hortulus, ī** *m* little garden.
**hortus, ī** *m* garden; *pl.* park.
**hospes, itis** *m* a) visitor, guest; b) entertainer, host; c) stranger, foreigner; d) one unacquainted with (*in re* or with *gen.*).
**hospita, ae** *f* hostess; visitor, guest, friend.

**hospitālis, e** hospitable, of a guest, of a host.

**hospitālitās, ātis** f hospitality.

**hospitium, ī** n hospitality; a) hospitable reception, entertainment; b) lodging, quarters, guest-chamber.

**hospitor** 1 to lodge.

**hospitus** 3 a) hospitable; b) strange, foreign.

**hostia, ae** f victim, sacrifice.

**hostiātus** 3 provided with victims.

**hosticus** 3 hostile; strange, foreign.

**hosti-ficus** 3 hostile, malicious.

**hostīlis, e** hostile, inimical.

**hostīmentum, ī** n compensation, requital.

**hostiō** 4 to recompense.

**hostis, is** m (and f) a) stranger, foreigner; b) enemy, foe.

**HS.** abbr. (for **IIS**) = **sestertius.**

**hūc** adv. to this place hither; to this point, so far; **hūcine** hitherto? to this? so far?

**hui** int. ha! ho! oh!

**hūiusce-modī, hūius-modī** adv. of this sort, such.

**hūmānitās, ātis** f human nature, humanity, human race, mankind; a) philanthropy, kindness, gentleness, sympathy; b) good breeding, education, civilization, elegance, refinement, good manners.

**hūmānitus** adv. 1. according to the common lot of humanity; 2. kindly.

**hūmānus** 3 human, belonging to man; **res hūmānae** human affairs, things happening to man, events of life; a) humane, kind, gentle, obliging, polite; b) well educated, refined, civilized, learned; — adv. **hūmānē** and **hūmāniter.**

**humātiō, ōnis** f burial.

**humātor, ōris** m one who buries.

**hūmectō, hūmeō,** see um...

**humerus, ī** m, see um...

**hūmēscō, hūmidus,** see um...

**humilis, e** low, lowly; a) small, slight, petty; b) shallow; c) mean, humble, poor, obscure; d) insignificant; e) base, abject, servile, low-spirited.

**humilitās, ātis** f lowness; meanness, insignificance; a) low birth; b) weakness; c) baseness, abjectness.

**humō** 1 to bury, inter.

**hūmor, ōris** m, see **umor.**

**humus, ī** f a) earth, soil, ground; b) country, region; loc. **humī** on the ground, to the ground.

**hyacinthinus** 3 of the hyacinthus; crimson, purple.

**hyacinthus, ī** m kinds of red or purple flower (lilies, corn-flags [?]).

**Hyades, um** f/pl. the Hyades, a group of seven stars.

**hyaena, ae** f hyena.

**hyalus, ī** m glass.

**hybrida, ae** m and f, see **hibrida.**

**hydra, ae** f water-serpent.

**hydr-aulēs, ae** m player on the water-organ.

**hydr-aulicus** 3 belonging to the water-organ.

**hydr-aulus, ī** m water-organ.

**hydria, ae** f jug, ewer, urn.

**hydrōpicus** 3 dropsical.

**hydrōps, ōpis** m dropsy.

**hydrus, ī** m water-serpent.

**Hymēn, (and Hȳmēn), enis** m the god of marriage; marriage-song.

**hymenaeus, ī** m marriage-song, nuptial hymn; a wedding, nuptials; the god of marriage.

**hyper-bolē, ēs** f exaggeration.

**hypo-caustum, ī** n underground vault for heating a house.

**hypo-critēs, ae** m mime who accompanied the delivery of an actor by his gestures.

**hypo-didascalus, ī** m under-teacher.

**hypo-mnēma, atis** n memorandum, note.

**hystericus** 3 hysterical.

# I

**iaceō, uī, (iacitūrus)** 2 to lie, lie down; **a)** to lie sick, lie at rest, recline at table; **b)** to lie dead, have fallen; **iacentēs, ium** *m/pl.* the fallen, slain; **c)** to lie prostrate, in ruins; **d)** to be inactive, to linger, tarry, stop; **e)** to hang loose; **f)** to lie low, be flat; **g)** to lie idle, neglected, unemployed; **h)** to be low, despised, discouraged.

**iaciō, iēcī, iactum** 3 **1.** to throw, cast, fling, hurl (*alqd in alqd*), hit, push; to send forth, emit; **2.** to throw up, to set, to establish, build, construct; **fundamenta** to lay foundations.

**iactāns, tis** boastful.

**iactantia, ae** *f* a boasting, vainglory.

**iactātiō, ōnis** *f* **a)** a throwing to and fro, tossing, shaking, agitation, violent motion, emotion; **b)** ostentation, display, vanity.

**iactātor, ōris** *m* boaster.

**iactātus, ūs** *m* = iactatio.

**iactitō** 1 to utter frequently, bandy.

**iactō 1 1.** to throw, cast, hurl often; **a)** to throw out, emit, spread; **b)** to pronounce, utter, speak; **c)** to mention frequently, speak often about; **d)** to assert in a boastful way, to boast (*re, in re*); **se iactāre** to make a display, to brag; **2.** to throw *or* toss about, drive about, shake; **se iactāre** to be active in (*in re*), devote oneself to.

**iactūra, ae** *f* a throwing away, throwing overboard; **a)** loss, damage, detriment, sacrifice; **iactūram facere** to suffer a loss, to lose, omit (*gen.*); **b)** expense, cost.

**iactus, ūs** *m* a throwing, casting, hurling, throw, cast; **intra iactum** within range.

**laculābilis, e** that can be thrown *or* hurled.

**iaculātor, ōris** *m* thrower, javelin--thrower.

**iaculātrix, īcis** *f* huntress.

**iaculor** 1 to throw, cast, hurl, throw the javelin; to throw at, strike at, hit (*alqm*); to aim at, strive after (*alqd*).

**iaculum, ī** *n* dart, javelin; fishing--net.

**iaculus** 3 that is thrown: *subst. m* a darting serpent; *n* a casting-net.

**iāientāculum, ī** *n* = ientaculum.

**iam 1.** *adv.* **a)** already; **b)** now, **iam ... iam** now ... now; **c)** forthwith, immediately, presently; **iam iam** (-que) every moment; **non iam** *or* **iam non** not from this time, not now, no longer; **2. a)** now, further, moreover; **b)** now at last.

**iambēus** 3 iambic.

**iambus, ī** *m* iambus; iambic poem.

**iānitor, ōris** *m*, **iānitrix, īcis** *f* door--keeper.

**ianthinus** 3 violet-coloured.

**iānua, ae** *f* door, house-door; entrance.        [January.]

**Iānuārius** 3 of January; *subst. m*]

**iānus, ī** *m* arched passage.

**iaspis, idis** *f* jasper.

**iātr-alīptēs, ae** *m* physician who heals by unguents.

**ibī** (*and ibĭ*) *adv.* in that place, there; **a)** then, thereupon; **b)** in that matter, on that occasion.

**ibī-dem** (*and ibĭ-*) *adv.* **a)** in the same place, in that very place, just there; **b)** at that very moment.

**ibis, is** *and* **idis** *f* the ibis.

**iccircō** = idcirco.

**ichneumōn, onis** *m* ichneumon (*Egyptian rat*).

**īcō, īcī, ictum** 3 to strike, hit, smite, stab; **foedus** to make a covenant *or* league; **ictus** 3 struck, smitten, tormented.

**iconicus** 3 copied from life.

**iconismus, ī** *m* portrayal.

**ictericus** 3 jaundiced.

**ictus, ūs** *m* blow, stroke, stab, cut, thrust; **a)** beat, impulse; **b)** attack; shock.

**icuncula, ae** *f* little portrait.

**id-circō** *adv.* on that account, therefore.

**idea, ae** *f* Platonic idea, archetype.

**ī-dem, eadem, idem** the same; **idem ac** the same as; at the same time, likewise, also.

**identidem** *adv.* repeatedly, several times.

**id-eō** *adv.* on that account, therefore.

**idiōta** *and* **-tēs, ae** *m* ignorant person, outsider.

**īdōlum** *and* **on, ī** *n* image; apparition.

**idōneus** 3 fit, proper, suitable, apt, capable, sufficient (with *dat.*, *ad alqd;* with *qui* and *subj.*); responsible, worthy.

**īdos** *n* form, appearance.

**īdūs, uum** *f/pl.* the ides, middle of the month.

**iecur, oris** (*and* **iocineris**) *n* the liver.

**iecusculum, ī** *n* a little liver.

**ieientāculum, ī** *n* = **ientaculum.**

**iēiūnitās, ātis** *f* a) a fasting; b) dryness, poverty, meagreness.

**iēiūnium, ī** *n* a fasting; a) hunger; b) leanness, poorness.

**iēiūnus** (rarely **iēiūniōsus**) 3 fasting, hungry; a) dry, barren; b) scanty, poor, insignificant; c) feeble, spiritless.

**ientāculum, ī** *n* breakfast.

**ientō** 1 to breakfast.

**igitur** *cj.* then, therefore, accordingly, consequently.

**ī-gnārus** 3 a) ignorant, not knowing, inexperienced, unacquainted with (*gen.*), unaware; b) not known, unknown, strange.

**ignāvia, ae** *f* a) inactivity, laziness; b) cowardice.

**ī-gnāvus** 3 a) inactive, lazy, slothful, idle; b) cowardly; *adv.* **ignāvē** (*and* **ignāviter**).

**ignēscō, —, —** 3 to take fire, kindle.

**igneus** 3 fiery, burning hot, glowing.

**igniculus, ī** *m* little flame, spark.

**igni-fer** 3 fire-bearing.

**igni-gena, ae** *m* fire-born.

**igni-pēs, edis** fiery-footed.

**igni-potēns, tis** mighty in fire.

**ignis, is** *m* fire; a) conflagration; b) firebrand, signal-fire, watch-fire, torch, lightning, thunderbolt, star; c) brightness, splendour, brilliancy, lustre, redness; d) glow, rage, fury; e) flame of love, beloved object, flame; f) destruction.

**ī-gnōbilis, e** unknown, unrenowned, obscure; of low birth, base-born, ignoble.

**ignōbilitās, ātis** *f* want of fame, obscurity; low birth.

**ī-gnōminia, ae** *f* disgrace, dishonour, ignominy.

**ignōminiōsus** 3 disgraceful, degraded.

**ignōrābilis, e** unknown.

**ignōrantia, ae** *f* ignorance, want of knowledge.

**ignōrātiō, ōnis** *f* = **ignorantia.**

**ī-gnōrō** 1 not to know (*alqd*), to be ignorant, unacquainted with; **ignōrātus** 3 unknown.

**ī-gnōscō, gnōvī, gnōtum** 3 to pardon, forgive, excuse, overlook, indulge (*alci alqd*).

**ī-gnōtus** 3 a) unknown, strange; low-born, base, ignoble; b) ignorant of, unacquainted with.

**īle** *n,* see **ilia.**

**īlex, icis** *f* holm-oak, ilex.

**īlia, ium** *n/pl.* groin, flanks; entrails.

**ī-licet** *adv.* a) one may go, let us go! b) all is over! all is lost!; d) immediately, at once.

**īlicētum, ī** *n* grove of holm-oaks.

**īliceus** 3 of holm-oak.

**ī-licō** *adv.* on the spot, instantly, directly.

**īlignus** 3 of the holm-oak, oaken.

**illā** *adv.,* see **ille.**

**il-labefactus** 3 unshaken, unbroken.

**il-lābor** 3 to fall, slip, glide *or* flow into (*ad alqd*); to fall to ruins.

**il-labōrātus** 3 not worked out.

**il-labōrō** 1 to work at *or* upon.

**illāc** *adv.* that way, on that side, there.

**il-lacerābilis, e** that cannot be torn *or* rent.

**il-lacessītus** 3 unprovoked.

**il-lacrimābilis, e** a) unwept, unlamented; b) inexorable.

**il-lacrimō** *and* **-mor** 1 a) to weep at *or* over (*dat.*), to lament; b) to drip, drop, distil.

**il-laesus** 3 unhurt, uninjured.

**il-laetābilis, e** cheerless, sad.

**il-lāpsus, ūs** *m* a gliding *or* passing onto something.

**il-laqueō** 1 to ensnare, entrap.

**il-laudābilis, e** not worthy of praise.

**il-laudātus** 3 a) unpraised; b) detestable.

**il-lautus** 3, see **illotus.**

**ille, a, ud** that; **hic ... ille** this ... that, the one ... the other; **ille et ille** such and such, one and another;

a) he, she, it; b) the well-known, the ancient, the famous, the former; — *adv.* **illā** on that side, there; **illŏ** to that place, thither.

**illecebra, ae** *f* enticement, inducement, bait.

**illecebrōsus** 3 enticing.

**il-lēctus**[1] 3 unread.

**il-lectus**[2] 3 allured.

**il-lectus**[3], **ūs** *m* allurement.

**il-lepidus** 3 impolite, unmannerly, rude.

**il-lēx**[1], **ēgis** lawless.

**illex**[2], **icis** alluring, seducing.

**illī** *adv.* = **illic.**

**il-lībātus** 3 undiminished, unimpaired.

**il-liberālis, e** ignoble, ungenerous; sordid, mean.

**il-liberālitās, ātis** *f* meanness, stinginess.

**illic**[1], **aec, uc** that, yonder; he, she, it.

**illī(c)**[2] *adv.* in that place, there; in that place.

**il-liciō, lexi, lectum** 3 to allure, entice; to seduce, mislead.

**il-licitātor, ōris** *m* sham-bidder, mock-purchaser.

**il-licitus** 3 forbidden, unlawful.

**il-licō** *adv.* = **ilico.**

**il-lidō, sī, sum** 3 a) to strike *or* dash against; b) to dash to pieces, to crush.

**il-ligō** 1 to tie, bind *or* fasten on, attach; a) to fetter, bind, oblige, encumber; b) to entangle, impede.

**illim** *adv.* = **illinc.**

**il-līmis, e** without mud.

**illinc** *adv.* from that place, thence; there.

**il-linō** 3 a) to smear over, to spread *or* lay on (*alqd alci rei*); b) to bedaub, anoint (*alqd re*).

**il-liquefactus** 3 melted, liquefied.

**il-lisus, ūs** *m* a dashing against.

**il-litterātus** 3 unlearned, unlettered.

**illō(c)** = **illuc.**

**il-locābilis, e** that cannot be disposed of in marriage.

**il-lōtus** 3 unwashed, unclean, dirty.

**illūc** *adv.* to that place *or* point.

**il-lūceō** 2 to blaze upon.

**il-lūcēscō, lūxī,** — 3 to grow light; to dawn, break.

**il-luctāns, tis** struggling on *or* against.

**il-lūdō** 3 to play at *or* with (*dat.*), to sport with; a) to make sport with

writing (*chartis*), to mock at, laugh at, jeer at, ridicule; b) to violate, abuse, disgrace, ruin.

**illūminātē** *adv.* distinctly.

**il-lūminō** 1 a) to light up, light, illuminate; b) to set off, adorn.

**il-lūnis, e** moonless.

**il-lūsiō, ōnis** *f* mockery.

**il-lūstris, e** full of light, lighted, bright, brilliant; a) clear, plain, distinct, evident; b) distinguished, remarkable; c) celebrated, renowned, famous, illustrious; noble.

**il-lūstrō** 1 to light up, make light; a) to bring to light; b) to make clear, explain, illustrate; c) to adorn, make famous *or* illustrious.

**il-lūtilis, e** not to be washed out.

**il-lūtus** 3 = **illotus.**

**il-luviēs, ēī** *f* a) inundation; b) dirt, filth.

**imāginārius** 3 fancied, seeming.

**imāginātiō, ōnis** *f* imagination, fancy.

**imāginor** 1 to imagine, fancy.

**imāginōsus** 3 pertaining to an image; **aes -um** mirror.

**imāgō, inis** *f* image, representation; a) portrait, figure, bust; b) waxen figure, portrait of an ancestor; c) likeness, counterfeit; d) shade, ghost of a dead man, dream, phantom, apparition, vision; e) echo; f) pretence, appearance; g) simile, similitude, comparison; h) idea, conception.

**imāguncula, ae** *f* little image.

**imbēcillitās, ātis** *f* a) weakness, feebleness; b) imbecility.

**im-bēcillus** 3 (*and* **-is, e**) a) weak, feeble; b) weak in mind.

**im-bellis, e** unwarlike; a) cowardly; b) peaceful.

**imber, bris** *m* shower of rain, violent rain; a) storm, raincloud; b) water, waves; c) shower, fall.

**im-berbis, e** *and* **-bus** 3 beardless.

**im-bibō, bibī,** — 3 to drink in, imbibe; a) to conceive; b) to determine, resolve (*alqd*).

**im-bītō** 3 to go in.

**imbrex, icis** *f* hollow tile, gutter-tile.

**imbricus** 3 bringing rain.

**imbri-fer** 3 rain-bringing.

**im-buŏ, uī, ūtum** 3 to wet, moisten; steep (*alqd re*); a) to stain, taint, infect; b) to fill; c) to train, educate, instruct.

imitābilis, e imitable.
imitāmen, inis *and* imitāmentum,
ī *n* imitation.
imitātiō, ōnis *f* a copying, imitation.
imitātor, ōris *m* imitator.
imitātrix, īcis *f* she that imitates.
imitor 1 a) to imitate, copy (*acc.*);
b) to resemble, be like.
im-maculātus 3 unstained.
im-madēscō, duī, — 3 to become
moist *or* wet.
im-mānis, e enormous, immense,
monstrous; frightful, savage, horrible.
immānitās, ātis *f* hugeness; savageness, barbarity, frightfulness; barbarians.
im-mānsuētus 3 untamed, savage.
im-mātūritās, ātis *f* untimely
haste.                    [untimely.]
im-mātūrus 3 unripe; premature,]
im-medicābilis, e incurable.
im-memor, oris unmindful (*gen.*),
forgetful, heedless.
im-memorābilis, e a) unworthy to
be repeated; indescribable; b) silent.
im-memorātus 3 unmentioned,
new.
immēnsitās, ātis *f* immensity.
im-mēnsus 3 immeasurable, immense, boundless.
im-merēns, tis not deserving, innocent.
im-mergō 3 to dip *or* plunge into
(*alqd in rem*); se immergere to
plunge into.
im-meritus 3 a) not deserving,
innocent; b) undeserved, unmerit-
ed; *adv.* immeritō.
im-mersābilis, e not to be sunk *or*
overwhelmed.
im-mētātus 3 unmeasured.
im-migrō 1 to migrate, remove into
(*in alqd*).
im-mineō, —, — 2 to project over,
bend, incline over, overhang (*dat.*);
a) to be imminent, threaten; to be
near to, be at hand; c) to strive
eagerly after, be intent upon.
im-minuō 3 to diminish, lessen; to
abate (*alqd de re*); to curtail; to
weaken, injure, destroy; to slight.
im-minūtiō, ōnis *f* a diminishing,
lessening; mutilation.
im-misceō 2 to mix in, mingle with
(*alqd alci rei*), entwine; to join,
associate.

im-miserābilis, e unpitied.
im-misericors, dis pitiless.
im-missiō, ōnis *f* a letting grow.
im-mītis, e a) harsh, unripe, sour;
b) rough, cruel, pitiless, stern,
inexorable.
im-mittō 3 1. to send in, let in;
a) to dispatch, let go, let loose
against (*in* or *ad alqd*); P. *and* se
immittere to throw oneself into,
to advance, attack; b) to discharge,
shoot, cast among; c) to put into
possession, to install; d) to let into,
insert, sink into; e) to instigate, suborn; f) to cause (*alci alqd*); 2. to let
grow; immissus 3 long, flowing
(*hair*).
immō *adv.* a) no indeed, nay rather,
on the contrary, by no means;
b) indeed, assuredly.
im-mōbilis, e immovable, unmoved.
im-moderātiō, ōnis *f* want of moderation, excess.
im-moderātus 3 a) without measure, immeasurable; b) immoderate,
unrestrained, intemperate.
im-modestia, ae *f* intemperate
conduct; insubordination.
im-modestus 3 intemperate, excessive, unrestrained.
im-modicus 3 a) immoderate, excessive; b) unrestrained.
im-modulātus 3 inharmonious.
immolātiō, ōnis *f* a sacrificing.
immolātor, ōris *m* sacrificer.
im-mōlītus 3 built.
im-molō 1 to sacrifice (*alci alqd*).
im-morior 3 to die in *or* upon.
im-moror 1 to stay, linger at a place.
im-morsus 3 bitten; stimulated.
im-mortālis, e a) undying, immortal; *m/pl.* the gods; b) imperishable,
eternal.
im-mortālitās, ātis *f* immortality,
everlasting renown, imperishable-
ness.
im-mōtus 3 unmoved, motionless,
immovable, unshaken, steadfast.
im-moveō 2 to move in.
im-mūgiō 4 to roar, resound inwardly.
im-mulgeō 2 to milk into.
im-munditia, ae *f* uncleanness.
im-mundus 3 unclean, impure.
im-mūniō 4 to fortify.
im-mūnis, e not bound, free from
obligation; a) exempt from taxes

(*with abl.* or *gen.*), from military service, from work; **b)** without gifts; **c)** inactive, doing nothing; **d)** not sharing *or* partaking in, devoid of (*alcis rei*).

**im-mūnitās, ātis** *f* exemption from public burdens, immunity, privilege.          [paved.]

**im-mūnītus** 3 unfortified; un-│

**im-murmurō** 1 to murmur in, at *or* against (*dat.*).

**im-mūtābilis**[1], **e** unchangeable, unalterable.

**im-mūtābilis**[2], **e** changed.

**im-mūtābilitās, ātis** *f* immutability.

**im-mūtātiō, ōnis** *f* change, alteration; metonymy.

**im-mūtātus** 3 unchanged.

**im-mūtēscō, tuī,** — 3 to become silent.

**im-mūtō** 1 to change, alter, transform.

**im-pācātus** 3 disinclined to peace, warlike.

**im-pallēscō, palluī** 3 to grow pale at *or* over.

**im-pār, aris** unequal; **a)** uneven, odd, awry; **b)** unequal in strength, inferior (*alci*); **c)** inferior in birth.

**im-parātus** 3 unprepared, unprovided with.

**im-pāstus** 3 unfed, hungry.

**im-patiēns, tis** unable to bear *or* to endure (*gen.*); **a)** impatient; **b)** without feeling.

**im-patientia, ae** *f* inability to endure.

**im-pavidus** 3 fearless, intrepid.

**impedimentum, ī** *n* hindrance, impediment; *pl.* heavy baggage, travelling equipage.

**im-pediō** 4 to entangle, involve, hold fast, wrap round (*alqd re*); **a)** to make impassable; **b)** to embarrass; to hinder, impede, prevent, obstruct, detain, check (*alqm re, a re, in re; ne, quominus, quin*).

**impedītiō, ōnis** *f* a hindering, hindrance.

**impedītō** 1 to impede.

**impedītus** 3 hindered, impeded; **a)** impassable, inaccessible; **b)** embarrassed, encumbered, burdened, not ready for battle; **c)** difficult, intricate.

**im-pellō, pulī, pulsum** 3 to strike, strike upon; **a)** to push forward,

set in motion, drive on; to impel, propel, wield; **b)** to put to rout, to complete one's ruin, to throw to the ground; **c)** to incite, urge, instigate, persuade, move (*alqm ad* or *in alqd; ut, ne, inf.*).

**im-pendeō, —, —** 2 to hang over, overhang (*dat.*); to impend, threaten, be near, at hand (*alci, in alqm*).

**impendiōsus** 3 extravagant.

**impendium, ī** *n* expense, outlay, cost; loss; interest, usury; *adv.* **impendiō** much, very much.

**im-pendō, ndī, ēnsum** 3 to expend, lay out (*in alqd*); to devote, employ, apply; **impēnsus** 3 **a)** dear, at a high price, expensive; **b)** earnest, great, vehement.

**im-penetrābilis, e** impenetrable, inaccessible, unconquerable.

**impēnsa, ae** *f* expense, outlay, cost; contribution, waste.

**imperātor, ōris** *m* ruler, lord; **a)** commander; **b)** emperor.

**imperātōrius** 3 **a)** relating to a general; **b)** imperial.

**imperātrix, īcis** *f* female ruler *or* commander.

**imperātum, ī** *n, see* **impero.**

**im-perceptus** 3 unperceived.

**im-percō** 3 to spare.

**im-percussus** 3 noiseless.

**im-perditus** 3 not killed.

**im-perfectus** 3 unfinished, **in**complete; undigested.

**im-perfossus** 3 unpierced.

**imperiōsus** 3 far-ruling, powerful; imperious, arbitrary.

**im-perītia, ae** *f* inexperience.

**imperitō** 1 to govern, rule, command.

**imperītus** 3 inexperienced, ignorant (*gen.*).

**imperium, ī** *n* **1.** command, order, direction; **2.** might, power; **a)** rule; **b)** command, control, authority; **c)** supreme power, sway, command-in-chief, highest office; **d)** magistrate, commander; **e)** dominion, empire, realm.

**im-periūrātus** 3 that is not sworn falsely by.

**im-permissus** 3 unlawful, forbidden.

**imperō** 1 **a)** to command, order, enjoin (*alci alqd; ut, ne*); **imperātum, ī** *n* command, order; **b)** to give orders for, make requisition for, levy, demand (*alci naves, obsides*); **c)** to rule, control, govern, be supreme master (*alci*).

**im-perpetuus** 3 not permanent.

**im-perspicuus** 3 not perspicuous, obscure.

**im-perterritus** 3 undaunted.

**im-pertiō** *and* **-ior** 4 to share with, communicate, bestow, present with (*alci alqd; alqm re*).

**im-perturbātus** 3 undisturbed, calm.

**im-pervius** 3 impassable.

**impete** *archaic abl. of* **impetus.**

**impetibilis, e** unbearable.

**impetis** *archaic genit. of* **impetus.**

**im-petō** 3 to attack (*alqm*).

**impetrābilis, e** 1. attainable; 2. able to obtain.

**impetrātiō, ōnis** *f* an obtaining by request.

**impetriō** 4 to seek to obtain by good omens.

**im-petrō** 1 to accomplish, effect, bring to pass; to obtain, procure, get (*by request*) (*alqd ab alqo; ut*).

**impetus, ūs** *m* violent impulse *or* motion, vehemence, rush, vigour; **a)** attack, assault, onset; **b)** impetuosity, ardour, passion, pressure, instinct; **c)** inclination, desire.

**im-pexus** 3 uncombed; unpolished, uncouth.

**im-pietās, ātis** *f* irreverence, undutifulness; treason.

**im-piger** 3 diligent, active, quick.

**impigritās, ātis** *f* activity, indefatigableness.

**im-pingō, pēgī, pāctum** 3 to drive, strike at *or* into, to fasten upon (*alqd alci rei, in alqd*); to thrust, strike, dash against; to force upon.

**im-piō** 1 to defile with sin.

**im-pius** 3 ungodly, wicked, impious, unpatriotic, undutiful.

**im-plācābilis, e** implacable, irreconcilable.

**im-plācātus** 3 unappeased, unastisfied.

**im-placidus** 3 ungentle, savage, fierce.

**im-plexus** 3 entwined, involved.

**im-pleō, ēvī, ētum** 2 to fill up *or* full, to make full, to fill (*alqd with abl. or gen.*); **a)** to satisfy, satiate; **b)** to make pregnant; **c)** to make full (*a certain measure or number*), complete; **d)** to finish, end, accom-

plish; **e)** to fulfil, discharge; **f)** to infect.

**implicātiō, ōnis** *f* an entwining, entanglement, embarrassment.

**im-plicīscor** 3 to get confused.

**im-plicō, uī** (*and* **āvī**), **ātum** *and* **itum** 1 **a)** to enfold, involve, entangle, enwrap, envelop; **b)** to attach, unite, join; **c)** to engage in, to confound, perplex, embarrass; **d)** to twine *or* weave around (*alqa re*); **implicātus, implicitus** 3 entangled, involved, confused.

**im-plōrābilis, e** that may be invoked to aid. [(*for help*).]

**im-plōrātiō, ōnis** *f* an imploring}

**im-plōrō** 1 to implore, beseech, entreat (*alqm, alqd ab alqo; ut, ne*).

**im-plūmis, e** unfledged; bald.

**im-pluō, uī,** — 3 to rain into *or* upon.     [*impluvium*, square.]

**impluviātus** 3 in the shape of an}

**im-pluvium, ī** *n* small court open to the sky in the middle of a Roman house, with a cistern.

**im-polītus** 3 **a)** unpolished, unrefined, rude; **b)** unfinished.

**im-pollūtus** 3 unstained.

**im-pōnō** 3 to place, set, put into, upon *or* in a place (*alqd in re, in rem, dat.*); **a)** to put on board, embark; **b)** to set over, constitute; **c)** to impose, lay upon, put upon, inflict (*alci alqd*); **d)** to impose upon, deceive, cheat; **e)** to assign, assess, exact; to apply, give, add; **f)** to cause (*alci alqd*).

**im-portāticius** 3 imported.

**im-portō** 1 to bring, carry *or* convey into; **a)** to import; **b)** to occasion, cause (*alci alqd*).

**importūnitās, ātis** *f* importunity, rudeness, ruthlessness.

**im-portūnus** 3 unsuitable; **a)** troublesome, distressing; **b)** rude, cruel, savage.

**im-portuōsus** 3 without a harbour.

**impos, otis** not master of (*gen.*).

**im-potēns, tis a)** powerless, weak, feeble; **b)** not master of, unable to control (*gen.*); **c)** without self-control, unbridled, headstrong, violent, insolent, excessive, despotic.

**im-potentia, ae** *f* **a)** inability, poverty; **b)** want of moderation, ungovernableness, passionateness, fury.

**im-praesentiārum** (= *in praesentia rerum*) for the present, in present circumstances.

**im-prānsus** 3 without breakfast, fasting.

**im-precātiō, ōnis** *f* curse.

**im-precor** 1 to call down upon, imprecate.

**im-pressiō, ōnis** *f* a) beat, emphasis, impression; b) onset, attack, assault.

**im-prīmis** *adv.* chiefly, especially.

**im-primō, pressī, pressum** 3 a) to press into *or* upon (*alqd in re, dat.*); b) to imprint, mark, stamp (*alqa re*); P. to take impressions.

**im-probābilis, e** not to be approved.

**im-probātiō, ōnis** *f* disapproval.

**im-probitās, ātis** *f* wickedness, dishonesty.

**im-probō** 1 to disapprove, reject.

**im-probus** 3 a) bad, dishonest, disloyal, wicked; b) relentless, merciless, shameless, naughty; *dimin.* **improbulus.**

**im-prōcērus** 3 of small stature.

**im-prōdictus** 3 not postponed.

**im-professus** 3 not professing adherence.

**im-prōmptus** 3 not ready, not quick; hesitating.

**im-proper(āt)us** 3 not hasty.

**im-prosperus** 3 unfortunate.

**im-prōvidus** 3 a) not foreseeing, not anticipating; b) heedless, improvident.

**im-prōvīsus** 3 unforeseen, unexpected; (**de, ex**) **imprōvīsō** unexpectedly.

**im-prūdēns, tis** not foreseeing *or* expecting; a) without knowing, unaware, ignorant (*gen.*); b) unwise, rash, inconsiderate.

**im-prūdentia, ae** *f* a) want of foresight; b) imprudence, ignorance; c) inconsiderateness.

**im-pūbēs, eris** (*and* **impūbis, e**) a) under age, youthful, beardless; b) unmarried, chaste.

**im-pudēns, tis** shameless, impudent.

**im-pudentia, ae** *f* shamelessness, impudence.

**im-pudīcitia, ae** *f* unchastity, lewdness.

**im-pudīcus** 3 unchaste. lewd.

**impugnātiō, ōnis** *f* assault, attack.

**im-pugnō** 1 to fight against, attack, assail, to oppose.

**im-pulsiō, ōnis** *f* = **impulsus.**

**impulsor, ōris** *m* inciter, instigator.

**im-pulsus, ūs** *m* push, pressure, shock; incitement; impulse, instigation.

**impūne** *adv.* a) with impunity, unpunished; b) safely, without danger.

**impūnitās, ātis** *f* a) impunity, safety; b) licence, licentiousness.

**im-pūnītus** 3 a) unpunished; b) unrestrained.

**impūrātus** 3 dirty, vile, infamous, abominable.

**impūritās, ātis** *f* impurity, pollution.

**im-pūritia, ae** *f* = **impuritas.**

**im-pūrus** 3 unclean, filthy, foul; defiled, infamous, shameful, impure.

**imputātor, ōris** *m* one who makes up an account.

**im-putātus** 3 unpruned.

**im-putō** 1 to reckon, attribute, ascribe, charge (*alci alqd*).

**īmulus** 3 lowest.

**imus** 3, *see* **inferus.**

**in** *prep.* **1.** *with abl.* in; a) *of space:* in, on, upon, over, among, before, under; b) *of time:* in, during, within, in the course of, at, on the point of; c) *of other relations:* in the condition of, in the case of, in relation to, subject to, affected by, engaged *or* involved in; **2.** *with acc.* into; a) *of space:* into, up to, down to, towards; b) *of time:* to, till, for; c) *of other relations:* in relation to, about, respecting, towards, against, with a view to, according to.

**in-abruptus** 3 unbroken.

**in-accēnsus** 3 unkindled.

**in-accessus** 3 inaccessible.

**in-acēscō, acuī,** — 3 to turn sour; to become bitter.

**in-adsuētus** 3, *see* **inassuetus.**

**in-adustus** 3 unsinged.

**in-aedificō** 1 a) to build in *or* upon (*in re, in rem*); b) to build up, wall *or* block up, barricade.

**in-aequābilis, e** unequal, uneven.

**in-aequālis, e** a) unequal, uneven, unlike; b) varying, changeable; c) making unequal.

**in-aequālitās, ātis** *f* unevenness.

**in-aequātus** 3 unequal.

**in-aequō** 1 to make even, level.
**in-aestimābilis, e** priceless, inestimable; **a)** valueless, worthless; **b)** unaccountable.
**in-aestuō** 1 to boil *or* rage within.
**in-affectātus** 3 unaffected.
**in-agitābilis, e** immovable.
**in-agitātus** 3 unmoved.
**in-alpīnus** 3 living on the Alps.
**in-amābilis, e** repulsive, odious.
**in-amārēscō, ruī,** — 3 to become bitter.
**in-amātus** 3 unloved.
**in-ambitiōsus** 3 unambitious, unassuming.
**in-ambulātiō, ōnis** *f* a walking up and down.
**in-ambulō** 1 to walk up and down.
**in-amoenus** 3 unpleasant.
**ināniae, ārum** *f|pl.* emptiness.
**inānilogista, ae** *m* idle talker.
**(in-animālis, e** *and*) **in-animus** 3 lifeless, inanimate.
**inānimentum, ī** *n* emptiness.
**ināniō** 4 to make empty.
**in-ānis, e** empty, void, vacant; **a)** stripped, deserted, abandoned, unoccupied; **b)** empty-handed; **c)** useless, worthless, vain, groundless; **d)** conceited, puffed up; *subst.* **ināne, is** *n* empty space, vanity.
**inānitās, ātis** *f* emptiness, empty space; vanity, worthlessness.
**in-apertus** 3 not exposed.
**in-arātus** 3 unploughed.
**in-ārdēscō, ārsī,** — 3 to kindle, take fire, burn, glow.
**in-ārēscō, ruī,** — 3 to become dry.
**in-ascēnsus** 3 not ascended.
**in-aspectus** 3 unseen.
**in-assuētus** 3 unaccustomed.
**in-attenuātus** 3 undiminished, unimpaired.
**in-audāx, ācis** timid, fearful.
**in-audiō** 4 to hear tell, be told of (esp. a secret).
**in-audītus** 3 **a)** unheard of, unusual; **b)** unheard, without a hearing.
**in-augurō** 1 **a)** to practise augury; **b)** to inaugurate, consecrate.
**in-aurēs, ium** *f|pl.* ear-rings.
**in-aurō** 1 to overlay with gold.
**in-auspicātus** 3 done without auspices; *adv.* -**ō.**
**in-ausus** 3 not ventured, not attempted.
**inb..., see imb...**

**in-caeduus** 3 uncut, unfelled.
**in-calēscō, luī,** — 3 to grow warm *or* hot, to glow.
**in-calfaciō** 3 to warm, heat.
**in-callidus** 3 unskilful, unintelligent.
**in-candēscō, udī,** — 3 to grow hot, to glow.
**in-cānēscō, nuī,** — 3 to become white *or* grey.
**in-cantō** 1 to consecrate with charms.
**in-cānus** 3 quite white.
**in-cassum, see cassus.**
**in-castigātus** 3 unpunished.
**in-cautus** 3 **a)** incautious, inconsiderate, heedless; **b)** unforeseen, unexpected; **c)** unguarded, unsafe.
**in-cēdō, ssī, ssum** 3 to go, step, march along; **a)** to advance, proceed, march (*in, ad alqd*); **b)** to come to, happen, befall, attack, approach, appear; **c)** to go *or* come into (*alqd*).
**in-celebrātus** 3, **in-celeber, bris, bre** not made known, not famed.
**in-cēnātus** 3 dinnerless.
**incendiārius, ī** *m* incendiary.
**incendium, ī** *n* fire, conflagration; **a)** fire, flame, heat, glow; **b)** vehemence, passion; **c)** destruction.
**in-cendō, ndī, ēnsum** 3 to kindle, set fire to, set on fire; **a)** to light up, brighten, illumine; **b)** to inflame, fire, rouse, excite, enrage; **c)** to enhance, increase; **d)** to ruin.
**in-cēnō** 1 to dine in *or* at.
**in-cēnsiō, ōnis** *f* a setting on fire.
**in-cēnsus¹** 3, *part. of* **incendo.**
**in-cēnsus²** 3 not assessed, unregistered.
**inceptiō, ōnis** *f* = **inceptum.**
**in-ceptō** 1 to begin, undertake.
**inceptor, ōris** *m* beginner.
**inceptum, ī** *n and* -**tus, ūs** *m* a beginning, undertaking, attempt, enterprise, design.
**in-cernō** 3 to sift.
**in-cērō** 1 to smear with wax.
**incertō** 1 to make uncertain.
**in-certus** 3 **a)** uncertain, unreliable, unsettled, vague, obscure; **b)** doubtful, dubious, doubting, hesitating (*gen.*); *subst.* **incertum, ī** *n* uncertainty.
**in-cessō, (īv)ī,** — 3 to assault, assail, attack (*acc.*).

**in-cessus, ūs** *m* a) a walking, pace, gait; **b)** attack, invasion; **c)** entrance.

**incesti-ficus** 3 acting uncleanly.

**incestō** 1 to pollute, defile.

**in-cestus**[1] 3 polluted, impure, defiled, sinful, unchaste, lewd; **in-cestum, ī** *n* unchastity, incest.

**in-cestus**[2] **ūs** *m* = **incestum**, *see* **incestus**[1].

**in-choō,** *see* **incoho.**

**in-cidō**[1], **cidī, cāsum** 3 to fall into *or* upon (*in alqd, dat.*); **a)** to rush at, flow into; **b)** to attack, assault (*in alqm*); **c)** to incur, become involved, fall in with, come upon (*in alqd, dat.*); **d)** to fall out, happen, occur; to come upon, befall (*alci*).

**in-cidō**[2], **cidī, cīsum** 3 a) to cut into, cut through; **b)** to cut upon, engrave (*in rem, re*); **c)** to break off, interrupt, stop; **d)** to cut off, remove (*spem*).

**incīle, is** *n* canal for carrying off water.

**incilō** 1 to rebuke. [water.

**in-cingō** 3 to gird, gird about, surround.

**in-cinō** 3 to begin to sing.

**in-cipiō,** *pf.* **coepī, coeptum** *and* **inceptum** 3 a) to take in hand, begin, commence, undertake (*alqd, a re;* with *inf.*); to have a beginning, arise.

**in-cipissō** 3 to begin. [arise.

**incīsē, -sim** *adv.* in short phrases.

**in-cīsiō, ōnis** *f*, **in-cīsum, ī** *n* section, division, clause.

**incitāmentum, ī** *n* incitement, inducement, incentive.

**incitātiō, ōnis** *f* an inciting, rousing; a) violent motion; b) ardour, energy.

**in-citō** 1 to set in rapid motion; **a)** to incite, urge, rouse, spur on; **b)** to excite, stir up, stimulate; **c)** to enhance, increase; **incitātus** 3 hurried, rapid, swift.

**in-citus**[1] 3 rapid, swift.

**in-citus**[2] 3 immovable (of pieces in a game); **ad incitās** (*sc. calcēs*) **redigere** to bring to a standstill, checkmate.

**in-cīvīlis, e** uncivil, hard, cruel.

**in-clāmitō** 1 to cry against, scold.

**in-clāmō** 1 to cry out to, call upon; to scold.

**in-clārēscō, ruī,** — 3 to become known *or* famous.

**in-clēmēns, tis** unmerciful, harsh.

**in-clēmentia, ae** *f* harshness, unkindness, rigour.

**in-clīnābilis, e** inclined, prone to (*ad alqd*).

**in-clīnātiō, ōnis** *f* a leaning, bending, inclining; a) inclination, favour; b) alteration, change, inflexion.

**in-clīnātus** 3 inclined; **a)** bent down, sunken, fallen; **b)** disposed, prone, favourable (*ad alqd, ad*).

**in-clīnis, e** bending. [*alqm*).

**in-clīnō** 1 1. *trans.* to lean, bend, incline, direct, turn; a) to drive back; b) to sink; c) to change, alter, change for the worse, bring down, cause to decline; d) to give a decisive turn to; 2. *intr.* (*and* P.); a) to turn, incline, sink; b) to yield, give way; c) to change.

**inclitus** 3 = **inclutus.**

**in-clūdō, sī, sum** 3 a) to shut up *or* in, to confine, enclose, keep in (*alqm in rem, in re*); **b)** to insert, embrace, comprehend; **c)** to obstruct, hinder.

**in-clūsiō, ōnis** *f* confinement.

**in-clutus** 3 famous, renowned.

**in-coāctus** 3 not compulsory.

**in-coctus** 3 uncooked, raw.

**in-cōgitābilis, e, in-cōgitāns, tis** inconsiderate.

**in-cōgitantia, ae** *f* thoughtlessness.

**in-cōgitātus** 3 unstudied; unthinkable; thoughtless.

**in-cōgitō** 1 to contrive, design against.

**in-cognitus** 3 a) unknown; b) unexamined, untried; c) unclaimed.

**in-cohō** 1 to begin, commence; *part.* **in-cohātus** 3 only begun, unfinished. [resident.

**incola, ae** *m* (*and f*) inhabitant.

**in-colō** 3 (*trans. and intr.*) to dwell, abide in, inhabit (*alqd*).

**in-columis, e** uninjured, safe and sound, unharmed.

**incolumitās, ātis** *f* safety, soundness, good condition.

**in-comitātus** 3 unaccompanied.

**in-comitiō** 1 to insult publicly.

**in-commendātus** 3 given up, abandoned.

**in-commodesticus** 3 = **incommodus.** [venience.

**in-commoditās, ātis** *f* incon-

**in-commodō** 1 to be troublesome, to annoy (*dat.*).

**in-commodum, ī** *n* a) inconvenience, trouble; **b)** disadvantage, detriment, injury; **c)** damage, misfortune.

**in-commodus 3** inconvenient, unsuitable, unfit; unreasonable; troublesome, disagreeable.

**in-commūtābilis, e** unchangeable.

**in-compertus 3** unascertained, unknown.

**in-compositus 3** not arranged, disordered, irregular, artless, rough.

**in-comprehēnsibilis, e** not to be seized; incomprehensible; unattainable.

**in-cōmptus 3** untended, unkempt, unadorned; artless, rude.

**in-concessus 3** not allowed, forbidden.

**in-conciliō 1** to ensnare; to get by trickery.

**in-concinnus 3** awkward, inelegant, absurd.

**in-concussus 3** unshaken.

**in-conditus 3** confused, unorganized, disorderly; artless, rough.

**in-cōnfūsus 3** not disconcerted.

**in-congruēns, tis** not agreeing, inconsistent.

**in-cōnsīderantia, ae** *f* thoughtlessness.

**in-cōnsīderātus 3** thoughtless, inconsiderate.

**in-cōnsōlābilis, e** inconsolable.

**in-cōnstāns, tis** changeable, inconstant, fickle, capricious.

**in-cōnstantia, ae** *f* inconsistency, fickleness.

**incōnsultū** *meo* without consulting me.

**in-cōnsultus 3** a) not consulted; **b)** without advice; **c)** inconsiderate, indiscreet.

**in-cōnsūmptus 3** unconsumed; imperishable.

**in-contāminātus 3** undefiled.

**in-contentus e** unstretched.

**in-continēns, tis** incontinent, intemperate.

**in-continentia, ae** *f* incontinence, intemperance.

**in-conveniēns, tis** not agreeing with, dissimilar.

**in-coquō 3** to boil in *or* with; to dye, imbue.

**in-corporālis, e** unsubstantial.

**in-corrēctus 3** unamended, uncorrected.

**in-corruptus 3** not corrupted, unspoiled, uninjured; a) unadulterated, genuine; **b)** pure, upright; **c)** unbribed.

**in-crēbrāvit** (?) has visited frequently.

**in-crēb(r)ēscō, b(r)uī, — 3** to become prevalent *or* strong; to grow, increase.

**in-crēdibilis, e** incredible, extraordinary.

**in-crēdulus 3** unbelieving, incredulous.

**in-crēmentum, ī** *n* growth, increase; seed, progeny.

**in-crepitō 1** a) to call loudly to; **b)** to reproach, rebuke.

**in-crepō, uī, itum 1 1.** *intr.* to make a noise; a) to rustle, rattle, roar; **b)** to be noised abroad; **2.** *trans.* a) to utter aloud, call upon; **b)** to cause to sound; **c)** to thunder at, to upbraid, chide, rebuke, reproach.

**in-crēscō, crēvī, — 3** to grow in *or* upon; to grow, increase.

**in-crētus 3,** *part. of* **incerno.**

**in-cruentātus 3** not stained with blood.

**in-cruentus 3** without bloodshed, unwounded.

**in-crustō 1** to cover, incrust.

**in-cubitō 1** to defile.

**in-cubō, uī, itum 1** to lie in *or* upon; a) to pass the night in a temple; **b)** to hatch, brood over; **c)** to watch earnestly over.

**in-cūdō, dī, sum 3** to forge, shape.

**in-culcō 1** to trample in; to mix in; a) to impress, inculcate; **b)** to force upon (*alci alqd*).

**in-culpātus 3** unblamed, blameless.

**in-cultus¹ 3** uncultivated, untilled; a) unarranged, disordered; **b)** unpolished, unrefined; **c)** rude, without education; **d)** waste, desert; rough.

**in-cultus², ūs** *m* neglect.

**in-cumbō, cubuī, cubitum 3** to lie upon, recline *or* lean upon (*in alqd; dat.*); a) to rush towards, throw oneself upon; **b)** to burst upon; **c)** to apply, devote oneself to, exert oneself upon; **d)** to incline towards; **e)** to fall upon forcibly.

**in-cūnābula, ōrum** *n/pl.* cradle clothes; a) birth-place, cradle; **b)** origin, beginning.

**in-cūrātus** 3 unhealed, incurable.
**in-cūria, ae** f want' of care, carelessness, negligence, indifference.
**in-cūriōsus** 3 a) careless, negligent; b) neglected.
**in-currō, (cu)currī, cursum** 3 to run to or against, run into (in alqd; dat.); a) to rush at or upon, assail, to make an inroad; b) to extend to, border on; c) to meet, stumble on; to fall into (an evil), to incur; d) to fall on, coincide with.
**in-cursiō, ōnis** f a) a running against; b) onset, assault, attack; c) inroad, incursion.
**in-cursitō** 1 to run against, attack.
**in-cursō** 1 to run or strike against (dat.); a) to attack, to make an incursion into (in alqd); b) to meet, fall upon.
**in-cursus, ūs** m = incursio.
**in-curvēscō and -īscō** 3 —, — to bend, curve.
**in-curvō** 1 to bend (inwards), curve.
**in-curvus** 3 bent, curved, crooked.
**in-cūs, ūdis** f anvil.
**in-cūsātiō, ōnis** f accusation, blame, reproach.
**in-cūsō** 1 to accuse, find fault with.
**in-cussus, ūs** m a dashing against, shock.
**in-cūstōdītus** 3 a) unwatched, unguarded; b) unconcealed.
**in-cutiō, cussī, cussum** 3 to strike, dash or beat against (alqd in alqd); a) to throw, hurl; b) to strike into, inspire with, inflict, (alci alqd).
**indāgātiō, ōnis** f inquiry, investigation.
**indāgātor, ōris** m investigator, explorer.
**indāgātrix, īcis** f she who searches or explores.
**ind-āgō**[1] 1 to trace out; to search, explore.
**indāgō**[2]**, inis** f an encircling, enclosing (esp. in hunting).
**ind-audiō** = in-audiō.
**in-de** adv. from there, thence, a) on that side; b) from that time forth, after that, thereupon; c) from that cause.
**in-dēbitus** 3 not owed, not due.
**in-decēns, tis** unbecoming, improper, indecent.
**in-deceō** 2 to be unbecoming.
**in-dēclīnābilis, e** inflexible.
**in-dēclīnātus** 3 unchanged; firm.

**in-decoris, e** without honour, shameful.
**in-decorō** 1 to disfigure, disgrace, dishonour.
**in-decōrus** 3 unbecoming, unseemly, ugly, disgraceful.
**in-dēfatigābilis, e, in-dēfatigātus** 3 untiring.
**in-dēfēnsus** 3 unprotected.
**in-dēfessus** 3 unwearied; indefatigable.
**in-dēflētus** 3 unwept.
**in-dēiectus** 3 not thrown down.
**in-dēlēbilis, e** imperishable.
**in-dēlibātus** 3 untouched.
**in-demnātus** 3 uncondemned.
**in-demnis, e** uninjured.
**in-dēplōrātus** 3 unwept, unlamented.
**in-dēprāvātus** 3 uncorrupted.
**in-dēprēnsus** 3 undetected.
**in-dēsertus** 3 not forsaken; imperishable.
**in-dēspectus** 3 unfathomable.
**in-dēstrictus** 3 unhurt.
**in-dētōnsus** 3 unshorn.
**in-dēvītātus** 3 unavoided; unavoidable.
**in-dex, icis** m (and f) informer; a) betrayer, indicator; b) the forefinger; c) title, inscription; d) touch--stone; e) index.
**indicātiō, ōnis** f a valuing, setting a price upon a thing.
**indīcente mē** without my saying.
**indicium, ī** n discovery, disclosure, evidence; a) permission to or reward for giving evidence; b) mark, proof.
**in-dīcō**[1] 1 to disclose, point out, show, declare; a) to make known, tell; b) to put a price on, to value.
**in-dīcō**[2] 3 a) to announce, proclaim, declare, to make publicly known; b) to impose, enjoin (alci alqd).
**in-dictiō, ōnis** f (proclamation of) a tax.
**in-dictus** 3 unsaid; indictā causā without a hearing.
**ind-idem** adv. from the same place.
**in-differēns, tis** indifferent.
**ind-igem** (acc.) needy.
**indi-gena, ae** m and f native, indigenous.
**indigentia, ae** f need, want, insatiableness.
**ind-igeō, uī, —** 2 to need, want, be in need of (abl. or gen.); to long for; **indigēns, tis** needy.

**indiges, etis,** indigenous; native god, deified hero.

**in-digestus** 3 unarranged.

**in-dignābundus** 3 full of indignation, indignant.

**in-dignāns, tis** impatient, indignant.

**in-dignātiō, ōnis** f indignation, displeasure, disdain.

**indignātiuncula, ae** f little indignation.

**in-dignitās, ātis** f a) unworthiness, shamefulness, degrading treatment; b) indignation.

**in-dignor** 1 to consider as unworthy or improper, to be offended or indignant at (alqd).

**in-dignus** 3 unworthy, not deserving (with abl.; with qui and subj.); undeservedly suffering; a) innocent; b) unbecoming, shameful; undeserved; **indignē ferre** to take ill.

**indigus** 3 needy, in want of.

**in-dīligēns, tis** careless.

**in-dīligentia, ae** f carelessness, negligence.

**ind-ipīscor (and -ō), deptus sum** 3 to attain, obtain.

**in-dīreptus** 3 unplundered.

**in-discrētus** 3 a) undivided; b) without distinction, indistinguishable.

**in-disertus** 3 not eloquent.

**in-dispēnsātus** 3 unregulated.

**in-dispositus** 3 unarranged.

**in-dissolūbilis, e** indissoluble.

**in-distinctus** 3 confused.

**in-dīviduus** 3 indivisible; subst. **in-dīviduum, ī** n an atom.

**in-dīvīsus** 3 held in common.

**in-dō, didī, ditum** 3 to put into, set or place in or on, insert (alqd in rem or alci rei); a) to give, apply, impose; b) to introduce; c) to cause, occasion.

**in-docilis, e** a) unteachable; ignorant; b) hard to learn.

**in-doctus** 3 untaught; unskilful.

**in-dolentia, ae** f freedom from pain, insensibility.

**ind-olēs, is** f natural constitution, inborn quality, nature; disposition, talents.

**in-dolēscō, luī, —** 3 to feel pain, be grieved.

**in-domābilis, e** untamable.

**in-domitus** 3 a) untamed, unrestrained, wild; b) untamable, invincible.

**in-dormiō** 4 to sleep in or upon; to be asleep; to sleep over.

**in-dōtātus** 3 without a dowry, without gifts.

**in-dubitātus** 3 undoubted.

**in-dubitō** 1 to distrust (dat.).

**in-dubius** 3 not doubtful.

**in-dūcō** 3 to draw over, overlay (alqd re), to draw on; a) to strike out; b) to repeal, cancel, make invalid; c) to bring in, introduce; d) to lead in, lead up, bring forward; e) to bring upon the stage, produce, represent in speaking or writing; f) to set down in an account; g) to move, excite, persuade, induce, seduce (alqm ad or in alqd; ut); (in) **animum indūcere** to bring one's mind to, to resolve; to be convinced.

**in-ductiō, ōnis** f a) a bringing in, leading to; b) introduction; c) intention, inclination; d) induction, reasoning from instances.

**inductor, ōris** m chastiser.

**in-ductus**[1], **ūs** m inducement, incitement.

**in-ductus**[2] 3 imported; foreign.

**indūcula, ae** f a woman's undergarment.

**indu-gredior = ingredior.**

**indulgēns, tis** kind, tender, indulgent.

**indulgentia, ae** f kindness, indulgence, forbearance; tenderness, affection.

**in-dulgeō, lsī, (ltum)** 2 to be complaisant, forbearing, to yield, incline, allow, gratify (dat.); a) to give oneself up to; b) to care for; to concede, permit, grant.

**ind-ūmentum, ī** n covering, skin.

**ind-uō, uī, ūtum** 3 to put on, dress in (alci alqd); a) to cover, wrap, clothe, array; b) to entangle, involve (alqm re); to engage in; to assume.

**indu-perātor, ōris** m = imperator.

**in-dūrēscō, ruī, —** 3 to become hard; to be hardened.

**in-dūrō** 1 to make hard, harden.

**indusiārius, ī** m maker of upper tunics (?).

**indusiātus** 3 wearing an upper tunic (?).

**industria, ae** f diligence, activity, assiduity, industry; (de) **industriā** purposely, intentionally.

**industrius** 3 diligent, active, zealous, assiduous.

**indūtiae, ārum** f/pl. truce, armistice.

**indūtus, ūs** m a putting on; attire.

**induviae, ārum** f/pl. clothes.

**in-ēbriō** 1 to intoxicate; to deafen with talk.

**in-edia, ae** f abstinence from food, fasting.

**in-ēditus** 3 not published.

**in-efficāx, ācis** ineffective.

**in-ēlabōrātus** 3 unstudied.

**in-ēlegāns, tis** inelegant, tasteless, not fine.

**in-ēluctābilis, e** inevitable.

**in-ēmendābilis, e** irremediable.

**in-ēmorior** 3 to die in or at (dat.).

**in-ēmptus** 3 unbought.

**in-ēnārrābilis, e** indescribable.

**in-ēnōdābilis, e** inexplicable.

**in-eō, iī, itum, īre** 1. intr. to go in, enter (in alqd); to begin, commence; **iniēns aetas** youth; 2. trans. a) to enter; b) to commence a period of time, to begin (office, business), to undertake; **ratiōnem reī inīre** to make an estimate, to calculate, consider; **gratiam ab alqo** to obtain the favour of.

**ineptia, ae** f (mostly pl.) silliness, absurdity.

**ineptiō** 4 to play the fool.

**in-eptus** 3 a) unsuitable, unfit, improper; b) silly, awkward, absurd.

**in-ermis, e** and **-mus** 3 unarmed, defenceless; harmless.

**in-errāns, tis** not wandering, fixed.

**in-errō** 1 to wander in, haunt.

**in-ers, tis** without skill; a) inactive, lazy, idle, cowardly, indolent; b) numbing; dull, insipid.

**inertia, ae** f unskilfulness; inactivity, laziness.

**in-ēruditus** 3 unlearned, illiterate.

**in-ēscō** 1 to allure with a bait.

**in-euschēmē** adv. unbecomingly.

**inēvectus** mounted high.

**in-ēvītābilis, e** inevitable.

**in-ēvolūtus** 3 not unrolled, unopened,

**in-excitābilis, e** from which one cannot be roused.

**in-excitus** 3 unmoved, quiet.

**in-excūsābilis, e** inexcusable, without excuse.

**in-exercitātus** 3 untrained.

**in-exhaustus** 3 unexhausted, inexhaustible.

**in-exōrābilis, e** a) inexorable; b) unobtainable by entreaty.

**in-expedītus** 3 entangled.

**in-experrēctus** 3 not awakened.

**in-expertus** 3 a) inexperienced, unpractised, unacquainted with; b) untried, untested.

**in-expiābilis, e** inexpiable; implacable.

**in-explēbilis, e** insatiable.

**in-explētus** 3 insatiable.

**in-explicābilis, e** inextricable, intricate; a) impracticable, impassable (via); b) with no result, endless.

**in-explicitus** 3 obscure.

**in-explōrātus** 3 unexplored; adv. **-ō** without reconnoitring.

**in-expugnābilis, e** impregnable, unconquerable.

**in-cxspectātus** 3 unlooked for.

**in-exstinctus** 3 unextinguished; insatiable.

**in-exsuperābilis, e** insurmountable, insuperable.

**in-extricābilis, e** inextricable.

**in-fabrē** adv. unskilfully.

**in-fabricātus** 3 unwrought, unfashioned.

**īn-facētiae, ārum** f/pl. coarse jests, absurdities.

**īn-facētus** 3 without wit, dull, stupid, coarse.

**in-fācundus** 3 not eloquent.

**īnfāmia, ae** f ill fame, ill report, shame, disgrace, reproach.

**īn-fāmis, e** disreputable, infamous; disgraceful.

**īn-fāmō** 1 to bring into ill repute; to accuse, charge.

**īn-fandus** 3 unspeakable, unutterable; shocking, abominable.

**īn-fāns tis** a) speechless; b) poor of speech, not eloquent; c) young, little, infant; childish, foolish, silly; subst. **īnfāns, tis** m and f (little) child.

**īnfantārius** 3 fond of children.

**īnfantia, ae** f lack of eloquence; infancy.

**in-fatigābilis, e** tireless.

**in-fatuō** 1 to befool, infatuate.

**īn-faustus** 3 unlucky, unpropitious.

**īn-fector, ōris** m dyer.

**īn-fectus[1]** 3 dyed.

**īn-fectus[2]** 3 not done, not made, unfinished, unaccomplished; **in-**

fectā rē without effecting one's purpose; **a)** impracticable, impossible; **b)** uncoined.

**in-fēcunditās, ātis** *f* barrenness.

**in-fēcundus** 3 barren, unfruitful.

**in-fēlicitās, ātis** *f* ill-luck, unhappiness.

**in-fēlicō** 1 to bring bad luck to.

**in-fēlix, īcis a)** unfruitful; **b)** unhappy, unlucky, miserable; ill-boding.

**in-fēnsō** 1 to treat as an enemy.

**in-fēnsus** 3 hostile, ready to attack.

**in-fērciō, rsī, rsum** 4 to stuff in, cram in.

**inferiae, ārum** *f/pl.* sacrifices in honour of the dead.

**inferior, ius,** *see* **inferus.**

**infernus** 3 lower, of the underworld.

**in-ferō, intulī, illātum** 3 to bring, bear, carry in *or* to (*alqd in alqd*, or with *dat.*); **a)** to put *or* place on; **b)** to offer, sacrifice, render; to bring forward, introduce, produce; **c) bellum alci** to make war on, make an attack; **signa** to advance to the attack; **d)** to produce, cause, occasion, inspire; **P.** *or* **se inferre** to fall into, to rush, hasten.

**inferus** 3 below, beneath; *subst.* **inferī, ōrum** *m/pl.* the dead, the lower world; — *comp.* **īnferior, ius** lower, further down; subsequent, later, latter; inferior, weaker, meaner; — *superl.* **infimus** 3 *and* **īmus** 3 lowest, last, worst, meanest; **īmum, ī** *n* lowest part, bottom.

**in-fervēscō, ferbuī,** — 3 to begin to boil.

**in-festō** 1 to annoy, attack.

**in-festus** 3 **a)** unsafe, insecure, molested; **b)** hostile, inimical, dangerous, troublesome, ready for battle.

**in-ficētus** 3 *and* **īnficētiae,** *see* **infacetus, infacetiae.**

**in-ficiō, fēcī, fectum** 3 **a)** to dye, colour; to steep; **b)** to poison, stain, taint, infect, corrupt. [less.]

**in-fidēlis, e** unfaithful, faithless.

**in-fidēlitās, ātis** *f* faithlessness.

**in-fidus** 3 faithless, treacherous, false.

**in-figō** 3 to fasten in *or* to, drive in, affix (*alqd in rem; dat.*); to imprint, impress, fix in (*alqd in re, dat.*). [rank.]

**infimātis, is** *m* person of the lowest

**infimus** 3, *see* **inferus.**

**in-findō** 3 to cut into.

**in-finitās, ātis** *f* endlessness.

**in-finītiō, ōnis** *f* infinity.

**in-finītus** 3 boundless; **a)** endless, unceasing, countless; **b)** indefinite, general.

**in-firmātiō, ōnis** *f* invalidation.

**in-firmitās, ātis** *f* weakness, infirmity; **a)** want of courage *or* spirit; **b)** unsteadiness, instability.

**in-firmō** 1 to weaken; **a)** to shake; **b)** to refute; to annul.

**in-firmus** 3 weak, feeble; **a)** invalid, ill; **b)** timorous, superstitious, inconstant; **c)** trivial, inconclusive.

**in-fit** he (she) begins.

**infitiae, ārum** *f/pl.* a denying; **infitiās īre** to deny.

**infitiālis, e** negative, containing a denial.

**īnfitiātiō, ōnis** *f* a denying.

**īnfitiātor, ōris** *m* denier.

**īnfitior** 1 to deny, disown (*alqd*).

**in-flammātiō, ōnis** *f* a kindling; conflagration; an inflaming.

**in-flammō** 1 **a)** to kindle, set on fire; **b)** to inflame, excite, stir up, rouse. [flatulence.]

**in-flātiō, ōnis** *f* a blowing up,

**in-flātus¹** 3 blown into; **a)** swollen; **b)** puffed up, pompous, haughty; **c)** scornful.

**in-flātus², ūs** *m* a blowing into, blast; inspiration.

**in-flectō** 3 to bend, curve; **a)** to modulate (*the voice*); **b)** to change, alter; **c)** to move, affect.

**in-flētus** 3 unwept.

**in-flexibilis, e** inflexible.

**in-flexiō, ōnis** *f* a bending.

**in-flexus, ūs** *m* bending; change.

**in-flīgō, xī, ctum** 3 to strike against, dash into (*alci rei alqd*); to inflict, impose (*alci alqd*).

**in-flō** 1 to blow into; **a)** to puff out, swell; **b)** to produce by blowing; **c)** to puff up, make proud; **d)** to inspire, encourage.

**in-fluō, uxī,** — 3 to flow *or* stream in; to steal into.

**in-fodiō** 3 to dig in, bury.

**in-fōrmātiō, ōnis** *f* representation, idea, conception.

**in-formīdātus** 3 not feared.

**in-fōrmis, e** shapeless; deformed, hideous.

**in-fŏrmŏ** 1 to form, shape, fashion; a) to form an idea, to conceive; b) to represent, describe; c) to instruct, educate.

**ĭn-fŏrŏ** 1 a) to summon to court; b) to penetrate.

**in-fortūnātus** 3 unfortunate, unhappy.

**infortūnium,** ī *n* misfortune, calamity.

**infrā** 1. *adv.* below, beneath; 2. *prep.* with *acc.* a) below, beneath; b) later than; c) inferior to.

**in-frāctĭō, ōnis** *f* a breaking.

**in-frāctus** 3 a) exhausted, dejected; b) disconnected.

**in-fragilis,** e unwearied, strong.

**in-fremŏ** 3 to growl, bellow.

**in-frēnātus**[1] 3 without a bridle.

**in-frēnātus**[2] 3, *part. pf.* P. *of* **in-freno**.

**in-frendŏ** 3 to gnash (*the teeth*).

**in-frēnis,** e (*and* **-us** 3) unbridled.

**in-frēnŏ** 1 to bridle, harness; to restrain.

**in-frequēns, tis** infrequent, in small numbers, seldom doing; a) thinly attended, not forming a quorum; b) scantily populated, not filled with, not well provided with.

**in-frequentia, ae** *f* a) small number, scantiness; b) solitude, loneliness.

**in-fringŏ, frēgī, frāctum** 3 to break off, break in pieces; to weaken, impair, subdue.

**in-frŏns, dis** without foliage, treeless.

**in-frūctuōsus** 3 fruitless, useless.

**in-frūnitus** 3 unsatisfactory; uninteresting, silly.

**in-fūcātus** 3 highly coloured.

**infula, ae** *f* bandage; (*sacred*) fillet; ornament.

**infulātus** 3 wearing an *infula*.

**in-fulciŏ** 4 to stuff *or* cram in.

**infumus, ĭnfumātis** = **infi...**

**in-fundŏ** 3 to pour in *or* on (*alqd in alqd*); a) to administer, pour out; b) to cause to enter, let stream in *or* on; to spread over; **infūsus** 3 spread, lying on (*dat.*).

**in-fuscŏ** 1 to make dark *or* black; to stain, tarnish, disfigure, corrupt, spoil.

**in-gemēscŏ** 3 = **ingemisco**.

**in-geminŏ** 1 to (re)double, repeat, reiterate; *intr.* to be redoubled.

**in-gemiscŏ, muī,** — 3 to groan over, sigh at; lament (*alqd, alqm*).

**in-gemŏ** 3 = **ingemisco**.

**in-generŏ** 1 to implant; to produce.

**ingeniātus** 3 disposed by nature.

**in-geniōsus** 3 naturally gifted, talented; requiring talent; naturally suited.

**in-genium,** ī *n* innate *or* natural quality; a) disposition, temper, character; natural bent; b) natural capacity, mental power, talents, abilities, parts, genius, fancy; c) man of genius; d) clever thought.

**in-gēns, tis** vast, huge, immense, enormous.

**in-genuī** (*pf. indic.*) to implant; **ingenitus** inborn.

**ingenuitās, ātis** *f* a) condition of one freeborn; b) uprightness, frankness, noble-mindedness.

**in-genuus** 3 native; a) freeborn; b) like a freeman, noble, honourable; upright, frank; c) weak, delicate.

**in-gerŏ** 3 to carry, put, throw *or* heap into *or* on; a) to inflict; b) to obtrude, force upon (*alci alqd*).

**in-glomerŏ** 1 to pile up.

**in-glōrĭ(ōs)us** 3 inglorious.

**in-gluvĭēs, ēī** *f* gullet, crop of birds, maw; gluttony.

**in-grātē** unwillingly; ungratefully.

**ingrāti-ficus** 3 unthankful.

**in-grāt(i)īs** *adv.* unwillingly.

**in-grātus** 3 a) unpleasant; b) ungrateful; thankless, unprofitable.

**in-gravēscŏ,** —, — 3 to become heavier; to grow worse *or* more oppressive.

**in-gravŏ** 1 to make heavy, oppress, molest, make worse.

**in-gredior, gressus sum** 3 a) to go into, enter (*intra* or *in alqd*); b) to go along, walk, proceed; c) to enter upon, engage in (*alqd*); d) to attack; to begin, to undertake; to commence speaking.

**in-gressĭō, ōnis** *f* = **ingressus**.

**in-gressus, ūs** *m* a) an entering, marching in, entrance; b) inroad; c) a walking, gait, pace; d) a beginning.

**in-gruŏ, uī,** — 3 to break in, fall upon violently, assail (*in alqd*).

**inguen, inis** *n* (*mostly pl.* **inguina, um**) the groin; a) the privy parts; b) tumour.

**in-gurgitō** 1 to pour in, swill; **se ingurgitāre** to plunge in; to gormandize.

**in-gustātus** 3 not tasted before.

**in-habilis, e** unmanageable, unwieldy; unfit, ill adapted to.

**in-habitābilis, e** uninhabitable.

**in-habitō** 1 to inhabit, dwell in.

**in-haereō, sī, (sum)** 2 a) to stick in or fast, to cling, adhere, remain fast to; b) to be inherent, connected (ad alqd, in re, dat.). [**inhaereo.**]

**in-haerēscō, haesī, haesum** 3 = }

**in-hālō** 1 to breathe at or upon.

**in-hibeō, uī, itum** 2 to hold back or in; a) to row backwards, to cease rowing; b) to check, restrain, hinder; c) to practise, use, employ (alqd alci or in alqm).

**in-hibitiō, ōnis** f a restraining; backward movement.

**in-hiō** 1 to gape, to open the mouth wide; a) to gape at or for; b) to regard longingly.

**in-honestō** 1 to dishonour.

**in-honestus** 3 a) dishonourable, shameful, disgraceful; b) unseemly, ugly.

**in-honōrātus** 3 a) not honoured, disregarded; b) unrewarded.

**in-honōri-ficus** 3 dishonourable.

**in-honōrus** 3 unsightly.

**in-horreō, —, —** 2 to stand erect, bristle.

**in-horrēscō, ruī, —** 3 a) to rise erect, bristle up; b) to shake, shudder, tremble.

**in-hospitālis, e** inhospitable.

**in-hospitālitās, ātis** f inhospitality.

**inhospitus** 3 inhospitable.

**in-hūmānitās, ātis** f inhumanity, cruelty; a) barbarity, rudeness; b) incivility, brutality, unkindness; c) niggardliness.

**in-hūmāniter** uncivilly.

**in-hūmānus** 3 rude, savage, cruel, barbarous, inhuman; a) uncultivated; b) uncivil, uncourteous.

**in-humātus** 3 unburied.

**in-ibi** adv. in that place, there; near (of time); therein.

**in-icio, iēcī, iectum** 3 a) to throw, cast or put in or into (alqd in alqd or dat.); **se inicere** to throw oneself into; b) to inspire (alci alqd), infuse, occasion, to cause; c) to mention, let drop; d) to throw on or over; to lay on (alci manum), to seize.

**in-iectiō, ōnis** f a laying on.

**in-iectō** 1 to lay on.

**in-iectus, ūs** m a throwing on or over.

**in-igō, ēgī, āctum** 3 to drive, incite.

**inimīcitiae, ārum** f/pl. (rarely sing.) enmity, hostility.

**inimīcō** 1 to make hostile.

**in-imīcus** 3 hostile, inimical; subst. ~, ī m, -ca, ae f enemy, foe; hurtful, injurious.

**inīquitās, ātis** f unevenness; a) unfavourableness, difficulty, adverseness; b) unfairness, injustice, unreasonableness.

**in-īquus** 3 uneven, unequal, steep; a) unfavourable, disadvantageous; b) excessive, not of the right measure; c) unfair, unjust; d) inimical, hostile, adverse; e) unwilling, impatient.

**initiātiō, ōnis** f (and **initiāmenta, ōrum** n/pl.) initiation, consecration.

**in-itiō** 1 to initiate, admit.

**initium, ī** n a going in; beginning, commencement; a) pl. constituent parts, elements; b) first principles, elements of science; c) secret mysteries.

**in-itus, ūs** m arrival; beginning.

**in-iūcunditās, ātis** f unpleasantness.

**in-iūcundus** 3 unpleasant, harsh.

**in-iūdicātus** 3 undecided.

**in-iungō** 3 a) to join or fasten into (alqd in alqd); b) to join with, attach to (alci alqd); to inflict, bring upon; to impose upon, enjoin.

**in-iūrātus** 3 unsworn.

**iniūria, ae** f injury, injustice, wrong; a) outrage, insult, damage, harm; b) unjust acquisition; c) revenge for an affront.

**in-iūrior** 1 to do an injury.

**iniūriōsus** 3 unjust, wrongful, hurtful (in alqm).

**in-iūr(i)us** 3 wrongful, unjust.

**in-iussū** without orders or command.

**in-iussus** 3 uncommanded, unbidden.

**in-iūstitia, ae** f injustice.

**in-iūstus** 3 unjust, wrongful; harsh, severe, oppressive.

**inl..., inm...,** see **ill..., imm...**

**in-nābilis, e** that cannot be swum in.

**in-nāscor** 3 to be born, grow in or upon; **innātus** 3 inborn.

**in-natō** 1 a) to swim into; **b)** to swim *or* float in *or* upon.

**in-nāvigābilis, e** not navigable.

**in-nectō** 3 to tie, join, fasten about, together *or* to.

**in-nītor** 3 to lean, depend upon.

**in-nō** 1 a) to swim into; **b)** to swim upon, sail upon (*alqd*).

**in-nocēns, tis** a) guiltless, innocent, blameless; **c)** harmless, inoffensive, upright.

**innocentia, ae** *f* innocence; **a)** inoffensiveness; **b)** uprightness, disinterestedness.

**in-nocuus = innoxius.**

**in-nōtēscō, tuī, —** 3 to become known.

**in-novō** 1 to renew; **se** to return to (*ad*).

**in-noxius** 3 harmless; innocent; unhurt, free from injury.

**in-nūbilus** 3 (*and* **in-nūbis, e**) cloudless.

**in-nūbō** 3 to marry into (*with dat.*).

**in-nubus** 3 = **innuptus.**

**in-numerābilis, e** innumerable.

**in-numerābilitās, ātis** *f* countless number.

**in-numerus** 3 (*and* -**rālis, e**) numberless.

**in-nuō, uī, —** 3 to nod to *or* at.

**in-nuptus** 3 unmarried, virgin; (*nuptiae*) unhappy (*marriage*).

**in-nūtriō** 4 to bring up in.

**in-oblītus** 3 mindful.

**in-obrutus** 3 not overwhelmed.

**in-obsequēns, tis** disobedient.

**in-observābilis, e** untraceable.

**in-observantia, ae** *f* carelessness, disorder.

**in-observātus** 3 unobserved.

**in-occiduus** 3 never setting *or* closing.

**in-odōrus** 3 unscented.

**in-offēnsus** 3 untouched, unobstructed, undisturbed.

**in-officiōsus** 3 careless of obligations.

**in-olēns, entis** without smell.

**in-olēscō, lēvī, litum** 3 to grow upon *or* into (*dat.*).

**in-ōminātus** 3 ill-omened.

**in-opertus** 3 naked.

**inopia, ae** *f* want, lack; need, poverty, scarcity, helplessness.

**in-opināns, tis** not expecting, unaware.

**in-opinātus** (*and* **in-opīnus**) 3

**1.** (*seldom*) = **inopinans; 2.** unexpected, unsuspected.

**in-opiōsus** 3 in need of (*alcis*).

**in-ops, opis** a) helpless, poor, needy, lacking (*alcis rei or alqa re*); **b)** powerless, weak; **c)** poor in words *or* thoughts, mean, pitiful.

**in-ōrātā rē** without pleading.

**in-ōrdinātus** 3 not arranged.

**in-ōrnātus** 3 unadorned, uncelebrated.

**inp..., see imp...**

**inquam** (*defective vb.*) to say.

**in-quiēs, ētis** restless, unquiet.

**in-quiētō** 1 to disquiet, disturb.

**in-quiētus** 3 restless, unquiet.

**inquilinus, ī** *m* tenant, lodger.

**in-quinō** 1 to stain, pollute, defile; **inquinātus** 3 polluted, defiled, foul.

**in-quirō, sīvī, sītum** 3 to seek after, search for; **a)** to inquire into, examine; **b)** to seek grounds of accusation (*in alqm*).

**in-quīsītiō, ōnis** *f* a searching after; investigation, inquiry.

**in-quīsītor, ōris** *m* inquirer, spy; investigator.

**in-quīsītus** unexamined.

**inr..., see irr...**

**in-saepiō** 4 to fence round.

**in-salūbris, bre** unhealthy.

**in-salūtātus** 3 ungreeted.

**in-sānābilis, e** incurable.

**insānia, ae** *f* insanity, madness; frenzy; **a)** rapture, inspiration; **b)** senseless extravagance, excess.

**in-sāniō** 4 to be mad, insane; to rage, rave.

**in-sānitās, ātis** *f* unsoundness.

**in-sānus** 3 insane, mad, raging, raving; **a)** enthusiastic, enraptured, inspired; **b)** monstrous, excessive.

**in-satiābilis, e** a) insatiable; **b)** not surfeiting.

**in-satiātus** 3 insatiate.

**in-satietās, ātis** *f* insatiableness.

**in-saturābilis, e** insatiable.

**in-scendō, ndī, ēnsum** 3 to climb up, mount (*alqd*).

**in-scēnsiō, ōnis** *f* embarkation.

**in-sciēns, tis** not knowing, unaware; ignorant, silly, stupid.

**in-scientia, ae** *f* ignorance, want of knowledge; inexperience.

**īnscītia, ae** *f* a) awkwardness, unskilfulness; **b)** ignorance; = **inscientia.**

**in-scītus** 3 unskilful, blundering.

**in-scius** 3 not knowing, ignorant.

**in-scrībō** 3 **a)** to write in *or* upon (*in re; dat.*), to inscribe; **b)** to ascribe, assign (*alci alqd*); **c)** to furnish with an inscription *or* title (*alci alqd*); **d)** to mark, characterize.

**in-scriptiō, ōnis** *f* **a)** a writing upon; **b)** inscription, title.

**in-sculpō** 3 to engrave, cut *or* carve in *or* upon, to impress (*alqd in re*).

**in-secābilis, e** indivisible.

**in-secō¹, uī, ctum** 1 to cut into, cut to pieces. [the story of (*acc.*).]

**in-secō², (sexī)** to tell of, relate

**in-sectātiō, ōnis** *f* pursuit; a railing at.

**in-sectātor, ōris** *m* persecutor; censurer.

**in-sector** (*and* -ō) 1 to pursue, attack; to reproach, rail at.

**in-sēdābiliter** unceasingly.

**in-segestus** not sown.

**in-senēscō, nuī,** — 3 to grow old in *or* at (*dat.*).

**in-sēnsilis, e** imperceptible.

**in-sēparābilis, e** inseparable.

**in-sepultus** 3 unburied.

**in-sequor** 3 to follow after (*acc.*), come next; **a)** to pursue; **b)** to censure, reproach, attack; **c)** to strive after; **d)** to overtake.

**in-serēnus** 3 overcast.

**in-serō¹, sēvī, situm** 3 to sow *or* plant in (*in alqd; dat.*); **a)** to ingraft; **b)** to implant; **insitus** 3 innate, natural.

**in-serō², ruī, rtum** 3 to put, place *or* set in, insert (*alqd in alqd; dat.*); **a)** to introduce, intermingle with; **se inserere** to meddle with; **b)** to incorporate with, place among.

**in-serpō** 3 to steal upon.

**in-sertō** 1 to put into.

**in-serviō** 4 to serve; **a)** to be a slave *or* serviceable; **b)** to be devoted *or* attached to; to take care of, attend to (*dat.*).

**in-servō** 1 to observe.

**in-sībilō** 1 to hiss *or* whistle in.

**in-siccātus** 3 not dried.

**in-sideō, sēdī, sessum** 2 **a)** to sit in *or* upon (*in re*), to be settled, seated, fixed, stamped in; **b)** to keep possession of, occupy; to inhabit (*acc.*).

**insidiae, ārum** *f/pl.* ambush, ambuscade; plot, artifice, snare, trap, deceit, treachery.

**insidiātor, ōris** *m* soldier in ambush, waylayer, lurker.

**insidior** 1 to lie in ambush, in wait for; to wait for; to plot against (*dat.*).

**insidiōsus** 3 deceitful, artful, cunning, treacherous; dangerous.

**in-sīdō, sēdī, sessum** 3 **a)** to sit down upon (*in re; dat.*); to settle, become fixed, rooted in; **b)** to occupy, beset.

**insigne, is** *n* token, mark, signal; official badge, decoration, distinction; flag, standard.

**in-signiō** 4 to make conspicuous, distinguish.

**in-signis, e** distinguished by a mark, noted; **a)** remarkable, distinguished; **b)** extraordinary, excellent, notorious.

**insignītus** 3 marked; **a)** noticeable, plain; **b)** notable, distinguished, conspicuous; *adv.* **insignītē**.

**insilia** *n/pl.* treadles (of a loom).

**in-siliō, luī,** — 4 to leap, spring, jump in *or* on (*in alqd; dat.* or *acc.*).

**insimul** = **simul**.

**in-simulātiō, ōnis** *f* accusation, charge.

**in-simulō** 1 to charge, accuse, blame (*alqm* with *gen.*).

**in-sincērus** 3 impure, tainted.

**in-sinuātiō, ōnis** *f* a winning favour.

**in-sinuō** 1 to push forward into a gap; **P.** *or* **se īnsinuāre** to penetrate (*inter* or *in alqd*), work one's way in; to insinuate oneself (*alci*).

**in-sipiēns, tis** unwise, foolish.

**insipientia, ae** *f* folly, stupidity.

**in-sistō, stitī,** — 3 **1.** to stand *or* tread upon, set foot on (*in re; dat.*); **a)** to step on; **b)** to enter, enter on (*alqd*); **c)** to pursue, press on (*alci*); **d)** to persist, insist, apply oneself, be busy about (*alqd*); **2.** to stand still, pause, stop, be fixed *or* obstinate in (*inf.*).

**insitīcius** 3 ingrafted, foreign.

**insitiō, ōnis** *f* a grafting; time of grafting.

**insitīvus** 3 grafted, ingrafted; pretended, foreign, spurious, bastard.

**insitor, ōris** *m* grafter.

**in-situs** 3, *part. pf.* **P** of **insero¹**.

**in-sociābilis, e** with whom no alliance is possible.

**in-sōlābiliter** inconsolably.

**in-solēns, tis a)** unaccustomed (*alcis rei, in re*); **b)** unusual, extravagant, excessive, immoderate; **c)** proud, haughty, arrogant, insolent.

**in-solentia, ae** *f* **a)** strangeness, novelty; **b)** extravagance, excess; **c)** pride, arrogance.

**in-solēscō, —, —** 3 to become haughty *or* insolent.

**in-solidus** 3 weak, tender.

**in-solitus** 3 **a)** unaccustomed; **b)** unusual.

**in-solūbilis, e** that cannot be paid.

**in-somnia, ae** *f* sleeplessness.

**in-somnis, e** sleepless.

**in-somnium, ī** *n* 1. dream; 2. = insomnia.

**in-sonō, uī, —** 1 to sound (*also alqd*), resound, make a noise, roar, rustle, crack.

**in-sōns, tis** innocent, guiltless.

**in-sōpītus** 3 sleepless.

**in-sopor, -ōris** sleepless.

**in-spectiō, ōnis** *f* investigation.

**in-spectō** 1 to look at, view.

**in-spector, ōris** *m* observer.

**in-spectus, ūs** *m* contemplation.

**in-spērāns, tis** not hoping, not expecting.

**in-spērātus** 3 unhoped for, unexpected.

**in-spergō, rsī, rsum** 3 to sprinkle on *or* over, strew on.

**in-spiciō, spexī, spectum** 3 to look into *or* upon (*in alqd; rem*); **a)** to read; **b)** to examine, to inspect, view, observe; **c)** to investigate.

**in-spīcō** 1 to make pointed, sharpen.

**in-spīrō** 1 **a)** to breathe into (*dat.*), blow upon; **b)** to inspire, rouse, inflame; to instil, implant (*alci alqd*).

**in-spoliātus** 3 not plundered.

**in-spuō** 3, **in-spūtō** 1 to spit on.

**in-spurcō** 1 to defile.

**in-stabilis, e** unstable, unsteady, not firm, inconstant.

**in-stāns, tis a)** present, immediate; **b)** pressing, threatening.

**instantia, ae** *f* **a)** presence; **b)** perseverance.

**instar** *n* (*indecl.*) image, likeness, resemblance; **a)** equal size, number, value; **b)** *with gen.* in the form of, like, as large as, equivalent to.

**instaurātiō, ōnis** *f* renewal.

**instaurātīvus** 3 renewed.

**in-staurō** 1 **a)** to establish, set about, prepare; **b)** to renew, repeat; to repair, restore.

**in-sternō** 3 to cover over, spread upon; to lay upon.

**instīgātor, ōris** *m* (*f* **-trīx, īcis**) stimulator, instigator.

**in-stīgō** 1 to incite, stimulate.

**in-stillō** 1 to drop in, instil.

**in-stimulātor, ōris** *m* instigator.

**in-stimulō** 1 to stimulate, arouse, incite.

**in-stinctor, ōris** *m* inciter.

**in-stinctus, ūs** *m* incitement.

**in-stinguō, īnxī, īnctum** 3 to incite, impel.

**in-stipulor** 1 to stipulate.

**instita, ae** *f* border of a lady's robe.

**in-stitiō, ōnis** *f* a standing still.

**institor, ōris** *m* hawker, pedlar.

**institōrium, ī** *n* trade of a hawker.

**in-stituō, uī, ūtum** 3 **1.** to put *or* place into; **a)** to plant, fix, set; **b)** to build, construct, erect, found, establish; **c)** to draw up in order (*troops*); **d)** to designate, appoint; **2.** to undertake, begin, commence; **a)** to purpose, determine, resolve upon; **b)** to introduce, institute; **c)** to ordain, regulate; **3.** to teach, instruct, educate (*alqm alqa re, ad alqd*).

**institūtiō, ōnis** *f* = institutum.

**institūtum, ī** *n* arrangement, disposition; **a)** old-established custom, usage; **b)** undertaking, purpose; **c)** instruction; *pl.* principles, method.

**instō, stitī, (stātūrus)** 1 **1.** to stand in *or* on, to enter (*viam*); **2.** to press upon (*dat.*); **a)** to urge, insist, pursue; **b)** to be at hand, approach, impend; **c)** to be intent upon, work hard at, strive after (with *dat.* or *acc., ut, ne, acc. c. inf.*).

**in-strātus**[1] 3 uncovered.

**in-strātus**[2] 3, *part. pf.* P. of in-sterno.

**in-strēnuus** 3 inactive, lazy, idle.

**in-strepō** 3 to rattle, creak.

**in-strīdō** 3 to hiss in *or* on.

**in-stringō** 3 to bind round.

**in-structiō, ōnis** *f* a drawing up in order, array; construction.

**instructor, ōris** *m* preparer.

**instructus**[1] 3 **a)** ordered, drawn up; **b)** provided with, furnished; **c)** taught, instructed (*in re, re*).

**īn-structus²**, ūs *m* equipment.

**īnstrūmentum, ī** *n* tool, implement, instrument, apparatus, material; **a)** dress, apparel; **b)** ornament, embellishment; **c)** document; **d)** means.

**īn-struō 3 1.** to build in *or* into; **a)** to build, erect; **b)** to draw up in order, set in order; **c)** to prepare, make ready; **2.** to provide, procure, furnish, equip (*alqa re*), to teach, instruct.

**īnsuāsum (?), ī** *n* = suasum

**īn-suāvis, e** unpleasant, disagreeable.

**īn-sūdō 1** to sweat on.

**īnsuē-factus 3** accustomed to.

**īn-suēscō 3 a)** to accustom oneself to (*ad alqd; inf.*); **b)** to accustom (*alqm*).

**īn-suētus 3 1.** *part. pf.* P. *of* **in-suesco; 2. a)** unaccustomed (*gen., dat., ad alqd, inf.*); **b)** unusual.

**īnsula, ae** *f* **a)** island; **b)** tenement house, block of flats.

**īnsulānus, ī** *m* islander.

**īnsulsitās, ātis** *f* absurdity, bad taste.

**īn-sulsus 3 a)** unsalted, without taste; **b)** insipid, absurd.

**īn-sultō 1 a)** to leap upon, bound, jump; **b)** to scoff at, taunt, insult (*dat.; in alqd*).

**īn-sultūra, ae** *f* a leaping on.

**īn-sum, īnfuī, inesse** to be in *or* on, be contained in, belong to (*in re; dat.*).

**īn-sūmō 3** to take for, apply, expend (*alqd in re* or *alci rei*).

**īn-suō 3** to sew in *or* into.

**īn-super** *adv.* above, on the top; from above; over and above, moreover.

**īn-superābilis, e** insurmountable; unconquerable.

**īn-surgō 3** to rise (up), lift oneself; to rise against.

**īn-susurrō 1** to whisper in *or* to.

**īn-tābēscō, buī, — 3** to melt; to pine away.

**īn-tāctilis, e** intangible.

**īn-tāctus 3** untouched, uninjured; **a)** untried, unattempted; **b)** undefiled, chaste.

**īn-tāminātus 3** unsullied.

**īn-tēctus 3 1.** *part. pf.* P. *of* intego; **2.** uncovered, unarmed; frank.

**īn-tegellus 3** undefiled; uninjured.

**īn-teger, gra, grum** untouched; **a)** unhurt, uninjured; **b)** unimpaired; fresh, sound, vigorous; entire, whole, complete; **c)** undecided, undetermined, open; **d)** inexperienced, ignorant; **e)** healthy, sane, unbiassed; **f)** spotless, blameless, pure, honest, virtuous, impartial, unbribed; — **ab, de, ex integro** afresh.

**īn-tegō 3** to cover, to protect.

**integrāscō 3** to start afresh.

**integrātiō, ōnis** *f* a renewing, restoring.

**integritās, ātis** *f* unimpaired condition; **a)** completeness, soundness; **b)** purity, chastity; **c)** honesty, innocence, integrity.

**integrō 1** to make whole, restore, repair; to renew, repeat, begin again.          [guise.]

**īn-tegumentum, ī** *n* covering, disguise.

**intellēctus, ūs** *m* **a)** perception, discernment, understanding; **b)** sense, meaning.

**intellegēns, tis** intelligent, discerning, well acquainted with (*gen.*); *subst.* connoisseur.

**intellegentia, ae** *f* intelligence, discernment; **a)** understanding; knowledge, skill, taste; **b)** perception.

**intellegibilis, e** understandable.

**intel-legō, ēxī, ēctum 3** to perceive; **a)** to understand, comprehend (*alqd; acc. c. inf.*), have skill in, be master of; **b)** to judge, think, be of opinion; **c)** to be a connoisseur.

**in-temerandus 3** inviolable.

**in-temerātus 3** inviolate, pure.

**in-temperāns, tis** intemperate, immoderate, unrestrained, profligate.

**in-temperantia, ae** *f* want of moderation, intemperance; insolence, insubordination.

**in-temperātus 3** immoderate, extravagant.

**in-temperiae, ārum** *f/pl.* distemper (of mind).

**in-temperiēs, ēī** *f* excess, intemperateness; **a)** inclement weather; **b)** intemperate behaviour.

**in-tempestīvus 3** untimely, unseasonable.

**in-tempestus 3 a)** timeless; **nox -a** the dead of night; **b)** unhealthy; **c)** stormy.

**in-temptātus** 3 untried.

**in-tendō, ndī, ntum** 3 **1.** to stretch, strain; to stretch forth, exert; **2.** to extend; a) to lay *or* put upon (*alci alqd*); to direct, bend, turn, aim (*alqd in* or *ad alqd*); to assail with; b) to direct one's course to, to intend, purpose, endeavour; c) to direct with hostile intention (*alqd alci* or *in alqm*); d) to increase, magnify.

**intentātiō, ōnis** *f* a stretching out towards.

**in-tentātus** 3 **1.** *part. pf.* P. of *intento*; **2.** = **intemptatus**.

**in-tentiō, ōnis** *f* a stretching, straining; a) exertion, effort; b) attention, application; c) attack, accusation.

**in-tentō** 1 to stretch *or* hold out threateningly (*alqd in alqm* or *alci*).

**intentus¹, ūs** *m* a stretching out.

**in-tentus²** 3 stretched, strained; a) intent, attentive (*alci rei, in* or *ad alqd*), anxious, eager; vigorous; active.

**in-tepeō, —, —** 2 to be warm.

**in-tepēscō, puī, —** 3 to become warm.

**inter** *prep.* with *acc.* a) *of space:* between, among, amid; b) *of time:* between, during, in the course of; c) *denoting relation:* between, among.

**inter-aestuō** 1 to be inflamed at intervals (*or* in places).

**interāmenta, ōrum** *n/pl.* interior woodwork *of a ship*.

**inter-aptus** 3 joined together.

**inter-ārēscō, —, —** 3 to become

**interātim** = **interim**. [dry.]

**inter-bibō** 3 to drink up.

**inter-bītō** 3 to perish.

**inter-calāris, e** *and* **-ius** 3 inserted, intercalary.

**inter-calō** 1 to insert, intercalate; to put off, defer.

**inter-capēdō, inis** *f* interruption, interval.

**inter-cēdō** 3 to go between, come between; a) to stand *or* lie between; b) to intervene, pass, happen between; c) to protest against, interfere, interpose a veto (with *dat.; quominus*); d) to occur, happen.

**interceptiō, ōnis** *f* a taking away.

**interceptor, ōris** *m* interceptor, embezzler.

**inter-cessiō, ōnis** *f* intervention.

**inter-cessor, ōris** *m* a) vetoer, preventer; b) mediator, surety.

**inter-cīdō¹, cīdī, cīsum** 3 to cut through *or* asunder, cut down.

**inter-cīdō², cidī, — 3** a) to fall between; to happen; b) to perish, decay; c) to drop out, be forgotten.

**inter-cinō, —, —** 3 to sing between.

**inter-cipiō, cēpī, ceptum** 3 to take by the way, intercept; a) to embezzle, steal; b) to interrupt, hinder; c) to snatch away, carry off prematurely.

**intercisē** *adv.* disconnectedly.

**inter-clūdō, sī, sum** 3 a) to shut out *or* off, block up, hinder (*alci alqd*); c) to cut off, separate.

**inter-clūsiō, ōnis** *f* a stopping, hindering.

**inter-columnium, ī** *n* space between two columns.

**inter-currō, (cu)currī, cursum** 3 to run between; a) to step between, intercede; b) to run to in the meanwhile.

**inter-cursō** 1 = **intercurro**.

**inter-cursus, ūs** *m* intervention.

**inter-cus, cutis** under the skin.

**inter-dīcō** 3 a) to forbid, prohibit, interdict; **alci aquā et igni** to banish; b) to make a provisional decree; — *subst.* **interdictum, ī** *n* a) prohibition; b) a prætor's decree, interdict.

**inter-dictiō, ōnis** *f* a prohibiting.

**inter-diū(s)** *adv.* by day.

**inter-dō** 1 to interpose; to diffuse; **non interduim** (*subj.*) I would not give anything, I do not care.

**inter-ductus, ūs** *m* punctuation.

**inter-dum** *adv.* sometimes.

**inter-eā** *adv.* a) in the meantime, meanwhile; b) nevertheless, however.

**inter-ēmptor, ōris** *m* murderer.

**inter-eō, iī, itum, īre** to be lost, perish, go to ruin.

**inter-equitō** 1 to ride between.

**inter-fātiō, ōnis** *f* interruption in speaking.

**inter-fectiō, ōnis** *f* a slaying.

**inter-fector, ōris** *m* murderer.

**inter-fectrix, icis** *f* murderess.

**inter-ficiō, fēcī, fectum** 3 to destroy, kill, slay.

**inter-fīō** to pass away; **to be** destroyed.

**inter-fluō** 3 to flow between.
**inter-fodiō** 3 to pierce.
**inter-for** 1 to interrupt *(alqm)*.
**inter-fugiō** 3 to flee among.
**inter-fulgeō** 2 to gleam among.
**inter-furō** 3 to rage between *or* through.
**inter-fūsus** 3 flowing between; interposed; stained.
**inter-iaceō**, —, — 2 to lie between.
**inter-ibi** *adv.* in the meantime.
**inter-iciō, iēcī, iectum** 3 to throw, cast, put, place between *or* among; **P.** to intervene; — **interiectus** 3 interposed.
**inter-iectus, ūs** *m* a putting between, intervention; interval.
**interim** *adv.* meanwhile, sometimes, however.
**inter-imō, ēmī, ēmptum** 3 to take from the midst, take away; to destroy, kill, slay.
**interior, ius** inner, interior; **a)** inland; **b)** more confidential, intimate, secret.
**inter-itiō, ōnis** *f* destruction, ruin.
**inter-itus, ūs** *m* destruction, ruin, fall, annihilation.
**inter-iungō** 3 **a)** to join together, unite; **b)** to unyoke, rest.
**inter-lābor** 3 to glide *or* fall between.
**inter-legō** 3 to pluck off here and there.
**inter-ligō** 1 to bind together.
**inter-linō** 3 to smear *or* daub between; to falsify by erasure.
**inter-loquor** 3 to interrupt in speaking.
**inter-lūceō, xī**, — 2 to shine forth (from its surroundings); to show gaps.
**inter-lūnium, ī** *n* time of new moon.
**inter-luō**, —, — 3 to flow between.
**inter-maneō** 2 to remain among.
**inter-mēnstruus** 3 between two months; *subst.* **-um, ī** *n* time of the new moon, change of moon.
**inter-micō** 1 to gleam (amid).
**in-terminātus**[1] 3 unbounded.
**inter-minātus**[2] 3, *part. pf.* **P.** of **interminor.**
**inter-minor** 1 to threaten, forbid with threats.
**inter-misceō** 2 to mix among, mingle.
**inter-missiō, ōnis** *f* a leaving off, interval.

**inter-mittō** 3 to place between; **P.** to lie between; **a)** to leave a space between, separate, isolate; **b)** to leave off, discontinue, interrupt, neglect; **P.** to be discontinued for an interval; **c)** to let pass, suffer to elapse.
**inter-morior** 3 to die off, perish; to faint away, to wither away; **intermortuus** 3 half-dead, almost perished.
**inter-mundia, ōrum** *n/pl.* spaces between the worlds.
**inter-mūrālis, e** between two walls.
**inter-nātus** 3 grown between.
**inter-necīnus** 3 annihilating.
**inter-neciō, ōnis** *f* massacre, utter destruction.
**internecīvus** 3 murderous, destructive.
**inter-necō** 1 to destroy utterly.
**inter-nectō** 3 to bind together.
**inter-nigrāns, ntis** black in places (on a white ground).
**inter-niteō, uī**, — 2 to shine forth.
**inter-nōdium, ī** *n* space between two joints.
**inter-nōscō, nōvī**, — 3 to distinguish between.
**inter-nūntiō** 1 to negotiate.
**inter-nūntius, ī** *m and* **-tia, ae** *f* negotiator, go-between.
**internus** 3 inward, internal.
**in-terō** 3 to pound *or* mash together.
**interpellātiō, ōnis** *f* interruption, disturbance.
**interpellātor, ōris** *m* disturber.
**inter-pellō** 1 to interrupt a speaker; **a)** to urge as an objection; **b)** to molest by remarks; **c)** to prevent, hinder, disturb, obstruct.
**inter-plicō** 1 to weave in, insert; to enfold.
**interpolis, e** furbished, repaired.
**interpolō** 1 to furbish, repair; to interpolate, falsify.
**inter-pōnō** 3 to put, place, lay *or* set between; **a)** to insert, interpose, intermix, falsify; **b)** to let pass, permit to elapse; **P.** to pass between, **spatiō interpositō** some time after; **c)** to introduce, bring forward, admit, **se interpōnere** to engage in, have to do with, meddle, interfere; **d)** to allege as a reason *or* pretext; **fidem interpōnere** to pledge one's word.

**inter-positiō, ōnis** f an introducing, insertion.

**inter-positus, ūs** m interposition.

**inter-pres, etis** m and f negotiator, mediator; **a)** explainer, expounder, interpreter, soothsayer; **b)** translator.

**interpretātiō, ōnis** f explanation, interpretation; translation.

**interpretor 1 a)** to assist, aid (alci); **b)** to explain, expound, interpret; **c)** to translate; **d)** to understand, comprehend; **e)** to decide, determine.

**inter-primō, pressī, pressum** 3 to squeeze, crush.

**inter-punctiō, ōnis** f division by points.

**inter-pungō, (nxī), nctum** 3 to divide by points; **interpunctus** 3 well divided; subst. **-tum, ī** n mark of punctuation.

**inter-quiēscō, ēvī, —** 3 to pause, rest a while.

**inter-rēgnum, ī** n interval between two reigns.

**inter-rēx, rēgis** m regent, interrex.

**in-territus** 3 undaunted.

**inter-rogātiō, ōnis** f question; **a)** interrogation; **b)** examination (of witnesses); **c)** argument, syllogism.

**interrogātiuncula, ae** f short argument.

**inter-rogō** 1 to ask, question (alqm; alqm alqd or de re); **a)** to examine judicially; **b)** to accuse, bring an action against.

**inter-rumpō** 3 to interrupt; **a)** to break asunder or to pieces; **b)** to separate; **c)** to disturb.

**interruptē** adv. interruptedly.

**inter-saepiō** 4 to hedge or fence in, shut off; **a)** to block up; **b)** to cut off, separate (alqd a re; alci alqd).

**inter-scindō** 3 to tear asunder, separate.

**inter-scrībō** 3 to write between.

**inter-serō¹, sēvī, situm** 3 to sow or plant between.

**inter-serō², (seruī, sertum)** 3 to put or place between.

**inter-sistō, stitī, —** 3 to pause, stop in the middle.

**inter-sonō** 1 to sound among.

**inter-spīrātiō, ōnis** f a breathing between.

**inter-stinctus** 3 checkered, spotted.

**inter-stinguō** 3 to extinguish.

**inter-stringō** 3 to strangle.

**inter-struō** 3 to connect.

**inter-sum, fuī, esse** to be between (inter alqd); to intervene; **a)** to be different, distinguished from; **b)** to be present at, take part in (in re or with dat.); **interest** it concerns, it is of importance, of interest (alcis, with inf., acc.c.inf., indirect question; ad alqd).

**inter-texō** 3 to intertwine, interweave.

**inter-trahō** 3 to take away, draw out.

**inter-trīmentum, ī** n loss by attrition, waste, damage.

**inter-turbātiō, ōnis** f disturbance.

**inter-turbō** 1 to interrupt.

**inter-vallum, ī** n space between; **a)** distance, interval; **b)** interval of time, pause; **c)** difference.

**inter-vellō** 3 to pull out here and there.

**inter-veniō** 4 to come between, intervene (with dat.); **a)** to break in upon, interrupt (dat.); **b)** to interfere, put a stop to.

**interventor, ōris** m visitor, intruder.

**interventus, ūs** m intervention.

**inter-vertō** 3 to embezzle; **a)** to intercept; **b)** to defraud.

**inter-viās** on the way.

**inter-vireō** 2 to show green among.

**inter-visō, sī, sum** 3 to take a look; to visit from time to time.

**inter-vol(it)ō** 1 to fly among or through.

**inter-vomō** 3 to throw up among.

**inter-vortō** 3 = **interverto**.

**in-testābilis, e a)** incapable of bearing witness, infamous; **b)** = **intestatus²**.

**in-testātus¹** 3 **a)** intestate; **b)** not convicted by evidence.

**in-testātus²** 3 castrated.

**intestīnus** 3 inward, internal; subst. **-a, ōrum** n/pl. (rarely sing.) intestines, entrails.

**in-texō** 3 **a)** to weave or plait in, interweave; **b)** to wind or weave around; **c)** to surround.

**intibum, ī** n endive.

**intimus** 3 inmost; **a)** deepest, most profound, most secret; **b)** most familiar, intimate; subst. **~, ī** m intimate friend.

**in-tingō** 3 to dip in.

**in-tolerābilis, e** a) unable to bear; b) unbearable.

**in-tolerandus** 3 unbearable.

**in-tolerāns, tis** a) unable to bear, impatient of (gen.), intolerant; immoderate; b) intolerable.

**in-tolerantia, ae** f insolence.

**in-tonō, uī,** — 1 to thunder; to resound, make a noise.

**in-tōnsus** 3 unshorn, with long hair and beard; uncombed.

**in-torqueō** 2 a) to twist or turn round, to wind; b) to hurl, launch, cast; c) to distort.

**intrā** 1. adv. within; 2. prep. with acc. within, into; a) within, in the space of, during, before the lapse of; b) less than, fewer than.

**intrābilis, e** accessible.

**in-tractābilis, e** unmanageable, intractable, rude, fierce.

**in-tractātus** 3 not handled; unattempted.

**in-tremō** and **-mīscō, -uī,** — 3 to tremble.

**in-trepidus** 3 undaunted, undisturbed.

**in-tribuō** 3 to contribute.

**in-trīcō** 1 to entangle, perplex.

**intrīn-secus** adv. inside, inwardly.

**in-trītus** 3 unexhausted.

**intrō¹** adv. inside, within.

**intrō²** 1 to go into, enter (in, ad alqd; alqd); to penetrate into.

**intrō-dūcō** 3 to lead or conduct into (alqd in alqd); a) to bring into, introduce; b) to bring forward, maintain (alqd; acc.c.inf.).

**intrō-ductiō, ōnis** f introduction.

**intro-eō, iī, itum, īre** to go into, enter.

**intrō-ferō, —, lātum** 3 to carry in.

**intrō-gredior, gressus sum** 3 to enter.

**intro-itus, ūs** m an entering, entrance; a) beginning; b) introduction; passage.

**intrō-mittō** 3 to send in, let in.

**intrōrsum** and **-sus** adv. a) towards the inside; b) inside, within; internally.

**intrō-rumpō** 3 to break into; enter by force.

**intrō-spectō** 1 to look into.

**intrō-spiciō, spexī, spectum** 3 to look into or upon; to observe; to inspect, examine (alqd or in alqd).

**intubum, ī** n = intibum.

**in-tueor** 2 (and **in-tuor** 3) to look at attentively (in alqd), gaze at (alqd); to consider, contemplate, observe, regard.

**in-tumēscō, muī,** — 3 to swell up; to swell with, be puffed up.

**in-tumulātus** 3 unburied.

**intumus** 3 = intimus.

**in-tuor** 3, see intueor.

**in-turbidus** 3 undisturbed, quiet.

**intus** adv. a) within, inside, in the heart; b) to the inside.

**in-tūtus** 3 unguarded, unsafe.

**inula, ae** f (a plant) elecampane.

**inuleus, ī** m = hinnuleus.

**in-ultus** 3 unavenged, unpunished.

**in-umbrō** 1 to overshadow, darken.

**in-undātiō, ōnis** f inundation, flood.

**in-undō** 1 a) to overflow, inundate; b) to flow over (re), spread.

**in-ung(u)ō** 3 to anoint; to besmear.

**in-urbānus** 3 rustic, unmannerly, rude, unpolished; unrefined, inelegant, not witty.

**in-urgeō** 2 to thrust at.

**in-ūrō** 3 to burn in; to brand, imprint indelibly; b) to inflict.

**in-ūsitātus** 3 unusual.

**in-ustus** 3 unburnt (?).

**in-ūtilis, e** useless, unserviceable; hurtful, injurious.

**in-ūtilitās, ātis** f uselessness; injuriousness.

**in-vādō** 3 1. to go or come into (in rem, rem); a) to set foot upon; b) to undertake, begin; 2. to rush upon; a) to attack, invade; b) to fall upon, seize, befall.

**in-valēscō, luī,** — 3 to become strong or stronger; to increase; to prevail.

**in-validus** 3 weak, feeble, infirm; inefficient.

**invectīcius** 3 imported; insincere.

**in-vectiō, ōnis** f importation; a sailing in.

**in-vehō** 3 1. to carry or bear in or into (alqd in alqd or alci rei); to occasion, bring upon; 2. with reflex. pron., or P. to burst into, attack; to attack with words, inveigh against; to ride, drive, sail in or into.

**in-vendibilis, e** unsalable.

**in-veniō** 4 to come or light upon (alqd), meet with; a) to find out, discover, learn, become acquainted with; **b)** to acquire, earn; **c)** to devise, contrive.

**inventiō, ōnis** f (faculty of) invention.

**inventor, ōris** m and **-trīx, īcis** f inventor, contriver, discoverer.

**inventum, ī** n invention, discovery, contrivance.

**inventus, ūs** m discovery.

**in-venustus** 3 without charm, ungraceful.

**in-vērē** (?) untruthfully.

**in-verēcundus** 3 shameless, immodest.

**in-vergō, —, —** 3 to pour upon.

**in-versiō, ōnis** f inversion; irony; allegory.

**in-vertō** 3 to turn upside down, turn about; **a)** to turn or plough up; **b)** to pervert; **c)** to change, alter, reverse.

**in-vesperāscit, —,—** 3 it becomes evening.

**investigātiō, ōnis** f an inquiring into, investigation.

**investigātor, ōris** m inquirer, investigator.

**in-vestīgō** 1 to trace out, search into, investigate, find out.

**in-vestiō** 4 to clothe or surround with.

**in-veterāscō, āvī, —** 3 to grow old: to become fixed, established, rooted, or obsolete.

**in-veterātiō, ōnis** f an inveterate fault.

**in-veterō** 1 to establish; **inveterātus** 3 long-established, inveterate.

**in-vetitus** 3 unrestrained.

**in-vicem** adv. **a)** by turns; **b)** mutually, on both sides; **c)** on the other hand.

**in-victus** 3 unconquered; unconquerable.

**invidentia, ae** f envy.

**in-videō** 2 to look askance at (alqd); to envy, grudge (alci, alci rei alcis); **invidendus** 3 enviable.

**invidia, ae** f envy, grudge, jealousy, ill-will; **a)** cause of envy; **b)** odium, unpopularity.

**invidiōsus** 3 **a)** envious; **b)** exciting ill-feeling, enviable, envied; **c)** hateful, hated.

**invidus** 3 envious, jealous.

**in-vigilō** 1 to be awake, watch at,

over or on account of; to be watchful over.

**in-violābilis, e** inviolable, invulnerable.

**in-violātus** 3 unhurt; inviolable.

**in-vīsitātus** 3 unseen; new, strange.

**in-vīsō, sī, (sum)** 3 to go to see, to visit; to get a sight of.

**in-vīsus¹** 3 unseen.

**in-vīsus²** 3 **a)** hated, hateful; **b)** malicious.

**invītāmentum, ī** n allurement, incitement.

**invītātiō, ōnis** f invitation; challenge.

**invītātus, ūs** m (only abl. sg.) = invitatio.

**in-vītō** 1 to invite (alqm in or ad alqd; with abl.); **a)** to entertain; **se invītāre** to take one's fill; **b)** to summon, challenge; **c)** to allure, entice, attract.

**in-vītus** 3 unwilling, reluctant.

**in-vius** 3 impassable.

**in-vocātiō, ōnis** f invocation.

**in-vocātus** 3 uncalled, uninvited.

**in-vocō** 1 to call upon.

**in-volātus, ūs** m a flying, flight.

**in-volitō** 1 to float or wave over.

**in-volō** 1 **a)** to fly into; **b)** to fly at, rush upon; to attack, invade.

**involūcrum, ī** n veil, covering.

**in-volūtus** 3 involved, intricate.

**in-volvō** 3 **a)** to roll to, into or upon; **b)** to wrap up, envelop; to cover, overwhelm (alqd re).

**in-volvolus, ī** m leaf-curling caterpillar.

**in-vors-, -vort-** = **in-vers-, -vert-.**

**in-vulnerābilis, e** invulnerable.

**in-vulnerātus** 3 unwounded.

**iō** int. ho! hurrah!

**iocātiō, ōnis** f a joking.

**iocor** 1 to jest, joke.

**iocōsus** 3 jocose, humorous, facetious.

**ioculāris, e** = iocōsus; **ioculāria, ium** n/pl. jests, jokes.

**ioculārius** 3 ludicrous.

**ioculātor, ōris** m jester, joker.

**ioculor** 1 = iocor.

**ioculus, ī** m little jest.

**iocus, ī** m jest, joke; **a)** pastime; **b)** trifle; **c)** child's play.

**iōta** n the Greek letter I.

**ipse, a, um** self; himself, herself, itself; the master, mistress, teacher, the chief person; **per se ipse** of himself, by himself; a) just, very, exactly, identical; b) of one's own accord, spontaneously; *comic superl.* **ipsissumus.**

**ira, ae** *f* anger, wrath, rage.

**irācundia, ae** *f* irascibility, wrath, anger.

**irācundus 3** irascible, angry.

**irāscor, — 3** to grow angry.

**irātus 3** angry, enraged (*dat.*).

**irim** (*acc.*) *m* hedgehog.

**irōnia, ae** *f* irony.

**ir-radiō 1** to irradiate.

**ir-rāsus 3** unshorn; unsmoothed.

**ir-ratiōnālis, e** irrational, unscientific.

**ir-raucēscō, rausī, — 3** to become hoarse.

**ir-redux, ucis** that does not bring one back.

**ir-religātus 3** unbound.

**ir-religiōsus 3** impious.

**ir-remeābilis, e** from which there is no return.

**ir-remediābilis, e** irreconcilable.

**ir-reparābilis, e** irrecoverable.

**ir-repertus 3** undiscovered.

**ir-rēpō 3** to creep into.

**ir-reprehēnsus 3** blameless.

**ir-rēptō 1** to creep upon, steal over.

**ir-requiētus 3** restless.

**ir-resectus 3** uncut, unpared.

**ir-resolūtus 3** not loosed.

**ir-restinctus 3** unquenched.

**ir-rētiō 4** to catch in a net; to entangle (*alqm re*).

**ir-retortus 3** not turned back.

**ir-reverēns, tis** irreverent, disrespectful.

**ir-reverentia, ae** *f* disrespect.

**ir-revocābilis, e** irrevocable; implacable.

**ir-revocātus 3** not called again.

**ir-rīdeō 2** to laugh at.

**ir-rīdiculē** *adv.* without wit.

**ir-rīdiculum, ī** *n* laughing-stock.

**ir-rigātiō, ōnis** *f* a watering.

**ir-rigō 1** a) to conduct water to; b) to water, irrigate, to inundate; to bathe, flood.

**irriguus 3** a) supplying water; b) well-watered, soaked.

**ir-rīsiō, ōnis** *f* = **irrisus.**

**ir-rīsor, ōris** *m* derider, mocker.

**ir-rīsus, ūs** *m* a scoffing, mockery, derision.

**ir-rītābilis, e** irritable, excitable.

(**irrītāmen, inis** *n and*) **irrītāmentum, ī** *n* incitement, incentive.

**irrītātiō, ōnis** *f* incitement, irritation.

**irrītātor, ōris** *m* inciter.

**irrītō 1** to excite, incite, stimulate, to provoke, exasperate.

**ir-ritus 3** a) invalid, void; b) vain, useless, ineffectual.

**ir-rogātiō, ōnis** *f* an imposing.

**ir-rogō 1** a) to propose against one; b) to impose, inflict, ordain (*alci alqd*).

**ir-rōrō 1** to bedew, moisten, trickle down upon.

**ir-rubēscō, buī, — 3** to grow red.

**ir-ructō 1** to belch at.

**ir-rūgō 1** to wrinkle, fold.

**ir-rumō 1** to treat obscenely *or* foully; to defile; *hence* **irrumātiō, ōnis** *f*; **irrumātor, ōris** *m.*

**ir-rumpō 3** to break *or* rush in *or* into; to intrude, invade.

**ir-ruō, uī, — 3** to rush in, invade; to fling in.

**irruptiō, ōnis** *f* invasion, incursion.

**ir-ruptus 3** unbroken.

**is, ea, id** he, she, it; a) **is quī** he who; b) this *or* that (*man, woman, thing*); c) such, of such a sort *or* kind; d) the one mentioned; **isque, et is, atque is** and that too, and indeed.

**ischnon** (ἰσχνόν) slender.

**is-elasticus 3** *adj.* applied to competitions which entitled winners to a triumphal entry into their town; **-um, ī** *n* present given to the winners.

**issula** *f* (*from ipse*) little mistress.

**istāc** *adv.* there, by that way.

**istāc-tenus** thus far.

**iste, a, ud** that (of yours) (*referring to the person spoken to, or to something mentioned by him*); your client (*in a lawsuit*).

**istī** *adv.* = **istic².**

**istic¹, aec, oc** *or* **uc** = **iste.**

**istic²** *adv.* there, in that place, here; in this affair.

**istim** *adv.* = **istinc.**

**istinc** *adv.* from there, thence.

**istius-modī** of that kind, such.

**istō(c)** *adv.* thither, that way.

**istōrsum** *adv.* thitherwards, in that direction.

**istuc¹** *neutr. of* **istic¹.**

**istūc²** *adv.* thither.

**ita** *adv.* thus, so, in such manner; **ut ... ita** as ..., so; although ..., yet; **itane?** is it so? really? **quid ita?** why so? how is that?; a) and so, consequently, and then; b) yes, just so; c) accordingly, under these circumstances; d) **ita ... ut** so ... that, on the condition that, in so far, only in so far as; **non ita** *or* **haud ita** not very, not especially.

**ita-que 1.** = **et ita;** 2. *cj.* and so, therefore, for that reason.

**item** *adv.* likewise, besides, also; a second time.

**iter, itineris** *n* 1. a going, walk, way; 2. journey, march, passage; **in itinere** on the march; a) a day's journey; b) legal right of way; c) passage, road, path; d) course, method, custom, means.

**iterātiō, ōnis** *f* repetition.

**iterō 1** to do a second time; a) to repeat; b) to plough again.

**iterum** *adv.* a second time, again.

**itidem** *adv.* in like manner.

**itiner, eris** *n* = **iter.**

**itiō, ōnis** *f* = **itus.**

**itō 1** to go.

**itus, ūs** *m* a walking, going (away), departure.

**iuba, ae** *f* mane; crest (*of a helmet or serpent*).

**iubar, aris** *n* beaming light, radiance; morning star, light of the sun.

**iubātus 3** with a mane *or* crest.

**iubeō, iussī, iussum 2** to order, command, bid, tell (*alqm, de re, acc.c.inf.*); a) to decree, ratify; b) to designate, appoint.

**iubilum, ī** *n* glad cry, shout.

**iūcunditās, ātis** *f* pleasantness; a) delight; cheerfulness; b) good office, favour.

**iūcundus 3** pleasant, agreeable, delightful.

**iūdex, icis** *m* (*f*) judge; juryman; critic.

**iūdicātiō, ōnis** *f* judgment.

**iūdicātus, ūs** *m* office of judge.

**iūdiciālis, e** *and* **iūdiciārius 3** judicial, judiciary, juridical.

**iūdicium, ī** *n* 1. judicial investigation (*de re, alcis rei*), trial; a) court of justice; b) body of judges; c) jurisdiction; 2. sentence, decision; a) opinion, judgment;

b) power of judging, discernment; c) consideration, discretion.

**iūdicō 1** to be a judge, to judge, decide, pass judgment; a) to pass sentence against b) to resolve, determine, settle; c) to consider, hold, think; d) to suppose, conclude; e) to declare openly.

**iugālis, e** yoked together; matrimonial, nuptial.

**iugātiō, ōnis** *f* a binding to rails.

**iūgerum, ī** *n* a land measure (about $^2/_3$ of an acre).

**iūgis, e** perpetual, never failing.

**iūges,** *only:* **iūges auspicium** joined auspice.

**iūglāns, dis** *f* walnut (-tree).

**iugō 1** to bind, connect; to marry.

**iugōsus 3** mountainous.

**iugulae, ārum** *f* Orion's belt.

**iugulātiō, ōnis** *f* a murdering.

**iugulō 1** to cut the throat; a) to slay, murder; b) to ruin, destroy.

**iugulum, ī** *n* (*and* **-us** *m*) throat.

**iugum, ī** *n* yoke; a) yoke, span, pair, team; b) yoke of slavery, of matrimony; c) arch of spears; d) the constellation Libra; e) beam of a weaver's loom; rowers' bench; f) ridge, mountain heights.

**Iūlius 3** belonging to July; *m* (*mensis*) July.

**iūmentum, ī** *n* yoked animal, beast for drawing *or* carrying.

**iunceus 3** made of rushes; as thin as a rush.

**iuncōsus 3** full of rushes.

**iūnctim** *adv.* successively.

**iūnctiō, ōnis** *f* a joining, uniting.

**iūnctūra, ae** *f* a joining; a) joint, juncture, connection; b) relationship.

**iuncus, ī** *m* (bul)rush.

**iungō, iūnxī, iūnctum 3** to yoke, harness (*ad alqd*); a) to attach, fasten; b) to join, unite, connect); **fluvium ponte** to throw a bridge over a river; c) to make by joining, bring together, associate; **iūnctus 3** joined together, connected, united, intimate; **iūnctissimī** *m/pl.* nearest relations.

**iūnior, ōris** comparatively young.

**iūniperus, ī** *f* juniper-tree.

**Iūnius 3** belonging to June; *m* (*mensis*) June.

**iūnix, icis** *f* heifer.    [a censor.)

**iūrātor, ōris** *m* sworn assistant of)

**iūrgium, ī** *n* quarrel, altercation.
**iūrgō** 1 to quarrel, brawl, scold.
**iūri-diciālis, e** relating to right *or* justice.
**iūris-dictiō, ōnis** *f* administration of justice; jurisdiction.
**iūrō** 1 to swear, take an oath (*per alqm, in alqd*); **a)** to affirm on oath, swear to; **b)** to deny on oath; **iūrā-tus** 3 on oath.
**iūs¹, iūris** *n* broth, soup.
**iūs², iūris** *n* **a)** right, statutes, law, justice; **b)** privilege, permission, liberty, conceded right; **iūre** rightfully, justly; **c)** legal power, authority; **d)** court of justice.
**iūs iūrandum, iūris iūrandī** *n* oath.
**iussū** by order.
**iussum, ī** *n* order, command, ordinance; prescription.
**iūsti-ficus** 3 acting justly.
**iūstitia, ae** *f* justice, equity.
**iūstitium, ī** *n* judicial vacation; suspension, holiday.
**iūstus** 3 just, equitable; **a)** fair, upright, righteous; **b)** regular, lawful, rightful, proper; *subst.* **iūstum, ī** *n* justice; **iūsta, ōrum**

*n/pl.* rights; due forms and observances; **c)** justified.
**iuvenālis, e** youthful.
**iuvenca, ae** *f* heifer; young woman.
**iuvencus, ī** *m* young bullock; young man; *adj.* young.
**iuvenēscō, —, — 3 a)** to grow up to youth; **b)** to grow young again.
**iuvenīlis, e** youthful, juvenile.
**iuvenis, is** young; *subst. m* young man, youth; *f* maiden.
**iuvenix, īcis** *f* young cow.
**iuvenor** 1 to act indiscreetly, to wanton.
**iuventa, ae** (*and* **iuventās, ātis**) *f* age of youth; **a)** youthful vigour; **b)** the young, young people; **c)** downy beard.
**iuventūs, ūtis** *f* **a)** time of youth; **b)** young people; young men in the army.
**iuvō, iūvī, iūtum** 1 to delight, gratify, please; to help, aid.
**iuxtā 1.** *adv.* near, close, hard by; in like manner, equally; **2.** *prep.* with *acc.* near to, close to, hard by; **a)** immediately after; **b)** along with; **c)** approaching, bordering on.
**iuxtim** *adv.* close beside; alike.

# K

**K** *abbr.* = **Kaeso.**     |     **Kal.** = **Kalendae** (*see* **Calendae**).

# L

**L** *abbr.* 1. = **Lūcius;** 2. *as a numeral* = 50.

**labāscō,** —, — 3 to waver, yield.

**labea, ae** *f* lip. [disgrace.]

**lābēcula, ae** *f* little stain, slight]

**labe-faciō** 3 = **labefacto.**

**labe-factō** 1 to cause to totter, to shake, to weaken, impair, ruin, destroy.

**labellum¹, ī** *n* little lip.

**lābellum², ī** *n* small basin.

**labeōsus** 3 with large lips.

**lābēs, is** *f* a) a falling; downfall; ruin, destruction; b) spot, stain; disgrace, ignominy.

**labium, ī** *n* lip.

**labō** 1 to totter, waver, be unsteady; to be undecided.

**lābor¹, lāpsus sum** 3 to glide, slide, slip; a) to fall down, sink; b) to glide *or* float down; c) to glide along *or* off; d) to slip, stumble; e) to escape, vanish, pass away, elapse; f) to fall into (*ad* or *in alqd*); g) to be mistaken, err, commit a fault.

**labor², ōris** *m* work, labour, toil, exertion; a) drudgery, hardship; b) laboriousness, effort; c) trouble, distress, need, difficulty, pain.

**labōrātus** 3 toilsome.

**labōri-fer** 3 toil-enduring.

**labōriōsus** 3 a) full of toil *or* hardship; b) industrious.

**labōrō** 1 1. a) to work, toil, exert oneself, strive (*in* or *de re; ut, ne, inf.*); b) to suffer, be troubled, vexed; to be in distress, difficulty *or* danger (*ex, ab, in re, re*); 2. to work out, elaborate, produce with effort (*alqd*).

**labōs, ōris** *m* = **labor².**

**labrum¹, ī** *n* lip, edge.

**lābrum², ī** *n* bathing-tub, basin.

**labrusca, ae** *f* wild vine.

**labruscum, ī** *n* wild grape.

**labyrinthēus** 3 labyrinthine.

**labyrinthus, ī** *m* labyrinth.

**lac, lactis** *n* milk; milky juice.

**lacer, era, erum** a) mangled, lacerated, torn; mutilated; b) lacerating.

**lacerātiō, ōnis** *f* mangling, lacerating.

**lacerna, ae** *f* cloak.

**lacernātus** 3 cloaked.

**lacerō** 1 to mangle, tear to pieces; a) to censure, wound; b) to waste, squander, ruin.

**lacerta, ae** *f* lizard.

**lacertōsus** 3 muscular.

**lacertus¹, ī** *m* lizard.

**lacertus², ī** *m* a) muscle; b) upper arm; c) strength, vigour.

**lacessō, īvī** *and* **iī, ītum** 3 to excite, provoke (*alqm ad alqd, re*), irritate, exasperate; to move, arouse, produce.

**lachanizō** 1 to be weak.

**lacinia, ae** *f* flap, corner.

**Lacōnicus** 3 Spartan; *subst.* **-um, ī** *n* sweating-room (in baths).

**lacrima, ae** *f* tear; drop.

**lacrimābilis, e** lamentable.

**lacrimābundus** 3 weeping.

**lacrimō** 1 to weep; to drop, distil.

**lacrimōsus** 3 full of tears; lamentable; plaintive.

**lacrimula, ae** *f* little tear.

**lacruma, -mō** = **lacrima, mō.**

**lactēns, tis** a) sucking (milk), young; b) sappy, juicy; c) milk-white.

**lacteolus** 3 milk-white.

**lactēs, ium** *f*/*pl.* small guts.

**lactēscō,** —, — 3 to turn to milk.

**lacteus** 3 milky; a) full of milk; b) milk-white.

**lactō¹** 1 a) to contain milk; b) to suck milk.

**lactō²** 1 to allure, deceive with flattery.

**lactūca, ae** *f* (**lactūcula, ae** *f*) garden-lettuce.

**lacūna, ae** *f* hole, pit; a) pool, pond; b) gap, void, defect.

**lacūnar, āris** *n* panelled ceiling.

**lacūnō** 1 to panel.

**lacūnōsus** 3 full of hollows.

**lacus, ūs** *m* a) basin, tank, (wine-)vat, cistern; b) lake; pool.

**laedō, sī, sum** 3 a) to strike at, hurt, wound, injure, afflict; b) to insult, offend, annoy.

**laena, ae** f cloak, mantle.
**laesiō, ōnis** f hurt, provocation.
**laetābilis, e** joyful, glad.
**laetātiō, ōnis** f a rejoicing.
**laeti-ficō** 1 to cheer, gladden; to fertilize; to be glad.
**laeti-ficus** 3 pleasing.
**laetitiā, ae** f joy, gladness, delight; beauty, grace.
**laetō** 1 to delight, gladden.
**laetor** 1 to be glad, rejoice (re, de or in re; quod; acc. c. inf.).
**laetus** 3 glad, joyful, cheerful, joyous; a) pleasing, prosperous; b) fertile, rich, copious.
**laevus** 3 left, on the left side; subst.
**laeva, ae** f left hand; a) awkward, foolish; b) lucky, propitious; c) unfavourable, unfortunate.
**laganum, ī** n cake of flour and oil.
**lagēna, ae** f = **lagoēna**.
**lagēos, ī** f species of vine.
**lagoena, ae** f flagon.
**lagōis, idis** f grouse.
**lagōna, ae** f, see lagoena.
**laguncula, ae** f flask.
**lalisiō, ōnis** m foal of a wild ass.
**lallō** 1 to sing a lullaby.
**lāma, ae** f bog, fen.
**lamberō** 1 to lick.
**lambō** 3 to lick, lap, wash.
**lāmella, ae** f metal plate, coin.
**lāmenta, ōrum** n/pl. lamentation.
**lāmentābilis, e** lamentable; a) mournful; b) deplorable.
**lāmentārius** 3 causing lament.
**lāmentātiō, ōnis** f a lamenting.
**lāmentor** 1 to wail, moan, weep; lament; (alqd.) to bewail.
**lamia, ae** f witch; vampire.
**lām(i)na** and **lammina, ae** f thin plate, leaf, layer; a) plate of iron used for torture; b) blade; c) money, coin; d) peel.
**lampas, adis** f torch, light, lamp; daylight, day.
**lāna, ae** f wool, woollen thread; a) working in wool; b) down, cotton, fleecy cloud.
**lānārius, ī** m worker in wool.
**lānātus** 3 woolly; subst. -a, ae f sheep.
**lancea, ae** f lance, spear.
**lancinō** 1 to rend to pieces, to squander.
**lāneus** 3 woollen; soft.
**langue-faciō** 3 to make languid or faint.

**langueō, guī,** — 2 to be faint, weak, languid, weary.
**languēscō, guī,** — 3 to become faint, weak, languid.
**languid(ul)us** 3 faint, weak, languid, dull; sluggish, inactive.
**languor, ōris** m weariness, feebleness; inactivity, dullness.
**laniātus, ūs** m (and **laniātiō, ōnis** f) a mangling; anguish.
**laniēna, ae** f a butcher's stall.
**lāni-ficium, ī** n wool-work.
**lāni-ficus** 3 working in wool.
**lāni-ger** 3 wool-bearing; subst. m and f ram, sheep, lamb.
**laniō** 1 to tear to pieces, mangle.
**laniōnius** 3 of a butcher.
**lanista, ae** m trainer of gladiators; inciter, instigator.
**lānitium, ī** n wool.
**lanius, ī** m butcher; executioner.
**lanterna, ae** f lantern, lamp.
**lanternārius, ī** m lantern-bearer.
**lānūgō, inis** f down of plants or of the beard.
**lanx, cis** f a) plate, platter, dish; b) scale of a balance.
**lapathus, ī** m sorrel.
**lapi-cīda, ae** m stone-cutter.
**lapicīdinae, arum** f/pl. quarries.
**lapidārius** 3 relating to stone.
**lapidātiō, ōnis** f a throwing of stones, stoning. [stones.]
**lapidātor, ōris** m thrower of]
**lapideus** 3 of stone.
**lapidō** 1 to throw stones at; **lapidat** it rains stones.
**lapidōsus** 3 full of stones, stony.
**lapillus, ī** m little stone, pebble; precious stone.
**lapis, idis** m stone; a) marble; b) milestone; c) boundary-stone; d) tombstone; e) precious stone; jewel; f) auctioneer's block; g) blockhead.
**lappa, ae** f goose-grass.
**lāpsiō, ōnis** f a gliding; tendency.
**lāpsō** 1 to stumble or totter.
**lāpsus, ūs** m a gliding, sliding, flowing; a) flight; b) a falling, fall; c) fault, error.
**laqueāre, āris** n = lacunar.
**laqueātus** 3 panelled.
**laqueus, ī** m noose, snare, trap.
**Lār, Laris** m tutelary god of a house or city; home, hearth.
**lārdum, ī** n = laridum.
**largi-ficus** 3 copious.

**largi-fluus** 3 flowing copiously.
**largi-loquos** 3 talkative.
**largior** 4 to give abundantly, bestow, impart (alci alqd); to bribe; to grant; to forgive.
**largitās, ātis** f liberality, bounty.
**largitiō, ōnis** f a giving freely, bestowing, lavishing, liberality; a) bribery; b) a granting.
**largītor, ōris** m bestower, granter; briber; squanderer.
**largus** 3 a) liberal in giving, bountiful; b) abundant, plentiful; adv. **largē** and **largiter**.
**lāridum, ī** n bacon.
**larix, icis** f larch.
**(lārua** and) **lārva, ae** f spectre, mask.
**lāruātus** 3 bewitched.
**lārvālis, e** ghostly.
**lasanum, ī** n cooking-pot; commode.
**lāsarpīci-fer** = **lāserpīci-fer.**
**lascīvia, ae** f a) playfulness, jollity, wantonness; b) licentiousness, insolence.
**lascīvībundus** 3 frolicsome.
**lascīviō** 4 a) to be wanton, insolent, licentious; b) to sport.
**lascīvus** 3 a) playful, jolly, wanton; b) licentious, unrestrained, insolent.
**lāserpīci-fer** 3 producing laserpicium.
**lāserpīcium, ī** n the juice of a North African plant (silphium or sirpe).
**lassitūdō, inis** f weariness.
**lassō** 1 to make weary, tire.
**lassulus** 3 somewhat tired.
**lassus** 3 wearied, tired, faint.
**latebra, ae** f hiding-place, retreat; a) concealment; refuge; b) subterfuge, pretext.
**latebricola, ae** frequenting low haunts.
**latebrōsus** 3 full of hiding-places; full of holes.
**latēns, tis** hidden, secret.
**lateō, uī,** — 2 to lie hid or concealed; a) to be retired, sheltered; b) to remain unknown.
**later, eris** m brick, tile.
**laterāmen, inis** n earthenware.
**laterculus, ī** m small brick; cake, biscuit.
**latericius** 3 made of bricks; subst. **-ium, ī** n brickwork.
**latericulus, ī** m small brick.

**latēscō** 3 to hide oneself.
**latex, icis** m a liquid, fluid; water, wine, oil.
**latibulum, ī** n = **latebra.**
**lāti-clāvius** 3 having a broad purple stripe.
**lāti-fundium, ī** n large estate.
**latinitās, ātis** f a) pure Latinity; b) Latin rights (limited citizen-rights).
**lātiō, ōnis** f a bringing; **auxilii** a rendering assistance; **legis** a proposing; **suffragii** a voting.
**latitō** 1 to be hidden, concealed.
**lātitūdō, inis** f breadth, width; extent; broad pronunciation; richness of expression.
**lātomiae** f/pl. = **lautumiae.**
**lātor, ōris** m mover, proposer.
**lātrātor, ōris** m barker; dog.
**lātrātus, ūs** m a barking.
**lātrīna, ae** f privy.
**lātrō**[1] to bark, bark at; to growl, grumble, roar, rage.
**latrō**[2], **ōnis** m a) hired servant, mercenary soldier; b) freebooter, highwayman, robber; c) hunter; d) piece in a game.
**latrōcinium, ī** n a) robbery, piracy; b) villany, roguery, fraud; c) band of robbers.
**latrōcinor** 1 to practise robbery or piracy; to serve as a mercenary.
**latrunculārius** 3 for playing a game resembling draughts.
**latrunculus, ī** m a) robber; b) piece in a game.
**lātumiae, ārum** f/pl. = **lautumiae.**
**lātūra, ae** f a carrying of burdens.
**lātus**[1] 3 a) broad, wide, spacious, extended; b) diffuse, copious.
**latus**[2], **eris** n side, flank; **latus dare alci** to expose oneself to; the lungs; the body; flank of an army.
**latusculum, ī** n (little) side.
**laudābilis, e** praiseworthy.
**laudātiō, ōnis** f praise, eulogy, panegyric; funeral oration.
**laudātor, ōris** m, **laudātrix, īcis** f praiser, eulogizer; funeral orator; witness to character.
**laudicēnī, ōrum** m/pl. persons who applaud an orator in order to get a dinner.
**laudō** 1 to praise, laud, commend; to deliver a funeral oration; to cite, quote; **laudātus** 3 praiseworthy, excellent.

**laurea, ae** *f* = **laurus**.
**laureātus** 3 crowned with bay.
**laureola, ae** *f* laurel (bay) wreath.
**laureus** 3 of bay.
**lauri-comus** 3 covered with bay-
-trees.
**lauri-fer** *and* **-ger** 3 crowned *or*
decked with bay.
**laurus, ī** (*and* **-ūs**) *f* bay-tree;
a) laurel (bay) wreath; b) triumph.
**laus, dis** *f* praise, glory; a) commendation, eulogy; b) praiseworthy action, merit.
**lautia, ōrum** *n/pl.* public entertainment of ambassadors.
**lautitia, ae** *f* splendour, elegance,
magnificence.
**lautumiae, ārum** *f/pl.* stone-
quarry; prison, dungeon.
**lautus** 3 washed; neat; a) elegant,
splendid, sumptuous; b) distinguished, refined.
**lavābrum, ī** *n* bath.
**lavātiō, ōnis** *f* a washing, bathing;
bath; bathing-apparatus.
**lavō, lāvī, lautum, lōtum** *or*
**lavātum** 1 (*and* 3) a) to wash,
bathe; b) to wet; c) to wash away.
**laxāmentum, ī** *n* mitigation, alleviation, respite.
**laxitās, ātis** *f* wideness, spa-
ciousness.
**laxō** 1 to unloose, slacken; a) to
extend, expand, stretch out; b) to
relax, release, relieve, ease, refresh.
**laxus** 3 a) loose, lax, relaxed;
b) wide, open, extended.
**lea** *and* **leaena, ae** *f* lioness.
**lebēs, ētis** *m* basin, kettle, cauldron.
**lectica, ae** *f* a) litter; b) bier.
**lecticāriola, ae** *f* litter-bearer's
lover.
**lecticārius, ī** *m* litter-bearer.
**lecticula, ae** *f* litter, bier, couch.
**lēctiō, ōnis** *f* a) a selecting; b) a
reading, perusal; a reading aloud.
**lecti-sterniātor, ōris** *m* slave who
prepares couches for a *lectisternium*.
**lecti-sternium, ī** *n* feast offered to
the gods.
**lēctitō** 1 to read often.
**lēctiuncula, ae** *f* a reading.
**lēctor, ōris** *m* reader.
**lectulus, ī** *m*, *dim. of* **lectus¹**.
**lectus¹, ī** *m* a) bed, couch; b) sofa;
dining-couch; c) bier.
**lēctus²** 3 chosen, picked, selected;
choice.

**lēgātārius, ī** *m* legatee.
**lēgātiō, ōnis** *f* a) embassy, public
commission; message of an ambassador; b) office of a lieutenant;
deputy command; command of a
legion.
**lēgātor, ōris** *m* testator.
**lēgātōrius** 3 of a deputy.
**lēgātum, ī** *n* legacy, bequest.
**lēgātus, ī** *m* a) ambassador; b) deputy, lieutenant, lieutenant-ge-
neral.
**lēge-rupiō, ōnis** *f* law-breaking.
**lēgi-fer** 3 law-giving.
**legiō, ōnis** *f* a Roman legion; army.
**legiōnārius** 3 belonging to a
legion; *subst.* ~, **ī** *m* legionary.
**lēgi-rupa, ae** *m* breaker of the
law.
**lēgitimus** (*or* **-umus**) 3 lawful,
legal, legitimate; right, just, proper,
fit, appropriate.
**legiuncula, ae** *f* a small legion.
**lēgō¹** 1 a) to depute, despatch, send
as an ambassador; b) to commission (*alci alqd*); c) to choose as
one's lieutenant; d) to bequeath.
**legō², lēgī, lēctum** 3 a) to collect,
gather, pick; b) to wind up, spin;
c) to receive, pick up; d) to trace
out, catch up; e) to coast, pass
along *or* over; f) to choose, select,
pick out; g) to read, peruse; to read
aloud, recite.
**lēgulēius** 3 pettifogger.
**legūmen, inis** *n* pulse, bean.
**lembunculus, ī** *m* small boat.
**lembus, ī** *m* cutter. boat.
**lēmma, atis** *n* a) theme, subject;
b) (title of) a short poem.
**lēmniscātus** 3 adorned with rib-
bons.
**lēmniscus, ī** *m* ribbon (*attached to
a victor's crown*).
**lemurēs, um** *m/pl.* spirits of the
dead, ghosts, spectres; **lemūria,
ōrum** *n/pl.* festival for appeasing
the spirits of the dead.
**lēna, ae** *f* procuress, bawd; she that
entices.
**lēnīmen, inis** *and* **-mentum, ī** *n*
alleviation, mitigation, solace.
**lēniō** 4 to alleviate, mitigate, soften,
soothe.
**lēnis, e** soft, smooth, mild, gentle;
a) moderate, gradual; b) calm, kind.
**lēnitās, ātis** *f* mildness, softness,
gentleness, smoothness.

lēnitūdō, inis f = lenitas.

lēnō, ōnis m pander, procurer.

lēnōcinium, ī n a pandering; enticement; allurement; finery; flattery.

lēnōcinor, 1 to flatter (alci); to stimulate, aid.

lēnōnius 3 belonging to a procurer.

lēns, tis f lentil.

lentēscō 3 to become sticky or pliant; to slacken.

lentisci-fer 3 bearing mastictrees.

lentiscus, ī f (and -um, ī n) mastic tree or wood.

lentitūdō, inis f slowness; dullness, apathy.

lentō 1 to make flexible, to bend.

lentulus 3 rather slow.

lentus 3 tenacious, sticky; a) tough, pliant, flexible; b) slow, sluggish, lingering, lazy, drawling; c) indifferent, phlegmatic.

lēnullus (and lēnunculus), ī m = leno.

lēnunculus, ī m = lembunculus.

leō, ōnis m lion.

leōnīnus 3 of a lion, leonine.

lepas, adis f limpet.

lepidus 3 pleasant, charming, elegant; witty.

(lepor, ōris and) lepōs, ōris m pleasantness, charm; wit.

lepus, oris m hare.

lepusculus, ī m little hare.

lessus m funeral lamentation.

lētālis, e deadly, fatal.

lēthargicus 3 drowsy, lethargic.

lēthargus, ī m drowsiness.

lēti-fer = letalis.

lētō 1 to kill.

lētum, ī n death; ruin.

leuc-aspis, idis bearing white shields.

leucophaeātus 3 clothed in grey.

Leuc-ophryna, ae f with white eyebrows (Diana).

levāmen, inis and -mentum, ī n alleviation.

levātiō, ōnis f alleviation; a diminishing.

leviculus 3 somewhat vain.

levidēnsis, e thin, slight, poor.

levi-fidus 3 worthy of little belief.

levi-pēs, pedis light-footed.

lēvis[1], e smooth, smoothed; beardless, slippery, youthful, delicate; flowing (speech).

levis[2], e light, not heavy; a) gentle, soft, mild; b) quick, rapid, swift; c) trifling, unimportant, insignificant, small; d) light-minded, unsteady, capricious, fickle, inconstant.

levi-somnus 3 sleeping lightly.

lēvitās[1], ātis f smoothness.

levitās[2], ātis f lightness; a) mobility; b) groundlessness; c) levity, inconstancy.

lēvō[1] 1 to smooth, polish.

levō[2] 1 1. to make light, lighten, diminish (alci alqd); a) to relieve (alqm re); b) to lessen; 2. to raise, lift up; a) to support; b) to console.

lēvor, ōris m smoothness.

lēx, lēgis f 1. formula; a) compact, agreement, covenant; b) stipulation, terms; 2. proposal of a law, bill; a) law, legal enactment; pl. constitution; b) precept, regulation, rule.

(lībāmen, inis and) lībāmentum, ī n libation, offering; first-fruits.

lībārius, ī m pastry-cook.

lībātiō, ōnis f drink-offering.

lībella, ae f a) small coin ($^1/_{10}$ dēnārius); hērēs ex lībellā heir to one tenth of an estate; b) builder's level.

libellus, ī m little book, pamphlet; a) (answer to) a petition; b) memorandum-book; journal; c) letter; d) libel, satire; e) programme; f) announcement, placard.

libēns, tis willing, with goodwill, with pleasure; adv. libenter.

liber[1], brī m 1. bark of a tree; 2. book, writing; a) letter; b) list, catalogue.

liber[2], era, erum free; a) unrestricted, unlimited; b) free from care, debt or tax; aedes uninhabited; c) frank, open; d) free socially and politically, independent (re, a re).

līberālis, e a) belonging to freedom; b) worthy of a free man, gentlemanly, decorous, noble, noble-minded; kind, generous, liberal, plentiful, bountiful.

līberālitās, ātis f a) noble or kind disposition or character; b) liberality, generosity; c) gift, present.

līberātiō, ōnis f a releasing, delivering, acquittal, discharge.

līberātor, ōris m deliverer, liberator.

**liberi**, ōrum *or* um *m/pl.* children.

**liberō** 1 to set free, liberate (*alqm re*, *ab* or *ex re*); **a**) to manumit; **b**) to free, deliver, release; **c**) to cancel, render void; **d**) to free from taxes; **e**) **fidem** to keep one's word; **nomina** to settle debts; **f**) to absolve, acquit.

**liberta**, ae *f* freedwoman.

**libertās**, ātis *f* freedom, liberty; **a**) civil *or* political freedom, independence; **b**) frankness.

**libertinus** 3 of the class of freedmen; *subst. m*, *f* freedman, -woman.

**libertus**, ī *m* freedman.

**libet**, **libuit** *and* **libitum est** 2 it pleases, is agreeable; *subst.* **libita**, **ōrum** *n/pl.* pleasure, liking.

**libidinor** 1 to indulge lust.

**libidinōsus** 3 **a**) luxurious, licentious, lustful; **b**) wilful, wanton.

**libidō**, **inis** *f* desire, pleasure, longing; **a**) wilfulness, caprice; **b**) lust, sensual desire, lewdness.

**libita**, **ōrum** *n/pl.*, *see* **libet.**

**libitinārius**, ī *m* undertaker.

**libō** 1 to take a little away from (*alqd ab* or *ex re*); **a**) to touch, taste; **b**) to diminish; **c**) to sacrifice, offer, consecrate, make a libation (*alci alqd*).

**libra**, ae *f* 1. balance, pair of scales; **libra et aes** due legal form; builder's level; 2. the Roman pound.

**librāmentum**, ī *n* **a**) weight, gravity; **b**) level surface, horizontal plane.

**librāria**, ae *f* weigher of wool.

**librāriolus**, ī *m* = **librarius.**

**librārium**, ī *n* book-case.

**librārius**, ī *m* belonging to books; *subst. m* copyist, scribe; bookseller.

**librātor**, ōris *m* **a**) leveller, surveyor; engineer; **b**) = **libritor.**

**librātus** 3 hurled, poised.

**librilis**, e of a pound weight.

**libritor**, ōris *m* hurler, thrower.

**librō** 1 to poise, balance; to swing, hurl.

**libum**, ī *n* cake (*for offering*).

**liburn(ic)a**, ae *f* light warship.

**licēns**, **tis** unrestrained, bold, licentious.

**licentia**, ae *f* freedom, licence; licentiousness, lawlessness, uncontrolled power.

**liceō**, **uī**, — 2 to be valued, fetch a price.

**liceor**, **itus sum** 2 to bid, offer a price for.

**licet**, **licuit** *and* **licitum est** 2 it is allowed, permitted (*alci* with *inf.*; *acc.* with *inf.*), one may, one is at liberty; *cj.* with *subj.* even if, although.

**lichēn**, **ēnis** *m* ringworm.

**licitātiō**, **ōnis** *f* a bidding (*at a sale*).

**licitātor**, **ōris** *m* bidder.

**licitor** 1 = **liceor.**

**licitus** 3 permitted, allowed.

**licium**, ī *n* (*usu. plur.*) loops for raising any desired number of warp-threads, in order to pass the woof in front of *or* behind them; thread; woven material.

**lictor**, **ōris** *m* lictor, official attendant of a magistrate.

**liēn**, **ēnis** *m* spleen.

**liēnōsus** 3 suffering from a disorder of the spleen.

**ligāmen**, **inis** *and* **-mentum**, ī *n* band, tie, bandage.

**lignārius**, ī *m* carpenter, joiner.

**lignātiō**, **ōnis** *f* a procuring of wood.

**lignātor**, **ōris** *m* wood-cutter.

**ligneolus** *and* **ligneus** 3 wooden.

**lignor** 1 to procure wood.

**lignum**, ī *n* **a**) wood, firewood; **b**) tree; **c**) spearshaft; **d**) puppet; **e**) writing-table.

**ligō**[1], **ōnis** *m* mattock, hoe.

**ligō**[2] 1 to tie, to bind.

**ligula**, ae *f* = **lingula.**

**ligūr(r)iō** 4 **a**) to lick, lick up; to pick at; to feed daintily; to prey on; to lust after.

**ligūr(r)itiō**, **ōnis** *f* daintiness.

**ligustrum**, ī *n* privet.

**lilium**, ī *n* lily.

**lima**, ae *f* file; a polishing.

**limāt(ul)us** 3 filed, polished.

**limāx**, **ācis** *f* (*and m*) slug.

**limbulārius**, ī *m* maker of fringes.

**limbus**, ī *m* hem, edge, border.

**limen**, **inis** *n* threshold; **a**) door, entrance; **b**) starting-point, beginning; **c**) dwelling.

**limes**, **itis** *m* cross-path (*between fields*); **a**) boundary-line, boundary--wall; **b**) path, way, passage, road.

**limō**[1] 1 to file, polish; **a**) to rub; **b**) to examine accurately; **c**) to file off, diminish.

**limō**[2] 1 to cover with mud.

**limōsus** 3 miry, muddy.

**limpidus** 3 clear, limpid.

**limulus** 3 slightly aslant.

**limus¹, ī** *m* mud, mire, dirt.

**limus²** 3 aslant, sideways.

**limus³, ī** *m* priest's apron.

**līnea, ae** *f* linen thread; a) plumb-line; b) line, stroke; c) bound, limit; d) fishing-line.

**lineāmentum, ī** *n* line, stroke; *pl.* outline, sketch; features.

**lineō** 1 to make straight.

**lineus** 3 flaxen, linen.

**lingō, linxī, linctum** 3 to lick.

**lingua, ae** *f* the tongue; a) speech, language; eloquence; b) a language *or* tongue, dialect; c) tongue of land.

**linguārium, ī** *n* fine for thoughtless speaking.

**lingula, ae** *f* a) tongue of land; b) shoe-strap; c) ladle.

**lingulāca, ae** *f* chatterbox.

**liniāmentum, ī** *n* = lineamentum.

**lini-ger** 3 linen-wearing.

**linō, lēvī** *or* **līvī, litum** 3 to be-smear, anoint; to erase; to bedaub, cover.

**linquō, līquī,** — 3 to leave, quit; to forsake; abandon, omit (*alqd*).

**linteātus** 3 clothed in linen.

**linteō, ōnis** *m* linen-weaver.

**linteolum, ī** *n* small linen cloth.

**linter, tris** *f* (*m*) boat, skiff; trough, tub.

**linteus** 3 of linen; *subst.* **linteum, ī** *n* linen cloth, sail.

**lintriculus, ī** *m* small boat.

**linum, ī** *n* flax, linen; a) thread, cord, fishing-line; b) linen cloth *or* garment; c) rope; d) hunter's *or* fisher's net.

**lippiō** 4 to have sore eyes; to burn.

**lippitūdō, inis** *f* inflammation of the eyes.

**lippus** 3 with sore eyes; blind; running with juice.

**lique-faciō** (*and* **liquē-**) 3 to melt, dissolve; to weaken.

**liquēns** (*and* **li-**), **tis** liquid.

**liqueō, liquī** *or* **licuī,** — 2 to be clear, evident.

**liquēscō,** —, — 3 to become clear *or* fluid, to melt (away); a) to become effeminate; b) to putrefy.

**liquidiusculus** 3 milder, softer.

**liquidus** (*and* **li-**) 3 flowing, fluid, liquid; *subst.* **liquidum, ī** *n* a

liquid; a) clear, bright, limpid; b) pure; c) clear, evident, certain; *subst.* **liquidum, ī** *n* certainty; *adv.* **liquidō** clearly, certainly.

**liquō** 1 to melt, liquefy; to strain, purify.

**liquor¹** (*and* **li-**), **ōris** *m* a) fluidity, liquidity; b) a fluid; c) the sea.

**liquor²,** —, — 3 to flow; to melt away.

**līs, lītis** *f* contention, quarrel; a) controversy, dispute; b) lawsuit.

**litāmen, inis** *n* sacrifice.

**litātiō, ōnis** *f* auspicious sacrifice.

**lītera, ae** *f*, *see* **littera**.

**liti-cen, inis** *m* clarion-blower.

**lītigātor, ōris** *m* party in a lawsuit.

**lītigiōsus** 3 a) quarrelsome, full of dispute, contentious; b) disputed, contested.

**lītigium, ī** *n* = lis.

**lītigō** 1 to dispute, quarrel.

**litō** 1 a) to sacrifice under favour-able auspices, to obtain favourable omens; b) to propitiate.

**litorālis, e** relating to the shore.

**litoreus** 3 belonging to the shore.

**littera, ae** *f* 1. letter of the alphabet, *pl.* the alphabet; a handwriting; 2. *pl.* a writing; a) letter, epistle; b) document, record, deed; c) li-terature; d) learning, culture, liberal education.

**litterārius** 3 relating to reading and writing.

**litterātor, ōris** *m* elementary teacher.

**litterātūra, ae** *f* writing; alphabet; grammar.

**litterātus** 3 inscribed with letters; a) literal; b) learned, lettered, liberally educated.

**litterula, ae** *f* a) small letter (*of the alphabet*); b) *pl.* short letter, note; (knowledge of) literature.

**litūra, ae** *f* erasure; blot.

**litus, oris** *n* sea-shore, coast, beach; bank.

**lituus, ī** *m* a) curved staff of an augur; b) clarion, trumpet.

**līveō,** —, — 2 to be bluish, dark, livid; to envy (*with dat.*).

**līvēscō** 3 to turn blue.

**līvidulus** 3 envious.

**līvidus** 3 bluish, blue-grey; blue--black, black; livid; envious.

**līvor, ōris** *m* bluish colour, livid spot; envy, malice.

**lixa, ae** *m* sutler, camp-follower.
**locārius, ī** *m* seller of theatre seats.
**locātiō, ōnis** *f* a) a placing; **b)** a letting out, leasing; contract.
**locātor, ōris** *m* landlord.
**locitō** 1 to hire out.
**locō** 1 to place, put, lay, set (*alqd in re*); **a)** to give in marriage (*women*); **b)** to let, lease, hire, farm out; to lend money at interest; **c)** to give out on contract. [-hole.|
**loculāmentum, ī** *n* case, pigeon-|
**loculus, ī** *m* a) small place; **b)** receptacle, coffer, satchel.
**locuplēs, ētis** rich, wealthy, opulent, richly supplied; trustworthy, reliable, credible.
**locuplētātor, ōris** *m* one who enriches.
**locuplētō** 1 to enrich; to adorn (*alqm re*).
**locus, ī** *m* place, spot, locality (*pl.* **loca, ōrum** *n*) 1. a) the right *or* proper place, (**in**) **loco** in the right place; b) special, appointed place, station, post, position; c) dwelling, residence; d) locality, district, region; e) place in the order of succession (**primo loco** firstly); f) passage in a book (*pl.* **locī**); topic, matter, subject, point, head, division; **loci communes** passages of a general import; g) position, rank, degree, birth (**nobili** *or* **summo loco natus**), **loco** *with gen.* in the condition of (**filii loco esse** *or* **amare** as a son, in the place of, instead of); **2.** time, right time; a) opportunity, occasion; b) condition, situation.
**locusta, ae** *f* locust; crayfish.
**locūtiō, ōnis** *f* a speaking, pronunciation, speech.
**lōdīcula, ae** *f* blanket.
**lōdīx, īcis** *f* blanket.
**logī, ōrum** *m/pl.* words; empty talk; jest.
**logica, ōrum** *n/pl.* logic.
**lolium, ī** *n* darnel.
**lolligō, inis** (*and* **lolliguncula, ae**) *f* cuttle-fish.
**lōmentum, ī** *n* cleansing-cream.
**long-aevus** 3 aged, old.
**longē** *adv.* **1.** (*of space*) a long way off, far off, at a distance; a) far, from afar; b) by far, very much; c) at length, diffusely; **2.** (*of time*) long, for a long time (*longe ante*).

**longinquitās, ātis** *f* length, extent, long duration.
**longinquus** 3 long; a) distant, far, remote, foreign, strange; b) long in duration, tedious, long deferred, distant.
**longiter** far.
**longitūdō, inis** *f* length; long duration.
**longiusculus** 3 rather long.
**longulus** 3 somewhat long.
**longurius, ī** *m* long pole.
**longus** 3 1. (*of space*) long; **navis longa** man-of-war; a) tall, vast, spacious; b) far off, remote, distant; prolix; **2.** of long duration, tedious.
**lopas, adis** *f* limpet.
**loquācitās, ātis** *f* talkativeness.
**loquāx, ācis** *and* **loquāculus** 3 talkative, garrulous.
**loquēla** (*and* **-ella**), **ae** *f* speech, discourse, language.
**loquentia, ae** *f* readiness of speech.
**loquitor** 1 to speak.
**loquor, cūtus sum** 3 1. to speak (*cum, pro alqo, de re*); **2.** to indicate clearly; a) to say (*alqd*); b) to mention.
**lōrārius, ī** *m* flogger of slaves.
**lōrātus** 3 bound with thongs.
**lōreus** 3 made of thongs.
**lōrīca, ae** *f* a) leather cuirass; b) breast-work.
**lōrīcātus** 3 armed with a cuirass.
**lōrīcula, ae** *f* small breastwork.
**lōri-pēs, edis** with deformed feet.
**lōrum, ī** *n* thong; a) rein; b) whip; c) leather amulet.
**lōtium, ī** *n* urine.
**lōtos** *and* **-us, ī** *f* (*and m*) lotus; flute (*of lotus-wood*).
**lōtus** 3 = **lautus** (*lavo*).
**lubēns, lubet, lubīdō,** *see* **libens, libet, libido.**
**lubentia, ae** *f* pleasure.
**lūbricō** 1 to make slippery.
**lūbricus** 3 slippery; a) quickly moving, fleeting; b) uncertain, critical, hazardous; c) deceitful, tricky.
**lūca bōs** *f* (Lucanian cow) elephant.
**lūcānica, ae** *f* smoked sausage.
**lūcar, āris** *n* salary (*of actors*).
**lucellum, ī** *n* small gain, little profit.
**lūceō, xī,** — 2 a) to be bright, shine; b) to be conspicuous, clear; **lūcet** it is day.

**lucerna, ae** *f* lamp, oil-lamp.

**lūcēsco, lūxī,** — **3** to grow light, become day.

**lūcidus 3** clear, bright, shining; perspicuous.

**lūci-fer 3** light-bringing; *m* the morning-star; day.

**lūci-fuga, ae** *m* one who shuns daylight.

**lūci-fugus 3** light-shunning.

**lūciscō 3** = **lucesco.**

**lucrātīvus 3** lucrative, profitable.

**lucri-ficābilis, e, lucri-fer 3** profitable.

**lucri-fuga, ae** *m and f* gain-shunning.

**lucri-peta, ae** *m and f* greedy of gain.

**lucror 1** to gain, win, acquire.

**lucrōsus 3** profitable, lucrative.

**lucrum, ī** *n* gain, profit, advantage; **(in) lucro esse** to be profitable; **lucri facere** *alqd* to gain, to reap the benefit of; **a)** love of gain, avarice; **b)** riches.

**luctāmen, inis** *n* effort, exertion.

**luctātiō, ōnis** *f* a wrestling, struggling, contest, fight.

**luctātor, ōris** *m* wrestler.

**lūcti-ficus 3, lūcti-fer 3, lūcti-ficābilis, e** mournful, doleful.

**lūcti-sonus 3** sad-sounding.

**luctor** (*and* **luctō) 1** to wrestle, struggle, strive.

**lūctuōsus 3** mournful, sorrowful, lamentable.

**lūctus, ūs** *m* sorrow, mourning; mourning apparel.

**lūcubrātiō, ōnis** *f* a working by lamp-light.

**lūcubrātōrius 3** serving for studies at night.

**lūcubrō 1** to work by night.

**lūculentus 3 a)** full of light, bright; **b)** distinguished, splendid; *adv.* **lūculentē** *and* **lūculenter.**

**lucunzulus, ī** *m* a kind of pastry.

**lūcus, ī** *m* grove, wood.

**lūcusta, ae** *f* = **locusta.**

**lūdia, ae** *f* **a)** stage-dancer; **b)** gladiator's wife.

**lūdibrium, ī** *n* derision, mockery; laughing-stock, plaything.

**lūdibundus 3 a)** playful, sportive, wanton; **b)** without effort *or* danger.

**(lūdicer), cra, crum a)** sportive, playful; **b)** belonging to public games *or* stage-plays; *subst.* **lū-**

**dicrum, ī** *n* **a)** plaything, toy; **b)** public games, scenic show.

**lūdi-faciō 3** to make sport of.

**lūdi-ficābilis, e** used in mockery.

**lūdificātiō, ōnis** *f* a deriding, rallying, mockery.

**lūdi-ficātor, ōris** *m* mocker.

**lūdi-ficātus, ūs** *m* mockery.

**(lūdi-ficō** *and*) **lūdi-ficor 1 a)** to deride, make game of, turn into ridicule, mock; **b)** to thwart, frustrate.

**lūdiō, ōnis** *and* **lūdius, ī** *m* stage-player.

**lūdō, sī, sum 3** to play, sport (*alqd; alqa re*); **a)** to frolic; **b)** to practise as a pastime, play with; **c)** to baffle, ridicule, deceive.

**lūdus, ī** *m* play, game, pastime; **a)** (*pl.*) public games, spectacles, shows, exhibitions; **b)** stage-play; **c)** child's play, mere sport; trifle; jest, joke; **d)** gladiatorial school; **e)** elementary school.

**luella, ae** *f* expiation.

**luēs, is** *f* plague, pestilence; ruin, destruction.

**lūgeō, xī,** — **2** to mourn, lament.

**lūgubris, e** belonging to mourning; **a)** mournful, doleful, plaintive; **b)** disastrous; *subst.* **lūgubria, ium** *n/pl.* mourning attire.

**lumbi-fragium, ī** *n* rupture of the loins.

**lumbrīcus, ī** *m* earthworm.

**lumbus, ī** *m* the loin.

**lūmen, inis** *n* light; **a)** lamp, candle, torch; **b)** daylight, day; **c)** the light of life; **d)** eye, the light of the eye; **e)** window; **f)** splendour, glory, ornament; **g)** salvation, help.

**lūmināria, ium** *n/pl.* window-shutters.

**lūminōsus 3** full of light; conspicuous.

**lūna, ae** *f* the moon; moonshine; **a)** crescent; **b)** month.

**lūnāris, e** lunar; moonlike.

**lūnō 1** to bend into a crescent.

**lūnula, ae** *f* crescent-shaped ornament.

**luō[1] 3** to wash, cleanse.

**luō[2], luī,** — **3** to expiate, atone for (*alqd*); **a)** to avert by expiation *or* punishment; **b)** to pay, to suffer punishment.

**lupa, ae** *f* she-wolf; harlot.

**lupănar, ăris** *n* brothel.

**lupātus** 3 with wolf's teeth; **lu-
pāta, ōrum** n/pl. and **-tī, ōrum**
m/pl. curb armed with sharp teeth.
**Lupercālia, i(or)um** n/pl. festival
of Lupercus.
**lupillus, ī** m lupin.
**lupīnus** 3 of a wolf, wolf's; subst.
**lupīnus, ī** m and **lupīnum, ī** n a)
lupin; b) counter in a game.
**lupus, ī** m a) wolf; b) voracious fish,
pike; c) hook; d) a horse's bit
armed with sharp teeth.
**lurcō, ōnis** m glutton.
**lūreō** 2 to be ghastly pale.
**lūridus** 3 (making) sickly yellow,
ghastly, lurid.
**lūror, ōris** m paleness.
**luscinia, ae** f (and **-ius, ī** m, **-iola,
ae** f) nightingale.
**luscitiōsus** 3 dim-eyed.
**luscus** 3 one-eyed.
**lūsiō, ōnis** f playing, game.
**lūsitō** 1 to play, sport.
**lūsor, ōris** m player; playful writer;
humourist.
**lūsōrius** 3 used for play or pleasure.
**lūstrālis, e** a) relating to expiation;
b) quinquennial.
**lūstrātiō, ōnis** f a) purification by
sacrifice; b) a wandering, travers-
ing, going about.
**lūstricus** 3 = lustralis.
**lūstrō**[1] 1 to light up, illuminate.
**lūstrō**[2] 1 a) to purify by expiation;
b) to review, survey, examine; to go
over or about, to traverse.
**lustror** 1 to frequent brothels.
**lustrum**[1], **ī** n a) bog, morass; b) den
or lair of wild beasts; c) brothel;
d) debauchery.
**lūstrum**[2], **ī** n a) expiatory sacrifice;
b) period of (five) years; quinquennial festival.
**lūsus, ūs** m play, game, sport,
amusement, dalliance.
**lūteolus** 3 yellow.

**luteus**[1] 3 of mud or clay; worthless;
dirty.
**lūteus**[2] 3 orange, yellow.
**lut(it)ō** 1 to make dirty.
**lutulentus** 3 muddy, dirty.
**lutum**[1], **ī** n mud, mire, dirt; loam,
clay.
**lūtum**[2], **ī** n dyer's weed, yellow
colour.
**lūx, lūcis** f (m) light; a) splendour,
brightness; b) daylight, day; **prīmā
lūce** at dawn; **lūce** or **lūcī** in the
daytime; c) light of life; d) light of
the eye; e) clearness, elucidation;
f) publicity, the sight of men;
g) help, succour, encouragement,
ornament.
**luxō** 1 to dislocate.
**luxor** 1 to revel, feast.
**luxuria, ae** f and **-iēs, ēī** f rankness,
luxuriant growth; riotous living,
extravagance.
**luxuriō** and **-or** 1 to be rank, luxuriant, abundant in growth; a) to be
playful, sportive; b) to abound in,
swell, increase; c) to revel, run riot.
**luxuriōsus** 3 rank, luxuriant, exuberant; a) dissolute, luxurious, voluptuous; b) excessive.
**luxus, ūs** m rankness; a) luxury,
debauchery, sensual excess, extravagance; b) splendour.
**lychno-bius, ī** m one who lives
by lamp-light.
**lychnūchus, ī** m lamp-stand, candlestick.
**lychnus, ī** m light, lamp.
**lygdos, ī** f white marble.
**lympha, ae** f clear water.
**lymphāticus** and **lymphātus** 3 insane, mad, frantic.
**lymphō** 1 to make mad.
**lynx, cis** m and f lynx.
**lyra, ae** f lyre, lute; lyric poetry, song.
**lyricus** 3 lyric; m lyric poet.
**lyristēs, ae** m lyre-player.

# M

**M** *abbr.* **1.** = **Marcus; 2.** *as a numeral* = 1000; **M'** = **Mānius.**

**macellārius, ī** *m* victualler.

**macellum, ī** *n* (*and* **-us, ī** *m*) food-market.

**maceō** 2 to be lean.

**macer, cra, crum** lean, meagre.

**māceria, ae** *f* wall.

**mācerō** 1 to soak, make soft; to weaken, emaciate, enervate; to tease, torment.

**macēscō** 3 to become lean.

**machaera, ae** *f* sword.

**machaerophorus, ī** *m* swordbearer; halberdier, satellite.

**māchina, ae** *f* machine, engine (windlass, crane, catapult); device, artifice.

**māchināmentum, ī** *n* machine, instrument.

**māchinātiō, ōnis** *f* a) mechanism, machinery; b) = **māchina.**

**māchinātor, ōris** *m* (*and* **-trīx, icis** *f*) maker of machines, engineer; contriver, inventor.

**māchinor** 1 to contrive, devise, invent; to scheme, plot.

**māchinōsus** 3 ingeniously contrived.

**maciēs, ēī** *f* leanness, thinness.

**macilentus** 3 thin, lean.

**macrēscō, —, —** 3 to grow lean *or* thin.

**macritūdō, inis** *f* leanness.

**macro-cōl(l)um, ī** *n* large-sized paper, royal paper.

**mactābilis, e** deadly.

**mactātor, ōris** *m* killer.

**mactātus, ūs** *m* sacrifice.

**macte** (*voc. of* **mactus**), *pl.* **mactī** magnified, glorified; **macte virtute** hail to thee!, good-luck!, be honoured!, well done!

**mactō** 1 **1.** to magnify, glorify; honour; **2.** to afflict, punish; to sacrifice, kill.

**mactus** 3 wounded.

**macula, ae** *f* a) spot, mark; blot, stain, blemish, fault; b) mesh (*of a net*).

**maculō** 1 to stain, pollute, disgrace.

**maculōsus** 3 a) spotted; b) stained, polluted; disgraced; abominable.

**made-faciō** 3 (*and* **-factō** 1) to wet, moisten.

**madeō** 2 to be wet; a) to be made soft by boiling; b) to be soaked in (*re*).

**madēscō, duī, —** 3 to become wet *or* moist.

**madidus** 3 wet, moist, steeped.

**mador, ōris** *m* moisture.

**madulsa, ae** *m* drunkard.

**maelēs, is** *f* marten, badger.

**maena, ae** *f* small sea-fish.

**maenas, adis** *f* bacchante.

**maeniānum, ī** *n* balcony.

**maereō, —, —** 2 a) to mourn, grieve, lament; b) to bemoan, bewail (*acc.*).

**maeror, ōris** *m* mourning, sadness, grief.

**maestiter** *adv. of* **maestus.**

**maestitia, ae** *f* sadness, sorrowfulness, grief, dejection.

**maestitūdō, inis** *f* = **maestitia.**

**maestus** 3 a) sad, sorrowful, dejected; b) causing sorrow, gloomy.

**māgālia, ium** *n/pl.* huts, cottages.

**mage** = **magis.**

**magicus** 3 magical, magic.

**magis** *adv.* a) more, in a higher degree; **non magis quam** not so much ... as, not so ... but rather; b) rather, with better reason, more truly.

**magister, trī** *m* master, chief, ruler, director; a) superintendent; b) teacher, leader, adviser.

**magisterium, ī** *n* direction, superintendency, tutorship, guardianship.

**magistra, ae** *f* mistress, directress, leader, instructress.

**magistrātūs, ūs** *m* dignity *or* office of a magistrate, civil office, magistracy; a magistrate, high civil officer, public functionary.

**magmentārius** 3 for additional offerings. [nimity.]

**magn-animitās, ātis** *f* magna-]

**magn-animus** 3 high-minded, high-spirited.

**magnēs, ētis** *m* (*lapis*) loadstone, magnet.

**magni-dicus** 3 boastful.

**magnificentia, ae** *f* grandeur, splendour, magnificence; **a)** loftiness, greatness; **b)** a boasting, pompousness.

**magni-ficō** 1 to esteem highly.

**magni-ficus** 3 splendid, fine, costly, sumptuous; **a)** fond of display; **b)** boasting, pompous; **c)** noble, distinguished.

**magni-loquentia, ae** *f* elevated language, lofty style; boasting.

**magni-loquus** 3 boastful; sublime.

**magnitūdō, inis** *f* greatness, size; **a)** number, quantity; **b)** importance, vastness, extent.

**magn-opere** (*and* **magnō opere**, *superl.* **maximō opere**) *adv.* very much, greatly, exceedingly, particularly; earnestly, urgently.

**magnus** 3 (*comp.* **māior, ius;** *superl.* **maximus**) **1.** a) (*of size*) large, great, big, high, tall, long, broad, extensive, spacious; b) (*of number or quantity*) considerable, abundant, much, numerous; c) (*of value*) high; **magnī aestimāre, magnō vendere; māior pars** majority; **2.** (*of time*) a) great, long, extended; b) aged, old, advanced; **māior** (*natu*) elder, **maximus** eldest; **māiōrēs** *pl.* fathers, ancestors; **3.** (*of force*) a) strong, powerful, vehement, loud (*vox*); b) considerable, great, mighty, important, weighty; c) high, eminent, noble, powerful; d) haughty, proud, boastful; e) high-minded; f) excessive, intense.

**magus, ī** *m* magician; *adj.* 3 magic.

**magȳdaris** *f* seed (*or* stalk?) of the plant *sirpe* or *silphium*.

**māiālis, is** *m* hog.

**māiestās, ātis** *f* majesty, grandeur, greatness, elevation, dignity; high-treason.

**māior, māius,** *see* **magnus**.

**Māius** 3 of the month of May; (*mensis*) *m* May.

**māiusculus** 3 somewhat greater *or* older.

**māla, ae** *f* cheek-bone, jaw; cheek.

**malacia, ae** *f* calm at sea.

**malacissō** 1 to render soft.

**malacus** 3 soft; luxurious; nimble.

**malaxō** 1 to soften, to make flexible.

**male** *adv.* (*comp.* **pēius,** *superl.* **pessimē**) **a)** badly, ill, wrong, wickedly; **b)** unfortunately, unsuccessfully; **c)** unseasonably; **d)** excessively, very much, greatly; imperfectly, scarcely, not at all.

**male-dicāx, ācis** abusive.

**male-dīcō** 3 to speak ill of, abuse, revile (*alci*).

**male-dictiō, ōnis** *f* a reviling, abuse.

**male-dictum, ī** *n* abusive language, curse. [ous.]

**male-dicus** 3 abusive, slander-]

**male-faciō** 3 to do evil; **male-factum, ī** *n* evil deed, injury.

**male-factor, ōris** *m* evil-doer.

**maleficium, ī** *n* evil deed, offence; wickedness, injury.

**male-ficus** 3 evil-doing; vicious, wicked; mischievous.

**male-suādus** 3 ill-advising.

**male-volēns, tis** = **malevolus**.

**malevolentia, ae** *f* ill-will, malevolence. [vious, malevolent.]

**male-volus** 3 ill-disposed, en-]

**māli-fer** 3 apple-bearing.

**malignitās, ātis** *f* ill-will, malice, envy; niggardliness.

**malignus** 3 ill-disposed, wicked, malicious; **a)** barren, unfruitful; **b)** niggardly, scanty.

**malitia, ae** *f* malice, roguery.

**malitiōsus** 3 ill-disposed, wicked, knavish, malicious.

**malivolentia, malivolus,** *see* **male-**.

**malleātor, ōris** *m* one who hammers, beater.

**malleolus, ī** *m* fire-dart.

**malleus, ī** *m* hammer, mallet.

**mālō, mālui, mālle** to choose rather, prefer; to be more favourable (*alci*).

**mālobathron, ī** *n* a costly (cinnamon-) oil *or* ointment.

**mālum¹, ī** *n* apple, quince, citron, pomegranate.

**malum², ī** *n* evil; **a)** fault; **b)** misfortune, calamity, mischief; **c)** punishment, hurt, harm, injury; **d)** wrong-doing, vice; *int.* plague!, wretch.

**malus¹** 3 (*comp.* **pēior, us,** *superl.* **pessimus**) 3) bad; **a)** evil, wicked, mischievous, wrong, criminal, depraved, malicious; (*subst.*) **malī, ōrum** *m/pl.* unpatriotic citizens;

**b)** ugly, hideous; **c)** unlucky, unfortunate, miserable; **d)** injurious, pernicious, destructive.

**mālus², ī 1.** *m* upright pole, mast, prop; **2.** *f* apple-tree; citron.

**malva, ae** *f* mallow.

**mamilla, ae** *f* breast; darling.

**mamillāre, is** *n* brassière.

**mamma, ae** *f* breast, pap; teat.

**mammeātus** (*and* **mammōsus**) 3 full-breasted.

**mammia** *n/pl.* little mothers.

**mammicula, ae** *f* = mamilla.

**mānābilis, e** penetrating.

**manceps, cipis** *m* purchaser, renter, contractor; surety.

**mancipātiō, ōnis** *f* transfer of property, purchase.

**mancipium, ī** *n* **a)** a taking possession of; legal purchase; **lex mancipii** contract of sale; right of possession; **b)** slave obtained by legal transfer.

**mancipō 1** to transfer by formal sale, to sell, give up to.

**mancup-** *see* **mancip-** *and* **manceps.**

**mancus 3** maimed, defective.

**mandātor, ōris** *m* suborner.

**mandātū** *abl.* by order.

**mandātum, ī** *n* charge, order, commission, injunction.

**mandō¹ 1** to commit to the charge of (*alci alqd; de re*), to order, commission (*alci*).

**mandō², ndī, ānsum 3** to chew, masticate; to eat, consume.

**mandra, ae** *f* **a)** drove of cattle; **b)** squares on a game-board.

**mandūcō 1** to chew, to eat.

**mandūcus, ī** *m* mask representing a glutton.

**māne 1.** *n* (*abl.* -**ī**) the early morning; **2.** *adv.* early in the morning.

**maneō, mānsī, mānsum 2 1.** to stay, remain, abide; **a)** to pass the night; **b)** to last, endure, continue; to persist, adhere to (*in re*); **2.** to await, expect (*acc.*).

**mānēs, ium** *m/pl.* ghosts *or* shades of the departed; **a)** corpse; **b)** the lower world, infernal regions.

**mangō, ōnis** *m* slave-dealer.

**mangōnicus 3** of a slave-dealer.

**manicae, ārum** *f/pl.* **a)** long sleeves; **b)** handcuffs; grapple.

**manicātus 3** with long sleeves.

**manicula, ae** *f* little hand.

**manifestārius 3** clear; caught in the act, red-handed.

**manifestō 1** to show clearly, manifest, reveal.

**mani-festus 3** palpable; **a)** convicted of, manifestly betraying (*gen.*); **b)** clear, plain.

**maniplāris, -plus,** *see* **manipul-.**

**manipulāris, e** (*and* -**ius 3**) manipular, of a company; *subst.* common soldier.

**manipulātim** *adv.* in maniples.

**manipulus, ī** *m* a handful, bundle; maniple *or* company of foot-soldiers.

**mann(ul)us, ī** *m* small Gallic horse.

**mānō 1** to flow, run, drop, trickle (*re*); **a)** to flow; **b)** to proceed (*ab, ex, de re*); **c)** to spread; to pass away.

**mānsiō, ōnis** *f* a remaining, stay, sojourn.

**mānsitō 1** to stay, abide, remain.

**mānstrūca, ae** *f* = mastrūca.

**mānsuē-faciō 3** to make tame.

**mānsuēs, ētis** = mansuetus.

**mānsuēscō, suēvī, suētum 3 a)** to become tame *or* gentle; **b)** to tame.

**mānsuētūdō, inis** *f* tameness, mildness, gentleness, clemency.

**mānsuētus 3** tame; gentle, soft, mild, quiet, tranquil.

**mānsūrus 3,** *part. fut.* of maneo.

**mantēle, is** *n* towel, napkin.

**mantellum, ī** *n* cloak, cover.

**mantica, ae** *f* wallet.

**mantis-cinor 1** *meaning doubtful:* *either* to help oneself liberally *or* to prophesy.

**mantō 1** to wait (for).

**manuālis, e** thrown by the hand.

**manubiae, ārum** *f/pl.* money obtained by the sale of booty, prize-money; spoils, plunder.

**manubiālis, e, manubiārius 3** coming from *or* producing booty.

**manubrium, ī** *n* handle, hilt, haft.

**manuf-** *see* **manif-; manufestārius 3** plain.

**manuleārius, ī** *m* maker of long sleeves.

**manuleātus 3** provided with long sleeves.

**manū-missiō, ōnis** *f* a setting free.

**manū-mittō 3** to set free.

**manu-pretium, ī** *n* pay, wages, hire; reward.

**manus, ūs** *f* the hand; **in manibus habēre** to be engaged on; **a)** armed hand, fist; **b)** personal valour; **c)** hand to hand fight, close combat; **manum conferre** *or* **conserere** to come to close quarters; **d)** force, violence, power; jurisdiction (*of a father, of a husband*); **in manū alcis esse** to be in one's power; **e)** work, work of the artist *or* craftsman, workmanship; handwriting; **f)** a handful, band, body of men, corps, armed force; **g)** trunk of an elephant; grappling-iron.

**mapālia, ium** *n/pl.* huts, cottages, movable dwellings.

**mappa, ae** *f* napkin; signal-flag.

**marceō, —, — 2** to wither, droop; to be faint, feeble, languid.

**marcēscō, —, — 3** to begin to droop; to become languid, weak, feeble.

**marcidus 3** withered, faded; weak, feeble, languid.

**marcor, ōris** *m* withering, languor.

**marculus, ī** *m* small hammer.

**mare, is** *n* the sea, ocean; **terrā marīque** by sea and land; sea-water.

**margarīta, ae** *f* (*and* **-tum, ī** *n*) pearl.

**marginō 1** to enclose with a margin.

**margō, inis** *m* (*and f*) border, edge, boundary.

**marīnus 3** = **maritimus.**

**marisca, ae** *f* **a)** fig; **b)** haemorrhoid.

**marīta, ae** *f, see* **maritus.**

**marītālis, e** matrimonial, nuptial.

**maritimus (-umus) 3** relating to the sea, marine, maritime, on the sea, on the sea-coast; *subst.* **maritima, ōrum** *n/pl.* coast.

**marītō 1** to wed, marry.

**marītus 3** matrimonial, nuptial, wedded; *subst.* **~, ī** *m* husband, **-a, ae** *f* wife.

**marmor, oris** *n* marble; **a)** marble block, marble work, statue; **b)** surface of the sea.

**marmorārius (faber)** worker in marble.

**marmorātus 3** covered with marble.

**marmoreus 3** made of marble; marble-like, smooth, shining.

**marra, ae** *f* hoe.

**Mārs, tis** *m* Mars, the God of War; **a)** war, battle, contest, engagement; **b)** manner of fighting, issue of battle, fortune of war; **aequo** (*or* **ancipiti**) **Marte** without decision.

**marsuppium** (*and* **-sūpium**), **ī** *n* money-bag, purse.

**Mārtiālis, e** relating to Mars.

**Mārtius 3** belonging to Mars; (*mensis*) *m* March.

**mās, maris a)** *m* man, male being; **b)** *adj.* male, masculine; manly, brave.

**masculīnus 3** male, masculine.

**masculus 3** male; manly, vigorous.

**massa, ae** *f* dough; lump, mass.

**mastīgia, ae** *m* gallows-bird, scoundrel, good-for-nothing.

**mastrūca, ae** *f* (garment of) sheepskin.

**mastrūcātus 3** clothed in sheepskins.

**masturbor 1** to masturbate; *hence* **masturbātor, ōris** *m.*

**matara, ae** *f* *and* **-ris, is** *f* Gallic javelin.

**matella, ae** *f* (chamber-)pot.

**matelliō, ōnis** *m* small pot, vessel.

**māter, tris** *f* mother; parent, producer, origin, source.

**mātercula, ae** *f* little mother.

**māteria, ae** *and* **-iēs, ēī** *f* matter, stuff; **a)** materials, wood, timber; **b)** provisions, store, resource; **c)** subject, subject-matter, topic, ground, theme; **d)** occasion, opportunity, cause; **e)** natural disposition, abilities.

**māteriārius, ī** *m* timber-merchant.

**māteriātus 3** timbered.

**māterior 1** to fetch timber.

**māternus 3** a mother's, maternal, motherly.

**mātertera, ae** *f* mother's sister, maternal aunt.

**mathēmatica, ae** *f* mathematics; astrology.

**mathēmaticus, ī** *m* mathematician; astrologer.

**mātri-cīda, ae** *m* matricide, a mother's murderer.

**mātricīdium, ī** *n* matricide, the murder of a mother.

**mātrimōnium, ī** *n* wedlock, marriage; matrimony; *pl.* wives.

**mātrimus** (*and* **-īmus**) **3** having a mother still living.

**mātrix, īcis** *f* **a)** womb; **b)** parent stem of plants.

**mātrōna, ae** *f* wife, matron; woman of rank, lady.

**mātrōnālis, e** belonging to a matron or married woman.

**mattea, ae** f dainty bit.

**matula, ae** f vessel, (chamber-)pot; simpleton.

**mātūrātē** in good time.

**mātūrēscō, ruī,** — 3 to become ripe, ripen; to come to maturity.

**mātūritās, ātis** f ripeness; a) full time, perfection; b) proper time; c) promptness.

**mātūrō** 1 1. to make ripe; P. to become ripe; a) to do early, betimes; b) to hasten, accelerate, dispatch; to hurry, precipitate (alqd; alci alqd); 2. intr. to make haste.

**mātūrus** 3 a) ripe, mature; developed, mellow; grown up, marriageable, of age, advanced in life; b) seasonable, timely, early, speedy; premature.

**mātūtīnus** 3 of the morning, early in the morning.

**maxilla, ae** f jaw.

**maximē (-umē)** adv. in the highest degree, most of all; quam ~ as much as possible; a) particularly, especially; b) essentially, principally, just, precisely; c) certainly, very well.

**maximitās, ātis** f greatness.

**maximus (-umus)** 3, superl. of magnus.

**māzo-nomus, ī** m large dish.

**meātus, ūs** m a) a going, passing, course, flight; b) way, path, channel.

**mē-castor** int. by Castor!

**mēchanicus, ī** m engineer.

**meddix,** see medix.

**medeor,** — 2 to heal, cure (with dat.); to relieve, amend, correct, restore.

**mediastīnus, ī** m common servant, menial, drudge.

**mēdica, ae** f lucerne.

**medicābilis, e** curable.

**(medicāmen, inis** and**) medicāmentum, ī** n remedy; a) medicament, medicine, plaster; b) drug, poison; c) dye, paint; d) charm; artificial means; antidote.

**medicātus, ūs** m charm.

**medicīna, ae** f a) the healing art, medicine; b) surgery; c) remedy, medicine.

**medicō** 1 to add drugs or poison to; to dye; to produce by drugs or charms.

**medicor** 1 to heal, cure (with dat.).

**medicus** 3 healing; subst. ~, ī m physician, surgeon.

**medietās, ātis** f the middle, mean.

**medimnum, ī** n (and **-us, ī** m) Greek bushel.

**mediocris, e** middling; a) moderate, inferior, inconsiderable; b) tolerable, ordinary.

**mediocritās, ātis** f the middle state; moderation; mean; mediocrity.

**medioxumus** 3 in the middle.

**meditāmentum, ī** n (and **-āmen, inis** n) preparation, practice.

**meditātiō, ōnis** f a thinking over, contemplation (with gen.); preparation, exercise.

**medi-terrāneus** 3 inland.

**meditor** 1 to think over, contemplate, reflect; to plan, design; to study, practise; **meditātus** 3 thought upon, considered, studied, devised, prepared.

**medius** 3 1. mid, mean, middle, in the middle, in the midst; (in) **mediō forō** in the midst of the Forum; **medium tempus** intervening time; **mediā nocte** at midnight; 2. standing between two extremities; a) middling, tolerable, common, moderate; b) neutral, undecided; ambiguous; c) mediating; 3. subst. **medium, ī** n the middle, the midst, the middle point, centre; a) the public, community, publicity, human society; b) common weal; **de medio tollere** to put out of the way; **de medio recedere** to go away; **in medio relinquere** to leave undecided; **in medio ponere** to place in the sight of all; **in medium proferre** to publish; **in medium procedere** to come forward, appear in public; **in medium vocare** to summon before the public; **in medium consulere** to care for the public good.

**mēdius fidius,** see fidius.

**medix tuticus** m the highest magistrate of the Oscans.

**medulla, ae** f marrow, the inmost part, kernel, heart.

**medullitus** adv. from the marrow, inwardly, heartily.

**medullula, ae** *f* soft marrow.

**mefitis,** *see* **mephitis.**

**megistānēs, um** *m/pl.* grandees, magnates.

**meherclē** (*and* **meherc(u)lēs**) *int.* by Hercules!

**mēiō, —, —** 3 to make water.

**mel, mellis** *n* honey; sweetness.

**melan-cholicus** 3 melancholy.

**melandryum, ī** *n* salted tunny-fish.

**melculum, ī** *n* little honey.

**melichrūs** (μελίχρους) honey-complexioned.

**melicus** 3 lyrical, melodious.

**meli-lōtos, ī** *m* sweet clover.

**meli-mēlum, ī** *n* sweet apple.

**Mēlinum, ī** *n* pipeclay.

**melior,** *comp. of* **bonus.**

**melisphyllum, ī** *n* balm.

**melius,** *see* **bonus.**

**meliusculus** 3 rather better.

**mell(in)a, ae** *f* mead; sweetness.

**melli-fer** 3 honey-bearing.

**mellilla, ae** *f* little honey.

**mellina, ae** *f* bag of marten-skin.

**mellitus** 3 sweet with honey; lovely, darling.

**melos** (*pl.* **melē**) *n* tune, song.

**membrāna, ae** *f* skin, membrane; parchment.

**membrānula, ae** *f* (thin) parchment.

**membrātim** *adv.* by pieces.

**membrum, ī** *n* limb, member; part, portion, division.

**mē-met,** *see* **met.**

**meminī, —, isse** to remember, recollect a) to think of (*with gen.* or *acc.*; *acc.c.inf.*); b) to make mention of, mention.

**memor, oris** 1. mindful, remembering (*gen.*); a) thankful; unrelenting, relentless; b) having a good memory; 2. recalling, mentioning.

**memorābilis, e** memorable, remarkable, famous.

**memorandus** 3 = **memorabilis.**

**memorātor, ōris** *m*, **-trix, īcis** *f* narrator.

**memorātus, ūs** *m* mention.

**memoria, ae** *f* memory; a) remembrance, recollection; **post hominum memoriam** since the memory of man; b) record, historical account; c) period of recollection, time; history.

**memoriālis, e** relating to memory.

**memoriola, ae** *f* memory.

**memoriter** *adv.* with a good memory.

**memorō** 1 to call to mind, mention, recount, relate (*alqd*).

**menda, ae** *f* = **mendum.**

**mendāci-loquus** 3 lying, mendacious.

**mendācium, ī** (*dimin.* **-iunculum**) *n* lie, untruth; fiction, falsehood.

**mendāx, ācis** given to lying, *m* a liar; a) false, deceptive; b) feigned, counterfeit.

**mendīcābulum, ī** *n* beggar (?).

**mendīcātiō, ōnis** *f* begging.

**mendīcitās, ātis** *f* beggary, pauperism.

**mendīcō** *and* **-or** 1 to beg, ask alms.

**mendīculus** 3 beggarly.

**mendīcus** 3 beggarly, needy; *subst.*
~ **ī** *m* beggar; poor, paltry, pitiful.

**mendōsus** 3 full of faults, faulty, incorrect; blundering.

**mendum, ī** *n* fault, error, blunder.

**mēns, tis** *f* mind, intellect, understanding; a) judgment, discernment; b) disposition, feeling, character, heart, soul; spirit, courage, boldness, passion, impulse; c) thought, idea, opinion; d) plan, purpose.

**mēnsa, ae** *f* table; a) meal, food, course; table; ~ **secunda** dessert; b) sacrificial table; c) counter of a money-changer.

**mēnsārius, ī** *m* banker; finance commissioner.

**mēnsiō, ōnis** *f* a measuring, measure.

**mēnsis, is** *m* month.

**mēnsor, ōris** *m* measurer, surveyor.

**mēnstruālis, e** monthly.

**mēnstruus** 3 monthly, lasting a month; *subst.* **-um, ī** *n* a month's provisions; monthly term of office.

**mēnsula, ae** *f* little table.

**mēnsūra, ae** *f* a measuring, measure, standard; extent, capacity, limit.

**ment(h)a, ae** *f* mint.

**mentiō, ōnis** *f* a calling to mind, mention; suggestion, hint.

**mentior, ītus sum** 4 a) to lie, be a liar, to invent; b) to assert falsely, feign; c) to fail in a promise, break one's word, deceive, cheat; **mentītus** 3 counterfeit, feigned.

**mentula, ae** *f* penis.

**mentum, ī** *n* chin.

**meō** 1 to go, pass.

**mephītis, is** *f* noxious vapour, malaria.

**merāc(u)lus** 3 unmixed, strong.

**merācus** 3 unmixed, pure.

**mercābilis, e** purchasable.

**mercātor, ōris** *m* a) trader, merchant; b) buyer.

**mercātōrius** 3 of a merchant.

**mercātūra, ae** *f* trade, commerce; goods.

**mercātus, ūs** *m* a) trade, traffic; b) market, fair.

**mercēdula, ae** *f* small wages; small rent.

**mercēn(n)ārius** 3 hired, serving for pay; paid, mercenary, bribed; *m* hireling, hired servant, mercenary.

**mercēs, ēdis** *f* reward, price, hire, pay; a) wages, fee, salary; b) punishment, injury; c) rent, revenue, income.

**mercimōnium, ī** *n* merchandise.

**mercor** 1 to trade, traffic, buy.

**merda, ae** *f* dung, excrement.

**merenda, ae** *f* afternoon meal.

**mereō** 2 *and* **mereor, ritus sum** 2 a) to deserve, merit; to earn, gain, acquire, obtain (*alqd*); **stipendia** to serve as a soldier; **equo** as a horse-soldier; b) to incur (*poenam, odium*); to deserve well *or* ill (*bene, male de alqo*); **merēns, tis** deserving, meriting; **meritus** 3 deserved, fit, just, right.

**meretrīcium, ī** *n* trade of a prostitute.

**meretrīcius** 3 relating to a harlot *or* prostitute.

**meretrīcula, ae** *f* prostitute, courtesan.

**meretrīx, īcis** *f* prostitute.

**mergae, ārum** *f/pl.* reaping-fork.

**merges, itis** *f* reaping-fork; forkful.

**mergō, rsī, rsum** 3 to dip in, immerse, plunge into water (*alqd in rem, in re*), sink, bury; a) to thrust *or* drive into; b) to cover, conceal, overwhelm.

**mergus, ī** *m* diver, gull.

**meridiānus** 3 of midday, of noon; southerly.                   [siesta.]

**merīdiātiō, ōnis** *f* midday-rest,]

**merīdiēs, ēī** *m* midday, noon; south.

**merīdiō** 1 to take a midday sleep.

**meritō[1]** 1 to earn, deserve.

**meritō[2]** *adv.* deservedly, justly.

**meritōrius** 3 earning money; hired, paid; *subst.* -ia *n/pl.* lodgings.

**meritum, ī** *n* desert; merit, worth; benefit, kindness, service; fault, offence.

**mero-bibus** 3 drinking unmixed wine.

**merops, opis** *m* bee-eater.

**mersō** 1, *intens. of* **mergo.**

**merula, ae** *f* a) blackbird; b) a fish.

**meruleus** 3 as black as a blackbird.

**merus** 3 unmixed, pure; a) nothing but, mere; b) genuine, unadulterated, true, real; *subst.*

**merum, ī** *n* unmixed wine.

**merx, cis** (*nomin. also* **mers**) *f* goods, merchandise.

**meso-chorus, ī** *m* leader of a claque; hired applauder.

**messis, is** *f* harvest, gathering; a) harvest-time; b) crops.

**messor, ōris** *m* mower, reaper.

**messōrius, ** 3 of a reaper.

**met** (*enclitic suffix*) self, own.

**mēta, ae** *f* a) turning post, goal; b) end, extremity; c) turning point, critical point.

**metalli-fer** 3 productive of *or* rich in metals.

**metallum, ī** *n* metal; mine.

**meta-morphōsis, is** *f* transformation.

**mētātor, ōris** *m* measurer.

**mētior, mēnsus sum** 4 to measure; a) to measure out, distribute (*alci alqd*); b) to pass over, traverse; c) to estimate, value (*alqd re*).

**metō, (messui,) messum** 3 to reap, mow; a) to gather, collect, harvest; b) to cut down, destroy.

**metōpo-scopus, ī** *m* forehead-inspector, soothsayer.

**mētor** (*and* **mētō**) 1 to measure out, mark out, lay out.

**metrēta, ae** *f* a Greek measure (8—9 gallons).

**metrum, ī** *n* metre.

**metūculōsus** 3 a) afraid; b) frightening.

**mētula, ae** *f* little conical pillar.

**metuō, uī, — 3** to fear (*alci, de re, alqd; ne, ne non, ut*).

**metus, ūs** *m* fear, apprehension, dread, anxiety.

**meus** 3 my, mine, my own, my dear; *pl.* **mei** my friends, relations, adherents, followers.

mĭca, ae *f* grain, crumb, bit.

mĭcō, cuī, — 1 a) to quiver, shake, tremble, beat, palpitate; b) to sparkle, shine, flicker, flash; c) (*digitis*) to hold up a number of the fingers for a moment and challenge someone to say how many fingers are raised (*a game, used also as a method of casting lots*).

micturĭō 4 to want to make water.

migrātĭō, ōnis *f* removal, migration; change of meaning.

migrō 1 a) to remove, depart, emigrate (*ab, ex, de re in* or *ad alqd*); b) *trans.* to transport; to transgress.

mīles, itis *m* (*f*) soldier; a) foot-soldier, common soldier; b) soldiery, army; c) piece on a game board; d) follower.

mīlia, mīliārius, mīliēs, *see* mill...

mīlitāris, e of a soldier, of war, military; warlike, martial; res mīlitāris (art of) warfare.

mīlitārius 3 military.

mīlitia, ae *f* military service, warfare; a) war, expedition; b) soldiers, militia.

mīlitō 1 to perform military service, be a soldier.

milium, ī *n* millet.

mīlle *indecl.* (*pl.* mīlia, ium) *n* a thousand; innumerable; mīlle (passuum) a mile.

millēsimus 3 the thousandth.

milliārius 3 containing a thousand; *subst.* mīlliārium, ī *n* mile-stone, mile.

millĭē(n)s *adv.* a thousand times.

mīluīnus (mīlvīnus) 3 resembling a kite; rapacious.

mīluus (mīlvus) ī *m* (*and f*) a) bird of prey, kite; b) a fish of prey.

mīma, ae *f* mime actress.

mīmiambī, ōrum *m/pl.* mimic verse in iambics.

mīmicus 3 farcical; *adv.* -cē like a mime-actor.

mīmula, ae *f dim. of* mima.

mīmus, ī *m* a) mime-actor; b) mime, farce.

mina, ae *f* a mina (*Greek money,* 100 *denarii*).

mināciae, ārum *f/pl.* threats.

minae, ārum *f/pl.* a) pinnacles; b) threats, menaces.

mĭnanter *adv.* threateningly.

mĭnātĭō, ōnis *f* a threatening.

mĭnāx, ācis a) overhanging; b) threatening.

mĭneō 2 to project.

mingō, nxī, (n)ctum 3 to make water.

mĭniāt(ul)us 3 coloured red.

mĭnimus 3, *superl. of* parvus; mĭnimē *superl.* of parum.

mĭnister, trī *m* attendant, servant; helper, assistant, agent, accomplice.

mĭnisterium, ī *n* a) attendance, service, employment, office; b) suite, train, helpers.

mĭnistra, ae, *fem. of* minister.

mĭnistrātōr, ōris *m* attendant, helper.

mĭnistrātōrius 3 for servants' use.

mĭnistrātrīx, īcis *f* female attendant.

mĭnistrō 1 to attend, wait upon, serve (*wine*); a) to furnish, supply, provide (*alci alqd*); b) to execute, carry out.

mĭnitābundus 3 threatening.

mĭnitor (*and* -ō) 1, *intens. of* minor¹.

mĭnium, ī *n* red lead, vermilion.

mĭnor¹ 1 a) to project, overhang; b) to threaten (*alci alqd, alqa re; acc.c.inf. fut.*).

mĭnor², us, *comp. of* parvus; minus *comp.* of parum.

mĭnuō, uī, ūtum 3 a) to make smaller, lessen, diminish; P. to grow less, decrease; b) to reduce, weaken, abate, break.

mĭnusculus 3 rather little.

mĭnūtal, ālis *n* minced food.

mĭnūtātim *adv.* little by little, bit by bit, gradually.

mĭnūtia, ae *f* fineness.

mĭnūtŭlus 3, *dim. of* minutus.

mĭnūtus 3 diminished; little, small, minute, trifling; res mĭnūtae trifles.

mīrābilis, e a) wonderful, marvellous; admirable; b) extraordinary, strange, singular.

mīrābundus 3 astonished.

mīrācula, ae *f* monstrosity.

mīrāculum, ī *n* wonder, marvel, miracle; wonderful thing.

mīrandus 3 wonderful.

mīrātĭō, ōnis *f* wonder, admiration.

mīrātor, ōris *m and* -trīx, īcis *f* admirer.

mīri-ficus 3 = mirabilis.

mīri-modīs wonderfully.

**mirmillō, ōnis** *m* gladiator with Gallic arms.

**mīror** (*and* **-ō**) 1 a) to wonder at; b) to admire, esteem.

**mīrus** 3 = **mirabilis**.

**mis = mei** (*gen.*).

**miscellānea, ōrum** *n/pl.* hashed food.

**miscellus** 3 mixed.

**misceō, cuī, xtum (stum)** 2 to mix, mingle, intermingle (*alqd re, cum re, alci rei*); a) to join, unite; b) to disturb, confound, throw into confusion.

**misellus** 3, *dim. of* **miser**.

**miser, era, erum** wretched, unfortunate, poor; a) pitiable, lamentable; b) worthless.

**miserābilis, e** pitiable, miserable, wretched; plaintive.

**miserandus** 3 = **miserabilis**.

**miserātiō, ōnis** *f* pity, compassion; pathetic speech.

**misereor** (rarely **-eō**), ritus sum 2 to feel pity *or* compassion, to commiserate (*gen.*).

**miserēscō, —, —** 3 = **misereor**.

**miseret** (*and* **-ētur**, rarely **-ēscit**), **-itum est** *me alcis* I feel pity for.

**miseria, ae** *f* wretchedness, misery, misfortune, distress.

**misericordia, ae** *f* compassion, sympathy, mercy.

**miseri-cors, dis** pitiful, compassionate, merciful.

**miseror** 1 to lament; to pity.

**missīcius** 3 discharged.

**missiculō** 1 to send often.

**missilis, e** that may be thrown, missile; *subst.* **missile, is** *n* missile, javelin.

**missiō, ōnis** *f* a sending away; a) release; b) discharge from service; c) quarter; d) cessation.

**missitō** 1 to send repeatedly.

**missus, ūs** *m* a sending, dispatching; throwing; bow-shot; round *or* heat (in a race).

**mitella, ae** *f*, *dim. of* **mitra**.

**mitellītus** 3 wearing a *mitella*; **-a cena** dinner at which *mitellae* were provided for guests.

**mītēscō** *and* **-īscō, —, —** 3 to grow mild, soft, gentle, ripe.

**mīti-ficō** 1 to make mild; to ripen; to digest.

**mīti-ficus** 3 gentle.

**mītigātiō, ōnis** *f* an assuaging, soothing, appeasing.

**mitigō** 1 to soften; a) to make mild, tender, soft; b) to soothe, assuage, appease.

**mītis, e** mild; a) mellow, ripe, soft; b) gentle, kind.

**mitra, ae** *f* head-band, turban.

**mitrātus** 3 wearing a *mitra*.

**mitto, mīsī, missum** 3 to send; a) to throw, hurl, cast; b) to send, cause to go; **sub iugum** under the yoke; **ad alqm** *or* **alci** to send word, send orders; **librum ad alqm** to dedicate; c) to yield, produce, furnish; to let out, put forth, emit, utter; d) to let go, drop, release, dismiss; to forgo, omit, pass over; to forget, put away.

**mītulus, ī** *m* mussel.

**mixtim** in combination.

**mixtūra, ae** *f* blending.

**mnēmosynum, ī** *n* keepsake.

**mōbilis, e** movable, quick; a) pliant, pliable, excitable; b) changeable, inconstant.

**mōbilitās, ātis** *f* movableness, mobility; a) agility, quickness; b) changeableness, fickleness.

**mōbilitō** 1 to impart motion to.

**moderābilis, e** moderate.

**moderāmen, inis** *n* a) rudder, helm; b) government.

**moderanter** with control.

**moderātim** gradually.

**moderātiō, ōnis** *f* guidance, government; moderation; self-control, temperance.

**moderātor, ōris** *m* manager, governor, ruler, controller.

**moderātrix, īcis** *f* controller.

**moderātus** 3 a) moderate, temperate; b) within bounds, restrained.

**moderor** (*and* **-ō**) 1 a) to set bounds, restrain, to limit (*with dat.*); b) to govern, regulate, manage, direct.

**modestia, ae** *f* moderation; a) discretion, sobriety; b) unassuming behaviour, shyness, modesty; c) obedience, subordination; d) correctness of conduct, propriety.

**modestus** 3 moderate, keeping within bounds; a) calm, gentle; b) modest, forbearing; c) sober, discreet, orderly, virtuous.

**modiālis, e** containing a *modius*.

**modicus** 3 moderate; a) middling, small, mean, scanty; b) calm, temperate; c) unpretending.

**modi-ficātiō, ōnis** *f* measuring, scansion (*of verse*).

**modi-ficō** 1 to measure off.

**modius, ī** *m* (*a measure, about 2 gallons*).

**modo** (*and* **modō**) **1.** *adv.* only, but; **non modo ... sed etiam** not only ... but also; **non modo (non) ... sed ne ... quidem** not only not ... but not even; **2.** *with subj.* if only, provided that; **modo ne** provided that not; **3.** (*of time*) now, but now, just now, lately; presently; **modo ... modo** now ... now, sometimes ... sometimes.

**modulātor, ōris** *m* musician.

**modulātus**[1] 3 musical.

**modulātus**[2], **ūs** *m* playing, music.

**modulor** 1 to measure rhythmically, to modulate, sing, play.

**modulus, ī** *m* measure.

**modus, ī** *m* measure, standard measure; a) size, extent, quantity; b) time, rhythm, metre, melody; c) bound, limit; d) moderation, due measure; e) way, manner; **modo, in modum, ad modum** in the manner of; **nullo modo** by no means; **mirum in modum** wonderfully; **quodam modo** in a certain manner, somehow; **huius (eius) modi** of this *or* that kind.

**moecha, ae** *f* adulteress.

**moechissō** 1 to seduce.

**moechor** 1 to commit adultery.

**moechus, ī** *m* fornicator, adulterer.

**moenerō** = **munero**.

**moenia**[1], **ium** *n/pl.* defensive walls, city-walls, bulwarks, ramparts, fortifications; a) city enclosed by walls; b) the buildings of a city.

**moenia**[2], **ium** *n/pl.* = **munia**.

**moenimentum** = **munimentum**.

**mola, ae** *f* a) millstone, grindstone; *pl.* mill; b) spelt coarsely ground and mixed with salt.

**molāris, is** *m* a) millstone; b) molar tooth.

**mōlēs, is** *f* huge, heavy mass, bulk; a) massive structure *or* apparatus, colossus, large building; b) dam, pier, mole, foundation; c) great quantity, multitude; weight, power; d) difficulty, labour, trouble.

**molestia, ae** *f* molestation, trouble; a) annoyance, vexation; b) affectation.

**molestus** 3 burdensome, troublesome, grieving, annoying; stiff, affected.

**mōlimen, inis** *and* **mōlimentum, ī** *n* a) exertion, effort; b) weight, importance.

**mōlior** 4 **1.** to set in motion, displace, remove (*alqd*); a) to hurl, weigh (*anchor*), wield; b) to set about, attempt (any thing difficult *or* laborious); to build, make, cause; c) to undertake, devise; **2.** to toil, exert oneself.

**mōlitiō, ōnis** *f* a) a removing, demolishing; b) a making (with labour).

**mōlitor, ōris** *m* builder, contriver, author.

**mōlitrix, īcis** *f* she who contrives.

**mollēscō, —, —** 3 to become soft, effeminate.

**molliculus** 3 rather soft *or* voluptuous.

**mollimentum, ī** *n* means of mitigation.

**molliō** 4 to soften, make pliant *or* supple; a) to mitigate, moderate; b) to render effeminate.

**molli-pēs, pedis** soft-footed.

**mollis, e** soft, impressionable; a) pliant, flexible, supple; b) mild, tender, delicate; c) quiet, calm, gentle; d) movable, fickle; e) effeminate, unmanly, weak; f) amatory, voluptuous.

**mollitia, ae** *f and* **mollitiēs, ēī** *f* softness; a) pliability, flexibility; b) tenderness, gentleness, mildness; c) weakness, effeminacy, voluptuousness.

**mollitūdō, inis** *f* = **mollitia**.

**molō, uī, itum** 3 to grind.

**molocinārius, ī** *m* dyer of mauve-coloured garments.

**mōly, yos** *n* a magic herb.

**mōmen, inis** *n* a) momentum; b) moving mass.

**mōmentum, ī** *n* **1.** moving power; a) weight; b) that which turns the scales; influence, impulse; cause, circumstance, importance, turning point; **2.** motion; a) alteration; b) moment, minute, instant; c) period.

**mon-aulos, ī** *m* single flute.

monēdula, ae *f* daw, jackdaw.

moneō, uī, itum 2 to remind, admonish (*alqm de re* or *gen.*); a) to warn; exhort, advise; b) to teach, instruct, punish; c) to announce, predict, foretell.

monēris, is *f* galley with one bank of oars.

monērula = monēdula.

monēta, ae *f* a) mint; b) coined money, coin; c) stamp, die.

monētālis, e of *or* relating to the mint; *subst. m* mint-master.

monetrīx, īcis *f* instructress.

monīle, is *n* necklace.

monimentum, ī *n* = monumentum.

monitiō, ōnis *f* a warning, admonition, advice.

monitor, ōris *m* admonisher, reminder; prompter; teacher.

monitum, ī *n* admonition, advice; prophecy.

monitus, ūs *m* = monitum.

mono-grammus 3 outlined, sketched.

mono-podium, ī *n* table with one foot.

mono-pōlium, ī *n* monopoly.

mono-tropus, ī *m* all alone.

mōns, tis *m* mountain, mount, range of mountains; rock.

mōnstrābilis, e remarkable.

mōnstrātiō, ōnis *f* a showing.

mōnstrātor, ōris *m* shower, pointer out, introducer, inventor.

mōnstrātus 3 distinguished, conspicuous.

mōnstri-fer 3 producing monsters.

mōnstri-ficus 3 working wonders, magic.

mōnstrō 1 to show, point out (*alci alqd*); a) to ordain, appoint, indicate; b) to inform against.

mōnstrōsus 3 = monstruosus.

mōnstrum, ī *n* omen; a) monster, monstrosity; b) miracle.

mōnstruōsus 3 wonderful, monstrous.

montānus 3 belonging to a mountain, of a mountain, mountainous; *subst. ~, ī m* mountain dweller.

monti-cola, ae *m* mountain dweller.

monti-fer 3 bearing (*i. e.* buried under) mountains.

monti-vagus 3 wandering over the mountains.

mont(u)ōsus 3 mountainous.

monumentum, ī *n* remembrance, a) memorial, monument; statue; memorial offering, sepulchre, tomb; b) tradition, chronicle, record.

mora¹, ae *f* division of Spartan infantry, battalion.

mora², ae *f* delay, procrastination; a) pause on a march; b) space of time; c) obstruction, hindrance.

mōrālis, e of morals, moral.

morātor, ōris *m* delayer, loiterer.

mōrātus 3 a) mannered, constituted; b) characteristic, expressive of character.

morbidus 3 unhealthy.

morbōsus 3 diseased, morbid.

morbus, ī *m* sickness, disease; distress.

mordāx, ācis biting; stinging, sharp, piercing.

mordeō, momordī, morsum 2 to bite, chew; a) to gnaw at; b) to clasp, take hold of; e) to indent, wash away; d) to bite, pain, hurt.

mordicibus *abl.* with bites (?).

mordicus *adv.* a) by biting, with the teeth; b) tenaciously.

mōrē *adv.* foolishly.

morētum, ī *n* a rustic dish, salad.

moribundus 3 dying; mortal.

mōri-geror (*or* -ō) 1 to comply with, humour (*alci*).

mōri-gerus 3 complying.

mōriō, ōnis *m* fool, jester.

morior, mortuus sum 3 to die; mortuus 3 dead, dead person; to die away, die out, decay, pass away.

mōro-logus 3 foolish.

moror¹ 1 a) to stay, delay, (*trans.* and *intr.*), to linger, loiter; b) to hold the attention of; to hinder; nihil moror I have nothing to say to, I do not heed, I do not care for.

moror² 1 to be a fool.

mōrōsitās, ātis *f* peevishness, fretfulness, morosity.

mōrōsus 3 peevish, fretful, fastidious, morose, stubborn.

mors, tis *f* death; a) mode of death; b) dead body, corpse.

morsa, ōrum *n/pl.* small pieces.

morsiuncula, ae *f* a biting of the lips.

morsus, ūs *m* a biting, bite; a) an eating, corrosion; b) a seizing, holding; c) malicious attack; d) sting, pain, vexation.

**mortālis, e** mortal; *subst. m* man, mortal, human being; **a)** temporary, transient; **b)** earthly, human; **mortālia, ium** *n/pl.* human affairs.

**mortālitās, ātis** *f* mortality; **a)** mortal destiny; **b)** mortals.

**mortārium, ī** *n* mortar.

**morticīnus 3** dead (*body*).

**morti-fer 3** death-bringing, deadly.

**mortuālia, ium** *n/pl.* funeral songs.

**mortuus 3,** *see* **morior.**

**mōrum, ī** *n* **a)** mulberry; **b)** blackberry.

**mōrus¹, ī** *f* mulberry-tree.

**mōrus² 3** foolish, silly.

**mōs, mōris** *m* habit, manner, custom, fashion; **a)** will, humour, precept, law; **mōrem gerere alci = morigerari; b)** quality, nature, mode, fashion; *pl.* conduct, behaviour, manners, morals, character.

**mōtiō, ōnis** *f* = **motus.**

**mōtiuncula, ae** *f* slight attack of fever.

**mōtō 1** to move about.

**mōtor, ōris** *m* one who moves *or* rocks.

**mōtus, ūs** *m* a moving; motion; **terrae** earth-quake; **a)** movement, change; **b)** gesticulation, dancing; **c)** evolution; **d)** impulse, gesture, passion, agitation, emotion; **e)** thought, inspiration; **f)** political movement, tumult, commotion.

**moveō, mōvī, mōtum 2** to move, set in motion; **1.** to stir, shake, disturb, remove; **arma** to take up arms; **se movēre** *and* **P.** to move *or* bestir oneself, to dance; **a)** to ponder; **b)** to change; **c)** to move, excite, affect, inspire, influence; **d)** to shake, cause to waver, to disturb, concern, trouble, torment; **e)** to occasion, cause, produce, begin; **2.** to remove, put out of its place (*alqd loco; re, de, ex, ab re in* or *ad alqd*); **castra movēre** to break up camp, march away; *intr.*, **se movēre** *or* **P.** to move from a place, betake oneself; to drive away, dislodge, expel.

**mox** *adv.* soon, directly, presently; then, thereupon.

**mūcidus 3 a)** running at the nose; **b)** mouldy.

**mūcrō, ōnis** *m* sharp point, edge; sword; sharpness.

**mūcus, ī** *m* nasal mucus.

**mūgil(is), is** *m* mullet.

**mūginor 1** to dally, hesitate.

**mūgiō 4** to low, bellow; to sound, roar.

**mūgītor, ōris** *m* bellower.

**mūgītus, ūs** *m* a lowing, bellowing; roaring.

**mūla, ae** *f* she-mule.

**mulceō, sī, sum 2** to stroke, touch lightly; **a)** to soothe, appease, soften; **b)** to charm, delight, caress.

**Mulciber, eris** *and* **erī** *m* Vulcan; fire.

**mulcō 1** to beat, cudgel, maltreat.

**mulctra, ae** *f and* **-trum, ī** *n and* **mulctrārium, ī** *n* milk-pail.

**mulgeō, lsī, — 2** to milk.

**muliebris, e a)** of a woman, womanly, feminine; **b)** womanish, effeminate.

**mulier, eris** *f* woman, female, wife.

**mulierārius 3** of a woman.

**muliercula, ae** *f* (weak) woman.

**mulierōsitās, ātis** *f* passionate love of women.

**mulierōsus 3** fond of women.

**mūlīnus 3** mulish.

**mūliō, ōnis** *m* muleteer.

**mūliōnius 3** of a muleteer.

**mullus, ī** *m* red mullet.

**mulsus 3** honey-sweet; *subst.* **mulsum, ī** *n* honey-wine.

**multa, ae** *f* penalty, fine, loss.

**mult-angulus 3** having many angles.

**multātīcius 3** accruing from fines.

**multātiō, ōnis** *f* penalty, fine.

**multēsimus 3** very small, trifling.

**multi-bibus 3** fond of drinking.

**multi-cavus 3** many-holed, porous.

**multicia, -ōrum** *n/pl.* fine-spun garments.

**multifāriam** *adv.* in many places.

**multi-fidus 3** (much) split.

**multi-fōrmis, e** multiform, manifold.

**multi-forus 3** pierced with many holes.

**multi-generis, e** *and* **multi-genus 3** of many kinds.

**multi-iugus 3** *and* **-gis, e** (yoked) many together.

**multi-loquium, ī** *n* much talk.

**multi-loquos 3** talkative.

**multi-modīs** *adv.* in many ways, variously.

**multi-plex, icis** having many folds *or* windings; **a)** manifold; **b)** numerous, various; **c)** many times as large; **d)** many-sided; versatile, changeable.

**multiplicābilis, e** manifold.

**multiplicātiō, ōnis** *f* a multiplying.

**multiplicō** 1 to multiply, increase.

**multi-potēns, tis** very mighty.

**multi-sonus** 3 loud sounding.

**multitūdō, inis** *f* large number, multitude; crowd, mob.

**multi-vagus** 3 wandering much.

**multi-volus** 3 desiring much.

**multō** 1 to punish.

**multum** 1. *as subst. n* a great part, much; *abl.* **multō** by much, by far, a great deal; 2. *adv.* much, very much, greatly, often, frequently, far; 3. *comp.* **plūs, plūris** *n* more, a greater part; a) **plūris** of more value, at a higher price; b) *adv.* **plūs** more, in a higher degree; 4. *superl.* **plūrimum, ī** *n* very much, a great deal, most; a) *gen.* **plūrimī** of the greatest value or importance; at a very high price; b) *adv.* **plūrimum** very much, for the most part.

**multus** 3 1. much, many, numerous; **multī, ōrum** *m/pl.* many, the multitude, common people; **multa, ōrum** *n/pl.* many things; a) considerable, abundant, extensive, vigorous, zealous; b) far advanced (*multa nocte*); c) copious; 2. *comp.* **plūrēs, a** more, in greater number; 3. *superl.* **plūrimus** 3 very much, very many, most.

**mūlus, ī** *m* mule.

**mundānus, ī** *m* citizen of the world, cosmopolitan.

**munditia, ae** (*and* **-tiēs, ēī**) *f* a) cleanliness, cleanness; b) neatness, elegance.

**mundulus** 3 neat, elegant.

**mundus**[1] 3 a) clean, cleanly; b) nice, neat, elegant, fine, genteel; *adv.* **-ē** *and* **-iter; in mundō** prepared, in readiness.

**mundus**[2] **, ī** *m* a) toilet-outfit; b) the universe, the world; c) mankind.

**mūnerārius, ī** *m* arranger of public games. [ents.]

**mūneri-gerulus** 3 carrying pres-│ (**mūnerō** *and*) **mūneror** 1 to reward, bestow, present.

**mūnia** *n/pl.* duties, functions.

**mūni-ceps, cipis** *m* (*and f*) citizen of a *municipium* or free town; fellow-citizen.

**mūnicipālis, e** belonging to a *municipium*, provincial.

**mūnicipātim** by *municipia*.

**mūnicipium, ī** *n* self-governing town (*esp.* in Italy).

**mūnificentia, ae** *f* liberality, bountifulness.

**mūni-ficō** 1 to present.

**mūni-ficus** 3 liberal, bountiful.

(**mūnimen, inis** *and*) **mūnimentum, ī** *n* a) defence; b) fortification.

**mūniō** 4 to wall, wall round; a) to build with walls; b) to fortify, defend, secure; c) (*viam*) to build *or* pave.

**mūnis, e** ready to serve.

**mūnitiō, ōnis** *f* a fortifying, entrenching; a) paving of roads; b) fortification, rampart.

**mūnitō** 1 to pave, make passable (*viam*).

**mūnitor, ōris** *m* fortifier, engineer, sapper.

**mūnitus** 3 fortified, protected.

**mūnus, eris** *n* a) duty, office, function; b) service, favour; the last service (*burial*); c) present, gift; public show.

**mūnusculum, ī** *n* small gift.

**mūraena, ae,** *f* = **murena**.

**mūrālis, e** of a wall, mural.

**mūrēna, ae** *f* (*a sea-fish*) muræna.

**mūrex, icis** *m* a) purple-fish; b) purple dye; c) projecting rock; d) spiked trap.

**muria, ae** *f* brine, pickle.

**muriāticum, ī** *n* pickled fish.

**mūri-cīdus, ī** *m* mouse-killer, coward.

**murmillō, ōnis** *m* = **mirmillo**.

**murmur, uris** *n* murmur, a murmuring, humming, buzzing, roaring, crashing, sounding.

**murmurātiō, ōnis** *f* murmuring.

**murmurillum, ī** *n* = **murmur**.

**murmurō** 1 to murmur, mutter, roar.

**murra, ae** *f* 1. myrrh-tree, myrrh; 2. fluor-spar.

**murreus** 3 1. myrrh-coloured (pale yellow); perfumed with myrrh; 2. of fluor-spar.

**murrinus** 3 = **murreus; murrina, ae** *f* wine flavoured with myrrh.

**murtētum, ī** *n* grove of myrtles.

**murteus** 3 of myrtle; adorned with myrtle (*or* as dark as myrtle).

**murtum, ī** *n* myrtle-berry.
**murtus, ī** (*and* **ūs**) *f* myrtle; spear of myrtle-wood.
**mūrus, ī** *m* wall, rim; protection, defence.
**mūs, mūris** *m* mouse, rat.
**Mūsa, ae** *f* a muse; song, poem, poetry, sciences.
**musca, ae** *f* a fly; intruder.
**muscārium, ī** *n* fly-brush (also used as a clothes-brush).
**mūs-cipula, ae** *f and* **-um, ī** *n* mouse-trap.
**muscōsus** 3 mossy.
**mūsculus, ī** *m* a little mouse; a) muscle; b) shed; c) mussel.
**mūscus, ī** *m* moss.
**mūsica, ae** *f* (*or* **-cē, ēs** *f*) *and* **mūsica, ōrum** *n/pl.* music; poetry; fine art.
**mūsicus** 3 belonging to the muses, to music, musical; *subst.* ~, **ī** *m* musician; **mūsicē** elegantly.
**mussitō** 1 = **musso** a), b).
**mussō** 1 a) to murmur, mutter, buzz; b) to bear in silence; c) to wonder *or* brood in silence.
**mustāceum, ī** *n* wedding-cake.
**mustēla, ae** *f* weasel.
**mustēlinus** 3 of a weasel.
**musteus** 3 must-like, quite new.
**mustum, ī** *n* must; vintage.
**mūtābilis, e** mutable, changeable.
**mūtābilitās, ātis** *f* mutability.
**mūtātiō, ōnis** *f* change, alteration; interchange.
**mūtātor, ōris** *m* one who changes *or* barters.
**mutilō** 1 to maim, mutilate.

**mutilus** 3 maimed, mutilated.
**mūtiō** 4, *see* **muttio.**
**mūtō**[1] 1 1. to move, remove, to move from its place; 2. to change, alter; **vestem mūtāre** to put on mourning; a) to exchange; b) to take in exchange (*alqd alqa re*).
**mūtō**[2], **ōnis** *m* penis; *hence* **mūtūniātus** 3.
**muttiō** 4 to mutter, mumble.
**muttitiō, -ōnis** *f* muttering.
**mūtuātiō, ōnis** *f* a borrowing.
**mūtuitō** 1 to seek to borrow.
**mūtuō,** *adv. of* **mutuus.**
**mūtuor** 1 to borrow; to obtain, get (*alqd ab alqo*).
**mūtus** 3 dumb, mute, speechless; silent, still.
**mūtuus** 3 borrowed; lent; a) mutual, reciprocal, on both sides; *subst.* **mūtuum, ī** *n* a) a return of like for like; b) loan.
**myo-parō, ōnis** *m* a pirate's vessel.
**myrica, ae** *f* tamarisk.
**myrmillō, ōnis** *m, see* **mirmillo.**
**myrobalanum, ī** *n* balsam.
**myro-pōla, ae** *m* perfume-dealer.
**myro-pōlium, ī** *n* perfumer's shop.
**myro-thēcium, ī** *n* unguent-box.
**myrrha, ae** *f* = **murra** (1).
**myrtum, myrtus** etc., *see* **murt...**
**myst-agōgus, ī** *m* a guide to mysteries *or* temples, cicerone.
**mystērium, ī** *n* secret, mystery; *pl.* **-ia, iōrum** secret rites *or* worship.
**mystēs, ae** *m* priest at the mysteries.
**mysticus** 3 mystic, secret.
**myxa, ae** *f* curved spout of a lamp; lamp-wick.

# N

**nablium, ī** *n* lute, mandolin.
**nae** *int.* = **nē¹.**
**naenia, ae** *f, see* **nenia.**
**naevus, ī** *m* birth-mark, mole.
**Nāias, adis** *and* **Nāis, idis** *f* water-nymph, Naiad.
**nam** *cj.* for, for instance; *as enclitic with an interrogative:* **quisnam** who?; **ubinam** where?
**nam-que** *cj.* = **nam.**
**nancīscor, nactus** *and* **nanctus sum** 3 to light (up)on, meet with, find, get, obtain, incur.
**nānus, ī** *m* dwarf.
**Napaeae, -ārum** *f/pl.* nymphs of woodland valleys.
**nāpus, ī** *m* swede.
**narcissus, ī** *m* narcissus, daffodil.
**nardinum, ī** *n* nard-wine.
**nardum, ī** *n and* **nardus, ī** *f* nard, nard-oil.
**nāris, is** *f* nostril, *pl.* the nose; perception, sagacity.
**nārrābilis, e** that can be told *or* related.                    [ing, relating.]
**nārrātiō, ōnis** *f* a telling, narrat-
**nārrātiuncula, ae** *f* anecdote.
**nārrātor, ōris** *m* relater, narrator.
**nārrātus, ūs** *m* narration, narrative.
**nārrō** 1 **a)** to tell, narrate, relate; **b)** to say, mention.
**narthēcium, ī** *n* ointment-box.
**nārus** 3 = **gnarus.**
**nāscor, nātus sum** 3 to be born, be produced, (*abl.; ex alqo*); **a)** to spring from, proceed, rise (*ab, ex re*); **ex hoc nāscitur, ut** hence it follows that; **b)** to grow, be found; — **nātus** 3 born (*abl.; ex alqo*); **a)** destined, designed, intended (*dat.; ad* or *in alqd*); **b)** constituted by nature, fitted; **c)** (*with an expression of time*) old; *subst. m* son, *f* daughter, *pl. m* children, young ones.
**nassa, ae** *f* trap, net, snare.
**nassiterna, ae** *f* watering-pot.
**nāsturtium** *or* **-cium, ī** *n* cress.
**nāsus, ī** *m* (*and* **-um** *n*) nose; sense of smell, perception.
**nāsūtus** 3 large-nosed; sarcastic.

**nāta, ae** *f* daughter.
**nātālicius** 3 relating to a birthday; *subst.* **-ia, ae** *f* birthday entertainment.
**nātālis, e** pertaining to birth, of birth; **dies** *or subst. m* birthday; *pl.* origin, family.
**natātiō, ōnis** *f,* **natātus, ūs** *m* swimming.
**natātor, ōris** *m* swimmer.
**nātiō, ōnis** *f* 1. birth; 2. **a)** nation, people; **b)** race, species, class, set, kind, breed.
**natis, is** *f* (*usu. pl.*) buttocks.
**nātivus** 3 born; inborn, innate, natural.
**natō** 1 to swim, float; **a)** to be flooded, be full of; **b)** to fluctuate, waver.
**natrix, icis** *f* (*and m*) water-snake.
**nātūra, ae** *f* 1. birth; 2. nature; **a)** natural quality, constitution; disposition, character, inclination, bent, temper; **b)** human nature; **c)** the order of the world, course of things, laws of nature; **d)** the world, universe; **e)** element, substance, essence; **f)** organ of generation.
**nātūrālis, e** natural, by birth; **a)** produced by nature, according to nature; **b)** relating to nature.
(**nātus, ūs** *m* birth, age); **magnus** *or* **grandis nātū** old, aged; **minimus nātū** the youngest.
**nau-archus, ī** *m* captain of a vessel.
**nauclēricus** 3 belonging to a skipper.
**nau-clērus, ī** *m* skipper.
**naucula** = **navicula.**
**nauculor** 1 to sail.
(**naucum** *n*); **non nauci esse** to be of no value.
**nau-fragium, ī** *n* shipwreck; **a)** storm; **b)** ruin, loss; **c)** remnants, remains.
**nau-fragus** 3 **a)** shipwrecked, wrecked; ruined; **b)** causing shipwreck.
**naulum, ī** *n* passage-money.
**nau-machia, ae** *f* mock sea-fight; place in which such fights were held.

**naumachiārii, ōrum** *m/pl.* fighters in a mock naval battle.

**nausea, ae** *f* sea-sickness, vomiting, nausea.

**nauseō 1 a)** to be sea-sick, to vomit **b)** to cause disgust.

**nauseola, ae** *f* squeamishness.

**nausia, ae** *f* = **nausea**.

**nausiābundus 3** sea-sick, bilious.

**nausiātor, ōris** *m* one subject to sea-sickness.

**nauta, ae** *m* **a)** sailor, seaman, mariner; **b)** trader, merchant, ship-owner; **c)** passenger.

**nautea, ae** *f* a stinking liquid.

**nauticus 3** nautical, naval; *subst. m* = **nauta**.

**nāvālis, e** relating to ships, nautical, naval; **socii nāvālēs** seamen, marines; *subst.* **nāvāle, is** *n* a) station for ships, harbour; **b)** *pl.* dockyard, tackling, rigging.

**nāvicula, ae** *f* little ship, boat.

**nāviculāria, ae** *f* business of shipping.

**nāviculārius, ī** *m* ship-owner.

**nāvi-fragus 3** causing shipwreck.

**nāvigābilis, e** navigable.

**nāvigātiō, ōnis** *f* a sailing, navigation, voyage.

**nāvi-ger 3** bearing ships.

**nāvigiolum, ī** *n* = **navicula**.

**nāvigium, ī** *n* vessel, ship.

**nāvigō 1 a)** to sail, voyage, cruise; **b)** to sail over *or* through (*alqd*), to navigate; **c)** to earn by navigation.

**nāvis, is** *f* vessel, ship; boat; ~ **longa** man-of-war, ~ **onerāria** transport-ship.

**nāvita, ae** *m* = **nauta**.

**nāvitās, ātis** *f* assiduity, zeal.

**nāviter,** *adv. of* **navus.**

**nāvō 1** to do zealously, assiduously, diligently; **operam nāvāre alci** to render assistance; to accomplish, effect (*alqd in alqm*).

**nāvus 3** active, busy, diligent, assiduous.

**nē[1]** *int.* verily, truly.

**-ne[2]** *interrog. particle:* **1.** *in simple direct or indirect questions* (*sometimes* = **nonne**), **videsne, videmusne** do you (we) see?; do you not see?; **2.** *in compound questions* (*direct or indirect*): **-ne ... an** = **utrum ... an; nec-ne** or not.

**nē[3]** *particle of negation and cj.;* **1. nē ... quidem** noteven; **2.** *with* *subj.* (*or imperat.*) *to express a negative desire, purpose, command, etc.:* not, that not, lest, so that not.

**nebris, idis** *f* fawn-skin worn by worshippers of Bacchus.

**nebula, ae** *f* mist, cloud; smoke.

**nebulō, ōnis** *m* paltry, worthless fellow; idler.

**nebulōsus 3** misty, foggy, cloudy.

**nec** *and* **neque 1.** = **non; 2.** and not, nor, neither; **neque quisquam** and no one, **neque umquam** and never; **neque vero** and indeed not; **neque enim** for not; **neque tamen** and yet not; **nec-nōn** and besides; **neque aut ... aut** and neither ... nor; **nec ... nec, neque ... neque** neither ... nor; **nec-ne** or not.

**nec-dum** *adv.* and not yet.

**necessāriō** *and* **-ē** *adv.* necessarily.

**necessārius 3** necessary; **a)** indispensable; **b)** unavoidable, inevitable; **c)** pressing, compulsory, essential; **d)** connected, related; *subst.* ~, **ī** *m* relation, kinsman, friend.

**necesse** (*and* **-sum**) **esse** to be necessary, indispensable, inevitable (*with inf., acc. c. inf., dat. c. inf., subj.; ut*); ~ **habēre** to consider necessary.

**necessitās, ātis** *f* necessity; **a)** inevitableness; **b)** compulsion, force, exigency; **c)** fate, destiny; **d)** need, poverty, want; *pl.* necessaries, necessary expenses; **e)** connection, relationship, friendship.

**necessitūdō, inis** *f* **1.** necessity, compulsion, want, need, distress; **2.** close connection, relationship, friendship; relations, friends.

**necessum** (*obsolete*) = **necesse**.

**nec-ne** or not.

**nec-nōn** (*see* **nec**).

**necō 1** to kill, slay.

**nec-opīnāns, tis** not expecting, unaware.

**nec-opīnātus 3** unexpected; *adv.* **-ō**.

**nec-opīnus 3** not expecting; unexpected.

**nectar, aris** *n* nectar, drink of the gods.

**nectareus 3** of nectar; delicious.

**nectō, nex(u)ī, nexum 3** to tie, bind, fasten, connect (*alqd re*), weave together; **a)** to fetter, confine; **b)** to attach (*alqd ex re*); **c)** to devise; *subst.* **nexus, ī** *m* prisoner for debt; **nexum, ī** *n* personal obligation, voluntary assignment of the person for debt.

**në-cubi** *cj.* with *subj.* lest anywhere.

**në-cunde** *cj.* with *subj.* lest from anywhere.

**në-dum 1.** *cj.* with *subj.* much less, still less, not to speak of; **2.** *adv.* not to say, much more.

**ne-fandus** = **nefarius**.

**ne-fārius 3** abominable, impious, execrable; *subst.* **-ium, ī** *n* = **nefas.**

**ne-fās** *n* (*indecl.*, only *nom.* and *acc. sg.*) unlawful, criminal, sinful thing; abominable wretch.

**ne-fāstus 3 1.** forbidden, unholy; **2.** a) unlucky, inauspicious; b) sinful, profane, wicked.

**negantia, ae** *f* negation.

**negātiō, ōnis** *f* a denying, negation.

**negitō 1** to persist in denying.

**neglēctiō, ōnis** *f*, **neglēctus, ūs** *m* a neglecting, neglect.

**neglēctus 3** *and* **neglegēns, tis,** *see* **neglego.**

**neglegentia, ae** *f* a) carelessness, negligence; b) coldness, disrespect.

**neg-legō, lēxī, lēctum 3** to neglect, disregard, slight, take no heed of; a) to despise, contemn; b) to overlook, pass over; **neglegēns, tis** negligent, careless, indifferent; prodigal, extravagant; **neglēctus 3** neglected, disregarded.

**negō 1** a) to say no; b) to deny, to maintain *or* assert that a thing is not; c) to refuse.

**negōtiālis, e** relating to business.

**negōtiātiō, ōnis** *f* wholesale business, banking business.

**negōtiātor, ōris** *m* wholesale dealer, merchant, banker.

**negōtiolum, ī** *n* little business.

**negōtior 1** to carry on (a wholesale) business, to trade, traffic; **negōtiāns, tis** *m* trader, merchant, banker.               [busy, occupied.]

**negōtiōsus 3** full of business,]

**neg-ōtium, ī** *n* business, employment, occupation; a) affair, undertaking; b) difficult affair, difficulty, pains, trouble, labour; ⁓ **alci facessere** *or* **exhibēre** to cause trouble to; **nullo negōtio** easily; c) public business, affairs of state; d) trade, banking business; e) domestic af-

fairs, management of a household; f) matter, thing.

**nēmō (nūllius, nēminī, nēminem, nūllō** no man, no one, nobody; with **non nēmō** some one, **nēmō non** every one.

**nemorālis** (*and* **-ēnsis**), e of a grove *or* wood, sylvan.

**nemori-cultrix, icis** *f* inhabitant of]

**nemori-vagus 3** wandering in the woods.                          [trees.]

**nemorōsus 3** full of woods *or*]

**nem-pe** *adv.* truly, certainly, of course, indeed; namely.

**nemus, oris** *n* wood, grove, forest; plantation.

**nēnia, ae** *f* a) funeral song, dirge; mournful song; b) magic song, incantation; c) song, nursery song, lullaby.

**neō, nēvī, nētum 2** to spin, weave.

**nepa, ae** *f* scorpion; crab.

**nepōs, ōtis** *m* a) grandson; b) descendant, nephew; c) spendthrift.

**nepōtātus, ūs** *m* prodigality.

**nepōtor 1** to squander.

**nepōtulus, ī** *m* little grandson.

**neptis, is** *f* granddaughter.

**nē-quam** (*indecl.*, *comp.* **nēquior,** *superl.* **nēquissimus**) good-for-nothing, worthless, useless, bad, wicked.

**nē-quāquam** *adv.* by no means.

**ne-que,** *see* **nec.**

**neque-dum,** *see* **necdum.**

**ne-queō, īvī** *and* **iī, itum, īre** to be unable (*with inf.*).

**nē-quiquam** *adv.* in vain, to no purpose, without good reason; for nothing.

**nēquiter, *adv.* of** **nequam.**

**nēquitia, ae** (*and* **nēquitiēs, ēī**) *f* worthlessness, badness, wickedness, profligacy.

**nervōsus 3** sinewy, wiry, energetic.

**nervulus, ī** *m* vigour, strength.

**nervus, ī** *m* sinew, tendon; a) cord, string, *pl.* stringed instrument; b) bowstring; c) leather cover of a shield; d) thong, fetter, prison; e) vigour, force, strength, energy; f) penis.

**ne-sciō 4** a) not to know, to be ignorant; **nesciō an** I know not whether, perhaps, probably; **nescio (-)quis** I know not who, some one; **nescio-quōius 3** someone's; b) to be unacquainted with.

**ne-scius 3 a)** unknowing, ignorant, unaware; **b)** unable, incapable; **c)** unknown.

**neu** = neve.

**neuter, tra, trum** neither of the two; of neither sex *or* gender.

**ne-uti-quam** *adv.* by no means.

**neutrō** *adv.* to neither side.

**neutr-ubi** *adv.* in neither place.

**nē-ve** *and* **neu** *cj.* **a)** and not, nor, or not, and that not, and lest; **neu ... neu** neither ... nor.

**ne-vult** etc. = **nōn vult** etc.

**nex, necis** *f* murder, violent death; the blood of the slain.

**nexilis, e** tied *or* bound together.

**nexum, ī** *n*, *see* necto.

**nexus, ūs** *m* a binding together, interlacing, entwining; **a)** a bond; **b)** personal obligation of a debtor, assignment of the person for debt.

**nī** *cj.* **1.** unless, if not; **2.** = nē³ not, that not.

**nīcātor, ōris** *m* victor.

**nīcētērium, ī** *n* prize of victory.

**nictō 1** to wink; to flicker.

**nīdāmentum, ī** *n* materials of a nest.

**nīdi-ficus 3**: -um ver the season of nesting.

**nīdor, ōris** *m* vapour, steam, smell.

**nīdulus, ī** *m* little nest.

**nīdus, ī** *m* nest; nestling; dwelling, home; book-case.

**niger, gra, grum** black, dark, dusky; **a)** gloomy; **b)** unlucky, unpropitious; **c)** wicked, bad.

**nigrēscō, gruī,** — **3** to become black.

**nigrō 1 a)** to be black; **b)** to blacken.

**nigror, ōris** *m* blackness.

**nihil** (*indecl.*, only *nom.* and *acc.*; *gen.* **nūllīus reī**, *dat.* **nūllī reī**, *abl.* **nūllā rē**) nothing, a nothing, of no value; **non nihil** something, **nihil non** everything, **nihil aliud nisi** *or* **quam** nothing else but; **nihil** *adv.* in nothing, in no respect, not at all.

**nihil-dum** *adv.* nothing as yet.

**nihilum, ī** *n* nothing; **nihilī** for nothing, of no account; **ad nihilum recidere**, **in nihilum occidere** come to nothing; **nihilō** (*abl.*) by nothing, not at all; **pro nihilo** for nothing; **de nihilo** without cause; **nihilō(-)minus** *adv.* nevertheless.

**nīl** = nihil; **nīlum** = nihilum.

**nimbātus 3** (shrouded in rain-clouds); humbugging (?).

**nimbi-fer 3** storm-bringing.

**nimbōsus 3** cloudy, stormy.

**nimbus, ī** *m* cloud, rain-cloud; **a)** stormy rain, rain-storm, heavy shower; **b)** cloud, mass, multitude.

**nī-mīrum** *adv.* without doubt, certainly, surely, to be sure, forsooth.

**nimis** *adv.* **a)** too much, overmuch, excessively; **non nimis** not very much, not particularly; **b)** greatly, very much.

**nimius 3** too great, too much, excessive, beyond measure; *adv.* (**nimiō** *and*) **nimium a)** = nimis; **b)** by far; **nimium quantum** very much indeed, as much as can be.

**ningues** *f/pl.* snow.

**ning(u)it, ninxit,** — **3** it snows.

**ni-si** *cj.* if not, unless; **a)** (*after negatives*) except, but, only; **nihil** (aliud) nisi nothing but; **non ... nisi** *or* **nisi ... non** only; **b) nisi si, nisi quod** except, unless, save only; **nisi forte, nisi vero** unless perhaps.

**nīsus, ūs** *m* a pressing *or* resting upon *or* against; **a)** a striving, exertion; **b)** step, flight, push, ascent; **c)** a giving birth.

**nītēdula** *and* **nītēl(l)a, ae** *f* small mouse, dormouse.

**nīteō, uī,** — **2** to shine, glitter, be bright; **a)** to be well-fed, in good condition, to thrive; **b)** to flourish, abound; **c)** to be illustrious.

**nītēscō, tuī,** — **3** to begin to shine, become sleek.

**nitidiusculus 3** a little more shiny.

**nitidus 3** shining, glittering, bright; **a)** sleek, fat, healthy-looking; **b)** handsome, neat, elegant; **c)** flourishing, blooming; **d)** cultivated, refined.

**nitor¹, ōris** *m* brightness, splendour, lustre, sheen; **a)** beauty, elegance, charm, grace; **b)** dignity, excellence.

**nītor², nīxus** *or* **nīsus sum 3** to rest, lean *or* support oneself upon (*alqā re*, *in alqd*); **a)** to tread, press forward; to climb, ascend, push up towards a height; **b)** to strive, exert oneself, endeavour; **c)** to rest, rely, depend upon.

**nitrātus** 3 containing soda.

**nitrum, ī** n natural carbonate of soda.

**nivālis, e** snowy; snow-white, covered with snow; cold.

**nivārius** 3 filled with snow.

**nivātus** 3 cooled with snow.

**ni-ve** cj. or if not; or lest.

**niveus** 3 = nivalis.

**nivōsus** 3 full of snow, snowy.

**nix, nivis** f snow; white hair.

**nixor** 1 = nitor².

**nixus, ūs** m = nisus.

**nō** 1 to swim, sail, flow, fly.

**nōbilis, e** knowable; a) well-known, noticeable, celebrated, renowned, famous, notorious; b) of noble birth, noble, highborn; c) excellent, superior.

**nōbilitās, ātis** f fame, renown, celebrity; a) noble birth, nobility; b) the nobility, the nobles; c) excellence, superiority.

**nōbilitō** 1 to make known, famous, notorious.

**nocēns, tis** a) hurtful, injurious; b) culpable, criminal.

**noceō, uī, itum** 2 to harm, hurt, injure (alci).

**nocīvus** 3 hurtful, injurious.

**nocti-fer ī** m evening-star.

**nocti-lūca, ae** f the moon.

**nocti-vagus** 3 night-wandering.

**noctū** adv. at night, by night.

**noctua, ae** f night-owl, owl.

**noctuābundus** 3 (travelling) in the night-time.

**noctuīnus** 3 of an owl.

**nocturnus** 3 by night, nocturnal.

**noctu-vigilus** 3 awake at night.

**nocuus** 3 injurious.

**nōdō** 1 to tie in a knot, to knot, fetter.

**nōdōsus** 3 knotty; intricate.

**nōdus, ī** m knot; a) knot or knob on the joint of an animal, knot in the wood of plants; b) bud; c) band, grip, girdle, bond, obligation; d) entanglement, difficulty, impediment.

**noenu(m)** (obsolete) = non.

**nōlō, luī, —, nōlle** not to wish, to be unwilling (with inf., acc.c.inf.); to wish ill, be adverse (alci).

**nōmen, inis** n name, appellation; nōmen mihi est Gaio or Gaius I am called G.; nōmen dare alci to give a name, to call; nōmen

dare, edere, profiteri to give in one's name, to enlist; nōmen alcis deferre to give information against, to accuse judicially; a) title; b) gentile name, race, family, nation; person; c) fame, repute, renown; d) the mere name, pretext, pretence; e) name of a debtor in an account-book, bond, obligation, security for a debt; nōmen solvere to pay a debt; nōmina exigere to collect one's debts; nōmine by name, under the name, in the name of, on the ground, on account or behalf of; meo nōmine in my name, on my behalf.

**nomen-clātiō, ōnis** f a calling by name.

**nōmen-c(u)lātor, ōris** m name-caller.

**nōminātim** adv. by name, expressly.

**nōminātiō, ōnis** f a naming, nomination.

**nōminitō** 1 to name.

**nōminō** 1 to name, call by name; P. to be called; a) to name, mention, make famous; b) to nominate for office; c) to accuse, arraign.

**nomisma, atis** n coin.

**nomos, ī** m song.

**nōn** aov. a) not; b) (in answers) no.

**Nōnae, ārum** f/pl. the nones (the fifth or seventh day of a month).

**nōnāgēsimus** 3 the ninetieth.

**nōnāgiē(n)s** adv. ninety times.

**nōnāgintā** ninety.

**nōnānus** 3 belonging to the ninth legion.

**nōnāria, ae** f prostitute.

**nōn-dum** adv. not yet.

**nōngentī** 3 nine hundred.

**nōn-ne** adv. interr. not?

**nōn-nēmō** someone, many a one.

**nōn-nihil** something; somewhat.

**nōn-nūllus** 3 some, several; considerable.

**nōn-numquam** adv. sometimes.

**nōnus** 3 the ninth; subst. nōna, ae f the ninth hour.

**norma, ae** f carpenter's square, measure, standard, rule; precept.

**nōs** we; I.

**nōscitō** 1 to observe, perceive; to recognize.

**nōscō, nōvī, nōtum** 3 to become acquainted with, to learn to know; *perf.* to know; a) to recognize; b) to acknowledge, allow, admit; c) to investigate a case.

**noster, tra, trum** our, ours; **nostrī, ōrum** *m/pl.* our friends, troops, countrymen; a) favourable to us; b) = **meus.**

**nostrās, ātis** of our country, native.

**nota, ae** *f* mark, token, sign; a) written character, cipher; note, criticism; mark of punctuation; b) mark on a cask of wine; c) branded mark, brand; mark of ignominy; d) reproach, disgrace, official censure; e) nod, sign.

**notābilis, e** remarkable, noteworthy, extraordinary.

**notārius, ī** *m* shorthand-writer; secretary.

**notātiō, ōnis** *f* a marking, noting; a) degradation by a censor; b) a noticing, observing; c) analysis of meaning.

**notātus** 3 a) marked, recognizable; b) perceptible (*alci*).

**nōtēscō, tuī, —** 3 to become known.

**nothus** 3 bastard; counterfeit.

**nōtiō, ōnis** *f* a becoming acquainted with; a) examination, investigation, inquiry; b) idea, conception, notion.

**nōtitia, ae** (*and* -iēs, ēī) *f* acquaintance; a) a being known; fame; b) knowledge; c) conception, idea.

**notō** 1 to mark, designate with a mark; a) to note down, write; b) to denote, indicate, signify; c) to observe; d) to blame, censure, reprimand.

**nōtor, ōris** *m* witness to identity

**notus[1], ī** *m* the south wind.

**nōtus[2]** 3 known; *subst. m* an acquaintance; a) familiar, friendly; b) common, customary; c) notorious, of ill repute.

**novācula, ae** *f* razor.

**novālis, is** *f and* **novāle, is** *n* fallow land; cultivated land; crop.

**novātrix, īcis** *f* she that renews.

**novellō** 1 to plant young vines.

**novellus** 3 new, young, fresh.

**novem** (*indecl.*) nine.

**November, bris, bre** belonging to November; (*mensis m*) November.

**noven-diālis, e** a) of nine days,

lasting nine days; b) on the ninth day.

**novēnī** 3 nine each.

**noverca, ae** *f* step-mother.

**novercālis, e** of a step-mother.

**novīcius** 3 new, fresh; new comer, novice.

**noviē(n)s** *adv.* nine times.

**novitās, ātis** *f* newness, novelty; rareness, strangeness; a) new acquaintance; b) newness of rank, upstart condition.

**novō** 1 to make new, renew, renovate; a) to invent; b) to change, alter, fashion anew; **res novāre** to effect a revolution, overthrow the government.

**novus** 3 new, fresh, recent; **novae res** political innovations, revolution; **homo novus** upstart, the first of a family to hold a curule office, newly ennobled; a) new, novel, strange, singular, unusual, unheard of; b) inexperienced, unaccustomed, unused, unacquainted with; *superl.* **novissimus** 3 the latest, last, extreme; **agmen novissimum** the rear; *adv.* **novē**, in a new fashion; **novissimē** lately, recently, a short time ago; lastly, finally.

**nox, noctis** *f* night; darkness; a) death; b) sleep, dream; c) the lower world; d) confusion, gloom, blindness.

**noxa, ae** *f* harm, injury, damage; a) crime, fault, offence; b) punishment.

**noxia, ae** *f* a) guilt, crime; b) hurt, damage, injury.

**noxiōsus** 3 injurious.

**noxius** 3 a) hurtful, noxious; b) criminal, guilty; *m* a criminal.

**nūbēcula, ae** *f* little cloud.

**nūbēs, is** *f* cloud; a) multitude; b) darkness, obscurity, concealment, veil; c̄) sad condition, gloom, misfortune; d) phantom.

**nūbi-fer** 3 cloud-bringing; cloud-capped.

**nūbi-gena, ae** *m, f* cloud-born.

**nūbilis, e** marriageable.

**nūbilus** 3 cloudy, overcast; *subst.* -um, ī *n* cloudy weather, *pl.* clouds; a) dark, gloomy; b) unfavourable; unhappy.

**nūbi-vagus** 3 wandering in the clouds.

**nūbō, nūpsī, ptum** 3 to veil; *(of a bride)* to be married, to marry *(alci)*; **nupta, -ae** *f* wife, spouse, bride.

**nucētum, ī** *n* plantation of nut trees.

**nuci-frangibulum, ī** *n* nutcracker, tooth.

**nuc(u)leus, ī** *m* kernel, nut.

**nu-diūs** it is now the ... day; ~ **tertius** the day before yesterday.

**nūdō** 1 to bare, uncover, strip, *(alqd re)*; **a)** to leave undefended; **b)** to rob, spoil, plunder; **c)** to expose, disclose.

**nūdus** 3 naked, bare, unclothed; **a)** in light attire; **b)** unarmed, unprotected; **c)** deprived of, destitute; **d)** needy, poor; **e)** bare, mere, alone, only; **f)** simple, unadorned.

**nūgae, ārum** *f/pl.* jests, trifles, nonsense, silly things, trumpery; foolish, trifling fellow.

**nūgātor, ōris** *m* babbler, trifler.

**nūgātōrius** 3 trifling, silly, worthless, frivolous.

**nūgāx, ācis** jesting, trifling.

**nūgi-gerulus, ī** *m* dealer in trumpery.

**nūgi-vendus, ī** *m* seller of trumpery.

**nūgor** 1 to trifle, be frivolous; to lie.

**nūllus** 3 none, no, not any, nobody; **nūllo ordine** without (any) order; **nūllus non** every one; **non nūllus** some; **a)** non-existent; **b)** insignificant, of no account, worthless.

**nūllus-dum** none as yet.

**num** *interrog. particle* **a)** introducing a direct question, *gen. suggesting a negative answer*; really? surely not?; **numne = num; b)** *in indirect questions*: whether.

**numella, ae** *f* fetter *(for slaves)*.

**nūmen, inis** *n* nod, command; **a)** divine will, divine command, divine authority, divinity, divine majesty, god, goddess; **b)** oracle.

**numerābilis, e** that can be counted; easily counted.

**numerātiō, ōnis** *f* payment.

**numerō** 1 to count, reckon, number; **a)** to count out, pay down; **numerātus** 3 in ready money; *subst.* **-um, ī** *n* ready money, cash; **b)** to reckon under *(alqd in re, inter alqos)*, class under, consider, hold; **c)** to recount, relate.

**numerōsus** 3 **a)** numerous, manifold, populous; **b)** measured, rhythmical.

**numerus, ī** *m* **1.** measure, rhythm, melody, harmony, numbers, verse, metre; **2.** number, certain number; calculation; **a)** class, category, estimation; **in hostium numero ducere** to count as enemies; **b)** rank, place, condition, position; **c)** mass, heap; quantity, body, party, collection; **d)** a mere number, nothing; *abl. as adv.* **numerō** at the proper time; too soon.

**nummārius** 3 belonging to money; bribed.

**nummātus** 3 provided with money.

**nummulāri(ol)us, ī** *m* money-changer.

**nummulus, ī** *m* paltry money.

**nummus, ī** *m* coin, piece of money; *pl.* money; **a)** sesterce; **b)** penny, trifle.

**num-ne**, *see* **num.**

**numquam** *adv.* never; **non ~** sometimes; **~ non** always.

**num-quī** *interrog. adv.* in any way? at all?

**num-quid 1.** *in direct questions:* **a)** anything? **b)** *simply as an interrog. particle;* **2.** *in indirect questions:* whether.

**nunc** *adv.* **a)** now, at present; **nunc ipsum** at this very moment; **nunc ... nunc** now ... now, at one time ... at another; **b)** under these circumstances, as matters are; **nunc autem, ~ vero** but now, now however.

**nunciam = nunc.**

**nuncupātiō, ōnis** *f* public proclamation.

**nuncupō** 1 to call by name, name; to pronounce publicly, utter, vow, nominate as heir.

**nūndinae, ārum** *f/pl.* (ninth day) market-day, market, trade, traffic, business.

**nūndinālis cocus** a nine-day cook (once-a-week cook).

**nūndinātiō, ōnis** *f* a trafficking, trade, buying and selling.

**nūndinor** 1 **a)** to go to market, trade, traffic; **b)** to purchase.

**(nūndinus** of nine days) **a)** *see* **nundinae; b) trīnum nūndinum** period of three market-days *(about 20 days)*.

**nunquam**, *see* **numquam**.

**nŭntia, ae** *f* she that announces, female messenger.

**nŭntiātiō, ōnis** *f* augur's right of announcing his observations.

**nŭntiō** 1 to announce, report, make known, give orders.

**nŭntius, 3** announcing, bringing news; *subst.* **~, ĭ** *m* a) messenger, announcer; b) (*also* **-ium** *n*) message, news, tidings; command, order.

**nū-per** *adv.* (*superl.* **nŭperrimē**) newly, lately, not long ago.

**nŭperus 3** newly arrived.

**nuptiae, ārum** *f/pl.* (*and* **nuptus, ūs** *m*) nuptials, marriage, wedding.

**nuptiālis, e** relating to a marriage, nuptial.

**nurus, ūs** *f* daughter-in-law; young married woman.

**nusquam** *adv.* a) nowhere; b) to no place; c) on no occasion, in nothing; d) for nothing.

**nūtāmen, inis** *n* a waving.

**nūtātiō, ōnis** *f* a tottering, going to ruin.

**nūtō** 1 to nod, move up and down, totter, waver.

**nūtrīcātus, ūs** *m* a suckling, bringing up.

**nūtrīcium, ĭ** *n* nursing.

**nūtrīcius, ĭ** *m* foster-father.

(**nūtrīcō** *and*) **nūtrīcor** 1 to nourish; to sustain.

**nūtrīcula, ae** *f* nurse.

(**nūtrīmen, inis** *and*) **nūtrīmentum, ĭ** *n* a) nourishment; b) fuel; training.

**nūtriō** (*and* **-or**) 4 a) to suckle, nourish, feed, bring up; b) to tend, take care of, cherish, cultivate.

**nūtrītor, ōris** *m* breeder, rearer.

**nūtrix, īcis** *f* nurse, foster-mother; breast.

**nūtus, ūs** *m* a nodding, inclination; a) downward tendency, gravity; b) command, will, hint.

**nux, nucis** *f* nut; nut-tree; almond-tree.

**nympha, ae** *and* **nymphē, ēs** *f* a) bride, young woman; b) nymph; water.

# O

**ō** *int.* o! oh!

**ob** *prep.* with *acc.* a) towards, to; b) at, before, in front of, over against, **ob oculos versari**; c) on account of, for, because of, for the sake of.

**ob-aerātus** 3 involved in debt.

**ob-agitō** 1 to disturb.

**ob-ambulō** 1 to walk before *or* near; to walk up and down.

**ob-ārdēscō, ārsī, — 3** to blaze up.

**ob-armō** 1 to arm against.

**ob-arō** 1 to plough up.

**obba, ae** *f* a vessel for holding wine.

**ob-brūtēscō** 3 to become stupid.

**ob-dō, didī, ditum 3** a) to set, put, place before *or* against (*alqd* with *dat.*); b) to expose; c) to shut, close. [mīvī, — 3 to fall asleep.]

**(ob-dormiō 4 and) ob-dormiscō,**

**ob-dūcō** 3 1. to lead against, bring forward; 2. a) to draw over (*alqd* with *dat.*), draw in front; b) to cover over, overspread; c) to swallow; to pass (time); **obductus** 3 overspread, clouded, scarred over, wrinkled.

**ob-ductiō, ōnis** *f* a covering.

**ob-ductō** 1 to bring in as a rival.

**ōb-dūrēscō, ruī, — 3** to become hard *or* insensitive.

**ob-dūrō** 1 to hold out, persist.

**obeliscus, ī** *m* obelisk.

**ob-eō, iī (īvī), itum, īre** 1. *intr.* to go to (*in alqd*); a) to go to meet, go against; b) to go down, set, to die, perish; 2. *trans.* to reach, betake oneself to, to visit, travel over, wander through (*alqd*); a) to run over, survey, review; b) to surround; c) to engage in, apply oneself to, to perform, execute, accomplish; **mortem** *or* **diem (supremum)** to die.

**ob-equitō** 1 to ride up to (*dat.*).

**ob-errō** 1 to wander about; blunder. [ness.]

**ob-ēsitās, ātis** *f* fatness, stout-

**ob-ēsus** 3 fat, plump; coarse.

**ōbex, icis** *m and f* bolt, bar; barrier, barricade, obstacle.

**ob-f..., ob-g...,** *see* **off..., ogg...**

**ob-fuī,** *see* **obsum.**

**ob-haereō 2, ob-haerēscō 3** to stick fast, cleave to.

**ob-iaceō 2** to lie against, in the way (*dat.*).

**ōb-iciō (and ŏb-), iēcī, iectum 3** 1. to throw against *or* in the way of, to oppose (*alci alqd*); 2. to throw before, throw to, cast, offer, present (*alci alqd*); a) to expose; b) to hold before as a defence *or* protection; c) to cast up at (as an accusation *or* reproach).

**obiectātiō, ōnis** *f* reproach.

**ob-iectō** 1 to set against, throw at (*alqd alci rei*); a) to abandon, expose; b) to cast up at (as a reproach).

**ob-iectus, ūs** *m* a) a placing *or* putting before *or* against; b) a lying against *or* opposite.

**ob-iiciō,** *see* **obicio.**

**ob-īrāscor** 3 to grow angry at.

**ob-iter** *adv.* on the way; by the way, incidentally.

**ob-itus, ūs** *m* a) meeting; b) ruin, destruction, death.

**ob-iūrgātiō, ōnis** *f* a chiding, reproof, scolding.

**ob-iūrgātor, ōris** *m* chider, blamer.

**ob-iūrgātōrius** 3 reproachful.

**ob-iūrgitō** 1 to chide, rebuke.

**ob-iūr(i)gō** 1 to chide, scold, reprove; to deter by reproof; to chastise.

**(ob-languēscō), guī, — 3** to become languid.

**ob-lātrātrīx, īcis** *f* she who barks at.

**ob-lātrō** 1 to bark at *or* against.

**(oblectāmen, inis** *and*) **oblectāmentum, ī** *n* delight, amusement, pleasure.

**oblectātiō, ōnis** *f* a delighting, pleasing, delight.

**ob-lectō** 1 to delight, please, amuse.

**ob-lēniō 4** to soothe.

**ob-līdō, sī, sum 3** to squeeze together, compress.

**ob-ligātiō, ōnis** *f* a pledging, obligation.

**ob-ligō** 1 **a)** to bind *or* fasten; **b)** to bind up, bandage; **c)** to put under obligation, make liable; to involve in (*alqm alqa re*); **d)** to pledge, mortgage; **obligātus** 3 bound, under an obligation, indebted, devoted, mortgaged.

**ob-līmō** 1 to cover with slime *or* mud; to lavish, squander.

**ob-linō** 3 to daub, smear over, besmear, bedaub; **a)** to cover over, load; **b)** to stain, pollute, defile.

**oblīquō** 1 to turn sideways *or* aside, turn awry.

**ob-līquus** 3 **a)** slanting, sideways, oblique; **b)** indirect, covert; envious.

**ob-litēscō, tuī,** — 3 to hide oneself.

**ob-litterō** 1 to erase; to blot out of memory; to cancel.

**oblitus** *part. pass.* of **oblino; oblitus** of **obliviscor.**

**oblīviō, ōnis** *f* **a)** forgetfulness, oblivion; **b)** amnesty.

**oblīviōsus** 3 **a)** forgetful; **b)** causing forgetfulness.

**ob-līvīscor, oblītus sum** 3 to forget (*with gen.* or *acc.*).

**oblīvium, ī** *n* = **oblivio.**

**ob-locūtor, ōris** *m* contradictor.

**ob-longus** 3 oblong.

**ob-loquor** 3 to speak against, reproach; to accompany in song, to sound in accompaniment.

**ob-luctor** 1 to struggle *or* strive against.

**ob-lūdiō** (?) 1 to jest.

**ob-mōlior** 4 to build *or* pile against (as a defence *or* obstruction).

**ob-murmurō** 1 to murmur at *or* against.

**ob-mūtēscō, tuī,** — 3 to become dumb; to cease.

**ob-nātus** 3 growing on.

**ob-nītor** 3 to press against, resist; **obnīxus** 3 steadfast, firm, resolute.

**ob-noxiōsus** 3 slavish.

**ob-noxius** 3 **a)** liable to, addicted to (*dat.*), guilty of (with *dat.* or *gen.*); **b)** subject, exposed to (*dat.*); submissive, servile; **c)** obliged, indebted, responsible (*dat.*).

**ob-nūbilus** 3 clouded over.

**ob-nūbō** 3 to cover, veil.

**ob-nūntiātiō, ōnis** *f* announcement of evil omens.

**ob-nūntiō** 1 to announce bad omens *or* news.

**oboediēns, tis** obedient, compliant (*dat.*).

**oboedientia, ae** *f* obedience.

**ob-oediō, īvī, ītum** 4 to give ear, hearken, listen; to obey (*dat.*).

**ob-oleō** 2 to emit a smell, smell of (*acc.*); to attract by smell (*dat.*).

**ob-orior** 4 to arise, appear, spring up (before someone).

**ob-p..., see opp...**

**ob-rēpō, rēpsī, rēptum** 3 to creep up; to approach stealthily, come up suddenly.

**ob-rēptō** 1 = **obrepo.**

**ob-rētiō** 4 to entangle.

**ob-rigēscō, guī,** — 3 to become stiff *or* hard.

**ob-rōdō** 3 to gnaw at.

**ob-rogō** 1 to repeal a law by another.

**ob-ruō** 3 to cover over (*alqd re*); **a)** to hide, bury, sink; **b)** to overwhelm, conceal, eclipse, obscure; **c)** to overload, weigh down, oppress.

**obrussa, ae** *f* the testing of gold by fire.

**ob-saepiō** 4 to hedge in, fence in, enclose.

**ob-saturor** 1 to have more than enough of.

**obscaenus** 3, see **obscenus.**

**ob-scaevō** 1 to give bad omens.

**obs-cēnitās, ātis** *f* impurity, unchastity, lewdness.

**obs-cēnus** 3 filthy, repulsive, offensive; **a)** impure, indecent, lewd, obscene; **b)** ill-omened, inauspicious.

**obscūrātiō, ōnis** *f* a darkening.

**obscūritās, ātis** *f* darkness, obscurity; **a)** indistinctness, unintelligibility; **b)** low birth.

**obscūrō** 1 to darken, obscure; **a)** to hide, conceal; **b)** to make indistinct, unintelligible; **c)** to make unknown, forgotten, to eclipse.

**ob-scūrus** 3 dark, obscure; **a)** hidden, concealed, secret; **b)** indistinct, unintelligible; **c)** reserved; **d)** unknown, not celebrated, ignoble, mean.

**ob-secrātiō, ōnis** *f* earnest entreaty; **a)** public prayer *or* supplication; **b)** appeal.

**ob-secrō** 1 to entreat earnestly (*alqm; ut*), to implore, supplicate, conjure.

**ob-secundō** 1 to be compliant, subservient, to yield (*dat.*).

**ob-sēpiō** 4, *see* obsaepio.

**obsequēl(l)a, ae** *f* = obsequium.

**ob-sequēns, tis** compliant, obedient, yielding (*dat.*).

**obsequentia, ae** *f* = obsequium.

**obsequiōsus** 3 compliant, obsequious.

**obsequium, ī** *n* compliance, complaisance, obedience, indulgence, submission.

**ob-sequor** 3 to comply with, obey, submit, indulge in (*with dat.*).

**ob-serō¹** 1 to bolt, bar, fasten, shut up.

**ob-serō², sēvī, situm** 3 to sow, plant, cover over, fill (*alqd re*).

**ob-servābilis, e** remarkable.

**ob-servāns, tis** attentive, respectful.

**observantia, ae** *f* respect, esteem.

**observātiō, ōnis** *f* a) an observing, watching; b) accuracy, circumspection.                              [server.]

**ob-servātor, ōris** *m* watcher, observitō 1 to watch, observe diligently.

**ob-servō** 1 to observe, watch; a) to attend to, guard, keep, regard; b) to respect, esteem, honour.

**ob-ses, idis** *m*, *f* hostage; surety, pledge, security.

**ob-sessiō, ōnis** *f* = obsidio.

**ob-sessor, ōris** *m* besieger, blockader, haunter.

**ob-sideō, sēdī, sessum** 2 to sit at (*acc.*); a) to sit *or* stay by; b) to beset, besiege, invest, blockade; to occupy, fill, haunt; c) to look out for, watch for.

**obsidiālis, e** relating to a siege *or* blockade.

**obsidiō, ōnis** *f* siege, blockade; pressing danger.            [hostage.]

**obsidium¹, ī** *n* condition of a]

**obsidium², ī** siege, blockade; danger.

**ob-sīdō, sēdī, sessum** 3 to beset, to occupy.

**ob-signātor, ōris** *m* sealer, witness.

**ob-signō** 1 a) to seal; b) to attest under seal; c) to impress.

**ob-sipō** 1 to sprinkle over.

**ob-sistō, stitī, —** 3 to stand in the way; to withstand, resist (*dat.*); *subst.* obstita, ōrum *n/pl.* things struck by lightning.

**obsole-fīō, factus sum, fierī** 3 = obsolesco.

**obsolēscō, lēvī, (lētum)** 3 to decay, wear out, fall into disuse, grow old *or* shabby; **obsolētus** 3 worn out; decayed, shabby; a) common, mean; b) obsolete.

**obsōnātor, ōris** *m* buyer of victuals.

**obsōnātus, ūs** *m* purchase of provisions.

**obsōnium, ī** *n* relish, victuals; fish.

**ob-sonō¹,** 1 to interrupt in speech.

**obsōnō² and -or** 1 to buy provisions.

**ob-sorbeō** 2 to swallow, gulp down.

**ob-stetrix, īcis** *f* midwife.

**obstinātiō, ōnis** *f* firmness, steadfastness, persistence, obstinacy.

**obstinātus** 3 firmly resolved, persistent, stubborn, obstinate.

**ob-stinō** 1 to resolve, determine firmly, persist (*alqd;* with *inf.*).

**ob-stipēscō** = obstupesco.

**ob-stīpus** 3 inclined, bent, turned aside.

**obstita, ōrum** *n/pl.*, *see* obsisto.

**ob-stō, stitī, (stātūrus)** 1 to stand against, to be in the way; to resist; hinder, obstruct (*alci; ne, quominus*).

**ob-strepō** 3 to make a noise at *or* against (*dat.*); to interrupt with a noise, drown with clamour, shout down.

**ob-strigillō** 1 to be a hindrance.

**ob-stringō** 3 a) to bind, fasten, tie to; b) to bind, fetter, put under an obligation; c) to entangle, involve, make guilty of (*alqm re*).

**ob-structiō, ōnis** *f* hindrance, obstruction.

**obs-trūdō** = obtrudo.

**ob-struō** 3 to build before *or* against; **lumīnibus alcis** to block up the light, build before the windows; to block up, close, hinder.

**ob-stupefaciō** 3 to astonish, astound, amaze, stupefy.

**ob-stupēscō, puī, —** 3 to become senseless, astounded, amazed.

**ob-stupidus** 3 amazed, stupefied.

**ob-sum, fuī, esse** to be in the way, hinder, injure.

**ob-suō** 3 to sew on *or* up.      [deaf.]

**ob-surdēscō, duī, —** 3 to become]

**ob-taedēscit** it starts to weary.

**ob-tegō** 3 to cover; a) to protect; b) to conceal, veil, hide.

**ob-temperātiō, ōnis** *f* compliance, obedience.

**ob-temperō** 1 to comply, obey, submit (*dat.*).

**ob-tendō, ndī, ntum** 3 to stretch *or* spread before; **a)** to plead as an excuse; **b)** to hide, conceal; **P.** to lie opposite (*dat.*).

**ob-tentus, ūs** *m* **a)** a stretching *or* spreading before; **b)** pretext, pretence, excuse.

**ob-terō** 3 to trample, crush, to bruise; **a)** to destroy; **b)** to put down, degrade.

**ob-testātiō, ōnis** *f* adjuration, earnest entreaty.

**ob-testor** 1 to call to witness; **a)** to assert solemnly (*alqd; acc. c. inf.*); **b)** to conjure, implore, entreat (*alqm; ut*).

**ob-texō** 3 to overspread.

**ob-ticeō** 2 to be silent.

**ob-ticēscō, cuī, —** 3 to become silent.

**ob-tineō, tinuī, tentum** 2 to hold fast; **a)** to occupy, possess, keep; **b)** to assert, maintain; **c)** to obtain; *intr.* to stand, continue.

**ob-tingō, tigī, —** 3 to fall to the lot of, happen (*alci; ut*).

**ob-torpēscō, puī, —** 3 to grow stiff, torpid, insensible.

**ob-torqueō** 2 to twist *or* turn round; to wrench.

**ob-trectātiō, ōnis** *f* detraction, disparagement.

**ob-trectātor, ōris** *m* detractor, disparager, rival.

**ob-trectō** 1 to disparage.

**ob-trūdō** 3 to thrust upon; to gulp down.

**ob-truncō** 1 to kill, slaughter.

**ob-tueor** 2 to gaze on, see clearly.

**ob-tundō, tudī, tū(n)sum** 3 to beat upon (*alqd*); **a)** to make blunt *or* dull, to stun, deafen; **b)** to annoy, tire; **obtū(n)sus** 3 blunt, dulled, stupid, weak.

**ob-turbō** 1 to disturb, disorder, confuse; **a)** to trouble; **b)** to interrupt, distract.

**ob-turgēscō** 3 to swell.

**ob-tūrō** 1 to stop up, close.

**ob-tūtus, ūs** *m* a looking at, beholding, gaze.

**ob-umbrō** 1 to overshadow; **a)** to darken; **b)** to conceal, cover; **c)** to cast into the shade.

**ob-uncus** 3 hooked.    [by fire.�

**ob-ustus** 3 burnt into, hardened⎱

**ob-vāgiō** 4 to whimper at.

**ob-vallō** 1 to wall round.

**ob-veniō** 4 **a)** to come up to, come to meet; **b)** to occur; **c)** to fall to the lot of.

**ob-versor** 1 to move up and down before; to hover before; to appear (*dat.; ante alqm*).

**ob-versus** 3 **a)** turned towards; **b)** inclined to; *subst.* opponent.

**ob-vertō** 3 to turn towards *or* against (*alqd in* or *ad alqd*); **P.** to face, turn oneself to.

**ob-viam** *adv.* in the way, towards, against, meeting (*dat.*); **obviam īre** to come to meet; to oppose, resist, contend against, prevent.

**ob-vigilō** 1 to be watchful.

**obvius** 3 in the way, meeting, to meet (*dat.*); **a)** exposed to, open to, subject to; **b)** ready, at hand; **c)** affable, courteous.

**ob-volvō** 3 to wrap round *or* up, envelop.    [-vert-.⎱

**ob-vors-, -vort- = ob-vers-,⎰**

**oc-caecō** 1 to make blind; **a)** to darken, obscure, overcloud; **c)** to hide from sight.

**oc-callātus** 3 indurated.

**oc-callēscō, luī, —** 3 to become thick-skinned, callous.

**oc-canō, nuī, —** 3 to sound for action.

**occāsiō, ōnis** *f* opportunity, favourable moment; surprise attack.

**occāsiuncula, ae** *f* opportunity.

**oc-cāsus, ūs** *m* setting; the west; downfall.

**occātiō, ōnis** *f* a harrowing.

**occātor, ōris** *m* harrower.

**oc-cēdō** 3 to go up to.

**oc-centō** 1 to sing a (satirical) song to *or* at.

**oc-ceptō** 1 to begin.

**occidēns, tis** *m* the west.

**occidiō, ōnis** *f* massacre, complete slaughter, extermination.

**oc-cidō¹, cidī, (cāsūrus)** 3 to fall down; **a)** to go down, set; **b)** to fall, perish, die, be ruined, be lost.

**oc-cidō², cidī, cīsum** 3 to strike down; **a)** to cut down, kill; **b)** to plague to death, to undo; **occīsissumus** most completely ruined.

**occiduus** 3 sinking; setting, western.

**occillō** 1 to batter, smash.

**oc-cinō, cinuī (cecinī), —** 3 to sing inauspiciously, to croak.

oc-cip io, cēpī, ceptum 3 to begin

oc-cipitium, ī (and occiput, itis) n back of the head. [slaughter.]

oc-cīsiō, ōnis f massacre,)

oc-cīsor, ōris m killer.

oc-clāmitō 1 to cry aloud.

oc-clūdō, sī, sum 3 to shut up, close.

ocō 1 to harrow, till. [dead.)

cc-cubō, —, — 1 to lie down, lie)

oc-culcō 1 to trample down.

oc-culō, culuī, cultum 3 to hide, conceal, keep secret.

occultātiō, ōnis f concealing.

occultātor, ōris m concealer.

occultō 1, intens. of occulo.

occultus 3 hidden, concealed, secret, imperceptible; reserved, close; subst. occultum, ī n secret; hiding-place.

oc-cumbō, cubuī, cubitum 3 to fall down, fall in death, die.

occupātiō, ōnis f a) a seizing, taking possession of; b) business, employment, affairs.

occupātus 3 busy, engaged.

occupō 1 to take possession of, seize; a) to fill, occupy with (alqd re); b) to fall upon, attack (before an enemy); c) to anticipate, do anything first (inf.); d) to put out or invest money.

oc-currō, (cu)currī, cursum 3 to run to meet, hasten to meet (alci); a) to attack; b) to come to, be present at; c) to come in the way of, present itself, meet the eye, come into the thoughts, appear, occur, happen; d) to resist, oppose, counteract; to come to the help of, assist, prevent; e) to reply, answer (dat.).

occursātiō, ōnis f a running to meet; greeting, attention.

occursiō, ōnis f assault.

oc-cursō 1 to go to meet (dat.); a) to attack; b) to approach; c) to forestall; d) to occur to (the mind).

oc-cursus, ūs m a meeting, falling in with; movement.

ocellātus 3 marked with eyes, spotted (dice or marbles).

ocellus, ī m little eye.

ōcimum, ī n basil (a plant).

ōcior, us (comp.) swifter; comp. adv. ōcius (more) swiftly; superl. ōcissimē.

ocliferius 3 striking the eye.

ocrea, ae f metal greave.

ocreātus 3 wearing greaves.

octāvus 3 the eighth.

octiē(n)s adv. eight times.

octingentēsimus 3 eight hundredth.

octingentī 3 eight hundred.

octi-pēs, edis eight-footed.

octō (indecl.) eight.

October, bris, bre belonging to October; (mensis) m October.

octō-decim (indecl.) eighteen.

octōgēnārius 3 containing eighty; eighty years old.

octōgēnī 3 eighty each.

octōgēsimus 3 the eightieth.

octōgiē(n)s adv. eighty times.

octōgintā (indecl.) eighty.

octō-iugis, e eight together.

octōnī 3 eight each.

octō-phoros, on carried by eight bearers; subst. -on, ī n litter carried by eight bearers.

octuplicātus 3 multiplied by eight.

octuplus 3 eightfold; subst. octuplum, ī n eightfold payment.

octussis, is m eight asses.

oculātus 3 having eyes, seeing; conspicuous.

oculeus 3 having many eyes.

oculissumus 3 dearest (apple of my eye).

oculus, ī m eye; a) bud; b) pearl (metaph.).

ōdēum (and ōdīum), ī n concert-hall.

ōdī, ōdisse (ōsūrus) to hate, dislike, be displeased with.

odiōs(s)icus 3 = odiōsus.

odiōsus 3 hateful, odious, annoying.

odium, ī n hatred, enmity; a) aversion; b) object of hatred.

odor (and odōs), ōris m smell, odour; a) perfume, spice; b) scent, suspicion.

odōrātiō, ōnis f a smelling smell.

odōrātus[1], ūs m sense of smell.

odōrātus[2] 3 fragrant.

odōri-fer 3 fragrant; producing perfumes.

odōrō 1 to make fragrant.

odōror 1 a) to smell at or out, scent; b) to aspire to; c) to get a smattering of (acc.).

odōrus 3 a) sweet-smelling; b) keen-scented.

odōs, ōris m (obsolete) = odor.

oeno-phorum, ī n wine-basket.

oeno-pōlium, ī n wine-shop.

oenus 3 (obsolete) = unus.

**oestrus, ī** *m* gadfly; frenzy.
**oesus, ūs** *m* (*obsolete*) = **usus.**
**oesypum, ī** *n* cosmetic made from wool-grease.
**ofella, ae** *f* bit, mouthful.
**offa, ae** *f* a) ball of meal; **b)** cutlet; **c)** tumour; **d)** abortion, shapeless mass.
**offātim** by bits.
**offendiculum, ī** *n* stumbling-block, obstacle.
**of-fendō, endī, ēnsum** 3 to hit, strike, knock, dash against; **1.** a) to come upon, meet with (*in re*); b) to suffer disaster, receive an injury; c) to offend, make a mistake, blunder; **2.** to offend, shock, displease; **offēnsus** 3 a) offended, displeased; b) offensive, odious.
**offensa, ae** *f* a striking against; a) offence, affront, enmity; **b)** disfavour, displeasure.
**of-fēnsātiō, ōnis** *f* blunder.
**offēnsiō, ōnis** *f* a striking against; **a)** indisposition, illness, complaint; **b)** a stumbling; offence, injury; **c)** hatred, enmity, aversion, disgust, dislike, disfavour; **d)** accident, misfortune, failure, defeat.
**offēnsiuncula, ae** *f* a) slight offence; **b)** slight failure.
**offēnsō** 1 to strike against.
**offēnsus** 3, *see* offendo.
**of-fēnsus, ūs** *m* shock; disfavour.
**of-ferō, obtulī, oblātum, offerre** to bring to, place before, present, show, exhibit (*alci alqd*); **a)** to offer, bring forward; **b)** to expose; **c)** to cause, occasion, bestow, inflict; — **P.** *or* se offerre to present oneself, oppose oneself.
**offerumentae, ārum** *f*/*pl.* presents (= blows).
**officina, ae** *f* workshop, manufactory.
**of-ficiō, fēcī, fectum** 3 to be in the way of, hinder, oppose, obstruct, thwart (*dat.*).
**officiōsus** 3 obliging, courteous, serviceable; dutiful.
**officium, ī** *n* **1.** service, kindness; a) attention, complaisance, friendly service; b) respect, courtesy, deference; c) office, service, employment, work; **2.** duty, obligation, business, function; a) sense of duty, dutifulness, conscience; b) obedience, allegiance.

**of-fīgō, —, —** 3 to fix, fasten.
**of-firmō** 1 to hold fast to; **offirmā-tus** 3 firm; obstinate.
**of-flectō** 3 to turn round.
**of-fōcō** 1 to choke.
**of-frēnātus** 3 bound, fettered.
**of-fūcia, ae** *f* paint; deceit.
**offula, ae** *f* bit, morsel.
**of-fulgeō, -lsī, —** 2 to shine upon, appear.
**of-fundō** 3 to pour before *or* round; to spread over, cover.
**og-gannio** 4 to growl at.
**og-gerō** 3 to bring to, press upon.
**oh!** *int.* oh! ah!
**ōhē** (*and* ō, ĕ) *int.* hi there! stop!
**oi, oiei** alas!
**olea, ae** *f* = **oliva.**
**oleāginus** 3 of the olive-tree.
**oleārius** 3 of oil; *subst.* oil-dealer.
**oleaster, trī** *m* wild olive-tree.
**olēns, tis** smelling; **a)** fragrant; **b)** stinking.
**oleō, oluī, —** 2 (*and* olō 3) to emit a smell, smell; to smell of (*alqd*), indicate, betray.
**olētum, ī** *n* faeces, excrement.
**oleum, ī** *n* oil; wrestling-school; rhetorical exercise. [*alqd*).\
**ol-faciō** 3 to smell, to scent out\
**ol-factō** 1 to smell.
**olidus** 3 smelling; stinking.
**ōlim** *adv.* **a)** formerly, some time ago, of old; **b)** one day, hereafter, at a future time; **c)** at times, often, for some time past.
**olitor, ōris** *m* kitchen-gardener.
**olitōrius** 3 relating to vegetables.
**oliva, ae** *f* a) olive; **b)** olive-tree; olive-branch; staff of olive-wood.
**olivētum, ī** *n* olive-garden.
**olīvi-fer** 3 olive-bearing.
**olīvum, ī** *n* olive-oil; unguent; wrestling-school.
**ōlla, ae** *f* pot, jar.
**ōllāris, e** preserved in a jar.
**olle** *and* **ollus** (*obsolete*) = **ille.**
**olor, ōris** *m* swan.
**olōrinus** 3 relating to a swan.
**olus, eris** *n* kitchen-herbs, vegetables, cabbage.
**olusculum, ī** *n* = olus.
**omāsum, ī** *n* bullock's tripe; paunch.
**ōmen, inis** *n* omen, sign, augury, token, foreboding; solemn usage, ceremony.
**ōmentum, ī** *n* a) fat; **b)** bowels.
**ōminātor, ōris** *m* prophet.

**ōminor** 1 to forebode, presage, predict, prophesy.

**ōminōsus** 3 ominous.

**o-mittō** 3 to let go, let alone, let loose, let fall; a) to give up, leave off; b) to leave unmentioned, to omit, overlook.

**omni-genus** 3 of all sorts.

**omni-modīs** in every way.

**omnīnō** adv. a) altogether, wholly, entirely, totally; b) in general, in all; c) to be sure; **omnīnō non** not at all.

**omni-parēns, tis** all-producing.

**omni-potēns, tis** all-powerful.

**omnis, e** all, each, every; a) all, whole, complete; b) of all kinds.

**omni-tuēns, ntis** all-seeing.

**omni-vagus** 3 wandering everywhere.

**omni-volus** 3 all-wishing.

**onager** and **onagrus, ī** m wild ass.

**onāgos, ī** m ass-driver.

**onerārius** 3 of burden; subst. -a, ae f merchant-vessel, transport.

**onerō** 1 to load, burden; a) to weigh down, oppress, overload; b) to pile up, aggravate; c) to stow away.

**onerōsus** 3 heavy, burdensome.

**onocrotalus, ī** m pelican.

**onus, eris** n load, burden, freight, cargo; weight; a) trouble, charge, difficulty; b) public burden, tax, expense, debt.

**onustus** 3 loaded, burdened (re), freighted; filled; weighed down.

**onyx, ychis** m and f onyx; onyx box, perfume-box.

**opācitās, ātis** f shadiness.

**opācō** 1 to shade, overshadow.

**opācus** 3 shaded, shady; dark, obscure.

**opella, ae** f a little work.

**opera, ae** f pains, effort, exertion, work; **operam dare** to see to, attend to, deal with (alci rei or ut); **operae pretium est** it is worth while; a) service, help; b) leisure, spare time; c) a day's work; workman, hired assistant; plur. hired mob, gang.

**operārius** 3 working; subst. ~, ī m day-labourer, workman.

**operculum, ī** n lid, cover.

**operīmentum, ī** n a covering, cover.

**operiō, eruī, ertum** 4 to cover, cover over; a) to bury; b) to cover, shut, overwhelm; c) to hide, conceal, dissemble; **opertus** 3 hidden, covered; subst. -um, ī n secret; secret place.

**operor** 1 to work, labour, be busied (alci rei); to be engaged in worship or sacrifice.

**operōsus** 3 a) painstaking, active, busy; efficacious; b) troublesome, toilsome, difficult; c) elaborate, artfully constructed.

**opertōrium, ī** n covering.

**opēs, um** f/pl., see **ops.**

**ophītēs, ae** m serpentine.

**opicus** 3 uncivilized.

**opi-fer** 3 helpful, helping.

**opi-fex, icis** m, f a) worker, framer; b) mechanic, artisan.

**opi-ficīna, ae** f workshop.

**ōpiliō, ōnis** m shepherd. [dance.]

**opīmitās, ātis** f richness, abun-)

**opīmus** 3 fat, well-fed; a) fruitful, fertile; b) rich, copious; c) sumptuous, splendid; overloaded (speech).

**opīnābilis, e** conjectural.

**opīnātiō, ōnis** f conjecture, opinion.

**opīnātor, ōris** m one who holds an opinion.

**opīnātus** 3 supposed, fancied.

**opīnātus, ūs** m supposition.

**opīniō, ōnis** f opinion, conjecture, supposition, belief; a) impression; b) expectation; c) reputation; d) fame, report.

**opīnor** (and -ō) 1 to be of opinion, believe, think, suppose.

**opi-parus** 3 splendid, sumptuous.

**opistho-graphus** 3 covered with writing on the back.

**opitulor** 1 to help, aid.

**opo-balsamum, ī** n balsam.

**oportet, uit,** — 2 it is necessary, proper, becoming.

**op-pangō, pēgī,** — 3 to impress.

**op-pectō** 3 to pick (food).

**op-pēdō, —, —** 3 to insult (alci).

**op-perior, pertus** (rarely **perītus**) **sum** 4 to wait (for).

**op-petō** 3 to go to meet; to encounter, suffer (alqd).

**oppidānus** 3 belonging to a (small) town; subst. ~, ī m inhabitant of a (small) town.

**oppidātim** in each town.

**oppidō** adv. quite, exceedingly, exactly (also **oppidō quam**).

**oppidulum, ī** n little town.

**oppidum, ī** n fortification; a) town, provincial town; b) fortified place.

**op-pignerō** 1 to pledge, pawn.
**op-pilō** 1 to shut up, block up.
**op-pingō, pēgī,** — 3 to impress.
**op-pleō, ēvī, ētum** 2 to fill, fill up (*alqd re*).
**op-pōnō** 3 to set against, put *or* place opposite *or* before (*alqd alci rei, ad alqd*); **a)** to oppose, interpose, expose, **b)** to bring forward, present, adduce, allege; **c)** to place in comparison; **d)** to pledge, mortgage.
**opportūnitās, ātis** *f* fitness, convenience, appropriateness, suitability; **a)** right time, opportunity; **b)** advantage.
**op-portūnus** 3 fit, suitable, appropriate; **a)** opportune, favourable, serviceable, advantageous, useful (*dat.; ad alqd*); **b)** exposed to, liable to.
**op-positus, ūs** *m* a setting *or* placing against *or* opposite, opposition.
**op-pressiō, ōnis** *f* force; violent seizure; overthrow.
**oppressiuncula, ae** *f* a slight touching *or* feeling.
**oppressor, ōris** *m* suppressor.
**op-pressus, ūs** *m* pressure.
**op-primō, pressī, pressum** 3 **1.** to press down *or* together, to sink; **a)** to crush, stifle, extinguish, close; **b)** to weigh down; **c)** to suppress, conceal, hide; **d)** to overpower, overthrow, prostrate, subdue; **2.** to fall upon, surprise, seize, catch.
**opprobrāmentum, ī** *n* reproach.
**op-probrium, ī** *n* reproach, abuse; disgrace, scandal, dishonour.
**op-probrō** 1 to reproach, taunt (*alci alqd*). [attack, assault.]
**op-pugnātiō, ōnis** *f* a storming;
**op-pugnātor, ōris** *m* attacker.
**op-pugnō** 1 to strike with the fist; to storm; to attack, assault, fight against.
**ops ..., opt ...,** *see* obs ..., obt ...
**ops, opis** *f* **a)** might, power, strength; **b)** assistance, help, aid, succour; *pl.* **opēs, um a)** means, property, wealth, riches, resources; **b)** forces, troops; **c)** influence, power. [desirable.]
**optābilis, e** to be wished for,
**optātiō, ōnis** *f* wish.
**opthalmiās, ae** *m* a fish.
**optimās, ātis** one of the best; *subst.* (*gen.* **optimātēs, ium** *pl.*) *m* aristocrat(s).

**optimus** 3 *and* **optimē,** *superl. of* **bonus** *and* **bene.**
**optiō[1], ōnis** *f* free choice, option.
**optiō[2], ōnis** *m* adjutant, assistant.
**optivus** 3 chosen.
**optō** 1 **a)** to choose, select; **b)** to wish for, desire (*alqd; ut*); **optandus** 3 desirable; **optātus** 3 wished for, desired, dear, welcome; **optātum, ī** *n* wish; **optātō** as desired.
**optumus** 3 (*obsolete*) = **optimus.**
**opulēns, tis** = **opulentus.**
**opulentia, ae** (*and* **-titās, ātis**) *f* riches, wealth; power, greatness.
**opulentō** 1 to enrich.
**opulentus** 3 rich, wealthy (with *abl.* or *gen.*); **a)** splendid, sumptuous; **b)** powerful, mighty.
**opus, eris** *n* work; **1.** labour; **a)** action, deed, achievement, performance, business, undertaking; **b)** artistic work, workmanship, art; **2.** product of labour; **a)** work, book, composition; **b)** building, structure; **c)** military work, fortification, entrenchment; siege-apparatus; **3. opus est** there is need, it is required, useful (*alci res* or *re*; *inf.* or *acc. c. inf.*).
**opusculum, ī** *n* a little work.
**ōra[1], ae** *f* ship's cable.
**ōra[2], ae** *f* edge, border, margin, end; **a)** sea-coast; **b)** region, country, clime, zone.
**ōrāc(u)lum, ī** *n* **a)** oracle, divine announcement, prophecy, wise speech; **b)** place where oracles are given.
**ōrāmentum, ī** *n* (?) coaxing.
**ōrārius** 3 belonging to the sea-coast.
**ōrātiō, ōnis** *f* **1.** a speaking; **a)** speech, use of language, faculty of speech, language; **b)** manner of speech, style, expression; **c)** a language; prose; **d)** subject, theme; **2.** set speech; **a)** harangue, oration; **b)** eloquence; **c)** imperial message, rescript.
**ōrātiuncula, ae** *f* short speech.
**ōrātor, ōris** *m* **a)** speaker, orator; **b)** negotiator, spokesman.
**ōrātōrius** 3 oratorical.
**ōrātrīx, īcis** *f* female suppliant.
**ōrātus, ūs** *m* request, entreaty.
**orbātiō, ōnis** *f* deprivation.
**orbātor, ōris** *m* one who deprives of children.
**orbiculātus** 3 circular, round.

**orbis, is** m circle, ring, orbit; circuit; **a)** a winding, circular motion; **b)** routine; **c)** rotation; **d)** rounded period of speech; **e)** circular surface, shield, wheel, table, eye, quoit; disk of the sun or moon, the heavens; **f)** (*terrae, terrarum*) the earth, the universe; region, territory; mankind.

**orbita, ae** f (wheel-)rut, track.

**orbitās, ātis** f bereavement, childlessness; want.

**orbitōsus** 3 full of cart-ruts.

**orbō** 1 to bereave of children or parents, to deprive (*alqm re*).

**orbus** 3 deprived; **a)** bereft, destitute (*re, a re*); **b)** bereaved of parents or children, widowed; ~, ī m and **orba, ae** f orphan, widow.

**orca, ae** f jar, barrel; dice-box.

**orchas, adis** f a kind of olive.

**orchēstra, ae** f place where the senate sat in the theatre.

**orcīnus** (*or* -īvus) 3 of the underworld.

**Orcus, ī** m (the god of) the underworld; death.

**ōrdia prima** n/pl. = **primordia.**

**ōrdinārius** 3 ordinary, regular.

**ōrdinātim** adv. in succession, in good order.

**ōrdinātiō, ōnis** f a regulating, arranging, appointment.

**ōrdinātor, ōris** m one who sets in order (*a law-suit*).

**ōrdinō** 1 to set in order, arrange; **a)** to settle, regulate; **b)** to appoint; — **ōrdinātus** 3 arranged, orderly.

**ōrdior, ōrsus sum** 4 to begin, to commence; subst. **ōrsa, ōrum** n/pl. **a)** a beginning, undertaking; **b)** speech.

**ōrdō, inis** m series; **a)** line, row, order, rank; **b)** array, file; **c)** band, troop, company, centuria; **d)** centurionship, command, centurion; **e)** order, rank, class, degree; **f)** order, succession; **g)** regularity, rule, usage, custom.

**orēas, adis** f mountain-nymph, oread.

**orexis, is** f appetite.

**organicus, ī** m musician.

**organum, ī** n instrument.

**orgia, ōrum** n/pl. orgies, secret festival, nocturnal festival of Bacchus. [brass.]

**ori-chalcum, ī** n yellow copper,

**ōricilla, ae** f = **auricilla.**

**ōricula, ae** f = **auricula.**

**oriēns, tis** m the rising sun; the east, orient; the sun-god.

**orīgō, inis** f origin, source, descent, lineage, birth; record of early history.

**orior, ortus sum** (**oritūrus**) 4 **a)** to rise, arise, become visible; **b)** to spring from, come forth, take origin (*ab, ex re*); to be born from (*ab, ex alqo, alqo*), descend, originate; to grow; **c)** to begin.

**oriundus** 3 descended, springing from (*ab alqo; ab, ex re*).

**ōrnāmentum, ī** n equipment, accoutrement; **a)** furniture; **b)** ornament, decoration; **c)** honour, ornament, distinction.

**ōrnātrīx, īcis** f lady's maid.

**ōrnātus, ūs** m equipment, outfit, accoutrements, furniture; **a)** dress, attire; **b)** ornament, decoration, embellishment.

**ōrnō** 1 to equip, fit out, provide, supply (*alqd re*); **a)** to adorn, embellish, decorate, set off; **b)** to honour, distinguish, praise, extol; — **ōrnātus** 3 fitted out, provided; **a)** adorned, decorated, embellished, handsome, beautiful; **b)** honoured, distinguished; **c)** admirable, excellent, eminent, illustrious.

**ornus, ī** f mountain-ash.

**ōrō** 1 to speak (*alqd*); **a)** to speak as an orator, treat, plead, argue; **b)** to beg, pray, entreat (*alqm alqd; ut, ne*).

**ōrsa, ōrum** n/pl., see **ordior.**

**ōrsus, ūs** m a beginning, undertaking.

**ortho-graphia, ae** f orthography.

**ortho-pȳgium, ī** n the raised tail of a bird.

**ortus, ūs** m a rising, sunrise; **a)** east; **b)** birth, origin, source.

**oryx, ygis** m wild goat.

**oryza, ae** f rice.

**ōs[1], ōris** n the mouth, jaws, (bird's or ship's) beak; **a)** tongue, lips, speech, talk; **b)** opening, mouth; **c)** face, look, expression, presence; mask; impudence, boldness.

**os[2], ossis** n bone; marrow; inmost part, heart.

**os-cen, inis** m (f) bird of augury.

**ōscillum, ī** n little mask (*of Bacchus*).

**ōscitanter** *adv.* drowsily; negligently.

**ōscitātiō, ōnis** *f* yawning.

**ōs-citō** (*and* **ōs-citor**) 1 to open the mouth, gape, yawn; to be sleepy, listless, negligent.

**ōsculābundus** 3 kissing repeatedly.

**ōsculātiō, ōnis** (*and* **-lentia**[?]**, ae**) *f* a kissing.

**ōsculor** 1 to kiss; to caress.

**ōsculum, ī** *n* little mouth; kiss.

**ōsor, ōris** *m* hater.

**osseus** 3 of bone, bony.

**ossi-fraga, ae** *f* (bone-breaker) sea-eagle, osprey; *or* the bearded vulture.

**os-tendō, ndī, ntum** (*and* **nsum**) 3 to stretch out (*alci alqd*); **a)** to show, expose to view, exhibit, display, lay open, disclose, betray, make known, promise; **b)** to express, indicate, declare; **se ostendere** *and* P. to become visible.

**ostentātiō, ōnis** *f* a showing, displaying, revealing; **a)** boasting, ostentation; **b)** pomp, false show, pretence, simulation.

**ostentātor, ōris** *m* displayer, boaster, vaunter.

**os-tentō** 1 to hold out, present to view, show, point out, indicate; **a)** to display, exhibit; **b)** to boast of (*alqd*); **c)** to promise, offer, threaten; **d)** to declare, make known, disclose (*alqd; acc.c.inf.*).

**ostentuī** (*dat.*) for a show, sign *or* pretence.

**ostentum, ī** *n* prodigy, portent.

**ōstiārium, ī** *n* door-tax.

**ōstiārius, ī** *m* doorkeeper, porter.

**ōstiātim** *adv.* from door to door.

**ōstium, ī** *n* door; entrance, mouth.

**ostrea, ae** *f and* **-um, ī** *n* mussel, oyster.

**ostreātus** 3 (covered with oyster-shells) covered with weals.

**ostri-fer** 3 producing oysters.

**ostrīnus** 3 purple.

**ostrum, ī** *n* purple(-dye); purple dress *or* covering.

**ōtiolum, ī** *n* a little leisure.

**ōtior** 1 to be idle, at leisure.

**ōtiōsus** 3 idle, at leisure, disengaged, unoccupied; **a)** free from public affairs and duties; **b)** quiet, calm, undisturbed; **c)** passionless, indifferent, neutral, unconcerned.

**ōtium, ī** *n* leisure, idleness, ease; **a)** literary work, study, fruit of leisure; **b)** rest, repose, quiet; **c)** peace.

**ovātus, ūs** *m* rejoicing, triumph.

**ovīle, is** *n* sheepfold, fold for goats; enclosure for voting in the Campus Martius.

**ovillus** 3 of sheep.

**ovis, is** *f* sheep; wool; simpleton.

**ovō** 1 **a)** to rejoice, exult; **b)** to celebrate a lesser triumph.

**ōvum, ī** *n* egg; egg-shaped ball.

**oxy-garum, ī** *n* mixture of vinegar and fish-sauce.

# P

**P.** *abbr.* = Publius.
**pābulătiō, ōnis** *f* a foraging.
**pābulātor, ōris** *m* forager.
**pābulor** 1 to forage.
**pābulum, ī** *n* fodder; food, nourishment.
**păcālis, e** relating to peace, peaceful.
**păcātor, ōris** *m* pacifier, conqueror.
**păcātus** 3 pacified, quieted, peaceful; *subst.* **păcātum, ī** *n* friendly country.
**păci-fer** 3 peace-bringing.
**păci-ficătiō, ōnis** *f* a peacemaking, pacification.
**păci-ficător, ōris** *m* peace-maker.
**păcificătōrius** 3 peace-making.
**(păci-ficō** *and)* **păci-ficor** 1 to make peace, reconcile, appease.
**păci-ficus** 3 peace-making.
**paciscor, pactus sum** 3 a) to make a contract *or* agreement, to agree (*cum alqo; ut; inf.*); b) to stipulate, bargain for (*alqd*); c) to barter, exchange; **pactus** 3 agreed upon, stipulated, settled; betrothed; **pacta, ae** *f* betrothed woman.
**păcō** 1 to reduce to peace, to pacify, subdue.
**pacta, ae** *f, see* paciscor.
**pactiō, ōnis** *f* a) agreement, contract, covenant, treaty; underhar i agreement; b) (*verborum*) form of words.
**pactor, ōris** *m* negotiator.
**pactum, ī** *n* 1. = pactio; 2. (*abl. only*) way, means; **nullo, aliquo, alio, hoc pacto.**
**paeān, ānis** *m* a) hymn (to Apollo); b) = paeon.
**paedagōgium, ī** *n* training school for page-boys; page-boys.
**paed-agōgus, ī** *m* slave in charge of children; guardian, leader.
**paedīcō** 1 to practise unnatural vice.
**paedīcō, ōnis** (*and* **paedīcātor, ōris**) *m* practiser of unnatural vice.
**paedor, ōris** *m* dirt, filth.
**paegniărius** 3 belonging to sport.

**paelex, icis** *f* concubine, mistress.
**paelicătus, ūs** *m* concubinage.
**paene** *adv.* nearly, almost.
**paen-īnsula, ae** *f* peninsula.
**paenitentia, ae** *f* repentance.
**paeniteō, uī, — 2 a)** to repent, regret; to displease; **paenitendus** regrettable, to be ashamed of; b) **me paenitet** (*alcis rei* or with *inf.* or *quod*) it repents me, grieves, makes sorry, I am displeased *or* vexed; it offends, dissatisfies; **non paenitet** I am content, satisfied.
**paenula, ae** *f* travelling-cloak, mantle.
**paenulātus** 3 clothed in the *paenula*.
**paeōn, ōnis** *m* a *metrical foot.*
**paetus** (*and* **-tulus**) 3 having a slight squint *or* cast in the eye.
**păgānicus** 3 = paganus; *subst.* **-a** (*sc. pila*), ae *f* ball stuffed with feathers.
**păgānus** 3 belonging to a village, rustic; *subst.* **~, ī** *m* villager, peasant, countryman; civilian.
**păgātim** *adv.* by villages.
**păgella, ae** *f* = pagina.
**păgina, ae** *f* page, leaf of paper; sheet; tablet, poem.
**păginula, ae** *f* (little) page.
**păgus, ī** *m* a) district, canton, region; b) village; villagers, country people.
**păla, ae** *f* spade; socket *or* bezel of a ring.
**palaestra, ae** *f* wrestling-school, wrestling-place, gymnasium; a) wrestling; b) rhetorical exercise; c) brothel.
**palaestricus** 3 of the *palaestra.*
**palaestrīta, ae** *m* director of a *palaestra.*
**palam** 1. *adv.* openly, publicly, plainly, without concealment; 2. *prep.* with *abl.* in the presence of, before.
**Palātīnus** 3 of the Palatine hill; of the imperial house.
**Palātium, ī** *n* the Palatine hill; palace.

**palātum,** ī *n and* **palātus,** ī *m* the palate; a) taste, judgment; b) vault.

**palē, ēs** *f* wrestling.

**palea, ae** *f* chaff.

**palear, āris** *n* dew-lap (*of an ox*).

**palim-psēstus,** ī *m* palimpsest, parchment rewritten after erasure.

**pālitor** (?) 1 to wander.

**paliūrus,** ī *m* Christ's thorn.

**palla, ae** *f* long robe, outer garment, mantle; curtain.

**pallaca, ae** *f* concubine.

**Palladium,** ī *n* image of Pallas.

**pallēns, tis** a)pale, wan; pale-yellow, pale-green; **b)** causing paleness; **c)** sickly.

**palleō, uī,** — 2 to be pale, be faded; to be anxious, fearful (of).

**pallēscō, luī,** — 2 to turn pale, grow yellow; to become afraid.

**palliātus** 3 dressed in a long Greek robe; Greek.

**pallidulus** 3 pale.

**pallidus** 3 = **pallens.**

**palliolātus** 3 covered with a *pallium; adv.* **palliolātim.**

**palliolum,** ī *n* little Greek mantle; hood.

**pallium,** ī *n* Greek cloak; coverlet.

**pallor, ōris** *m* paleness; fear, alarm.

**pallula, ae** *f, dim. of* **palla.**

**palma[1], ae** *f* palm, flat hand, hand; oar-blade.

**palma[2], ae** *f* palm-tree; a) date; b) palm-branch; c) palm-wreath, token of victory, prize, reward, victory; d) broom of palm-twigs; e) branch, twig.

**palmāris, e** deserving the palm, excellent.

**palmārium,** ī *n* masterpiece.

**palmātus** 3 embroidered with palm--twigs.

**palmes, itis** *m* vine-shoot; vine; branch.

**palmētum,** ī *n* palm-grove.

**palmi-fer** 3 palm-bearing.

**palmōsus** 3 full of palm-trees.

**palmula, ae** *f* oar(-blade); date.

**pālor** 1 to wander about, to roam, be dispersed; straggle.

**palpātiō, ōnis** *f* caress.

**palpātor, ōris** *m* flatterer.

**palpebra, ae** *f* (*usu. pl.*) eyelid.

**palpitō** 1 to quiver, throb.

(**palpō** *and*) **palpor** 1 to stroke, touch gently; to flatter.

**palpō, ōnis** *m* flatterer.

**palpum** (*or* **-us?**), ī *n* a stroking, flattering.

**palūdāmentum,** ī *n* military cloak.

**palūdātus** 3 clothed in a military cloak.

**palūdōsus** 3 marshy, boggy.

**palumbēs, is** *m, f* (*and* **-us,** ī *m*) woodpigeon, ring-dove.

**pālus[1],** ī *m* stake.

**palūs[2], ūdis** *f* swamp, marsh, bog, pond, pool.

**palūx, ūcis** *f* = **balux.**

**palūster, tris, tre** marshy, swampy.

**pampineus** 3 of vine (shoots).

**pampinus,** ī *m* (*f*) shoot, tendril (of vines, &c.).

**panaca, ae** *f* wine-glass.

**pan-acēa, ae** *f* a plant said to heal all diseases; panacea.

**pānāri(ol)um,** ī *n* bread-basket.

**pan-chrēstus** 3 useful for everything.

**pan-craticē** like an athlete.

**pan-cration** *and* **-cratium,** ī *n* gymnastic contest (*wrestling and boxing*).

**pandiculor** 1 to stretch oneself.

**pandō, pandī, passum** 3 to extend, spread out; to open, throw open, disclose.

**pandus** 3 bent, curved.

**pāne** *n* = **panis.**

**pan-ēgyricus,** ī *m* eulogy.

**pangō, pepigī (panxī), pāctum** 3 to fasten, fix, drive in; a) to make, compose, write; b) to settle, agree upon, contract.

**pāniceus** 3 of bread.

**pāniculus,** ī *m* thatch.

**pānīcum,** ī *n* wild millet.

**pāni-ficium,** ī *n* (the making of) bread, cakes.

**pānis, is** *m* bread, loaf. [cloth.)

**pannāria, ōrum** *n/pl.* presents of)

**panniculus,** ī *m* small garment.

**pannōsus** 3 ragged; shrivelled.

**pannūceus** (*and* **-ius**) 3 tattered; shrivelled.

**pannus,** ī *m* piece of cloth, garment; rag, patch.

**pānsa, ae** *adj.* broad-footed.

**pantex, icis** *m* belly, bowels.

**panthēra, ae** *f* panther.

**panthērīnus** 3 like a panther; mottled(?).

**panto-mīmicus** 3 of a pantomimus.

**panto-mīmus,** ī *m,* **-mīma, ae** *f* dumb-show actor, actress.

panto-pōlium, ī n general store.
papae int. indeed! 'strange!
pāpās m father; tutor.                  [(seed).\
papāver, eris n (and m) poppy∫
papāvereus 3 of poppies.
pāpiliō, ōnis m butterfly, moth.
papilla, ae f nipple, teat, breast.
pappō 1 to eat.
pappus, ī m old man; (thistle) down.
papula, ae f pimple, pustule.
papȳri-fer 3 producing papyrus.
papȳrus, ī f and -um, ī n papyrus, paper-reed, paper.
pār, paris 1. equal, like, equally strong, a match; adequate, suitable, proper; 2. subst. m and f comrade, mate; n a pair.
parābilis, e procurable.
para-bolē, ēs f comparison.
parārius, ī m agent, broker.
parasīta, ae f (female) parasite.
parasītaster, trī m mean parasite.
parasītātiō, ōnis f parasitism.
parasīticus 3 parasitic.
parasītor 1 to play the parasite.
para-situs, ī m guest, parasite.
parātiō, ōnis f a procuring, striving after (gen.).
para-tragoedō 1 to speak in tragic style or pompously.
parātus[1] 3 a) prepared, ready, provided, furnished, fitted, equipped, skilled; easy; b) bought.
parātus[2], ūs m preparation, provision; outfit; clothing.
parce-prōmus 3 niggardly.
parcitās, ātis f sparingness.
parcō, pepercī, (parsūrus) 3 a) to spare, be sparing, use moderately (alci rei); b) to preserve by sparing (with dat.); to abstain, forbear, leave off, desist, cease (dat.).
parcus 3 a) sparing, frugal, thrifty; moderate; scanty, small, little, slight; b) narrow-minded, niggardly.
pardus, ī m panther.
pārēns[1], tis obedient; subst. pā-rentēs, ium m/pl. subjects.
pārēns[2], tis m and f parent, father, mother, pl. parents; a) ancestor, progenitor, pl. relations, kindred; b) father, founder, inventor, author.
parentālis, e a) of parents, parental; b) belonging to the festival in honour of dead parents; subst.

parentālia, ium n/pl. festival in honour of dead parents.
parenti-cīda, ae m parricide.
parentō 1 to offer a sacrifice in honour of parents or relatives (alci); to revenge, appease, satisfy (alci).
pārēō, uī, (pāritūrus) 2 1. to appear, be visible; pāret it is clear, evident, manifest; 2. to obey, be obedient; to submit to, comply with, gratify, yield (alci).
pāri-cīda, ae m, see parricida.
pariēs, etis m wall of a building.
parietinae, ārum f/pl. fallen walls, ruins.
parilis, e similar, like, equal.
pariō, peperī, partum (paritūrus) 3 a) to bring forth, bear, beget; b) to produce; c) to get, win, acquire, procure (alqd; sibi alqd ab alqo); to occasion; subst. parta, ōrum n/pl.acquisitions, possessions.
pariter adv. a) equally, in like manner, as well, alike; b) at the same time, together (~ cum re).
paritō 1 to prepare; to be about to (inf.).
parma, ae f small round shield, target.                          [shield.∫
parmātus 3 armed with a round∫
parmula, ae f little round shield.
parmulārius, ī m partisan of gladiators armed with the parmula.
parō 1 to prepare, furnish, provide, contrive, design, dispose (alqd; alci alqd); a) to intend, be on the point of, be about, prepare oneself, make arrangements (inf.); b) to procure, acquire, get, obtain, buy.
par-ochus, ī m purveyor; host, entertainer.
par-opsis, idis f (dessert) dish.
parra, ae f owl.
parri-cīda, ae m and f a) parricide, murderer of a parent or near relative; b) traitor, rebel.
parricīdium, ī n a) murder of a parent or relation, of a citizen; b) high treason, rebellion.
pars, tis f part; magnam, maximam partem for the most part, in great part = magnā, maximā ex parte; (ex) aliquā parte to some extent; omni (ex) parte entirely, in every respect; a) portion, share; prō virīlī parte to the best of one's abilities; b) part, place, region, district; c) direction,

relation, respect; **in utramque partem disputāre** for and against; **in omnēs partēs** in every respect; altogether; **d)** division, section, species, branch; **e)** party, faction, side; **f)** *pl.* part, character (*on the stage*); office, duty, function.

**parsimōnia, ae** *f* thriftiness, parsimony.

**parthenicē, ēs** *f* an unknown plant.

**parti-ceps, cipis** sharing, partaking (*with gen.*); *subst. m* sharer, partaker, partner.

**participō** 1 to give a share to (*alqm alcis rei*), to impart; to share with (*alqd cum alqo*); to partake of (*alqd*).

**particula, ae** *f* small part, little bit, particle.

**particulātim** piecemeal.

**partim a)** = **partem; b)** *adv.* partly; **c) partim ... partim** one part ... another part.

**partiō, ōnis** *f* a giving birth.

**partior** (*and* **partiō**) 4 **a)** to divide (*alqd in partes*); **b)** to distribute, apportion, share, part.

**partītē** *adv.* with proper divisions.

**partitiō, ōnis** *f* **a)** a sharing, partition; **b)** division; **c)** distribution.

**partitūdō, inis** *f* = **partio.**

**parturiō** 4 to be in travail *or* labour; **a)** to teem with; **b)** to be pregnant with, brood over, meditate (*alqd*); **c)** to be anxious *or* concerned.

**partus, ūs** *m* a bringing forth, bearing, birth; **a)** time of delivery; **b)** beginning; **c)** offspring, child, young one.

**parum** *adv.* too little, not enough, not sufficiently; *as subst.* a little, too little, not enough; *comp.* **minus** less; not at all, not; **non minus** no less, just as much; *superl.* **minimē** least of all, in the smallest degree; by no means, not at all.

**parum-loquium, ī** *n* talking too little.

**parum-per** *adv.* for a little while.

**parvitās, ātis** *f* smallness.

**parvulus** 3 very little *or* small, slight; very young; **a parvulo** *or* **-is** from childhood.

**parvus** 3 *adj.* little, small (*comp.* **minor, us,** *superl.* **minimus** 3); **a)** young; (natu) **minor** younger; **minimus** youngest; **b)** short, brief; **c)** insignificant, trifling, petty, un-

important; **d)** low, mean, poor; *subst.* **a) parvus, ī** *m* boy, child; **a parvo** *or* **-is** from childhood; **b) minōrēs, um** *m/pl.* descendants, posterity; **c) parvum, ī** *n* a little, trifle; *adv.* **minimum** very little.

**pasceolus, ī** *m* little money-bag.

**pāscō, pāvi, pāstum** 3 to feed, supply with food; **a)** to feed cattle, lead to pasture; **b)** to feed, nourish, maintain, support; to let grow, cultivate; to feast, satisfy, gratify; **c)** to use (land) as pasture; (of animals) to graze (on); **P. pāscor, pāstus sum** 3 **a)** to feed, eat, graze on, browse, to feed on; **b)** to feast oneself.

**pāscuus** 3 fit for pasture, for grazing; *subst.* **pāscua, ōrum** *n/pl.* pastures.

**passer, eris** *m* **a)** sparrow; **b)** a flat fish; **c) ~ marinus** ostrich.

**passerculus, ī** *m* little sparrow.

**passim** *adv.* scattered about, here and there, far and wide, in every direction, confusedly, at random, promiscuously.

**passum, ī** *n* raisin-wine.

**passus** 3 (*pf. part.* P. of **pandō**) spread out; dried; curdled.

**passus, ūs** *m* step, stride, pace; footstep.

**pāstillus, ī** *m* lozenge, pastille.

**pāstiō, ōnis** *f* a pasturing, pasture.

**pāstor, ōris** *m* herdsman, shepherd.

**pāstōrālis, e** *and* **pāstōricius** 3 (*also* **pāstōrius** 3) relating to a shepherd, pastoral.

**pāstus, ūs** *m* food, pasture.

**patagiārius, ī** *m* maker of fringes.

**patagiātus** 3 furnished with fringes.

**pate-faciō** 3 to open, throw open; to make visible, disclose, expose, display, reveal, detect.

**patefactiō, ōnis** *f* a throwing open.

**patella, ae** *f* pan, dish, platter; sacrificial dish.

**patellārii dī** platter-gods, Lares.

**patēns, tis** open, unobstructed, accessible, passable; evident.

**pateō, uī, — 2** to be open, stand open, lie open to (*alci*); **a)** to be accessible *or* passable; **b)** to stretch out, extend; **c)** to be exposed to; **d)** to be visible, manifest.

**pater, tris** *m* father, *pl.* fathers, parents, forefathers; **a)** *pl.* senators; **b)** creator, author, chief, head.

**patera, ae** f sacrificial dish.
**paternus** 3 fatherly, paternal; native, ancestral.
**patēscō, tuī,** — 3 to be opened, lie open; a) to extend; b) to become visible or manifest.
**pathicus** 3 submitting to unnatural lust; licentious.
**patibilis, e** a) endurable, tolerable; b) sensitive.
**patibulātus** 3 fastened on a gallows, crucified.           [cross.]
**patibulum, ī** n gibbet, gallows.
**patiēns, tis** bearing, enduring, suffering (with gen.); a) patient; b) firm, hard, unyielding.
**patientia, ae** f endurance, patience; a) perseverance; b) want; of spirit; c) forbearance, indulgence; d) submission to lust; humility, subjection.
**patina, ae** f dish, pan.
**patinārius** 3 pertaining to a dish.
**patiō** (archaic) = **patior.**
**patior, passus sum** 3 to suffer, bear, endure, undergo; to allow, permit, let (alqd; with acc.c.inf.; ut); to submit to lust.
**qatrātor, ōris** m accomplisher, achiever.
**patrātus, ī** m, see **patro.**
**patria, ae** f fatherland, native land, native town, home.
**patricē** adv. in a fatherly manner.
**patriciātus, ūs** m the status of patrician.
**patricius** 3 patrician, noble; subst. ~, **ī** m a patrician, nobleman.
**patrimōnium, ī** n inherited property, inheritance, patrimony, estate.
**patrimus** (and **īmus**) 3 whose father still lives.
**patrissō** 1 to be like one's father.
**patrītus** 3 paternal.
**patrius** 3 of a father, paternal; inherited, ancestral; relating to one's country.
**patrō** 1 to accomplish, achieve, perform, execute; **pater patrātus** m the chief of the fetiales.
**patrōcinium, ī** n a) protection, defence, patronage; b) defence in a court of law.
**patrōcinor** 1 to protect, defend.
**patrōna, ae** f protectress, patroness.
**patrōnus, ī** m a) protector, defender, patron; b) advocate before a court of justice

**patruēlis, e** of a father's brother; of a cousin; m cousin.
**patruus, ī** m a father's brother, paternal uncle; severe censor; adj. 3 of an uncle.
**patulus** 3 standing open; spreading; extended.
**pauci-loquium, ī** n talking little.
**paucitās, ātis** f small number, fewness.
**pauculī** 3 very few.
**paucus** 3 a) small; b) pl. few, a few; a select few; c) **pauca** n/pl. a few things, little, a few words.
**paul(l)ātim** adv. gradually, little by little.
**paul(l)īs-per** adv. a little while.
**paul(l)ulus** 3, dim. of **paul(l)us.**
**paul(l)us** 3 small, little; subst. **paulum, ī** n a little, trifle, a little while; **paulō post** a little later.
**pauper, eris** poor, not wealthy; scanty, meagre; subst. m a poor man.
**pauperculus** 3 poor.
**pauperiēs, ēī** f = **paupertas.**
**pauperō** 1 to impoverish.
**paupertās, ātis** f poverty.
**pausa, ae** f pause, cessation, end.
**pausārius, ī** m time-keeper for rowers.
**pausea** and **-ia, ae** f a kind of olive.
**pauxillātim** adv. gradually.
**pauxillis-per** adv. in a very little time.
**pauxill(ul)us** 3 very small.
**pave-factus** 3 frightened, alarmed.
**paveō,** —, — 2 to tremble, quake with fear, be afraid, terrified.
**pavēscō,** —, — 3 = **paveo.**
**pavidus** 3 a) quaking, frightened, excited; b) causing fear, making timorous.
**pavimentātus** 3 furnished with a pavement.
**pavimentum, ī** n pavement.
**paviō** 4 to beat, strike.
**pavitō** 1 to tremble with fear (at).
**pāvō, ōnis** (and **pāvus, ī**) m peacock.
**pāvōninus** 3 made of, or coloured like, a peacock's tail.
**pavor, ōris** m a trembling, quaking, terror, fear, dread; excitement.
**pāx, pācis** f peace; treaty of peace, time of peace; **pāce tuā** with your good leave; a) goddess of peace; b) peace of mind, tranquillity; assistance or favour (of the gods).

**P.C.** = **patres conscripti.**

**peccātum, ī** *n* (*and* **-us, ūs** *m*) fault, error, sin, transgression, crime.

**peccō** 1 to commit a fault, to sin, transgress, offend (*alqd; in re; in alqm*); to go wrong, *or* astray.

**pecorōsus** 3 abounding in cattle.

**pecten, inis** *m* comb; a) reed (i.e. toothed bar) of a loom; loom; weaver's shuttle (?); comb for carding wool, &c.; b) a kind of shell-fish; c) quill for striking the strings of a lyre; d) rake; e) a kind of dance.

**pectō, pexī, pexum** 3 to comb (hair, wool, flax, .&c.).

**pectus, oris** *n* breast; a) heart, soul, courage, feelings; b) mind, understanding, character.

**pecū** *plur.* **pecua** *n* a) flocks, herds; b) money.

**pecuārius** 3 of cattle *or* sheep; *subst.* a) ~, ī *m* cattle-breeder, grazier; b) **-ia, ae** *f* cattle-breeding; c) **-ia, ōrum** *n/pl.* herds of cattle *or* sheep.

**pecūlātor, ōris** *m* embezzler of public money.

**pecūlātus, ūs** *m* embezzlement of public money.

**pecūliāris, e** as private property, one's own; special.

**pecūliātus** 3 provided with money.

**pecūliō** 1 to give a present to.

**pecūliōsus** 3 possessing savings.

**pecūlium, ī** *n* savings, personal property (of slaves, *or* other members of a household;) small sum of money.

**pecūnia, ae** *f* a) property (*in cattle*), riches, wealth; b) money.

**pecūniārius** 3 relating to money, pecuniary.

**pecūniōsus** 3 rich, wealthy.

**pecus¹, oris** *n* cattle, swine, sheep; flock.

**pecus², udis** *f* domestic animal (head of cattle, sheep &c.); wild animal; brute (as term of abuse).

**pedālis, e** of the length *or* breadth of a foot.

**pedārius (senator)** senator of inferior rank.

**pedātus¹, ūs** *m* an advance, attack.

**pedātus²** 3 provided with feet.

**pedes, itis** *m* walker; (*as adj.*) on foot; foot-soldier, infantry.

**pedester, tris, tre** on foot, pedestrian; a) of infantry, on land; b) simple, plain; in prose, prosaic.

**pede-temptim** *adv.* step by step; slowly; cautiously.

**pedica, ae** *f* fetter, snare.

**pēdis, is** *m and f* louse.

**pedi-sequus, ī** *m and* **-a, ae** *f* servant, attendant, lackey, footman, waiting-woman.

**peditāstellus, ī** *m* poor little infantryman.

**peditātus, ūs** *m* infantry.

**pēdō, pepēdī, pēditum** 3 to break wind.

**pēdor, ōris** *m* = **paedor.**

**pedum, ī** *n* a shepherd's crook.

**pēgma, atis** *n* a) book-case, shelf; b) stage machine, movable platform.

**peii...,** *see* **peri...**

**pē-i(i)erō** 1 to swear falsely, forswear oneself; **iūs pēierātum** false oath.

**pēior, pēius,** *see* **malus.**

**pelagius** 3 relating to the sea, of the sea.

**pelagus, ī** *n* (*plur.* **-gē**) the open sea, ocean.

**pēlamys, ydis** *f* young tunny-fish.

**pēlex, icis** *f* = **paelex.**

**pell-,** *see also* **perl-.**

**pellācia, ae** *f* enticement.

**pellāx, ācis** deceitful.

**pellecebrae, ārum** *f/pl.* inducements.

**pel-lēctiō, ōnis** *f* a reading through, perusal.

**pel-legō** = **perlego.**

**pel-liciō, lexī, lectum** 3 to allure, entice, seduce, decoy; to win over.

**pellicula, ae** *f* small skin *or* hide.

**pelliō, ōnis** *m* furrier, skinner.

**pellis, is** *f* hide, skin, felt, pelt; leather, leather cover, leather tent.

**pellītus** 3 clothed in hides.

**pellō, pepulī, pulsum** 3 to set in motion, strike, push; a) to beat, knock (*alqd*); b) to move, touch, make an impression on; c) to drive out *or* away, expel; to put to flight, drive back; to banish.

**pelōris, idis** *f* giant mussel.

**pelta, ae** *f* light crescent-shaped shield.

**peltastēs, ae** *m* soldier armed with the *pelta.*

**peltātus** (*and* **pelti-fer**) 3 armed with the *pelta.*

**pelvis, is** *f* basin.
**penārius** 3 relating to provisions.
**penātēs, ium** *m/pl.* the Penates (*guardian gods of the household store-cupboard and the state stores*); a dwelling, home.
**penāti-ger** 3 carrying the Penates.
**pendeō, pependī,** — 2 a) to hang, hang down (*in, ex, ab, de re*); b) to be flabby, weak; c) to hover, be suspended *or* poised; d) to depend upon (*re, ex re*); e) to be in suspense, undecided, unfinished; to be ready to fall.
**pendō, pependī, pēnsum** 3 to suspend; a) to weigh, weigh out; to pay (out); b) to ponder, consider; c) to value, esteem (*alqd magni, parvi,* &c.); d) to have a certain weight; — **pēnsus** 3 weighed, valued; **nihil pēnsī habēre** to attach no value to, care nothing about; **pēnsum, ī** *n* portion (*of wool*) weighed out, day's work, task.
**pendulus** 3 hanging down; in suspense.
**penes** *prep.* with *acc.* a) in the possession *or* power of; b) belonging to, with.      [ing.]
**penetrābilis, e** penetrable; pierc-]
**penetrālis, e** a) inward, inner, internal; **penetrāle, is** *n* (*mostly pl.* **-ālia, ium**) inner part, inner room, secret place, sanctuary; b) piercing.
**penetrō** 1 a) to set *or* place in; to enter, penetrate, betake (oneself) (*in, ad alqd*); b) *trans.* to pierce, to penetrate.
**pēnicillus, ī** *m* (*and* **-um, ī** *n*) painter's brush.
**pēniculus, ī** *m* a) brush; b) sponge; c) thatch (?).
**pēnis, is** *m* tail; the penis; lust.
**penitus**[1] 3 inner, inmost.
**penitus**[2] (*also* **-tē**) *adv.* inwardly, internally, deeply; a) far within; b) accurately, thoroughly; c) wholly, entirely.
**penna, ae** *f* feather; a) wing; plumage; b) flight; c) (feather on an) arrow.
**pennātus** 3 winged.
**penni-ger** 3 feathered, winged.
**penni-pēs, edis** wing-footed.
**penni-potēns, entis** winged.
**pēnsilis, e** hanging, suspended.
**pēnsiō, ōnis** *f* a paying, payment; instalment; rent.

**pēnsitō** 1 to weigh out; a) to weigh, consider, think over; b) to pay (*alci alqd*).
**pēnsō** 1 to weigh, weigh out; a) to compare; b) to counterbalance, compensate, repay, requite, atone for (*alqd re*); c) to ponder, consider, examine, judge (*alqd ex re*).
**pēnsum** *and* **pēnsus,** *see* pendo.
**pentēris, idis** *f* = **quinqueremis.**
**penuārius,** *see* penarius.
**pēnūria, ae** *f* want, scarcity.
**penus, oris** *n and* **penus, ūs** *f and* **ī** *m or* **penum, ī** *n* provisions, victuals, store of food.
**peplum, ī** *n and* **-us, ī** *m* robe of state of Athene at Athens.
**per** *prep.* with *acc.* **1.** (*of space*) through, through the midst of, throughout, along, over (*per medios hostes, per Alpes proficisci, vigiles disponere per urbem, per oram, per muros, per municipia; per manus tradere* from hand to hand; *cives per domus invitati* from house to house); **2.** (*of time*) through, during, in the course of, within (*per idem tempus, multos per annos, per noctem*); **3.** (*of agency*) a) through, by, by means of, by the hands of, by the agency of (*per speculatores cognoscere, per servum nuntiare; per se* in person, alone, for oneself); b) under pretence of, by the pretext of, in the name of (*per fidem fallere, decipere aliquem per indutias*); (*in entreaties, oaths*) *per deos immortales* by the immortal gods; d) for, for the sake of, on account of, by, as far as concerns (*per metum, per ambitionem; per leges non licet, per me licet*); e) (*of manner*) by, through, with, in (*per vim* violently, *per iocum* in sport, *per iniuriam, per dolum, per speciem*).
**pēra, ae** *f* bag, wallet.
**per-absurdus** 3 very absurd.
**per-accommodātus** 3 very convenient.
**per-ācer, cris, cre** very sharp.
**per-acerbus** 3 very harsh.
**per-acēscō, acuī,** — 3 to become much vexed.
**per-āctiō, ōnis** *f* a finishing, completion.
**per-acūtus** 3 very sharp, clear.
**per-adulēscēns, tis** *and* **peradulēscentulus, ī** *m* very young (man).

**per-aequē** *adv.* equally.
**per-agitō** 1 to harass; to excite.
**per-agō** 3 1. to pierce through; 2. to drive about, harass; a) to stir up, cultivate; b) to bring to an end, complete, finish, accomplish; to pass through, traverse; to live through, pass (*a time*); to play (*a part*) through; to prosecute till a conviction is obtained; c) to set forth, go through, go over.
**per-agrātiō, ōnis** *f* travelling.
**per-agrō** 1 to go over, travel through, traverse.
**per-amāns, tis** very loving.
**per-ambulō** 1 to travel through.
**per-amoenus** 3 very pleasant.
**per-amplus** 3 very large.
**per-angustus** 3 very narrow.
**per-annō** 1 to live through a year.
**per-antīquus** 3 very old.
**per-appositus** 3 very fit *or* suitable.
**per-arduus** 3 very difficult.
**per-argūtus** 3 very acute *or* clever.
**per-armātus** 3 well-armed.
**per-arō** 1 to furrow; to write down; to write on.
**pērātus** 3 in a wallet.
**per-attentus** 3 very attentive.
**per-audiendus** 3 that must be heard to the end.
**per-bacchor** 1 to revel through.
**per-beātus** 3 very happy.
**per-bellē** *adv.* very prettily.
**per-bene** *adv.* very well.
**per-benevolus** 3 very friendly.
**per-benignē** *adv.* very kindly.
**per-bibō** 3 to drink up, swallow.
**per-bītō** 3 to perish.
**per-blandus** 3 very charming.
**per-bonus** 3 very good.
**per-brevis, e** very short.
**perca, ae** *f* perch (the fish).
**per-calefactus** thoroughly warmed.
**(per-calēscō** 3) **-caluī** to become heated through.
**(per-callēscō** 3) **-calluī** a) to become quite hardened; b) to get to know thoroughly.
**per-cārus** 3 very dear.
**per-cautus** 3 very cautious.
**per-celebrō** 1 to speak of frequently.
**per-celer, is, e** very swift, sudden.
**per-cellō, culī, culsum** 3 to strike, hit, beat; a) to throw down, strike

down, overthrow, shatter; b) to ruin, destroy; to scare, unnerve; c) to thrill.
**per-cēnseō** 2 a) to count through *or* over, to enumerate; b) to survey; review, examine; c) to judge, criticize; d) to travel through.
**perceptiō, ōnis** *f* gathering, harvesting; comprehension; concept.
**per-cīdō** 3 to strike, beat; to cut to pieces.
**per-cieō** 2 (*and* **-ciō** 4) to stir, excite; **percitus** 3 a) aroused, excited; b) excitable, irritable.
**per-cipiō, cēpī, ceptum** 3 to seize, lay hold of, catch; a) to take to oneself, assume; b) to get, receive, gather, harvest; c) to perceive, be sensible of, hear, feel; d) to learn, know, comprehend, understand; — *subst.* **perceptum, ī** *n* principle, rule.　　　　　[teous.)
**per-cīvīlis, e** very polite, cour-)
**per-cognōscō** 3 to become acquainted with thoroughly.
**per-cōlō** 1 to allow to pass through.
**per-colō** 3 to adorn, honour exceedingly, crown.
**per-cōmis, e** very friendly.
**per-commodus** 3 very convenient *or* suitable.
**per-cōnor** 1 to persist in effort.
**percontātiō, ōnis** *f* inquiry.
**percontātor, ōris** *m* inquirer.
**per-contor** 1 to ask, inquire, question (*alqd ab, ex alqo; alqm de re; alqm alqd*).
**per-contumāx, ācis** very obstinate.
**per-cōpiōsus** 3 full of invention.
**per-coquō** 3 to cook *or* heat thoroughly; to ripen; to scorch.
**per-crēb(r)ēscō, b(r)uī, — 3 to become very frequent, spread abroad.
**per-crepō** 1 to resound, ring with.
**per-crucior** 1 to be in great anxiety.
**per-cunctor** 1 = **percontor.**
**per-cupidus** 3 very fond of.
**per-cupiō** 3 to desire greatly.
**per-cūriōsus** 3 very inquisitive.
**per-cūrō** 1 to heal thoroughly.
**per-currō, (cu)currī, cursum** 3 a) to run along *or* over, to traverse; to run *or* hasten through, run over.
**per-cursātiō, ōnis** *f* a running *or* travelling through.
**per-cursiō, ōnis** *f* a running through, rapid survey.

**per-cursō** 1 to wander about.

**percussiō, ōnis** f a) a striking against, beating; b) measure of time, a beating time.

**percussor, ōris** m murderer.

**percussus, ūs** m = percussio.

**per-cutiō, cussī, cussum** 3 a) to strike through, pierce, cut (alqd re); b) to strike, beat, hit; c) to wound, kill, slay; to execute, behead; d) to affect, move, shock, astound.

**per-decōrus** 3 very seemly or becoming.

**per-dēlirus** 3 very foolish.

**per-depsō** 3 to knead well.

**per-difficilis, e** very difficult.

**per-dignus** 3 very worthy.

**per-diligēns, tis** very careful.

**per-discō** 3 to learn thoroughly.

**per-disertē** adv. very eloquently.

**perditor, ōris** m ruiner, destroyer.

**perditus, ūs** m ruin.

**per-diū** adv. a very long time.

**per-diuturnus** 3 lasting very long.

**per-dives, itis** very rich.

**perdix, īcis** f partridge.

**per-dō, didī, ditum** 3 to destroy, ruin, undo; a) to waste, squander; b) to throw away, lose; — **perditus** 3 lost, ruined, wretched, miserable, desperate, hopeless; immoderate; abandoned, profligate, incorrigible.

**per-doceō** 1 to teach or instruct thoroughly.

**per-doctus** 3 very learned.

**per-dolēscō, luī,** — 3 to feel great pain or grief.

**per-domō** 1 to tame thoroughly; to subdue thoroughly.

**per-dormiscō** 3 to sleep through.

**per-dūcō** 3 **1.** to lead or bring to (alqd ad or in alqd); a) to seduce (a woman); b) to carry on, continue, prolong; c) to persuade, induce, win over; **2.** to spread over, smear over (alqd re).

**per-ductō** 1 to lead to or round.

**per-ductor, ōris** m a) guide; b) pander.

**per-dūdum** adv. very long ago.

**per-duelliō, ōnis** f high-treason.

**per-duellis, is** m enemy.

**perduim, perduint,** subj. of perdo.

**per-dūrō** 1 to last, endure.

**per-edō** 3 to eat up, consume, devour.

**per-egrē and -ī** adv. a) away from home, abroad, in a foreign country; from abroad; b) to foreign parts.

**peregrīnābundus** 3 travelling about.

**peregrīnātiō, ōnis** f sojourn abroad, travelling. [veller.]

**peregrīnātor, ōris** m habitual tra-)

**peregrīnitās, ātis** f foreign manners and customs; the status of a foreigner.

**peregrīnor** 1 to be or live abroad, to travel about; to be a stranger, alien, foreigner.

**peregrīnus** 3 a) foreign, strange, subst. ~, ī m foreigner, stranger, alien; b) unversed, inexperienced in.

**per-ēlegāns, tis** very pretty, neat, elegant.

**per-ēloquēns, tis** very eloquent.

**per-emnia, ium** n/pl. auspices taken on crossing a river or spring.

**per-ēmptor, ōris** m killer.

**perendiē** adv. on the day after to-morrow.

**perendinus** 3 after to-morrow.

**per-ennis, e** lasting throughout the year; lasting, everlasting, ever-flowing; unceasing, perpetual.

**perenni-servus, ī** m slave for life-time. [tinuance.]

**perennitās, ātis** f duration, con-)

**perennō** 1 to last, endure.

**per-eō, iī, itum, īre** to pass away, be lost, perish, die; a) to be desperately in love (with acc. or abl.); b) to be wasted, spent in vain.

**per-equitō** 1 to ride through, ride about.

**per-errō** 1 to wander through, roam over, look over.

**per-ērudītus** 3 very learned.

**per-excelsus** 3 very high.

**per-exiguus** 3 very small, very little, very short.

**per-expedītus** 3 very easy.

**per-fabricō** 1 to deceive, cheat.

**per-facētus** 3 very witty.

**per-facilis, e** very easy; very willing.

**per-familiāris, e** very intimate, familiar; m intimate friend.

**perfectiō, ōnis** f perfection, completion.

**perfector, ōris** m one who perfects.

**perfectus** 3 perfect, complete, finished.

**per-ferō** 3 to carry through, bear or bring to a certain place (alqd ad or in alqd); a) to bring, convey;

**b)** to bring news, announce; **c)** to bring to an end, carry out, complete, accomplish, to carry through (*legem*); **d)** to bear, suffer, endure.

**per-fica, ae** *f adj.* perfecting.

**per-ficiō, fēcī, fectum** 3 to complete; **a)** to make perfect, bring about, effect, execute, carry out, accomplish, achieve; **b)** to finish, bring to an end; **c)** to carry through, cause.

**per-fidēlis e** very faithful.

**perfidia ae** *f* faithlessness, perfidy, treachery.

**perfidiōsus** 3 = **perfidus**.

**per-fidus** 3 faithless, perfidious, treacherous.

**per-fīgō** 3 to pierce.

**per-flābilis, e** that can be blown through.

**per-flāgitiōsus** 3 very shameful.

**per-flō** 1 to blow through, blow over.

**per-fluctuō** 1 to surge through.

**per-fluō** 3 to flow to waste, leak out.

**per-fodiō** 3 to dig through, pierce through, perforate.

**per-forō** 1 to bore *or* pierce through.

**per-fortiter** very bravely.

**per-fossor, ōris** *m* housebreaker.

**per-fremō** 3 to roar *or* snort along.

**per-frequēns, tis** much visited, frequented.

**per-fricō** 1 to rub over, scratch; **ōs** to lay aside shame.

**per-frigefaciō** 3 to make very cold, to terrify.

**per-frigēscō, frixī** 3 to catch cold.

**per-frigidus** 3 very cold.

**per-fringō, frēgī, frāctum** 3 to break through; **a)** to break to pieces, shiver, shatter; **b)** to violate; **c)** to overpower.

**per-fruor** 3 to enjoy fully (*abl.*).

**per-fuga, ae** *m* deserter, fugitive.

**per-fugiō** 3 to flee away, to flee for refuge; to go over, desert.

**perfugium, ī** *n* place of refuge, asylum, shelter.

**per-fūnctiō, ōnis** *f* a performing, discharging.

**per-fundō** 3 ᴧ) to soak, wet, flood, dye (*alqd re*); **b)** to besprinkle, bathe, anoint; **c)** to bestrew, scatter over; **d)** to inspire, fill, imbue

**per-fungor** 3 to perform, discharge, accomplish, execute (*abl.*); **a)** to undergo, endure; **b)** to come to the end of.

**per-furō** 3 to rage on furiously (through, *acc.*).

**per-fūsōrius** 3 **a)** superficial; **b)** trumped-up, vexatious.

**per-gaudeō** 2 to be very glad.

**pergō, perrēxī, perrēctum** 3 to continue, proceed with, go on (*alqd; inf.*); **a)** to (continue to) speak; **b)** to proceed, go, march. [fashion.]

**per-graecor** 1 to revel in Greek]

**per-grandis, e** very large, very great, very old.

**per-graphicus** 3 very artful.

**per-grātus** 3 very pleasant, very agreeable.

**per-gravis, e** very heavy; very important.

**pergula, ae** *f* shed, loggia; observatory, school; brothel.

**per-hauriō** 4 to devour greedily.

**per-hibeō** 2 to bring forward, adduce; to say, assert (*alqd; acc.c.inf.*).

**perhilum** *adv.* very little.

**per-honōrificus** 3 very honourable; very respectful.

**per-horrēscō** 3 to shudder, shake with terror; to shudder at (*alqd*).

**per-horridus** 3 very dreadful.

**per-hūmānus** 3 very kind; *adv.* **-niter.**

**periclitātiō, ōnis** *f* experiment.

**periclitor** 1 to try, test; **a)** to risk, hazard, endanger; **b)** to be in danger, run risk.

**periculōsus** 3 dangerous, perilous, hazardous, threatening.

**periculum** (*and* **periclum**), **ī** *n* **1.** trial, experiment, test; **periculum facere alcis rei** to make a trial of, experience; attempt in authorship, essay; **2. a)** danger, peril, risk, hazard, dangerous deed; **b)** trial, action, suit; **c)** judicial record, register.

**per-idōneus** 3 very suitable.

**perierātiuncula, ae** *f* a little false swearing.

**per-ierō** 1, *see* **peiero.**

**per-illūstris, e** very evident; very distinguished.

**per-imbēcillus** 3 very weak.

**per-imō, ēmī, ēmptum** 3 **a)** to destroy, annihilate, to kill; **b)** to prevent, frustrate.

**per-impedītus** 3 very much obstructed.

**per-incommodus** 3 very inconvenient, very troublesome.

**per-inde** *adv.* in the same manner; **perinde ac** or **ut** or **quam** just as.

**per-indignē** *adv.* very indignantly.

**per-indulgēns, tis** very indulgent.

**per-infāmis, e** very infamous.

**per-infirmus** 3 very weak.

**per-ingeniōsus** 3 very clever.

**per-ingrātus** 3 very ungrateful.

**per-inīquus** 3 a) very unfair; b) very much upset, displeased.

**per-insignis, e** very conspicuous or remarkable.

**per-invalidus** 3 very weak.

**per-invīsus** 3 much hated.

**per-invītus** 3 very unwilling.

**peri-odus, ī** *f* (rhetorical) period.

**peri-patēticus** 3 Peripatetic, Aristotelian. [stroma.]

**peri-petasma, atis** *n* = **peri-**

**peri-phrasis, is** *f* circumlocution.

**per-īrātus** 3 very angry.

**peri-scelis, idis** *f* knee-band, garter.

**peri-strōma, atis** *n* coverlet curtain, carpet.

**peri-stȳl(i)um, ī** *n* court surrounded by a colonnade, peristyle.

**perītia, ae** *f* experience, knowledge, skill.

**perītus** 3 experienced, skilled, practised, expert, trained (with *gen.* or *abl.*, *ad alqd*, *de re*).

**per-iūcundus** 3 very agreeable.

**per-iūriōsus** 3 full of perjury.

**per-iūrium, ī** *n* perjury.

**per-iūrō** = **peiero.**

**per-iūrus** 3 perjured, lying.

**perl...,** *see also* **pell...**

**per-labor** 3 to glide over or through; to travel, make one's way.

**per-laetus** 3 very joyful.

**per-lātē** *adv.* very widely.

**per-lateō** 2 to remain hidden.

**per-lātus** 3, *part. of* **perfero.**

**per-lēctiō, ōnis** *f* perusal.

**per-legō** 3 to survey thoroughly, examine all over; to read through, peruse.

**per-lepidē** very nicely.

**per-levis, e** very (s)light.

**per-libēns, tis** very willing.

**per-līberālis, e** well-bred; *adv.* **-iter** very liberally, graciously.

**per-librō** 1 a) to weigh; b) to whirl, hurl.

**per-liciō** 3 = **pellicio.**

**per-litō** 1 to sacrifice with favourable omens.

**per-longinquus** 3 very lengthy.

**per-longus** 3 very long, tedious; *adv.* **-gē** very far.

**per-lubēns, tis** = **perlibens.**

**per-lubet** it pleases much.

**per-lūceō** 2 to shine through; to be transparent, clear.

**per-lūcidulus** 3 transparent.

**per-lūcidus** 3 translucent; very bright.

**per-lūctuōsus** 3 very mournful.

**per-luō** 3 to wash off, bathe.

**per-lūstrō** 1 to wander through; to examine, survey.

**per-madefaciō** 3 to drench.

**per-madēscō, maduī** 3 to become wet or soft.

**per-magnus** 3 very great.

**per-male** *adv.* very badly.

**per-mānanter** *adv.* by flowing through.

**per-mānāscō** 3 to flow through.

**per-maneō** 2 to remain, stay, abide (*in re*); a) to endure, continue; b) to persist.

**per-mānō** 1 to flow through or to (*in* or *ad alqd*); to penetrate.

**per-mānsiō, ōnis** *f* a remaining.

**per-marīnus** 3 accompanying through the sea.

**per-mātūrēscō, ruī,** — 3 to become quite ripe.

**per-mediocris, e** very moderate.

**per-meditātus** 3 well prepared or trained.

**per-meō** 1 to go through, pass through or over; to penetrate.

**per-mereō** 2 to perform military service (of a country, *acc.*).

**per-mētior** 4 to measure out; to traverse.

**per-mingō, minxī,** — 3 to make water upon, defile.

**per-mīrus** 3 very wonderful.

**per-misceō** 2 to mix together, intermingle; a) to throw into confusion; b) to unite.

**per-missiō, ōnis** *f* leave, permission; surrender.

**per-missū** *m, only abl.* by permission (of ...).

**permitiālis, e** destructive.

**permitiēs,** *f* ruin.

**per-mittō** 3 to let go, let loose; **equum, se permittere** to gallop, rush; a) to give up, yield, leave, surrender, intrust, commit (*alci alqd*); to use without restraint; b) to sacrifice; **c)** to permit, allow, grant (*ut; inf.*); **permissum, ī** *n* permission.

**permixtē** *and* **-tim** *adv.* confusedly.

**per-mixtiō, ōnis** *f* a mixing together, mixture; confusion.

**per-modestus** 3 very modest, very moderate.

**per-modicus** 3 very small.

**per-molestus** 3 very troublesome; *adv.* **-tē** with much vexation.

**per-molō** 3 to grind; to debauch.

**per-mōtiō, ōnis** *f* movement, agitation; emotion.

**per-moveō** 2 to move thoroughly, excite, rouse; **a)** to induce, influence, prevail on; **b)** to agitate, disturb.

**per-mulceō** 2 **a)** to stroke, touch gently; **b)** to flatter, please, charm; **c)** to soothe, appease, soften.

**per-multus** 3 very much, very many.

**per-mūniō** 4 to fortify completely; to finish fortifying.

**per-mūtātiō, ōnis** *f* change, alteration; exchange.

**per-mūtō** 1 to change, alter; to exchange.

**perna, ae** *f* leg of pork, ham.

**per-necessārius** 3 **a)** very necessary; **b)** very intimate.

**per-necesse est** it is very necessary.

**per-negō** 1 to deny obstinately.

**per-neō** 2 to spin to an end.

**perniciābilis, e** = perniciosus.

**per-niciēs, ēī** *f* destruction, ruin, death.

**perniciōsus** 3 destructive, ruinous, pernicious, dangerous.

**pernīcitās, ātis** *f* swiftness, briskness.

**per-niger** 3 quite black.

**per-nimium** *adv.* too much, very much.

**pernix, īcis** swift, brisk, nimble.

**per-nōbilis, e** very famous.

**per-noctō** 1 to pass the night.

**pernōnidēs, ae** *m* son of a ham.

**per-nōscō** 3 to learn throughly, become thoroughly acquainted with.

**per-nōtēscō, tuī,** — 3 to become generally known.

**per-nōtus** 3 well known.

**per-nox, ctis** through the night.

**pernula, ae** *f* = perna.

**per-numerō** 1 to count out.

**pērō, ōnis** *m* rustic boot.

**per-obscūrus** 3 very obscure.

**per-odiōsus** 3 very annoying.

**per-officiōsē** *adv.* very courteously.

**per-oleō** 2 to emit a penetrating odour.

**pērōnātus** 3 wearing the *pero*.

**per-opportūnus** 3 very seasonable, convenient.

**per-optātō** *adv.* very much to one's wish.

**per-opus** *indecl.* very necessary.

**per-ōrātiō, ōnis** *f* conclusion of a speech, peroration.

**per-ōrnō** 1 to adorn much.

**per-ōrō** 1 to speak to the end, plead throughout; to end, conclude, finish.

**per-ōsculor** 1 to kiss repeatedly.

**per-ōsus** 3 hating (*acc.*).

**per-pācō** 1 to pacify completely.

**per-parcē** *adv.* very sparingly.

**per-parvulus** 3 very small.

**per-parvus** 3 very little.

**per-pāstus** 3 well fed.

**per-paucī** 3 very few.

**per-pauculī** 3 very few.

**per-paul(l)um, ī** *n* a very little.

**per-pauper, eris** very poor.

**per-pauxillum, ī** *n* a very little.

**per-pavefaciō** 3 to terrify.

**per-pellō** 3 to drive on, urge, compel, prevail upon (*alqm; ut, ne*).

**perpendiculum, ī** *n* plumb-line.

**per-pendō, pendī, pēnsum** 3 to weigh carefully.

**perperam** *adv.* wrongly, falsely, untruly.

**perpes, petis** uninterrupted.

**perpessīcius** 3 patient.

**perpessiō, ōnis** *f* a suffering.

**per-petior, pessus sum** 3 to bear *or* suffer steadfastly.

**per-petrō** 1 to complete, achieve, effect, execute, perform.

**perpetuārius** 3 continually at work.

**perpetuitās, ātis** *f* uninterrupted duration, continuity, succession.

**perpetuō**[1] 1 to cause to continue, perpetuate.

**perpetuō**[2] *adv.* uninterruptedly, for ever.

**perpetuus** 3 **a)** uninterrupted, continuous, whole, entire; **b)** constant, perpetual, lasting, permanent; **in perpetuum** for ever; **c)** universal, general.

**per-placeō** 2 to please greatly.
**perplexābilis, e** obscure.
**per-plexor** 1 to cause confusion.
**per-plexus** 3 entangled, intricate, involved, confused; ambiguous, obscure; *adv.* **-xē** *and* **-xim.**
**per-plicātus** 3 entangled.
**per-pluō** 3 to let the rain through; to pour itself into.
**per-poliō** 4 to polish thoroughly, to make perfect; **perpolītus** 3 accomplished, refined.
**per-populor** 1 to ravage *or* devastate completely.
**per-pōtātiō, ōnis** *f* drinking-bout.
**per-pōtō** 1 to continue drinking; to drink off (*alqd*).
**per-primō, pressī, pressum** 3 to press hard *or* continually.
**per-propinquus** 3 very nearly related.
**per-prūrīscō** 3 to itch all over.
**per-pugnāx, ācis** very pugnacious.
**per-pulcher** 3 very beautiful.
**per-pūr(i)gō** 1 to cleanse thoroughly; **a)** to clear up, explain; **b)** to confute, refute.
**per-pusillus** 3 very small, very little.
**per-putō** 1 to explain.
**per-quam** *adv.* exceedingly.
**per-quīrō, quīsīvī, quīsītum** 3 to search for eagerly, inquire diligently, examine.
**per-quīsītius** *comp. adv.* more critically.
**per-quīsītor, ōris** *m* seeker out.
**per-rārus** 3 very rare.
**per-reconditus** 3 very hidden.
**per-rēpō** 3 to creep along.
**per-rēptō** 1 to crawl (over).
**per-rīdiculus** 3 very ridiculous.
**per-rogātiō, ōnis** *f* enactment of a law. [(*alqd*).]
**per-rogō** 1 to ask in succession]
**per-rumpō** 3 to break through, force a way through; to shatter; to overcome.
**per-saepe** *adv.* very often.
**per-salsus** 3 very witty.
**per-salūtātiō, ōnis** *f* general salutation. [sion.]
**per-salūtō** 1 to greet in succes-]
**per-sānctē** 3 very solemnly.
**per-sapiēns, tis** very wise.
**per-scienter** *adv.* very knowingly.
**per-scindō** 3 to tear to pieces.
**per-scītus** 3 very clever.

**per-scrībō** 3 to write down explicitly, at length; **a)** to note down, enter in a register, to record; **b)** to enter in an account-book; **c)** to assign money by writing, pay by draft; **d)** to announce, recount, detail.
**per-scrīptiō, ōnis** *f* a writing down, entry; draft (of money).
**per-scrīptor, ōris** *m* book-keeper.
**per-scrūtātiō, ōnis** *f* a searching.
**per-scrūtor** (*and* -ō) 1 to search through, examine.
**per-secō** 1 **a)** to dissect, lay bare; **b)** to cut out.
**per-sector** 1 **a)** to pursue; **b)** to investigate.
**per-sedeō** 2 to sit continuously.
**per-sēgnis, e** very sluggish *or* inactive.
**per-sentiō** 4 to feel deeply; to perceive distinctly.
**per-sentiscō** 3 = **persentiō.**
**per-sequor** 3 to follow constantly, follow after, pursue (*acc.*); to press upon, chase; **a)** to pursue hostilely, punish; **b)** to prosecute judicially; **c)** to note down, record, register; **d)** to pursue eagerly; to busy oneself with; **e)** to imitate, copy, be a follower of; **f)** to search over *or* through; **g)** to continue, carry on, carry out, perform, execute, accomplish; **h)** catch up, overtake; **i)** to set forth, relate, expound, describe, explain.
**persevērāns, tis,** persistent, persevering.
**persevērantia, ae** *f* perseverance, persistence.
**per-sevērō** 1 to remain steadfast, persevere in, persist, proceed with, continue (*in rē; inf.*).
**per-sevērus** 3 very severe, strict.
**per-sīdō, sēdī, sessum** 3 to settle down; to penetrate through.
**per-signō** 1 to note down carefully.
**per-similis, e** very like.
**per-simplex, icis** very simple.
**per-sistō** 3 to persist.
**persōlla, ae** *f* (a little mask) an ugly fright.
**per-sōlus** 3 quite alone.
**per-solvō** 3 **a)** to pay, pay off, pay out (*alci alqd*); **b)** to render, fulfil, discharge an obligation; **c)** to suffer *or* to inflict (punishment); **d)** to explain.

**persōna, ae** *f* mask (*worn by actors*); **a)** character, part (*in a play or in life*), person; **b)** station, rank, condition.

**persōnātus 3** in a mask, masked; in an assumed character.

**per-sonō 1 a)** to resound, re-echo; to make a loud noise; **b)** to fill with sound (*alqd*); **c)** to cry aloud, shout.

**per-sonus 3** resounding.

**per-spectē** intelligently.

**per-spectō 1** to inspect; to see to the end.

**perspectus 3** clearly perceived, well known.

**per-speculor 1** to explore thoroughly.

**per-spergō 3** to besprinkle.

**perspicāx, ācis** sharp-sighted, acute.

**perspicientia, ae** *f* clear perception, full knowledge.

**per-spiciō, spexī, spectum 3** to look through; to see clearly; **a)** to look at, examine, view, inspect; **b)** to read through; **c)** to mark, observe, perceive.

**perspicuitās, ātis** *f* clearness, perspicuity.

**perspicuus 3** transparent; clear, evident, manifest, conspicuous.

**per-spissō** *adv.* very slowly.

**per-sternō 3** to pave throughout.

**per-stimulō 1** to stimulate incessantly.

**per-stō, stitī (stātūrus) 1** to remain standing, stand firm; **a)** to remain unchanged, last; **b)** to persist in, persevere (*in re*).

**per-strepō 3** to make a great noise.

**per-stringō 3** to touch lightly, graze; **a)** to affect deeply, strike, move; to dazzle; to deafen; **b)** to scold, blame, reproach; **c)** to touch on in speaking.

**per-studiōsus 3** very eager, *or* fond.

**per-suādeō 2** (*with dat.*) **a)** to persuade, induce, prevail upon (with *ut* or *ne*); **mihi persuādētur** I am persuaded, prevailed upon; **b)** to convince (of a fact) (*alci de re* or with *acc.* and *inf.*); **mihi persuāsum est** I am convinced.

**persuāsiō, ōnis** *f* persuasion; conviction, belief, opinion.

**per-suāstrix, īcis** *f* she who persuades.

**persuāsus, ūs** *m* = persuasio.

**per-subtīlis, e** very subtle; very fine.

**per-sultō 1** to leap about; to range through (*alqd*).

**per-tābēscō, buī, — 3** to waste away.

**per-taedet, taesum est 2** it wearies, disgusts.

**pertaesus 3** disgusted at (*acc.*).

**per-tegō 3** to cover all over.

**per-temptō 1 a)** to prove thoroughly, try, put to the test; **b)** to penetrate, affect deeply, try severely.

**per-tendō, tendī, (tēnsum** *or*) **tentum 3** to push on, proceed; to carry through.

**per-tentō 1** = pertempto.

**per-tenuis, e** very weak, very slight.

**per-terebrō 1** to bore through.

**per-tergeō 2** to wipe; to touch *or* brush lightly.

**per-terreō 2** to terrify.

**perterri-crepus 3** sounding terribly. [to complete.]

**per-texō 3** to weave throughout.

**pertica, ae** *f* pole, (measuring) rod, staff.

**per-timefactus 3** greatly frightened.

**per-timēscō, muī, — 3** to be very much afraid, fear exceedingly.

**pertinācia, ae** *f* stubbornness; perseverance.

**per-tināx, ācis** tenacious; **a)** persevering, firm; **b)** obstinate, stubborn; stingy.

**per-tineō, tinuī, — 2** to reach *or* extend to, stretch to; **a)** to belong, relate, pertain, concern, refer to; **b)** to be applicable *or* suitable, tend, lead, conduce to (*ad alqd*).

**per-tingō, —, — 3** to reach, extend.

**per-tolerō 1** to endure to the end.

**per-torqueō 2** to distort.

**per-tractātē** in a hackneyed style.

**per-tractātiō, ōnis** *f* a being busy with (*gen.*).

**per-tractō 1** to touch, handle; to busy oneself with, treat, study.

**per-trahō 3** to draw along, drag; to entice *or* allure to a place

**per-trectō 1** = pertracto.

**per-tribuō 3** to give.

**pertrīcōsus 3** hard to understand (*or* trifling?).

**per-trīstis, e** very sad *or* gloomy.

**per-trītus 3** trite.

**per-tumultuōsē** *adv.* with much agitation.

**per-tundō, tudī, tūsum** 3 to thrust *or* bore through.

**per-turbātiō, ōnis** *f* confusion, disorder; a) disturbance, revolution; b) passion, emotion.

**per-turbātrīx, īcis** *f* disturber.

**per-turbō** 1 a) to confuse, disturb, throw into disorder; b) to disquiet, discompose, embarrass; — **perturbātus** 3 confused, troubled, disturbed; agitated; discomposed.

**per-turpis, e** very disgraceful.

**pērula, ae** *f* little wallet.

**per-ungō** 3 to besmear, anoint.

**per-urbānus** 3 very polite, refined, witty.

**per-urgeō** 2 to urge strongly.

**per-ūrō** 3 to burn up; a) to inflame, rub sore; b) to consume; to nip (with cold).

**per-ūtilis, e** very useful.

**per-vādō** 3 to go, come, pass through, to extend; to reach, arrive at.

**per-vagor** 1 a) to rove *or* wander over *or* about (*alqd*); b) to spread out, extend (*in re*); **pervagātus** 3 wide-spread, well known.

**per-vagus** 3 wandering about.

**per-variē** *adv.* very variously.

**per-vāstō** 3 to devastate.

**per-vehō** 3 a) to carry *or* convey through; b) to lead, conduct, bring, convey to; P. to pass through, to travel, sail to.

**per-vellō** 3 to pull, pluck; to pinch, hurt; to excite; to revile, disparage.

**per-veniō** 4 to come, arrive; to reach, attain (*ad, in alqd*).

**per-vēnor** 1 to hunt through.

**per-versāriō** *adv.* crazily.

**perversitās, ātis** *f* perversity.

**per-versus** 3 turned the wrong way, awry, perverse; wrong.

**per-vertō** 3 to turn upside down, overthrow, throw down; to destroy, ruin, undo.

**per-vesperi** *adv.* very late in the evening.

**per-vestīgātiō, ōnis** *f* investigation.

**per-vestīgō** 1 to track out; to investigate, search into.

**per-vetus, eris** *and* **per-vetustus** 3 very old.

**per-vicācia, ae** *f* persistence; stubbornness.

**per-vicāx, ācis** unyielding, persevering; obstinate, headstrong, wilful.

**per-videō** 2 a) to behold, survey, review; b) to look through, perceive, discern.

**per-vigeō, uī,** — 2 to flourish continually; to remain strong.

**per-vigil, is** ever watchful.

**per-vigilātiō, ōnis** *f* vigil.

**per-vigilium, ī** *n* a) a remaining awake throughout the night; b) vigil.

**per-vigilō** 1 to remain awake throughout the night.

**per-vīlis, e** very cheap.

**per-vincō** 3 to conquer completely; a) to prevail upon; b) to carry one's point, to effect (*ut*), to outbid; to prove.

**per-vius** 3 passable, accessible, unobstructed; *subst.* **pervium, ī** *n* thoroughfare, passage.

**per-vīvō** 3 to live on.

**per-volitō** 1 to fly through.

**per-volō**[1] 1 a) to fly through *or* about (*alqd*); b) to fly *or* hasten to (*in alqd*).

**per-volō**[2]**, voluī, velle** to wish greatly, be very desirous.

**per-volūtō** 1 to roll over and over; to unroll, read.

**per-volvō** 3 a) to roll over; b) to unroll, read through; c) P. to make oneself familiar with (*in re*).

**per-vors-, -vort- = per-vers-, -vert-.**

**per-vulgō** 1 to make common *or* public, to publish, make known; to prostitute oneself; to visit often, haunt; **pervulgātus** 3 well known, common.

**pēs, pedis** *m* foot; **pedibus** on foot; by land; **pedem ferre** to go *or* come; **conferre** to come to close quarters; **referre** to return, go back; **in sententiam pedibus īre** to vote for a motion in the senate; — a) foot (*of animals*), talon, hoof; b) step, gait, course; c) sheet, sail-rope; d) foot (*as a measure*); e) metrical foot, kind of verse.

**pessimus** 3, *superl. of* **malus.**

**pessulus, ī** *m* bolt (*of a door*).

**pessum** *adv.* to the ground, to the bottom, downwards; ~ **īre** to be ruined, to perish; ~ **dare** to destroy, ruin.

**pesti-fer** 3 destructive, fatal, injurious.

**pestilēns, tis** unhealthy, pestilential; deadly, fatal.

**pestilentia, ae** (and **pestilitās, ātis**) f unhealthy air or weather; plague, pestilence.

**pestis, is** f a) plague, pestilence; b) destruction, ruin, death; c) injurious person, curse, bane.

**petasātus** 3 wearing a *petasus* or travelling cap.

**petasō, ōnis** (dimin. -**sunculus, ī**) m shoulder of pork.

**petasus, ī** m traveller's hat.

**petaurum, ī** n acrobat's apparatus (? = spring-board, see-saw, wheel).

**petessō, —, —** 3 to long for, strive after.

**petītiō, ōnis** f a) attack, blow; b) a soliciting, requesting; c) application for office, candidature; d) claim, suit.

**petitor, ōris** m a) seeker; candidate; b) plaintiff.

**petīturiō** 4 to desire to be a candidate.

**petītus, ūs** m a falling towards.

**petō, tīvī** (or **tiī**), **tītum** 3 to seek, aim at; a) to make for, go to (acc.); b) to fall upon, attack, assail; c) to go to seek, fetch; d) to pursue, aim at; to demand, exact, desire; e) to ask, request (ut); to solicit, be a candidate for; f) to demand at law, sue for, claim.

**petorritum, ī** n open four-wheeled carriage.

**petra, ae** f rock, stone.

**petrō, ōnis** m old ram.

**petulāns, tis** forward, pert, petulant; wanton, impudent.

**petulantia, ae** f impudence, forwardness; heedlessness.

**petulcus** 3 butting.

**pexātus** 3 dressed in a garment of new wool.

**pexus** 3 of new wool.

**phaecasium, ī** n white shoe worn by priests; hence **phaecasiātus** 3.

**phalanga, ae** f wooden roller.

**phalangītēs, ae** m heavy-armed soldier (of the phalanx).

**phalanx, angis** f band of soldiers; Macedonian phalanx, heavy-armed men in close array.

**phalārica, ae** f = **falarica**.

**phalerae, ārum** f/pl. metal ornament worn on the breast.

**phalerātus** 3 wearing the *phalerae*; fine-sounding.

**phantasma, atis** n ghost, spectre.

**pharetra, ae** f quiver.

**pharetrātus** 3 and **pharetriger** 3 wearing a quiver.

**pharmaco-pōla, ae** m seller of drugs, quack.

**phasēlus, ī** m and f kidney-bean; swift-sailing yacht.

**phengītēs, ae** m transparent crystal.

**phiala, ae** f shallow cup.

**philēma, atis** n kiss.

**Philipp(ē)us** (**nummus**) m gold coin worth 20 drachmae.

**philitia, ōrum** n/pl. public meals of the Lacedemonians.

**philo-logia, ae** f (love of) learning; literary exposition.

**philo-logus, ī** m learned man.

**philo-sophia, ae** f philosophy; phi osophical question, sect.

**philosophor** 1 to study philosophy.

**philo-sophus, ī** m philosopher; adj. 3 philosophical.

**philtrum, ī** n love-potion.

**philyra, ae** f inner bark of a linden--tree.

**phimus, ī** m dice-box.    [seal.]

**phōca, ae** (and -**ē, ēs**) f sea-calf, phoenico-pterus, ī m flamingo.

**phoenix, icis** m phœnix.

**phōn-ascus, ī** m voice-teacher.

**phrenēsis, is** f madness.

**phrenēticus** 3 mad, frantic.

**phrygiō, ōnis** m gold-embroiderer.

**phthisis, is** f tuberculosis.

**phylaca, ae** f prison.

**phȳl-archus, ī** m chief of a tribe, prince, sheik.

**phyrgiō = phrygiō.**

**phȳsētēr, ēris** m a kind of whale.

**physicus** 3 relating to nature, natural, physical; subst. **~, ī** m natural philosopher; -**a, ae** f and -**a, ōrum** n/pl. natural philosophy, physics.

**physio-gnōmōn, onis** m physiognomist.    [losophy.]

**physio-logia, ae** f natural phi-

**piābilis, e** expiable.

**piāculāris, e** atoning, expiating.

**piāculum, ī** n means of expiating, expiatory sacrifice; a) expiation, expiatory victim; b) sin, guilt, guilty person.

**piāmen, inis** n = **piaculum**.

pīca, ae *f* magpie.
picāria, ae *f* pitch-works.
picea, ae *f* pitch-pine.
piceus 3 pitchy, pitch-black.
picō 1 to pitch; picātus 3 with a pitchy taste.
pictor, ōris *m* painter.
pictūra, ae *f* art of painting, painting; a) a painting, picture; b) a painting in words.
pictūrātus 3 painted; embroidered.
picus, ī *m* wood-pecker; griffin.
pietās, ātis *f* dutifulness, sense of duty; a) piety, religiousness, devotion; b) filial love, affection, patriotism; c) justice; d) kindness, tenderness.
piger, gra, grum slow, dull, lazy (*ad alqd*), indolent, inactive; sluggish; unfruitful.
piget, uit (*and* itum est) 2 a) it grieves, troubles, displeases (*alqm alcis rei*; *inf.*); b) = paenitet.
pigmentārius, ī *m* dealer in paints *or* unguents.
pigmentum, ī *n* paint, colour, pigment; decoration, ornament.
pignerātor, ōris *m* one who takes a pledge.
pignerō 1 to pledge, pawn, mortgage; -or 1 to take as a pledge; to appropriate, make one's own.
pignus, oris (*or* eris) *n* pledge, pawn, security; a) mortgage; b) hostage; c) wager, stake; d) assurance, proof; e) *pl.* pledges of love (*children*).
pigritia, ae (*and* -iēs, ēī) *f* sloth, laziness, indolence.
pigror (*and* -ō) 1 to be slow, sluggish.
pīla¹, ae *f* mortar.
pīla², ae *f* pillar; pier.
pila³, ae *f* (game of) ball.
pīlānus, ī *m* soldier of the third line (= triarius).
pīlātus 3 closely packed (*or* armed with the *pilum*).
pīleātus 3 = pilleatus.
pīlentum, ī *n* carriage, coach.
pīleus, *see* pilleus.
pili-crepus, ī *m* ball-player.
pilleātus 3 wearing a felt cap.
pilleolus, ī *m* small felt cap.
pilleus, ī *m and* -um, ī *n* felt cap (a token of freedom).
pilō 1 to depilate.
pilōsus 3 hairy, shaggy.

pīlum, ī *n* a) heavy javelin of the legionaries; b) primum pīlum the first maniple of the *triarii*.
pilus¹, ī *m* hair; trifle.
pilus², ī *m* = pīlum pīlum b).
pin(n)a, ae *f* a shell-fish.
pinētum, ī *n* pine-wood.
pīneus 3 of pine.
pingo, pinxī, pictum 3 to paint; to stain, dye, colour; a) to represent, depict, portray; b) to embroider; c) to tattoo; d) to decorate, variegate; to colour, embellish; — pictus 3 a) painted, coloured; b) variegated, tattooed; c) adorned; unreal.
pinguêscō, —, — 3 to grow fat *or* fertile.
pinguiārius, ī *m* a lover of fat.
pinguis, e fat, plump, thick, well fed; oily, greasy; *subst.* pingue, is *n* fat, grease; a) rich, fertile; b) dull, heavy, awkward, stupid; c) bombastic; d) calm, quiet, comfortable.
pīni-fer 3 pine-bearing.
pīni-ger 3 pine-bearing.
pinna¹, ae *f* = penna.
pinna², ae *f* fin; pinnacle, battlement.
pinnātus 3 feathered, winged.
pinni-ger 3 a) = pinnatus; b) provided with fins.
pinni-pēs, edis = pennipes.
pinni-rapus, ī *m* crest-seizer, a kind of gladiator.
pinnula, ae *f* little wing.
pino-tērēs, ae *m* small crab.
pīnsātiō, ōnis *f* pounding.
pīnsitō 1 to grind.
pīnsō, (pīnsuī, pīstum) 3 to pound.
pīnus, ūs *and* ī *f* a) pine, fir; b) ship; c) torch; d) wreath of pine-leaves; e) oar.
piō 1 to appease, propitiate; to atone for, expiate, purify.
piper, eris *n* pepper.
piperātus 3 peppered; thievish.
pīpilō 1 to chirp, twitter.
pipulum, ī *n* outcry.
pīrāta, ae *m* sea-robber, pirate.
pīrāticus 3 of pirates, piratical; *subst.* -ca, ae *f* piracy.
pirum, ī *n* pear.
pirus, ī *f* pear-tree.
piscārius 3 belonging to fish.
piscātor, ōris *m* fisherman, fishmonger.

**piscātōrius** 3 of fishermen, fishing- -... [fish.]

**piscātus, ūs** *m* fishing, catch of

**pisciculus, ī** *m* little fish.

**piscīna, ae** *f* fish-pond, swimming- -pool.

**piscīnārius, ī** *m* owner of a fish- pond.

**piscis, is** *m* fish.

**piscor** 1 to fish.

**piscōsus** 3 abounding in fish.

**pisculentus** 3 full of fish.

**pistillum, ī** *n* pestle.

**pistor, ōris** *m* miller, baker.

**pistōrius** 3 pertaining to a baker.

**pistrilla, ae** *f* little pounding-mill.

**pistrīnēnsis, e** belonging to a pounding-mill.

**pistrīnum, ī** *n* (*and* **-na, ae** *f*) corn- -mill; bakery..

**pistrix, īcis** *f* sea-monster (*also* **pristis** *and* **pistris, is**).

**pithēcium, ī** *n* little ape.

**pītuīta, ae** *f* phlegm, catarrh, cold.

**pītuītōsus,** 3 full of phlegm.

**pius** 3 dutiful; a) pious, religious; *pl.* the blessed, departed; b) affec- tionate, filial, loving, devoted; pa- triotic; c) holy, sacred, just, right.

**pix, picis** *f* pitch.

**plācābilis, e** 1. easily appeased, pla- cable; 2. effective in appeasing.

**plācābilitās, ātis** *f* placability.

**plācāmen, inis** *and* **plācāmentum, ī** *n* means of appeasing.

**plācātiō, ōnis** *f* an appeasing.

**plācātus** 3, *see* placo.

**placenta, ae** *f* cake.

**placeō, uī** *and* **placitus sum, itum** 2 to please, be pleasing, agreeable, acceptable (*alci*); **sibi placēre** to flatter oneself, be satisfied with one- self; a) to find favour; b) **placet** (*perf.* **placuit** *or* **placitum est**) it seems good, is settled, resolved; **si placet** if you please.

**placidus** 3 gentle, quiet, calm, peaceful, placid; kind, mild.

**placitō** 1 to please.

**placitus** 3 a) pleasing, agreeable; b) agreed on; *subst.* **placitum, ī** *n* that which is agreeable; opinion, doctrine.

**plācō** 1 a) to quiet, soothe, calm, appease; b) to reconcile; **plācātus** 3 soothed, calmed, reconciled; quiet, gentle, still.

**plāga¹, ae** *f* blow, stroke; a) cut,

thrust, wound; b) loss, injury, misfortune, disaster.

**plaga², ae** *f* (mesh of a) net, snare, trap. [trict, zone.]

**plaga³, ae** *f* tract, region, dis-

**plagiārius, ī** *m* kidnapper; plagia- rist.

**plāgi-ger** 3, **-gerulus** 3, **plāgi- patida, ae** *m* one who is flogged.

**plāgōsus** 3 fond of flogging.

**plagula, ae** *f* curtain.

**plagūsia, ae** *f* a kind of fish.

**planctus, ūs** *m* = **plangor**.

**plango, anxī, anctum** 3 to strike, beat; to make a noise by beating; to lament aloud, bewail; **-or** to beat one's breast.

**plangor, ōris** *m* a striking, beating, loud lamentation, wailing.

**plāni-loquus** 3 plain-speaking.

**plāni-pēs, pedis** *m* bare-footed mime-actor.

**plānitās, ātis** *f* distinctness.

**plānitia, ae** *and* **plānitiēs, ēī** *f* level ground, plain.

**planta¹, ae** *f* shoot for propagation, cutting.

**planta², ae** *f* sole of the foot.

**plantāria, ium** *n/pl.* a) young plants *or* trees; b) sandals; c) hair; **plantāris, e** on the soles of the feet.

**planus¹, ī** *m* vagabond, impostor.

**plānus²** 3 a) level, flat, even; b) plain; distinct; *subst.* **plānum, ī** *n* plain; *adv.* **plānē** clearly, distinctly; entire- ly, quite; by all means, to be sure.

**plasma, atis** *n* affected modulation of the voice.

**platalea, ae** *f* spoonbill; pelican.

**platanōn, ōnis** *m* grove of plane- trees.

**platanus, ī** (*and* **ūs**) *f* plane-tree.

**platēa** (*and* **platēa**) **ae** *f* street.

**plaudō, sī, sum** 3 a) to clap, slap, beat, to stamp; to strike together; b) to clap the hands, applaud, ap- prove.

**plausibilis, e** worthy of applause.

**plausor, ōris** *m* applauder.

**plaustrum, ī** *n* wagon, cart.

**plausus, ūs** *m* a clapping, noise; a clapping of hands, applause.

**plēbēcula, ae** *f* rabble, mob.

**plēbēius** 3 of the common people, plebeian; common, vulgar.

**plēbēs, (e)ī** *f* = **plebs.**

**plēbi-cola, a**, *m* friend of the com- mon people.

**plēbs, is** *f* a) the common people, commons; **b)** populace, lower class,\
**plectilis, e** plaited. [mob.]

**plector,** — 3 to be beaten *or* punished.

**plēctrum, ī** *n* a) plectrum for striking the chords of a stringed instrument; **b)** lyre, lute; **c)** rudder.

**plēnus** 3 full, filled *(with gen.; abl.)*; a) stout; **b)** strong, sonorous; **c)** pregnant; **d)** filled, satisfied, sated; **e)** abundant, copious, substantial; full, at full length; **f)** much frequented, numerous; **g)** entire, complete, whole, finished.

**plērus** 3 = **plerusque.**

**plērus-que, plēraque, plērumque** a very great part, most; a) **plērumque** *subst. n* the greatest part, *adv.* for the most part, mostly, commonly; **b)** **plērique** 3 the greater part, majority, very many; **in plērisque** in the majority of cases.

**plexus** 3 plaited.

**plicātrix, īcis** *f* one who folds clothes.

**plicō, —, ātum** 1 to fold together, coil up.

**plōdō, sī, sum** 3 = **plaudo.**

**ploerēs** = **plures.**

**ploerus** 3 = **plerus.**

**plōrābilis, e** lamentable.

**plōrābundus** 3 lamenting.

**plōrātor, ōris** *m* mourner.

**plōrātus, ūs** *m* lamentation.

**plōrō** 1 to cry aloud, wail, lament, weep; to bewail *(acc.)*.

**plōstellum, ī** *n* small wagon.

**plōstrum, ī** *n* = **plaustrum.**

**ploxenum (-inum), ī** *n* the frame of a Gallic cart (?).

**pluit, pluit (plūvit)** 3 it rains.

**plūma, ae** *f* soft feather, down.

**plūmātile, is** *n* robe with feather-trimming.

**plūmātus** 3 covered with feathers; embroidered.

**plumbeus** 3 of lead; lead-coloured; a) dull; poor; **b)** heavy, oppressive.

**plumbum, ī** *n* lead, leaden ball; (leaden) pipe *or* pencil.

**plūmeus** 3 filled with feathers; like feathers.

**plūmi-pēs, edis** feather-footed.

**plūmōsus** 3 feathered.

**plūrēs, plūrimus, plūs,** *see* **multus.**

**plūrifāriam** *adv.* in many places.

**plūsculus** 3 a little more.

**pluteus, ī** *m* (*and* **pluteum, ī** *n*) a) penthouse, shed; **b)** parapet, breastwork; **c)** (the back of) a couch; **d)** desk; shelf; **e)** bier.

**pluvia, ae** *f* rain.

**pluviālis, e** = **pluvius.**

**pluvius** 3 rainy; causing *or* bringing rain.

**P. M.** *abbr.* = **pontifex maximus.**

**pōcillum, ī** *n* small cup.

**pōc(u)lum, ī** *n* drinking vessel, cup; drink, drinking-bout; draught.

**podagra, ae** *f* gout in the feet.

**podagrōsus** *and* **podagricus** 3 gouty.

**pōdex, icis** *m* fundament, anus.

**podium, ī** *n* balcony; terrace.

**poēma, atis** *n* poem.

**poēmatium, ī** *n* short poem.

**poena, ae** *f* indemnification, compensation, recompense, expiation; a) punishment, penalty *(poenas alcis rei dare* to be punished for*)*; **b)** hardship, suffering, pain; **c)** the goddess of vengeance.

**poeniceus** = **pūniceus.**

**poeniō** *and* **-ior** = **punio(r).**

**poenitentia, ae** *f and* **poenitet,** *see* **paenitentia** *and* **paenitet.**

**poenitiō, ōnis** *f, see* **punitio.**

**poēsis, is** *f* poetry, poesy; poem.

**poēta, ae** *m* poet.

**poēticus** 3 poetic, poetical; *subst.* **-ca, ae** *and* **-cē, ēs** *f* the poetic art.

**poētria, ae** (*and* **-tris, idis**) *f* poetess.

**pol** *int.* by Pollux! indeed! truly!

**polenta, ae** *f* peeled barley, barley-groats.

**polentārius** 3 of barley-groats.

**poliō** 4 to smooth, polish; a) to whitewash; **b)** to embellish, adorn, decorate, refine; — **polītus** 3 polished; refined, accomplished, polite.

**politicus** 3 of *or* belonging to the state *or* government.

**politūra, ae** *f* polishing.

**pollen, inis** *n* (*and* **pollis, inis** *m, f*) fine flour.

**pollēns, entis,** *see* **polleo.**

**pollentia, ae** *f* might, power.

**polleō, (uī),** — 2 to be strong, mighty, powerful, able, efficacious; to prevail, avail; **pollēns, tis** strong, mighty.

**pollex, icis** *m* the thumb; the big toe.

**pol-liceor, licitus sum** 2 to offer, promise *(alci alqd; acc. c. inf.)*; *subst.* **pollicitum, ī** *n* promise.

**pollicitātiō, ōnis** f promise.
**pollicitor** 1 to promise repeatedly.
**pollinārius** 3 for fine flour.
**polli(n)ctor, ōris** m washer and anointer of corpses.
**pollingō, inxi, inctum** 3 to wash and anoint a corpse.
**pollūceō, xi, ctum** 2 to present as a sacrifice; to serve up; to serve, entertain.
**pollūcibiliter** adv. sumptuously.
**pollūctūra, ae** f splendid dinner.
**pol-luō, uī, ūtum** 3 to defile, pollute, contaminate, dishonour, violate; **pollūtus** 3 defiled; vicious, unchaste.
**polus, ī** m pole of the earth; the sky, the heavens.
**poly-phagus, ī** m gormandizer.
**pōlypōsus** 3 with a polypus in the nose.
**pōlypus, ī** m polypus; greedy person; polypus in the nose.
**pōmārium, ī** n orchard.
**pōmārius, ī** m fruiterer.
**pōm(o)ērium, ī** n open space on each side of the walls of a city.
**pōmi-fer** 3 fruit-bearing.
**pōmōsus** 3 abounding in fruit.
**pompa, ae** f solemn procession; retinue; **a)** funeral procession; **b)** display, ostentation, pomp.
**pōmum, ī** n fruit; fruit-tree.
**pōmus, ī** f fruit-tree.
**ponderō** 1 to weigh; to ponder, consider (alqd ex re, re).
**ponderōsus** 3 weighty.
**pondō a)** (abl. sg.) in weight; **b)** (with libra, &c. understood) pound, pounds.
**pondus, eris** n weight, heaviness; **a)** balance, equilibrium; **b)** burden, load, heavy body; **c)** mass, quantity, sum; a pound weight; **d)** consequence, importance; stability.
**pōne 1.** adv. behind; **2.** prep. with acc. behind.
**pōnō, posuī** (and **posīvī**), **positum** (and **postum**) 3 to put, place, set, lay; **1. a)** to put or set down (alqd in re) librum in mensa, sellam sub quercu; **b)** to plant (trees); **b)** to set before (to eat and drink); **c)** to lay out; to bury; **d)** to invest, put out at interest; **e)** to propose as a prize; **f)** to wager, stake; **g)** to spend, employ (time, trouble); **h)** to dedicate (a votive offering); **i)** to station

(troops); to put a person in some position or office, to appoint; to erect, set up (statuam in foro), build (domum, castellum in monte), **castra pōnere** to pitch a camp; **j)** to represent, picture; **k)** to lay down or aside, take off, remove, give up (vestem, arma, librum de manu); **2.** to put, place (omnem spem in consule or in fuga); **a) P. positus esse in re** to be based or founded upon, to rest upon, depend on; **b)** to apply (omnem curam in salute); **c)** to fix, give (nomen alci); to ordain (laws); **d)** to reckon, count, consider, regard; **e)** to lay down as true, assert, maintain, assume; **f)** to put away, dismiss, forgo, leave off, lay down, surrender.
**pōns, tis** m bridge; **a)** gangway; **b)** passage; **c)** drawbridge; **d)** deck of a ship.
**ponticulus, ī** m little bridge.
**ponti-fex, icis** m high priest.
**pontificālis, e** and **-ficius** 3 pontifical, relating to the high priest.
**pontificātus, ūs** m office of a high priest, pontificate.
**pontō, ōnis** m large flat boat; transport.
**pontus, ī** m the sea.
**popa, ae** m priest's attendant at sacrifices.
**popanum, ī** n sacrificial cake.
**popellus, ī** m the common people, rabble.
**popīna, ae** f cook-shop, eating-house, low tavern; food sold at a cook-shop.
**popīnō, ōnis** m frequenter of eating-houses, glutton.
**poples, itis** m hollow of the knee; knee.
**poplus, ī** m = **populus**.
**poppysma, atis** n a clicking with the tongue (sign of approval).
**populābilis, e** that can be devastated.    [ravaging.)
**populābundus** 3 laying waste,)
**populāris, e** relating to the people, popular, designed for the people; **a)** agreeable to the people; **b)** democratic, demagogic; **c)** of the same people or country, native; — subst. m fellow-countryman, associate, pl. the popular party, democrats; n/pl. the common people's seats in the theatre.

**populāritās, ātis** f a) fellow-citizenship; b) desire to please the people.

**populātiō, ōnis** f devastation.

**populātor, ōris** m and **-trix, īcis** f devastator, plunderer.

**populātus, ūs** m devastation.

**pōpuleus 3** of a poplar.

**pōpuli-fer 3** poplar-bearing.

**pōpulnus 3** of poplar wood.

**populor** and **-lō 1** to lay waste, devastate, plunder, destroy.

**populus¹, ī** m a people, political community, the citizens; multitude, crowd, throng.

**pōpulus², ī** f poplar.

**porca, ae** f sow.

**porcellus, ī** m little pig.

**porcinārius, ī** m dealer in pork.

**porcīnus 3** of pigs; *subst.* **-īna, ae** f pork.

**porclēna, ae** f little sow.

**porculus, ī** m little pig.

**porcus, ī** m hog, pig.

**porgō = porrigo².**

**porphyrēticus 3** purple-red.

**por-rēctiō, ōnis** f a stretching out, extension.

**por(r)iciō, —, rēctum 3** to offer as a sacrifice; **inter caesa et porrēcta** between the killing of a victim and the laying of its entrails on the altar, i. e. at the last moment.

**porrīgō¹, inis** f scurf, scab.

**por-rigō², rēxī, rēctum 3** to stretch out, reach out, extend; a) to stretch on the ground, lay at full length; b) to lengthen; c) to offer, present, hold out to (*alci alqd*).

**porrō** *adv.* forward; a) onward, to or at a distance; b) henceforward, furthermore; c) besides, moreover, again.

**porrum, ī** n and **-us, ī** m leek.

**porta, ae** f gate; avenue, entrance, passage.

**portātiō, ōnis** f a carrying, conveying.

**por-tendō, ndī, ntum 3** to point out, indicate, foretell, presage, portend (*alqd; acc. c. inf.*).

**portenti-ficus 3** creating monsters (*or* wonder-working).

**portentōsus 3** prodigious, portentous, monstrous.

**portentum, ī** n marvel, prodigy, portent; a) monster, monstrosity; b) strange tale, wonderful story, fiction.

**porthmeus** (*dissyllabic*) m ferryman.

**porticula, ae** f little gallery or portico.

**porticus, ūs** f colonnade, arcade, portico; a) entrance; b) gallery (*in a siege*); c) the Stoic school.

**portiō, ōnis** f share, portion; instalment; proportion.

**portisculus, ī** m coxswain's hammer (for beating time).

**portitor, ōris** m a) ferryman; waggoner (*constellation*); b) custom-house officer.

**portō 1** to carry, convey.

**portōrium, ī** n tax, toll, duty.

**portula, ae** f small gate.

**portuōsus 3** having many harbours.

**portus, ūs** m harbour, haven; refuge; river-mouth.

**pōsca, ae** f drink made of egg, vinegar, and water.

**poscō, poposcī, — 3** to beg, demand, request, desire (*alqd ab alqo* or *alqm alqd*); a) to require, need; b) to inquire, ask (*alqd*); c) to challenge to fight; d) to offer a price, bid for; e) to call, call upon, invoke.

**positiō, ōnis** f placing, position, situation; affirmation.

**positor, ōris** m founder, builder.

**positūra, ae** f situation, structure.

**positus, ūs** m position, place, situation; arrangement.

**possessiō, ōnis** f a) a taking possession, possessing; b) possession, property, estate.

**possessiuncula, ae** f small property or estate.

**possessor, ōris** m possessor.

**pos-sideō, sēdī, sessum 2** to possess, have, hold.

**pos-sīdō, sēdī, sessum 3** to occupy, take possession of.

**possum, potuī, posse** a) to be able; I can (*with inf.*); b) to avail, have influence or efficacy (*multum*).

**post 1.** *adv.* behind; afterwards, after, subsequently; **2.** *prep.* with *acc.*; a) behind; b) after, since.

**post-eā** *adv.* after, after that, afterwards.

**posteā-quam** *cj.* = postquam.

**posteritās, ātis** f after-ages, posterity, future generations.

**posterus 3** coming after, following, next, future; **in posterum** for the future, for the next day; *subst.* **posterī, ōrum** m/pl. descendants, posterity; — *comp.* **posterior, ius** following after, later, posterior, inferior, worse; — *sup.* **postrēmus** 3 hindmost, last, lowest, meanest, worst; *adv.* **postrēmum** for the last time; **postrēmō** at last, finally; **postumus** 3 last born, posthumous.

**post-ferŏ** 3 = **postpono.**

**post-genitī, ōrum** *m/pl.* posterity, descendants.

**post-habeō** 2 = **postpono.**

**post-hāc** *adv.* henceforth, after this, in future.

**post-ibi** *adv.* after that, afterwards.

**posticulum, ī** *n* back-premises.

**postīcus** 3 hinder, back; *subst.* **postīcum, ī** *n* back-door.

**postid(eā)** *adv.* = **postea.**

**postilēna, ae** *f* crupper.

**postiliō, ōnis** *f* claim of a god for a forgotten sacrifice.

**post-illā(c)** afterwards.

**postis, is** *m* door-post; door, gate.

**post-liminium, ī** *n* right to return home with citizen-rights.

**pos(t)-merīdiānus** 3 in the afternoon. [after, presently.]

**post-modo** *and* **-modum** *adv.* soon

**post-partor, ōris** *m* subsequent acquirer, descendant.

**post-pōnō** 3 to put after, esteem less, disregard.

**post-prīncipiō** in the sequel.

**post-putō** 1 to esteem less.

**post-quam** *cj.* after, when.

**postrēmus** 3, *see* **posterus.**

**postrī-diē** (*and* **postrī-duō**) *adv.* on the following day.

**post-scaenia, ōrum** *n/pl.* that which is behind the scenes.

**post-scrībō** 3 to write after *or* under.

**postulātīcius** 3 demanded, requested.

**postulātiō, ōnis** *f* claim, demand; a) complaint, expostulation; b) application to the prætor to admit a complaint.

**postulātor, ōris** *m* claimant.

**postulātum, ī** *n* demand.

**postulātus, ūs** *m* complaint, (law-) suit.

**postulō** 1 to demand, claim; a) to request (*alqd ab alqo; alqm alqd, de re; ut, ne*); b) to summon, prosecute (*alqm de re*); c) to ask leave to prosecute.

**postumus** 3, *see* **posterus.**

**pōtātiō, ōnis** *f* drinking-bout.

**pōtātor, ōris** *m* drinker.

**pote,** *see* **potis.**

**potēns, tis** mighty, powerful, ruling over; able, capable, efficacious; possessed of, master of, in control of.

**potentātus, ūs** *m* power *or* command in a state, dominion.

**potentia, ae** *f* power, might, force; a) (unconstitutional) political power, rule, dominion, command; b) influence, efficacy.

**pōtērium, ī** *n* drinking-vessel.

**potestās, ātis** *f* ability, capacity, power to do something; a) legal power, control; b) political power, authority, dominion, rule, sovereignty; official authority, office, magistracy, magistrate; c) opportunity, ability, leave, permission; **potestātem sui facere alci** to give an opportunity of speaking to *or* fighting with one.

**potīcius** 3 childish (?).

**potin?** = **potes-ne?, potest-ne?**

**pōtiō, ōnis** *f* a drinking, drink; magic potion, love-potion, poisonous draught.

**pōtiō** 4 to put into the power of (*alqm alcis*).

**pōtiōnātus** 3 having been given a draught *or* potion.

**potior¹, ius,** *comp.* of **potis.**

**potior², titus sum** 4 to become master of, take possession of, obtain, acquire (*with gen., abl., acc.*); to possess, hold, occupy, enjoy.

**potis, pote** able, capable, possible; **potis sum** = **possum; potis** *or* **pote est** = **potest** it may be, can be, is possible; — *comp.* **potior, us** better, preferable, more important; *adv.* **potius** rather, preferably, more; — *superl.* **potissimus** 3 chief, principal, most important; *adv.* **potissimum** especially, above all, of all people, of all things.

**pōtitō** 1 to drink often.

**pōtiuncula, ae** *f* small potion.

**pōtō, āvi, pōtum** *or* **pōtātum** 1 to drink, absorb; — **pōtus** 3 a) drunk, drunk up; b) drunken, intoxicated.

**pōtor, ōris** *m* drinker, drunkard.

**pōtrix, īcis** *f* female tippler.

**pōtulentus** 3 a) drinkable; **-um, ī** *n* drink; b) drunken.

**pōtus¹** 3, *see* **poto.**

**pōtus², ūs** *m* a drinking, drink.

**P. R.** *abbr.* = **populus Romanus.**

**prae 1.** *adv.* before, in front; **praeut, praequam** *cj.* in comparison with (what); **2.** *prep.* with *acc.* a) before, in front of; **prae manu** at hand; **prae se ferre** to display, boast of; b) in comparison with; c) because of, on account of, for **prae lacrimis loqui non posse.**

**prae-acūtus** 3 sharp, pointed.

**prae-altus** 3 very high *or* deep.

**prae-beō, uī, itum** 2 to hold forth, reach out (*alci alqd*); a) to proffer, offer, present, furnish, afford; b) to give, occasion, cause (c) to show, exhibit, represent (*se virum, se misericordem praebere*).

**prae-bibō, bibī, —** 3 to drink to (*alci*).

**praebitor, ōris** *m* furnisher, purveyor.

**prae-calidus** 3 very warm *or* hot

**prae-calvus** 3 very bald.

**prae-cantrix, īcis** *f* sorceress.

**prae-cānus** 3 quite white (*or* prematurely white?).

**prae-caveō** 2 a) to use precaution, take care, be on one's guard (*a re; ne*); b) to take care for (*with dat.*).

**prae-cēdō** 3 to go before, precede; to surpass, outdo.

**prae-celer, eris, ere** very swift.

**prae-celerō** 1 to hurry forward (*intrans. or trans.*).

**prae-cellō, —, —** 3 to surpass, excel (*alqm re*), distinguish oneself; **praecellēns, tis** excellent, eminent, distinguished.

**prae-celsus** 3 very high, very lofty.

**prae-centiō, ōnis** *f* prelude.

**prae-centō** 1 to utter incantations before (*alci*).

**prae-ceps, cipitis** head-foremost, headlong; a) steep, precipitous, abrupt; *subst.* steep place, precipice; danger, critical circumstances; b) hasty, rapid; rash, reckless; c) inclined, prone (*in alqd*); **praeceps** (*as adv.*) down headlong; into peril.

**praeceptiō, ōnis** *f* a) precept; b) preconception; c) legacy paid before the winding-up of an estate.

**praeceptīvus** 3 didactic.

**praeceptor, ōris** *m* teacher, instructor.

**praeceptrix, īcis** *f* preceptress.

**praeceptum, ī** *n* precept, order, injunction; rule, maxim.

**prae-cerpō, psī, ptum** 3 to pluck

*or* gather prematurely; to forestall, intercept.

**prae-cīdō, cīdī, cīsum** 3 a) to cut off; b) to refuse; c) to cut short, abridge; d) to cut in pieces; e) to break off suddenly.

**prae-cingō** 3 to gird about; to surround, encircle (*alqd re*).

**prae-cinō, cinuī** (*and* **cecinī**), **centum** 3 a) to recite *or* play before; b) to foretell, predict.

**praecipes, ipis** = **praeceps**.

**prae-cipiō, cēpī, ceptum** 3 a) to take *or* obtain in advance, to anticipate, to enjoy in anticipation; b) to conjecture; c) to advise (*alci alqd; ut, ne, inf.*), warn, instruct, prescribe, command, give rules.

**praecipitātiō, ōnis** *f* a headlong fall.

**praecipitium, ī** *n* precipice.

**praecipitō** 1 1. to cast down headlong; a) to destroy, ruin; b) to hurry, hasten (*alqd; inf.*); 2. *intr.* to throw oneself down, to rush headlong, fall down, sink to ruin; — **praecipitanter** headlong.

**praecipuē** *adv.* chiefly, principally, especially.

**praecipuus** 3 a) received in advance; b) particular, peculiar, especial; principal, distinguished, eminent; — *subst.* **praecipuum, ī** *n* desirable *or* important thing.

**prae-cīsus** 3 broken off, steep, abrupt, precipitous; short; *adv.* concisely, positively.

**prae-clārus** 3 very clear, very bright; a) splendid, noble, excellent, admirable; b) famous, celebrated.

**prae-clūdō, sī, sum** 3 to shut off, shut, close.

**praecō, ōnis** *m* crier, herald; auctioneer; publisher, eulogist.

**prae-cōgitō** 1 to think *or* consider beforehand.

**prae-cognōscō** 3 to know *or* see beforehand.

**prae-colō** 3 to cultivate beforehand; to honour prematurely.

**prae-compositus** 3 arranged beforehand.

**praecōnius** 3 of a public crier; *subst.* **praecōnium, ī** *n* office of a public crier; proclamation, publication; laudation.

**prae-cōnsūmō** 3 to waste *or* spend beforehand.

**prae-contrectō** 1 to feel *or* handle beforehand.

**prae-cordia, ōrum** *n/pl.* 1. midriff, diaphragm; 2. internal organs; a) breast; b) heart, feeling, mind.

**prae-corrumpō** 3 to bribe beforehand.

**prae-cox, -cocis** *and* **-coquis, e** premature; precocious.

**prae-cultus** 3 highly ornamented.

**prae-cupidus** 3 very fond of.

**prae-currō, (cu)currī, cursum** 3 to run before, hasten on before; a) to precede, anticipate (*alqd*); b) to exceed, surpass, excel (*alqm re*).

**prae-cursiō, ōnis** *f* a) previous occurrence; b) preliminary skirmish.

**prae-cursor, ōris** *m* forerunner; advanced guard; scput.

**prae-cursōrius** 3 sent in advance.

**prae-cutiō, cussī, cussum** 3 to shake *or* brandish before.

**praeda, ae** *f* booty, spoil, plunder; a) prey, game; b) gain, profit, advantage.     [dering.]

**praedābundus** 3 ravaging, plun-*f*

**prae-damnō** 1 to condemn beforehand; to give up in advance.

**praedātiō, ōnis** *f (and* **-dātus, ūs** *m)* a pillaging.

**praedātor, ōris** *m and* **-trīx, īcis** *f* plunderer; hunter; greedy person.

**praedātōrius** 3 plundering, predatory.     [forehand.]

**prae-dēlassō** 1 to weary out be-*f*

**prae-dēstinō** 1 to decree beforehand (*alci alqd*).

**praediātor, ōris** *m* dealer in estates.

**praediātōrius** 3 relating to the sale of estates.

**praedicābilis, e** praiseworthy.

**praedicātiō, ōnis** *f* proclamation, publication; a) praise, commendation; b) declaration.

**praedicātor, ōris** *m* commender.

**prae-dicō**[1] 1 to publish, proclaim; a) to declare publicly, assert, announce, boast of; b) to praise, commend.

**prae-dicō**[2] 3 to say *or* mention before; a) to foretell, predict, prophesy; b) to prearrange; to order beforehand.

**prae-dictiō, ōnis** *f* prediction.

**prae-dictum, ī** *n* a) prediction; b) order, command; c) agreement, concert.

**praediolum, ī** *n* small farm *or* estate.

**prae-discō** 3 to learn beforehand.

**prae-dispositus** 3 arranged beforehand.

**prae-ditus** 3 endowed, gifted *or* provided with; possessed of (*abl.*).

**praedium, ī** *n* farm, estate.

**prae-dīves, itis** very rich.

**prae-dīvīnō** 1 to have a presentiment.

**praedō, ōnis** *m* plunc erer, robber; pirate.

**prae-doceō** 2 to instruct befc rehand.

**prae-domō** 1 to overcome beforehand.

**praedor** 1 1. to make booty, plunder; 2. *trans.* to carry off as prey; to plunder, rob.

**prae-dūcō** 3 to draw *or* construct in front of (*dat.*).

**prae-dulcis, e** very sweet.

**prae-dūrus** 3 very hard, very tough.

**prae-ēmineō, 2 = praemineo.**

**prae-eō** to go before (*alci*), lead the way; to dictate (a formula); to order, dictate.

**prae-fātiō, ōnis** *f* religious form of words, formula; preface, introduction.

**praefectūra, ae** *f* office of a *praefectus*; a) command, administration; b) district, province; city governed by a prefect; prefecture.

**praefectus, ī** *m* overseer, superintendent; a) commander, governor; b) prefect.

**prae-ferō** 3 to bear *or* carry before, in front (*alci alqd*); a) to show, display; manifest, betray; b) to put before; c) to prefer, choose rather (*alci alqd*); d) to anticipate; **P.** to ride *or* march past.

**prae-ferōx, ōcis** very defiant *or* headstrong.

**prae-ferrātus** 3 in irons.

**prae-fervidus** 3 very hot, glowing.

**prae-festīnō** 1 a) to hasten too much; b) to hasten past.

**prae-fica, ae** *f* woman hired to lament at a funeral.

**prae-ficiō, fēcī, fectum** 3 to set *or* place over, place in authority over (*alqm alci rei*), appoint to command.

**prae-fidēns, tis** over-confident.

**prae-fīgō** 3 a) to fix *or* fasten in front *or* on the end; b) to point with; c) to pierce.

**prae-fīniō** 4 to determine beforehand, prescribe; **praefīnītō** (*as adv.*) as prescribed.

**prae-fiscinē** (-nī) *adv.* may no evil befall us!; meaning no harm, without offence.

**prae-flōrō** 1 to rob of its bloom beforehand.          [past (*alqd*).]

**prae-fluō**, —, — 3 to flow by *or*

**prae-fōcō** 1 to choke.

**prae-fodiō** 3 a) to dig in front of (*alqd*); **b)** to bury beforehand.

**prae-for** 1 to say beforehand, utter in advance; a) to utter a preliminary prayer; **b)** to preface; **c)** to invoke; **d)** to foretell, prophesy.

**prae-frāctus** 3 abrupt; stern, harsh.

**prae-frīgidus** 3 very cold.

**prae-fringō, frēgī, frāctum** 3 to break off at the end.

**prae-fulciō** 4 to prop up; to use as a prop; to fence round; to secure.

**prae-fulgeō** 2 to shine forth, beam, glitter; to be conspicuous; to outshine.

**prae-fulgurō** 1 to flash forth; to fill with brightness (*acc.*).

**prae-furō** 3 to rage violently.

**prae-gaudeō** 2 to rejoice greatly.

**prae-gelidus** 3 very cold.

**prae-gestiō** 4 to desire greatly.

**prae-gnā(n)s, (n)tis** pregnant, with child, big with, full of.

**prae-gracilis, e** very slender.

**prae-grandis, e** very large; very powerful *or* great.

**prae-gravis, e** very heavy; a) burdensome; **b)** wearisome.

**prae-gravō** 1 to oppress with, encumber, burden; to depress, weigh down.

**prae-gredior, gressus sum** 3 a) to go before *or* in advance; **b)** to pass by, go past (*acc.*).

**praegressiō, ōnis** *f* a preceding, precedence.          [velopment.]

**praegressus, ūs** *m* previous de-

**prae-gustātor, ōris** *m* one who tastes first, taster.

**prae-gustō** 1 to taste beforehand.

**prae-hibeō** 2 = **praebeo.**

**prae-iaceō**, —, — 2 to lie before *or* in front of (*acc.*).

**prae-iūdicium, ī** *n* previous judgment, preliminary decision; a) precedent, example; **b)** premature decision; **c)** prejudice, disadvantage.

**prae-iūdicō** 1 to judge *or* decide beforehand (*de re*); **praeiūdicātus** 3 decided previously, prejudged; **opinio praeiūdicāta** prejudice.

**prae-lābor** 3 to glide *or* flow past *or* along (*acc.*).

**prae-lambō**, —, — 3 to lick *or* taste before.

**prae-largus** 3 very prodigal of.

**prae-lautus** 3 very sumptuous.

**prae-legō** 3 a) to sail past; **b)** to lecture on.

**prae-libō** 1 to taste beforehand.

**prae-ligō** 1 to bind in front; to bind up; **praeligātus** 3 obdurate.

**prae-longus** 3 very long.

**prae-loquor** 3 to speak before someone else; to speak by way of preface.

**prae-lūceō** 2 to shine before; to outshine, surpass (*alci*).

**prae-lūdō** 3 to say by way of preface.

**prae-lūsiō, ōnis** *f* prelude.

**prae-lūstris, e** magnificent.

**prae-mandō** 1 to order beforehand; *subst.* **praemandātum, ī** *n* warrant of arrest.

**prae-mātūrus** 3 too early, untimely, premature.

**prae-medicātus** 3 protected by medicines *or* charms.

**prae-meditātiō, ōnis** *f* a considering beforehand.

**prae-meditor** 1 to consider *or* meditate beforehand.

**prae-mercor** 1 to buy before.

**prae-metuō**, —, — 3 to fear beforehand; **praemetuenter** anxiously.

**prae-mineo**, —, — 2 to surpass, excel (*acc.*).

**praemior** 1 to stipulate for a reward.

**prae-mittō** 3 to send in advance; to send out; to say first.

**praemium, ī** *n* **1.** profit, advantage, gain; prerogative, distinction; **2.** reward, recompense; prize; exploit; booty.

**prae-molestia, ae** *f* trouble beforehand, apprehension.

**prae-mōlior** 4 to prepare.

**prae-moneō** 2 a) to forewarn, admonish beforehand (*ut, ne*); **b)** to foretell, presage.          [ing.]

**prae-monitus, ūs** *m* a forewarn-

**prae-mōnstrātor, ōris** *m* guide.

**prae-mōnstrō** 1 to show, guide, warn; to predict, presage.

**prae-mordeō** 2 to bite off.

**prae-morior** 3 to die prematurely.
**prae-mūniō** 4 a) to fortify, protect, secure; b) to place before as a defence; c) to say beforehand to obviate objections.
**prae-mūnītiō, ōnis** f preparation.
**prae-nārrō** 1 to relate beforehand.
**prae-natō** 1 to swim before or past, to flow by.
**prae-nāvigō** 1 to sail past; to pass through.
**prae-niteō** 2 to outshine (alci).
**prae-nōmen, inis** n first or personal name; title.
**prae-nōscō** 3 to learn beforehand, foreknow.
**prae-nōtiō, ōnis** f preconception, innate idea.    [dark.\
**prae-nūbilus** 3 very cloudy, very∫
**prae-nūntiō** 1 to announce, foretell.
**prae-nūntius, ī** m and **-nūntia, ae** f foreteller, foreboder; **-nūntium, ī** n sign, omen.
**prae-occupātiō, ōnis** f a seizing beforehand.
**prae-occupō** 1 to seize or take possession of before; a) to anticipate, prevent; b) to hasten to do sooner.
**prae-olit mihi** I smell in advance.
**prae-optō** 1 to prefer.
**prae-pandō, —, —** 3 to spread out before, extend; to open.
**prae-parātiō, ōnis** f preparation.
**prae-parō** 1 to prepare, make ready, provide (alqd ad alqd).
**prae-pedimentum, ī** n hindrance, impediment.
**prae-pediō** 4 to tether, shackle, fetter; to hinder, obstruct.
**prae-pendeō, pendī, —** 2 to hang down in front.
**prae-pes, petis** quick in flight, fleet; auspicious; subst. m and f bird; bird of good omen.
**prae-pilātus** 3 tipped with a ball.
**prae-pinguis, e** very fat, rich.
**prae-polleō** 2 to be very powerful, exceed in power.
**prae-ponderō** 1 to preponderate; to outweigh, surpass.
**prae-pōnō** 3 to put or set before; a) to put over, set over, place at the head of (alqm alci rei); b) to prefer; subst. **praepositus, ī** m = **praefectus; praepositum, ī** n preferable, desirable thing.
**prae-portō** 1 to carry in front; to show.

**prae-positiō, ōnis** f a) preference; b) preposition.
**prae-posterus** 3 reversed, inverted, perverse, preposterous; unseasonable.
**prae-potēns, tis** very mighty or powerful.
**prae-properus** 3 too hasty, precipitate; adv. **-rē** and **-ranter.**
**prae-pūtium, ī** n foreskin.
**praequam,** see **prae.**
**prae-queror** 3 to complain beforehand.
**prae-radiō** 1 to outshine.
**prae-rapidus** 3 very rapid.
**prae-rigēscō,** 3 to become very stiff.
**prae-ripiō, ripuī, reptum** 3 a) to seize first or prematurely; to forestall; b) to frustrate.
**prae-rōdō** 3 to gnaw (off).
**prae-rogātīvus** 3 voting before others; subst. **praerogātīva, ae** f a) century that voted first (also n/pl. the votes of the first centuries); b) previous choice; c) sign, omen.
**prae-rumpō** 3 to break off short.
**prae-ruptus** 3 steep, precipitous; headstrong; harsh.
**praes, praedis** m surety, bondsman; property of a surety.
**praesaepe, is** n (and **-saepēs** or **-saepis, is** f) a) manger; b) stall, stable, fold; home; c) beehive.
**prae-saepiō** 4 to barricade.
**prae-sāgiō** (and **-ior**) 4 to have a presentiment; to forebode.
**praesāgītiō, ōnis** f presentiment, foreboding.
**praesāgium, ī** n presentiment, foreboding, presage, prediction.
**prae-sāgus** 3 foreboding; predicting.
**prae-sciō** 4 to know beforehand.
**prae-sciscō, īvī, (iī), —** 3 to learn or find out beforehand.
**prae-scius** 3 knowing beforehand.
**prae-scrībō** 3 to prefix in writing; a) to use as a pretext; b) to dictate; c) to order, direct, prescribe (alci alqd; ut, ne); d) to outline in advance.
**prae-scrīptiō, ōnis** f title; a) pretext, excuse; b) order, rule; c) captious objection.
**prae-scrīptum, ī** n prescribed limit; task; order, rule.
**prae-secō** 1 to cut off short.

**prae-segmen, inis** *n* clippings.
**praesēns, tis 1.** present, in person;
**2.** at hand, immediate, instant;
a) ready, prompt, efficacious, powerful; b) pressing, urgent; c) aiding;
propitious; d) determined, resolute;
— **in praesēns** (*tempus*) for the
present, for the moment; **in praesentī** at present, now; *subst.* **praesentia, ium** *n/pl.* the present,
present circumstances.
**prae-sēnsiō, ōnis** *f* presentiment;
preconception. [effect.]
**praesentāneus 3** having a quick
**praesentārius 3** = **praesens.**
**praesentia, ae** *f* presence, a being
present; effect, efficacy.
**prae-sentiō 4** to feel *or* perceive
beforehand.
**praesēpe, is** *n, see* **praesaepe.**
**praesertim** *adv.* especially, chiefly.
**prae-serviō 4** to serve by preference.
**prae-ses, sidis** presiding, protecting, guarding; *subst.* *m* and *f* a) protector, guardian, defender; b) chief,
ruler.
**prae-sideō, sēdī, (sessum) 2** to sit
before; to protect, guard; to preside
over, govern.
**praesidiārius 3** serving as a guard
*or* garrison.
**praesidium, ī** *n* protection, defence;
a) aid, assistance, support; b) escort, convoy; c) guard, garrison,
patrol, post, picket, troops; d) station, camp, fortification.
**prae-significō 1** to indicate beforehand.
**prae-signis, e** remarkable before
others.
**prae-solidō 1** to solidify.
**prae-sonō 1** to sound first.
**prae-spargō 3** to strew before.
**praestābilis, e** = **praestans.**
**praestāns, tis** distinguished, excellent, superior, pre-eminent.
**praestantia, ae** *f* excellence, superiority.
**praestātiō, ōnis** *f* guarantee.
**prae-sternō 3** to strew before; to
lay in front; to deck, make ready;
to smooth the way.
**prae-stes, itis** protecting.
**praest(r)igiae, ārum** *f/pl.* deceptions, illusions, trickery.
**prae-st(r)igiātor, ōris** *m*, **-trīx,
īcis** *f* conjurer, cheat.

**praestinō 1** to buy.
**prae-stituō, uī, ūtum 3** to determine beforehand (*alci alqd*).
**prae-stō**[1] *adv.* at hand, ready, present, here, at one's service (*alci, ad
alqd*); present in a hostile manner.
**prae-stō**[2], **stitī, stitum (stātūrus)
1 1.** to stand out, stand before; a) to
distinguish oneself, excel (*alci re;
alqm re*), be superior; b) **praestat**
it is preferable *or* better (*dat.; dat.
c. inf.*); **2.** *trans.* to perform, execute, fulfil; **fidem** to keep one's
word; a) to give, offer, furnish (*alci
alqd*); b) to show, exhibit, prove,
evince, manifest; **se praestare** to
show *or* prove oneself (*constantem,
fortem*); c) to answer, be responsible
for, warrant (*alqm or alqd, de re;
alci alqd; acc. c. inf.*).
**praestōlor 1** to wait for (*alqd*), stand
ready for (*alci*).
**prae-stringō 3** to draw together,
fasten up, bind fast; to blunt, dazzle,
weaken.
**prae-struō 3** to build before, block
up; a) to secure beforehand; b) to
prepare. [greatly.]
**prae-sūdō 1** to sweat *or* labour
**prae-sul, ulis** and **-sultātor, ōris**
*m* leader in a dance *or* procession.
**prae-sultō 1** to leap *or* dance before.
**prae-sum, fuī, (futūrus), esse** to
be leader, be set over, preside, rule,
command, superintend (*with dat.*).
**prae-sūmō 3** to take beforehand;
a) to enjoy beforehand, anticipate;
b) to imagine beforehand, to suppose, take for granted, presume,
presuppose.
**prae-sūmptiō, ōnis** *f* expectation,
hope. [to cover (*alqd re*).]
**prae-suō, —, sūtum 3** to sew up;
**prae-tegō 3** to cover, shelter.
**prae-temptō 1** to feel, try *or* test
beforehand.
**prae-tendō, ndī, ntum 3** to stretch
forth *or* forward; a) to place, hold
*or* spread before (*alqd alci rei*); **P.** to
lie before *or* in front; b) to pretend,
hold before as a pretext.
**prae-tentō 1,** *see* **praetempto.**
**(prae-tepēscō), praetepuī, — 3**
to grow warm before.
**praeter 1.** *adv.* (*used as cj.*) unless it
be, except; **2.** *prep.* with *acc.* past, in
front of, along; a) except; b) above,
besides; c) beyond, contrary to.

**praeter-agō** 3 to drive past.

**praeter-bītō** 3 to go by.

**praeter-dūcō** 3 to lead by.

**praeter-eā** *adv.* besides, beyond this, further; a) moreover; b) henceforth, thereafter.

**praeter-eō** to go by, pass by (*alqd*); a) to pass, elapse; b) to flow past *or* along; c) to escape the notice of, be unknown to; d) to neglect, omit, not to mention, leave unnoticed *or* unpractised; e) to go beyond, surpass, excel; to pass in a race; **praeteritus** 3 gone by, past, departed.

**praeter-equitō** 1 to ride past.

**praeter-feror** to go past (*alqd*).

**praeter-fluō** 3 to flow by *or* past (*alqd*); to pass away.

**praeter-gredior, gressus sum** 3 to walk by; to surpass.

**praeter-hāc** *adv.* further.

**praeter-itus** 3, *see* praetereo.

**praeter-lābor** 3 to glide past (*alqd*).

**praeter-meō** 1 to go by.

**praeter-missiō, ōnis** *f* omission, neglect.

**praeter-mittō** 3 to let pass; a) to omit, neglect, leave undone; b) to overlook.

**praeter-nāvigō** 1 to sail past.

**prae-terō** 3 to rub off.

**praeter-quam** *cj.* more than; except, beyond, unless it be; ~ **quod** except that, apart from the fact that.

**praeter-vectiō, ōnis** *f* a place where people sail by.

**praeter-vehor** 3 to pass, drive, ride, sail by (*alqd*).

**praeter-volō** 1 to fly by *or* past; to slip by, escape; to pass over cursorily.

**prae-texō** 3 a) to fringe, border, edge; b) to adorn in front; **praetextus** 3 bordered with purple (*also* = praetextātus); c) to cover, conceal (*alqd re*); d) to pretend, allege as an excuse.

**praetexta, ae** *f* a) (*toga*) purple-bordered toga (worn by the higher magistrates and by free-born boys); b) (*fabula*) tragedy dealing with Roman life.

**praetextātus** 3 wearing a *toga praetexta*; under age; indecent.

**praetextum, ī** *n* pretence, pretext; ornament.

**praetextus, ūs** *m* outward appearance, show, adornment; pretence, pretext.

**prae-timeō** 2 to fear beforehand.

**prae-tinctus** 3 moistened beforehand.

**praetor, ōris** *m* leader, chief, president; a) commander, general; b) praetor, magistrate; c) governor.

**praetōriānus** 3 prætorian, belonging to the imperial bodyguard; *subst. m* one of the imperial body-guard.

**praetōricius** 3 of a prætor.

**praetōrius** 3 a) relating to a prætor, of a prætor; b) of a general; **cohors praetōria** a general's *or* emperor's body-guard; **porta, -ia** the gate near the general's tent; c) belonging to a propraetor; — *subst.* a) **-ius, ī** *m* a past prætor; b) **-ium, ī** *n* a general's tent; council of war; place before the general's tent; residence of a governor; palace, imposing residence; imperial body-guard.

**prae-torqueō** 2 to twist, wring.

**prae-tractō** 1 to discuss beforehand.

**prae-trepidō** 1 to be excited.

**prae-trepidus** 3 palpitating; disquieted.

**prae-truncō** 1 to cut off.

**praetūra, ae** *f* prætorship.

**prae-umbrō** 1 to overshadow, to obscure.

**prae-ustus** 3 burned at the end *or* point; frost-bitten.

**praeut,** *see* prae.

**prae-vādō** 3 to obtain a discharge from (*acc.*).

**prae-valeō, uī, —** 2 to be very strong *or* powerful, to be stronger, have greater power *or* worth, be superior, prevail.

**prae-validus** 3 very strong *or* powerful; too strong.

**prae-vallō** 1 to fortify in front.

**praevāricātiō, ōnis** *f* collusion.

**praevāricātor, ōris** *m* collusive advocate, sham accuser.

**prae-vāricor** 1 to play a double part, be a false advocate.

**prae-vehor** 3 to drive, ride, fly, forward *or* in front; to flow past.

**prae-veniō** 4 to come before, get the start of, to forestall.

**prae-verrō** 3 to sweep.

**prae-vertō** *and* **-vertor** 3 a) to do first *or* in preference, attend to first; to be wholly occupied with, intent on; b) to go before, precede, outrun;

c) to interfere with, anticipate, prevent; d) to possess first; e) to be of more importance, outweigh.

**prae-vetitus** 3 forbidden.

**prae-videō** 2 to see first; to foresee.

**prae-vitiō** 1 to corrupt beforehand.

**prae-vius** 3 going before.

**prae-volō** 1 to fly before, in advance.

**prae-vortō**, *see* **prae-vertō.**

**prāgmaticus** 3 skilled in state business.

**prandeō, ndi, ānsum** 2 to lunch (on); **prānsus** 3 having lunched.

**prandium, ī** n lunch.

**prānsitō** 1 to lunch on.

**prānsor, ōris** m guest at lunch.

**prasinus** 3 (leek-)green.

**prātēnsis, e** growing in meadows.

**prātulum, ī** n small meadow.

**prātum, ī** n meadow; meadow grass; flat surface.

**prāvitās, ātis** f crookedness, deformity; a) perversity; b) viciousness, wickedness.

**prāvus** 3 crooked, distorted, deformed; a) perverse; b) bad, wicked, vicious.

**precārius** 3 a) obtained by begging *or* entreaty; b) uncertain, precarious; *adv.* **precāriō** by entreaty; on sufferance.

**precātiō, ōnis** f a begging, entreating, prayer.                     [cessor.₎

**precātor, ōris** m pleader, inter-₎

**precātus, ūs** m prayer.

**precēs, um** f/pl. (*sing. rare*) wish, entreaty; a) prayer; b) curse, execration.

**preciae, ārum** f/pl. a kind of vine.

**precor** 1 to beg, pray, beseech, entreat; to pray to, invoke (*alqm, alqd, alqd ab alqo; ut, ne*); to wish good *or* evil (*alci alqd*), curse.

**prehendō, ndi, ēnsum** 3 to grasp, seize, lay hold of; a) to catch, occupy; to reach; b) to arrest, detain.

**prehēnsō** 1 = prenso.

**prēlum, ī** n wine-press, olive-press; clothes-press.

**premō, pressī, pressum** 3 1. to press, compress; a) to press out, express, obtain by pressing; b) to press with the body, stand, sit *or* lie on (*torum, humum, currum*); **vestigia alcis** to follow in the footsteps of; c) to press down, burden, load, freight (*magno onere alqm*); d) to cover, conceal by covering; to bury;

e) to press hard upon, keep close to; to pursue closely, follow up; to importune, vex; f) to depress, lower; 2. to press into, force in; a) to plant; b) to impress, mark; c) to press down, weigh down, sink; to oppress, overwhelm; d) to degrade, humble, disparage, depreciate; e) to check, tighten, repress, restrain; f) to shorten, prune; g) to keep down, rule; h) to overshadow; to compress, close, shut; i) to abridge, condense.

**prēndō** = **prehendo.**

**prēnsātiō, ōnis** f a canvassing for office.

**prēnsō** 1 a) to grasp, seize, lay hold of; b) to canvass.

**pressiō, ōnis** f leverage; contrivance for raising a heavy mass.

**pressō** 1 to press.

**pressus**[1] 3 compressed; a) low (*voice*); moderate; b) concise; c) restrained, plain, without ornament; **pressē** *adv.* distinctly; concisely; simply; exactly.

**pressus**[2]**, ūs** m pressure.

**prēstēr, ēris** m a) fiery whirlwind; b) serpent whose bite causes burning thirst.

**pretiōsus** 3 valuable, precious, costly; extravagant.

**pretium, ī** n worth, value, price; **pretio** by purchase; bribe; ransom; wages, reward; punishment; **operae pretium est** it is worth while.

**precem, -ī, -e,** *see* **preces.**

**prīdem** *adv.* long ago, long since.

**prīdiānus** of the day before, yesterday's.

**prī-diē** *adv.* on the day before; a) **prīdiē quam** a day earlier than; b) **prīdiē eius diei** the day before.

**prīm-aevus** 3 youthful.

**prīmānus, ī** m soldier of the first legion.                     [cipal, excellent.₎

**prīmārius** 3 of the first rank, prin-₎

**prīmi-genus** 3 original, first.

**prīmi-pīlāris, is** m *and* **prīmipīlus, ī** m the first centurion of a legion.

**prīm-itiae, ārum** f/pl. firstlings, firstfruits; first attempt.

**prīmitus** *adv.* at first; for the first time.

**prīm-ōrdium, ī** n first beginning, origin, original element; beginning of a new reign.

**prīmōris, e a)** at the extreme edge *or* tip of; **b)** first, chief, principal (*also as subst.*).

**primulus 3** first, early; *adv.* -um first.

**prīmus 3** first; at the extremity of; **primum agmen** the van; **prīmā nocte** at the beginning of the night; **in prīmā prōvinciā** at the entrance of the province; the first, chief, principal, most excellent; — *subst.* **a) primae, ārum** *f/pl.* (*scil. partes*), the chief *or* leading part, first rank; **b) prīmum, ī** *n* the van, first part, beginning; — *adv.* **prīmum:** for the first time; firstly; **ubi prīmum** as soon as; **quam prīmum** as soon as possible; **prīmō** at first, at the beginning, firstly.

**prin-ceps, ipis 1.** *adj.* = **primus; 2.** *subst.* *m* **a)** author, founder; mover; **b)** leader, head, chief, master, superior, director, ruler, prince, sovereign, emperor; **principēs, um** *m/pl.* **a)** the first, most eminent, most noble; **b)** soldiers of the second line (*between the hastati and triarii*); *sing.* a company of the *principes*, centurion(ship) of the *principes*.

**principālis, e a)** first, original, primitive; **b)** princely, imperial; **c)** chief, principal.

**principātus, ūs** *m* the first place, pre-eminence; **a)** highest place, commandership; **b)** rule, reign, sovereignity, dominion, empire; **c)** principle; **d)** beginning.

**principiālis, e** in the beginning, earliest.

**principium, ī** *n* a beginning, commencement; (**in** *or* **a)** **prīncipiō** at the beginning, at first; **a)** foundation, element, principle; **b)** (*pl.*) the foremost rank, front line of soldiers; **c)** (*pl.*) head-quarters, principal place in a camp.

**prior, us** *comp.* **a)** former, previous, prior, first; **b)** better, superior; **c)** (in) front, fore; *subst.* **priōrēs, um** *m/pl.* ancestors; **prius** *adv.* earlier, previously.

**priscus 3** of former times, old, olden, ancient; **a)** antique, venerable; **b)** former, previous; **c)** old-fashioned, severe, strict.

**pristinus 3 a)** former, early, primitive, original; **b)** just past, previous.

**pristis, is** *f* **a)** a sea-monster, whale; **b)** ship of war.

**prius-quam** *cj.* before; **non prius quam** not until.

**prīvātim** *adv.* apart from state affairs, as an individual, for oneself, privately, separately; at home.

**prīvātiō, ōnis** *f* a freeing from (*gen.*).

**prīvātus 3** apart from the state, belonging to an individual, private, personal; **a)** common, out of office, not princely; **b)** *subst.* **., ī** *m* private individual; **-um, ī** *n* private property, private use, privacy.

**prīvigna, ae** *f* step-daughter.

**prīvignus, ī** *m* step-son.

**prīvi-lēgium, ī** *n* law relating to a single person only; privilege, prerogative.

**prīvō 1** to bereave, deprive of (*alqm re*); to free, release.

**prīvus 3** single, each, every, one each; private, peculiar, particular.

**prō¹** *int.* oh! ah! alas! (with *voc.:* pro sancte Juppiter; with *acc.:* pro deum hominumque fidem).

**prō²** *prep.* with *abl.* **1.** (*of place*) **a)** before, in front of, in face of (*aciem pro castris instruere, pro templis praesidia collocare*); **b)** from, on (the front of) (*pro tectis* or *pro litore stare, orationem habere pro rostris*); **2.** (*of relation*) **a)** for, on behalf of, for the benefit of, in the service of (*pro patria pugnare, pro libertate mori, oratio pro Milone*); **b)** in the place of, instead of, for, as good as (*Cato unus mihi est pro centum milibus, pro vallo carros obiecerant, aliquem pro deo colere, se pro cive gerere, Volsci pro victis abierunt*); **c)** as a reward, in exchange *or* return for (*pro beneficiis gratiam referre*); **d)** in proportion to, according to, by virtue of (*proelium atrocius quam pro numero pugnantium, alqm pro dignitate laudare, pro viribus agere, consilium pro tempore et pro re capere, pro mea parte* for my part, *pro se quisque* each one according to his strength). **prō quam = proquam.**

**pro-āgorus, ī** *m* chief magistrate of a place (*in Sicily*).

**pro-auctor, ōris** *m* ancestor.

**pro-avia, ae** *f* great grandmother.

**pro-avītus 3** ancestral.

**pro-avus, ī** *m* great grandfather; ancestor.

**probābilis, e** that may be believed *or* approved; pleasing, acceptable; probable, credible, likely.

**probābilitās, ātis** *f* probability, credibility.

**probātiō, ōnis** *f* proving, examination; a) approval, assent; b) proof, demonstration.

**probātor, ōris** *m* approver.

**probātus 3** a) approved, tried and found good; b) pleasing, acceptable.

**prōbet** = **prohibet**.

**probitās, ātis** *f* honesty, uprightness.

**probō 1** 1. to try, test, prove, examine, inspect; a) to judge; b) to approve, esteem good; 2. a) to represent *or* commend as good *or* serviceable; **P.** *or* se probāre alci to render oneself acceptable, to recommend oneself to; b) to show, prove, demonstrate (*alci alqd*).

**pro-boscis, idis** *f* trunk (*of an elephant*).

**probriperlecebrae, ārum** *f/pl.* enticements to vice.

**probrōsus 3** shameful, ignominious, infamous, abusive.

**probrum, ī** *n* a) shameful *or* disgraceful deed; unchastity, lewdness; b) disgrace, infamy; reproach, abuse, insult.

**probus 3** good, proper, excellent; a) upright, honest, virtuous, honourable; b) modest.

**procācitās, ātis** *f* impudence.

**procāx, ācis** importunate, bold, insolent, shameless, forward.

**prō-cēdō 3** to go forth *or* before; a) to proceed, advance, go forward; b) to appear, show oneself, step forward; c) to advance, make progress; to run on, pass, elapse; to continue, remain; to go on; **eo prōcēdere** to go so far; d) to turn out, result, succeed well, prosper.

**procella, ae** *f* storm, tempest; onset, charge, stormy attack.

**prō-cellō 3** to throw forward.

**procellōsus 3** stormy.

**procerēs, um** *m/pl.* (*and sing.* **-rem**) chiefs, nobles, princes. [length.]

**prōcēritās, ātis** *f* tallness, height,)

**prō-cērus 3** tall, long, extended.

**prōcessiō, ōnis** *f* advance.

**prōcessus, ūs** *m* advance, progress.

**prō-cidō, cidī,** — **3** to fall down *or* forward.

**prōciduus 3** fallen, prostrate.

**(prō-cinctus m) in prōcinctū** on the battle-field, ready for action.

**prō-clāmātor, ōris** *m* shouter, noisy advocate.

**prō-clāmō 1** to call out, cry out.

**prō-clīnō 1** to turn, incline; **-nātus** turned in someone's favour; going downhill.

**prō-clīvis, e** sloping down, steep; a) inclined, prone to (*ad alqd*); b) easy; *subst.* **-clīve, is** *n* descent; *adv.* **-clīve, -clīvī** downhill, easily, readily.

**prō-clīvitās, ātis** *f* slope; inclination, tendency.

**prō-clīvus 3** = **proclivis; planus ex prōclivō** flat instead of steep; easy instead of difficult, plain instead of obscure.

**procoetōn, ōnis** *m* anteroom.

**prō-cōnsul, ulis** *m* proconsul.

**prōcōnsulāris, e** proconsular.

**prōcōnsulātus, ūs** *m* proconsulship.

**procor 1** to ask, demand.

**prōcrāstinātiō, ōnis** *f* a putting off from day to day.

**prō-crāstinō 1** to put off till tomorrow.

**prō-creātiō, ōnis** *f* procreation.

**prō-creātor, ōris** *m* begetter (*pl.* parents); creator, producer.

**prō-creātrīx, īcis** *f* she who brings forth, mother. [make.]

**prō-creō 1** to beget; produce, cause,)

**prō-crēscō 3** to spring; to grow.

**prō-cubō 1** to lie stretched out.

**prō-cūdō 3** to forge, hammer out, produce.

**procul** *adv.* far off, far away, at a distance; from afar; **procul dubio** without doubt.

**prō-culcō 1** to tread down, trample upon; *hence* **prōculcātiō, ōnis** *f.*

**proculēna, ae** *f* little sow.

**prō-cumbō, cubuī, cubitum 3** to lean, bend *or* fall forward; a) to fall *or* sink down, prostrate oneself; b) to fall to ruin.

**prōcūrātiō, ōnis** *f* a taking care of; a) administration, management, charge; b) office of a procurator; c) expiatory sacrifice, expiation.

**prōcūrātiuncula, ae** *f* a trifling post *or* duty.

**prō-cūrātor, ōris** *m* manager, administrator; a) agent, deputy; b) imperial finance-officer *or* governor.

**prŏcŭrātrix, īcis** *f* governess, pro-tectress.

**prō-cūrō** (*and* **prŏ-**) 1 **a**) to take care of, attend to, look after, ad-minister (as an agent or procurator); **b**) to expiate.

**prō-currō, (cu)currī, cursum** 3 to run *or* rush forward; to project.

**prō-cursātiō, ōnis** *f* sally, skirmi-shing.

**prŏcursātor, ōris** *m* skirmisher.

**prō-cursō** 1 to run forth, to skir-mish.

**prō-cursus, ūs** *m* a running for-ward, sally, attack.

**prō-curvō** 1 to bend forwards.

**prō-curvus** 3 bent *or* curved for-ward.

**procus, ī** *m* wooer, suitor; canvasser.

**prō-deambulō** 1 to walk out.

**prōd-eō** to go *or* come forth (*ex re in alqd*); **a**) to appear, show oneself, to appear in public; **b**) to advance, go forward.

**prō-dīcō** 3 to put off, defer.

**prō-dictātor, ōris** *m* vice-dictator.

**prōdigentia, ae** *f* profusion, pro-digality.

**prōdigiālis, e a**) averting unnatural portents; **b**) unnatural, monstrous.

**prōdigiōsus** 3 wonderful, strange, unnatural.

**prōdigium, ī** *n* **a**) prodigy, portent, omen, token, sign; **b**) monster.

**prōd-igō, ēgī, — 3** to drive forth; to use up, squander.

**prōdigus** 3 wasteful, prodigal; **a**) rich, generous; **b**) not sparing.

**prōditiō, ōnis** *f* betrayal, treachery, treason.

**prōditor, ōris** *m* betrayer, traitor.

**prō-dō, didī, ditum** 3 to give *or* bring forth; **a**) to produce, bear; **b**) to put forth in writing, to hand down, transmit (*alci alqd*); **c**) to publish, proclaim relate, report; **d**) to appoint; **e**) to discover, reveal, betray; **f**) to betray perfidiously, surrender, abandon (*alci alqd*); **g**) to prolong.

**prō-doceō** 2 to teach, inculcate.

**prō-dromus, ī** *m* forerunner, mes-senger; wind blowing before the rising of the Dog-star.

**prō-dūcō** 3 **1.** to lead forth, to bring out (in front of), conduct; **a**) to produce, introduce; **b**) to cause to appear; **c**) to promote, advance;

**d**) to induce; **2.** to draw *or* stretch out, lengthen; **a**) to beget; **b**) to protract, put off; **c**) to bring up, cultivate.

**prō-ductiō, ōnis** *f* a lengthening, prolonging, a putting off.

**prō-ductō** 1 to spin out.

**prō-ductus** 3 lengthened, prolong-ed, drawn out; **prōducta, ōrum** *n/pl.* = **proegmena.**

**pro-ēgmena, ōrum** *n/pl.* preferable things.

**proeliāris, e** pertaining to a battle.

**proeliātor, ōris** *m* warrior.

**proelior** 1 to fight (*cum alqo*).

**proelium, ī** *n* battle, fight, combat; *plur.* warriors.

**pro-fānō** 1 to desecrate, profane.

**pro-fānus** 3 not sacred, profane; common; impious; ill-boding.

**pro-fātus, ūs** *m* an uttering.

**profectiō, ōnis** *f* a setting out, de-parture; source, origin.

**pro-fectō** *adv.* truly, surely, really, indeed.

**prōfectus, ūs** *m* advance, progress, increase, profit.

**prō-ferō** 3 **1.** to carry forward *or* bring forth; **a**) to extend, stretch out; **b**) to make known, produce in public, discover, reveal, invent; **c**) to bring to light, perform, produce; **d**) to utter, quote, mention; **2. a**) to advance, move forward, extend, lengthen; **b**) to put off, postpone.

**professiō, ōnis** *f* **a**) public acknow-ledgment, declaration, return (of name, property, &c.); **b**) business, profession.

**professor, ōris** *m* public teacher.

**professōrius** 3 of a school-master.

**pro-fēstus** 3 not festival, common.

**prō-ficiō, fēcī, fectum** 3 to ad-vance; **a**) to make progress, to ef-fect *or* gain something (*alqd in re, ad alqd*); **b**) to be useful, serviceable (*ad alqd*).

**pro-ficīscor** (*and* **-cō;** *also* **prōfi-cīscor**), **fectus sum** 3 **a**) to set out, march, depart, go, travel; **b**) to set out from, begin with, go on; **c**) to spring *or* arise from.

**pro-fiteor** (*and* **prō-**), **fessus sum** 2 to declare publicly, ac-knowledge, confess, avow; **a**) to profess an art *or* science (*philo-sophiam, ius*); **b**) se **profitērī** to profess to be something (*se philo-*

*sophum*) **c**) to offer, propose, promise; **d**) to give in one's name (for service), make a return (of property, &c.);— **professus** 3 acknowledged.

**prō-flātus, ūs** *m* breathing forth, snoring.

**prōflīgātor, ōris** *m* spendthrift.

**prōflīgātus** 3 **a**) degraded, abandoned; **b**) advanced (age).

**prō-flīgō** 1 to strike to the ground, overthrow, overcome; **a**) to ruin, destroy; **b**) to lower, debase; **c**) to bring nearly to an end.

**prō-flō** 1 to blow *or* breathe forth.

**prō-fluēns, tis,** *see* **profluo.**

**prō-fluentia, ae** *f* a flowing forth.

**prō-fluō** 3 to flow forth; to issue, proceed; **prōfluēns, tis** flowing along; *subst. f* running water, stream.

**prō-fluvium, ī** *n* a flowing forth.

**pro-for** 1 to say *or* speak out.

**prō-fringō** 3 to break up, to till.

**pro-fugiō** 3 to flee away, escape; to flee before *or* from (*acc.*).

**pro-fugus** 3 fleeing, fugitive; banished.

**pro-fundō** (*and* **prō-**) 3 to pour *out or* forth; **P.** *or* **se profundere** to gush forth, to burst forth; **a**) to utter; **b**) to bring forth, produce; **c**) to spend, sacrifice, lavish, squander; **d**) to stretch *or* lay out.

**pro-fundus** 3 deep, profound, bottomless, immoderate, inexhaustible; *subst.* **-um, ī** *n* depth, the deep, sea.

**pro-fūsiō, ōnis** *f* profusion, prodigality.

**pro-fūsus** 3 lavish, excessive; extravagant, profuse; **profūsē** *adv.* in disorder.

**prō-gener, erī** *m* granddaughter's husband.

**prō-generō** 1 to beget, generate.

**prōgeniēs, ēī** *f* descent, lineage, race; progeny, offspring.

**prō-genitor, ōris** *m* ancestor, progenitor.

**prō-gignō** 3 to beget, bear, produce.

**prō-gnāriter** *adv.* expertly, properly.

**prō-gnātus** 3 born, descended.

**prō-gredior, gressus sum** 3 **a**) to go forth *or* out (*ex re, in alqd*); to go forward, advance; **b**) to go on, proceed (*in speech*).

**prōgressiō, ōnis** *f, fig.* ⸗ **progressus.**

**prō-gressus, ūs** *m* **a**) advance, progression, progress; **b**) a beginning; **c**) growth, increase, advancement.

**progymnastēs, ae** *m* a slave who teaches gymnastics.

**pro-hibeō, uī, itum** 2 **1.** to hold back, keep in check, keep off, verta (*alqm or alqd re, a re*); **commeatu** to cut off from supplies; **senatu** to exclude from the senate; **a**) to prevent, hinder (*inf.; acc. c. inf.; ne, quominus, quin*); **b**) to forbid, prohibit; **2.** to preserve, defend, protect (*alqd a re*).

**prohibitiō, ōnis** *f* a forbidding.

**prō-iciō, iēcī, iectum** 3 **a**) to throw forth *or* before (*alci alqd*); **b**) to throw, thrust, drive *or* put out, to stretch out, extend (*bracchium, pedem, hastam*); **P.** to project; **c**) to cast out, expel, exile, banish; **d**) to throw down *or* away, let go, abandon; to give up, yield, resign, neglect.

**prō-iectīcius** 3 cast out, exposed.

**prō-iectiō, ōnis** *f* a stretching out.

**prō-iectō** 1 to blame.

**prō-iectus**[1] 3 stretched out, jutting out, projecting; **a**) prominent, conspicuous; **b**) inclined, prone (*in alqd*); **c**) abject, contemptible; downcast.

**prō-iectus**[2]**, ūs** *m* stretching-out.

**prō-iiciō,** *see* **proicio.**

**proin, proinde** *adv.* **a**) therefore, so; **b**) just so; ~ **ac, ut** just as; ~ **quasi** just as if.

**prō-lābor** 3 **1.** to glide forward, to slide *or* slip along; **a**) to go on, proceed; **b**) to fall into (a feeling *or* state); **2.** to slip out, escape; **a**) to fall down; **b**) to fall into decay; **c**) to fail, err; **d**) to sink, decline, go to ruin.

**prō-lāpsiō, ōnis** *f* a slipping, falling.

**prō-lātiō, ōnis** *f* a bringing forward, mentioning, citing; **a**) extension, enlargement; **b**) a putting off, delay.

**prō-lātō** 1 **a**) to extend, enlarge; **b**) to put off, delay, postpone.

**prō-lectō** 1 to allure, entice.

**prōlēs, is** *f* offspring, progeny, race, stock; **a**) descendants; **b**) young men.

**prōlētārius** 3 common, vulgar; *subst. m* citizen of the lowest class.

**prō-liciō, —, —** 3 to allure forth, to excite.

**prō-lixus** 3 a) extended, wide, broad; b) willing, well-disposed; favourable, fortunate.

**prō-logus, ī** *m* preface, prologue; the deliverer of a prologue.

**prō-loquor** 3 to speak out, utter, declare.

**prō-lubium, ī** *n* desire, inclination.

**prō-lūdō** 3 to practise beforehand (*ad alqd*); to rehearse.

**prō-luō, uī, ūtum** 3 a) to wash, wet, moisten; b) to wash off *or* away.

**prō-lūsiō, ōnis** *f* preliminary exercise.

**prō-luviēs, ēī** *f* a) overflow, inundation; b) refuse, filth.

**prō-mercālis, e** on sale.

(**prō-mereō** *and*) **prō-mereor** 2 a) to deserve, merit, be worthy of (*alqd; ut*); b) to deserve well (*de alqo*); c) to earn (the good-will of).

**prō-meritum, ī** *n* desert, merit (*in alqm*); guilt.

**prō-mineō, —, —** 2 to stand out, jut, project, overhang; to reach out, extend; *subst.* **prōminēns, tis** *n* projection.

**prō-miscuus** (*and* **-cus**) 3 mixed, not distinct *or* separate, indiscriminate, in common; mean, ordinary; *adv.* -c(u)ē, -cam.

**prō-missiō, ōnis** *f* a promising.

**prōmissor, ōris** *m* promiser, boaster.

**prōmissum, ī** *n* promise.

**prō-missus** 3 hanging down, long.

**prō-mittō** 3 1. to let grow, let hang down; 2. to promise, give hope of (*alci alqd, de re, acc. c. inf.*); a) to promise to come, engage oneself to dine (*ad alqm*); b) to foretell, predict.

**prōmō, mpsī, mptum** 3 a) to take out, bring forth (*alqd ex re*), produce, put *or* draw forth; b) to bring to light, disclose; c) to utter, tell, express (*alqd*).

**prō-moneō, —, —** 2 to remind.

**prōmontorium, ī** *n* = promunturium.

**prōmōta, ōrum** *n/pl.* = proegmena *or* producta.

**prō-moveō** 2 to move forward, push onward; a) to cause to advance; b) to extend; c) to bring to light; d) to promote; e) to postpone.

**prōmptāria cella** *f* store-chamber; prison.

**prōmptō** 1 to distribute; to have the disposal of.

**prōmptus[1]** 3 1. visible, apparent, manifest; 2. at hand, ready; a) inclined, disposed; b) enterprising; resolute, courageous; c) easy, practicable.

**prōmptus[2], ūs** *m; only* in **prōmptū** a) public, open, visible, before the eyes; b) ready, at hand; c) easy.

**prōmulgātiō, ōnis** *f* public announcement.

**prō-mulgō** 1 to publish, promulgate.

**prō-mulsis, idis** *f* a relish taken before a meal, hors d'œuvre.

**prōmunturium, ī** *n* headland, promontory. [keeper.]

**prōmus, ī** *m* steward, butler;

**prō-mūtuus** 3 advanced, lent beforehand.

**prō-nectō** 3 to spin out.

**pro-nepōs, ōtis** *m* great grandson.

**pro-neptis, is** *f* great granddaughter.

**pro-noea, ae** *f* providence.

**prō-nuba, ae** *f* bride's attendant, brides-woman; patroness of marriage.

**prō-nūntiātiō, ōnis** *f* publication, proclamation; a) decision of a judge; b) proposition (*in logic*); c) utterance, delivery.

**prō-nūntiātor, ōris** *m* narrator, relater. [axiom.]

**prōnūntiātum, ī** *n* proposition,

**prō-nūntiō** 1 a) to publish, proclaim, announce, make known, disclose (*alci alqd*); b) to relate, report; c) to order; d) to recite, declaim, deliver; e) to decide, pronounce a judgment.

**prō-nūper** = nūper.

**prō-nurus, ūs** *f* a grandson's wife.

**prōnus** 3 inclined forward, hanging down, face downwards; a) stooping; flying headlong; setting, sinking; b) sloping, precipitous, steep; c) inclined, well disposed, favourable; d) easy; *subst.* **prōnum, ī** *n* slope.

**pro-oemior** 1 to make a preface *or* introduction.

**pro-oemium, ī** *n* introduction, preface.

**propāgātiō, ōnis** *f* a) an extending, enlarging, prolonging; b) propagation.

**propāgātor, ōris** *m* enlarger, extender.

**pro-pāgō[1]** (*and* **prō-**), **inis** *f* sucker, layer, shoot; **a)** offspring, child; **b)** progeny, posterity.

**pro-pāgō[2]** (*and* **prō-**)1 to propagate; **a)** to enlarge, extend; **b)** to prolong.

**prō-palam** *adv.* publicly, openly.

**prō-patulus** 3 open *or* uncovered in front; **in prōpatulō** in the open air; publicly.

**prope** (*comp.* **propius**, *superl.* **proximē** *and* **-umē**) **1.** *adv.* near, nigh; **a)** not far distant; **b)** at hand; **c)** nearly, almost; **2.** *prep.* with *acc.* **a)** (*of place*) near, near by, hard by; **b)** (*of time* *and other relations*) close to, near to, about (*res prope secessionem venit*); **3. a)** *comp. adj.* **propior, ius** nearer, nigher; **propiora** *n/pl.* places lying nearer; later, more recent; more nearly related, more like, more intimate, concerning more nearly; **b)** *superl.* **proximus** (*and* **-umus**) 3 the nearest, next, very near; *subst.* **proximum, ī** *n* neighbourhood, nearest place *or* point; next preceding *or* following (**proximē** shortly before *or* after); the next in value *or* quality, most like *or* similar, most closely related; *subst.* **proximī, ōrum** *m/pl.* nearest relatives, those standing next.

**prope-diem** *adv.* very soon.

**prō-pellō** (*and* **prō-**), **puli, pulsum** 3 to drive, push *or* urge forward (*alqd ex re in rem*); **a)** to drive out *or* away; **b)** to drive on, move, impel; **c)** to keep off (*alqd ab alqo*).

**prope-modum** *and* **-modo** *adv.* nearly, almost.

**propempticon, ī** *n* farewell address.

**prō-pendeō, pendī, pēnsum** 2 to hang down; **a)** to preponderate, weigh more; **b)** to be inclined *or* disposed.

**prō-pēnsiō, ōnis** *f* inclination, propensity.

**prō-pēnsus** 3 hanging down; **a)** heavy (*i.e.* rich); important; **b)** coming near, approaching; **c)** inclined, disposed, ready, willing (*in* or *ad alqd*).

**properanter** *adv.* hastily, speedily, quickly.

**properantia, ae** *and* **properātiō, ōnis** *f* haste, speed.

**properātō** *adv.* = **properanter**.

**propcri-pēs, pedis** swift-footed.

**properō** 1 **a)** to do in haste, hasten; **b)** *intr.* to make haste, be quick.

**properus** 3 hastening, quick, speedy.

**prō-pexus** 3 combed forward, hanging down.

**propinātiō, ōnis** *f* a drinking to someone's health, a toast.

**prō-pīnō** (*and* **prō-**) 1 to drink to one's health; to deliver, yield up.

**propinquitās, ātis** *f* a) nearness; **b)** relationship.

**propinquō** 1 **a)** to come near, draw near, approach; **b)** to hasten, accelerate.

**propinquus** 3 near, nigh, neighbouring; **a)** near in time, at hand; **b)** similar; **c)** kindred, related; *subst.* **propinquus, ī** *m and* **-a, ae** *f* relation, kinsman, kinswoman; **propinquē** *adv.* near.

**propior, ius**, *comp. of* **prope**.

**propitiō** 1 to appease, propitiate.

**propitius** 3 favourable, inclined, well disposed, gracious (*alci*).

**pro-pnigēum, ī** *n* fire-place (*of a bath*).

**prō-pōla, ae** *m* retailer of eatables.

**prō-polluō** 3 to defile *or* pollute.

**prō-pōnō** 3 to put *or* set forth, lay out, expose to view; **a)** to expose for sale, offer; **b)** to make known, publish; **c)** to bring forward, declare, state a proposition; **d)** to propose, promise, offer as a reward (*alci alqd*); **P.** to threaten, menace; to set before the mind, imagine, conceive (*sibi spem*); to propose, make a proposal; **e)** to purpose, intend, design, resolve.

**prōporrō** furthermore, moreover.

**prō-portiō, ōnis** *f* proportion, symmetry, analogy.

**prō-positiō, ōnis** *f* = **propositum**.

**prō-positum, ī** *n* **1. a)** design, purpose, intention; **b)** notion; conception; **c)** manner *or* course of life; **2.** main point, principal subject, theme; **3.** first proposition in a syllogism.

**prō-praetor, ōris** *m* proprætor.

**propriē** *adv.* personally, as one's own, individually; **a)** peculiarly, characteristically; **b)** especially; **c)** properly, accurately, in the proper sense.

**proprietās, ātis** *f* a property, peculiar quality; ownership.

**proprius** 3 lasting, permanent; a) one's own, peculiar, proper; *subst.* **proprium, ī** *n* property; b) characteristic, essential, especial; c) exclusive, personal, individual.

**prōprōmptū, in ~ = in prōmptū.**

**propter 1.** *adv.* near, hard by; **2.** *prep.* with *acc.* a) near, close to; b) on account of, because of, for.

**propter-eā** *adv.* therefore, on that account. [mous.]

**pro-pudiōsus** 3 shameful, infa-

**pro-pudium, ī** *n* a) shameful act; b) shameful person, villain, rascal.

**prōpugnāculum, ī** *n* bulwark, rampart, fort; a) defence, protection; b) grounds of defence.

**prō-pugnātiō, ōnis** *f* defence.

**prō-pugnātor, ōris** *m* defender, protector.

**prō-pugnō 1** a) to fight in the front, go forth to fight; b) to fight in defence.

**prō-pulsātiō, ōnis** *f* a repelling.

**prō-pulsō 1** to drive back, repel, ward off, avert (*alqd a re*). [ing as.]

**prōquam** in proportion as, accord-

**prōra, ae** *f* forepart of a ship, prow, bow; ship.

**prō-rēpō 3** to creep forward, crawl out. [prow of a ship.]

**prōrēta, ae** *m* watchman at the

**prō-ripiō, ripuī, reptum 3** to snatch, drag, tear forth; **se prō-ripere** to rush forward, hurry away.

**prō-rītō 1** to attract.

**prō-rogātiō, ōnis** *f* prolongation; a deferring.

**prō-rogō 1** to prolong, protract (*alci alqd*); to put off, defer.

**prō(r)sus** (*and* **prō(r)sum**) *adv.* straight forward; a) utterly, entirely, wholly, absolutely; b) in a word, in short.

**prō-rumpō 3** a) *intrans.* (*and* **P.**) to break *or* burst forth; to break out; b) *trans.* to cause to break forth.

**prō-ruō 3** a) to rush forth; b) to tumble down; c) *trans.* to throw down, pull down; d) **se ~** to rush.

**prōsa** (*sc. oratio*) *f* prose.

**prō-sāpia, ae** *f* family, race.

**pro-scaenium, ī** *n* the stage.

**prō-scindō 3** a) to rend, to plough; b) to revile, censure.

**prō-scrībō 3** to make public; a) to offer publicly for sale, advertise; b) to confiscate; c) to proscribe, outlaw.

**prō-scriptiō, ōnis** *f* a) advertisement of sale; b) proscription.

**prōscrīpturiō 4** to desire a proscription.

**prō-secō 1** to cut off; to plough; *subst.* **prōsecta, ōrum** *n/pl.* parts cut off for sacrifice, entrails.

**prō-seda, ae** *f* prostitute.

**prō-sēminō 1** to sow, to propagate.

**prō-sentiō 4** to perceive beforehand.

**prō-sequor 3** to follow, accompany, attend, escort (*acc.*); a) to pursue, attack; b) to go on *or* proceed with; c) to honour, present *or* treat with, wait upon; d) to go on, continue, follow up, describe at length.

**prō-serō¹ 3** to extend, thrust out.

**prō-serō² 3** to produce by sowing.

**prō-serpō 3** to creep forward.

**proseucha, ae** *f* Jewish place of prayer.

**prō-sicō = prō-secō.**

**prō-siliō, siluī** (*and* **silīvī, silīi**), — 4 to spring *or* leap forth, burst forth, start out; to rush, hasten to a place.

**prō-socer, erī** *m* a wife's grandfather.

**prō-spectō 1** to look forth, see afar off; a) to look at *or* out; b) to look for, await, expect.

**prōspectus, ūs** *m* (distant) view, prospect; a) (faculty of) sight; b) a sight.

**prō-speculor 1 = prospecto.**

**prosperitās, ātis** *f* good fortune, prosperity, success.

**prosperō 1** to make successful, happy, prosperous (*alci alqd*).

**prosperus 3** a) fortunate, according to one's wishes; b) favourable, lucky, prosperous, propitious.

**prōspicientia, ae** *f* foresight, precaution.

**prō-spiciō, spexī, spectum 3 1.** to look forward, into the distance, look out; to exercise foresight, take care of, provide for (*alci; ut, ne*); **2.** to see afar, command a view of; a) to have a wide prospect; b) to foresee; c) to provide, procure (*alci alqd*).

**prō-sternō 3** to strew before, throw to the ground, cast down; to overthrow, destroy, ruin. [prostitute.]

**prō-stibilis, is** *f*, **-stibulum, ī** *n*

**prō-stituō, uī, ūtum 3** to prostitute; **-ūta, ae** *f* prostitute.

**prō-stō, stitī, —** 1 to be on sale.

**prō-subigō** 3 to dig up.
**prō-sum, prōfui, (prōfutūrus), prōdesse** to be useful, to be of use (*alci*).
**prō-tegō** 3 to cover in front; to protect, defend; to ward off.
**prō-tēlō** 1 to drive away.
**prōtēlum, ī** *n* line, succession.
**prō-tendō, ndī, ntum** 3 to stretch forth *or* out.
**prō-tenus** *adv.* = **protinus.**
**prō-terō** 3 to tread upon, trample down, crush, maltreat.
**prō-terreō** 2 to frighten away.
**protervitās, ātis** *f* boldness, impudence, wantonness.
**protervus** (*and* **prō-**) 3 vehement; a) bold, forward; b) impudent, wanton.
**pro-thȳmē** *adv.* willingly.
**pro-thȳmia, ae** *f* readiness, willingness.
**prō-tinam** = **prōtinus.**
**prō-tinus** *adv.* a) forward, further on; b) straightway, on the spot; immediately, at once; c) continuously, uninterruptedly.
**prō-tollō** 3 to stretch forth; to prolong; to defer.
**prō-tonō** 1 to thunder forth.
**prōto-prāxia, ae** *f* priority in a claim.
**prōto-tomus** 3 cut first; *subst. m* early greens.
**prō-trahō** 3 to draw *or* drag forth; a) to compel, force; b) to bring forth, produce, bring to light, reveal; to drag on, defer.
**prō-trūdō** 3 to thrust forth, push forward; to put off, defer.
**prō-turbō** 1 to drive on *or* away; to throw down.
**pro-ut** *cj.* according as, just as.
**prō-vehō** 3 to carry forward *or* away; a) to conduct, lead on, carry; b) to promote, advance, exalt, raise; P. to go on, ride, drive, *or* sail on; to advance, make progress; **prōvectus aetāte** advanced in life.
**prō-veniō** 4 to come forth, appear; a) to grow up, arise; to go on, advance; b) to thrive, prosper, flourish.
**prōventus, ūs** *m* growth, produce, harvest;-issue, result, success.
**prō-verbium, ī** *n* old saying, proverb. [dent.]
**prō-vidēns, tis** foreseeing, pru-/
**prōvidentia, ae** *f* foresight; a) precaution, forethought; b) providence.

**prō-videō** 2 to see from afar; a) to foresee; b) to look out, take care, care for (*dat.; de re; ut, ne*); c) to provide; **prōvīsō** with foresight.
**prōvidus** 3 foreseeing (*gen.*); a) cautious, provident, prudent; b) caring for (*gen.*).
**prōvincia, ae** *f* 1. official duty, sphere of duty; business, office; 2. province, administration of a province.
**prōvinciālis, e** of a province, provincial; *subst. m* provincial, inhabitant of a province.
**prōvinciātim** *adv.* province by province.
**prō-visiō, ōnis** *f* = **providentia.**
**prō-vīsō** 3 a) to go to see; b) to be on the look-out for.
**prōvīsor, ōris** *m* foreseer; provider.
**prō-vīsus, ūs** *m* = **providentia.**
**prō-vīvō** 3 to go on living.
**prō-vocātiō, ōnis** *f* appeal (in law).
**prō-vocātor, ōris** *m* challenger; a kind of gladiator.
**prō-vocō** 1 to call forth *or* out; a) to summon, invite, incite; b) to challenge; to emulate; c) to appeal (in law); to appeal to.
**prō-volō** 1 to fly forth; to rush forth.
**prō-volvō** 3 to roll forward *or* along; P. *and* se **prōvolvere** a) to throw oneself down, prostrate oneself; b) to be expelled.
**prō-vomō** 3 to vomit forth.
**prō-vulgō** 1 to make known publicly.
**proxenēta, ae** *m* agent, broker.
**proximē** *adv., see* **prope.**
**proximitās, ātis** *f* nearness, similarity; near relationship.
**proximus** 3, *superl. of* **prope.**
**prūdēns, tis** 1. knowing, with intention; foreseeing; 2. a) skilled, experienced, practised (*gen.*); b) wise, discreet, prudent.
**prūdentia, ae** *f* 1. a foreseeing; 2. a) knowledge, skill; b) prudence, practical wisdom, discretion.
**pruīna, ae** *f* hoar-frost, rime; a) snow; b) winter.
**pruīnōsus** 3 covered with hoar-frost.
**prūna, ae** *f* burning *or* live coal.
**prūniceus** 3 of plum-tree wood.
**prūnum, ī** *n* plum.
**prūnus, ī** *f* plum-tree.
**prūrigō, inis** *f* itch; itching desire.
**prūriō** 4 to itch; to long for.

**prytanĕum** *and* **-ĭum, ī** *n* town hall, council-hall.

**prytanis, is** *m* prytanis (*Greek magistrate*).

**psallō, lī,** — 3 to play on *or* sing to the cithara.

**psaltērium, ī** *n* a stringed instrument.

**psaltria, ae** *f* female player on the cithara.

**psecas, adis** *f* hair-dresser.

**psēphisma, atis** *n* decree of a Greek popular assembly.

**Pseudo-catō, ōnis** *m* a sham Cato.

**pseudomenos, ī** *m* sophistical syllogism.

**pseudo-thyrum, ī** *n* secret door.

**psīlo-citharistēs, ae** *m* one who plays on the cithara without singing.

**psīlōthrum, ī** *n* a depilatory.

**psithia (vītis)** *f* a kind of vine.

**psittacus, ī** *m* parrot.

**psȳcho-mantĭum, ī** *n* place where the souls of the dead were interrogated.

**psythia** = **psithia.**

**-pte** (*suffix*) self, own.

**ptisanārium, ī** *n* decoction of barley-groats.

**pūbens, tis** mature, exuberant.

**pūbertās, ātis** *f* maturity, puberty; manhood; downy beard.

**pūbēs¹, is** *f* a) the genitals; b) young men; men, people.

**pūbēs², eris** adult, grown up; downy.

**pūbēscō, buī,** — 3 to arrive at the age of puberty; a) to grow up, arrive at maturity; b) to be covered *or* clothed (of plants).

**pūblicānus, ī** *m* farmer of state-revenues; **muliercula -a** wench of a tax-farmer.

**pūblicātĭō, ōnis** *f* confiscation.

**pūblicē** *adv.* a) in the name, at the command of the state; b) in the interest of the state; c) at the cost of the state; d) all together, in a body.

**pūblicitus** *adv.* a) = **publice;** b) publicly, in public.

**pūblicō** 1 to make public; a) to appropriate to the public use; to confiscate; b) to give over to the public use; to prostitute; to publish.

**pūblicus** 3 belonging to the people, to the state, to the community; a) in the name, on account, at the cost of the state; b) public, common, general, universal; — *subst.* a) **rēs pūblica** public affair, state business, commonwealth, republic, state; public property, state treasury; the public interest; b) **pūblicum, ī** *n* state property; public revenue, treasury, money; public place, street; **in pūblicō** publicly, openly, in the street.

**pudeō** 2 a) to be ashamed; b) to make ashamed; mostly *impers.* **pudet** (*perf.* **puduit** *or* **puditum est**) **me alcis rei** I am ashamed of;

**pudēns, tis** bashful, modest, chaste; **pudendus** 3 shameful, disgraceful, scandalous.

**pudibundus** 3 shamefaced, bashful.

**pudīcitia, ae** *f* bashfulness, modesty, chastity, virtue.

**pudīcus** 3 bashful, modest, chaste, virtuous.

**pudor, ōris** *m* sense of shame, shyness, bashfulness; a) honour; b) modesty, decency, sense of propriety; c) chastity; d) shame, disgrace.

**puella, ae** *f* girl, maiden; a) daughter; b) mistress, sweetheart; c) young woman.

**puellāris, e** girlish, maidenly.

**puellula, ae** *f, dim. of* **puella.**

**puellus, ī** *m* = **puerulus.**

**puer, erī** *m* a) child; boy; b) youth, young man; c) servant, slave; d) bachelor.

**puera, ae** *f* girl.

**puerāscō** 3 to grow up into boyhood.

**puerculus, ī** *m* little boy.

**puerīlis, e** boyish, childish, youthful.

**puerīlitās, ātis** *f* childishness.

**pueritia, ae** *f* boyhood, childhood.

**puer-pera, ae** *f* woman in childbirth.

**puerperium, ī** *n* childbirth.

**puer-perus** 3 aiding childbirth.

**puertia, ae** *f* = **pueritia.**

**puerulus, ī** *m* little boy.

**pūga, ae** *f* rump, buttocks.

**pugil, ilis** *m* boxer, pugilist.

**pugilātōrius follis** punching-ball.

**pugilātus, ūs** *m and* **-ātĭō, ōnis** *f* boxing.

**pugilicē** like a boxer.

**pugillārēs, ium** *m/pl.*, **pugillāria, ium** *n/pl.* little writing-tablets.

pūgiō, ōnis *m* dagger, poniard.

pūgiunculus, ī *m* small dagger.

pugna, ae *f* a) fight, battle, combat; b) contention, quarrel; c) line of battle.

pugnācitās, ātis *f* desire of fighting.

pugnāculum, ī *n* fortified place, fort.

pugnātor, ōris *m* fighter, combatant.

pugnātōrius 3 of a fighter.

pugnāx, ācis fond of fighting, combative, warlike; obstinate.

pugneus 3 pertaining to the fist.

pugnō 1 to fight; a) to contradict; b) to struggle, contend.

pugnus, ī *m* the fist; boxing.

pulcer, cra, crum = pulcher.

pulchellus 3 pretty little.

pulcher, chra, chrum beautiful, fair, handsome; fine, excellent, glorious, noble; fortunate.

pulchritūdō, inis *f* beauty; excellence.

pūlēium, ī *n* an aromatic plant.

pūlex, icis *m* flea.

pullārius, ī *m* feeder of fowls.

pullātī, ōrum *m/pl.* persons in mourning dress; the common people.

pulleiāceus 3 = pullus[2].

pullulō 1 to shoot up, sprout; to swarm with (*abl.*).

pullus[1], ī *m* young animal, chicken.

pullus[2] 3 dark grey, very dark, gloomy; *subst.* pullum, ī *n* dark *or* grey stuff.

pulmentārium, ī *n* = pulpamentum.

pulmentum, ī *n* portion of food.

pulmō, ōnis *m* the lung.

pulmōneus 3 of the lungs.

pulpa, ae *f* flesh.

(pulpāmen, inis *and*) pulpāmentum, ī *n* flesh, meat; a relish, tasty food.

pulpitum, ī *n* platform, stage, tribune.

puls, tis *f* thick pap, porridge.

pulsātiō, ōnis *f* a striking.

pulsātor, ōris *m* striker, player (*of a lyre*).

pulsō 1 to beat, strike, knock; to move, agitate, alarm.

pulsus, ūs *m* a beating, striking; impulse, influence.

pultātiō, ōnis *f* knocking (at a door).

pulti-phagus 3 porridge-eating (*i.e.* Roman).

pultō 1 = pulsō.

pulvereus 3 full of dust, dusty; raising dust.

pulverulentus 3 dusty.

pulvillus, ī *m* small cushion.

pulvīnar, āris *n* couch of the gods (*pl.* feast of the gods); cushioned seat.

pulvīnārium, ī *n* ship's berth.

pulvīnus, ī *m* cushion, pillow.

pulvis, eris *m* (*f*) dust, sand, ashes; a) dust of the circus, arena, field; toil; b) scene of action.

pulvisculus, ī *m* dust; cum pulvisculo dust and all, completely.

pūmex, icis *m* (*and f*) pumice-stone; porous stone, lava bed.

pūmiceus 3 of pumice; dry as a stone. [-stone.]

pūmicō 1 to smooth with pumice-

pūmiliō, ōnis *m and f* (*and* pūmilus, ī *m*) dwarf.

punctim *adv.* by stabbing. [pain.]

punctiuncula, ae *f* prick; pricking

punctum, ī *n* puncture; a) point, voting-mark; b) small portion of time, moment; c) brief clause, short section.

pungō, pupugī, punctum 3 to prick, puncture; to sting, vex, grieve, disturb, afflict, annoy.

pūniceus 3 bright red.

pūniō *and* pūnior 4 to punish; to avenge (*alqm*; *alqd*).

pūnītor, ōris *m* punisher, avenger.

pūpa, ae *f* a) girl; b) doll.

pūpilla, ae *f* orphan-girl; pupil of the eye.

pūpillāris, e of an orphan.

pūpillus, ī *m* orphan-boy; ward.

puppis, is *f* stern *or* poop; ship, vessel; back.

pūpula, ae *f* (pupil of) the eye.

pūpulus, ī *m* (pūpus, ī *m*) little boy, child.

pūrgāmen, inis *and* pūrgāmentum, ī *n* a) filth, dirt, sweepings; b) means of purgation *or* expiation.

pūrgātiō, ōnis *f* a cleansing; a) a purging; b) justification.

pūrgitō 1 to make clean.

pūrgō (*and* -rigō) 1 to cleanse; a) to purge, free oneself from; b) to cleanse morally, purify, expiate; c) to excuse, justify, exculpate; to disprove; to clear up.

pūri-ficō 1 to cleanse, purify.

pūriter, *adv. of* purus.

**purpura, ae** *f* purple dye, purple; **a)** purple garment; **b)** purple robe of a king, high dignity.

**purpurātus 3** clad in purple; *subst. m* high officer, courtier.

**purpureus 3 a)** violet, crimson, purple (of many shades); **b)** clad in purple; **c)** shining, bright, beautiful.

**purpurissātus 3** dyed with purple.

**purpurissum, ī** *n* purple dye.

**pūrulentus 3** discharging pus, festering.

**pūrus 3** (*adv.* **-ē** *and* **-iter**) pure, clean; **a)** clear, bright, serene; **b)** purifying; **c)** purified, expiated; **d)** spotless, unspotted; undefiled; **e)** unadorned, simple, plain, unmixed, unadulterated; **f)** pure, honest; chaste; **g)** unconditional, absolute.

**pūs, pūris** *n* matter from a sore, pus; gall, bitter speech.

**pusillus 3** tiny, petty.

**pūsiō, ōnis** *m* little boy.

**pūs(s)ula** *and* **pustula, ae** *f* pimple, pustule; refined silver (melted so as to form bubbles).

**pustulātus 3** blistered; refined.

**puta** (imperative of *puto*) suppose, for instance.

**putāmen, inis** *n* husk, nut-shell.

**putātiō, ōnis** *f* a pruning.

**putātor, ōris** *m* pruner.

**puteal, ālis** *n* stone-enclosure of a well; stone-enclosure.

**puteālis, e** of a well.

**puteārius, ī** *m* well-digger.

**pūtēfaciō 3** (?) to make rotten.

**pūteō 2** to stink; to rot.

**puter, tris, tre** rotten, decaying, stinking, putrid; **a)** crumbling, soft, flabby; **b)** languishing.

**pūtēscō, tuī, — 3** to rot, decay, putrefy.

**puteus, ī** *m* **a)** pit; dungeon; **b)** well, cistern; **c)** spring.

**pūtidiusculus 3** rather disgusting *or* tedious.

**pūtidus** (*and* **pūtidulus**) **3** rotten, decaying, putrid; **a)** withered; **b)** disgusting, affected, unnatural.

**putillus, ī** *m* little boy.

**putō 1 1.** to prune; **2. a)** to estimate, reckon, value, consider; **b)** to think, reflect; **c)** to believe, suppose.

**pūtor, ōris** *m* stench.

**putre-faciō 3** to make rotten, cause to putrefy; to soften.

**putrēscō 3** to rot.

**putridus 3** *and* **putris, e** = **puter**.

**putus 3** pure, complete, out and out.

**pyctēs** *and* **-ta, ae** *m* boxer, pugilist.

**pyelus, ī** *m* bath-tub.

**pȳga, ae** *f* = **puga**.

**pȳgargus, ī** *m* antelope.

**pyra, ae** *f* funeral pile, pyre.

**pȳramis, idis** *f* pyramid.

**pyrethrum, ī** *n* a plant.

**pyrōpus, ī** *m* gold-bronze.

**pyrrhicha, ae** *f* war-dance.

**pȳthaulēs, ae** *m* one who accompanies an actor on a flute.

**pȳtisma, atis** *n* wine spit out after tasting.

**pȳtissō 1** to spit out (wine, after tasting).

**pyxis, idis** *f* small box, casket.

# Q

**Q.** *abbr.* = **Quintus** *or* **que.**

**quā** (*interrog. and relat.*) **a)** by what way, on which side, where; **b)** in so far as; **quā ... quā** partly ... partly, as well ... as; **c)** in what manner, in any manner.

**quā-cumque** by *or* in whatever way, wherever.

**quādam ... tenus** *adv.* to a certain point, so far.

**quadra, ae** *f* a quarter (of a circular loaf, cake, cheese, &c.).

**quadrāgēnārius** 3 forty years old.

**quadrāgēnī** 3 forty each.

**quadrāgēsimus** 3 the fortieth.

**quadrāgiē(n)s** *adv.* forty times.

**quadrāgintā** forty.

**quadrāns, tis** *m* fourth part, quarter; quarter of an as, *or* of a pint.

**quadrantal, ālis** *n* a liquid measure of 8 *congii* (= *amphora*).

**quadrantārius** 3 **a)** reduced to a fourth part; **b)** costing a quarter of an as.

**quadrātus** 3 squared, square; *subst.* **quadrātum, ī** *n* a square; quartile aspect (*in astrology*).

**quadrī-duum, ī** *n* space of four days.

**quadri-ennium, ī** *n* period of four years.

**quadri-fāriam** *adv.* into four parts.

**quadri-fidus** 3 split into four parts.

**quadrigae, ārum** *f/pl.* (*sing. rare*) team of four; four-horse chariot.

**quadrīgārius** 3 (*and subst. m*) (of a) chariot-racer.

**quadrīgātus** 3 stamped with a quadriga.

**quadrīgulae, ārum** *f/pl.* small quadrigae.

**quadri-iugus** 3 (*and* **-iugis, e**) of a team of four; *subst.* **quadriiugī, ōrum** *m/pl.* four-horse chariot.

**quadri-lībris, e** weighing four pounds.

**quadri-mēstris, e** of four months.

**quadrim(ul)us** 3 four years old.

**quadringēnārius** 3 consisting of four hundred each.

**quadringēnī** 3 four hundred each.

**quadringentēsimus** 3 the four hundredth.

**quadringentī** 3 four hundred.

**quadringentiē(n)s** *adv.* four hundred times.

**quadri-partītus** *or* **-pertītus** 3 divided into four parts.

**quadri-pedāns, -pēs, -plex,** *see* **quadru-.**

**quadri-rēmis, e** with oars worked by four rowers; *subst. f* quadrireme.

**quadri-vium, ī** *n* cross-roads.

**quadrō** 1 **a)** to make full *or* complete; **b)** to arrange properly; **c)** *intr.* to agree, fit, to accord, correspond with.

**quadrum, ī** *n* square.

**quadru-pedāns, tis** galloping; *subst.* horse, steed.

**quadru-pedō** at a trot.

**quadru-pēs, pedis** four-footed; *subst. m* and *f* quadruped, horse.

**quadrup(u)lātor, ōris** *m* **a)** informer; **b)** fraudulent arbitrator; **c)** exaggerator.

**quadru-plex, icis** = **quadruplus.**

**quadru-plicō** 1 to quadruple.

**quadrup(u)lor** 1 to be a public informer.

**quadru-plus** 3 fourfold; *subst.* **-um, ī** *n* four times as much.

**quadru-vium, ī** *n*, *see* **quadrivium.**

**quaeritō** 1 to seek eagerly.

**quaerō, sīvī** *and* **siī, sītum** 3 to seek, search for (*alqd*); **a)** to miss, want; **b)** to seek to obtain *or* procure; to get, earn, acquire (*alqd; alci alqd*); **c)** to wish to know, ask, inquire, demand (*alqd; de re: alqd ab, ex, de alqo*); **d)** to investigate, examine, make inquiry; **e)** to inquire into judicially, to examine under torture (*de alqo in alqm*).

**quaesītiō, ōnis** *f* inquisition.

**quaesītor, ōris** *m* president of a criminal investigation.

**quaesītus** 3 **a)** far-fetched, affected; **b)** sought out, uncommon, extraordinary; — *subst.* **quaesītum, ī** *n* question; gain.

**quaesō, 3 1.** = quaero; **2.** to beg, beseech, entreat (*alqd ab alqo; ut, ne*); **quaeso** I pray, please; **quaesumus** we beg.

**quaesticulus, ī** *m* small profit.

**quaestiō, ōnis** *f* an asking, seeking; question, inquiry, examination; **a)** judicial inquiry, investigation with torture; subject of investigation, evidence; commission of inquisition, criminal court; **b)** scientific inquiry, subject of debate, matter, case, cause, dispute. [tion.]

**quaestiuncula, ae** *f* little question.

**quaestor, ōris** *m* quæstor **a)**; financial and administrative assistant to a magistrate *or* provincial governor; **b)** officer of the treasury; **c)** investigator of capital crimes.

**quaestōrius 3** of a quæstor; *subst.* **a) quaestōrius, ī** *m* ex-quæstor; **b) quaestōrium, ī** *n* tent *or* dwelling of a quæstor.

**quaestuāria, ae** *f* prostitute.

**quaestuōsus 3 a)** gainful, profitable; **b)** greedy of gain, eager for profit; **c)** having much gain, rich.

**quaestūra, ae** *f* office of a quæstor, quæstorship.

**quaestus, ūs** *m* gain, profit, advantage; source of gain; business, trade.

**quā-libet** *and* **quā-lubet** *adv.* where you will; anyhow.

**quālis, e 1.** (*interr.*, *exclam.*) of what sort, kind *or* nature; **2.** (*rel.*) of such a kind as, such as; **3.** (*indef.*) having some quality *or* other.

**quālis-cumque 2 a)** of whatever kind *or* sort; **b)** any whatever.

**quālis-libet 2** of what sort you will.

**quālis-nam 2** of what kind then?

**quālitās, ātis** *f* quality, property, condition.

**quāliter** *adv.* just as.

**quālus, ī** *m* (*and* **-um, ī** *n*) wicker-basket, wool-basket.

**quam 1.** (*interrog.* or *exclamatory*) how greatly, how much, how; **2.** (*rel.*) as; **tam ... quam** as (much) ... as; (with *superl. adj.* or *adv.*) **quam maximus** as great as possible, **quam celerrime** as quickly as possible; — (*after comp.*) than.

**quam-diū** how long? as long as.

**quam-libet** *adv.* however much.

**quam-ob-rem a)** on what account? why?; **b)** wherefore; **c)** therefore.

**quam-prīmum** *adv.* as soon as possible.

**quam-quam** *cj.* though, although; (*in transitions*) however, yet.

**quam-vīs 1.** *adv.* as you will, however (much), ever so much; **2.** *cj.* however (much), although.

**quā-nam** by what way.

**quandō 1.** *adv.* **a)** at what time?; when?; **b)** at any time, ever; **2.** *cj.* when (*v. rare*); since, as (*causal*).

**quandō-cumque a)** whenever, as often as; **b)** at some time *or* other.

**quandō-que** *cj.* whenever; since, as; *adv.* at some time.

**quando-quidem** *cj.* since, as.

**quanquam** = quamquam.

**quantillus 3** = quantulus.

**quantitās, ātis** *f* greatness, quantity.

**quantopere a)** how greatly, how much; to what an extent; **b)** as much as.

**quantulus 3** how little, how small.

**quantulus-cumque 3** however small *or* little.

**quantus 3** (*interr.*, *exclam.*, *relat.*) **a)** how great; how much; **b)** as great as, as much as; — **quantum** how much; as much as, as far as; — **quantī** of what value, at what price; **quantō** (*abl.*) by how much, by as much as; **quantō ... tantō** the more ... the more.

**quantus-cumque 3** however great; however small; **quantumcumque** as much as ever; **quanticumque** at whatever price.

**quantus-libet** = quantusvis.

**quantus-quantus 3** = quantuscumque.

**quantus-vīs 3** as great as you will.

**quantumvīs** as much as you please.

**quā-propter** wherefore?; therefore.

**quāquā** by whatever way, wherever.

**quāque,** *see* usque.

**quā-rē** (*interr.* and *rel.*) **a)** whereby (?); **b)** wherefore (?) why (?); **c)** therefore.

**quārtadecumānī, ōrum** *m/pl.* soldiers of the fourteenth legion.

**quārtānus 3** of the fourth day; *subst.* **quārtāna, ae** *f* quartan fever; **quārtānī, ōrum** *m/pl.* soldiers of the fourth legion.

**quārtārius, ī** *m* the fourth part; quarter of a sextarius.

**quārtus 3** the fourth.

**qua-si** *cj.* as if, as though, as; *adv.* as it were, so to speak; nearly, almost.

**quasillum, ī** *n (and* -us, ī *m)* wool--basket *(for spinning).*

**quassābilis, e** that can be shaken.

**quassātiō, ōnis** *f* a shaking.

**quassō 1 a)** *intens.* of **quatio; b)** *intrans.,* to shake; to rattle.

**quassus, ūs** *m* a shaking.

**quate-faciō 3** to shake, weaken.

**quā-tenus a)** how far?; up to what point?; **b)** as far as; **c)** in so far as, inasmuch as; **d)** since, as.

**quater** *adv.* four times.

**quaternī 3** four each.

**quatiō, —, quassum 3** to shake, wield, brandish; **a)** to beat, strike; **b)** to drive, chase; **c)** to crush, batter, shatter, beat to pieces; **d)** to agitate, touch, affect, trouble, vex, harass, plague.

**quattuor** *(indecl.)* four.

**quattuor-decim** fourteen.

**quattuor-virātus, ūs** *m* office of the *quattuorviri.*

**quattuor-virī, ōrum** *m/pl.* commission of four members.

**-que** *cj.* and; **que ... que** *(or* **et, ac)** as well ... as, both ... and.

**quem-ad-modum a)** in what manner, how; **b)** as, just as, as for instance.

**queō, quīvī,** *(or* **iī, itum), īre** to be able, I can.

**quercētum, ī** *n* an oak-wood.

**querceus 3** of oak.

**quercus, ūs** *f* oak; garland of oak--leaves.

**querēl(l)a, ae** *f* complaint; **a)** wailing, cry; **b)** physical complaint.

**queribundus 3** complaining, plaintive.

**querimōnia, ae** *f* = **querela.**

**queritor 1** to complain vehemently.

**quern(e)us 3** of oak.

**queror, questus sum 3** to complain, lament, bewail *(alqd; de re);* **a)** to make complaint; **b)** to lament, sing plaintively.

**querquētulānus 3** of an oak-wood.

**querulus 3 a)** complaining, querulous; **b)** plaintive.

**questus, ūs** *m* a complaining, complaint.

**quī¹, quae, quod 1.** *interrog.* what?; what kind of a?; **2.** *relat.* **a)** who, which, what, that; **b)** he who, that

which; **c)** such as; **quō ... eō** the more ... the more.

**quī², qua** *(and* **quae), quod** *indef.* any, some, any one.

**quī³ 1.** *(abl.* = **quō), quīcum** = **cum quō; 2. a)** *interrog.* how?; why?; **b)** *relat.* by which, with which; **c)** somehow; **d)** oh that! (in wishes).

**quia** *cj.* because; **quianam?** why?; **quiane?** because?

**quic-quam,** *see* **quisquam.**

**quic-quid,** *see* **quisquis.**

**quīcum,** *see* **quī³.**

**quī-cumque, quae-, quod- a)** whoever, whatever, whichever, all that; **b)** any, every possible.

**quī-dam, quae-dam, quiddam** *(subst.) and* **quoddam** *(adj.)* a certain, a certain one; **a)** somebody, one, something; *pl.* some, certain ones; **b)** a kind of, so to speak.

**quidem** *adv.* assuredly, certainly, in fact, indeed, at least, in truth; for instance, for example; **ne ... quidem** not even; not ... either.

**quid-nī** *adv.* why not?

**quiēs, ētis** *f* rest, repose, quiet; **a)** sleep; **b)** sleep of death; **c)** dream; **d)** silence; peace, neutrality; **e)** resting-place.

**quiēscō, ēvī, ētum 3** to rest, repose, keep quiet; **a)** to sleep, be asleep; **b)** to be silent, still, calm; **c)** to be at peace, be neutral; **d)** to do nothing, to be inactive; to cease, refrain from; **e)** to come to rest, to be quiet, undisturbed, free from trouble.

**quiētus 3** quiet; **a)** sleeping, resting; **b)** inactive; **c)** free from trouble *or* agitation, peaceful; **d)** retired, taking no part in politics; neutral; **e)** undisturbed, restful; **f)** calm, mild; indolent.

**quī-libet, quae-libet, quid-libet** *(subst.) and* **quod-libet** *(adj.)* any one, any thing you please; any without distinction, the first that comes.

**quīn 1.** *adv.* **a)** why not?; wherefore not?; how not?; **b)** rather, nay, indeed, verily, in fact; **2.** *cj.* **a)** that not, without; **b)** that, but that *(only after negatives).*

**quī-nam 3** who, which, what?

**quīnavicēnārius 3, -ia lēx** relating to minors under twenty-five.

**Quīnctīlis, e,** *see* **Quintilis.**

**quīnctus 3** = **quintus.**

**quinc-ūnx, ūncis** *m* a) five twelfths of a whole, of an *as*; b) a quincunx (five objects arranged like the five pips on dice or playing-cards).

**quin-deciē(n)s** *adv.* fifteen times.

**quin-decim** (*indecl.*) fifteen.

**quindecimvirālis, e** of a commission of fifteen members.

**quindecim-virī, ōrum** *m/pl.* commission of fifteen members.

**quingēni 3** five hundred each.

**quingentēsimus 3** the five hundredth.

**quingenti 3** five hundred.

**quingentiē(n)s** *adv.* five hundred times.

**quini 3** five each.

**quinquāgēni 3** fifty each.

**quinquāgēsimus 3** the fiftieth; *subst.* **-a, ae** *f* the fiftieth part.

**quinquāgintā** (*indecl.*) fifty.

**quinquātrūs, uum** *f/pl.* (and **-tria, ium** *n/pl.*) festival in honour of Minerva.

**quinque** (*indecl.*) five.

**quinquennālis, e** occurring every five years; lasting five years.

**quinqu-ennis, e** five years old; *subst.* **-ia** *n/pl.* games held every fifth year.                              [years.]

**quinqu-ennium, ī** *n* period of five

**quinque-partītus** *and* **-pertītus 3** divided into five parts.

**quinque-rēmis, e** with oars worked by five rowers; (**navis**) quinquereme.

**quinque-vir, ī** *m* one of a commission *or* college of five.

**quinque-virātus, ūs** *m* office of a *quinquevir*.

**quinquiē(n)s** *adv.* five times.

**quinqui-plex, icis** fivefold, with five leaves.

**quinqui-plicō 1** to make fivefold.

**quintadecimāni, ōrum** *m/pl.* soldiers of the fifteenth legion.

**quintāna, ae** *f* (*sc. via*) road in a Roman camp; market.

**quintāni, ōrum** *m/pl.* soldiers of the fifth legion.

**Quintīlis, e** belonging to July, *subst.*, ~ (*sc. mensis.*) July.

**quintus 3** the fifth.

**quintus-decimus 3** the fifteenth.

**quippe** *adv.* a) of course, to be sure, obviously, naturally, indeed; b) **quippe qui** since he, inasmuch as he.

**quippiam = quidpiam**, *see* **quispiam.**

**quippini** why not?; certainly, to be sure.

**Quirīs, ītis** *m* Roman citizen.

**quirītātiō, ōnis** *f* and **-tus, ūs** *m* shriek, scream, cry of distress.

**quirītō 1** to shriek, wail; to cry aloud.

**quis** (*subst. and adj.*), **quid** (*subst.*) **1.** (*interr.*) who?; which one?; what?; a) **quid** for what purpose?; why?; b) **quid** what!; how!; why!; **quid ita** why so?; how so?; **quid quod** what of the fact that ...?; moreover; **2.** (*indef.*) anyone, anybody, anything; someone, something (mostly after *ne, num, si, nisi, cum*).

**quis-nam, quid-nam** who then?; what then?

**quis-piam, quae-piam** (*subst. and adj.*), **quid-piam** (*subst.*) *and* **quod-piam** (*adj.*) someone, something.

**quis-quam, quid-quam** *or* **quic-quam** (*subst.* only) anyone, anything (*in negative sentences*); **nec quisquam** and no one.

**quis-que, quae-que, quid-que** (*subst.*) *and* **quod-que** (*adj.*) each, every, every one, every thing; a) **decimus quisque** every tenth; **quinto quōque anno** every fifth year, every four years; **primus quisque** the first possible, the very first; b) (*with superl.*) **optimus quisque** all the best, every good man; **optima quaeque** all the best things.

**quisquiliae, ārum** *f/pl.* rubbish, sweepings, refuse.

**quisquis, quidquid** *or* **quicquid** (*subst.*) whoever, whatever; also rarely = *quisque*; *adv.* **quidquid** however much *or* far.

**qui-vīs, quae-vīs, quid-vīs** (*subst.*) *and* **quod-vīs** (*adj.*) whoever you will, whatever you please, any (one), anything.

**quivīscumque, quae-, quod-** any whatsoever.

**quō 1.** *adv.* a) *interrog.* and *relat.* whither, to what place, where; to whom, into what family; to what purpose; by what *or* which means, whereby; b) *indef.* to any place, anywhere; **2.** *cj.* (in order) that, that thereby, that ... the more; **non quō** not because, not that; **quō ... eo** the more ..., the more.

**quoad a)** how long?; **b)** as long as, until, as far as.

**quō-circā** *adv.* therefore.

**quō-cumque** whithersoever.

**quod** (*relat. pron.* and *cj.*) (as to) the fact that, in so far as, because, on the ground that; **quod sī** and if, but if.

**quōdam-modo** *adv.* in a certain manner *or* measure.

**quodsī**, *see* **quod.**

**quoiās, ātis** (*also nomin.* **quoiātis**) = **cuiās.**

**quōius; quoi** (archaic) = **cūius; cui.**

**quōius(nam)** 3 = **cūius** 3.

**quō-libet** *adv.* to any place whatever.

**quom** (*archaic*) = **cum.**

**quō-minus** *cj.* with *subj.* used after verbs of preventing and refusing (by which ... not, so that ... not).

**quō-modo a)** how (*interrog., exclam., relat.*); **b)** just as.

**quōmodo-cumque** in whatever way.

**quōmodo-nam** *adv.* how then?

**quō-nam** *adv.* whither? how far? how long?

**quondam** *adv.* **a)** at one time, once, formerly; **b)** sometimes; **c)** at some future time.

**quon-iam** *cj.* now that, since, seeing that.

**quō-piam** *adv.* to some *or* any place.

**quoppiam** = **quodpiam**, *see* **quispiam.**

**quō-quam** *adv.* to any place.

**quoque** *adv.* also, too.

**quōque-versus** = **quoquoversus.**

**quō-quō** whithersoever.

**quōquō-versus** *and* **-versum** *adv.* in every direction.

**quōr** (archaic) = **cūr.**

**quōrsum** *and* **-us** *adv.* **a)** whither, to what place?; **b)** to what purpose?

**quot** (*indecl.*) **a)** how many? **b)** as many as.

**quot-annīs** *adv.* every year, yearly.

**quot-cumque** (*indecl.*) however many.

**quotēnī** 3 how many each.

**quotīdiānus, quotīdiē,** *see* **cot...**

**quotiē(n)s** *adv.* **a)** how often?, how many times?; **b)** (*rel.*) as often as.

**quotiē(n)s-cumque** *adv.* however often, as often as.

**quot-quot** (*indecl.*) however many.

**quotumus** 3 = **quotus.**

**quotus** 3 which? (in the series 1st, 2nd, 3rd, &c.); **quota hōra?** what hour?; **quota pars?** what fraction?; **quotus quisque est?** how few there are!; **quotacumque pars** what a small fraction!, the smallest possible part.

**quo-usque** *adv.* **a)** how far?; **b)** how long?; until when?

**quō-vīs** *adv.* to any place, anywhere.

**quum** an incorrect spelling of **cum** (*cj.*).

**qūr** = **cūr.**

# R

**R.** *abbr.* = **Romanus** *or* **Rufus.**

**rabidus** 3 furious, raving, enraged, mad; inspired.

**rabiēs**, (ēi) *f* rage, madness, frenzy; a) anger, fury; b) fierceness; c) inspiration.

**rabiō**, —, — 3 to rave, be mad.

**rabiōsulus** 3 a little mad.

**rabiōsus** 3 = **rabidus.**

**rabula**, ae *m* ranter.

**racēmi-fer** 3 cluster-bearing.

**racēmus**, ī *m* cluster of grapes, bunch of berries; wine.

**radiātus** 3 shining, emitting rays; irradiated.

**rādicēscō** 3 to strike root.

**rādicitus** *adv.* with the root; radically, utterly.

**rādicula**, ae *f* little root.

**radiō** *and* **radior** 1 to shine; *subst.* **radiāns, tis** *m* the sun.

**radiōs(s)us** 3 beaming.

**radius**, ī *m* staff, stake; a) spoke of a wheel; b) measuring-rod; c) radius of a circle; d) weaver's shuttle; e) a kind of long olive; f) beam, ray of light.

**rādix**, īcis *f* root; a) radish; b) lower part, foot (*of a hill*) (*mostly plur.*); c) ground, basis, origin, source; d) foundation.

**rādō**, sī, sum 3 to scrape, scratch, shave; a) to rub, smooth; b) to lacerate; c) to shave off, erase; d) to touch in passing, graze.

**raeda**, ae *f* travelling-carriage.

**raedārius**, ī *m* coachman.

**rallus** 3 thin.

**rāmālia, ium** *n/pl.* (*sing.* **rāmāle** *rare*) branches, twigs, brushwood.

**rāmentum**, ī *n* (*and* -ta, ae *f*) chip, bit, morsel.

**rāmes, itis** *m* small tube of the lung.

**rāmeus** 3 of boughs *or* branches.

**rāmex, icis** *m* varicose veins, varicocele.

**rāmōsus** 3 full of boughs, branching.

**rāmulus**, ī *m* twig, sprig.

**rāmus**, ī *m* branch, bough; club; tree.

**rāna**, ae *f* a) frog; b) a sea-fish.

**rancēns, tis** = **rancidus.**

**rancid(ul)us** 3 stinking, tainted; disgusting.

**rānunculus**, ī *m* little frog.

**rapācida**, ae *m* 'son of a robber'.

**rapācitās**, ātis *f* greediness, rapacity.

**rapāx**, ācis grasping, rapacious; a) prone to grasp; b) greedy, insatiable; *m* robber.

**raphanus**, ī *m* radish.

**rapiditās**, ātis *f* rapidity.

**rapidus** 3 snatching, seizing, carrying off, hurrying away; consuming, rapacious; impetuous, whirling, rapid.

**rapina**, ae *f* robbery, plundering; prey, booty.

**rapiō, puī, ptum** 3 **1.** to snatch to oneself, seize and carry off, seize hastily; a) to lead away with haste, hurry away *or* off; b) to tear, pluck, drag; **2.** to snatch away, carry off; a) to rob, ravish, plunder, ravage, carry off as plunder; b) to lay waste; c) to carry away, lead astray, transport, draw irresistibly; d) to seize by violence, steal; *subst.* **raptum**, ī *n* plunder, booty.

**raptim** *adv.* hastily, hurriedly.

**raptiō, ōnis** *f* seizing, abduction.

**raptō** 1 a) to carry away, hurry away, drag away *or* along; b) to rob, plunder.

**raptor, ōris** *m* robber, plunderer; abductor.

**raptum**, ī *n*, *see* **rapio.**

**raptus, ūs** *m* a) a carrying off, abduction, rape; b) a rending, tearing off; c) plunder.

**rāpulum**, ī *n* turnip.

**rāpum**, ī *n* turnip; knob of tree-roots.

**rārē-faciō** 3 to make thin, rarefy.

**rārēscō**, —, — 3 to grow thin, lose density; to widen out.

**rāritās**, ātis *f* want of density, looseness of texture; fewness, thinness.

**rārus** 3 (*adv.* **rārō**) loose in texture, thin, wide apart, with large meshes;

a) with large intervals, scattered, scanty, dispersed; b) few in number, rare, nor frequent; c) uncommon, extraordinary, remarkable, distinguished in its kind.

**rāsilis, e** polished, smoothed.

**rāsitō** 1 to shave.

**rāstellus, ī** m = rastrum.

**rāstrum, ī** n and **rāster, trī** m toothed hoe.

**ratiō, ōnis** f a reckoning; 1. account, computation, calculation; **ratiō constat** the account is correct; **ratiōnem inire** or **habere** to make a computation; **conficere** or **(com)putare** to settle an account; **in ratiōnem inducere** to bring into one's account; **ratiōnem reddere alci** to give an account; **ratiōnem repetere ab alqo** to call to account; — a) roll, register, list; b) money-transaction, business, affair; connection, relation, reference; **ratiōnem habere cum alqo** to have to do with; 2. respect, regard, consideration, concern; **ratiōnem habere** or **ducere alcis rei**, to consider, have regard for; **ratiōnem habere hominis** to accept a man as a candidate (at an election); interest, advantage (*alcis ratiōnibus consulere, ratiōnēs meas vestrae saluti antepono*); 3. judgment, understanding; a) reason; b) way, manner, course, method (**ratiō belli gerendi; vitae ratiōnēs** plan of life; **ratiōne** methodically); procedure, plan; c) reason, motive, ground, principle; d) argument, reasoning; 4. system; a) theory, doctrine, science, knowledge, philosophy; b) rule, order, principle; c) fashion, manner, way (**omni ratiōne** by all means).

**ratiōcinātiō, ōnis** f a) deliberate consideration, reasoning; b) syllogism.

**ratiōcinātīvus** 3 belonging to reasoning or syllogisms.

**ratiōcinātor, ōris** m reckoner, computer.

**ratiōcinor** 1 to reckon, compute, calculate; to deliberate; to argue, reason, conclude.

**ratiōnābilis, e** endowed with reason.

**ratiōnālis, e** a) endowed with reason; b) rational, logical.

**ratiōnārium, ī** n statistical survey.

**ratis, is** f raft, pontoon; float (for swimming on); boat, ship.

**ratiuncula, ae** f a) little reckoning or account; b) slight reason or ground; c) petty syllogism.

**ratus** 3 reckoned, calculated; a) fixed, defined, settled, established; b) confirmed, sure, certain; valid; **prō ratā (parte)** proportionately.

**rauci-sonus** 3 hoarse-sounding.

**raucus** 3 hoarse; hollow-sounding, deep-voiced; roaring, ringing, growling.

**raudus, eris** n, see **rudus** 2.

**raudusculum, ī** n small sum of money.

**rāviō** 4 to talk oneself hoarse.

**rāvis, is** f hoarseness.

**rāvus** 3 yellowish-grey.

**rea, ae** f, see **reus**.

**reāpse** adv. indeed, really.

**reātus, ūs** m state of an accused person.

**rebellātiō, ōnis** f = rebellio.

**reballātrix, īcis** f = rebellis.

**rebelliō, ōnis** f renewal of war; revolt, rebellion.

**rebellis, e** insurgent, rebellious; refractory.

**re-bellō** 1 to renew a war; to revolt, rebel.

**re-bītō** 3 to go back, return.

**re-boō** 1 to (make to) resound, echo.

**re-calcitrō** 1 to kick back; to reject advances.

**re-caleō, —, —** 2 to be warm again.

**re-calēscō, luī, —** 3 a) to grow warm again; b) to regain one's heat, to be rekindled.

**re-calfaciō** 3 to make warm again.

**re-calvus** 3 with a bald forehead.

**re-candēscō, duī, —** 3 a) to begin to glow; b) to grow white.

**re-canō** 3 to resound.

**re-cantō** 1 a) to recall, recant, revoke; b) to charm away; c) to re--echo.

**re-cēdō** 3 a) to go back, retire, withdraw, recede, retreat, be distant; b) to go away, depart, vanish, disappear (*ab, ex re in alqd*); c) to depart from, abandon (*a re*); to resign, yield, desist; d) to be removed, cut off.

**re-cellō, —, —** 3 to spring or fly back.

**recēns, tis** a) just come, lately arisen, modern; subsequent to, fresh from (*a re, re*); **b**) fresh, vigorous, young, recent; — *adv.* (**recēns**) lately, recently, newly, just.

**re-cēnseō, suī, sum** (*or* **situm**) 2 to count, number, muster, survey, review, *examine*; **a**) to go over, reckon up; **b**) to consider; **c**) to recount (*in words*).

**recēnsio, ōnis** *f* a numbering, mustering.

**recēnsus, ūs** *m* a reviewing, mustering.

**receptāculum, ī** *n* **a**) reservoir, magazine, receptacle; **b**) place of refuge, retreat, shelter.

**re-ceptiō, ōnis** *f* receiving.

**re-ceptō** 1 **a**) to take back, draw back; **b**) to receive habitually, to harbour.

**receptor, ōris** *m* concealer.

**receptrix, īcis** *f* concealer.

**receptum, ī** *n* obligation.

**receptus, ūs** *m* **a**) a taking back; **b**) a retiring, retreat; place of retreat, refuge; withdrawal.

**re-cessim** *adv.* backwards.

**recessus, ūs** *m* a going back, retiring; **a**) retreat, escape, withdrawal; **b**) nook, corner, recess, retired spot, inner room; solitude.

**recidīvus** 3 restored; constantly renewed.

**re(c)cidō, re(c)cidī, recāsūrus** 3 **a**) to fall back, return, recoil; to be thrown back, relapse; **b**) to sink, be subdued, be reduced, fall into (*ex re, in* or *ad alqd*); to fall into a certain time (*in tempus*).

**re-cīdō, cīdī, cīsum** 3 to cut away, down *or* off; to hew (*a*) to extirpate; **b**) to lop off, cut away, prune away.

**re-cingō** 3 to ungird; **P.** to ungird *or* divest oneself of (*alqd*).

**re-cinō, —, —** 3 **a**) to resound, echo; to keep on hooting (*or* to hoot in warning tones); **b**) to cause to resound; to celebrate, praise in song.

**reciperō** 1 = **recupero**.

**re-cipiō, cēpī, ceptum** 3 **1.** to take, draw, get, bring, fetch back (*alqd ab* or *ex re, in* or *ad alqd*); **se recipere** to withdraw, retire, retreat; **a**) to draw back (*troops*), cause to retreat; **signum recipiendi** signal for retreat; **b**) to save, deliver (*alqm ex re*); **2.** to get back, rescue, receive again, regain, recover, (re)conquer, take possession of, occupy; **se re-**

**cipere** to recover *or* collect oneself, regain courage; **3.** to admit, accept; **a**) to take to oneself, take in, receive, welcome (*tecto* or *domum suam*); **b**) to admit (*to a class*) (*alqm in ordinem senatorium, in civitatem, in amicitiam, in fidem*); **c**) to receive *or* entertain a charge against one; **d**) to admit, allow; **e**) to take upon oneself, assume (*mandatum, officium*); **f**) to guarantee, to promise, be responsible for.

**reciprocō** 1 **a**) to move backwards and forwards, to turn back, move back, reverse; **b) P.** *and intr.* to ebb and flow, alternate.

**reciprocus** 3 returning, ebbing.

**recitātiō, ōnis** *f* a reading aloud.

**recitātor, ōris** *m* reader, reciter.

**re-citō** 1 to read aloud.

**re-clāmātiō, ōnis** *f* shout of disapproval.                    [oppose.]

**re-clāmitō** 1 to contradict loudly,

**re-clāmō** to cry out against; **a**) to contradict loudly; **b**) to resound.

**re-clīnis, e** leaning back.

**re-clīnō** 1 to bend back, cause to lean back; to relieve; to rest.

**re-clūdō, sī, sum** 3 to unclose, open; to disclose; (*rarely*) to close.

**re-cōgitō** 1 to think over again.

**re-cognitiō, ōnis** *f* inspection.

**re-cognōscō** 3 to know again; **a**) to recall to mind; to recognize; **b**) to inspect, review, examine, revise.

**re-colligō** 3 to collect again, to regain; **se recolligere** to collect oneself, take courage (again); to reconcile.

**re-colō** 3 to cultivate again; **a**) to practise again; **b**) to restore, renew; to revisit; to reinvest; **c**) to think over again.

**re-commentor** 1 to recall to mind.

**re-commīniscor** 3 to remember.

**re-compōnō** 3 to readjust; to appease.

**re-conciliātiō, ōnis** *f* a reconciling; restoration.

**re-conciliātor, ōris** *m* restorer.

**re-conciliō** 1 to restore, repair; **a**) to re-unite, reconcile; **b**) to win over again.

**re-concinnō** 1 to repair, set right again.

**re-conditus** 3 put out of the way; **a**) hidden, concealed, far removed; sequestered; **b**) profound, abstruse.

**re-condō** 3 to put back *or* away (*alqd in alqd*); **oculos** to shut again; **a)** to lay up, store away, hoard; **b)** to hide, conceal (*alqd in re, re*).

**re-cōnflō** 1 to rekindle.

**re-coquō** 3 to cook *or* boil again; to melt *or* forge again.

**re-cordātiō, ōnis** *f* recollection, remembrance.

**re-cordor** 1 to remember, recollect (*alqd; de re; acc. c. inf.*), to think over.

**re-corrigō** 3 to reform.

**re-creō** 1 to make *or* create anew; to revive, restore, refresh, invigorate.

**re-crepō, —** 1 to resound.

**re-crēscō** 3 to grow again.

**re-crūdēscō, duī, —** 3 to break open afresh (*vulnera*); to break out again.

**rēctā** (*sc.* **viā**) *adv.* straight, right on.

**rēctiō, ōnis** *f* a ruling, direction.

**rēctor, ōris** *m* (*and* **-trīx, īcis** *f*) controller, director, governor; steersman, tutor.

**rēctus** 3 straight; **a)** upright; erect; **b)** right, correct, proper, appropriate, suitable, due; **c)** plain, simple, natural; **d)** honest, upright, virtuous, good; — *subst.* **rēctum, ī** *n* the right, the good, virtue; *adv.* **rēctē** straight; rightly, duly, well; (*in answers*) all right.

**re-cubō, —, —** 1 to lie on the back, to recline.

**rēcula, ae** *f* small property.

**re-cumbō, cubuī, —** 3 to lie backwards, recline (*at table*), lie down; to fall, sink down.

**recuperātiō, ōnis** *f* a regaining, recovery.

**recuperātor, ōris** *m* **a)** regainer, recoverer; **b)** judicial umpire, arbitrator.

**recuperātōrius** 3 of umpires.

**recuperō** 1 to regain, recover.

**re-cūrō** 1 to cure, restore.

**re-currō, currī, cursum** 3 to run back, hasten back (*in or ad alqd*); **a)** to come back to, return; **b)** to have recourse to.

**re-cursō** 1 to run back, return.

**re-cursus, ūs** *m* a running back, return, retreat.

**re-curvō** 1 to bend *or* curve backward.

**re-curvus** 3 bent back.

**re-cūsātiō, ōnis** *f* a declining, refusal; counter-plea; objection.

**re-cūsō** 1 to decline, refuse, reject (*alqd; de re; inf.; ne, quominus, quin*); to object, protest.

**re-cutiō, —, cussum** 3 to shake, cause to rebound *or* reverberate.

**recutītus** 3 circumcised; chafed.

**red-ambulō** 1 to come back.

**red-amō** 1 to love in return.

**red-ārdēscō** 3 to blaze up again.

**red-arguō, uī, —** 3 to confute, refute, contradict (*acc.*).

**red-auspicō** 1 to take return-auspices, to go back.

**red-dō, didī, ditum** 3 **1.** to bring back; **P.** *and* **se reddere** to return; **2.** to give *or* put back, restore, return; **a)** to recite, rehearse; **b)** to render, make, cause to be (*mare tutum, servitutem lenem, alqm iratum*); **3.** **a)** to repay (*beneficium, gratiam*); **b)** to take vengeance for (*hostibus cladem*); **c)** to pay back (*debts*), suffer (*punishment*); **d)** to deliver, assign, bestow, grant, to render, give what is due; **rationem reddere** to render an account; **ius reddere** to administer justice; **e)** to give out *or* forth, to reply; **f)** to imitate, represent, express; to translate, render (*alqd Latine*).

**red-dūcō = reduco**

**red-ēmptiō, ōnis** *f* a buying back, ransoming; **a)** a bribing; **b)** farming.

**red-ēmptō** 1 to ransom, redeem.

**red-ēmptor, ōris** *m* contractor, farmer, purveyor.

**redēmptūra, ae** *f* a contracting, farming.

**red-eō** to go *or* come back, return; **ad se redire** to recover one's senses; to return to one's natural bent; **in gratiam cum alqo** to be reconciled with; **a)** to return, recur (*to a former topic*); **b)** to come in (*as revenue*); **c)** to come to, be brought to, betake oneself to, have recourse to.

**red-hālō** 1 to breathe out again.

**red-hibeō** 2 to give back.

**red-igō, ēgī, āctum** 3 to drive, bring *or* lead back; **a)** to collect, raise, call in (*money*); to confiscate; **b)** to bring *or* reduce to a state *or* condition, force (*Galliam in potestatem, in dicionem, sub imperium*), to make, render; **in provinciam** to reduce to a province; **ad vanum et irritum** to make fruitless, to frustrate; c) to lessen, reduce.

**redimiculum, ī** *n* band, fillet, bond.

**redimiō** 4 to bind *or* wreathe round, to crown.

**red-imō, ēmī, ēmptum** 3 a) to buy back; to redeem, ransom, set free; b) to buy off, avert; c) to buy, procure by purchase; farm, hire, contract for, undertake.

**red-integrō** 1 to make whole again; a) to restore, renew; b) to refresh, revive.

**red-ipiscor** 3 to get back.

**red-itiō, ōnis** *f* return.

**red-itus, ūs** *m* a coming back, return; a) revolution, circuit; b) income, revenue.

**redivia, ae** *f* = **reduvia**.

**redivīvus** 3 used again; *subst.* **-um, ī** *n* old building materials used as new.

**red-oleō, uī,** — 2 to smell of (*alqd*); to be discernible (by smell).

**re-domitus** 3 subdued again.

**re-dōnō** 1 to give back; to resign.

**re-dormiō** 4 to sleep again.

**re-dūcō** 3 a) to bring, lead *or* draw back, to call back; b) to restore; to re-marry.

**re-ductiō, ōnis** *f* a bringing back.

**re-ductor, ōris** *m* one who leads back; restorer.

**re-ductus** 3 a) drawn back; b) retired, sequestered, remote.

**red-uncus** 3 bent *or* curved back.

**redundantia, ae** *f* superfluity, superabundance.

**red-undō** 1 to stream over, overflow; to be swimming with (*re*); a) to flow forth freely; b) to abound in, to be in excess.

**reduvia, ae** *f* hangnail.

**re(d)-dux, ucis** a) bringing back; b) brought back, returned.

**re-fectiō, ōnis** *f* a repairing, restoring.

**re-fector, ōris** *m* restorer.

**re-fellō, fellī,** — 3 to refute, confute, rebut.

**re-ferciō, rsī, rtum** 4 to stuff full, fill up; **refertus** 3 crammed, filled (with *abl.* or *gen.*).

**re-feriō,** —, — 4 to strike back.

**re-ferō, rettulī, relātum, referre** 3 1. to bear, carry, bring back (*alqd*

*in* or *ad alqd*); a) to bring back as a trophy, booty, present; b) to bring back a message, to report, announce, relate; c) to move back, remove backwards (*castra; pedem* or *se referre* or **P.** to go back, retreat, withdraw, return); d) to call to mind, think over; to refer to, assign to, give credit for; to judge by, measure according to a certain standard; e) to pay back, repay, pay in return, give back; f) **gratiam** to make a return, to show one's gratitude; g) to reply, return, answer; to repeat; to echo, resound; h) to restore, renew, revive; i) to call back to memory; to represent, recall; 2. to bring, deliver, transmit (*pecuniam in aerarium*); a) to note down, register, record; b) to tell, say, assert, relate; c) to bring before *or* refer to (*ad senatum*); to include (in a list), enter (*nomen in tabulas, alqm in proscriptos*).

**rē-fert, rē-tulit, rē-ferre** it matters, concerns, is of advantage *or* importance (*meā, tuā, suā*; with *gen.*; with *inf.* or *acc. c. inf.*).

**refertus** 3, see **refercio**.

**re-ferveō,** —, — 2 to boil up *or* over again.

**re-fervēscō** 3 to bubble up.

**re-ficiō, fēcī, fectum** 3 to make again; a) to choose again; b) to restore, repair, re-establish; c) to make up to full strength; d) to refresh, revive; e) to get back (*money*), get in return.

**re-fīgō** 3 to unfasten, unloose; to abolish, abrogate, repeal.

**re-fingō** 3 to form anew.

**re-flāgitō** 1 to demand back.

**re-flātus, ūs** *m* contrary wind.

**re-flectō** 3 to bend *or* turn backward; to turn about, to change, to bring back.

**re-flō** 1 to blow against *or* contrary; to breathe out again.

**re-fluō** 3 to flow back.

**refluus** 3 flowing back.

**re-fodiō** 3 to dig up.

**re-fōrmātiō, ōnis** *f* reformation.

**re-fōrmātor, ōris** *m* reformer.

**re-fōrmīdātiō, ōnis** *f* dread.

**re-fōrmīdō** 1 to dread, shun.

**re-fōrmō** 1 to form again, remould, transform.

**re-foveō** 2 to refresh, revive.

**refrāctāri(ol)us** 3 stubborn, over bearing.

**re-frāgor** 1 to oppose, withstand (*dat.*).

**re-frēnātiō, ōnis** *f* a restraining.

**re-frēnō** 1 to bridle, check.

**re-fricō, cuī, cātum** 1 to rub *or* scratch open again; to renew.

**re-frīgerātiō, ōnis** *f* a cooling.

**re-frīgerō** 1 to make cool; **P.** to cool oneself, grow cool.

**re-frīgēscō, frīxī, — 3** to grow cool (again); to lose vigour *or* interest, to abate, fail.

**re-fringō, frēgī, frāctum** 3 to break up, off, *or* open; to break in pieces, check, destroy.

**re-fugiō** 3 to flee back; **a)** to flee away, escape, take to flight (*ex or a re*); **b)** to turn away from, avoid, shun (*alqd*).

**refugium, ī** *n* place of refuge.

**re-fugus** 3 receding; fugitive.

**re-fulgeō, fulsī, — 2** to shine *or* gleam back.

**re-fundō** 3 to cause to flow back *or* overflow.

**refūtātiō, ōnis** *f* (**refūtātus, ūs** *m*) refutation.

**re-fūtō** 1 to drive back; **a)** to repel, resist; to contemn; **b)** to confute, refute.

**rēgāliolus, ī** *m* (*a little bird*) wren.

**rēgālis, e** kingly, princely.

**re-gelō** 1 to thaw.

**re-gemō** 3 to groan.

**re-gerō** 3 to bear, carry *or* bring back; to return.

**rēgia, ae** *f* royal palace, castle, residence; **a)** royal city *or* tent; **b)** court, courtiers; **c)** basilica, public hall.

**rēgi-ficus** = **regius a).**

**re-gignō** 3 to reproduce.

**rēgillus** 3 royal, splendid.

**regimen, inis** *n* a guiding, direction; **a)** government; **b)** rudder; **c)** ruler, governor.

**rēgina, ae** *f* queen, princess, lady.

**regiō, ōnis** *f* 1. direction, line, situation; **e regiōne** in a straight line, directly, opposite; 2. boundary line, boundary; **a)** region of the heavens *or* of the earth; **b)** tract, territory, neighbourhood; **c)** district, province; **sphere**; **d)** quarter of a city.

**regiōnātim** *adv.* by districts.

**rēgius** 3 of a king, royal, regal; **a)**

splendid, magnificent; **b)** despotic, tyrannical; **c)** = **regalis**; *subst.*

**rēgii, ōrum** *m/pl.* royal troops; courtiers, satraps.

**re-glūtinō** 1 to unglue, separate.

**rēgnātor, ōris** *m* = **rex.**

**rēgnātrīx, īcis** *f* ruling, imperial.

**rēgnō** 1 to be king, to rule, reign; **a)** to rule as a king; **b)** to be master, to domineer.

**rēgnum, ī** *n* royal power, monarchy; sovereignty, absolute power, despotism; kingdom, realm.

**regō, rēxī, rēctum** 3 to guide, conduct, direct (*acc.*); **a)** to rule, govern, control; **b)** to regulate.

**re-gredior, gressus sum** 3 to go back, retreat, march back, withdraw.

**re-gressus, ūs** *m* return; **a)** retreat; **b)** going back; **c)** recourse.

**rēgula, ae** *f* **a)** straight piece of wood, board; ruler, rule; **b)** model, pattern, example.

**rēgulus, ī** *m* petty king, chieftain; prince.

**re-gustō** 1 to taste repeatedly.

**rē-iciō, iēcī, iectum** 3 to throw back; **a)** to repel, drive back, cast back, cast up *or* away (*a ship*); **b)** to reject, refuse, scorn, disdain; **c)** to throw away, remove; **d)** to expel, relegate; **e)** to put off, defer (*in alqd*); **f)** to refer.

**rēiculus** 3 **a)** worthless; **b)** misspent, wasted.

**rēiecta** *and* **rēiectānea, ōrum** *n/pl.* rejectable things.

**rēiectiō, ōnis** *f* rejection.

**rē-iectō** 1 to throw back.

**re-lābor** 3 to slide, glide, sink back; to glide *or* flow down.

**re-languēscō, guī, — 3** to grow languid *or* faint.

**re-lātiō, ōnis** *f* report, proposition, motion; throwing back; returning; repetition.

**re-lātor, ōris** *m* mover, proposer.

**relātus, ūs** *m* report; recital.

**rē-laxātiō, ōnis** *f* relaxation, easing, alleviation.

**re-laxō** 1 to loosen, open; **a)** to relax, abate; **b)** to ease, relieve, mitigate; to release.

**relēgātiō, ōnis** *f* banishment.

**re-lēgō**[1] 1 to send away, dispatch; **a)** to banish; **b)** to put aside, reject; **c)** to refer.

**re-legŏ²** 3 to gather together, collect again; a) to travel over *or* traverse again; b) to read again; c) to consider again.

**re-lentēscō**, —, — 3 to slacken.

**re-levŏ** 1 to lift up, raise; to relieve, alleviate, mitigate; to free from (*abl.*); to lighten.

**relictiō, ōnis** *f* a forsaking, abandoning.

**relicuos (-cuus)** 3 = **reliquus.**

**religātiō,ōnis** *f* a binding *or* tying up.

**religiō, ōnis** *f* 1. a) scrupulousness; superstitious awe, scrupulous fear; religious scruples, scruples of conscience; **religiōnī mihi est** it is a matter of conscience; b) anxiety, punctiliousness, conscientiousness; 2. a) religious feeling, reverence of the gods, fear of god, religion, piety, devoutness; superstition; b) worship of the gods; religious observance, ceremony; c) religious system, mode of worship, faith, cult; 3. sacredness, sanctity; a) sacred obligation; b) holy object, sacred place, consecrated things; c) religious liability, sin, curse.

**religiōsus** 3 a) careful, anxious, scrupulous; b) conscientious, pious, devout, religious; superstitious; c) holy, sacred; d) forbidden by religious scruples.

**re-ligŏ** 1 to bind back *or* fast.

**re-linŏ, lēvī**, — 3 to unseal, open; to take out.

**re-linquŏ, līquī, lictum** 3 1. to leave behind; a) to leave; to leave behind by death, bequeath; b) to let remain, suffer to be (*alqm insepultum, alqd in medio*); 2. to leave remaining, leave over, leave to (*alci alqd*); *subst.* **relictum, ī** *n* remains, remnant; 3. to go away from, abandon, forsake, desert, give up; a) to leave in the lurch; b) to neglect, slight; to leave unpunished; c) to pass over, not to mention.

**reliquiae, ārum** *f/pl.* remainder, remains, relics, rest, fragments; ashes.

**reliquus** 3 a) left behind *or* over, remaining; *subst.* **reliquum, ī** *n* rest, remainder; b) outstanding, in arrear; *subst.* **-um, ī** *n* residue, remaining debt; c) other, rest; **reliquī** *pl.* 3 the others, the rest; d) subsequent, future.

**rellig-, relliqu-,** *see* **relig-, reliqu-.**

**re-lūceŏ, xī**, — 2 to shine back.

**re-lūcēscŏ, lūxī**, — 3 to become bright again. [against (*dat.*).]

**re-luctor** 1 to strive *or* struggle]

**re-macrēscŏ, cruī**, — 3 to grow lean again.

**re-maledīcŏ** 3 to revile back.

**re-maneŏ** 2 a) to stay behind; b) to be left, remain.

**re-mānŏ** 1 to flow back.

**re-mānsiō, ōnis** *f* a staying behind, remaining.

**re-meābilis, e** continually returning.

**remediābilis, e** curable.

**re-medium, ī** *n* remedy, medicine; means of healing *or* aid.

**remeligŏ, inis** *f* dawdler.

**re-meŏ** 1 to go *or* come back, return.

**re-mētior** 4 to go over again, to retrace, traverse again; to give back in equal quantity.

**rēmex, igis** *m* rower.

**rēmigātiō, ōnis** *f* a rowing.

**rēmigium, ī** *n* a rowing; oars; rowers.

**rēmigŏ** 1 to row.

**re-migrō** 1 to wander back, return.

**re-miniscor**, — 3 to call to mind, recollect, remember.

**re-misceŏ** 2 to mix up, mingle.

**re-missiō, ōnis** *f* a) a sending back; b) a letting down, lowering; c) a relaxing, slackening; remission; d) recreation; e) mildness, laxness.

**re-missus** 3 relaxed, languid; a) mild, gentle, indulgent, soft, yielding; b) gay, cheerful, merry; c) slack, careless.

**re-mittŏ** 3 1. to send back; to dismiss; a) to throw back; b) to give back, give out, yield, return (*beneficium*); c) to give back from oneself, give up, reject, resign; 2. to loosen, relax, slacken; to melt; thaw; a) to leave off, abate, remit; **se remittere** to leave off work, refresh oneself; to become milder, to cease; b) to pardon, remit; c) to give up, allow, concede, grant; d) to cease, omit.

**re-mōlior** 4 to press *or* push back.

**re-mollēscŏ**, —, — 3 to become soft again; a) to be touched, moved, influenced; b) to be enervated.

**re-mollŏ** 4 to make weak *or* effeminate.

**re-mora, ae** *f* delay.

**re-morāmen, inis** *n* hindrance.

**re-mordeō, mordī, morsum** 2 to bite back; to torment, vex.

**re-moror** 1 a) to stay, tarry, linger; b) *trans.* to detain, delay, hinder.

**re-mōtiō, ōnis** *f* removal.

**re-mōtus** 3 removed; distant, far off; a) remote; free from, disconnected; b) rejectable.

**re-moveō** 2 to move back *or* away, withdraw, remove, lay aside, put away, abolish.

**re-mūgiō** 4 a) to bellow again; b) to bellow back; to resound.

**re-mulceō** 2 to stroke; to put (a tail) between the legs.

**remulcum, ī** *n* towing cable.

**remūnerātiō, ōnis** *f* recompense, reward.

**re-mūneror** 1 to repay, reward, recompense (*alqm re*).

**re-murmurō** 1 to murmur back.

**rēmus, ī** *m* oar.

**re-nārrō** 1 to relate again.

**re-nāscor** 3 to be born again, to rise *or* grow again.

**re-nāvigō** 1 to sail back.

**re-neō** 2 to unspin, unravel.

**rēnēs, um** *and* **ium** *m/pl.* the kidneys.

**re-nīdeō, —, —** 2 to shine *or* gleam back; to beam with joy, smile.

**re-nīdēscō** 3 to reflect light.

**re-nītor** 3 to withstand, resist.

**re-nō**[1] 1 to swim back.

**rēnō**[2]**, ōnis** *m* reindeer skin, fur-cloak.

**re-nōdō** 1 a) to tie back; b) to untie.

**re-novāmen, inis** *n* renewal, new form.

**re-novātiō, ōnis** *f* a renewing.

**re-novō** 1 a) to renew, restore, repeat; b) to refresh, revive, recreate; **se renovāre** *or* P. to recover, be renewed in strength. [up.]

**re-numerō** 1 to pay back; to count]

**re-nūntiātiō, ōnis** *f* proclamation, declaration, report.

**re-nūntiō** 1 to bring back a message (*alci alqd*); a) to report, announce; b) to proclaim, declare elected; c) to revoke, recall, renounce.

**re-nūntius, ī** *m* bringer-back of news.

**re-nuō, uī, —** 3 to deny (*by nodding*), to refuse.

**re-nūtō** 1 to refuse.

**re-nūtus, ūs** *m* refusal.

**reor, ratus sum** 2 to think, believe, suppose, judge (*alqd; acc. c. inf.*).

**repāgula, ōrum** *n/pl.* bars *or* bolts of a door; barrier.

**re-pandus** 3 bent upwards.

**re-parābilis, e** reparable, retrievable. [from.]

**re-parcō** 3 to spare; to abstain]

**re-parātor, ōris** *m* restorer, renewer.

**re-parō** 1 1. to get back, a) to restore, repair, renew; b) to retrieve; c) to refresh, revive; 2. to take in exchange.

**re-pastinātiō, ōnis** *f* a digging up again.

**re-pectō, —, pexum** 3 to comb again.

**re-pellō, reppulī, repulsum** 3 a) to drive *or* thrust back; b) to drive away; c) to keep off, remove; d) to reject, repulse, spurn, scorn; e) to refute.

**re-pendō, pendī, pēnsum** 3 to weigh back; a) to weigh in return, pay in equal weight; b) to repay, purchase, ransom, redeem; c) to requite, recompense.

**repēns, tis** a) sudden, unexpected (*adv.* **-te** *and* **repēns**); b) fresh, recent.

**re-pēnsō** 1, *intens. of* **rependo**.

**repentīnus** 3 unexpected, sudden, hasty; upstart.

**re-percō** 3 = **re-parcō**.

**repercussus, ūs** *m* a rebounding, reverberation.

**re-percutiō** 3 to strike, push *or* drive back; P. a) to rebound, echo; b) to be reflected.

**re-periō, repperī, repertum** 4 a) to find again; b) to find out, discover; c) to perceive, learn, ascertain; d) to acquire, obtain; e) to invent, devise.

**repertor, ōris** *m* discoverer, inventor, deviser, author.

**repetentia, ae** *f* recollection.

**re-petītiō, ōnis** *f* repetition.

**repetītor, ōris** *m* one who asks back.

**re-petō** 3 1. a) to attack *or* fall upon again; b) to seek again, go to again, return; 2. a) to fetch back; to repeat, renew, begin again; **memoriam** (*rei*) to call to mind again; to repeat by words *or* writing; to think over again; to reckon again; b) to ask back, to demand restitution or satisfaction (res repetere); (pecuniae) repetundae, ārum f/pl. (property which is being sought back) the crime of extortion; to claim, demand as one's right; poenam to punish; to derive, to trace from; to begin, to undertake.

**re-pleō, plēvī, plētum** 2 a) to fill again, fill up; to replenish, complete; b) to make full; satisfy, supply.

**re-plicātiō, ōnis** f a folding back.

**re-plicō** 1 to fold back, unroll, open.

**rēpō, rēpsī,** — 3 to crawl, creep.

**re-pōnō** 3 a) to put or place back; to lay up, store, preserve; b) to lay aside, store up, put away; to lay in the earth, bury; c) to give back, restore, requite, retaliate, make compensation (alci alqd pro re); d) to place back, replace; to restore to a former condition; e) to repeat, renew; to answer again; f) to place, lay, put (in the proper or natural place); to place, count, reckon, class; g) to cause to rest on (alqd in re).

**re-portō** 1 to bear, carry or bring back; a) to bring back information, to report (alqd alci); b) to carry home.

**re-poscō,** —, — 3 to demand back; to claim.

**re-positōrium, ī** n dinner-wagon, tray.

**repostor, ōris** m restorer.

**repos(i)tus** 3 remote, distant.

**repōtia, ōrum** n/pl. a revelling on the day after an entertainment.

**re-praesentātiō, ōnis** f payment in cash.

**re-praesentō** 1 to make present or manifest, to display, show; a) to pay in ready money; b) to perform immediately, realize, accomplish instantly, hasten.

**re-prehendō** 3 to hold fast, detain, check; to blame, censure; to refute; to restore.

**reprehēnsiō, ōnis** f blame, censure; check; refutation. [peatedly.]

**re-prehēnsō** 1 to hold back, re-]

**reprehēnsor, ōris** m blamer, censurer; reformer.

**re-prēndō** 3 = reprehendo.

**re-pressor, ōris** m restrainer.

**re-primō, pressī, pressum** 3 to press or hold back; a) to restrain, check; se reprimere to restrain oneself; b) to limit, confine.

**re-prōmissiō, ōnis** f counter-promise.

**re-prōmittō** 3 to promise in return.

**rēptābundus** 3 creeping.

**rēptō** 1 to crawl, walk slowly.

**repudiātiō, ōnis** f refusal.

**re-pudiō** 1 to reject, refuse, disdain, scorn, repudiate.

**repudiōsus** 3 shocking, offensive, objectionable.

**repudium, ī** n a casting off; putting away; divorce, separation.

**re-puerāscō,** —, — 3 to become a boy again.

**re-pugnāns, tis** contrary, opposed.

**re-pugnantia, ae** f contradiction.

**re-pugnō** 1 a) to resist, oppose, withstand (dat.); b) to be inconsistent, incompatible.

**re-pullulō** 1 to sprout again.

**repulsa, ae** f rejection, repulse; refusal, denial.

**re-pulsō** 1 a) to re-echo; b) to reject.

**re-pulsus, ūs** m reflection of light, echo. [again.]

**re-pungō,** —, — 3 to prick or goad]

**re-pūrgō** 1 to cleanse again; to clear away.

**reputātiō, ōnis** f consideration, thinking over.

**re-putō** 1 to reckon, count; to think over, consider.

**re-quiēs, ētis** (also **requiem, requiē**) f rest, repose, recreation.

**re-quiēscō, quiēvī,** — 3 to rest, repose, to sleep; to be relieved; rarely trans. to lay to rest.

**re-quiētus** 3 rested, refreshed.

**re-quīritō** 1 to inquire after.

**re-quīrō, sīvī** or **siī, sītum** 3 a) to seek again, search for; b) to miss, want, require, demand, desire; c) to ask for, inquire after (alqd; de re; alqd ab or ex alqo); to investigate.

**rēs, rēī** (and **rěī**) f 1. thing, matter, affair; a) pl. the world, the universe, nature; b) condition, position, circumstances; respect, relation; **in omnibus rēbus** in every respect, from every point of view; **rem renuntiare** to relate the state of affairs; **rēs secundae** or **prosperae** (adversae) good (bad) fortune; fate, lot; ground, reason; c) business, affair, matter of business; **rēs mili-**

taris *or* bellica military affairs; **r. maritima** *or* **navalis** naval affairs; **frumentaria** corn-supply, **rustica** agriculture,*pl.* **rēs divinae** religion; **rem suscipere** to undertake a task; d) lawsuit, action; commonwealth, state, republic, public interest *or* power, government, = **rēs publica** (*see* **publicus**); e) benefit, profit, advantage, interest (*rebus suis consulere, in rem meam est* it is useful for me);**2.** property, possessions, estate, wealth; **rēs familiaris** private affairs *or* property; **3.** deed, action; a) exploit, battle, engagement,affair; b) event, occurrence, facts, history; **rērum scriptor** historian; c) actual thing, reality, truth; nature of a thing; d) contents, substance.

**re-sacrō** 1 to free from a curse.
**re-saeviō** 4 to rage again.
**re-salūtātiō, ōnis** *f* responsive greeting.
**re-salūtō** 1 to greet in return.
**re-sānēscō, nuī, —** 3 to become sound again.
**re-sarciō** 4 to patch up *or* mend again; to repair.
**re-scindō** 3 a) to tear open again; **b)** to break up, tear off *or* away, to force open; **c)** to annul, repeal.
**re-sciscō** 3 to find out, ascertain.
**re-scrībō** 3 a) to write back; to answer in writing; to rewrite; **b)** to re-enlist; **c)** to transfer; **d)** to place (money) to someone's credit, to pay back.
**re-scriptum, ī** *n* imperial rescript.
**re-secō** 1 to cut a part off, cut back; to curtail, check.
**re-secrō** 1 to adjure repeatedly.
**re-sēminō** 1 to sow *or* produce again.
**re-sequor** 3 to answer, reply.
**re-serō** 1 to unlock, unclose; to open, reveal, begin.
**re-servō** 1 to keep back, reserve (*alqd ad* or *in alqd*); a) to save, preserve; **b)** to retain.
**re-ses, idis** inactive, lazy.
**re-sideō, sēdī, sessum** 2 to be seated; a) to rest, keep a festival *or* holiday; **b)** to reside, be left, remain.
**re-sīdō, sēdī, sessum** 3 to sit down, settle; a) to sink, fall; **b)** to abate, grow calm, subside.
**residuus** 3 remaining, left behind; *subst.* **-um, ī** *n* remainder, residue.

**re-signō** 1 a) to unseal, open; to reveal; **b)** to annul, destroy; **c)** to pay back, resign.
**re-siliō, luī, —** 4 to leap *or* spring back; to contract, shrink.
**re-sīmus** 3 turned up.
**rēsīna, ae** *f* resin.
**rēsīnātus** 3 smeared *or* flavoured with resin.
**re-sipiō, —, —** 3 to taste *or* smack of.
**re-sipīscō, pīvī (piī *and* puī), —** 3 to recover one's senses.
**re-sistō, stitī, —** 3 a) to stand back, to halt, stop; to remain behind; to pause, stay; to recover a footing; **b)** to resist, oppose, withstand (*alci, contra alqd; ne, quin*).
**re-solvō** 3 to untie, unbind, loosen; a) to open; **b)** to relax, unnerve; **c)** to annul, cancel, abolish; **d)** to free, dispel, dissolve, melt; **e)** to pay (back).
**re-sonābilis, e** resounding.
**re-sonō** 1 to resound, echo; a) to sound; **b)** to fill with sound, cause to resound.
**re-sonus** 3 resounding.
**re-sorbeō, —, —** 2 to suck back, swallow again.
**re-spectō** 1 to look back, round *or* about (*ad alqd*); a) to gaze at, look upon (*alqd*); **b)** to regard, care for; **c)** to look for, expect (*alqd ab alqo*).
**respectus, ūs** *m* a looking back *or* about; a) regard, respect, consideration; **b)** refuge, retreat.
**re-spergō, rsī, rsum** 3 to besprinkle, bestrew (*alqd re*).
**respersiō, ōnis** *f* a besprinkling.
**re-spiciō, exī, ectum** 3 a) to look back, behind *or* about (*ad alqd*); to have respect to; **b)** to look back at (*alqd*), to see behind; **c)** to reflect upon, think of, to consider, care for, regard, have a care for (*alqd*).
**re-spīrāmen, inis** *n* windpipe.
**re-spīrātiō, ōnis** *f* a breathing out, breathing; exhalation; a taking breath.
**re-spīrō** 1 a) to breathe out; **b)** to take *or* recover breath, to recover, revive, be refreshed; **c)** to abate, cease.
**re-splendeō, uī, —** 2 to shine back, glitter.
**re-spondeō, ndī, ōnsum** 2 to promise in return; a) to answer, reply, make answer (*alci alqd; de re; acc. c.*

*inf.*); **b)** to give decisions, to give advice (*ius, de iure*); **c)** to answer to one's name, to appear, be present; **d)** to answer, correspond, agree, be equal *or* a match for (*dat.*); to requite, return; to be punctual in paying.

**re-spōnsiō, ōnis** *f* answer, reply.

**respōnsitō** 1 to give advice professionally.

**respōnsō** 1 **a)** to answer, echo; **b)** to withstand, defy.

**re-spōnsor, ōris** *m* one who gives an expert's opinion.

**respōnsum, ī** *n* **a)** answer; **b)** answer of a lawyer, priest, *or* oracle.

**rēs-pūblica, ae** *f*, *see* publicus.

**re-spuō** 3 to spit back *or* out; to reject, refuse, spurn.

**re-stāgnō** 1 to overflow; to be inundated.

**re-staurō** 1 to restore, repair.

**resticula, ae** *f* cord, line.

**restinctiō, ōnis** *f* a quenching.

**re-stinguō, īnxī, īnctum** 3 to quench, extinguish; to mitigate, appease; to destroy.

**restiō, ōnis** *m* rope-maker; one who is whipped with ropes.

**re-stipulātiō, ōnis** *f* counter-obligation.

**re-stipulor** 1 to stipulate in return.

**restis, is** *f* rope, cord.

**restitō** 1 to tarry, hesitate.

**restitrīx, īcis** *f* she who remains behind.

**re-stituō, uī, ūtum** 3 **1.** to replace; **a)** to bring *or* call back; **b)** to give back, restore, deliver up (*alci alqd*); **2.** to reinstate, restore to the former state, bring back; **a)** to renew, rebuild, revive, repair; **b)** to make restitution of, make good again, compensate; **c)** to revoke, make void, reverse.

**restitūtiō, ōnis** *f* a replacing, reinstating; restoring; recalling.

**restitūtor, ōris** *m* restorer.

**re-stō, stitī, —** 1 **a)** to stay back *or* behind; **b)** to withstand, resist; **c)** to be left, remain alive; **restat ut** it remains that; to be in store for; **quod restat** for the future.

**re-strictus** 3 bound fast, tight, close; **a)** strict, stern; **b)** niggardly, stingy; **c)** moderate.

**re-stringō** 3 to bind back *or* fast; **a)** to tighten; **b)** to confine, restrict.

**re-sūdō** 1 to sweat out.

**re-sultō** 1 to rebound, spring back; **a)** to resound; **b)** to be repugnant.

**re-sūmō** 3 to take again *or* back; **a)** to renew, repeat; **b)** to obtain again.

**re-supīnō** 1 to throw down (on the back).

**re-supīnus** 3 lying on the back; arrogant ('with his nose in the air').

**re-surgō** 3 to rise up again, to reappear.

**re-suscitō** 1 to rouse again.

**re-sūtus** 3 unstitched, come apart.

**re-tardātiō, ōnis** *f* a retarding, delaying.

**re-tardō** 1 to retard, delay, detain, hinder.

**re-taxō** 1 to censure in return.

**rēte, is** *n* net.

**re-tegō** 3 to uncover, make bare; to open; to reveal.

**re-temptō** 1 to try again.

**re-tendō, ndī, ntum** *or* **ēnsum** 3 to unbend (*a bow*).

**re-tentiō, ōnis** *f* a keeping back.

**re-tentō¹** 1 to hold back *or* fast; to preserve.

**re-tentō²** 1 = retempto.

**re-texō** 3 **a)** to unweave, unravel; to annul, cancel, reverse; **b)** to weave anew, to renew, repeat.

**rētiārius, ī** *m* fighter furnished with a net.

**reticentia, ae** *f* silence, a keeping silence; pause.

**re-ticeō, cuī, —** 2 **a)** to be silent; **b)** to keep secret.

**rēticulum, ī** *n* fishing-net; net-bag; hair-net.

**retināculum, ī** *n* band, halter, rope, cable.                    [cious (*gen.*).\

**re-tinēns, tis** holding fast, tena-/

**re-tinentia, ae** *f* a remembering.

**re-tineō, tinuī, tentum** 2 to hold back *or* fast, to detain (*alqm in re*); **a)** to hold in check, restrain; **b)** to fetter; **c)** to keep, preserve, retain, maintain.

**re-tinniō** 4 to resound.

**re-tonō, —, —** 1 to thunder back.

**re-torqueō** 2 to twist, bend *or* turn back; to change.

**re-torridus** 3 parched up, withered; old, cunning.

**re-tractātiō, ōnis** *f* **a)** recollection; **b)** drawing back, refusal.

**retractātus** 3 revised, corrected.

**re-tractō** 1 a) to draw back, take back, recall, retract; to refuse; b) to handle again, take in hand again, go over again, retouch, renew; to consider again, revise.

**retractus** 3 retired, remote.

**re-trahō** 3 a) to draw, drag, fetch back; to keep back, prevent, detain from (*alqm a re*); **se retrahere** to withdraw oneself; b) to draw *or* drag again; to draw forth again; c) to draw towards again (*alqm in alqd*).

**re-trectō** 1 = retracto.

**re-tribuō** 3 to give again *or* back; to return, restore, repay.

**re-trītus** 3 rubbed down.

**retrō** *adv.* backwards, back, behind; in the past.

**retro-agō** 3 to turn back *or* aside.

**retrōrsum** (*and* **-us**) *adv.* = retro.

**retrō-versus** 3 turned backwards.

**re-trūdō** 3 to push back; to thrust into a corner; to hide.

**re-tundō, rettudī, retū(n)sum** 3 to beat back; a) to blunt, make dull; b) to check; **retū(n)sus** 3 blunt, dull.

**reus, ī** *m* and **rea, ae** *f* a party in a law-suit; accused person, defendant; one who is bound *or* answerable for something (*gen.*).

**re-valēscō, luī,** — 3 to become well again, to recover, be restored.

**re-vehō** 3 to carry back; **P.** to come, sail, ride back.

**re-vellō** 3 to tear, pull *or* pluck off *or* away; to do away with, abolish; to tear up, open.

**re-vēlō** 1 to unveil, uncover.

**re-veniō** 4 to come back, return.

**rē-vērā** *adv.* indeed, in truth, truly.

**re-verberō** 1 to beat back; to cause to rebound.

**re-verēns, tis** respectful, reverent.

**reverentia, ae** *f* reverence, awe, respect.          [to fear, be afraid of.]

**re-vereor** 2 to feel awe *or* respect,

**re-verrō** 3 to sweep back again.

**re-versiō, ōnis** *f* a turning back; return, recurrence.

**re-vertor** (rarely **-ō**), *perf.* **revertī, reversum** 3 to turn back, return, come back; *part.* **reversus** having returned.

**re-videō** 2 to go back to see.

**re-vilēscō** 3 to become cheap.

**re-vinciō** 4 a) to bind back; b) to bind fast, fasten; to bind around, fetter.

**re-vincō** 3 to conquer, subdue; to convict, refute.

**re-virēscō, ruī,** — 3 to become green again; to become young *or* vigorous again.

**re-vīsō, sī,** — 3 to revisit; to go back to see.

**re-vīvīscō, vixī, victum** 3 to come to life again, revive.

**re-vocābilis, e** revocable.

**re-vocāmen, inis** *n* a calling back, warning.

**re-vocātiō, ōnis** *f* a calling back.

**re-vocō** 1 1. to call back, recall (*alqm de, ex, a re in or ad alqd*); a) to draw, turn, fetch back; b) to call off, withdraw, check; divert; c) to demand back; to recall; d) to renew, restore; e) to revoke, retract, cancel; f) to apply, reduce, refer; 2. to call anew, ask again, invite in return; a) to recall (*players*), to encore; b) to summon again.

**re-volō** 1 to fly back.

**re-volūbilis, e** that may be rolled back.

**re-volvō** 3 to roll back; a) to unroll, open again, read over, repeat, think over; b) P. to return, recur; — **re-volūtus** 3 returning, elapsed.

**re-vomō** 3 to vomit up.

**re-vorr-, -vors-, -vort-** = re-verr-, -vers-, -vert-.

**rēx, rēgis** *m* king, monarch, prince; *adj.* ruling, supreme; — a) *pl.* royal family, princes; b) arbitrary ruler; despot, tyrant; c) high priest; d) leader, head, chief, master, lord; e) mighty person, great man, patron, protector.

**rhadinē** *f adj.* (ῥαδινή) delicate.

**rhaps-ōdia, ae** *f* lay, book (*of a poem*).

**rhētor, oris** *m* a) teacher of rhetoric; b) = orator.

**rhētoricus** 3 rhetorical, of an orator; *subst.* **-a, ae** *f* and **ōrum** *n/pl.* art of rhetoric.

**rhino-cerōs, ōtis** *m* rhinoceros; vessel made of rhinoceros horn.

**rhō** *n* (*indecl.*) the Greek letter r.

**rhombus, ī** *m* a) a magician's circle; b) turbot.

**rhonchus, ī** *m* a) snore; b) grunt of contempt, sneer.

**rhythmicus, ī** *m* one who teaches the art of preserving rhythm in poetry.

**rhythmus (-os), ī** *m* rhythm.

**rhytium, i** *n* drinking-horn.

**rīca, ae** *f* veil.

**rīcinium, ī** *n* small veil, kerchief.

**rictum, ī** *n and* **rictus, ūs** *m* wide open mouth.

**rīdeō, sī, sum** 2 to laugh; to smile; a) to look cheerful, be favourable, to smile at (*alci; ad alqm*); b) to beam; c) to laugh at (*acc.*), deride, mock.

**rīdibundus** 3 laughing.

**rīdiculāria, ōrum** *n/pl.* fun, drollery.

**rīdiculus** 3 exciting laughter, funny, amusing, droll; *subst.* **-um, ī** *n* jest, joke.

**rigēns, tis** = **rigidus.**

**rigeō, guī,** — 2 a) to be stiff *or* numb; b) to stand on end, bristle up.

**rigēscō, riguī,** — 3 to become stiff.

**rigidō** 1 to stiffen, confirm.

**rigidus** 3 stiff, hard, inflexible; a) rigid; rocky; b) stern, rough, cruel.

**rigō** 1 to conduct (*water*); to wet, moisten, water.

**rigor, ōris** *m* stiffness; a) cold, chilliness; b) hardness, severity, sternness.

**riguus** 3 watering; watered.

**rīma, ae** *f* chink, fissure, cleft.

**rīmor** 1 to lay open, cleave; a) to turn over, pry into, search; b) to examine, investigate thoroughly.

**rīmōsus** 3 full of chinks *or* fissures.

**ringor,** — 3 to show the teeth; to snarl.

**rīpa, ae** *f* bank of a river (*rarely*, sea-coast).

**rīpula, ae** *f* small bank.

**riscus, ī** *m* trunk, chest.

**rīsiō, ōnis** *f* a laughing, laughter.

**rīsor, ōris** *m* mocker.

**rīsus, ūs** *m* laughter, laughing, laugh; a) object of laughter; b) mockery.

**rīte** *adv.* according to (*religious*) usage *or* ceremonies, according to rites; a) properly, fitly, justly, rightly, duly; b) fortunately, luckily.

**rītus, ūs** *m* religious usage, ceremony, rite; custom, usage, manner, mode; **rītū** (*with gen.*) in the manner *or* fashion of.

**rīvālis, is** *m* rival, competitor.

**rīvālitās, ātis** *f* rivalry.

**rīvulus, ī** *m* rivulet, streamlet.

**rīvus, ī** *m* brook, stream.

**rixa, ae** *f* quarrel, brawl, dispute.

**rixor** 1 to quarrel, brawl, dispute.

**rōbigīnōsus** 3 rusty; corroding, envious.

**rōbigō, inis** *f* rust; a) blight, mildew tartar (*or* decay?) on the teeth; rustiness (through lack of use).

**rōboreus** 3 oaken.

**rōborō** 1 to strengthen, invigorate.

**rōbur, oris** *n* hard-wood, oakwood, oak-tree; a) things made of hard wood, bench, club, lance; b) underground dungeon in the prison at Rome; c) hardness, firmness, strength; d) the best *or* strongest part, the pick; the flower of troops; stronghold.

**rōbus** 3 red.

**rōbustus** 3 oaken; hard, firm, solid, strong, vigorous, robust.

**rōdō, sī, sum** 3 to gnaw; to eat away, consume, corrode; to slander, disparage.

**rogālis, e** of a funeral pile.

**rogātiō, ōnis** *f* a) proposed law, bill; b) entreaty; request; question, interrogation.

**rogātiuncula, ae** *f* little question; little bill.

**rogātor, ōris** *m* a) proposer of a bill; b) collector of votes; beggar.

**rogātus, ūs** *m* request, entreaty.

**rogitātiō, ōnis** *f* proposed law.

**rogitō** 1 to ask (repeatedly).

**rogō** 1 1. to ask, question; **rogātum, ī** *n* question; a) **alqm sententiam** to ask an opinion, call upon to vote; b) **populum** *or* **lēgem** to propose a law; **magistrātum** to propose for election; 2. to ask for, beg, entreat, request (*alqd ab alqo; alqm; ut, ne*); to invite.

**rogus, ī** *m* funeral pile; grave.

**rōrāriī, ōrum** *m/pl.* skirmishers.

**rōridus** 3 = **roscidus.**

**rōri-fer** 3 dew-bringing.

**rōrō** 1 a) to drop dew; **rōrat** dew falls; to trickle, drip, be moist; b) to bedew, moisten.

**rōs, rōris** *m* dew, dewdrops; moisture, water; **rōs marīnus, ī** *m* rosemary.

**rosa, ae** *f* a) rose-bush; b) rose, wreath of roses.

**rosārius** 3 of roses; *subst.* **-ium, ī** *n* = **rosētum.**

**rōscidus** 3 a) full of dew, dewy, dripping; b) moistened, wet.

**rosētum, ī** n rose-garden.

**roseus 3** of roses; rosy.

**rōsidus 3** = roscidus.

**rōstrātus 3** having a beak; **columna** (or **corōna**) **-a** adorned with beaks of vessels.

**rōstrum, ī** n bill, beak, snout; **a)** beak of a ship; **b)** pl. platform for speakers in the Forum (adorned with ships' beaks).

**rota, ae** f wheel; **a)** potter's wheel; **b)** wheel for torture; **c)** roller; **d)** wheel of a chariot, chariot; **e)** vicissitude, alternation, fickleness.

**rotātus, ūs** m whirling motion.

**rotō 1** to turn, whirl or swing round; intr. to roll round.

**rotula, ae** f little wheel.

**rotundō 1** to make round; to round off.

**rotundus 3** round; **a)** rounded, circular, spherical; **b)** rounded, perfect, elegant.

**rube-faciō 3** to make red.

**rubellus 3** pale red.          [blush.]

**rubeō, uī,** — 2 to be red; to redden,

**ruber, bra, brum** red, ruddy.

**rubēscō, buī,** — 3 to grow or turn red.          [ous toad.]

**rubēta, ae** f a species of venom-

**rubētum, ī** n bramble-thicket.

**rubeus 3** of a bramble-bush.

**rubicund(ul)us 3** red.

**rubidus 3** blackish red.

**rubor, ōris** m redness; **a)** flush, blush; **b)** bashfulness, modesty; **c)** shame, disgrace.          [law.]

**rubrīca, ae** f red ochre; (title of) a

**rubus, ī** m bramble-bush; blackberry.

**rūctābundus 3** belching frequently.

**rūctō** (and **-or**) 1 to belch.

**rūctus, ūs** m a belching.

**rudēns** (and **rū-**), **tis** m and f rope, cable.

**rudiārius, ī** m discharged gladiator.

**rudimentum, ī** n first attempt, trial, essay, beginning, novitiate.

**rudis¹, is** f gladiator's practice-foil (presented to gladiators on retirement).

**rudis², e** unwrought, roughly made; untilled; unskilled, untrained, inexperienced (gen.; in re); uncultured.

**rudō** (and **rūdō**), **īvī,** — 3 to roar, bellow, bray.

**rūdus, eris** n 1. rubbish, debris, broken stone, plaster; — 2. formless piece of metal used as money.

**rūf(ul)us 3** dull yellowish or brownish red; red-haired.

**rūga, ae** f wrinkle, frown, gloomy look.

**rūgō 1** to be wrinkled.

**rūgōsus 3** wrinkled.

**ruīna, ae** f a tumbling, falling down, fall; **a)** disaster, calamity, overthrow, ruin; **b)** slip; **c)** destruction, death; **d)** fallen building, ruins.

**ruīnōsus 3 a)** going to ruin; **b)** fallen, ruined.

**rumex, icis** m and f sorrel.

**rūmi-ferō 1** to praise publicly.

**rūmināātiō, ōnis** f a chewing the cud, rumination; reflection.

**rūminō 1** to chew again.

**rūmor, ōris** m vague sound; **a)** cry of applause; **b)** common talk, report, hearsay; **c)** popular voice, common opinion, fame.

**rumpia, ae** f long sword.

**rumpō, rūpī, ruptum 3** to break, burst, tear, rend, break asunder; **a)** to burst to pieces, break open, break through; **viam** to force a way (also **sē rumpere** and **P. rumpī**); **b)** to cause to break forth; **c)** to violate, destroy, annul, interrupt, cut short.

**rūmusculus, ī** m idle talk, gossip.

**runcō 1** to depilate.

**ruō, ruī, rutum (ruitūrus) 3 1.** to hasten, hurry, run, rush; **a)** to fall with violence, tumble down, go to ruin; **b)** to rush, hasten, hurry, dash (in alqd); **c)** to fall, be ruined; **2.** trans. to cause to fall, cast down, to throw up in a heap.

**rūpēs, is** f rock, cliff, cavern.

**ruptor, ōris** m breaker, violator.

**rūri-cola, ae** m and f inhabiting the country, rural, rustic.

**rūri-gena, ae** m and f countryman, -woman.

**rūrō 1** to be in the country.

**rūrsus** and **rūrsum** adv. turned back, back, backwards; **a)** again, anew; **b)** on the contrary, on the other hand, in return.

**rūs, rūris** n the country, fields; **a)** country-seat, farm; **b)** rusticity; **rūs** into the country; **rūrī** and **rūre** in the country; **rūre** from the country.

**rūscum, ī** n butcher's-broom.

**russātus 3** dressed in red.

**russus 3** red.

**rūsticānus** 3 of the country, rustic.
**rūsticātiō, ōnis** *f* rural life.
**rūsticitās, ātis** *f* rustic behaviour,
boorishness; simplicity.
**rūsticor** 1 to live in the country.
**rūsticulus** 3 = **rūsticus**; *subst. m*
countryman; *f* grouse.
**rūsticus** 3 of the country, rural,
rustic; *m* countryman, peasant;
**a)** simple, plain; **b)** boorish, awkward, rude; coarse.

**rūsum** *and* **-us** = **rūrsum**, **-us**.
**rūta**[1], **ae** *f* rue (*a herb*); bitterness.
**rūta**[2] (et) **caesa** *n/pl.* minerals and
timber.
**rutābulum, ī** *n* poker, fire-rake.
**rūtātus** 3 garnished with rue.
**rutilō** 1 **a)** to colour reddish; **b)** to
shine with a reddish gleam. [red.]
**rutilus** 3 reddish yellow, golden
**rutrum, ī** *n* shovel, spade.
**rūtula, ae** *f* a little piece of rue.

# S

**sabbata, ōrum** *n/pl.* Sabbath; Jewish festival.

**sabbatāriae, ārum** *f/pl.* Sabbath-keepers, Jewesses.

**sabulum, ī** *n* coarse sand, gravel.

**saburra, ae** *f* sand; ballast.

**saburrō** 1 to fill (with ballast; with food).

**sacci-pērium, ī** *n* cover for a purse.

**saccō[1], ōnis** *m* 'bagman', i.e. usurer.

**saccō[2]** 1 to strain, filter.

**sacculus, ī** *m* small bag.

**saccus, ī** *m* sack, bag, purse.

**sacellum, ī** *n* little sanctuary, chapel.

**sacer, cra, crum** holy, sacred, consecrated (with *gen.* or *dat.*); accursed, execrable.

**sacerdōs, ōtis** *m* and *f* priest, priestess.

**sacerdōtālis, e** priestly.

**sacerdōtium, ī** *n* priesthood.

**sacrāmentum, ī** *n* a) money deposited by the parties in a suit, forfeit-money; b) civil suit; dispute; c) military oath of allegiance; d) oath, obligation.

**sacrārium, ī** *n* a) shrine, sacristy; b) chapel, sanctuary.

**sacrēs** = **sacrī** (sacer).

**sacri-cola, ae** *m* sacrificing priest.

**sacri-fer** 3 bearing sacred things.

**sacrificālis, e** belonging to sacrificing.

**sacrificātiō, ōnis** *f* a sacrificing.

**sacrificium, ī** *n* sacrifice.

**sacrificō** 1 to sacrifice, offer a sacrifice (*alci re* or *rem*).

**sacrificulus, ī** *m* sacrificing priest.

**sacri-ficus** 3 sacrificial.

**sacrilegium, ī** *n* temple-robbery, sacrilege.

**sacri-legus** 3 a) stealing sacred things; robbing a temple, sacrilegious; b) impious, godless, wicked.

**sacrō** 1 to consecrate, dedicate, devote; a) to render sacred or inviolable; b) to immortalize, render imperishable; c) to devote to the infernal gods.

**sacrō-sānctus** 3 most holy, inviolable.

**sacruficō** = **sacrificō**.

**sacrum, ī** *n* a) sacred *or* holy thing; sanctuary; b) sacrifice, holy rite; victim; worship, divine service; festival; mystery; poetry.

**saeculāris, e:** a) **-ēs (lūdī)** centennial games; b) **-e carmen** hymn composed for such games.

**saec(u)lum, ī** *n* a) generation, age, lifetime; b) a hundred years, century; long period; the times, spirit of the age.

**saepe** *adv.* often, frequently.

**saepe-numerō** *adv.* often.

**saepēs, is** *f* hedge, fence; enclosure.

**saepiculē** pretty often.

**saepimentum, ī** *n* hedge, enclosure.

**saepiō, psī, ptum** 4 to hedge in, fence in, enclose; to protect.

**saeptum, ī** *n* (*usu. pl.*) fence, enclosure, fold; barrier.

**saeta, ae** *f* stiff hair, bristle; part of a fishing-line.

**saeti-ger** 3 bristle-bearing; *subst. m*⎫
**saetōsus** 3 bristly.       [boar.⎰

**saevi-dicus** 3 spoken angrily.

**saeviō** 4 to rage, rave, be furious *or* fierce.

**saevitia, ae** *f* (*and* **-tūdō** *f*) rage, fury, fierceness, savageness, severity.

**saevus** 3 raging, furious, mad; fierce, cruel, savage, ferocious; *adv.* **-vē**, **-viter**.

**sāga, ae** *f* female soothsayer.

**sagācitās, ātis** *f* keenness (*of perception*), sagacity, acuteness.

**sagātus** 3 clothed in a military cloak.

**sagāx, ācis** keen in the scent; keen, acute, sagacious, clever.

**sagīna, ae** *f* a feeding, fattening: food, nourishment.

**sagīnō** 1 to feed, fatten, cram.

**sāgiō** 4 to perceive keenly.

**sagitta, ae** *f* arrow, bolt.

**sagittārius, ī** *m* archer.

**sagittātus** barbed.

**sagitti-fer** 3 arrow-bearing.

**sagitti-potēns, tis** mighty with arrows.

**sagittō** 1 to shoot with arrows.

**sagmina, um** *n/pl.* tuft of sacred grass.

**sagulātus 3** wearing a *sagulum.*

**sagulum, ī** *n* = **sagum.**

**sagum, ī** *n* (military) cloak.

**sāgus 3** prophetic.

**sāl, salis** *m* (*n*) salt; **a)** salt-water, brine, sea; **b)** acuteness, cunning, wit, good sense, elegance, brilliance; sarcasm.

**salacō, ōnis** *m* braggart.

**salamandra, ae** *f* salamander.

**salapūtium, ī** *n* little man, manikin.

**salārius 3** of salt; *subst.* ~, **ī** *m* dealer in salted fish; **salārium, ī** *n* salt- -money, pension, salary, stipend.

**salāx, ācis** lustful, lecherous; provoking lust.

**salebra, ae** *f* rough *or* uneven road; roughness. [even.]

**salebrōsus 3** rough, rugged, un-]

**saliātus, ūs** *m* appointment *or* dignity of the *Salii.*

**salictum, ī** *n* willow plantation.

**salignus 3** of willows.

**Salii, (ōr)um** *m/pl.* the priests of Mars.

**salillum, ī** *n* salt-cellar.

**salinae, ārum** *f/pl.* salt-works, salt-pits.

**salinum, ī** *n* salt-cellar.

**saliō, luī** *or* **liī, — 4** to leap, spring, bound, jump; *subst.* **salientēs, ium** *m/pl.* springs, fountains.

**saliunca, ae** *f* wild nard.

**saliva, ae** *f* spittle, saliva; taste, appetite.

**salix, icis** *f* willow.

**salsāmentārius, ī** *m* salt-fish dealer.

**salsāmentum, ī** *n* salted fish; brine.

**salsi-potēns, ntis** ruling the salt sea.

**salsūra, ae** *f* a salting, pickling.

**salsus 3** salted, salt; **a)** biting, sharp; **b)** witty, satirical.

**saltātiō, ōnis** *f* a dancing, dance.

**saltātor, ōris** *m* dancer.

**saltātōrius 3** of dancing.

**saltātrix, īcis** *f* dancing-girl.

**saltātus, ūs** *m* = **saltatio.**

**saltem** (*and* **saltim**) *adv.* at least.

**saltō 1** to dance, to represent in dancing.

**saltuōsus 3** well-wooded.

**saltus¹, ūs** *m* forest- *or* mountain- pasture, wooded upland; mountain- -pass; tight corner.

**saltus², ūs** *m* a leaping, leap.

**salūbris, e** (*and* **salūber, bris, bre**) **a)** healthful, wholesome, salubrious, salutary, serviceable; **b)** sound, vigorous.

**salūbritās, ātis** *f* healthfulness, wholesomeness; healthiness, health; means of deliverance.

**salum, ī** *n* open sea, sea; tossing at sea; river current.

**salūs, ūtis** *f* health; **a)** welfare, well- -being, weal, good fortune; **b)** se- curity, safety, deliverance, life; **c)** salutation, greeting; **salūtem di- cere** to greet, to bid farewell.

**salūtāris, e** healthful, wholesome, beneficial.

**salūtātiō, ōnis** *f* a greeting, salut- ing; a waiting upon, visit.

**salūtātor, ōris** *m* one who salutes; caller.

**salūtātrix, īcis** *f* (*as adj.*) (of) greeting; of callers.

**salūti-fer 3** health-bringing.

**salūti-gerulus 3** carrying greetings.

**salūtō 1** to greet, salute; **a)** to greet as, to name; **b)** to wait upon, to call upon, visit.

**salveō, —, — 2** to be well, be in good health; **salvē, salvēte** greet- ing!; hail!; good day!; farewell!

**salvus 3** safe, unhurt, preserved, sound, still alive; *adv.* **-vē** in good health, well, all right.

**sambūca, ae** *f* harp(-player).

**sambūcistria, ae** *f* female harpist.

**sānābilis, e** curable, healable.

**sānātiō, ōnis** *f* a healing, curing.

**sanciō, sanxī, sānctum 4** to make sacred *or* inviolable; **a)** to appoint, order, establish, decree (*alqd; ut, ne*); **b)** to confirm, ratify; **c)** to for- bid under penalty *or* punishment.

**sānctimōnia, ae** *f* = **sanctitas.**

**sānctiō, ōnis** *f* ordinance; penal clause, declaration of a penalty.

**sānctitās, ātis** *f* sacredness, sanc- tity; **a)** inviolability; **b)** holiness, purity, virtue, integrity, chastity; piety.

**sānctitūdō, inis** *f* = **sanctitas.**

**sānctor, ōris** *m* ordainer.

**sānctus 3** sacred, inviolable; **a)** ve- nerable, august, divine; **b)** virtuous, holy, pious; innocent, pure: chaste, just.

**sandali-gerula, ae** *f* female slave who carried her mistress' sandals.

**sandalium, ī** *n* slipper, sandal.

**sandapila, ae** *f* bier for poor people.
**sandyx, ycis** *f* vermilion.
**sānē** *adv.* **1.** soberly, sensibly, reasonably; **2.** a) indeed, truly, forsooth, well, by all means; b) to be sure, certainly: c) *(with imperative)* then, if you will; d) exceedingly, extremely; **sānē quam** very much indeed, uncommonly.
**sanguen, inis** *n* = **sanguis.**
**sanguināns, antis** blood-stained; blood-thirsty.
**sanguinārius** 3 blood-thirsty.
**sanguineus** 3 bloody, of blood; **a)** stained with blood; **b)** bloodred; **c)** blood-thirsty.
**sanguinolentus** *and* **sanguinulentus** 3 = **sanguineus.**
**sanguis** *(and -is)*, **inis** *m* blood; a) bloodshed; **b)** vigour, strength, life; c) consanguinity, race, family, blood; **d)** descendant, offspring.
**saniēs, ēi** *f* corrupted blood, bloody matter, venom, poison.
**sānitās, ātis** *f* health; a) soundness of mind, good sense, reasonableness; **b)** solidity, propriety.
**sanna, ae** *f* grimace.
**sanniō, ōnis** *m* buffoon.
**sānō** 1 to heal, cure, make sound; to restore, repair.
**sānus** 3 sound, healthy, whole; sober, reasonable, discreet.
**sapa, ae** *f* must, new wine boiled thick.
**sāperda, ae** *m* a cheap kind of salt fish.
**sapiēns, tis** wise, knowing, sensible, judicious, discreet; *subst.* *m* a wise man, philosopher.
**sapientia, ae** *f* good sense, prudence, discretion, wisdom; philosophy.
**sapienti-potēns, tis** mighty in wisdom.
**sapiō, iī, — 3** a) to taste of *(alqd)*; **b)** to have taste; c) to be sensible *or* wise; **d)** to understand.
**sāpō, ōnis** *m* soap.
**sapor, ōris** *m* taste, flavour; a) delicacy, pleasant odour; **b)** good taste, elegance.
**saprophagō** 3 to eat putrid food.
**sarcina, ae** *f* bundle, soldier's pack; load, burden; burden of the womb.
**sarcinārius** 3 belonging to baggage.
**sarcinātor, ōris** *m* one who patches *or* mends clothes.

**sarcinātus** 3 burdened with baggage. [gage.|
**sarcinula, ae** *f* bundle, small bag-|
**sarciō, rsī, rtum** 4 to patch, mend, repair; to make good, make amends for; **sartus** 3 in good condition, in good repair.
**sarco-phagus, ī** *m* coffin.
**sarculum, ī** *n* hoe.
**sardonyx, ychis** *m* and *f* sardonyx.
**sargus, ī** *m* a sea-fish.
**sariō** 4 to hoe, weed.
**saris(s)a, ae** *f* Macedonian lance.
**sarīso-phorus, ī** *m* Macedonian lancer.
**sarmen, inis** *n* = **sarmentum.**
**sarmentum, ī** *n (pl.)* twigs, brushwood, faggots.
**sarrācum, ī** *n* = **serracum.**
**sartāgō, inis** *f* frying-pan.
**sartor, ōris** *m* one who hoes.
**sartūra, ae** *f* patching, patch.
**sartus** 3, *see* **sarcio.**
**sat** *adv.* = **satis.**
**sata, ōrum** *n/pl.* standing corn, crops.
**sat-agius** 3 over-anxious.
**sat-agō** 3 (= *satis agō*) a) to pay debts; **b)** to have enough to do, be in trouble.
**satelles, itis** *m* and *f* attendant, escort, life-guard; a) *pl.* train, retinue; **b)** follower, partner, accomplice.
**satiās, (ātis)** *f* = **satietas.**
**satietās, ātis** *f* a) sufficiency, abundance; **b)** satiety, fulness; c) loathing, disgust.
**satillum** *n* a small trifle.
**satin'** *and* **satine** = **satisne.**
**satiō[1]** 1 to fill *(alqm re)*; a) to satisfy, satiate, appease; **b)** to overfill, disgust.
**satiō[2], ōnis** *f* a) a sowing, planting; **b)** sown field.
**satira, ae** *f* = **satura.**
**satis** enough, sufficiently, sufficient; **satis superque** more than enough; a) tolerably, moderately, well enough, pretty well, somewhat; **b) satis esse** to suffice; **satis habēre** to think sufficient, be satisfied, content; **satis agere**, *see* **satago**; **satis dare**, *see* **satisdo**; *comp.* **satius** better, preferable, more advantageous.
**satis-datiō, ōnis** *f* a giving of bail *or* security.
**satis-dō** 1 to give bail *or* security.

**satis-faciō** 3 to satisfy, give satisfaction; **a)** to pay (*a creditor*); **b)** to apologize, make excuse (*alci de re*); **c)** to make amends; **d)** to prove sufficiently (*alci acc. c. inf.*).

**satis-factiō, ōnis** *f* reparation, amends; apology.

**sator, ōris** *m* sower, planter; begetter, father, creator.

**satrapēa** *and* **-īa, ae** *f* satrapy, province of Persia.

**satrapēs, is** *and* **-pa, ae** *m* satrap, governor.

**satur, ra, rum** full, sated, satiated (*abl.* or *gen.*); fat, rich, fertile, abundant.

**satura¹, ae** *f* **a)** dish of various fruits, mixture, medley; **per saturam** confusedly; **b)** discursive composition; satire.

**satura²** *f* female satyr.

**saturēia, ōrum** *n/pl.* a herb.

**saturiō** *m* a well-fed man.

**saturitās, ātis** *f* fulness, repleteness; abundance.

**saturō** 1 = **satiō¹**.

**satus¹, ūs** *m* a sowing, planting; **a)** seed; **b)** a begetting, producing, origin, race.

**satus²** 3, *see* **sero²**.

**satyriscus, ī** *m* little Satyr.

**satyrus, ī** *m* Satyr; Satyric drama.

**sauciātiō, ōnis** *f* a wounding.

**sauciō** 1 to wound, hurt; to cut.

**saucius** 3 wounded, hurt, damaged, weakened.

**sāv-**, *see* **suāv-**.

**saxātilis, e** (found) among rocks.

**saxētum, ī** *n* rocky place.

**saxeus** 3 rocky, stony.

**saxi-fer** 3 bearing *or* casting stones.

**saxi-ficus** 3 turning into stone, petrifying.

**saxi-fragus** 3 stone-breaking.

**saxōsus** 3 stony, rocky.

**saxulum, ī** *n* (little) rock.

**saxum, ī** *n* large stone, fragment of rock; rock; stone-wall.

**S.C.** *abbr.* = **senatūs cōnsultum.**

**scabellum, ī** *n* percussion instrument used at dramatic performances.

**scaber, bra, brum** rough, scurfy, untidy, scabby, mangy.

**scabiēs, ēī** *f* roughness, scurf; **a)** scab, mange, leprosy; **b)** an itching, longing, pruriency.

**scabillum, ī** *n* = **scabellum.**

**scabiōsus** 3 scabby, scurfy; mildewy, spoilt (*grain*).

**scabō, scābī,** — 3 to scratch.

**scaena, ae** *f* stage, theatre; **a)** scene; **b)** publicity, public; **c)** parade, show; **d)** pretext, pretence.

**scaenālis, e** = **scaenicus.**

**scaenicus** 3 of the stage, scenic, dramatic, theatrical; *subst.* ~, **ī** *m* actor, player.

**scaeva, ae** *f* omen (*on the left hand*), portent.

**scaevus** 3 left.

**scālae, ārum** *f/pl.* flight of steps, staircase; ladder.

**scalmus, ī** *m* peg to hold an oar, thole, rowlock.

**scalpellum, ī** *n* scalpel, lancet.

**scalpō, psī, ptum** 3 to scratch, cut, carve; to tickle.

**scalprum, ī** *n* chisel, knife.

**scalptūra, ae** *f* carving.

**scalpurriō** 4 to scratch.

**scambus** 3 bandy-legged.

**scammōnia** (*and* **-ea**), **ae** *f* scammony.

**scamnum, ī** *n* bench, stool; throne.

**scandō, ndī, (ānsum)** 3 to climb, mount, ascend, mount into.

**scandula, ae** *f* roofing-lath.

**scapha, ae** *f* boat, skiff.

**scaphium, ī** *n* drinking-vessel, basin; chamber-pot.

**scapulae, ārum** *f/pl.* the shoulder-blades, shoulders.

**scāpus, ī** *m* rod forming part of a loom.

**scarus, ī** *m* (*a savoury sea-fish*).

**scatebra, ae** *f* a bubbling, spring-water.

**scateō** 2 (*and* **scatō** 3) to bubble *or* gush up; to swarm, abound (*abl.*).

**scatur(r)īgō, inis** *f* bubbling water, spring-water.

**scatur(r)iō** 4 to bubble.

**scaurus** 3 club-footed.

**scazōn, ontis** *m* 'limping' iambic line.

**scelerātus** 3 polluted by crime, defiled, profaned; **a)** wicked, vicious; **b)** annoying, troublesome.

**scelerō** 1 to pollute, defile.

**scelerōsus** (*and* **scelerus?**) 3 wicked.

**scelestus** 3 wicked, villanous, accursed, infamous, knavish; *m* rogue, scoundrel.

**scelus, eris** *n* wicked deed, crime, offence; **a)** wickedness, impiety; **b)** villain, scoundrel, rascal; **c)** misfortune. [-bearing.]

**scēptri-fer** *and* **-ger** 3 sceptre-]

**scēptrum, ī** *n* sceptre; dominion, kingdom, rule.

**scēptūchus, ī** *m* sceptre-bearer.

**scheda, ae** *f* = **scida**.

**schĕma, ae** *f and* **schēma, atis** *n* figure, fashion, manner.

**schoenicula** *f* scented with rush-perfume.

**schoeno-batēs, ae** *m* rope-dancer.

**schoenus, ī** *m* aromatic reed, perfume.

**schola, ae** *f* learned lecture *or* dispute; school; sect.

**scholasticus** 3 of a school, rhetorical; *subst.* ~, **ī** *m* teacher *or* student of rhetoric; grammarian.

**scida, ae** *f* strip of papyrus bark, leaf of paper.

**sciēns, tis** knowing; **a)** knowingly, purposely, intentionally; **b)** skilled, versed, expert.

**scientia, ae** *f* knowledge; science, skill.

**scī-licet** *adv.* of course, obviously, naturally, no doubt, certainly, to be sure; doubtless; namely.

**scilla, ae** *f* squill (a plant).

**scīn'** = **scisne**.

**scindō, idī, issum** 3 to cut, tear, rend, split, cleave, divide, break asunder; to destroy.

**scindula, ae** *f* = **scandula**.

**scintilla, ae** *f* spark.

**scintillō** 1 to sparkle, flash.

**scintillula, ae** *f* little spark.

**sciō, scīvī** *and* **scii, scītum** 4 **a)** to know, have knowledge, perceive; **b)** to understand, be skilled in.

**scipiō, ōnis** *m* staff.

**scirpea, ae** *f* basket-work made of rushes to form the body of a wagon.

**scirpeus** 3 of rushes.

**scirpiculus, ī** *m* rush-basket.

**scirpus, ī** *m* rush, bulrush.

**scīscitātor, ōris** *m* inquirer.

**scīscitor** (*and* **-ō**) 1 to seek to know, to inquire, question, examine (*alqd ex alqo, alqm de re*).

**scīscō, scīvī, scītum** 3 to decree, ordain (*alqd; ut*); to assent to, vote for (*alqd*); to inquire, ascertain.

**scissus** 3 rent, split, cleft; furrowed; harsh.

**scītāmentum, ī** *n* dainty.

**scītor** 1 = **sciscitor**.

**scītulus** 3 = **scitus²** (b).

**scītum, ī** *n* decree, ordinance.

**scītus¹, ūs** *m* (*only abl.*) = **scitum**.

**scītus²** 3 **a)** knowing, clever, shrewd, skilful (*gen.*), experienced, adroit; **b)** pretty, fine, elegant.

**sciūrus, ī** *m* squirrel.

**scobis, is** *f* sawdust, filings.

**scomber, brī** *m* mackerel.

**scōpae, ārum** *f/pl.* twigs; broom, besom.

**scopulōsus** 3 rocky, craggy.

**scopulus, ī** *m* rock, crag, cliff; difficulty, danger.

**scordalus, ī** *m* brawler.

**scorpiō, ōnis** *and* **scorpius, ī** *m* scorpion; a military engine; a sea-fish.

**scortātor, ōris** *m* fornicator.

**scorteus** 3 leathern; *subst.* **-ea, ae** *f* coat of leather.

**scortillum, ī** *n dim. of* **scortum** (b).

**scortor** 1 to whore.

**scortum, ī** *n* **a)** skin, hide; **b)** whore, prostitute.

**screō** 1 to hawk, clear the throat noisily; *hence* **screātor, ōris** *m*; **screātus, ūs** *m*.

**scrība, ae** *m* clerk, secretary.

**scrib(i)lita, ae** *f* cheese tart.

**scrībō, psī, ptum** 3 **a)** to scratch, engrave, draw; **b)** to write (*alqd alci, ad alqm, de re*); to beg, entreat, command by letter; **c)** to compose, draw up; **d)** to write of, describe; **e)** to enroll (*soldiers*).

**scrīnium, ī** *n* chest, box, case.

**scrīptiō, ōnis** *f* a writing; written composition, text.

**scrīptitō** 1 to write often *or* continually, to compose.

**scrīptor, ōris** *m* **a)** writer, scribe, copyist; **b)** author, composer; historian, poet.

**scrīptula, ōrum** *n/pl.* lines on a board for playing *duodecim scripta*.

**scrīptum, ī** *n* something written; writing, composition, essay, treatise, book, work, letter; **duodecim scripta** a game resembling draughts.

**scrīptūra, ae** *f* **a)** = **scriptio**; **b)** tax paid on public pastures.

**scrīptus, ūs** *m* office of a scribe.

**scrīpulum, ī** *n* = **scrupulum**.

**scrobis, is** *m and f* ditch, trench.

**scrōfa, ae** f a sow.
**scrōfi-pāscus, ī** m breeder of pigs.
**scrūpeus** 3 stony, rugged.
**scrūpōsus** 3 rugged; hard.
**scrūpulōsus** 3 full of sharp stones, rough, rugged; careful, anxious, scrupulous.
**scrūpulum, ī** n the 24th part of an ounce. [xiety, scruple.]
**scrūpulus, ī** m uneasiness, an-
**scrūpus, ī** m = **scrupulus.**
**scrūta, ōrum** n/pl. trash, trumpery.
**scrūtātiō, ōnis** f search.
**scrūtātor, ōris** m searcher, examiner.
**scrūtor** 1 to search carefully, examine thoroughly, explore, investigate, find out, search out.
**sculpō, psī, ptum** 3 to carve, cut, chisel; to form, fashion. [shoes.]
**sculpōneae, ārum** f/pl. wooden]
**sculptilis, e** carved, sculptured.
**sculptor, ōris** m stone-cutter sculptor.
**sculptūra, ae** f sculpture.
**scurra, ae** m buffoon, jester; dandy, man about town.
**scurrīlis, e** buffoon-like, scurrilous.
**scurrīlitās, ātis** f buffoonery.
**scurror** 1 to play the buffoon, be a parasite.
**scūtāle, is** n thong of a sling.
**scūtārius, ī** m shield-maker.
**scūtātus** 3 armed with a shield.
**scutella, ae** f little flat dish.
**scutica, ae** f lash, wip.
**scūti-gerulus** 3 shield-bearer.
**scutra, ae** f flat dish.
**scutula¹, ae** f wooden roller, cylinder.
**scutula², ae** f lozenge-shaped dish; patch over the eye.
**scutulāta, ōrum** n/pl. check-patterned garments.
**scūtulum, ī** n small shield.
**scūtum, ī** n shield, oblong shield.
**scymnus, ī** m whelp.
**scyphus, ī** m cup, goblet.
**scytalē, ēs** f a kind of snake.
**S.D.** abbr. = **salutem dicit.**
**sē** acc., abl. himself, herself, itself.
**sēbum, ī** n suet; tallow.
**sē-cēdō** 3 to go away or apart, to separate, withdraw, retire.
**sē-cernō** 3 to sunder, sever, divide, put apart, separate, disjoin (alqd a re); to discern.
**secespita, ae** f sacrificial knife.

**sē-cessiō, ōnis** f a) a going aside, withdrawal, retirement; b) secession, schism.
**sē-cessus, ūs** m retirement, solitude; retreat, hiding-place.
**sē-clūdō, sī, sum** 3 to shut off; to shut up or apart, to seclude, separate, remove (alqd a re).
**sēclum, ī** n, see **saeculum.**
**secō, cuī, ctum** 1 to cut; to cut off, up, down; a) to tear, wound, hurt; b) to divide, cleave, separate; c) to cut or pass through, traverse; d) to decide.
**sēcrētiō, ōnis** f separation.
**sē-crētus** 3 severed, separated; a) retired, remote, lonely, solitary; b) secret, hidden, concealed; c) deprived of, lacking; — subst. **sēcrētum, ī** n retirement, solitude, secrecy; secret; adv. **sēcrētō** in secret, apart, secretly, without witnesses, in private.
**secta, ae** f path, way; mode, manner, method; a) party, side; b) school, sect, faction.
**sectārius** 3 leading (the flock).
**sectātor, ōris** m follower, attendant, adherent, pl. train, retinue.
**sectilis, e** (that can be) cut, divided.
**sectiō, ōnis** f buying of confiscated goods; confiscated property.
**sector¹, ōris** m cutter; purchaser at a sale of confiscated goods.
**sector²** 1 to follow continually, attend, accompany (acc.); to follow after, pursue, chase.
**sectūra, ae** f a digging, mine.
**sē-cubitus, ūs** m a lying or sleeping alone.
**sē-cubō, buī,** — 1 to sleep or live alone.
**sēculāris, sēculum, ī** n = **saec-.**
**secundānī, ōrum** m/pl. soldiers of the second legion.
**secundārius** 3 of second quality or importance.
**secundō¹** 1 to favour, further.
**secundō²** adv. secondly.
**secundum** adv. behind; prep. with acc. behind; along; besides; after; next to; in accordance with; in favour of.
**secundus** 3 following, next, second; **secundae (partes)** second part, inferior part, second rank; a) secondary, subordinate, inferior; b) following, accompanying, downward; **secundo flumine** down

stream, with the current; c) favourable, propitious, fortunate; **secundo populo** with the consent of the people; **res secundae** good fortune.

**secūricula, ae** f little axe.

**secūri-fer** and **-ger** 3 axe- or hatchet-bearing.

**secūris, is** f a) axe, hatchet; b) blow, wound, injury; c) pl. authority, power, sovereignty.

**sēcūritās, ātis** f a) freedom from care, peace of mind; confidence; b) safety, security.

**sē-cūrus** 3 free from care, fearless, untroubled, composed, quiet; a) cheerful, bright, serene; b) careless, negligent; c) safe, free from danger; d) dispelling care.

**secus**¹ n (indecl.) sex.

**secus**² adv. otherwise, not·so; **non secus** even so, just so (with atque or quam); not well, wrongly; comp. **sequius** otherwise than good, ill, discreditable (sometimes written **secius**; see also **sētius**).

**secūtor, ōris** m pursuer; a kind of gladiator.

**sed** cj. a) (after a negative) but, but on the contrary; b) but, yet, however; c) (in resuming a discourse) but.

**sēdāmen, inis** n alleviation.

**sēdātiō, ōnis** f an allaying, assuaging.

**sēdātus** 3 composed, quiet, calm.

**sē-decim** (indecl.) sixteen.

**sēdēcula, ae** f little seat, stool.

**sedentārius** 3 sitting.

**sedeō, sēdī, sessum** 2 to sit (in loco); a) to sit in council, in judgment; b) to remain in a place, stay; to sit still or idle, to be inactive; c) to sit down, remain encamped; d) to hold fast, be fixed or established; e) to sink, subside.

**sēdēs, is** f seat; a) dwelling-place, residence, home; resting-place; b) place, spot, seat; foundation; c) station, rank.

**sedile, is** n seat, stool, chair.

**sēd-itiō, ōnis** f a going apart; separation, dissension, quarrel; insurrection, rebellion, mutiny, military revolt.

**sēditiōsus** 3 factious, seditious, mutinous, turbulent.

**sēdō** 1 to soothe, still, allay, assuage, appease, stop, check.

**sē-dūcō** 3 to lead aside, take apart; to turn aside, separate, sever; **sē-ductus** 3 remote, withdrawn.

**sē-ductiō, ōnis** f a leading aside.

**sēdulitās, ātis** f a) assiduity, zeal, application; b) officiousness, obtrusiveness.

**sēdulus** 3 a) busy, diligent, zealous, assiduous, earnest, unremitting; b) officious, obtrusive; adv. **sēdulō**.

**seges, etis** f a) cornfield, standing corn; crop; b) multitude. [menta.)

**segmentātus** 3 adorned with seg-)

**segmentum, ī** n strip of brocade, &c., used as a border or trimming.

**sēgnipes, edis** slow-footed.

**sēgnis, e** slow, sluggish, inactive, lazy, dilatory; lingering, languid.

**sēgnitia, ae** (and **sēgnitās, ātis** and **-tiēs, ēī**) f slowness, sluggishness, tardiness, inactivity.

**sē-gregō** 1 to separate from the flock; to set apart, separate, sever, remove, segregate.

**sē-grex, gregis** separate.

**sei = sī.**

**sē-iugātus** 3 separated.

**sē-iugis, e** drawn by six horses; pl. **sēiugēs** m chariot drawn by six horses.

**sē-iūnctim** adv. separately.

**sē-iūnctiō, ōnis** f a separating.

**sē-iungō** 3 to disjoin, sever, separate; to distinguish.

**sē-lēctiō, ōnis** f selection. [pound.)

**se-lībra** (and **sē-**), **ae** f half a)

**sē-ligō, lēgī, lēctum** 3 to choose out, select, single out.

**sella, ae** f seat, chair; a) teacher's chair; b) official chair of a magistrate; c) sedan-chair.

**sellāria** n/pl. lounge.

**sellāriolus** 3 for lounging in.

**sellārius, ī** m voluptuary.

**selli-sternium, ī** n banquet in honour of goddesses.

**sellula, ae** f little sedan-chair.

**sellulārius, ī** m sedentary mechanic.

**sēmanimis, -us,** see **sēmi...**

**semel** adv. a) a single time, once; **non semel** more than once; **semel atque iterum** once and again, repeatedly; b) once for all; c) first, the first time.

**sēmen, inis** n seed; a) shoot, seedling; b) stock, race; c) descendant, offspring; d) origin, ground, cause, element.

**sēmenti-fer** 3 fruitful.
**sēmentis, is** f a sowing; young crops.
**sēmentivus** 3 of seed or sowing.
**sēmermis, e** and **-mus** 3, see se-miermis.
**sē-mē(n)stris, e** of six months, half-yearly.
**sēm-ēsus** 3 half-consumed.
**sē-met** = **se** (strengthened).
**sēmi-adapertus** 3 half-opened.
**sēmi-ambustus** 3 half-burned.
**sēmianimis, e** and **-mus** 3 half--alive; half-dead.
**sēmi-apertus** 3 half-open.
**sēmi-barbarus** 3 half-barbarian.
**sēmi-bōs, bovis** m half-ox (the Minotaur).
**sēmi-caper, prī** m half-goat (= Pan, faun).
**sēmi-cremātus** and **-cremus** 3 half-burned.
**sēmi-crūdus** 3 half-raw; half-digested.
**sēmi-cubitālis, e** half a cubit long.
**sēmi-deus** 3 half-divine; m demigod.
**sēmi-doctus** 3 half-taught.
**sēmiermis, e** (and **-mus** 3) half-armed.
**sēmiēsus** 3 = semesus.
**sēmi-factus** 3 half-finished.
**sēmi-fer** 3 half-man and half-beast; half-savage.
**sēmi-fultus** 3 half-supported.
**sēmi-germānus** 3 half-German.
**sēmi-graecus, e** half-Greek.
**sēmi-gravis, e** half-drunken.
**sē-migrō** 1 to go away, remove.
**sēmi-hiāns, tis** half-open.
**sēmi-homō, inis** half-human; half--man and half-beast.
**sēmi-hōra, ae** f half-hour.
**sēmi-lacer** 3 half-mangled.
**sēmi-lautus** 3 half-washed.
**sēmi-liber, era, erum** half-free.
**sēmi-lixa, ae** m half-sutler.
**sēmi-marinus** 3 half in the sea.
**sēmi-mās, maris** m half-male, hermaphrodite; castrated.
**sēmi-mortuus** 3 half-dead.
**sēminārium, ī** n nursery-garden, nursery.                [author.)
**sēminātor, ōris** m sower, producer,
**sēmi-nex, necis** half-dead.
**sēminium, ī** n seed; race, breed.
**sēminō** 1 to sow, beget, produce.
**sēmi-nūdus** 3 half-naked.
**sēmi-pāgānus** 3 half a yokel.

**sēmi-perfectus** 3 half-finished.
**sēmi-plēnus** 3 half-manned.
**sēmi-putātus** 3 half-pruned.
**sēmī-rāsus** 3 half-shaven.
**sēmi-reductus** 3 half-bent back.
**sēmi-refectus** 3 half-repaired.
**sēmi-rutus** 3 half-ruined.
**sēmis, issis** m a half-unit, half an as; a half.
**sēmi-senex, senis** m elderly man.
**sēmi-sepultus** 3 half-buried.
**sēmi-somnus** 3 (and **-nis, e**) half--asleep.
**sēmi-supīnus** 3 half on one's back.
**sēmita, ae** f narrow way, footpath; way, lane.
**sēmitālis, e** of footpaths.
**sēmitārius** 3 found in lanes.
**sēmi-tēctus** 3 half-covered.
**sēmi-ustulātus** or **-ustilātus** 3 = semustulatus.
**sēmi-ustus** 3 = semustus.
**sēmi-vir, ī** m half-man (half-beast); a) half-male, hermaphrodite; castrated; b) womanish, effeminate.
**sēmi-vīvus** 3 half-alive; half-dead.
**sē-modius, ī** m half-modius.
**sē-move** ō2 to move apart or away, to sever; **sēmōtus** 3 remote, distant; confidential.
**semper** adv. always, ever.
**sempiternus** 3 everlasting, perpetual, eternal.
**semul** = **simul**.
**sēm-uncia, ae** f half an ounce; the 24th part (of an as); a trifle.
**sēmunciārius** 3 containing the 24th part.
**sēm-ustulātus, -ustilātus,** and **sēm-ustus** 3 half-burned.
**senāculum, ī** n meeting-place of the senate.
**senāriolus, ī** m, dim. of senarius.
**sēnārius** 3 consisting of six each; (**versus**) ~ m verse of six feet.
**senātor, ōris** m senator.
**senātōrius** 3 senatorial.
**senātus, ūs** m senate, council of state; a) body of senators; b) meeting of the senate; **senātūs consultum** decree of the senate; **senātūs auctoritas** resolution of the senate.
**senecta, ae** f = senectus[2].
**senectus[1]** 3 = senilis.
**senectūs[2], ūtis** f old age; a) old men; b) gray hair; c) moroseness; d) maturity.

**seneō, —, —** 2 to be old.

**senēscō, nui, —** 3 to grow old, become aged; to grow old in strength, to decay, waste away.

**senex, senis** old, aged (*comp.* **senior, ius**); *subst.* **senex** *m* and *f* old man *or* woman; **seniōrēs, um** *m*/*pl.* elderly persons (*between 45 and 60*)

**sēni** 3 six each. [*years.*)

**senilis, e** of an old man, of old age, senile.

**sēniō, ōnis** *m* the number six.

**senium, i** *n* weakness *or* decay of old age; a) trouble, affliction; b) gloom, moroseness.

**senius, i** *m* old man.

**sēnsibilis, e** perceptible by the senses.

**sēnsifer** 3 producing sensation.

**sēnsilis, e** having sensation.

**sēnsim** *adv.* gradually, by degrees, gently, slowly.

**sēnsus, ūs** *m* perception; **1.** power of perceiving, sensation, sense (*sēnsus videndi* or *oculorum*); consciousness; **2.** understanding, mind; a) feeling, common-sense; b) opinion, thought, view, notion; c) meaning, signification; **3.** sentiment, emotion, inclination, disposition, habit of mind, mode of thinking.

**sententia, ae** *f* opinion, thought, meaning, purpose; **ex animi sententiā** to the best of one's belief; a) way of thinking, judgment; b) determination, decision, sentence, vote (*of senators*); c) meaning, signification (*of a word*), purport of a speech; d) maxim, aphorism, axiom, saying.

**sententiola, ae** *f* short sentence, maxim.

**sententiōsus** 3 full of meaning, sententious.

**senticētum, i** *m* thorn-bush.

**sentīna, ae** *f* bilge-water; ship's hold; sewer; dregs, refuse, rabble.

**sentiō, sēnsi, sēnsum** 4 to feel, perceive, discern by sense (*alqd, de re; acc. c. inf.*), be sensible of; a) to feel the effects of, to experience, learn, suffer; b) to understand, observe, notice, remark; c) to think, judge, imagine, suppose, believe, mean; d) to give an opinion, to vote, declare; **sēnsa, ōrum** *n*/*pl.* thoughts, opinions.

**sentis, is** *m* (*f*) thorn-bush, briar.

**sentīscō** 3 to perceive, observe.

**sentus** 3 rough, overgrown with thorns, uncared for.

**se-orsum** *and* **-sus** *adv.* asunder, apart, separately.

**sē-par, paris** separate, different.

**sēparābilis, e** separable.

**sēparātim,** *adv.* of **separatus.**

**sēparātiō, ōnis** *f* a severing, separation.

**sēparātus** 3 separated, severed, apart, distinct, particular, different; far off, remote.

**sē-parō** 1 to separate, divide.

**sepelibilis, e** that may be hidden.

**sepeliō, pelīvi, pultum** 4 to bury, inter (*also* to cremate); a) to destroy, ruin, suppress; b) to immerse, sink.

**sēpēs, sēpiō,** see **saepes, saepio.**

**sēpia, ae** *f* cuttle-fish; ink.

**sēpiola, ae** *f* little cuttle-fish.

**sē-pōnō** 3 to put *or* lay aside, apart; a) to keep back, reserve; b) to separate, pick out; to distinguish; c) to keep far off, exclude; **sēpositus** 3 choice, select; reserved; distant.

**sēps, sēpis** *m* and *f* poisonous snake--like lizard.

**sēpse** = **se ipse.**

**sēpta, ōrum** *n*/*pl.*, see **saepta.**

**septem** (*indecl.*) seven.

**September, bris, bre** belonging to September; (*mensis*) *m* September.

**septem-decim** = **septendecim.**

**septem-fluus** 3 with seven streams *or* mouths.

**semptem-geminus** 3 sevenfold (with seven mouths, with seven hills).

**septem-pedālis, e** seven feet long.

**septem-plex, icis** sevenfold.

**septem-triō,** see **septentrio.**

**septem-vir, i** *m* one of a college of seven.

**septemvirālis, e** of the *septemviri.*

**septem-virātus, ūs** *m* office of a *septemvir.*

**septēnārius** 3 consisting of seven; *subst. m* line containing seven (and a half) feet, septenarius.

**septen-decim** (*indecl.*) seventeen.

**septēni** 3 seven each; seven at once; *sing.* sevenfold.

**septentriō, ōnis** *m* (*usu. pl.*) the seven stars of the Great *or* Little Bear; the north; (*sg.*) north-wind.

**septentriōnālis, e** northern.

**septiē(n)s** *adv.* seven times.

**septimānī, ōrum** *m/pl.* soldiers of the seventh legion.

**septi-montiālis, e** relating to the festival of the seven hills.

**septimus 3** the seventh.

**septingentēsimus 3** the seven hundreth.

**septingentī 3** seven hundred.

**septuāgēsimus 3** seventieth.

**septuāgintā** *(indecl.)* seventy.

**septu-ennis, e** seven years old.

**septumus 3 = septimus.**

**sept-unx, uncis** *m* seven ounces, seven twelfths.

**sepulcrālis, e** funeral.

**sepulcrētum, ī** *n* burial place.

**sepulcrum, ī** *n* burial-place; grave, tomb, sepulchre; dead person.

**sepultūra, ae** *f* a burying, burial, interment, cremation.

**sequāx, ācis** following quickly, pursuing penetrating.

**sequester, tris, tre, (and tra, trum)** mediating; *subst.* *m* mediator, go--between; *n* deposit, security.

**sequius** *adv.*, *comp. of* **secus²**.

**sequor, cūtus sum 3** to follow, come after; to accompany; **a)** to pursue; **b)** to come next, succeed, ensue; **c)** to go to, have for a destination; to aim at, seek to gain; **d)** to accede to, imitate, take as a guide; **e)** to follow naturally, come of itself; **f)** to follow logically; **g)** to fall to, fall to the share of.

**Ser.** *abbr.* = **Servius.**

**sera, ae** *f* bar, bolt.

**serēnitās, ātis** *f* clearness, fair weather; favourableness.

**serēnō 1** to make clear *or* bright.

**serēnus 3** clear, bright, serene; *subst.* -**um, ī** *n* clear sky, fair weather; cheerful, glad.

**serēscō** to dry *(intrans.)*.

**sēria, ae** *f* earthen vessel, jar.

**sēricātus 3** dressed in silk.

**sēricus 3** of silk; *subst.* -**ca, ōrum** *n/pl.* silk garments.

**seriēs, ēī** *f* row, succession, chain, series; lineage.

**sēriola, ae** *f* small jar.

**sērius¹ 3** serious, earnest; *subst.* **sēria, ōrum** *n/pl.* serious things, earnestness; *adv.* **sēriō** in earnest, earnestly.

**sērius²** *adv.*, *comp. of* **serus.**

**sermō, ōnis** *m* talk, conversation; **a)** learned talk, discourse, discus-

sion; **b)** subject of conversation; **c)** ordinary speech, conversational language; familiar style; **d)** manner of speaking, language, expression, diction; dialect; **e)** common talk, report, rumour.

**sermōcinātiō, ōnis** *f* discussion

**sermōcinor 1** to talk, converse.

**sermunculus, ī** *m* report, rumour, gossip.

**serō¹, (ruī,) rtum 3** to join together, interweave, entwine; **serta, ōrum** *n/pl.* (*and* **sertae, ārum** *f/pl.*) garlands, wreaths; to connect, combine, compose.

**serō², sēvī, satum 3 a)** to sow, plant; *subst.* **sata, ōrum** *n/pl.* cornfields, standing crops; **b)** to beget, engender, bring forth; **satus** begotten, sprung, born *(abl.)*; **c)** to spread abroad, disseminate, cause, occasion.

**serō³,** *adv. of* **serus.**

**serpēns, tis** *f and m* snake, serpent.

**serpenti-gena, ae** *m* sprung from a serpent.

**serpenti-pēs, edis** serpent-footed.

**serperastra, ōrum** *n/pl.* bandages, knee-splints.

**serpillum, ī** *n* = **serpyllum.**

**serpō, psī, — 3** to crawl, creep; to move slowly, proceed imperceptibly; to extend gradually, spread abroad.

**serpyllum, ī** (*and* **serpullum, ī**) *n* wild thyme.

**serra, ae** *f* saw. [on, cart.]

**serrācum, ī** *n* two-wheeled wag-]

**serrātus 3** notched on the edge; indented.

**serrula, ae** *f* little saw.

**serta, ōrum** *n/pl.*, *see* **sero¹.**

**serum¹, ī** *n* whey, watery part of curdled milk.

**sērus 3** (*adv.* **sērō**) late, belated, too late; *subst.* **sērum², ī** *n* late time; **sērō diei** late in the day, at a late hour; *comp.* **sērius** later, too late.

**serva, ae** *f* female slave, servant--maid.

**servābilis, e** that can be saved.

**servantissimus 3** most observant.

**servātor, ōris** *m* preserver, saviour.

**servātrix, īcis,** *fem. of* **servator.**

**servilicola, ae** *f* low prostitute.

**servilis, e** servile; of slaves.

**serviō 4** to serve, be a slave *or* servant, be in service (*apud alqm, alci*);

a) (*of land*) to be subject to burdens *or* obligations; b) to comply with, gratify, subserve, assist, be governed, enslaved by (*alci*).

**servitium, ī** *n* = **servitus** (a), (c).

**servitrīcius** 3 of slaves.

**servitūs, ūtis** *f* condition of a slave; a) slavery, servitude, service, subjection; b) (*of land*) liability to obligations; c) servants, slaves, body of servants.

**servō** 1 to observe, pay heed to, watch (*alqd*); a) to keep, preserve, guard, maintain; b) to keep for the future, lay up, reserve, retain, store; c) to keep safe; to rescue; d) to keep to, stay in (a place).

**servolus, ī** *m* = **servulus**.

**servula, ae** *f* servant maid.

**servulus, ī** *m* young slave.

**servus** 3 servile, slavish, subject; (*of lands*) subject to obligations; *subst.* **servus, ī** *m*, **serva, ae** *f* slave, servant.

**sēsamum, ī** *n* sesame.

**sescēnāris** *adj.* (meaning unknown).

**ses-cēnārius** 3 consisting of six hundred.

**ses-cēni** (*and* **-centēni**) six hundred each.

**ses-centēsimus** 3 the six hundredth.

**ses-centī** 3 six hundred; countless.

**ses-centiē(n)s** *adv.* six hundred times.

**sēsē** = **sē**.

**seselis, is** *f* (*a plant*).

**sēsqui** *adv.* one half more, half as much again.

**sēsqui-alter** 3 one and a half.

**sēsqui-hōra, ae** *f* one hour and a half.

**sēsqui-modius, ī** *m* a modius and a half.

**sēsqui-octāvus** 3 of nine eighths.

**sēsqui-opus, eris** *n* the work of a day and a half.

**sēsqui-pedālis, e** one foot and a half long.

**sēsqui-pēs, edis** *m* a foot and a half.

**sēsqui-plāga, ae** *f* a blow and a half.

**sēsqui-plex, icis** one and a half times.

**sēsqui-tertius** 3 of one and a third.

**sessibulum, ī** *n* seat.

**sessilis, e** fit for sitting upon; dwarf (of plants).

**sessiō, ōnis** *f* a sitting; seat; session.

**sessitō** 1 to sit much.

**sessiuncula, ae** *f* small circle for conversation.

**sessor, ōris** *m* one who sits; rider; inhabitant.

**sēstertiolum, ī** *n* = **sestertium**.

**sēs-tertius, ī** *m* (*genit. pl.* **-tium**) sesterce (*a small silver coin, originally worth two and a half* asses): **decies sēstertium** (= *decies centena milia sēstertium*) a million sesterces; **sēstertium, ī** *n* (*usu. pl.* **sēstertia**) a thousand sesterces.

**sēsuma, ae** *f* sesame.

**set** *cj.* = **sed**.

**sēta, ae** *f* = **saeta**.

**sētiger** 3 = **saetiger**.

**sētius** *adv.* (confused with *sequius*, *see* **secus**) otherwise; not well, ill; **nōn sētius** none the less.

**sētōsus** 3 = **saetosus**.

**seu** = **sīve**.

**sevēritās, ātis** *f* seriousness, severity, sternness, strictness.

**sevēritūdō, inis** *f* = **sevēritās**.

**sevērus** 3 serious, grave, strict, austere, stern; harsh, hard.

**sē-vocō** 1 to call aside *or* away; to call off, withdraw (*alqd a re*).

**sēvum, ī** *n* = **sebum**.

**Sex.** *abbr.* = **Sextus**.

**sex** (*indecl.*) six.

**sexāgēnārius** 3 sixty years old.

**sexāgēni** 3 sixty each.

**sexāgēsimus** 3 the sixtieth.

**sexāgiē(n)s** *adv.* sixty times.

**sexāgintā** (*indecl.*) sixty.

**sex-angulus** 3 hexagonal.

**sexc...**, *see* **sesc...**

**sex-decim** = **sedecim**.

**sex-ennis, e** of six years.

**sex-ennium, ī** *n* period of six years.

**sexiē(n)s** *adv.* six times.

**sex-prīmī, ōrum** *m/pl.* a board of six magistrates in provincial towns.

**sextā-decimānī, ōrum** *m/pl.* soldiers of the sixteenth legion.

**sextāns, tis** *m* the sixth part (*of an as, iugerum, sextarius,* &c.).

**sextārius, ī** *m* (*a liquid measure*) pint.

**Sextilis, e** belonging to August; (*mensis*) *m* August.

**sextula, ae** *f* the sixth part of an *uncia*.

**sextus** 3 the sixth.

**sexus, ūs** *m* sex.

**sī** *cj.* if, if only, if ever, even if; in case, in the hope that, on the chance that.

**sībilō** 1 to hiss, whistle; to hiss at (*acc.*).

**sībilus**[1] 3 hissing, whistling.

**sībilus**[2], **ī** *m* (*plur. also* **sībila** *n*) a hissing, whistling, rustling; contemptuous hissing.

**Sibylla** *and* **Sibulla, ae** *f* prophetess, female soothsayer.

**Sibyllīnus** 3 Sibylline.

**sīc** *adv.* so, thus, in this manner; in this case, on this condition; **a)** **ut** ... **sic** as ..., so ...; **b)** so much, to such a degree; **c)** just so, yes.

**sīca, ae** *f* dagger, poniard; assassination.

**sīcārius, ī** *m* assassin, murderer.

**siccitās, ātis** *f* dryness, drought; **a)** firm, healthy condition; **b)** jejuneness, simplicity.

**siccō** 1 to dry, dry up; to drain.

**sicc-oculus** 3 having dry eyes.

**siccus** 3 dry; *subst.* **-um, ī** *n* dry land; **a)** thirsty; sober; **b)** firm, healthy; **c)** plain, insipid, dull.

**sīcilicula, ae** *f* small sickle.

**sīcilicissitō** 1 to be in the Sicilian manner.

**sīcine** *adv.* (*sīc* + *ne*) thus? indeed?

**sī-cubi** *cj.* if anywhere.

**sīcula, ae** *f* (small dagger) penis.

**sī-cunde** *cj.* if from anywhere.

**sīc-ut(ī)** *adv.* so as, just as, as; **sicuti ... ita** just as ... so; as it were, just as if, as for instance.

**sīdereus** 3 starry, of stars; **a)** bright, glittering; **b)** heavenly, divine.

**sīdō, sēdī** *and* **sīdī, sessum** 3 to sit down, settle; **a)** to sink down; **b)** to become fixed.

**sīdus, eris** *n* constellation; **a)** star; heavenly body; **b)** sky, heavens; **c)** time of year, day; **d)** climate, region; **e)** weather, storm; **f)** pride, glory.

**sigillātus** 3 adorned with little figures. [image; **b)** seal.)

**sigillum, ī** *n* **a)** small figure *or*)

**sigma** *n* the Greek letter *Σ*; semicircular dining-couch.

**signātor, ōris** *m* one who seals; witness to a will *or* contract.

**signi-fer** 3 bearing figures, starry; **orbis** zodiac; *subst. m* standard-bearer.

**significanter** *adv.* plainly, clearly.

**significātiō, ōnis** *f* a pointing out, indicating, showing, sign, token; **a)** sign of assent, approbation, applause; **b)** meaning, signification (*of a word*).

**signi-ficō** 1 to give a sign *or* indication; **a)** to indicate, point out, make known; **b)** to foreshow, indicate future things; **c)** to mean, signify.

**signō** 1 to mark, mark out, designate; **a)** to engrave; to seal, seal up; **b)** to stamp, coin, impress, imprint; **c)** to observe, notice; **d)** to adorn, decorate.

**signum, ī** *n* **1.** sign, mark, token; **a)** signal, order, command, watchword, pass-word; **b)** standard, flag, banner; **signa movēre** *or* **convellere** to march away, **inferre** to attack, **signa conferre** to fight, come to close quarters; **c)** a small division of troops, company, maniple; **2.** figure, image, statue, picture; **a)** seal, signet; **b)** group of stars, constellation.

**sīlānus, ī** *m* fountain.

**silentium, ī** *n* silence, stillness; **a)** freedom from disturbance in taking the auspices; **b)** repose, tranquillity, leisure.

**sileō, uī, — 2 1.** *intr.* **a)** to be still, silent, noiseless; *subst.* **silentēs, um** *m/pl.* the silent, the dead; Pythagoreans; **b)** to be inactive, to rest, cease; **2.** *trans.* to be silent about (*acc.*); *subst.* **silenda, ōrum** *n/pl.* secrets, mysteries.

**siler, eris** *n* a pliant plant.

**silēscō, luī, — 3** to become silent.

**silex, icis** *m* (and *f*) flint, pebble; rock, crag.

**silicernium, ī** *n* funeral feast; old man.

**siligineus** 3 of fine wheaten flour.

**siligō, inis** *f* white flour.

**siliqua, ae** *f* husk, pod, shell, *pl.* pulse.

**sillybus, ī** *m* = sittybus.

**silua, ae** *f* = silva.

**silūrus, ī** *m* a river-fish.

**sīlus** 3 snub-nosed, flat-nosed.

**silva, ae** *f* wood, forest; **a)** grove, shrubbery; **b)** tree, undergrowth; **c)** crowded mass, crop, growth; plentiful supply; materials.

**silvēscō, —, — 3** to grow wild.

(**silvester, tris, tre** *and*) **silvestris, e** of a wood *or* forest, wooded; **a)** living in the woods; **b)** growing wild, wild; rural, pastoral.

**silvi-cola, ae** *m* inhabitant of the woods.

**silvi-cultrīx, īcis** *f* living in the woods.

**silvifragus 3** breaking trees.

**ilvōsus 3** wooded.

**sīmia, ae** *f (and* **-ius, ī** *m)* ape, monkey.

**simila, ae** *f* fine wheaten flour.

**similis, e** like, resembling, similar (with *gen.* or *dat.*); **veri similis** likely, probable; *subst.* **simile, is** *n* comparison, simile.

**similitūdō, inis** *f* likeness, resemblance; imitation; sameness; a) analogy; b) comparison, simile.

**simiolus, ī** *m* little ape.

**simītū** (archaic) = **simul.**

**sīmius, ī** *m*, see **simia.**

**sim-plex, icis** simple; a) uncompounded, unmixed; b) single, one; c) plain, simple, natural; d) open, frank, guileless, artless, sincere; *adv.*

**simpliciter** plainly, directly, openly, artlessly, simply.

**simplicitās, ātis** *f* simplicity; candour.

**simplum, ī** *n* an original sum *or* number (*without multiplication*).

**simpulum, ī** *n* sacrificial ladle.

**simpuvium, ī** *n* sacrificial bowl.

**simul 1.** *adv.* at once, at the same time, together; **simul cum** together with; **simul ... simul** partly ... partly, as well ... as; **2.** *cj.* **simul ac, simul atque, simul ut, simul** as soon as.

**simula, ae** *f* = **simila.**

**simulācrum, ī** *n* likeness; a) image, figure, portrait, statue; b) vision in a dream; shadow, shade; c) portraiture, characterization; d) phantom, mere image, appearance; e) imitation, reflection.

**simulāmen, inis** *n* copy.

**simulātiō, ōnis** *f* false show, feigning, shamming; pretence, deceit, hypocrisy.

**simulātor, ōris** *m* imitator; feigner, pretender, hypocrite.

**simulātrīx, īcis** *f* one who transforms (*men into the image of beasts*).

**simulō 1** to make like (*alqd alci rei*); a) to imitate, copy, represent; b) to pretend, feign, counterfeit, simulate, assume the appearance of; **simulātus 3** feigned, counterfeit, pretended.

**simultās, ātis** *f* jealousy, rivalry, enmity, quarrel.

**simulter** = **similiter**, in a similar way.

**sīmus** (*and* **-ulus**) **3** flat-nosed.

**sin** *cj.* if however, but if; **sīn minus** but if not.

**sināpi**, *indecl. n and* **-pis, is** *f* mustard.

**sincēritās, ātis** *f* soundness, purity, integrity, uprightness.

**sincērus 3** unadulterated; a) pure, unmixed, uninjured, whole; b) sound, candid, sincere; real, genuine.

**sincipitāmentum, ī** *n* pig's cheek.

**sinciput, itis** *n* a) pig's cheek; b) brain.

**sindōn, onis** *f* fine linen, muslin.

**sine** *prep.* with *abl.* without.

**singillātim** *adv.* one by one, singly; severally.

**singulāris, e** one by one, alone, single; a) singular; *subst. m* picked horseman; b) single in its kind, matchless, unique, extraordinary, exceptional; *adv.* **sing(u)lāriter.**

**singulārius 3** single.

**singulī, ae, a** one each; single, several, one alone.

**singultim** *adv.* sobbingly; stammeringly.

**singultiō 4** to throb.

**singultō 1** to sob, gasp (out).

**singultus, ūs** *m* a sobbing, panting, gasping.

**singulus 3**, see **singuli.**

**sinister, tra, trum** left, on the left hand; *subst.* **sinistra, ae** *f* left hand, left side; a) awkward, wrong, perverse; b) unfavourable, unlucky, inauspicious; c) favourable, lucky. auspicious.

**sinisteritās, ātis** *f* awkwardness.

**sinistrōrsum** *and* **-sus** *adv.* to the left.

**sinō, sīvī, situm 3** a) to lay, place, *or* put down; b) to let, suffer, allow, permit (*inf.; acc. c. inf.*); *imperative* **sine** let, be it so.

**sīnum, ī** *n* (*and* **sīnus, ī** *m*) vessel, pot, bowl, basin.

**sinuō 1** to bend, wind, curve, swell out in curves.

**sinuōsus 3** full of bendings *or* curves, sinuous.

**sinus, ūs** *m* curve, fold, hollow, coil; a) bay, gulf; hollow, valley; b) shore of a bay; c) fold of the toga, of a garment, bosom, lap; purse; **d)** wind-filled sail; **e)** love, affection, intimacy, protection; **f)** interior, inmost part, heart; **g)** place of refuge.

**sīparium, ī** *n* small theatre-curtain; comedy.

**sīparum, ī** *n* = **supparum.**

**siphō, ōnis** *m* **a)** siphon; **b)** fireengine.          [pipe.]

**sīphunculus, ī** *m* little tube or}

**si-quidem** *cj.* **a)** if indeed; **b)** since, inasmuch as.

**siremps(e)** exactly the same.

**Sīrius, ī** *m* the Dog-star.

**sirp... = scirp...**

**sirpe, is** *n* a North African plant.

**sis** = **si vis** if you will, please.

**siser, eris** *n* a salad plant.

**sistō, stitī and stetī, statum** 3 **1.** to cause to stand, to place, put (*alqm* or *alqd in loco* or *loco*); **a)** to set up, to convey, bring, lead to; **b)** to erect, build; **c)** to cause to appear before a court; **se sistere** to appear, present oneself; **d)** to make stand still, to stop, check, arrest, detain; **se sistere** to halt, make a stand; **status** 3 set, fixed, appointed; **2.** *intr.* to stand; **a)** to appear; **b)** to stand still; **c)** to stand firm, continue, endure, remain.

**sīstrātus** 3 provided with a *sīstrum.*

**sīstrum, ī** *n* metal rattle.

**sisymbrium, ī** *n* a fragrant herb.

**sitella, ae** *f* urn for lots, ballot-box.

**siticulōsus** 3 thirsty, dry, parched.

**sitienter** *adv.* greedily, eagerly.

**sitiō** 4 to thirst, be thirsty; to be dry, parched, arid; **sitiēns, tis a)** thirsty, dry; **b)** eager, greedy.

**sitis, is** *f* thirst; **a)** dryness, drought; **b)** eager desire, greediness.

**sitītor, ōris** *m* one who thirsts.

**sittybus, ī** *m* book-label.

**situla, ae** *f* bucket; urn used for drawing lots.

**situs¹, ūs** *m* **a)** situation, position, site; construction; **b)** want of cultivation, neglect; mould, dirt, rust; inactivity, sloth.

**situs²** 3 **a)** placed, lying, situated; **b)** built, erected; **c)** buried; **situm esse in re** to rest *or* depend upon.

**sī-ve** *or* **seu** *cj.* or if; or; **sīve potius** or rather; **sīve ... sīve** if ..., or if ...; whether ..., or ...

**smaragdus, ī** *m* and *f* emerald (*and other jewels*).

**smilax, acis** *f* (*a plant*) bindweed.

**smyrna, ae** *f* myrrh.

**sōbrietās, ātis** *f* sobriety.

**sōbrīnus, ī** *m and* **-a, ae** *f* cousin (*on the mother's side*).

**sōbrius** 3 not intoxicated; **a)** sober; moderate, continent; **b)** sensible; cautious.

**soccātus** 3 wearing *socci.*

**socculus, ī** *m, dim. of* **soccus.**

**soccus, ī** *m* light shoe; comedy.

**socer** (*and* **-erus**), **erī** *m* father-inlaw; *pl.* parents-in-law.

**sociābilis, e** sociable, easily united.

**sociālis, e** of allies *or* partners; **a)** conjugal; **b)** sociable, social.

**sociālitās, ātis** *f* fellowship.

**sociātrix, īcis** *f* uniting.

**sociennus, ī** *m* = **socius.**

**societās, ātis** *f* union, society; fellowship, association; **a)** political league, alliance, confederacy; **b)** partnership, association in business.

**sociō** 1 to join, unite, associate (*alqd cum alqo*); to hold in common, share, take part in.

**socio-fraudus** 3 one who deceives his comrades.

**socius** 3 united, associated, allied; shared, joint; *subst.* **socius,** *ī m and* **-ia, ae** *f* companion, associate, fellow, partner; ally, confederate.

**socordia, ae** *f* dulness, stupidity, indolence.

**so-cors, rdis** weak-minded; stupid; indolent.

**socrus, ūs** *f* mother-in-law.

**sodālicius** 3 relating to fellowship *or* companionship; *subst.* **-ium, ī** *n* = **sodalitas.**

**sodālis, e** of companions, friendly; *subst. m* **a)** comrade, companion, mate; **b)** member of a club, of a college of priests; **c)** table companion, boon companion; accomplice.

**sodālitās, ātis** *f* companionship, fellowship, friendship; **a)** association; **b)** religious brotherhood; **c)** club for feasting; **d)** secret, illegal society, political club.

**sōdēs** = **si audes** if you please.

**sōl, sōlis** *m* the sun; **a)** the sun-god; **b)** sunlight, sunshine, heat of the sun, sunny day; **c)** day; **d)** publicity, appearance in public; **e)** sun, star = distinguished person.

**sōlāciolum, ī** *n* a little comfort.

sōlācium, ī *n* consolation, comfort, relief, solace; **a)** an assuaging, means of help, refuge; **b)** amends, compensation; **c)** consoler. [tion.]

sōlāmen, inis *n* comfort, consola-]

sōlāris, e relating to the sun.

sōlārium, ī *n* **a)** sun-dial; clock; **b)** flat roof, balcony.

sōlātium, ī *m* = solacium.

sōlātor, ōris *m* consoler, comforter.

soldurii, ōrum *m/pl.* vassals, liege-]

soldus 3 = solidus. [men.]

solea, ae *f* **a)** sole, sandal; fetter for the feet; **b)** (*kind of fish*) sole.

soleārius, ī *m* sandal-maker.

soleātus 3 wearing sandals.

solemnis *and* solennis, e = sollemnis.

soleō, solitus sum 2 **a)** to be accustomed *or* wont (*inf.*); **ut solet** as is his custom; **b)** to cohabit with; — **solitus** 3 usual, customary; *subst.* **solitum, ī** *n* what is usual, the customary, custom.

soliditās, ātis *f* solidity.

solidō 1 to make dense *or* solid, to make firm, strengthen.

solidus 3 dense; **a)** massive, compact, firm, solid, hard; *subst.* **solidum, ī** *n* something firm, solid body, firm ground, mass, solidity; **b)** whole, complete, entire; **solidum, ī** *n* the whole sum, the total; **c)** true, real, enduring, substantial, trustworthy.

sōli-fer 3 sun-bringing.

sōli-gena, ae *m* child of the sun-god.

sōlitārius 3 solitary, alone, lonely, unsocial.

sōlitūdō, inis *f* loneliness, solitude; **a)** desert, wilderness; **b)** destitution, deprivation; **c)** retirement; **d)** helplessness.

solitum, ī *n and* solitus 3, *see* soleo.

solium, ī *n* seat, chair; **a)** throne, royal seat, royal dignity *or* power; **b)** arm-chair; **c)** coffin; **d)** bathing-tub.

sōli-vagus 3 wandering alone; lonely, single.

soll-emnis *and* -ennis, e annual; periodic; **a)** established; ceremonial, religious, solemn; **b)** usual, customary; *subst.* **sollemne, is** *n* festival, solemnity, sacrifice; custom, rite, ceremony.

soll-ers, rtis clever, skilful, adroit, expert, ingenious.

soll-ertia, ae *f* skill, cleverness, adroitness, ingenuity, expertness, shrewdness; trick.

sollicitātiō, ōnis *f* an inciting to mutiny *or* rebellion.

sollicitō 1 to move violently, stir, agitate, shake; **a)** to plough; **b)** to disturb, trouble, harass, annoy; **c)** to stir up, incite, instigate to revolt.

sollicitūdō, inis *f* uneasiness, disquiet, anxiety, care, trouble.

solli-citus 3 tossed, stirred up, agitated; **a)** troubled, disturbed, anxious, uneasy (*de re, pro alqo*); **b)** causing trouble, disquieting, painful; **c)** careful, busy.

solli-ferreum, ī *n* javelin of iron.

sollistimus 3 most perfect *or* auspicious.

sollus whole, entire.

sōlō 1 to empty; to lay waste.

soloecismus, ī *m* solecism.

sōlor 1 to comfort, console; **a)** to soothe, assuage, lessen; **b)** to compensate.

sōlstitiālis, e relating to the summer solstice, of midsummer, of summer heat; solar.

sōl-stitium, ī *n* (summer) solstice, summer time, heat of summer.

solum[1], ī *n* the lowest part, bottom, ground, foundation; **a)** floor, pavement; **b)** sole of a foot; **c)** earth, soil; land, country; **d)** basis.

sōlum[2] *adv.*, *see* solus.

sōlus 3 alone, only, single, sole; **a)** lonely, solitary, deserted, widowed; **b)** unfrequented, uninhabited; *adv.* **sōlum** only, merely, barely; **non sōlum ... sed etiam** not only ... but also, **non sōlum (non) ... sed ne ... quidem** not only not ... but not even. [der.]

solūtilis, e easily coming asun-]

solūtiō, ōnis *f* **a)** a loosening; (dis-) solution; **b)** payment.

solūtus 3, *see* solvo.

solvō, solvī, solūtum 3 to loosen, untie, unbind (*alqd a or de re*), unfetter, release, open; **navem** to weigh anchor, to sail; **a)** to pay *or* discharge a debt; **solvendō non esse** to be insolvent; to pay, fulfil, perform a duty *or* promise (*alqd; alci alqd*); **poenam** to suffer punishment; **b)** to set free, release, relieve, acquit, absolve (*alqm re*); **c)** to detach, remove, disjoin, break up (*pontem*), separate; to relax, weaken; **d**) to dissolve, bring to an end; to solve, explain; — **solūtus** 3 loosened; **a**) unbound, free; unburdened, independent, free from debt, care, *or* punishment; **b**) unrestrained, unchecked, wanton, disorderly, lax, remiss, careless; **c**) without metre, prose, loose, irregular; **d**) fluent, ready (*in speaking*).

**somnīculōsus** 3 sleepy, drowsy.

**somni-fer** 3 sleep-bringing.

**somniō** 1 to dream (*de alqo, alqm, alqd*); to talk foolishly.

**somnium, ī** *n* dream; vain imagination, fancy, nonsense.

**somnus, ī** *m* sleep, slumber; **a**) sleep of death; night; **b**) drowsiness, laziness, inactivity.

**sonābilis, e** = **sonans**.

**sonāns, tis** sounding, resounding, sonorous.

**soni-pēs, pedis** *m* horse, steed.

**sonitus, ūs** *m* sound, noise, din; thunder.

**sonīvius** 3 = **sonans; tripudium sonīvium** noise of the corn dropped by the sacred chickens (in augury).

**sonō, nuī, (sonātūrus)** 1 (*and* 3) **1.** *intr.* to make a noise, sound, resound, roar; **2.** *trans.* to speak, sound; to sing, celebrate; to mean.

**sonor, ōris** *m* = **sonitus**.

**sonōrus** 3 = **sonans**.

**sōns, sontis** guilty; *subst.* *m* criminal, sinner.

**sonticus** 3 serious, weighty.

**sonus, ī** *m* sound, noise; voice; tone.

**sophia, ae** *f* wisdom.

**sophisma, atis** *n* false conclusion, fallacy.

**sophistēs** *and* **-a, ae** *m* sophist.

**sophos** *and* **-us, ī** *m* wise (man).

**sophōs** *int.* bravo!, well done!

**sōpiō¹** 4 to lull asleep, put to sleep; **P.** to fall asleep; **a**) to stun, stupefy; **b**) to calm, assuage, still, quiet.

**sōpiō², ōnis** penis (?).

**sopor, ōris** *m* deep sleep; **a**) sleepiness, lethargy; **b**) sleeping-potion; **c**) the god of sleep; **d**) death; **e**) temple of the head.

**sopōrātus** 3 **a**) put to sleep, stilled; **b**) soporific, stupefying.

**sopōri-fer** 3 causing deep sleep.

**sopōrus** 3 sleep-bringing; drowsy.

**sōracum, ī** *n* hamper.

**sorbeō, buī,** — 2 to suck in, swallow.

**sorbillō** 1 to suck in, sip.

**sorbilō** *adv.* in little drops, on a low diet.

**sorbitiō, ōnis** *f* draught, drink; broth.

**sorbum, ī** *n* sorb, service-berry.

**sordeō, (uī),** — 2 to be dirty; to be mean *or* despised (*alci*).

**sordēs, is** *f* (*usu. pl.*) dirt, filth; **a**) dirty clothes, mourning; **b**) meanness, low condition, baseness, stinginess, niggardliness, covetousness; **c**) rabble, dregs of the people.

**sordēscō, duī,** — 3 to become dirty.

**sordidātus** 3 in mourning attire.

**sordidulus** 3 dirty, mean.

**sordidus** 3 dirty, foul, filthy; **a**) in mourning attire; **b**) mean, despicable, vile; poor; base, disgraceful; niggardly, stingy.

**sorditūdō, inis** *f* = **sordes**.

**sōrex, icis** *m* shrew-mouse.

**sōricīnus** 3 of a shrew-mouse.

**sōrītēs, ae** *m* (*in logic*) conclusion drawn from accumulated arguments.

**soror, ōris** *f* sister; cousin.

**sororcula, ae** *f* little sister.

**sorōri-cīda, ae** *m* murderer of a sister.

**sorōrius** 3 of, for a sister.

**sors, rtis** *f* lot; *pl.* oracle; **a**) a casting lots; **b**) oracular response, prophecy; **c**) lot, share, money, capital; fate, destiny, chance; **d**) official duty.

**sorsum** *and* **-us** *adv.* = **seorsum**.

**sorticula, ae** *f* small tablet.

**sorti-fer** *and* **-ger** 3 oracular.

**sorti-legus** 3 foretelling, prophetic; *subst.* ~, **ī** *m* soothsayer.

**sortior** (*and* **-ō**) 4 to cast *or* draw lots; **a**) to assign by lot; **b**) to cast lots for, get by lot; to gain by fate, get, receive, obtain; **c**) to choose, select; — **sortītus** 3 gained by lot, appointed by lot.

**sortis, is** *f* = **sors**.

**sortītiō, ōnis** *f* a casting lots.

**sortītō** by lot, by destiny.

**sortītor, ōris** *m* one who draws lots.

**sortītus, ūs** *m* = **sortitio**.

**sospes, itis** safe and sound, unhurt, fortunate, happy.

**sospita, ae** *f* she who saves.

**sospitālis, e** bringing deliverance.
**sospitō** 1 to save, protect.
**sōtēr, ēris** m saviour.
**sōtēria, ōrum** n/pl. presents given on recovery from illness.
**spādix, īcis** reddish brown.
**spadō, ōnis** m eunuch.
**spargō, rsī, rsum** 3 to strew, scatter, sprinkle; **a)** to scatter seeds, to sow; **b)** to throw, hurl, cast; **c)** to spread abroad, disseminate, disperse; **d)** to dissipate, squander; **e)** to distribute, divide, tear in pieces; **f)** to besprinkle; **sparsus** 3 dispersed; speckled, freckled.
**sparsiō, ōnis** f scattering.
**spartum, ī** n esparto (grass).
**sparulus, ī** m sea-bream.
**sparus, ī** m hunting-spear.
**spatha, ae** f broadsword; weaver's batten (for tightening the threads).
**spatior** 1 to walk about, take a walk; to spread out.
**spatiōsus** 3 roomy, of great extent, wide, spacious; lasting long.
**spatium, ī** n room, extent; **a)** size, length, breadth; **b)** interval, distance; **c)** race-course; lap; walk, promenade; open space, public place; **d)** space of time, interval, period; time, respite, leisure, opportunity; length of time; metrical time, measure.
**speciālis, e** individual, particular.
**speciēs, ēī** f 1. a seeing, sight, look, view; 2. appearance, mien, exterior, outside; **a)** vision, dream; **b)** beautiful form, beauty, splendour, display, show; **c)** likeness, image, statue; **d)** semblance, seeming, resemblance; **speciē** in appearance; **ad speciem** for the sake of outward show; 3. idea, notion, conception; **a)** ideal, model; **b)** species, kind, sort.
**specillum, ī** n probe.
**specimen, inis** n mark, token; **a)** pattern, model, specimen, example, proof; **b)** ideal.
**speciō, xī, (ctum)** 3 to see, behold.
**speciōsus** 3 showy, fair, fine, beautiful, handsome, splendid; **a)** respectable; **b)** imposing, for show; specious, plausible.
**spectābilis, e a)** visible; **b)** worth seeing, admirable.
**spectāculum** (and **spectāclum**), **ī** n 1. spectator's seat in a theatre;

theatre; 2. show, sight, spectacle; stage-play.
**spectāmen, inis** n proof, sign.
**spectātiō, ōnis** f a looking at, beholding; testing of money.
**spectātor, ōris** m looker-on; **a)** beholder, observer, spectator; **b)** examiner, connoisseur.
**spectātrix, īcis** f female beholder.
**spectātus** 3 well tried or tested; excellent.
**spectiō, ōnis** f the right of observing or determining the auspices.
**spectō** 1 to look; to behold, view, observe, gaze at, contemplate (*alqd*); **a)** to attend as a spectator; **b)** to examine, try, prove; to keep in view, bear in mind, aim at, look for (*alqd*; *ut*); **c)** to intend, tend towards; **res ad arma spectat** things look like war; **d)** to look or face towards (*ad* or *in alqd*).
**spectrum, ī** n image; phantom.
**spēcula**[1], **ae** f slight hope.
**specula**[2], **ae** f height, eminence, watch-tower; **esse in speculis** to be on the watch.
**speculābilis, e** visible.
**speculābundus** 3 watching, on the watch.
**speculāria, gen. -iōrum, abl. -ibus** n/pl. window panes.
**speculātor, ōris** m watcher, spy, scout; explorer, examiner.
**speculātōrius** 3 relating to spies, of scouts; **-ia (navis)** scouting-ship.
**speculātrix, īcis** f female spy or watcher.
**speculor** 1 **a)** to look around, spy; **b)** to look out, spy out, watch, explore, wait for.
**speculum, ī** n **a)** mirror; **b)** image.
**specus, ūs** m (n) cave, cavern, grotto; **a)** ditch, pit, canal, excavation; **b)** hollow.
**spēlaeum, ī** n cave, hole, den.
**spēlunca, ae** f cave, grotto.
**spērābilis, e** that may be hoped for.
**spernāx, ācis** contemptuous.
**spernō, sprēvī, sprētum** 3 **a)** to separate, sever, remove; **b)** to reject, disdain, despise.
**spērō** 1 to expect; to hope (*alqd*; *acc. c. inf.*); to trust in.
**spēs, ēī** f expectation; 1. hope (*alcis rei*); **a)** object of hope; **b)** goddess of hope; 2. fear, apprehension; anticipation.

**sphaera, ae** *f* ball, sphere.
**sphaeristērium, ī** *n* place for playing ball.
**sphaeromachia, ae** *f* boxing with padded iron balls fastened to the hands.
**Sphinx, ingis** *f* Sphinx.
**spīca, ae** *f* ear of corn, point, spike.
**spīceus 3** of ears of corn.
**spīci-fer 3** bearing ears of corn.
**spīciō 3** = **speciō**.
**spīculum, ī** *n* point, sting; arrow, dart, javelin.
**spīcum, ī** *n* = **spīca**.
**spīna, ae** *f* thorn, prickle; a) thornbush; b) spine, backbone; c) subtlety, perplexity; d) difficulty, pain, anxiety.
**spīnētum, ī** *n* thorn-hedge.
**spīneus 3** thorny.
**spīni-ger 3** thorn-bearing.
**spīnōsus 3** thorny, prickly; galling; crabbed, obscure.
**spinter, eris** *n* metal armlet.
**spintria, ae** *m* male prostitute.
**spinturnicium, ī** *n* bird of (ill) omen.
**spīnus, ī** *f* blackthorn, sloe.
**spīra, ae** *f* coil, twist, fold.
**spīrābilis, e** that can be breathed; life-giving.
**spīrāculum, ī** *n* air-hole, vent.
**spīrāmen, inis** *n* a) air-hole; b) puff of air.
**spīrāmentum, ī** *n* air-hole, pore; pause, breathing-time.
**spīritus, ūs** *m* a) breath, air, breeze; b) breath of life, life; c) spirit, soul, mind, inspiration, courage; haughtiness, pride.
**spīrō 1** a) to breathe, draw breath; to be alive; b) to blow, pant; c) to exhale, emit odour, to smell; breathe out; d) to be full of, inspired with, to intend, aim at; to express, imitate.
**spissāmentum, ī** *n* stopper, plug.
**spissātiō, ōnis** *f* a packing tight, ramming.
**spissēscō 3** to grow thick, condense.
**spissi-gradus 3** walking slowly.
**spissō 1** to condense.
**spissus 3** thick, crowded, dense, close; tardy, slow, tiresome.
**splēn, ēnis** *n* spleen.
**splendeō, (uī),** — **2** to shine, glitter, be bright; to be distinguished *or* glorious.

**splendēscō, duī,** — **3** to become bright, begin to shine.
**splendidus 3** bright, shining, brilliant; a) splendid, magnificent, noble, fine; b) sumptuous, showy; c) distinguished, illustrious, renowned; d) clear.
**splendor, ōris** *m* brightness, clearness; a) splendour, magnificence, honour; b) ornament.
**splēniātus 3** having a face-patch on.
**splēnium, ī** *n* face-patch.
**spoliārium, ī** *n* stripping-room in the amphitheatre; den of plunder.
**spoliātiō, ōnis** *f* a plundering, robbing, deprivation, robbery.
**spoliātor, ōris** *m* plunderer.
**spoliātrīx, īcis,** *fem. of* **spoliator**.
**spoliō 1** to rob one of his clothes, to strip (*acc.*); to plunder, rob, despoil, deprive (*alqm re*).
**spolium, ī** *n* skin, hide; a) (*pl.*) plunder, booty, arms taken from an enemy, spoil; b) victory.
**sponda, ae** *f* a) frame of a couch, bedstead; b) bed, sofa; c) bier.
**spondālia** (*or* **-aulia**), **ōrum** *n/pl.* sacrificial song accompanied by the flute.
**spondeō, spopondī, spōnsum 2** to promise solemnly, engage, pledge oneself (*alqd; alci alqd*); a) to warrant, be a security (*pro alqo, alqd pro alqo*); b) to betroth, promise in marriage; c) to vow; d) to forebode, to promise; *subst.* **spōnsus, ī** *m* bridegroom; **spōnsa, ae** *f* bride.
**spondēus** *and* **-īus, ī** *m* spondee (- -).
**spondylus, ī** *m* a shell-fish (? mussel).
**spongia** (*and* **-ea**), **ae** *f* sponge; open-worked coat of mail.
**spōnsa, ae** *f*, *see* **spondeo**.
**spōnsālia, gen. -iōrum, abl. -ibus** *n/pl.* betrothal.
**spōnsiō, ōnis** *f* solemn promise, engagement, pledge, surety, formal stipulation *or* treaty; legal wager.
**spōnsor, ōris** *m* surety.
**spōnsum, ī** *n* solemn promise *or* engagement.
**spōnsus[1], ī** *m*, *see* **spondeo**.
**spōnsus[2], ūs** *m* engagement, contract.
**sponte** *f* (*abl. sing.*) a) of one's own accord, voluntarily, willingly, freely; b) without aid, alone; c) of itself, for its own sake.
**sporta, ae** *f* a hamper, basket.

**sportella, ae** f = sportula.

**sportula, ae** f little basket; **a)** provision-basket; **b)** gift, present (gen. to clients).

**S.P.Q.R.** abbr. = senatus populusque Romanus the Senate and Roman people.

**sprētiō, ōnis** f a despising, contempt.

**sprētor, ōris** m despiser.

**spūma, ae** f foam, froth, scum; pomade for dyeing hair.

**spūmātus, ūs** m serpent's slaver.

**spūmēscō, —, —** 3 to begin to foam.

**spūmeus** 3 foaming.

**spūmi-fer** and **-ger** 3 foaming.

**spūmō** 1 to foam, froth; **spūmātus** 3 covered with foam.

**spūmōsus** 3 foaming, frothy.

**spuō, uī, ūtum** 3 to spit (out).

**spurci-dicus** 3 obscene.

**spurci-ficus** 3 polluting.

**spurcitiēs, ēī** and **-tia, ae** f filth.

**spurcō** 1 to defile, pollute; **spurcātus** 3 = spurcus.

**spurcus** 3 filthy, dirty, foul, obscene, impure.

**spūtātilicus** 3 despicable, detestable.

**spūtātor, ōris** m spitter.

**spūtō** 1 to spit out.

**spūtum, ī** n spittle.

**squāleō, —, —** 2 to be rough, scaly, stiff, or bristly (alqa re); **a)** to be dirty, neglected, foul, waste; **b)** to mourn in squalid garments.

**squālidus** 3 rough, stiff, scaly; **a)** unadorned, unpolished; **b)** dirty, filthy, squalid, neglected; **c)** in mourning attire.

**squālor, ōris** m roughness; **a)** filthiness, foulness; **b)** mourning attire.

**squālus** 3 stiff with dirt.

**squāma, ae** f scale; pl. scale-armour.

**squāmeus** 3, **squāmi-fer** 3, **squāmi-ger** 3, **squāmōsus** 3 scaly; subst. **-gerī** (genit. **-gerum**) m/pl. fishes.

**squatus, ī** m angel-fish.

**squilla, ae** f a shell-fish (? prawn).

**st!** int. hush!; 'sh!

**stabilīmen, inis** n stay, support.

**stabilīmentum, ī** n = stabilimen.

**stabiliō** 4 to make firm, to prop, support, establish.

**stabilis, e** standing; **a)** stable, firm; **b)** steadfast, constant, lasting, durable, immutable.

**stabilitās, ātis** f stability, steadfastness, durability, firmness.

**stabilitor, ōris** m establisher.

**stabulārius, ī** m tavern-keeper.

**stabulor** and **-lō** 1 to stand in a stable; to abide, dwell.

**stabulum, ī** n standing-place, abode; **a)** stable, stall, fold; **b)** tavern, brothel.

**stacta, ae** f juice of myrrh.

**stadium, ī** n **a)** race-course; **b)** stade (about 600 feet).

**stāgnō** 1 **a)** to form a pool of water; **b)** to overflow, inundate (alqd); **c)** to be inundated.

**stāgnōsus** 3 full of pools.

**stāgnum[1], ī** n standing water; **a)** lake, pond, pool; **b)** water (in general); sea.

**stagnum[2], ī** n alloy of silver and lead.

**stalagmium, ī** n ear-pendant.

**stāmen, inis** n **a)** warp of a web; thread; **b)** cloth; fillet; **c)** string of a lyre.

**stāmineus** 3 provided with threads.

**stannum** = stagnum[2].

**statārius** 3 standing firm; quiet; **~ia, ae** f (sc. cōmoedia) standing-still comedy (with little action); **~ius, ī** m actor in statāria.

**statēra, ae** f balance; yoke-pole.

**staticulus, ī** m a slow dance.

**statim** adv. **a)** firmly, steadily; **b)** on the spot, at once, immediately.

**statiō, ōnis** f **a)** a standing; **b)** station, position, abode, quarters; **c)** post, outpost, watch, picket, guard, sentinels; **d)** roadstead, anchorage.

**statīvus** 3 fixed, standing still; subst. **statīva, ōrum** n/pl. permanent camp.

**stator, ōris** m **a)** attendant of a magistrate; **b) Stator** (title of Jupiter) stayer of flight, supporter.

**statua, ae** f statue, image.

**statuārius, ī** m statuary, sculptor.

**statūmen, inis** n prop, support; rib of a ship.

**statuō, uī, ūtum** 3 to set up, cause to stand; to stop; **a)** to erect, build, raise, found; **b)** to fix, appoint, determine, decide, ordain (alqd; ut); to resolve, purpose (inf.; ut); **c)** to believe, be convinced, judge, consider.

**statūra, ae** f height, size, stature.

**status[1]** 3, see sisto.

**status²**, ūs *m* a standing; a) position, posture, attitude; b) condition, state, circumstances, arrangement; c) standing, position in life; d) system *or* line of defence (in oratory).

**statūtus** 3 big, sturdy.

**stega**, ae *f* deck of a ship.

**stēliō**, ōnis *m* = stellio.

**stēlla**, ae *f* star; constellation; the sun.

**stēllāns**, tis a) starry; b) shining.

**stēllātus** 3 a) starry; b) placed in the heavens as a constellation; c) shining, bright.

**stēlli-fer** *and* **-ger** 3 star-bearing.

**stēlliō**, ōnis *m* lizard with spots.

**stemma**, atis *n* a) wreath hung on an ancestor's image; b) pedigree; c) antiquity.

**stercoreus** 3 dirty, filthy.

**stercorō** 1 to dung, manure.

**sterculinum**, ī *n* dung-pit.

**stercus**, oris *n* dung, manure.

**sterilis**, e barren; a) empty, vain; b) making unfruitful.

**sterilitās**, ātis *f* unfruitfulness, barrenness.

**sternāx**, ācis throwing off the rider.

**sternō**, strāvī, strātum 3 a) to stretch out, spread out, extend, strew, scatter; b) to throw down, stretch on the ground; c) to level, pave (*a road*); d) to bestrew, cover; to cover with carpets, to saddle; to smooth over.

**sternū(tā)mentum**, ī *n* a sneezing.

**sternuō**, uī, — 3 to sneeze; to crackle.

**sterquilinum**, ī *n* dung-pit.

**stertō**, —, — 3 to snore, snort.

**stibadium**, ī *n* semicircular couch.

**stigma**, atis *n* brand; mark of disgrace; cut.

**stigmatiās**, ae *m* branded slave.

**stigmōsus** 3 branded.

**stilla**, ae *f* drop.

**stillārium**, ī *n* a drop; gratuity, tip.

**stilli-cidium**, ī *n* dripping water (*esp.* from eaves of buildings).

**stillō** 1 a) to fall in drops, drip; b) to let drop, to distil.

**stilus**, ī *m* pointed instrument for writing, style; a) writing, composition; b) manner of writing, style; c) pointed stake.

**stimulātiō**, ōnis *f* incitement.

**stimulātrīx**, īcis *f* she who goads.

**stimuleus** 3 relating to the goad, of goads.

**stimulō** 1 to goad, prick; a) to torment, vex, trouble; b) to incite, spur, stimulate.

**stimulus**, ī *m* prick, goad; a) pointed stake; b) sting, torment, pain; spur, incentive, incitement.

**stinguō**, —, — 3 to extinguish.

**stipātiō**, ōnis *f* throng, retinue.

**stipātor**, ōris *m* attendant, satellite.

**stipendiārius** (stī-?) 3 a) serving for pay; b) liable to tribute, tributary.

**stipendium**, ī *n* a) pay of a soldier; military service, campaign, a year's service; b) tax, tribute, contribution; penalty.

**stipes**, itis *m* log, stump, trunk of a tree; a) tree; branch; b) blockhead, dunce.

**stipō** 1 a) to press *or* crowd together, compress; b) to cram, stuff, fill full; c) to surround, attend, accompany.

**stips**, ipis *f* contribution in money; a) gift, alms; b) fee.

**stipula**, ae *f* stalk, stem, straw, stubble; reed-pipe.

**stipulātiō**, ōnis *f* agreement, covenant, stipulation.

**stipulātiuncula**, ae *f* a little stipulation.

**stipulātor**, ōris *m* bargainer.

**stipulor** 1 to stipulate, make a bargain *or* contract (*alqd*).

**stiria**, ae *f* icicle.

**stirpēs** *and* **stirpis**, is *f* = stirps.

**stirpitus** *adv.* by the roots, utterly.

**stirps** (stirpēs, stirpis), is *f* (*m*) lowest part of a tree, the trunk with the root; a) plant, shrub, tree; b) root, stem; shoot; c) family, origin, lineage; d) root, source, beginning; e) descendant, offspring.

**stīva**, ae *f* plough-handle.

**stlāt(t)ārius** 3 carried in ships, imported (?).

**stlīs**, ītis *f* (*archaic*) = lis.

**stloppus**, ī *m* the noise of a slap on the cheek.

**stō**, stetī (stātūrus) 1 1. to stand, be upright, remain standing; a) to be stationed (*troops*); to be at anchor; b) to stand on end, bristle up (*abl.*); c) to stand out with, to be full of, loaded with; d) to cost; e) to stand by, at the side of, adhere to (*cum* or *ab alqo, pro re* or *adversus alqm*); to rest upon, depend on; **per**

me stat it stands to my account, is my fault (*quominus, ne*); **2.** to stand firm, to endure, persist, remain; a) to be fixed, determined; b) to keep the stage (*of plays*).

**stola, ae** *f* gown, long robe of a woman; noble matron.

**stolātus 3** in a woman's dress; befitting a matron.

**stolidus 3** stupid, foolish, dull, rude.

**stomachicus 3** suffering from disease of the stomach.

**stomachor 1** to be angry, irritated, indignant.

**stomachōsus 3** angry, irritable.

**stomachus, ī** *m* a) gullet; b) stomach; c) taste, liking; d) anger, irritation; e) **bonus ∼** good humour.

**storea** *and* **-ia, ae** *f* straw-mat, rush--mat.

**strabō, ōnis** *m* a squinting one, squinter.

**strāgēs, is** *f* a throwing down, overthrow, ruin; a) defeat, slaughter, massacre; b) fallen mass, confused heap.

**strāgulus 3** fit for spreading out; **strāgula vestis** *and* **strāgulum, ī** *n* blanket, carpet.

**strāmen, inis** *n* straw, litter.

**strāmenticius 3** of straw.

**strāmentum, ī** *n* a) straw, litter; b) pack-saddle.

**strāmineus 3** made of *or* covered with straw.

**strangulō 1** to throttle, choke, strangle; to torment, torture.

**strang-ūria, ae** *f* difficulty in passing urine.

**stratēgēma, atis** *n* military artifice, stratagem.

**stratēgus, ī** *m* commander; president of a banquet.

**stratiōticus 3** soldierly.

**strātum, ī** *n* covering, blanket; a) bed, couch; b) horsecloth, saddle; c) pavement.

**strātūra, ae** *f* a paving.

**strēna, ae** *f* omen, portent; new year's gift.

**strēnuitās, ātis** *f* quickness, activity, promptness.

**strēnuus 3** a) active, quick, ready, prompt, brave; b) turbulent, restless.

**strepitō 1** to make a loud noise.

**strepitus, ūs** *m* noise, din, rustling; sound.

**strepō, puī, (pitum) 3** to make a noise, to rustle, rattle, roar; to sound, ring, resound.

**striātus 3** ribbed, fluted.

**strictim** *adv.* closely; briefly, superficially.

**strictūra, ae** *f* mass of hot metal.

**strictus 3** drawn together, narrow, close, tight; concise.

**strīdeō, —, — 2** *and* **strīdō, dī, — 3** to creak, hiss, hum, rustle, whistle.

**strīdor, ōris** *m* a creaking, hissing, humming, whistling, grunting, braying, whispering.

**strīdulus 3** rustling, hissing, creaking, whistling, crackling.

**strigilis, is** *f* skin-scraper.

**strigō 1** to stop; to jib.

**strigor, ōris,** *a word of doubtful sense; perhaps =* **strigosus.**

**strigōsus 3** lean, thin, meagre.

**stringō, strinxī, strictum 3** a) to touch lightly, graze upon; to wound; to touch, move; b) to draw *or* strip off, pluck; to draw, unsheath; c) to draw tight together, tie together.

**stringor, ōris** *m* shock, twinge.

**strix, igis** *f* screech-owl.

**stropha, ae** *f* trick.

**strophiārius, ī** *m* maker of breast--bands.

**strophium, ī** *n* breast-band; garland.

**structilis, e** of, for building.

**strūctor, ōris** *m* builder, mason; head-waiter.

**structūra, ae** *f* structure, building, construction; arrangement.

**struēs, is** *f* heap; heap of offering--cakes; phalanx of soldiers.

**struix, īcis** *f* pile.

**strūma, ae** *f* tuberculous tumour.

**strūmōsus 3** suffering from a tuberculous tumour.

**struō, -uxī, -uctum 3** to heap up, pile, join together; a) to erect, build, construct, fabricate; b) to prepare, get ready; c) to arrange, put in order; d) to contrive, design, cause, occasion.

**strūthea, ōrum** *n/pl.* a kind of quinces.

**studeō, uī, — 2** to give attention to, take pains with, apply oneself to, be busy with, strive after, pursue, desire (*alci rei; inf.; acc. c. inf.*); a) to be favourable *or* attached to, to side with; b) to study (*with dat.*).

**studiōsus** 3 zealous, eager, diligent, careful; **a)** devoted to, studious, fond of (*gen.*); **b)** partial, friendly, favourable, inclined to.

**studium, ī** *n* zeal, eagerness, application, enthusiasm, exertion, desire, study (*alcis rei*); **a)** favour, inclination, attachment, devotion, interest; **b)** partiality, partisanship, prejudice; **c)** employment, pursuit, propensity, favourite study; literary occupation, research.

**stulti-loquentia, ae** *f,* **-loquium, ī** *n* silly talk.

**stulti-loquus** 3 speaking foolishly.

**stultitia, ae** *f* folly, foolishness; silliness, stupidity.

**stulti-vidus** 3 seeing mistakenly.

**stultus** 3 foolish, stupid, silly, infatuated; *subst.* ~, ī *m* fool.

**stupe-faciō** 3 to stun, stupefy, astonish.

**stupeō, uī,** —, 2 **a)** to be insensible, to be stunned, benumbed; **b)** to be amazed, surprised; **c)** to gaze at with wonder (*alqd*).

**stupēscō,** —, — 3 to be struck with wonder or awe.

**stupiditās, ātis** *f* insensibility; dulness, stupidity.

**stupidus** 3 senseless; amazed; stupid, foolish.

**stupor, ōris** *m* senselessness, dulness; **a)** astonishment, amazement; **b)** stupidity, foolishness.

**stuppa, ae** *f* coarse flax, tow.

**stuppeus** 3 of tow, flaxen.

**stuprātor, ōris** *m* ravisher.

**stuprō** 1 to defile, deflower, ravish.

**stuprum, ī** *n* a debauching; unchastity.

**sturnus, ī** *m* starling.

**Stygius** 3 of the river Styx; of the nether world; infernal.

**Styx, ygis** *f* a river in Hades (the abode of the dead).

**suādēla, ae** *f* a persuading.

**suādeō, sī, sum** 2 to advise, counsel, exhort, suggest, recommend (*alci alqd, ut, ne*); **a)** to impel, induce; **b)** to promote, support; **c)** to persuade.

**suādus** 3 persuasive.

**suāsiō, ōnis** *f* a recommending; advocacy, persuasive eloquence.

**suāsor, ōris** *m* adviser, exhorter; promoter (*gen.*).

**suāsōria, ae** *f* speech of advice.

**suāsum, ī** *n* dark dye.

**suāsus, ūs** *m* a persuading, exhorting.

**suāve-olēns, tis** sweet-smelling.

**suāviātiō, ōnis** *f* a kissing.

**suāvi-dicus** 3 speaking sweetly.

**suāvi-loquēns, tis** speaking sweetly.

**suāvi-loquentia, ae** *f* agreeable speech.

**suāviolum, ī** *n* little kiss.

**suāvior** 1 to kiss.

**suāvis, e** sweet, agreeable, pleasant, delightful, attractive.

**suāvi-sāviātiō, ōnis** *f* sweet kissing.

**suāvitās, ātis** *f* sweetness, pleasantness, agreeableness.

**suāvitūdō, inis** *f* = **suavitas.**

**suāvium, ī** *n* kiss.

**sub** 1. *prep.* with *acc.* a) (*of place, to express motion*) under; up towards; close up to, **sub iugum mittere, sub montem succedere, sub imperium** *or* **potestatem redigere;** b) (*of time*) about, close upon, just before, **sub noctem, sub idem tempus;** 2. *prep.* with *abl.* a) (*of place, to express position*) under, beneath, at the bottom of, at the foot of, **sub terra habitare, sub monte considere;** just behind; b) (*of condition*) under, beneath, **sub imperio, sub regno, sub dicione alcis esse, sub conditionibus;** c) (*of time*) at, at the same time as, **sub ipsa profectione, sub decessu suo.**

**sub-absurdus** 3 rather absurd or foolish.

**sub-accūsō** 1 to blame a little.

**sub-āctiō, ōnis** *f* training.

**sub-aerātus** 3 with bronze underneath.

**sub-agrestis, e** rather rustic.

**sub-ālāris, e** under the armpits.

**sub-amārus** 3 somewhat bitter.

**sub-aquilus** 3 dull black.

**sub-arroganter** somewhat arrogantly.

**sub-auscultō** 1 to listen secretly.

**sub-basilicānu:, ī** *m* loafer, idler.

**sub-bibō** 3 to drink a little.

**sub-blandior** 4 to flatter or caress a little.

**sub-c...,** *see also* **succ...**

**sub-cavus** 3 hollow underneath.

**sub-contumēliōsē** somewhat insultingly.

**sub-crispus** 3 somewhat curled.

**subcustōs, ōdis** m under-guard.
**sub-dēbilis, e** somewhat crippled.
**sub-difficilis, e** rather difficult.
**sub-diffīdō** 3 to distrust a little.
**subditīvus** 3 substituted, not genuine, false, spurious.
**sub-dō, didī, ditum** 3 to put, place, or set under; to apply (*alqd alci rei*); **P.** to lie under or near; **a)** to subdue; **b)** to substitute, forge, suborn.
**sub-doceō** 2 to give supplementary lessons to.
**sub-dolus** 3 cunning, crafty, deceitful.
**sub-domō** 1 to tame, break in.
**sub-dubitō** 1 to doubt a little.
**sub-dūcō** 3 **1.** to draw up; to draw or take away; **a)** to draw away, remove, lead away, steal; **se subducere** or **P.** to withdraw secretly, steal away; **b)** to balance, calculate, compute; **2.** to draw up on high, lift up, draw ashore.
**sub-ductiō, ōnis** f a drawing a ship ashore; reckoning.
**sub-dūrus** 3 somewhat hard.
**sub-edō** 3 to eat away underneath.
**sub-eō 1.** to go under, come under (*alqd*); **a)** to enter, take cover in; **b)** to take upon oneself, to undergo, submit to, to sustain, undertake, encounter, endure; **2. a)** to go or come up, ascend, climb (*in, ad alqd*); **b)** to go to, approach, advance; to approach secretly or gradually (*alqd, ad alqd*); to steal into; to assail; **c)** to come into one's mind; **d)** to come immediately after, take the place of, follow (*alci* or *in locum alcis*).
**sūber, eris** n cork-oak; cork.
**sub-f...,** see **suff...**
**sub-g...,** see **sugg...**
**sub-horridus** 3 somewhat rough.
**sub-iaceō** 2 to lie below.
**sŭb-iciō** (*and* **sŭb-**), **iēcī, iectum** 3 **1.** to throw, put, lay under (*alqd alci rei, sub alqd*); **a)** to subject, subdue; **P.** to be subject; to expose, make liable; **b)** to substitute, forge; to suborn; **2.** to place near or by, advance near (*alqd alci rei*); **a)** to present; **b)** to suggest, bring to mind, prompt, propose, whisper to (*alci alqd*); **c)** to put after; **d)** to connect, append, subjoin; to range or reckon under, subordinate, comprise in; **e)** to answer, reply; **3.** to throw from under, throw up on high, raise,

lift up (*alqd in alqd*); **se sŭbicere** to rise; — **subiectus** 3 lying under or near; **a)** adjacent; **b)** subjected, subject; **c)** exposed to; *subst.* **subiectī, ōrum** m/pl. subjects.
**sub-iectiō, ōnis** f a placing under; substitution, forgery.
**sub-iectō** 1 to throw up; to place underneath; to apply.
**sub-iector, ōris** m forger.
**sub-iectus** 3, *see* **subicio.**
**subigitātiō, ōnis** f touching, love-making.
**subigitātrīx, īcis** f woman who makes love.
**sub-igitō** 1 to touch, make love.
**sub-igō, ēgī, āctum** 3 **1.** to drive or bring up; **2.** to bring under; **a)** to force, compel, impel, oblige, constrain (*alqm ad* or *in alqd; inf.*); **b)** to overcome, conquer, subdue; **c)** to 'work up' in any way (to plough or dig soil, to plough through water, to propel a boat, to sharpen a tool); **d)** to discipline, train.
**sub-iiciō,** *see* **subicio.**
**sub-impudēns, tis** somewhat shameless.
**sub-inānis, e** rather vain.
**sub-inde** *adv.* **a)** immediately after, just after; **b)** from time to time, repeatedly.
**sub-insulsus** 3 somewhat insipid.
**sub-invideō** 2 to envy a little (*dat.*).
**sub-invīsus** 3 somewhat hated.
**sub-invītō** 1 to give a hint.
**sub-īrāscor,** — 3 to be a little angry (*dat.*).
**sub-īrātus** 3 somewhat angry.
**subitārius** 3 collected or built hastily, done in haste.
**subitus** 3 (*adv.* **subitō**) **a)** sudden, unexpected; *subst.* **subitum, ī** n sudden occurrence, surprise; **b)** = **subitarius.**
**sub-iungō** 3 to add, join, subjoin; to yoke, harness (*curru*); to subdue, subject (*alqd alci, sub alqd*).
**sub-lābor** 3 **a)** to glide imperceptibly; **b)** to fall down, sink.
**sub-lātiō, ōnis** f exaltation.
**sub-lātus** 3 elated, proud, haughty.
**sub-lectō** 1 to allure, decoy.
**sub-legō** 3 **a)** to gather, pick up; **b)** to take away secretly; to listen to secretly; **c)** to choose instead.
**sublestus** 3 weak, slight.
**sub-levātiō, ōnis** f alleviation.

**sub-levō** 1 to lift up, raise up, hold up; **a)** to support, assist, encourage; **b)** to lessen, to diminish, mitigate.

**sublica, ae** f stake, pile.

**sublicius** 3 resting upon piles.

**sub-ligāculum, ī** and **-ligar, āris** n loin-cloth, under-pants.

**sub-ligō** 1 to bind below.

**sublīmis, e** high, lofty; in the air, aloft; adv. **sublime** (and **sublīmen** [?]) aloft, on high, upwards; **a)** elevated, exalted, sublime; **b)** distinguished.

**sublīmitās, ātis** f loftiness, sublimity.

**sub-lingulō, ōnis** m under-licker, cook's boy.

**sub-linō** 3 to besmear; ~ **ōs** (alci) to cheat.

**sub-lūceō, —, — 2** to shine forth from below, glimmer.

**sub-luō** 3 to wash underneath.

**sub-lūstris, e** glimmering.

**sub-m...**, see also **summ...**

**sub-merus** 3 almost unmixed.

**sub-molestus** 3 somewhat vexatious; **-tē** adv. with some annoyance. [vish or fretful.]

**sub-mōrōsus** 3 somewhat peevish.

**sub-nāscor** 3 to grow up under.

**sub-natō** 1 to swim underneath.

**sub-nectō** 3 to tie or bind on (under); to fasten.

**sub-negō** 1 to deny partly.

**sub-niger, gra, grum** dull black.

**sub-nimium** a pun on subparum (= supparum).

**sub-nīsus** and **-nīxus** 3 resting or leaning on (abl.); propped up; relying on. [notate.]

**sub-notō** 1 to note (down); to annotate.

**sub-nuba, ae** f rival.

**sub-nūbilus** 3 somewhat cloudy.

**subō** 1 to be in heat or lustful.

**sub-obscēnus** 3 somewhat obscene.

**sub-obscūrus** 3 somewhat dark.

**sub-odiōsus** 3 somewhat odious.

**sub-offendō** 3 to give some offence.

**sub-olēs, is** f offspring, descendant.

**sub-olēscō, —, — 3** to grow up.

**sub-olet mihi** I smell, have an inkling.

**sub-orior** 4 to spring up (as a replacement); hence **subortus, ūs** m replenishment.

**sub-ōrnō** 1 to furnish, provide, supply (secretly) (alqm re); to instruct privately, suborn.

**sub-p...**, see **supp...**

**sub-rancidus** 3 slightly tainted.

**sub-raucus** 3 somewhat hoarse.

**sub-rēmigō** 1 to paddle (under water).

**sub-rēpō** 3 to creep or crawl up (to), steal upon.

**sub-rīdeō** 2 to smile.

**sub-rīdiculē** adv. rather laughably.

**sub-rigō** 3 to raise up.

**sub-ringor, —, — 3** to grin with annoyance.

**sub-ripiō** 3, see **surripio**.

**sub-rogō** 1, see **surrogo**.

**sub-rōstrānī, ōrum** m/pl. loungers (round the rostra).

**sub-rubeō** 2 to be reddish, to blush.

**sub-rubicundus** 3 somewhat red.

**sub-rūfus** 3 reddish.

**sub-ruō** 3 to dig under, undermine, overthrow, demolish; to subvert, destroy.

**sub-rūsticus** 3 somewhat clownish.

**sub-rutilus** 3 reddish.

**sub-scrībō** 3 to write beneath (alqd alci rei); **a)** to sign a charge; **b)** to subscribe, sign, support, assent to (dat.).

**sub-scrīptiō, ōnis** f a writing beneath; **a)** a noting down; **b)** register; **c)** a joining in an accusation.

**sub-scrīptor, ōris** m joint accuser.

**subscūs, ūdis** f the tenon of a dovetail.

**sub-secīvus** 3 = **subsicivus**.

**sub-secō** 1 to cut off, clip.

**sub-sellium, ī** n bench, seat; pl. court, tribunal.

**sub-sentiō** 4 to feel, notice, discover secretly.

**sub-sequor** 3 to follow, come after (acc.); **a)** to attend, accompany; **b)** to follow up, support.

**sub-serviō** 4 to serve, to accommodate oneself to (alci).

**sub-sicivus** 3 left over, remaining; (of time) odd, spare; (of work) done in odd moments.

**subsidiārius** 3 belonging to a reserve; pl. m reserve-troops.

**subsidior** 1 to act as a reserve.

**sub-sidium, ī** n a) reserve line, reserve forces; **b)** aid, help, relief; **c)** place of refuge.

**sub-sīdō, sēdī, sessum** 3 to sit down, crouch down; **a)** to settle, sink, subside; **b)** to settle down, stop (in a place); **c)** to lie in wait for.

**sub-signānī, ōrum** m/pl. reserve-
-troops.

**sub-signō** 1 to enter in a register;
to undertake, guarantee.

**sub-siliō, siluī, — 4** to leap up.

**sub-sistō, stitī, — 3** to stand still,
remain standing, to stop, halt (*in
loco*); a) to cease; b) to remain, stay;
c) to resist, withstand (*alci*).

**sub-sortior** 4 to substitute by lot.

**sub-sortītiō, ōnis** f a choosing of
substitutes by lot.

**sub-stantia, ae** f substance, essence;
support, backing.

**sub-sternō** 3 a) to spread under or
in front; to place under oneself or
someone else; to place at someone's
disposal, yield.

**sub-stituō, uī, ūtum 3** a) to put
under, next, or in front of; to present; b) to put instead, substitute.

**sub-stō** 1 to stand firm, hold out.

**sub-strāmen, inis** n something put
underneath; rollers for transporting
ships.

**sub-stringō** 3 to bind or draw up,
**aurem** to prick the ear, listen attentively; to hold in.

**sub-structiō, ōnis** f foundation,
substructure.

**sub-struō** 3 to build beneath; a) to
lay the foundation of; b) to pave.

**sub-sultim** adv. by leaps and
bounds.

**sub-sultō** 1, *intens. of* **subsilio**.

**sub-sum,—,sub-esse** to be under or
behind (*dat.*); a) to be concealed in;
b) to be subject to; c) to lie at the
bottom, be underneath, near, at
hand.

**sub-sūtus** 3 trimmed at the bottom.

**sub-tēmen, inis** n woof, weft;
thread, yarn.

**subter 1.** adv. below, beneath;
**2.** prep. with acc. and abl. below,
beneath, under.

**subter-dūcō** 3 to withdraw secretly.

**subter-fugiō, fūgī, — 3** to flee in
secret, escape, evade, shun.

**subter-lābor** 3 to glide or flow
under; to escape (*acc.*).

**sub-terō** 3 to wear away underneath.

**subter-rāneus** 3 underground.

**subter-volō** 1 to fly beneath.

**sub-texō** 3 to draw in front; to
cover, veil; to weave into, connect,
join together, add.

**subtīlis, e** fine, thin; a) precise,

exact, accurate; b) keen, delicate,
acute, refined; c) plain, simple, unadorned.

**subtīlitās, ātis** f fineness, thinness;
a) accuracy, exactness; b) discernment, subtlety; c) plainness, simplicity.

**sub-timeō** 2 to be a little afraid.

**sub-trahō** 3 **1.** to draw away from
under (*dat.*); **2.** to take away secretly, remove, withdraw (*alci alqd*);
**se subtrahere** or **P.** to withdraw,
retire.

**sub-trīstis, e** somewhat sad.

**sub-turpiculus** 3 and **sub-turpis,
e** somewhat disgraceful.

**subtus** adv. under, beneath.

**sub-tūsus** 3 somewhat bruised.

**sub-ūcula, ae** f under-tunic.

**sūbula, ae** f awl; small spear.

**subulcus, ī** m swineherd.

**sub-urbānitās, ātis** f nearness to
the city.

**sub-urbānus** 3 near the city, sub-
urban; subst. **-um, ī** n estate near
Rome; **-ī, ōrum** m/pl. inhabitants
of towns near Rome.

**sub-urbium, ī** n suburb.

**sub-urgeō** 2 to press to, drive close
to.

**sub-ūrō** 3 to burn a little, to singe.

**sub-vectiō, ōnis** f a carrying, conveying.

**sub-vectō** 1 to carry, convey, bring
to.

**sub-vectus, ūs** m a conveying.

**sub-vehō** 3 to carry or bring up; to
convey, transport.

**sub-veniō** 4 a) to come to help, to
assist, aid; b) to relieve, remedy,
cure (*dat.*).

**sub-ventō** 1, *intens. of* **subvenio**.

**sub-vereor** 2 to fear a little.

**sub-versor, ōris** m overthrower,
subverter.

**sub-vertō** 3 to overturn, upset,
overthrow, to ruin, destroy.

**sub-vexus** 3 sloping upward.

**sub-volō** 1 to fly up.

**sub-volturius** 3 coloured like a vulture.

**sub-volvō** 3 to roll up.

**sub-vortō** 3 = **subverto**.

**succēdāneus** 3 substituted, taking
the place of.

**suc-cēdō** 3 **1.** to go up under; a) to
pass under, submit oneself to; b) to
go to, approach, advance, march on

*or* up; to go into, enter; c) to turn out well, be successful, prosper, succeed; **2.** to go up, ascend (*ad alqd*; *dat.*); **3.** to come after, follow after *or* close upon, come into the place of, succeed; to supply the place of, relieve (*alci*).

**suc-cendō, ndī, ēnsum** 3 to set on fire, kindle; to inflame.

**succēnseō** 2 = suscenseo.

**suc-centuriō¹,ōnis** *m* subcenturion.

**suc-centuriō²** 1 to enlist as a replacement; **-iātus,** placed in reserve.

**suc-cernō** 3 to sift.

**suc-cessiō, ōnis** *f* a succeeding, succession.

**successor, ōris** *m* successor, heir.

**successus, ūs** *m* a) advance; b) good progress, success.

**succīdāneus** 3 = succedaneus.

**suc-cīdia, ae** *f* flitch of bacon.

**suc-cīdō¹, cīdī, cīsum** 3 to cut off below *or* from below; to cut down *or* through.

**suc-cīdō², cīdī, —** 3 to sink down.

**succiduus** 3 sinking down.

**suc-cinctus** 3 concise.

**suc-cingō** 3 a) to tuck up the clothes; b) to gird round, surround (*alqd re*); to furnish, provide, equip.

**suc-cingulum, ī** *n* girdle.

**suc-cinō, —, —** 3 to sing with, chime in with.

**suc-cipiō** 3 = suscipio.

**suc-clāmātiō, ōnis** *f* a shouting, acclamation.

**suc-clāmō** 1 to shout to (*alci*).

**suc-collō** 1 to take upon the shoulders.

**suc-contumēliōsē** = sub-c...

**suc-crēscō** 3 to grow from below, grow up; to succeed to (*dat.*).

**suc-crispus** 3 = sub-c...

**suc-cumbō, cubuī, cubitum** 3 to sink down, to be overcome, to succumb, yield.

**suc-currō, currī, cursum** 3 to run under; a) to run to help, hasten to the aid of, to assist (*dat.*); b) to come into one's mind, suggest itself.

**succussus, ūs** *m* a shaking, jolting.

**suc-custōs, ōdis** *m* assistant watchman.

**suc-cutiō, cussī, cussum** 3 to shake up.

**sūcidus** 3 juicy, fresh.

**sūcinum, ī** *n* amber.

**sūcinus** 3 of amber.

**sucula, ae** *f* a) windlass; b) little sow; c) the constellation *Hyades*.

**sūcus, ī** *m* juice, sap, moisture; a) medicinal drink; b) taste, flavour; c) vigour, force.

**sūdārium, ī** *n* handkerchief.

**sūdātiō, ōnis** *f* sweating.

**sūdātōrius** 3 of *or* for sweating; *subst.* **-ium** *n* sweating-room.

**sūdātrīx, īcis** causing perspiration.

**sudis, is** *f* stake; bristle, fin(?).

**sūdō** 1 to sweat; to drip, be wet; to toil hard.

**sūdor, ōris** *m* sweat; moisture; exertion.

**suduculum, ī** *n* stick (*dimin. of* sudis).

**sūdus** 3 clear, serene; *subst.* **sūdum, ī** *n* bright sky, fair weather.

**suēscō, ēvī, ētum** 3 a) to become accustomed, *perf.* to be wont; **suētus** 3 accustomed, wont (*dat.*), customary, usual; b) to accustom to (*alqm re*).

**sūfes, etis** *m* judge, chief magistrate (*in Carthage*).

**suf-farciō** 1 to stuff full, cram.

**suf-ferō, sufferre** to bear, support, endure, suffer.

**suf-ficiō, fēcī, fectum** 3 **1.** a) to afford, supply, furnish; b) to put in the place of another, substitute, choose as a substitute; **2.** to be sufficient, suffice, be adequate, avail; to stain.

**suf-fīgō** 3 to fix beneath, to fasten up(on).

**(suffīmen, inis** *and*) **suffīmentum, ī** *n* fumigation, incense.

**suf-fiō** 4 to perfume, fumigate.

**sufflāmen, inis** *n* drag, brake.

**sufflāminō** 1 to brake, check.

**suf-flāvus** 3 greyish yellow.

**suf-flō** 1 to blow (up), inflate.

**suffōcātiō, ōnis** *f* suffocation.

**suf-fōcō** 1 to throttle, choke, strangle.

**suf-fodiō** 3 to dig under, undermine; to pierce from below.

**suffossiō, ōnis** *f* undermining, mine.

**suffrāgātiō, ōnis** *f* a) a voting; b) favourable vote, support.

**suffrāgātor, ōris** *m* a) voter; b) favourer, supporter.

**suffrāgātōrius** 3 belonging to the support of a candidate.

**suffrāgium, ī** *n* voting-tablet; vote, suffrage; **suffrāgium ferre** to vote; **a)** right of voting; **b)** judgment, opinion; **c)** approbation, assent.

**suf-frāgor** 1 to vote for, support, favour, recommend, promote (*alci*).

**suf-fringō, frēgī, frāctum** 3 to break below.

**su-fugiō, fūgī, — 3** to flee.

**suf-fugium, ī** *n* place of refuge.

**suf-fulciō** 4 to support beneath.

**suf-fundō** 3 to pour under, out, into, *or* upon, to overspread, suffuse, infuse; **suffūsus** 3 a) flowing; **b)** intermingled, bedewed, coloured, stained.

**suf-fūror** 1 to pilfer, filch.

**suf-fuscus** 3 brownish.

**suffūsus** 3, *see* **suffundo.**

**sug-gerō** 3 **a)** to put under; **b)** to pile up, erect; **c)** to put immediately after; **d)** to furnish, afford, supply, add, subjoin; **e)** to suggest, prompt.

**suggestum, ī** *n* and **-us, ūs** *m* elevated place; platform, stage.

**suggillātiō, suggillō,** *see* **sugi...**

**sug-grandis, e** pretty large *or* spacious.

**sug-gredior, gressus sum** 3 to come up, approach.

**sūgillātiō, ōnis** *f* affront, insult.

**sūgillō** 1 to beat black and blue; to taunt, insult, revile.

**sūgō, xī, ctum** 3 to suck, suck in.

**suillus** 3 of swine.

**sulcātor, ōris** *m* one who ploughs *or* cuts through.

**sulcō** 1 to furrow, plough, to sail over.

**sulcus, ī** *m* furrow; **a)** a ploughing; **b)** a cutting, trench, ditch; **c)** track, trail; **d)** wrinkle; **e)** vulva.

**sulfur, uris** *n* = **sulpur.**

**sullāturiō** 4 to want to play the part of Sulla.

**sulphur, uris** *n* = **sulpur.**

**sulpur, uris** *n* brimstone, sulphur.

**sulpurātus** 3 impregnated with sulphur; **-ta** *n/pl.* sulphur matches.

**sulpureus** 3 sulphurous, sulphur-yellow.

**sultis** = si vultis (*compare* **sīs**).

**sum, fuī, esse** 1. **a)** to be, exist, live; **b)** to happen, befall, occur, take place; **c)** to be present, be found, stay, abide; **d)** to be possible, to be the case that ... (*ut*); 2. (*perf. tense*)

to be a thing of the past, to be no more; 3. *as a copula:* to be; a) *with gen. poss.* to belong *or* pertain to, be of, be peculiar to, characteristic of, be the duty of; b) *with gen. or abl. qualit.* to be of, be possessed of, belong to, have; c) *with numbers:* to be of, consist of; d) *with gen. or abl. of value:* to be valued at, cost; e) *with dat.* to have, possess (*patri est ampla domus*).

**sumbolus, -um** = **symbolus, -um.**

**sūmen, inis** *n* breast, teat, udder (*of a sow*); sow.

**summa, ae** *f* 1. the sum, amount, contents, substance, quantity, number; a) sum of money; b) the whole, the chief point, chief thing, principal matter; **ad summam** on the whole, generally, in short; **summa imperii** chief command; **summa rerum** supreme power, the most vital issues *or* interests; 2. pre-eminence, first place, first rank.

**sum-mānō** 1 to trickle over, wet.

**summārium, ī** *n* epitome of chief points, summary.

**summās, ātis** *m* and *f* of high birth, noble.

**summātim** *adv.* generally, summarily.

**summātus, ūs** *m* supremacy.

**summē** *adv.* exceedingly, very much.

**sum-mergō** 3 to dip *or* plunge under water, overwhelm, drown, submerge.

**sumministrātor, ōris** *m* supplier, abettor.

**sum-ministrō** 1 to furnish, supply (*alci alqd*).

**summissim** softly.

**sum-missiō, ōnis** *f* a) a letting down, lowering; lessening, diminishing; b) depression.

**sum-missus** 3 lowered; a) low, soft, gentle, calm, composed; b) mean, abject, crouching; humble, submissive.

**sum-mittō** 3 1. to let *or* put down, to lower, sink, drop; a) to relax, moderate, lessen, abate; b) to place under, submit, bring down, humble; 2. to send privately, dispatch secretly (*alci alqd*), to send as aid *or* reinforcement, to send as a substitute; 3. to let grow long; to rear, put forth, produce.

**sum-moneō** 2 to remind secretly.

**sum-moveŏ** 2 to move up *or* away, remove out of the way (*alqm a re*); **a)** to clear away, dislodge; **b)** to banish; **c)** to keep away from, withdraw, withhold, force from, induce to abandon (*alqm re, a re*).

**summula, ae** *f* trifling sum.

**summus** 3, *superl. of* **superus.**

**sum-mūtŏ** 1 to exchange, substitute.

**sūmŏ, mpsī, mptum** 3 to take, take up *or* in hand (*alqd ab alqo*); **a)** to take for use, put on; to wear, eat, consume, (**supplicium de alqo** to exact punishment); **b)** to take for granted, suppose, assert, affirm, maintain, cite, mention, adduce; **c)** to assume, choose, select, purchase, hire; **d)** to undertake, begin, enter upon; **ē)** to claim, arrogate, appropriate; **f)** to wear out, harass.

**sūmptiō, ōnis** *f* premise of a syllogism.

**sūmptuārius** 3 pertaining to expense.

**sūmptuōsus** 3 **a)** expensive, costly; **b)** extravagant, prodigal.

**sūmptus, ūs** *m* charge, expense, cost; extravagance.

**suŏ, suī, sūtum** 3 to sew, stitch, to fasten together; *subst.* **sūtum, ī** *n* joint.

**su-ove-taurīlia, ium** *n/pl.* sacrifice of a pig, a sheep and a bull.

**supellex, ectilis** *f* household goods, movables, chattels, furniture.

**super** **1.** *adv.* over; **a)** above, on the top, from above; **b)** besides, moreover; **c)** over and above; **2.** *prep.* **a)** *with abl.* over, above; (*of time*) during; about, concerning; **b)** *with acc.* over, above; beyond; during; more than (*super modum, super decem milia, super omnia* above all).

**superā** = **suprā.**

**superābilis, e** that may be surmounted *or* overcome.

**super-addŏ** 3 to add over and above.

**superāns, antis** prevailing, in the ascendant.

**superātor, ōris** *m* conqueror.

**superbia, ae** *f* pride, haughtiness, insolence, lofty spirit, noble pride.

**superbi-ficus** 3 acting proudly.

**superbi-loquentia, ae** *f* arrogant speech.

**superbiŏ, —, —** 4 to be proud, haughty; to boast (*abl.*); to look magnificent.

**superbus** 3 **a)** haughty, proud, arrogant, tyrannical; **b)** fastidious, nice; **c)** excellent, distinguished, splendid, magnificent.

**superciliōsus** 3 disdainful, censorious.

**super-cilium, ī** *n* eyebrow; **a)** severity, sternness, austerity; **b)** pride, haughtiness; **c)** ridge, summit of a hill.

**super-currŏ** 3 to exceed (in value).

**super-ēmineŏ** 2 to overtop, surmount.

**super-ēvolŏ** 1 to fly away over.

**superficiārius** 3 one who builds on another man's land.

**super-ficiēs, ēī** *f* surface; building with its ground.

**super-fiŏ** 3 to be left over, remain.

**super-fixus** 3 fixed on the top.

**super-fluŏ, —, —** 3 to run over, overflow, to be in superfluity.

**superfluus** 3 **a)** overflowing; **b)** superfluous.

**super-fugiŏ** 3 to flee over.

**super-fulgeŏ** 2 to shine forth over.

**super-fundŏ** 3 **a)** to pour upon *or* over; **se superfundere** *and* P. to overflow, spread itself; **b)** to cover.

**super-gredior, gressus sum** 3 to go over, overstep; to surpass.

**super-iaciŏ, iēcī, iectum (iactum)** 3 **a)** to cast *or* throw over *or* upon; **b)** to surmount; to exceed, outdo (*acc.*).

**super-immineŏ** 2 to hang over.

**super-impendeŏ** 2 to overhang.

**super-impōnŏ** 3 to place *or* put upon.

**super-incendŏ** 3 to inflame still more.

**super-incidŏ** 3 to fall upon from above.

**super-incubŏ** 1 to lie upon.

**super-incumbŏ, cubuī, —** 3 to lay oneself down upon.

**super-induŏ** 3 to put on over.

**super-ingerŏ** 3 to pile on top.

**super-iniciŏ** 3 to throw *or* cast over.

**super-insternŏ** 3 to spread over.

**super-instrepŏ** 3 to sound over.

**super-iūmentārius, ī** *m* inspector. of the drivers of beasts of burden.

**super-lābor** 3 to glide over.

**super-lātiō, ōnis** *f* exaggeration.

**super-lātus** 3 exaggerated, hyperbolical.

**superne** *adv.* a) from above; b) above.

**supernus** lying above, on high, upper; celestial.

**superō** 1 1. to be above, to project; a) to be superior, prevail, to have the upper hand, be conqueror, surpass; b) to abound, be in abundance; c) to remain, be left, be still alive, survive; 2. *trans.* to surmount, pass over, mount, ascend; a) to overtop, surpass, excel, exceed; b) to sail past, go by; c) to conquer, overcome, vanquish, subdue.

**super-obruō** 3 to cover over, overwhelm.

**super-occupō** 1 to take by surprise.

**super-pendeō** 2 to overhang.

**super-pōnō** 3 to lay, place, put over or upon.

**super-scandō** 3 to climb over.

**super-scrībō** 3 to write over.

**super-sedeō** 2 a) to sit on; b) to forbear, desist, leave off, refrain (*abl.; inf.*).

**super-stāgnō** 1 to overflow.

**super-sternō** 3 to strew or spread over.

**super-stes, stitis** a) standing by (of a witness actually present); b) surviving, outliving, remaining.

**super-stitiō, ōnis** *f* superstition, superstitious rite; excessive religious awe; object of dread.

**superstitiōsus** 3 a) superstitious; anxious; b) prophetic.

**superstitō** 1 to be over and above; to preserve.

**super-stō, —, —** 1 to stand over or upon.

**super-struō** 3 to build upon or over.

**super-sum, -fuī, -esse** to remain, be left; a) to exist still; b) to survive, outlive; c) to be over and above, abound, be superfluous, be equal to (*dat.*); d) to protrude.

**super-tegō** 3 to cover over.

**super-urgeō** 2 to press from above.

**superus** 3 what is above, upper, higher; a) **superī, ōrum** *m/pl.* the celestial gods, men upon earth; b) **supera, ōrum** *n/pl.* the upper world; *comp.* **superior, us** a) higher, upper; b) past, gone by, former, last, first, older; c) superior, nobler, more important, conqueror;

— *superl.* **suprēmus** 3 a) highest, uppermost, supreme; b) extreme, last; **suprēmus diēs** the day of death; *subst.* **suprēma, ōrum** *n/pl.* death, funeral rites, last will; — *superl.* **summus** 3 highest, topmost, highest part, top of, surface of; **summum, ī** *n* top, surface (also as *adv.* at the utmost, at most); a) extreme, last; **summa aestas** midsummer, height of summer; b) greatest, most important, most excellent or distinguished, most valuable, best, chief; **summa rēs** the chief thing or point; **summum ius** strictest right, rigour of the law; **summa rēs** crisis, decisive point; **summō tempore** at a critical juncture, in an emergency; **summō opere** with all one's might (*adv.* **summē** in the highest degree, extremely); c) most perfect, whole, complete, entire; **summa rēs pūblica** the general welfare, the general cause.

**super-vacāneus** 3 over and above, superfluous, needless, useless, unnecessary.

**super-vacuus** 3 = **supervacāneus**.

**super-vādō** 3 to climb or pass over.

**super-vehor** 3 to ride, sail, pass beyond.

**super-veniō** 4 to follow up, overtake; a) to appear unexpectedly, come on by surprise, come on the scene; b) to be added; c) to surpass.

**super-ventus, ūs** *m* a coming up, arrival.

**super-vīvō** 3 to survive.

**super-volitō** 1 to fly over.

**super-volō** 1 to fly over.

**supīnō** 1 to turn up or over.

**supīnus** 3 a) lying on the back, face upwards; indolent; b) sloping or flowing up; c) (of verses) readable backwards.

**sup-paenitet** 2 it causes a little regret.

**sup-palpor** 1 to stroke a little, to flatter.

**sup-pār, paris** almost equal or contemporary.

**sup-parasītor** 1 to flatter a little like a parasite.

**supparum, ī** *n* a) woman's garment of linen; b) small sail.

**suppeditātiō, ōnis** *f* abundance.

**sup-pedĭtō 1 a)** to furnish, afford, supply, procure (*alci alqd*); **b)** *intr.* to be available, be at hand, abound, be sufficient, suffice (*alci*).

**sup-pēdō 3** to break wind a little.

**sup-pernātus 3** hewn down.

**suppetiae, ārum** *f*|*pl.* aid, assistance.

**suppetĭor 1** to aid, help, succour (*alci*).

**sup-petō 3** *intr.* = suppedito b).

**sup-pīlō 1** to steal; to rob.

**sup-pingō 3** to fasten beneath.

**sup-plantō 1** to trip up.

**sup-plaudō 3** = supplodo.

**sup-plēmentum, ī** *n* a filling up; **a)** supply, supplement; **b)** recruiting, reinforcement.

**sup-pleō, ēvī, ētum 2** to fill up, supply, complete, make full, repair, recruit.

**sup-plex, ĭcis** bending the knee, kneeling; **a)** supplicating, suppliant. entreating (*alci; ut*); **b)** humble, submissive; *subst. m* humble petitioner.

**sup-plicātĭō, ōnis** *f* public thanksgiving.

**supplicĭum, ī** *n* a kneeling down; **a)** humble entreaty, petition, supplication, prayer; **b)** = supplicatio; **c)** (capital) punishment, execution; penalty, torture, pain, distress.

**sup-plĭcō 1** to kneel down to, pray *or* beseech humbly (*alci*); to pray, worship (*diis*).

**sup-plōdō, sī, sum 3** to stamp (*pedem*).

**supplōsĭō, ōnis** *f* a stamping.

**sup-pōnō 3** to put, place *or* lay under (*alqd alci rei*); **a)** to make subject, submit; **b)** to put under something, annex, subjoin (*alci rei alqd*); **c)** to substitute (*alqd in locum, pro alqo*), forge.

**sup-portō 1** to carry, bring up, convey.

**supposĭtīcĭus 3** substituted, spurious.

**sup-posĭtĭō, ōnis** *f* substitution of a child.

**sup-postrix, ĭcis** *f* she who substitutes.

**sup-pressĭō, ōnis** *f* a keeping back, embezzlement.

**sup-prĭmō, pressī, pressum 3** to press down, press under; **a)** to hold back, check, restrain; to stop, sink (*a ship*); **b)** to suppress, conceal, hide, keep secret; to embezzle; — suppressus 3 subdued, low.

**sup-prōmus, ī** *m* under-butler.

**sup-pŭdet 2 me** I am somewhat ashamed (*alcis rei*).

**suppūrātĭō, ōnis** *f* suppuration, abscess.

**sup-pūrō 1** to suppurate, fester (*lit.* or *metaph.*).

**suppus 3** upside down.

**sup-putō 1** to count up, reckon, calculate.

**suprā 1.** *adv.* above, on the upper side, over, on the top; **a)** before, previously; **b)** more, further, beyond; **2.** *prep.* with *acc.* above, over; **a)** beyond; **b)** before; **c)** more than, above.

**suprālātĭō, suprālātus,** *see* superlatio, superlatus.

**suprā-scandō 3** to climb over.

**suprēmus 3,** *superl. of* superus.

**supter, suptus = subter, -tus.**

**sūra, ae** *f* calf of the leg.

**surculus, ī** *m* shoot, sprout, spring, sucker.

**surdaster, tra, trum** somewhat deaf.

**surdĭtās, ātis** *f* deafness.

**surdus 3** deaf (*ad alqd*); **a)** unheeding, regardless; **b)** not understanding (*in re*); **c)** silent, noiseless; **d)** faint, weak.

**surgō, surrēxī, surrēctum 3 a)** to rise, arise, get up; **b)** to grow up, appear, rise, spring up; **c)** to mount up, ascend; to increase.

**surpĭculus = scirpiculus.**

**surpite, surpuit, = surripite, surripuit.**

**sur-rēpō 3,** *see* subrepo.

**sur-reptĭcius = sur-rupticius.**

**surrēxe, surrigō = surrexisse, subrigo.**

**sur-rĭpĭō, rĭpuī, reptum 3** to snatch *or* take away secretly, to steal, filch, pilfer (*alqd alci or ab alqo*); **se surrĭpere** to steal away, withdraw privily.

**sur-rogō 1** to cause to be chosen as substitute.

**sur-ruptĭcĭus 3** stolen.

**sūrsum (and sūrsus)** *adv.* **a)** upwards; **b)** above, on high.

**sūs[1], suis** *f* and *m* **a)** sow, swine, pig, hog; **b)** a fish.

**sus²** *adv., see* susque.

**sus-cēnseō, uī,** — 2 to be angry, enraged (*alci; quod, acc. c. inf.*).

**susceptiō, ōnis** *f* an undertaking.

**sus-cipiō, cēpī, ceptum** 3 1. to catch (something as it falls), to support; a) to take up a new-born child, acknowledge; b) to have *or* beget a child from one (*ex alqa*); 2. to take, accept, receive; a) to undertake, begin, take up (*alqd*); to submit to; b) to assume; c) to enter upon; d) to answer, take up a discourse.

**sus-citō** 1 to raise *or* stir up, raise on high, lift up; a) to cause to stand up, awake, excite, incite; b) to rekindle; c) to cause.

**su-spectō** 1 a) to look up at (*alqd*); b) to suspect, mistrust.

**su-spectus¹, ūs** *m* a looking up *or* upwards; height; admiration, esteem, respect.

**su-spectus²** 3 suspected, causing suspicion, mistrust *or* fear.

**sus-pendium, ī** *n* a hanging, hanging oneself.

**sus-pendō, ndī, ēnsum** 3 to hang up, hang (*alqd re, ex, de* or *a re*); a) to raise, lift up, to prop up; b) to keep in suspense, make doubtful *or* uncertain, leave undecided.

**sus-pēnsūra, ae** *f* vault; floor supported on pillars.

**sus-pēnsus** 3 suspended, hanging; poised, touching lightly, light; a) resting *or* depending upon (*ex re*); b) uncertain, doubtful, wavering, floating; c) fearful, anxious, timid.

**suspicāx, ācis** distrustful.

**su-spiciō¹, exī, ectum** 3 to look up (at, *acc.*); a) to look up to; b) to esteem, honour, admire; c) to suspect (v. rare; see *suspectus*).

**su-spiciō², ōnis** *f* a) suspicion, mistrust; **in suspiciōne esse alci** to be suspected by; **alqm in suspiciōnem adducere** to make one suspected; b) opinion, notion, conception, idea.

**suspiciōsus** 3 a) full of suspicion, mistrustful; b) causing suspicion, suspected.

**suspicor** (*and* -ō) 1 to suspect, conjecture, suppose (*alqd; acc. c. inf.*).

**suspirātus, ūs** *m* a sighing, deep breath.

**su-spiritus, ūs** *m* deep breath, sigh, groan.

**suspīrium, ī** *n* a) deep breath, sigh; b) shortness of breath, panting; c) breath, respiration.

**su-spirō** 1 to breathe deeply, heave a sigh, to long for (*alqd*); to exhale.

**susque dēque** *adv.* (up and down); of no importance; ~ **habeō** I don't care.

**sustentāculum, ī** *n* prop, stay.

**sustentātiō, ōnis** *f* a deferring, delay.

**sus-tentō** 1 to hold up, keep upright, sustain; a) to maintain, preserve, sustain with food; b) to hold out, bear, suffer, endure; c) to hold up, resist, check, put off, delay.

**sus-tineō, nuī,** — 2 to hold up, keep up, support, sustain; a) to bear, endure; to withstand, hold out against; to tolerate; b) to undertake, be equal to; c) to maintain, feed, nourish, sustain; d) to hold back, check, restrain, defer, delay, prolong.

**sus-tollō,** —, — 3 to raise *or* lift up; to take away, carry off.

**sūsum = sūrsum.**

**susurrātor, ōris** *m* whisperer.

**susurrō** 1 to whisper, murmur.

**susurrus¹, ī** *m* a whispering, murmuring, humming.

**susurrus²** 3 whispering.

**sūtēla, ae** *f* cunning trick.

**sūtilis, e** sewed together, fastened together.

**sūtor, ōris** *m* shoemaker.

**sūtōrius** 3 of a shoemaker.

**sūtrinus** 3 = **sutorius**; *subst.* **sūtrīnum, ī** *n* shoemaking.

**sūtūra, ae** *f* a sewing, seam.

**suus** 3 *poss. adj.* his, her, its, their (own); *subst.* a) **suī, ōrum** *m/pl.* one's own troops, friends, dependents, countrymen; b) **suum, ī** *n* one's own property; proper, peculiar, suitable; appointed; favourable, propitious; independent, one's own master, free.

**sȳcophanta, ae** *m* false accuser, slanderer; cheat; flatterer, sycophant.

**sȳcophantia, ae** *f* cheating, deceit.

**sȳcophantiōsē** deceitfully.

**sȳcophantor** 1 to trick, deceive.

**syllaba, ae** *f* syllable; *pl.* verses.

**syllabātim** *adv.* syllable by syllable.

**syllogismus, ī** *m* syllogism.

**sym-bola, ae** *f* contribution, share of the cost of a meal; *pl.* 'feast' (*i.e.* a beating).

**symbolus, ī** *m and* **-um, ī** *n* token, sign.

**sym-phōnia, ae** *f* concerted music (vocal *or* instrumental).

**symphōniacus** 3 musical.

**symplegma, atis** *n* embrace.

**syn-edrus, ī** *m* councillor.

**syn-grapha, ae** *f* written agreement to pay, bond.

**syn-graphus, ī** *m* a) contract; b) passport.

**syn-odūs, ontis** *m* a sea-fish.

**synthesina, ae** *f* dressing-gown.

**synthesis, is** *f* a) dinner-service; b) suit of clothes; c) dressing-gown, house-coat.

**syrma, atis** *n* (tragic actor's) robe with a train; tragedy.

**syrtis, is** *and* **idos** *f* sandbank in the sea; *esp.* two dangerous shoals off the coast of North Africa.

# T

**T.** = Titus; **Ti.** = Tiberius.

**tabella, ae** *f* small board, panel; **a)** gaming-board; **b)** little painting; **c)** fan; **d)** writing-tablet; letter; document, contract, deed, record; **e)** votive tablet; **f)** voting-tablet.

**tabellārius** 3 relating to voting; mail-carrying; *subst.* ~, **ī** *m* letter--carrier.

**tābeō, —, —** 2 **a)** to melt, waste away, fall away, be consumed; **b)** to drip.

**taberna, ae** *f* hut, shed; **a)** tavern, shop, stall, workshop; **b)** arcade (?) in the circus.

**tabernāc(u)lum, ī** *n* tent; place for observing the auspices.

**tabernārius, ī** *m* shopkeeper.

**tabernula, ae** *f* little shop *or* tavern.

**tābēs, is** *f* a melting away, putrefaction, decay; **a)** moisture of decay *or* melting; noxious fluid; **b)** wasting disease, pestilence, plague; **c)** decline.

**tābēscō, buī, —** 3 **a)** to melt gradually, waste away, be dissolved, decay; **b)** to pine away.

**tābidulus** 3 consuming.

**tābidus** 3 melting, wasting, decaying; corrupting, destructive.

**tābi-ficus** 3 dissolving, consuming.

**tabula, ae** *f* board, plank; **a)** gaming-board; **b)** picture, painting; **c)** writing-tablet; table of the law; **d)** auction; **e)** writing, document, record, note; register, list; contract; will; account-book.

**tabulārium, ī** *n* archives.

**tabulārius, ī** *m* revenue official.

**tabulātiō, ōnis** *f* a flooring, story.

**tabulātus** 3 boarded, floored; *subst.* **-um, ī** *n* a flooring, floor, story.

**tābum, ī** *n* **a)** corrupt moisture, matter, putrid gore; **b)** plague, pestilence.

**taceō, uī, itum** 2 **a)** to be silent, still; **b)** to pass over in silence (*alqd*).

**taciturnitās, ātis** *f* silence, taciturnity.

**taciturnus** 3 silent, taciturn; still, quiet.

**tacitus** 3 **a)** silent, not speaking, quiet; mute, noiseless; **b)** kept secret, passed over in silence, unmentioned; **c)** secret, concealed, hidden, silently assumed.

**tāctilis, e** tangible.

**tāctiō, ōnis** *f* a touching; sense of touch.

**tāctus, ūs** *m* **a)** a touching, touch; operation, influence; **b)** sense of touch, feeling.

**taeda, ae** *f* pine-tree; **a)** chip *or* plank of pine-wood; **b)** torch; nuptial torch; wedding.

**taedet, uit** *or* **taesum est** 2 to cause weariness *or* disgust; **taedet me** I am disgusted, weary (*alqm alcis rei; inf.*).

**taedi-fer** 3 torch-bearing.

**taedium, ī** *n* disgust, loathing, weariness.

**taenia, ae** *f* band, fillet, ribbon.

**taeter, tra, trum** nasty, foul, hideous, shocking, abominable.

**tagāx, ācis** thievish.

**tālāris, e** reaching *or* belonging to the ankles; *subst.* **tālāria, ium** *n/pl.* ankles; winged sandals *or* shoes; long garment reaching to the ankles; an instrument of torture.

**tālārius** 3 relating to dice.

**tālea, ae** *f* stake, bar.

**talentum, ī** *n* talent (*as a weight =* ½ cwt, *and as a sum money =* some hundreds of pounds).

**tāliō, ōnis** *f* punishment in kind ('an eye for an eye').

**tālis, e** such, of such a kind; **a)** of such a distinguished, remarkable kind; **b)** so bad *or* blamable; **c)** the following.

**tālitrum, ī** *n* rap with the knuckles.

**talpa, ae** *f* (*m*) mole.

**tālus, ī** *m* **a)** ankle, ankle-bone; heel; **b)** kind of dice.

**tam** *adv.* so, so very, to such a degree; **quam ... tam** as ... so; **tam ... quam** as much ... as, as well ... as; **non tam ... quam** not so much ... as.

**tamarix, īcis** *f* tamarisk.

**tam-diŭ** *adv.* so long.

**tamen** *adv.* nevertheless, notwithstanding; yet at least, still.

**tamendem** (?) = **tamen.**

**tamen-etsī** *cj.* = **tametsi.**

**tam-etsī** *cj.* though, although.

**tam-quam** *adv.* as, just as; *cj.* with *subj.* as if, as though (= *tamquam si*); to the effect that, on the ground that.

**tandem** *adv.* at last, finally; *in interrogations:* pray, then, now.

**tangō, tetigī, tāctum** 3 to touch; a) to come to, arrive at, reach, enter; b) to border on, be connected with; c) to taste, eat, drink; d) to besprinkle, moisten, dye; e) to strike, hit; f) to move, touch, affect, impress; g) to touch upon, mention; h) to catch, cheat.

**tan-quam** = **tamquam.**

**tantillus** 3 = **tantulus.**

**tantīs-per** *adv.* just so long.

**tant-opere** *adv.* so much, so earnestly, to such a degree.

**tantulus** 3 so little, so small; *subst.* **-um, ī** *n* such a trifle.

**tantus** 3 so great, so much, so important; a) (*rarely*) so small, so slight; b) (*rarely*) *pl.* **tantī** so many; c) *subst.* **tantum, ī** *n* so much, such a quantity *or* number, so high a degree; **alterum tantum** as much again, twice as much; so little, such a trifle; **tantī** (*gen. of value*) of such value, worth so much, for so much; **tanti est** it is worth while; **tanto** by so much, so much the; **quanto ... tanto** the ... the; d) *adv.* **tantum** so much, so greatly, so far; only so much, so little; only, merely; **non tantum ... sed etiam** not only ... but also; **tantummodo** only, merely; **tantum non** nearly, almost; **tantum quod** only, only just, hardly.

**tantus-dem** 3 just so great *or* large; *subst.* **tantundem** *n* just as much; *adv.* just as far.

(**tapēs**), **ētis** *m and* **tap(p)ēte, is** *n* (*abl. pl. also* **tapētis**) carpet, coverlet, tapestry.

**tardēscō** 3 to grow sluggish.

**tardi-gradus** 3 slowly stepping.

**tardi-loquus** 3 slow-speaking.

**tardi-pēs, edis** slow-footed.

**tarditās, ātis** *f* slowness, tardiness; dulness, stupidity.

**tarditūdō, inis** *f* slowness.

**tardiusculus** 3 rather slow.

**tardō** 1 a) to retard, stop, hinder; b) *intr.* to delay.

**tardus** 3 slow, tardy, sluggish; a) long, lasting; b) slow of approach, late; c) making slow; d) dull, heavy, stupid.

**tarmes, itis** *m* wood-worm.

**tarpezīta, ae** *m* money-changer, banker.

**tata, ae** *m* daddy.

**tat(ae)** *excl.*

**taureus** 3 of a bull *or* bull's hide; *subst.* **-ea, ae** *f* a whip of hide.

**tauri-fer** 3 producing bulls.

**tauri-fōrmis, e** bull-shaped.

**taurīnus** 3 of bulls *or* oxen.

**taurus, ī** *m* bull, ox.

**taxātiō, ōnis** *f* estimation.

**taxeus** 3 of yew-trees.

**taxillus, ī** *m* small dice.

**taxō** 1 a) to reproach; b) to appraise, estimate.

**taxus, ī** *f* yew-tree; javelin of yew-wood.

**tech(i)na, ae** *f* trick, artifice.

**tēctor, ōris** *m* plasterer.

**tēctōriolum, ī** *n* little plaster *or* stucco-work.

**tēctōrium, ī** *n* plaster, stucco, fresco-painting; paste for use on the face; hypocritical speech.

**tēctōrius** 3 for covering a roof.

**tēctum, ī** *n* roof; a) ceiling of a room; b) room, dwelling, house, temple, den, grotto.

**tēctus** 3 covered; a) roofed, decked; b) concealed, secret; c) close, reserved, cautious.

**teges, etis** *f* mat.

**tegeticula, ae** *f* small mat.

**tegillum, ī** *n* little cover, hood.

**tegimen, inis** *n* cover; protection.

**tegimentum, tegmentum, ī** *n* cover, covering; protection.

**tegmen, inis** *n* = **tegimen.**

**tegō, tēxī, tēctum** 3 to cover (*alqd re*); a) to hide, conceal; to keep secret, cloak, dissemble; b) to protect, defend.

**tēgula, ae** *f* tile; tiled roof.

**tegumen, tegumentum** = **tegimen(tum).**

**tegus, oris** *n* = **tergus.**

**tēla, ae** *f* web; a) warp; b) loom; c) design, plan.

**tēlinum, ī** *n* a costly perfume

**tellūs, ūris** *f* the earth, globe; **a)** soil, ground; land, country, district, territory; **b)** estate; **c)** goddess of the Earth.

**tēlum, ī** *n* missile weapon; spear, javelin; weapon; sword, dagger; shaft of light.

**temerārius** 3 **a)** accidental; **b)** rash, inconsiderate, thoughtless, foolhardy.

**temerātor, ōris** *m* seducer, ravisher.

**temere** *adv.* by chance, accidentally, casually, without purpose; **a)** without reason, inconsiderately, rashly; **b) non temere** not easily, hardly.

**temeritās, ātis** *f* **a)** chance, accident; **b)** rashness, haste, thoughtlessness, indiscretion, foolhardiness.

**temerō** 1 to violate, defile, dishonour, disgrace.

**tēmētum, ī** *n* wine, intoxicating drink.

**temnō, —, —** 3 to contemn, despise (= **contemno**).

**tēmō, ōnis** *m* pole *or* beam of a wagon; wagon; *the constellation* Charles's Wain.

**temperāmentum, ī** *n* right proportion, measure, moderation; middle way.

**temperāns, tis** moderate, continent, sober, temperate.

**temperantia, ae** *f* moderation, temperance, continence.

**temperātiō, ōnis** *f* due admixture, just proportion, composition; proper regulation, order.

**temperātor, ōris** *m* one who regulates *or* moderates; tempering (metal).

**temperātūra, ae** *f* proper balance; temperature; constitution (*of the body*).

**temperātus** 3 **a)** properly arranged *or* prepared; **b)** moderate, temperate, mild, quiet, calm.

**temperī** *adv.* in due time.

**temperiēs, ēi** *f* = **temperatio;** moderate temperature.

**temperō** 1 **a)** to mingle in due proportion, to observe proper limits *or* measure; to compound properly (*vinum*); to arrange, order, regulate, govern, manage; **c)** to use with moderation, act temperately, to soften, qualify, temper; **d)** to keep back, restrain (*sibi, irae*); **c)** to be moderate, restrain oneself, forbear, abstain, spare.

**tempestās, ātis** *f* weather; **a)** bad weather, storm, tempest; **b)** storm, attack, fury; calamity, misfortune, danger; **c)** space *or* period of time, season.

**tempestivitās, ātis** *f* fit time, seasonableness.

**tempestīvus** 3 happening *or* done at the proper time; **a)** seasonable, opportune, appropriate, timely, fitting, ripe; **b)** early.

**templum, ī** *n* space cut off, sacred space; **a)** space in the sky *or* on the earth marked out by the augur for observing the birds; open space; **b)** sanctuary, temple, chapel, shrine.

**temporārius** 3 proper for the time; temporary, changeable.

**temporī** *adv.* = **temperi.**

**temptābundus** 3 attempting.

**temptāmen, inis** *and* **temptāmentum, ī** *n* = **temptatio a).**

**temptātiō, ōnis** *f* **a)** trial, essay, proof; **b)** attack (*of disease*).

**temptātor, ōris** *m* tempter, assailant.

**temptō** 1 to touch, handle, feel; **a)** to attack, assail; **b)** to try, prove, test; to try, attempt, essay; **c)** to tempt, incite, disturb, sound, tamper with, work upon; **d)** to intend, purpose, undertake.

**tempus**[1]**, oris** *n* time, division of time, section of time, period of time, space of time, distinct point of time; **anni tempus** season; **ex tempore** without preparation; **a)** right, proper, fit time, right occasion, opportunity; **tempus est** it is high time, it is the right time; **tempore** at the proper time; **b)** circumstances of time, the times, state *or* condition of things; **ex tempore** according to circumstances; dangerous *or* unfortunate circumstances, crisis, misfortune, calamity; emergency, extremity; **c)** time of life, years; **d)** measure (*of syllables*), quantity.

**tempus**[2]**, oris** *n*, *mostly pl.*, temple on the forehead; head.

**tēmulentus** 3 drunken, intoxicated.

**tenācitās, ātis** *f* a holding fast, tenacity; avarice, niggardliness.

**tenāx, ācis** holding fast, gripping; **a)** tenacious, fast, firm, tough, sticky; **b)** constant, steadfast, persevering, persisting (*with gen.*); obstinate; **c)** stingy, niggardly, sordid.

**tendicula, ae** *f* **a)** snare, trap; **b)** clothes-stretcher.

**tendō, tetendī, tentum** (*and* **tēnsum**) 3 **1.** to stretch, stretch out, make tense (*alqd*); **a)** to distend, extend, **manūs alci** *or* **ad alqd;** to pitch (*a tent*); **b)** to hold out, offer, present, reach, extend (*alci alqd*); **insidias** to lay snares; **c)** to direct, turn; **2.** *intr.* **a)** to be encamped, be in tents, to encamp; **b)** to travel, run, sail, hold a course, direct oneself, move, march (*in* or *ad alqd*); **c)** to aim at, attack; **d)** to extend, stretch, reach to; **e)** to be inclined to, to tend; **f)** to strive, endeavour, struggle, contend, fight; to resist, withstand (*contra* or *adversus*).

**tenebrae, ārum** *f/pl.* darkness; **a)** night; blindness, swoon, darkness of death; dark place, lurking place, haunts; **b)** obscurity, low station *or* condition.

**tenebricōsus** 3 full of darkness, dark, gloomy, obscure.

**tenebricus** *and* **tenebrōsus** 3 dark, gloomy, obscure.

**tenellulus** 3 (*and* **tenellus** 3) very tender *or* delicate.

**teneō, tenuī, (tentum)** 2 to hold, keep, grasp, hold fast. **1.** to have in the hand, mouth etc., keep, seize, comprehend; **a)** to hold in mind, understand, conceive, comprehend, know; **b)** to hold one's way *or* course; to follow up, sail, steer, reach a place, land on, arrive at; **c)** to gain, acquire, obtain, attain; **d)** to convict, catch, detect; **2.** to hold in one's possession, have, possess, be master of; **a)** to inhabit, occupy, garrison; **b)** to comprise, comprehend; to include; **c)** to possess, master; to hold fast, keep in, hold back, bind, fetter, control; **d)** to preserve, maintain, retain, guard; to remember; **3.** **a)** to keep to, not to swerve from, remain true to; **b)** to last, endure, keep on; **c)** to charm, amuse, inspire; **d)** to bind, oblige; to maintain one's right; **4.** **a)** to hold back, repress, check, restrain, suppress; **b)** to de-

tain, delay; **c)** to keep a thing away from (*alqd ab alqo*).

**tener, era, erum** soft, delicate, tender, smooth; soft; **b)** tender, effeminate, sensitive; voluptuous; **c)** amorous; yielding.

**tenerāscō** 3 to grow soft.

**teneritās, ātis** *f* softness, tenderness.

**teneritūdō, inis** *f* = **teneritas**.

**tēnesmos, ī** *m* constipation.

**tennō** = **tendo**.

**tenor, ōris** *m* uninterrupted course, continuance, a keeping on, duration, career; **uno tenōre** uninterruptedly.

**tēnsa, ae** *f* chariot bearing the images of the gods.

**tentābundus** 3, *see* **temptabundus**.

**tentāmen, inis** *n*, *see* **temptamen**.

**tentigō, inis** *f* passion, lust.

**tentō** 1, *see* **tempto**.

**tentōrium, ī** *n* tent.

**tenuiculus** 3 very thin, mean, *or* poor.

**tenuis, e** thin; **a)** slender, fine, slight; **b)** small, narrow; **c)** shallow; **d)** fine, subtle, exact, nice, ingenious; **e)** insignificant, unimportant, trifling, weak; **f)** miserable, poor, mean, bad; **g)** plain, simple, without ornament.

**tenuitās, ātis** *f* thinness, fineness; **a)** slenderness, leanness; **b)** poverty, indigence; **c)** simplicity, plainness.

**tenuō** 1 to make thin, fine, weak; to lessen, diminish, enfeeble.

**tenus[1], oris** *n* snare.

**tenus[2]** *prep.* with *abl.* and *gen.* up to, as far as, unto; **verbō tenus** in words, nominally.

**tenvis, e** = **tenuis**.

**tepe-faciō** (*and* **tepē-**) 3 to make warm *or* tepid.

**tepeō, uī,** — 2 to be warm, tepid; to be in love (*algo* with one); to be lukewarm (in love).

**tepēscō, puī,** — 3 **a)** to grow warm *or* tepid; **b)** to cool off.

**tepidus** 3 **a)** tepid, warm; **b)** cooling, cool; **c)** faint, languid.

**tepor, ōris** *m* **a)** lukewarmness, moderate heat; **b)** want of fire, languor.

**ter** *adv.* thrice, three times.

**ter-deciē(n)s** *adv.* thirteen times.

**terebinthus, ī** *f* turpentine-tree.

**terebrō** 1 to bore, pierce, perforate; to scrape out; to worm one's way in.

**terēdō, inis** *f* wood-worm.

**teres, etis** rounded off, polished; smooth; a) well-turned; b) finely shaped, graceful, refined, elegant.

**ter-geminus** 3, *see* **trigeminus**.

**tergeō, sī, sum** 2 to wipe off, dry, *or* clean; to tickle; to scrape, grate on; to polish.

**tergīnum, ī** *n* whip, leather scourge.

**tergiversātiō, ōnis** *f* evasion, subterfuge.

**tergiversor** 1 to make excuses, to practise evasion.

**tergō** 3 = **tergeo**.

**tergum, ī** *n* back, rear; a) ridge; b) surface; c) hide, leather; shield, bag, *or* other thing made of leather.

**tergus, oris** *n* = **tergum**.

**termentum, ī** *n* hurt, injury (?).

**termes, itis** *m* cut branch.

**Terminālia, ium** *and* **iōrum** *n/pl.* festival of the god Terminus.

**terminātiō, ōnis** *f* a fixing of limits; ending, clausula; sense of rhythm.

**terminō** 1 to bound, limit; a) to circumscribe, confine; b) to determine, define (*alqd re*); c) to end, terminate.

**terminus, ī** *m* boundary-mark, boundary-stone; a) boundary, limit; b) the god of boundaries; c) limit, end, term.

**ternī** 3 three each; threefold, triple.

**terō, trivī, trītum** 3 to rub; a) to rub off; to polish, burnish, to turn at a lathe; b) to rub away, wear away; c) to thrash out, to grind, pound; d) to consume, waste, wear out, overdo with labour; e) to use often, tread often, frequent; f) to spend, pass (*tempus*).

**terra, ae** *f* the earth; a) land; **terrā marique** by land and sea; ground, soil; b) land, country, region, district; *pl.* the world; **orbis terrārum** the earth, the world.

**terrāneola, ae** *f* crested lark.

**terrēnus** 3 a) of earth, earthen, earthy; *subst.* **terrēnum, ī** *n* earth, soil, ground; b) of the earth, terrestrial.

**terreō, uī, itum** 2 to frighten, terrify, alarm (*alqm; ne*) a) to chase with terror, frighten *or* scare away; b) to deter (*alqm a re; quominus*).

**terrestris, e** belonging to the earth, terrestrial, earthly, of the land.

**terreus** 3 of the earth.

**terrebilis, e** terrible, frightful, dreadful.

**terriculum, ī** *n* something that causes fright, bugbear, phantom.

**terri-ficō** 1 = **terreo**.

**terri-ficus** 3 = **terribilis**.

**terri-gena, ae** *m and f* earthborn.

**terri-loquus** 3 terror-speaking.

**territō** 1 to frighten, terrify, alarm greatly.

**territōrium, ī** *n* territory, district.

**terror, ōris** *m* terror, fright, fear, dread; object of fear, cause of alarm.

**terruncius, ī** *m* = **teruncius**.

**tersus** 3 wiped; clean, neat; elegant.

**tertia-decumānī, ōrum** *m/pl.* soldiers of the thirteenth legion.

**tertiānus** 3 recurring every other day; *subst.* ~, **ī** *m* soldier of the third legion.

**tertius** 3 the third; *adv.* **tertiō** *and* **-um** for the third time, thirdly.

**tertius-decimus** 3 the thirteenth.

**ter-uncius, ī** *m* (three ounces) a quarter of an *as* (= ¹/₄₀ of a *dēnārius*); **hērēs ex teruncio** heir to ¹/₄₀ of an estate; **nullus** ~ not a farthing.

**ter-venēficus, ī** *m* arch-poisoner, arch-villain.

**tesqua** (*or* **tesca**), **ōrum** *n/pl.* deserts, wastes.

**tessella, ae** *f* small stone cube.

**tessellātus** 3 set with small square stones, tessellated.

**tessera, ae** *f* a) cube of stone *or* wood, dice; b) tablet containing watchword *or* orders; c) token, tally (for identification).

**tesserārius, ī** *m* officer who carried the watchword from the general through the camp.

**tesserula, ae** *f* = **tessera**.

**testa, ae** *f* a) tile, brick; b) earthen vessel, pot, urn, lamp; c) potsherd; d) shell of shell-fish, shell-fish; e) covering.

**testāceus** 3 of tiles *or* brick.

**testāmentārius** 3 belonging to a testament *or* will; *subst.* ~, **ī** *m* forger of a will.

**testāmentum, ī** *n* testament, last will.

**testātiō, ōnis** *f* a calling to witness.

**testātor, ōris** *m* testator.
**testātus** 3 attested; notorious, manifest, evident.
**testiculus, ī** *m* testicle, virility.
**testificātiō, ōnis** *f* a bearing witness; proof, evidence.
**testi-ficor** 1 a) to call to witness; b) to bear witness, testify, attest; c) to show, prove, demonstrate, declare.
**testimōnium, ī** *n* a) testimony, evidence; b) proof.
**testis**[1]**, is** *m and f* witness; spectator.
**testis**[2]**, is** *m* (*mostly pl.* **testēs, ium**) testicle.
**testor** 1 a) = **testificor**; b) *intr.* to make a will *or* testament.
**testū** (*indecl.*), **testum, ī** *n* earthenware cover *or* covered pot (for cooking).
**testūdineus** 3 like a tortoise; made of tortoise-shell.
**testūdō, inis** *f* tortoise; a) shell of the tortoise; b) arched room, arch, vault; c) ⚔ shed, shelter; covering of shields; d) stringed instrument, lyre; e) comb; f) a hedgehog's spines.
**testula, ae** *f* potsherd used as a voting-tablet.
**tēter** 3 = **taeter**.
**tetrachmum, ī** *n* four-drachma piece.
**tetraō, ōnis** *m* grouse, heath-cock.
**tetrarchēs, ae** *m* tetrarch.
**tetrarchia, ae** *f* tetrarchy.
**tetrastichon, ī** *n* poem of four lines.
**tetricus** 3 gloomy, harsh, grim, morose, severe.
**texō, xuī, xtum** 3 a) to weave, plait; b) to frame, construct, fabricate, make, compose.
**textilis, e** woven; *subst.* **textile, is** *n* web, stuff, cloth.
**textor, ōris** *m*, **textrīx, icis** *f* weaver.
**textōrius** 3 woven; (*metaph.*) fine-spun, far-fetched.
**textrīnum, ī** *n* a weaver's shop; the art of weaving; ship-yard.
**textum, ī** *n* web, stuff, cloth; texture, construction.
**textūra, ae** *f* web, texture.
**textus, ūs** *m* web, texture; structure, connexion.
**thalamēgus, ī** *f* (barge) fitted with a cabin.
**thalamus, ī** *m* a) bedchamber;

b) women's apartment, bridal bed, marriage; c) dwelling, habitation, abode.
**thalassicus** 3 of the sea.
**thalassinus** 3 purple (?).
**thallus, ī** *m* green twig.
**theātrālis, e** theatrical.
**theātrum, ī** *n* theatre, playhouse; a) the spectators, audience; b) place of exhibition, stage, sphere for any action.
**thēca, ae** *f* case, envelope, sheath, covering.
**thema, atis** *n* horoscope.
**thensaurārius** 3 of treasure.
**thēnsaurus, ī** *m* = **thesaurus**.
**theo-logus, ī** *m* theologian.
**thermae, ārum** *f/pl.* warm springs; warm baths.
**thermo-pōlium** (*and* **thermi-**)**, ī** *n* shop where warm drinks are sold.
**thermo-pōtō** 1 to refresh with warm drinks.
**thermulae, ārum** *f/pl.* = **thermae**.
**thēsaurus, ī** *m* treasure, hoard, store; treasury, storehouse; repository, magazine.
**thiasus, ī** *m* Bacchic dance *or* troop of dancers.
**tholus, ī** *m* (round building with a) dome.
**thōrāx, ācis** *m* breastplate, cuirass.
**thronus, ī** *m* elevated seat, throne.
**thunnus, ī** *m* = **thynnus**.
**thūs, ūris** *n* = **tus**.
**thȳias, adis** *f* Bacchant.
**thyius** 3 (?) of citrus wood.
**thȳlacistae** *m/pl.* bag in hand, i.e. asking for money (?).
**thymbra, ae** *f* savory(*a kitchen herb*).
**thymum, ī** *n* thyme.
**thynnus, ī** *m* tunny(-fish).
**thyrsi-ger** 3 bearing the thyrsus.
**thyrsus, ī** *m* stalk, stem; staff of Bacchus twined with ivy and vine; goad, incitement.
**Ti.** *abbr.* = **Tiberius**.
**tiāra, ae** *f and* **tiārās, ae** *m* turban, tiara, diadem.
**tibia, ae** *f* shin-bone; flute, pipe.
**tibiāle, is** *n* legging.
**tibi-cen, inis** *m* a) piper, flute-player; b) pillar, prop.
**tibīcina, ae** *f* female fluteplayer.
**tibīcinium, ī** *n* a playing on the flute.
**tigillum, ī** *n* little beam of wood.

**tignārius** 3 relating to timber; **faber** ~ carpenter.

**tignum, ī** *n* beam, log of timber.

**tigris, idis** *or* **is** *m and f* tiger, tigress; tiger skin.

**tilia, ae** *f* linden- *or* lime-tree.

**time-facio** 3 to terrify.

**timeō, uī,** — 2 to fear, be afraid of, dread, apprehend, be anxious (*alqd, alqm, de re; alci* for one; *with ne; ne non, ut; inf.*).

**timidītās, ātis** *f* fearfulness, timidity.

**timidus** 3 full of fear, timid, faint-hearted, cowardly.

**timor, ōris** *m* fear, dread, apprehension (*alcis rei*), alarm; cause *or* object of fear, terror.

**tinctilis, e** used for dipping.

**tinea, ae** *f* larva, grub, worm.

**ting(u)ō, tinxī, tinctum** 3 to moisten, wet, imbue (*alqd re*); **a)** to dip in, plunge; **b)** to stain, dye.

**tinnīmentum, ī** *n* a tinkling.

**tinniō** 4 to ring, tinkle, jingle.

**tinnītus, ūs** *m* a ringing, tinkling, jingling; jingle of words.

**tinnulus** 3 ringing, tinkling.

**tintinnābulum, ī** *n* bell.

**tintinnāculus** 3 tinkling, jingling.

**tintinō** 1 to ring, jingle.

**tinus, ī** *f* laurustinus (?).

**tippula, ae** *f* water-spider; very light thing.

**tīrō, ōnis** *m* young soldier, recruit; beginner, novice, learner.

**tīrōcinium, ī** *n* first service of a soldier; **a)** young troops, recruits; **b)** inexperience; **c)** first trial *or* effort, first attempt.

**tīrunculus, ī** *m* young recruit, novice.

**tis** = **tui** (*gen.*).

**titillātiō, ōnis** *f* a tickling.

**titillō** 1 to tickle.

**tittibilicium, ī** *n* trifle.

**titubāns, tis** wavering, faltering.

(**titubantia, ae** *f*), **titubātiō, ōnis** *f* a staggering, wavering.

**titubō** 1 to totter, stagger, reel; **a)** to stammer, falter; **b)** to hesitate, be perplexed; **c)** to blunder.

**titulus, ī** *m* inscription, superscription; **a)** title of a book; **b)** bill, placard; **c)** title of honour, rank *or* dignity; **d)** pretext, pretence.

**toculliō, ōnis** *m* usurer.

**tōfinus** 3 of tufa.

**tōfus, ī** *m* tufa, volcanic stone.

**toga, ae** *f* the toga (*upper garment of a Roman citizen in time of peace*); **a)** garment of peace; peace; **b)** political life; **c)** prostitute.

**togātārius, ī** *m* actor in a national Roman play.

**togātulus, ī** *m* humble citizen, client.

**togātus** 3 wearing the toga, clothed in a toga; **a)** in Roman dress, national; *subst.* ~, **ī** *m* Roman citizen; **b)** in the garb of peace; **c) togāta, ae** *f* prostitute.

**togula, ae** *f* little toga.

**tolerābilis, e** bearable, tolerable, passable; enduring.

**tolerāns, tis** bearing, enduring, patient (*alcis rei*). [ing.]

**tolerantia, ae** *f* a bearing, endur-/

**tolerātiō, ōnis** *f* = tolerantia.

**tolerō** 1 a) to bear, endure, sustain; **b)** to maintain, support, nourish.

**tollēnō, ōnis** *m* see-saw, swingbeam.

**tollō, sustulī, sublātum** 3 **1.** to lift *or* take up, raise; **a) signa tollere** to take up the standards, break up camp; **ancoras** to weigh anchor; **puerum, puellam** to accept, acknowledge, bring up; **sortes** to draw lots; **b)** to raise, exalt, elevate, extol; **animum** to cheer, encourage, animate, excite, make proud; **clamōrem** to raise a cry; **2. a)** to take away, remove, take *or* carry off, make away with, kill, destroy, ruin; **b)** to annul, cancel, abolish.

**tolūtārius** 3 trotting.

**tolūtim** *adv.* at a trot.

**tomāc(u)lum, ī** sausage.

**tōmentum, ī** *n* a stuffing, filling (*of cushions, matresses*).

**tomus, ī** *m* piece cut off; piece of writing-material.

**tondeō, totondī, tōnsum** 2 to shear, clip, shave; **a)** to mow, cut; **b)** to reap, pluck off, crop, graze, browse upon.

**tonitrālis, e** thundering.

**tonitruālis, e** pertaining to thunder.

**tonitrus, ūs** *m and* **tonitruum, ī** *n* thunder.

**tonō, uī,** — 1 to thunder; **a)** to sound, resound, roar; **b)** to thunder out.

**tōnsa, ae** *f* oar.

**tōnsilis, e** clipped.

**tōnsillae, ārum** *f/pl.* tonsils.
**tōnsitō** 1 to shear regularly.
**tōnsor, ōris** *m* hair-cutter, barber.
**tōnsōrius** 3 pertaining to shearing *or* shaving, of a barber.
**tōnstrícula, ae** *f* hairdresser.
**tōnstrína, ae** *f* barber's shop.
**tōnstrix, ícis** *f* hairdresser.
**tōnsūra, ae** *f* a clipping, shearing, shaving.
**tōnsus, ūs** *m* style of hair-cutting.
**tŏphus, í** *m* = tofus.
**topiārius** 3 relating to landscape-gardening; *subst.* ~, í *m* landscape-gardener; **topiāria, ae** *f* landscape-gardening.
**topper** (*archaic adv.*) **a)** quickly; **b)** perhaps.
**toral, ālis** *n* couch-covering, sofa-cloth.
**torculum, í** *n* wine-press; oil-press.
**toreuma, atis** *n* embossed work, work in relief.
**tormentum, í** *n* windlass, pulley; **a)** engine for hurling, missile, shot; **b)** inducement, compulsion; **c)** torment, torture, rack, anguish, pain.
**tormina, um** *n/pl.* colic, gripes.
**torminōsus** 3 suffering from colic.
**tornō** 1 to turn in a lathe, to round off.
**tornus, í** *m* lathe; chisel.
**torōsus** 3 muscular, brawny.
**torpēdō, inis** *f* **a)** = torpor; **b)** torpedo fish, electric ray.
**torpeō, —, —** 2 to be stiff, inert, immovable; to be benumbed, stupefied, dull, languid.
**torpēscō, puí, —** 3 to become stiff, inert, dull.
**torpidus** 3 stiff, benumbed, torpid.
**torpor, ōris** *m* numbness, stiffness, torpor; languor, indolence, dulness.
**torquātus** 3 adorned with a necklace.
**torqueō, torsí, tortum** 2 to wind, twist, turn round; **a)** to curl (*hair*); **b)** to throw with force, hurl, fling, whirl; **c)** to twist awry, wrest, distort, sprain, to put to the rack, torture; **d)** to turn, wrench, pervert; **e)** to put to the test, examine; **f)** to plague, harass, distress.
**(torquēs** *and*) **torquis, is** *m* (*and f*) twisted neck-chain, necklace, collar; **a)** coupling-collar for oxen; **b)** wreath, garland.

**torrēns, tis a)** burning, hot, heated; rushing, boiling, roaring; **b)** *subst.* *m* mountain stream, torrent.
**torreō, torruí, tostum** 2 to dry, parch; **a)** to burn, roast, singe; **b)** to inflame, fire.
**torrēscō** 3 to be burnt.
**torridus** 3 dried up, parched, dry, arid; frost-bitten.
**torris, is** *m* firebrand, piece of dry wood.
**tortilis, e** twisted.
**tortō** 1 to torture.
**tortor, ōris** *m* torturer; one who whirls.
**tortuōsus** 3 full of turns and windings, tortuous; intricate, perplexed, involved.
**tortus¹, ūs** *m* a winding; whirling.
**tortus²** 3 crooked, twisted.
**torulus, í** *m* tuft of hair.
**torus, í** *m* a swelling, protuberance; **a)** muscle; **b)** pillow, cushion, couch, sofa, bed; **c)** bridal-bed, marriage, amour; **d)** bier; **e)** knot on a garland; **f)** bank, mound.
**torvitās, ātis** *f* sternness, fierceness.
**torvus** 3 stern, grim, fierce, wild, frightful.
**tōsillae, ārum** *f/pl.* = tonsillae.
**tot** (*indecl.*) so many.
**toti-dem** (*indecl.*) just so many.
**totiē(n)s** *adv.* so often, so many times.
**tōtus** (*gen.* -íus *and* -ĭus, *dat.* -í) 3 whole, entire, all; *subst.* **tōtum, í** *n* the whole, all.
**tŏtus** 3 tŏta pars as large a fraction.
**toxicum, í** *n* poison (*for arrows*).
**trabālis, e** relating to beams of wood, of beams; beam-like.
**trabea, ae** *f* robe of state, robe of kings; the equestrian order.
**trabeātus** 3 in a robe of state.
**trabs, abis** *f* beam of wood; **a)** (trunk of) a tree; **b)** ship; **c)** battering-ram; spear-shaft; club; table.
**tractābilis, e** that can be handled, manageable, tractable; pliant, yielding, gentle.
**tractātiō, ōnis** *f* a handling, feeling; **a)** management, treatment; **b)** a using, use, usage.
**tractātor, ōris** *m* masseur.
**tractātrix, ícis** *f* masseuse.
**tractātus, ūs** *m* = tractatio.
**tractim** *adv.* with a gentle stroke; gradually, continuously.

**tractō** 1 1. to drag along *or* about, to pull; 2. to touch, handle, stroke, take in hand; a) to manage, work, exercise, practise (*alqd*); b) to treat, use; c) to handle, examine; to discuss; to negotiate.

**tractum, ī** *n* flock of wool drawn out for spinning.

**tractus**[1] 3 a) derived; b) flowing (*speech*).

**tractus**[2], **ūs** *m* a drawing, dragging, draught; track, course; a) extent, district, tract; b) a protracting; delay; slow movement; c) drawling.

**trāditiō, ōnis** *f* a) a giving up, delivering up, surrender; b) narrative.

**trāditor, ōris** *m* traitor.

**trā-dō, didī, ditum** 3 to give up, hand over (*alci alqd*); **per manūs** from hand to hand; a) to deliver, commit, intrust; b) to surrender, deliver up, betray; c) **se tradere** to devote oneself to (*alci rei, in alqd*); d) to leave behind, bequeath; e) to hand down to posterity, record, relate, transmit, recount; f) to teach.

**trā-dūcō** 3 to bring, carry, lead over (*alqm in alqd, ad alqm*); to lead *or* conduct across (*trans flumen*), **exercitum flumen** to transport over a river; a) to transfer, promote, advance, to win over, draw over, convert; b) to lead by (*alqm praeter, per, in alqd*); c) to spend, pass; d) to expose to ridicule.

**trā-ductiō, ōnis** *f* a) a carrying over, transferring, removal; b) course *or* lapse of time; c) exposure to disgrace.

**trā-ductor, ōris** *m* transferrer (*ad plebem*).

**trā-dux, ucis** *m* vine-branch, vine-layer.

**tragi-cōmoedia, ae** *f* drama composed of tragedy & comedy.

**tragicus** 3 of tragedy, tragic; a) in tragic style, lofty, sublime, grand; b) horrible; *subst. m* tragic dramatist *or* actor.

**tragoedia, ae** *f* tragedy; a) tragic scene, great tumult, disturbance, spectacle; b) tragic pathos, lofty diction.

**tragoedus, ī** *m* tragic actor, tragedian.

**trāgula, ae** *f* javelin (*of the Gauls and Iberians*).

**tragus, ī** *m* a) a fish; b) body-odour.

**trahāx, ācis** acquisitive.

**trahea, ae** *f* drag, sledge (for threshing).

**trahō, traxī, tractum** 3 to draw (*alqm or alqd ad, in, per alqd*) 1. to drag, haul, trail, pull forth, drag away; to drag about; a) to dissipate, squander; b) to take into consideration, to consider, weigh; 2. to draw to oneself; a) to allure, attract, influence; b) to draw *or* bring on, induce, cause; c) to appropriate, ascribe, refer; d) to interpret, ex, plain, construe; 3. a) to drag away violently, carry off, plunder; b) to draw along, lead on, be followed by; c) to draw apart, distract (*a re*); d) to draw in, take in, quaff, inhale; to take on, assume, acquire, get (*alqd ex, a re; nomen ex* or *a facinore*); to take to oneself, appropriate; e) to draw out, draw from, to deduce, derive (*ex, a re*); f) to draw together, contract; 4. to draw out in length; a) to lengthen, protract, prolong, delay; b) to wear away, spend, pass.

**trā-iciō, iēcī, iectum** 3 1. to throw, cast, shoot over (*alqd ex loco in locum*); a) to bring *or* carry across *or* over; to transfer; **copias flumen** to transport across; b) *intr. or* **se trāicere** *or* **P.** to cross, pass over; 2. to pass through, go over (*fluvium, mare*); 3. to thrust through, shoot through, transfix, pierce (*alqd re, alci alqd*).

**trā-iectiō, ōnis** *f* transposition; passage; **stellae** shooting-star; exaggeration.

**trā-iectus, ūs** *m* = **traiectio.**

**trā-l...,** *see* **trans-l...**

**trā-lātus** 3, *see* **transfero.**

**trā-loquor** 3 to relate.

**trā-m...,** *see* **trans-m...**

**trāma, ae** *f* warp-thread, when raised by the *licium*; bit of thread, trifle.

**trāmes, itis** *m* by-way, by-path; way, path, road, course.

**trā-natō** *and* **trā-nō** 1 to swim over, across, through; to fly through; to pass through; penetrate, permeate.

**tranquillitās, ātis** *f* quietness, stillness; a) calmness of the sea, still weather; b) rest, peace; c) mental calmness.

**tranquillō** 1 to calm, still, allay.

**tranquillus** 3 quiet, calm, still; *subst.* **tranquillum, ī** *n* = **tranquillitas.**

**trāns** *prep.* with *acc.* a) across, over; b) beyond, to *or* on the other side.
**trāns-abeō** 3 to pass by; to pierce.
**trāns-āctor, ōris** *m* manager.
**trāns-adigō** 3 to thrust, drive *or* pierce through.
**trāns-alpīnus** 3 beyond the Alps, Transalpine.
**trāns-bitō** 3 to go *or* come across.
**trānscendō, ndī, ēnsum** 3 to climb *or* pass over, cross, overstep, surmount; *trans.* to overstep, transcend; to transgress, violate.
**trāns-cīdō, cīdī, cīsum** 3 to cut through.
**trānscrībō** 3 a) to transcribe, copy; b) to transfer in writing; to make over, assign, give over (*alqd in alqm*); to transfer (*alci alqd*), remove.
**trāns-currō, (cu)currī, cursum** 3 a) to run over *or* across; to pass over (*ad alqd*); b) to run *or* hasten through, traverse; to sail *or* travel past.
**trāns-cursus, ūs** *m* a running past *or* through.
**trāns-dō** 3, **trāns-dūcō** 3, *see* trado, traduco.
**trānsenna, ae** *f* fowler's net, snare; grille, lattice.
**trāns-eō** 1. to go *or* pass over; a) to go over to the enemy, desert; b) to be transformed *or* turned; c) to pass over (*in reading or writing*) (*ad alqd*); d) to pass by, elapse; e) to pass, go, sail through; 2. to go through, pervade, penetrate (*alqd*); a) to pass beyond, transgress, violate; b) to outstrip, surpass; c) to go through briefly (*in speaking*); to touch lightly on (*in speaking*); to go *or* pass by; to omit, leave unnoticed.
**trānserō, — ertum** 3 (*compound of* sero) to graft.
**trāns-ferō** 3 1. to carry, bring, convey over *or* across (*alqd ad alqm, in alqd*); a) to transfer, transport; to transform; b) to copy, transcribe; to translate; c) to turn, direct, apply to (*alqd in alqd, ad alqm*); to use figuratively; d) to put off, defer, delay; 2. to carry along *or* in procession.
**trāns-figō** 3 to pierce *or* thrust through, transfix.
**trāns-figūrō** 1 to transform.
**trāns-fodiō** 3 = transfigo.
**trāns-fōrmis, e** transformed.

**trāns-fōrmō** 1 to transform.
**trāns-forō** 1 to pierce.
**trāns-fretō** 1 to cross the sea.
**trāns-fuga, ae** *m* deserter.
**trāns-fugiō, fūgī, — 3** to flee over, desert.
**trāns-fugium, ī** *n* desertion.
**trāns-fūmō** 1 to penetrate like smoke.
**trāns-fundō** 3 to pour from one vessel into another; to transfer (*alqd ad or in alqm*). [gling.]
**trāns-fūsiō, ōnis** *f* an intermin-
**trāns-gredior, gressus sum** 3 a) to step *or* pass over *or* across; to proceed, go over to; b) to go beyond, surpass (*alqd*).
**trāns-gressiō, ōnis** *f* a going over, passage; transposition.
**trāns-gressus, ūs** *m* crossing.
**trāns-iectiō, -iectus,** *see* **trā- i...**
**trāns-igō, ēgī, āctum** 3 to drive through; a) to thrust *or* run through, pierce, transfix; b) to carry through, bring to an end, perform, finish, accomplish, transact; to settle a difference, adjust, agree; c) to pass, spend (*time*).
**trāns-iciō** 3, *see* **tra-icio.**
**trānsiliō, siluī** (*and* **silīvī** *or* **siliī**), — 4 a) to leap *or* spring over, leap across; b) to spring over something (*alqd*); to exceed, transgress, go beyond; to pass by, neglect.
**trāns-itiō, ōnis** *f* a passing over, passage; desertion; infection.
**trānsitō** 1 to pass through (?).
**trānsitōrius** 3 provided with a passage.
**trāns-itus, ūs** *m* a) a passing over, passage; b) desertion; c) gradual transition of shaded colours; d) a passing through; place to pass through, ford, pass; e) a passing by; change, transition.
**trāns-lāticius** 3 traditional, customary, usual, common.
**trāns-lātiō, ōnis** *f* a transferring; transporting; a) metaphor, trope, b) a shifting, diversion, exchange.
**trānslātīvus** 3 that may be transferred.
**trāns-lātor, ōris** *m* transferrer.
**trāns-lātus, ūs** *m* a carrying past, procession.
**trāns-legō** 3 to read through.
**trāns-lûceō** 2 to shine *or* glimmer through; to be reflected.

**trāns-marīnus** 3 beyond sea, trans-marine.

**trāns-meō** 1 to go over or across.

**trāns-migrō** 1 to migrate.

**trāns-mineō** 2 to pierce right through.

**trāns-missiō, ōnis** f and **-missus, ūs** m a passing over, passage.

**trāns-mittō** 3 to send over or across; **a)** to convey across, transmit, transfer; **b)** to let pass; **c)** to give over, entrust; resign, yield (alci alqd); **d)** to go, travel, pass over (alqd); to leave unnoticed, neglect; to pass (time); to endure.

**trāns-montānus** 3 beyond the mountains.

**trāns-moveō** 2 to remove, transfer.     [transpose.

**trāns-mūtō** 1 to change, shift,

**trāns-natō, trāns-nō** 1, see **tra-nato**.     [name of.

**trāns-nōminō** 1 to change the

**trāns-padānus** 3 beyond the Po.

**trānspectus, ūs** m seeing through.

**trānspiciō** 3 to see through.

**trāns-pōnō** 3 to remove, transfer (alqd in locum).

**trāns-portātiō, ōnis** f removal.

**trāns-portō** 1 to carry, convey or bring over, transport (copias flumen).

**trāns-rhēnānus** 3 beyond the Rhine.

**trāns-scendō, -scrībō, -siliō,** see **tran-...**

**trāns-tiberīnus** 3 beyond the Tiber.

**trāns-tineō** 2 to pass through.

**trānstrum, ī** n **a)** cross-beam; **b)** bench for rowers.

**trānsultō** 1 to leap over or across.

**trānsūmō** 3 to take up, assume.

**trānsuō** 3 to stitch through, pierce.

**trāns-vectiō, ōnis** f a carrying over or across; riding past.

**trāns-vehō** 3 **a)** to carry or convey over or to the other side, to transport; **b)** to carry by or along; **P.** to travel or sail over, go or pass by, pass away.

**trāns-verberō** 1 to strike through, pierce, wound.

**trāns-versārius** 3 lying across.

**trāns-versus** 3 lying across, transverse, athwart, crosswise; astray, in a wrong direction; subst. **trānsversum, ī** n cross direction or situation, **ex** or **de -ō** transversely; unexpectedly.

**trāns-volitō** 1 to fly through.

**trāns-volō** 1 **a)** to fly over, across, beyond; **b)** to fly past or by (alqd).

**trāns-vorsus** 3 (archaic) = **transversus**.

**trapētus, ī** m oil-press.    [banker.

**trapezīta, ae** m money-changer,

**trapezo-phorum, ī** n foot of a table.

**trāsenna** = **trānsenna**.

**traulizī** (τραυλίζει) she lisps.

**trā-v...,** see **trans-v...**

**tre-cēnī** 3 three hundred each.

**tre-centēsimus** 3 three hundredth.

**tre-centī** 3 three hundred.

**trecentiē(n)s** adv. three hundred times.

**trechedīpnum, ī** n light garment worn when hastening to a dinner-party.

**tre-decim** (indecl.) thirteen.

**tremebundus** 3 trembling, shaking.     [or quake.

**treme-faciō** 3 to cause to tremble

**tremendus** 3 terrible, frightful.

**tremēscō** and **-īscō, —, —** 3 to tremble, quake for fear (at).

**tremibundus** 3 = **tremebundus**.

**tremō, uī, —** 3 to tremble (at), quake, quiver.

**tremor, ōris** m a trembling, quaking; earthquake; terror.

**tremulus** 3 trembling, quaking, quivering, tremulous.

**trepidanter** adv. in agitation.

**trepidātiō, ōnis** f confused hurry, agitation, anxiety, alarm.

**trepidō** 1 to hurry with alarm, hasten about, be agitated, be in alarm, in confusion; **a)** to be busy; **b)** to tremble at; **c)** to waver, hesitate.

**trepidus** 3 agitated, alarmed, restless, disturbed, anxious; **a)** boiling, bubbling (of things); **b)** perilous, critical, alarming; **in re trepida, in rebus trepidis** at a critical juncture.

**trēs, tria, ium** three; a few.

**tressis, is** m three asses.

**trēs-virī, triumvir(ōr)um** m/pl. board of three men.

**tri-angulum, ī** n triangle.

**tri-angulus** 3 triangular.

**triāriī, ōrum** m/pl. soldiers of the third rank in battle-order, the reserve.

**tribas, adis** f woman who practises homosexualism.

**tribolus, ī** m = **tribulus**.

**tribuārius** 3 relating to a tribe.

**tribūlis, is** *m* fellow tribesman; (at Athens) member of the same deme; proletarian.

**tribulum, ī** *n* threshing-sledge.

**tribulus, ī** *m* a kind of thistle.

**tribūnal, ālis** *n* raised platform for magistrates, judgment seat, tribunal; monumental mound.

**tribūnātus, ūs** *m* office of a tribune, tribuneship.

**tribūnicius** 3 of a tribune, tribunicial; *subst.* ⁓, ī *m* one that has been a tribune.

**tribūnus, ī** *m* tribune, the title of various Roman magistrates and officers, *esp.* a) tribune of the people; b) military tribune.

**tribuō, uī, ūtum** 3 a) to divide (*alqd in partes*); b) to distribute, assign, bestow, confer (*alci alqd*); to give, present, impart; c) to concede, grant, yield, allow; d) to ascribe, attribute, impute; e) to bestow, spend, devote.

**tribus, ūs** *f* tribe; third part of the Roman people; a) local division of the people, district (*31 rusticae* and *4 urbanae*); b) votes of a tribe.

**tribūtārius** 3 subject to tribute; -ae tabellae a note promising payment of money.

**tribūtim** *adv.* by tribes.

**tribūtiō, ōnis** *f* distribution.

**tribūtum, ī** *n* (*and* -us, ī *m*) tribute, tax, contribution.

**tribūtus** 3 arranged in tribes.

**trīcae, ārum** *f/pl.* nonsense; tricks.

**tricēnī** 3 thirty each.

**tri-ceps, cipitis** three-headed.

**tricēsimus** (*or* -cēns-) 3 thirtieth.

**trichila, ae** *f* arbour, bower.

**trichōrum, ī** *n* room divided into three parts.

**trīciē(n)s** *adv.* thirty times.

**tri-clīnium, ī** *n* a) table-couch, table-sofa; b) dining-room.

**tricor** 1 to make difficulties, to shuffle, play tricks.

**tri-corpor, oris** having three bodies.

**tri-cuspis, idis** three-pointed.

**tri-dēns, entis** three-pronged; *subst.* *m* trident.

**tridenti-fer** 3 *and* -ger 3 trident-bearing.

**tridenti-potēns, ntis** ruling with the trident.

**trī-duum, ī** *n* space of three days.

**triennia, ium** *n/pl.* triennial festival.

**tri-ennium, ī** *n* space of three years.

**triēns, tis** *m* third part (esp. of an *as* or a *sextarius*).

**trientābulum, ī** *n* equivalent in land for the third part of a debt.

**triēr-archus, ī** *m* commander of a trireme.

**triēris, is** (**nāvis**) *f* trireme, ship propelled by groups of three oars.

**trietēricus** 3 happening every third year.

**trietēris, idis** *f* a) space of three years; b) triennial festival.

**trifāriam** *adv.* in three places, on three sides.

**tri-faux, cis** having three throats.

**tri-fidus** 3 split into three parts, three-forked.

**tri-filis, e** with three hairs.

**tri-fōrmis, e** having three shapes.

**tri-fūr, is** *m* arch-thief.

**tri-furcifer, erī** *m* arch-villain.

**tri-geminus** 3 a) threefold; **fratres trigemini** three brothers born together; b) triform.

**trigēsimus** 3 = **tricesimus**.

**trigintā** (*indecl.*) thirty.

**trigōn, ōnis** *m* playing-ball.

**tri-libris, e** weighing three pounds.

**tri-linguis, e** three-tongued.

**tri-līx, īcis** woven with three threads.

**tri-mē(n)stris, e** of three months old.

**tri-metrus** (*and* -os) 3 of three measures; *subst.* ⁓, ī *m* trimeter.

**tri-modium, ī** *n* vessel containing three modii.

**trīmulus** 3 = **trimus**.

**trīmus** 3 three years old.

**trīnī** 3 a) three each; b) triple, threefold.

**tri-noctiālis, e** of three nights.

**tri-nōdis, e** having three knots.

**trīnum nūndinum** *n*, *see* **nundinum**.

**triō, ōnis** *m* threshing ox; *pl.* the constellations of the two Bears.

**triōbolus, ī** *m* coin worth three obols (= half-drachma).

**tri-parcus** 3 very niggardly.

**tri-partītus** 3 divided into three parts, threefold; *adv.* **tripartītō** in three parts.

**tri-pectorus** 3 triple-breasted.

**tri-pedālis, e** three feet long.

**tri-pertītus** 3 = **tripartitus**.

**tri-pēs, pedis** three-footed.

**tri-plex, icis** threefold, triple; a) *subst.* **triplex** *n* threefold portion; b) *subst.* **triplicēs** *m/pl.* writing-tablet with three leaves.

**triplus** 3 threefold, triple.

**tripudiō** 1 to beat the ground with the feet; to dance.

**tri-pudium, ī** *n* a) a dancing in three measures; solemn dance; b) **tripudium sollistimum** favourable omen in augury.

**tripūs, odis** *m* three-footed vessel *or* seat, tripod; (the Delphic) oracle.

**tri-quetrus** 3 triangular; Sicilian.

**tri-rēmis, e** propelled by groups of three oars; *subst. f* trireme.

**trīs** *acc.* = **tres.**

**tri-scurria, orum** *n/pl.* gross buffooneries.

**trīsticulus** 3 somewhat sorrowful, rather sad.                           [ing.]

**trīsti-ficus** 3 making sad, sadden-]

**trīstimōnia, ae** *f* sadness.

**tristis, e** a) sad, sorrowful, mournful, melancholy; b) bringing sorrow, saddening, doleful, dismal; c) gloomy, sullen, morose, severe, stern, harsh; d) distasteful, disagreeable.

**trīstitia, ae** (*and* **-tiēs, ēi**) *f* a) sadness, sorrow, melancholy; grief; b) moroseness, sternness, severity, harshness.

**tri-sulcus** 3 with three furrows, threefold, three-pronged.

**trit-avus, ī** *m* the father of an *atavus*, ancestor.

**trīticeus** (*and* **-cēius**) 3 of wheat, wheaten.

**trīticum, ī** *n* wheat.

**trītor, ōris** *m* one who rubs.

**trītūra, ae** *f* a threshing.

**trītus**[1] 3 rubbed; a) trodden, beaten, worn, frequented; b) much used, usual, commonplace; c) practised, expert.

**trītus**[2], **ūs** *m* a rubbing.

**triumphālis, e** of a triumph, triumphal; having had a triumph; **-ālia, -ium** *n/pl.* triumphal insignia.

**triumphō** 1 to celebrate a triumph, to triumph over (*ex* or *de alqo*); a) to exult, rejoice; b) to conquer completely (*alqm*); to obtain as booty.

**triumphus, ī** *m* triumph, triumphal procession; **triumphum agere ex** *or* **de alqo** to celebrate a triumph over; victory.

**trium-vir, ī** *m* triumvir, one of three associates in office, member of a board of three; *pl.* three joint commissioners.

**triumvirālis, e** of the triumvirs, triumviral.

**triumvirātus, ūs** *m* triumvirate, office of a triumvir.

**tri-venēfica, ae** *f* a thorough witch.

**tri-viālis, e** ordinary, commonplace.

**trivium, ī** *n* place where three roads meet, street-corner.

**tri-vius** 3 of the cross-roads; **Trivia, ae** *f* Diana *or* Hecate.

**trochaeus, ī** *m* trochee (*metrical foot consisting of one long and one short syllable*).

**trochus, ī** *m* boy's hoop.

**troclea, ae** *f* pulley.

**Trōg(l)o-dytae, ārum** *m/pl.* cave-dwellers.

**tropa** *adv.* at a game played with dice.

**tropaeum, ī** *n* trophy, memorial of victory; a) victory; b) monument, sign.                                   [wine.]

**tropis** (*acc.* **-in**) the sediment of]

**trucīdātiō, ōnis** *f* a slaughtering, massacre.

**trucīdō** 1 to cut down, slaughter, massacre, to ruin cruelly; to extinguish (*fire*).

**truculentia, ae** *f* fierceness, roughness, inclemency.

**truculentus** 3 grim, rough, harsh; savage, fierce, cruel.

**trudis, is** *f* pole, pike.

**trūdō, sī, sum** 3 to thrust, push, press on, drive forward; to put forth (*buds*); to force, impel (*alqm ad* or in *alqd*).

**trulla, ae** *f* a) ladle; b) fire-pan.

**truncō** 1 to cut off, maim, mutilate.

**truncus**[1], **ī** *m* a) trunk, stem of a tree; b) trunk of a body; side of meat; c) blockhead.

**truncus**[2] 3 maimed, mutilated, mangled, cut short; imperfect.

**trūsō** 1 to push violently.

**trutina, ae** *f* balance, pair of scales.

**trutinor** 1 to weigh.

**trux, ucis** fierce, ferocious, grim rough, savage, wild, furious.

**tryblium, ī** *n* dish.

**trȳgōnus, ī** *m* sting-ray.

**tū** thou, you.

**tuātim** *adv.* in your manner.

**tuba, ae** *f* trumpet.

**tūber, eris** *n* swelling, bump, hump, tumour; truffle (?).

**tubi-cen, inis** *m* trumpeter.

**tubi-lūstrium, ī** *n* festival for the purification of trumpets.

**tubula, ae** *f dimin. of* tuba.

**tubulātus** 3 provided with tubes.

**tubur, uris** *or* **eris** *m* a tree-fruit.

**tuburcinor** 1 to devour greedily.

**tubus, ī** *m* pipe.

**tuccētum, ī** *n* spiced meat-roll.

**tuditāns, antis** striking, beating.

**tueor** (*and* **tueō**), **tuitus sum** 2 to look at, view, behold, gaze upon (*alqd*); **a)** to care for, watch over, protect, defend; **b)** to maintain, uphold, preserve, keep up; **c)** to keep in mind; **d)** to keep in repair; **e)** to support, maintain, feed.

**tugurium, ī** *n* hut, cottage.

**tuitiō, ōnis** *f* protection.

**tum** *adv.* **a)** then, at that time; **b)** thereupon; then, afterwards; **c)** in the next place, next (*primum ... deinde ... tum ... postremo*); **d)** **tum ... tum** now ... now, as well ... as; **e)** **cum ... tum** in general .. and in particular, both ... and.

**tume-faciō** 3 to cause to swell; to puff up.

**tumeō, —, —** 2 to be swollen, blown *or* puffed up; **a)** to be puffed up with pride; **b)** to swell with anger, be excited; **c)** to be bombastic.

**tumēscō, muī, —** 3 to begin to swell; to swell with anger *or* pride; to begin to break out.

**tumidus** 3 swelling, swollen; **a)** puffed up, inflated, proud; **b)** pompous, bombastic; **c)** ambitious, arrogant, ready to break out; **d)** causing to swell.

**tumor, ōris** *m* a swelling, tumour; **a)** elevation; **b)** commotion, excitement, anger, wrath; **c)** pride, arrogance.

**tumulō** 1 to bury, inter.

**tumulōsus** 3 hilly.

**tumultuārius** 3 done *or* made in haste, confused, disorderly; brought together hastily, levied suddenly.

**tumultuātiō, ōnis** *f* confusion, bustle, tumult.

**tumultuor** (*and* **-ō**) 1 to be in confusion, in an uproar, to revolt; **tumultuātur** there is disorder.

**tumultuōsus** 3 confused, noisy, tumultuous; causing disturbance.

**tumultus, ūs** *m* noise, uproar, bustle, tumult, confusion; **a)** sedition, insurrection, revolt, mutiny; **b)** alarm, approaching war, civil war; **c)** disturbance, storm.

**tumulus, ī** *m* mound of earth, hill; sepulchral mound, grave.

**tunc** *adv.* **a)** then, at that time; **b)** thereupon, afterwards.

**tundō, tutudī, tū(n)sum** 3 to beat, strike; **a)** to thresh; **b)** to pound, bruise; **c)** to importune.

**tunica, ae** *f* under garment, shirt; coating, skin, peel.

**tunicātus** 3 clothed in a tunic; covered with skin.

**tunicula, ae** *f* little tunic.

**tuor** 3 = tueor.

**turba, ae** *f* tumult, noise, disturbance, confusion; **a)** crowd, throng, press, swarm; **b)** great number, multitude, band, mob.

**turbāmentum, ī** *n* means of disturbance.

**turbātiō, ōnis** *f* confusion, disorder, disturbance.

**turbātor, ōris** *m* disturber, stirrer-up.

**turbātrīx, īcis** *f* disturbing.

**turbātus** 3 troubled, disturbed, angered; confused, disorderly.

**turbellae, ārum** *f/pl.* disturbance, row.

**turben, inis** *m* (*and n?*) top.

**turbidus** 3 confused, disturbed, stormy; muddy, turbid; dishevelled; **a)** impetuous, excited, enraged; **b)** troubled, surprised, astonished, perplexed; **c)** mutinous, turbulent.

**turbineus** 3 cone-shaped.

**turbō[1], inis** *m* whirling *or* spinning motion, revolution; **a)** whirlwind, storm; **b)** eddy; whirl; coil; **c)** spinning-top; wheel; reel; whorl; spindle.

**turbō[2]** 1 to throw into disorder *or* confusion, to disturb, disorder, trouble; **a)** to agitate, make turbid; **b)** to stir up, derange, put to the rout; **c)** to amaze, confound, trouble.

**turbulentus** 3 (*adv.* -tē *and* -ter) restless, full of commotion, stormy; turbid; **a)** disturbed, confused; **b)** causing disturbance, seditious.

**turdus, ī** *m (and* **turda, ae** *f)* thrush.

**tūreus 3** of frankincense.

**turgeō, (rsī),** — 2 to be swollen; to be turgid *or* bombastic.

**turgēscō, —,** — 3 to begin to swell; to swell with passion.

**turgidulus 3,** *dim. of* **turgidus.**

**turgidus 3** swollen, inflated; bombastic.

**tūribulum, ī** *n* censer, incensepan.

**tūri-cremus 3** incense-burning.

**tūri-fer 3** incense-bearing.

**tūri-legus 3** incense-gathering.

**turma, ae** *f* division of cavalry; squadron, troop, band, body.

**turmālis, e** of the same squadron; equestrian.

**turmātim** *adv.* by squadrons.

**turpiculus 3** ugly; shameful.

**turpi-ficātus 3** made foul, corrupted.

**turpi-lucri-cupidus 3** greedy of dishonest gain.

**turpis, e** ugly, deformed; a) filthy, foul, nasty; b) disgraceful, shameful; infamous, base, indecent, obscene, scandalous.

**turpitūdō, inis** *f* ugliness, deformity; a) baseness; b) disgrace, dishonour, infamy.

**turpō 1** to make ugly, to deform, pollute, defile.

**turrĭcula, ae** *f* dice-box shaped like a tower.

**turri-ger 3** tower-bearing, turreted.

**turris, is** *f* tower; a) castle, palace; b) siege-tower; c) dovecote; d) howdah.

**turrītus 3** a) furnished *or* fortified with towers; b) adorned with a tower-crown; c) towering, lofty.

**turtur, uris** *m* turtle-dove.

**turturilla, ae** *f* (little turtle-dove); weakling.

**tūs, tūris** *n* incense, frankincense.

**tūsculum, ī** *n* a bit of incense.

**tussĭcula, ae** *f* fit of coughing.

**tussiō 4** to cough.

**tussis, is** *f* cough.

**tūtāmen, inis** *n and* **tūtāmentum, ī** *n* means of protection.

**tū-te** *(emphatic)* = **tu.**

**tūtē,** *adv. of* **tutus.**

**tūtēla, ae** *f* care, charge, protection, defence, patronage; a) wardship, guardianship; b) thing protected, charge; c) guardian, tutor, protector; ward; d) property of a) **tuticus,** *see* **medix.** [ward.f

**tūtō,** *adv.* **tutus.**

**tūtor[1], ōris** *m* protector, defender; guardian, tutor.

**tūtor[2]** *(and* **tūtō)** 1 to guard, protect, defend *(alqd a re; contra, adversus, ad alqm)*; a) to keep, keep safe, preserve, watch; b) to ward off, avert *(alqd).*

**tūtus 3** *(adv.* **tūtō** *and* **tūtē)** a) safe, secure, protected, guarded *(a re; adversus* or *ad alqd); subst.* **tūtum, ī** *n* safety, security, safe place, shelter; b) watchful, cautious, prudent; c) protecting.

**tuus 3** thy, thine, your, yours; *subst.* **tuī** *m/pl.* your friends, people, *or* party; **tua** *n/pl.* your property.

**tuxtax** (imitation of the sound of blows).

**tympanizō 1** to beat the tambourine.

**tympano-triba, ae** *m* one who plays on a tambourine; weakling.

**ty(m)panum, ī** *n* a) drum, tambourine; b) wheel without spokes, drum.

**typus, ī** *m* figure, image.

**tyranni-cīda, ae** *m* tyrant-slayer.

**tyrannicus 3** of a tyrant, tyrannical, despotic.

**tyrannis, idis** *f* tyranny, arbitrary *or* despotic power.

**tyranno-ctonus, ī** *m* tyrant-killer, regicide.

**tyrannus, ī** *m* monarch, absolute ruler, king, prince; tyrant, arbitrary ruler, despot.

**tyrianthina, ōrum** *n/pl.* purpleviolet robes.

**tyro-tarĭchum, ī** *n* ragout of cheese and salt-fish.

# U

**über¹, eris** *n* teat, udder, breast; **a)** fruitfulness, fertility, richness; **b)** fruitful field.

**über², eris** fertile, fruitful, productive (*with abl.*); rich, abounding, plentiful, copious.

**übertās, ātis** *f* fruitfulness, fertility; copiousness, fulness, plenty, richness.

**übertim** *adv.* copiously.

**übertō** 1 to make fruitful.

**ubi** (*and* **ubī**) **1.** *interr. adv.* where?; **2.** *rel. cj.* a) where; b) when, as soon as; c) whenever, as often as; **ubi-ubi** wherever.

**ubi-cumque** (*or* **-cunque**) **a)** wherever, wheresoever; **b)** anywhere, everywhere.

**ubi-libet** *adv.* anywhere.

**ubi-nam** *interr.* where?

**ubi-quāque** *adv.* anywhere; whenever(?).

**ubi-que** *adv.* everywhere, anywhere.

**ubi-quomque** = ubicumque.

**ubi-vīs** *adv.* where you will, everywhere.

**ūdō, ōnis** *m* shoe of felt *or* skin.

**ūdus** 3 moist, wet; sappy; drunk.

**ulcerātiō, ōnis** *f* sore, ulcer.

**ulcerō** 1 to cause to ulcerate, to make sore; to wound.

**ulcerōsus** 3 full of sores; wounded.

**ulcīscor, ultus sum** 3 to avenge (*acc.*); to avenge oneself; to take vengeance on, to punish, requite (*acc.*).

**ulcus, eris** *n* ulcer, sore; painful spot, sore place; *dimin.* **ulculum, ī** *n.*

**ūlīgō, inis** *f* moisture of the soil, dampness.

**ūllus** 3 any, any one.

**ulmeus** 3 of elm.

**ulmi-triba, ae** *m* elm-rubber, flogged slave.

**ulmus, ī** *f* elm, elm-tree.

**ulna, ae** *f* a) elbow; arm; b) ell.

**ulpicum, ī** *n* garlick.

(**ulter, tra, trum**) (*not used*); **1.** *comp.*

**ulterior, ius** farther, on the further side; a) at a greater distance, more remote *or* distant; b) beyond, farther on, farther; **2.** *superl.*

**ultimus** 3 farthest; a) most distant, most remote, last, extreme; b) earliest, oldest, first; last, latest, final; c) utmost, greatest, highest, worst; d) lowest, meanest.

**ultiō, ōnis** *f* an avenging, revenge.

**ultor, ōris** *m* avenger, punisher.

**ultrā 1.** *adv.* farther on; a) beyond; b) further, moreover, besides, longer (*comp.* **ulterius**); **2.** *prep.* with *acc.* a) on the farther side of, beyond, past, over, across; b) more than, above.

**ultrīx, īcis** *f* avenging.

**ultrō** *adv.* **1.** a) to the farther side; beyond, on the other side; **ultrō et citrō** up and down, to and fro; b) even, moreover, actually; **2.** of one's own accord, of oneself, voluntarily, spontaneously.

**ulula, ae** *f* screech-owl.

**ululātus, ūs** *m* a howling, shrieking, wailing.

**ululō** 1 to howl, shriek, yell, wail; to call upon with howling (*acc.*); to ring with cries.

**ulva, ae** *f* sedge.

**umbella, ae** *f* sunshade.

**umbilicus, ī** *m* navel; a) middle, centre; b) (end of a) stick on which a manuscript was rolled; c) a shellfish.

**umbō, ōnis** *m* knob, boss of a shield; shield; elbow; fullness (of a garment).

**umbra, ae** *f* shade, shadow; **1.** darkness; a) shadow in painting; b) shaded place; c) uninvited guest; **2.** shade, departed spirit, ghost; *pl.* the infernal regions, lower world; **3.** a) shelter, cover, protection; b) rest, leisure, retired *or* private life; c) shadow, phantom, semblance, show, pretext; d) a fish.

**umbrāculum, ī** *n* a) shady place; bower, arbour; school-room; b) parasol.

**umbrāticulus** = umbrāticus.

**umbrāticus** 3 (living, spent, *or* done) in the shade.

**umbrātilis, e** in the shade; **a)** private, retired, contemplative; **b)** scholastic, of the rhetorical schools.

**umbri-fer** 3 shady; shade-bearing.

**umbrō** 1 to shade, overshadow, cover.

**umbrōsus** 3 shady, giving shade.

**ūmectō** 1 to moisten, wet.

**ūmectus** 3 moist.

**ūmeō, —, —** 2 to be moist, wet, damp.

**umerus, ī** *m* shoulder, upper arm.

**ūmēscō** 3 to become moist.

**ūmiditās, ātis** *f* dampness.

**ūmid(ul)us** 3 moist, wet.

**ūmi-fer** 3 moist.

**ūmor, ōris** *m* moisture, liquid, fluid, dew, rain, tears, ocean.

**umquam** *adv.* ever, at any time; **nec umquam** and never.

**ūna** *adv., see* unus.

**ūn-animāns, tis** = unanimus.

**ūnanimitās, ātis** *f* unanimity, concord.

**ūn-animus** 3 of one mind, unanimous, concordant.

**uncia, ae** *f* twelfth part of a whole; ounce.

**unciārius** 3 containing a twelfth.

**unciātim** *adv.* by ounces.

**uncīnātus** 3 furnished with hooks, barbed.

**unciola, ae** *f* a paltry twelfth.

**unctiō, ōnis** *f* a besmearing, anointing.

**unctitō** 1 to anoint frequently.

**unctiusculus** 3 a little more oily.

**unctor, ōris** *m* anointer.

**unctōrium, ī** *n* anointing-room.

**unctūra, ae** *f* an anointing (*of the dead*).

**unctus** 3 **a)** anointed; **b)** oiled, greasy; **c)** rich; **d)** luxurious, sumptuous, voluptuous.

**uncus¹, ī** *m* hook, barb.

**uncus²** 3 hooked, crooked, curved.

**unda, ae** *f* wave; **a)** stream, water, fluid; **b)** moving air *or* smoke; **c)** agitation, surge; throng.

**unde** (*interr.* and *rel.*) from which place, whence; from whom; **unde unde** from somewhere or other.

**ūn-deciē(n)s** *adv.* eleven times.

**ūn-decim** (*indecl.*) eleven.

**ūn-decimus** 3 the eleventh.

**unde-cumque** from whatever point.

**ūn-dēnī** 3 eleven each.

**ūn-dē-vīcēsimānī, ōrum** *m/pl.* soldiers of the nineteenth legion.

**ūn-dē-vīcēsimus** 3 the nineteenth.

**ūn-dē-vīgintī** (*indecl.*) nineteen.

**undique** *adv.* from all parts *or* sides; on all sides, everywhere; in all respects.

**undi-sonus** 3 wave-sounding.

**undi-vagus** 3 wandering on waves.

**undō** 1 to rise in waves, to surge, swell; to wave, undulate; to overflow with (*alqo*); *trans.* to inundate.

**undōsus** 3 full of waves.

**ūn-et-vīcēsimānī, ōrum** *m/pl.* soldiers of the twenty-first legion.

**ungō, unxī, unctum** 3 to anoint.

**unguen, inis** *n* = **unguentum.**

**unguentārius** 3 of unguents; *m* dealer in ointments, *n* money to buy unguent.

**unguentātus** 3 anointed.

**unguentum, ī** *n* ointment, unguent, perfume.

**unguiculus, ī** *m* finger-nail, toe-nail.

**unguis, is** *m* finger-nail, toe-nail; claw, hoof, talon; **ad** *or* **in unguem** to a nicety, exactly; **unguis transversus** a finger's breadth.

**ungula, ae** *f* hoof; **a)** claw, talon; **b)** horse.

**unguō** 3 = **ungo.**

**ūni-color, ōris** of one colour.

**ūnicus** 3 one only, single; alone in its kind, singular, unique, unparalleled.

**ūni-fōrmis, e** uniform.

**ūni-gena, ae** only-begotten; born of the same parentage.

**ūni-manus** 3 one-handed.

**ūniō, ōnis** *m* single great pearl.

**ūnitās, ātis** *f* oneness, unity.

**ūniter** in(to) one.

**ūni-versālis, e** general, universal.

**ūniversitās, ātis** *f* the whole; the whole world, universe.

**ūni-versus** (*and* **-vorsus**) 3 **a)** combined into one, whole, entire, all together, collective; **b)** *subst.* **ūniversum, ī** *n* = **universitas;** **c)** *adv.* **ūniversē** *or* **in ūniversum** as a whole, in general.

**ūn-oculus** 3 one-eyed.

**ūnorsum** = **ūniversum.**

**unquam** *adv., see* **umquam.**

**ūnus** 3 one, a single, only one; **ad ūnum omnes** all to a man, without exception; **in ūnum** into one place; **ūnus quisque** each single, every one; **a)** one and the same, the same, common; **b)** *adv.* **ūnā** at the same place, at the same time, together, at once.

**ūpĭliō, ōnis** *m* = opilio.

**upupa, ae** *f* hoopoe; pick-axe.

**urbānĭtās, ātis** *f* life in Rome; **a)** city manners, city fashion, refinement, elegance, politeness, urbanity; **b)** wit, humour, pleasantry.

**urbānus** 3 belonging to the city (*Rome*), of the city, urban; *subst.* ~, ī *m* city man, *pl.* townsfolk, citizens; **a)** Roman; **b)** in city fashion, refined, elegant, cultivated, polished; **c)** witty, pleasant; **d)** bold, forward.

**urbi-capus, ī** *m* taker of cities.

**urbĭcus** 3 belonging to the city, to Rome.

**urbs, urbis** *f* city, walled town, capital; city of Rome; the citizens.

**urce(ol)us, ī** *m* pitcher, water-pot.

**ūrēdō, ĭnis** *f* blight (*upon plants*).

**urgeō, ursī, — 2** to push, press, drive, urge (*acc.*); **a)** to press upon, bear hard upon, oppress, weigh down, burden, to press hard, beset; **b)** to crowd, hem in, confine; **c)** to insist upon, lay stress upon; **d)** to stick to, apply oneself to diligently, to push on with.

**ūrīna, ae** *f* urine; semen.

**ūrīnātor, ōris** *m* diver.

**ūrīnor** 1 to dive.

**ūrios** 3 giver of favourable wind.

**urna, ae** *f* pitcher, water-pot, jug, jar, urn; voting-urn, urn for lots; urn for the ashes of the dead; a liquid measure.

**urnula, ae** *f, dim. of* urna.

**ūrō, ussī, ustum** 3 to burn, destroy by fire; **a)** to burn in (*of encaustic painting*); **b)** to waste by burning, destroy, harass, distress, plague, vex, disquiet; **c)** to dry up, parch, scorch; **d)** to pinch with cold, chafe, gall, rub sore; **e)** to burn with passion; inflame.

**ursa, ae** *f* she-bear; (*constellation*)⎫
**ursus, ī** *m* bear.             [the Bear.⎰

**urtīca, ae** *f* (stinging-)nettle; sea--nettle; itching desire.

**ūrus, ī** *m* a kind of wild ox.

**ūsĭtātus** 3 usual, customary, wonted, common, familiar.

**uspiam** *adv.* anywhere.

**usquam** *adv.* **a)** anywhere, at any place; in any thing, in any way; **b)** to any place.

**usque** *adv.* all the way, right (up), continuously, without interruption, all the while; **a)** *with prep.* **ab, ex, ad**; **b)** *rarely as prep. with acc.* right up to, as far as; **c)** *with adv.* (**usque eō** to such a point; **usque quāque** everywhere, on all occasions); **d)** *with cj.* (**usque dum, dōnec**).

**ustor, ōris** *m* burner of dead bodies.

**ustulō** 1 to burn.

**ūsū-capiō**[1] 3 to acquire by use *or* prescription.

**ūsū-capiō**[2]**, ōnis** *f* acquisition by use.

**ūsūra, ae** *f* a using, use, enjoyment; **a)** use of money lent; **b)** interest, usury.

**ūsūrārius** 3 **a)** borrowed; **b)** lent.

**ūsūrpātiō, ōnis** *f* a making use of; employment.

**ūsūrpō** 1 to take into use, employ, apply, practise, enjoy (*alqd*); **a)** to seize, usurp, assume; **b)** to take possession of, acquire; **c)** to name, call; **d)** to have experience of; to perceive.

**ūsus, ūs** *m* a using, making use of, use, application, practice, exercise; **a)** use and enjoyment, usufruct; **b)** frequent use, acquired skill, experience, expertness; **ūsū venit** it happens, occurs; **c)** usage, custom; **d)** intercourse, familiarity, intimacy; **e)** usefulness, advantage, profit; **ex ūsū alcis esse = alci ūsuī esse** to be useful *or* advantageous; **f)** occasion, want, need, necessity.

**ūsus-frūctus** (*acc.* **ūsum-frūctum**) *m* use and enjoyment, usufruct.

**ut 1. a)** (*interr.*) how? **b)** (*exclam.*) how! **c)** *in indirect questions and exclamations, with subj. and indic.* (*vides ut ...?* do you see how ...?); **d)** *in indignant or repudiating questions, with subj.* (*te ut ulla res frangat?* can anything prevail upon you?); **e)** *rarely in wishes =* utinam; **f)** (*relat.*) as, just as (*perge, ut instituisti; ut potui, tuli*); *α)* (*in parenthesis*) **ut aiunt, ut supra demonstravimus, ut dixi, ut fit;**

*β*) (*in comparisons*) *with correlative*
sic, ita, eodem modo: ut initium,
sic finis est; ut quisque ... sic
(ita) the more ... the more (*ut
quisque est vir optimus, ita difficillime
alios improbos esse suspicatur*); ut ...
ita indeed ... but, although ... yet,
ut nihil boni est in morte, ita
certe nihil mali; *γ*) (*in attestations*)
as it is true that: ita vivam, ut
maximos sumptus facio; *δ*) (*to
introduce an explanation or reason
or limitation*) as, as being, inasmuch
as, quod non decet, poeta iugit
ut maximum vitium; Diogenes
liberius ut Cynicus locutus est;
eloquens erat ut homo Theba-
nus (for a Theban); *ε*) ut si *with
subj.* as if; *ζ*) ut qui *with subj.*
seeing that, since, multa de me
questus est Caesar, ut qui a
Crasso in me esset incensus;
*η*) (*to introduce examples*) as, as for
example, multi gloriose mortui
sunt, ut Leonidas; 2. *cj.* a) *with
ind.* (*of time*) when, as soon as,
repente, ut Roman venit, praetor factus est; since, ut Brun-
disio profectus es, nullas postea
litteras a te accepi; b) *with subj.*
*α*) (*in final clauses*) that, in order
that, for the purpose of (*neg.* ne);
*with verbs of fearing* = ne non that
not; *β*) (*to express a consequence*)
that, so that (*neg.* ut non); *γ*) (*in
concessive clauses*) although, granting that, ut desint vires, tamen
est laudanda voluntas; *δ*) (*in
indirect commands*) that; *ε*) (eā
condiciōne) ut on condition that.
ut-cumque in whatever way, however; somehow; whenever.
ūtēns, tis using; *comp.* ūtentior
better able to spend (?).
ūtēnsilia, ium *n/pl.* necessaries,
materials, utensils.
uter¹, tris *m* leather bag *or* bottle.
uter², utra, utrum which of two,
which; either.
uter-cumque 3 whichever of the
two.
uter-libet 3 which of the two you
please, either of the two.
uter-que 3 each of two, both.

uterus, ī *m* (*and* uterum, ī *n*) belly,
paunch; womb; unborn child;
inside.
uter-vis 3 which of the two you
will, either of the two.
utī = ut.
ūtibilis, e useful, serviceable.
ūtilis, e useful, serviceable, suitable, fit, proper, profitable (*alci,
alci rei, ad alqd*).
ūtilitās, ātis *f* usefulness, service-
ableness, use, profit, advantage.
uti-nam (*with subj.*) would that!
oh that! utinam ne would that
not!
utiquam, ne ~ = neutiquam.
uti-que *adv.* in any case, at any
rate, by all means, certainly; at
least; especially.
ūtor, ūsus sum 3 to use, make use
of, employ (*with abl.*); a) to enjoy,
partake of; to have, possess, avail
oneself of, take advantage of; b) to
practise, exercise, perform; c) to
be intimate with, associate with.
ut-pote *adv.* seeing that, inasmuch
as, as being, as.
utrārius, ī *m* water-carrier.
utriculārius, ī *m* bagpiper.
utrim-que *adv.* from both sides;
on both sides.
utrō *adv.* to which of the two sides?
utrobīque *adv.* = utrubīque.
utrō-que *adv.* to both sides; in both
directions.
utrubī (*and* -ī) on which side?
utrubīque *adv.* on each of the two
sides, on both sides.
utrum (*in disjunctive questions*)
whether; utrum ... an whether
... or.
ut-ut = utcumque.
ūva, ae *f* grape; cluster of grapes
(*or other fruits, or bees*); vine.
ūvēns, ntis wet.
ūvēscō, —, — 3 to become moist
*or* wet; to refresh oneself.
ūvid(ul)us 3 moist, wet; a) well-
watered; b) drunken.
ūvi-fer 3 producing grapes.
uxor, ōris *f* wife, mate.
uxorcula, ae *f* little wife.
uxŏrius 3 of a wife; devoted to
one's wife, uxorious.

# V

**vacātiō, ōnis** f freedom from, immunity, exemption; **a)** exemption from military service; **b)** price paid for exemption from military service.

**vacca, ae** f cow.

**vaccinium, ī** n a purple flower (perhaps = *hyacinthus*).

**vaccula, ae** f little cow, heifer.

**vacerrōsus** 3 mad, crazy.

**vacillātiō, ōnis** f a reeling, wavering.

**vac(c)illō** 1 to waver, totter, reel, stagger, hesitate.

**vacē-fiō** to be made empty.

**vacivitās, ātis** f emptiness.

**vacīvus** 3 empty, void.

**vacō** 1 to be empty *or* void; **a)** to be vacant, unoccupied; **b)** to be uncultivated, uninhabited; **c)** to have no master, be without a possessor; **d)** to be free from, to be without (*re, a re*); to be free from duties, be disengaged; to be at leisure for (*dat.*) have time for, be devoted to; *impers.* **vacat** there is time, leisure for (*inf., dat. and inf.*).

**vacuē-faciō** 3 to make empty *or* free; **vacuē-factus** 3 empty, unoccupied.

**vacuitās, ātis** f **a)** freedom (from), exemption; **b)** vacancy.

**vacuō** 1 to empty.

**vacuus** 3 **a)** void, empty, free from, without, exempt (*re, a re, ab alqo*; with *gen.*); *subst.* **vacuum, ī** n empty space, void, vacuum; **b)** free from care; heart-whole; **c)** single, unmarried, widowed; **d)** vacant, without an owner, unoccupied; **e)** free from duty, disengaged, at leisure, idle; quiet, calm; **f)** worthless, useless, vain.

**vadimōnium, ī** n bail, security, recognizance; (day of) appearance in court.

**vādō** 3 to go, walk.

**vador** 1 to bind over to appear in court; **vadātus** (as *pass.*) bound.

**vadōsus** 3 full of shallows.

**vadum, ī** n shallow water, shoal; ford; **a)** dangerous water (to ships);

**b)** safe water (to swimmers); **c)** mass of water, sea, stream.

**vae** *int.* woe!, ah!, oh!; **vae tibi** (or **te**, *acc.*) alas for thee!

**vae-cors, vae-grandis, vaesānus,** *see* **ve-...**

**vafer, fra, frum** cunning, crafty, sly, artful, subtle.

**vagātiō, ōnis** f a wandering about.

**vāgīna, ae** f scabbard, sheath; husk; vagina.

**vāgiō** 4 to cry, scream, whimper.

**vāgītus, ūs** (*and* **vāgor, ōris**) m a crying, screaming.

**vagor** (*and* **vagō**) 1 to rove, ramble, roam, wander about.

**vagus** 3 wandering, strolling, rambling, roving; **a)** unsteady, inconstant, unsettled; **b)** aimless, indefinite, vague.

**vāh** *int.* ah! oh!

**valdē** *adv.* vehemently, strongly, very much.

**valē-dīcō** 3 to say good-bye, bid farewell.

**valēns, tis** strong, powerful; in good health, robust, vigorous, effective.

**valentulus** 3, *dim. of* **valens.**

**valeō, uī, itūrus** 2 to be strong; **a)** to be well *or* in health; **valē** (*as a farewell greeting*) farewell, good--bye; **b)** to be powerful, mighty, have weight *or* influence (*re, apud alqm; multum, plus, plurimum*) to prevail, have efficacy, avail, be effectual, succeed; **c)** to be able *or* capable; **d)** to be worth, valued at; to mean, signify.

**valēscō, luī, —** 3 to grow strong, gain strength.

**valētūdinārius** 3 invalid; **.ium** n hospital.

**valētūdō, inis** f state of health, bodily condition; **a)** good health; **b)** ill health, sickness, weakness.

**valgus** 3 bandy-legged.

**validus** 3 strong, vigorous; **a)** healthy, sound, robust; **b)** firm, fortified; **c)** powerful, mighty, influential, efficacious.

**valitūdō, inis** f, see **valetudo.**

**vallāris, e** of a rampart; ~ **corōna** wreath awarded for valour at an enemy's rampart.

**(vallēs** and) **vallis, is** f valley, vale.

**vallō** 1 to fortify with a rampart, entrench; to protect, defend (alqd).

**vallum, ī** n palisade; palisaded rampart, fortification; protection.

**vallus, ī** m stake, pole; **a)** palisade; **b)** rampart with palisades, stockade; **c)** tooth (of a comb).

**valvae, ārum** f/pl. leaves of a folding door.

**vānēscō, —, —** 3 to fade away, vanish, disappear.

**vāni-dicus** 3 bragging, lying.

**vāni-loquentia, ae** f a prating, vaunting.

**vāni-loquidōrus, ī** m liar.

**vāni-loquus** 3 lying; boasting.

**vānitās, ātis** f emptiness, unreality, mere show, vanity, untruth, deception; **a)** uselessness; failure; **b)** a boasting, vaunting, vainglory, lying, quackery.

**vānitūdō, inis** f lying talk.

**vannus, ī** f winnowing-fan.

**vānus** 3 empty, void, hollow; **a)** containing nothing, vain, unreal; without effect, fruitless, to no purpose; **b)** false, lying, untrue, deceitful, boastful, ostentatious, braggart; groundless, unreal; subst. **vānum, ī** n emptiness, groundlessness, mere show.

**vapidus** 3 mouldy, flat; spoilt, bad.

**vapor** (and **-ōs**), **ōris** m vapour, steam, smoke; **a)** exhalation; **b)** heat, warmth.

**vapōrārium, ī** n hot-air pipe.

**vapōri-fer** 3 giving out steam or heat.

**vapōrō** 1 to heat with steam, vapour, or smoke; to warm; to be hot, burn.

**vappa, ae** f spoiled or flat wine; a good-for-nothing.

**vāpulāris, e** of flogging.

**vāpulō** 1 to be flogged or whipped.

**vāra, ae** f forked pole (for stretching nets).

**variātiō, ōnis** (and **variantia, ae**) f diversity, difference.

**varicōsus** 3 with varicose veins.

**vāricus** 3 with legs wide apart.

**varietās, ātis** f **a)** variety, difference, diversity; **b)** vicissitude, change; difference in opinion; **c)** fickleness, inconstancy.

**variō** 1 **a)** to diversify, variegate, make particoloured, spot (alqd); to change, alter, interchange, make different, diverse, manifold; **b)** intr. to be particoloured; to be different, manifold, diverse; to differ in opinion; to waver, to differ, change, vary.

**varius** 3 variegated, particoloured; **a)** spotted, mottled; **b)** different, diverse, varying, manifold, changing, changeable; **c)** many-sided, versatile; fickle, inconstant, changeable.

**varix, icis** f and m dilated vein.

**vārus** 3 bent, crooked; **a)** with legs bent inward, knock-kneed; **b)** different, contrary.

**vas**[1], **vadis** m surety, bail.

**vās**[2], **vāsis** (and **vāsum**) n vessel, tool, utensil; **vāsa, ōrum** n/pl. luggage, baggage, military equipment.

**vāsārium, ī** n furniture-money, outfit.

**vāsculārius, ī** m worker in precious metals.

**vāsculum, ī** n small vessel.

**vāstātiō, ōnis** f a laying waste.

**vāstātor, ōris** m (and **-trīx, īcis** f) ravager, devastator.

**vāsti-ficus** 3 ravaging, devastating.

**vāstitās, ātis** (and **vāstitiēs, ēi**) f desolation, devastation, ruin, waste, desert.

**vāstō** 1 to make empty or void; **a)** to lay waste, desolate, ravage; **b)** to harass.

**vāstus**[1] 3 **a)** waste, desert, desolate, uncultivated, empty; **b)** devastated; **c)** rough, rude, uncouth, uncivilized.

**vastus**[2] 3 **a)** vast, huge, enormous; **b)** shapeless; monstrous.

**vātēs** (and **vātis**), **is** m and f soothsayer, diviner, seer, prophet; singer, bard, poet.

**vāticinātiō, ōnis** f prediction, prophecy.

**vāticinātor, ōris** m soothsayer, prophet.

**vāticinor** 1 to foretell, prophesy, divine; to utter teaching or warning; to rave, talk idly.

**vāti-cinus** 3 prophetic.

**vatillum, ī** n fire-pan.

**ve** cj. enclitic or, or perhaps; **ve ... ve** either ... or.

**vēcordia, ae** *f* madness, foolishness.

**vē-cors, rdis** mad, foolish, frantic.

**vectātiō, ōnis** *f* a riding, driving.

**vectigal, ālis** *n* tax, impost, duty; a) contribution paid to a magistrate; b) private income, rents.

**vectigālis, e** a) paid in taxes; b) liable to taxes, tributary; c) bringing in profit.

**vectiō, ōnis** *f* a carrying, conveyance.

**vectis, is** *m* lever; a) crowbar; b) bar, bolt.

**vectō** 1 to carry, convey.

**vector, ōris** *m* a) bearer, carrier; b) one who is carried, passenger, rider.

**vectōrius** 3 relating to conveying *or* transporting.

**vectūra, ae** *f* a carrying, conveying; conveyance, transport; passage-money, freight.

**vegeō** 2 to rouse, set in motion.

**vegetus** 3 vigorous, quick, active.

**vē-grandis, e** a) small, tiny; b) very great.

**vehemēns, tis** a) violent, vehement, furious, impetuous; b) strong, forcible, powerful, vigorous; *adv.* **vehementer** vehemently, violently, strongly, exceedingly, extremely, very much.

**vehiculum, ī** *n* vehicle, conveyance; litter, ship, wagon.

**vehō, vēxī, vectum** 3 to carry, bear, convey; to drive, draw; **P.** to be carried *or* conveyed; to ride, drive, sail, travel.

**vel** (*particle*) a) or, or rather; **vel ... vel** either ... or; b) even, actually; for example.

**vēlāmen, inis** *n* veil, covering, garment, clothing.

**vēlāmentum, ī** *n* a) = velamen; b) olive-branch wound round with wool.

**vēlārium, ī** *n* awning.

**vēles, itis** *m* skirmisher.

**vēli-fer** 3 sail-bearing.

**vēlificātiō, ōnis** *f* a sailing.

**vēli-ficor** (*and* **-ficō**) 1 to sail (through); to be zealous for (*with* dat.).

**vēlitāris, e** pertaining to skirmishers.

**vēlitātiō, ōnis** *f* a skirmishing.

**vēlitor** 1 to skirmish.

**vēli-volāns, tis** *and* **-volus** 3 flying *or* winged with sails.

**vellicātiō, ōnis** *f* taunting, fault-finding.

**vellicō** 1 to pluck, twitch; to criticize, rail at, taunt.

**vellō, vellī** (*and* **vulsī, volsī**), **vulsum** *and* **volsum** 3 to pluck, pull, twitch; to pluck out *or* off, to tear down.

**vellus, eris** *n* wool; a) fleece, sheepskin; b) skin of an animal; c) woollen band; d) silk; cloud; snow.

**vēlō** 1 to veil, cover; a) to wind about, encircle, surround; b) to hide, conceal, cloak.

**vēlōcitās, ātis** *f* quickness, swiftness, rapidity.

**vēlōx, ōcis** quick, swift, rapid.

**vēlum¹, ī** *n* sail; **vēla dare** to set sail.

**vēlum², ī** *n* drapery, curtain, awning, veil.

**vel-ut(ī)** a) as, even as, just as; b) for instance; c) **velut(sī)** (*with* subj.) just as if.

**vēmēns, tis** = **vehemens.**

**vēna, ae** *f* vein, blood-vessel; penis; a) water-course; b) vein in wood *or* stone; c) metallic vein; d) inmost nature, inmost *or* vital part, interior; e) vein of talent, disposition, natural bent, poetic genius.

**vēnābulum, ī** *n* hunting-spear.

**vēnālicius** 3 for sale; *subst.* ~, **ī** *m* slave-dealer.

**vēnālis, e** on sale; to be sold; *subst.* *m* slave; venal, that may be bribed.

**vēnāticus** 3 of the chase, for hunting.

**vēnātiō, ōnis** *f* a hunting, chase; hunting spectacle; wild beast fight; game.

**vēnātor, ǀōris** *m* hunter; explorer, searcher.

**vēnātōrius** 3 = venaticus.

**vēnātrīx, īcis** *f* huntress.

**vēnātūra, ae** *f* = vēnātus.

**vēnātus, ūs** *m* a hunting, chase; fishing.

**vendibilis, e** on sale, salable; popular, acceptable.

**venditātiō, ōnis** *f* a boasting, vaunting.

**venditātor, ōris** *m* boaster, vaunter.

**venditiō, ōnis** *f* a selling, sale, sale by auction; goods sold.

**venditō** 1 to offer for sale; a) to barter away, give for a bribe; b) to make traffic of; c) to praise, recommend.

**venditor, ōris** *m* seller.

**vendō, didī, ditum** 3 to sell; to have on sale; **a)** to sell by auction, to let out, farm out; **b)** to betray for money, give for a bribe; **c)** to cry up, praise, recommend.

**venē-fica, ae** *f* poisoner, sorceress, witch.

**venēficium, ī** *n* a poisoning, a preparing of poison; poisoned drink; magic, sorcery.

**venē-ficus** 3 mixing poison, magical; *subst.* ~, **ī** *m* poisoner, sorcerer.

**venēnārius, ī** *m* poisoner.

**venēnātus** 3 **a)** poisoned, poisonous; **b)** bewitched, enchanted.

**venēni-fer** 3 poisonous.

**venēnō** 1 to poison.

**venēnum, ī** *n* **a)** dye, drug; **b)** poison, poisoned drink; **c)** ruin, destruction, bane; **d)** magic potion, charm, philtre, sorcery.

**vēn-eō, iī, —, īre** to be on sale, be sold.

**venerābilis, e** reverend, venerable.

**venerābundus** 3 respectful, reverent.

**venerātiō, ōnis** *f* reverence, respect, worship.

**venerātor, ōris** *m* reverer, adorer.

**venereus** *and* **-ius** 3, *see* **venus.**

**veneror** (*and* **venerō**) 1 to revere, worship, adore; to implore, pray reverently to *or* for; to beseech humbly.

**venetus** 3 (Venetian); blue.

**venia, ae** *f* favour, grace, indulgence, permission; **bonā tuā veniā** by your indulgence, by your leave; **a)** pardon; **b)** forgiveness, indulgence to faults.

**veniō, vēnī, ventum** 4 to come, come to, arrive; **a)** to advance, approach; **ventūrus** 3 coming, future; **b)** to come into, fall into a state *or* condition (*in periculum, in calamitatem, in potestatem alcis*); **c)** to come forth, appear; to grow; — **vēnit mihi in mentem** (*alcis*) I thought of.

**vennū(n)cula, ae** *f* = **vēnūcula.**

**vēnō,** *see* **vēnum.**

**vēnor** 1 to hunt; to chase, pursue, strive after (*acc.*).

**vēnōsus** 3 full of veins; over-exuberant, turgid (?).

**venter, tris** *m* belly, paunch; **a)** stomach; **b)** womb, fœtus; **c)** a swelling, protuberance; **d)** appetite, gluttony.

**ventilō** 1 to wave in the air; **a)** to winnow (*grain*), fan; **b)** to incite.

**ventiō, ōnis** *f* a coming.

**ventitō** 1 to come often.

**ventōsus** 3 full of wind, windy; of the wind; **a)** swift *or* light as the wind; **b)** vain, empty; conceited; **c)** unsteady, fickle, inconstant, changeable.

**ventriculus, ī** *m* belly; **cordis** ventricle of the heart.

**ventriōsus** 3 big-bellied.

**ventulus, ī** *m* breeze.

**ventus, ī** *m* wind; **a)** fortune, circumstances; **b)** favour of the people, vain applause; **c)** storm, disturbance; **d)** rumour.

**vēnūcula, ae** *f* a kind of grape.

**vēnum** (*acc.*), **vēnō** (*dat.*) sale; **vēnum dō** = **vendō; vēnum eō** = **vēneō; vēnō pōnō** to expose for sale.

**venus, eris** *f* **a)** love, pleasures of love; beloved person; **b)** loveliness, beauty, charm, attractiveness; **c)** **Venus** the goddess of love; the planet Venus; the highest throw in dice-play; *adj.* **venereus** *and* **venerius** 3 dedicated to Venus; relating to sexual love; *subst. m, n* highest throw in dice-play.

**venustās, ātis** *f* loveliness, charm, beauty; **a)** attractiveness, gracefulness, sweetness; **b)** elegance, politeness.

**venustulus** 3, *dim. of* **venustus.**

**venustus** 3 charming, lovely, beautiful; attractive, fine.

**vē-pallidus** 3 very pale.

**veprēcula, ae** *f* little thorn-bush.

**veprēs, is** *m* (*and* *f*) thorn-bush, brier, bramble.

**vēr, vēris** *n* spring-time.

**vērātrum, ī** *n* hellebore.

**vērāx, ācis** truthful.

**verbēna, ae** *f* vervain; *pl.* sacred herbs *or* branches.

**verbēnātus** 3 decked with sacred twigs.

**verber, eris** *n* blow, lash; **a)** blows with a whip, a thrashing, flogging; **b)** cudgel, whip, scourge; **c)** thong of a sling.

**verberābilis, e** *and* **verbereus** 3 deserving to be flogged.

**verberābundus** 3 dealing blows.

**verberātiō, ōnis** f a beating, punishment.

**verberō**[1], **ōnis** m scoundrel.

**verberō**[2] 1 to beat, strike; **a)** to whip, scourge; **b)** to chastise, assail, harass, plague.

**verbi-vēlitātiō, ōnis** f skirmishing with words.

**verbōsus** 3 wordy, verbose.

**verbum, ī** n word, expression, pl. words, talk, discourse, speech; **verba facere** to speak, make a speech; **a)** utterance, saying, maxim, proverb; **b)** mere word, mere talk, stuff; **alci verba dare** to deceive, cheat; **c)** formula, incantation; — **verbō** in name, in theory; **ad verbum** word for word; **verbī causā** or **gratiā** for instance; **verbīs alcis** in the name of, in behalf of.

**vērculum, ī** n little spring.

**vērē,** adv. of **verus**.

**verēcundia, ae** f respect, awe, shyness, modesty; **a)** reverence, veneration; **b)** shame.

**verēcundor** 1 to be bashful, ashamed, shy.

**verēcundus** 3 bashful, modest; **a)** respectful; **b)** moderate.

**verēdus, ī** m swift horse.

**vereor, veritus sum** 2 **a)** to fear (alqd, ne, ut); **b)** to shrink from; hesitate (inf.), feel shame; **c)** to reverence, respect, stand in awe of; **verendus** 3 inspiring awe; n/pl. genital organs.

**veretrum, ī** n genital organs.

**vergiliae, ārum** f/pl. the seven stars (= Pleiades).

**vergō, (rsī), —3 a)** to incline or turn oneself to (ad or in alqd); **b)** to lie towards, be situated towards; **b)** to decline; **c)** trans. to pour in (alqd in rem); to incline, turn.

**vēri-dicus** 3 = **verax**.

**vēri-loquium, ī** n etymology.

**vēri-similis, e** probable, likely.

**vēri-similitūdō, inis** f probability.

**vēritas, ātis** f truth; **a)** reality, actual nature, real life; **b)** sincerity, candour, truthfulness; **c)** honesty, integrity.

**vēri-verbium, ī** n a speaking the truth.

**vermiculātus** 3 made in worm-pattern (mosaic).

**vermiculus, ī** m small worm, grub.

**vermina, um** n/pl. abdominal pains.

**verminātiō, ōnis** f pricking or itching pain.

**verminō** (and **-or**) 1 to itch; to have pricking or shooting pains.

**vermis, is** m worm.                    [slave.]

**verna, ae** m (and f) home-born]

**vernāculus** 3 born in the house, domestic; subst. m house-jester, wit; **a)** native, indigenous, Roman; **b)** invented by an accuser (crimen).

**vernīlis, e a)** slavish, servile; **b)** abject, crouching; **c)** forward, saucy.

**vernīlitās, ātis** f a) fawning; **b)** pertness, sauciness.

**vernō** 1 to become spring-like, be renewed, grow green; to be youthful.                    [verna: adj. native.]

**vernula, ae** m (and f) dimin. of]

**vernus** 3 relating to spring, spring-like.

**vērō,** adv. of **verus**.

**verpa, ae** f penis.

**verpus, ī** m a circumcised man.

**verrēs, is** m boar, male swine.

**verrīnus** 3 of a boar.

**verrō, —versum** 3 to sweep, brush; **a)** to sweep clean, to clean, to sweep out or together; **b)** to drag or sweep along, take away; **c)** to trail on the ground.

**verrūca, ae** f wart; small fault.

**verrūcōsus** 3 full of warts.

**verruncō** 1 to turn, **bene** to turn out well.

**verrūtum, ī** n = **verutum**.

**versābilis, e** movable, changeable.

**versābundus** 3 revolving.

**versātilis, e** turning round, revolving; versatile, adroit.

**versātiō, ōnis** f change.

**versi-capillus** 3 with greying hair.

**versi-color, ōris** changing in colour; particoloured.

**versiculus, ī** m little verse.

**versi-pellis, e a)** changed in appearance; **b)** subtle, crafty.

**versō** 1 1. to turn about often, to turn hither and thither, to turn round, roll; **a)** to turn, bend, shift, agitate, move about, drive round; **b)** to disturb, discompose, harass, vex; **c)** to handle, deal with; **d)** to revolve, consider, meditate; —**2. P. versor** 1 to turn oneself round; **a)** to stay, dwell, live; **b)** to be in a certain condition; **c)** to be occupied, busied, engaged in (in re), pay attention to, practise.

**versum** *adv.* = **versus²**.

**versūra, ae** *f* a) the borrowing of money to pay a debt; b) a borrowing, loan.

**versus¹** 3, *part. of* **verto** *and* **verro**.

**versus²** *adv.* towards, in the direction of, **in Italiam versus, ad mare versus**.

**versus³, ūs** *m* a turning; a) furrow; b) row, line; c) verse, poetry; d) turn *or* step in a dance.

**versūtia, ae** *f* cunning, craftiness.

**versūti-loquus** 3 craftily-speaking.

**versūtus** 3 cunning, crafty, dexterous.

**vertebra, ae** *f* joint.

**vertex, icis** *m* whirl, whirlpool, eddy; a) whirlwind; b) coil of flame, pillar of fire; c) top *or* crown of the head, top, summit, head; d) the pole of the heavens; e) height, hill, elevation; **a vertice** from above.

**verticōsus** 3 full of whirlpools.

**vertīgō, inis** *f* a turning *or* whirling round; a) revolution; b) giddiness, dizziness.

**vertō, rtī, rsum** 3 (*archaic* **vortō**) **1.** to turn, turn round, up, back (*acc.*); a) to turn, direct, convert; **ad se** to appropriate (*pecuniam*); b) to ascribe, refer, construe as, impute; c) to change to, cause to pass to; d) to turn away (*lumina, vultum*); e) to turn round *or* back (*pedem, gradum*), to put to flight (*alqm in fugam*); **terga vertere** to flee; f) to turn up, dig up, plough (*terram aratro*); to overthrow, overturn, subvert, destroy, ruin; g) to alter, change, exchange, transform, metamorphose; to translate; **2.** *intr. and* **P.** to turn *or* direct oneself; a) to turn out, result; b) to move about, roll round, revolve; c) to be in a certain condition *or* state, lie in a certain direction; d) (*of time*) revolve, come round; e) to depend, rest upon, belong to; f) to be changed, change to, become.

**vertragus, ī** *m* greyhound.

**verū, ūs** (*and* **verum**) *n* spit; javelin.

**veruina, ae** *f* small spit.

**vērum,** *see* **verus.**

**vērum enim-vērō** but truly.

**vērum-tamen** but yet, however, nevertheless.

**vērus** 3 true, real, actual, genuine, well-grounded, *subst.* **vērum, ī** *n*

truth, reality, fact; a) truthful, true, veracious, upright; b) fitting, reasonable, just, proper; *subst.* **vērum, ī** *n* duty; c) *adv.* **vērē** truly, truthfully, rightly, in fact, really, actually; d) *adv.* **vērō** in truth, really, indeed, (*in answers*) certainly, to be sure; (*as adversative particle*) but in fact, but indeed; (*in climax*) even, indeed; e) **vērum** (as *adv.*) yes, certainly; (as *cj.*) but, but in truth, but still.

**verūtum, ī** *m* javelin.

**verūtus** 3 armed with a javelin.

**vervēx, ēcis** *m* wether; dolt.

**vēsānia, ae** *f* madness, insanity.

**vēsāniēns, tis** furious, raging.

**vē-sānus** 3 mad, insane, frantic, raging.

**vescor, —, —** 3 to feed on, eat (*alqa re*; rarely *alqd*); to use, enjoy.

**vēscus** 3 a) consuming, corroding; b) thin, slender, feeble, wretched.

**vēsīca, ae** *f* bladder; a) vulva; b) cap; c) lantern; d) bombast.

**vēsicula, ae** *f* little bladder.

**vespa, ae** *f* wasp.

**vesper, erī** (*and* **-eris**) *m* a) the evening-star; b) evening, evening meal; c) the west; **vesperī** *and* **-e** in the evening.

**vespera, ae** *f* the evening.

**vesperāscō, rāvī, —** 3 to become evening, grow dark.

**vespertīliō, ōnis** *m* bat.

**vespertīnus** 3 of the evening; western.

**vesperūgō, inis** *f* evening-star.

**vespillō, ōnis** *m* corpse-bearer for the poor.

**Vesta, ae** *f* the goddess Vesta; a) hearth, fire on the hearth; b) temple of Vesta; *adj.* **Vestālis** belonging to Vesta; *subst. f* priestess of Vesta, Vestal virgin.

**vester, tra, trum** your, yours.

**vestiārium, ī** *n* clothing.

**vestibulum, ī** *n* a) entrance court, court-yard; porch, vestibule; b) entrance.

**vestīgātor, ōris** *m* spy.

**vestīgium, ī** *n* a) foot-print, foot-step, track; trace, mark, sign, *pl.* ruins; step, pace; b) sole of the foot; c) station, position, post; d) moment, instant; **e** *or* **in vestīgiō** on the spot, instantly.

**vestigō** 1 a) to track, follow the trail of; b) to investigate, search out.

**vestimentum, ī** *n* garment, article of clothing, *pl.* clothes.

**vestiō** 4 a) to clothe, dress; b) to cover, deck, adorn.

**vesti-p(l)ica, ae** *f* wardrobe-woman.

**vestis, is** *f* clothes, clothing, dress; a) carpet, tapestry; b) veil; c) spider's web; d) snake-skin.

**vestītus, ūs** *m* clothing; a) clothes, dress, attire; b) covering.

**veterāmentārius** 3, **~ sūtor** mender of old shoes.

**veterānus** 3 (*and subst. m*) veteran.

**veterārium, ī** *n* (*sc. vinum*) old vintage wine.

**veterāscō, āvī, —** 3 to become old.

**veterātor, ōris** *m* old hand, old fox.

**veterātōrius** 3 cunning, crafty.

**veterīnus** 3 of a draught-horse.

**veternōsus** 3 sleepy, dreamy.

**veternus, ī** *m* a) old age; b) lethargy, drowsiness, laziness.

**vetō, uī, itum** 1 to forbid, prohibit (*alqm; acc.c.inf.*); a) to interpose a veto; b) to check, prevent.

**vetulus** 3 old.

**vetus, eris** (*comp.* **vetustior,** *superl.* **veterrimus**) old, aged, advanced in years; of long standing, ancient; *subst.* **veterēs, um** *m/pl.* the ancients, forefathers, men of old; *f* the old booths of money-changers in the Forum.

**vetustās, ātis** *f* old age, long existence, length of time; a) friendship of long standing; b) antiquity; c) late posterity.

**vetustus** 3 old, aged, ancient, old-fashioned, antique.

**vexāmen, inis** *n* shaking.

**vexātiō, ōnis** *f* a shaking; a) hardship, trouble; b) ill-treatment, vexation.

**vexātor, ōris** *m* harasser, disturber.

**vexillārius, ī** *m* a) standardbearer, ensign; b) *pl.* reserve of veterans; detachment of soldiers.

**vexillātiō, ōnis** *f* detachment of soldiers.

**vexillum, ī** *n* standard, flag; a) signal-flag; b) company of soldiers, troop; detachment.

**vexō** 1 to move violently, shake; a) to harass, trouble, plague; disturb, molest; b) to damage,

maltreat, attack, abuse, annoy, injure, ruin.

**via, ae** *f* way, road; a) highroad; b) street in a town, lane; way, path, course; c) the right way, straight road; d) way, march, journey; way, manner, means, method.

**viālis, e** of the roads.

**viārius** 3 relating to highways.

**viāticātus** provided with travelling-money.

**viāticus** 3 relating to a journey; *subst.* **-cum, ī** *n* money for a journey; soldier's savings.

**viātor, ōris** *m* a) traveller, wayfarer; b) messenger of a magistrate.

**vībix, īcis** *f* weal.

**vibrō** 1 to shake, brandish; a) to cause to vibrate, move to and fro; **P.** to tremble; to hurl; b) *intr.* to tremble, quiver; to flash, glitter, gleam.

**viburnum, ī** *n* a kind of tree, wayfaring-tree.

**vīcānus** 3 of a village; *subst.* **~, ī** *m* villager.

**vicārius** 3 substituted, vicarious; *subst.* **~, ī** *m* substitute, deputy; under-slave.

**vicātim** *adv.* a) from street to street; b) in villages.

**vice** *and* **vicem,** *see* **vicis.**

**vicēnī** 3 twenty each.

**vicēnsimus** 3 = vicesimus.

**vicēs,** *see* **vicis.**

**vicēsimānus, ī** *m* soldier of the twentieth legion.

**vicēsimārius** 3 derived from a five per cent tax.

**vicēsimus** 3 the twentieth; *subst.* **-a, ae** *f* five per cent tax.

**vicia, ae** *f* vetch.

**viciē(n)s** *adv.* twenty times.

**vicīnālis, e** neighbouring.

(**vicīnia, ae** *f and*) **vicīnitās, ātis** *f* neighbourhood; the neighbours.

**vicīnus** 3 1. neighbouring, near; a) *subst.* **~, ī** *m*, **-a, ae** *f* neighbour; b) **-um, ī** *n* neighbourhood, vicinity; 2. a) near, approaching; b) similar, like.

**vicis** (*gen.*), *acc.* **em,** *abl.* **e,** *pl.* **vicēs,** *abl.* **vicibus** *f* change, interchange, alternation, turn; a) reply, answer, requital, compensation, equivalent, retaliation; b) lot, fate, fortune, destiny; c) position, place, office, post, duty, part; **d)** *adv.* **vicem** *and* **vice** for the sake of, on account of, as, like; **(in) vicem** by turns; mutually; instead of.

**vicissātim** *adv.* = **vicissim.**

**vicissim** *adv.* **a)** in turn, again; **b)** on the other hand.

**vicissitūdō, inis** *f* change, interchange, alternation, vicissitude.

**victima, ae** *f* beast for sacrifice, victim; sacrifice.

**victimārius, ī** *m* assistant at sacrifices.

**victitō** 1 to live *or* feed upon (*alqa re*).

**victor, ōris** *m* conqueror, victor; victorious.

**victōria, ae** *f* victory, conquest; the goddess of victory.

**victōriātus, ī** *m* silver coin with the figure of Victory.

**Victōriola, ae** *f* small statue of Victory.

**victrīx, īcis** *f* (*and n*) victorious.

**victus, ūs** *m* **a)** means of living, nourishment, food, victuals; **b)** manner of life, mode of living.

**viculus, ī** *m* hamlet.

**vīcus, ī** *m* **a)** village, hamlet; estate, farm; **b)** district of a town, street.

**vidē-licet** *adv.* **a)** clearly, plainly, obviously, manifestly; **b)** of course, to be sure; **c)** namely.

**videō, vīdī, vīsum** 2 **1.** to see; **a)** to have the power of seeing; **b)** to see, perceive, discern, to see again; to live to see, to experience; **c)** to look at, observe, behold; to go to see, visit; **d)** to see patiently, let pass, permit; **e)** to perceive mentally, observe, think, know, understand, comprehend; consider, reflect upon; **f)** to see to, take care, provide for, look after with care; **2. P. videor, vīsus sum** 2 **a)** to be seen, be looked upon, become visible, appear, to be evident *or* manifest; **b)** to seem, be regarded; **alci vidētur** it seems proper, right, good, it pleases; **sī vidētur** if you please.

**vidua, ae** *f* widow; unmarried woman.

**viduitās, ātis** *f* widowhood; lack.

**vidulus, ī** *m* wicker trunk.

**viduō** 1 to deprive *or* bereave of, deprive of a husband.

**viduus** 3 widowed; unmarried,

single, *see* **vidua; a)** deprived, bereft, destitute, without (*with abl. or gen.*); **b)** mateless, solitary.

**viētus** 3 shrivelled, withered.

**vigeō, uī,** — 2 to be lively, vigorous, strong, active; to flourish, bloom, be in repute, be esteemed; to prevail, be in vogue.

**vigēscō,** —, — 3 to become vigorous.

**vigēsimus** 3 = **vicesimus.**

**vigessis, is** *m* twenty *asses.*

**vigil, ilis** *m* watchman, sentinel; *adj.* watching, watchful, awake.

**vigilāns, tis** watchful, careful.

**vigilantia, ae** *f* wakefulness; watchfulness.

**vigilāx, ācis** watchful, wakeful.

**vigilia, ae** *f* a being awake, sleeplessness; **a)** a watching, keeping watch, watch, guard; **b)** watchmen, sentinels; **c)** a watch (a fourth part of the night); **d)** watchfulness, vigilance, attention.

**vigil(i)ārium, ī** *n* watch-tower.

**vigilō** 1 **a)** to keep awake, be wakeful; to watch, be vigilant *or* attentive; **b)** to watch through, to perform watching, execute by night.

**vigintī** (*indecl.*) twenty.

**vigintī-virātus, ūs** *m* office of *vigintīvirī.*

**vigintī-virī, ōrum** *m/pl.* commission *or* board of twenty men.

**vigor, ōris** *m* life, vigour, energy, liveliness.

**vīlica, ae** *f* female overseer; steward's wife.

**vīlicō** 1 to superintend, act as overseer.

**vīlicus, ī** *m* overseer, steward.

**vīlis, e** cheap, of little value, low, paltry, worthless, mean.

**vīlitās, ātis** *f* cheapness, low price; **a)** trifling value, worthlessness; **b)** disregard, contempt.

**vīlla, ae** *f* country-house, farm.

**vīllica, -cō, -cus,** *see* **vīlica, -co, -cus.**

**vīllōsus** 3 hairy, shaggy, rough.

**vīllula, ae** *f* small country house *or* villa.

**vīllum, ī** *n* a little wine, tipsiness.

**vīllus, ī** *m* shaggy hair, tuft of hair; nap of cloth.

**vīmen, inis** *n* pliant twig; **a)** withe, osier; **b)** wickerwork.

**vīmentum, ī** *n* osier, twig.

**vīmineus** 3 made of osiers, of wicker-work.

**vīn'** ( = **visne**) wilt thou? will you?

**vīnāceus, ī** *m* grape-stone.

**vīnālia, ium** *n/pl.* wine festival.

**vīnārius** 3 of wine, for wine; *subst.* ~, **ī** *m* wine-merchant; **-um, ī** *n* wine-pot, wine-flask.

**vincibilis, e** easily won.

**vinciō, vinxī, vinctum** 4 to bind, tie, fetter; a) to surround, encircle (*alqd alqa re*); **b)** to wind round; **c)** to bind, pledge, oblige; **d)** to restrain, confine.

**vinclum, ī** *n* = **vinculum.**

**vincō, vīcī, victum** 3 to conquer, overcome; a) to be victorious (*re*); **Olympia** (*acc.*) in the Olympian games; to prevail, get the mastery over, succeed, win; **b)** to overcome, overwhelm, subdue (*acc.*); **c)** to win over, cause to yield *or* give way; **d)** to outdo, surpass, exceed, excel; **e)** to show conclusively, carry a point.

**vinculum, ī** *n* band, tie; a) cord, rope, fetter; *pl.* fetters, bonds, prison; **b)** tie, band, restraint.

**vīn-dēmia, ae** *f* vintage; grapes, wine.                    [-gatherer.]

**vīndēmiātor, ōris** *m* grape-

**vīndēmiolae, ārum** *f/pl.* little vintage; small income.

**vīndēmitor, ōris** *m* the vintager (the name of a star).

**vindex, icis** *m* a) protector, champion, deliverer; **b)** avenger, punisher.

**vindicātiō, ōnis** *f* claim; protection; punishment.

**vindiciae, ārum** *f/pl.* thing *or* person claimed at law; legal claim; protection; **vindicias decernere** *or* **dare** to pronounce judgment concerning a claim.

**vindicō** 1 a) to assert a claim, demand formally, ask judgment for; to claim, arrogate, demand as one's own, assume; **b)** to champion, rescue, deliver (*alqm* or *alqd in libertatem, ab alqo*); to defend, protect, save; **c)** to avenge, punish, inflict punishment, take vengeance on.

**vindicta, ae** *f* a) the freeing of a slave, deliverance, rescue; liberating-rod; **b)** vengeance, revenge, punishment.

**vīnea, ae** *f* a) vine; **b)** vineyard; **c)** roof, shed for shelter, penthouse.

**vīnētum, ī** *n* vineyard.

**vīneus** 3 of vine-wood.

**vīnitor, ōris** *m* vine-dresser.

**vinnulus** 3 charming, pleasant.

**vīnolentia, ae** *f* wine-drinking, intoxication.

**vīnolentus** 3 a) drunken with wine, given to wine; **b)** mixed with wine.

**vīnōsus** 3 full of wine; a) drunken; **b)** given to wine; **c)** like wine.

**vīnulentia, vīnulentus,** *see* **vīno...**

**vīnum, ī** *n* wine; a) grape; **b)** vine.

**viola, ae** *f* a) violet; violet-colour; **b)** gillyflower, stock.

**violābilis, e** easily injured, **nōn** ~ inviolable.

**violārium, ī** *n* bed of violets.

**violārius, ī** *m* one who dyes violet.

**violātiō, ōnis** *f* a violating, profaning.

**violātor, ōris** *m* violator, profaner.

**violēns, tis** = **violentus.**

**violentia, ae** *f* violence, vehemence; impetuosity, ferocity, fury.

**violentus** 3 violent, impetuous, boisterous, harsh.

**violō** 1 to treat with violence, maltreat, injure, hurt, outrage, dishonour, violate (*acc.*); a) to defile, profane; **b)** to transgress, break; **c)** to offend.

**vīpera, ae** *f* viper, adder, snake.

**vīpereus** 3 of a viper *or* snake; a) snaky-haired; **b)** poisonous.

**vīperinus** 3 = **vīpereus.**

**vir, virī** *m* a man, male person, adult male; a) husband; **b)** man of character *or* courage, worthy man, hero; **c)** soldier, warrior; **d)** a single man, individual; *pl.* = **homines** human beings, men, mortals.

**virāgō, inis** *f* a manlike woman, female warrior.

**virectum, ī** *n* green place, turf.

**vireō, uī,** — 2 to be green; to be blooming, fresh, vigorous.

**virēscō, ruī,** — 3 to grow green.

**virētum, ī** *n* = **virectum.**

**virga, ae** *f* twig, rod, wand, staff; a) graft, scion; **b)** *pl.* = *fascēs;* **c)** magic wand; **d)** branch of a pedigree; **e)** coloured stripe.

**virgātor, ōris** *m* flogger.

**virgātus** 3 a) made of twigs; **b)** striped.

virgētum, ī n osier-thicket.

virgeus 3 of rods or twigs.

virgi-dēmia, ae f rod-harvest, sound cudgelling.

virginālis, e (and virginārius 3) maidenly, of a maiden; subst. -āle, is n the vulva.

virginēs-vendōnidēs, ae m seller of maidens.

virgineus 3 of a maiden, of a virgin, maidenly.

virginitās, ātis f maidenhood, virginity, chastity.

virgō, inis f maiden, virgin; young woman; the constellation Virgo; a Roman aqueduct.

virgula, ae f, dim. of virga.

virgultum, ī n thicket, shrubbery, shrub; slip for planting.

virguncula, ae f young girl.

virid(i)ārium, ī n pleasure-garden.

viridis, e green; fresh, youthful.

viriditās ātis f greenness, verdure; freshness.

viridō 1 a) to be green; b) to make green.

virilis, e of a man, like a man, manly, male; a) courageous, vigorous; b) adult; c) prō virilī parte to the best of one's power.

virilitās, ātis f manly age, manhood; virility.

viripotēns, ntis all-powerful.

virītim adv. man for man, singly, separately.

virōsus 3 stinking, fetid.

virtūs, ūtis f manhood, manliness, virility; a) firmness, strength; b) courage, bravery, valour; constancy, resolution; gallant deeds; c) excellence, worth; d) virtue, goodness, moral perfection, good quality; pl. accomplishments.

virus, ī n slime: poison; strong smell; saltiness.

vīs (acc. vim, abl. vī; pl. vīrēs, ium) f 1. sg. force, power, strength; a) energy; b) hostile strength, violence, force, attack, impetuosity, fury, compulsion; c) power, might, influence, potency; force, meaning, nature, essence, sense, import; d) quantity, number, abundance; 2. pl. vīrēs, ium powers, bodily strength; a) military forces, troops; b) means, resources; c) mental power, vigour.

viscātus 3 smeared with bird-lime;

deceptive, ensnaring; laying under an obligation.

viscerātiō, ōnis f public distribution of meat.

viscō 1 to smear, plaster, glue together.

viscum, ī n (and viscus, ī m) mistletoe; bird-lime.

viscus, eris n (usually pl.) a) flesh, meat; b) internal organs; c) womb; one's own flesh, children; d) the inmost part, heart, centre, life e) bosom-friend, favourite.

visiō, ōnis f apparition, appearance; idea, conception.

visitō 1 to see often; to visit.

visō, sī, — 3 a) to look at carefully or attentively, to view; b) to go to see, visit; visendus 3 worth seeing.

vispillō, ōnis m = vespillo.

visum, ī n sight, appearance, vision; perception, image.

visus, ūs m a) a seeing, look, sight; b) appearance, thing seen.

vīta, ae f life, lifetime; a) soul, shade; b) way or manner of life, conduct of life, manners; c) life, biography; d) men living, the world.

vitābilis, e to be shunned.

vitābundus 3 avoiding, shunning, evading (alqd).

vitālis, e of life, vital; living, long-lived; life-sustaining; subst. -lia n/pl. a) vital parts; b) grave-clothes.

vitātiō, ōnis f an avoiding.

vitellus, ī m a) little calf; b) yolk of an egg.

viteus 3 of the vine.

viti-cola, ae m cultivator of vines.

viticula, ae f little vine.

vitifer 3 vine-bearing.

vitigenus 3 produced from vines.

vitiō 1 to spoil, mar, corrupt, injure, damage, vitiate; a) to defile, debauch, ravish; b) to falsify, forge; c) to declare (a day) unfit for public business (on account of bad omens).

vitiōsitās, ātis f viciousness.

vitiōsus 3 full of faults, faulty, defective, bad, corrupt; a) vicious, wicked, depraved; b) contrary to the auspices.

vītis, is f vine, vine-branch: a) wine; b) centurion's staff; c) alba (a plant) bryony.

**vīti-sator, ōris** *m* planter of vines.
**vitium, ī** *n* fault, defect, blemish, imperfection; **a)** a failing, error, offence, crime; **b)** moral fault, vice.
**vitō** 1 to shun, avoid.
**vitor, ōris** *m* basket-maker.
**vitreārius, ī** *m* glass-blower.
**vitreus** 3 of glass; *subst. n/pl.* glass--ware; **a)** glassy, transparent, brilliant; **b)** brittle, precarious; **c)** blue--green.
**vitricus, ī** *m* stepfather.
**vitrum¹, ī** *n* glass.
**vitrum², ī** *n* (*a vegetable dye*) woad.
**vitta, ae** *f* ribbon, band, fillet.
**vittātus** 3 adorned with a fillet.
**vitula, ae** *f* calf, heifer.
**vitulīnus** 3 of a calf; *subst.* **-a, ae** *f* veal.
**vitulor** 1 to rejoice; to offer thanks.
**vitulus, ī** *m* **a)** calf; **b)** foal; **c)** ⁓ **marīnus** seal.
**vituperābilis, e** blamable.
**vituperātiō, ōnis** *f* a blaming, blame; blamable conduct.
**vituperātor, ōris** *m* blamer, censurer.
**vituperō** 1 **a)** to spoil (*an omen*); **b)** to blame, scold, censure.
**vīvācitās, ātis** *f* vital strength, longevity.
**vīvārium, ī** *n* park, preserve, aviary, fishpond.
**vīvātus** 3 lively, animated.
**vīvāx, ācis** long-lived; lively, vigorous; lasting.
**vīvēscō** 3 to grow lively *or* strong.
**vīvidus** 3 full of life, lively, animated, vigorous; life-like.
**vīvi-rādīx, īcis** *f* cutting with root.
**vīvō, vīxī, vīctūrus** 3 to live, to live; **a)** to have *or* enjoy life; **b)** to live on, last, continue; **c)** to live upon (*abl.*), support life; **d)** to live in a certain manner, to live at a certain place.
**vīvus** 3 living, alive, having life; **mē vīvō** in my lifetime; **a)** fresh, active, lasting; **b)** natural, unwrought; *subst.* **vīvum, ī** *n* that which is alive, living flesh; capital of money, principal.
**vix** *adv.* with difficulty, hardly, scarcely, barely; (*of time*) scarcely, just.
**vix-dum** *adv.* scarcely yet.
**vocābulum, ī** *n* name, appellation.
**vōcālis, e** uttering sounds, sounding, sonorous, singing; *subst.* *f* vowel; conferring the power of speech.
**vocāmen, inis** *n* name.
**vocātiō, ōnis** *f* an inviting.
**vocātor, ōris** *m* inviter.
**vocātus, ūs** *m* a calling to *or* upon, invoking; invitation.
**vōciferātiō, ōnis** *f* an exclaiming, outcry, clamour.
**vōciferor** (*and* **-rō**) 1 to cry aloud, exclaim, shout, scream (*acc.c.inf.; ut*).
**vocitō** 1 to (be wont to) call; to shout loudly.
**vocō** 1 to call, summon (*acc.*); **a)** to cite; **b)** to invite; **c)** to challenge, defy, entice, urge, stimulate (*alqm ad alqd*); **d)** to call by name, to name; **e)** to bring into a certain condition (*alqm in odium, in periculum; alqd in dubium* to call in question).
**vōcula, ae** *f* weak voice; *pl.* soft notes, tones; spiteful remarks.
**volaemum, ī** *n* a kind of large pear.
**volāticus** 3 flying, volatile, fickle.
**volātilis, e** flying, winged; swift, transitory.
**volātus, ūs** *m* a flying, flight.
**volēmum, ī** *n* = **volaemum.**
**volēns, tis** willing; **a)** with purpose; **b)** of one's own accord, ready; **c)** well-disposed, kind, favourable, propitious, gracious; **d)** acceptable, pleasing.
**volgus, volgāris** (*archaic*) = **vulgus, vulgaris.**
**volitō** 1 to fly about *or* to and fro; to flit, hover.
**volnerō, volnus** (*archaic*) = **vulnerō, vulnus.**
**volō¹** 1 to fly, *subst.* **volantēs, ium** *f/pl.* birds; to fly, hasten.
**volō², luī, velle** to be willing, to wish, to choose, purpose, intend, desire; **a)** **velim, vellem** I should like, should be glad; **b)** **aliquem alqd velle** to want something of someone; **c)** **bene** (**male**) **alci velle** to wish well; **d)** **quid tibi vis?** what are you driving at? what is your aim?; **e)** to command, ordain, appoint, determine; **f)** to believe, pretend, contend, maintain, say; **g)** to prefer, choose rather; **h)** to mean, signify, intend to say.
**volō³, ōnis** *m* volunteer.

**volpēcula, volpēs** (*archaic*) = **vulpecula, vulpes.**

**volsella, ae** *f* pair of tweezers.

**voltur-, voltus** (*archaic*) = **vultur-, vultus.**

**volūbilis, e** that may be turned; **a)** turning, rolling, revolving; **b)** changeable, fickle, unstable; **c)** fluent, rapid (*of speech*).

**volūbilitās, ātis** *f* the power of being turned round easily; **a)** a rapid turning, whirling; **b)** mutability, inconstancy; **c)** fluency, volubility.

**volucer** (*and* -**cris**), **cris, cre** flying, winged; *subst.* **volucris** *f* (*and m*) bird, winged insect; **a)** rapid, quick, fleet; **b)** transient, changeable.

**volūmen, inis** *n* **a)** coil, whirl, fold; **b)** revolution; **c)** book, roll, volume.

**voluntārius** 3 willing, of freewill, voluntary; *subst.* volunteer.

**voluntās, ātis** *f* will, free-will; **a)** wish, desire, purpose, aim, resolution; **b)** good-will, favour, affection, readiness; **voluntāte** willingly; **c)** last will, testament; **d)** inclination, disposition.

**volup** *adv.* pleasantly, agreeably.

**voluptābilis, e** pleasing, pleasant.

**voluptārius** 3 relating to pleasure; **a)** giving enjoyment, pleasurable; **b)** devoted to pleasure, voluptuous; *subst.* ~, **ī** *m* voluptuary, Epicure.

**voluptās, ātis** *f* pleasure, enjoyment, delight; **a)** desire, passion, sensual pleasures; **b)** *pl.* public shows, sports, spectacles, games; **c) mea voluptas** my darling.

**voluptuōsus** 3 agreeable, delightful.

**volūtābrum, ī** *n* hog-pool.

**volūtābundus** 3 wallowing about.

**volūtātiō, ōnis** *f* a rolling, wallowing; restlessness.

**volūtō** 1 to roll, turn; **a)** to roll about; **P.** to wallow, luxuriate; **b)** to turn over in the mind, consider, weigh.

**volva, ae** *f* womb (*esp. of a sow*).

**volvō, lvī, lūtum** 3 to roll, turn round *or* about, whirl round; **a)** to unroll (*books*), to read; **b)** to roll along, bring on, roll forth *or* down; **c) orbem** to form a circle; **d)** to pour forth (*words*), utter fluently; **e)** to revolve in the mind, to cher-

ish, to consider, weigh, ponder, meditate; **f)** to roll on (*time*), bring on *or* round; **P.** to turn round, revolve, roll oneself round *or* about.

**vōmer, eris** *m* ploughshare.

**vomica, ae** *f* abscess, ulcer.

**vōmis, eris** *m* = **vomer.**

**vomitiō, ōnis** *f and* -**tus, ūs** *m* a vomiting.

**vomitō** 1 to vomit.

**vomitor, ōris** *m* one who vomits.

**vomō, uī, itum** 3 to vomit; to vomit up, throw up (*alqd*).

**vorāginōsus** 3 full of chasms *or* pits.

**vorāgō, inis** *f* **a)** chasm, abyss; **b)** whirlpool.

**vorāx, ācis** greedy, voracious, gluttonous.

**vorō** 1 to devour, swallow; to read eagerly.

**vorrō** 3 = **verrō.**

**vors-,** *see* **vers-.**

**vorsōria, ae** *f* sail-rope; -**am capiō** to tack.

**vortex, vortō** (*archaic*) = **vertex, verto.**

**vōs** you (*pl.*).

**voster** (*archaic*) = **vester.**

**vōti-fer** 3 bearing a votive offering.

**vōtivus** 3 vowed, votive, promised by a vow, devoted.

**votō** 1 = **vetō.**

**vōtum, ī** *n* **a)** that which is vowed *or* promised by a vow, offering, gift; **b)** vow, promise to a god; **vōti damnātus** *or* **reus** having attained one's prayer; **c)** wish, desire, longing, prayer.

**voveō, vōvī, vōtum** 2 **a)** to vow, promise solemnly, pledge (*alqd; acc.c.inf.*); **b)** to wish, desire.

**vōx, vōcis** *f* voice; **a)** sound, tone, utterance, cry, call; **b)** word, saying, speech, remark, proverb, maxim; language; formula; **c)** tone, accent.

**vulgāris, e** common, usual, vulgar, extending to all.

**vūlgātor, ōris** *m* publisher, divulger.

**vulgātus** 3 common, public, known to all, notorious.

**vulgi-vagus** 3 roving, inconstant.

**vulgō¹,** *see* **vulgus.**

**vulgō²** 1 **a)** to spread among the multitude, make common, communicate; **b)** to prostitute; **c)** to publish, divulge.

**vulgus, ī** *n* (*acc*. also **vulgum** *m*) the people, the great multitude, the public, mob, rabble; **a)** the common soldiers; **b)** mass, crowd, throng, multitude; **c) vulgō** before all the world, openly, everywhere, generally, indiscriminately.

**vulnerātiō, ōnis** *f* a wounding, wound, injury.

**vulnerō** 1 to wound; to hurt, injure, grieve.

**vulni-ficus** 3 inflicting wounds.

**vulnus, eris** *n* wound; **a)** hurt, cut, blow, stroke; **b)** injury, misfortune, calamity, defeat, disaster; **c)** grief, pain, anguish, wound of love.

**vulpēcula, ae** *f* little fox.

**vulpēs, is** *f* fox.

**vulpīnus** 3 of a fox.

**vulsus** 3 with the hair plucked out, bald; effeminate.

**vulticulus, ī** *m* a mere look.

**vultuōsus** 3 making faces, full of grimaces; affected.

**vultur, uris** *m* vulture; avaricious man.

**vulturīnus** 3 of a vulture.

**vulturius, ī** *m* vulture; avaricious man; an unlucky throw at dice.

**vultus, ūs** *m* face, visage, countenance, features, looks, air, mien; **a)** bold, stern *or* angry look; **b)** look, appearance.

**vulva, ae** *f* = **volva**.

# X

**xenium, ī** *n* present (given to a guest).

**xērampelinae, ārum** *f/pl*. dark red clothes.

**xiphiās, ae** *m* sword-fish.

**xysticus, ī** *m* athlete.

**xystus, ī** *m* (*and* **-um, ī** *n*) walk in a garden, promenade.

# Z

**zāmia, ae** *f* damage, injury.

**zēlotypus** 3 jealous.

**zephyrus, ī** *m* west-wind.

**zmaragdus, ī** *m, f* = **smaragdus.**

**zōdiacus, ī** *m* the zodiac.

**zōna, ae** *f* girdle, belt (*of women*); **a)** money-belt; **b)** zone of the earth, climatic region.

**zōnārius** 3 of a belt; *subst. m* maker of girdles.

**zōnula, ae** *f* little girdle.

**zō-thēca, ae** *f*, **zō-thēcula, ae** *f* rest-room.

# English-Latin Dictionary

# A

**a: twice a day** bis in die.
**abandon** (*a person*) relinquo 3, desero 3; (*a task*) omitto 3; **~ed** perditus.
**abase** summitto 3.
**abash** ruborem inicio 3 (*alci*).
**abate** *v/t.* imminuo 3; *v/i.* remitto 3; **~ment** remissio *f*.
**abbey** abbatia *f*.
**abbreviat|e** imminuo 3; **~ion** contractio *f*.
**abdicat|e** abdico 1 (*me magistratu*); **~ion** abdicatio *f*.
**abduct** rapio 3.
**aberration** error *m*.
**abet** adiuvo 1; **~tor** minister *m*.
**abeyance: be in ~** iaceo 2 (*leges*).
**abhor** abhorreo 2 (ab); **~rence** odium *n*; **~rent (to)** alienus (ab).
**abide** habito 1, maneo 2; **~ by** sto 1 (*abl.*, *in re*).
**ability** facultas *f*, ingenium *n*.
**abject** humilis.
**abjure** eiuro 1.
**able** potens, potis, pote; ingeniosus; **~-bodied** validus; **be ~** possum.
**aboard** in nave; **go ~** navem conscendo 3.
**abode** domicilium *n*.
**abolish** tollo 3, aboleo 2.
**abomin|able** infandus, detestabilis; **~ate** abominor 1; **~ation** nefas *n*.
**aboriginal** indigena *m and f*.
**abortion** abortus, us *m*.
**abortive** irritus.
**abound** abundo 1, circumfluo 3 (*abl.*); **~ing in** abundans (*abl.*).
**about** *prep.* circ *ε*, circum (*acc.*); de (*abl.*); *adv.* circa, fere.
**above** *prep.* super, supra (*acc.*); **~ all** ante omnia; *adv.* supra.
**abreast** a latere (*alcis*).
**abridge** contraho 3; **~ment** epitoma *f and* -e *f*.
**abroad** foris, peregre; **be ~** peregrinor 1.
**abrogat|e** abrogo 1, rescindo 3; **~ion** abrogatio *f*.
**abrupt** repentinus, subitus; **~ly** subito.
**abscess** vomica *f*.

**abscond** lateo 2, latito 1.
**absence** absentia *f*; **leave of ~** commeatus, us *m*.
**absent** absens; **~-minded** obliviosus; **be ~** absum.
**absolute** purus, absolutus; **~ power** infinita potestas *f*; **~ly** plane, prorsus.
**absolve** absolvo 3.
**absorb** bibo 3; **~ent** bibulus; **~ed** occupatus.
**abstain** abstineo 2 (*abl.*).
**abstemious** abstemius.
**abstinen|ce** abstinentia *f*; **~t** abstinens.
**abstract** separo 1; *adj.* cogitatione perceptus.
**abstruse** reconditus, abstrusus.
**absurd** absurdus, ineptus; **~ity** ineptia *f*.
**abundan|ce** affluentia *f*, abundantia *f*; **~t** amplus, largus.
**abus|e** abutor 3 (*abl.*); maledico 3 (*alci*); contumelia *f*; **~ive** contumeliosus.
**abut** adiaceo 2 (*ad alqd, dat.*); **~ting** finitimus.
**abyss** vorago *f*, barathrum *n*.
**accede** assentior 4 (*alci*).
**accelerate** accelero 1.
**accent** sonus *m* (vocis); **~uate** syllabam acuo 3.
**accept** accipio 3; **~able** gratus, acceptus; **~ance** approbatio *f*.
**access** aditus, us *m*; **~ible** pervius (*dat.*); facilis (*homo*).
**accessory** adiunctus; conscius *m*.
**accident** casus, us *m*; **by ~** casu; **~al** fortuitus.
**acclamation** clamor *m*.
**accommodat|e** accommodo 1 (*alqd alci, ad alqd*); **~ing** comis; **~ion** deversorium *n*; accommodatio *f*.
**accompaniment: to the ~ of** ad (*acc.*).
**accompany** comitor 1, prosequor 3.
**accomplice** conscius *m*.
**accomplish** conficio 3, efficio 3; **~ed** politus; **~ments** artes *f/pl*.
**accord** *v/t.* concedo 3; *v/i.* consentio 4; *subst.* consensus, us *m*; **of**

**one's own** ~ sua sponte, ultro); **in ~ance with** ex (*abl.*); ~**ing to** pro (*abl.*); ~**ingly** itaque.

**accost** appello 1.

**account** numero 1, duco 3; ~ **for** causam affero 3; ratio *f*; narratio *f*; **on** ~ **of** ob, propter (*acc.*); **on no** ~ nullo modo; ~**ant** ratiocinator *m*; ~-**book** tabulae *f/pl.*

**accoutrements** arma *n/pl.*

**accrue** cedo 3 (*alci, in alqm*).

**accumulat|e** cumulo 1; ~**ion** congestus, us *m*.

**accura|cy** subtilitas *f*; ~**te** subtilis; ~**tely** accurate.

**accursed** sacer, exsecratus.

**accus|ation** accusatio *f*; ~**e** accuso 1 (*alqm rei*); ~**ed** reus *m*; ~**er** accusator *m*.

**accustom** assuefacio 3 (*alqm re*); **be** ~**ed** soleo 2.

**acerbity** acerbitas *f*.

**ache** doleo 2; dolor *m*.

**achieve** perficio 3; ~**ment** res *f* gesta.

**acid** acidus.

**acknowledge** fateor 2 (*acc. c. inf.*); agnosco 3 (*acc.*); ~**ment** confessio *f*.

**acme** culmen *n*.

**acorn** glans *f*.

**acquaint** certiorem facio 3 (*alqm*); ~**ance** consuetudo *f*, cognitio *f*.

**acquiesce** acquiesco 3 (*abl.*), contentus sum.

**acqui|re** acquiro 3; ~**sition** comparatio *f*.

**acquit** absolvo 3 (*de re*); ~**tal** absolutio *f*.

**acre** iugerum *n* (= ²/₃ *acre*).

**acrimonious** acerbus.

**across** trans (*acc.*).

**act** ago 3, me gero 3; *thea.* ago (*play or part*); factum *n*; *thea.* actus, us *m*; ~ **of Parliament** lex *f*; ~**ion** actio *f* (*also jur.*).

**activ|e** impiger, industrius; ~**ity** industria *f*.

**actor** histrio *m*; **actress** mima *f*.

**actual** verus; ~**ly** re vera.

**acumen** ingenii acies *f*.

**acute** acer.

**adage** proverbium *n*.

**adapt** accommodo 1.

**add** addo 3.

**adder** vipera *f*.

**addicted to** deditus (*dat.*).

**addition** accessio *f*.

**address** alloquor 3; alloquium *n*.

**adduce** profero 3.

**adept** peritus.

**adequate** par, satis magnus.

**adhere** haereo 2 (*in, ad*); sto 1 (*ab*); ~**nt** assectator *m*.

**adhesive** tenax.

**adieu** vale(te).

**adjacent** finitimus.

**adjoin** adiaceo 2 (*dat., ad*).

**adjourn** *v/t.* differo 3 (**till** *in* + *acc.*)

**adjudge** adiudico 1 (*alci alqd*).

**adjure** obsecro 1.

**adjust** accommodo 1, compono 3.

**adjutant** optio *m*.

**administer** administro 1; ~ **an oath** (*alqm*) iure iurando adigo 3.

**administrat|ion** procuratio *f*; ~**or** procurator *m*.

**admir|able** admirabilis; ~**ation** admiratio *f*; ~**e** admiror 1.

**admiral** praefectus *m* classis.

**admit (of)** recipio 3; ~**tance** aditus, us *m*.

**admonish** admoneo 2; ~**ment** monita *n/pl.*

**ado** negotium *n*.

**adolescent** adulescens *m*.

**adopt** adopto 1; ~**ion** adoptio *f*; ~**ive** adoptivus.

**adore** veneror 1.

**adorn** decoro 1.

**adrift: be** ~ fluctuo 1.

**adroit** callidus; ~**ness** sollertia *f*.

**adulation** assentatio *f*.

**adult** adultus.

**adulterate** corrumpo 3.

**adulter|er** adulter *m*; ~**ess** adultera *f*; ~**y** adulterium *n*; **commit** ~**y** adultero 1.

**advance** *v/t.* promoveo 2; *v/i.* progredior 3; ~**ed** (*time*) provectus; ~**ment** honor *m*.

**advantage** bonum *n*, commodum *n*; ~**ous** utilis; **be** ~**ous** prosum 1.

**adventure** casus, us *m*.

**advers|ary** adversarius *m*; ~**e** adversus; ~**ity** res *f/pl.* adversae.

**advert to** attingo 3 (*acc.*).

**advertise** proscribo 3; ~**ment** proscriptio *f*.

**advice** consilium *n*.

**advise** suadeo 2, moneo 2; ~**dly** consulto; ~**r** consiliarius *m*.

**advoca|cy** suasio *f*; *jur.* patrocinium *n*; ~**te** suadeo 2; *jur.* patronus *m*.

**aedile** aedilis *m*; ~**ship** aedilitas *f*.

**aegis** aegis *f*.

**aerial** aerius, aetherius.

**afar** procul.

**affab|ility** comitas *f*; **~le** comis.

**affair** res *f*, negotium *n*; **love ~** amor *m*.

**affect** afficio 3, moveo 2; simulo 1; **~ation** simulatio *f*; **~ed** molestus.

**affection** affectus, us *m*, amor *m*; **~ate** amans.

**affiance** spondeo 2.

**affinity** cognatio *f*.

**affirm** affirmo 1.

**affix** affigo 3.

**afflict** afflicto 1; **~ed with** affectus (*abl.*); **~ion** miseria *f*.

**affluen|ce** divitiae *f/pl.*; **~t** dives.

**afford** praebeo 2.

**affront** offendo 3; contumelia *f*.

**afloat: be ~** navigo 1.

**afoot** pedibus; **set ~** moveo 2.

**aforesaid** supra commemoratus.

**afraid** timidus, pavidus; **be ~ (of)** timeo 2; metuo 3.

**afresh** de integro.

**after** *prep.* post, secundum (*acc.*); *cj.* postquam; **~noon** post meridiem; *adj.* postmeridianus; **~wards** post, postea.

**again** iterum, rursus, rursum; **~ and ~** etiam atque etiam.

**against** contra, adversus, in (*acc.*).

**agape** hians.

**age** aetas *f*, saeculum *n*; (*of things*) vetustas *f*; **old ~** senectus, utis *f*; **4 years of ~** quattuor annos natus.

**aged** senex, provectae aetatis.

**agen|cy** opera *f* (*chiefly in abl.*); **~t** actor *m*; minister *m*.

**aggrandize** augeo 2.

**aggravate** aggravo 1.

**aggregate** summa *f*.

**aggress|ion** incursio *f*; **~ive** infestus; **be the ~or** ultro arma infero 3.

**aggrieve** laedo 3.

**aghast** attonitus.

**agil|e** pernix; **~ity** pernicitas *f*.

**agitat|e** agito 1, perturbo 1; **~ed** sollicitus; **~ion** agitatio *f*, perturbatio *f*.

**ago** abhinc (*acc.*); **long ~** iam pridem, iam dudum; **some time ~** dudum.

**agony** cruciatus, us *m*, acerbissimus dolor *m*.

**agrarian** agrarius.

**agree** consentio 4 (*cum alqo, de re*); congruo 3, assentior 4; **~ upon** compono 3; **~able** gratus, commodus, suavis; **be ~d** constat; **be ~d upon** convenit; **~ment** consensus, us *m*, conventum *n*; pactio *f*.

**agricultur|al** rusticus, agrestis; **~e** agri cultura *f*, res *f/pl.* rusticae.

**aground: run ~** sido 3.

**ague** febris *f*.

**ah** *int.* ah, a, heu.

**ahead: go ~** antecedo 3 (*dat., acc.*); anteeo (*dat., acc.*).

**aid** adiuvo 1 (*acc.*), succurro 3 (*dat.*); auxilium *n*.

**aide-de-camp** optio *m*.

**ail** doleo 2, aegroto 1; **~ing** aegrotus, aeger; **~ment** morbus *m*.

**aim** intendo 3 (*alqd, in alqd, alci*), peto 3 (*alqm*); *fig.* affecto 1, peto 3; finis *m*, consilium *n*.

**air** aer *m*, aether *m*, aura *f*; species *f*, modus *m*; **in the open ~** sub divo; **take the ~** deambulo 1; **put on ~s** me iacto 1; **~ing** ambulatio *f*; **~y** aerius.

**aisle** ala *f*.

**akin** finitimus (*dat.*).

**alacrity** alacritas *f*.

**alarm** terreo 2; **be ~ed** perturbor 1; trepidatio *f*, tumultus, us *m*, terror *m*.

**alas** heu, eheu, hei.

**albeit** etsi.

**alcove** angulus *m*; recessus, us *m*.

**alder** alnus, i *f*.

**ale** fermentum *n*.

**alert** alacer, vigil.

**alien** externus, alienus; peregrinus *m*; **~ate** (ab)alieno 1; **~ation** alienatio *f*.

**alight** descendo 3 (ad pedes); desilio 4; **set ~** incendo 3.

**alike** par, similis; *adv.* pariter.

**aliment** alimentum *n*.

**alive** vivus; **be ~** vivo 3.

**all** omnis, cunctus, totus; **~ together** universus; **~ the better** tanto melius; **nothing at ~** nihil omnino; **in ~** omnino.

**allay** levo 1, sedo 1.

**alleg|ation** affirmatio *f*; **~e** praetendo 3 (*acc.*); refero 3 (*acc. c. inf.*).

**allegiance** fides *f*; **take oath of ~** in verba alicuius iuro 1.

**allegory** translationes *f/pl.*

**alleviat|e** levo 1; **~ion** levatio *f*.

**alley** angiportus, us *m*.

**alli|ance** societas *f*, foedus *n*, coniunctio *f*; **~ed** socius, foederatus.

**allot** distribuo 3, assigno 1, do 1; ~ment assignatio *f*.

**allow** confiteor 2; patior 3 (*acc. c. inf.*; *ut*), sino 3 (*inf.*; *acc. c. inf.*), permitto 3 (*ut, inf.*); ~able permissus; ~ance diarium *n*; **make** ~ances for ignosco 3 (*dat.*); **it is** ~ed licet 2.

**alloy** corrumpo 3, misceo 2.

**allude to** tango 3, designo 1.

**allur|e** allicio 3; ~ement blanditia *f*; ~ing blandus.

**ally** socio 1; socius *m*.

**almanac** fasti *m/pl.*

**almighty** omnipotens.

**almond** amygdala *f*.

**almost** paene, fere, ferme.

**alms** stips *f*.

**aloft** sublime, in sublime, alte.

**alone** solus, unus; **let** ~ abstineo 2 (*ab*).

**along** praeter (*acc.*), secundum (*acc.*), per (*acc.*).

**aloof** procul; **keep** ~ removeo 2 me (*ab algo*).

**aloud** clare.

**alphabet** litterae *f/pl.*

**alpine** alpinus.

**already** iam.

**also** etiam, quoque.

**altar** ara *f*, altaria *n/pl.*

**alter** *v/t.* muto 1; *v/i.* mutor 1; ~ation mutatio *f*.

**altercation** iurgium *n*.

**alternat|e** vario 1; alternus; ~ely alternis, invicem; ~ion vicissitudo *f*; **have an** ~ive optio est (*alci*).

**although** quamquam, quamvis, (tam)etsi.

**altogether** omnino.

**always** semper.

**amalgamate** misceo 2.

**amanuensis** librarius *m*.

**amass** coacervo 1.

**amatory** amatorius.

**amaz|e** obstupefacio 3; **be** ~ed stupeo 2; ~ement stupor *m*; ~ing mirus.

**ambassador** legatus *m*.

**amber** sucinum *n*.

**ambigu|ity** ambiguitas *f*; ~ous ambiguus.

**ambitio|n** ambitio *f*; ~us cupidus gloriae.

**ambrosia** ambrosia *f*.

**ambuscade, ambush** insidior 1 (*dat.*); insidiae *f/pl.*

**amenable** oboediens (*dat.*).

**amend** corrigo 3, emendo 1; **make** ~s satisfacio 3 (*alci de re*).

**amiab|ility** suavitas *f*; ~le suavis.

**amicable** amicus.

**amid(st)** inter (*acc.*).       [fero 3.]

**amiss** perperam; **take** ~ moleste

**amity** amicitia *f*.

**ammunition** apparatus, us *m*; arma *n/pl.*

**amnesty** venia *f*.

**among** inter (*acc.*); apud (*acc.*).

**amorous** amatorius.

**amount** summa *f*; ~ **to** efficio 3, summa est.

**amphitheatre** amphitheatrum *n*.

**ampl|e** amplus; ~ify dilato 1; ~y abunde.

**amputate** seco 1.

**amuse** oblecto 1, delecto 1; ~ **one-self** ludo 3; ~ment delectatio *f*.

**analogy** similitudo, inis *f*, comparatio *f*.

**analyse** subtiliter dissero 3.

**anarch|ical** turbulentus; ~y licentia *f*.

**ancest|or** avus *m*, proavus *m*; *pl.* maiores *m/pl.*; ~ral avitus.

**anchor** ancora *f*; **weigh** ~ ancoram tollo 3; ~age statio *f*.

**ancient** antiquus, vetus, priscus.

**and** et, ac, atque, ...que.

**anecdote** fabula *f*.

**anew** denuo, de integro.

**angel** angelus *m*.

**anger** irrito 1; ira *f*.

**angle** piscor 1; angulus *m*; ~r piscator *m*.

**angr|ily** iracunde; ~y iratus; **be** ~y irascor 3.

**anguish** angor *m*.

**angular** angulatus.

**animadver|sion** animadversio *f*; ~t animadverto 3.

**animal** animal *n*; pecus, udis *f*, fera *f*.

**animat|e** animo 1, excito 1; ~ed alacer; ~ion animatio *f*, vis *f*.

**animosity** odium *n*.

**ankle** talus *m*.

**annals** annales *m/pl.*

**annex** addo 3, subicio 3.

**annihilat|e** deleo 2; ~ion internecio *f*.

**anniversary** dies *m* anniversarius.

**annotate** commentarium scribo 3 (*in alqd*).

**announce** (pro)nuntio 1; ~ment pronuntiatio *f*.

**annoy** offendo 3, vexo 1; ~ance molestia *f*, vexatio *f*; **be ~ed** moleste fero 3; ~ing molestus.

**annual** anniversarius, annuus; ~ly quotannis.

**annuity** annua *n/pl*.

**annul** tollo 3; ~ment abrogatio *f*.

**anoint** ungo 3; ~ing unctio *f*.

**anon** statim, mox.

**anonymous** sine auctoris nomine.

**another** alius; **one after ~** alius ex alio; **at ~ time** alias; **one ~** inter se; ~'s alienus.

**answer** respondeo 2 (*alci alqd*; *de re*), rescribo 3; ~ **for** praesto 1 (*alqm*; *alqd alci*); responsum *n*.

**ant** formica *f*.

**antagonis|m** odium *n*; ~t adversarius *m*.

**antechamber** atriolum *n*.

**anthem** carmen *n*.

**anticipate** antevenio 4 (*dat.*; *acc.*); anteverto 3 (*dat.*); praecipio 3.

**antics** ineptiae *f/pl*.

**antidote** remedium *n*.

**antipathy** odium *n*.

**antiquarian** antiquarius.

**antiqu|e** antiquus, priscus; ~ity antiquitas *f*.

**antithesis** *rhet.* contentio *f*.

**antler** cornu, us *n*.

**anvil** incus, udis *f*.

**anxi|ety** sollicitudo *f*, cura *f*; ~ous anxius, sollicitus; **be ~ous to** laboro 1 (*ut*, *inf.*).

**any** ullus; qui, qua *or* quae, quod; aliqui, aliqua, aliquod; ~**how** saltem, certe; ~**one** aliquis; quis; quisquam; ~**onesoever** quilibet, quivis; ~**thing** aliquid; quid; quidquam.

**apart** separatim, seorsum; ~ **from** praeter (*acc.*), extra (*acc.*); ~ment conclave *n*.

**apath|etic** languidus; ~y stupor *m*.

**ape** simia *f*.

**aperture** foramen *n*, hiatus, us *m*.

**aphorism** sententia *f*.

**apiary** alvus, i *f*.

**apolog|ist** defensor *m*; ~ise excuso 1 (*me*, *aldq*); veniam peto 3 (*gen.*, *quod*); ~y excusatio *f*.

**appal** exterreo 2.

**apparatus** apparatus, us *m*.

**apparel** vestio 4; vestis *f*.

**apparent** apertus, manifestus; simulatus, fictus; **be ~** appareo 2; ~ly specie.

**apparition** simulacrum *n*.

**appeal** appello 1, provoco 1 (*also jur.*); obsecro 1, testor 1; obsecratio *f*; *jur.* appellatio *f*, provocatio *f*.

**appear** appareo 2; me ostendo 3; *jur.* adsum, me sisto 3; videor 2; ~ance species *f*, aspectus, us *m*.

**appease** placo 1, sedo 1.

**appellant** appellator *m*.

**append** addo 3; ~age appendix *f*.

**appertain** pertineo 2 (*ad alqd*).

**appetite** appetitus, us *m*; cupiditas *f*, fames *f*.

**applau|d** (ap)plaudo 3, faveo 2; ~se plausus, us *m*; clamor *m*.

**apple** malum *n*.

**applica|ble** commodus (*dat.*); ~nt petitor *m*; ~tion petitio *f*; studium *n*.

**apply** *v/t.* adhibeo 2, admoveo 2; me confero 3 (*ad alqd*); *v/i.* pertineo 2 (*ad*); aggredior 3 (*alqm*).

**appoint** creo 1, facio 3, praeficio 3 (**to** *dat.*), constituo 3; ~ment creatio *f*, constitutum *n*.

**apportion** divido 3.

**apposite** aptus.

**appraise** aestimo 1.

**appreciate** aestimo 1.

**apprehen|d** comprehendo 3, percipio 3; metuo 3; ~sive timidus.

**apprentice** discipulus *m*.

**apprize** certiorem facio 3.

**approach** accedo 3 (*ad*, *acc.*, *dat.*); appropinquo 1 (*ad alqd*, *dat.*); accessus, us *m*; aditus, us *m*.

**approbation** approbatio *f*.

**appropriate** mihi arrogo 1, mihi ascisco 3, sumo 3; proprius, congruens (*dat.*).

**approv|al** approbatio *f*; ~e laudo 3, approbo 1.

**approximate** accedo 3 (*ad*, *dat.*); proximus.

**April** Aprilis (*mensis*) *m*.

**apt** aptus, idoneus, pronus (*ad*); ~itude ingenium *n*.

**aquatic** aquatilis.

**aqueduct** aquae ductus, us *m*.

**aquiline** aduncus.

**arable land** arvum *n*.

**arbiter** arbiter *m*.

**arbitrar|ily** ad libidinem (*alcs*); ~y libidinosus.

**arbitrat|e** discepto 1; ~or arbiter *m*.

**arbour** umbraculum *n*.

**arc** arcus, us *m*.

**arcade** porticus, us *f*.

**arch** fornix *m*, arcus, us *m*; lascivus; **~ed** fornicatus.

**archer** sagittarius *m*.

**architect** architectus *m*; **~ure** architectura *f*.

**archives** tabulae *f/pl*.

**archon** archon *m*.

**arctic** septentriones *m/pl*.; septentrionalis.

**ard|ent** ardens, vehemens; **~our** ardor *m*.

**arduous** arduus.

**area** area *f*; regio *f*.

**arena** arena *f*.

**argu|e** disputo 1, dissero 3; **~ment** argumentum *n*, ratio *f*, disputatio *f*.

**aria** canticum *n*.

**arid** aridus; **~ity** ariditas *f*.

**aright** recte.

**arise** (con)surgo 3; exorior 4 (*ex*); nascor 3.

**aristocra|cy** optimates *m/pl*.; **~tic** nobilis.

**arithmetic** arithmetica *n/pl*.

**ark** arca *f*.

**arm** *v/t.* armo 1; *v/i.* arma capio 3; bracchium *n*, lacertus *m*; **~s** arma *n/pl*., tela *n/pl*.; **be under ~s** sum in armis; **lay down ~s** arma pono 3.

**armature** copiae *f/pl*.

**armistice** induliae *f/pl*.

**armour** arma *n/pl*.; **~-bearer** armiger *m*; **~er** faber *m*; **~y** armamentarium *n*.

**armpit** ala *f*, axilla *f*.    [acies *f*.\]

**army** exercitus, us *m*; agmen *n*;\]

**aroma** odor *m*; **~tic** odoratus *m*.

**around** *prep.* circum, circa (*acc.*); *adv.* circa.

**arouse** suscito 1, excito 1.

**arraign** accuso 1.

**arrange** instruo 3, dispono 3, compono 3, ordino 1; **~ment** collocatio *f*, institutio *f*.

**array** instruo 3; **battle-~** acies *f*.

**arrears** reliqua *n/pl*.

**arrest** comprehendo 3; comprehensio *f*.

**arriv|al** adventus, us *m*; **~e** advenio 4, pervenio 4 (*in*, *ad*).

**arrogan|ce** arrogantia *f*, superbia *f*; **~t** arrogans.

**arrogate** sumo 3 (*mihi*).

**arrow** sagitta *f*; **~-head** cuspis, idis *f*.

**arsenal** armamentarium *n*.

**arson** incendium *n*.

**art** ars *f*; artificium *n*; opus *n*.

**artery** vena *f*.

**artful** callidus, vafer; **~ness** calliditas *f*.

**artic|le** res *f*, merx *f*, articulus *m*; **~ulate** distinctus; articulo 1; **~ulation** explanatio *f*.

**artifice** dolus *m*; **~r** artifex *m and f*.

**artificial** artificiosus, manu factus.

**artillery** tormenta *n/pl*.

**artisan** opifex *m and f*.

**artist** artifex *m and f*; pictor *m*; **~ic** artificiosus.

**artless** simplex.

**as** (*in comparisons*) atque, et, quam, ut; **~ ... ~** tam ... quam; **just ~** velut, tamquam, sicut; (*temporal*) dum; (*causal*) cum, quoniam; **~ regards** de (*abl.*), quod.

**ascen|d** ascendo 3 (*in*, *ad*); **~dency** potentia *f*; **~t** ascensus, us *m*.

**ascertain** comperio 4, cognosco 3.

**ascetic** austerus; **~ism** austeritas *f*.

**ascribe** ascribo 3, assigno 1.

**ash(-tree)** fraxinus, i *f*; **mountain ash** ornus, i *f*.

**ashamed: be ~** pudet 2 (*alqm*, *alcis rei*).

**ashes** cinis, eris *m*.

**ashore** in terram, in terra.

**ask** rogo 1 (*alqd ab alqo*; *ut*); peto 3 (*ut*); quaero 3 (*alqd*; *de re*).

**askance** limus, obliquus.

**aslant** obliquus.

**asleep: be ~** dormio 4; **fall ~** obdormio 4.

**aspect** facies *f*, aspectus, us *m*, vultus, us *m*.

**aspen** populus, i *f*.

**asperity** acerbitas *f*.

**aspersions: cast ~ on** calumnior 1.

**aspir|ation** studium *n*; **~e** aspiro 1 (*in*, *ad alqd*); peto 3; **~ing** appetens (*alcis rei*).

**ass** asinus *m*.

**assail** oppugno 1; invehor 3; **~ant** oppugnator *m*.

**assassin** percussor *m*, sicarius *m*; **~ate** caedo 3; **~ation** caedes *f*.

**assault** adorior 4; oppugnatio *f*, vis *f*.

**assembl|e** *v/t.* cogo 3, convoco 1; *v/i.* convenio 4; **~y** coetus, us *m*.

**assent** assentior 4; assensus, us *m*.

**assert** affirmo 1, vindico 1; **~ion** affirmatio *f*.

**assess** aestimo 1; **~ for taxes** censeo 2; **~ment** aestimatio *f*, census, us *m*; **~or** *jur.* assessor *m*.

**assets** bona *n/pl.*

**asseverate** assevero 1.

**assidu|ity** diligentia *f*; **~ous** sedulus.

**assign** (at)tribuo 3; *jur.* delego 1; **~ation** constitutum *n*; **~ment** assignatio *f*.

**assist** (ad)iuvo 1; **~ance** auxilium *n*, (ops,) opis *f*; **~ant** adiutor *m*, minister *m*.

**assizes** conventus, us *m*.

**associate** *v/t.* consocio 1; *v/i.* **~ with** utor 3 (*abl.*); socius *m*.

**association** societas *f*.

**assort** *v/i.* congruo 3; **~ment** varietas *f*.

**assuage** levo 1.

**assum|e** suscipio 3, induo 3, sumo 3 (*mihi*; *acc. c. inf.*); **~ption** arrogantia *f*; opinio *f*.

**assur|ance** fides *f*, fiducia *f*; **~e** confirmo 1, promitto 3; **be ~ed** confido 3; **~edly** profecto.

**astern** in puppi.

**asthma** anhelitus, us *m*.

**astonish** obstupefacio 3; **be ~ed** admiror 1, obstupesco 3; **~ment** admiratio *f*, stupor *m*.

**astound** obstupefacio 3; **be ~ed** obstupesco 3.

**astray: go ~** erro 1; **lead ~** in errorem induco 3.

**astringent** asper.

**astrolog|er** astrologus *m*; **~y** astrologia *f*.

**astronomer** astrologus *m*.

**astute** callidus.

**asunder: burst ~** dissilio 4.

**asylum** perfugium *n*.

**at** ad; apud; in (*abl.*); **~ the house of** apud (*alqm*); **~ home** domi; **~ Rome** Romae; **~ daybreak** prima luce; **~ the age of five** quinque annos natus; **~ a high price** magno pretio.

**atheist** impius.

**athlet|e** athleta *m*; **~ic** robustus.

**atmosphere** aer *m*, caelum *n*.

**atom** atomus, i *f*; corpora individua *n/pl.*

**atone** expio 1 (*alqd*); luo 3 (*alqd*); **~ment** piaculum *n*.

**atroci|ous** immanis; **~ty** atrocitas *f*.

**attach** adiungo 3, applico 1 (*ad alqd*, *alci rei*); **~ importance to** mea interest; **~ed to** devinctus(*alci*); **~ed by** alligatus (*abl.*); **~ment** caritas *f*.

**attack** adorior 4, oppugno 1, aggre-

**dior** 3; *fig.* invehor 3 (*in alqm*); *med.* tempto 1; impetus, us *m*.

**attain** consequor 3, pervenio 4 (*ad*, *in alqd*); adipiscor 3.

**attempt** conor 1, molior 4; conatum *n*.

**attend** prosequor 3 (*acc.*); intersum (*in re*, *dat.*); **~ to** animadverto 3, curo 1; **~ance** assectatio *f*; **~ant** assectator *m*.

**attent|ion** attentus animus *m*; observantia *f*; **pay ~ to** operam do 1, studeo 2 (*dat.*); **~ive** attentus, observans.

**attenuate** extenuo 1.

**attest** testificor 1.

**attic** cenaculum *n*.

**attire** vestio 4; vestitus, us *m*.

**attitude** status, us *m*; **adopt an ~** me gero 3.

**attorney** cognitor *m*.

**attract** (at)traho 3; **~ion** illecebrae *f/pl.*; **~ive** blandus.

**attribute** (at)tribuo 3; **be an ~ of** insum (*in re*; *dat.*); proprium est (*gen.*).

**auburn** fulvus.

**auction** auctio *f*; **sell by ~** sub hasta vendo 3; **~eer** praeco *m*.

**audac|ious** audax, confidens; **~ity** audacia *f*, confidentia *f*.

**audible** clarus.

**audience** audientes *m/pl.*, auditores *m/pl.*; **grant ~ to** admitto 3.

**audit** dispungo 3.

**auditor** auditor *m*.

**augment** augeo 2; **~ation** incrementum *n*.

**augur** auguror 1, vaticinor 1; augur *m*; **~y** augurium *n*; **take the ~ies** auguror 1.

**august** augustus.      [stus *m.*]

**August** (mensis) Sextilis *m*, Augu-]

**aunt** (*paternal*) amita *f*; (*maternal*) matertera *f*.

**auspices** auspicium *n*; **take the ~** auspicor 1.

**auspicious** faustus.

**auster|e** severus, austerus; **~ity** severitas *f*.

**authentic** verus; **well ~ated** quod constat.

**author** auctor *m*, scriptor *m*; **~ity** auctoritas *f*, potestas *f*; **~ities** magistratus *m/pl.*; **~ize** potestatem do 1 (*alci*).

**autograph** chirographum *n*.

**autonomy** libertas *f*.

**autumn** autumnus *m*; ~al autumnus.

**auxiliar|y** auxiliaris; ~ies auxilia *n/pl.*

**avail| o.s. of** utor 3 (*abl.*); **it ~s** prodest; **be of no ~** nihil valeo 2; ~able expeditus, in expedito.

**avaric|e** avaritia *f*; ~ious avarus.

**aveng|e** ulciscor 3 (*acc.*); ~er ultor *m*; ~ing ultrix.

**avenue** aditus, us *m*; xystus *m.*

**average: on the ~** circa.

**averse** aversus (*dat.*); **be ~ to** abhorreo 2 (*a re*).

**aver|sion** odium *n*; ~t averto 3; ~t from prohibeo 2 (*abl.*).

**avidity** aviditas *f.*

**avocation** officium *n.*

**avoid** vito 1, (de)fugio 3; ~ance fuga *f.*

**avow** confiteor 2; ~al confessio *f.*

**await** exspecto 1, maneo 2 (*acc.*).

**awake** *v/t.* excito 1, exsuscito 1; *v/i.* expergiscor 3; **be ~** vigilo 1.

**award** adiudico 1; addictio *f.*

**aware** gnarus; **be ~ of** sentio 4; **become ~ of** cognosco 3.

**away: be ~** absum; **~ with you!** abi!

**awe** reverentia *f*; **stand in ~ of** vereor 2; ~-struck pavidus.

**awful** verendus; terribilis.

**awhile** paulisper.

**awkward** laevus, rusticus; ~ness inscitia *f.*

**awning** velum *n.*

**awry** perversus.

**axe** securis *f.*

**axiom** sententia *f*, pronuntiatum *n.*

**axis, axle** axis *f.*

**aye** ita, semper.

**azure** caeruleus.

# B

**baa** balo 1.

**babbl|e** garrio 4; **~ing** garrulus.

**baboon** simia *f*.

**baby** infans *m*, parvulus *m*; **~hood** infantia *f*; **~ish** infans.

**bacchan|al** Bacchanalia *n/pl.*; **~te** Baccha *f*.

**bachelor** caelebs.

**back** *v/t.* adsum, adiuvo 1; *v/i.* pedem refero 3; **~ water** inhibeo 2 (*navem*); tergum *n*, dorsum *n*; **behind one's ~** clam (*alqm*); *adv.* retro, retrorsum; **~bite** rodo 3; **~bone** spina *f*; **~-door** posticum *n*; **~slide** deficio 3; **~ward** piger; **~wardness** pigritia *f*; **~wards** retro, retrorsum.

**bacon** laridum *n*.

**bad** malus, improbus, pravus.

**badge** insigne *n*.

**badger** maeles *f*.

**badness** malitia *f*, nequitia *f*.

**baffle** eludo 3.

**bag** saccus *m*, culleus *m*; **~gage** sarcinae *f/pl.*

**bail** spondeo 2 (*pro alqo*); vadimonium *n*.

**bailiff** vilicus *m*.

**bait** esca *f*.

**bake** coquo 3, torreo 2; **~r** pistor *m*.

**balance** libro 1; compenso 1; **~ accounts** rationes dispungo 3; libra *f*, trutina *f*.

**balcony** maenianum *n*.

**bald** calvus; *fig.* aridus; **~ness** calvitium *n*.

**baldric** balteus *m*.

**bale** egero 3; fascis *m*; **~ful** funestus.

**balk** frustror 1.

**ball** globus *m*, pila *f*.

**ballad** nenia *f*.

**ballast** saburra *f*.

**ballot** suffragium *n*, tabella *f*; **~-box** cista *f*.

**balm** balsamum *n*, solatium *n*; **~y** suavis.

**balustrade** cancelli *m/pl.*

**ban** interdico 3; interdictio *f*.

**band** vinculum *n*, manus, us *f*, caterva *f*; **~ together** coniuro 1.

**bandage** alligo 1; fascia *f*.

**bandit** latro *m*.

**bandy-legged** valgus.

**bane** venenum *n*, pernicies *f*; **~ful** perniciosus.

**bang** percutio 3, verbero 1; sonitus, us *m*.

**banish** aqua et igni interdico 3, eicio 3, pello 3; **~ment** eiectio *f*; exsilium *n*.

**banister** cancelli *m/pl.*

**bank** ripa *f*, tumulus *m*; argentaria *f*; **~ money** pecunias depono 3; **~er** argentarius *m*; **~rupt** decoctor *m*; **be ~rupt** conturbo 1, decoquo 3.

**banner** vexillum *n*.

**banquet** epulor 1; convivium *n*, epulae *f/pl.*

**banter** cavillor 1, iocor 1; iocus *m*.

**bar** obsero 1, intercludo 3, obsto 1; claustra *n/pl.*; vectis *m*; *fig.* impedimentum *n*; *jur.* cancelli *m/pl.*; **at the ~** forensis (*adj.*).

**barb** uncus *m*, hamus *m*; **~ed** hamatus.

**barbar|ian** barbarus *m*; **~ic** barbarus; **~ous** immanis, ferus.

**barber** tonsor *m*.

**bard** vates *m and f*.

**bare** nudus; *v/t.* aperio 4, nudo 1; **~faced** impudens; **~foot** nudo pede; **~ly** vix.

**bargain** paciscor 3; pactio *f*, pactum *n*.

**barge** linter, tris *f*.

**bark** latro 1; latratus, us *m*; cortex *m and f*, liber *m*.

**barley** hordeum *n*.

**barm** fermentum *n*.

**barn** horreum *n*, granaria *n/pl.*

**baron** princeps *m*.

**barque** ratis *f*.

**barracks** castra *n/pl.*

**barrel** dolium *n*, cupa *f*.

**barren** sterilis; **~ness** sterilitas *f*.

**barricade** obstruo 3; munimentum *n*.

**barrier** saepta *n/pl.*; claustra *n/pl.*

**barrister** advocatus *m*; patronus *m*.

**barrow** ferculum *n*; tumulus *m*.

**barter** muto 1 (*alqd alqa re*); paciscor 3; permutatio *f*.

**base** humilis, turpis; ~ **money** nummus *m* adulterinus; basis *f*; fundamentum *n*; **be** ~d **on** nitor 3; ~**less** vanus; ~**ness** turpitudo *f*.

**bashful** verecundus, pudens; ~**ness** pudor *m*.

**basilica** basilica *f*.

**basin** crater *m*.

**bask** apricor 1.

**basket** canistrum *n*, fiscina *f*.

**bas-relief** toreuma *n*.

**bass** *mus.* gravis.

**bastard** nothus.

**baste** verbero 1.

**bastion** castellum *n*.

**bat** vespertilio *m*.

**bath** balneum *n*, lavatio *f*; ~**keeper** balneator *m*; ~**tub** alveus *m*.

**bathe** *v/t.* lavo 1; *v/i.* lavor 1.

**battalion** cohors *f*.

**batter** percutio 3; ~**ing-ram** aries *m*.

**battle** pugna *f*, proelium *n*, acies *f*; **join** ~ proelium committere; ~**cry** clamor *m*; ~**field** acies *f*; ~**ment** pinna *f*.

**bawd** lena *f*.

**bawl** clamito 1.

**bay** badius; latro 1; sinus, us *m*; laurus, i *f*.

**be** sum; exsisto 3, me habeo 2.

**beach** litus *n*.

**beacon** ignis *m*.

**bead** lapillus *m*.

**beak** rostrum *n*; ~**ed** rostratus; ~**er** poculum *n*.

**beam** refulgeo 2; iubar *n*, radius *m*; tignum *n*, trabs *f*; ~**ing** lucidus.

**bean** faba *f*.

**bear** fero 3; patior 3; pario 3; ~ **with** morem gero 3 (*alci*); ursus *m*.

**beard** barba *f*; ~**ed** barbatus; ~**less** imberbis.

**bear|er** baiulus *m*; ~**ing** gestus, us *m*; **have** ~**ing on** pertineo 2 ad.

**beast** belua *f*, bestia *f*, fera *f*; ~**ly** immundus.

**beat** *v/t.* caedo 3, verbero 1; supero 1; *v/i.* palpito 1; ~ **against** incutio 3; ~**ing** ictus, us *m*; verbera *n/pl.*

**beauti|ful** pulcher, formosus; ~**fy** orno 1.

**beauty** pulchritudo *f*.

**beaver** castor *m*.

**because** quia, quod; ~ **of** propter (*acc.*).

**beck** nutus, us *m*; ~**on** innuo 3 (*alci*).

**becom|e** fio 3; *impers.* decet 2 (*alqm*); convenit 4; ~**ing** decorus, decens.

**bed** cubile *n*, lectus *m*; **go to** ~ cubitum eo 4; ~**chamber** cubiculum *n*; ~**clothes** stragulum *n*; ~**post** fulcrum *n*.

**bedeck** orno 1.

**bedew** perfundo 3.

**bee** apis *f*; ~**hive** alvearium *n*.

**beech** fagus, i *f*.

**beef** bubula *f*.

**beer** fermentum *n*.

**beet** beta *f*.

**beetle** scarabaeus *m*.

**befall** contingo 3 (*alci*); evenio 4 (*alci; ut*).

**befit** deceo 2.

**befool** ludificor 1.

**before** *prep.* ante, ob (*acc.*); prae (*acc.*), pro (*abl.*); apud (*acc.*); coram (*abl.*); *adv.* ante, antea, antehac.

**befoul** inquino 1.

**befriend** adiuvo 1.

**beg** oro 1 (*alqm alqd; ut*); rogo 1 (*alqd ab alqo; ut*); peto 3 (*ut*); mendico 1.

**beget** gigno 3; procreo 1.

**beggar** mendicus *m*; egens; ~**ly** mendicus.

**begin** coepi 3; incipio 3; exorior 4; ~**ner** tiro *m*; ~**ning** initium *n*; principium *n*.

**begone** abi!

**begrudge** invideo 2 (*alci, alci rei*).

**beguile** fallo 3.

**behalf: on** ~ **of** pro (*abl.*).

**behave** me gero 3; ~ **towards** utor 3 (*abl.*).

**behaviour** mores *m/pl.*

**behead** securi ferio 4, percutio 3.

**behind** *prep.* post (*acc.*); *adv.* post, a tergo.

**behold** conspicio 3, tueor 2; *exclam.* ecce, en.

**behove** oportet 2 (*acc. c. inf.*).

**being** homo *m*.

**belabour** mulco 1.

**belch** (e)ructo 1.

**beleaguer** obsideo 2.

**belie** dissimulo 1.

**belie|f** opinio *f*; fides *f*; ~**ve** credo 3 (*alci, acc. c. inf.*); puto 1; fidem habeo 2 (*dat.*).

**bell** tintinnabulum *n*.

**belligerent** bellicosus.

**bellow** mugio 4; ~**ing** mugitus, us *m*.

**bellows** follis *m*.

**belly** venter, tris *m*, alvus, i *f*; **~ out** tumeo 2.

**belong|to** esse (*alcs, alci*); **~ings** bona *n/pl*.

**beloved** dilectus.

**below** infra (*acc.*); subter (*acc.*).

**belt** cinctus, us *m*; cingulum *n*.

**bemoan** gemo 3.

**bench** subsellium *n*; transtrum *n*; *jur.* subsellia *n/pl*.

**bend** *v/t.* flecto 3, curvo 1; *v/i.* flector 3; flexus, us *m*, flexio *f*.

**beneath** sub (*abl.*); infra, subter (*acc.*).

**benefaction** donum *n*.

**benefi|cence** beneficentia *f*; **~cent** beneficus; **~cial** salutaris; **~t** prosum (*dat.*); beneficium *n*; **for the ~t of** gratia (*gen.*).

**benevolen|ce** benevolentia *f*; **~t** benevolus.

**benign** benignus.

**bent** curvus; **~ on** attentus (*dat.*).

**benumb** stupefacio 3; **be ~ed** torpeo 2.

**bequeath** lego 1; **~est** legatum *n*.

**ber|eave** orbo 1; **~eft** orbus (*abl.*).

**berry** baca *f*.

**berth** statio *f*.

**beseech** oro 1, obsecro 1.

**beset** obsideo 2, circumvenio 4.

**beside** ad, prope, iuxta (*acc.*); **~s** *prep.* praeter (*acc.*); *adv.* praeterea.

**besiege** obsideo 2, circumsedeo 2; **~er** obsessor *m*.

**besom** scopae *f/pl*.

**besotted** demens.

**bespatter** aspergo 3.

**besprinkle** aspergo 3, irroro 1.

**best** optimus.

**bestir oneself** expergiscor 3.

**bestow** dono 1, largior 4; confero 3 (*in alqm*), impertio 4.

**bet** pignus do 1; pono 3; pignus *n*; sponsio *f*.

**betake oneself** me confero 3.

**bethink oneself** respicio 3.

**betimes** mature.

**betoken** denuntio 1.

**betray** prodo 3; **~al** proditio *f*; **~er** proditor *m*.

**betroth** (de)spondeo 2 (*alci alqm*); **~al** sponsalia *n/pl*.; **~ed** sponsa *f*; pactus.

**better** melior; **it is ~** praestat; satius est; **get the ~ of** vinco 3.

**between** inter (*acc.*).

**beverage** potio *f*.

**bevy** grex *m*.

**bewail** deploro 1.

**beware** caveo 2 (*acc.*; *ab re*; *ut*, *ne*).

**bewildered** perturbatus.

**bewitch** fascino 1.

**beyond** *prep.* ultra (*acc.*), extra (*acc.*), supra (*acc.*), praeter (*acc.*); *adv.* ultra, supra.

**bias** inclino 1; inclinatio *f*.

**bicker** rixor 1; **~ing** altercatio *f*.

**bid** iubeo 2; **~ a price** liceor 2; voco 1; **~ farewell** valedico 3; **~ding** licitatio *f*; **at the ~ding of** iussu.

**bier** ferculum *n*.

**big** ingens, magnus.

**bilberry** vaccinium *n*.

**bile** bilis *f*.

**bilge-water** sentina *f*.

**bilk** fraudo 1.

**bill** rostrum *n*; libellus *m*; syngrapha *f*; rogatio *f*; lex *f*; titulus *m*.

**billet** hospitium *n*.

**bill-hook** falx *f*.

**billow** fluctus, us *m*; **~y** undosus.

**bin** arca *f*.

**bind** vincio 4, necto 3; *fig.* obligo 1, obstringo 3; **~ over** vador 1; **~ing** fascia *f*.

**birch** betula *f*.

**bird** avis *f*; ales *m and f*; volucris *f*; **~-cage** cavea *f*; **~-catcher** auceps *m*; **~-lime** viscum *n*; **~'s nest** nidus *m*.

**bireme** biremis *f*.

**birth** ortus, us *m*; genus *n*; partus, us *m*; **give ~ to** pario 3; **~day** dies *m* natalis.

**bit** frenum *n*; frustum *n*; offa *f*.

**bit|e** mordeo 2; morsus, us *m*; **~ing** asper.

**bitter** amarus, acerbus; **~ness** amaritudo *f*; acerbitas *f*.

**blab** vulgo 1.

**black** niger, ater; **~ and blue** lividus; **~-berry** rubus *m*; morum *n*; **~bird** merula *f*; **~en** maledico 3 (*alci*); **~ing** atramentum *n*; **~smith** faber *m* (ferrarius).

**bladder** vesica *f*.

**blade** herba *f*; lamina *f*.

**blame** reprehendo 3; accuso 1; culpa *f*; reprehensio *f*; **~less** innocens, integer; **~worthy** noxius.

**bland** mitis.

**blandishment** blanditia *f*; lenocinium *n*.

**blank** purus; vacuus.

**blanket** stragula *f*, vestis *f*.
**blaspheme** maledico 3 (*alci*).
**blast** uro 3; perdo 3; flatus, us *m*.
**blaze** ardeo 2, flagro 1; ignis *m*.
**bleach** candidum facio 3.
**bleak** tristis, frigidus.
**blear-eyed** lippus.
**bleat** balo 1.
**bleed** *v/t.* sanguinem mitto 3; *v/i.* sanguis fluit.
**blemish** macula *f*; vitium *n*.
**blend** commisceo 2.
**bless** benedico 3; fortuno 1; ～ed beatus; ～ing bonum *n*.
**blight** lues *f*; uredo *f*.
**blind** caecus; caeco 1; velum *n*; ～-fold oculos obligo 1; ～ly temere; ～ness caecitas *f*.
**blink** nicto 1.
**bliss** beatitudo *f*; ～ful beatus.
**blister** pustula *f*.
**blithe** hilarus.
**bloat** tumefacio 3; ～ed tumidus.
**block** moles *f*; massa *f*; ～ up obstruo 3; ～ade obsideo 2; obsessio *f*; ～head stipes *m*.
**blood** sanguis *m*; cruor *m*; ～less exsanguis, incruentus; ～-red sanguineus; ～shed caedes *f*; ～-stained cruentus; ～-thirsty cruentus; ～-vessel vena *f*.
**bloom** floreo 2; flos *m*; ～ing florens.
**blot** litura *f*; labes *f*; macula *f*; ～ out deleo 2, exstinguo 3.
**blow** flo 1; spiro 1; inflo 1; ～ one's nose emungo 3; ～ up inflo 1; ～ upon afflo 1; plaga *f*, ictus, us *m*.
**bludgeon** fustis *m*.
**blue** caeruleus.
**bluff** impolitus; abruptum *n*.
**bluish** lividus.
**blunder** erro 1; error *m*; ～ing mendosus.
**blunt** hebes; inurbanus; *v/t.* hebeto 1; retundo 3.
**blush** erubesco 3; ～ at pudet (*alqm, alcs rei*); rubor *m*.
**bluster** declamito 1; declamatio *f*.
**boar** verres *m*; aper, apri *m*.
**board** tabula *f*; mensa *f*, victus, us *m*; consilium *n*, collegium *n*; go on ～ navem conscendo 3; ～ over contabulo 1.
**boast** glorior 1 (*de re, re*); me iacto 1; iactatio *f*; ～ful gloriosus.
**boat** scapha *f*; navicula *f*; ～man nauta *m*.
**bode** vaticinor 1.

**bodily** corporeus.
**body** corpus *n*; globus *m*; manus, us *f*; collegium *n*; ～-guard stipatores *m/pl.*, satellites *m/pl.*
**bog** palus, udis *f*; ～gy paluster.
**boil** *v/t.* (aqua ferventi) coquo 3; *v/i.* ferveo 2; aestuo 1; vomica *f*; ～ed elixus.
**boisterous** turbidus.
**bold** audax, ferox; ～ness audacia *f*.
**bolster** pulvinus *m*; ～ up fulcio 4.
**bolt** obsero 1; fulmen *n*; telum *n*; repagula *n/pl.*; claustra *n/pl.*; clavus *m*.
**bombastic** tumidus.
**bond** vinculum *n*; nodus *m*; syngrapha *f*; ～age servitus, utis *f*.
**bone** os *n*.
**bonnet** mitra *f*.
**bony** osseus.
**book** liber, bri *m*; libellus *m*; volumen *n*; codex *m*; ～-binder glutinator *m*; ～case foruli *m/pl.*; ～seller librarius *m*.
**boom** mugio 4.
**boon** beneficium *n*; ～-companion sodalis *m*.
**boorish** agrestis.
**boot** calceus *m*; caliga *f*.
**booth** taberna *f*.
**booty** praeda *f*.
**booze** poto 1.
**border** ora *f*; margo *m and f*; finis *m*; ～ on attingo 3, contingo 3; ～ed with praetextus; ～ing finitimus.
**bor|e** perforo 1; obtundo 3; foramen *n*; ～ing importunus, odiosus.
**born** natus; be ～ nascor 3, orior 4.
**borough** municipium *n*.
**borrow** mutuor 1; ～ed mutuus; alienus; ～ing mutuatio *f*.
**bosom** sinus, us *m*; gremium *n*; pectus *n*.
**boss** bulla *f*; umbo *m*.
**both** ambo; uterque; in ～ directions utroque.
**both ... and** et ... et; cum ... tum.
**bother** vexo 1.
**bottle** ampulla *f*, amphora *f*.
**bottom** fundus *m*; imus, infimus.
**bough** ramus *m*; frons *f*.
**boulder** saxum *n*.
**bounce** salio 4.
**bound** *v/i.* exsilio 4; *v/t.* finio 4, termino 1; finis *m*; modus *m*; terminus *m*; be ～ to debeo 2; be ～ for tendo 3 (*in, ad*); ～ary finis *m*; ～less infinitus.

**bount|iful** benignus, liberalis; **~y** liberalitas *f*; praemium *n*.

**bout** certamen *n*.

**bow** flecto 3; inclino 1; demitto 3; saluto 1; arcus, us *m*; **~ed** curvus; **~-legged** valgus; **~man** sagittarius *m*.

**bowels** alvus, i *f*; viscera *n/pl*.

**bower** umbraculum *n*.

**bowl** crater *m*; patera *f*; **~ along** volvo 3.

**bows** prora *f*.

**box** arca *f*; cista *f*; colaphus *m*; pugnis certo 1; **~er** pugil *m*; **~ing glove** caestus, us *m*; **~-tree** buxus, i *f*.

**boy** puer, eri *m*; **~-hood** pueritia *f*.

**brace** firmo 1; fibula *f*; fascia *f*.

**bracelet** armilla *f*.

**brag** glorior 1; **~gart** gloriosus.

**braid** necto 3; intexo 3; limbus *m*.

**brain** cerebrum *n*; **~less** socors.

**brake** dumetum *n*.

**bramble** dumus *m*; sentis *m*.

**bran** furfur *m*.

**branch** ramus *m*; frons *f*; **~ into** dividor 3; **~ing** ramosus.

**brand** inuro 3; noto 1; torris *m*; stigma *n*.

**brandish** vibro 1; iacto 1.

**brass** aes *n*; orichalcum *n*.

**brav|e** fortis, acer; experior 4; **~ery** fortitudo *f*, virtus, utis *f*.

**brawl** rixor 1; rixa *f*.

**brawn** lacertus *m*; **~y** lacertosus.

**bray** rudo 3.

**brazen** aeneus, aeratus; impudens.

**breach** discutio 3; frango 3; violo 1; violatio *f*.

**bread** panis *m*; victus, us *m*.

**breadth** latitudo *f*.

**break** frango 3; rumpo 3; violo 1; **~ down** *v/i.* haereo 2; *v/t.* frango 3; **~ in** domo 1; **~ into** irrumpo 3; **~ off** dirumpo 3; **~ up** dissolvo 3; **~fast** prandium *n*; **~-water** moles *f*.

**breast** mamma *f*; pectus *n*; **~plate** lorica *f*.

**breath** spiritus, us *m*, anima *f*; **out of ~** exanimatus; **~e** spiro 1; anhelo 1; **~ing** respiratio *f*; **~ing-space** respirandi spatium *n*.

**breeches** bracae *f/pl*.

**breed** pario 3; genero 1; alo 3; genus *n*.

**breeze** aura *f*.

**brevity** brevitas *f*.

**brew** coquo 3.

**brib|e** (pecunia) corrumpo 3; largior 4; **~ery** largitio *f*; praemium *n*, donum *n*.

**brick** later *m*; **~-layer** structor *m*; **~work** latericium *n*.

**bridal** nuptialis; nuptiae *f/pl*.

**bride** nupta *f*; sponsa *f*; **~groom** sponsus *m*.

**bridge** pons *m*; pontem facio 3 (*in flumine*).

**bridle** infreno 1; frenum *n*.

**brief** brevis; *jur.* causa *f*; **in ~** ne multa.

**brier** vepres *m*.

**brigade** legio *f*.

**brigand** latro *m*; **~age** latrocinium *n*.

**bright** clarus, lucidus, nitidus, **~en** splendesco 3; **~ness** fulgor *m*, candor *m*.

**brillian|cy** splendor *m*, nitor *m*; **~t** splendidus, luculentus.

**brim** ora *f*; labrum *n*.

**brimstone** sulpur *n*.

**brine** muria *f*.

**bring** affero 3; adveho 3; **~ about** efficio 3; **~ forth** prodo 3; **~ forward** (a law) fero 3; **~ out** effero 3; **~ up the rear** agmen claudo 3.

**brink** margo *m*.

**brisk** alacer.

**bristl|e** horreo 2; seta *f*; **~y** setiger, hirsutus.

**brittle** fragilis.

**broad** latus, amplus.

**broil** torreo 2.

**broken** confectus.

**broker** interpres *m*.

**bronze** aes *n*; aeneus, aeratus.

**brooch** fibula *f*.

**brood|(over)** incubo 1 (*alci rei*); agito 1 (*rem*); fetus, us *m*.

**brook** rivus *m*; patior 3.

**broom** scopae *f/pl*.

**broth** ius *n*.

**brothel** lustrum *n*.

**brother** frater *m*; **~hood** sodalitas *f*; **~ly** fraternus.

**brow** supercilium *n*; frons *f*.

**brown** fuscus.

**browse upon** pascor 3; tondeo 2.

**bruise** contundo 3; contusum *n*.

**bruit abroad** vulgo 1.

**brush** detergeo 3; verro 3; scopae *f/pl.*; peniculus *m*; **~wood** virgulta *n/pl*.

**brut|al** saevus, inhumanus; **~ality** inhumanitas *f*; **~e** fera *f*.

**bubble** bulla *f*; **~ up** scateo 2.

**buck** cervus *m*.
**bucket** hama *f*.
**buckle** fibula *f*.
**bucolic** rusticus.
**bud** gemma *f*; gemmo 1.
**budge** me moveo 2.
**buffet** colaphus *m*; tundo 3.
**buffoon** scurra *m*.
**bug** cimex *m*; ~**bear** terricula *n/pl*.
**bugle** tuba *f*; bucina *f*.
**build** aedifico 1; construo 3; condo 3; ~ **upon** confido 3 (*alci*); ~**er** aedificator *m*; ~**ing** aedificium *n*.
**bulb** bulbus *m*.
**bulge** tumeo 2; tumor *m*.
**bulk** magnitudo *f*, moles *f*; maior pars *f*; ~**y** magnus.
**bull** taurus *m*; ~**ock** iuvencus *m*.
**bulrush** iuncus *m*.
**bulwark** munimentum *n*, propugnaculum *n*.
**bump** offendo 3; tuber *n*.
**bumpkin** rusticus *m*.
**bunch** racemus *m*.
**bundle** fascis *m*; sarcina *f*.
**bung** obturamentum *n*.
**buoy** fulcio 4; ~**ancy** levitas *f*; ~**ant** levis.
**bur** lappa *f*.
**burden** onero 1, opprimo 3; onus *n*; **beast of ~** iumentum *n*; ~**some** gravis, molestus.
**burgher** municeps *m*.
**burglar** fur *m*.
**burial** funus *n*; sepultura *f*; ~**-place** sepulcrum *n*.

**burn** *v/t*. uro 3, incendo 3; *v/i*. flagro 1, ardeo 2; ~**ing** ardens.
**burnish** polio 4.
**burnt-offering** hostia *f*.
**burrow** cuniculus *m*; ~ **under** suffodio 4.
**burst** *v/t*. (di)rumpo 3; *v/i*. dissilio 4; ~ **into** *fig*. effundo 3 in (*alqd*).
**bury** sepelio 4, humo 1; condo 3.
**bush** dumus *m*; frutex *m*.
**bushel** medimnum *n*.
**bushy** fruticosus.
**business** negotium *n*; res *f*; occupatio *f*; quaestus, us *m*; ars *f*.
**buskin** cothurnus *m*.
**bust** imago *f*.
**bustle** trepido 1; tumultus, us *m*.
**busy** occupatus, negotiosus.
**but** sed, at, verum, autem; **all ~** tantum non.
**butcher** lanius *m*; obtrunco 1; ~**y** caedes *f*.
**butler** promus *m*.
**butt** *fig*. ludibrium *n*.
**butter** butyrum *n*.
**butterfly** papilio *m*.
**buy** emo 3, paro 1; ~ **back, off** redimo 3; ~**er** emptor *m*.
**buzz** bombus *m*.
**by** ad (*acc*.), secundum (*acc*.), praeter (*acc*.); ab (*abl*.); per (*acc*.); **day ~ day** in dies; ~ **night** denocte; ~ **the gods** per deos; ~ **your leave** bona tua venia; ~**gone** praeteritus, priscus; ~**-road** deverticulum *n*; ~**standers** circumstantes *m/pl*.

# C

**cab** cisium *n.*
**cabal** coniurati *m/pl.*
**cabbage** brassica *f;* caulis *m.*
**cabin** casa *f;* cella *f.*
**cabinet** conclave *n;* armarium *n;* consilium *n.*
**cable** ancorale *n;* funis *m;* rudens *m and f.*
**cackle** strideo 2; strepitus, us *m.*
**cadaverous** cadaverosus.
**cage** cavea *f;* claustra *n/pl.;* includo 3 (*in*).
**cajole** blandior 4; **~ry** blanditia *f.*
**cake** libum *n;* placenta *f; v/i.* concresco 3.
**calamit|ous** funestus, exitiosus; **~y** calamitas *f,* clades *f;* malum *n.*
**calculat|e** computo 1; subduco (rationem) 3; **~ion** ratio *f;* calculus *m.*
**calendar** fasti *m/pl.*
**calends** Calendae *f/pl.*
**calf** vitulus *m;* sura *f.*
**call** appello 1, nomino 1; (ad)voco 1; **be ~ed** audio 4; **~ in** advoco 1; vox *f;* salutatio *f;* **pay a ~** saluto 1; **~ing** quaestus, us *m;* artificium *n.*
**callo|sity** callum *n;* **be ~us** obduresco 3, occalesco 3.
**callow** rudis.
**calm** placidus, tranquillus; sedo 1; tranquillitas *f;* malacia *f.*
**calumn|iate** criminor 1, calumnior 1; **~y** criminatio *f.*
**camel** camelus *m.*
**camp** castra *n/pl.;* **break up ~** castra moveo 2; **pitch ~** castra pono 3.
**campaign** expeditio *f;* stipendium *n.*
**can** possum; queo 4; scio 4; hama *f.*
**canal** fossa *f.*
**cancel** induco 3; tollo 3.
**cancer** cancer, cri *m.*
**candid** apertus, sincerus.
**candidat|e** candidatus *m;* **be a ~e for** peto 3; **~ure** petitio *f.*
**candle** candela *f;* cereus *m;* **~stick** candelabrum *n.*
**candour** candor *m.*
**cane** harundo *f;* virga *f;* verbero 1.
**canine** caninus.
**canister** pyxis *f.*

**canker** robigo *f.*
**cannon** tormentum *n.*
**cannot** non possum, nequeo 4; nescio 4.
**canoe** scapha *f.*
**canon** norma *f.*
**canopy** aulaea *n/pl.*
**canton** pagus *m.*
**canvas** linteum *n.*
**canvass** ambio 4; ambitio *f.*
**cap** pilleus *m.*
**capab|ility** facultas *f;* **~le** capax.
**capaci|ous** amplus, capax; **~ty** captus, us *m.*
**cape** promontorium *n;* sagum *n.*
**caper** exsulto 1; capparis *f.*
**capital** princeps; capitalis; caput *n;* sors *f.*
**capitol** capitolium *n.*
**capitulat|e** me dedo 3; **~ion** deditio *f.*
**capon** capo *m.*
**capric|e** libido *f;* **~ious** inconstans.
**capsize** evertor 3.
**captain** centurio *m;* praefectus *m;* nauarchus *m;* magister, tri *m.*
**captious** captiosus.
**captivate** delenio 4.
**captiv|e** captivus; **~ity** captivitas *f.*
**capture** capio 3.
**car** currus, us *m.*
**caravan** commeatus, us *m.*
**carcass** cadaver, eris *n,* corpus *n.*
**card** pecto 3; pecten *m.*
**care** cura *f,* sollicitudo *f;* curatio *f;* **take ~ (of)** caveo 2 (*alqd*); **take ~ (lest)** caveo 2 (*ne*); **~ for** curo 1; **I don't ~ for (about)** nihili facio 3 (*alqd*).
**career** cursus, us *m.*
**care|ful** diligens, attentus, curiosus; **~less** securus; neglegens; **~lessness** incuria *f,* neglegentia *f.*
**caress** blandior 4; mulceo 2; blanditia *f.*
**cargo** onus *n.*
**carnage** strages *f.*
**carol** carmen *n.*
**carouse** poto 1; comissor 1; **~r** comissator *m.*
**carp at** carpo 3, vellico 1.

**carpenter** faber *m* tignarius.
**carpet** stragulum *n*.
**carriage** raeda *f*, vehiculum *n*.
**carry** fero 3, gero 3, veho 3; porto 1; ~ **away** aufero 3; ~ **on** gero 3; ~ **out** exsequor 3; ~ **through** perfero 3.
**cart** plaustrum *n*.
**carve** caelo 1, sculpo 3; seco 1; ~**r** carptor *m*.
**carving** caelatura *f*; ~-**knife** culter, tri *m*.
**cascade** deiectus, us *m* aquae.
**case** res *f*, causa *f*; tempus *n*; involucrum *n*; **it is the ~ that** accidit ut.
**casement** fenestra *f*.
**cash** nummi *m/pl.*; pecunia *f*; numeratum *n*.
**cashier** exauctoro 1.
**cask** cupa *f*; ~**et** arcula *f*.
**cast** iacio 3, conicio 3; fundo 3; ~ **off** exuo 3; ~ **upon** confero 3; iactus, us *m*.
**castanet** crotalum *n*.
**castaway** naufragus.
**caste** ordo *m*.
**castigate** castigo 1.
**castle** castellum *n*; arx *f*.
**casual** fortuitus; ~**ty** casus, us *m*.
**cat** felis *f*.
**cataract** cataracta *f*.
**catarrh** gravedo *f*.
**catastrophe** ruina *f*.
**catch** capio 3; deprehendo 3; excipio 3; ~ **fire** ignem concipio 3; ~ **a disease** morbum contraho 3; praeda *f*.
**cater** obsono 1; ~**er** obsonator *m*.
**cattle** boves *m and f*; pecus *n*; pecudes *f/pl.*
**cauldron** lebes *m*; cortina *f*.
**cause** facio 3, efficio 3 (*alqd*, *ut*, *ne*); curo 1; creo 1; pario 3; causa *f*, materia *f*, effectio *f*; **with good ~** iure; **be the ~ of** per (*alqm*) fit ut, stat quominus; ~**less** vanus; ~**way** agger, eris *m*.
**caustic** acerbus.
**cauterize** aduro 3.
**cauti|on** cautio *f*; cura *f*; moneo 2; ~**ous** cautus, consideratus.
**cavalry** equitatus, us *m*; equites *m/pl.*; equestris; ~-**squadron** turma *f*; ~**man** eques *m*.
**cave** specus, us *m*; spelunca *f*; antrum *n*.
**cavil at** vellico 1.

**cavity** caverna *f*.
**caw** crocio 4.
**cease** desino 3 (*alcis rei*, *inf.*); desisto 3 (*re*, *inf.*); omitto 3 (*alqd*, *inf.*); consisto 3; ~**less** perpetuus.
**cedar** cedrus, i *f*.
**ceiling** lacunar *n*, tectum *n*.
**celebrat|e** celebro 1; ~**ed** celeber; ~**ion** celebratio *f*.
**celery** apium *n*.
**celestial** caelestis.
**celiba|cy** caelibatus, us *m*; ~**te** caelebs.
**cell** cella *f*.
**cellar** cella *f*.
**cement** ferrumen *n*; ~ **together** conglutino 1.
**cemetery** sepulcra *n/pl.*
**censor** censor *m*; noto 1; ~**ship** censura *f*.
**censure** vitupero 1; vituperatio *f*.
**census** census, us *m*; **hold the ~** censum habeo 2.
**centaur** centaurus *m*.
**centr|al** medius; ~**e** medium *n*; ~**e upon** situm esse (*in re*).
**centurion** centurio *m*; ~**ship** centuriatus, us *m*; ordo *m*.
**century** centuria *f*; ordo *m*; saeculum *n*.
**ceremon|ial** sollemnis; ~**y** caerimonia *f*; ritus, us *m*.
**certain** certus, exploratus; **a ~** quidam; **consider as ~** pro certo habeo 2; **be ~** certo scio 4; ~**ly** sane, profecto.
**certify** recognosco 3; certiorem facio 3.
**cessation** intermissio *f*.
**chafe** *v/t.* attero 3; *v/i.* stomachor 1.
**chaff** palea *f*; acus *n*; *fig.* quisquiliae *f/pl.*
**chagrin** dolor *m*.
**chain** catena *f*; vinculum *n*; *fig.* series *f*; **throw into ~s** catenas inicio 3 (*alci*).
**chair** sella *f*; cathedra *f*; ~**man** magister, tri *m*.
**chalk** creta *f*.
**challenge** provoco 1.
**chamber** conclave *n*; cubiculum *n*; cella *f*; ~-**servant** cubicularius *m*; ancilla *f*.
**champion** propugnator *m*.
**chance** fors *f*; casus, us *m*; spes *f*; **by ~** forte, casu; **it ~d** accidit (*ut*).
**chandelier** candelabrum *n*.
**change** *v/t.* (com)muto 1; verto 3;

*v/i.* mutor 1; me verto 3; (com-)mutatio *f*; vicis (*gen.*) *f*; vicissitudo *f*; **~able** mutabilis; **~ling** subditus.

**channel** canalis *m*; fretum *n*.

**chant** canto 1; cantus, us *m*.

**chapel** aedicula *f*; sacellum *n*.

**chaplet** sertum *n*.

**chapter** caput *n*.

**char** amburo 3.

**character** littera *f*; mores *m/pl.*; habitus, us *m*; *thea.* persona *f*; partes *f/pl.*; **of good ~** honestus; **~istic** proprius (*gen.*).

**charcoal** carbo *m*.

**charge** incurro 3; signa infero 3 (*in*); mando 1, committo 3 (*alci ut*); arguo 3 (*alqm alcis rei*; *acc. c. inf.*); impetus, us *m*; mandatum *n*; cura *f* (*gen.*); crimen *n*; sumptus, us *m*; **be in ~ of** praesum.

**chariot** currus, us *m*; **~eer** auriga *m*; quadrigarius *m*.

**charit|able** benignus, mitis; **~y** benignitas *f*; stips *f*.

**charm** fascino 1; delenio 4; cantio *f*; dulcedo *f*; **~ing** suavis, lepidus.

**chart** tabula *f*.

**chase** caelo 1; sector 1; agito 1; venatio *f*; venatus, us *m*.

**chasm** hiatus, us *m*.

**chaste** castus, pudicus, purus.

**chastise** castigo 1.

**chastity** castitas *f*.

**chat** garrio 4; **~ter** effutio 4; clamor *m*; crepitus, us *m*.

**cheap** vilis; **~ly** bene; **~ness** vilitas *f*.

**cheat** fraudo 1; circumvenio 4; fraudator *m*.

**check** cohibeo 2, contineo 2, retineo 2; comprimo 3; incommodum *n*.

**cheek** gena *f*, mala *f*, bucca *f*.

**cheer** *v/t.* erigo 3, hilaro 1; *v/i.* plaudo 3; clamorem tollo 3; clamor *m*; **be of good ~** bono animo sum; **~ful** alacer, hilaris.

**cheese** caseus *m*.

**chequer** vario 1; **~ed** varius.

**cherish** foveo 2; colo 3.

**cherry** cerasus, i *f*.

**chess-board** latruncularia tabula *f*.

**chess-man** latrunculus *m*.

**chest** arca *f*; armarium *n*; pectus *n*.

**chestnut** castanea *f*.

**chew** mando 3.

**chicanery** calumnia *f*.

**chicken** pullus *m*.

**chick-pea** cicer *n*.

**chide** obiurgo 1.

**chief** princeps, praecipuus, summus; princeps *m*; procer *m*; dux *m*.

**child** puer, eri *m*; infans *m*; **~birth** partus, us *m*; **~hood** pueritia *f*; **~ish** puerilis; **~ren** liberi *m/pl.*

**chill** refrigero 1; frigidus; frigus *n*.

**chime** sono 1.

**chimera** commentum *n*.

**chimney** caminus *m*.

**chin** mentum *n*.

**china** fictilia *n/pl.* tenuia.

**chine** tergum *n*.

**chink** rima *f*.

**chip** assula *f*.

**chirp** pipilo 1.

**chisel** scalprum *n*.

**choice** delectus, us *m*; conquisitus.

**choir** chorus *m*.

**choke** strangulo 1; suffoco 1.

**choleric** iracundus.

**choose** deligo 3, eligo 3; **~ rather** malo.

**chop** dolo 1; caedo 3; **~ off** detrunco 1; **~per** securis *f*.

**chord** chorda *f*; nervus *m*.

**chorus** chorus *m*.

**Christian** christianus; **~ name** praenomen *n*.

**chronic** diuturnus.

**chronicles** annales *m/pl.*

**chuckle** rideo 2.

**church** ecclesia *f*; aedes *f*.

**churlish** inhumanus, agrestis.

**cinder** cinis, eris *m*.

**cipher** numerus *m*; nota *f*.

**circle** orbis *m*; circulus *m*; corona *f*.

**circuit** ambitus, us *m*; **make a ~** circumeo 4.

**circula|r** rotundus; **~te** diffundo 3; percrebresco 3.

**circumcise** circumcido 3.

**circum|ference** ambitus, us *m*; **~locution** ambages *f/pl.*; **~navigate** circumvehor 3; **~scribe** circumscribo 3; **~spect** cautus; **~stance** res *f*; tempus *n*; **~vent** circumscribo 3.

**circus** circus *m*.

**cistern** cisterna *f*.

**citadel** arx *f*.

**cite** profero 3.

**cithern** cithara *f*.

**citizen** civis *m and f*; **~ship** civitas *f*.

**city** urbs *f*; urbanus.

**civil** civilis; comis; **~ian** civis, is *m and f*; civilis; **~ization** cultus, us *m*; **~ized** humanus.

**clad** vestitus (*abl.*).
**claim** postulo 1; exigo 3; vindico 1; postulatio *f*; ~ant petitor *m*.
**clamber** scando 3.
**clammy** umidus.
**clamour** clamor *m*; ~ **for** flagito 1.
**clamp** confibula *f*.
**clan** gens *f*.
**clandestine** clandestinus.
**clang** strepo 3; clangor *m*.
**clansman** gentilis *m*.
**clap** plaudo 3; ~**ping** plausus, us *m*.
**clarify** explano 1.
**clash** concrepo 1; confligo 3; crepitus, us *m*.
**clasp** complector 3; necto 3; fibula *f*; amplexus, us *m*.
**class** genus *n*; ordo *m*; ~ification discriptio *f*; ~ify discribo 3.
**clause** articulus *m*; incisum *n*; caput *n*.
**claw** unguis *m*.
**clay** lutum *n*; argilla *f*.
**clean** mundus, purus; (per)purgo 1; detergeo 2; ~liness munditia *f*.
**clear** liquidus, serenus; clarus; purus; apertus; expedio 4, purgo 1; ~ **oneself** me purgo 1; **it is** ~ **apparet**; ~ **up** explano 1; ~ness claritas *f*.
**cleave** findo 3, scindo 3; ~ **to** adhaereo 2.
**cleft** hiatus, us *m*; rima *f*.
**clemency** clementia *f*.
**clench** comprimo 3.
**clerk** scriba *m*.
**clever** sollers, callidus, ingeniosus; vafer; ~ness calliditas *f*.
**click** crepo 1.
**client** cliens *m and f*; consultor *m*.
**cliff** cautes *f*; scopulus *m*.
**climate** caelum *n*.
**climax** gradatio *f*.
**climb** scando 3, ascendo 3.
**cling** adhaereo 2 (*dat.*).
**clip** tondeo 2.
**clique** factio *f*; globus *m*.
**cloak** pallium *n*; lacerna *f*; dissimulo 1.
**clock** horologium *n*; clepsydra *f*.
**clod** glaeba *f*.
**clog** impedio 4; sculponeae *f/pl.*
**cloister** porticus, us *f*.
**close** claudo 3; comprimo 3; coeo 4; confertus, densus, creber; *adv.* prope, iuxta; finis *m*; exitus, us *m*; ~ **to** iuxta (*acc.*), prope (*acc.*).
**closet** cella *f*.

**clot** concresco 3.
**cloth** textile *n*; ~e vestio 4; induo 3; ~ed in amictus; ~es vestis *f*; vestitus, us *m*; vestimenta *n/pl.*
**cloud** nubes *f*; nubila *n/pl.*; **storm-~** nimbus *m*; ~ **over** nubem induco 3; ~y nubilus.
**cloven** bisulcus.
**clown** scurra *m*.
**club** fustis *m*; clava *f*; sodalitas *f*; collegium *n*.
**clue** *fig.* indicium *n*.
**clums|iness** inscitia *f*; ~y inscitus; rusticus.
**cluster** racemus *m*.
**clutch** arripio 3; ~es manus, us *f*.
**coach** currus, us *m*; raeda *f*; ~**man** raedarius *m*.
**coagulate** concresco 3.
**coal** carbo *m*.
**coalition** societas *f*; coitio *f*.
**coarse** crassus, rudis; incultus.
**coast** ora *f*; litus *n*; ~ **along** lego 3; praetervehor 3.
**coat** lacerna *f*; tegmentum *n*; illino 3.
**coax** palpo 1; blandior 4; ~**ing** blandimentum *n*.
**cobble** sarcio 4; ~r sutor *m*.
**cobweb** aranea *f*.
**cock** gallus *m*; **game ~** gallus *m* rixosus; mas; erigo 3; ~**roach** blatta *f*; ~**scomb** crista *f*.
**code** leges *f/pl.*
**coerce** cogo 3.
**coeval** aequalis (*dat.*).
**coffer** arca *f*.
**coffin** sarcophagus *m*.
**cog** dens *m*.
**cogent** gravis.
**cognizance** cognitio *f*.
**cognomen** cognomen *n*.
**cohere** cohaereo 2; ~**nce** contextus, us *m*.
**cohort** cohors *f*.
**coil** spira *f*; ~ **up** glomero 1.
**coin** nummus *m*; signo 1; novo 1; ~**age** moneta *f*.
**coincide** concurro 3; congruo 3; **by** ~**nce** forte.
**colander** colum *n*.
**cold** frigidus; frigus *n*; gravedo *f*; **be** ~ frigeo 2.
**collapse** concido 3.
**collar** collare *n*; monile *n*; comprehendo 3.
**colleague** collega *m*.
**collect** colligo 3, congero 3; ~**ion**

congeries *f*; collatio *f*; **~ive** universus; **~or** exactor *m*.

**college** collegium *n*.

**colli|de** confligo 3, concurro 3; **~sion** concursus, us *m*.

**colloquial** familiaris, vulgaris.

**collu|de** colludo 3; **~sion** collusio *f*; praevaricatio *f*.

**colonel** praefectus *m*; tribunus *m*.

**colon|ial** colonicus; **~ist** colonus *m*; **~izing** deductio *f*.

**colonnade** porticus, us *f*.

**colony** colonia *f*; **found a ~** coloniam deduco 3.

**colossal** vastus.

**colour** color *m*; pigmentum *n*; *fig.* species *f*; **~s** signum *n*; coloro 1; inficio 3; rubesco 3; **~ed** coloratus.

**colt** eculeus *m*.

**column** columna *f*; *mil.* agmen *n*.

**comb** pecto 3; pecten *m*.

**combat** repugno 1; pugna *f*; proelium *n*; certamen *n*.

**combin|ation** coniunctio *f*; conspiratio *f*; **~e** (con)iungo 3; confero 3 (in unum); conspiro 1.

**come** (per)venio 4; advehor 3; **~!** age, agite; **~ about** fieri; **~ down** descendo 3; **~ forth** prodeo 4; **~ in** incedo 3; **~ up with** consequor 3.

**comed|ian** comoedus *m*; **~y** comoedia *f*.

**comely** pulcher.

**comet** cometes, ae *m*.

**comfort** consolor 1; solatium *n*; consolatio *f*; **~able** commodus; **~er** consolator *m*.

**comic** comicus; ridiculus.

**command** impero 1 (*dat.*); iubeo 2 (*acc.*); praesum (*dat.*); imperium *n*, mandatum *n*, iussum *n*; **put in ~** praeficio 3; **~er** imperator *m*, dux *m*.

**commemorate** celebro 1.

**commence** incipio 3; exordior 4; **~ment** initium *n*.

**commend** commendo 1 (*alci alqd*); laudo 1 (*acc.*); **~able** laudabilis.

**commensurate** dignus (*abl.*).

**comment** sententia *f*; dictum *n*; **~ary** commentarii *m/pl*.

**commerce** mercatura *f*, mercatus, us *m*; commercium *n*.

**commission** mandatum *n*; mando 1 (*alci*).

**commit** mando 1, committo 3 (*alci alqd*); **~ (a crime)** committo 3; **be ~ted to** obligor 1 (*dat.*).

**commodity** merx *f*.

**common** communis; publicus; vulgaris; **in ~** in commune; communiter; **~s** plebs *f*; populus *m*; **~wealth** res *f* publica; civitas *f*.

**commotion** motus, us *m*; tumultus, us *m*; turba *f*.

**commune** colloquor 3.

**communica|te** impertio 4; communico 1; **~tion** communicatio *f*; commercium *n*.

**commun|ion** communio *f*; societas *f*; **~ity** commune *n*; civitas *f*.

**compact** solidus, compactus; pactum *n*, foedus *n*.

**companion** socius *m*; comes *m and f*; **~ship** sodalitas *f*.

**company** coetus, us *m*; convivae *m/pl.*; *mil.* manipulus *m*; societas *f*.

**compar|e** comparo 1, confero 3 (*alqd cum re*; *dat.*); **~ison** comparatio *f*; **in ~ison with** ad, adversus (*acc.*).

**compartment** pars *f*.

**compass** spatium *n*; **~es** circinus *m*.

**compassion** misericordia *f*; **~ate** misericors.

**compatible** conveniens.

**compatriot** civis *m and f*, popularis *m and f*.

**compel** cogo 3, subigo 3.

**compendium** summarium *n*.

**compensat|e** compenso 1 (*alqd re*); **~ion** compensatio *f*.

**compete** certo 1; contendo 3; **~ for** peto 3; **~nt** capax; locuples.

**competit|ion** certamen *n*; **~or** competitor *m*.

**compile** compono 3.

**complain** (con)queror 3 (*alqd, de re*); **~t** querela *f*, querimonia *f*.

**complaisan|ce** obsequium *n*; **~t** commodus.

**complement** supplementum *n*.

**complete** plenus, integer; perfectus; compleo 2, expleo 2; **~ly** omnino, prorsus.

**complex** multiplex; **~ion** color *m*.

**complian|ce** obtemperatio *f*; **~t** facilis.

**complicat|ed** involutus; **~ion** implicatio *f*.

**complicity** conscientia *f*.

**compliment** laudo 1; officium *n*; **pay one's ~s to** saluto 1.

**comply with** pareo 2, obtempero 1 (*dat.*).

**component** pars *f*; elementum *n*.

**compos|e** compono 3; sedo 1; **be ~ed of** consto 1 (*ex, in; abl.*); **~ed** placidus; **~er** auctor *m*; **~ition** compositio *f*; scriptio *f*; scriptum *n*; **~ure** aequus animus *m*.

**compound** misceo 2; **~ interest** anatocismus *m*.

**comprehen|d** percipio 3, intellego 3, comprehendo 3; **~sion** intellectus, us *m*.

**compress** concludo 3, coarto 1.

**comprise** comprehendo 3; contineo 2.

**compromise** implico 1; transigo 3 (*rem*).

**compulsion** vis *f*, necessitas *f*.

**compunction** paenitentia *f*.

**compute** computo 1.

**comrade** sodalis *m*, contubernalis *m*.

**concave** (con)cavus.

**conceal** celo 1 (*alqd, alqm*); abdo 3; occulto 1; **~ment** occultatio *f*; latebra *f*.

**concede** permitto 3, concedo 3.

**conceit** superbia *f*; **~ed** superbus.

**conceive** concipio 3; comprehendo 3.

**concentrate** cogo 3, contraho 3; operam do 1; intendo 3 animum.

**concept, conception** imago *f*, notio *f*.

**concern** attinet, pertinet (*ad*); interest, refert; **~ oneself about** curo 1 (*alqd*); **be ~ed in** versor 1; **be ~ed about** sollicitus sum; negotium *n*; cura *f*; sollicitudo *f*; **~ing** de (*abl.*).

**concert** concentus, us *m*.

**concession** concessio *f*.

**conciliate** concilio 1.

**concise** brevis, concisus; **~ness** brevitas *f*.

**conclu|de** concludo 3; perficio 3; **~sion** conclusio *f*; finis *m*; **~sive** certus.

**concord** concordia *f*.

**concourse** concursus, us *m*; frequentia *f*.

**concubine** concubina *f*, paelex *f*.

**concur** concurro 3; assentior 4.

**condemn** damno 1, condemno 1 (*alcis rei, de re*); improbo 1; **~ation** damnatio *f*.

**condense** spisso 1; premo 3; **~d** densus.

**condescend** descendo 3; me demitto 3.

**condition** status, us *m*; sors *f*, fortuna *f*; condicio *f*; lex *f*; **on ~ that** ea condicione ut.

**condole** consolor 1; **~nces** consolatio *f*.

**condone** condono 1.

**conduc|e to** conducit (*dat.*); proficit (*ad*); **~ive** utilis (*ad*).

**conduct** adduco 3, perduco 3; **~ oneself** me gero 3; mores *m/pl.*; vita *f*; administratio *f*; **~or** dux *m*.

**conduit** aquaeductus, us *m*; canalis *m*.

**cone** conus *m*.

**confectioner** pistor *m*; libarius *m*; **~y** crustum *n*.

**confedera|cy** foedus *n*; foederatae civitates *f/pl.*; **~te** foederatus; socius *m*.

**confer** *v/t.* confero 3, tribuo 3 (*alci alqd*); *v/i.* colloquor 3; **~ence** colloquium *n*; congressus, us *m*.

**confess** confiteor 2, fateor 2; **~ion** confessio *f*.

**confid|ant** conscius *m*; familiaris; **~e** *v/i.* confido 3 (*dat., abl.*); *v/t.* committo 3; **~ence** fides *f*; fiducia *f*; confidentia *f*; **~ent** confidens; **~ential** secretus.

**confine** includo 3, coerceo 2, contineo 2; **~d** artus; **~ment** vincula *n/pl.*; partus, us *m*.

**confirm** confirmo 1; comprobo 1.

**confiscat|e** proscribo 3; publico 1; **~ion** proscriptio *f*.

**conflagration** incendium *n*.

**conflict** certamen *n*; pugna *f*; **~ with** repugno 1.

**confluence** confluens *m*.

**conform|(to)** accommodo 1 (*me ad, dat.*); **~ity** convenientia *f*; **in ~ity with** ex (*abl.*), secundum (*acc.*).

**confound** confundo 3, misceo 2; obstupefacio 3.

**confront** compono 3; me oppono 3.

**confus|e** confundo 3; **~ion** perturbatio *f*; stupor *m*.

**confute** confuto 1.

**congeal** concresco 3.

**congenial** commodus.

**congratulat|e** gratulor 1; **~ion** gratulatio *f*.

**congregat|e** (me) congrego 1; **~ion** coetus, us *m*.

**congress** conventus, us *m*.

**conjectur|al** opinabilis; **~e** conicio 3; coniectura *f*.

**conjugal** coniugalis; maritus.

**conjuncture** discrimen *n*.

**conjur|ation** carmen *n*; obsecratio *f*; ~e obtestor 1; ~er praestigiator *m*.

**connect** conecto 3, coniungo 3 (*cum re, dat.*); **be ~ed with** contingo 3 (*alqm*); ~**ion** colligatio *f*; necessitudo *f*.

**connive** coniveo 2 (*in alqa re*).

**connoisseur** intellegens *m and f*.

**conquer** vinco 3, supero 1; ~**or** victor *m*, victrix *f*.

**conquest** victoria *f*.

**conscien|ce** conscientia *f*; religio *f*; ~**tious** religiosus; diligens.

**conscious** conscius (*alcis rei, alci rei*); ~**ness** conscientia *f*.

**conscript** tiro *m*; ~**ion** dilectus, us *m*.

**consecrate** consecro 1, dedico 1.

**consecutive** continuus.

**consent** annuo 3; **~ to** accipio 3; **~ that** permitto 3 (*ut*); consensus, us *m*.

**consequence** eventus, us *m*; **it is of no ~** nihil refert; **be the ~ of** consequor 3.

**consequently** ergo, igitur.

**consider** cogito 1 (*de*); considero 1 (*alqd, de*); delibero 1 (*alqd, de*); rationem habeo 2 (*alcis rei*); ~**able** aliquantus; ~**ate** humanus; ~**ation** respectus, us *m*; deliberatio *f*.

**consign** committo 3.

**consist** consto 1 (*ex, in re*); *abl.*); consisto 3 (*in*); ~**ency** constantia *f*; ~**ent** consentaneus (*dat.*); **be ~ent with** consentio 4.

**consol|ation** solatium *n*; ~**e** consolor 1.

**consolidate** stabilio 4.

**consort** coniunx *m and f*; **~ with** utor 3 (*abl.*).

**conspicuous** insignis, conspectus.

**conspir|acy** coniuratio *f*; ~**ator** coniuratus *m*; ~**e** coniuro 1.

**constable** vigil *m*.

**constan|cy** constantia *f*; fides *f*; ~**t** constans; fidelis; perpetuus.

**constellation** sidus *n*.

**consternation** pavor *m*; perturbatio *f*.

**constitut|e** constituo 3; statuo 3; compono 3; ~**ion** habitus, us *m*; natura *f*; res *f* publica; civitas *f*; ~**ional** legitimus, innatus.

**constrain** cogo 3; ~**t** necessitas *f*.

**construct** (con)struo 3; facio 3; ~**ion** constructio *f*; structura *f*.

**construe** interpretor 1.

**consul** consul *m*; ~**ar** consularis; ~**ate** consulatus, us *m*.

**consult** *v/t.* consulo 3 (*alqm de re*); *v/i.* consulto 1; ~**ation** deliberatio *f*.

**consum|e** consumo 3; abutor 3; conficio 3; edo 3; ~**er** emptor *m*.

**consummate** perficio 3; perfectus.

**consumption** tabes *f*.

**contact, contagion** contagio *f*.

**contain** capio 3; contineo 2.

**contaminate** contamino 1.

**contemplat|e** intueor 2; considero 1; ~**ion** contemplatio *f*.

**contemporary** aequalis.

**contempt** contemptio *f*; ~**ible** abiectus, contemptus; ~**uous** fastidiosus.

**contend** contendo 3; certo 1; **~ against** adversor 1.

**content** contentus (*abl.*); **be ~** satis habeo 2 (*inf., si*).

**content|ion** discordia *f*; controversia *f*; ~**ious** pugnax.

**contentment** aequus animus *m*.

**contest** contendo 3 (*cum alqo de re*); certamen *n*; contentio *f*; **be ~ed** in controversiam venio 4.

**contiguous** confinis (*dat.*).

**continen|ce** continentia *f*; ~**t** continens; continens *f*.

**contingen|cy** casus, us *m*; ~**t** fortuitus.

**continu|al** perpetuus; assiduus; ~**ance** perpetuitas *f*; ~**ation** continuatio *f*; ~**e** *v/i.* persevero 1 (*inf., in re*); permaneo 2 (*in*); pergo 3; *v/t.* continuo 1; prorogo 1; ~**ous** continens, perpetuus; ~**ously** continenter.

**contort** contorqueo 2.

**contour** forma *f*.

**contraband** illicitus.

**contract** contraho 3; astringo 3; **~ a debt** aes alienum contraho 3; **~ for** loco 1; conduco 3; locatio *f*; pactio *f*; ~**or** conductor *m*; redemptor *m*.

**contradict** adversor 1 (*dat.*); repugno 1; ~**ion** repugnantia *f*; ~**ory** repugnans.

**contrary** contrarius, diversus, adversus; **~ to** contra (*acc.*); contrarium *n* (*gen.*); **on the ~** contra; immo.

**contrast** confero 3; discrepo 1 (*cum, a re*); discrepantia *f*.

**contravene** violo 1.

**contribut|e** confero 3; affero 3 (*ad*); **~ion** collatio *f*; collecta *f*; stips *f*.

**contriv|ance** excogitatio *f*; ars *f*; machina *f*; **~e** struo 3; machinor 1; invenio 4; **~er** machinator *m*.

**control** moderor 1 (*dat.*); coerceo 2; moderatio *f*; potestas *f*.

**controversy** concertatio *f*, controversia *f*.

**contumacious** contumax.

**contumel|ious** contumeliosus; **~y** contumelia *f*.

**convalesce** convalesco 3; **~nt** convalescens.

**convene** (con)voco 1.

**convenien|ce** commoditas *f*; opportunitas *f*; utilitas *f*; **at your, his ~ce** commodo tuo, suo; **~t** commodus; opportunus.

**convention** conventus, us *m*; pactio *f*; mos *m*; **~al** usitatus.

**converge** in unum tendo 3.

**convers|ant** peritus (*gen.*); **~ation** colloquium *n*; sermo *m*; **~e** colloquor 3 (*cum*); congressus, us *m*; contrarium *n*.

**convert** (com)muto 1.

**convex** convexus.

**convey** (ad)veho 3; conveho 3; deporto 1; significo 1; **~ance** vehiculum *n*.

**convict** convinco 3 (*alqm alcs rei*); condemno 1; **~ion** damnatio *f*; opinio *f*.

**convince** persuadeo 2 (*alci*); **be ~d** persuasum habeo 2.

**conviviality** convivia *n/pl*.

**convoy** commeatus, us *m*.

**convuls|e** concutio 3; **~ion** perturbatio *f*.

**coo** queror 3.

**cook** coquo 3; coquus *m*; coqua *f*.

**cool** frigidus; impavidus; *v/t.* refrigero 1; *v/i.* refrigesco 3; **~ness** frigus *n*; impudentia *f*.

**coop** cavea *f*; **~ up** includo 3.

**cooperat|e** adiuvo 1; operam confero 3; **~ion** auxilium *n*; opera *f*.

**coot** fulica *f*.

**cope (with)** contendo 3 (*cum*).

**copious** largus, uber, abundans.

**copper** aes *n*; aenum *n*; aeneus.

**copse** fruticetum *n*, dumetum *n*.

**copulate** coeo 4.

**copy** describo 3, exscribo 3; imitor 1; exemplar *n*; similitudo *f*; **~ist** librarius *m*.

**coral** corallium *n*.

**cord** funis *m*; constringo 3; **~age** rudentes *m/pl*.

**cordial** benignus.

**cordon** corona *f*.

**core** medulla *f*.

**cork** suber, eris *n*; cortex *m*.

**corn** frumentum *n*; frumentarius; **standing ~** seges *f*; **~-merchant** frumentarius *m*; **~ supply, price of ~** annona *f*.

**corner** angulus *m*; recessus, us *m*.

**cornet** bucina *f*.

**coronet** diadema *n*.

**corpor|ation** collegium *n*; municipium *n*; **~eal** corporeus.

**corpse** cadaver, eris *n*, corpus *n*.

**corpulen|ce** opimus habitus, us *m*; **~t** pinguis.

**correct** rectus, accuratus; corrigo 3; emendo 1; **~ion** correctio *f*; castigatio *f*.

**correspond** congruo 3 (*cum, inter se, dat.*); respondeo 2 (*dat.*); litteras scribo 3; **~ence** convenientia *f*; litterae *f/pl.*; **~ing** par (*dat.*).

**corroborate** confirmo 1.

**corrode** erodo 3.

**corrugate** corrugo 3.

**corrupt** corrumpo 3; depravo 1; putridus; corruptus; **~er** corruptor *m*; **~ible** venalis; **~ion** corruptio *f*; corruptela *f*; largitio *f*.

**corselet** lorica *f*; thorax *m*.

**cosmetics** medicamina *n/pl.*; fucus *m*.

**cosmopolitan** mundanus *m*.

**cost** (con)sto 1; pretium *n*; impensa *f*; damnum *n*; **at what ~?** quanti?; **~ly** pretiosus; carus.

**costume** vestitus, us *m*.

**cot** lectulus *m*.

**cottage** casa *f*.

**couch** lectus *m*; cubile *n*; subsido 3; (*in language*) dico 3.

**cough** tussis *f*; tussio 4.

**council** concilium *n*, consilium *n*; **~ of war** praetorium *n*; **town-~lor** decurio *m*.

**counsel** moneo 2; consilium *n*; patronus *m*; **~lor** consiliarius *m*.

**count** numero 1; duco 3; **~ upon** fidem habeo 2 (*alci*).

**countenance** vultus, us *m*; facies *f*; indulgeo 2.

**counter** calculus *m*; mensa *f*; **run ~ to** repugno 1; **~act** occurro 3; **~balance** compenso 1 (*alqd cum*);

**~feit** simulo 1; adulterinus; fictus; **~pane** stragulum n.

**countless** innumerabilis.

**countrified** agrestis.

**country** rus n; agri m/pl.; terra f; fines m/pl.; **native ~** patria f; **in the ~** ruri; **~-house, ~ seat** villa f; **~man** rusticus m; homo m agrestis.

**coup d'état** res f/pl. novae.

**couple** copulo 1; par n; iugum n; bini, ae, a (adj.).

**courage** virtus, utis f; animus m; **~ous** fortis, animosus.

**courier** nuntius m.

**course** venor 1; curro 3; cursus, us m; iter, ineris n; curriculum n; ratio f, consilium n; **race-~** circus m; **in the ~** of in (abl.), inter (acc.); **of ~** sane; scilicet; videlicet.

**court** peto 3; ambio 4; capto 1; aula f; atrium n; regia f; **law-~** basilica f; subsellia n/pl.; iudicium n; **~eous** comis; **~esy** comitas f; **~esan** meretrix f; **~ier** comes m; **~ing** ambitio f.

**cousin** consobrinus m; consobrina f.

**cove** sinus, us m.

**covenant** stipulor 1; pactum n.

**cover** (in)tego 3; operio 4; obduco 3; velo 1; operculum n; praesidium n; **~ing** tegmen n, tegimentum n; **~let** stragulum n; **~t** occultus; obliquus; dumetum n.

**covet** concupisco 3; **~ous** avarus; **~ousness** avaritia f.

**cow** vacca f, bos f; terreo 2; **~-herd** pastor m, armentarius m.

**coward|ice** ignavia f; **~ly** ignavus,
**cower** tremo 3. [timidus.]

**coxcomb** crista f (galli); nugator m.

**coy** verecundus.

**crab** cancer, cri m; **~bed** morosus.

**crack** findo 3; dissilio 4; concrepo 1; rima f; crepitus, us m.

**cradle** cunae f/pl.; incunabula n/pl.; foveo 2.

**craft** ars f; artificium n; dolus m; scapha f; **~sman** artifex m, opifex m; **~y** callidus.

**crag** scopulus m; **~gy** asper.

**cram** refercio 4; stipo 1; sagino 1.

**cramp** comprimo 3.

**crane** grus, gruis f; tolleno m.

**crash** fragor m; **~ down** ruo 3.

**crate** corbis f.

**crater** crater, eris m.

**crav|e** oro 1, obsecro 1 (alqm alqd); **~en** ignavus; **~ing** desiderium n.

**crawl** repo 3; serpo 3.

**craz|iness** furor m; **~y** imbecillus.

**creak** strideo 2; concrepo 1.

**cream** flos m lactis.

**crease** corrugo 1; ruga f.

**creat|e** creo 1; pario 3; fingo 3; **~ion** mundus m; opus n; **~or** genitor m; (pro)creator m; auctor m; **~ure** animal n; animans m and f.

**creden|ce** fides f; **~tials** auctoritates f/pl.

**credible** credibilis.

**credit** fides f; existimatio f; gratia f; **be to one's ~** honori esse alci; fidem habeo 2 (alci); **~able** honestus; **~or** creditor m.

**credul|ity** credulitas f; **~ous** credulus.

**creek** aestuarium n.

**creep** serpo 3, repo 3; **~ up on** obrepo 3 (dat., ad, in).

**cremate** cremo 1.

**crescent** luna f; lunatus.

**crest** crista f; iuba f; vertex m; **~ed** cristatus; **~fallen** demissus.

**crevice** rima f.

**crew** nautae m/pl.; remiges m/pl.; remigium n.

**crib** praesaepe n; lectulus m.

**cricket** cicada f.

**crier** praeco m.

**crim|e** facinus n; scelus n; **~inal** nefarius; sons m.

**crimson** coccineus; coccum n.

**cring|e** adulor 1 (alqm, alci); **~ing** proiectus.

**cripple** fig. accido 3; **~d** claudus; mancus.

**crisis** discrimen n; tempus n.

**criterion** obrussa f.

**criti|c** iudex m, criticus m; **~cal** intellegens; dubius; **~cism** iudicium n; **~cise** iudico 1 (de); reprehendo 3.

**croak** cano 3; crocio 4; occino 3; **~ing** clamor m.

**crock** olla f; **~ery** fictilia n/pl.

**crocodile** crocodilus m.

**crone** anus, us f.

**crook** pedum n; **~ed** pravus.

**crop** seges f; fruges f; carpo 3; tondeo 2.

**cross** transeo 4; me traicio 3; obsto 1 (alci); **~ the mind** occurro 3 (animo); crux f; quincunx m; transversus; difficilis; **~-examination** interrogatio f; **~ing** transitus, us m; trivium n.

**crouch** subsido 3.
**crow** cornix *f*; cano 3.
**crowd** turba *f*; vulgus, i *n*; frequentia *f*; stipo 1; compleo 2; ~ **around** circumfundor 3 (*alci*); ~ **together** conglobo 1 (me); ~ed celeber; frequens.
**crown** corona *f*; diadema *n*; *fig.* cumulus *m*; diadema impono 3 (*capiti*); cingo 3.
**crucify** cruce afficio 3.
**crude** rudis.
**cruel** crudelis, atrox; ~ty crudelitas *f*.
**cruise** (per)vagor 1.
**crumb** frustum *n*; ~le frio 1; contero 3; corruo 3.
**crumpled** rugosus.
**crush** opprimo 3; frango 3.
**crust** crusta *f*; ~ **of bread** frustum *n*.
**crutch** baculum *n*.
**cry** clamo 1; fleo 2; vagio 4; ~ **out at** acclamo 1; clamor *m*; vox *f*.
**crystal** crystallum *n*.
**cub** catulus *m*.
**cuckoo** cuculus *m*.
**cucumber** cucumis *m*.
**cudgel** fustis *m*; baculum *n*; fuste verbero 1.
**cue** signum *n*; **give a** ~ innuo 3.
**cuff** colaphus *m*.
**cuirass** lorica *f*.
**cull** lego 3.
**culmination** fastigium *n*; summum *n*.
**culp|able** nocens; ~rit noxius *m*.
**cultivat|e** colo 3; ~ed cultus; ~ion cultura *f*; cultus, us *m*; ~or cultor *m*.
**culture** cultura *f* (animi).
**cumbersome** inhabilis.
**cumin** cuminum *n*.
**cunning** callidus, dolosus; astutia *f*.
**cup** poculum *n*, calix *m*; ~board armarium *n*.

**cupidity** cupiditas *f*.
**cur** canis *m*.
**curable** sanabilis.
**curator** curator *m*.
**curb** (re)freno 1; coerceo 2; frenum *n*; crepido *f*.
**curdle** *v/t.* coagulo 1; *v/i.* concreso 3.
**cure** medeor 2 (*dat.*); sano 1; sanatio *f*; remedium *n*.
**curio|sity** curiositas *f*; cura *f*; ~us curiosus; elaboratus; rarus.
**curl** torqueo 2; cincinnus *m*; cirrus *m*; ~y crispus, cincinnatus; ~ing iron calamister *m*.
**currant** acinus *m*.
**curren|cy** moneta *f*; ~t vulgaris, usitatus; **be** ~t vigeo 2; percrebresco 3; flumen *n*; aestus, us *m*; ~t of air aura *f*.
**curse** exsecror 1; exsecratio *f*; preces *f/pl.*
**curtail** coarto 1.
**curtain** aulaeum *n*.
**curve** sinus, us *m*; flexus, us *m*; flecto 3; curvo 1; ~d curvatus; sinuosus.
**cushion** pulvinus *m*.
**custod|ian** curator *m*; ~y custodia *f*.
**custom** mos *m*; consuetudo *f*; institutum *n*; commercium *n*; ~ary translaticius; usitatus; ~er emptor *m*.
**cut** caedo 3; seco 1; ~ **down** excido 3; ~ **off** praecido, intercludo 3; vulnus *n*; **a short** ~ via *f* compendiaria.
**cutter** celox *f*.
**cutting** acerbus.
**cuttle-fish** sepia *f*.
**cycle** orbis *m*.
**cylinder** cylindrus *m*.
**cymbal** cymbalum *n*.
**cynical** mordax.
**cypress** cupressus, i *f*.

# D

**dabble** tingo 3.

**dagger** pugio *m*, sica *f*.

**daily** cotidianus, diurnus; *adv.* cotidie; in dies.

**daint|iness** fastidium *n*; **~ies** cuppedia *n/pl.*; **~y** fastidiosus; delicatus. [moror 1.)

**dall|iance** lusus, us *m*; **~y** ludo 3;)

**dam** moles *f*; mater *f*; **~ up** obstruo 3.

**damage** laedo 3; affligo 3; damnum *n*; incommodum *n*; **~s** *jur.* damnum *n*.

**dame** matrona *f*.

**damp** umidus; umor *m*; restinguo 3.

**damsel** virgo *f*.

**dance** salto 1; saltatus, us *m*; **~r** saltator *m*; saltatrix *f*.

**dandruff** porrigo *f*.

**dandy** (homo) delicatus *m*.

**danger** periculum *n*; discrimen *n*; **~ous** periculosus; gravis.

**dangle** pendeo 2 (*ab, de re*).

**dank** umidus.

**dappled** varius; maculosus.

**dare** *v/i.* audeo 2; *v/t.* provoco 1 (*alqm in pugnam*).

**daring** audax; audacia *f*.

**dark** obscurus; ater; **it grows ~** advesperascit 3; **after ~** de nocte; **keep in the ~** celo 1 (*alqm alqd*); **~en** obscuro 1, occaeco 1; **~ness** tenebrae *f/pl.*; caligo *f*.

**darling** deliciae *f/pl.*

**darn** sarcio 4.

**dart** iaculor 1; provolo 1; emico 1; telum *n*, iaculum *n*.

**dash** ruo 3; **~ against** affligo 3 (*ad*); **~ to pieces** elido 3; **have one's hopes ~ed** spe depellor 3; impetus, us *m*; **~ing** animosus.

**dastardly** ignavus.

**date** dies *m and f*; tempus *n*; (*fruit*) palmula *f*; diem ascribo 3; **~ from** incipio 3 (*abl.*).

**daub** illino 3 (*alqd re*).

**daughter** filia *f*; **~-in-law** nurus, us *f*.

**daunt** percello 3; **~less** ferox, impavidus.

**dawdle** cesso 1.

**dawn** (prima) lux *f*; aurora *f*; dilucesco 3.

**day** dies *m and f*; lux *f*; **~ after ~** diem ex die; **every ~** in dies; **every other ~** alternis diebus; **the ~ before** pridie; **the ~ after** postridie; **~light** dies *m and f*, lux *f*.

**dazz|le** perstringo 3; **~ling** splendidus.

**dead** mortuus; **the ~** manes *m/pl.*; inferi *m/pl.*; **~ of night** nox *f* intempesta; **~en** obtundo 3; **~ly** funestus; capitalis.

**deaf** surdus; **~en** obtundo 3; **~ness** surditas *f*.

**deal** infligo 3 (*alci*); **~ out** dispertio 4; **~ with** tracto 1 (*alqm*); **~er** negotiator *m*, mercator *m*; **~ings** commercium *n*.

**dear** carus; pretiosus; **~ness** caritas *f*.

**dearth** inopia *f*.

**death** mors *f*; letum *n*; obitus, us *m*.

**debar** prohibeo 2.

**debase** adultero 1.

**debate** disputo 1 (*alqd, de re*); controversia *f*.

**debauch** stupro 1; perdo 3; **~ery** stuprum *n*.

**debilitate** debilito 1.

**debit** expensum fero 3 (*alci*).

**debt** aes *n* alienum; debitum *n*; **be in ~** in aere alieno sum; **~or** debitor *m*.

**decant** diffundo 3.

**decapitate** securi ferio 4; detrunco 1.

**decay** tabesco 3; putesco 3; minuor 3; tabes *f*; senium *n*.

**decease** obitus, us *m*; **~d** demortuus.

**deceit** fraus *f*; dolus *m*; **~ful** fallax, dolosus.

**deceive** decipio 3; fallo 3.

**December** (mensis) December, bris *m*.

**decemvir** decemvir *m*; **~ate** decemviratus, us *m*.

**decen|cy** pudor *m*; honestas *f*; **~t** honestus; decens.

**deception** fraus *f*; dolus *m*.

**decide** *v/t.* decerno 3; diiudico 1; *v/i.* constituo 3.

**decimate** decimo 1.

**decisi|on** decretum *n*, arbitrium *n*,

iudicium *n*; ~ve supremus (*proe-lium*); certus.

**deck** orno 1; pons *m*.

**declaim** declamo 1; ~ **against** invehor 3 (*in*); ~er declamator *m*.

**declar|ation** professio *f*; ~e *v/t.* declaro 1; renuntio 1; *v/i.* affirmo 1; ~e war bellum indico 3.

**decline** *v/i.* senesco 3, deficio 3; *v/t.* recuso 1 (*alqd*; *inf.*); deminutio *f*.

**decompose** putesco 3.

**decorat|e** (ex)orno 1; ~ion decus *n*; ornamentum *n*; insigne *n*.

**decorous** decorus.

**decoy** illicio 3.

**decrease** (de)minuor 3; imminutio *f*.

**decree** decerno 3; censeo 2; decretum *n*; ~ **of the senate** senatus consultum *n*.

**decrepit** decrepitus.

**decry** obtrecto 1.

**dedicat|e** dedico 1 (*dat.*); ~ion dedicatio *f*.

**deduce** concludo 3.

**deduct** deduco 3; ~ion deductio *f*; conclusio *f*.　　　　[tabula *f*.]

**deed** factum *n*; res *f*; facinus *n*;]

**deem** existimo 1.

**deep** altus, profundus; altum *n*; ~en altiorem facio 3; ~ly penitus.

**deer** cervus *m*.

**deface** deformo 1.

**defam|ation** obtrectatio *f*; ~e maledico 3 (*dat.*).

**defeat** vinco 3; supero 1; frustror 1; clades *f*; repulsa *f*.

**defect** vitium *n*; ~ion defectio *f*; ~ive vitiosus.

**defence** defensio *f*; tutela *f*; *jur.* patrocinium *n*; praesidium *n*; ~less inermis.

**defend** defendo 3; tueor 2; ~ant reus *m*; rea *f*; ~er propugnator *m*.

**defer** differo 3 (*alqd in*); ~ **to** obtempero 1; ~ence observantia *f*.

**defian|ce: in ~ce of** contra (*acc.*); ~t ferox.

**deficien|cy** inopia *f*; **be ~t** desum; deficio 3.

**defile** contamino 1; angustiae *f/pl.*

**defin|e** circumscribo 3; definio 4; ~ite definitus, certus; ~ition definitio *f*.

**deflect** deflecto 3.

**deform** deformo 1; ~ed pravus; ~ity pravitas *f*.

**defraud** fraudo 1 (*alqm, alqa re*).

**defray** suppedito 1.

**deft** scitus.

**defy** provoco 1; contemno 3.

**degenerate** degenero 1 (*ab*); perditus.

**degrad|ation** ignominia *f*; ~e moveo 2 (*abl.*); abicio 3; ~ing indignus.

**degree** gradus, us *m*; **in some ~** aliquantum; **by ~s** gradatim.

**deign** dignor 1 (*inf.*).

**deity** deus *m*; dea *f*; numen *n*.

**dejected** demissus.

**delay** moror 1; cunctor 1; mora *f*.

**delegat|e** defero 3 (*ad*); legatus *m*; ~ion legatio *f*.

**delete** deleo 2.

**deliberat|e** consulo 3, delibero 1 (*de*); cogitatus; ~ely consulto; ~ion deliberatio *f*.

**delica|cy** humanitas *f*; cuppedia *n/pl.*; ~te subtilis, tener, suavis.

**delicious** suavis.

**delight** *v/t.* delecto 1; *v/i.* gaudeo 2 (*abl., inf., quod*); delectatio *f*; voluptas *f*; ~ful iucundus.

**delineate** describo 3.

**delinquent** noxius *m*.

**deliver** libero 1; eripio 3; reddo 3, trado 3; ~ **a speech** orationem habeo 3; ~ance salus, utis *f*; ~y *rhet.* actio *f*; *med.* partus, us *m*.

**dell** vallis *f*.

**delude** decipio 3.

**deluge** inundatio *f*; inundo 1.

**delusi|on** error *m*; ~ve fallax.

**demagogue** contionator *m*.

**demand** postulo 1, flagito 1; postulatio *f*.

**demean** me demitto 3; ~our habitus, us *m*.

**demented** demens.

**demesne** ager, gri *m*.

**demigod** semideus *m*.

**demise** obitus, us *m*.

**democra|cy** civitas *f* popularis; ~tic popularis.

**demolish** demolior 4.

**demonstrat|e** demonstro 1; ~ion indicium *n*.　　　　[tatio *f*.]

**demur** dubito 1; haesito 1; dubi-]

**demure** verecundus.

**den** latibulum *n*.

**denial** negatio *f*.

**denizen** incola *m*.

**denote** indico 1, significo 1.

**denounce** defero 3 (*nomen alcis*).

**dense** densus, confertus.

**dent** vulnus *n.*

**denude** (de)nudo 1.

**denunciation** delatio *f;* accusatio *f.*

**deny** nego 1; infitior 1; abnuo **8**.

**depart** abeo 4, discedo 3 (*ab, ex, de*); *fig.* descisco 3 (*ab*); ~ment provincia *f;* munus *n;* ~ure discessus, us *m.*

**depend** pendeo 2 (*abl., ex*); nitor 3 (*abl.*); consisto 3 (*in re*); ~ant cliens *m;* ~ent (on) obnoxius (*dat.*).

**depict** (de)pingo 3; describo 3.

**deplor|able** miserabilis; ~e deploro.

**deploy** explico 1.

**depopulat|e** vasto 1; depopulor 1; ~ion vastatio *f.*

**deport** relego 1; ~ation relegatio *f;* exsilium *n;* ~ment habitus, us *m.*

**depose** abrogo 1 (*magistratum alci*); moveo 2; testificor 1.

**deposit** depono 3 (*apud alqm*); depositum *n;* pignus *n.*

**depot** horreum *n.*

**deprav|ed** corruptus; ~ity pravitas *f.*

**deprecate** deprecor 1 (*alqd ab alqo*).

**depreciate** detraho 3 (*de*).

**depredation** direptio *f.*

**depress** deprimo 3; ~ed fractus; ~ion tristitia *f.*

**deprive** privo 1 (*abl.*); adimo 3 (*alqd alci*); ~d of orbus (*abl.*).

**depth** altitudo *f;* ~s altum *n;* in ~ in agrum.

**deput|ation** legatio *f;* ~e mando 1 (*dat.*); ~y procurator *m;* legatus *m.*

**derange** perturbo 1; ~d insanus.

**deri|de** derideo 2; ~sion irrisus, us *m.*

**deriv|ation** declinatio *f;* ~e duco 3, traho 3 (*originem ab, ex*).

**derogatory** indignus.

**descend** descendo 3 (*de, ex, in, ad*); degredior 3; pervenio 4; ~ant progenies *f;* ~ants posteri *m/pl.;* ~ed ortus (*abl.*).

**descent** descensus, us *m;* genus *n.*

**describe** describo 3; exprimo 3; expono 3.

**descry** conspicio 3.

**desecrate** violo 1.

**desert** desero 3, relinquo 3; desertus, vastus; deserta *n/pl.;* ~s meritum *n;* ~er desertor *m,* perfuga *m.*

**deserve** mereor 2; dignus sum; ~dly merito, iure.

**design** describo 3; formo 1; cogito 1; descriptio *f;* consilium *n;* ~ate

designo 1; ~edly consulto; ~er architectus *m;* auctor *m.*

**desir|able** optabilis; ~e cupio 3; (ex)opto 1; gestio 4; cupiditas *f;* studium *n;* libido *f;* ~ous cupidus (*gen.*).

**desist** desisto 3 (*re, inf.*).

**desk** scrinium *n.*

**desolat|e** vastus, desertus; orbus; vasto 1; ~ion vastatio *f;* solitudo *f.*

**despair** despero 1 (*de; alqd; acc. c. inf.*); desperatio *f.*

**despatch** mitto 3; perficio 3, conficio 3; litterae *f/pl.*

**desperate** desperatus, periculosus.

**despise** contemno 3, sperno 3.

**despite** *prep.* etiamsi; *cj.* quamvis.

**despoil** spolio 1.     [mitto 3.]

**despond** despero 1, animum de-]

**despot** tyrannus *m;* ~ic tyrannicus.

**dessert** bellaria *n/pl.*

**destin|e** destino 1; ~ed fatalis (*ad*); ~y fatum *n.*

**destitut|e** inops, egens, expers; ~ion egestas *f,* inopia *f.*

**destroy** deleo 2, everto 3, perdo 3; ~er perditor *m.*

**destruct|ion** pernicies *f;* exitium *n;* ~ive exitialis.

**desultory** inconstans.

**detach** eximo 3, abripio 3; disiungo 3; removeo 2; ~ment manus, us *f.*

**detail** enarro 1; ~s singula *n/pl.;* in ~ singillatim.

**detain** teneo 2; retineo 2.

**detect** deprehendo 3; comperio 4.

**deter** deterreo 2 (*a re, ne*).

**deteriorate** corrumpo(r) 3.

**determin|ate** certus; ~ation sententia *f;* constantia *f;* ~e statuo 3, constituo 3 (*inf., ut*); decerno 3 (*alqd; acc. c. inf.; ut*); ~ed firmus, constans.

**detest** odi; abominor 1; ~able foedus, detestabilis.

**dethrone** regno expello 3.

**detonation** fragor *m.*

**detour** circuitus, us *m.*

**detract** detraho 3, derogo 1 (*de*); ~or obtrectator *m.*

**detriment** damnum *n,* detrimentum *n.*

**devastat|e** vasto 1, populor 1; ~ion vastatio *f.*

**develop** *v/t.* dilato 1, explico 1; amplifico 1; alo 3; *v/i.* cresco 3; ~ment incrementum *n.*

**deviat|e** declino 1 (*de*); **~ion** declinatio *f*.

**device** insigne *n*; artificium *n*.

**devil** diabolus *m*.

**devise** excogito 1; fingo 3.

**devoid** expers (*gen.*); vacuus (*abl.*).

**devolve** *v/t.* defero 3 (*alci*); *v/i.* pervenio 4 (*ad*); obvenio 4 (*dat.*).

**devot|e** devoveo 2 (*dat.*); confero 3 (*dat.*); **~e oneself to** incumbo 3 (*in, ad*); **~ed** sacer; studiosus (*gen.*); **~ion** studium *n*; **~ions** preces *f/pl.*

**devour** devoro 1.

**devout** pius.

**dew** ros *m*; **dew-lap** palearia *n/pl.*; **~y** roscidus. [dus.]

**dexter|ity** calliditas *f*; **~ous** calli-]

**diadem** diadema *n*.

**diagram** descriptio *f*.

**dial** solarium *n*.

**dialect** lingua *f*; **~ical** dialecticus; **~ics** dialectica *f*.

**dialogue** sermo *m*; dialogus *m*.

**diamond** adamas *m*.

**diaphragm** praecordia *n/pl.*

**diary** ephemeris *f*.

**dice** tali *m/pl.*; tesserae *f/pl.*; **game of ~** alea *f*; **~-board** alveus *m*; **~-box** fritillus *m*.

**dictat|e** impero 1; praescribo 3; dicto 1; praeceptum *n*; **~ion** praescriptum *n*; **~or** dictator *m*; **~orial** arrogans; **~orship** dictatura *f*.

**diction** dictio *f*.

**die** talus *m*; tessera *f*; morior 3; obeo 4; pereo 4; **~ out** obsolesco 3.

**diet** cibus *m*; victus, us *m*; diaeta *f*.

**differ** differo 3, discrepo 1, disto 1 (*ab, inter se*); **~ence** differentia *f*, distantia *f*; **it makes a ~ence** interest (*utrum ... an*); **~ent** diversus, varius, alius, dispar.

**difficult** difficilis, arduus; **~y** difficultas *f*; angustiae *f/pl.*; **with ~y** aegre, vix.

**diffident** verecundus.

**diffuse** diffundo 3; diffusus, verbosus.

**dig** fodio 3.

**digest** concoquo 3.

**dignif|ied** gravis; **~y** honesto 1.

**dignity** dignitas *f*, maiestas *f*.

**digress** digredior 3, declino 1; **~ion** digressio *f*.

**dike** fossa *f*; agger, eris *n*.

**dilapidated** ruinosus.

**dilate (upon)** dilato 1.

**dilatory** tardus.

**dilemma** complexio *f*; angustiae *f/pl.*

**diligen|ce** diligentia *f*, industria *f*; **~t** diligens, industrius.

**dilute** diluo 3.

**dim** obscurus, hebes; obscuro 1; **grow ~** hebesco 3.

**dimension** modus *m*; amplitudo *f*.

**dimin|ish** minuo 3; levo 1; **~utive** parvus, exiguus.

**dimness** obscuritas *f*.

**dimple** gelasinus *m*.

**din** sonitus, us *m*; strepitus, us *m*.

**dine** ceno 1.

**dingy** squalidus.

**dining|-couch, ~-room** triclinium *n*.

**dinner** cena *f*.

**dint** ictus, us *m*; **by ~ of** per (*acc.*).

**dip** *v/t.* tingo 3; mergo 3 (*abl.*); *v/i.* me inclino 1; **~ into** perstringo 3.

**diplomatist** legatus *m*.

**dire** dirus.

**direct** rectus; dirigo 3; intendo 3 (*in, ad*); doceo 2; rego 3; iubeo 2; **~ion** cursus, us *m*; iter, ineris *n*; administratio *f*; praeceptum *n*; inscriptio *f*; **in all ~ions** passim; **in the ~ion of** in, ad, ... versus; **~ly** recta; statim; **~or** magister, tri *m*; curator *m*.

**dirge** nenia *f*.

**dirt** sordes *f*; caenum *n*, lutum *n*; **~y** sordidus, squalidus; foedo 1.

**disable** debilito 1; **~d** mancus, debilis.

**disabuse** errorem tollo 3.

**disadvantage** incommodum *n*; **~ous** incommodus, iniquus.

**disaffect** alieno 1; **~ion** alienatio *f*; seditio *f*.

**disagree** dissentio 4, dissideo 2 (*ab, cum, inter se*); **~able** molestus, difficilis; **~ment** dissensio *f*; discordia *f*.

**disappear** evanesco 3; dilabor 3.

**disappoint** fallo 3; **~ing** fallax.

**disapprov|al** reprehensio *f*; **~e** improbo 1.

**disarm** exuo 3 armis.

**disarrange** turbo 1.

**disast|er** clades *f*; calamitas *f*; **~rous** calamitosus.

**disavow** infitior 1 (*alqd*).

**disband** dimitto 3.

**disbelieve** fidem non habeo 2.

**disburse** expendo 3; **~ment** erogatio *f*.

**discard** excutio 3.

**discern** discerno 3 (*alqd a re*); dispicio 3; **~ing** acutus; **~ment** iudicium *n*.

**discharge** evomo 3; (im)mitto 3; *mil.* dimitto 3, exauctoro 1; (per-)fungor 3 (*abl.*); coniectus, us *m*, missio *f*; *jur.* absolutio *f*.

**disciple** discipulus *m*.

**discipline** disciplina *f*; **good ~** modestia *f*; coerceo 2.

**disclaim** infitior 1.

**disclos|e** patefacio 3; ostendo 3; **~ure** indicium *n*.

**dis|colour** infusco 1; **~comfit** perturbo 1; **~comfort** vexatio *f*; **~composed** commotus; **~concert** perturbo 1; **~consolate** maerens.

**discontent** molestia *f*; **~ed** iniquus (*animus*).

**discontinue** desisto 3 (*abl., inf.*).

**discord** discordia *f*; **~ant** discors.

**discount** deduco 3; decessio *f*.

**discountenance** perturbo 1.

**discourage** animum frango 3; deterreo 2 (*alqm a re, ne*); **be ~d** animum demitto 3.

**discourse** sermo *m*; oratio *f*; **~ upon** dissero 3 (*de*).

**discourteous** inhumanus.

**discover** invenio 4; reperio 4; deprehendo 3; **~er** inventor *m*; **~y** inventum *n*.

**discredit** invidia *f*; fidem non habeo 2 (*alci*); **~able** inhonestus.

**discreet** prudens.

**discrepancy** discrepantia *f*.

**discretion** prudentia *f*; arbitratus, us *m*; arbitrium *n*; **at his ~** arbitratu, arbitrio suo.

**discriminat|e** diiudico 1 (*acc.,inter*); **~ing** acutus; **~ion** discrimen *n*.

**discuss** disputo 1, dissero 3 (*de*). **~ion** disceptatio *f*.

**disdain** despicio 3; contemno 3; fastidium *n*; **~ful** fastidiosus.

**disease** morbus *m*; **~d** aeger, morbo affectus.

**disembark** *v/t.* expono 3; *v/i.* egredior 3 (ex navi).

**disengage** expedio 4.

**disentangle** explico 1.

**disfavour** offensio *f*.

**disfigure** deformo 1.

**disfranchise** civitatem adimo 3 (*alci*).

**disgorge** evomo 3.

**disgrace** dedecoro 1; ignominia *f*,

turpitudo *f*; dedecus *n*; **be ~d** infamiam habeo 2, capio 3; **~ful** turpis, foedus.

**disguise** dissimulo 1; persona *f*; simulatio *f*.

**disgust** fastidium *n*, taedium *n*; fastidium pario 3, affero 3; taedet (*me alcis rei*); **~ing** foedus.

**dish** patina *f*, lanx *f*.

**dishearten** exanimo 1.

**dishevelled** passus.

**dishonest** fraudulentus, mendax; **~y** fraus *f*, improbitas *f*.

**dishonour** dedecoro 1; stupro 1; ignominia *f*; stuprum *n*; **~able** inhonestus.

**disinclined: be ~** abhorreo 2 (*a re*).

**disinherit** exheredo 1.

**disinterested** integer.

**disjointed** disiunctus.

**dislike** odi; abhorreo 2 (*ab*).

**dislocate** extorqueo 2.

**dislodge** (sum)moveo 2; deicio 3.

**disloyal** perfidus.

**dismal** tristis, maestus.

**dismay** percello 3; perturbo 1; perturbatio *f*; pavor *m*.

**dismember** discerpo 3.

**dismiss** (di)mitto 3; moveo 2; **~al** missio *f*.                [desilio 4.]

**dismount** descendo 3 (*ex equo*);|

**disobey** non pareo 2.

**disobliging** inhumanus.

**disorder** perturbo 1; perturbatio *f*, turba *f*; **~ly** inordinatus, turbulentus.

**disown** infitior 1.

**disparage** detraho 3 (*de*).

**dispel** dispello 3.

**dispens|ation** immunitas *f*; **~e** tribuo 3; **~e with** remitto 3.

**disperse** *v/t.* dissipo 1; *v/i.* dilabor 3.

**displace** summoveo 2.

**display** praebeo 2; ostendo 3; ostentatio *f*.

**displeas|e** displiceo 2; **be ~ed** aegre fero 3; **~ure** offensio *f*.

**dispos|al** dispositio *f*; dicio *f*; **~e** ordino 1; **~ed** propensus (*in, ad*); inclinatus (*ad*); **~ition** natura *f*; indoles *f*.

**dispossess** expello 3.

**disproportionate** inaequalis.

**dispute** discepto 1 (*de*); altercor 1 (*cum alqo*); controversia *f*.

**disqualif|ication** impedimentum *n*; **~y** impedio 4; impedimento est (*alci*).

**disquiet** sollicito 1; sollicitudo f.
**dis|regard** neglego 3; **~reputable** infamis; **~repute** infamia f; **~respectful** contumeliosus; **~robe** vestem detraho 3.
**dissatisf|action** molestia f; **be ~ied** me paenitet (*alcis rei*).
**dissemble** dissimulo 1; obtego 3.
**disseminate** dissemino 1.
**dissen|sion** dissensio f; **~t** dissentio 4 (*ab alqo*).
**dissertation** schola f.
**dissimilar** dissimilis (*gen.*, *dat.*).
**dissipat|e** dissipo 1; **~ed** dissolutus; **~ion** libidines f/pl.
**dissociate** separo 1.         [ve 3.]
**dissol|ute** dissolutus; **~ve** (dis)sol-]
**dissuade** dissuadeo 2 (*ne*).
**distan|ce** spatium n; **at a ~ce** longe, procul; **~t** disiunctus; longinquus; **be ~t** absum; disto 1 (*ab*).
**distaste** fastidium n; **~ful** odiosus.
**distend** distendo 3.
**distil** stillo 1.
**distinct** clarus, distinctus; alius (*ac*, *atque*); **~ion** discrimen n; distinctio f; honor m; **~ive** proprius; **~ly** clare; diserte.
**distinguish** discerno 3; distinguo 3 (*alqd ab alqo*); **~ oneself** emineo 2; **~ed** insignis, egregius.
**distort** detorqueo 3.
**distract** distraho 3; **~ed** amens; **~ion** perturbatio f.
**distress** affligo 3; ango 3; dolor m, angor m; **~ing** miser.
**distribut|e** distribuo 3; dispertio 4; **~ion** partitio f.
**district** regio f; tractus, us m; ager, gri m.
**distrust** diffido 3 (*dat.*); diffidentia f.
**disturb** perturbo 1; sollicito 1; **~ance** turba f; tumultus, us m; perturbatio f.
**disunite** dissocio 1.
**disuse** desuetudo f; **fall into ~** obsolesco 3.
**ditch** fossa f.
**ditty** nenia f.
**dive** mergo(r) 3 (*in rem*, *in re*); **~r** urinator m.
**diverg|e** decedo 3 (*de via*); deflecto 3 (*a*, *de*); **~ing** diversus.
**divers|e** varius, diversus; **~ion** derivatio f; oblectamentum n.
**divert** derivo 1; averto 3; oblecto 1; *mil.* distringo 3; **~ing** festivus, facetus.

**divest** exuo 3, depono 3; **~ oneself of** exuo 3 (*alqd*).
**divide** seco 1; divido 3; dispertio 4.
**divin|ation** divinatio f; **~e** divino 1 (*alqd*, *acc. c. inf.*); conicio 3; divinus; sacer; **~ely** divinitus; **~ity** numen n, deus m.
**division** partitio f; discidium n; pars f; (*for voting*) discessio f.
**divorce** divortium n; divortium facio 3 (*cum*).
**divulge** divulgo 1.
**dizziness** vertigo f.
**do** facio 3; ago 3; **have to ~ with** rationem habeo 2 (*cum*); **how ~ you ~?** quid agis?; **~ without** careo 2.
**docile** tractabilis.
**dock** navalia n/pl.; cancelli m/pl.; subduco 3 navem; praecido 3.
**doctor** medicus m.
**doctrine** ratio f; disciplina f.
**document** tabula f.         [(*alqd*).]
**dodge** elabor 3 (*ex*); declino 1]
**doe** cerva f.
**dog** canis m and f; investigo 1; **~ged** pertinax; **~matic** arrogans; **~star** Sirius m.
**doing** factum n.
**dole** diurnum n; diurnus cibus m; stips f; **~ out** divido 3; **~ful** maestus.
**doll** pupa f.
**dolphin** delphinus m.
**dolt** baro m.
**domain** regnum n; dicio f.
**dome** tholus m.
**domestic** domesticus, familiaris; famulus m; famula f.
**domicile** domus, us f; domicilium n.
**dominat|e** regno 1, dominor 1 (*in*); **~ion** dominatio f.
**domineering** imperiosus.
**dominion** imperium n; potestas f.
**donation** stips f.
**done: well ~!** euge!
**donkey** asinus m.
**doom** fatum n; exitium n; condemno 1; **~ed** fatalis.
**door** ianua f; fores f/pl.; ostium n; **in~s** domi; **out of ~s** foris; **back-~** posticum n; **~keeper** ianitor m; **~way** limen n.
**dose** medicamentum do 1.
**dot** punctum n.
**dot|age** deliratio f; **~ard** senex m delirus; **~e upon** depereo 4.
**double** duplex, geminus; duplum n;

duplico 1; flecto 3; **~-dealing** fraus *f*; versutus.

**doubt** dubito 1 (*de re*; *quin*); dubitatio *f*; **without ~** sine dubio; **~ful** dubius, incertus; anceps; **~less** nimirum; scilicet.

**dove** columba *f*.

**down**[1] lanugo *f*; plumae *f/pl.*

**down**[2] *prep.* de (*abl.*); **~ stream** secundum flumen; *adv.* deorsum; **~cast** demissus; **~fall** ruina *f*; **~hill** declivis; **~right** merus; plane, prorsus.

**dowry** dos *f*; **having a ~** dotata.

**doze** dormito 1.

**drag** traho 3; **~on** draco *m*.

**drain** sicco 1; (ex)haurio 4; cloaca *f*.

**drama** fabula *f*; **~tic** scaenicus; **~tist** poeta *m*.

**drapery** amictus, us *m*.

**draught** potio *f*; **game of ~s** latrunculi *m/pl.*

**draw** traho 3; educo 3 (*gladium*); haurio 4 (*aquam*); duco 3 (*spiritum*); **~ near** appropinquo 1; **~ up (in words)** concipio 3; *mil.* instruo 3; **~ing** tabula *f*; descriptio *f*.

**dread** formido 1; formido *f*; **~ful** terribilis, atrox.

**dream** somnio 1; somnium *n*.

**dreary** vastus; tristis.

**dregs** taex *f*; sentina *f*.

**drench** perfundo 3.

**dress** induo 3 (*sibi, alci, alqd*); vestio 4 (*alqm veste*); como 3 (*capillos*); obligo 1 (*vulnera*); vestis *f*; vestitus, us *m*; habitus, us *m*; **~ing** fomentum *n*.

**drift** defero 3 vento.

**drill** perforo 1; exerceo 2; terebra *f*; exercitium *n*.

**drink** bibo 3; **~ to** propino 1 (*alci*); potio *f*; potus, us *m*; **~er** potor *m*; **~ing-bout** potatio *f*.

**drip** stillo 1; mano 1 (*alqa re*); **~ping (with)** madidus (*abl.*).

**drive** *v/t.* ago 3; *v/i.* vehor 3; **~ away** abigo 3; **~ back** repello 3; **~ from, out** exigo 3; pello 3; **~r** agitator *m*, auriga *m*.

**droll** ridiculus.

**drone** fucus *m*; bombus *m*.

**droop** *v/i.* pendeo 2; langueo 2; *v/t.* demitto 3; **~ing** languidus, fractus.

**drop** *v/t.* demitto 3; stillo 1; delabor 3; decido 3; **~ in on** venio 4 (*ad*); gutta *f*.

**dropsy** hydrops *m*.

**drought** siccitas *f*.

**drove** grex *m*; **~r** pastor *m*; armentarius *m*.

**drown** summergo 3; *fig.* mergo 3.

**drows|iness** somnus *m*; **~y** somniculosus.

**drudge** mediastinus *m*; **~ry** labor *m*.

**drug** medicamentum *n*, venenum *n*; medico 1 (*alqd*).

**druids** Druides *m/pl.*

**drum** tympanum *n*.

**drunk** ebrius; **~ard** ebriosus *m*; **~enness** ebrietas *f*.

**dry** siccus, aridus; **~ land** aridum *n*; *v/t.* sicco 1; abstergeo 2; *v/i.* aresco 3; **~ness** siccitas *f*.

**dubious** dubius.

**duck** anas *f*; summergo 3.

**due** debitum *n*; vectigal *n*, portorium *n*; debitus, meritus; **in ~ time** tempore, tempori.

**duel** certamen *n*.

**dug** uber, eris *n*.

**dull** hebes; tardus; obtusus; subnubilus; frigidus; obtundo 3; hebeto 1; **~ness** tarditas *f*.

**dumb** mutus; **~founded** obstupefactus.

**dun** fuscus.

**dung** stercus *n*.

**dungeon** carcer, eris *n*.

**dunghill** sterquilinum *n*.

**dupe** ludifico 1; credulus homo *m*.

**duplicate** exemplar *n*.

**duplicity** fraus *f*.

**dura|ble** firmus, stabilis; **~tion** spatium *n*; tempus *n*; **of long, short ~tion** diuturnus, brevis.

**during** per (*acc.*), inter (*acc.*); in (*abl.*); *cj.* dum.

**dusk** crepusculum *n*; **~y** fuscus, obscurus.

**dust** pulvis *m*; tergeo 2; verro 3; **~y** pulverulentus.

**dutiful** pius; officiosus; **~ness** pietas *f*.

**duty** officium *n*; munus *n*; *mil.* **on ~** in statione (*esse*); **pay ~** vectigal pendo 3; **it is my ~** debeo 2.

**dwarf** pumilio *m and f*.

**dwell** habito 1 (*in*); incolo 3; **~ upon** commoror 1 (*alqd*); **~ing** domicilium *n*; habitatio *f*.

**dwindle** decresco 3, minuor 3.

**dye** tingo 3; inficio 3; color *m*; **~r** infector *m*.

**dynasty** domus, us *f*.

# E

**each** quisque; ~ **and every** unus quisque; ~ **of two** uterque; ~ **other** inter se; **one** ~ singuli.

**eager** avidus, cupidus (**for** *gen.*); acer; ~**ness** aviditas *f*; studium *n*.

**eagle** aquila *f*; ~**-bearer** aquilifer *m*.

**ear** auris *f*; **give** ~ **to** aures do 1, praebeo 2 (*alci*); ~ **of corn** spica *f*.

**earliness** maturitas *f*.

**early** matutinus, maturus; antiquus; *adv.* mane, mature.

**earn** mereo(r) 2; consequor 3.

**earnest** acer; serius; arrhabo *m*; ~**ly** magnopere, vehementer.

**earnings** merces *f*.

**earth** terra *f*, tellus *f*; ~**en** fictilis; ~**enware** fictilia *n/pl.*; ~**ly** terrestris; humanus; ~**quake** terrae motus, us *m*; ~**work** agger, eris *m*.

**ease** remitto 3; relaxo 1; levo 1; otium *n*; quies *f*; facilitas *f*; **at** ~ otiose.

**east** oriens *m*; solis ortus, us *m*; ~**er** pascha *f*; ~**ern** Eous; ~ **wind** eurus *m*.

**easy** facilis; expeditus; commodus.

**eat** edo 3; vescor 3 (*abl.*); ~ **up** comedo 3; consumo 3; ~**ables** cibaria *n/pl.*; ~**ing-house** popina *f*.

**eaves-drop** subausculto 1.

**ebb** recedo 3; *fig.* decresco 3; (aestus) recessus, us *m*; **be at a low** ~ iaceo 2.

**ebony** ebenum *n*.

**echo** imago *f*; refero 3; resono 1; itero 1.

**eclipse** defectio *f*; obscuro 1; **be** ~**d** deficio 3.

**eclogue** ecloga *f*.

**econom|ical** parcus; ~**y** parsimonia *f*.

**ecsta|sy** insania *f*; laetitia *f*; ~**tic** insanus.

**eddy** vertex *m*.

**edge** ora *f*; margo *m*; **cutting** ~ acies *f*; praetexo 3.

**edible** esculentus.

**edict** edictum *n*.

**edifice** aedificium *n*.

**edify** excolo 3.

**edit** edo 3.

**educat|e** educo 1; instituo 3; ~**ion** educatio *f*; disciplina *f*.

**eel** anguilla *f*.

**efface** deleo 2; oblittero 1.

**effect** efficio 3; effectus, us *m*; eventus, us *m*; vis *f*; **in** ~ reapse, re vera; **have** ~ **on** valeo 2 (*apud*); ~**ive** efficax; ~**s** bona *n/pl.*

**effeminate** effeminatus, mollis, muliebris.

**effervesce** effervesco 3; ~**nce** fervor *m*.

**efficac|ious** efficax; ~**y** vis *f*.

**efficient** idoneus.

**effigy** imago *f*.

**effort** conatus, us *m*; labor *m*.

**effrontery** impudentia *f*; os *n*.

**egg** ovum *n*; ~ **on** incito 1; ~**-shell** ovi putamen *n*.

**egregious** insignis.

**eight** octo; ~**een** duodeviginti; ~**eenth** duodevicesimus; ~**-fold** octuplus; ~**h** octavus; ~ **hundred** octingenti; ~**y** octoginta.

**either** alteruter; utervis, uterlibet; **on** ~ **side** utrimque; ~ ... **or** aut ... aut; vel ... vel.

**ejaculate** exclamo 1.

**eject** deicio 3.

**eke out** parco 3.

**elaborate** expolio 4; elaboratus, accuratus.

**elapse** praetereo 4.

**elated** elatus (gaudio, superbia).

**elbow** cubitum *n*.

**elder** maior natu; ~**ly** aetate provectus; **the** ~**ly** seniores *m/pl.*

**elect** creo 1; deligo 3; designatus; ~**ion** suffragium *n*; comitia *n/pl.*; ~**ioneering** petitio *f*, ambitio *f*; ~**or** suffragator *m*.

**elegan|ce** munditia *f*; urbanitas *f*; ~**t** elegans, urbanus.

**eleg|iacs** elegi *m/pl.*; ~**y** elegia *f*.

**element** elementum *n*; ~**s** principia *n/pl.*; elementa *n/pl.*; ~**ary** simplex.

**elephant** elephantus *m*.

**elevat|e** effero 3; excolo 3; ~**ed** celsus, elatus; ~**ion** elatio *f*.

**eleven** undecim; ~**th** undecimus.

**elicit** elicio 3.
**eligible** optabilis.
**eliminate** tollo 3.
**ell** ulna *f*.
**elm** ulmus, i *f*.
**elocution** pronuntiatio *f*.
**elope** (ef)fugio 3.
**eloquen|ce** eloquentia *f*, facundia *f*; ~t eloquens, disertus, copiosus.
**else** alioqui(n); aliter; **some one ~** alius; ~where alibi.
**elucidate** illustro 1.
**elu|de** effugio 3; elabor 3 (*abl.*); eludo 3; ~sive fallax.
**emaciat|e** macero 1; ~ion macies *f*.
**emanate** emano 3.
**emancipat|e** manumitto 3; libero 1; ~ion manumissio *f*.
**emasculate** enervo 1.
**embalm** condio 4.
**embankment** agger, eris *m*; moles *f*.
**embargo** prohibitio *f*.
**embark** *v/t.* impono 3 (*in navem*); *v/i.* navem conscendo 3; ~ **upon** ineo 3 (*alqd*).
**embarrass** impedio 4; implico 1; **be ~ed** haereo 2; perturbor 1; ~ment scrupulus *m*; angustiae *f/pl.*
**embassy** legatio *f*.
**embellish** orno 1; ~ment ornamentum *n*.
**embers** cinis, eris *m*.
**embezzle** averto 3; ~ment peculatus, us *m*; ~r peculator *m*.
**embitter** exacerbo 3.
**emblem** indicium *n*.
**embolden** confirmo 1.
**embrace** amplector 3, complector 3; complexus, us *m*.
**embroider** pingo 3.
**embroil** implico 1.
**emerald** smaragdus, i *m and f*.
**emerge** emergo 3, exsisto 3 (*ex*); ~ncy tempus *n*, discrimen *n*.
**emigrat|e** (e)migro 1; ~ion migratio *f*.
**eminen|ce** tumulus *m*; praestantia *f*; ~t praeclarus; nobilis.
**emissary** legatus *m*.
**emit** emitto 3; iacio 3.
**emotion** motus, us *m*; commotio *f*.
**emperor** imperator *m*, princeps *m*.
**empha|sis** vis *f*; ~size vehementer dico 3.
**empire** imperium *n*; regnum *n*.
**employ** utor 3; adhibeo 2; ~ment quaestus, us *m*.
**empower** potestatem do 1 (*alci*).

**empt|iness** inanitas *f*; ~y vacuus; inanis; vanus; exinanio 4; exhaurio 4.
**emulat|e** aemulor 1 (*acc.*); ~ion aemulatio *f*.
**enable** facultatem do 1 (*alci*).
**enact** sancio 4 (*legem, lege alqd, ut*); scisco 3 (*alqd, ut*); constituo 3; **get ~ed** perfero 3; ~ment lex *f*; scitum *n*.
**enamoured: be ~** depereo 2 (*alqm*).
**encamp** castra pono 3; consido 3.
**enchant** fascino 1; capio 3; ~ing venustus; ~ment, carmen *n*; ~ress venefica *f*.
**encircle** cingo 3; circumdo 1 (*alqd re*).
**enclos|e** includo 3; ~ure saepta *n/pl.*
**encore** revoco 1.
**encounter** offendo 3; congredior 3; oppeto 3 (*mortem*); experior 4 (*periculum*); congressus, us *m*.
**encourage** confirmo 1; hortor 1; ~ment cohortatio *f*.
**encroach upon** occupo 1; imminuo 3 (*ius etc.*).
**encumb|er** impedio 4; ~rance impedimentum *n*.
**end** finis *m*; **make an ~** finem facio 3 (*gen.*); **put an ~ to** finem affero 3 (*dat.*); dirimo 3; **in the ~** postremo; **to no ~** frustra; **to this ~** ideo; extremus; *v/t.* finio 4; *v/i.* desino 3.
**endanger** periclitor 1.
**endeavour** conor 1; conatum *n*.
**end|ing** exitus, us *m*; ~less infinitus.
**endow** dono 1 (*alqm re*); instruo 3; ~ed praeditus.
**endur|ance** patientia *f*; fortitudo *f*; ~e patior 3; (per)fero 3; duro 1; ~ing patiens (*gen.*); perennis.
**enemy** hostis *m and f*, inimicus *m*.
**energ|etic** acer; strenuus; ~y vis *f*; impetus, us *m*.
**enervate** enervo 1.
**enfeeble** debilito 1.
**enforce** exerceo 2.
**enfranchise** civitatem do 1 (*alci*).
**engage** *v/t.* conduco 3; *v/i.* congredior 3 (*cum hostibus*); (*in me*) recipio 3; promitto 3 (*acc. c. inf.*); ~ **in** suscipio 3; ~d occupatus (*in re*); sponsus; ~ment sponsio *f*; negotium *n*; proelium *n*.
**engender** gigno 3.
**engin|e** machina *f*; tormentum *n*; ~eer machinator *m*.

**engrave** incido 3; caelo 1; ~r sculptor *m*, sculptor *m*.
**engross** occupo 1.
**engulf** devoro 1.
**enhance** amplifico 1; augeo 2; ~ment amplificatio *f*.
**enigma** aenigma *n*.
**enjoin** praecipio 3 (*alci alqd*).
**enjoy** fruor 3, utor 3 (*abl.*); delector 1 (*abl.*); ~ment gaudium *n*; voluptas *f*.
**enlarge** augeo 2; dilato 1; ~ **upon** uberius loquor 3, dico 3.    [cio 3.]
**enlighten** erudio 4; certiorem fa-]
**enlist** *v/t.* conscribo 3; *v/i.* nomen do 1, edo 3, sacramentum dico 3.
**enliven** exhilaro 1.
**enmity** inimicitia *f*; simultas *f*.
**enorm|ity** immanitas *f*; scelus *n*; ~ous ingens; immanis.
**enough** satis; ~ **and to spare** satis superque; **not** ~ parum.
**enrage** exaspero 1.
**en|rapture** delecto 1; ~rich locupleto 1; ~rol ascribo 3 (*in, dat.*); ~sconce oneself consido 3.
**ensign** signum *n*; vexillum *n*.
**enslave** in servitutem abduco 3, abstraho 3; ~ment servitus, utis *f*.
**ensnare** irretio 4.
**ensue** sequor 3.
**ensure** curo 1; provideo 2 (*ut, ne*).
**entail** affero 3.
**entangle** implico 1.
**enter** ingredior 3 (*intra, in*); venio 4 (*in*); intro 1 (*alqd, in, ad*); refero 3 (*alqd in libellum*); ~ **upon** ineo 4 (*alqd*); ~prise inceptum *n*, consilium *n*; audacia *f*; ~prising promptus, audax.
**entertain** excipio 3; invito 1; oblecto 1; ~ment hospitium *n*; epulae *f/pl.*
**enthusias|m** studium *n*; ardor *m*; ~tic studiosus (*gen.*); **be** ~tic ardeo 2 (*studio*).
**entic|e** allicio 3, illicio 3; ~ement illecebra *f*; ~ing blandus.
**entire** totus; integer; universi; ~ly omnino; plane.
**entitle** inscribo 3; **be** ~d **to** ius habeo 2 (*gen.*); dignus sum (*abl., qui*).
**entrails** viscera *n/pl.*
**entrance** introitus, us *m*; aditus, us *m*; capio 3.
**entreat** oro 1, obsecro 1; flagito 1; ~y preces *f/pl.*; obsecratio *f*.

**entrust** credo 3 (*alqd alci*).
**entry** introitus, us *m*; aditus, us *m*; **make an** ~ refero 3 (*in*).
**entwine** implico 1 (*alqd alqa re*).
**enumerate** enumero 1.
**envelop** involvo 3; ~e involucrum *n*.
**env|iable** fortunatus; ~ious invidus; ~oy legatus *m*; ~y invidia *f*; invideo 2 (*dat.*).
**ephemeral** caducus, brevis.
**epic** epos *n*; epicus.
**epigram** epigramma *n*.
**epistle** epistula *f*.
**epitaph** elogium *n*.
**epoch** tempus *n*; saeculum *n*.
**equable** aequus.
**equal** aequus; aequalis; par; (ad-) aequo 1; aequipero 1; ~ity aequabilitas *f*; ~ize aequo 1.
**equanimity** aequus animus *m*.
**equestrian** equester; eques *m*.
**equinox** aequinoctium *n*.
**equip** orno 1; instruo 3; ~ment arma *n/pl.*; apparatus, us *m*; instrumentum *n*.
**equit|able** aequus; ~y aequitas *f*.
**equivocal** ambiguus.
**equivocate** tergiversor 1.
**era** tempus *n*.
**eradicate** exstirpo 1.
**eras|e** deleo 2; induco 3; ~ure litura *f*.
**ere** prius, ante quam.
**erect** exstruo 3; statuo 3; erectus; ~ion aedificatio *f*; aedificium *n*.
**erotic** amatorius.
**err** erro 1; pecco 1.
**errand** mandatum *n*; ~-**boy** nuntius *m*.
**err|atic** vagus; ~oneous falsus; ~or error *m*; erratum *n*; peccatum *n*.
**erudit|e** doctus, eruditus; ~ion eruditio *f*.
**eruption** eruptio *f*.
**escape** effugio 3; elabor 3 (*ex*); **it** ~s **one's notice** fallit; praeterit; effugium *n*.
**escort** prosequor 3; deduco 3; praesidium *n*; comitatus, us *m*.
**especial** praecipuus; ~ly praecipue; praesertim.
**espy** conspicor 1.
**essay** tento 1; periculum *n*.
**essen|ce** substantia *f*; ~tial necessarius.
**establish** instituo 3, statuo 3; stabilio 4; ~ **that** vinco 3 (*acc. c. inf.*); ~ment constitutio *f*; familia *f*.

**estate** status, us *m*; ager *m*; fundus *m*.

**esteem** diligo 3; magni facio 3; existimatio *f*.

**estimat|e** aestimo 1; iudicium *n*; aestimatio *f*; **~ion** existimatio *f*; opinio *f*.

**estrange** alieno 1; **~ment** alienatio *f*.

**estuary** aestuarium *n*.

**etern|al** aeternus; sempiternus; **~ity** aeternitas *f*.

**ether** aether, eris *m*; **~eal** aetherius.

**ethic|al** moralis; **~s** philosophia *f* moralis.

**etiquette** mos *n*.

**eulog|ize** laudo 1; **~y** laudatio *f*; laus *f*.

**eunuch** eunuchus *m*.

**evacuate** vacuefacio 3; *mil.* deduco 3 praesidium; excedo 3 (*abl.*).

**evade** subterfugio 3; fraudem facio 3 (*legi*).

**evaporate** exhalo 1.

**evasion** ambages *f/pl.*; **practise ~** tergiversor 1.

**eve: on the ~ of** pridie (*gen.*).

**even** aequus, planus; *adv.* etiam; vel; **not ... ~** ne ... quidem; **~ if** etiamsi.

**evening** vesper *m*; **good ~!** salve; **in the ~** vesperi; vespertinus; **~ star** Hesperus *m*.

**evenness** aequitas *f* (animi).

**event** res *f*; eventus, us *m*; **at all ~s** certe; **~ful** memorabilis; **~ually** postremo; ad postremum.

**ever** semper; **if ~** si quando; **nor ... ~** nec ... umquam; **~ since** ex eo tempore quo; **~lasting** sempiternus.

**every** quisque; omnis; **any and ~** quivis; **~ day** cotidie; **~ year** quotannis; **~body** quisque; omnes; nemo ... non; **~thing** quidque; omnia *n/pl.*; **~where** ubique; passim.

**evidence** testimonium *n*; indicium *n*; argumentum *n*; **give ~** testificor 1.

**evident** manifestus; apertus; evidens; **it is ~** apparet 2; **~ly** aperte; scilicet.

**evil** malus; improbus; pravus; malum *n*; incommodum *n*.

**evince** praesto 1.

**evoke** evoco 1.

**ewe** ovis *f*.

**ewer** urceus *m*.

**exact** exigo 3; impero 1; sumo 3 (*poenas*); subtilis; accuratus; diligens; **~itude** diligentia *f*.

**exaggerate** augeo 2; exaggero 1; in maius (vero) fero 3, extollo 3.

**exalt** effero 3; augeo 2; **~ed** celsus.

**examin|ation** investigatio *f*; interrogatio *f*; probatio *f*; **~e** investigo 1; interrogo 1; quaero 3; probo 1.

**example** exemplum *n*; exemplar *n*; documentum *n*; **for ~** verbi causa.

**exasperate** irrito 1.

**excavat|e** (ex)cavo 1; **~ion** cavum *n*.

**exceed** egredior 3 (*extra, acc.*); **~ingly** valde.

**excel** praesto 1 (*dat.*); excello 3 (*dat.*); **~lence** virtus, utis *f*; excellentia *f*; **~lent** optimus; praestans.

**except** excipio 3; nisi quod; nisi ut; praeter (*acc.*); **~ing you two** exceptis vobis duobus; **~ion** exceptio *f*; **without ~ion** omnes; **~ional** rarus; eximius.

**excess** nimium *n*; luxuria *f*; **~ive** nimius; immoderatus.

**exchange** muto 1 (*alqd alqa re*); inter se dare; permutatio *f*; **~ of money** collybus *m*.

**exchequer** aerarium *n*; fiscus *m*.

**excise** vectigalia *n/pl.*

**excit|able** fervidus; **~e** commoveo 2; excito 1, concito 1 (*ad*); **~ement** commotio *f*; perturbatio *f*.

**exclaim** exclamo 1; conclamo 1; **~ against** acclamo 1 (*dat.*).

**exclamation** vox *f*; exclamatio *f*.

**exclu|de** prohibeo 2; excludo 3; **~sion** interdictio *f*; **~sive** proprius.

**excrement** stercus *n*.

**excruciating** acerbissimus.

**exculpate** purgo 1.

**excus|able** venia dignus; **~e** me purgo 1, excuso 1 (*alci*); veniam do 1; ignosco 3; excusatio *f*; venia *f*.

**execrate** exsecror 1.

**execut|e** exsequor 3; perficio 3; supplicium sumo 3 (*de*); supplicio afficio 3; **~ion** supplicium *n*; mors *f*; **~ioner** carnifex *m*.

**exempl|ary** egregius; **~ify** exemplum do 1, prodo 1.

**exempt** libero 1; solvo 3 (*alqm alqa re*); immunitatem tribuo 3; immunis (*abl.*); **~ion** immunitas *f*; vacatio *f*.

**exercise** exerceo 2; exercitatio *f*; **take ~** ambulo 1.

**exert** exerceo 2; utor 3; **~ oneself** nitor 3; laboro 1; **~ion** contentio *f*.

exhal|ation exhalatio *f*; ~e exhalo 1.
exhaust exhaurio 4; defatigo 1; debilito 1; **be ~ed** deficio 3; ~ed confectus; defessus; effetus; ~ion lassitudo *f*.
exhibit propono 3; expono 3; exhibeo 2; praesto 1; ostento 1; ~ion spectaculum *n*; munus *n*.
exhilarate exhilaro 1.
exhort (ad-, co-)hortor 1; ~ation hortatio *f*.
exigency necessitas *f*.
exile eicio 3; aqua et igni interdico 3; pello 3; exsilium *n*; exsul *m and f*; extorris; **be an ~, live in ~** exsulo 1; **go into ~** solum verto 3.
exist sum; exsisto 3; exsto 1; ~ence vita *f*.
exit exitus, us *m*.
exonerate libero 1 (*culpa*).
exorbitant immodicus.
exordium exordium *n*.
expan|d pando 3; extendo 3; ~se spatium *n*.
expect exspecto 1 (*alqd*); spero 1 (*alqd, acc. c. inf.*); credo 3 (*acc. c. inf.*); ~ation exspectatio *f*; spes *f*; **contrary to ~ation** praeter spem.
expedien|cy utilitas *f*; ~t utilis; **be ~t** expedit.
expedit|e maturo 1; ~ion expeditio *f*.
expel (ex)pello 3; eicio 3.
expen|d impendo 3; ~se impensa *f*; sumptus, us *m*; ~sive sumptuosus; carus.
experience experior 4; patior 3; usus, us *m*; peritia *f*; ~d peritus (*gen.*).
experiment periculum *n*; experimentum *n* (facio 3).
expert peritus (*gen.*), sciens (*gen.*); ~ness peritia *f*.
expiat|e expio 1 (*alqd alqa re*); ~ion expiatio *f*.
expire exspiro 1; animam, vitam edo 3; exeo 2.
expl|ain explico 1; explano 1; expono 3; ~anation explanatio *f*; ratio *f*; ~icit apertus.
explode dirumpor 3; explodo 3 (*sententiam*).
exploit res *f* gesta; facinus *n*.
explore exploro 1; speculor 1.
explosion fragor *m*.
export exporto 1.
expos|e expono 3; profero 3 (*rem*); nudo 1; ~e to obicio 3; ~ed aper-
tus; obnoxius (*dat.*); ~ition explicatio *f*; ~tulate expostulo 1 (*cum alqo de, acc. c. inf.*); ~ure frigus *n*.
expound expono 3.
express effero 3; dico 3; significo 1; ~ion verba *n/pl.*; oratio *f*; vultus, us *m*; significatio *f*; ~ive significans; ~ly diserte.
exquisite conquisitus, exquisitus.
extant: **be ~** exsto 1.
extempor|ary subitus; ~e subito.
extend extendo 3, distendo 3; porrigo 3; propago 1.
extens|ion propagatio *f*; ~ive amplus, latus.
extent spatium *n*; **to this ~, that** hactenus ... ut; **to what ~** quatenus.
extenuate levo 1.
exterior exterior; species *f*.
exterminate ad internecionem deleo 2, redigo 3; deleo 2.
external externus; **~ things** quae extra sunt.
extinct mortuus; ~ion interitus, us *m*.
extinguish exstinguo 3.
extirpate exstirpo 1.
extol laudo 1; laudibus effero 3.
extort extorqueo 2; exprimo 3; **crime of ~ion** (pecuniae) repetundae *f/pl.*; ~ionate rapax.
extra praecipuus; *adv.* praeterea.
extract extraho 3; exprimo 3; **make an ~** excerpo 3; ~ion evulsio *f*; genus *n*.
extraneous alienus.
extraordinar|ily extra ordinem *or* modum; ~y extraordinarius; insolitus.
extravagan|ce luxuria *f*; sumptus *m/pl.*; ~t immodicus; prodigus, profusus.
extreme extremus; summus; ultimus; ~s extrema *n/pl.*
extricate (me) expedio 4, extraho 3.
exuberan|ce hilaritas *f*; ~t laetus; luxuriosus.
exude sudo 1.
exult gestio 4; exsulto 1; gaudeo 2 (*abl.*); ~ant laetus; ~ation laetitia *f*.
eye oculus *m*; lumen *n*; **before one's ~s** ante oculos, in oculis, in conspectu; aspicio 3; ~ball pupula *f*; ~brow supercilium *n*; ~lid palpebra *f*; ~sight acies *f*; ~-witness arbiter, tri *m*.

# F

**fable** fabula f; ~d fabulosus.

**fabric** textile n; textum n; fabrica f; ~ate *fig.* comminiscor 3; ~ation commentum n.

**fabulous** commenticius, fabulosus.

**face** os n; facies f; vultus, us m; frons f; ~ **to** ~ coram (*abl.*); **in the** ~ **of** in (*abl.*); obviam eo 4 (*dat.*); me oppono 3, offero 3 (*dat.*); ~ **(towards)** aspecto 1 (*acc.*); vergo 3 (*in, ad*); ~ **about** signa converto 3.

**facetious** facetus.

**facil|itate** facilius reddo 3; ~ity facilitas f; facultas f.

**facing** adversus (*acc.*).

**fact** res f; factum n; **in** ~ re vera.

**facti|on** factio f; pars f; ~ous factiosus.

**factor** procurator m; ~y officina f.

**faculty** facultas f; ingenium n.

**fade** palleo 2; pallesco 3; cado 3.

**faggot** fascis m; sarmenta n/pl.

**fail** v/i. deficio 3; desum (*dat.*); cado 3; male evenit; v/t. destituo 3; **without** ~ certe; ~ure defectio f.

**fain: I would** ~ velim, vellem.

**faint** hebes; languidus; confectus; intermorior 3; animus relinquit (*alqm*); ~hearted ignavus; ~ness languor m.

**fair** candidus; pulcher; sudus, serenus (*tempestas*); mediocris; secundus (*ventus*); aequus; nundinae f/pl.; ~ly satis; ~ness aequum n; candor m; ~ **weather** sudum n.

**faith** fides f; **put** ~ **in** fidem habeo 2 (*dat.*); **keep good** ~ fidem servo 1; **break** ~ fidem violo 1; **in good** ~ ex bona fide; ~ful fidelis; fidus; ~less perfidus.

**fall** cado 3; labor 3; praecipito 1; ruo 3; ~ **away** descisco 3 (*ab*); ~ **in with** incido 3 (*in c. acc.*); ~ **out** dissideo 2 (*inter se*); ~ **short of** desum (*dat.*); ~ **to** obtingit (*sors, etc., alci*); accidit (*alci*); ~ **upon** invado 3 (*in c. acc.*); casus, us m; lapsus, us m; ruina f; deminutio f.

**fallac|ious** fallax; ~y captio f.

**fallow** novalis, inaratus; ~ **land** novalis f; novale n; **lie** ~ cesso 1.

**fals|e** falsus; fictus; mendax; perfidus; ~ehood mendacium n; commentum n; ~ify corrumpo 3; vitio 1.

**falter** titubo 1; haereo 2.

**fame** gloria f; fama f; nomen n.

**familiar** familiaris (**with** *dat.*); notus; **be on** ~ **terms with** familiariter utor 3 (*alqo*); ~ity familiaritas f; usus, us m; ~ize assuefacio 3 (*alqm alqa re*).

**family** domus, us f; mei, tui, sui; familia f (*of common descent*); domesticus; gentilis.

**famine** fames f.

**famished** fame confectus.

**famous** clarus, praeclarus, celeber, nobilis.

**fan** flabellum n; ventilo 1.

**fancy** fingo 3 (cogitatione, animo); puto 1; cogitatio f; somnium n; species f; libido f; **as I** ~ ut libet (*mihi*).

**fang** dens m.

**fantastic** commenticius; vanus.

**far** procul; longe; **by** ~ longe, multo; **be** ~ **(removed) from** longe absum (ab); **as** ~ **as** tenus (*abl.*); *adv.* quatenus, quoad; **thus** ~ hactenus; ~-fetched arcessitus; ~-off longinquus.

**farce** mimus m.

**fare** me habeo 2 (*bene, male*); mihi evenit; cibus m; vectura f; ~well vale.

**farm** fundus m; praedium n; ager, gri m; colo 3; conduco 3 (*vectigalia*); ~ **out** loco 1; ~er agricola m; colonus m; ~house villa f; ~ing agri cultura f.

**farthing: not a** ~ nullus teruncius m; **I don't care a** ~ non flocci facio 3.

**fasces** fasces m/pl.

**fascinat|e** capio 3; delenio 4; ~ion blanditiae f/pl.

**fashion** fabricor 1; effingo 3; forma f; mos m; **after the** ~ **of** more (*gen.*); ~able elegans; **it is** ~able moris est.

**fast** firmus; stabilis; celer; velox;

**fasten** ieiunus sum; ieiunium *n*; **make ~** deligo 1; **be ~ asleep** arte dormio 4.
**fasten** figo 3 (*alqd in re*); annecto 3 (*ad alqd; dat.*); deligo 1 (*ad*); **~ing** claustra *n/pl.*; vinculum *n*.
**fastidious** fastidiosus.
**fat** pinguis; opimus; obesus; pingue *n*; adeps *m and f.*
**fatal** fatalis; funestus; perniciosus; **~ity** fatum *n*.
**fate** fatum *n*; **~d** fatalis (*ad*).
**father** pater *m*; parens; **~-in-law** socer *m*; **~less** orbus; **~ly** paternus.
**fathom** *fig.* mente comprehendo 3; **~less** profundus.
**fatigue** fatigo 1; (de)fatigatio *f.*
**fatness** pinguitudo *f*, obesitas *f.*
**fatt|en** sagino 1; farcio 4; **~y** pinguis.
**fatuous** fatuus.
**fault** culpa *f*; delictum *n*; peccatum *n*; vitium *n*; **find ~ with** accuso 1; **commit a ~** pecco 1; **it is my ~** per me stat (*quominus, ne*); **~less** emendatus; perfectus; **~y** mendosus, vitiosus.
**favour** faveo 2, foveo 2, studeo 2 (*dat.*); gratia *f*; studium *n*; beneficium *n*; **confer a ~** beneficium confero 3; **win the ~ of** gratiam ineo 4 (*ab, apud*); **in ~ of** pro (*abl.*); **~able** prosperus; secundus; **~ite** gratus; carus; dilectus; deliciae *f/pl.*; **~itism** studium *n.*
**fawn** hinnuleus *m*; **~ upon** adulor 1 (*alqm*).
**fear** timeo 2, metuo 3; vereor 2; **~ for** diffido 3 (*dat.*); metus, us *m*, timor *m*; **~ful** timidus; atrox; **~less** fidens.
**feast** convivium *n*; epulae *f/pl.*; dies *m* festus; epulor 1; convivor 1.
**feat** factum *n*; res *f.*
**feather** penna *f*, pluma *f.*
**feature** proprium *n*; **~s** vultus, us *m*; lineamenta *n/pl.*
**February** Februarius (mensis) *m.*
**fecundity** fecunditas *f.*
**federation** civitates *f/pl.* foederatae.
**fee** merces *f.*
**feeble** infirmus; imbecillus; **~ness** infirmitas *f*, imbecillitas *f.*
**feed** *v/t.* alo 3; nutrio 4; pasco 1; *v/i.* vescor 3 (*abl.*); pascor 1.
**feel** tento 1; tango 3; contrecto 1; sentio 4; percipio 3; **~ing** tactus, us *m*; sensus, us *m*; **~ings** animus *m.*

**feign** fingo 3; simulo 1.
**felicitate** gratulor 1 (*alci de re, quod*).
**fell** dirus; caedo 3.
**fellow** socius *m*; homo *m*; **~citizen** civis *m and f*; **~countryman** popularis *m*; **~slave** conservus *m*; **~ship** societas *f*; sodalitas *f*; **~soldier** commilito *m.*
**felt** coactum *n.*
**female** femineus; femina *f.*
**feminine** muliebris; femineus.
**fen** palus, udis *f.*
**fence** saepes *f*; saepta *n/pl.*; rudibus certare; **~ in** saepio 4.
**ferment** fermentum *n*; *fig.* aestus, us *m*; **be in a ~** ferveo 2; fermentor 1.
**fern** filix *f.*
**feroci|ous** trux; **~ty** atrocitas *f.*
**ferret out** eruo 3.
**ferry** transveho 3; **~man** portitor *m.*
**fertil|e** fertilis; fecundus; **~ity** fecunditas *f*; **~ize** laetifico 1.
**ferv|ent** ardens; **~our** ardor *m.*
**fester** suppuro 1.
**festiv|al** dies *m* festus; sollemne *n*; feriae *f/pl.*; **~e** festus; festivus; **~ity** sollemnia *n/pl.*
**festoon** serta *n/pl.*
**fetch** fero 3; arcesso 3.
**fetid** fetidus.
**fetter** compes *m*; vinculum *n*; catena *f*; catenas inicio 3 (*alci*).
**feud** simultas *f.*
**fever** febris *f*; **~ish** *fig.* furiosus.
**few** pauci; aliquot; rarus.
**fibre** fibra *f.*
**fickle** levis; mobilis; **~ness** levitas *f.*
**ficti|on** commentum *n*; fabula *f*; **~tious** fictus.
**fidelity** fidelitas *f.*
**field** ager, gri *m*; arvum *n*; *fig.* campus *m*; locus *m*; **~ of battle** acies *f*; **in the ~** militiae.
**fiendish** inhumanus.
**fierce** atrox; saevus; acer; **~ness** atrocitas *f.*
**fiery** igneus, ardens; ferox.
**fif|teen** quindecim; **~teenth** quintus decimus; **~th** quintus; **~tieth** quinquagesimus; **~ty** quinquaginta.
**fig** ficus, i *and* us *f.*
**fight** pugno 1; dimico 1; (con)certo 1; **~ a battle** proelium committo 3; pugna *f*; certamen *n*; **~er** pugnator *m.*

**figur|ative** translatus; ~e figura *f*; forma *f*; signum *n*; ~e of speech translatio *f*.

**filament** filum *n*.

**filch** surripio 3.

**file** lima *f*; *mil.* ordo *m*; **rank and ~** gregarii milites *m/pl.*; limo 1.

**filial** pius.

**fill** impleo 2, compleo 2 (*alqd alqa re*); celebro 1 (*locum, aures etc.*); inicio 3 (*spem, etc. alci*).

**fillet** vitta *f*; fascia *f*.

**film** membrana *f*.

**filter** liquo 1; colum *n*.

**filth** sordes *f/pl.*; caenum *n*; illuvies *f*; ~**iness** squalor *m*; ~**y** sordidus; spurcus; foedus.

**final** ultimus, extremus; ~**ly** ad extremum; postremo; denique.

**finance** pecuniam solvo 3 (*pro re*); **(public) ~s** aerarium *n*.

**find** invenio 4; reperio 4; nanciscor 3; ~ **guilty** damno 1; ~ **out** comperio 4; ~**ing** inventum *n*.

**fine** praeclarus; pulcher; bellus; tenuis; subtilis; multo 1 (*alqm pecunia*); multa *f*; ~**ness** tenuitas *f*; ~**sse** argutiae *f/pl.*

**finger** digitus *m*; attrecto 1; ~**-tips** extremi digiti *m/pl.*

**finish** conficio 3, perficio 3; perago 3; finio 4; ~ **off** absolvo 3; absolutio *f*; ~**ed** perfectus.

**fir** abies *m*; pinus, us *f*; **of ~-wood** abiegnus.

**fire** ignis *m*; incendium *n*; ardor *m*; **set on ~** incendo 3; **be on ~** ardeo 2; **~catch ~** exardesco 3; ~**brand** fax *f*; ~**-place** focus *m*; ~**wood** ligna *n/pl.*

**firm** firmus, stabilis; constans; societas *f*; **make ~** firmo 1; **stand ~** sto 1; ~**ament** caelum *n*; ~**ness** firmitas *f*; constantia *f*.

**first** primus; princeps; **at ~** primo; ~**ly, in the ~ place** primo, primum; **for the ~ time** primum; ~**-fruits** primitiae *f/pl.*

**fish** piscis *m*; piscor 1; ~ **for** capto 1; ~**erman** piscator *m*; ~**ing boat** piscatoria navis *f*; ~**ing rod** harundo *f*; ~**monger** cetarius *m*; ~**pond** piscina *f*.

**fist** pugnus *m*.

**fit** aptus (*alci; ad alqd*); idoneus; accommodatus; *v/t.* accommodo 1 (*alci ad alqd*); *v/i.* convenio 4 (*ad*); ~ **out** instruo 3; impetus, us *m*;

~**ful** incertus; ~**ting** decens; **it is** ~**ting** oportet.

**five** quinque; ~ **hundred** quingenti, ~ **times** quinquies.

**fix** figo 3; constituo 3; destino 1; defigo 3 (*oculos in alqd*); ~**ed** certus; constans.

**flabby, flaccid** mollis; enervatus.

**flag** languesco 3; refrigesco 3; vexillum *n*, signum *n*.

**flagon** lagoena *f*.

**flame** flamma *f*; flagro 1; ~**-coloured** flammeus.

**flamen** flamen *m*.

**flank** latus *n*; ilia *n/pl.*; *mil.* **on the ~s** a lateribus.

**flap** *v/t.* plaudo 3 (*pennis etc.*); *v/i.* fluito 1; lacinia *f*.

**flare** flagro 1.

**flash** fulgeo 2; corusco 1; mico 1; fulgor *m*; **lightning ~** fulgur *n*.

**flask** ampulla *f*.

**flat** aequus; planus; campester; pronus; *fig.* frigidus; campus *m*; ~**ness** planities *f*; ~**ten** complano 1.

**flatter** adulor 1 (*acc.*); blandior 4, assentor 1 (*dat.*); ~**er** assentator *m*; ~**ing** blandus; ~**y** adulatio *f*.

**flatulent** inflatus.

**flaunt** ostento 1.

**flavour** sapor *m*; **have a ~** sapio 3 (*acc.*).

**flaw** vitium *n*, mendum *n*; ~**less** emendatus.

**flax** linum *n*; carbasus, i *f*; ~**en** flavus.

**flay** pellem deripio 3.

**flea** pulex *m*.

**flee** fugio 3; in fugam me do 1, confero 3.

**fleec|e** vellus *n*; expilo 1; ~**y** laniger.

**fleet** celer; classis *f*; ~**ing** fugax; ~**ness** velocitas *f*.

**flesh** caro *f*; corpus *n*.

**flexib|ility** mollitia *f*; ~**le** flexibilis; lentus.

**flicker** mico 1; corusco 1.

**flight** volatus, us *m*; lapsus, us *m*; fuga *f*; **put to ~** in fugam do 1, conicio 3 (*alqm*); ~ **of stairs** scalae *f/pl.*; ~**y** levis.

**flimsy** subtilis; pertenuis.

**flinch** abhorreo 2 (*ab*).

**fling** iacio 3; ~ **away** pro-, ab-icio 3.

**flint** silex *m*; ~**y** *fig.* ferreus.

**flippant** nugax.

**flit** volito 1.

**float** fluito 1; inno 1; fluo 3; ratis *f*.

**flock** grex *m*; pecus *n*; floccus *m*; ~ **to, towards, together** confluo 3; congregor 3.

**flog** verbero 1; **~ging** verberatio *f*; verbera *n/pl.*

**flood** diluvies *f*, diluvium *n*; unda *f*; *fig.* flumen *n*; inundo 1.

**floor** solum *n*; pavimentum *n*; contignatio *f*.

**florid** rubicundus; floridus.

**flounce** instita *f*.

**flounder** mergor 3; haereo 2.

**flour** farina *f*.

**flourish** floreo 2; vigeo 2; iacto 1; flos *m*; clangor *m* (*tubarum*).

**flout** contemno 3.

**flow** fluo 3; mano 1; ~ **down, into, past** de-, in-, praeter-fluo 3; flumen *n*; lapsus, us *m*; accessus, us *m* (*aestus*).

**flower** flos *m*; flosculus *m*; floreo 2; **~y** floreus; floridus.

**fluctuate** me iacto 1; nato 1.

**fluen|cy** copia *f*, facultas *f* dicendi; **~t** volubilis, copiosus.

**fluid** liquidus; liquor *m*.

**flurry** trepidatio *f*; trepido 1.

**flush** rubeo 2; rubor *m*; flos *m*; planus.

**flute** tibia *f*; **~-player** tibicen *m*.

**flutter** volito 1; trepidatio *f*.

**fly** volo 1; fugio 3; ~ **at** involo 1; ~ **open** dissilio 4; musca *f*; **~ing** volucer.

**foal** eculeus *m*.

**foam** spumo 1; spuma *f*; **~ing** spumeus, spumosus.

**fodder** pabulum *n*.

**foe** hostis *m*; inimicus *m*.

**fog** caligo *f*, nebula *f*; **~gy** caliginosus.

**foil** eludo 3; rudis *f*; lamina *f*.

**fold** complico 1; ruga *f*, sinus, us *m* (*vestis*); saepta *n/pl.*; ovile *n*; **~ing--doors** valvae *f/pl.*

**foliage** frondes *f/pl.*

**folk** vulgus, i *n*.

**follow** (con-, in-)sequor 3; insisto 3 (*rationem, etc.*); utor 3 (consiliis); **as ~s** in hunc modum; **it ~s that** sequitur ut; **~er** assectator *m*; **the ~ing** proximus; **~ing** comitatus, us *m*.

**folly** stultitia *f*.

**foment** *fig.* concito 1.

**fond** amans, studiosus (*gen.*); indulgens (*in alqm; dat.*); **be ~ of** amo 1 (*acc., inf.*); **~le** mulceo 2; blandior 4.

**food** cibus *m*; alimentum *n*; pabulum *n*; victus, us *m*.

**fool** stultus *m*; ludificor 1 (*alqm*), ludo 3 (*alqm*); **~ery** ineptiae *f/pl.*; **~-hardy** temerarius, **~ish** stultus, ineptus.

**foot** pes *m*; *mil.* pedes *m/pl.*; pedites *m/pl.*; imum *n* (*adj.* imus); **at the ~ of** sub (*abl.*); **on ~** pedibus; pedestris; pedes; **~ing** status, us *m*; **~man** pedisequus *m*; **~path** semita *f*; **~print** vestigium *n*; **~stool** scamnum *n*.

**foppish** delicatus.

**for** *prep.* pro (*abl.*); ob, propter (*causam*); in, ad (*acc.*); **~ my part** pro mea parte; **leave ~ dead** pro occiso relinquo 3; *cj.* nam; enim; quippe.

**forage** pabulor 1; frumentor 1; pabulum *n*.

**forbear** mitto 3, desino 3 (*inf.*); **~ance** patientia *f*.

**forbid** veto 1 (*acc. c. inf.*); impero 1 (*ne*).

**force** vis *f*; **be in ~** valeo 2; *v/t.* cogo 3 (*ut, inf.*); **~ a way through, out of** perrumpo 3 per, erumpo 3 ex; **~ out of** extorqueo 2; **~d** arcessitus; **~s** copiae *f/pl.*

**forcible** vehemens; gravis.

**ford** vadum *n*; vado transeo 4.

**fore|bode** portendo 3; praesentio 4; **~cast** praevideo 2; **~fathers** maiores *m/pl.*; **~finger** digitus *m* index; **~go** dimitto 3; **~head** frons *f*.

**foreign** externus; peregrinus; **~ to** abhorrens ab; **~er** advena *m*; peregrinus *m*.

**fore|knowledge** providentia *f*; **~man** procurator *m*; **~most** princeps, primus; **~see** provideo 2; **~sight** providentia *f*.

**forest** silva *f*.

**fore|stall** anteverto 3 (*dat.*); **~tell** praedico 3.

**forfeit** multor 1 (*abl.*); multa *f*; commissus.

**forge** fabricor 1 (*gladium*); subicio 3; fornax *f*.

**forget** obliviscor 3 (*gen., acc.*); **~ful** immemor (*gen.*); obliviosus.

**forgive** ignosco 3 (*alci alqd*); **~ness** venia *f*.

**fork** furca *f*; **~ed** bifurcus.

**forlorn** destitutus; miser.

**form** forma *f*, figura *f*, species *f*; genus *n*; ritus, us *m*; scamnum *n*;

**for** ~'s **sake** dicis causa; (con-)formo 1; fingo 3; instruo 3 (*aciem*); ineo 4 (*consilium*).

**formal|ities** ritus *m/pl.*; iusta *n/pl.*; ~**ly** rite.

**former** prior; superior; pristinus; **the** ~ ille; ~**ly** olim, quondam.

**formidable** gravis.

**formula** formula *f*; carmen *n*; praefatio *f*.

**forsake** desero 3.

**forsooth** scilicet, nempe.

**forswear** eiuro 1 (*alqd*); ~ **oneself** periuro 1.

**fort** castellum *n*.

**forth** foras; **from that time** ~ inde; ~**with** protinus.

**fortieth** quadragesimus.

**fortif|ication** munitio *f*; munimentum *n*; moenia *n/pl.*; ~**y** munio 4.

**fortress** castellum *n*; arx *f*.

**fortuitous** fortuitus, ~**ly** fortuito, forte.

**fortun|ate** felix; fortunatus; ~**e** fortuna *f* (*secunda, adversa*); fors *f*; **good** ~**e** felicitas *f*; res *f/pl.* secundae; divitiae *f/pl.*, fortunae *f/pl.*; res *f* (*familiaris*); ~**e-teller** hariolus *m*.

**forty** quadraginta.

**forum** forum *n*.

**forward** porro, ante; **thence-**~ iam inde; protervus; promptus; adiuvo 1; perfero 3 (*litteras*); ~**ness** protervitas *f*.

**foster** foveo 2; nutrio 4; ~**-child** alumnus *m*; ~**-mother** nutrix *f*.

**foul** foedus; taeter; inquino 1; ~**ness** foeditas *f*.

**found** condo 3, constituo 3; deduco (*coloniam*); ~**ation** fundamentum *n*; sedes *f*; ~**er** conditor *m*; auctor *m*; summergor 3.

**foundry** fornax *f*.

**fountain** fons *f*.

**four** quattuor; ~ **each** quaterni; ~ **times** quater; ~ **hundred** quadringenti; ~**fold** quadruplus; quadruplum *n*; ~**footed** quadrupes; ~**teen** quattuordecim; ~**teenth** quartus decimus; ~**th** quartus; ~**thly** quarto.

**fowl** volucris *f*; gallina *f*; ~**er** auceps *m*; ~**ing** aucupium *n*.

**fox** vulpes *f*; **old** ~ veterator *m*; vulpinus.

**fract|ion** pars *f*; ~**ure** frango 3.

**fragile** fragilis.

**fragment** fragmentum *n*.

**fragran|ce** suavis odor *m*; ~**t** odorus, suavis.

**frail** infirmus, fragilis.

**frame** compages *m*; forma *f*; ~ **of mind** affectio *f*; animus *m*; compono 3; fabricor 1; formo 1; concipio 3 (*ius iurandum*); forma includo 3 (*tabulam*).

**franchise** civitas *f*; suffragium *n*.

**frank** liber; simplex; sincerus; ~**ness** libertas *f*.

**frantic** fanaticus; insanus.

**fratern|al** fraternus; ~**ity** sodalitas *f*.

**fraud** fraus *f*; dolus *m*; ~**ulent** fraudulentus.

**fray** rixa *f*; detero 3.

**freak** monstrum *n*; ~**ish** inconstans.

**freckle** macula *f*.

**free** liber (*re, a re*); vacuus (*a re*); expers (*gen.*); **be** ~ **from** careo 2 (*abl.*); ~ **from blame** extra culpam; ~ **from care** securus; **of one's own** ~ **will** sua sponte; libero 1 (*alqm re, a re*); manumitto 3 (*servum*); vindico 1 (*ab*); ~**booter** latro *m*; ~**born** ingenuus; ~**dman** libertus *m*; ~**dom** libertas *f*; vacuitas *f*.

**freeze** congelo 1; concresco 3; conglacio 1.

**freight** onus *n*; navem onero 1.

**frenz|ied** furiosus, insanus; ~**y** furor *m*.

**frequen|cy** crebritas *f*; frequentia *f*; ~**t** creber; frequens; celebro 1; ~**ted** celeber; ~**tly** crebro.

**fresh** recens; integer; **a**~ de integro; ~**en** increbresco 3 (*ventus*); ~**ness** viriditas *f*.

**fret** sollicito 1; doleo 2; ~**ful** morosus.

**friction** tritus, us *m*.

**friend** amicus *m*; familiaris *m*; ~**ly** comes; benevolus, amicus (*erga, dat.*); ~**ship** amicitia *f*; familiaritas *f*.

**fright** terror *m*; ~**en** (per)terreo 2; ~**ful** terribilis; atrox.

**frigid** frigidus.

**frill** segmenta *n/pl.*

**fringe** fimbriae *f/pl.*; limbus *m*.

**fritter away** dissipo 1.

**frivol|ity** levitas *f*; ~**ous** levis; nugax.

**fro: to and** ~ ultro citroque.

**frock** stola *f*.

**frog** rana *f*.

**frolic** ludo 3; lascivio 4; lascivia *f*.

**from** a, ab (*abl.*); de (*abl.*); e, ex (*abl.*); ~ **all sides** undique; ~ **day to day** in dies; ~ **that time** inde; ~ **this, that place** hinc, illinc.

**front** frons *f*; ~ **of a column** primum agmen *n*; **in** ~ a fronte; **in** ~ **of** pro (*abl.*); ante (*acc.*); **in** ~ (*adj.*) adversus; obviam eo 4 (*alci*); aspecto 3 (*alqd*); ~**ier** finis *m*; ~**ing** adversus (*acc.*).

**frost** gelu *n*; pruina *f*; ~**bitten** praeustus; ~**y** gelidus.

**froth** spuma *f*; spumo 1.

**frown** frontem contraho 3; contractio *f* frontis.

**frozen** glacie, frigore concretus.

**frugal** frugi; parcus; ~**ity** parsimonia *f*.

**fruit** fructus, us *m*; pomum *n*; fruges *f/pl.*; baca *f*; ~**erer** pomarius *m*; ~**ful** fructuosus; frugifer; fecundus; ~**less** irritus; ~**tree** pomum *n*.

**frustrate** dirimo 3; disturbo 1.

**fry** frigo 3; ~**ing-pan** sartago *f*.

**fuel** ligna *n/pl.*; **gather** ~ lignor 1; *fig.* **add** ~ **to** faces subicio 3 (*dat.*).

**fugitive** caducus; fugax; profugus *m*; fugitivus *m*.

**fulfil** expleo 2; perfungor 3; exsequor 3.

**full** plenus (*abl.*); refertus (*abl.*, *gen.*); frequens; satur (*cibo*); ~**y** copiose.

**fulminate** intono 1.

**fume** fumus *m*; stomachor 1.

**fumigate** fumigo 1; vaporo 1.

**fun** iocus *m*; ludus *m*.

**function** officium *n*, munus *n*; ~**ary** magistratus, us *m*.

**fund** copia *f* (pecuniae); ~**amental** ultimus.

**funeral** funus *n*; exsequiae *f/pl.*; funebris.

**funnel** infundibulum *n*.

**funny** ridiculus.

**fur** pellis *f*; villi *m/pl.*, pili *m/pl.*

**furbish** interpolo 1.

**furious** iratus; furibundus.

**furlong** stadium *n*.

**furlough** commeatus, us *m*.

**furnace** fornax *f*.

**furnish** praebeo 2; suppedito 1; orno 1 (*alqd re*).

**furniture** supellex *f*.

**furrow** sulcus *m*; sulco 1.

**furry** villosus.

**further** ulterior; consulo 3 (*dat.*); *adv.* longius; praeterea; amplius; ~**more** porro.

**furtive** furtivus.

**fury** furor *m*; rabies *f*; furia *f*.

**fuse** fundo 3; *fig.* confundo 3.

**fuss** perturbatio *f*.

**fustian** *fig.* tumor *m*; tumidus.

**futile** futilis; vanus.

**future** futurus; **in, for the** ~ in futurum, in posterum; futura *n/pl.*

# G

**gable** fastigium *n.*

**gad-fly** asilus *m.*

**gag** praeligo 1; obturamentum *n.*

**gage** pignus *n.*

**gaiety** hilaritas *f.*

**gain** lucror 1; consequor 3, pario 3; paro 1; lucrum *n*; quaestus, us *m*; **~ful** lucrosus.

**gainsay** nego 1; contra dico 3.

**gait** incessus, us *m.*

**gale** ventus *m.*

**gall** fel *n*; bilis *m*; mordeo 2.

**gallant** fortis; amator *m*; **~ry** virtus, utis *f.*

**gallery** porticus, us *f*; pinacotheca *f.*

**galley** navis *f* longa.

**galling** mordax.

**gallop: at a ~** citato equo.

**gallows** crux *f*; patibulum *n.*

**gambl|e** alea ludo 3; **~er** aleator *m*; **~ing** alea *f.*

**gambol** lascivio 4.

**game** ludus *m*; lusus, us *m*; venatio *f.*

**gaming** alea *f.*

**gammon** perna *f.*

**gander** anser, eris *m.*

**gang** caterva *f*; operae *f/pl.*

**gaol** carcer, eris *m*; **~er** custos *m.*

**gap** lacuna *f*; **~e** dehisco 3; hio 1; stupeo 2 (at *alqd*).

**garb** vestitus, us *m.*

**garbage** quisquiliae *f/pl.*

**garden** hortus *m*; **~er** hortulanus *m.*

**garland** corona *f*; sertum *n.*

**garlic** allium *n.*

**garment** vestimentum *n.*

**garnish** decoro 1.

**garret** cenaculum *n.*

**garrison** praesidium *n*; praesidio confirmo 1.

**garrulous** loquax.

**garter** periscelis, idis *f.*

**gash** plaga *f*; vulnus *n*; seco 1.

**gasp** anhelo 1; anhelitus, us *m.*

**gate** porta *f*; **~post** postis *m*; **~way** limen *n.*

**gather** colligo 3; confero 3; cogo 3; lego 3; *fig.* conicio 3 (*ex re*); **~ in** meto 3; **~ing** coetus, us *m.*

**gaudy** versicolor.

**gauge** metior 4; modulus *m.*

**gauntlet** caestus, us *m.*

**gay** hilaris, hilarus; festus.

**gaze** intueor 2; contemplo 1; obtutus, us *m.*

**gazette** acta *n/pl.* diurna.

**gear** instrumentum *n.*

**gelding** canterius *m.*

**gem** gemma *f.*

**gender** genus *n.*

**general** generalis; communis; universus; **become ~** increbresco 3; **in ~** ad summam; dux *m*, imperator *m*; **~ities** loci *m/pl.* communes; **~ize** universe loquor 3; **~ly** plerumque; vulgo.

**generat|e** pario 3; genero 1; **~ion** saeculum *n*; aetas *f.*

**gener|osity** liberalitas *f*; **~ous** liberalis, generosus.

**genial** benignus, comis.

**genius** ingenium *n.*

**genteel** politus.

**gentile** gentilis.

**gentle** lenis, mitis; nobilis; **~man** generosus *m* (homo); **~manly** honestus; **~ness** lenitas *f*; mansuetudo *f.*

**genuine** sincerus, verus, merus.

**geography** geographia *f.*

**geomet|er** geometres, ae *m*; **~ry** geometria *f.*

**germ** germen *n*; semen *n*; **~ane** affinis; **~inate** germino 1.

**gest|iculate** gestum ago 3; **~iculation** gestus, us *m*; iactatio *f*; **~ure** gestus, us *m*; motus, us *m.*

**get** adipiscor 3; nanciscor 3; pario 3; percipio 3 (*fructus*); impetro 1 (*quod postulo*); **~ something done** curo 1 alqd faciendum; *v/impers.* fit; **~ abroad** percrebresco 3; **~ along, on** procedo 3; **~ back** recupero 1; **~ out** descendo 3 (*e curru*); **~ to** pervenio 4 (*ad*); **~ up** surgo 3.

**ghastly** pallidus; foedus.

**ghost** umbra *f*; Manes *m/pl.*; larva *f.*

**giant** vir *m* eximia corporis magnitudine; gigas, ntis *m*; praegrandis.

**gibbet** furca *f*; patibulum *n.*

**gidd|iness** vertigo *f*; **~y** levis.

**gift** donum *n*; munus *n*; facultas *f*; **~ed** praeditus (*alqa re*); ingeniosus.
**gig** cisium *n*.
**gigantic** immanis.
**giggle** cacchinno 1.
**gild** inauro 1.
**gill** quartarius *m*.
**gilt** aureus, inauratus.
**gimlet** terebra *f*.
**gin** pedica *f*, plaga *f*.
**gingerly** pedetemptim.
**gird** cingor 3 (*alqa re*); **~le** cingulum *n*.
**girl** puella *f*; virgo *f*; **~ish** virginalis.
**girth** cingula *f*.
**gist** summa *f*.
**give** do 1; dono 1; tribuo 3; **~ one's word** fidem interpono 3; **~ place, way to** (de)cedo 3 (*alci*); **~** largior 4; **~ back** reddo 3; **~ in** me dedo 4 (*alci*); **~ out** me fero 3; **~ up** trado 3; dimitto 3; **~ way to** indulgeo 2 (*dat.*).
**glad** laetus; **be ~** gaudeo 2; **~den** hilaro 1.
**glade** saltus, us *m*; nemus *n*.
**gladiator** gladiator *m*; **of a ~** gladiatorius.
**gladly** libenter.
**glance** oculos adicio 3 (*dat.*); aspectus, us *m*.
**gland** glandula *f*.
**glar|e** torvis oculis aspicio 3; fulgor *m*; **~ing** fulgens; *fig.* manifestus.
**glass** vitrum *n*; **drinking ~** poculum *n* (vitreum); **looking ~** speculum *n*; **~ware** vitrea *n/pl.*; **of ~** vitreus.
**gleam** fulgeo 2; fulgor *m*, nitor *m*; **~ing** nitidus.
**glean** spicas lego 3; colligo 3.
**glee** hilaritas *f*.
**glen** convallis *f*.
**glib** blandus; volubilis.
**glide** labor 3.
**glimmer** subluceo 2.
**glimpse** conspicio 3; aspectus, us *m*.
**glitter** fulgeo 2; corusco 1; fulgor *m*.
**gloat** pascor 3 (*alqa re*).
**globe** globus *m*; orbis *m* (terrarum).
**gloom** tenebrae *f/pl.*; caligo *f*; **~y** tenebricosus, tenebrosus; tristis; ater.
**glori|fy** celebro 1; augeo 2; **~ous** praeclarus, amplus.
**glory** gloria *f*; decus *n*; **~ in** glorior 1 (*in re*).
**gloss** nitor *m*; interpretatio *f*; **~y** nitidus.

**gloves** manicae *f/pl.*
**glow** candeo 2, caleo 2; *fig.* ardeo 2; calor *m*; ardor *m*; **~worm** cicindela *f*.
**glue** gluten *n*; **~ together** coagmento 1.
**glut** satio 1; satietas *f*; **~ton** helluo *m*; lurco *m*; **~tony** edacitas *f*; gula *f*.
**gnarled** nodosus.
**gnash** frendeo 2.
**gnat** culex *m*.
**gnaw** rodo 3.
**go** eo 4; vado 3; **~ well** bene procedit 3 (*alci*); **let ~** dimitto 3, omitto 3; **~ astray** erro 1; **~ away** discedo 3; **~ before** anteeo 4 (*dat., acc.*); **~ by** praetereo 4; sequor 3; **~ on** fio 3; **~ over** transeo 4; **~ up to** subeo 4.
**goad** stimulus *m*; **~ on** stimulo 1 (*ad, in, ut*).
**goal** meta *f*; calx *f*.
**goat** caper, pri *m*; capra *f*.
**go-between** internuntius *m*.
**gobble** devoro 1.
**goblet** poculum *n*; scyphus *m*.
**god** deus *m*; numen *n*; **~dess** dea *f*; **~less** impius; **~like** divinus.
**gold** aurum *n*; aureus; **~leaf** brattea *f*; **~smith** aurifex *m*.
**good** bonus; probus; utilis (*ad*); bonum *n*, commodum *n*; **~s** bona *n/pl.*; merx *f*; **a ~ deal** aliquantum (*gen.*); **a ~ many** complures; **do ~ to** prosum (*dat.*); **make ~** sarcio 4; **~-bye** vale; **~ day** salve; **~-for-nothing** nequam; **~-natured** comis; **~-will** benevolentia *f*.
**goose** anser, eris *m*.
**gore** cruor *m*.                         [(*me re*).
**gorge** fauces *f/pl.*; ingurgito 1
**gorgeous** magnificus.
**gormandise** helluor 1.
**gory** cruentus.
**gossip** rumor *m*; sermo *m*; sermonem confero 3 (*cum alqo*); garrio 4; **~ing** garrulus.
**gourd** cucurbita *f*.
**gout** podagra *f*; **~y** arthriticus.
**govern** impero 1 (*dat.*); rego 3, guberno 1, moderor 1 (*acc.*); **~ment** administratio *f*; imperium *n*; res *f* publica; qui rei publicae praesunt; **~or** gubernator *m*; proconsul *m or* pro consule; praetor *m*; legatus *m*; praefectus *m*; **be ~or** praesum (*dat.*).

**gown** stola *f*; palla *f*.

**grace** gratia *f*; venia *f*; elegantia *f*; decoro 1 (*alqd alqa re*); **get into the good ~s of** gratiam concilio 1 (*alcs*); **~ful** decorus, venustus.

**gracious** propritius, benignus.

**grade** gradus, us *m*; locus *m*.

**gradually** gradatim; paulatim; sensim.

**graft** insero 3; surculus *m*.

**grain** frumentum *n*; granum *n*, mica *f*.

**grammar** grammatica *f*; **~ian** grammaticus *m*.

**granary** horreum *n*.

**grand** grandis; magnificus; sublimis; **~daughter** neptis *f*; **~eur** maiestas *f*; **~father** avus *m*; **~iloquent** grandiloquus; **~mother** avia *f*; **~son** nepos *m*.

**grange** villa *f*.

**grant** concedo 3; permitto 3; tribuo 3.

**grape** uva *f*; acinus *m and* -um *n*; **~vine** vitis *f*.

**graphic** vividus.

**grappl|e** luctor 1 (*cum*); **~ing-iron** manus *f* ferrea.

**grasp** comprehendo 3, complector 3 (*also fig.*); complexus, us *m*; manus, us *f*; **~ at** appeto 3; **~ing** avarus.

**grass** gramen *n*; herba *f*; **~y** herbidus, herbosus.

**grate** (con)tero 3; strideo 2; focus *m*.

**grateful** gratus; **be ~** gratiam habeo 2 (*alci*).

**grati|fication** expletio *f*; voluptas *f*; **~fy** gratificor 1 (*alci*); morem gero 3 (*alci*); expleo 2; **~fying** gratus; **~tude** gratia *f*.

**gratuit|ous** gratuitus; **~y** corollarium *n*.

**grave** gravis, serius; austerus; sepulcrum *n*; **from the ~** ab inferis.

**gravel** glarea *f*.

**grave|stone** monumentum *n*; **~-yard** sepulcra *n/pl*.

**gravity** gravitas *f*; severitas *f*; momentum *n*.

**gravy** ius *n*.

**graze** *v/t.* pasco 3; perstringo 3 (*alqd alqa re*); *v/i.* pascor 3.

**grease** adeps *m and f*; pingue *n*; ungo 3.

**great** magnus; ingens; grandis; **as, how ~** quantus; **so ~** tantus; **~-**

**-grandfather** proavus *m*; **~ly** magnopere; valde; **~ness** magnitudo *f*, amplitudo *f*.

**greed** avaritia *f*; edacitas *f*; **~y** avarus, avidus; cupidus (*gen.*).

**green** viridus; prasinus; crudus; **~s** olus *n*; **be ~** vireo 2; **~horn** tiro *m*; **~ness** viriditas *f*; cruditas *f*; **~sward** herba *f*; caespes *m*.

**greet** saluto 1; **~ing** salutatio *f*.

**grey** canus, albus; glaucus; **~ hair** cani capilli *m/pl.*; canities *f*.

**grief** dolor *m*; luctus, us *m*; maeror *m*.

**griev|ance** querel(l)a *f*; iniuria *f*; **~e** *v/t.* dolore afficio 3 (*alqm*); ango 3; *v/i.* doleo 2 (*acc., abl., quod*); piget 2 (*me alcs rei*); **~ous** acerbus, gravis.

**grill** torreo 2.

**grim** torvus, atrox.

**grimace** os torqueo 2.

**grimy** squalidus.

**grin** rideo 2.

**grind** (con)tero 3; molo 3; frendeo 2 (*dentibus*); **~ down** opprimo 3; **~stone** cos *f*.

**grip** comprehendo 3; manus, us *f*.

**grisly** horridus.

**grizzled** canus.

**groan** (in)gemo 3 (*alqd*); gemitus, us *m*.

**groin** inguen *n*.

**groom** agaso *m*.

**groove** canalis *m*.

**grope** praetento 1 (*iter*).

**gross** crassus; indecorus; **~ness** magnitudo *f*; turpitudo *f*.

**grotto** antrum *n*.

**ground** terra *f*; solum *n*; humus, i *f*; locus *m* (*aequus etc.*); **~s** causa *f*, ratio *f*; **on, to the ~** humi; **gain ~** percrebresco 3 (*rumor*); proficio 3; **~less** vanus, inanis; **~work** fundamentum *n*.

**group** circulus *m*; globus *m*; dispono 3.

**grove** lucus *m*; nemus *n*.

**grovel** me abicio 3 (*ad pedes*); **~ling** humilis.

**grow** *v/i.* cresco 3; adolesco 3; nascor 3; *fig.* fio 3; *v/t.* colo 3, sero 3; **~ long** promitto 3 (*capillos etc.*).

**growl** fremo 3; fremitus, us *m*.

**grow|n up** adultus; **~th** incrementum *n*; auctus, us *m*.

**grub** vermiculus *m*; **~ up** eruo 3.

**grudge** invideo 2 (*dat.*); simultas *f*;

**bear a ~ against** succenseo 2 (*alci*).
**gruel** puls *f*.
**gruff** asper.
**grumble** murmuro 1.
**guarantee** fides *f*; pignus *n*; fidem do 1 (*alci*); satisdo 1.
**guard** custodio 4; tueor 2; praesideo 2 (*dat.*); custodia *f*; praesidium *n*; custos *m*; vigiliae *f/pl.* (*by night*); **mount ~** custodiam ago 3; **be on one's ~** caveo 2 (*alqd*); **off one's ~** incautus; **~ed** cautus; **~ian** praeses *m and f*; tutor *m*.
**guess** conicio 3; divino 1; coniectura *f*.
**guest** hospes *m*; hospita *f*; conviva *m*.
**guidance** consilium *n*.
**guide** duco 3; rego 3; dux *m*.
**guild** sodalitas *f*, societas *f*; collegium *n*.

**guile** dolus *m*; **~ful** dolosus.
**guilt** noxa *f*; scelus *n*; culpa *f*; **~less** innocens; **~y** noxius, sons, nocens.
**guise** species *f*.
**gulf** sinus, us *m*, gurges *m*.
**gull** mergus *m*; ludificor 1.
**gullet** gula *f*.
**gullible** credulus.
**gully** fauces *f/pl.*
**gulp** singultus, us *m*; **~ down** absorbeo 2.
**gum** gingiva *f*; gummi *n*; lacrima *f*.
**gurgle** murmuro 1.
**gush** me profundo 3; emico 1.
**gust** aura *f*; flatus, us *m*; **~y** ventosus.
**gut** exintero 1.
**guts** intestina *n/pl.*, viscera *n/pl.*
**gutter** fossa *f*; cloaca *f*; imbrex *f*.
**gymnas|ium** palaestra *f*, gymnasium *n*; **~tic** gymnicus; **~tics** palaestra *f*.

# H

**habit** mos *m*; consuetudo *f*; habitus, us *m*; **be in the ~ of** soleo 2; **~ation** domicilium *n*; **~ual** usitatus.

**hack** concido 3; caballus *m*; **~neyed** tritus.

**haft** manubrium *n*.

**hag** anus, us *f*; **~gard** macie confectus.

**hail** saluto 1; salvere iubeo 2 (*alqm*); *int.* salve; grando *f*; **it ~s** grandinat.

**hair** capillus *m*; crinis *m*; pilus *m*; **~dresser** tonsor *m*; cinerarius *m*; **~less** glaber, calvus; **~y** pilosus, villosus.

**hale** validus.

**half** dimidius; dimidia pars *f*; dimidium *n*; **~-breed** hibrida *m* and *f*; **~ hour** semihora *f*; **~-moon** luna *f* dimidia; **~-pound** selibra *f*; **~-witted** stultus; **~yearly** semestris.

**hall** atrium *n*.

**hallow** sacro 1; **~ed** sanctus.

**hallucination** error *m* (mentis); somnium *n*.

**halo** corona *f*.

**halt** *v/t.* constituo 3; *v/i.* consisto 3; haesito 1; claudico 1; claudus; **~er** capistrum *n*.

**ham** perna *f*; poples *m*.

**hamlet** viculus *m*.

**hammer** malleus *m*; tundo 3 (malleo).

**hamper** qualus *m*; impedio 4.

**hamstring** poplites succido 3 (*alci*).

**hand** manus, us *f*; palma *f*; **right, left ~** dext(e)ra, laeva; **at ~** praesto, ad manum; **be at ~** adsum (*dat.*); **by ~** manu; **in ~** in manibus; **on the one ~, on the other ~** quidem ... sed, at ... contra; **~ to ~** comminus (*pugnare*); **come to ~** venire ad manum; **have a ~ in** intersum (*dat.*); **~ down, over** trado 3; **~ in** profiteor 2 (*nomen etc.*); **~ round** circumfero 3; **~book** libellus *m*; **~cuffs** manicae *f/pl.*; **~ful** manipulus *m*.

**handi|craft** artificium *n*; **~work** opus *n*.

**handkerchief** sudarium *n*.

**handle** tracto 1; ansa *f*; manubrium *n*.

**hand|maid** ancilla *f*; **~some** pulcher, decorus, speciosus; liberalis; **~writing** chirographum *n*; manus, us *f*; **~y** habilis, dexter.

**hang** *v/t.* suspendo 3 (*alqm, alqd, re, ex, de, in re*); affigo 3 (*ad, dat.*); *v/i.* pendeo 2; **~ back** dubito 1; **~ over** immineo 2 (*dat.*); **let ~** demitto 3; **~er-on** assecla *m*; **~ing** suspendium *n*; **~ings** aulaea *n/pl.*; **~man** carnifex *m*.

**hanker after** cupio 3.

**hap|hazardly** temere; **~less** infelix; **~ly** fortasse.

**happen** accido 3 (**that** *ut*); contingo 3 (*dat.*); evenio 4; fio.

**happ|iness** felicitas *f*; **~y** felix, beatus, fortunatus.

**harangue** contionor 1 (*apud*); contio *f*.

**harass** sollicito 1; vexo 1; fatigo 1.

**harbinger** (prae)nuntius *m*.

**harbour** portus, us *m*; *fig.* refugium *n*; excipio 3.

**hard** durus; asper; difficilis, arduus; *adv.* valde, sedulo; **~ by** prope, iuxta; **be ~ pressed** premor 3; **~en** duro 1; **become ~ened** obduresco 3; **~hearted** ferreus; **~ly** vix, aegre; **~ness** duritia *f*; **~ship** iniuria *f*; labor *m*; **~ware** ferramenta *n/pl.*; **~y** robustus.

**hare** lepus, oris *m*.

**harlot** meretrix *f*.

**harm** laedo 3; noceo 2 (*dat.*); iniuria *f*; incommodum *n*; **~ful** nocens; **~less** innocens.

**harmon|ious** concors; **~ise** concino 3; consentio 4; **~y** concentus, us *m*; concordia *f*.

**harness** freni *m/pl.*; frenos impono 3.

**harp** cithara *f*; **~ upon** canto 1.

**harrow** rastrum *n*; occo 1.

**harsh** asper, austerus, durus.

**hart** cervus *m*.

**harvest** messis *f*; demeto 3, percipio 3; **~er** messor *m*.

**hast|e** propero 1, festino 1; festinatio *f*; celeritas *f*; ⁓en accelero 1, maturo 1; ⁓ily propere, raptim; ⁓y properus, praeceps; iracundus.

**hat** petasus *m*.

**hatch** excludo 3; coquo 3 (*consilium*).

**hatchet** securis *f*.

**hate** odi; ⁓ful invisus, odiosus; be ⁓ful to odio sum (*alci*).

**hatred** odium *n*.

**haught|iness** superbia *f*, arrogantia *f*; ⁓y superbus, arrogans.

**haul** traho 3, rapio 3; ⁓ down, up de-, sub-duco 3 (*naves*); praeda *f*.

**haunch** clunis *f or m*.

**haunt** celebro 1, frequento 1; inquieto 1; latebra *f*.

**have** habeo 2; teneo 2; est mihi; utor 3; I ⁓ to do this hoc mihi faciendum est.

**haven** refugium *n*.

**havoc** caedes *f*, clades *f*.

**hawk** accipiter *m*; *v/i.* exscreo 1; *v/t.* vendito 1; ⁓er institor *m*.

**hay** faenum *n*; ⁓-loft faenilia *n/pl*.

**hazard** in discrimen committo 3, voco 1; in aleam do 1; periculum *n*; alea *f*; ⁓ous periculosus.

**haze** nebula *f*.

**hazel** corylus, i *f*.

**he** ille; ⁓ who is qui; ⁓ himself ipse.

**head** caput *n*; vertex *m*; princeps *m*; be ⁓ of praesum (*dat.*); *mil.* ⁓ of a column primum agmen *n*; ⁓ foremost pronus; be brought to a ⁓ in discrimen adducor 3; hang over one's ⁓ supra caput est; lay ⁓s together capita conferre; make ⁓way proficio 3; ⁓ache capitis dolor *m*; ⁓band vitta *f*; ⁓land promontorium *n*; ⁓long praeceps; ⁓quarters principia *n/pl.*; ⁓strong pervicax.

**heal** sano 1; medeor 2 (*dat.*); coeo 4 (*vulnera*); ⁓er medicus *m*; ⁓ing sanatio *f*; salutaris.

**health** sanitas *f*, valetudo *f*; good, bad ⁓ bona, infirma valetudo *f*; drink one's ⁓ propino 1 (*salutem alci*); ⁓ful salubris, salutaris; ⁓y sanus, validus.

**heap** acervus *m*; cumulus *m*; ⁓ up coacervo 1; ⁓ upon congero 3 (*in alqm*).

**hear** audio 4 (*acc., acc. c. inf.*); percipio 3; *fig.* cognosco 3; ⁓ing auditus, us *m*; audientia *f*; give a ⁓ing aures praebeo 2 (*alci*).

**hearken** ausculto 1 (*alci*).

**hearsay** auditio *f*; rumor *m*.

**heart** cor *n*; *fig.* pectus *n*; animus *m*; viscera *n/pl.*; know by ⁓ memoria teneo 2; ⁓-breaking miserabilis; ⁓felt sincerus; ⁓en confirmo 1.

**hearth** focus *m*.

**heart|ily** summo studio; vehementer; ⁓iness studium *n*; ⁓less ferreus; ⁓y sincerus, comis.

**heat** calor *m*, ardor *m*; aestus, us *m*; calefacio 3.

**heath** planum *n*; loca *n/pl.* virgultis obsita.

**heathen** paganus; barbarus.

**heave** *v/i.* tumeo 2; tumesco 3; *v/t.* tollo 3; ⁓ a groan, sigh gemitum, suspirium do 1, duco 3.

**heaven** caelum *n*; *fig.* superi *m/pl.*; di *m/pl.* immortales; ⁓ly caelestis, divinus.

**heav|iness** gravitas *f*; ⁓y gravis; crassus; aeger (*animi*) magnus (*imber etc.*).

**hecatomb** hecatombe *f*.

**hectic** febriculosus; *fig.* incitatus.

**hedge** saepes *f*; saepio 4; ⁓hog erinaceus *m*.

**heed** oboedio 4 (*dat.*); take ⁓ curo 1; caveo 2; ⁓ful memor, cautus; ⁓less immemor (*gen.*); incautus.

**heel** calx *f*; take to one's ⁓s me in pedes conicio 3.

**heifer** iuvenca *f*.

**height** altitudo *f*; proceritas *f*; locus *m* editus, superior; *fig.* fastigium *n*; summus; ⁓en amplifico 1; augeo 2.

**heinous** atrox, nefarius.

**heir** heres *m and f*.

**hell** inferi *m/pl.*; ⁓ish infernus; nefandus.

**helm** gubernaculum *n*; clavus *m*.

**helmet** galea *f*, cassis *f*; ⁓ed galeatus.

**helmsman** gubernator *m*.

**help** adiuvo 1; subvenio 4 (*dat.*); opem fero 3; porrigo 3 (*cibus*); I can't ⁓ facere non possum quin; auxilium *n*, ops *f*; ⁓er adiutor *m*; ⁓ful utilis; ⁓less inops.

**hem** ora *f*, insita *f*; ⁓ in circumsedeo 2; claudo 3.

**hemlock** cicuta *f*.

**hemp** cannabis *f*.

**hen** gallina *f*.

**hence** hinc; ita; ex quo; ⁓forth dehinc, posthac.

**her** suus; eius.

**herald** praeco *m*; praenuntio 1.
**herb** herba *f*.
**herd** grex *m*; pecus *n*; **~sman** pastor *m*.
**here** hic; **~ and there** passim; **be ~** adsum; **~abouts** hic alicubi; **~after** posthac, aliquando.
**hereditary** hereditarius; paternus.
**here|sy** prava opinio *f*; **~tical** pravus.
**hereupon** hic.
**heritage** hereditas *f*.
**hermit** homo *m* solitarius.
**hero** heros *m*; vir *m* fortissimus; **~ic** heroicus; **~ine** heroina *f*, herois *f*; **~ism** virtus *f*, fortitudo *f*.
**heron** ardea *f*.
**herself** ipsa.
**hesita|ncy** haesitatio *f*; **~te** dubito 1; haesito 1, cunctor 1; **~tion** haesitatio *f*.
**hew** caedo 3; dolo 1.
**hiccup** singulto 1; singultus, us *m*.
**hide** *v/t.* celo 1; abdo 3, condo 3; dissimulo 1; *v/i.* lateo 2; corium *n*; pellis *f*.
**hideous** foedus, taeter, informis.
**hiding** verbera *n/pl.*; **~place** latebrae *f/pl.*
**high** altus; (ex)celsus; sublimis; *fig.* summus, amplus; magnus (*price, etc.*); **~-born** generosus; **~lands** loca *n/pl.* montuosa; **~ly** magni (*aestimo*); **~-priest** pontifex *m*; **~-spirited** ferox; **~way** via *f*; **~wayman** latro *m*.
**hilarity** hilaritas *f*.
**hill** collis *m*; clivus *m*; tumulus *m*; **~y** clivosus.
**hilt** manubrium *n*.
**himself** ipse; se(met); **by ~** solitarius, solus.
**hind** cerva *f*; posterior.
**hind|er** impedio 4 (*alqm a re*; *ne, quin, quominus*); obsto 1 (*alci*; *ne, quominus*); **~rance** impedimentum *n*, mora *f*.
**hinge** cardo *m*; **~ on** vertor 3 (*in re*).
**hint** significo 1; significatio *f*; signum *n*.
**hip** coxendix *f*.
**hire** conduco 3; merces *f*; **~ling** mercenarius *m*.
**his** suus; eius.
**hiss** sibilo 1; **~ off** explodo 3; **~ing** sibilus, us *m*.
**histor|ian** rerum scriptor *m*; **~ical**

**historicus; ~y** historia *f*; res *f/pl.* (gestae).
**hit** ferio 4; percutio 3; **~ upon** invenio 4; plaga *f*.
**hitch** impedimentum *n*; **~ up** succingo 3.
**hither** huc; **~to** adhuc; antehac.
**hive** alvearium *n*.
**hoard** recondo 3; thesaurus *m*.
**hoar|frost** pruina *f*; **~iness** canities *f*.
**hoarse** raucus.
**hoary** canus; priscus.
**hoax** fallo 3; fallacie *f/pl.*
**hobble** claudico 1.
**hobby** studium *n*.
**hoe** sarculum *n*.
**hog** porcus *m*.
**hoist** tollo 3; **~ sail** vela do 1.
**hold** teneo 2; gesto 1; capio 3; habeo 2, possideo 2; gero 3 (*magistratum*); **~ the belief that** existimo 1, censeo 2; **~ good** convenit 4 (*ad*); **~ one's tongue** conticesco 3; **~ out** sustineo 2; **~ with** consentio 4; caverna *f*; manus, us *f*; **catch ~ of** comprehendo 3; arripio 3.
**hole** cavum *n*; foramen *n*.
**holiday** feriae *f/pl.*; dies *m* festus; **keep ~** ferior 1; ferias ago 3.
**holiness** sanctitas *f*; numen *n*.
**hollow** cavus; *fig.* vanus; fucatus; caverna *f*, cavum *n*; **~ out** (ex-) cavo 1.
**holy** sanctus, divinus.
**homage** observantia *f*, veneratio *f*.
**home** domus, us *f*; domicilium *n*; **at ~** domi; **~(wards)** domum; **from ~** domo; **drive, strike ~** adigo 3; domesticus; **~ly** rusticus; **~sickness** suorum desiderium *n*.
**honest** probus, sincerus; **~y** probitas *f*.
**honey** mel *n*; **~comb** favus *m*; **~ed** mellitus.
**honorary** honorarius.
**honour** honor *m*; dignitas *f*; honestas *f*; **word of ~** fides *f*; **~s** iusta *n/pl.*; honoro 1; honesto 1; in honore habeo 2; orno 1, colo 3; **~able** honestus.
**hood** cucullus *m*; **~wink** ludificor 1.
**hoof** ungula *f*.
**hook** hamus *m*; uncus *m*; hamo capio 3; **~ed** aduncus.
**hoop** circulus *m*.
**hoot** cano 3; *fig.* obstrepo 3 (*alci*).
**hop** salio 4.

**hope** spero 1 (*alqd, acc. c. inf.*); ex-specto 1 (*alqd*); spes *f*; **lose, give up** ~ despero 1.

**horizon** prospectus, us *m*; ~tal aequus.

**horn** cornu *n*; bucina *f*; corneus; ~ed cornutus.

**horri|ble** horribilis, atrox, foedus; ~fy terreo 2; percello 3.

**horror** horror *m*, pavor *m*.

**horse** equus *m*; **on** ~back (in) equo; ~man eques *m*; ~-race certamen *n* equorum; ~shoe solea *f*; ~-whip flagellum *n*.

**hose** tibiale *n*.

**hospit|able** hospitalis; ~al valetudinarium *n*; ~ality hospitium *n*; liberalitas *f*.

**host** hospes *m*; multitudo *f*; ~age obses *m*; ~elry caupona *f*; ~ess hospita *f*.

**hostil|e** hostilis; inimicus, infestus, infensus; ~ity inimicitiae *f/pl.*; ~ities bellum *n*.

**hot** calidus; aestuosus; **be** ~ caleo 2; aestuo 1; ~-headed fervidus, calidus.

**hound** canis *m or f* (venaticus); ~ **on** stimulo 1, agito 1.

**hour** hora *f*; **half an** ~ semihora *f*; **from** ~ **to** ~ in horas; ~-glass horologium *n*.

**house** domus, us *f*; domicilium *n*; aedes *f*; tectum *n*; **at my** ~ apud me; domo excipio 3; condo 3; ~-breaker fur *m*; ~hold familia *f*; ~hold gods Lares *m/pl.*, Penates *m/pl.*; ~keeper dispensator *m*; ~-maid ancilla *f*; ~wife materfamilias *f*.

**hovel** gurgustium *n*.

**hover** (circum)volito 1; *fig.* obversor 1 (*alci; ante alqm*).

**how** quomodo, quemadmodum; *int.* quam, ut; ~ **much** quantus; ~ **many** quot; ~ever utcumque; tamen.

**howl** ululo 1; ululatus, us *m*.

**hubbub** clamor *m*.

**huckster** institor *m*.

**huddled together** confertus.

**hue** color *m*.

**huff: be in a** ~ stomachor 1.

**hug** amplector 3; complexus, us *m*.

**huge** ingens, vastus, immanis.

**hull** alveus *m* (navis).

**hum** murmuro 1; musso 1; bombus *m*; fremitus, us *m*.

**human** humanus; ~ **beings** homines *m/pl.*; ~e humanus; ~ity humanitas *f*; genus *n* humanum.

**humble** humilis; demissus; deprimo 3.

**humbug** tricae *f/pl.*

**humid** umidus.

**humili|ate** deprimo 3; ~ation dedecus *n*; ~ating indignus; ~ty modestia *f*.

**humorous** facetus, festivus.

**humour** ingenium *n*; facetiae *f/pl.*; **be in the** ~ **to** libet 2 (*alci c. inf.*); morem gero 3 (*alci*); gratificor 1.

**hump** gibba *f*.

**hunchbacked** gibber.

**hundred** centum 1; **a** ~ **times** centies; ~th centesimus.

**hunger** fames *f*; inedia *f*; esurio 4.

**hungry** ieiunus.

**hunt** venor 1; venatus, us *m*, venatio *f*; ~er venator *m*; ~ing spear venabulum *n*; ~ress venatrix *f*.

**hurdle** crates f.

**hurl** conicio 3 (*in*); iaculor 1.

**hurricane** procella *f*.

**hurr|ied** praeceps; praeproperus; ~iedly raptim; ~y *v/i.* festino 1, propero 1, curro 3; *v/t.* rapio 3; festinatio *f*.

**hurt** noceo 2; laedo 3; doleo 2; **be** ~ acerbe fero 3 (*alqd*); ~ful noxius.

**husband** maritus *m*; vir *m*; ~man agricola *m*; ~ry agri cultura *f*; parsimonia *f*.

**hush** st!, tace, tacete; sedo 1; ~ **up** celo 1.

**husk** folliculus *m*; vagina *f*.

**husky** raucus.

**hustle** trudo 3.

**hut** tugurium *n*; casa *f*.

**hutch** cavea *f*.

**hyena** hyaena *f*.

**hymeneal** nuptialis.

**hymn** carmen *n*; cano 3.

**hyperbole** superlatio *f*.

**hypocri|sy** (dis)simulatio *f*; ~te (dis)simulator *m*; ~tical simulatus, fictus.

**hypothesis** sumptio *f*; **on this** ~ hoc posito.

# I

**I** ego.

**ic|e** glacies *f*; **~icle** stiria *f*; **~y** glacialis, gelidus.

**idea** notio *f*; notitia *f*; imago *f*; **~l** perfectus; exemplum *n*.

**identi|cal** idem; **~fy** agnosco 3.

**ides** idus, uum *f/pl.*

**idiocy** fatuitas *f*.

**idiom** proprietas *f* (linguae); **~atic** proprius.

**idiot** imbecillus, fatuus (homo *m*).

**idle** otiosus, vacuus; deses, ignavus; (*of things*) vanus, irritus; **be ~** cesso 1, vaco 1; **~ness** pigritia *f*, desidia *f*.

**idol** simulacrum *n*; *fig.* deliciae *f/pl.*; **~ise** veneror 1.

**if** si; **~ not** sin, si minus; **~ ... not** nisi; **~ only** dummodo; **but, even ~** quod si, etiamsi; **I ask ~** rogo 1 num.

**ignite** *v/t.* accendo 3; *v/i.* exardesco 3.

**ignoble** ignobilis; turpis.

**ignominious** turpis.

**ignor|ance** ignoratio *f*, ignorantia *f*; inscitia *f*; **~ant** ignarus, imprudens (*gen.*); rudis; **be ~ant** ignoro 1; nescio 4; **~e** praetereo 4; neglego 3.

**ill** aeger, aegrotus; malus; malum *n*; **be ~** aegroto 1; laboro 1; morbo afficior 3; **speak ~ of** maledico 3 (*alci*); **~-advised** temerarius; **~-bred** inhumanus, agrestis.

**illegal** contra leges.

**illegitimate** spurius, haud legitimus.

**ill-|fated** infelix; **~ health** valetudo *f*.

**illiterate** illiteratus, indoctus.

**ill|natured** malevolus; **~ness** morbus *m*; valetudo *f*; **~omened** dirus, infaustus; **~ temper** stomachus *m*; **~-tempered** iracundus, difficilis.

**illuminate** illustro 9.

**illus|ion** error *m*; species *f*; **~ory** vanus.

**illustrat|e** illustro 1; **~ion** exemplum *n*.

**illustrious** praeclarus, illustris.

**image** imago *f*; simulacrum *n*; effigies *f*; species *f*.

**imagin|ary** commenticius; **~ation** cogitatio *f*; **~e** animo fingo 3; puto 1.

**imbue** imbuo 3, inficio 3 (*alqd alqa re*).

**imitat|e** imitor 1; effingo 3; **~ion** imitatio *f*; imago *f*; **~or** imitator *m*.

**immaculate** integer.

**immature** crudus.

**immeasurable** immensus.

**immediate** praesens; proximus; **~ly** statim, protinus, continuo.

**immense** ingens, immanis.

**immerse** mergo 3.

**immigrant** advena *m*.

**imminent** praesens; **be ~** immineo 2.

**immoderate** immoderatus, nimius.

**immodest** impudicus.

**immoral** pravus, turpis; **~ity** pravitas *f*; luxus, us *m*.

**immortal** immortalis; aeternus; **~ity** immortalitas *f*.

**immovable** immobilis.     [tas *f*.]

**immun|e** immunis; **~ity** immuni-}

**immure** includo 3.

**impair** infringo 3; imminuo 3; elevo 1.

**impart** impertio 4 (*alci alqd*); communico 1 (*cum alqo*).

**impartial** aequus, integer; **~ity** aequitas *f*.

**impassable** invius.

**impatien|ce** ardor *m*; **~t** impatiens (*gen.*); avidus (**for** *gen.*); **be ~t for** gestio 4 (*inf.*).

**impeach** accuso 1; postulo 1.

**impediment** impedimentum *n*; **~ of speech** haesitantia *f* (linguae).

**impel** impello 3 (*ad alqd, ut*).

**impend** impendeo 2; **~ing** praesens, futurus.

**impenetrable** invius, inaccessus.

**imperative** necessarius.

**imperceptibly** sensim.

**imperfect** imperfectus; mancus, mendosus; **~ion** vitium *n*.

**imperial** imperatorius; augustus.

**imperious** imperiosus.

**imperishable** immortalis.

**impersonate** partes sustineo 2 (*alcs*).

**impertinen|ce** contumelia *f*; os *n*; ~t contumeliosus.

**imperturbable** tranquillus.

**impervious (to)** surdus (ad).

**impetuous** acer, fervidus.

**impetus** vis *f*.

**impious** nefarius, impius.

**implacable** implacabilis; atrox.

**implant** insero 3.

**implement** instrumentum *n*.

**implicate** implico 1; **be ~d** affinis, conscius sum.

**implicit** tacitus.

**implore** oro 1, obsecro 1.

**impl|y: be ~ied in** inest (in).

**impolite** inhumanus.

**import** importo 1 (*in*); significatio *f*; ~s merces *f/pl*. (importaticiae).

**importan|ce** momentum *n*, pondus *n*; **be of ~ce interest (to me** mea); ~t gravis, magnus; amplus.

**importun|ate** improbus; ~e flagito 1.

**impos|e** impono 3 (*alqd alci*); ~e **upon** impono 3 (*alci*); ~ition fraus *f*.

**impossible: it is** ~ fieri non potest (*quin*).

**impostor** planus *m*.

**imprecation** preces *f/pl*.

**impregna|ble** inexpugnabilis; ~te inicio 3.

**impress** (per)moveo 2; inculco 1; imprimo 3; ~ion impressio *f*; opinio *f*; ~ive gravis.

**imprison** in vincula, carcerem conicio 3; includo 3; ~ment vincula *n/pl*.

**improbable** haud veri similis.

**improper** indecorus.

**improve** *v/t*. corrigo 3; meliorem facio 3, reddo 3; *v/i*. melior fio; proficio 3.

**improvident** improvidus.

**imprudence** temeritas *f*, imprudentia *f*.

**impuden|ce** impudentia *f*; os *n*; ~t impudens.

**impugn** impugno 1.

**impulse** impulsus, us *m*; impetus, us *m*.

**impunity: with ~** impune.

**impure** impurus.

**impute** do 1, attribuo 3, imputo 1 (*alci qlqd*).

**in** in (*abl.*); ~ **Rome** Romae; ~ **summer** aestate; ~ **the writings of** apud (*alqm*); ~ **that** quod.

**in|accessible** invius; difficilis; ~ac**curate** parum diligens; ~action otium *n*; ~active iners; ~activity inertia *f*.

**in|adequate** impar (*dat.*); ~ad**vertently** per imprudentiam; ~**animate** inanimus; ~**appropriate** parum aptus.

**inasmuch as** quoniam; ~ **he** quippe qui.

**in|attentive** parum attentus; ~**augural** aditialis; ~**augurate** inauguro 1; ~**auspicious** dirus; ~**can****tation** carmen *n*.

**incapa|ble: be ~ble of** non possum; alienus sum (ab); ~**city** inscitia *f*.

**in|cautious** incautus; ~**cense** tus *n*; incendo 3 (*ira*); ~**centive** incitamentum *n*; ~**cessant** continuus, assiduus; ~**cest** incestum *n*.

**inch** uncia *f*.

**incident** casus, us *m*; res *f*; ~**ally** casu.

**incite** incito 1; ~**ment** stimulus *m*.

**in|civility** inhumanitas *f*; ~**clement** asper.

**inclin|ation** voluntas *f*; animus *m*; studium *n*; ~**e** inclino 1; induco 3; clivus *m*; **be favourably ~ed to** inclinor 1 ad; **I am ~ed to think** haud scio 4 an, nescio 4 an.

**include** includo 3; ascribo 3.

**incom|e** vectigal *n*; ~**parable** singularis; ~**patible** repugnans; ~**petence** inscitia *f*; ~**plete** imperfectus.

**incon|clusive** infirmus; **be ~gru****ous** discrepo 1; ~**siderate** inconsideratus; ~**sistent** inconstans; absonus, alienus (ab); ~**stant** inconstans, levis; ~**venience** incommodum *n*; incommodo 1 (*alci*); ~**venient** incommodus.

**in|corporate** contribuo 3; ascribo 3; ~**correct** falsus, mendosus; ~**correctly** perperam, prave; ~**corrigible** perditus; ~**corruptible** integer.

**increase** *v/t*. augeo 2; amplifico 1; *v/i*. cresco 3; incrementum *n*.

**incred|ible** incredibilis; ~**ulous** incredulus.

**in|criminate** culpam (*in alqm*) transfero 3; ~**culcate** inculco 1.

**incur** suscipio 3; incurro 3 (*alqd*).

**in|curable** insanabilis; ~**cursion** incursio *f*.

**indebted** obnoxius; be ~ pecuniam debeo 2 (*alci*); *fig.* acceptum refero 3 (*alqd alci*).

**indecen|cy** turpitudo *f*; ~t turpis.

**indeci|sion** dubitatio *f*; ~sive dubius, anceps.

**indeed** quidem; vero; ain' (vero)? 

**inde|fatigable** impiger; ~finable nescio quis; ~finite infinitus.

**indelicate** putidus.  [muneror 1.]

**indemnify** damnum sarcio 4; re-]

**independen|ce** libertas *f*; ~t liber, solutus; sui iuris (*homo*).

**inde|structible** perennis; ~terminate** anceps, dubius.

**index** index *m*.

**indicat|e** indico 1, significo 1; ~ion indicium *n*; signum *n*.

**indict** accuso 1; reum facio 3; ~ment** accusatio *f*; crimen *n*.

**indifferen|ce** aequus animus *m*; neglegentia *f*; ~t neglegens; (*of things*) indifferens; be ~t to parvi facio 3 (*alqd*).

**indi|genous** indigena *f*; ~gent inops; ~gestible** gravis; ~gestion** cruditas *f*.

**indign|ant:** be ~ indignor 1 (*alqd*); stomachor 1 (*alqa re*); ~ation indignatio *f*; ira *f*; ~ity contumelia *f*, indignitas *f*.

**indirect** obliquus.

**indis|creet** imprudens; ~criminate** promiscuus; *adv.* passim.

**indispos|ed** aegrotus; ~ition valetudo *f*.

**indis|putable** certus; ~tinct obscurus, obtusus.

**individual** proprius; singuli.

**indolen|ce** inertia *f*; ~t iners.

**indomitable** invictus.

**indoor** domesticus; ~s domi.

**induce** adduco 3, induco 3 (*alqm ut*); persuadeo 2 (*alci ut*); ~ment praemium *n*; illecebra *f*.

**indulge** indulgeo 2 (*dat.*); morem gero 3 (*alci*); expleo 2 (*alqd*); ~nce indulgentia *f*; venia *f*; ~nt indulgens, remissus.

**industr|ious** industrius, sedulus, navus; ~y industria *f*.

**inebriated** ebrius.

**in|effectual** irritus; ~efficient invalidus; ~ept ineptus; ~ert segnis, immobilis; ~ertness segnitia *f*; ~evitable necessarius; ~exhaustible** infinitus; ~exorable inexorabilis, durus; ~expensive vilis.

**inexper|ience** imperitia *f*; ~ienced imperitus, rudis (*gen.*); ~t inscitus.

**in|explicable** inexplicabilis; ~expressible** infandus; ~fallible certus.

**infam|ous** infamis; flagitiosus; ~y flagitium *n*.

**infan|cy** (prima) pueritia *f*, infantia *f*; ~t infans *m and f*; ~tile infans; ~try pedes *m/sg. and pl.*, pedites *m/sg. and pl.*; peditatus, us *m*; pedester.

**infatuat|ed** demens; ~ion dementia *f*.

**infect** inficio 3; ~ion contagio *f*.

**infer** colligo 3; ~ence coniectura *f*.

**inferior** inferior, deterior; impar (*dat.*).

**infernal** infernus; ~ **regions** inferi *m/pl.*

**infinit|e** infinitus, immensus; ~y infinitas *f*.

**infirm** infirmus, imbecillus; ~ity infirmitas *f*.

**inflam|e** in-, ac-cendo 3; be ~ed flagro 1; ~matory** turbulentus.

**inflat|e** inflo 1; be ~ed turgeo 2; ~ion tumor *m*.

**inflexib|ility** pertinacia *f*; ~le obstinatus, rigidus.

**inflict** infero 3; impono 3 (*alqd alci*); ~ **punishment** poenam sumo 3 (*de alqo*).

**influen|ce** momentum *n*; auctoritas *f*; **have ~ce with** possum apud; moveo 2; ~tial gravis, amplus.

**inform** certiorem facio 3 (*alqm*); doceo 2; **be ~ed** cognosco 3; ~ **against** nomen defero 3 (*alcs*); ~ation nuntius *m*; ~er delator *m*, index *m*.

**infringe** violo 1, imminuo 3; ~ment imminutio *f*.

**infuse** infundo 3.

**ingen|ious** sollers; ~uity sollertia *f*; ~uous ingenuus.

**inglorious** inglorius, turpis.

**ingrained** insitus.

**ingrati|ate** gratiam ineo 4 (*apud alqm*); ~tude ingratus animus *m*.

**inhabit** teneo 2, incolo 3; habito 1; ~able habitabilis; ~ant incola *m and f*.

**inhere** inhaereo 2 (*re, in re*); insum.

**inherit** hereditatem adeo 4, capio 3; ~ance hereditas *f*; ~ed hereditarius.

**inhospitable** inhospitalis; inhumanus.

**inhuman** immanis, crudelis.
**iniquit|ous** improbus; **~y** scelus n.
**initia|l** primus; **~te** initio 1 (*alqm alci rei*).
**injudicious** inconsultus.
**injunction** mandatum n.
**injur|e** noceo 2, obsum (*dat.*); laedo 3; **~ious** noxius, gravis; **~y** damnum n, incommodum n; vulnus n; iniuria f.
**injustice** iniustitia f; iniuria f.
**ink** atramentum n̄.
**inland** mediterraneus, interior.
**inlet** aestuarium n.
**inmate** inquilinus m.
**inmost** intimus.
**inn** caupona f; deversorium n.
**innate** insitus, innatus.
**inner** interior.
**innkeeper** caupo m.
**innocen|ce** innocentia f; **~t** innocens; insons; castus.
**innovat|e** novo 1; **~ion** res f/pl. novae.
**innumerable** innumerabilis.
**inoffensive** innocens.
**inopportune** inopportunus.
**inordinate** immoderatus.
**inquir|e** quaero 3 (*alqd ab, de, alqo*); percontor 1 (*alqd ab alqo; alqm de re*); interrogo 1 (*alqm*); **~e into** inquiro 3 (*in alqd*); **~y** percontatio f, interrogatio f; quaestio f.
**inquisitive** percontator m.
**inroad** incursio f; **make an ~** incurro 3 (*in*).    [sania f.\
**insan|e** insanus, vecors; **~ity** in-\
**insatiable** insatiabilis.
**inscri|be** inscribo 3 (*alqd in re*); **~ption** inscriptio f; titulus m.
**insect** insectum n.
**insecure** instabilis.
**insensib|ility** lentitudo f; **~le** lentus.
**insert** insero 3 (*alqd in alqd, dat.*); includo 3 (*in re, in rem*).
**inside** intra (*acc.*); *adv.* intus; interiora n/pl.
**insight** cognitio f.
**insignia** insignia n/pl.
**in|significant** exiguus; nullius momenti; **~sincere** fictus, simulatus.
**insinuate** me insinuo 1 (*alci*); significo 1.
**insipid** insulsus, frigidus.
**insist** flagito 1; urgeo 2; insto 1.
**insolen|ce** insolentia f, contumacia f; **~** superbus.

**insolvent: be ~** decoquo 3.
**insomuch** adeo (*ut*).
**inspect** inspicio 3; recenseo 2 (*exercitum*); **~ion** recensio f, recognitio f; **~or** curator m.
**inspir|ation** afflatus, us m; instinctus, us m; **~e** *fig.* inicio 3, incutio 3 (*alci alqd*); **~ed** instinctus (*re*).
**instal|l** inauguro 1; **~ment** pensio f.
**instance** n exemplum n; **for ~** verbi gratia.
**instant** praesens; momentum n (*temporis*); **~ly** continuo, statim.
**instead of** pro (*abl.*); loco (*gen.*).
**instigat|e** instigo 1; **at your ~ion** instigante, auctore te.
**instil** instillo 1.
**instinct** impetus, us m; natura f; **~ive** naturalis.
**institut|e** in-, con-stituo 3; **~ion** institutum n.
**instruct** instituo 3; doceo 2; praecipio 3; mando 1 (*alci ut*); **~ion** institutio f; mandatum n; **~ive** utilis; **~or** magister m.
**instrument** instrumentum n; organum n; machina f; **~ality: by your ~** tua opera.
**insubordinate** seditiosus.
**insufferable** intolerabilis.
**insufficien|cy** inopia f; **~t** non satis (magnus).
**insulate** segrego 1.
**insult** probrum n; contumelia f; contumeliam impono 3 (*alci*), iacio 3 (*in alqm*); **~ing** contumeliosus.
**insupportable** intolerabilis.
**insure** caveo 2 (*ut*).
**insur|gent** turbulentus, seditiosus; **~rection** tumultus, us m; defectio f.
**intact** integer, incolumis.
**integr|al** necessarius; **~ity** integritas f, innoc̄ itia f.
**intell|ect** mens f; ingenium n; **~igence** mens f; intellegentia f; ingenium n; sollertia f; **~igent** intellegens; ingeniosus.
**intempera|nce** intemperantia f; **~te** intemperans, immoderatus.
**intend** in animo habeo 2, in animo est (mihi) (*inf.*); destino 1 (*alqd*).
**intense** magnus, acer.
**intens|ify** incendo 3; **~ity** vis f; ardor m.
**intent** intentus (*re, in re*); totus (*in re*); **be ~ on** animum intendo 3 in (*re*); **~ion** consilium n; **~ionally**

consulto; de industria; **~ness** intentio *f*.

**inter** sepelio 4.

**intercalary** intercalarius.

**intercede** deprecor 1 (**for** alqm; *ut*, *ne*).

**intercept** intercipio 3; excipio 3.

**intercession** deprecatio *f*.

**interchange** commuto 1 (*inter se*); vices *f/pl.*; vicissitudo *f*.

**intercourse** usus, us *m*; consuetudo *f*; commercium *n*.

**interdict** interdico 3 (*alci alqa re*, *alci alqd*).

**interest** delecto 1; capio 3; **~ one-self** incumbo 3 (*dat.*); utilitas *f*; commodum *n*; **it is of ~ interest** (*alcs, ad alqd*); studium *n*; faenus *n* (**on** money); **gain the ~ of** gratiam concilio 1 (*alcs*); **~ing** iucundus.

**interfere** me interpono 3 (*dat.*, *in alqd*); intercedo 3, intervenio 4 (*dat.*); **~nce** intercessio *f*.

**interim: in the ~** interim.

**interior** interior; pars *f* interior; interiora *n/pl.*

**interlude** *thea.* embolium *n*.

**intermedia|ry** internuntius *m*; **~te** medius.

**interment** sepultura *f*.

**intermingle** misceo 2.

**intermission** intermissio *f*; **without ~** assidue.

**internal** intestinus, domesticus; interior.

**interpose** interpono 3; intercedo 3.

**interpret** interpretor 1; explano 1; **~ation** interpretatio *f*; **~er** interpres *m*.

**interrogat|e** interrogo 1; **~ion** interrogatio *f*; quaestio *f*.

**interrupt** interrumpo 3 (*orationem*, *etc.*); interpello 1 (*alqm*); **~ion** interpellatio *f*.

**intersperse** misceo 2.

**interval** spatium *n* (*inter*); intervallum *n*; **after an ~ of a year** anno interiecto; **in the ~** interim.

**interven|e** intercedo 3, intersum; interpello 1; intervenio 4; **~ing** medius; **~tion** intercessio *f*.

**interview** admitto 3; colloquor 3 (*cum alqo, inter se*); colloquium *n*.

**intestate** intestatus.

**intestines** intestina *n/pl.*

**intima|cy** familiaritas *f*, necessitudo *f*; **~te** familiaris; intimus *m*; significo 1; **~tion** denuntiatio *f*.

**intimidat|e** terreo 2; **~ion** minae *f/pl.*

**into** in (*acc.*).

**intolera|ble** intolerabilis; **~nt** intolerans.

**intoxicat|ed** ebrius; **~ion** ebrietas *f*.

**intrench** vallo et fossa munio 4; **~ment** vallum *n*, munimentum *n*.

**intrepid** intrepidus, fortis; **~ity** fortitudo *f*.

**intricate** implicatus.

**intrigue** dolus *m*; fallaciae *f/pl.*

**introduc|e** intro-, in-duco 3; inveho 3; **~tion** inductio *f*; *liter.* prooemium *n*, exordium *n*; praefatio *f*; **give an ~ion** commendo 1 (*alqm alci*); **letter of ~ion** litterae *f/pl.* commendaticiae.

**intrude** inculco 1 (*me alci*).

**inundat|e** inundo 1; **~ion** diluvies *f*, diluvium *n*.

**inure** duro 1.

**invade** invado 3 (*in*); bellum infero 3 (*dat.*).

**invalid** aegrotus (*homo*); irritus; **~ate** infirmo 1; labefacto 1.

**invaluable** inaestimabilis.

**invariable** constans.

**invasion** irruptio *f*.

**invective** convicium *n*.

**inveigh against** invenor 3 (*in*); insector 1, incesso 3.

**inveigle** pellicio 3.

**invent** reperio 4; excogito 1; **~ion** inventum *n*; commentum *n*; **~or** inventor *m*, auctor *m*.

**invert** inverto 3.

**invest** inauguro 1 (*alqm magistratum*); addo 3 (*alqd alci rei*); circumsedeo 2 (*urbem, etc.*); colloco 1 (*pecuniam in re*).

**investigat|e** investigo 1; quaero 3; **~ion** investigatio *f*; quaestio *f*.

**inveterate** inveteratus.

**invidious** invidiosus, invisus.

**invigorate** corroboro 1; confirmo 1.

**in|vincible** invictus; **~violate** inviolatus, sacrosanctus; **~visible** obscurus, caecus.

**invit|ation** invitatio *f*; **~e** invito 1, voco 1 (*alqm in, ad*); accesso 3; **~ing** gratus, blandus.

**invoke** invoco 1, imploro 1.

**involuntar|y** coactus; **~ily** imprudenter; haud sponte.

**involve** contineo 2; affero 3; admisceo 2; **be ~d in** versor 1, implicor 1 (*abl.*).

**inward** interior; **~ly** penitus.
**irascible** iracundus.
**ire** ira *f.*
**irk** piget 2 (*me alcs rei*); **~some** molestus.
**iron** ferrum *n;* ferreus; **~s** vincula *n/pl.;* **~mongery** ferramenta *n/pl.*
**irony** ironia *f;* dissimulatio *f.*
**irrational** fatuus; brutus.
**irreconcilable** repugnans.
**ir|recoverable** irreparabilis; **~refutable** certissimus.
**irregular** inaequabilis, incompositus, tumultuarius (*milites*).
**irrelevant: be ~** nihil attinet.
**ir|religious** impius; **~reparable** irreparabilis; **~reproachable** integer; **~resistible** invictus; **~re-**

**solute** dubius; **~revocable** irrevocabilis.
**irrigat|e** irrigo 1; **~ion** irrigatio *f.*
**irrita|ble** stomachosus; **~te** stomachum moveo 2 (*alci*); irrito 1; **~tion** stomachus *m.*
**island** insula *f;* **~er** insulanus *m.*
**isolate** intercludo 3; secerno 3.
**issue** *v/i.* evenio 4; *v/t.* edo 3; metior 4 (*frumentum*); **~ forth** egredior 3; eventus, us *m;* exitus, us *m;* egressus, us *m;* res *f;* liberi *m/pl.;* **the main ~** summa *f.*
**it** id.
**itch** prurio 4; *fig.* gestio 4; prurigo *f.*
**iterat|e** itero 1; **~ion** iteratio *f.*
**itinerant** vagus.
**ivory** ebur *n;* eburneus.
**ivy** hedera *f.*

# J

**jackdaw** monedula *f*.
**Jack-of-all-trades** omnis Minervae homo *m*.
**jaded** defessus.
**jagged** scopulosus.
**jail** carcer, eris *n*; **~er** custos *m*.
**jam** conditae baccae *f/pl*.
**jamb** postis *m*.
**January** Ianuarius (mensis) *m*.
**jar** discrepo 1; olla *f*; cadus *m* (*wine*); **a~** semiapertus; **~ring** discors, dissonus.
**jaunty** hilaris.
**javelin** pilum *n*, iaculum *n*.
**jaw** malae *f/pl*.; maxilla *f*; *fig*. fauces *f/pl*.
**jealous** invidus, aemulus; **be ~ of** invideo 2 (*alci*); **~y** invidia *f*, aemulatio *f*.
**jeer** cavillor 1, derideo 2; irrisio *f*.
**jeopard|ise** periclitor 1; **~y** periculum *n*.
**jest** iocor 1; cavillor 1; iocus *m*; **in ~** per iocum; **~er** cavillator *m*, sannio *m*, scurra *m*.
**jet:** **~ of water** aqua *f* saliens; **~black** niger; **~ty** moles *f*, crepido *f*.
**Jew** Iudaeus *m*.
**jewel** gemma *f*; **~led** gemmeus; **~ler** aurifex *m*.
**Jewish** Iudaicus.
**jibe** convicium *n*.
**jilt** repudio 1.
**jingle** tinnio 4.
**job** opus *n*; negotium *n*.
**jockey** eques *m*.
**joc|ose** iocosus; **~und** hilaris.
**join** (con)iungo 3; connecto 3; me adiungo 3 (*alci, ad*); **~ in** intersum (*dat.*); **~ together** coeo 4; **~er** faber, bri *m*.
**joint** commissura *f*; articulus *m*; nodus *m*; communis.
**joist** tignum *n*.
**joke** iocus *m*; iocatio *f*; iocor 1 (*de*); cavillor 1.
**jolly** hilaris, festivus.

**jolt** quasso 1, iacto 1; iactatio *f*.
**jostle** trudo 3.
**jot:** **not a ~** ne pilus quidem; **I don't care a ~** non pili facio 3 (*alqd*).
**journal** ephemeris *f*; commentarii *m/pl*.
**journey** iter, ineris *n*; iter facio 3; proficiscor 3.
**jovial** hilaris.
**joy** gaudium *n*; laetitia *f*; gaudeo 2; **~ful** laetus.
**jubilant** exsultans.
**judge** iudico 1; reor 2, existimo 1, aestimo 1; iudex *m*, quaesitor *m*; existimator *m*; **~ment** iudicium *n*; arbitrium *n*; **pronounce ~ment** ius dico 3; **good ~ment** consilium *n*.
**judic|ial** iudicialis, iudiciarius, forensis; **~ious** prudens.
**juic|e** sucus *m*; **~y** sucosus.
**jug** urceus *m*.
**juggl|er** praestigiator *m*; **~ing** praestigiae *f/pl*.
**July** Quintilis (mensis) *m*; Iulius (mensis) *m*.
**jumble** confundo 3.
**jump** salio 4; saltus, us *m*.
**juncture** tempus *n*.
**June** (mensis) Iunius *m*.
**jungle** loca *n/pl*. obsita (*virgultis etc.*).
**junior** minor natu.
**juniper** iuniperus, i *f*.
**juris|consult** iuris consultus *m*; **~diction** iurisdictio *f*; **~t** iuris consultus *m*.
**jur|or** iudex *m*; **~y** iudices *m/pl*.
**just** iustus, aequus; meritus; *adv*. vix; modo; **~ as** perinde ac; **~ when** cum maxime; commodum ... cum.
**just|ice** iustitia *f*; **~ifiably** iure; **~ification** purgatio *f*; **~ify** purgo 1, excuso 1.
**jut| out** exsto 1; promineo 2; **~ting** proiectus.
**juvenile** iuvenilis.

# K

**keel** carina *f.*

**keen** acer, sagax; studiosus; ~ness sagacitas *f*, acies *f.*

**keep** teneo 2, retineo 2; servo 1 (*fidem etc.*); habeo 2; custodio 4; condo 3 (*frumentum etc.*); ~ accounts tabulas conficio 3; ~ away abstineo 2 (*me, alqm*); ~ company congregor 1 (*cum*); ~ holiday festum diem celebro 1; ~ in the dark celo 1 (*alqd alqm*); ~ off arceo 2; ~ up tueor 2; ~up with subsequor 3; arx *f*; ~er custos *m*; ~ing custodia *f*; in ~ing with conveniens (*dat.*); ~sake pignus *n.*

**keg** cadus *m.*

**kennel** cubile *n.*

**kerchief** sudarium *n.*

**kernel** nucleus *m.*

**kettle** olla *f.*

**key** clavis *f*; ~hole foramen *n.*

**kick** calce ferio 4, peto 3; calx *f.*

**kid** haedus *m.*

**kidnap** surripio 3.

**kidneys** renes *m/pl.*

**kill** interficio 3, occido 3, caedo 3; neco 1; ~ing caedes *f.*

**kiln** fornax *f.*

**kin** propinqui *m/pl.*, necessarii *m/pl.*

**kind** benignus, comis; genus *n*; of this ~ huiusmodi; of such a ~ talis ... (qualis).

**kindle** *v/t.* ac-, in-cendo 3; inflammo 1; *v/i.* exardesco 3.

**kindness** benignitas *f*, comitas *f*; beneficium *n*; officium *n.*

**kindred** propinqui *m/pl.*, necessarii *m/pl.*; cognatus, consanguineus; *fig.* finitimus.

**king** rex *m*; be ~ regno 1; ~dom regnum *n*; ~ly regius.

**kinsman** necessarius *m.*

**kiss** suavior 1, osculor 1; suavium *n*, osculum *n.*

**kitchen** culina *f.*

**kite** milvus *m.*

**knack** sollertia *f.*

**knapsack** sarcina *f.*

**knav|e** nebulo *m*, furcifer *m*, scelestus *m*; ~ery nequitia *f*; ~ish nequam, improbus.

**knead** subigo 3.

**knee** genu *n*; ~l nitor 3 genibus.

**knife** culter *m.*

**knight** eques *m*; ~ly equester.

**knit:** ~ the brows supercilium contraho 3.

**knob** bulla *f*; umbilicus *m*; nodus *m.*

**knock** pulso 1; ferio 4; ~ at the door fores pulso 1; ~ down sterno 3; (*at an auction*) addico 3 (*alqd alci*); pulsatio *f*; ~-kneed varus.

**knot** nodus *m*; *fig.* vinculum *n*; (*of people*) circulus *m*; nodo 1; ~ty nodosus.

**know** scio 4; (cog)nosco 3; not to ~ nescio 4, ignoro 1; be ~n constat 1; make ~n declaro 1; ~ledge scientia *f*; cognitio *f*; doctrina *f*; without the ~ledge of clam (*abl.*); to my ~ledge quod sciam; well-~n notus, celeber.

# L

**label** titulus *m.*

**laborious** operosus.

**labor** laboro 1; contendo 3 (*inf.*); labor *m*; opera *f*; partus, us *m*; **~er** operarius *m*, mercenarius *m.*

**lace** necto 3; alligo 1.

**lacerate** lacero 1.

**lack** egeo 2, careo 2; mihi deest; inopia *f*; defectio *f.*

**lackey** pedisequus *m.*

**lacking: be ~** deficio 3, desum.

**lad** puer *m.*

**ladder** scalae *f/pl.*

**lade** onero 1; **~n** onustus, gravis.

**ladle** trulla *f.*

**lady** matrona *f*, mulier *f*; **~ship** domina *f*, era *f.*

**lag** cesso 1; **~gard** cessator *m.*

**lake** lacus, us *m*; stagnum *n.*

**lamb** agnus *m*; (*meal*) agnina *f.*

**lame** claudus; **be ~** claudico 1; **~ness** claudicatio *f.*

**lament** lugeo 2; miseror 1; lamentor 1; **~able** miserandus; **~ation** lamentatio *f*; plangor *m.*

**lamp** lucerna *f.*

**lampoon** versus *m/pl.* probrosi, famosi.

**lamprey** murena *f.*

**lampstand** lychnuchus *m.*

**lance** hasta *f*, lancea *f*; telum *n*; incido 3.

**land** terra *f*, tellus, uris *f*; solum *n*; ager, gri *m*; terrestris; *v/t.* expono 3; *v/i.* egredior 3 (e nave).

**land|ing** egressus, us *m*; **~lady** caupona *f*; **~lord** caupo *m*; **~mark** lapis *m*; **~owner** (agri) possessor *m*; **~slide** lapsus, us *m* terrae; **~tax** vectigal *n.*

**lane** angiportus, us *m.*

**language** lingua *f*; oratio *f*, verba *n/pl.*, sermo *m.*

**langu|id** languidus; **be ~id** langueo 2; **~ish** tabesco 3; **~or** lassitudo *f.*

**lank** strigosus.

**lantern** lanterna *f.*

**lap** gremium *n*; sinus, us *m*; lambo 3.

**lapse** labor 3; error *m*; **~ of time** spatium *n.*

**larceny** furtum *n.*

**lard** adeps *m*; laridum *n*; **~er** carnarium *n.*

**large** magnus, grandis, amplus, ingens; **~ss** donativum *n*; largitio *f.*

**lark** alauda *f.*

**lascivious** libidinosus.

**lash** flagello 1; flagellum *n*; verbera *n/pl.*

**lass** puella *f.*

**lassitude** lassitudo *f.*

**last** ultimus, postremus; extremus; **~ night** proxima nocte; **in the ~ three days** his tribus diebus; **~ but one** proximus a postremo; forma *f*; **at ~** postremo, ad extremum, demum, denique; duro 1; maneo 2; **~ing** diuturnus; **~ly** denique.

**late** serus; **~ at night** sera, multa nocte; **~ in life** provecta iam aetate; **the ~** (de)mortuus (*alqs*), recens (*alqd*); *adv.* sero; **~ly** nuper, modo, recens.

**lath** tignum *n.*

**lathe** tornus *m.*

**lather** spuma *f.*

**Latin** Latinus; **speak ~** Latine loquor 3.

**latitude** libertas *f.*

**latter** posterior; **the ~** hic; **~ly** nuper.

**lattice** cancelli *m/pl.*

**laudable** laudabilis.

**laugh** rideo 2; cachinno 1; **~ at** irrideo 2 (*acc.*); risus, us *m*; **~able** ridiculus; **~ing-stock** ludibrium *n.*

**launch** deduco 3 (*naves*); **~ at** iaculor 1 (*in*); inmitto 3 (*in*).

**laurel** laurus, i *f* (*tree and wreath*); laureus.

**lavish** pro-, ef-fusus; profundo 3; largior 4 (*alqd alci*).

**law** lex *f*; **the ~** ius *n*; **go to ~** litem intendo 3 (*alci*); **propose, enact a ~** fero 3, scisco 3 legem; **~ful** legitimus; **~less** seditiosus; **~lessness** licentia *f.*

**lawn** pratum *n.*

**lawsuit** lis *f.*

**lawyer** iuris consultus *m.*

**lax** dissolutus, remissior, neglegens; **~ness** neglegentia *f.*

**lay** pono 3; loco 1; edo 3 (*ova*); ~ **aside** repono 3; ~ **before** defero 3, propono 3; ~ **down arms** ab armis discedo 3; ~ **hold of** prehendo 3; ~ **plans** consilium capio 3, ineo 4; ~ **siege to** obsideo 2; ~ **upon** impono 3; ~ **waste** vasto 1; cantus, us *m*.

**layer** tabulatum *n*.

**laz|iness** pigritia *f*; ~**y** ignavus, piger.

**lead**[1] plumbum *n*; plumbeus.

**lead**[2] duco 3; ~ **back, out, round** re-, e-, circum-duco 3; ~ **a life** vitam ago 3; ~**er** dux *m*; be ~**er** praesum (*dat.*).

**leading** primus, princeps; ~ **men** principes *m/pl*.

**leaf** folium *n*; (*of book*) scheda *f*, pagina *f*; (*of door*) foris *f*; be in ~ frondesco 3; ~**y** frondosus.

**league** societas *f*; be in ~ conspiro 1, coniuro 1.

**leak** perfluo 3; rima *f*; ~**y** rimosus.

**lean** macer; (in)nitor 3 (*abl.*); incumbo 3 (*in alqd*); ~**ness** macies *f*.

**leap** salio 4; saltus, us *m*.

**learn** disco 3; cognosco 3, certior fio; ~**ed** doctus, eruditus; ~**ing** doctrina *f*, eruditio *f*.

**lease** conduco 3; loco 1; locatio *f*.

**least** minimus; at ~ saltem, certe.

**leather** corium *n*; scorteus.

**leave** relinquo 3, destituo 3 (*acc.*); discedo 3 (*ab, ex*); excedo 3 (*ex loco*); (*at death*) lego 1; ~ **off** desino 3; ~ **out** omitto 3; potestas *f*; ~ **of absence** commeatus, us *m*; **by your** ~ bona tua venia.

**lecherous** salax.

**lecture** schola *f*, acroasis *f*; scholas habeo 2; ~**room** schola *f*.

**ledge** tabula *f*; pluteus *m*; ~**r** codex *m*.

**leech** hirudo *f*.

**leek** porrum *n*.

**lees** faex *f*.

**left** laevus, sinister; ~ **over** reliquus; be ~ **over** resto 1.

**leg** crus, uris *n*.

**legacy** legatum *n*; ~-**hunter** captator *m*.

**legal** legitimus; ex lege.

**legate** legatus *m*; legatio *f*.

**legend** fabula *f*; ~**ary** commenticius.

**legion** legio *f*; ~**ary** legionarius *m*.

**legislate** leges scribo 3.

**legitimate** legitimus; germanus.

**leisure** otium *n*; at ~ otiosus, vacuus; be at ~ vaco 1; ~**ly** lentus.

**lend** mutuum (*alqd*) do 1 (*alci*); commodo 1 (*alqd alci*).

**length** longitudo *f*; diurnitas *f* (*temporis*); at ~ tandem; demum; late, fuse (*loqui*); ~**en** produco 3; ~**wise** in longitudinem.

**lenient** mitis, lenis.

**lentil** lens *f*.

**less** minor; *adv.* minus; **much, still** ~ nedum (*subj.*); ~**ee** conductor *m*; ~**en** minuo 3.

**lesson** *fig.* documentum *n*; **take** ~**s** disco 3; audio 4 (*alqm*).

**lessor** locator *m*.

**lest** ne.

**let** permitto 3; sino 3; loco 1 (*agrum etc.*); ~ **alone** abstineo 2 (*me re*); ~ **down** demitto 3; ~ **loose, go** emitto 3.

**lethargy** veternus *m*.

**letter** littera *f*; epistola *f*, litterae *f/pl.*; ~-**carrier** tabellarius *m*.

**lettuce** lactuca *f*.

**level** planus, aequus; ~ **place** planities *f*; *fig.* gradus, us *m*; **make** ~ **with** exaequo 1 (*alqd alci rei*); sterno 3 (*muros*).

**lever** vectis *m*.

**levity** iocatio *f*.

**levy** delectus, us *m*; delectum habeo 2, scribo 3; impero 1 (*alqd alci*).

**lewd** incestus.

**liable** obnoxius (*dat.*).

**liar** (homo *m*) mendax.

**libation** libamentum *n*; **make** ~ libo 1.

**libel** diffamo 1; libellus *m* (*famosus*).

**liberal** liberalis, benignus; ~**ity** liberalitas *f*.

**liberat|e** solvo 3; libero 1; ~**ion** liberatio *f*.

**liberty** libertas *f*; be at ~ to licet 2 (*dat. c. inf.*).

**library** bibliotheca *f*.

**licen|ce** potestas *f*; venia *f*; licentia *f*; ~**se** potestatem do 1 (*alci*); ~**tious** libidinosus.

**lick** lambo 3, lingo 3.

**lictor** lictor *m*.

**lid** operculum *n*; **eye~** palpebra *f*.

**lie** mentior 4 (*in alqa re*); iaceo 2; cubo 1, recumbo 3; (*of places*) situm esse; **as far as in me** ~**s** quantum in me est; ~ **in wait** insidior 1 (*dat.*); mendacium *n*.

**lieu: in ~ of** loco (*gen.*).
**lieutenant** legatus *m.*
**life** vita *f*; anima *f*; vigor *m*, viriditas *f*; **~(time)** aetas *f*; **in his ~time** vivus (*adj.*); **~less** exanimis; frigidus.
**lift** tollo 3; levo 1; sublevo 1; effero 3.
**ligature** ligamentum *n.*
**light** lux *f*; lumen *n*; **see in a good, unfavourable ~** in mitiorem, deteriorem partem accipio 3 (*alqd*); **set ~ to** accendo 3; illustris; levis; **grow ~** lucesco 3; **make ~** illustro 1; **make ~ of** contemno 3; **~ upon** offendo 3 (*acc.*); **~-armed troops** levis armatura *f*; velites *m/pl.*
**lighten** *v/t.* levo 1; *v/i.* fulguro 1, fulgeo 2.
**light|house** pharus, i *f*; **~ness** levitas *f*; **~ning** fulmen *n.*
**like** similis (*gen.*); par (*dat.*); *adv.* similiter (*ac*); modo, ritu (*gen.*); velut(i); me iuvat 1; amo 1 (*inf.*); mihi libet 2, placet 2; **~ly** veri similis; **it is ~ly** fieri potest (*ut*); **~n** comparo 1; **~ness** similitudo *f*; effigies *f*; **~wise** item.
**liking** animus *m.*
**lily** lilium *n.*
**limb** membrum *n*; articulus *m.*
**lime** calx *f*; **bird-~** viscum *n*; **~ tree** tilia *f.*
**limit** finis *m*; modus *m*; terminus *m*; finio 4; circumscribo 3; **~ed** circumscriptus, certus; **~less** infinitus.
**limp** claudico 1; languidus; **~et** lepas *f.*
**limpid** liquidus.
**line** linea *f*; (*battle*) acies *f*; (*of march*) agmen *n*; (*poetry*) versus, us *m*; **~s** ordines *m/pl.*; **~ up** in ordinem instruo 3, dispono 3.
**line|age** genus *n*; **~ament** lineamentum *n.*
**linen** linteum *n*; linteus, lineus.
**linger** moror 1, cunctor 1; **~ing** tardus.
**link** connecto 3; iungo 3; vinculum *n.*
**lion** leo *m*; **~ess** leaena *f.*
**lip** labrum *n*; *fig.* os *n.*
**liqu|efy** liquefacio 3; **~id** liquidus; liquidum *n*; liquor *m.*
**lisping** blaesus.
**list** tabula *f*; index *m.*
**listen** ausculto 1; audio 4; **~er** auditor *m.*

**listless** languidus.
**litera|lly** ad litteram; **~ture** litterae *f/pl.*
**litigate** litigo 1.
**litter** lectica *f*; fetus, us *m.*
**little** parvus, exiguus; (*time*) brevis; **for a ~ time** paulisper; **a ~** paulum; **too ~** parum.
**live** vivo 3, spiro 1; vitam ago 3; **~ in** habito 1 (*acc.*); **~ on, off** vescor 3 (*abl.*); vivus.
**livel|ihood** victus, us *m*; **~iness** alacritas *f*; **~y** alacer, laetus.
**liver** iecur *n.*
**livid** lividus.
**living** vivus; victus, us *m.*
**lizard** lacerta *f.*
**lo** ecce, en.
**load** onero 1 (*abl.*); *fig.* congero 3 (*alqd in alqm*); onus *n*; **~ed** onustus.
**loaf** panis *m.*
**loam** lutum *n.*
**loan: make a ~** mutuum do 1 (*alqd*); **obtain a ~** mutuor 1 (*alqd*).
**loath** invitus.
**loath|e** odi; fastidio 4; **~ing** fastidium *n*; **~some** foedus, taeter.
**lobby** vestibulum *n.*
**lobster** locusta *f.*
**locality** locus *m.*
**lock** obsero 1; sera *f*; floccus *m*; **~ out** excludo 3; **~ up** concludo 3; **~s** crines *m/pl.*
**locust** locusta *f.*
**lodge** deversor 1, deverto 3 (*in, apud*); maneo 2; **~r** inquilinus *m*; deversor *m.*
**lodging** deversorium *n*, hospitium *n.*
**loft** cenaculum *n*; **~iness** excelsitas *f*; **~y** excelsus, altus, sublimis.
**log** tignum *n*; stipes *m.*
**loggerheads: be at ~** discordo 1 (*ab, inter se*).
**logic** dialectica *f*; **~al** dialecticus; **~ian** dialecticus *m.*
**loin** lumbus *m.*
**loiter** cunctor 1, cesso 1.
**lonel|iness** solitudo *f*; **~y** solus, solitarius.
**long** longus; procerus; (*time*) diuturnus; promissus (*capillus*); *adv.* diu; **~ ago** iam pridem; **~ after, before** multo ante, post; **how ~** quamdiu; **~ to** aveo 2, gestio 4 (*inf.*); **~ for** desidero 1; **~ed-for** exspectatus; **~ing** desiderium *n.*
**look** speciem habeo 2, praebeo 2 (*honesti, ridentis, etc.*); **~ (at)**

aspicio 3; intueor 2 (*alqd*); ~ **after** colo 3; ~ **down (on)** despicio 3 (*acc.*); ~ **for** quaero 3; ~ **forward** exspecto 1; ~ **out!** cave; ~ **round** circumspicio 3; ~ **towards** specto 1; ~ **up (to)** suspicio 3; aspectus, us *m*; obtutus, us *m*; vultus, us *m*; ~**er-on** spectator *m*; ~**ing-glass** speculum *n*.

**loom** tela *f*.

**loop** retinaculum *n*; ~**hole** fenestra *f*; locus *m*.

**loose** laxus, solutus; mobilis; *fig.* dissolutus; **let ~** emitto 3; ~**n** laxo 1; remitto 3; solvo 3; ~**ness** pravitas *f*.

**lop** amputo 1; ~**-sided** inaequalis.

**loquacious** loquax.

**lord** dominus *m*; ~ **it over** dominor 1 (*in*); ~**ly** regius, superbus.

**lore** doctrina *f*.

**lose** amitto 3; perdo 3; ~ **heart** animo deficio 3; ~ **an opportunity** tempori desum; ~ **the day** vincor 3.

**loss** damnum *n*, detrimentum *n*; **be at a ~** haereo 2.

**lot** sors *f*; *fig.* fortuna *f*; **by ~** sorte, sortito; **cast ~s (for)** sortibus utor 3; sortior 4 (*acc.*); **it falls to my ~** mihi contingit 3.

**loud** magnus, clarus.

**lounge** otior 1; desideo 2.

**louse** pediculus *m*; pedis *m*.

**love** amo 1, diligo 3; me iuvat 1, cordi est mihi (*alqd, inf.*); amor *m*; studium *n*; caritas *f*; **fall in ~ with** adamo 1; ~**-affair** amor *m*; ~**liness** venustas *f*; ~**ly** venustus, amabilis; ~**r** amator *m*; amans *m*.

**loving** amans.

**low** humilis, demissus; gravis; summissus; obscurus; sordidus, abiectus; mugio 4; ~**-born** ignobilis; ~**er**

inferior; demitto 3; abicio 3; ~**ering** minax; ~**est** infimus, imus; ~**ing** mugitus, us *m*; ~**lands** loca *n/pl.* campestria; ~**-spirited** demissus.

**loyal** fidelis, fidus; ~**ty** fides *f*.

**lozenge** pastillus *m*.

**lubricate** ungo 3.

**lucid** lucidus, clarus.

**luck** fors *f*, fortuna *f*; **good ~** felicitas *f*; ~**less** infelix; ~**y** felix, fortunatus; faustus.

**lucrative** fructuosus.

**ludicrous** ridiculus.

**luggage** impedimenta *n/pl.*; sarcinae *f/pl.*

**lukewarm** tepidus; frigidus.

**lull** sedo 1; sopio 4; ~**aby** nenia *f*.

**lumber** scruta *n/pl.*

**lumin|ary** lumen *n*; ~**ous** lucidus.

**lump** massa *f*; glaeba *f*; ~**ish** crassus.

**lun|acy** insania *f*; ~**ar** lunaris; ~**atic** insanus.

**lunch** prandium *n*; ~ **(on)** prandeo 2.

**lung** pulmo *m*.

**lurch: leave in the ~** derelinquo 3.

**lure** pellicio 3; esca *f*; illecebrae *f/pl.*

**lurk** lateo 2; latito 1.

**luscious** praedulcis.

**lust** libido *f*; ~**ful** libidinosus.

**lustra|l** lustralis; ~**tion** lustratio *f*.

**lustre** nitor *m*, splendor *m*.

**lusty** validus.

**luxuri|ant** luxuriosus; ~**ous** lautus, delicatus.

**luxury** luxuria *f*, lautitia *f*; luxus, us *m*.

**lying** mendax; ~**-in** puerperium *n*.

**lynx** lynx *m and f*; ~**-eyed** lynceus.

**lyre** lyra *f*, cithara *f*; fides *f/pl.*; ~**-player** citharoedus *m*.

**lyric** lyricus; carmen *n* lyricum.

# M

machin|ations fallaciae *f*/*pl.*, artes *f*/*pl.*; ~e machina *f*; ~ery machinatio *f*.

mackerel scomber, bri *m*.

mad insanus; be ~ furo 3.

madam domina *f*.

mad|den mentem alieno 1 (*alci*); irrito 1; ~man homo *m* furiosus; ~ness insania *f*; furor *m*.

magazine armamentarium *n*.

maggot vermiculus *m*.

magic magicus; magica ars *f*; ~ian magus *m*.

magist|erial imperiosus; ~racy magistratus, us *m*; ~rate magistratus, us *m*.

magnanim|ity magnanimitas *f*; ~ous magnanimus.

magnet lapis *m* magnes.

magnificen|ce magnificentia *f*; ~t splendidus, lautus.

magni|fy amplifico 1; ~tude magnitudo *f*.

magpie pica *f*.

maid virgo *f*, puella *f*; ~enly virginalis, puellaris; ~servant ancilla *f*.

mail squamae *f*/*pl.*; spongia *f*; litterae *f*/*pl.*; tabellarius.

maim mutilo 1; ~ed mancus, truncus.

main praecipuus, primus; ~ point summa *f*; ~ road via *f*; pontus *m*; ~land continens *f*; ~ly plerumque, praecipue.

maintain conservo 1; sustineo 2; contendo 3, affirmo 1 (*alqd, acc. c. inf.*).  [maiestas *f*.]

majest|ic augustus, regius; ~y]

major|-domo dispensator *m*; ~ity plerique *m*/*pl.*; maior pars *f*.

make facio 3; fingo 3; reddo 3 (*mare tutum, alqm iratum*); cogo 3 (*alqm alqd facere*); ~ as if simulo 1 (*acc. c. inf.*); ~ away with tollo 3; ~ for peto 3; ~ good sarcio 4; ~ light of contemno 3; ~ much of magni facio 3; ~ up expleo 2 (*numerum*); ~ up one's mind certum est (*inf.*); ~ war bellum infero 3; ~ way decedo 3 (*alci*); ~r fabricator *m*, creator *m*.

malady morbus *m*.

male mas, virilis.

malediction dirae *f*/*pl.*

malevolen|ce malevolentia *f*; ~t malevolus.

malice malitia *f*.

malign obtrecto 1.

malleable ductilis, lentus.

mallet malleus *m*.

maltreat vexo 1.

man homo *m*; genus *n* humanum, mortales *m*/*pl.*; vir *m*; our men nostri *m*/*pl.*; compleo 2 (*naves*); ~servant servus *m*.

manacle manica *f*.

manage curo 1; administro 1; gero 3; tracto 1; ~able tractabilis; ~ment cura *f*, administratio *f*; ~r (pro)curator *m*; magister, tri *m*.

mane iuba *f*.

manful fortis.

manger praesaepe *n*.

mangle lanio 1.

manhood: reach ~ togam virilem sumo 3; in ~ iuvenis, vir.

mania insania *f*.

manifest manifestus, apertus; declaro 1, ostendo 3.

manifold multiplex, varius.

maniple manipulus *m*.

manipulate tracto 1.

man|kind genus *n* humanum; ~liness fortitudo *f*; ~ly fortis.

manner modus *m*; ratio *f*; mos *m*; ~s mores *m*/*pl.*; ~ed affectatus.

manœuvre decursio *f*.

manor praedium *n*.

mansion domus, us *f*.

manslaughter caedes *f*.

mantle palla *f*.

manual libellus *m*.

manufacture fabrica *f*; fabricor 1.

manumi|ssion manumissio *f*; ~t manumitto 3.

manure stercus *n*.

many multi, plerique; a good ~ complures; how ~ quot.

map tabula *f*; ~ out describo 3.

maple acer, eris *n*.

mar deformo 1, corrumpo 3.

marauding praedatorius.

**marble** marmor *n*; marmoreus.
**March** (mensis) Martius *m*.
**march** iter facio 3; progredior 3; incedo 3; iter, ineris *n*; agmen *n*; **on the ~** in itinere.
**mare** equa *f*.
**margin** margo *f*.
**marigold** caltha *f*.
**mari|ne** marinus; (miles *m*) classicus; **~ner** nauta *m*; **~time** maritimus.
**mark** noto 1, operam do 1 (*dat.*); nota *f*; signum *n*, indicium *n*; **~ out** denoto 1; **~ed** gravis.
**market** forum *n*, macellum *n*; mercatus, us *m*; **~** (**day**) nundinae *f*/*pl.*; nundinor 1; obsono 1.
**marriage** coniugium *n*; matrimonium *n*; nuptiae *f*/*pl.*; **~able** nubilis; **~-contract** pactio *f* nuptialis.
**marrow** medulla *f*.
**marry** (in matrimonium) duco 3 (*alqm uxorem*); nubo 3 (*alci viro*); colloco 1 (in matrimonium)(*filiam*); matrimonio iungor 3.
**marsh** palus, udis *f*; **~y** paluster.
**marshal** instruo 3.
**martial** bellicosus, bellicus.
**marvel** miror 1 (**at** *alqd*); **~lous** mirus.
**masculine** virilis, masculinus.
**mash** farrago *f*; contundo 3.
**mask** persona *f*; *fig.* integumentum *n*; dissimulo 1.
**mason** structor *m*.
**mass** moles *f*; multitudo *f*; vulgus, i *n*; congrego(r) 1.
**massacre** trucido 1; caedes *f*.
**massive** solidus.
**mast** malus *m*; glans *f*.
**master** dominus *m*, erus *m*; magister, tri *m* (*societatis, ludi, navis*); potens (*gen.*); peritus (*in re*); **be ~ of** potior 4 (*abl.*); domo 1; **~ful** imperiosus; **~ly** artificiosus; **~y** potestas *f*, victoria *f*.
**masticate** mando 3.
**mat** teges *f*; storea *f*.
**match** (ex)aequo 1, comparo 1; par sum; certamen *n*; **~less** singularis.
**mate** socius *m*; coeo 4.
**material** corporeus; materia *f*; textile *n*.
**maternal** maternus.
**mathematic|al** mathematicus; **~ian** mathematicus *m*.
**matrimony** matrimonium *n*.
**matron** matrona *f*; **~ly** matronalis.

**matter** corpus *n*; res *f*; materia *f*; **what is the ~?** quid est?; **it ~s** refert 3 (*parvi, magni, etc.*).
**mattress** culcita *f*.
**matur|e** adultus; maturus; maturo 1; **~ity** maturitas *f*.
**maxim** sententia *f*; praeceptum *n*.
**May** (mensis) Maius *m*.
**may** licet 2 (*alci*); possum (*inf.*); **~be** forsitan, fortasse.
**mayor** praefectus *m* urbi(s).
**maze** labyrinthus *m*.
**me** me; **to ~** mihi.
**meadow** pratum *n*.
**meagre** exilis, exiguus.
**meal** prandium *n*; farina *f*; **chief ~** cena *f*.
**mean** humilis; illiberalis; medius; in animo est (*mihi inf.*); significo 1, volo (mihi) (*verba etc.*); dico 3; medium *n*; mediocritas *f*; **~s** modus *m*; **by all ~s** omnino; **by no ~s** haudquaquam, nullo modo; **by ~s of** per (*acc.*); **~ing** significatio *f*; sententia *f*; **~ness** sordes *f*; humilitas *f*; **~while** interea, interim.
**measure** metior 4; mensura *f*; modus *m*; consilium *n*; **in some ~** aliqua ex parte; **take ~s** provideo 2 (*ut, ne*); **~d** moderatus; **~ment** mensura *f*.
**meat** caro, carnis *f*.
**mechani|c** faber, bri *m*; **~sm** machina *f*.
**meddle** me immisceo 2 (*alci rei*).
**mediat|e** me interpono 3; **~or** deprecator *m*; intercessor *m*.
**medic|al** medicinus; **~ate** medico 1; **~ine** medicina *f*; medicamentum *n*, medicamen *n*.
**mediocr|e** mediocris; **~ity** mediocritas *f*.
**meditat|e** volvo 3; cogito 1 (*de*); in animo est mihi (*inf.*); **~ion** cogitatio *f*.
**medium** medius, mediocris; modus *m*.
**medley** farrago *f*.
**meed** praemium *n*.
**meek** mitis, demissus; **~ness** animus *m* demissus.
**meet** aptus, accommodatus (*ad*); obviam fio (*alci*); convenio 4 (*alqm*); incido 3 (*alci*); oppeto 3 (*mortem etc.*); **go to ~** obviam eo 4 (*alci*); **~ together** convenio 4; **~ing** coetus, us *m*; conventus, us *m*; contio *f*.
**melancholy** tristis; tristitia *f*.

**mellow** mitis, maturus, lenis; maturesco 3.

**melod|ious** canorus; **~y** modus m; cantus, us m.

**melon** melopepo m.

**melt** v/t. liquefacio 3; v/i. liquefio, liquesco 3; **~ away** dilabor 3.

**member** membrum n; socius m.

**memor|able** memorabilis; insignis; **~ial** monumentum n; **~y** memoria f; recordatio f.

**menac|e** minor 1 (alci alqd); minae f/pl.; **~ing** minax.

**mend** v/t. sarcio 4; emendo 1; corrigo 3; v/i. melior fio.

**mendacious** mendax.

**mendicant** mendicus.

**menial** sordidus; mediastinus m.

**mention** (com)memoro 1; mentionem facio 3 (gen., de); **not to ~** ne dicam; mentio f.

**mercenary** mercenarius, conductus (miles m).

**merchan|dise** merx f; res f/pl. venales; **~t** mercator m; **~t-ship** navis f oneraria.

**merc|iful** clemens, misericors; **~i-less** durus; **~y** misericordia f, venia f; **show ~y** ignosco 3.

**mere** merus, unus; lacus, us m.

**merge** confundo 3.

**merit** mereo(r) 2; meritum n; virtus utis f; **~ed** meritus.

**merry** hilarus, festivus.

**mesh** macula f; plaga f.

**mess** squalor m.

**mess|age** nuntius m; **~enger** nuntius m; tabellarius m.

**metal** metallum n.

**metamorphose** transformo 1; verto 3.

**metaphor** translatio f; **~ical** translatus.

**meteor** fax f.

**methinks** ut mihi videtur.

**method** ratio f; modus m; **~ically** disposite.

**metonymy** immutatio f.

**metr|e** numerus m; **~ical** metricus.

**metropolis** caput n; urbs f.

**mettle** ferocitas f; **~some** ferox, animosus.

**mews** stabula n/pl.

**mid** medius; **~day** meridies m; meridianus.

**middle** medius; medium n; **~-aged** senior.

**middling** mediocris.

**midge** culex m.

**mid|land** mediterraneus; **~night** media nox f; **~riff** praecordia n/pl.

**midst** medius.

**mid|summer** media aestas f; **~wife** obstetrix f; **~winter** bruma f.

**might** vis f, potestas f; **~y** validus, (prae)potens.

**migrate** migro 1.

**mild** mitis, clemens, facilis; tepidus.

**mildew** robigo f; situs, us m.

**mildness** lenitas f, mansuetudo f.

**mile** mille passuum; **~stone** milliarium n.

**military** militaris, bellicus; militares copiae f; **~ service** militia f.

**militate against** contra facio 3 (alqm).

**milk** mulgeo 2; lac n; **~y** lacteus.

**mill** tero 3; mola f; pistrinum n; **~er** pistor m; **~stone** mola f.

**millet** milium n.

**million** decies centena milia.

**mime** imitor 1; mimus m.

**mince** conseco 1; **not to ~ matters** ut plane aperteque dicam; **~d meat** minutal n.

**mind** curo 1; **~ one's own business** meum negotium ago 3; mens f; animus m; ingenium n; sensus, us m; sententia f; **be out of one's ~** insanio 4; **bear in ~** memini; **call to ~** recordor 1; **change one's ~** sententiam muto 1; **have a ~ to** mihi libet; mihi in animo est; **to my ~** ex mea sententia; **~ful** memor (gen.).

**mine** meus; (ef)fodio 4; mil. cuniculos ago 3; metallum n; cuniculus m; **~r** metallicus m; **~ral** metallum n.

**mingle** (im)misceo 2 (alqd alci rei); confundo 3 (alqd in alqd).

**miniature** minutus.

**minimum** minimus.

**minion** minister, tri m; satelles m.

**minister** praefectus m; **~ to** servio 4 (dat.); prosum (dat.).

**ministry** ministerium n.

**minor** minor; filius m familias; **~ity** minor pars f; aetas f nondum adulta.

**minstrel** vates m.

**mint** cudo 3; moneta f; mentha f.

**minus** sine (abl.).

**minute** minutus, pusillus; subtilis; momentum n (temporis); commentarius m.

**mirac|le** miraculum *n*, prodigium *n*; **~ulous** mirus.
**mire** lutum *n*.
**mirror** specu|um *n*; imaginem reddo 3.
**mirth** hilaritas *f*, laetitia *f*; **~ful** hilarus.
**misadventure** casus, us *m*.
**misanthropic** inhumanus.
**misapply** abutor 3.
**mis|apprehension** error *m*; **~behave** indecore me gero 3.
**miscalculat|e** erro 1; **~ion** error *m*.
**miscarriage** abortus, us *m*.
**miscellan|eous** promiscuus, varius; **~y** farrago *f*.
**mischance** incommodum *n*.
**mischie|f** incommodum *n*; maleficium *n*; pestis *f*; **~vous** improbus, noxius.
**miscon|duct** peccatum *n*; **~strue** male interpretor 1.
**misdeed** delictum *n*.
**miser** homo *m* avarus; **~able** miser; **~y** miseria *f*, angor *m*.
**misfortune** adversa *n/pl.*; incommodum *n*; calamitas *f*.
**misgivings: have ~** diffido 3.
**mis|govern** male administro 1; **~guided** demens; **~hap** incommodum *n*; **~interpret** male interpretor 1; male iudico 1; **~lay** amitto 3; **~lead** decipio 3; **~represent** in deteriorem partem interpretor 1; **~rule** male administro 1.
**miss** aberro 1 (*abl.*); frustra mittor 3 (*telum etc.*); amitto 3 (*occasionem etc.*); desidero 1 (*alqm*); requiro 3 (*alqd*); puella *f*; domina *f*.
**misshapen** deformis, pravus.
**missile** telum *n*, missile *n*.
**missing: be ~** desidero 1; desum.
**mission** legatio *f*; officium *n*.
**mist** nebula *f*; caligo *f*.
**mistake** error *m*; erratum *n*; mendum *n*; **by ~ for** pro (*abl.*); **be ~n** erro 1, fallor 3 (*in re*).
**mistletoe** viscum *n*.
**mistress** era *f*, domina *f*, mater *f* familias; puella *f*, amica *f*.
**mistrust** diffido 3; diffidentia *f*.
**misty** nebulosus.
**misunderstand** haud recte intellego 3; **~ing** error *m*.
**misuse** iniuriose tracto 1.
**mite** teruncius *m*.
**mitigat|e** mitigo 1; levo 1; **~ion** levamentum *n*.

**mix** (ad)misceo 2 (*alqd re*); commisceo 3 (*alqd cum re*); **~ed** promiscuus, varius; **~ture** mixtura *f*.
**moan** gemo 3; gemitus, us *m*.
**moat** fossa *f*.
**mob** turba *f*; multitudo *f*; vulgus, i *n*; circumfundor 3 (*dat.*).
**mobile** mobilis.
**mock** irrideo 2, derideo 2 (*acc.*); illudo 3 (*dat.*); fictus; **~er** derisor *m*; **~ery** irrisio *f*; irrisus, us *m*; ludificatio *f*.
**mode** modus *m*; ratio *f*.
**model** exemplum *n*, exemplar *n*; fingo 3.
**moderat|e** modicus, moderatus, modestus; tempero 1, mitigo 1; moderor 1 (*dat.*); **~ion** modus *m*; moderatio *f*, mediocritas *f*.
**modern** recens, novus.
**modest** modicus; verecundus, demissus; **~y** verecundia *f*; pudor *m*.
**modify** tempero 1; immuto 1; accommodo 1 (*alqd*; **to suit** ad *alqd*).
**modulat|e** flecto 3; **~ion** flexio *f*.
**moist** umidus; **~en** madefacio 3; rigo 1; **~ure** umor *m*.
**molar** molaris *m*.
**mole** talpa *f*; moles *f*; naevus *m*.
**molest** vexo 1, sollicito 1; **~ation** vexatio *f*.
**mollify** mitigo 1.
**moment** punctum *n*, momentum *n* (temporis); **in a ~** statim; **at the ~ when** cum maxime; **of great ~** magni momenti; **~ary** brevis; **~ous** maximi momenti; **~um** impetus, us *m*.
**monarch** rex *m*, princeps *m*; **~ical** regius; **~y** regnum *n*.
**monastery** monasterium *n*.
**money** pecunia *f*; nummi *m/pl.*; nummarius; **~-bag** fiscus *m*; **~-changer** nummularius *m*; **~-lender** faenerator *m*; **~ed** pecuniosus.
**mongrel** hibrida *m and f*.
**monkey** simia *f*.
**monograph** libellus *m*.
**monoton|ous** similis; **~y** similitudo *f*.
**monster, monstrosity** belua *f*; monstrum *n*.
**monstrous** monstruosus, portentosus; nefarius.
**month** mensis *m*; **~ly** menstruus.
**monument** monumentum *n*.

**mood** animus *m*; mens *f*; affectus, us *m* (*mentis etc.*); ~y morosus.

**moon** luna *f*; ~light lunae lumen *n*.

**moor** religo 1, deligo 1; loca *n/pl.* patentia; ~ings retinacula *n/pl.*; statio *f*.

**mop** detergeo 2.

**moral** moralis; probus; ~s mores *m/pl.*; officia *n/pl.*; **the ~ is** significat; ~ity honestas *f*.

**morbid** morbosus, insanus.

**more** plus, magis; ultra (*acc., quam*); amplius; **no ~** non iam, non diutius; ~over praeterea.

**morning** matutinum tempus *n*; **in the ~** mane; matutinus; **good morning!** salve.

**morose** tristis, difficilis.

**morrow** posterus dies *m*; crastinus dies *m*.

**morsel** offa *f*; frustum *n*.

**mortal** mortalis; mortifer, funestus; ~ity mortalitas *f*; mortes *f/pl.*

**mortar** mortarium *n*; calx *f*.

**mortgage** pignus *n*; pignero 1.

**mortif|ication** offensio *f*; indignitas *f*; ~y *v/t.* offendo 3 (*alqm*); *v/i.* putresco 3.

**mosaic** tessellatus (*opus, pavimentum, etc.*).

**mosquito** culex *m*.

**moss** muscus *m*; ~y muscosus.

**most** plurimus; plerique; *adv.* maxime, plurimum; **at the ~** summum; **for the ~ part** plerumque, fere, maximam partem.

**moth** blatta *f*.

**mother** mater *f*; **of a ~** maternus; ~-in-law socrus, us *f*; ~ **tongue** patrius sermo *m*.

**motion** motus, us *m*; agitatio *f*; rogatio *f*; sententia *f*; **adopt a ~ in** sententiam (*alcs*) discedo 3; innuo 3 (*dat.*); ~less immotus.

**motive** causa *f*, ratio *f*.

**motley, mottled** versicolor; varius, maculosus.

**motto** sententia *f*.

**mould** fingo 3; formo 1; forma *f*; robigo *f*; situs, us *m*; ~er putresco 3; ~ering, ~y puter, mucidus.

**moult** pennas exuo 3.

**mound** tumulus *m*; agger, eris *m*.

**mount** scando 3, conscendo 3 (*alqd*); ascendo 3 (*alqd, in alqd*); equum conscendo 3; ~ **guard** in statione sum.

**mountain** mons *m*; ~eer montanus (homo) *m*; ~ous montuosus; ~ **range** iugum *n*.

**mourn** lugeo 2, maereo 2, doleo 2 (*acc.*); ~ful tristis, luctuosus; lugubris; ~ing luctus, us *m*; squalor *m*; sordes *f/pl.*; **be in ~ing** squaleo 2; **go into ~ing** vestitum muto 1.

**mouse** mus *m*; ~-trap muscipula *f*.

**moustache** labri superioris capilli *m/pl.*

**mouth** os *n*; rostrum *n*; ostium *n*; ~ful bucca *f*.

**move** *v/t.* moveo 2; commoveo 2 (*alqm ad*); (re)fero 3 (*legem, rogationem, etc.*); *v/i.* moveor 2, me moveo 2; migro 1; ~ables bona *n/pl.* (mobilia); ~ment motus, us *m*.

**moving** miserabilis, flebilis.

**mow** seco 1, meto 3.

**much** multus; multum *n*; *adv.* multum; multo (*with comparatives*); **as ~ as** tantus ... quantus; **how ~** quantus; **too ~** nimius; nimium *n*; **~ less** nedum.

**mud** lutum *n*, caenum *n*; limus *m*; ~dle confundo 3; perturbo 1; ~dy lutulentus, limosus; turbidus.

**muffle** involvo 3, obvolvo 3.

**mug** poculum *n*; ~gy umidus.

**mulberry** morum *n*; ~-tree morus, i *f*.

**mule** mulus *m*; ~teer mulio *m*.

**mulish** pervicax.

**mullet** mullus *m*.

**multi|ply** *v/t.* multiplico 1, augeo 2; *v/i.* cresco 3; ~tude multitudo *f*; vis *f*; vulgus, i *n*.

**mumble** murmuro 1; musso 1.

**munch** mando 3.

**municipal** municipalis; ~ity municipium *n*.

**munificen|ce** liberalitas *f*; ~t liberalis.

**murder** neco 1; interficio 3; obtrunco 1; caedes *f*, nex *f*; ~er homicida *m*; sicarius *m*; percussor *m*; ~ous cruentus.

**murky** caliginosus, obscurus.

**murmur** murmuro 1; fremo 3 (*acc. c. inf.*); murmur *n*; fremitus, us *m*.

**musc|le** lacertus *m*; nervus *m*; ~ular lacertosus.

**muse** meditor 1, cogito 1; Musa *f*.

**mushroom** fungus *m*; boletus *m*.

**music** musica *f and n/pl.*; cantus, us *m*; modi *m/pl.*; ~al musicus, canorus; musicorum studiosus; ~ian musicus *m.*

**muslin** sindon *f.*

**must** debeo 2 (*inf.*); oportet me (*inf.*); necesse est mihi (*inf., ut*); **I ~ go** eundum est mihi; mustum *n.*

**mustard** sinapi *indecl. n*, sinapis *f.*

**muster** *v/t.* cogo 3; lustro 1; *v/i.* congregor 1; recensio *f.*

**musty** mucidus.

**mutability** inconstantia *f.*

**mute** mutus, tacitus.

**mutilate** mutilo 1, (de)trunco 1.

**mutin|ous** seditiosus, turbulentus; ~y seditio *f;* seditionem facio 3.

**mutter** murmuro 1, musso 1; murmur *n.*

**mutton** ovilla (caro) *f.*

**mutual** mutuus.

**muzzle** os *n;* fiscella *f.*

**my** meus.

**myriad** sescenti.

**myrrh** murra *f.*

**myrtle** myrtus, i *f;* myrteus.

**myself** (me) ipse.

**myster|ious** occultus, arcanus; ~y arcanum *n;* res *f* occulta.

**mystic** mysticus.

**mystification** ambages *f/pl.*

**myth** fabula *f;* ~ical fabulosus.

# N

**nag** caballus *m.*

**nail** unguis *m;* clavus *m;* clavis (con)figo 3 *(dat.).*

**naive** simplex.

**naked** nudus; apertus.

**name** nomen *n,* vocabulum *n;* **family ~, sur~** cognomen *n;* **first ~** praenomen *n;* **good ~** fama *f,* existimatio *f;* **in ~** nomine; **in my ~** meis verbis; **in the ~ of** per *(deos);* nomino 1, appello 1, nuncupo 1; dico 3; **~ly** dico, inquam.

**nap** villus *m;* brevis somnus *m.*

**nape** cervix *f.*

**napkin** mappa *f.*

**narcotic** somnifer.

**nard** nardum *n.*

**narrat|e** (e)narro 1; **~ion, ~ive** narratio *f;* historia *f;* **~or** narrator *m.*

**narrow** angustus, artus; angustior fio; **~ly** diligenter; haud multum abest quin ...; **~ness, ~s** angustiae *f/pl.*

**nasty** foedus, taeter.

**natal** natalis.

**nation** gens *f,* natio *f;* populus *m;* cives *m/pl.;* res *f* publica; **~al** communis; **~al assembly** concilium *n* populi.

**native** indigena *m and f;* **be a ~ of** natus sum; **~ land** patria *f;* **~ language** patrius sermo *m.*

**natural** naturalis; nativus; proprius *(gen.);* **~ parts** ingenium *n;* **~ize** civitatem do 1 *(alci);* **~ly** natura, naturaliter.

**nature** natura *f* (rerum); ingenium *n;* indoles *f;* vis *f.*

**naught** nihil; **set at ~** parvi facio 3, contemno 3; **~y** improbus.

**nause|a** nausea *f;* fastidium *n;* **~ate** fastidium facio 3; **~ating** taeter, foedus.

**nautical** nauticus.

**naval** navalis, maritimus.

**navel** umbilicus *m.*

**naviga|ble** navigabilis; **~te** navigo 1; **~tor** nauta *m,* gubernator *m.*

**navy** classis *f.*

**nay** immo; minime (vero).

**near** prope, ad; iuxta *(acc.);* propin-quus, vicinus; *adv.* prope, iuxta; appropinquo 1 *(ad; dat.);* **be ~ at hand** adsum; advento 1 *(tempus).*

**nearer** propior; *adv.* propius.

**nearest** proximus; *adv.* proxime.

**near|ly** prope, paene; fere, ferme; haud multum afuit quin ...; **~ness** propinquitas *f.*

**neat** mundus, nitidus; **~ness** mun-ditia *f.*

**necess|ary** necessarius; **it is ~ary** necesse est *(inf.);* opus est *(nom.; abl.);* **~aries** necessaria *n/pl.;* **~i-tate** cogo 3 *(inf.);* **~ity** necessitas *f;* egestas *f;* res *f* necessaria; tem-pus *n.*

**neck** cervix *f;* collum *n;* angustiae *f/pl.;* **~lace** monile *n.*

**nectar** nectar *n.*

**need** egeo 2 *(abl.);* requiro 3 *(alqd);* egestas *f,* inopia *f;* **there is ~ of** (mihi) opus est *(nom.; abl.);* **there is no ~** nihil attinet 2 *(inf.);* **~ful** opus; necessarius.

**needle** acus, us *f.*

**need|less** sine causa; **~y** egens.

**nefarious** nefarius.

**negat|ion** negatio *f;* **~ive** negans; **give a ~ive answer** nego 1; inter-cedo 3 *(dat.).*

**neglect** neglego 3, praetermitto 3; desum *(dat.);* incuria *f,* neglegentia *f;* **~ful of** neglegens *(gen.).*

**negligen|ce** neglegentia *f;* **~t** remis-sus.

**negotiat|e** ago 3 *(de re);* **~ion** pactio *f.*

**negro** Aethiops *m.*

**neigh** hinnio 1; hinnitus, us *m.*

**neighbour** vicinus *m; fig.* alter *m;* **~hood** vicinitas *f;* **~ing** vicinus, finitimus, propinquus.

**neither** neuter, neutri; **~ ... nor** neque ... neque, nec ... nec; neve ... neve.

**nephew** fratris *or* sororis filius *m.*

**nerv|e** nervus *m;* **~ous** anxius, tre-pidus; **~ousness** metus, us *m;* anxietas *f.*

**nest** nidus *m;* nidum facio 3.

**net** rete *n;* plaga *f;* plagis capio 3.

**nether** infernus; ~most infimus, imus.

**nettle** urtica f.

**neuter** neuter.

**neutral** medius; neutrius partis; **remain** ~ quiesco 3.

**never** numquam; **and** ~ nec umquam; **nevermore** numquam posthac; ~**theless** nihilominus, (at)tamen, verumtamen.

**new** novus, recens; ~**comer** advena m; ~**ly** nuper, modo, recens; ~**ness** novitas f.

**news** nuntius m; **what** ~? quid novi?; ~ **was brought** nuntiatum est (acc. c. inf.); ~**paper** acta n/pl. diurna.

**newt** lacertus m.

**next** proximus (dat.); insequens; posterus; **on the** ~ **day** postridie; adv. deinceps, proxime; ~ **before** proximus ante; ~ **after, to** secundum (acc.); iuxta (acc.); deinde, postea.

**nib** acumen n.

**nibble** rodo 3; ~ **at** arrodo 3.

**nice** subtilis, exquisitus; elegans; suavis, dulcis; **to a** ~**ty** ad unguem.

**niche** angulus m.

**nick** incido 3; **in the** ~ **of time** in ipso articulo temporis.

**nickname** cognomen n.

**niece** fratris or sororis filia f.

**niggardly** sordidus, parcus.

**night** nox f; **all** ~ pernox; **at** ~**fall** sub noctem; **by** ~ noctu, de nocte; nocturnus; ~**ingale** luscinia f; ~-**watch** vigiliae f/pl., excubiae f/pl.

**nimble** pernix.

**nine** novem; ~ **hundred** nongenti; ~ **times** novies; ~**teen** undeviginti; ~**teenth** undevicesimus; ~**tieth** nonagesimus; ~**ty** nonaginta; **ninth** nonus.

**nip** mordeo 2; vellico 1; uro 3; ~**pers** forceps f.

**nipple** papilla f.

**nitre** nitrum n.

**no** nullus; immo; minime (vero); ~ **one** nemo; **and** ~ **one** nec quisquam; ~ **more than** nihilo magis quam; ~ **news** nihil novi; ~ **sooner** ... **than** ubi primum.

**nob|ility** nobilitas f; nobiles m/pl.; generosus animus m; ~**le** nobilis, generosus, excelsus; praeclarus; ~**leman** vir m nobilis.

**nobody** nemo.

**nocturnal** nocturnus.

**nod** nuto 1; nutus, us m; ~ **(assent) to** annuo 3 (alci; alqd alci); ~**ding** nutans.

**nois|e** sonitus, us m; strepitus, us m; crepitus, us m; ~**e abroad** effero 3; ~**eless** tacitus, silens; ~**ome** taeter, foedus; ~**y** clamosus, tumultuosus, argutus.

**nomadic** vagus.

**nominally** nomine; verbo; specie (gen.).

**nominat|e** nomino 1, dico 3; ~**ion** nominatio f.

**none** nemo; nullus; ~ **the less** nihilominus.

**nones** nonae f/pl.

**nonsens|e** nugae f/pl., ineptiae f/pl.; ~**ical** absurdus, ineptus.

**nook** angulus m.

**noon** meridies m; ~**day** meridianus.

**noose** laqueus m.

**nor** neque, nec; neu.

**normal** solitus.

**north** septentrio m; septentriones m/pl.; septentrionalis; ~-**east** inter septentriones et orientem; ~-**east wind** aquilo m; ~-**west** inter septentriones et occasum solis; ~-**west wind** caurus m; ~-**wind** aquilo m.

**nose** nasus m; nares f/pl.; ~**gay** fasciculus m (florum).

**nostril** naris f.

**not** non; haud; minus; **and** ~ neque, nec; ~ **even** ne ... quidem; ~ **that** ... **but** non quod ... sed; ~ **yet** nondum.

**nota|ble** memorabilis; ~**ry** scriba m; ~**tion** notatio f.

**notch** incisura f.

**note** nota f; codicilli m/pl.; vox f; ~**s** commentarius m; noto 1; animadverto 3, intellego 3; ~**book** pugillares m/pl.; ~**d** insignis; ~**worthy** memorabilis.

**nothing** nihil; nihilum n.

**notice** animadverto 3; proscriptio f; titulus m; **attract** ~ conspicior 3; **escape** ~ fallo 3 (alqm; acc. c. inf.); lateo 2; **give** ~ denuntio 1, praenuntio 1; ~**able** notabilis.

**notif|ication** denuntiatio f; ~**y** denuntio 1.

**notion** notio f, suspicio f.

**notor|iety** infamia f; ~**ious** notus, infamis, famosus.

**notwithstanding** nihilominus, attamen.

**noun** nomen *n*.
**nourish** nutrio 4; alo 3; ~ment alimentum *n*; cibus *m*.
**novel** novus; ~ty novitas *f*, insolentia *f*.
**November** (mensis) November, bris *m*.
**novice** tiro *m*.
**now** nunc, iam, hodie; ~ ... ~ modo ... modo; ~ **(for a long time)** iam diu, iam pridem; *particle* quidem, nunc; ~adays nunc; hodie; ~ **and then** aliquando.
**no|where** nusquam; ~wise haudquaquam.
**noxious** nocens.
**nude** nudus.
**nudge** fodico 1.
**nuisance: be a ~** molestum est.

**null** irritus; ~ify infirmo 1; irritum facio 3.
**numb** torpens; **be ~** torpeo 2.
**number** numerus *m*; **a ~** pars *f*; **a considerable ~** aliquot; **large ~s, a large ~** multi *m/pl.*, complures *m/pl.*; multitudo *f*, copia *f*; **what, such a ~** quot?, tot; (e)numero 1; ~less innumerabilis.
**numbness** torpor *m*.
**numerous** multi, plurimi, plures.
**nuptial** nuptialis; ~s nuptiae *f/pl*.
**nurse** nutrix *f*; *fig.* altrix *f*; nutrio 4, alo 3; assideo 2 (*aegrotanti*); ~ry (*for plants*) seminarium *n*.
**nurture** educatio *f*.
**nut** nux *f*.
**nutri|ment, ~tion** alimentum *n*; cibus *m*; ~tious alibilis.

# O

**O, oh!** o.

**oak** quercus, us *f*; ilex *f*; aesculus, i *f*; quern(e)us; aesculeus; **~wood** robur *n*.

**oar** remus *m*; **~blade** palma *f*; **~s-man** remex *m*.

**oat** avena *f*; avenaceus.

**oath** ius *n* iurandum; **military ~** sacramentum *n*; **swear an ~ to** iuro 1 in verba (*alcs*); **tender, take an ~** ius iurandum defero 3 (*alci*), accipio 3.

**obdurate** obstinatus, durus.

**obedien|ce** oboedientia *f*; **~t** oboediens (*dat*.); dicto audiens (*alci*).

**obese** obesus.

**obey** pareo 2, oboedio 4, obtempero 1 (*dat*.).

**object| (to)** improbo 1, gravor 1 (*acc*.); repugno 1 (*dat*.); recuso 1 (*alqd, ne; after neg.: quin, quominus*); res *f*; consilium *n*; finis *m*; **I have no ~ion** per me licet (*inf., subj.*); **~ionable** ingratus; **~ive** externus.

**obligat|ion** officium *n*; **be under an ~ion** obnoxius, obligatus sum (*alci*); **lay under an ~ion** obligo 1, obstringo 3; **~ory** necessarius.

**oblig|e** cogo 3; gratificor 1 (*alci*); beneficium confero 3 (*in alqm*); gratum facio 3 (*alci*); **~ing** comis, facilis.

**oblique** obliquus.

**obliterate** deleo 2; oblittero 1.

**oblivi|on** oblivio *f*; **~ous** immemor, ignarus (*gen*.).

**obloquy** vituperatio *f*.          [cens.]

**obnoxious** ingratus, invisus; no-]

**obscen|e** obscenus, turpis; **~ity** obscenitas *f*.

**obscur|e** obscurus, reconditus; ignobilis; obscuro 1; **~ity** obscuritas *f*; tenebrae *f/pl*.

**obsequies** exsequiae *f/pl*.

**obsequious** obsequens, ambitiosus.

**observ|ance** conservatio *f*; mos *m*; **~ation** observatio *f*, contemplatio *f*; sententia *f*; **~e** observo 1, contemplor 1; dico 3; conservo 1.

**obsolete** obsoletus; **become ~** obsolesco 3.

**obstacle** impedimentum *n*.

**obstina|cy** pertinacia *f*, pervicacia *f*; **~te** pertinax, pervicax, obstinatus.

**obstruct** *v/t*. obstruo 3 (*dat*.); *v/i*. obsto 1 (*dat*.); **~ion** impedimentum *n*.

**obtain** adipiscor 3, consequor 3; nanciscor 3; obtineo 2; impetro 1.

**obtru|de** inculco 1 (*alqd, se, alci*); ingero 3 (*alqd alci*); **~sive** molestus.

**obtuse** hebes, obtusus.

**obviate** occurro 3 (*dat*.).

**obvious** apertus, manifestus.

**occasion** occasio *f*; tempus *n*; causa *f*; efficio 3; **~ally** per occasionem, aliquando.

**occult** arcanus.

**occup|ation** occupatio *f*, possessio *f*; negotium *n*; quaestus, us *m*; **~y** occupo 1; obsideo 2; obsido 3; teneo 2; **be ~ied with** versor 1 (*in re*); totum sum in (*re*).

**occur** accido 3, contingo 3; evenio 4; in mentem venio 4, occurro 3 (*dat*.); **~rence** res *f*.

**ocean** oceanus *m*.

**October** (mensis) October, bris *m*.

**odd** impar; insolitus, mirus; ridiculus; subsicivus (*tempus etc*.); **be at ~s with** dissideo 2 (*ab; inter se*).

**ode** carmen *n*.

**odi|ous** invisus, odiosus; **~um** invidia *f*.

**odour** odor *m*; **be in bad ~ with** invidiam suscipio 3 (*apud alqm*).

**of** de (*abl*.), ex (*abl*.); **each ~ you** uterque vestrum; **one ~ you** unus ex vobis.

**off: (the coast of)** prope, propter (*acc*.); **be well ~ for** abundo 1 (*abl*.); **far ~** longe (*ab*); **make ~** me conicio 3 (*in*); **some way ~** procul (*ab*).

**offal** quisquiliae *f/pl*.

**offen|ce** delictum *n*, peccatum *n*; offensio *f*; **~d** offendo 3 (*acc*.); laedo 3; pecco 1; **~d against** violo 1 (*ius etc*.); **~sive** odiosus, molestus; putidus; **take the ~sive** bellum, signa infero 3 (*in*).

**offer** offero 3, defero 3; porrigo 3;

adhibeo 2 (*preces etc.*); macto 1 (*hostia*); condicio *f*; ~ing donum *n*.

office officium *n*, munus *n*; magistratus, us *m*; ministerium *n*; hold ~ magistratum obtineo 2; ~r praefectus *m*.

official publicus, civilis; minister, tri *m*; lictor *m*.

officious molestus.

offset compenso 1 (*alqd alqua re, cum alqua re*).

offspring progenies *f*; liberi *m/pl.*

often saepe, saepenumero; as ~ as quotiescumque; how ~ quoties; so ~ toties.

ogre larva *f*.

oil oleum *n*; of ~ olearius.

ointment unguentum *n*; eye ~ collyrium *n*.

old vetus, antiquus, vetustus; senex, senior; four years ~ quattuor annos natus; ~ age senectus, utis *f*; ~er maior natu; ~-fashioned priscus, pristinus; obsoletus; ~ man senex *m*; ~ woman anus, us *f*.

olive (tree) olea *f*, oliva *f*; ~-oil oleum *n*.

omen omen *n*; auspicium *n*; obtain good ~s lito 1.

ominous infaustus, infelix.

omission praetermissio *f*.

omit praetermitto 3, omitto 3; praetereo 4; relinquo 3.

on in (*abl.*); super (*acc.*); ~ all sides undique; ~ foot pedibus; ~ the right a dextra parte; ~ the subject of de (*abl.*); *adv.* porro.

once semel; at ~ simul, uno tempore; ilico, statim; ~ (upon a time) olim, quondam.

one unus; ~ and all cuncti; ~ and the same idem; ~ another inter se; ~ by ~ singuli; singillatim; ~ day olim, aliquando; ~ of unus ex, quidam ex (*abl.*); ~ or two unus vel alter; ~ ... ~ alius ... alius; ~ who is qui; ~-eyed luscus; ~-sided inaequalis, iniquus.

onerous gravis.

onion caepa *f*, caepe *n*.

only unus, solus, unicus; *adv.* solum, modo, tantum.

onset, onslaught impetus, us *m*; incursus, us *m*.

onward porro.

ooze mano 1.

opaque caecus.

open apertus, patens; manifestus; simplex; patefacio 3; aperio 4; pando 3; *fig.* exordior 4 (*orationem*); be, lie ~ pateo 2; in the ~ air sub divo; ~ing exordium *n* (*orationis*); foramen *n*; os *n*; *fig.* ansa *f*, opportunitas *f*; ~ly palam, aperte.

operat|e ago 3, facio 3; *med.* seco 1; ~e upon moveo 2; ~ion res *f*; actio *f*; ~ive efficax.

opin|e opinor 1; ~ion opinio *f*, sententia *f*; good ~ion existimatio *f*; give an ~ion on censeo 2 (*de*).

opponent adversarius *m*.

opportun|e opportunus, idoneus, tempestivus; ~ity occasio *f*, opportunitas *f*; tempus *n*.

oppose *v/t.* oppono 3 (*alqd alci, alci rei*); *v/i.* adversor 1, repugno 1, obsto 1 (*dat.*).

opposit|e adversus, contrarius, diversus; ~e to contra (*acc.*); e regione (*gen.*); adversus (*acc.*); ~ion repugnantia *f*; adversarii *m/pl.*

oppress premo 3; affligo 3; vexo 1; ~ion vexatio *f*; iniuriae *f/pl.*; ~ive iniquus, gravis, acerbus.

opprobrious turpis.

option optio *f* (eligendi).

opulen|ce divitiae *f/pl.*; ~t locuples, dives.

or aut; either ... ~ aut ... aut; vel ... vel; whether ... ~ sive ... sive, seu ... seu; *interrog.* utrum ... an; ~ not annon (*direct*); necne (*indirect*).

oracle oraculum *n*; responsum *n*.

orally voce, verbis.

orange(-coloured) luteus.

orat|ion oratio *f*; contio *f*; ~or orator *m*; ~orical oratorius; ~ory rhetorica *f*; eloquentia *f*; facundia *f*.

orb orbis *m*; ~it orbis *m*; ambitus, us *m*.

orchard pomarium *n*.

orchestra symphoniaci pueri *m/pl.*, servi *m/pl.*

ordain sancio 4; statuo 3; decerno 3.

ordeal discrimen *n*.

order dispono 3; iubeo 2 (*acc. c. inf.*); impero 1 (*alci ut*); edico 3 (*ut*); ordo *m*, descriptio *f*; iussum *n*, mandatum *n*; imperium *n*, imperatum *n*; ~ of battle acies *f*; the equestrian ~ equester ordo *m*; the lower ~s vulgus, i *n*; by, without ~ of iussu, iniussu (*gen.*);

**money** ~ perscriptio f; **in good** ~ ordine, in ordinem, ex ordine; **~ly** compositus; modestus.
**ordinance** edictum n.
**ordinary** usitatus, cottidianus, vulgaris; mediocris.
**ore** metallum n.
**organ** pars f; membrum n; organum n; **~isation** descriptio f, temperatio f; **~ise** dispono 3, compono 3; tempero 1; **~ism** animal n; animans n.
**orgies** orgia n/pl.; fig. comissatio f.
**orient** oriens m.
**orifice** os n.
**origin** origo f; principium n; primordia n/pl.; genus n; **~al** pristinus; principalis; singularis; exemplar n, exemplum n; **~ate** v/t. instituo 3; v/i. orior 4 (ex, ab); principium, initium duco 3 (ab); nascor 3 (ex); **~ator** auctor m.
**ornament** ornamentum n; ornatus, us m; fig. decus n; lumen n.
**ornate** pictus.
**orphan** orbus.
**oscillat|e** agitor 1, iactor 1; **~ion** agitatio f.
**osier** vimen n; vimeneus.
**ostensibly** per speciem.
**ostentat|ion** ostentatio f; **~ious** gloriosus.
**ostler** agaso m.
**ostrich** struthiocamelus m.
**other** alius, (than atque); **the** ~ (of two) alter; **the ~s** ceteri m/pl., reliqui m/pl.; **of ~s** alienus; **~wise** aliter, secus; alioquin, sin aliter.
**otter** lutra f.
**ought** debeo 2 (inf.); oportet (acc. c. inf.).
**ounce** uncia f.
**our** noster; **~selves** (nos) ipsi.
**oust** eicio 3.
**out** foris (esse, cenare, etc.); foras (ire); ~ **of** e, ex (abl.); **(one)** ~ **of, (made)** ~ **of** de (abl.); ~ **of fear** per, propter metum; **~break** impetus, us m; **~cast** extorris; **~cry** clamor m; acclamatio f; **~do** supero 1; vinco 3; **~doors** foris, foras.
**outer** exterior; **~most** extremus.
**out|fit** apparatus, us m; **~house** tugurium n; **~landish** barbarus; **~law** proscribo 3; proscriptus m; latro m; **~lay** impensa f; **~let** exitus, us m; emissarium n; **~line** lineamenta n/pl.; **~live** supersum; **~look** prospectus, us m; **~number**

superiores esse (numero); **~post** statio f.
**outrage** vexo 1; violo 1; iniuria afficio 3; vexatio f; iniuria f; facinus n; **~ous** indignus, turpis.
**out|right** plane, prorsus; **~set** principium n; **~side** extra (acc.), adv. extrinsecus, foris; externus; species f; **~skirts** suburbanus; be **~spoken** aperte loquor 3; **~standing** reliquus; praestans; **~strip** supero 1; **~ward** externus; **~wardly** specie; **~weigh** praepondero 1; antiquius sum (alqd alci); **~wit** decipio 3; **~work** munitio f.
**oven** furnus m; fornax f.
**over** super (acc. and abl.); supra (acc.); trans (flumen, etc.); plus (numbers); per (Alpes, etc.); ~ **and above** praeter (acc.); ~ **and** ~ **(again)** saepenumero, identidem; be ~ praesum (dat.); **it is all** ~ **with** actum est de (alqo); **place, appoint** ~ praeficio 3 (alqm alci rei).
**over|awe** deterreo 2; **~bearing** insolens; **~burden** praegravo 1; **~cast** obscuratus, obductus; **~coat (cloak)** lacerna f; **~come** vinco 3; supero 1; **~flow** me effundo 3; redundo 1; **~grow** obsitus (abl.); **~hang** immineo 2 (dat.); **~head** insuper; **~hear** excipio 3; **~lay** induco 3 (alqd re); **~look** prospicio 3; conniveo 2; ignosco 3 (alci alqd); **~much** nimis; nimium; **~power** opprimo 3; **~reach** circumvenio 4; **~run** percurro 3 (alqd); potior 4 (abl.); **~seer** curator m; **~shadow** obscuro 1, obumbro 1; **~take** consequor 3 (alqm); fig. deprehendo 3, opprimo 3; **~throw** everto 3, prosterno 3; ruina f.
**overtly** aperte.
**overtures: make** ~ **of peace** condicionem fero 3; **make** ~ **to** sollicito 1 (alqm).
**over|turn** everto 3; **~whelm** obruo 3, opprimo 3.
**owe** debeo 2 (alqd alci).
**owl** bubo m, noctua f.
**owing to** propter (acc.); **be** ~ stat 1 (per alqm quominus).
**own** meus, tuus, suus, etc.; meus ipsius; (meus) proprius; possideo 2, teneo 2, habeo 2; ~ **that** confiteor 2 (acc. c. inf.); **~er** dominus m.
**ox** bos m.
**oyster** ostrea f.

# P

**pace** passus, us *m*; gradus, us *m*; spatior 1; incedo 3.
**pacify** paco 1, sedo 1.
**pack** colligo 3 (*sarcinas etc.*); stipo 1; sarcina *f*; grex *m*, turba *f*; ~et fasciculus *m*; ~horse iumentum *n*.
**pact** pactio *f*; pactum *n*.
**pad** farcio 4; ~ding tomentum *n*.
**paddle** remus *m*; remigo 1.
**paddock** saeptum *n*.
**page** pagina *f*; puer, eri *m*.
**pageant** spectaculum *n*.
**pail** hama *f*.
**pain** dolor *m*; **mental ~** aegritudo *f*; **be in ~** doleo 2; *v/t.* dolore afficio 3 (*alqm*); ~ful acerbus; ~s opera *f*; **take ~s** operam do 1 (*ut, ne*); elaboro 1 (*in alqa re; ut*); ~staking operosus, industrius.
**paint** pingo 3; fuco 1; pigmentum *n*; ~brush penicillus *m*; ~er pictor *m*; ~ing tabula *f*; **art of ~ing** pictura *f*.
**pair** par *n*; bini, ae, a; iungo 3; compono 3 (*combatants etc.*).
**palace** regia *f*.
**palat|able** iucundus; ~e palatum *n*.
**pale** pallidus, albus; palus *m*; obscuror 1; **grow, be ~** palleo 2.
**palisade** vallum *n*.
**pall** pallium *n*; satietatem pario 3.
**pallet** grabatus *m*.
**palliate** lenio 4; extenuo 1.
**pallor** pallor *m*.
**palm** palma *f*; ~ **off upon** suppono 3 (*alqd alci*).
**palpable** manifestus.
**palpitate** salio 4; palpito 1.
**palsy** paralysis *f*.
**paltry** vilis, exiguus.
**pamper** indulgeo 2 (*dat.*); foveo 2 (*acc.*).
**pamphlet** libellus *m*.
**pan** patina *f*, patella *f*; **frying-~** sartago *f*.
**pander** leno *m*.
**panegyric** laudatio *f*.
**panel** tabula *f*; ~**led** laqueatus; ~**led ceiling** lacunar *n*.
**pang** dolor *m*.

**panic** pavor *m*; ~**stricken** pavidus, exterritus.
**pannier** clitellae *f/pl.*
**pansy** viola *f*.
**pant** anhelo 1; ~**ing** anhelitus, us *m*.
**panther** panthera *f*.
**pantry** cella *f* (penaria).
**pap** puls *f*.
**paper** charta *f*; papyrus, i *f*; libellus *m*.
**papyrus** papyrus, i *f*.
**parade** pompa *f*; *mil.* decursus, us *m*; ostento 1; *mil.* decurro 3.
**paragon** specimen *n*.
**paralys|e** debilito 1; *fig.* percello 3; ~**is** paralysis *f*.
**paramount** summus; antiquissimus.
**paramour** adulter *m*; meretrix *f*.
**parapet** pluteus *m*.
**paraphernalia** apparatus, us *m*.
**paraphrase** interpretor 1.
**parasite** parasitus *m*.
**parasol** umbraculum *n*.
**parcel** fasciculus *m*; ~ **out** partior 4.
**parch** torreo 2; uro 3; ~**ed** torridus, aridus.
**parchment** membrana *f*.
**pardon** ignosco 3 (*alci alqd*); veniam do 1 (*alci*); venia *f*, excusatio *f*.
**pare** reseco 1; circumcido 3.
**parent** parens *m and f*; genitor *m*, genetrix *f*; ~**age** genus *n*; stirps *f*; ~**al** patrius.
**park** horti *m/pl.*; vivarium *n*.
**parlance** sermo *m*.
**parley** colloquor 3; colloquium *n*.
**parliament** concilium *n*; senatus, us *m*.
**parlour** conclave *n*.
**parody** per iocum imitor 1.
**parole** fides *f*.
**parricide** parricida *m*; parricidium *n*.
**parrot** psittacus *m*.
**parry** eludo 3; propulso 3.
**parsimon|ious** parcus; ~**y** parsimonia *f*; sordes *f/pl.*
**part** pars *f*; *thea.* partes *f/pl.*; persona *f*; ~**s** loca *n/pl.*; **in, to, foreign ~s** peregre; **for my ~** equidem;

**for the most** ~ plerumque; **in great** ~ magna ex parte; **do one's** ~ officium servo 1; **play a** ~ partes ago 3; **take** ~ **in good, bad,** ~ **in** bonam, malam, partem accipio 3 (*alqd*); **take** ~ **in** intersum 2 (*dat.*); me immisceo 2 (*dat.*); attingo 3 (*alqd*); **have no** ~ **in** expertem sum (*gen.*); **it is my** ~ meum est; **it is the** ~ **of a king** regis est; *v/t.* seiungo 3; separo 1; divido 3; *v/i.* ~ **from** discedo 3, digredior 3 (*ab*).

**partake** particeps sum (*gen.*); intersum (*dat.*).

**partial** cupidus; iniquus; ~ity studium *n*; ~ly ex aliqua parte.

**particip|ant** particeps; ~ate particeps sum.

**particle** particula *f*.

**particular** proprius; praecipuus; subtilis; ~ly praecipue, praesertim.

**parting** digressus, us *m*.

**partisan** fautor *m*; **be a** ~ **of** studiosus sum (*gen.*).

**partition** partitio *f*; paries *m*.

**partly** partim; (aliqua) ex parte.

**partner** socius *m*; consors; ~ship societas *f*.

**partridge** perdix *f*.

**party** pars *f*, factio *f*; convivium *n*; ~ **to** affinis (*dat.*).

**pass** *v/t.* ago 3, dego 3 (*tempus*); trado 3 (*alci alqd*); perfero 3 (*legem*); *v/i.* intercedo 3; transeo 4 (*dies, etc.*); pervenio 4 (*hereditas, etc.*); ~ **away** intereo 4; ~ **by** praetereo 4, praetervehor 3 (*acc.*); ~ **on** *v/t.* trado 3; *v/i.* pergo 3; ~ **over** transeo 4 (*alqd; ad*); praetermitto 3; **come to** ~ fio, evenio 4; angustiae *f/pl.*, fauces *f/pl.*; discrimen *n*.

**passable** tolerabilis.

**passage** transitus, us *m*; via *f*; iter, ineris *n*; transitio *f*; (*of book*) locus *m*.

**passenger** vector *m*.

**passer-by** qui praeterit.

**passion** (*animi*) motus *m/pl.*; cupiditas *f*; libido *f*; ira *f*; iracundia *f*; studium *n*; ~ate ardens, vehemens; iracundus.

**passive** iners, lentus.

**password** tessera *f*.

**past** praeteritus; praeterita *n/pl.*; praeteritum tempus *n*; *prep.* praeter, ultra (*acc.*).

**paste** gluten *n*.

**pastille** pastillus *m*.

**pastime** ludus *m*.

**pastoral** pastoralis.

**pastry** crustum *n*; ~-**cook** pistor *m*; crustularius *m*.

**pastur|age** pabulum *n*; pastus, us *m*; ~e pascuum *n*; pasco 3.

**pat** permulceo 2; palpo 1.

**patch** sarcio 4; pannus *m*; ~work cento *m*.

**patent** apertus, manifestus; diploma *n*, privilegium *n*.

**paternal** paternus, patrius.

**path** semita *f*; trames *m*; via *f*; iter, ineris *n*.

**pathetic** miser, miserabilis.

**pathless** invius.

**patien|ce** patientia *f*; **with** ~ce aequo animo; ~t patiens; aeger *m*, aegrotus *m*.

**patrician** patricius.

**patriot** bonus, optimus civis *m*; ~ic amans patriae.

**patrol** custodiae *f/pl.*, vigiliae *f/pl.*

**patron** patronus *m*; praeses *m*; ~age patrocinium *n*; clientela *f*; ~ize faveo 2 (*dat.*).

**pattern** exemplar *n*, exemplum *n* specimen *n*; signum *n*.

**paucity** paucitas *f*.

**paunch** venter, tris *m*.

**pauper** inops.

**pause** subsisto 3; intermitto 3; intermissio *f*.

**pave** munio 4; ~ment pavimentum *n*.

**pavilion** tabernaculum *n*.

**paw** pes *m*; pulso 1.

**pawn** (op)pignero 1; pignus *n*.

**pay** solvo 3; pendo 3 (*pecuniam pro*); ~ **down, out** numero 1; ~ **off** exsolvo 3 (*aes alienum, etc.*); ~ **penalty** poenas do 1; ~ **respects** saluto 1 (*alqm*); merces *f*; **soldier's** ~ stipendium *n*; ~master tribunus *m* aerarius; ~ment solutio *f*.

**pea** pisum *n*.

**peace** pax *f*; otium *n*; ~ **of mind** securitas *f*; ~able tranquillus; ~ful pacatus, placidus.

**peach** Persicum *n*.

**peacock** pavo *m*.

**peak** cacumen *n*; vertex *m*.

**peal** sono 1; fragor *m*.

**pear** pirum *n*; ~-**tree** pirus, i *f*.

**pearl** margarita *f*.

**peasant** rusticus, agrestis.

**pebble** calculus *m*.

**peck** vellico 1; modius *m.*

**peculation** peculatus, us *m.*

**peculiar** proprius; singularis; **~ity** proprium *n*; proprietas *f.*

**pedant** scholasticus *m*; **~ry** molestia *f.*

**peddle** vendito 1.

**pedestal** basis *f.*

**pedestrian** pedester.

**pedigree** stemma *n.*

**pediment** fastigium *n.*

**peel** cutis *f*; membrana *f*; reseco 1.

**peep** strictim aspicio 3 (**at** *alqd*).

**peer** rimor 1 (**at** *alqd*); par; **~less** unicus.

**peevish** stomachosus, morosus.

**peg** clavus *m.*

**pell-mell** passim.

**pelt** iacio 3 (*alqd in alqm*); peto 3 (*alqm telis, etc.*).

**pen** calamus *m*; (*for animals*) saepta *n/pl.*; scribo 3; includo 3.

**penalty** poena *f*; supplicium *n*, damnum *n*; **pay, exact the ~** poenas do 1, sumo 3.

**pencil** penicillus *m.*

**pending** dum.

**penetrat|e** pervado 3 (*ad, per*); penetro 1, pervenio 4 (*in, ad*); **~ion** sagacitas *f.*

**peninsula** paeninsula *f.*

**penitent: be ~** paenitet (*me alcs rei, quod, inf.*).

**pennant** vexillum *n.*

**penniless** inops.

**penny** as *m* (*a copper coin*).

**pension** annua *n/pl.*

**penthouse** vinea *f.*

**penur|ious** inops; **~y** egestas *f.*

**people** homines *m/pl.*; populus *m*; **common ~** plebs *f*; vulgus, i *n*; incolo 3; frequento 1; **of the ~** publicus.

**pepper** piper *n.*

**perceive** percipio 3; sentio 4; intellego 3.

**perch** insido 3 (*dat.*); sedile *n* (*avium*).

**perchance** forte.

**percussion** ictus, us *m.*

**perdition** exitium *n.*

**peremptorily** praecise.

**perfect** perfectus; integer; merus; perficio 3; **~ion** perfectio *f*, absolutio *f*; **~ly** plane, prorsus.

**perfid|ious** perfidus; **~y** perfidia *f.*

**perforate** perforo 1.

**perforce** per vim; invitus.

**perform** persequor 3; exsequor 3; fungor 3 (*abl.*); praesto 1 (*munus, fidem, etc.*); *thea.* ago 3; **~ance** functio *f.*

**perfume** odor *m*; unguentum *n*; **~d** odoratus.

**perhaps** fortasse; forsan, forsitan; forte; nescio an; haud scio an.

**peril** periculum *n*, discrimen *n*; **~ous** periculosus.

**period** tempus *n*; aetas *f*; spatium *n* temporis.

**perish** pereo 4, intereo 4; **~able** caducus.

**peristyle** peristylum *n.*

**perjur|ed** periurus; **~y** periurium *n*; **commit ~y** peiero 1.

**permanen|ce** stabilitas *f*; **~t** diuturnus, mansurus; **~tly** perpetuo.

**permeate** permano 1 (*in*).

**permission** potestas *f*; **with your ~** bona tua venia; **without the ~ of** iniussu (*alcs*); invito (*algo*); **give ~** potestatem facio 3 (*alci faciendi*); **have ~** licet (*per alqm*).

**permit** permitto 3 (*alci ut*); sino 3 (*inf.*; *acc. c. inf.*); **it is ~ted** licet (*alci inf.*; *acc. c. inf.*).

**pernicious** perniciosus.

**peroration** peroratio *f.*

**perpendicular** (di)rectus.

**perpetrate** committo 3; admitto 3 (*facinus; facinus in me*).

**perpetua|l** perennis, sempiternus, perpetuus; **~te** perpetuo 1.

**perplex** distraho 3; sollicito 1; **be ~ed** haereo 2; **~ity** dubitatio *f.*

**persecut|e** insector 1; **~ion** insectatio *f*; **~or** insectator *m.*

**persever|ance** perseverantia *f*; **~e** persevero 1, persto 1 (*in re*); **~ing** pertinax.

**persist** persto 1, persevero 1 (*in re*); permaneo 2; **~ent** pertinax.

**person** homo *m*; caput *n*; persona *f*; **in ~** ipse; **~age** persona *f*; **~al** privatus; proprius; **~al appearance** habitus, us *m*; **~ality** mores *m/pl.*

**perspicaci|ous** perspicax; **~ty** acumen *n.*

**perspir|ation** sudor *m*; **~e** sudo 1.

**persuade** persuadeo 2 (*alci ut, ne*); adduco 3 (*alqm in, ad, ut*).

**pert** procax.

**pertain** attineo 2, pertineo 2 (*ad*).

**pertinacious** pertinax.

**pertinent** aptus, appositus.

**pertness** procacitas *f.*

**perturb** (per)turbo 1; sollicito 1; **~ation** perturbatio f.

**perus|al** pellectio f; **~e** perlego 3.

**pervade** permano 1 (in, ad); pervado 3 (acc., in, per).

**perverse** perversus, pravus; pertinax.

**perver|sion** depravatio f; **~t** depravo 1; corrumpo 3.

**pest** pestis f; **~er** vexo 1; **~ilence** pestilentia f.

**pestle** pilum n.

**pet** deliciae f/pl.; amores m/pl.

**petition** preces f/pl.; libellus m; libellum do 1 (alci); **~er** supplex m.

**petrif|y** in lapidem me verto 3; fig. **be ~ied** obstupesco 3.

**petticoat** tunica f.

**pettish** stomachosus.

**petty** minutus, angustus.

**petulant** stomachosus.

**pew** subsellium n.

**phantom** simulacrum n.

**pheasant** phasianus m.

**phenomenon** res f (mirabilis, nova).

**phial** laguncula f.

**philanthrop|ic** beneficus, humanus; **~y** humanitas f.

**philolog|ical** grammaticus; **~ist** grammaticus m; **~y** grammatica f.

**philosoph|er** philosophus m; sapiens m; **~ize** philosophor 1; **~y** philosophia f.

**philtre** amatorium n.

**phlegm** pituita f; **~atic** lentus.

**phoenix** phoenix m.

**phrase** verba n/pl.; dico 3, loquor 3.

**physic** medicamentum n; **~al** physicus; **~al strength** corporis vires f/pl.; **~ian** medicus m; **~s** physica n/pl.

**physiognomy** vultus, us m; oris lineamenta n/pl.

**pick** carpo 3, lego 3; **~ out** vello 3; eligo 3; **~ up** tollo 3, colligo 3; **the ~ of the troops** robus m militum; **~axe** dolabra f; **~ed** lectus, electus; **~et** statio f; stationem dispono 3.

**pickle** condo 3; condio 4; muria f.

**pickpocket** fur m.

**picture** tabula f; depingo 3; fingo 3 (animo).

**pie** crustum n.

**piece** frustum n; thea. fabula f; mus. carmen n; sarcio 4; **~ of money** nummus m; **break in ~s** comminuo 3; **fall to ~s** dissolvor 3; **tear in ~s** discerpo 3; lanio 1.

**pied** versicolor.

**pier** moles f; pila f.

**pierc|e** confodio 4, traicio 3; perforo 1, terebro 1; fig. ango 3; **~ing** acutus, acer.

**piety** pietas f.

**pig** porcus m; sus f and m; porcinus.

**pigeon** columba f; palumbes m and f.

**pigmy** pumilio m and f.

**pigsty** hara f.

**pike** hasta f; (fish) lupus m.

**pile** acervus m; cumulus m; strues f; palus m; sublica f; funeral **~** rogus m; (of cloth) villus m; **~ up** congero 3, exstruo 3; coacervo 1.

**pilfer** surripio 3 (alqd alci); **~er** fur m.

**pill** pilula f.

**pillage** v/t. diripio 3; populor 1; v/i. praedor 1; rapina f, direptio f.

**pillar** columna f; fig. columen n.

**pillow** pulvinus m; cervical n.

**pilot** gubernator m; guberno 1.

**pimp** leno m.

**pimple** pusula f, pustula f.

**pin** acus, us f; fibula f; affigo 3 (alqd ad alqd, dat.).

**pincers** forceps f.

**pinch** vellico 1; uro 3 (frigus, calcei, etc.); urgeo 2 (inopia).

**pine** tabesco 3; consenesco 3; pinus, us f.

**pinion** vincio 4; pinna f.

**pink** roseus.

**pinnacle** fastigium n.

**pint** sextarius m.

**pious** pius, religiosus.

**pip** semen n; granum n.

**pipe** fistula f; tibia f; tubus m; tubulus m; **reed ~** calamus m; tibia cano 3; **~r** fistulator m; tibicen m.

**piquant** acer; salsus.

**pique** offensio f.

**pira|cy** latrocinium n; **~te** praedo m; pirata m; piraticus.

**pit** fovea f, fossa f; barathrum n; **arm~** ala f; excavo 1; **~ against** oppono 3 (dat.).

**pitch** pono 3 (castra); conicio 3; pix f; **to such a ~** eo (gen.); **highest ~** fastigium n; **musical ~** vox f; **~ed battle** universae rei dimicatio f; **~er** urceus m; **~fork** furca f; **~pipe** fistula f; **~y** piceus.

**piteous** miserabilis.

**pitfall** *fig.* laqueus *m*; plagna *f*.
**pith** medulla *f*; *fig.* summa *f*; ~y sententiosus.
**pit|iable, ~iful** miserabilis, afflictus; ~iless durus, ferreus.
**pittance** mercedula *f*.
**pity** misereor 2 (*gen.*); me miseret (*gen.*); misericordia *f*, miseratio *f*; ~ing misericors.
**pivot** cardo *m*.
**placard** libellus *m*.
**placate** placo 1.
**place** locus *m*; sedes *f*; gradus, us *m*; officium *n*; **in this, that** ~ hic, illic; **in the same** ~ ibidem; **in the** ~ **of** loco (*gen.*); **take** ~ fio, accido 3; **out of** ~ ineptus; pono 3; (col)loco 1; statuo 3.
**placid** placidus, tranquillus.
**plagiari|sm** furtum *n*; ~ze compilo 1 (*alqd*).
**plague** pestilentia *f*; pestis *f*; molestus sum, vexo 1.
**plain** planus, manifestus, apertus, clarus; inornatus, subtilis, purus, simplex; campus *m*; planities *f*; aequum *n*; ~ly simpliciter (*loqui, etc.*); ~ness simplicitas *f*.
**plaint** querela *f*.
**plaintiff** petitor *m*, actor *m*, accusator *m*.
**plaintive** querulus, miserabilis.
**plait** intexo 3, nodo 1.
**plan** consilium *n*; ratio *f*; descriptio *f*; consilium capio 3; excogito 1; describo 3.
**plane** tero 1; rado 3; lima *f*, runcina *f*; ~-tree platanus, i *f*.
**planet** stella *f* errans.
**plank** tabula *f*.
**plant** sero 3, consero 3; pono 3; herba *f*; ~ation arbustum *n*; ~er sator *m*.
**plaster** induco 3 (*alqd alci rei*); tectorium *n*.
**plate** lamina *f*; lanx *f*, patella *f*; **silver** ~ argentum *n*.
**platform** tribunal *n*; suggestus, us *m*; (*in Forum*) rostra *n/pl.*
**plaudits** plausus, us *m*.
**plausible** probabilis, speciosus.
**play** ludo 3; cano 3 (*abl.*); ago 3 (*fabulam*); ludus *m*; *thea.* fabula *f*; ~er histrio *m*; ~ful lascivus, iocosus; ~mate collusor *m*.
**plea** excusatio *f*; *jur.* exceptio *f*; ~d excuso 1, causor 1 (*alqd*); obsecro 1 (*ut*); defendo 3 (*acc. c. inf.*); ~d a

**case** causam dico 1, ago 3; ~der orator *m*.
**pleasant** iucundus, amoenus; suavis; ~ry facetiae *f/pl.*
**please** placeo 2 (*dat.*); delecto 1 (*acc.*); gratificor 1 (*alci*); ~! amabo te; **as you** ~ quod libet; **if you** ~ si libet.
**pleas|ing** gratus; **be** ~ing cordi est (*alci*); ~ure voluptas *f*; libido *f*; arbitratus, us *m*; **it is the** ~ure **of** placet 2, videtur 3 (*dat.*).
**plebeian** plebeius; ~ **order** plebs *f*.
**pledge** spondeo 2 (*alqd alci*; *acc. c. inf.*); promitto 3; oppignero 1, obligo 1 (*alqd*); pignus *n*; fides *f*.
**plent|iful** largus, uber; ~y copia *f*; ~y of satis (*gen.*).
**pliable** lentus; flexibilis.
**plight** obligo 1; miseria *f*.
**plot** coniuro 1; molior 4; coniuratio *f*; consilium *n*; *thea.* argumentum *n*; ~ **of land** agellus *m*.
**plough** aro 1; aratrum *n*; ~share vomer, eris *n*.
**pluck** carpo, lego 3; vello 3; ~ up courage bono animo sum, utor 3; ~y fortis.
**plug** obturo 1; obturamentum *n*.
**plum** prunum *n*; ~-tree prunus, i *f*.
**plumage** pinnae *f/pl.*, plumae *f/pl.*
**plumb(-line)** perpendiculum *n*.
**plume** penna *f*, pinna *f*; ~ oneself on me iacto 1 (*de*).
**plump** pinguis, nitidus.
**plunder** praedor 1; diripio 3; praeda *f*; ~ing rapina *f*; praedatorius.
**plunge** *v/t.* (im)mergo 3, summergo 3 (*in*); *v/i.* me mergo, etc. (*in*).
**plural** pluralis; ~ity multitudo *f*.
**ply** exerceo 2, urgeo 2.
**poach** furor 1; ~er fur *m*.
**pocket** sacculus *m*; intercipio 3; ~-book (tablets) pugillares *m/pl.*; ~-money peculium *n*.
**pod** siliqua *f*.
**poem** poema, atis *n*, carmen *n*.
**poet** poeta *m*; ~ess poetria *f*; ~ical poeticus; ~ry carmen *n*; poesis *f*; versus *m/pl.*
**poignant** acerbus.
**point** acumen *n*; mucro *m*; punctum *n*; locus *m*; res *f*; **the main** ~ summa *f*; caput *n*; **to this** ~ huc; **to such a** ~ eo; **on the** ~ **of speaking** locuturus; **be to the** ~ attineo 2; ~ **out** (de)monstro 1; designo 1;

significo 1; ostendo 3; ~ed (prae-)
acutus; salsus; ~er index *m*; ~less
frigidus, insulsus, ineptus.
**poise** libro 1.
**poison** venenum *n*; venenum do 1
(*alci*); veneno 1 (*alqd*); ~er vene-
ficus *m*; ~ing veneficium *n*; ~ous
venenatus.
**poke** fodio 3; fodico 1; ~r rutabu-
lum *n*.
**polar** septentrionalis.
**pole** contus *m*; axis *m*; ~cat feles *f*.
**polemics** controversiae *f/pl*.
**police** vigiles *m/pl*.
**policy** consilia *n/pl*.; ratio *f*.
**polish** polio 4; *fig*. limo 1; nitor *m*;
lima *f*; ~ed (per)politus.
**polite** comis, humanus; urbanus;
~ness comitas *f*; humanitas *f*.
**politic** prudens.
**politic|al** civilis, politicus; ~s res *f*
publica; **take part in** ~s in re
publica versor 1.
**poll** suffragium *n*.
**pollut|e** inquino 1, contamino 1;
polluo 3; ~ion colluvio *f*.
**pomp** pompa *f*; apparatus, us *m*;
~osity magnificentia *f*; ~ous inflatus.
**pond** stagnum *n*.
**ponder** considero 1; animo voluto
1; ~ous gravis.
**poniard** pugio *m*.
**pony** mannus *m*.
**pool** stagnum *n*; lacus, us *m*.
**poop** puppis *f*.        [exilis.]
**poor** pauper, inops, egens; miser;]
**pop** crepito 1; ~ **out** exsilio 4;
crepitus, us *m*.
**pope** pontifex *m*.
**poplar** populus, i *f*; populeus.
**poppy** papaver, eris *n*.
**populace** plebes *m/pl*.; vulgus, i *n*.
**popular** popularis; gratus, acceptus; vulgaris; ~ **party** populares
*m/pl*.; ~ity favor *m* (populi); studium *n*; ~ly populariter.
**population** populus *m*.
**populous** frequens, celeber.
**porcelain** fictilis.
**porch** vestibulum *n*; porticus, us *f*.
**porcupine** hystrix *f*.
**pore** foramen *n*; ~ **over** animum,
considerationem intendo 3 (*in
alqd*).
**pork** porcina *f*.
**porridge** puls *f*.
**port** portus, us *m*.

**portal** porta *f*.
**portcullis** cataracta *f*.
**portend** portendo 3; significo 1.
**portent** prodigium *n*, portentum *n*,
monstrum *n*; ~ous prodigiosus.
**porter** ianitor *m*; ostiarius *m*;
baiulus *m*.
**portfolio** scrinium *n*.
**portico** porticus, us *f*.
**portion** pars *f*; divido 3; partior 4;
**marriage** ~ dos *f*.
**portly** plenus.
**portmanteau** mantica *f*.
**portrait** imago *f*.
**portray** pingo 3; depingo 3, describo 3.
**pose** *v/t*. (pro)pono 3 (*quaestionem*);
*v/i*. simulo 1 (*acc. c. inf.*); status,
us *m*.
**position** locus *m*; situs, us *m*; *fig*.
status, us *m*; gradus, us *m*.
**positive** certus, firmus; **be** ~ **that**
pro certo habeo 2.
**possess** possideo 2, habeo 2, teneo
2; est mihi; ~ed insanus; ~ion
possessio *f*; **take** ~ion of occupo 1,
capio 3 (*locum, animum, etc.*); ~ions
bona *n/pl*.
**possible: it is** ~ fieri potest (*ut*);
**as quickly as** ~ quam celerrime.
**possibly** fortasse; fieri potest (*ut*).
**post** (col)loco 1; constituo 3 (*milites*);
do 1 (*litteras*); ~ **up** propono 3, figo
3 (*in publicum*); palus *m*; cippus *m*;
statio *f*, locus *m*, praesidium *n*; officium *n*; **door**~ postis *m*; tabellarius.
**posteri|or** posterior; ~ty posteri
*m/pl*.; posteritas *f*.
**postman** tabellarius *m*.
**postpone** differo 3, profero 3.
**postulate** pono 3.
**posture** status, us *m*.
**pot** olla *f*.
**poten|cy** vis *f*; ~t efficax, potens;
~tate princeps *m*, rex *m*.
**potion** potio *f*.
**potsherd** testa *f*.
**potter** figulus *m*; ~y fictilia *n/pl*.
**pouch** pera *f*; sacculus *m*.
**poultry** altiles *m/pl*.
**pounce upon** insilio 4; involo 1 (*in
alqm*).
**pound** tero 3; tundo 3; libra *f*.
**pour** fundo 3; ~ **down** *v/i*. me deicio
3; *v/t*. praecipito 1; ~ **forth, out**
*v/t*. profundo 3; *v/i*. me eicio 3,
effundor 3.

**poverty** paupertas *f*, egestas *f*.

**powder** pulvis *m*; tero 3 (*in pulverem*).

**power** vis *f*; ops *f*; potestas *f*, potentia *f*; imperium *n*, dicio *f*; **be in one's ~** in manu sum (*alcs*); **~ful** validus; potens, valens; efficax; **be very, most ~ful** multum, plurimum possum; **be ~less** nihil possum.

**practical experience, practice** usus, us *m*; tractatio *f*; exercitatio *f*.

**practise** exerceo 2; celebro 1; meditor 1; **~d** exercitatus, peritus.

**praetor** praetor *m*; **~ian guard** praetoriani *m/pl.*; praetorium *n*; **~ship** praetura *f*.

**praise** laudo 1; celebro 1 (*laudibus*); laus *f*; **~-worthy** laudabilis, laudandus.

**prance** exsulto 1.

**prank** iocus *m*.

**prate, prattle** garrio 4, blatero 1.

**pray** precor 1, obsecro 1; oro 1 (*alqm, alqd, ut*); quaeso 3 (*alqd ab alqo, ut*); **~ to the gods** adoro 1 (*acc.*); supplico 1 (*dat.*); **~er** preces *f/pl.*; precatio *f*.

**preach** doceo 2.

**preamble** praefatio *f*; exordium *n*.

**precarious** incertus.

**precaution: take ~s** praecaveo 2 (*ne*).

**precede** praeeo 4; antecedo 3 (*acc., dat.*); ante fio, sum (*quam*).

**precedence: give ~ to** cedo 3 (*alci*); praevertor 3 (*alqd, alci rei*).

**preced|ent** exemplum *n*; **~ing** proximus, superior.

**precept** praeceptum *n*.

**precinct** templum *n*.

**precious** pretiosus.

**precipi|ce** locus *m* praeceps, abruptus; **~tate** *v/i.* me praecipito 1, deicio 3; *v/t.* maturo 1 (*alqd*); praeceps, temerarius; **~tous** praeceps, praeruptus.

**precis|e** subtilis, exactus; **~ion** subtilitas *f*; cura *f*.

**preclude** prohibeo 2 (*inf., ne*).

**precocious** praecox.

**precon|ceived** praeiudicatus; **~ception** praeiudicata opinio *f*; **~certed** compositus.

**pre|decessor** proximus; **~determine** praefinio 4; **~dicament** angustiae *f/pl.*

**predict** praedico 3; **~ion** praedictum *n*; praedictio *f*.

**pre|dilection** studium *n*; **~dominate** plus, plurimum possum; superiores sunt; **~eminent** praecipuus.

**preface** praefatio *f*; praefor 1 (*pauca*).

**prefect** praefectus *m*; **~ure** praefectura *f*.

**prefer** malo (*alqd, inf.*); antepono 3, praepono 3 (*acc., dat.*); **~ a charge against** nomen defero 3 (*alcs de re*); **~able** potior, antiquior; **~ably** potius.

**prefix** praescribo 3, praepono 3.

**pregnan|cy** graviditas *f*; **~t** gravida, praegnans.

**prejud|ge** praeiudico 1; **~ice** praeiudicata opinio *f*; laedo 3.

**preliminary: ~ exercise** prolusio *f*; **make some ~ remarks** pauca praefor 1.

**prelude** proemium *n*; *fig.* prolusio *f*.

**premature** praematurus, immaturus.

**premeditate** praemeditor 1; **~dly** consulto, de industria.

**premier** princeps *m*.

**premise** propositio *f*, assumptio *f*; **~s** aedificia *n/pl.*

**premium** praemium *n*.

**premonition** augurium *n*.

**preoccupied** occupatus.

**prepar|ation** praeparatio *f*; **~e** (prae)paro 1; meditor 1; me comparo 1 (*ad alqd*).

**preponderate** plus, plurimum polleo 2.

**preposterous** praeposterus, absurdus.

**presage** portendo 3; significo 1.

**prescribe** praescribo 3.

**presence** praesentia *f*; conspectus, us *m*; **~ of mind** praesens animus *m*; praesentia *f* animi; **in the ~ of** coram (*abl.*); **in my ~ce** me praesente.

**present** praesens; **at the ~ in** praesenti; **for the ~ in** praesens; **at the ~ day** hodie; **be ~** adsum, intersum (*dat.*); introduco 3; offero 3, obicio 3; praebeo 2, dono 1 (*alqm dono*); **~ itself** occurro 3; obvenio 4; donum *n*, munus *n*; **~iment** augurium *n*; **~ly** mox, brevi.

**preserv|ation** conservatio *f*; **~e**

(con)servo 1; tueor 2; (*fruit*) condio 4; ~ed conditivus; ~er servator *m*.

**preside** praesideo 2 (*dat.*); ~nt praefectus *m*.

**press** premo 3 (*alqd, alqm*); ~ hard urgeo 2; insto 1 (*dat.*); ~ together comprimo 3; prelum *n* (*for wine, olives, clothes, etc.*); turba *f*; ~ing praesens; ~ingly vehementer, impense; ~ure pressus, us *m*.

**prestige** gloria *f*.

**presum|e** sumo 3 (*mihi ut*); audeo 2; ~ption arrogantia *f*; coniectura *f*; ~ptuous arrogans.

**preten|ce** simulatio *f*, species *f*; ~d simulo 1; dictito 1; fingo 3; ~der qui regnum affectat; ~sion ostentatio *f*; **have ~sions to** affecto 1 (*alqd*).

**preternatural** monstruosus; ~ly praeter modum.

**pretext** species *f*; **put forward as a ~** praetendo 3 (*alqd alci rei*).

**pretty** bellus, pulcher, lepidus.

**prevail** vinco 3; valeo 2; ~ upon impetro 1 (*alqd ab alqo; ut*).

**prevalent** creber, vulgatus; **become ~** increb(r)esco 3.

**prevaricate** tergiversor 1.

**prevent** prohibeo 2 (*alqm; quominus; acc. c. inf.*); obsto 1 (*dat.; quominus*).

**previous** proximus, superior, prior; ~ to prius quam; ~ly antea, antehac.

**prey** praeda *f*; ~ upon praedor 1; *fig.* sollicito 1.

**price** pretium *n*; ~ of corn, food annona *f*; **sell at a high, low ~** magno, parvo vendo 3; *v/t.* pretium constituo 3; ~less pretiosissimus.

**prick** pungo 3; *fig.* stimulo 1; ~ up one's ears aures erigo 3; stimulus *m*; aculeus *m*; ~le spina *f*; ~ly spinosus.

**pride** superbia *f*; fastidium *n*; ~ oneself on glorior 1 (*de, in re*).

**priest** sacerdos *m and f*; ~hood sacerdotium *n*.

**prima|cy** principatus, us *m*; ~ry primus.

**prime** optimus; erudio 4 (*alqm de*); **be in the ~** floreo 2, vigeo 2; ~val priscus.

**primitive** priscus, pristinus, antiquus, principalis.

**prince** rex *m*, princeps *m*; regulus *m*; ~ly regalis; ~ss regina *f*; regis filia *f*.

**principal** praecipuus, primus; magister, tri *m*; (*money*) caput *n*; ~ity regnum *n*.

**principle** principium *n*, elementum *n*; institutum *n*, decretum *n*; **man of ~** vir *m* probus, integer.

**print** imprimo 3 (*alqd in re*); nota *f* (*impressa*); tabula *f*.

**prior** potior; ~ to ante (*acc.*).

**prison** carcer, eris *n*; vincula *n/pl.*; ~er captivus *m*; *jur.* reus *m*; **take ~er** capio 3.

**priva|cy** solitudo *f*; secretum *n*; secessus, us *m*; ~te privatus; proprius; secretus; domesticus; **in ~te** privatim; secreto; ~te soldier miles *m* gregarius; ~tion inopia *f*.

**privet** ligustrum *n*.

**privilege** ius *n*; commodum *n*.

**privy** secretus; ~ to conscius (*dat.*).

**prize** praemium *n*; praeda *f*; magni facio 3.

**probab|ility** veri similitudo *f*; ~le veri similis; probabilis; ~ly nescio an.

**probation** rudimenta *n/pl.*; ~er tiro *m*.

**probe** scrutinor 1; tento .

**probity** probitas *f*.

**problem** quaestio *f*.

**procedure** ratio *f*.

**proceed** pergo 3; procedo 3, progredior 3; ~ against persequor 3 (*alqm iudicio*); *fig.* ~ from proficiscor 3; ~ing ratio *f*; ~ings acta *n/pl.*; ~s fructus, us *m*.

**process** *jur.* actio *f*; ~ion pompa *f*.

**procla|im** pronuntio 1; renuntio 1, declaro 1 (*alqm consulem, etc.*); edico 3; ~mation praedicatio *f*; edictum *n*.

**proconsul** proconsul *m*; pro consule.

**procrastinat|e** cunctor 1; ~ion mora *f*; cunctatio *f*.

**procur|ator** procurator *m*; ~e comparo 1, adipiscor 3; ~er leno *m*.

**prodigal** prodigus.

**prodig|ious** immanis; ~y portentum *n*, prodigium *n*; miraculum *n*.

**produce** profero 3, produco 3; pario 3; (ef)fero 3; efficio 3, moveo 2; fructus, us *m*; ferus, us *m*.

**product** fructus, us *m*; opus *n*; ~ive ferax; fecundus.

**profan|ation** violatio *f*; ~e profanus; impius; violo 1; polluo 3.

**profess** profiteor 2 *(alqd; acc. c. inf.)*; ~ion professio *f*; artificium *n*.
**proffer** polliceor 2.
**proficient** prudens, peritus *(gen.)*.
**profile** obliqua imago *f*.
**profit** prosum *(dat.)*; proficio 3 *(ad)*; commodum *n*, bonum *n*; emolumentum *n*, lucrum *n*; quaestus, us *m*; **get ~ from** proficio 3 *(abl.)*; ~able fructuosus, quaestuosus; ~less inutilis. [ditus.]
**profliga|cy** flagitia *n/pl.*; ~te per-
**profound** altus, profundus; ~ly penitus, valde.
**profus|e** prodigus, profusus; ~ion copia *f*.
**progeny** progenies *f*.
**programme** consilium *n*.
**progress** progredior 3; iter, ineris *n*; progressus, us *m*; progressio *f*; **make ~** proficio 3 *(in alqa re)*; progressus facio 3; ~ion progressio *f*.
**prohibit** veto 1, prohibeo 2 *(acc. c. inf.)*; interdico 3 *(alci alqd; ne)*; ~ion interdictum *n*.
**project** emineo 2 *(ex, in, super)*; consilium *n*; ~ile missile *n*; ~ing eminens, projectus.
**proletariat** vulgus, i *n*.
**prolific** fecundus.
**prolix** verbosus.
**prologue** prologus *m*.
**prolong** produco 3; prorogo 1 *(imperium)*; ~ation propagatio *f*; ~ed diuturnus.
**prominent** eminens; praestans.
**promise** promitto 3; polliceor 2, profiteor 2; promissum *n*; **keep, break a ~** fidem servo 1, fallo 3.
**promontory** promunturium *n*.
**promot|e** proveho 3, produco 3 *(alqm ad honorem)*; servio 4, consulo 3 *(alci rei)*; ~ion amplior honoris gradus, us *m*.
**prompt** promptus, paratus *(ad)*; impello 3 *(alqm in, ut)*; subicio 3 *(verba etc.)*; ~itude celeritas *f*.
**promulgate** promulgo 1.
**prone** pronus; ~ to pronus, propensus *(ad)*.
**prong** dens *m*.
**pronounce** pronuntio 1 *(sententiam etc.)*; enuntio 1, loquor 3 *(litteras)*.
**pronunciation** appellatio *f*.
**proof** documentum *n*, argumentum *n*, indicium *n*; **be a ~** documento sum; **make ~ of** experior 4; ~ **against** invictus *(ab, adversus)*.

**prop** adminiculum *n*, columen *n*; ~ **up** fulcio 4, sustineo 2.
**propagat|e** propago 1; dissemino 1; ~ion propagatio *f*.
**propel** impello 3.
**propensity** proclivitas *f*; **have a ~ to** propensus, pronus sum *(ad)*.
**proper** proprius; decorus; **it is ~** decet *(acc. c. inf.)*; ~ly proprie; recte, commode; ~ty proprium *n*; proprietas *f*; bona *n/pl.*; res *f*; fortunae *f/pl.*
**prophe|cy** praedictio *f*; praedictum *n*; oraculum *n*; ~sy vaticinor 1, ominor 1, divino 1; praedico 3; ~t vates *m and f*; ~tic divinus.
**propinquity** propinquitas *f*.
**propitiat|e** placo 1; ~ion placatio *f*; piaculum *n*.
**propitious** propitius, faustus, prosperus.
**proportion** ratio *f*; **in ~, ~ally** pro portione; **in ~ to** pro *(abl.)*; **sense of ~** modus *m*.
**propos|al** condicio *f*; consilium *n*; **carry a ~al** *(for a law)* rogationem perfero 3; ~e in animo est *(mihi)*, cogito 1 *(inf.)*; pono 3; fero 3, rogo 1 *(legem)*; ~er lator *m* *(legis)*; auctor *m*; ~ition condicio *f*; propositio *f*, propositum *n*.
**propound** expono 3, propono 3.
**propriet|or** dominus *m*; ~y decorum *n*.
**prorogue** differo 3; prorogo 1.
**proscri|be** proscribo 3; ~ption proscriptio *f*.
**prose** soluta oratio *f*; solutus.
**prosecut|e** nomen *(alcs)* defero 3; accuso 1 *(alqm ob, de re)*; exsequor 3, persequor 3; ~ion accusatio *f*, delatio *f*; ~or accusator *m*, actor *m*.
**prospect** prospectus, us *m*; spes *f*.
**prosper** *v/t.* adiuvo 1; *v/i.* secunda, prospera fortuna utor 3; floreo 2; bene procedit *(mihi)*; ~ity res *f/pl.* secundae, prosperae; ~ous secundus, prosperus, florens.
**prostitute** vulgo 1; meretrix *f*.
**prostrate** sterno 3; ~ **oneself** procumbo 3, me proicio 3, prosterno 3 *(humi, ad pedes alcs)*; **be ~d** iaceo 2, fractus sum.
**protect** defendo 3, tueor 2; protego 3; ~ion tutela *f*; praesidium *n*; ~or defensor *m*, praeses *m*.
**protest** obtestor 1 *(acc. c. inf.)*; ~ **against** recuso 1 *(ne, quominus)*.

**protract** (pro)duco 3; ~ed diuturnus.

**protrude** *v/t.* protrudo 3; *v/i.* emineo 2.

**protuberan|ce** tuber, eris *n*; ~t eminens.

**proud** superbus, arrogans; **be ~ of** glorior 1 (*de, in re*).

**prove** *v/t.* probo 1, confirmo 1, efficio 3; experior 4; *v/i.* me praesto 1, praebeo 2; evado 3.

**proverb** proverbium *n*.

**provide** (com)paro 1; praebeo 2; ~ **against** caveo 2, provideo 2 (*ne*); ~ **for** provideo 2 (*dat.*); ~d with instructus (*abl.*); ~d that dum(modo), modo.

**providen|ce** providentia *f*; ~t providus; ~tially divinitus.

**provinc|e** regio *f*; provincia *f* (*also fig.*); ~ial provincialis.

**provision: make ~ for** provideo 2; **make ~ that** caveo 2 (*ut, ne*); ~s frumentum *n*; res *f* frumentaria; commeatus, us *m*; cibaria *n/pl.*; ~ally ad tempus.

**provocation** contumelia *f*.

**provok|e** irrito 1, lacesso 3; moveo 2 (*alqd*); ~ing molestus.

**prow** prora *f*.

**prowess** virtus, utis *f*.

**prowl** vagor 1.

**proxim|ate** proximus; ~ity propinquitas *f*.

**proxy** procurator *m*; vicarius *m*.

**prude|nce** prudentia *f*; ~nt cautus, prudens; ~ntly pudor *m*.

**prun|e** (am)puto 1 (*also fig.*); ~ing knife falx *f*.

**pry into** rimor 1, exploro 1.

**puberty** pubes aetas *f*.

**public** publicus; ~ **affairs**, ~ **life** res *f* publica; **appear in ~** prodeo 4 in publicum; **in ~** in publico; **at ~ expense** publice; **make ~** vulgo 1; **the ~** populus *m*; vulgus, i *n*; ~ **house** caupona *f*; ~an caupo *m*; ~ity lux *f*.

**publish** effero 3; pervulgo 1; edo 3 (*librum etc.*).

**pudding** placenta *f*.

**puddle** lacuna *f*.

**puerile** puerilis, ineptus.

**puff** *v/t.* fio 1; *v/i.* anhelo 1; ~ **out** inflo 1; **be ~ed up** *fig.* me effero 3, tumeo 2.

**pugilist** pugil *m*.

**pugnacious** pugnax.

**pull** traho 3, vello 3, rapio 3; ~ **down** demolior 4, destruo 3; ~ **out** revello 3, evello 3, eripio 3; nisus, us *m*; ~ey troclea *f*; ~ing tractus, us *m*.

**pulp** caro *f*.

**puls|ate** agitor 1; ~e pulsus, us *m* venarum.

**pulverise** tero 3.

**pumice** pumex *m*.

**pump** antlia *f*; ~ **out** exhaurio 4 (*sentinam, aquam, etc.*); ~kin pepo *m*.

**pun** iocus *m*; iocor 1.

**punch** pertundo 3, terebro 1 (*alqd alqa re*); pulso 1, ferio 4 (*alqm*); ictus, us *m*.

**punctilious** religiosus.

**punctual** diligens; ~ly ad tempus, tempore.

**punctuat|e** interpungo 3; ~ion mark** interpunctum *n*.

**puncture** pungo 3; punctum *n*.

**pungent** acer.

**punish** punio 4; animadverto 3; poenas sumo 3, capio 3 (*de alqo*); ~ment poena *f*; supplicium *n*; animadversio *f*.

**puny** pusillus.

**pupil** discipulus *m*; ~ **of the eye** pupilla *f*, pupula *f*.

**puppet** pupa *f*.

**puppy** catellus *m*; catulus.

**purchase** emo 3; comparo 1; emptio *f*; merx *f*; ~r emptor *m*.

**pure** purus, merus; castus, integer.

**purge** purgo 1 (*alvum, urbem, etc.*).

**puri|fy** purgo 1; lustro 1; ~ty castitas *f*, integritas *f*.

**purloin** surripio 3.

**purple** purpureus, conchyliatus; purpura *f*; conchylium *n*.

**purport** volo (*esse etc.*); significatio *f*, sententia *f*; summa *f*; **what is the ~** quo spectat?

**purpose** propositum *n*, consilium *n*; animus *m*; finis *m*; voluntas *f*; **with this ~** eo, ideo (... *ut*); **on ~** consulto; de industria; **to no ~** frustra, nequicquam; **it is to the ~** multum refert (*si, utrum, etc.*); **in animo habeo 2, est**; consilium est (*inf.*); ~less vanus, inutilis, irritus; ~ly consulto.

**purse** crumena *f*; marsupium *n*; sacculus *m*; astringo 3.

**pursu|ance: in ~ance of** ex (*abl.*); secundum (*acc.*); ~e (per)sequor 3, insequor 3; insisto 3 (*acc.*, *dat.*); ~it studium *n.*

**purvey** comparo 1; praebeo 2; ~ **food** obsono 1.

**push** trudo 3, impello 3, expello 3; ~ **on** contendo 3, pergo 3; iter facio 3; impulsus, us *m*; impetus, us *m.*

**pusillanimous** timidus, ignavus.

**puss** feles *f.*

**put** pono 3; colloco 1; ~ **aside** *fig.* (de)pono 3; ~ **away** condo 3; ~ **back** repono 3; ~ **down** depono 3; comprimo 3 (*seditionem*); ~ **forth** summitto 3, effero 3; ~ **in** impono 3, insero 3 (*alqd in rem*); ~ **into shore** applico 1 (*navem ad terram*); ~ **off** *v/t.* differo 3 (*alqd in posterum diem*); *v/i.* navem solvo 3; ~ **on**

**impono** 3 (*alqd alci*, *in alqd*); induo 3 (*vestem alci*, *mihi*); ~ **out** eicio 3, exstinguo 3 (*ignem*); effodio 3 (*oculum*); *fig.* perturbo 1 (*alqm*); ~ **out of the way** tollo 3; ~ **to sea** navem solvo 3; ~ **up at** deverto 3 (*ad*, *apud*); ~ **up for** peto 3 (*consulatum*); ~ **up for sale** propono 3 (*alqd venale*); ~ **up with** tolero 1, devoro 1.

**putr|ify** putesco 3; ~**id** puter, putridus.

**puzz|le** aenigma *n*; quaestio *f*; dubium facio 3; perturbo 1; **be ~ed** haereo 2, dubito 1; ~**ing** obscurus, ambiguus, dubius.

**pygmy** pumilio *m.*

**pyramid** pyramis *f.*

**pyre** rogus *m.*

# Q

**quack** pharmacopola *m*, circulator *m*.

**quadrangle** quadratum *n*.

**quadruped** quadrupes *m and f*.

**quadruple: in ~** in quadruplum.

**quaff** haurio 4.

**quail** trepido 1; **~ before** pertimesco 3 (*alqd*); coturnix *f*.

**quaint** facetus, insolitus.

**quak|e** tremo 3; tremor *m*; **~ing** trepidus.

**quali|fication** potestas *f*; exceptio *f*; **~fied** idoneus, aptus (*ad*); dignus (*abl.*); **~fy** idoneum facio 3 (*alqm*); diminuo 3 (*alqd de voluptate, etc.*); **~ty** ingenium *n*; natura *f*; virtus, utis *f*.

**quandary** angustiae *f/pl*.

**quantity** magnitudo *f*; numerus *m*; vis *f*; **small ~** aliquantulum *n*.

**quarrel** rixor 1, altercor 1; iurgium *n*, altercatio *f*, rixa *f*; **~some** litigiosus, pugnax.

**quarry** lapicidinae *f/pl*.; praeda *f*; excido 3.

**quart** duo sextarii *m/pl*.

**quarter** in quattuor partes divido 3; in hospitia deduco 3 (*milites*); quarta pars *f*; quadrans *m*; locus *m*, regio *f*; (*of a town*) vicus *m*; **ask for ~** in deditionem venio 4; **fight without ~** sine missione pugno 1; **give ~** parco 3, veniam do 1; **~s** hospitium *n*; *mil.* castra *n/pl*.; **general's ~s** praetorium *n*; **come to close ~s** manum consero 3 (*cum alqo*); **at close ~s** comminus.

**quash** rescindo 3; irritum facio 3.

**quavering** vibrans, tremulus, tremens.

**quay** crepido *f*.

**queen** regina *f*.

**queer** insolitus; absurdus; mirificus.

**quell** comprimo 3; sedo 1.

**quench** exstinguo 3; expleo 2 (*sitim*).

**querulous** queribundus, querulus.

**query** quaestio *f*.

**quest** inquisitio *f*; **be in ~ of** quaero 3 (*acc.*).

**question** interrogo 1, percontor 1 (*alqm*); dubito 1 (*de re*); (inter)rogatum *n*; dubitatio *f*; quaestio *f*; res *f*; **the ~ is** quaestio est (*an*); **put someone to the ~** quaestionem habeo 2 (*de alqo*); **~able** anceps, incertus; **~ing** interrogatio *f*.

**quibbl|e** captio *f*; captiose dico 3; **~ing** captiosus.

**quick** celer, velox; alacer, impiger; promptus (*ad*); acutus, callidus; **be ~** propero 1; vivum *n*; **cut to the ~** mordeo 2; **~en** *v/t.* accelero 1; excito 1; *v/i.* vigeo 2; **~ness** celeritas *f*, alacritas *f*; acumen *n*; **~silver** argentum *n* vivum; **~tempered** iracundus; **~witted** acutus, sagax.

**quiet** quietus, tranquillus; tacitus, taciturnus; placo 1, sedo 1; quies *f*, tranquillitas *f*; otium *n*; **be ~** sileo 2, taceo 2; **~ness** otium *n*.

**quill** penna *f*.

**quince** cydonium *n*.

**quintessence** medulla *f*.

**quip** dictum *n*.

**quit** excedo 3 (*abl., ex*); relinquo 3 (*acc.*); **~ of** exemptus, solutus (*abl.*).

**quite** prorsus, plane, admodum; omnino; **not ~** parum.

**quiver** tremo 3, trepido 1; tremor *m*; (*for arrows*) pharetra *f*; **~ing** tremebundus, tremulus.

**quoit** discus *m*.

**quot|ation** dictum *n*; **~e** profero 3, laudo 1 (*auctores, testes*).

**quoth** ait, inquit.

# R

**rabbit** cuniculus *m*.
**rabble** turba *f*; colluvio *f*.
**rabid** rabidus.
**race** certo 1; gens *f*; genus *n*; stirps *f*; certamen *n* (*equorum etc*.); **chariot-~** curriculum *n*; **~-course** stadium *n*, curriculum *n*.
**rack** torqueo 2; equuleus *m*; tormentum *n*; carnificina *f*; cratis *f*; **be ~ed** (ex)crucior 1; **~et** strepitus, us *m*.
**racy** salsus.
**radia|nce** fulgor *m*, splendor *m*; **~nt** nitidus, fulgens, splendidus; **~te** fulgeo 2.
**radical** totus; *pol*. popularis; **~ly** penitus, omnino.
**radish** radix *f*.
**radius** radius *m*.
**raft** ratis *f*.
**rafter** trabs *f*.
**rag** pannus *m*; **~s** panni *m/pl*.
**rage** ira *f*; furor *m*; rabies *f*; furo 3, saevio 4.
**ragged** pannuceus (*vestis*); pannosus (*homo*).
**raid** incursio *f*; incursionem facio 3 (*in*).
**rail** palus *m*; longurius *m*; **~ at** maledico 3 (*dat*.); convicium facio 3 (*alci*); **~ing** pali *m/pl*., saepes *f*; convicium *n*; **~lery** iocatio *f*.
**raiment** vestis *f*.
**rain** pluvia *f*; imber *m*; **it ~s** pluit; **~bow** arcus, us *m* (pluvius); **~water** aquae *f/pl*. pluviae; **~y** pluvius, pluvialis.
**raise** tollo 3 (*alqd*; *clamorem*; *cachinnum*); (sub)levo 1; erigo 3 (*caput, oculos, animum*); effero 3 (*alqm ad dignitatem*); sero 3 (*fruges*); cogo 3 (*pecuniam*); conscribo 3 (*exercitum*).
**raisin** uva *f* passa.
**rake** rado 3; **~ up** excito 1; rastrum *n*; *fig*. ganeo *m*.
**rally** *v/t*. restituo 3 (*ordines, aciem*); irrideo 2 (*alqm*); *v/i*. me colligo 3; concurro 3 (*milites*).
**ram** aries *m*; arietinus; **~ down** fistuco 1.

**rambl|e** vagor 1, erro 1; **~ing** vagus.
**rampart** vallum *n*; agger, eris *m*; moenia *n/pl*.
**ranco|rous** infensus; **~ur** simultates *f/pl*.; invidia *f*.
**random** fortuitus; **at ~** temere.
**range** *v/t*. dispono 3; *v/i*. (per)vagor 1; ordo *m*; genus *n*; *fig*. campus *m*, area *f* (*orationis etc*.); **mountain ~** iugum *n*; **~ of a weapon** teli iactus, us *m*.
**rank** numero 1; habeo 2 (*alqm in numero*); ordo *m*; series *f*; gradus, us *m*; dignitas *f*; status, us *m*; luxuriosus; fetidus, rancidus; *fig*. merus.
**ransack** diripio 3; perscrutor 1.
**ransom** redimo 3; pretium *n*; redemptio *f*.
**rant** bacchor 1.
**rap** ferio 4; pulso 1; ictus, us *m*.
**rapaci|ous** rapax; **~ty** rapacitas *f*.
**rape** rapio 3; raptus, us *m*.
**rapid** celer, rapidus; **~ity** celeritas *f*, velocitas *f*.
**rapier** gladius *m*.
**rapine** rapina *f*.
**rapt** stupens; **~ure** laetitia *f*.
**rar|e** rarus; tenuis (*aer*); singularis; **~efy** extenuo 1; **~ely** raro; **~eness** raritas *f*, paucitas *f*.
**rascal** verbero *m*, furcifer *m*; **~ly** nequam, flagitiosus.
**rasp** *v/t*. rado 3; *v/i*. strideo 2; scobina *f*.
**rat** mus *m*.
**rate** aestimo 1 (*alqm, alqd, magni*); censeo 2; increpo 1; pretium *n*; vectigal *n*; **~ of interest** faenus *n*; **at a high ~** magno; **at any ~** utique, certe.
**rather** potius, prius, libentius; quin, immo; **I would ~** malo, mallem.
**ratif|ication** sanctio *f* (*foederis*); **~y** sancio 4; confirmo 1.
**rating** aestimatio *f*.
**ration** (diurnus) cibus *m*; **soldier's ~** cibaria *n/pl*.
**rational** rationis particeps (*homo*); consentaneus; **~ity** ratio *f*.

**rattle** crepitus, us *m*; crotalum *n*; crepo 1, crepito 1.

**ravage** vasto 1, populor 1; diripio 3.

**rave** furo 3, bacchor 1; saevio 4.

**raven** corvus *m*; ~ous rapax, edax.

**ravine** fauces *f/pl.*; vallis *f* praerupta.

**raving** furens, insanus, rabidus.

**ravish** rapio 3; stupro 1; ~ing suavissimus.

**raw** crudus 3; *fig.* rudis, imperitus; ~ **soldier** tiro *m*.

**ray** radius *m*; iubar *n*.

**raze to the ground** solo aequo 1 (*alqd*); funditus everto 3, deleo 2.

**razor** novacula *f*.

**reach** *v/i.* pervenio 4 (*ad*); attingo 3, tango 3 (*alqd*); *v/i.* pertineo 2 (*ad*); ~ **out** porrigo 3; spatium *n*; iactus, us *m* (*teli*); **beyond ~ of** extra (*acc.*).

**react upon** afficio 3 (*alqm, alqd, invicem*).

**read** lego 3 (*alqd, librum*); volvo 3 (*librum*); ~ **aloud** recito 1; ~ **through** perlego 3; ~er lector *m*; ~ing lectio *f*, recitatio *f*.

**readily** ultro, libenter.

**ready** paratus, promptus (*ad*); celer, facilis; **be ~** praesto sum; **get ~** (com)paro 1; ~ **money** praesens pecunia *f*.

**real** verus, germanus, solidus; ~ **property** fundus *m*; ~isation effectus, us *m*; ~ise *v/t.* perficio 3; redigo 3 (*pecuniam*); *v/i.* intellego 3; mente concipio 3; ~ity veritas *f*; verum *n*; **in ~ity** re vera.

**really** re vera; vero, profecto.

**realm** regnum *n*; *fig.* regio *f*.

**reanimate** recreo 1.

**reap** meto 3; *fig.* percipio 3 (*fructum ex re, rei*); ~er messor *m*.

**reappear** redeo 4.

**rear** *v/t.* educo 1 *and* 3; alo 3; *v/i.* me erigo 3; tergum *n*; **in the ~** a tergo; ~ **of a column** novissimum agmen *n*; **bring up the ~** agmen claudo 3.

**reason** ratio *f*, mens *f*; causa *f*; **with ~** ratione; **without ~** temere; **the ~ for ... is** idcirco (*alqd facio*) ... quod; **ask the ~ for** quaero 3 cur, quamobrem; **by ~ of** propter (*acc.*); ratiocinor 1; disputo 1 (*de re*); dissero 3 (*de re, cum alqo*); ~able prudens; probabilis (*coniectura*); aequus; mediocris, modicus; ~er disputator *m*; ~ing ratio *f*, ratiocinatio *f*.

**reass|emble** redeo 4; ~ure confirmo 1 (*animos etc.*).

**rebel** descisco 3 (*ab*); seditionem, rebellionem facio 3, commoveo 2; hostis *m*; ~lion seditio *f*, rebellio *f*; defectio *f*; tumultus, us *m*; ~lious seditiosus, turbulentus.

**rebound** resilio 4.

**rebuff** sperno 3, repello 3; repulsa *f*.

**rebuild** restituo 3, reficio 3.

**rebuke** increpo 1; reprehendo 3; reprehensio *f*.

**rebut** refello 3.

**recall** revoco 1 (*ad*; *in animum*); reduco 3; revocatio *f*; receptus, us *m*.

**recant** revoco 1 (*alqd*).

**recede** recedo 3.

**receive** accipio 3, excipio 3, recipio 3, capio 3.

**recent** recens; ~ly recens, nuper.

**recep|tacle** receptaculum *n*; ~tion aditus, us *m*; admissio *f*; congressus, us *m*; ~tive studiosus, capax.

**recess** recessus, us *m*; secessus, us *m*.

**reciproc|al** mutuus; ~ate refero 3.

**reci|tal** narratio *f*, enumeratio *f*; ~e recito 1, pronuntio 1.

**reckless** temerarius, incautus; incuriosus (*gen.*); ~ness temeritas *f*.

**reckon** duco 3; refero 3 (*alqm, alqd, in numero*); ascribo 3 (*in numerum*); ~ **up** (e)numero 1, computo 1, aestimo 1; ~ing ratio *f*; enumeratio *f*; numerus *m*; ~ing on fretus (*abl.*).

**reclaim** repeto 3, reposco 3; recupero 1.

**recline** recumbo 3, accumbo 3.

**recogni|se** cognosco 3, agnosco 3 (*alqm*); ~ **that** intellego 3 (*acc. c. inf.*); ~tion agnitio *f*.

**recoil** recido 3 (*in alqm*).

**recollect** memini; reminiscor 3; colligo 3 (*me, animum*); ~ion memoria *f*.

**recommence** instauro 1, redintegro 1.

**recommend** commendo 1 (*alqm, alqd, alci*); suadeo 2 (*alci ut*); ~ation commendatio *f*, laudatio *f*.

**recompense** remunero 1 (*alqm re*); praemium *n*, munus *n*; remuneratio *f*; merces *f*.

**reconcil|e** reconcilio 1; in gratiam restituo 3; accommodo 1 (*alqd ad alqd*); **be ~ed** in gratiam redeo 4 (*cum*); ~iation reconciliatio *f*.

**recondite** abditus, abstrusus.

**reconnoitre** exploro 1.
**reconsider** reputo 1, retracto 1 (*alqd*).
**reconstruct** restituo 3; *fig.* repeto 3 (*alqd memoria*).
**record** litteris mando 1; refero 3; historia *f*; narratio *f*; monumentum *n*; memoria *f*; tabula *f*; ~s acta *n/pl.*; fasti *m/pl*.
**recount** enarro 1, commemoro 1.
**recourse: have ~ to** decurro 3 (*ad*); descendo 3 (*ad*).
**recover** *v/t.* recupero 1; recipio 3; **~ oneself** colligo 3 (*me, animum*); *v/i.* convalesco 3; emergo 3 (*ex*); **~y** recuperatio *f* (*rei*); refectio *f*; salus, utis *f*.
**recreat|e** recreo 1; **~ion** remissio *f*; relaxatio *f*; requies *f*; vacatio *f*.
**recruit** reficio 3; *mil.* (con)scribo 3; comparo 1; sacramento adigo 3; tiro *m*.
**recti|fy** corrigo 3; emendo 1; **~tude** probitas *f*.
**recur** red•o 4; **~rence** reditus, us *m*; assiduitas *f*.
**red** ruber, rubens, rubicundus, rufus, rutilus; **be ~** rubeo 2; **~den** (e)rubesco 3.
**redeem** redimo 3; **~er** liberator *m*.
**red-handed: catch ~** manifesto deprehendo 3 (*alqm*).
**red|-hot** candens; **~ lead** minium *n*; **~ness** rubor *m*.
**redolent** redolens (*alqd*).
**redouble** ingemino 1.
**redress** corrigo 3; restituo 3.
**reduc|e** minuo 3; redigo 3 (*alqm in alqd*); subigo 3, vinco 3 (*alqm*); **be ~ed to** recido 3 (*in alqd*); redeo 4 (*ad*); **~tion** deminutio *f*.
**redundant** supervacaneus; **be ~** redundo 1.
**re-echo** refero 3.
**reed** harundo *f*; calamus *m*.
**reef** saxa *n/pl.*; scopuli *m/pl.*; contraho 3 (*vela*).
**reek** fumo 1.
**reel** vacillo 1, titubo 1; fusus *m*.
**re|elect** reficio 3; **~establish** restituo 3.
**refer** refero 3 (*rem ad alqm, ad alqd*); reicio 3 (*rem ad alqm; alqm ad rem*); **~ to** memoro 1; attingo 3 (*alqd*); **~ee** arbiter, tri *m*; **~ence** mentio *f*; locus *m*; **have ~ence to** attineo 2 (*ad*).
**refill** repleo 2.

**refine** defaeco 1 (*vinum etc.*); *fig.* expolio 4; excolo 3 (*alqd*); **~d** humanus, politus; **~ment** humanitas *f*, urbanitas *f*.
**reflect** reddo 3 (imaginem); **~ upon** reputo 1, considero 1, recordor 1 (*alqd*); **~ion** imago *f*; cogitatio *f*, deliberatio *f*; **cast a ~ion upon** reprehendo 3.
**reform** emendo 1; corrigo 3; restituo 3, reficio 3; correctio *f*; **~er** corrector *m*.
**refractory** contumax.
**refrain** (me) abstineo 2, tempero 1 (*re, a re, quin, quominus*); me contineo 2, contineor 2 (*re, a re*).
**refresh** recreo 1, renovo 1; reficio 3; **~ment** cibus *m*.
**refuge** perfugium *n*, refugium *n*, asylum *n*; **take ~ with** confugio 3 (*ad*); **~e** exsul *m*; profugus *m*.
**refund** reddo 3.
**refus|al** recusatio *f*, repudiatio *f*, repulsa *f*; **~e** recuso 1 (*acc., ne, quin, quominus*); abnuo 3 (*acc.*); nolo (*inf.*); nego 1 (*alqd alci, acc. c. inf.*); purgamentum *n*; *fig.* faex *f*; quisquiliae *f/pl*.
**refut|ation** reprehensio *f*, dissolutio *f*; **~e** refello 3, refuto 1, revinco 3 (*acc.*).
**regain** recipio 3.
**regal** regius; **~ia** insignia *n/pl.* regia.
**regard** specto 1, aspicio 3; intueor 2, respicio 3; habeo 2 (*alqm pro amico*); duco 3 (*alqm amicum etc.*); cura *f*, respectus, us *m*; honor *m*; **have ~ to** rationem habeo 2 (*gen.*); **~less** neglegens, incuriosus (*gen.*); **as ~s** quod.
**regen|cy** procuratio *f* regni; **~t** procurator *m* regni.
**regimen** victus, us *m*.
**regiment** legio *f*, cohors *f*.
**region** regio *f*; tractus, us *m*.
**regist|er** in tabulas refero 3; perscribo 3; tabulae *f/pl.*; album *n*; **~rar** actuarius *m*; **~ry** tabularium *n*.
**regret** piget 2, paenitet 2 (*me alcs rei, inf.*); doleo 2 (*acc., abl., acc. c. inf., quod*).
**regular** constans, certus; ordinarius; aequabilis; iustus (*bellum etc.*); status (*sacrificia, dies etc.*); **~ troops** legionarii milites *m/pl.*; **~ity** ordo *m*; constantia *f*.
**regulat|e** ordino 1, compono 3; moderor 1 (*dat.*); administro 1;

~ion administratio *f*; praeceptum *n*, institutum *n*.

**rehearse** meditor 1; narro 1.

**reign** regno 1; dominor 1 (*dat.*); regnum *n*, imperium *n*.

**reimburse** remuneror 1.

**rein** habena *f*; frenum *n*; **take, hold the ~s** habenas accipio 3, teneo 2; **~ in** coerceo 2, freno 1.

**reinforce** firmo 1; **~ments** subsidia *n/pl.*, auxilia *n/pl.*

**reiterate** itero 1.

**reject** reicio 3; repudio 1; sperno 3; **~ion** repudiatio *f*.

**rejoic|e** *v/i.* gaudeo 2 (*acc. c. inf.*; *quod*); laetor 1 (*abl., acc. c. inf.*); *v/t.* delecto 1; **~ing** laetitia *f*.

**rejoin** redeo 4 (*ad, in alqm, alqd*); respondeo 2 (*acc. c. inf.*); **~der** responsum *n*.

**rekindle** suscito 1.                    [*bum*).\

**relapse** recido 3 (*in graviorem mor-*\

**relate** (e)narro 1, expono 3, refero 3 (*alqd*); trado 3 (*acc. c inf.*); **~ to** attinet 2 (*ad*); spectat 1 (*ad*); **~d** propinquus, cognatus (*dat.*); finitimus.

**relation** propinquus *m*; cognatus *m*; narratio *f*; **~ship** cognatio *f*, coniunctio *f*; necessitudo *f*.

**relative** propinquus *m*; cognatus *m*; **~ly** mediocriter.

**relax** *v/t.* relaxo 1; remitto 3; *v/i.* relanguesco 3; **~ation** remissio *f*, relaxatio *f*; otium *n*.

**release** libero 1; (ex)solvo 3; liberatio *f*; missio *f* (*from service*).

**relent** iram mitigo 1, mollio 4; **~less** atrox, saevus.

**relevant** quod attinet 2 (*ad*).

**relia|ble** fidus, certus; locuples; **~nce** fiducia *f*; **place ~nce on** fidem habeo 2 (*alci*).

**relic** *fig.* monumentum *n*; **~s** reliquiae *f/pl.* (*alcs*).

**relief** levamen *n*, levamentum *n* (*gen.*); *mil.* subsidium *n*, auxilium *n*; **carve in ~** caelo 1.

**relieve** (sub)levo 1; mitigo 1, exonero 1; succurro 3, subvenio 4 (*alci*); (*on duty etc.*) succedo 3 (*dat.*); excipio 3 (*alqm*).

**religi|on** religio *f*; sacra *n/pl.*; **~ous** religiosus, sacer, sollemnis.

**relinquish** remitto 3, concedo 3, relinquo 3.

**relish** delector 1 (*re*); sapor *m*; condimentum *n*.

**reluctant** invitus; **be ~** nolo.

**rely** confido 3 (*dat., abl.*); fidem habeo 2 (*alci*); **~ing on** fretus (*abl.*).

**remain** (per)maneo 2; moror 1; resto 1; supersum; **it ~s that** restat 1 ut; **~der** reliquum *n*; **the ~der of** ceteri *m/pl.*; **~ing** reliquus, residuus, superstes; **~s** reliquiae *f/pl.*

**remark** animadverto 3; dico 3; dictum *n*; **~able** singularis, insignis.

**remedy** remedium *n*, medicamentum *n*; medicamentum do 1; sano 1; medeor 2 (*dat.*); corrigo 3.

**rememb|er** memini; reminiscor 3 (*gen., acc. c. inf.*); recordor 1 (*acc.; acc. c. inf.*); memor sum (*gen.*); **~er me to** saluta (*alqm*); **~rance** recordatio *f*, memoria *f*.

**remind** (ad)moneo 2, commoneo 2, commonefacio 3 (*alqm de re, gen.*).

**reminiscence** recordatio *f*.

**remiss** neglegens; **~ion** remissio *f*.

**remit** mitto 3 (*pecuniam*); remitto 3 (*poenam*); **~tance** pecunia *f*.

**remnant** reliquum *n*; reliquiae *f/pl.*; **the ~ of** reliquus, ceterus.

**remonstrate** reclamo 1; **~ with** obiurgo 1 (*alqm, quod*).

**remorse** conscientia *f* (**for** *gen.*); **feel ~ for** paenitet 2 (*me alcs rei, quod*); **~less** immisericors.

**remote** remotus, semotus (*abl.*); *fig.* alienus, disiunctus (*ab*); **~ness** longinquitas *f*.

**remov|al** amotio *f*; migratio *f*; **~e** *v/t.* removeo 2, amoveo 2; tollo 3; segrego 1; *v/i.* (e)migro 1, commigro 1.

**remunerat|e** remuneror 1 (*alqm*); **~ion** remuneratio *f*; praemium *n*.

**rend** scindo 3; lacero 3, lanio 1.

**render** reddo 3, trado 3, tribuo 3; ago 3 (*gratias*); (*with double acc.*) facio 3, efficio 3, reddo 3; **~ up** dedo 3, trado 3; **~ an account** rationes refero 3.

**rendezvous** constitutum *n*.

**renew** renovo 1, instauro 1, redintegro 1; **~al** renovatio *f*.

**renounce** renuntio 1, eiuro 1; abdico 1 (*me re*).

**renovate** renovo 1.

**renown** gloria *f*, fama *f*; **~ed** clarus.

**rent** conduco 3; **~ out** loco 1; merces *f*; vectigal *n*; **~er** conductor *m*.

**renunciation** abdicatio *f*.

**reopen** (iterum) recludo 3.

**repair** reficio 3, restituo 3; sarcio 4; ~ **to** me recipio 3 (*ad*); restitutio *f*, refectio *f*; **in good** ~ sartus; **in bad** ~ ruinosus.     [(*dat*.).]

**reparation: make** ~ satisfacio 3]

**repast** cena *f*; epulae *f*/*pl.*

**repay** refero 3 (*alqd alci*); remuneror 1 (*alqm*; *alqd*); ~**ment** remuneratio *f*; solutio *f*.

**repeal** abrogo 1; rescindo 3.

**repeat** itero 1, renovo 1; ~ **often** decanto 1; ~**edly** identidem; saepius, persaepe.

**repel** repello 3; propulso 1.

**repent** paenitet 2 (*me alcs rei*, *inf.*, *quod*); ~**ance** paenitentia *f*.

**repetition** iteratio *f*, repetitio *f*.

**repine** queror 3.

**replace** repono 3; ~ ... **with** substituo 3 (*alqm pro alqo*, *alci*); suppono 3 (*alqm pro alqo*); subrogo 1 (*alqm in locum alcs*).

**reple|nish** repleo 2; ~**te** repletus, plenus (*abl.*).

**reply** respondeo 2; responsum *n*.

**report** (re)nuntio 1, refero 3 (*alqd*; *acc. c. inf.*); rumor *m*, fama *f*; relatio *f*, renuntiatio *f*; ~**er** nuntius *m*, notarius *m*.

**repose** pono 3; quies *f*; ótium *n*; **enjoy** ~ otiosus sum.

**reprehen|d** reprehendo 3; ~**sible** vituperabilis.

**represent** repraesento 1, exprimo 3, imitor 1; propono 3 (*acc. c. inf.*); sto 1 (*pro alqo*, *alqa re*); ~**ation** imago *f*; ~**ative** vicarius *m*; procurator *m*.

**repress** reprimo 3; coerceo 2.

**reprieve** supplicium differo 3; veniam do 1; parco 3 (*dat.*); dilatio *f* (supplicii); venia *f*.

**reprimand** reprehendo 3.

**reprisals** ultio *f*.

**reproach** exprobro 1 (*alci alqd*; *quod*); obicio 3 (*alci alqd*; *acc. c. inf.*; *quod*); increpito 1 (*alqm*); opprobrium *n*, probrum *n*; vituperatio *f*; ~**ful** obiurgatorius.

**reprobate** perditus.

**reproduce** propago 1; *fig.* refero 3; imitor 1.

**repro|of** obiurgatio *f*, reprehensio *f*; ~**ve** reprehendo 3, obiurgo 1.

**reptile** serpens *f*.

**republic** res *f* publica; civitas *f* (libera, popularis); ~**an** popularis.

**repudiate** repudio 1.

**repugnan|ce** odium *n*; fastidium *n*; ~**t** aversus (*ab*); **be** ~**t to** odio sum; repugno 1 (*dat.*).

**repuls|e** repello 3; offensio *f*, repulsa *f*; ~**ive** odiosus, foedus.

**reput|able** honestus; ~**ation**, ~**e** fama *f*; **good** ~**e** existimatio *f*, laus *f*; honor *m*; **bad** ~**e** infamia *f*.

**request** peto 3, posco 3 (*alqd ab alqo*; *ut*); rogo 1 (*alqm alqd*; *ut*); rogatum *n*, postulatum *n*; preces *f*/*pl.*

**require** requiro 3 (*alqd*; *alqd ex alqo*); quaero 3; posco 3; desidero 1.

**requisite** necessarius.

**requit|al** remuneratio *f*, vicis *f* (*beneficii*); ultio *f* (*sceleris*); ~**e** vindico 1 (*scelus*); ulciscor 3 (*alqm pro scelere*; *scelus*); (com)penso 1 (*alqd alqa re*); remuneror 1 (*alqm alqa re*).

**rescind** rescindo 3; abrogo 1.

**rescue** libero 1, vindico 1, eripio 3 (*alqm ab*); **come to the** ~ subvenio 4 (*alci*).

**research** investigatio *f*.

**resembl|ance** similitudo *f*; ~**e** similis sum (*gen.*, *dat.*); accedo 3 (*ad*).

**resent** aegre, moleste fero 3 (*alqd*, *quod*); ~**ful** iracundus; ~**ment** ira *f*, invidia *f*; dolor *m*.

**reserv|ation** exceptio *f*; ~**e** (re)servo 1 (*alqd*, *alqm*, *ad*, *dat.*); sepono 3; taciturnitas *f*; ~**es** subsidia *n*/*pl.*; subsidiarii *m*/*pl.*; ~**ed** tectus, taciturnus.

**reservoir** cisterna *f*; lacus, us *m*.

**reside** habito 1; *fig.* consto 1 (*in*, *ex re*); ~**nce** mansio *f*, habitatio *f*; domicilium *n*; domus, us *f*; ~**nt** habitator *m*.

**resign** (con)cedo 3 (*alqd alci*); permitto 3, remitto 3, depono 3; summitto 3 (*me*, *animum*, *ad*, *dat.*); ~**ation** abdicatio *f*; aequus animus *m*; patientia *f*; ~**ed** patiens.

**resin** resina *f*.

**resist** resisto 3, obsisto 3, repugno 1 (*dat.*).

**resolut|e** firmus, fortis, obstinatus; ~**ion** constantia *f*, firmitas *f*; solutio *f*; sententia *f*; **pass a** ~**ion** (de-)cerno 3.

**resolve** (dis)solvo 3; dissipo 1; statuo 3 (*inf.*; *ut*); constituo 3, decerno 3 (*inf.*; *acc. c. inf.*); certum est, concilium est (*mihi*, *inf.*); consilium *n*, propositum *n*; sententia *f*.

**resort** locus *m* celeber; **~ to** decurro 3, descendo 3, confugio 3 (*ad*).

**resound** resono 1, persono 1 (*alqa re*).

**resource** auxilium *n*, subsidium *n*; **~s** opes *f/pl.*, copiae *f/pl.*

**respect** observo 1; suspicio 3, colo 3; vereor 2; observantia *f*, honor *m*; **pay one's ~s to** saluto 1 (*alqm*); **as ~s** quod attinet 2 (*ad*); **in both ~s** in utramque partem; **in every ~** omnino; **in other ~s** ceterum; **~ability** honestas *f*; **~able** honestus; **~ful** observans (*gen.*), verecundus; **~ing** de (*abl.*).

**respiration** spiritus, us *m*; respiratio *f*.

**respite** mora *f*, intermissio *f*.

**resplendent** splendidus.

**respond** respondeo 2 (*dat.*).

**responsib|ility** officium *n*; cura *f*; **be ~le for** praesto 1 (*alqd*); **hold, make ~le for** rationem reposco 3 (*ab alqo alcs rei*).

**rest** (re)quies *f*; otium *n*; adminiculum *n*; **the ~** (*adj.*) reliquus, ceterus; reliquum *n*; *v/t.* repono 3 (*alqd in re*); *v/i.* (re)quiesco 3; quietem capio 3; **~ upon** nitor 3 (*abl.*); **~ with** situm est (*in alqo; in re*).

**restitution: make ~** satisfacio 3 (*alci*); restituo 3 (*alqd*).

**rest|ive** ferox; **~less** turbidus, inquietus.

**restor|ation** refectio *f*; restitutio *f* (*bonorum*); **~e** renovo 1, redintegro 1; restituo 3, refero 3; reddo 3; **be ~ed** redeo 4; **~er** restitutor *m*.

**restrain** coerceo 2, retineo 2; comprimo 3; **~t** moderatio *f*; repagula *n/pl.*

**restrict** (de)finio 4 (*alqd*); circumscribo 3, includo 3 (*alqm*); **~ed** angustus; **~ion** modus *m*; finis *n*.

**result** evenio 4 (*ex re, ut*); evado 3 (*ex re*); fio 3 (*ut*); nascor 3 (*ab, ex*); eventus, us *m*; exitus, us *m*; fructus, us *m*.

**resume** repeto 3, recolo 3.

**retailer** venditor *m*.

**retain** retineo 2, teneo 2; servo 1; **~er** satelles *m and f*.

**retaliat|e** ulciscor 3 (*alqm, alqd*); **~ion** vicis *f* (*gen.*); ultio *f*.

**retard** retardo 1.

**reticent** taciturnus.

**retinue** comitatus, us *m*; satellites *m/pl.*

**retire** recedo 3, decedo 3; abeo 4; me recipio 3; **~d** remotus, quietus; **~ment** solitudo *f*; otium *n*.

**retouch** retracto 1.

**retrace** repeto 3; pedem refero 3.

**retract** renuntio 1.

**retreat** me recipio 3; pedem refero 3; recedo 3; receptus, us *m*; recessus, us *m*; latebrae *f/pl.*

**retribution** poena *f*; merces *f*.

**retrieve** recupero 1; sarcio 4.

**return** *v/i.* redeo 4; revertor 3; *v/t.* reddo 3; refero 3 (*gratiam*); remitto 3; renuntio 1 (*alqm consulem*); reditus, us *m*; regressus, us *m*; remuneratio *f*; quaestus, us *m*; fructus *m/pl.*

**reunite** reconcilio 1.

**reveal** patefacio 3; aperio 4; enuntio 1.

**revel** comissor 1; *fig.* bacchor 1, exsulto 1; comissatio *f*, bacchatio *f*.

**revelation** patefactio *f*.

**reveller** comissator *m*.

**revenge** ultio *f*; poena *f*; vicis *f* (*gen.*); **take ~ on** ulciscor 3 (*alqm*); **take ~ for** vindico 1 (*scelus in alqm*); **~r** vindex *m*.

**revenue** vectigal *n*; fructus, us *m*.

**revere** (re)vereor 2; veneror 1; **~nce** reverentia *f*; honor *m*; **~nd** venerabilis; **~nt** pius, reverens.

**revers|e** inverto 3; *fig.* recindo 3 (*legem, iudicium etc.*); infirmo 1; conversio *f*, commutatio *f*; *mil.* clades *f*; aversus, contrarius; **~t to** redeo 4 (*ad*).

**review** recenseo 2, recognosco 3, lustro 1; recensio *f*, recognitio *f* (*civium etc.*); **~er** censor *m*.

**revile** maledico 3 (*alci*).

**revis|e** corrigo 3, emendo 1; retracto 1 (*leges*); **~ion** emendatio *f*; lima *f*.

**revisit** reviso 3.

**reviv|al** renovatio *f*; **~e** *v/t.* reficio 3, recreo 1 (*alqm ex vulnere, morbo*); *fig.* excito 1, redintegro 1; *v/i.* me, animum recipio 3; renascor 3.

**revoke** renuntio 1, rescindo 3.

**revolt** deficio 3, descisco 3 (*ab alqo*); defectio *f*; tumultus, us *m*; **~ing** foedus.

**revolution** conversio *f*; circuitus, us *m*; commutatio *f*; *pol.* res *f/pl.* novae; **~ary** novus (*res*); seditiosus (*homo*); **~ise** novo 1.

**revolve** volvor 3, convertor 3; voluto 1 (*alqd animo*).

**revulsion** fastidium *n*.

**reward** praemium *n*; merces *f*; fructus, us *m*; praemio afficio 3 (*alqm*); remuneror 1.

**rhetoric** rhetorica *f*; ~al rhetoricus, oratorius; ~ian rhetor *m*.

**rheum** pituita *f*; ~atism dolor *m* artuum.

**rhinoceros** rhinoceros *m*.

**rhyme** versus *m/pl.*; carmen *n*.

**rhythm** numerus *m*; modus *m*; ~ical numerosus.

**rib** costa *f*.

**ribald** obscenus.

**ribbon** vitta *f*, taenia *f*.

**rice** oryza *f*.

**rich** dives, locuples, opulentus (*in abl.*); pretiosus; uber, fertilis (*terra etc.*); ~es divitiae *f/pl.*, opes *f/pl.*; ~ness ubertas *f*, copia *f*.

**rid** libero 1; **get ~ of** exuo 3, depono 3, tollo 3.

**riddle** aenigma *n*; ambages *f/pl.*; **be ~d with** confodior 3.

**ride** vehor 3 (*equo, curru*); ~r eques *m*.

**ridge** dorsum *n*, iugum *n*.

**ridicul|e** risus, us *m*; irrideo 2 (*acc.*); ~ous ridiculus.

**rife: be ~** increbresco 3.

**rifle** compilo 1.

**rift** rima *f*; hiatus, us *m*.

**rig** armo 1; ~ging armamenta *n/pl.*

**right** dexter (*manus etc.*); rectus, iustus, aequus; restituo 3, corrigo 3; fas *n*, iustum *n*; ius *n*; **on, to the ~** dextra, dextrorsum; **all ~** bene habet; **be ~** recte sentio 4, facio 3; **~ hand** dextra (manus) *f*; **~ on** recta; ~eous integer, probus; ~ful iustus, legitimus; ~ly recte, iuste, iure.

**rigid** rigidus; severus.

**rigo|rous** durus, severus; ~ur duritia *f*, asperitas *f*.

**rill** rivulus *m*.

**rim** labrum *n*; crepido *f*.

**rime** pruina *f*.

**rind** crusta *f*, cutis *f*; corium *n*.

**ring** tinnio 4, resono 1; circulus *m*; orbis *m*; (*of people*) corona *f*; (*for finger*) anulus *m*; (*for horses*) gyrus *m*; ~ing clarus (*vox etc.*); ~let cincinnus *m*.

**rinse** eluo 3.

**riot** turbae *f/pl.*; tumultus, us *m*; turbas efficio 3; **run ~** luxurior 1; ~ous turbulentus; dissolutus.

**rip** scindo 3; **~ up** rescindo 3.

**ripe** maturus, tempestivus, coctus; **~ for** paratus (*ad*); **~n** maturesco 3; ~ness maturitas *f*.

**ripple** trepido 1.

**ris|e** (ex)surgo 3; (ex)orior 4; me erigo 3; cresco 3; increbresco 3 (*ventus*); rebello 1; incrementum *n*; ortus, us *m*; collis *m*; tumulus *m*; **give ~e to** pario 3; ~ing ortus, us *m* (*solis*); tumultus, us *m*; seditio *f*, rebellio *f*.

**risk** periclitor 1 (*one's life caput or capite*); periculum *n*, discrimen *n*; **run a ~** periculum facio 3, adeo 4 (*capitis*); ~y periculosus.

**rite** ritus, us *m*.

**rival** aemulor 1 (*alqm*); aemulus *m*, competitor *m*; **~ in love** rivalis *m*; ~ry aemulatio *f*, rivalitas *f*.

**river** flumen *n*; amnis *m*; fluvius *m*; ~-bed alveus *m*.

**rivet** clavus *m*.

**rivulet** rivus *m*.

**road** via *f*; iter, ineris *n*; ~stead statio *f*.

**roam** vagor 1.

**roar** rudo 3; fremo 3; fremitus, us *m*; clamor *m*.

**roast** torreo 2; frigo 3; assus.

**rob** *v/t.* compilo 1 (*templum*); spolio 1 (*alqm re*); adimo 3 (*alqd alci*); *v/i.* latrocinor 1; ~ber latro *m*, fur *m*; ~bery latrocinium *n*.

**robe** vestis *f*, palla *f*; vestio 4.

**robust** validus, robustus.

**rock** *v/t.* agito 1; moveo 2; *v/i.* vacillo 1, nuto 1; rupes *f*, cautes *f*; scopulum *n*, saxum *n*; ~y saxosus, scopulosus.

**rod** virga *f*; **fishing ~** harundo *f*.

**roe** cerva *f*; (*of fish*) ova *n/pl.*; ~buck cervus *m*.

**rogue** veterator *m*, furcifer *m*.

**roll** *v/t.* volvo 3; *v/i.* volvor 3; volutor 1; globus *m*; (*of writing*) volumen *n*; (*of names*) album *n*; ~er (*for ships*) scutula *f*, phalangae *f/pl.*; cylindrus *m*.

**roman|ce** fabula *f*; ~tic commenticius.

**romp** lascivio 4; lascivia *f*.

**roof** tectum *n*, culmen *n*; tego 3.

**room** locus *m*; spatium *n*; conclave *n*; cella *f*; ~y amplus.

**roost** stabulor 1.

**root** radix *f*; *fig.* fons *f*; **take ~** coalesco 3; **become ~ed** inveterasco 3; **~ up** radicitus evello 3; **~ed** inveteratus.

**rope** funis *m*; restis *f*; rudens *m*; **~-walker** funambulus *m*.

**rose** rosa *f*.

**rostrum** rostra *n/pl.*

**rosy** roseus.

**rot** *v/i.* putesco 3; *v/t.* putrefacio 3; tabes *f*.

**rotat|e** volvor 3; me converto 3; convertor 3; **~ion** conversio *f*.

**rotten** put(r)idus.

**rotund** rotundus.

**rouge** fucus *m*; fuco 1.

**rough** asper, horridus; incultus, incomptus; **~ness** asperitas *f*.

**round** globosus, rotundus; flecto 3 (*promontorium*); ambitus, us *m*; orbis *m*; anfractus, us *m*; circuitio *f* (*vigiliarum*); *adv. and prep.* circum, circa (*acc.*); **~ about** circiter (*eandem horam*; *septuaginta*); ad (*centum*); **~ the year ~** toto anno; **~ off** torno 1; concludo 3.

**round|about** devius; **~about way** circuitio *f*; **~ly** libere, aperte.

**rouse** suscito 1, excito 1; **~ oneself** expergiscor 3.

**rout** turba *f*; fuga *f*; fundo 3, fugo 1.

**route** iter, ineris *n*.

**routine** usus, us *m*; consuetudo *f*.

**rove** vagor 1, erro 1.

**row** ordo *m*; versus, us *m*; turba *f*; tumultus, us *m*; **~ of seats** gradus, us *m*; remigo 1; **~er** remex *m*; **~ing** remigatio *f*.

**royal** regius, regalis, **~ty** regnum *n*.

**rub** (per)frico 1; tero 3; **~ off** detergeo 2; **~ out** deleo 2; induco 3.

**rubbish** quisquiliae *f/pl.*, nugae *f/pl.*

**rubble** rudus *n*.

**ruby** carbunculus *m*.

**rude** rudis, inconditus, rusticus; inhumanus, asper, insolens; **~ness** rusticitas *f*; inhumanitas *f*.

**rudiment|s** elementa *n/pl.*; **~ary** incohatus, rudis.

**rue** ruta *f*; paenitet 2 (*me alcs rei*); **~ful** maestus.

**ruffian** latro *m*; sicarius *m*.

**ruffle** agito 1.

**rug** stragulum *n*.

**rugged** asper, praeruptus.

**ruin** perdo 3; profligo 1; affligo 3; corrumpo 3; interitus, us *m*; exitium *n*; pernicies *f*; calamitas *f*, clades *f*; **~ed** ruinosus (*aedes*); afflictus; **~ous** exitiosus, funestus.

**rule** *v/t.* rego 3; impero 1 (*dat.*); moderor 1; *v/i.* praesum (*dat.*); regno 1; decerno 3, edico 3 (*ut*); (*for measuring*) regula *f*; *fig.* regula *f*, norma *f*; praescriptum *n*, praeceptum *n*, institutum *n*; lex *f*; dicio *f*, imperium *n*; **~r** moderator *m*, gubernator *m*, rector *m*; regula *f*.

**rumble** mugio 4; murmur *m*.

**rumour** rumor *m*; fama *f*.

**rumple** ruga *f*.

**run** curro 3; fluo 3 (*aqua*), labor 3, mano 1; **~ aground** eicior 3; **~ away** aufugio 3; **~ out** exeo 4; **~ over** *fig.* percurro 3; **~away** fugitivus *m*; **~ner** cursor *m*.

**rupture** rumpo 3; *fig.* dissidium *n*.

**rural** ruralis.

**rush** iuncus *m*; impetus, us *m*; incursio *f*; concursus, us *m*; ruo 3, curro 3; me praecipito 1; **~ at** me inicio 3 (*in*); occurso 1 (*dat.*); **~ out** evolo 1; me effundo 3; **~ing** praeceps; **~-basket** scirpiculus *m*; **~y** iunceus, scirpeus.

**russet** fulvus.

**rust** robigo *f*; *v/i.* robigine laedor 3; *v/t.* robigine laedo 3.

**rustic** agrestis; rusticus.

**rustle** crepo 1, crepito 1; crepitus, us *m*.

**rusty** robigine laesus.

**rut** orbita *f*.

**ruthless** immitis, saevus, crudelis.

# S

**Sabbath** sabbata *n/pl.*
**sable** niger, ater.
**sabre** gladius *m.*
**sack** saccus *m*; direptio *f* (*urbis*); diripio 3, populor 1; **~cloth** vestis *f* cannabina; **~er** direptor *m.*
**sacred** sacer, sanctus.
**sacri|fice** *v/t.* immolo 1; *fig.* profundo 3 (*alqd pro*); condono 1 (*alqd dat.*); *v/i.* sacrifico 1; (sacrifium) facio 3 (*alci hostiis*); sacrificium *n*; res *f* divina; *fig.* iactura *f*; **~lege** sacrilegium *n*; **~sty** sacrarium *n.*
**sad** maestus, tristis; **be ~** maereo 2; **~den** contristo 1.
**saddle** ephippium *n*; sterno 3; *fig.* **~ with** impono 3 (*alqd alci*); **pack-~** clitellae *f/pl.*
**sadness** tristitia *f*, maestitia *f.*
**safe** tutus, salvus, incolumis; cella *f*; (*for money*) arca *f*; **~-conduct** fides *f*; **~guard** cautio *f*; **~ty** salus, utis *f.*
**saffron** crocum *n and* crocus *m*; croceus.
**sagaci|ous** prudens, sagax; **~ty** sagacitas *f.*
**sage** sapiens *m.*
**sail** navigo 1; **~ round** circumvehor 3; velum *n*; **set ~** vela do 1; navem solvo 3; **~ing** navigatio *f*; **~or** nauta *m.*
**saintly** sanctus, pius.
**sake: for the ~ of** (*alcs, rei*) causa, gratia; pro (*abl.*).
**salamander** salamandra *f.*
**salary** merces *f.*
**sale** venditio *f*; **for ~** venalis; **offer for ~** venum do 1; **public ~** hasta *f*; **~sman** venditor *m.*
**salient** praecipuus.
**saline** salsus.
**saliva** saliva *f.*
**sallow** pallidus, luridus.
**sally** eruptio *f*; **make a ~** eruptionem facio 3.
**salmon** salmo *m.*
**salt** sal *m*; **~-cellar** salinum *n*; **~works** salinae *f/pl.*; **~y** salsus.
**salubrious** salubris.
**salutary** salutaris, utilis.

**salut|ation** salutatio *f*; salus, utis *f*; **~e** saluto 1.
**salvation** salus, utis *f.*
**salve** unguentum *n.*
**salver** scutella *f.*
**same** idem (**as** qui, *atque*).
**sample** exemplum *n.*
**sanct|ify** sacro 1, consecro 1; **~ion** ratum facio 3; sancio 4 (*legem etc.*); permitto 3 (*alci ut*); auctoritas *f*; confirmatio *f*; **~ity** sanctitas *f*; **~uary** asylum *n.*
**sand** arena *f*, saburra *f*; **~-pit** arenaria *f.*
**sandal** solea *f*, crepida *f.*
**sandy** arenosus.
**sane** sanus.
**sanguine: be ~** spero 1 (*acc. c. inf.*); magnam spem habeo 2.
**sanit|ary** purus, saluber; **~y** sanitas *f.*
**sap** sucus *m*; subruo 3, labefacto 1; **~ling** arbor *f* novella.
**sapper** munitor *m.*
**sapphire** sapphirus, i *f.*
**sarcas|m** cavillatio *f*; **~tic** dicax, acerbus.
**sardine** sarda *f.*
**sash** cingulum *n.*
**satchel** loculus *m.*
**sate, satiate** satio 1, saturo 1; expleo 2.
**satiety** saturitas *f.*
**satir|e** satura *f*; **~ical** satiricus; dicax; **~ist** saturarum scriptor *m.*
**satis|faction: give ~faction** satisfacio 3 (*dat.*); placet 2 (*dat.*); **~factorily** ex sententia (mea); **~factory** idoneus, probabilis; **~fy** expleo 2 (*alqd*); satisfacio 3 (*alci*); **be ~fied** satis habeo 2; mihi persuasum est (*acc. c. inf.*).
**satrap** satrapes *m.*
**saturate** saturo 1.
**satyr** satyrus *m.*
**sauce** ius *n*; condimentum *n*; **~pan** cacabus *m*; **~r** patella *f.*
**saucy** petulans, protervus.
**saunter** spatior 1.
**sausage** botulus *m*; tomaculum *n.*
**savage** ferus; immanis, saevus;

homo *m* incultus, barbarus; **~ry** feritas *f*, immanitas *f*, atrocitas *f*; barbaria *f*.

**sav|e** servo 1; eripio 3; salutem affero 3 (*alci*); **~e up** reservo 1; *adv. and prep.* praeter (*acc.*); nisi (*quod*); **~ing** compendium *n* (*alcs rei*); **~iour** servator *m*.

**savour** sapor *m*; **~ of** (red)oleo 2 (*alqd*); **~y** conditus; **be ~y** sapio 3.

**saw** serra *f*; proverbium *n*; *v/t.* serra seco 1 (*alqd*); *v/i.* serram, duco 3; **~dust** scobis *f*.

**say** dico 3; loquor 3 (*alqd*); **~ yes** aio; **~ that ... not** nego 1; **said I** inquam, aio; **said he** inquit, ait; **as Homer ~s** ut ait Homerus; **they (men) ~ that** ferunt 3, traditum est (*acc. c. inf.*); **he is said to be** traditur 3, dicitur 3 (esse); **~ing** dictum *n*, proverbium *n*; **as the ~ing is** ut aiunt.

**scab** scabies *f*.

**scabbard** vagina *f*.

**scaffold** machina *f*; *fig.* securis *f*, supplicium *n*.

**scal|e** conscendo 3; lanx *f*; squama *f* (*piscis etc.*); *fig.* gradus, us *m*; modus *m*; **pair of ~es** trutina *f*; **~ing-ladder** scalae *f/pl.*

**scalp** cutis *f* capitis.

**scalpel** scalpellum *n*.

**scaly** squamosus.

**scamp** verbero *m*, furcifer *m*.

**scan** intueor 2; contemplor 1, considero 1.

**scandal** opprobrium *n*, dedecus *n*; **~ise** offendo 3 (*dat.*); **~ous** probrosus, infamis, turpis.

**scant|iness** exiguitas *f*; inopia *f*; **~y** exiguus, tenuis.

**scapegoat** piaculum *n*.

**scar** cicatrix *f*.

**scarc|e** rarus; **~ely** vix; **~ely yet** vixdum; **~ity** inopia *f*, paucitas *f*.

**scare** terreo 2; **~crow** formido *f*.

**scarf** velamen *n*; rica *f*.

**scarlet** coccum *n*; coccinus.

**scarred** cicatricosus.

**scatter** *v/t.* spargo 3; dissipo 1; disicio 3; *v/i.* dissipor 1, disicior 3; **~ing** dissipatio *f*.

**scene** locus *m*; spectaculum *n*; *thea.* scaena *f*; **come on the ~** intervenio 4; **~ry** scaena *f*; species *f* loci.

**scent** odoror 1 (*cibum etc.*); odor *m*; **get ~ of** olfacio 3, odoror 1 (*alqd*); **~ed** odoratus.

**sceptical: be ~** dubito 1.

**sceptre** sceptrum *n*; scipio *m*.

**schedule** tabula *f*.

**scheme** consilium *n*; ars *f*; insidiae *f/pl.*; ratio *f*; molior 4.

**scholar** vir *m* doctus, eruditus; discipulus *m*; **~ly** doctus; **~ship** litterae *f/pl.*; doctrina *f*.

**school** schola *f* (philosophorum); (*for boys*) ludus *m*; *fig.* disciplina *f*, secta *f* (*Platonis etc.*); erudio 4; **~ed** expertus (*gen.*); **~fellow** condiscipulus *m*; **~master** magister *m*.

**schooner** actuaria *f*.

**scien|ce** scientia *f*, disciplina *f*, doctrina *f*; ars *f*, ratio *f*; **~ce of war** res *f* militaris; **~tific** physicus.

**scion** proles *f*, progenies *f*.

**scissors** forfex *f*.

**scoff at** irrideo 2, derideo 2 (*acc.*); **~ing** irrisio *f*; irrisus, us *m*.

**scold** increpo 1, obiurgo 1; **~ing** obiurgatio *f*.

**scoop** ligula *f*; **~ out** excavo 1 (*alqd*).

**scope** campus *m*; area *f*; locus *m*.

**scorch** amburo 3; torreo 2; **~ed, ~ing** torridus.

**score** noto 1; nota *f*; (*total*) summa *f*; viginti; **reckon the ~** rationem computo 1.

**scorn** contemno 3, sperno 3; **~er** contemptor *m*; **~ful** fastidiosus (*gen.*); arrogans, superbus.

**scorpion** scorpio *m*.

**scot-free** incolumis.

**scoundrel** nebulo *m*, furcifer *m*.

**scour** (de)tergeo 2; verro 3; *fig.* pervagor 1.

**scourge** virgis caedo 3; verbero 1; flagellum *n*.

**scout** explorator *m*, speculator *m*; exploro 1; repudio 1, sperno 3.

**scowl** frontem contraho 3; frontis contractio *f*; **~ing** trux.

**scraggy** strigosus.

**scramble (up)** conscendo 3, scando 3 (*arcem etc.*).

**scrap** frustum *n*.

**scrape** rado 3; angustiae *f/pl.*; **~r** strigilis *f*.

**scratch** rado 3; seco 1; nota *f*.

**scream** vociferor 1; clamo 1, clamito 1; ululo 1; clamor *m*; vociferatio *f*.

**screech** ululo 1; ululatus, us *m*.

**screen** tego 3; vela *n/pl.*; *fig.* species *f*.

**screw** clavus *m*.

**scribe** scriba *m*; librarius *m*.
**script** scriptio *f*, scriptura *f*.
**scrofula** struma *f*.
**scroll** volumen *n*.
**scrub** tergeo 2.
**scrup|le** scrupulus *m*; religio *f*; cunctor 1, dubito 1 (*inf.*); ~ulous religiosus, diligens; ~ulousness religio *f*, diligentia *f*.
**scrutinise** (per)scrutor 1.
**scuffle** rixa *f*.
**scull** palma *f*.
**sculp|tor** sculptor *m*; ~ture sculptura *f*; sculpo 3.
**scum** spuma *f*; *fig.* sentina *f*; quisquiliae *f/pl*.
**scurf** porrigo *f*.
**scurrilous** scurrilis, probrosus.
**scuttle** summergo 3.
**scythe** falx *f*.
**sea** mare *n*; pelagus, i *n*; **by ~ and land** terra marique; **be at ~** fluctuo 1; marinus, maritimus; ~ **board, coast** ora *f* (maritima); ~**gull** mergus *m*.
**seal** (ob)signo 1 (*epistolam, testamenta*); signum *n*; phoca *f*; ~**ed** obsignatus; ~**ing-wax** cera *f*.
**seam** sutura *f*.
**seaman** nauta *m*.
**sear** uro 3.
**search** (per)scrutor 1; ~ **for** quaero 3; indago 1; ~ **into** investigo 1; ~ **out** exploro 1; investigatio *f*; ~**ing** diligens.
**seasick** nauseabundus; **be ~** nauseo 1; ~**ness** nausea *f*.
**seaside** maritimus.
**season** tempus *n*; condio 4 (*cibum*); ~**able** tempestivus; ~**ably** ad tempus; ~**ing** condimentum *n*; sal *m*.
**seat** sedes *f*, sella *f*; (**rows of**) ~**s** subsellia *n/pl.*; ~ **oneself** consido 3; **be ~ed** sedeo 2.
**seaweed** alga *f*.
**secede** descisco 3 (*ab*).
**seclu|ded** secretus; ~**sion** solitudo *f*.
**second** secundus (*ad, ab*); alter; **a ~ time** iterum; momentum *n* (*temporis*); adiuvo 1; ~**ary** secundarius, posterior; ~**er** suasor *m*; ~**ly** deinde; ~**rate** inferior.
**secre|cy** secretum *n*; ~**t** occultus, tectus, arcanus; clandestinus; occultum *n*; commissa *n/pl.*; **keep a ~t** occultum teneo 2 (*alqd*); **keep ~t from** celo 1 (*alqd alqm*); ~**tary** scriba *m*.

**secrete** abdo 3.
**secretly** clam, occulte.
**sect** secta *f*, schola *f*.
**section** pars *f*.
**secure** tutus; confirmo 1; tueor 2; munio 4 (*me contra alqd*).
**security** salus, utis *f*; cautio *f*; pignus *n*, vas *m*; **give ~** caveo 2 (*alci de re*), cautionem praesto 1; **get ~ from** caveo 2 (*ab alqd*); **be ~ for** vas fio (*alci*).
**sedan-chair** lectica *f*.
**sedate** sedatus, gravis.
**sedentary** iners.
**sedge** ulva *f*.
**sediment** faex *f*.
**sediti|on** seditio *f*; tumultus, us *m*; ~**ous** seditiosus, factiosus.
**seduc|e** tempto 1; corrumpo 3; ~**er** corruptor *m*; ~**tion** corruptela *f*; stuprum *n*; ~**tive** blandus.
**sedulous** assiduus.
**see** video 2; cerno 3; conspicor 1; specto 1 (*fabulam, ludos*); (*mentally*) intellego 3; percipio 3; sentio 4; ~ **to** consulo 3 (*dat.*); video 2 (*alqd*); **go to ~** viso 3.
**seed** semen *n*.
**seeing that** quoniam, siquidem.
**seek** quaero 3; (ex)peto 3.
**seem** videor 2 (*inf.*); ~**ing** fictus; ~**ingly** ut videtur; ~**ly** decens, decorus; **it is ~ly** decet 2 (*acc. c. inf.*).
**seer** vates *m*.
**seethe** ferveo 2.
**segregate** secerno 3.
**seiz|e** rapio 3; comprehendo 3, deprehendo 3; *mil.* occupo 1; invado 3; ~**ure** comprehensio *f*.
**seldom** raro.
**select** deligo 3, eligo 3; lectus, exquisitus; ~**ion** delectus, us *m*.
**self** ipse; ~**-confidence** sui fiducia *f*; ~**-control** modestia *f*, moderatio *f*; **be ~ish** mea causa ago 3; mihi (soli) consulo 3.
**sell** *v/t.* vendo 3 (*alqd auro*); *v/i.* veneo, venum eo 4; ~**er** venditor *m*; ~**ing** venditio *f*.
**semblance** imago *f*, umbra *f*; simulacrum *n*.
**semicircle** hemicyclium *n*.
**senat|e** senatus, us *m*; patres *m/pl.*; ~**e-house** curia *f*; ~**or** senator *m*; ~**ors** patres *m/pl.* conscripti; ~**orial** senatorius.
**send** mitto 3; ~ **away** dimitto 3; ~ **back** remitto 3; ~ **for** accerso 3;

**~ word** nuntio 1; certiorem facio 3 (*alqm*); (re)scribo 3; **~ing** missio *f*.

**senil|e** senilis; **~ity** senium *n*.

**senior** maior natu (*quam alqs, alqo*); superior (*aetate, gradu*); **~ity** superior aetas *f*, gradus, us *m*.

**sensation** sensus, us *m*.

**sense** sensus, us *m*; mens *f*, prudentia *f*; sententia *f* (*legis*); **out of one's ~** mente captus; **~less** stultus, fatuus.

**sensible** prudens; **be ~** sentio 4 (*alqd*); intellego 3.

**sensitive** tener, mollis.

**sensual** voluptarius; **~ity** voluptates *f*/*pl*.

**sentence** sententia *f*; *jur*. iudicium *n*; damno 1, condemno 1, multo 1 (*alqm morte, exsilio*); **pass ~** sententiam fero 3.

**sentiment** sensus, us *m*; opinio *f*, sententia *f*; **hold the same ~s** eadem sentio 4.

**sentinel, sentry** vigil *m*, excubitor *m*; **sentinels** vigilia *f*, statio *f*; **be on sentry duty** in statione sum.

**separa|ble** separabilis; **~te** separo 1, disiungo 3 (*a re*); divido 3 (*alqd in partes*); (*mentally*) discerno 3, secerno 3; separatus, disiunctus; **~tion** disiunctio *f*.

**September** (*mensis*) September, bris *m*.

**sepulchre** sepulcrum *n*.

**sequence** ordo *m*; series *f*.

**sequestrate** sequestro pono 3, do 1 (*alqd*).

**serene** tranquillus, serenus.

**serf** servus *m*; **~dom** servitium *n*; servitus, utis *f*.

**series** series *f*; **a ~ of** continuus.

**serious** gravis (*homo, res*); severus (*homo*); serius (*res*); **~ matters** seria *n*/*pl*.; **~ness** gravitas *f*.

**sermon** oratio *f*.

**serpent** serpens *f*, anguis *m and f*; coluber, bri *m*, draco *m*; **~ine** sinuosus, multiplex.

**serrated** serratus.

**serried** confertus, densus.

**servant** famulus *m*, servus *m*; minister, tri *m*.

**serve** servio 4 (*dat*.); prosum (*dat*.); proficio 3 (*ad, in alqd*); *mil*. stipendia mereo(r) 2, milito 1; **~ for** sum (*pro re*); **~ up** appono 3 (*cibum alci*).

**service** ministerium *n*; opera *f*; officium *n*; **military ~** militia *f*;

stipendia *n*/*pl*.; **good ~s** merita *n*/*pl*.; **be of ~ to** prosum (*dat*.); **~able** utilis; aptus (*ad*).

**servi|le** servilis; abiectus, humilis; **~lity** humilitas *f*, adulatio *f*; **~tude** servitus, utis *f*; servitium *n*.

**session** sessio *f*; **~s** conventus *m*/*pl*.

**sesterce** sestertius *m*; **a thousand ~s** sestertium *n*.

**set** status, ratus; series *f*; circulus *m*, globus *m*; *v*/*t*. pono 3; (col)loco 1; statuo 3; *v*/*i*. occido 3 (*sol*); **~ about** incipio 3; **~ against** oppono 3 (*alqd alci rei*); **~ apart** sepono 3; **~ at naught** contemno 3, nihili facio 3; **~ on fire** incendo 3; **~ out** proficiscor 3; **~ up** statuo 3, constituo 3; **~tee** lectus *m*; **~ting** occasus, us *m*.

**settle** *v*/*t*. constituo 3 (*gentem, pretium*); compono 3 (*controversias*); solvo 3 (*nomen, aes alienum*); deduco 3 (*coloniam, colonos*); *v*/*i*. consido 3 (*in*); **~d** certus, ratus; **~ment** deductio *f* (*coloniae*); colonia *f*; compositio *f*; **~r** colonus *m*; advena *m*.

**seven** septem; **~fold** septemplex; **~ hundred** septingenti; **~teen** septendecim; **~th** septimus; **~tieth** septuagesimus; **~ty** septuaginta.

**sever** disiungo 3. [guli.}

**several** aliquot; (com)plures; sin-}

**sever|e** durus, austerus, severus; gravis, acerbus (*poena, morbus etc*.); **~ity** severitas *f*, gravitas *f*.

**sew** suo 3.

**sewer** cloaca *f*.

**sex** sexus, us *m*.

**shabby** obsoletus; pannosus (*homo*); sordidus.

**shackle** vinculum *n*; compes *f*.

**shade** umbra *f*; simulacrum *n*; **~s** manes *m*/*pl*., inferi *m*/*pl*.; opaco 1; **put in the ~** officio 3 (*alci; nomini*); **sun-~** umbraculum *n*.

**shadow** umbra *f*; **~y** inanis, vanus.

**shady** opacus, umbrosus, umbrifer.

**shaft** telum *n*; sagitta *f*; hastile *n*; temo *m*.

**shaggy** villosus, hirtus.

**shak|e** *v*/*t*. quatio 3, concutio 3; agito 1; labefacto 1, commoveo 2; *v*/*i*. quatior 3; *fig*. horreo 2, horresco 3; **~e one's head** abnuo 3; **~y** tremebundus, instabilis.

**shallow** brevis; *fig*. vanus, levis; vadum *n*.

**sham** simulatus, falsus; simulo 1.

**shame** pudor *m*, verecundia *f*; rubor *m*; dedecus *n*, probrum *n*; ruborem, pudorem incutio 3 (*alci*); dedecoro 1 (*acc.*); **feel ~** pudet 2 (*me alcs rei*); **~faced** verecundus; **~ful** turpis, probrosus, flagitiosus; **~less** impudens, improbus; **~lessness** impudentia *f*.

**shank** crus, uris *n*.

**shape** forma *f*, figura *f*, facies *f*; fingo 3; (con)formo 1; **~less** informis, deformis; **~ly** formosus.

**shard** testa *f*.

**share** pars *f*; partior 4, communico 1, consocio 1 (*alqd cum alqo*); **~ out** divido 3; **have a ~ of** in partem habeo 2; intersum (*dat.*); **~d** communis; **~r** particeps *m*, socius *m*.

**shark** pistrix *f*.

**sharp** acutus; acer (*sensus*); sagax, argutus; mordax; **~en** acuo 3; **~er** fraudator *m*; **~ness** asperitas *f*, acerbitas *f*; acumen *n*; subtilitas *f*.

**shatter** frango 3, elido 3; quasso 1.

**shav|e** rado 3, tondeo 2; **~ings** ramenta *n/pl.*

**shawl** palla *f*.

**she** ea, haec, illa.

**sheaf** manipulus *m*; fascis *m*.

**shear** tondeo 2; **~ing** tonsura *f*; **~s** forfices *f/pl.*

**sheath** vagina *f*; **~e** recondo 3 (*gladium in vaginam*).

**shed** profundo 3, effundo 3 (*lacrimas, sanguinem, etc.*); **be ~** decido 3 (*ex alqa re*); tectum *n*, tugurium *n*.

**sheen** fulgor *m*.

**sheep** ovis *f*; **~fold** saepta *n/pl.*

**sheer** abruptus, praeruptus; merus, germanus.

**sheet** (*linen*) linteum *n*; (*paper*) scida *f*; (*metal*) lamina *f*; *naut.* pes *m*.

**shelf** pluteus *m*; pegma *n*.

**shell** concha *f*, testa *f* (*ostreae etc.*); putamen *n*; crusta *f*; **~fish** concha *f*.

**shelter** tego 3, defendo 3; in tutelam recipio 3; perfugium *n*; hospitium *n*.

**shepherd** pastor *m*.

**shield** scutum *n*; clipeus *m*; *fig.* praesidium *n*; tego 3 (*alqd ab alqa re*).

**shift** *v/t.* moveo 2; (per)muto 1; *v/i.* moveor 2, mutor 1; consilium *n*; stropha *f*; tunica *f*; mutatio *f*; **make ~** provideo 2; **~y** versutus, subdolus.

**shin** crus, uris *n*; **~bone** tibia *f*.

**shine** luceo 2, fulgeo 2, niteo 2; nitor *m*.

**shingle** calculi *m/pl.*

**shining** lucidus, nitidus, fulgens.

**ship** navis *f*; **merchant ~** navis *f* oneraria; **war~** navis *f* longa; **in navem impono** 3; **~owner** navicularius *m*; **~ping** naves *f/pl.*; **~wreck** naufragium *n*; **~wrecked** naufragus.

**shirt** tunica *f*, subucula *f*.

**shiver** *v/t.* comminuo 3; *v/i.* horreo 2; tremo 3; fragmentum *n*; horror *m*, tremor *m*.

**shoal** examen *n* (*piscium*); vadum *n*; syrtis *f*.

**shock** conflictus, us *m*; concursus, us *m*; impetus, us *m*; *fig.* offensio *f*; offendo 3; **be ~ed** obstupesco 3; **~ing** foedus, atrox, nefarius.

**shoe** calceus *m*; **indoor ~, horse~** solea *f*; calceo 1; **~maker** sutor *m*; **~string** lingula *f*.

**shoot** planta *f*, virga *f*; *v/t.* (e)mitto 3, conicio 3 (*telum*); vulnero 1 (*alqm*); *v/i.* volo 1; **~ing star** fax *f*.

**shop** taberna *f*; obsono 1; **~keeper** tabernarius *m*; **~ping** obsonatio, us *m*.

**shore** litus *n*; ora *f*; **~ up** fulcio 4.

**short** brevis; **be ~ of** egeo 2 (*abl.*); **fall ~ of** non contingo 3 (*alqd*); **in ~** denique; **~age** inopia *f*; **~coming** delictum *n*; **~cut** compendiaria via *f*; **~en** contraho 3; **~hand** notae *f/pl.*; **~hand writer** notarius *m*; **~ly** brevi, mox; breviter; **~ness** brevitas *f*; **~sighted** hebes (*oculus*); *fig.* improvidus.

**shot** ictus, us *m*; **within, out of, ~** intra, extra ictum (teli).

**shoulder** umerus *m*; **in umeros tollo** 3 (*onus*).

**shout** clamo 1, vociferor 1; clamor *m*.

**shove** trudo 3.

**shovel** rutrum *n*; pala *f*.

**show** monstro 1 (*viam etc.*); praebeo 3, exhibeo 2, praesto 1 (*virtutem*; *me fortem*); **~ that** demonstro 1, doceo 2 (*acc. c. inf.*); **~ off** ostento 1 (*alqd, me*); ostentatio *f*, species *f*; spectaculum *n*.

**shower** imber, bris *m*; ingero 3, fundo 3 (*tela in alqm*); **~y** pluvius.

**showy** magnificus, speciosus.

**shred** conseco 1; fragmentum *n*.

**shrewd** sagax, acutus; **~ness** calliditas *f*.

**shrewish** importunus.

**shriek** ululo 1; ululatus, us *m*.

**shrill** (per)acutus.

**shrine** delubrum *n*, sacrarium *n*.

**shrink** me contraho 3; **~ from** refugio 3, abhorreo 2 (*ab*); detrecto 1, reformido 1 (*alqd*).

**shrivel** torreo 2; **~led** rugosus, torridus.

**shroud** involvo 3 (*alqd alqa re*).

**shrub** frutex *m*; **~bery** arbustum *n*.

**shudder** horreo 2; **~ at** perhorresco 3 (*alqd*); horror *m*, tremor *m*.

**shuffle** *v/t.* (per)misceo 2; *v/i.* tergiversor 1.

**shun** fugio 3; vito 1.

**shut** claudo 3, occludo 3; obsero 1 (*fores*); operio 4; **~ in** includo 3; **~ out** excludo 3; **~ter** foricula *f*.

**shuttle** radius *m*.

**shy** timidus, verecundus; consternor 1; **~ness** verecundia *f*.

**Sibyl** Sibylla *f*; **~line** Sibyllinus.

**sick** aeger, aegrotus; **be ~** aegroto 1; morbo afficior 3; vomo 3; nauseo 1; **be ~ of** taedet 2 (*me alcs rei*); **~en** *v/t.* fastidium moveo 2; *v/i.* in morbum cado 3, incido 3.

**sickle** falx *f*.

**sick|ly** aeger, invalidus; **~ness** morbus *m*; aegrotatio *f*.

**side** latus *n* (*corporis, collis*); pars *f*; factio *f*; **on this, that ~** hinc, illinc; **on this, that ~ of** citra (*acc.*), trans (*acc.*); **on both, all ~s** utrimque, undique; **on, at the ~** a latere (*alcs, exercitus etc.*); **be on the ~ of** sto 1 (*ab alqo*); **be on neither ~** nullius partis sum; **~long** obliquus, limus; **~ways** in obliquum.

**siege** obsidio *f*, obsessio *f*; **lay ~ to** obsideo 2 (*urbem*); oppugno 1; **~-works** opera *n/pl*.

**sieve** cribrum *n*.

**sift** perscrutor 1.

**sigh** suspiro 1; gemo 3; suspirium duco 3, traho 3; suspirium *n*; **~ing** suspiratus, us *m*.

**sight** visus, us *m*; acies *f* (*oculorum*); conspectus, us *m*; aspectus, us *m*; species *f*; spectaculum *n*; **at first ~** primo aspectu; **in ~ of** in conspectu (*alcs*); **catch ~ of** conspicio 3, conspicor 1 (*alqd*).

**sign** signum *n*, indicium *n*, nota *f*; vestigium *n*; **heavenly ~** omen *n*,

portentum *n*; subscribo 3 (*dat.*); **~ with a seal** signo 1.

**signal** signum *n*; insignis, egregius; **give a ~** signum do 1; annuo 3; *mil.* cano 3 (*receptui etc.*).

**sign|ature** nomen *n*; **~et** signum *n*; **~et-ring** anulus *m*.

**significan|ce** significatio *f*; **~t** significans (*verbum*).

**signify** significo 1; sibi vult.

**silen|ce** silentium *n*; refuto 1 (*alqm*); **keep ~ce** taceo 2, sileo 2; **~t** tacitus, silens; **~tly** tacite.

**silk** serica *n/pl.*; bombyx *m*; **~en** sericus.

**sill** limen *n*.

**sill|iness** stultitia *f*; **~y** stultus, ineptus, fatuus.

**silver** argenteus; argentum *n*; argento induco 3 (*alqd*).

**similar** similis, par (*gen., dat.*); **~ity** similitudo *f*.

**simile** similitudo *f*.

**simple** simplex, merus; **~-minded** ineptus, credulus; **~ton** stultus (homo) *m*.

**simpl|icity** simplicitas *f*; candor *m*; **~ify** dilucide, apertius narro 1; explano 1; **~y** solum, simpliciter.

**simulat|e** simulo 1; **~ion** simulatio *f*.

**simultaneously** eodem tempore; simul.

**sin** peccatum *n*, delictum *n*; pecco 1.

**since** ex (*abl.*), ab (*abl.*); post (*acc.*); *conj.* postquam (*perf. indic.*); **it is many years** abhinc multos annos; **long ~** iamdudum; (*causal*) cum (*subj.*), quoniam (*indic.*).

**sincer|e** simplex, candidus, sincerus; **~ity** probitas *f*, sinceritas *f*.

**sinew** nervus *m*; lacertus *m*; **~y** nervosus.

**sinful** impius, pravus.

**sing** cano 3, canto 1 (*alqd*).

**singe** aduro 3, amburo 3.

**sing|er** cantator *m*, cantatrix *f*; **~ing** cantus, us *m*.

**single** unus, solus; **~ out** eligo 3; **in ~ combat** comminus.

**singular** singularis, unicus, egregius; novus, mirabilis.

**sinister** dirus.

**sink** *v/t.* deprimo 3 (*navem*); *v/i.* consido 3, desido 3; mergor 3 (*in aquam*); ruo 3; collabor 3.

**sinner** peccator *m*.

**sinuous** sinuosus.

**sip** sorbillo 1, degusto 1.
**sire** pater, tris *m*, genitor *m*.
**Siren** Siren *f*.
**sister** soror *f*.
**sit** sedeo 2 (*in sede*); ~ **down** consido 3; ~ **up** vigilo 1 (*de nocte*).
**site** situs, us *m*; locus *m*.
**sitting** (con)sessio *f*.
**situat|ed** situs (*in*); **be ~ed** iaceo 2; **~ion** situs, us *m*; locus *m*.
**six** sex; ~ **hundred** sescenti; **~teen** sedecim; **~teenth** sextus decimus; **~tieth** sexagesimus; **~ty** sexaginta.
**size** magnitudo *f*, amplitudo *f*; **of what ~?** quantus?
**skein** spira *f*.
**skeleton** ossa *n/pl.*; *fig.* larva *f*.
**sketch** adumbro 1; describo 3; adumbratio *f*; lineamenta *n/pl.*
**skewer** veru *n*.
**skil|ful** sollers, habilis; **~l** sollertia *f*, peritia *f*; artificium *n*; **~led** peritus (*gen., abl.*); doctus, sciens (*gen.*).
**skim** despumo 1; ~ **over** percurro 3, perstringo 3, rado 3 (*alqd*).
**skin** cutis *f*; pellis *f*, tergum *n* (*bovis etc.*); pellem detraho 3 (*alci*); **dressed in ~s** pellitus; **~ny** macer.
**skip** exsulto 1; salio 4; lascivio 4 (*agnus etc.*); *fig.* praetereo 4, transilio 4; **~per** navicularius *m*; nauarchus *m*.
**skirmish** proelium *n* (leve); concursatio *f*; velitor 1, concurso 1; **~er** veles *m*, concursator *m*.
**skirt** limbus *m*; praetereo 4; *fig.* perstringo 3.
**skittish** lascivus.
**skulk** lateo 2; delitesco 3 (*in re*).
**skull** caput *n*.
**sky** caelum *n*; **~-blue** caeruleus; **raise to the skies** in caelum fero 3.
**slab** lapis *m*; tabula *f*.
**slack** laxus, remissus; piger; **~en** remitto 3; relaxo 1; **~ness** pigritia *f*, remissio *f*.
**slake** exstinguo 3, restinguo 3.
**slander** maledico 3 (*dat.*); criminor 1, obtrecto 1 (*alqm*); maledictio *f*, criminatio *f*, obtrectatio *f*; crimen *n*; **~er** obtrectator *m*; **~ous** maledicus.
**slanting** obliquus.
**slap** alapa *f*; pulso 1.
**slash** incido 3; plaga *f*.
**slate** (*roof*) tegula *f*; **writing-~** tabula *f*.

**slaughter** caedo 3, concido 3; trucido 1; caedes *f*, internecio *f*.
**slave** servus *m*; famulus *m*; **home-born ~** verna *m and f*; **female ~** ancilla *f*, serva *f*; (de)sudo 1; laboro 1; **~-dealer** venalicius *m*; **~ry** servitium *n*; servitus, utis *f*.
**slay** interficio 3, caedo 3, occido 3; neco 1; interimo 3; **~er** interfector *m*, percussor *m*.
**sledge** trahea *f*; **~hammer** malleus *m*.
**sleek** nitidus, nitens.
**sleep** dormio 4; quiesco 3; dormito 1, somnum capio 3; ~ **off** edormio 4; somnus *m*; quies *f*; sopor *m*; **go to ~** obdormisco 3; **during ~ in** somnis; **~iness** somni cupido *f*; **~ing-draught** sopor *m*; **~less** insomnis; **be ~less** vigilo 1; **~lessness** insomnia *f*; **~y** semisomnus, somniculosus.
**sleet** grando *f*.
**sleeve** manicae *f/pl.*
**sleigh** trahea *f*.
**sleight-of-hand** praestigiae *f/pl.*
**slender** gracilis, tenuis; exilis; **~ness** gracilitas *f*.
**slice** concido 3; segmentum *n*.
**slide** labor 3; lapsus, us *m*.
**slight** levis, exiguus, parvus; despicio 3, contemno 3, parvi facio 3; neglego 3; indignitas *f*, neglegentia *f*; **~ingly** contemptim.
**slim** gracilis, tenuis.
**slim|e** limus *m*; lutum *n*; **~y** limosus.
**sling** funda *f*; mitto 3, conicio 3; suspendo 3 (*alqd e re*); **~er** funditor *m*.
**slink away** me subduco 3.
**slip** labor 3; **let ~** amitto 3 (*opportunitatem*); ~ **away** me subduco 3; ~ **out of** elabor 3; lapsus, us *m*; *fig.* error *m*; **make a ~** erro 1; **~per** solea *f*, crepida *f*; **~pery** lubricus; **~shod** dissolutus.
**slit** incido 3, scindo 3.
**sloop** lembus *m*.
**slop|e** clivus *m*; fastigium *n*; vergo 3; **~ing** declivis, acclivis, proclivis.
**sloth** segnitia *f*, desidia *f*; **~ful** segnis, ignavus, piger.
**slovenly** neglegens.
**slow** tardus, lentus, segnis; **~ness** tarditas *f*, pigritia *f*.
**slugg|ard** homo *m* ignavus; **~ish** piger, ignavus.

**sluice** cataracta *f.*

**slumber** sopor *m*; dormio 4.

**slur** macula *f*; **cast a ~ upon** maculo 1 (*alqd*).

**slush** tabes *f.*

**sly** callidus, astutus, vafer.

**smack** alapa *f*; sonus *m*; **fishing-~** lenunculus *m*; ferio 4; verbero 1; **~ of** sapio 3 (*alqd*); (red)oleo 2 (*alqd*).

**small** parvus, tenuis, brevis, exiguus; **how ~?** quantulus?; **~ness** exiguitas *f*, brevitas *f.*

**smart** lautus, acer, acerbus; sagax; mordeor 2, doleo 2; poenam do 1; morsus, us *m*, dolor *m.*

**smash** comminuo 3, confringo 3.

**smear** lino 3 (*alqd alqa re*); illino 3 (*alqd alci rei*).

**smell** olfacio 3, odoror 1; **~ of** (red)oleo 2 (*alqd*); odor *m*; **sense of ~** odoratus, us *m*; **sweet-~ing** odoratus.

**smelt** (ex)coquo 3.

**smile** (sub)rideo 2, renideo 2; risus, us *m.*

**smite** ferio 4.

**smith** faber, *m*; ferrarius *m*; **~y** officina *f* (ferraria); fabrica *f.*

**smok|e** *v/i.* fumo 1; *v/t.* fumigo 1; fumus *m*; vapor *m*; **~y** fumosus, fumidus.

**smooth** levis, teres; glaber; placidus, tranquillus (*mare*); levo 1; polio 4; rado 3; **~ness** levitas *f*, lenitas *f*; **~-tongued** blandus.

**smother** opprimo 3; suffoco 1; *fig.* reprimo 3, comprimo 3.

**smoulder** fumo 1.

**smudge** litura *f.*

**smug** mihi placens.

**smuggle** furtim, contra leges importo 1 (*alqd*).

**smut** fuligo *f*; **~ty** *fig.* obscenus.

**snack** cenula *f.*

**snaffle** frenum *n.*

**snail** cochlea *f.*

**snak|e** anguis *m and f*; coluber, bri *m*; serpens *f*; **~y** anguineus, vipereus.

**snap** *v/t.* praefringo 3; *v/i.* frangor 3, rumpor 3; crepo 1; concrepo 1 (*digitis*); **~ up** corripio 3; crepitus, us *m.*

**snare** plaga *f*, pedica *f*; laqueus *m*; *fig.* insidiae *f/pl.*; irretio 4; laqueo capto 1.

**snarl** gannio 4; ringor 3.

**snatch** rapio 3, carpo 3; **~ at** capto 1; **~ away from** avello 3; **~ up** arripio 3; **in ~es** carptim.

**sneak** correpo 3 (*in intra*); arrepo 3 (*ad*).

**sneer** irrideo 2, derideo 2, naso suspendo 3 (*alqm, alqd*); irrisio *f*; irrisus, us *m.*

**sneez|e** sternuo 3; **~ing** sternumentum *n.*

**sniff** odoror 1.

**snip** praecido 3; segmentum *n.*

**snore** sterto 3.

**snort** fremo 3; fremitus, us *m.*

**snout** rostrum *n.*

**snow** nix *f*; **it ~s** ningit 3; **~-white** niveus, nivalis; **~y** nivosus.

**snub** contemno 3, sperno 3; **~-nosed** simus, silus.

**snuff** (out) exstinguo 3.

**snug** commodus.

**so** ita, tam, adeo (... ut); **just ~** sic; ita; **and ~** itaque, ergo, igitur; **and ~ on** et cetera.

**soak** *v/t.* madefacio 3; macero 1; *v/i.* mano 1; **~ed** madidus.

**soap** sapo *m.*

**soar** sublime feror 3; subvolo 1; me tollo 3.

**sob** singulto 1; singultus, us *m.*

**sob|er** sobrius, siccus; sanus; modestus, temperans; **~riety** sobrietas *f*; continentia *f*, temperantia *f.*

**sociab|ility** facilitas *f*; **~le** sociabilis; comis.

**social** communis, civilis.

**society** societas *f*, communitas *f*, commune *n*; civitas *f*; sodalitas *f*, collegium *n.*

**socket** cavum *n*; sedes *f.*

**socle** basis *f.*

**sod** caespes *m.*

**soda** nitrum *n.*

**sodden** madidus.

**sofa** lectulus *m.*

**soft** mollis, lenis, tener; mitis, mansuetus; **~en** *v/t.* (e)mollio 4; mitigo 1 (*cibum, severitatem*); lenio 4, placo 1; *v/i.* mitesco 3, mansuesco 3; **~ness** mollitia *f*, lenitas *f.*

**soil** terra *f*; solum *n*; humus, i *f*; inquino 1, foedo 1.

**sojourn** (com)moror 1; commoratio *f*, mansio *f.*

**solace** consolor 1; consolatio *f*; solatium *n.*

**solder** ferrumen *n*; ferrumino 1.

**soldier** miles *m*; **common ~** gregarius (miles) *m*; **~ly** militaris; **~y** miles *m*.

**sole** planta *f*; solum *n*; solus, unus, unicus; **~ly** solum, tantum.

**solemn** sollemnis, festus; augustus, religiosus; severus, gravis, serius; **~ity** sollemne *n*; gravitas *f*, severitas *f*; **~ize** celebro 1.

**solicit** peto 3 (*alqd ab alqo*); flagito 1, obsecro 1 (*alqm; ut*); **~ation** flagitatio *f*; **~or** cognitor *m*; iuris consultus *m*; **~ous** officiosus; **~ude** anxietas *f*.

**solid** solidus; firmus, robustus; solidum *n*; **~ify** concresco 3.

**soliloquize** mecum loquor 3.

**solit|ary** solitarius (*homo*); desertus, solus, secretus; **~ude** solitudo *f*.

**solo** solus.

**solstice: summer ~** solstitium *n*; **winter ~** bruma *f*.

**solution** dilutum *n*; explicatio *f*.

**solve** (dis)solvo 3; enodo 1; **be ~nt** solvendo sum.

**sombre** tristis, tenebrosus.

**some** aliqui, nonnullus; aliquot (*pl.*); aliquid, aliquantum *n*; **~ ... others** alii ... alii; **~body, ~one** aliquis, quidam, nescio quis; **~how** aliqua; **~thing** aliquid, nescio quid; **~time** aliquando; **~times** aliquando, interdum, nonnunquam; modo ... modo; **~where** alicubi.

**son** filius *m*; **~-in-law** gener, eri *m*.

**song** cantus, us *m*; carmen *n*.

**sonorous** sonorus, clarus.

**soon** mox, brevi, iam; **~ after** post paulo; **as ~ as** simul atque, ac; statim ut; cum primum, ubi primum; **as ~ as possible** quamprimum; **~er ante ... quam**; libentius.

**soot** fuligo *f*.

**soothe** mitigo 1, sedo 1, placo 1.

**soothsayer** augur *m*, haruspex *m*, vates *m*.

**sooty** fuliginosus, fumosus.

**sop** *fig.* delenimentum *n*.

**sophist** sophistes *m*; cavillator *m*; **~ical** captiosus; **~ry** captiones *f/pl.*; **~icated** urbanus.

**soporific** soporifer, somnificus.

**sorcer|er** veneficus *m*; magus *m*; **~ess** maga *f*, saga *f*; **~y** veneficia *n/pl.*

**sordid** sordidus.

**sore** ulcus *n*; acerbus, gravis (*dolor etc.*); **be ~** doleo 2 (*caput etc.*); *fig.* aegre fero 3 (*alqd; quod*); **~ly** graviter; **~ness** dolor *m*.

**sorrel** lapathus *m*.

**sorrow** dolor *m*, maeror *m*; luctus, us *m*; doleo 2, lugeo 2; **~ful** maestus, maerens, tristis.

**sorry** miser, miserabilis; **be ~** paenitet 2, piget 2 (*me alcs rei; inf.; quod*).

**sort** genus; **a ~ of** quidam; **of this, that ~** huiusmodi, eiusmodi; **of such a ~** is, talis; **of all ~s** omnis; digero 3, dispono 3; **~ with** consentio 4 (*cum*).

**sortie** eruptio *f*, excursio *f*; **make a ~** erumpo 3.

**sot** potator *m*.

**soul** animus *m*; anima *f*; **with all my ~** ex animo, toto pectore; **not a ~** nemo (omnium); **~less** hebes.

**sound** sanus; salvus, incolumis; artus (*somnus*); sonus *m*; sonitus, us *m*; vox *f*; *v/t.* cano 3 (*classicum*; *signum*; *fidibus*); tento 1 (*vadum*); scrutor 1 (*animos*); **~** the praises of celebro 1 (*laudem*; *alqm*); *v/i.* sono 1, cano 3; sonitum reddo 3; **~ness** sanitas *f*, gravitas *f*.

**soup** ius *n*.

**sour** acerbus; acidus; amarus; **turn ~** (co)acesco 3.

**source** fons *m*; caput *n*; origo *f*; **have its ~ in** orior 4 (*ab*).

**south** meridies *m*; australis, meridianus; **~ wind** auster, tri *m*; **~-east** inter meridiem et solis ortum; **~-east wind** eurus *m*; **~-pole** polus *m* australis; **~-west** inter meridiem et occasum solis; **~-west wind** Africus *m*.

**sovereign** rex *m*, princeps *m*; potentissimus; validus; **~ty** principatus, us *m*; regnum *n*; imperium *n*.

**sow** scrofa *f*, porca *f*; (con)sero 3; **~er** sator *m*; **~ing** sementis *f*, satio *f*.

**spac|e** locus *m*; spatium *n*, intervallum *n*; **~ious** amplus, latus, capax; **~iousness** amplitudo *f*.

**spade** pala *f*.

**span** palmus *m*; spatium *n* (*temporis*); iungo 3 (*flumen ponte*).

**spangled** distinctus (*stellis etc.*).

**spar|e** exilis; subsicivus (*tempus*, *opera*); parco 3 (*dat.*); parce utor 3 (*abl.*); **~ing** parcus (*in re*; *gen.*).

**spark** scintilla *f*; igniculus *m*; **~le** mico 1, corusco 1, scintillo 1; **~ling** micans, coruscus.

**sparrow** passer, eris *m*.

**sparse** rarus.

**spasm** convulsio *f*; **~odic** *fig.* rarus.

**spatter** aspergo 3.

**speak** dico 3, loquor 3 (*de re*); **~ out** eloquor 3; **~ to** alloquor 3, appello 1 (*alqm*); **~er** orator *m.*

**spear** hasta *f.*; telum *n.*; hasta transfigo 3 (*alqm*); **~man** hastatus *m.*; iaculator *m.*

**special** proprius, peculiaris; praecipuus, extraordinarius; **~ity** proprium *n.*; quod proprium est (*gen., dat.*); **~ly** praecipue.

**species** genus *n.*

**specif|ic** peculiaris; certus; **~ically** subtiliter; diserte.

**specimen** exemplum *n.*, exemplar *m.*; specimen *n.*

**specious** probabilis, speciosus.

**speck** macula *f.*; **~led** maculosus, varius.

**specta|cle** spectaculum *n.*; **~tor** spectator *m.*

**spectre** larva *f.*; simulacrum *n.*, imago *f.*

**speculat|e** cogito 1 (*de re*); inquiro 3 (*rem*); conicio 3; coniecturam facio 3; **~ion** coniectura *f.*

**speech** oratio *f.*, lingua *f.*; contio *f.*; sermo *m.*; verba *n/pl.*; **make a ~** orationem, contionem habeo 2; **~less** mutus.

**speed** celeritas *f.*, accelero 1, maturo 1; fortuno 1; **~y** celer, citus.

**spell** carmen *n.*; cantus, us *m.*; litteras ordino 1.

**spend** impendo 3, insumo 3. (*alqd in alqd*); ago 3, dego 3, consumo 3 (*tempus*); **~thrift** nepos *m.*; profusus (homo) *m.*

**spent: be ~** defervesco 3 (*ira, cupido etc.*).

**spew** vomo 3.

**sphere** sphaera *f.*; globus *m.*; *fig.* campus *m.*; provincia *f.*, area *f.*

**sphinx** Sphinx *f.*

**spice** odor *m.*; condimentum *n.*; condio 4; **~d** odoratus.

**spider's web** aranea *f.*

**spike** clavus *m.*; cuspis *f.*; spica *f.*

**spill** effundo 3; assula *f.*

**spin** *v/t.* neo 2; deduco 3; verso 1; *v/i.* versor 1; **~ out** duco 3; **~dle** fusus *m.*

**spine** spina *f.*

**spinster** innupta *f.*

**spiral** spira *f.*, coc(h)lea *f.*; **in a ~ shape** in cocleam.

**spirit** animus *m.*; anima *f.*; mens *f.*, ingenium *n.*; vigor *m.*; voluntas *f.*,

sententia *f.* (*legis*); **high ~s** animi *m/pl.*, spiritus *m/pl.*; **~s of the dead** Manes *m/pl.*; **~ed** animosus, ferox, acer; **~less** ignavus; abiectus (animo).

**spit** spuo 3; veru (con)figo 3 (*carnem*); veru *n.*

**spite** malevolentia *f.*, malignitas *f.*, invidia *f.*; laedo 3; malevolentia utor 3 (*in alqm*); **~ful** malevolus, infestus.

**spittle** sputum *n.*

**splash** aspergo 3 (*alqm alqa re*); sonitus, us *m.*

**spleen** lien *m.*; bilis *f.*; stomachus *m.*

**splend|id** splendidus, lautus, magnificus; praeclarus; **~our** splendor *m.*; lautitia *f.*

**splenetic** stomachosus.

**splinter** assula *f.*; fragmentum *n.*

**split** *v/t.* (dif)findo 3, scindo 3; *v/i.* dissilio 4; fissum *n.*; fissura *f.*

**splutter** crepo 1, crepito 1; balbutio 4.

**spoil** spolio 1; corrumpo 3; vitio 1; (nimium) indulgeo 2 (*dat.*); praeda *f.*; spolia *n/pl.*

**spoke** radius *m.*

**spokesman** interpres *m.*, orator *m.*

**spondee** spondeus *m.*

**sponge** spongia *f.*; spongia detergo 3.

**spontaneous** voluntarius; **~ly** sua sponte, ultro.

**spoon** cochlear *n.*

**sporadic** rarus.

**sport** ludo 3; ludus *m.*; lusus, us *m.*; ludibrium *n.*; **make ~ of** ludifico 1 (*alqm*); **be the ~** of ludibrio sum (*alcs*); **~ive** ludicer, iocosus; **~sman** venator *m.*

**spot** macula *f.*, nota *f.*; locus *m.*; **on the ~** ibidem; conspicio 3; **~less** integer, purus; **~ted** maculosus, varius.

**spouse** coniunx *f.* and *m.*

**spout** os *n.*; prosilio 4; emico 1.

**sprain** intorqueo 2.

**sprawl** fundor 3 (*humo*).

**spray** aspergo 3; aspergo *f.*; ramulus *m.*

**spread** extendo 3, pando 3; **~ abroad** *v/t.* sero 3, differo 3, divulgo 1; *v/i.* diffundor 3; serpo 3; evagor 1; increbresco 3, percrebresco 3, peragro 1 (*rumores etc.*); **~ing** patulus.

**sprig** ramulus *m.*

**sprightly** alacer, hilaris.

**spring** ver *n*; fons *m*; saltus, us *m*; vernus; salio 4, exsilio 4; **~ down** desilio 4; **~ from** nascor 3 (*ab, ex re*; *alqo*); **~ up** coorior 4 (*tempestas etc.*); exorior 4 (*seditio etc.*); exsilio 4 (*de sella*); **~-time** vernum tempus *n*.

**sprinkle** aspergo 3, inspergo 3 (*alqd alqa re*; *alqd alci rei*).

**sprout** cresco 3, emergo 3 (*ex*); surculus *m*.

**spruce** nitidus, lautus.

**spume** spuma *f*.

**spur** calcar *n*; (*of mountains*) iugum *n*; calcaribus concito 1; calcaria subdo 1 (*equo*); *fig.* concito 1.

**spurious** falsus.

**spurn** aspernor 1; reicio 3.

**spurt** emico 1; nisus, us *m*; impetus, us *m*.

**spy** explorator *m*, speculator *m*; **~ out** exploro 1.

**squabble** altercor 1, rixor 1; iurgium *n*.

**squadron** (**of cavalry**) turma *f*, ala *f*.

**squal|id** sordidus, squalidus; **~or** squalor *m*.

**squall** procella *f*; vagio 4.

**squander** effundo 3; dissipo 1; **~er** nepos *m*.

**square** quadratum *n*; quadratus; quadro 1; **~ with** consentio 4 (*cum*); **~ accounts** rationem subduco 3.

**squash** obtero 3.

**squat** subsido 3; consido 3; brevis, humilis.

**squeak** strideo 2; stridor *m*.

**squeamish** fastidiosus.

**squeeze** comprimo 3, premo 3.

**squint** strabonem sum; limis (oculis) intueor 2; **~ing** strabo, paetus.

**squire** armiger, eri *m*.

**squirrel** sciurus *m*.

**stab** (con)fodio 3, percutio 3; vulnus *n*.

**stability** stabilitas *f*.

**stable** stabilis, firmus, solidus; stabulum *n*.

**stack** coacervo 1; acervus *m*; strues *f*.

**staff** baculum *n*; scipio *m*; *fig.* columen *n*; **military ~** legati *m/pl*.

**stag** cervus *m*.

**stage** pulpitum *n*, proscaenium *n*; scaena *f*; gradus, us *m*.

**stagger** titubo 1, vacillo 1.

**stagnant** iners; *fig.* frigidus; **be ~** stagno 1; **~ water** stagnum *n*.

**stagnat|e** refrigesco 3, torpesco 3; **~ion** cessatio *f*; torpor *m*.

**staid** severus.

**stain** tingo 3, inficio 3; maculo 1, foedo 1; macula *f*; *fig.* labes *f*, nota *f*; **~less** purus.

**stair** scala *f*; gradus, us *m*; **~case** scalae *f/pl*.

**stake** palus *m*; stipes *m*; sudes *f*; pignus *n*; **be at ~** in discrimen venio 4; pono 3.

**stale** obsoletus, vulgaris; mucidus.

**stalk** stirps *f*, caulis *m*; *v/i.* incedo 3; *v/t.* (vestigiis) persequor 3.

**stall** stabulum *n*, tectum *n*; taberna *f*.

**stallion** (equus) admissarius *m*.

**stamina** robur *n*; vires *f/pl*.

**stammer** (lingua) haesito 1; balbutio 4; haesitatio *f*; **~ing** balbus.

**stamp** signo 1; imprimo 3; pedem supplodo 3; moneta *f*, forma *f*, nota *f*; (pedis) supplosio *f*.

**stand** *v/i.* sto 1; *v/t.* tolero 1; patior 3, perfero 3; statio *f*; **~ raised** ~ suggestus, us *m*; **be at, come to, a ~** consisto 3; **bring to a ~** constituo 3; **make a ~** resisto 3; **~ by** adsum (*dat.*); **~ firm** consisto 3; **~ for** peto 3 (*magistratum*); **~ round** circumsto 1 (*acc.*); **~ still** subsisto 3, consisto 3; **~ thus** se habet 2 (*res*); **it ~s to reason** dubitari non potest (*quin*); **~ up** (con)surgo 3; **~ up for** adsum (*dat.*).

**standard** signum *n*, vexillum *n*; norma *f*, regula *f*; **~-bearer** aquilifer, eri *m*; signifer, eri *m*.

**standing** status, us *m*; locus *m*.

**standstill: be at a ~** cesso 1; haereo 2.

**star** stella *f*; sidus *n*, astrum *n*; *fig.* lumen *n*.

**starboard** dextra *f*; **to ~** ad dexteram; dextera.

**starch** amylum *n*.

**stare** stupeo 2; **~ at** intueor 2 (*alqd*; *in alqd*); (oculorum) obtutus, us *m*.

**stark naked** plane nudus.

**starling** sturnus *m*.

**starry** sidereus, stellans.

**start** *v/i.* tremo 3; proficiscor 3; incipio 3 (*alqd*; *inf.*); coepi (*inf.*); *v/t.* instituo 3; aggredior 3 (*alqd, ad alqd*); **~ing-place** carcer, eris *n*.

**startle** terreo 2; timorem, metum inicio 3 (*alci*).

**starv|ation** fames *f*, inedia *f*; **~e**

fame conficior 3, consumor 3; *fig.* privo 1 (*alqm alqa re*).

**state** condicio *f*; status, us *m*; locus *m*; res *f* publica, civitas *f*; pompa *f*; publicus, civilis; profiteor 2; declaro 1, affirmo 1, explico 1; **~liness** lautitia *f*, gravitas *f*; **~ly** magnificus, gravis; **~ment** affirmatio *f*, professio *f*; testimonium *n*; **~sman** qui in re publica versatur; vir *m* rei publicae gubernandae peritus.

**station** locus *m*; condicio *f*; ordo *m*; statio *f*; (dis)pono 3; **~ary** fixus, immotus; **~ery** chartae *f*/*pl.*

**statue** statua *f*; signum *n*.

**stature** statura *f*.

**statute** lex *f*.

**stave** scipio *m*; **~ off** arceo 2, prohibeo 2.

**stay** *v/i.* maneo 2, commoror 1 (*apud, in*); *v/t.* moror 1; mora *f*; commoratio *f*; *fig.* columen *n*, praesidium *n*.

**stead: in his ~** pro eo; **~fast** constans; firmus; **~fastness** constantia *f*; **~iness** stabilitas *f*; **~y** firmus, stabilis; frugi, honestus.

**steak** frustum *n* (*carnis*); offa *f*.

**steal** furor 1; surripio 3; **~ away** me subduco 3; dilabor 3; **~ over, upon** irrepo 3 (*in alqd*); **~ up to** arrepo 3 (*ad*); **~ing** furtum *n*.

**stealth: by ~** clam; furtim; **~y** furtivus, clandestinus.

**steam** vapor *m*; *v/i.* fumo 1; *v/t.* vaporo 1.

**steed** equus *m* (bellator).

**steel** chalybs *m*; ferrum *n*; duro 1.

**steep** praeceps, arduus, praeruptus; madefacio 3; **~le** turris *f*.

**steer** guberno 1; rego 3; iuvencus *m*; **~ing** gubernatio *f*; **~sman** gubernator *m*.

**stem** stirps *f*; stipes *m*; obsisto 3, resisto 3 (*dat.*).

**stench** fetor *m*; foedus odor *m*.

**stenograph|er** notarius *m*; **~y** notae *f*/*pl.*

**step** gradus, us *m*; vestigium *n*; *fig.* **~s** consilium *n*; incedo 3, ingredior 3; **~ by ~** pedetemptim; **~-daughter** privigna *f*; **~-father** vitricus *m*; **~-mother** noverca *f*; **~-son** privignus *m*.

**steril|e** sterilis, inutilis; **~ity** sterilitas *f*.

**stern** severus, durus, rigidus; puppis *f*; **~ness** severitas *f*.

**stew** coquo 3; caro *f* elixa.

**steward** vilicus *m*; procurator *m*.

**stick** *v/t.* (de)figo 3 (*alqd in re*); *v/i.* haereo 2 (*re; in re*); adhaereo 2 (*in re*); adhaeresco 3 (*ad; in re*); baculum *n*; clava *f*; **~y** tenax, lentus.

**stiff** rigidus; durus, severus; **~en** rigeo 2; rigesco 3; **~ness** rigor *m*; duritia *f*.

**stifle** strangulo 1, suffoco 1; *fig.* reprimo 3.

**stigma** nota *f*; stigma *n*; **~tize** noto 1.

**still** immotus, tranquillus, quietus; placo 1, sedo 1; *adv.* adhuc, etiam; etiamnunc, etiamtum; semper, usque; nihilominus, (at)tamen, verumtamen; **~ness** quies *f*; silentium *n*.

**stilted** inflatus.

**stimul|ate** excito 1, incendo 3, stimulo 1; **~us** stimulus *m*; incitamentum *n*.

**sting** pungo 3; *fig.* mordeo 2, uro 3; aculeus *m*; morsus, us *m*.

**sting|iness** sordes *f*/*pl.*; **~y** sordidus, parcus.

**stink** male oleo 2; fetor *m*.

**stint** parco 3 (*dat.*); pensum *n*.

**stipend** merces *f*; annuum *n*.

**stipulat|e** (de)paciscor 3 (*ut*); statuo 3 (*ut*); **~ion** condicio *f*.

**stir** (com)moveo 2; motus, us *m*; tumultus, us *m*; turba *f*; **~ up** excito 1; misceo 2.

**stitch** suo 3.

**stock** stirps *f*; genus *n*; copia *f*; instrumentum *n*, merces *f*/*pl.*; pecus *n*; instruo 3, repleo 2 (*alqd alqa re*); tritus, usitatus; **well-~ed** abundans, frequens (*abl.*).

**stockade** vallum *n*.

**stocking** tibiale *n*.

**stocks** compedes *f*/*pl.*

**stoic** Stoicus; durus; Stoicus *m*.

**stole** palla *f*.

**stolid** hebes, stolidus.

**stomach** stomachus *m*; concoquo 3.

**stone** lapis *m*; saxum *n*; nucleus *m* (*olivarum etc.*); lapideus; lapidibus cooperio 4 (*alqm*); **~-quarry** lapicidinae *f*/*pl.*

**stony** lapidosus, saxosus, saxeus; **~-hearted** ferreus.

**stook** manipulus *m*.

**stool** scamnum *n*.

**stoop** demitto 3, summitto 3; *fig.* descendo 3 (*ad alqd*).

**stop** *v/t.* teneo 2, retineo 2; sisto 3; *fig.* cohibeo 2; comprimo 3, reprimo 3; *v/i.* consisto 3, insisto 3, subsisto 3; maneo 2; commoror 1 (*apud alqm*); desino 3, omitto 3 (*inf.*); ~ **up** obturo 1, obsaepio 4; interpunctum *n*; **put a ~ to** dirimo 3, comprimo 3; moram facio 3 (*alci rei*); ~**per** obturamentum *n*.

**store** condo 3, repono 3; copia *f*; ~**s** commeatus, us *m*; ~**house** apotheca *f*, cella *f*; horreum *n*; ~**keeper** cellarius *m*.

**storey** tabulatum *n*.

**stork** ciconia *f*.

**storm** tempestas *f*; procella *f*; *v/t.* expugno 1; *v/i.* saevio 4; ~**ing** expugnatio *f*; ~**y** turbulentus, turbidus.

**story** fabula *f*; res *f*; **there is a ~** ferunt 3 (*acc. c. inf.*); ~**-teller** narrator *m*.

**stout** pinguis, opimus; validus; ~**-hearted** impavidus, fortis; ~**ness** habitus, us *m* opimus (corporis).

**stove** caminus *m*; focus *m*.

**stow** repono 3, condo 3; ~ **away** me condo 3, abdo 3.

**straggle** vagor 1, palor 1.

**straight** rectus, directus; *adv.* recta; ~**en** corrigo 3; ~**forward** directus, sincerus, simplex; ~**way** statim, continuo.

**strain** *v/t.* contendo 3; intendo 3 (*aciem*); intorqueo 2 (*talum*); liquo 1, colo 1 (*vinum*); *v/i.* nitor 3, me intendo 3 (*ut, ne*); contentio *f*; nixus, us *m*; labor *m*; cantus, us *m*; modus *m*; ~**ed** accersitus (*dictum etc.*); ~**er** colum *n*.

**strait** fretum *n*; angustiae *f/pl.*; ~**-laced** rigidus.

**strand** litus *n*; **be ~ed** eicior 3 (in litore).

**strange** insolitus, inusitatus, mirus, novus; peregrinus, externus; alienus (*ab; dat.*); ~**ly** mirabiliter; nescio quo pacto; ~**ness** insolentia *f*; ~**r** peregrinus *m*; hospes *m*; homo *m* ignotus; *fig.* **a ~r to** ignarus, rudis, imperitus (*gen.*).

**strangle** strangulo 1.

**strap** lorum *n*; loris vincio 4; ~**ping** validus.

**stratagem** insidiae *f/pl.*; machina *f*; dolus *m*.

**strategy** consilium *n*; belli ratio *f*.

**straw** stramentum *n*; culmus *m*; *fig.* pilus *m*; stramenticius; ~**berry** fragum *n*.

**stray** (ab)erro 1, vagor 1, palor 1; errans.

**streak** linea *f*; ~**ed** virgatus.

**stream** rivus *m*; flumen *n*; **down ~** secundo flumine; **up ~** adverso flumine; labor 3; me effundo 3; ~**er** vexillum *n*.

**street** via *f*; vicus *m*; platea *f*.

**strength** vis *f*; vires *f/pl.*; robur *n*; firmitas *f*, firmitudo *f*; ~ **of mind** constantia *f*; **on the ~ of** fretus (*abl.*); ~**en** (con)firmo 1; stabilio 4.

**strenuous** acer, impiger.

**stress** vis *f*; impetus, us *m*; pondus *n*; **lay ~ on** (magni) momenti facio 3 (*alqd*).

**stretch** *v/t.* (in)tendo 3, contendo 3; *v/i.* pateo 2; patesco 3, pandor 3; ~ **forth, out** porrigo 3, extendo 3; contentio *f*, intentio *f*; tractus, us *m*; spatium *n*; ~**er** lectica *f*.

**strew** sterno 3, spargo 3.

**stricken**: ~ **in years** aetate confectus.

**strict** severus, durus; intentus, diligens.

**stricture** reprehensio *f*.

**stride** magnis gradibus incedo 3; magnus gradus, us *m*.

**strife** discordia *f*; iurgia *n/pl.*; lites *f/pl.*

**strigil** strigilis *f*.

**strike** *v/t.* ferio 4; percutio 3, caedo 3, ico 3; signo 1 (*nummos*); pello 3 (*lyram, nervos*); percello 3, percutio 3 (*animum, mentem*); incurro 3, incurso 1 (*in oculos, aures*); *v/i.* sono 1; ~ **against** infligo 3, offendo 3 (*alqd alci*); ~ **at, down** subverto 3, everto 3; ~ **camp** castra moveo 2; **it ~s me** mihi occurrit 3, venit 4 in mentem; ~ **out** induco 3.

**striking** insignis, gravis, mirus.

**string** linum *n*; nervus *m* (*lyrae, arcus*); chorda *f* (*lyrae*); **shoe~** corrigia *f*; ~ **together** conecto 3; ~**ed instrument** fides *f/pl.*

**stringent** severus.

**strip** *v/t.* spolio 1, nudo 1, exuo 3 (*alqm alqa re*); *v/i.* vestem depono 3; ~ **off** stringo 3, exuo 3, detraho 3 (*alqd*); ~ **of paper** (papyri) scida *f*; ~ **of cloth** fascia *f*.

**stripe** virga *f*; **purple ~** clavus *m* (latus, angustus); ~**s** verbera *n/pl.*, vulnera *n/pl.*; ~**d** virgatus.

**striv|e** (e)nitor 3 (*ut; ad, pro*); contendo 3 (*inf.; ut; ad alqd; contra alqm*); conor 1 (*inf.*); **~ing** contentio *f*, appetitio *f* (*gen.*).

**stroke** (per)mulceo 2; ictus, us *m*; plaga *f*; pulsus, us *m* (remorum); linea *f*.

**stroll** inambulo 1, spatior 1; ambulatio *f*.

**strong** validus, robustus, firmus, fortis; gravis, acer; potens; vehemens; **be ~** valeo 2; **~-box** arca *f*; **~hold** arx *f*; praesidium *n*.

**structure** compages *f*; aedificium *n*; *fig.* ratio *f*.

**struggle** luctor 1, pugno 1 (*cum*); nitor 3 (*ut*); contendo 3 (*inf.*); dimico 1 (*cum; de*); certamen *n*; dimicatio *f*.

**strut** magnifice incedo 3; magnifice me iacto 1.

**stubble** stipula *f*.

**stubborn** pertinax, pervicax, obstinatus; **~ness** pertinacia *f*.

**stud** equaria *f*; equi *m/pl.*

**studded** distinctus (*alqa re*).

**stud|ent** qui studet (*litteras, doctrinas etc.*); homo *m* litterarum studiosus; **~ent of rhetoric** scholasticus *m*; **~ied** meditatus, exquisitus; **~ious** studiosus (*litterarum, doctrinae*).

**study** studeo 2 (*dat.*); operam do 1, incumbo 3 (*dat.*); cognosco 3; meditor 1; meditatio *f*; studium *n*; opera *f*; litterarum studia *n/pl.*; ars *f*; bibliotheca *f*.

**stuff** materia *f*; textile *n*; farcio 4, refercio 4; sagino 1; **~ing** fartum *n*; (*of cushions*) tomentum *n*.

**stumble** offendo 3 (*pedem ad alqd*); labor 3; **~ upon** incido 3 (*dat.*).

**stump** stipes *m*.

**stun** (ob)stupefacio 3; consterno 1; **be ~ned** sopior 4.

**stunted** minutus.

**stupe|faction** stupor *m*; **~fy** (ob)stupefacio 3; consterno 1; **~ndous** permirus.

**stupid** stultus, stupidus, stolidus; **~ity** stultitia *f*.

**sturdy** robustus, validus, firmus.

**sturgeon** acipenser, eris *m*.

**stutter** balbutio 4; haesito 1; **~ing** balbus.

**sty** hara *f*.

**styl|e** ratio *f*; modus *m*; **literary ~e** genus *n*; oratio *f*; stilus *m*; sermo *m*;

apello 1, voco 1; dico 3; **~ish** lautus, magnificus.

**subaltern** optio *m*.

**subdue** subicio 3, subigo 3, redigo 3; domo 1.

**subject** subicio 3 (*alqm sub alqd; dat.*); oppono 3 (*alqm alci rei*); subiectus, dicto audiens; **~ to** obnoxius (*dat.*); civis *m*; privatus *m*; res *f*; argumentum *n*; materia *f*; quaestio *f*; **~ion** servitus, utis *f*.

**sub|join** subicio 3; **~jugate** subigo 3, redigo 3; domo 1.

**sublim|e** elatus, excelsus; **~ity** elatio *f*.

**submarine** marinus, summersus.

**submerge** summergo 3, demergo 3; inundo 1.

**submi|ssive** humilis, summissus, supplex; **~t** me summitto 3, subicio 3 (*dat.*); (con)cedo 3 (*dat.*); subeo 4; perfero 3 (*labores etc.*); refero 3 (*alqd ad alqm*).

**subordinate** subicio 3 (*alqd alci rei*); secundus, inferior; minister, tri *m*.

**suborn** suborno 1.

**subpoena** testimonium denuntio 1 (*alci*).

**subscri|be** subscribo 3; assentior 4 (*alci, sententiae*); confero 3 (*pecuniam*); **~ption** subscriptio *f*.

**subsequent** posterior, proximus; **~ly** postea, deinde.

**subsid|e** resido 3, remitto 3; cado 3; defervesco 3 (*ira etc.*); **~iary** secundus; subsidiarius (*cohortes etc.*); **~ise** pecunias praebeo 2; **~y** collatio *f*.

**subsist** sustineor 2; consto 1; sum; **~ence** victus, us *m*.

**substan|ce** res *f*; natura *f*; corpus *n*; summa *f*; **~tial** solidus; gravis, magnus; amplus; **~tiate** probo 1 (*crimen*); argumentis confirmo 1.

**substitute** vicarius *m*; **as a ~ for** pro (*alqo*); in vicem (*alcs*); substituo 3, suppono 3 (*alqm, alqd, in locum alcs, pro alqo*).

**subterfuge** tergiversatio *f*; dolus *m*.

**subterranean** subterraneus.

**subtle** subtilis, acutus, acer; callidus; **~ty** subtilitas *f*; acumen *n*; astutia *f*.

**subtract** deduco 3.

**suburb** suburbium *n*; **~an** suburbanus.

**subver|sion** eversio *f*; **~t** everto 3.

**succeed** v/t. succedo 3 (alci); excipio 3 (annus annum; regnum); v/i. succedit 3 (mihi); prospere evenit 4 (mihi); efficio 3 (ut); ~ in perficio 3 (alqd).

**success** res f/pl. secundae, prosperae; felicitas f; ~ful felix, fortunatus; secundus, bonus; ~ion continuatio f, series f; in ~ion ex ordine; ~ive continuus; ~or successor m.

**succinct** brevis.

**succour** subvenio 4, succurro 3 (dat.); auxilium n.

**succulent** sucosus.

**succumb** (con)cedo 3, succumbo 3 (dat.).

**such** talis, huiusmodi, eiusmodi; ~ a man as to is … qui; ~ a good man tam bonus vir; to ~ an extent adeo; in ~ a way ita.

**suck** sugo 3; sorbeo 2; bibo 3; ~ing lactens; ~le mammam do 1, praebeo 2 (dat.).

**sudden** subitus, repentinus, repens; ~ly repente, subito.

**sue** litem, actionem intendo 3 (alci); ~ for peto 3, rogo 1, precor 1 (alqd ab alqo).

**suet** sebum n.

**suffer** subeo 4, accipio 3, patior 3, perpetior 3, (per)fero 3 (labores etc.); permitto 3 (alci inf.; ut); sino 3 (acc. c. inf.; inf.; subj.); ~ from afficior 3 (abl.); laboro 1 (abl.); ~er aeger, gri m; ~ing miseria f; labor m; ~ing from afflictus (abl.).

**suffice** sufficio 3 (dat.; ad; ut); suppeto 3 (dat.); satis sum.

**sufficien|cy**, ~t satis (alcs rei).

**suffocate** suffoco 1, strangulo 1.

**suffrage** suffragium n.

**suffuse** suffundo 3 (alqd alqa re).

**sugar** saccharon n; mel n (lit. honey).

**suggest** subicio 3, inicio 3 (alqd alci); admoneo 2 (ut); ~ itself animo occurrit 3; ~ion admonitus, us m; consilium n; at my ~ion me auctore.

**suicid|al** funestus, fatalis; ~e mors f voluntaria; **commit** ~e mihi mortem conscisco 3.

**suit** v/t. accommodo 1 (alqd ad); v/i. convenio 4 (in, ad alqd; dat.; acc. c. inf.); congruo 3 (cum; dat.); decet 2 (alqm); placet 2 (alci); ~able idoneus, aptus (ad); commodus, opportunus; dignus.

**suite** comitatus, us m; satellites m/pl., comites m/pl.

**suitor** procus m.

**sulky** morosus, difficilis.

**sullen** tristis, severus, tetricus.

**sully** contamino 1.

**sulphur** sulfur n.

**sultr|iness** aestus, us m; ~y aestuosus.

**sum** summa f; pecunia f; caput n; ~ up subduco 3; ~marily sine mora; ~mary brevis, subitus; breviarium n; **give a ~mary** breviter describo 3.

**summer** aestas f; aestivus.

**summit** cacumen n, culmen n; vertex m; summus mons m.

**summon** voco 1 (also jur. in ius), accerso 3; appello 1; ~s accessitus, us m.

**sumptuous** sumptuosus, lautissimus.

**sun** sol m; ~ oneself apricor 1; ~beam solis radius m; ~burnt adustus; ~dial solarium n.

**sunken** depressus, humilis, cavus.

**sun|ny** apricus; ~rise solis ortus, us m; ~set solis occasus, us m; ~shine sol m; lux f.

**sup** ceno 1.

**superabundan|ce** abundantia f; ~t abundans.

**superannuated** qui annuum accipit 3; obsoletus.

**superb** magnificus, lautus.

**super|cilious** arrogans, superbus, fastidiosus; ~ficial levis; ~fluous supervacaneus; ~human (paene) divinus.

**superintend** praesum (dat.); curo 1 (alqd); ~ence cura f; administratio f; ~ent (pro)curator m; praefectus m.

**superior** superior, melior; amplior; praestans; **be ~ to** supero 1.

**super|lative** praestans, singularis; ~natural divinus; ~scription titulus m; ~stition superstitio f, religio f; ~stitious superstitiosus, religiosus; ~vision cura f, curatio f.

**supine** supinus, iners.

**supper** cena f.

**supple** flexibilis, lentus.

**supplement** accessio f, appendix f.

**suppli|ant** supplex m and f; ~cate supplico 1 (dat.); oro 1, obsecro 1 (alqm); ~cation preces f/pl.; ~catory supplex.

**suppl|y** praebeo 2, suppedito 1, ministro 1 (*alqd alci*); suppleo 2, (re)sarcio 4 (*damna*); copia *f*, facultas *f*; **~ies** commeatus, us *m*; copiae *f/pl.*

**support** sustineo 2, sublevo 1; perfero 3, tolero 1 (*labores*); alo 3, sustento 1 (*familiam*); adiuvo 1 (*alqm*); adsum (*alci*); firmamentum *n*, adminiculum *n*; *fig.* columen *n*; praesidium *n*; alimentum *n*; **~er** fautor *m*, adiutor *m*.

**suppos|e** pono 2; fingo 3 (animo), puto 1, opinor 1; **~ition** opinio *f*; **~itious** subditus, subditivus.

**suppress** reprimo 3, opprimo 3; supprimo 3, celo 1 (*famam etc.*).

**suprem|acy** principatus, us *m*; imperium *n*; **~e** summus, supremus.

**sure** certus; compertus (*res*); fidus (*homo*); **be ~** pro certo habeo 2; certe scio 4; compertum habeo 2; **be ~ to** cura 1 (*ut*)!; **~ly** certe, certo, nimirum; **~ty** vas *m*, sponsor *m*; **be ~ty for** spondeo 2 (*pro alqo*).

**surf** fluctus *m/pl.*

**surface** aequor *n*; summum *n*; *adj.* summus.

**surfeit** satietas *f*; satio 1.

**surge** fluctus, us *m*; aestus, us *m*; aestuo 1, surgo 3.

**surge|on** chirurgus *m*; **~ry** chirurgia *f*.

**surl|iness** morositas *f*; **~y** morosus, difficilis.

**surmise** suspicor 1; coniectura *f*.

**surmount** transcendo 3 (*alqd*); *fig.* (ex)supero 1; vinco 3.

**surname** cognomen *n*.

**surpass** (ex)supero 1; vinco 3; praesto 1.

**surplus** residuum *m*, reliquum *n*.

**surpris|e** admiratio *f*; res *f* improvisa; opprimo 3, adorior 4 (*alqm*); occupo 1 (*urbem etc.*); **be ~ed** miror 1 (*acc.*; *acc. c. inf.*; *quod*; *si*); **~ing** mirus, mirabilis.

**surrender** *v/t.* cedo 3, trado 3; *v/i.* me dedo 3, arma trado 3; deditio *f*, traditio *f*.

**surreptitious** furtivus, clandestinus; **~ly** furtim, clam.

**surround** circumsto 1 (*acc.*); circumdo 1, cingo 3 (*alqd, alqm, alqa re*); circumsedeo 2 (*urbem*); **~ed by** circumfusus, cinctus (*abl.*).

**survey** contemplor 1, considero 1;

contemplatio *f*; mensura *f* (*agri etc.*); **~or** finitor *m*, metator *m*.

**surviv|e** supersum, superstes sum (*dat.*); supero 1; **~ing** superstes.

**susceptib|ility** mollitia *f* (animi); **~le** obnoxius (*dat.*).

**suspect** suspicor 1 (*alqd*; *acc. c. inf.*); suspectum habeo 2 (*alqm*); **be ~ed** in suspicione sum (*alci alcs rei*); suspectus sum.

**suspend** suspendo 3 (*alqd re*; *e, de re*); intermitto 3 (*proelium etc.*); moveo 2 (*alqm magistratu*).

**suspense** dubitatio *f*; **in ~** suspensus, incertus, dubius.

**suspension** intermissio *f*.

**suspici|on** suspicio *f*; **~ous** suspiciosus (*in alqm*; *res*).

**sust|ain** sustineo 2; alo 3, sustento 1; patior 3; **~enance** victus, us *m*; alimentum *n*.

**swaddling-clothes** incunabula *n/pl.*

**swagger** magnifice incedo 3; magnifice me iacto 1.

**swallow** hirundo *f*; devoro 1; haurio 4.

**swamp** palus, udis *f*; inundo 1; deprimo 3 (*navem*); **~y** paludosus.

**swan** cygnus *m*.

**sward** caespes *m*.

**swarm** examen *n*; *fig.* turba *f*, multitudo *f*; congregor 1, glomeror 1; **~ out of** effundor 3 (*abl.*); **~ up** scando 3.

**swarthy** fuscus, adustus.

**swathe** fascia *f*.

**sway** *v/t.* agito 1; *v/i.* vacillo 1, fluito 1; *fig.* dirigo 3, rego 3; imperium *n*; dicio *f*.

**swear** iuro 1 (*per alqm*; *in alqd*; *acc. inf.*); iusiurandum accipio 3; **~ at** exsecror 1 (*alqm*); **~ in** iureiurando obstringo 3 (*alqm*); iusiurandum adigo 3 (*alqm*); **~ allegiance to** iuro 1 in nomen (*alcs*); **~ing** exsecrationes *f/pl.*

**sweat** sudor *m*; sudo 1.

**sweep** verro 3 (*vias, purgamenta, etc.*); (de)tergeo 2 (*vias*); percurro 3 (*alqd oculo*); **~ings** purgamenta *n/pl.*

**sweet** dulcis, suavis, iucundus; **~en** iucundum facio 3; **~heart** deliciae *f/pl.*; **~ness** dulcedo *f*, suavitas *f*.

**swell** *v/i.* tumeo 2; tumesco 3, turgesco 3; cresco 3; *v/t.* distendo 3; inflo 1; fluctus, us *m*; **~ing** tumor *m*.

**swerve** declino 1 (*ab, de*).
**swift** celer; velox, rapidus; **~ness** velocitas *f*.
**swim** nato 1; **~mer** natator *m*; **~ming** natatio *f*.
**swindle** fraudo 1 (*alqm pecunia*); decipio 3 (*alqm*); fraus *f*; **~r** fraudator *m*.
**swine** sus *f and m*; **~herd** subulcus *m*.
**swing** *v/t.* agito 1 (*huc illuc*); *v/i.* vacillo 1, fluito 1; *fig.* **~ round** me verto 3 (*in*).
**swirl** torqueor 2; vertex *m*.
**swish** strepitus, us *m*.
**switch** virga *f*; *v/t.* muto 1; *v/i.* mutor 1.
**swollen** tumidus, turgidus.
**swoon** collabor 3.
**swoop** lapsus, us *m*; impetus, us *m*; **~ down (on)** (de)labor 3 (*in*); **~ upon** involo 1, incurro 3 (*in*).

**sword** gladius *m*; ferrum *n*.
**sycophant** assentator *m*.
**syllable** syllaba *f*.
**symbol** signum *n*; imago *f*.
**symmetr|ical** aequalis, congruens; **~y** convenientia *f*.
**sympath|etic** misericors; **~ise** misereor 2 (*gen.*); **~y** misericordia *f*; concordia *f*.
**symphony** concentus, us *m*; symphonia *f*.
**symptom** indicium *n*, signum *n*.
**syndicate** societas *f*.
**synonymous** quod idem declarat 1 (*verbum*).
**synopsis** epitoma *f*.
**syntax** constructio *f* verborum.
**synthesis** coniunctio *f*.
**syringe** sipho *m*.
**system** ratio *f*, institutio *f*, descriptio *f*; disciplina *f* (*philosophiae*); **~atic** ordinatus; **~atise** ordino 1.

table — 462 — tear

# T

**table** mensa *f*; *fig.* cena *f*; index *m*.
**tablet** tabula *f*, tabella *f*, tessera *f*.
**tacit** tacitus; **~urn** taciturnus.
**tack** *v/t.* figo 3 (*alqd in re*); **~ together, up** (con)suo 3 (*alqd*); *v/i.* reciprocor 1; clavulus *m*.
**tackle** armamenta *n/pl.*, instrumenta *n/pl.*; obviam eo 4 (*dat.*).
**tact** prudentia *f*, humanitas *f*; **~ful** prudens.
**tactics** belli ratio *f*; consilium *n*.
**tag** pittacium *n*; **~ after** subsequor 3 (*alqm*).
**tail** cauda *f*.
**tailor** vestiarius (homo) *m*.
**taint** contamino 1, inquino 1; imbuo 3; contagio *f*; vitium *n*.
**take** capio 1, sumo 3, accipio 3; duco 3; **~ after** similis sum (*alcs*); **~ away** adimo 3, aufero 3, tollo 3 (*alqd*); **~ down** detraho 3; **~ for** ignem accipio 3, concipio 3; **~ for** habeo 2 (*pro amico etc.*); **~ hold of** comprehendo 3; **~ in** recipio 3, accipio 3 (*hospitem*); comprehendo 3, percipio 3 (*mente*); decipio 3 (*alqm dolo*); **~ off** depono 3 (*vestem*); **~ out** eximo 3, eripio 3; **~ (oneself) to** me confero 3; **~ place** fio 3; **~ up** sumo 3 (*arma*); consumo 3 (*tempus*); suscipio 3 (*bellum, partem alcs*).
**tale** fabula *f*, narratio *f*, historia *f*.
**talent** ingenium *n*; indoles *f*; **~ed** ingeniosus.
**talk** (col)loquor 3 (*cum alqo*); sermo *m*; colloquium *n*; **~ative** loquax, garrulus; **~ativeness** loquacitas *f*.
**tall** procerus; grandis; longus; **~ness** proceritas *f*.
**tallow** sebum *n*.
**tally** convenio 4 (*cum re*); tessera *f*; ratio *f*.
**talon** unguis *m*.
**tambourine** tympanum *n*.
**tame** mansuetus, cicur, domitus; ignavus; mansuefacio 3; domo 1; **~ness** lentitudo *f*; **~r** domitor *m*.
**tamper with** *fig.* sollicito 1 (*alqm*).
**tan** pelles conficio 3; coloro 1 (*corpus*).

**tangle** implico 1; implicatio *f*; nodus *m*.
**tank** lacus, us *m*; cisterna *f*; **~ard** cantharus *m*.
**tanner** coriarius *m*.
**tantamount** idem (*ac*); par (*dat.*).
**tap** leviter pulso 1; ictus, us *m*.
**tape** taenia *f*.
**taper** cereus *m*; fastigor 1; **~ing** fastigatus (*in cacumen etc.*).
**tapestry** tapetia *n/pl.*
**tar** pix *f*. [lentus.]
**tard|iness** tarditas *f*; **~y** tardus,
**tare** lolium *n*.
**target** *fig.* scopus *m*.
**tarnish** maculo 1, vitio 1.
**tarry** (com)moror 1.
**tart** scriblita *f*; acidus; mordax.
**task** opus *n*, negotium *n*, pensum *n*; onus impono 3 (*alci*); **~master** exactor *m* (*operis*).
**tassels** fimbriae *f/pl.*; cirri *m/pl.*
**taste** *v/t.* (de)gusto 1, (de)libo 1 (*alqd*); *v/i.* sapio 3 (*alqd; bene*); sapor *m*; gustatus, us *m*; *fig.* intellegentia *f*; iudicium *n*; elegantia *f*; **~ful** elegans, intellegens; **~less** insulsus.
**tast|er** praegustator *m*; **~y** sapidus, conditus.
**tatter** pannus *m*; **~ed** pannosus.
**tattle** garrio 4.
**tattoo** compungo 3.
**taunt** obicio 3 (*alqd alci*); opprobrium *n*, convicium *n*.
**tavern** caupona *f*.
**tawdry** fucosus.
**tawny** fulvus.
**tax** vectigal *n*; incuso 1 (*alqm alcs rei*); vectigal impono 3 (*alci*); censeo 2 (*alqm*); **~-collector** exactor *m*.
**teach** doceo 2 (*alqm alqd; inf.*); erudio 4, instruo 3 (*alqm alqa re*); **~er** magister, tri *m*; doctor *m*, praeceptor *m*; **~ing** doctrina *f*, institutio *f*; praecepta *n/pl.*
**team** iugum *n*.
**tear**[1] lacrima *f*; **shed ~s** lacrimas fundo 3; **~ful** lacrimans.
**tear**[2] scindo 3; **~ to pieces** lanio 1; discindo 3; convello 3; scissura *f*.

**tease** obtundo 3 (*alqm*); vexo 1.

**teat** mamma *f.*

**tedious** lentus, longus, molestus.

**teem** abundo 1, scateo 2 (*alqa re*).

**tell** (e)narro 1 (*rem alci*); dico 3 (*acc. c. inf.*); memoro 1 (*alqd*); iubeo 2 (*alqm alqd facere*); ~ing gravis, validus.

**temerity** temeritas *f.*

**temper** tempero 1; lenio 4; animus *m*; **bad ~** iracundia *f*; **bad-~ed** morosus, difficilis; ~ament habitus, us *m*; ~ance temperantia *f*, modestia *f*; ~ate temperatus, temperans.

**temperature** temperatura *f*; **high ~** calor *m*; **low ~** frigor *m.*

**tempest** tempestas *f*; ~uous procellosus.

**temple** templum *n*; aedes *f*; tempus *n* (*capitis*); ~-keeper aedituus *m.*

**tempor|arily** ad tempus; in tempus; ~ary temporarius; ~ise cunctor 1; tempori servio 4.

**tempt** tempto 1, sollicito 1; ~ation sollicitatio *f*; illecebra *f*; ~er temptator *m*; ~ing illecebrosus.

**ten** decem; ~ **times** decies.

**tenac|ious** pertinax, tenax; ~ity tenacitas *f*, pertinacia *f.*

**tenant** conductor *m*; incola *m.*

**tend** *v/t.* colo 3; curo 1; *v/i.* tendo 3; pertineo 2; specto 1; ~ency inclinatio *f.*

**tender** tener, delicatus, mollis; defero 3, offero 3; ~ness teneritas *f*; indulgentia *f.*

**tendon** nervus *m.*

**tendril** pampinus *m.*

**tenet** institutum *n*, dogma *n.*

**tenor** cursus, us *m*; ratio *f.*

**tens|e** tentus; intentus; tempus *n*; ~ion intentio *f.*

**tent** tabernaculum *n*; **general's ~** praetorium *n.*

**tentacle** bracchium *n.*

**tenth** decimus.

**tenuous** exiguus, rarus.

**tepid** tepidus.

**term** finis *m*; spatium *n*; tempus *n*; verbum *n*; nuncupo 1, appello 1; ~s condicio *f*; **be on good (bad) ~s (with)** est mihi amicitia (inimicitia) (*cum alqo*).

**termin|ate** finio 4; concludo 3; ~ation finis *m*; exitus, us *m*; ~ology vocabula *n/pl.*, verba *n/pl.*

**terrestrial** terrestris, terrenus.

**terrible, terrific** terribilis, horribilis.

**territory** fines *m/pl.*; ager, gri *m*; terra *f.*

**terror** terror *m*, pavor *m*; ~ize terreo 2.

**terse** pressus, astrictus; ~ness brevitas *f.*

**test** experior 4; tento 1, specto 1, periclitor 1; periculum *n*, experimentum *n*; obrussa *f.*

**testa|ment** testamentum *n*; ~tor testator *m.*

**testicle** testis *m.*

**testify (to)** testificor 1, testor 1, declaro 1 (*alqd*; *acc. c. inf.*).

**testimony** testimonium *n.*

**testy** stomachosus.

**tether** religo 1.

**text** verba *n/pl.*; oratio *f.*

**textile** textilis; textile *n.*

**texture** textus, us *m*; textum *n.*

**than** quam, atque.

**thank** gratias ago 3 (*alci*); ~ **you** benigne; ~ful gratus; ~less ingratus; ~s gratia *f*, gratiae *f/pl.*; ~sgiving supplicatio *f*, gratulatio *f.*

**that** ille; is; iste; *relat.* qui, quae, quod; *cj.* ut; ~ **not** ut non, ne; **oh ~!** utinam.

**thatch** stramentum *n.*

**thaw** *v/t.* (dis)solvo 3; *v/i.* tabesco 3, resolvor 3.

**the** ille; ~ **more** ... ~ **more** quo magis ... eo magis.

**theatr|e** theatrum *n*; scaena *f*, cavea *f*; spectaculum *n*; ~ical theatralis, scaenicus.

**theft** furtum *n.*

**their** suus, sua, suum.

**theme** propositum *n*, argumentum *n*; res *f.*

**then** tum, tunc; deinde, inde, post, postea; igitur, ergo; ~ **and there** ilico.

**thence** inde, illinc; hinc; ~forth ex eo tempore, inde.

**theolog|ian** theologus *m*; ~y theologia *f.*

**theor|etically** scientia; ~y ratio *f*; scientia *f.*

**there** ibi, illic; eo; ~abouts circa; ~after exinde; ~fore igitur, ergo, itaque; ~upon tum, subinde, inde.

**thesis** propositum *n*, argumentum *n.*

**thick** densus, crassus, artus; creber, confertus; **in the ~ of** in medio

(*proelio etc.*); ~en denso 1; ~et dumetum *n*; ~ness crassitudo *f*.
thie|f fur *m and f*; ~ve furor 1; ~vish furax.
thigh femur *n*.
thin tenuis; rarus; gracilis; subtilis; exilis, macer; attenuo 1, extenuo 1.
thing res *f*; negotium *n*.
think cogito 1; arbitror 1, opinor 1, puto 1, existimo 1; credo 3; censeo 2; ~ about, over cogito 1 (*alqd*; *de re*); reputo 1 (*alqd*); ~er philosophus *m*; ~ing cogitatio *f*.
third tertius; tertia pars *f*; ~ly tertio.
thirst sitis *f*; sitio 4 (*alqd*); ~y sitiens, siccus.
thirt|een tredecim; ~eenth tertius decimus; ~ieth trigesimus; ~y triginta.
this hic, haec, hoc.
thistle carduus *m*.
thither illuc, eo.
thong lorum *n*.
thorn spina *f*; ~bush sentis *m*; ~y spinosus.
thorough germanus, perfectus; ~bred generosus; ~fare pervium *n*; ~ly penitus, omnino, plane.
though quamquam, quamvis; etsi, etiamsi.
thought cogitatio *f*; cogitatum *n*; notio *f*; ~ful providus; ~fulness cura *f*; ~less inconsultus, neglegens; ~lessness temeritas *f*.
thousand mille, *pl.* milia; a ~ times miliens; ~th millesimus.
thrall servus *m*.
thrash tero 3, tundo 3 (*frumentum*); verbero 1; ~ing verbera *n/pl.*
thread filum *n*, linum *n*; cursus, us *m* (*verborum*); filum in acum conicio 3; ~ one's way me insinuo 1; ~bare obsoletus.
threat minae *f/pl.*; ~en *v/t.* minor 1 (*alqd alci*; *acc. c. inf.*); intendo 3 (*alqd alci, in alqm*); denuntio 1 (*alqd alci*); *v/i.* impendeo 2; insto 1; ~ening minax.
three tres, tria; ~ days triduum *n*; ~ each terni; ~ hundred trecenti; ~ times ter; ~ years triennium *n*; ~fold triplex; ~legged tripes.
thresh tero 3, tundo 3; ~ing tritura *f*; ~ing floor area *f*.
threshold limen *n*.
thrice ter.
thrift frugalitas *f*; ~y frugi; parcus.

thrill agito 1 (*alqm, mentem*); commoveo 2; stringor *m*, horror *m*; ~ed attonitus.
thriv|e vigeo 2, floreo 2, vireo 2; ~ing vegetus, vigens, laetus.
throat guttur *n*, iugulum *n*; fauces *f/pl.*; gula *f*; cut the ~ iugulo 1.
throb palpito 1; salio 4; pulsus, us *m*.
throes dolor *m*.
throne solium *n*; *fig.* regnum *n*.
throng frequentia *f*, multitudo *f*, turba *f*; *v/t.* frequento 1, celebro 1 (*locum*); *v/i.* confluo 3.
throttle strangulo 1, suffoco 1.
through per (*acc.*); propter (*acc.*); ~out per (*totam urbem, noctem etc.*); *adv.* penitus, semper.
throw iacio 3, conicio 3, mitto 3; iacto 1; excutio 3, deicio 3 (*equitem*); ~ across traicio 3; ~ away proicio 3, abicio 3; ~ oneself down me proicio 3; iactus, us *m*; coniectus, us *m*.
thrush turdus *m*.
thrust trudo 3, pello 3; plaga *f*.
thud fragor *m*.
thumb pollex *m*.
thump tundo 3.
thunder tonitrus, us *m*; tono 1; ~bolt fulmen *n*; ~ing tonans; ~struck attonitus, obstupefactus.
thus ita, sic.
thwart obsto 1 (*dat.*); disturbo 1 (*alqd*); transtrum *n*.
thyme thymum *n*.
thyrsus thyrsus *m*.
tiara tiara *f*.
tick crepito 1; pedis *m*.
ticket tessera *f*.
ticking crepitus, us *m*.
tick|le titillo 1; ~ling titillatio *f*; ~lish *fig.* lubricus.
tide aestus, us *m*.
tid|iness munditia *f*; ~y mundus.
tidings nuntius *m*.
tie (al)ligo 1; vincio 4; vinculum *n*; necessitudo *f*, coniunctio *f* (*amicitiae etc.*).
tier ordo *m*.
tiger tigris *m*.
tight strictus, contentus, astrictus, artus; ~en (a)stringo 3, contendo 3.
tile tegula *f*, imbrex *f*; later, eris *m*.
till colo 3; dum, donec, quoad; *prep.* (usque) ad (*acc.*); ~er cultor *m*, arator *m*; gubernaculum *n*; clavus *m*.

**tilt** proclino 1, inclino 1.

**timber** materia *f*, materies *f*; ligna *n/pl.*

**time** tempus *n*; tempestas *f*, aetas *f*; spatium *n*; **at that** ~ tum; ea tempestate; **at** ~**s** aliquando, interdum; **at the same** ~ simul; **at a good** ~, **in** ~ tempore, in tempore, ad tempus; **at another** ~ alias; **for the first** ~ primum; **what is the** ~? hora quota est?; **keep** ~ servo 1 numerum, modum; **in** ~ in numerum; **be in** ~ (tempus) metior 4; ~**ly** tempestivus, opportunus, maturus; ~**piece** horologium *n*.

**timid** timidus, trepidus; ~**ity** timiditas *f*.

**timorous** pavidus.

**tin** stannum *n*.

**tincture** color *m*; tingo 3.

**tinder** fomes *m*.

**tinge** tingo 3, imbuo 3.

**tingle** ferveo 2.

**tinkle** tinnio 4; crepito 1; crepitus, us *m*; tinnitus, us *m*.

**tinsel** brattea *f*; bratteatus.

**tint** color *m*; tingo 3.

**tiny** parvulus, pusillus, exiguus.

**tip** cacumen *n*; apex *m*; **finger**-extremus digitus *m*; praefigo 3 (*caput hastae*); ~ **up** inclino 1.

**tipple** poto 1; ~**r** potator *m*.

**tipsy** ebrius, temulentus.

**tiptoe: stand on** ~ in digitos me erigo 3.

**tirade** declamatio *f*.

**tire** (de)fatigo 1; **I am** ~**d of** taedet 2 me (*alcs rei*); ~**d** (de)fessus, lassus; ~**some** odiosus, molestus; laboriosus.

**tiro** tiro *m*.

**tissue** textus, us *m*.

**titbit** cuppedium *n*; mattea *f*.

**tithe** decima (pars) *f*.

**title** titulus *m*; inscriptio *f*; nomen *n*; ~**d** nobilis.

**to** ad (*acc.*), in (*acc.*); *final cj.* ut; ~ **and fro** huc illuc; **all** ~ **a man** omnes ad unum.

**toad** bufo *m*; ~**stool** fungus *m*.

**toady** assentor 1 (*alci*); adulor 1 (*alqm, alci*); assentator *m*.

**toast** torreo 2; frigo 3; propino 1 (*poculum alci*; *salutem*); propinatio *f*.

**today** hodie; hodiernus dies *m*.

**toe** digitus *m*.

**toga** toga *f*.

**together** simul, una; ~ **with** (una) cum (*abl.*).

**toil** labor *m*; laboro 1; ~**s** plagae *f/pl.*

**toilet** ornatus, us *m*; cultus, us *m*.

**toilsome** laboriosus.

**token** signum *n*.

**tolera|ble** tolerabilis; mediocris; ~**bly** satis; ~**nce** indulgentia *f*; ~**nt** patiens (*gen.*); indulgens; ~**te** tolero 1; patior 3, fero 3; indulgeo 2 (*dat.*).

**toll** vectigal *n*.

**tomb** sepulcrum *n*, monumentum *n*; ~**stone** lapis *m*.

**tomorrow** cras; crastinus dies *m*; **after** ~ perendinus.

**tone** sonus *m*, vox *f*; color *m*.

**tongs** forceps *f*.

**tongue** lingua *f*.

**tonight** hac nocte.

**tonsils** tonsillae *f/pl.*

**too** et, etiam; quoque; nimis; ~ **long** nimis longus; longior; ~ **much** nimis, nimium; ~ **little** parum.

**tool** instrumentum *n*, ferramentum *n*; *fig.* minister, tri *m*.

**tooth** dens *m*; ~**less** edentulus; ~**pick** dentiscalpium *n*.

**top** summus; summum cacumen *n*, fastigium *n*, caput *n*, culmen *n*; vertex *m*; turbo *m*; **on the** ~ **of the hill** in summo monte.

**toper** potator *m*.

**topic** res *f*; locus *m*; argumentum *n*.

**topmost** summus.

**topography** locorum descriptio *f*.

**topsy-turvy** sursum deorsum (*versare omnia*).

**torch** fax *f*; taeda *f*.

**torment** (ex)crucio 1; ango 3; vexo 1; cruciatus, us *m*.

**tornado** turbo *m*.

**torp|id** piger, iners; ~**or** inertia *f*, pigritia *f*; torpor *m*.

**torrent** torrens *m*.

**torrid** torridus.

**tortoise(-shell)** testudo *f*.

**torture** (ex)crucio 1; (ex)torqueo 2; tormenta *n/pl.*; quaestio *f*, cruciatus, us *m*; ~**r** carnifex *m*.

**toss** iacto 1; iactus, us *m*.

**total** totus, cunctus; summa *f*; ~**ly** omnino.

**totter** titubo 1, vacillo 1, labo 1.

**touch** tango 3, attingo 3; *fig.* moveo 2; flecto 3, afficio 3; ~ **in at** navem appello 3 (*ad*); ~ **upon** tango 3, attingo 3, perstringo 3; tactus us *m*; contagio *f*; ~ing quod ad; de (*abl.*); ~stone index *m*; *fig.* obrussa *f*; ~y difficilis, stomachosus.

**tough** lentus, durus; difficilis.

**tour** iter, ineris *n*; (*abroad*) peregrinatio *f*; circuitio *f*; iter facio 3, circumeo 4; ~ist peregrinator *m*.

**tow** stuppa *f*; (remulco) traho 3; ~-line remulcum *n*.

**towards** ad, adversus, in (*acc.*); sub (*noctem*); erga (*alqm*).

**towel** mantele *n*.

**tower** turris *f*; ~ up emineo 2.

**town** urbs *f*; oppidum *n*; municipium *n*; urbanus; ~ councillors decuriones *m/pl.*; ~ crier praeco *m*; ~hall curia *f*; ~sman oppidanus *m*, municeps *m*.

**toy** crepundia *n/pl.*; *fig.* ludicrum *n*, ludibrium *n*; ludo 3.

**trace** vestigium *n*, indicium *n*; significatio *f*; habena *f*, lorum *n* (*equi*); sequor 3; indago 1.

**track** vestigium *n*; callis *f*; ~ out, down odoror 1, indago 1, vestigo 1; ~less avius, invius.

**tract** tractus, us *m*; regio *f*; libellus *m*.

**tractable** tractabilis, docilis.

**trade** commercium *n*; mercatura *f*; negotium *n*; artificium *n*; negotior 1; ~r mercator *m*; ~sman caupo *m*.

**trading vessel** navis *f* oneraria.

**tradition** mos *m* (maiorum); fama *f*, memoria *f*; **there is a ~** traditur; tradunt; memoria proditum est (*acc. c. inf.*); ~al a maioribus traditus.

**traduce** maledico 3 (*dat.*); obtrecto 1 (*alqm*).

**traffic** commercium *n*; commercium habeo 2 (*cum alqo*); (merces) muto 1.

**trag|edian** tragoedus *m*; ~edy tragoedia *f*; ~ic tragicus; *fig.* tristis, miserabilis.

**trail** traho 3; vestigo 1, odoror 1; vestigia *n/pl.*

**train** instituo 3; doceo 2, exerceo 2; exercito 1; assuefacio 3 (*alqm alqa re*; *inf.*); pompa *f*; commeatus, us *m*; tractus, us *m*; ordo *m*; series *f*; ~er exercitor *m*; ~ing disciplina *f*, exercitatio *f*.

**trait** nota *f*.

**traitor** proditor *m*; ~ous perfidus.

**trample on** calco 1, conculco 1; obtero 3.

**tranquil** tranquillus, placidus; ~lity otium *n*.

**transact** transigo 3, conficio 3, ago 3; ~ion res *f*, negotium *n*.

**transcend** supero 1.

**transcri|be** transcribo 3; ~pt exemplar *n*.

**transfer** traduco 3, transfero 3; translatio *f*.

**transfix** traicio 3, transfigo 3; *fig.* ~ed (ob)stupefactus.

**transform** muto 1; verto 3.

**transgress** violo 1; transcendo 3; ~ion violatio *f*, delictum *n*.

**transient** fluxus, caducus, brevis.

**transit** transitus, us *m*.

**translat|e** converto 3, reddo 3; interpretor 1; ~or interpres *m*.

**trans|lucent** pellucidus; ~marine transmarinus; ~mit transmitto 3; ~parent pellucidus; ~plant transfero 3.

**transport** transporto 1; traicio 3, transveho 3; *fig.* **be ~ed** exardesco 3, efferor 3 (*gaudio etc.*); vectura *f*; navis *f* oneraria.

**transverse** transversus.

**trap** pedica *f*, plaga *f*; insidiae *f/pl.*; **mouse~** muscipulum *n*; irretio 4.

**trappings** ornatus, us *m*; insignia *n/pl.*

**trash** scruta *n/pl.*; quisquiliae *f/pl.*; ~y vilis.

**travail** dolor *m*, labor *m*.

**travel** iter facio 3; peregrinor 1; ~ over perlustro 1 (*acc.*); peregrinatio *f*; ~ler viator *m*, peregrinator *m*.

**traverse** obeo 4; perlustro 1.

**tray** ferculum *n*, repositorium *n*.

**treacher|ous** perfidus, perfidiosus; lubricus; ~y perfidia *f*.

**tread** insisto 3 (*in re*; *dat.*); ~ upon calco 1 (*alqd*); gradus, us *m*; vestigium *n*.

**treason** maiestas *f*; proditio *f*; **commit ~** maiestatem minuo 3, laedo 3.

**treasur|e** thesaurus *m*; gaza *f*; coacervo 1; plurimi facio 3, aestimo 1; ~er aerarii praefectus *m*; ~y aerarium *n*; fiscus *m*; thesaurus *m*.

**treat** tracto 1; accipio 3 (*alqm bene*); habeo 2 (*alqm pro amico, in honore*); utor 3 (*abl.*); curo 1 (*aegrotum*); dissero 3, disputo 1 (*de re*); ~ lightly parvi facio 3 (*rem*); ~ with ago 3, paciscor 3 (*cum alqo*); ~ise liber, bri *m*; ~ment tractatio *f*; curatio *f*; ~y foedus, *n*, pactio *f*; pactum *n*.

**treble** acutus (*sonus*); triplex.
**tree** arbor *f*.
**trellis** cancelli *m/pl*.
**trembl|e** tremo 3, contremisco 3 (*alqd*); **~ing** tremor *m*; tremens, tremulus.
**tremendous** immanis, ingens.
**trem|or** tremor *m*; **~ulous** tremulus.
**trench** fossa *f*; sulcus *m*.
**trepidation** trepidatio *f*.
**trespass** pecco 1; **~ upon** *fig.* praesumo 3 (*alqd*); imminuo 3.
**tress** crinis *m*; coma *f*.
**trial** experientia *f*; periculum *n*; probatio *f*; conatus, us *m*; *jur.* iudicium *n*; quaestio *f*; **make ~ of** periclitor 1; **put on ~** postulo 1 (*alqm de re*).
**triang|le** triangulum *n*; **~ular** triangulus, triquetrus.
**tribe** gens *f*, natio *f*; tribus, us *f*.
**tribunal** iudicium *n*; quaestio *f*.
**tribun|ate** tribunatus, us *m*; **~e** tribunus *m* (*plebis, militum*); **~icial** tribunicius.
**tribut|ary** stipendiarius, vectigalis; **~e** tributum *n*, vectigal *n*; *fig.* munus *n*.
**trice** momentum *n*.
**trick** dolus *m*; fallacia *f*; fallo 3; ludificor 1; **~ery** dolus *m*; artificium *n*.
**trickle** mano 1; stillo 1.
**tricky** difficilis.
**trident** tridens *m*.
**tried** spectatus, probatus.
**trifl|e** nugae *f/pl.*; nugor 1; ludo 3; **~e with** illudo 3 (*acc.*); **~ing** levissimus; inconstans; ineptiae *f/pl.*
**trill** vibro 1; **~ing** tremulus.
**trim** mundus, nitidus; tondeo 2; puto 1; como 3 (*capillos*); **~mer** qui temporibus servit.
**trip** offendo 3 (pedem); *fig.* erro 1; **~ up** supplanto 1 (*alqm*); iter, ineris *n*.
**tripartite** tripartitus.
**tripe** omasum *n*.
**tri|ple** triplex; **~pod** tripus, odis *m*; **~reme** triremis *f*.
**trite** tritus, pervulgatus.
**triumph** victoria *f*; **Roman general's ~** triumphus *m*; ovatio *f*; exsulto 1; triumpho 1; **~ over** supero 1; **~al** triumphalis; **~ant** victor.
**triumvir** triumvir *m*; **~ate** triumviratus, us *m*.

**trivial** levis.
**troop** caterva *f*, manus, us *f*; grex *m*; turma *f* (*equitum*); confluo 3; **~er** eques *m*; **~s** copiae *f/pl.*; milites *m/pl.*
**trophy** tropaeum *n*.
**troth** fides *f*.
**trouble** opera *f*; labor *m*; negotium *n*; molestia *f*; incommodum *n*; dolor *m*; res *f/pl.* adversae; sollicito 1, perturbo 1; molestiam exhibeo 2 (*alci*); **~ oneself** curo 1 (*alqd*; *ut*; *inf.*); **be ~d with, by** laboro 1 (*morbo etc.*); **~some** molestus, gravis.
**trough** alveus *m*.
**trousers** bracae *f/pl.*
**truant** vagus.
**truce** indutiae *f/pl.*
**truck** carrus *m*.
**trudge** pedibus eo 4.
**true** verus; germanus, sincerus; fidus; rectus; **be ~ of** cadit 3 (*in*); convenit 4 (*dat.*).
**truffle** tuber, eris *n*.
**truly** profecto.
**trump up** comminiscor 3.
**trumpet** bucina *f*; *mil.* tuba *f*; **~ abroad** celebro 1, vulgo 1; **~er** bucinator *m*, tubicen *m*.
**truncheon** scipio *m*.
**trunk** truncus *m*; stirps *f*; truncus *m* corporis; proboscis *f* (*elephanti*); arca *f*, cista *f*.
**truss** fascia *f*; fascis *m*.
**trust** confido 3 (*alci*; *alqa re*); fidem habeo 2 (*alci*); fides *f*; mandatum *n*, depositum *n*; **~ful** credulus; **~worthy** certus, fidus, gravis (*auctor, testis*); **~y** fidus, fidelis.
**truth** veritas *f*; vera *n/pl.*; fides *f*; **in ~** vero; **~ful** verax.
**try** conor 1, tento 1 (*inf.*); experior 4, periclitor 1 (*alqd*); *jur.* iudico 1; cognosco 3 (*causam*; *de re*); **~ing** incommodus, difficilis.
**tub** labrum *n*; cupa *f*.
**tube** fistula *f*; tubus *m*.
**tuck up** succingo 3.
**tuft** crista *f*; floccus *m*; **~ed** cristatus.
**tug** traho 3.
**tuition** institutio *f*.
**tumble** cado 3, concido 3; casus, us *m*; **~r** petaurista *m*; poculum *n*.
**tumbrel** plaustrum *n*.
**tumour** tumor *m*.
**tumult** tumultus, us *m*; turba *f*;

perturbatio *f*; ～**uous** tumultuosus, turbulentus.

**tun** dolium *n*.

**tune** cantus, us *m*; carmen *n*; numeri *m/pl.*; **keep in** ～ concentum servo 1; **be out of** ～ discrepo 1; **out of** ～ absonus; tendo 3; ～**ful** canorus.

**tunic** tunica *f*.

**tunnel** cuniculus *m*.

**turban** mitra *f*.

**turbid** turbidus.

**turbot** rhombus *m*.

**turbulent** turbulentus, tumultuosus.

**turf** caespes *m*; herba *f*.

**turgid** tumidus, turgidus.

**turmoil** tumultus, us *m*; turba *f*.

**turn** *v/t.* (con)verto 3; verso 1; torqueo 2; flecto 3 (*oculos, equum, cursum, promontorium*); intendo 3 (*oculos, iter, animum*); *v/i.* (con)vertor 3; me (con)verto 3; fio; ～ **against** descisco 3 (*ab*); ～ **aside** declino 1 (*de via etc.*); ～ **away** aversor 1 (*ab*); ～ **bad** vitior 1; ～ **in** devertor 3 (*apud*); ～ **into** *v/t.* verto 3, muto 1 (*alqd in, ad*); *v/i.* muto 1, mutor 1; me converto 3; ～ **off** averto 3; ～ **out** eicio 3, exigo 3; moveo 2; *v/i.* cado 3, evenio 4, accido 3 (*bene, male, etc.*); evado 3 (*sapiens, orator*); ～ **round** verso 1, contorqueo 2 (*rotam etc.*); ～ **sour** (co)acesco 3 (*vinum*); ～ **to use, one's advantage** utor 3 (*abl.*); ad utilitatem meam refero 3 (*alqd*); ～ **upon** vertor 3; situm est (*in alqo, alqa re*); ～ **upside down** everto 3; conversio *f*; flexus, us *m* (*viae*); commutatio *f*, vicissitudo *f*; ambulatio *f*; **a good, bad** ～ beneficium *n*, iniuria *f*; **in** ～ invicem; **by** ～**s** alternis; ～**ing point** discrimen *n*.

**turnip** rapum *n*.

**turnkey** ianitor *m* (carceris).

**turpentine** terebinthus, i *f*.

**turret** turris *f*.

**turtle-dove** turtur *m*.

**tusk** dens *m*.

**tutelary** praeses.

**tutor** magister, tri *m*; praeceptor *m*; doceo 2; instituo 3.

**twang** sonitus, us *m*; sono 1.

**twelfth** duodecimus.

**twelve** duodecim; ～ **each** duodeni; ～ **times** duodecies; ～**month** annus *m*.

**twentieth** vicesimus.

**twenty** viginti; ～ **each** viceni; ～ **times** vicies.

**twice** bis; ～ **as much** bis tantum; ～ **over** semel atque iterum.

**twig** surculus *m*; virga *f*.

**twilight** crepusculum *n*.

**twin** geminus.

**twine** linum *n*; *v/t.* circumplico 1, circumplector 3 (*alqd alqa re*); *v/i.* ～ **around** complector 3 (*alqd*).

**twinge** morsus, us *m* (doloris).

**twinkle** mico 1, corusco 1.

**twirl** verso 1.

**twist** (con)torqueo 2; intorqueo 2; spira *f*.

**twit** vellico 1; irrideo 2 (*acc.*).

**twitch** vellico 1; vello 3; motus, us *m*.

**twitter** pipilo 1; garrio 4.

**two** duo, duae, duo; bini; ～ **days** biduum *n*; ～ **hundred** ducenti; ～ **years** biennium *n*; ～**fold** duplex.

**typ|e** exemplar *n*, exemplum *n*; forma *f*; litterae *f/pl.*; ～**ical** proprius; ～**ify** exemplum sum.

**tyrann|ical** tyrannicus, superbus; ～**ize** dominor 1 (*alqd; in alqm*); opprimo 3; ～**y** tyrannis *f*; dominatus, us *m*, dominatio *f*.

**tyrant** tyrannus *m*; dominus *m*.

# U

**udder** uber, eris *n.*
**ugl|iness** deformitas *f*; foeditas *f*; ~y deformis, informis; pravus.
**ulcer** ulcus *n*; suppuro 1.
**ulterior** occultus.
**ultimate** ultimus, postremus; ~ly ad postremum.
**umbrage: take ~** offendor 3.
**umbrella** umbraculum *n.*
**umpire** arbiter, tri *m.*
**unabashed** intrepidus, impudens.
**unable: be ~** nequeo 4; non possum (*inf.*).
**un|acceptable** ingratus, invisus; ~accountable inexplicabilis.
**unaccustomed** insolitus (*ad*); insolens, insuetus (*gen.*).
**un|acquainted** ignarus, expers (*gen.*); ~affected simplex, sincerus; ~alterable immutabilis; ~ambitious modestus.
**unanim|ity** consensio *f*; consensus, us *m*; ~ously una voce; consensu omnium.
**un|armed** inermis; ~asked sponte, ultro; ~assuming modestus, humilis; ~authenticated sine auctore; incertus; ~availing irritus, vanus; ~avenged inultus; ~avoidable quod vitari non potest; necessarius.
**unaware** inscius, ignarus (*gen.*); ~s (de) improviso; **take ~s** imprudentem, inopinantem capio 3 (*alqm*).
**un|bar** resero 1; aperio 4; ~bearable intolerabilis; ~becoming indecorus; alienus (*abl.*); ~bend remitto 3; ~bending rigidus; ~biassed incorruptus; ~bidden iniussus; invocatus; ~bind (re)solvo 3; ~blemished purus, integer; ~bolt resero 1; ~born nondum natus; ~bosom oneself me patefacio 3; ~bounded infinitus; ~bridled effrenatus; ~broken continuus, perpetuus; ~burden oneself me patefacio 3; onus allevo 1; ~buried inhumatus, insepultus; ~button (re)solvo 3; ~ceasing continuus, perpetuus.
**uncertain** dubius, incertus; anceps; **be ~** dubito 1; haereo 2; **it is ~**

incertum est; ~ty dubium *n*; dubitatio *f.*
**unchange|able** immutabilis; **be ~d** permaneo 2.
**un|charitable** malevolus, iniquus; ~chaste impudicus; ~checked liber; ~civil inhumanus, rusticus; ~civilised barbarus, incultus.
**uncle** patruus *m* (*paternal*); avunculus *m* (*maternal*).
**un|clean** impurus; ~clouded serenus; ~coil evolvo 3; ~comfortable incommodus, gravis; ~common rarus, insolens, insolitus; ~concerned otiosus; ~connected disiunctus; ~conquered invictus.
**unconscious** inscius, ignarus (*gen.*); ~ness oblivio *f*; defectio *f* (*animi*).
**unconstitutional** non legitimus; illicitus; ~ly contra rem publicam.
**un|controlled** impotens, effrenatus; ~couple disiungo 3; ~couth incultus, rudis, inhumanus; ~cover recludo 3; aperio 4; ~cultivated incultus; ~damaged integer; ~daunted intrepidus, impavidus; ~deceive errorem tollo 3 (*dat.*); ~decided anceps; dubius; ~defended nudus; ~deniably certe.
**under** sub (*acc.*; *abl.*); subter, infra (*acc.*); per (*acc.*); **~ a pretence of** specie; **~ arms** armatus; **~ ten days** intra decem dies; ~garment subucula *f*; ~go subeo 4; perfero 3, patior 3; ~ground sub terra; subterraneus; ~growth virgulta *n/pl.*; ~hand clandestinus, perfidus; ~line noto 1; ~ling assecla *m*; ~mine labefacto 1; detraho 3 (*alqd de re*); ~neath infra, subter (*acc.*).
**understand** intellego 3, comprehendo 3; teneo 2; accipio 3, percipio 3; certior fio; audio 4; ~ing mens *f*; ingenium *n.*
**undertak|e** suscipio 3 (*alqd*); spondeo 2; recipio 3, promitto 3 (*alqd*; *acc. c. inf.*); ~er libitinarius *m*; ~ing inceptum *n*, facinus *n.*
**un|deserved** immeritus; ~developed immaturus; crudus; ~digested crudus; ~diminished integer; ~

disputed certus; ∼do (dis)solvo 3, resolvo 3; pessum do 1; irritum facio 3; be ∼done pereo 4; leave ∼done omitto 3; ∼doing dissolutio *f*; ∼doubted certus, haud dubius; ∼dress vestem exuo 3, detraho 3; ∼dressed nudus.

**undulate** fluctuo 1.

un|duly nimis; ∼earth detego 3; ∼earthly mirus, monstruosus; ∼easiness perturbatio *f*, aegritudo *f*; ∼educated indoctus, illitteratus, ineruditus; ∼employed vacuus, otiosus.

**unequal** impar, dispar; ∼led singularis, unicus.

un|equivocally plane; ∼erring certus; ∼even inaequabilis, asper; ∼exampled inauditus, unicus; ∼expected inopinatus, inexpectatus; necopinatus; improvisus; ∼failing perennis; ∼fair iniquus, iniustus.   [fidem fallo 3.]

**unfaithful** perfidus, infidus; be ∼]

un|familiar novus, insolitus; ∼fasten refigo 3; ∼favourable iniquus, alienus, adversus, inopportunus; ∼feeling durus; ∼finished imperfectus, rudis; ∼fit inutilis, inhabilis; indignus; ∼fold explico 1; evolvo 3; ∼foreseen improvisus; ∼forgiving implacabilis, atrox; ∼formed crudus, informis; ∼fortunate miser, infelix; ∼founded vanus; ∼friendly inimicus; ∼fulfilled inanis, vanus; ∼furl solvo 3, pando 3; ∼gainly imperitus, rusticus; ∼gentlemanly illiberalis; ∼godly impius; ∼gracious inhumanus; ∼grateful ingratus; immemor (beneficii); ∼guarded parum custoditus; incautus; ∼happy miser, infelix; ∼harmed incolumis; ∼healthy pestilens (*locus*); valetudine affectus; ∼heard (of) inauditus; ∼hesitatingly audacter; ∼holy impius, nefarius; ∼hurt incolumis.

**uniform** aequabilis; ornatus, us *m* militaris; ∼ity aequabilitas *f*.

un|impaired integer; ∼important nullius momenti; ∼inhabitable inhabitabilis; ∼inhabited desertus; ∼injured incolumis; ∼intelligible obscurus; ∼intentional haud meditatus, cogitatus.

**union** consociatio *f*; concilium *n*; societas *f*; coniunctio *f*.

**unique** unicus, singularis.

**unison: in** ∼ una voce.

**unit|e** *v/t.* (con)iungo 3; consocio 1; *v/i.* coniuro 1; consocior 1; ∼ed consociatus; ∼y consensus, us *m*; concordia *f*.

univers|al communis; ∼ally in universum, universe; ∼e mundus *m*; ∼ity academia *f*.

un|just iniquus, iniustus; ∼kempt horridus, incomptus; ∼kind haud benignus; crudelis, inhumanus; ∼known ignotus, incognitus; ∼lace solvo 3.

**unlawful** illicitus, vetitus; **it is** ∼ nefas est; ∼ly contra legem; contra ius.

**unless** nisi, ni.

un|like dissimilis, dispar (*gen.*, *dat.*); ∼limited infinitus; ∼load expono 3; ∼lock resero 1; ∼looked-for necopinatus, inexspectatus; ∼loose solvo 3; ∼lucky infelix; ∼manageable intractabilis; ∼manly mollis; ∼mannerly agrestis, inhumanus; ∼married caelebs; ∼mentionable infandus; ∼merciful immitis; ∼mindful immemor (*gen.*); ∼mistakeable certissimus; ∼mixed merus; ∼moved immotus.

**unnatural** immanis, nefarius; arcessitus (*oratio*); ∼ly praeter naturam.

un|necessary haud necessarius; supervacaneus; ∼nerve frango 3.

**unnoticed: pass** ∼ lateo 2.

un|occupied vacuus; ∼palatable *fig.* molestus; ∼patriotic improbus, malus; ∼pleasant iniucundus, molestus; ∼polished impolitus, rudis.

**unpopular** invidiosus, invisus, ingratus; ∼ity invidia *f*; offensio *f*.

un|practised inexpertus; ∼precedented inauditus, novus; ∼prepossessing iniucundus; ∼principled improbus; nequam; ∼propitious iniquus, infaustus; ∼provoked ultro (*adv.*); ∼punished impunitus; ∼questionably facile, certe; ∼ravel retexo 3; *fig.* enodo 1; ∼reasonable absurdus; contra rationem.

un|refined crudus; rudis; ∼relenting atrox; ∼remitting assiduus; ∼restrained effrenatus, liber; ∼ripe crudus; ∼rivalled unicus; praestantissimus; ∼roll evolvo 3; ∼ruffled aequus; ∼ruly impotens; ∼saddle stratum detraho 3; ∼safe infestus, lubricus, periculosus; ∼

**seal** resigno 1; aperio 4; ~season-able immaturus, ineptus; ~seemly indecorus; ~seen invisus; ~serviceable inutilis.

**unsettled** dubius; perturbatus; vagus; **leave ~** in medio relinquo 3.

**un|sheath** educo 3, eripio 3 (e vagina); ~sightly turpis, foedus; ~skilled imperitus (gen.); ~sociable difficilis; ~sophisticated simplex; ~sound infirmus, morbosus; ~sparing profusus, prodigus (gen.); ~speakable infandus; ~stable, ~steady instabilis, fluxus; ~successful infelix; adversus, irritus; ~suitable incommodus, ineptus; alienus (ab); ~suspecting incautus; ~thinking inconsideratus; ~tie (dis)solvo 3; laxo 1.

**until** ad, in (acc.); cj. dum, quoad, donec; **not ~** non prius (ante) ... quam.

**un|timely** immaturus; ~tiring assiduus; ~touched intactus, integer; ~toward adversus; ~tried inexpertus; ~troubled securus, tranquillus; ~true falsus; ~truth mendacium n; ~used insuetus (gen.); insolitus (ad; gen.); integer; ~usual insolitus, insolens, novus; ~varnished haud fucatus; ~veil detego 3; fig. patefacio 3, aperio 4; ~versed in imperitus (gen.); ~warlike imbellis; ~wary imprudens, incautus; ~wearied impiger; ~welcome iniucundus, ingratus; ~well aeger; ~wholesome gravis (cibus); noxius; ~wieldy inhabilis.

**unwilling** invitus; **be ~** nolo (inf.); ~ly invitus.

**un|wind** revolvo 3; ~wise insipiens; ~witting imprudens; ~wonted insuetus, insolitus; ~worthy indignus (abl.; qui); alienus (ab); ~wrap evolvo 3; explico 1; ~written non scriptus; ~yielding firmus, obstinatus.

**up** sursum; **~ and down** sursum deorsum; **~ in the air** sublime; **~ to** ad (acc.); in (acc.); **~ to this year** usque ad hunc annum.

**up|braid** obiurgo 1; ~country in interiora; ~hill acclivis, arduus; ~hold sustineo 2, sustento 1; ~land editus.

**upon** in, super (acc., abl.); **~ the right** a dextra.

**upper** superior, superus; ~most supremus, summus.

**upright** rectus; integer, honestus, bonus; ~ness probitas f.

**uproar** tumultus, us m; turba f.

**uproot** evello 3.

**upset** everto 3, subverto 3; sollicito 1 (alqm).

**upshot** exitus, us m.

**upside: turn ~ down** sursum deorsum verso 1.

**up|start** novus homo m; terrae filius m; ~stream adverso flumine; in adversum flumen.

**upwards** sursum; sublime; **~ of** amplius, plus.

**urge** suadeo 2 (alci ut; alqd alci); hortor 1 (alqm ut; alci alqd); impello 3 (alqm ad alqd); ~ **on** incito 1; impello 3; ~nt gravis, praesens; ~ntly vehementer.

**urn** urna f.

**usage** mos m.

**use** utor 3 (abl.); adhibeo 2 (alqd ad alqd; in re); tracto 1 (alqm); usus, us m; utilitas f; commodum n; **be of ~** prosum; usui sum; **make ~ of** utor 3 (alqa re); **in common ~** usitatus; ~ **up** consumo 3; ~d to assuetus, assuefactus; ~ful utilis, commodus; ~less inutilis, vanus, irritus; **it is ~less** nihil prodest; ~lessly frustra.

**usher in** introduco 3; fig. infero 3.

**usual** solitus, usitatus, consuetus; **be ~** soleo 2; ~ly plerumque; fere.

**usufruct** usus, us m.

**usurer** faenerator m; **be a ~** faeneror 1.

**usurp** invado 3 (in alqd; alqd); usurpo 1.

**usury** faeneratio f; faenus n.

**utensils** supellex f; instrumenta n/pl.

**utility** utilitas f.

**utmost** extremus, ultimus, summus; **to my ~** quantum in me est; omnibus viribus.

**utter** totus, merus, germanus; dico 3, emitto 3, loquor 3; ~ance dictum n; ~ly omnino, funditus; ~most ultimus, extremus.

# V

**vacan|cy** (vacuus) locus *m*; inane *n*; ~t vacuus, inanis.

**vacat|e** vacuefacio 3; ~ion feriae *f/pl.*

**vacillat|e** vacillo 1; ~ion dubitatio *f.*

**vacuum** inane *n*.

**vagabond** vagus; erro *m*.

**vagary** libido *f.*

**vagrant** vagus; erro *m*.

**vague** incertus, dubius; vagus; ~ness obscuritas *f.*

**vain** vanus, inanis, irritus, levis; gloriosus (*homo*); **in ~** frustra, nequiquam; ~**glorious** gloriosus.

**vale** vallis *f.*

**valet** cubicularius *m*.

**valiant** fortis.

**valid** firmus, certus, ratus; ~ity auctoritas *f*, gravitas *f.*

**valley** vallis *f.*

**valour** virtus, utis *f.*

**valu|able** pretiosus; magni (pretii); ~ation aestimatio *f.*

**value** aestimo 1, habeo 2, facio 3, duco 3, pendo 3 (*alqd magni, pluris, parvi, etc.*); diligo 3; pretium *n*; aestimatio *f*; virtus, utis *f*; honor *m*; **be of ~** prosum (*alci*); ~**less** minimi pretii.

**vampire** lamia *f.*

**van** *mil.* primum agmen *n.*

**vanish** evanesco 3, dilabor 3.

**vanity** vanitas *f*; iactatio *f*, gloria *f.*

**vanquish** vinco 3; supero 1.

**vapour** vapor *m*; halitus, us *m*; exhalatio *f.*

**variable** varius, mutabilis, mobilis.

**variance** discordia *f*; discrepantia *f*; **be at ~ with** pugno 1 cum; **at ~ with** discors.

**variation** varietas *f*, commutatio *f.*

**varicose** varicosus; ~ **vein** varix *f.*

**var|ied** varius, diversus; ~**iegate** vario 1; ~**iety** varietas *f*, diversitas *f*; ~**ious** varius, diversus, multiplex; ~**ious opinions were expressed** alius aliud dixit.

**varnish** *fig.* fucus *m.*

**vary** vario 1, muto 1; distinguo 3.

**vase** amphora *f.*

**vast** ingens, maximus, immensus.

**vat** dolium *n*.

**vault** salio 4; fornix *f*; camera *f*; saltus, us *m*; ~**ed** fornicatus.

**vaunt** iacto 1, ostento 1 (*alqd*); glorior 1 (*acc. c. inf.*); iactatio *f*, ostentatio *f.*

**veal** vitulina *f.*

**veer** (me) verto 3 (*in, ad*).

**vegetable** planta *f*; ~**s** olus *n.*

**vehemen|ce** vis *f*; ~t vehemens, ardens.

**vehicle** vehiculum *n.*

**veil** velum *n*, velamentum *n*; rica *f*; velo 1; tego 3.

**vein** vena *f.*

**velocity** velocitas *f*, celeritas *f.*

**venal** venalis.

**vend** vendo 3; ~**or** venditor *m*.

**venera|ble** venerabilis, gravis, augustus; ~**te** veneror 1; ~**tion** veneratio *f.*

**vengeance** ultio *f.*

**venison** ferina *f.*

**venom** virus, i *n*, venenum *n*; ~**ous** venenatus; mordax.

**vent** foramen *n*; **give ~ to** erumpo 3 (*abl.; alqd*); erumpo 3, effundo 3 (*alqd in alqm*).

**ventilat|e** *fig.* in medium profero 3; ~**ion** perflatus, us *m.*

**venture** audeo 2 (*alqd; inf.*); conor 1 (*alqd; inf.*); periclitor 1 (*alqd*); in periculum infero 3 (*alqm, alqd*); in aleam do 1; periculum *n*, discrimen *n*; alea *f*; **at a ~** temere; ~**some** audax, audens.

**verac|ious** verax, verus; ~**ity** fides *f*, veritas *f.*

**verb** verbum *n*; ~**ally** verbum pro verbo (*reddere etc.*); sermone (*iubere*); ~**atim** totidem verbis; ~**ose** verbosus.

**verdict** sententia *f*; iudicium *n*; **pronounce ~** pronuntio 1.

**verdure** viriditas *f.*

**verg|e** margo *m*; ora *f*; ~**ing on** proximus (*dat.*).

**verify** probo 1, confirmo 1.

**vermilion** miniatus.

**vernacular** patrius sermo *m.*

**vernal** vernus.

**versatile** varius, multiplex.
**vers|e** versus, us *m*; carmen *n*; ~ed in peritus (*gen.*), exercitatus (*in re*).
**vertebra** vertebra *f*.
**vertical** rectus, directus; ~ly ad lineam.
**very** *adv.* valde, maxime, admodum (*bonus etc.*); **not** ~ non ita; ~ **much** magnopere, vehementer; *adj.* germanus; **this** ~ hic ipse; **at that** ~ **moment** ea ipsa hora.
**vessel** vas *n*; navis *f*.
**vest** subucul ɔ *f*.
**vestal** vestalis (virgo) *f*.
**vestibule** vestibulum *n*.
**vestige** indicium *n*, signum *n*; nota *f*.
**vetch** vicia *f*.
**veteran** veteranus (miles) *m*; vetus.
**veto** intercessio *f*; intercedo 3 (*dat.*).
**vex** sollicito 1, vexo 1; ~ation stomachus *m*; ~atious molestus, odiosus.
**vibrate** tremo 3; vibro 1.
**vice** flagitium *n*, vitium *n*; pravitas *f*, turpitudo *f*; ~roy praefectus *m*.
**vicious** flagitiosus, pravus, nequam.
**vicinity** vicinitas *f*; vicinum *n*.
**vicissitudes** vices *f/pl.*, vicissitudines *f/pl*.
**victim** victima *f*, hostia *f*.
**victor** victor *m*, victrix *f*; ~ious victor; **be** ~ious vinco 3; ~y victoria *f*; triumphus *m*; **gain** ~y victoriam consequor 3.
**victuals** victus, us *m*; cibaria *n/pl*.
**vie with** certo 1, contendo 3 (*cum*).
**view** conspectus, us *m*; acies *f*; *fig.* sententia *f*, opinio *f*; iudicium *n*; ~ **down, over** despectus, us *m*; **be in** ~ sum in prospectu; **come into** ~ venio 4 in conspectum (*alcs*); **in** ~ in conspectu; ante oculos; *fig.* **in my** ~ meo iudicio; mihi videtur; **take the same** ~ idem sentio 4 (*quod, atque*); **with a** ~ **to** ut; gratia, causa (*alcs rei*); intueor 2, contueor 2; specto 1, contemplor 1.
**vigilan|ce** vigilantia *f*; ~t vigilans, providus.
**vigo|rous** acer, strenuus, ferox; ~ur ferocitas *f*; vis *f*.
**vile** turpis, perditus, nequam.
**vilify** maledico 3 (*dat.*).
**villa** villa *f*.

**village** pagus *m*, vicus *m*; ~r rusticus *m*, agrestis *m*.
**villain** verbero *m*, furcifer *m*; ~y nequitia *f*; flagitium *n*.
**vindicate** purgo 1.
**vine** vitis *f*; ~ **leaf** pampineus *m*.
**vinegar** acetum *n*.
**vin|eyard** vinea *f*; vinetum *n*; ~tage vindemia *f*.
**viol|ate** violo 1; ~ater violator *m*; ~ence vis *f*, violentia *f*; impetus, us *m*; ~ent violentus, vehemens.
**violet** viola *f*.
**viper** vipera *f*.
**virgin** virgo *f*; innupta *f*; virginalis; ~ity virginitas *f*.
**viril|e** virilis; mas; ~ity virilitas *f*.
**virtue** virtus, utis *f*; probitas *f*; **in** ~ **of** pro (*abl.*); per (*acc.*).
**virtuous** honestus, probus.
**virulen|ce** acerbitas *f*; vis *f*; ~t acerbus, gravis.
**visage** os *n*.
**viscous** lentus.
**visible** conspicuus, manifestus; **be** ~ appareo 2.
**vision** visus, us *m*; aspectus, us *m*; visum *n*; imago *f*.
**visit** (in)viso 1; saluto 1; salutatio *f*; ~or hospes *m and f*.
**vista** prospectus, us *m*; despectus, us *m*.
**vital** vitalis; necessarius; ~ity alacritas *f*.
**vitiate** vitio 1.
**vivaci|ous** alacer, acer; ~ty alacritas *f*.
**vivid** vivus, acer.
**vocal** sonorus.
**vociferously** magno clamore.
**vogue** mos *m*.
**voice** vox *f*; *fig.* sententia *f*, opinio *f*.
**void** inanis, vacuus; liber (*abl.*); irritus (*lex*); inane *n*; lacuna *f*; erumpo 3, evomo 3.
**volition** voluntas *f*.
**volley** *fig.* nubes *f*.
**voluble** loquax.
**volum|e** volumen *n*; liber, bri *m*; ~inous copiosus.
**volunt|arily** mea (sua) sponte, voluntate; ultro; ~ary voluntarius.
**volunteer** sponte, ultro offero 3 (*alqd*); *mil.* nomen do 1; (miles) voluntarius *m*.
**voluptuous** voluptarius, libidinosus.

**vomit** (e)vomo 3.
**voracious** avidus, vorax.
**votary** cultor *m*.
**vot|e** suffragium *n* (*populi*); sententia *f* (*iudicis*); *v/t.* censeo 2; decerno 3; *v/i.* suffragium fero 3; ~e for suffragor 1 (*alci*); ~ing-tablet tabella *f*; ~ing urn, box cista *f*.
**votive** votivus.
**vouch for** praesto 1, confirmo 1 (*alqd*).

**vouch|er** auctoritas *f*; ~safe concedo 3 (*alqd*); permitto 3 (*ut*).
**vow** (de)voveo 2; promitto 3; votum *n*.
**vowel** vocalis *f*.
**voyage** navigatio *f*; **make a ~** navigo 1.
**vulgar** vulgaris, communis; agrestis, insulsus, ineptus; ~ity ineptiae *f/pl.*; ~ly vulgo.
**vulture** vultur *m*.

# W

**waddle** vacillo 1.

**waft** fero 3.

**wag** quasso 1; moveo 2; ioculator *m*.

**wage** gero 3 (*bellum etc. cum alqo*).

**wager** spondeo 2; pono 3; sponsio *f*; pignus *n*.

**wages** merces *f/pl.*; praemium *n*.

**waggon** plaustrum *n*; carrus *m*; ~er bubulcus *m*; auriga, ae *m*.

**wail** ploro 1; fleo 2; ploratus, us *m*; fletus, us *m*.

**wain** plaustrum *n*.

**waist** medium corpus *n*.

**wait** exspecto 1, maneo 2, opperior 4 (*alqd*; *dum*); ~ on ministro 1 (*alci*); ~er puer, eri *m*; minister, tri *m*.

**waive** remitto 3 (*alqd*).

**wake** *v/t.* excito 1, suscito 1; *v/i.* expergiscor 3; vigilia *f*; ~ful vigilans.

**walk** pedibus eo 4; ambulo 1, spatior 1; ~ in inambulo 1 (*abl.*); ~er pedes *m*; ~ing stick baculum *n*.

**wall** murus *m*; city ~ moenia *n/pl.*; house~ paries *m*; munio 4; ~ed munitus; ~et pera *f*.

**wallow** volutor 1.

**walnut** (tree) iuglans *f*.

**wan** pallidus.

**wand** virga *f*; caduceus *m*.

**wander** erro 1, vagor 1, palor 1; ~ing vagus; erratio *f*.

**wane** decresco 3; minuor 3.

**wanness** pallor *m*.

**want** volo; aveo 2; careo 2 (*abl.*); desidero 1; inopia *f*, egestas *f*; there ~s deest; opus est (*nom.*; *abl.*); be ~ing deficio 3, desum, absum.

**wanton** libidinosus, protervus, procax; ~ness protervitas *f*.

**war** bellum *n*; militia *f*; make ~ on arma, bellum infero 3 (*alci*); wage ~ bellum gero 3; bello 1; declare ~ bellum indico 3 (*alci*); in ~ and peace pace belloque; ~-cry clamor *m*.

**warble** cano 3.   [*m*.]

**ward** custodia *f*; pupillus *m*, pupilla *f*; regio *f* (*urbis*); ~ off arceo 2; defendo 3, averto 3; ~en, ~er custos *m*, excubitor *m*; ~ship tutela *f*.

**wares** merces *f/pl.*

**war|fare** militia *f*; res *f* bellica; ~like bellicosus.

**warm** calidus, tepidus; *fig.* acer; tepefacio 3; foveo 2; ~th calor *m*, tepor *m*.

**warn** (ad)moneo 2 (*alqm alqd*; *ut*); ~ing monitus, us *m*; admonitum *n*.

**warp** stamen *n*; torqueo 2.

**warrant** auctoritas *f*; mandatum *n*; spondeo 2; praesto 1; promitto 3.

**warrior** bellator *m*.

**wary** cautus, providus.

**wash** *v/t.* lavo 1; *v/i.* lavor 1; ~ against alluo 3 (*acc.*); ~ing lavatio *f*.

**wasp** vespa *f*.

**waste** consumo 3; perdo 3, tero 3 (*tempus etc.*); dissipo 1, profundo 3 (*rem*); vastus, desertus; lay ~ vasto 1, populor 1; effusio *f*; vastitas *f*, solitudo *f*; ~ful prodigus, effusus; ~fulness luxuria *f*.

**watch** *v/t.* observo 1; custodio 4; exspecto 1; *v/i.* vigilo 1, excubo 1; vigilia *f*; excubiae *f/pl.*; custodia *f*; keep ~ over custodio 4; set a ~ vigilias dispono 3; ~ful vigilans; ~man vigil *m*; ~-tower specula *f*; ~word tessera *f*.

**water** (ir)rigo 1; aqua *f*; sea~ aqua *f* marina; by land and ~ terra marique; ~-carrier aquarius *m*; ~-clock clepsydra *f*; well ~ed irriguus; ~fall desiliens aqua *f*; ~ing-place aquatio *f*.

**wattle** crates *f*.

**wave** unda *f*; fluctus, us *m*; *v/t.* iacto 1, agito 1; *v/i.* fluctuo 1, fluito 1; ~r fluctuo 1, vacillo 1, dubito 1; ~ring dubius, incertus.

**wax** cera *f*; *v/t.* cero 1; *v/i.* cresco 3 (*luna*); ~en cereus.

**way** via *f*; cursus, us *m*; *fig.* modus *m*; ratio *f*; on the ~ ex itinere; out of the ~ devius, remotus, abstrusus; get under ~ ancoram solvo 3; ~farer viator *m*; ~lay insidior 1 (*dat.*); ~side ad viam; ~ward pertinax, levis.

**we** nos.

**weak** infirmus, debilis, imbecillus, fractus, tenuis; ~en infirmo 1; frango 3, comminuo 3; ~ness infirmitas *f*.

**weal** vibix *f*; **common** ~ bonum *n* publicum.

**wealth** divitiae *f/pl.*, opes *f/pl.*; copia *f*; ~y dives, opulentus, locuples.

**wean** lacte depello 3.

**weapon** telum *n*; iaculum *n*; ~s arma *n/pl.*

**wear** *v/t.* gero 3 (*vestem*); *v/i.* duro 1; ~ away (con)tero 3; ~ out conficio 3; tritus, us *m*; habitus, us *m*; ~ied defessus; ~iness lassitudo *f*; ~ing amictus (*alqa veste*); ~isome operosus, laboriosus.

**weary** defessus, defatigatus; (de-)fatigo 1; **be** ~ **of** taedet 2 me (*alcs rei*).

**weasel** mustela *f*.

**weather** tempestas *f*; caelum *n*; **fine** ~ serenitas *f*; **bad** ~ foeda tempestas *f*; *fig.* perfero 3; ~beaten adustus.

**weave** (con)texo 3; ~r textor *m*.

**web** tela *f*; textum *n*.

**wed** duco 3 (*uxorem*); nubo 3 (*maritum*); ~ded maritus, nupta; *fig.* ~ded to deditus (*dat.*); ~ding nuptiae *f/pl.*

**wedge** cuneus *m*.

**wedlock** matrimonium *n*.

**weed** lolium *n*; runco 1.

**week** septem dies *m/pl.*

**weep** fleo 2; lacrimor 1; ~ over defleo 2 (*alqd*), illacrimo 1 (*dat.*); ~ing fletus, us *m*.

**weevil** curculio *m*.

**weigh** (ex)pendo 3; penso 1; *fig.* pondero 1; ~ down premo 3, opprimo 3; gravo 1; ~t pondus *n*; momentum *n*; gravitas *f*; auctoritas *f*; **have great, no** ~t multum, nihil valeo 2 (*apud alqm*); ~ty gravis.

**welcome** gratus, acceptus; salvere iubeo 2; (benigne) excipio 3, accipio 3; saluto 1; *int.* salve!; salutatio *f*.

**weld** ferrumino 1.

**welfare** salus, utis *f*; bonum *n*, commodum *n*.

**well** puteus *m*; fons *m*; *adj.* valens, salvus; *adv.* bene, probe; **be** ~ valeo 2; ~-being felicitas *f*; ~-born nobilis; ~-bred urbanus, comis; ~-disposed to benevolus (*erga, in alqm*); ~earned (bene) meritus;

~-known celebratus; ~-versed peritus, versatus; ~-wisher amicus *m*.

**west** occidens *m*; occasus, us *m* (solis); ~ern *ad* occidentem; occidentalis; ~wards in occasum; ~ wind zephyrus *m*.

**wet** madefacio 3; umidus, udus, madidus; **be** ~ madeo 2; ~ness umor *m*.

**whale** balaena *f*, cetus *m*.

**wharf** crepido *f*.

**what** quid?, quod?; ~ **kind of a** quod?, *exclam.* qui, qualis; *relat.* quod; ~ever quicumque; quisquis.

**wheat** triticum *n*.

**wheedle** blandior 4 (*dat.*).

**wheel** rota *f*; ~ **round** *v/t.* circumago 3; *v/i.* circumagor 3.

**whelp** catulus *m*.

**when** quando?; *cj.* cum, ubi, postquam, ut; ~ce unde?; ~ever quandocumque, quotiescumque, cum.

**where** ubi?, quo?; *relat.* qua, ubi; ~ ... **from** unde?; ~ **on earth** ubi gentium?; ~as quoniam; ~by qua ratione; ~upon quo facto; ~ver ubicumque.

**whet** acuo 3.

**whether** *interrog.* num; utrum ... (*an*); -ne ... (*an*); *cj.* ~ ... **or** sive ... sive; seu ... seu.

**whetstone** cos *f*.

**which** quis?; *relat.* qui; ~ **(of two)** uter?; *relat.* quis; ~ever quicumque.

**while** *cj.* dum; donec, cum; tempus *n*; **for a little** ~ parumper; ~ **away** dego 3.

**whim** arbitrium *n*; libido *f*.

**whimper** vagio 4.

**whimsical** ridiculus.

**whine** vagio 4.

**whip** flagellum *n*; lora *n/pl.*; verbero 1.

**whirl** turbo *m*; ~ **round** torqueor 2; ~pool vorago *f*, vertex *m*; ~wind turbo *m*.

**whiskers** capilli *m/pl.*

**whisper** (in)susurro 1; susurrus *m*.

**whistle** sibilo 1; sibilus *m*; fistula *f*.

**white** albus, candidus; canus (*capilli*); album *n*; ~n albesco 3, canesco 3; ~ness candor *m*; ~wash dealbo 1.

**whither** quo?

**who** quis?; *relat.* qui; ~ever quicumque.

**whole** totus, cunctus, omnis; integer, solidus; totum *n*; **as a ~** in universum; **on the ~** ad summam; **~sale dealer** mercator *m*; **~some** salutaris.

**wholly** omnino; ex omni ratione; prorsus.

**whoop** ululo 1; ululatus, us *m*.

**whose** cuius.

**why** cur?, quare?, quam ob rem?; **~ not** quidni?

**wick** filum *n*.

**wicked** scelestus, improbus, nefarius; **~ness** scelus *n*, flagitium *n*; nequitia *f*.

**wicker** vimineus; **~work** vimen *n*.

**wide** latus, amplus; *adv.* late; **~spread** (per)vulgatus; **~spreading** patulus (*rami*); **~n** laxo 1, dilato 1.

**widow** vidua *f*; **~ed** viduus; **~er** viduus homo *m*.

**width** latitudo *f*, amplitudo *f*.

**wield** gero 3; utor 3.

**wife** uxor *f*, coniunx *f*.

**wig** capillamentum *n*.

**wild** ferus, incultus, vastus; insanus; **~erness** desertum *n*; vastitas *f*; **~ness** feritas *f*.

**wiles** dolus *m*; fallaciae *f/pl*.

**wilful** pertinax, pervicax.

**will** voluntas *f*; consilium *n*, arbitrium *n*; testamentum *n*; **against my ~** me invito; invitus (*adj.*); **as you ~** ut libet.

**willing** libens; promptus (*ad*); **~ly** libenter; **~ness** studium *n*.

**willow** salix *f*.

**wily** vafer, astutus, callidus.

**win** vinco 3 (*in pugna etc.*); consequor 3, pario 3 (*alqd*); concilio 1 (*gratiam etc.*).

**wind**[1] ventus *m*.

**wind**[2] volvo 3; glomero 1; **~ one's way into** me insinuo 1 (*in*); **~ed** anhelans; **~ing** flexuosus; ambages *f/pl.*; sinus, us *m*.

**window** fenestra *f*. [tosus.}

**wind|pipe** aspera arteria *f*; **~y** ven- }

**wine** vinum *n*; **~cellar** cella *f*; **~press** prelum *m*.

**wing** ala *f*, penna *f*; cornu *n* (*exercitus*); volo 1; **~ed** volucer, pinniger.

**wink** nictus, us *m*; nicto 1; **~ at** coniveo 2 (*dat.*).

**win|ner** victor *m*; **~ning** victor; blandus, suavis.

**winnowing fan** vannus, i *f*.

**winter** hiems *f*; hiemo 1, hiberno 1; **~ solstice** bruma *f*; **~quarters** hiberna *n/pl.*

**wintry** hiemalis, hibernus.

**wipe** (de)tergeo 2; **~ out** deleo 2.

**wisdom** sapientia *f*; consilium *n*.

**wise** sapiens, prudens, peritus.

**wish** volo (*inf.*); cupio 3, opto 1 (*inf.*); **~ for** volo, opto 1 (*alqd*); votum *n*, optatum *n*, desiderium *n*; optatio *f*; **against my ~es** me invito.

**wit** sal *m*; facetiae *f/pl.*; ingenium *n*, acumen *n*; **to ~** scilicet.

**witch** saga *f*; venefica *f*; **~craft** veneficium *n*; magicae artes *f/pl.*

**with** cum (*abl.*); **~ me** mecum; apud me; **it rests, lies ~ me** penes me est; **~draw** *v/t.* removeo 2; abduco 3, deduco 3; *v/i.* (re)cedo 3, me recipio 3.

**wither** *v/t.* torreo 2; *v/i.* languesco 3, aresco 3; **~ed** marcidus, rugosus.

**withhold** retineo 2; supprimo 3, recuso 1.

**within** in (*abl.*); intra, inter (*acc.*); cis, citra (*acc.*); *adv.* intus.

**without** sine (*abl.*); *cj.* quin; *adv.* extra, extrinsecus.

**withstand** obsto 1, resisto 3, obsisto 3 (*dat.*).

**witness** testis *m*; arbiter *m*, spectator *m*; video 2; conspicio 3; **bear ~, call to ~** testor 1, testificor 1 (*alqd; alqm; acc. c. inf.*); **bear ~ against** testimonium dico 3 (*in alqm*).

**witt|icism** dictum *n*; **~y** facetus, salsus.

**wizard** magus *m*.

**woad** vitrum *n*.

**woe** dolor *m*; **~ful** miser, tristis.

**wolf** lupus *m*.

**woman** mulier *f*, femina *f*; **old ~** anus, us *f*; **young ~** puella *f*; **~ish** muliebris, effeminatus; **~ly, ~'s** muliebris, femineus.

**womb** uterus *m*.

**wonder** admiratio *f*; miraculum *n*; (ad)miror 1 (*alqd; acc. c. inf.; quod*); **~ful** mirus, mirabilis, mirificus.

**wont** mos *m*; **be ~** soleo 2.

**woo** peto 3; *fig.* ambio 4.

**wood** lignum *n*; silva *f*; nemus *n*; **~cutter** lignator *m*; **~ed** silvestris; **~en** ligneus; **~pigeon** palumbes *m*; **~y** lignosus, silvosus.

**wooer** procus *m*.

**wool** lana *f*; **⁓len** laneus.

**word** verbum *n*, vocabulum *n*, nomen *n*; vox *f*; **⁓s** dicta *n/pl.*; **in a ⁓, few ⁓s** paucis, breviter; **have ⁓s with** altercor 1 (*cum alqo*); **send (back) ⁓** (re)nuntio 1; **keep, break one's ⁓** fidem servo 1, fallo 3; **⁓y** verbosus.

**work** opus *n*; labor *m*; opera *f*; pensum *n*; **⁓ of art** opus *n*; ars *f*; artificium *n*; **⁓s** machinatio *f*; *v/i.* (e)laboro 1; *v/t.* subigo 3, colo 3 (*terram*); **⁓ at** exerceo 2 (*rem*); versor 1 (*in re*); **⁓ upon** flecto 3 (*animum etc.*); **⁓er** opifex *m*, artifex *m*; **⁓house** ergastulum *n*; **⁓ing** cultus, us *m* (*terrae*); **⁓man** opifex *m*; **⁓shop** officina *f*.

**world** mundus *m*; orbis *m* terrarum; **all the ⁓** omnes (ad unum); nemo est quin (*subj.*); **where in the ⁓** ubi gentium?; **in the whole ⁓** usquam.

**worm** vermis *m*; tinea *f*; **⁓ one's way into** me insinuo 1 (*in*).

**worry** sollicito 1; exerceo 2; agito 1.

**worse** peior, deterior; **for the ⁓** in deterius; **grow ⁓, ⁓n** ingravesco 3.

**worship** colo 3; veneror 1; cultus, us *m*; veneratio *f*; **⁓per** cultor *m*.

**worst** pessimus, deterrimus, ultimus; **get the ⁓ of it** vincor 3.

**worth** dignus (*abl.*); pretium *n*; dignitas *f*; **it is ⁓ (while)** operae pretium est (*inf.*); **⁓less** nequam (*homo*); inutilis, vilis; **⁓y** dignus (*abl.*; *qui*); bonus.

**would that** utinam.

**wound** vulnus *n*; plaga *f*; vulnero 1; saucio 4.

**wrangle** altercor 1.

**wrap** involvo 3, obvolvo 3 (*alqd re*); **⁓per** involucrum *n*; tegumentum *n*.

**wrath** ira *f*.

**wreath** sertum *n*; corona *f*; volumen *n*; vertex *m*; **⁓e** necto 3 (*caput sertis*).

**wreck** frango 3, illido 3; naufragium *n*; **⁓ed** naufragus.

**wrench, wrest** extorqueo 2 (*alqd alci*).

**wrestl|e** luctor 1; **⁓er** luctator *m*; **⁓ing** luctatio *f*.

**wretch** homo *m* nequam, perditus, miser; **⁓ed** infelix, miserabilis; **⁓edness** miseria *f*.

**wriggle** torqueo 2 me.

**wring** torqueo 2, crucio 1; **⁓ from** extorqueo 2 (*alqd alci*).

**wrinkle** ruga *f*; **⁓d** rugosus.

**writ** litterae *f/pl.*; mandatum *n*.

**write** scribo 3; **⁓ back** rescribo 3; **⁓ out** perscribo 3; **⁓r** scriptor *m*, auctor *m*.

**writing** scriptio *f*, scriptura *f*; **⁓s** scripta *n/pl.*; **⁓-case** scrinium *n*; **⁓-paper** charta *f*.

**wrong** falsus; pravus, iniustus, iniquus; iniuriam infero 3 (*alci*); **be ⁓** erro 1; **⁓doer** maleficus *m*; **⁓ful** iniustus; **⁓ly** male, perperam, falso.

**wry** distortus.

# Y

**yacht** phaselus *m*; celox *f*.
**yard** area *f*, cohors *f*; antenna *f* (*navis*).
**yarn** linum *n*; fabula *f*.
**yawn** oscito 1; *fig.* hio 1, dehisco 3; oscitatio *f*.
**yea** ita, certe.
**year** annus *m*; ~ly anniversarius; *adv.* quotannis.
**yearn| for** desidero 1; ~ing desiderium *n*.
**yeast** fermentum *n*.
**yell** ululo 1; ululatus, us *m*.
**yellow** flavus, luteus, croceus.
**yelp** gannio 4.
**yes** ita (vero); sane, certe, etiam; **say** ~ aio.
**yesterday** heri; hesternus dies *m*.
**yet** tamen, vero, nihilominus, at;

(*of time*) etiam(-nunc), adhuc; **not** ~ nondum.
**yew** taxus, i *f*.
**yield** *v/t.* effero 3; *fig.* pario 3, affero 3; do 1, concedo 3, dedo 3; *v/i.* cedo 3, obsequor 3 (*dat.*); fructus, us *m*; ~ing mollis.
**yoke** iugum *n*; iungo 3.
**yolk** vitellus *m*.
**yonder** *adj.* ille; *adv.* ecce, illic.
**yore** olim, quondam.
**you** tu, vos.
**young** iuvenis, parvus, adolescens; partus, us *m*, fetus, us *m*; ~er iunior, minor natu.
**your** tuus, vester.
**youth** iuventus, utis *f*, adolescentia *f*; iuvenis *m*, adolescens *m*; ~ful iuvenilis, puerilis.

# Z

**zeal** studium *n*; ardor *m*; ~ous studiosus, acer.
**zephyr** zephyrus *m*.
**zero** nihil.

**zest** gustatus, us *m*; studium *n*.
**zigzag** anfractus, us *m* (*viae etc.*); tortuosus.
**zone** zona *f*; regio *f*.